Handwriting & Highlighting noted 6/24/04
NG

DATE DUE

JUL 15 2004	
MAY 0 9 2008	

BRODART, CO.   Cat. No. 23-221-003

Vetal Flores
Drawer M
Bronte, Texas 76933

AMERICAN
LITERARY
MASTERS

VOLUME TWO

❖ ❖ ❖ / JAMES / CRANE

ADAMS / O'NEILL / ROBINSON

FROST / DREISER / ANDERSON

ELIOT / STEVENS / FITZGERALD

HEMINGWAY / WOLFE / FAULKNER

HOLT, RINEHART AND WINSTON, INC.

New York / Chicago / San Francisco / Toronto

Contents

Novelist

Dramatist

O. K.

Poet

Now.

Begin
here.   Poet & Belief and skepticism   1869-1935

P o e t

No.

ROBERT FROST   *Introduction* 18 74 - 1963   567

P o e t P S k e p t i c i s m

Part

WALLACE STEVENS   *Introduction*

1879 - 1955

Short Story Writer

SCOTT FITZGERALD   *Introduction*

1896 - 1946

Novelist

ERNEST HEMINGWAY   *Introduction*   Primitivist

War   1960

Short story Writer

Novelists With Social Themes

Novelists

1897 - 1962

Preface

If you are going to study literature, why not the best? If there are to be introductions, why not essays that launch the reader directly into the literature that follows? Such were the challenges that prompted the making of this book and guided the editors at every stage of their work. The result is an anthology of masterpieces by twenty-two major American authors that will fill several needs now widely felt among teachers.

Here are presented (with only three exceptions) whole works by the few great writers rather than shorter pieces by the many—as in anthologies where the major writers are greatly outnumbered by minor ones. The texts are chosen for their literary excellence rather than as documents illustrating the American scene or the growth of American civilization. Instead of biography and cultural history for their own sake, the introductions provide interpretations of works of art as such, including only that part of their setting needed to make them as meaningful for readers today as they were to highly intelligent contemporaries of the authors.

An anthology of a different sort, with the focus shifted from literature to such topics as the expanding frontier or the decline of Puritanism, might well consume many pages with selections from Parkman's *Oregon Trail* and Garland's *Main Travelled Roads* or with a sheaf of lesser writings by Holmes, Theodore Parker, and the like. By contrast, these two themes, as far as they enter into literature, are here amply illustrated by the complete texts of *Huckleberry Finn* and *The Scarlet Letter* without deviating from the rule of excellence. Again, instructors might find it difficult to point out the literary value of such introductions as are frequently offered them on the rise of railroads and the growth of cities, or to make poetic capital out of the biographical fact that Frost was born in San Francisco or that Emerson had two wives. But Frost's relation to the pastoral tradition and Emerson's struggle to give a new form to the essay, as set forth in the present introductions, are highly relevant to the student of literature. After close familiarity with the selected masterpieces of major authors, as here pointed up by critical commentary, the potential enthusiasm of the undergraduate mind will be fixed by the best, not scattered by the miscellaneous.

Choosing the best is no easy task, yet the editors feel confident of general agreement with most of their choices. Of the older authors Poe, Hawthorne and Melville, Emerson and Whitman, Mark Twain, Henry James and Emily Dickinson are widely recognized as the best poets and novelists of the nineteenth century. And for sheer excellence Thoreau and Henry Adams have been added to this list, rather than writers in the second rank of achievement merely because they fit more neatly into some conventional "literary" slot. Among more recent writers it is harder to arrive at general agreement, but surely O'Neill, Hemingway and Faulkner, Frost and Eliot stand out pre-eminently among the moderns. These fifteen great originals will provide instructors with the staple of any college course in American Literature.

Seven additional authors have been included, however, so that the instructor can make choices of his own. In selecting these, the editors have given preference to writers who pioneered new directions in technique and opened up new areas of American experience for the creative imagination. Because of his originality, as well as for general superiority, Stevens clearly takes precedence over Sandburg, Fitzgerald over Sinclair Lewis, and a similar case can be made for Dreiser, Wolfe, and the others. However preferences may differ in twentieth-century literature, here is God's plenty to choose from—a dozen major moderns fully represented. Again, for the more recent authors it was not always possible to include full-scale masterpieces because of copyright limitations, but parts of longer works have been used very rarely and only when they are really separable and are significant in scope. Also, in two instances the author's greatest work was of such bulk as to burst the seams of even these ample volumes; so *Look Homeward, Angel* among the moderns, like *Moby Dick* among the older classics, had to yield to less voluminous choices. These outsize novels can be assigned as supplementary reading.

For those intent upon studying the best in American literature, a large part of it is here made available within the covers of a single anthology. In addition to broad coverage, we have aimed at proportion and variety. About half of the authors are chosen from the older period and half from our own century. There are eight poets and ten novelists; two masters of nonfiction prose; one master each in the drama and the short story—with some writers scoring in more than one genre, including the essay. In recent years many instructors, dissatisfied with the conventional anthology, have tried to concentrate on the masterpieces by using a large number of separate paperbacks as texts. AMERICAN LITERARY MASTERS provides the equivalent of more than twenty such volumes with a number of distinct advantages: the convenience of a single order instead of many, for a permanently available textbook, at a much lower cost; authoritative texts, study aids, and introductions of a quality not found in cheap reprints.

The editors have agreed upon a common approach and a common goal, but there has been no attempt to impose a strict uniformity. The problems vary from author to author, and the treatment is varied to fit these needs. Moreover, the editors have been chosen not because they belong to a particular school but because of their competence as critics and scholars who can speak with special authority in certain areas where they have been centering their interests. And they have been given a free hand to present their authors as they see best, within the flexible limits of a general plan. Each introduction surveys the author's total pattern and significance, relating him to tradition and milieu, then concentrates on a discussion of the major works selected—by asking challenging questions as to structure, language, imagery, themes, and ideas. Following each group of texts are Reading Suggestions (a summary evaluation of the best editions and studies of the author), then a brief Biography. Though the selections themselves have been chosen primarily for literary excellence, they were also chosen with an eye to their representativeness and their suitability to American college students. Every effort has been made to reproduce faithfully the most authoritative texts and to furnish them with such annotations as are needed to make them intelligible.

This book has been designed to meet the aims of several kinds of courses. For the introductory course in American Literature it achieves all the really important goals of the standard survey, while offering at the same time much more ample material for reading our best authors in depth. Either volume taken separately will serve as an admirable text for the one-semester course favored by some colleges and universities, whether it concentrates on the older or newer writers. The full contents of both volumes, supplemented by the suggestions for further reading, will provide all the texts needed in courses on the most advanced undergraduate level, whether taken by a student primarily interested in literature or one pursuing a program in American studies. For when literature is selected and studied on any other basis than its merit as a work of the creative imagination it immediately becomes something else, historical document or social tract, and so loses its value as a unique component of the total cultural pattern. For example, the poet of *Walden* is an artist, but the polemicist of "Civil Disobedience" is not. Again, as a special vision of the American experience *Leaves of Grass* differs vastly from *Democratic Vistas*. These differences are made explicit by the editorial commentary. The principles of selection and the approach adopted in these volumes seem to us the most rewarding ones for any study of American literature, either as a single aspect of our civilization or as an integral part of the whole.

CHARLES R. ANDERSON
GENERAL EDITOR

Johns Hopkins University
December 1964

✢   Though the anthology was a joint enterprise, the sections dealing with the twenty-two authors were edited as follows: Twain and O'Neill by Richard Adams; Whitman and Anderson by Roger Asselineau; Melville and Stevens by James Baird; Poe and Crane by Roy Male; Dreiser and Wolfe by Wallace Stegner; Emerson and Robinson by Carl Strauch; Hawthorne and Eliot by Hyatt Waggoner; Thoreau, Dickinson, James, Adams, Frost, Fitzgerald, Hemingway, and Faulkner by Charles Anderson.

AMERICAN
LITERARY
MASTERS

He is a critic, short story writer,
and novelist.

Literary criticism is acute.

S.S. show him at his best.

He began as writer of "international novel)

HENRY JAMES ✦
An expatriate 1843-1916

Began with Am. Renaissance & ante-
bellum Am. and ended with second
Am. Renaissance (about time of W.W. I)

Stages of artistic growth:

1. 1864 - 1879 - gifted apprentice
2. 1880 - 1889 - perfecting his fiction
   in the tradition of
   Balzacian realism

3. 1890 - 1899 - undergoing a re-apprenticeship
   in which he took stock of
   his past accomplishments
   and searched for a new
   kind of expression

4. 1900 - 1916 - achieving final period of
   accomplishment, the "major
   phase"

Product 135 short and long works
of fiction, criticism, travel accounts,
memoirs, letters.

Henry James stands in the forefront
of new literature following the Civil War.
James wrote about life as it
really was. A realist.
He was at his best in the area of
psychological realism.

His method was to prepare a
character in a difficult and complex social
situation and then show his growing
awareness with all of the subtleties and *refinements*

Introduction

If only because he was such a prodigious creator, James stands in the very top rank of American novelists. More than any of them he was the dedicated artist. Others who wrote a comparable quantity of fiction, like Howells, fall far below him in quality. Those who achieved a comparable excellence, such as Hawthorne, did so only occasionally, not in book after book as he did. Perhaps only Faulkner is a rival on both scores. In a writing career that spanned a full half century, from the last days of the Civil War to the first of World War I, he produced a body of novels and tales that fill thirty-six volumes yet maintain a remarkably high level of performance. Fully two thirds of this large shelf can be reckoned as first-rate, and half of these rank with the best fictions in English. They range from the slightest sketch to the full two-volume novel, and James proved himself a master time and again in each of the several forms. He has been most praised for his achievement in the outsized novel, running to six hundred or more pages in normal editions, and students should read at least one of his masterpieces on this ambitious scale (such as *The Portrait of a Lady* or *The Ambassadors*). He also has few peers in the standard-sized novel and the short story. Perhaps for sheer ability as a taleteller it was in the novelette that he chiefly distinguished himself.

In addition to this accomplishment in fiction, prolific as it was, he wrote an almost equal number of volumes of nonfictional prose. These include a number of travel books, which furnish a significant background to his fictions; three volumes of autobiography, remarkable for their attempt to trace the history of an imagination; more than a dozen books of criticism, covering the theater and painting as well as the craft of fiction; and several plays, of interest because of his application of the dramatic method to his later novels. Since his death there have also been published numerous volumes of his letters and his invaluable literary *Notebooks*. (If one added to these the fifty or more books that have been written about James, he would

3

have a small library.) His was indeed an indefatigable pen. Many of these miscellaneous writings have intrinsic value. All told, they add to the stature of his achievement and aid us in understanding it. This is a formidable task. James will never have a wide popular following, even in the appreciative reading of the novels and tales alone. But their very "difficulty" presents a challenge to serious students, and this is enhanced by the key role he played in the developing tradition of the novel. Though he never wrote a systematic body of criticism, his voluminous commentary on techniques makes him a pervasive force in all discussions of literary theory, quite in addition to his influence on the modern craft of fiction.

To survey the whole of Henry James's work, and generalize about it, is not easy. He had several styles and experimented in numerous genres, many of them overlapping. But for convenience his career may be divided into three stages. First came his early period, when he discovered the international theme and exploited it in a succession of books that reached their peak in *The Portrait of a Lady* (1881). Then followed the middle years, as he turned away from the subject of the American in Europe and explored many new themes and techniques, ending in his attempt to write for the stage during the 1890's. Finally, as he pulled himself out of this error with a renewed dedication to the art of fiction, there gradually emerged his famous "later manner," culminating in the powerful group of novels completed in his sixtieth year. These periods should not be thought of as rigid boundaries but as signposts along the path of his development through a life of extraordinary achievement.

The fifteen years of his writing career from 1865 until his first masterpiece can be thought of as a kind of apprenticeship. It was nearly as long as that of Hawthorne, who devoted twenty years to short fictions before producing *The Scarlet Letter*. But James experimented much more widely from story to novel length during his trial years. Hawthorne was his first master and his one link with the American tradition in fiction. Beginning his career just after the older novelist's death, James followed him not only in time but in his devotion to two important matters of theme and technique. Both writers, being concerned with inner values, place their emphasis on the effects of action rather than on the events of an outward plot. As a result, the focus of reader interest is shifted away from who-does-what-and-to-whom to the characters' unfolding awareness of who they are and where they stand in relation to their world. Secondly, both of them rely on the minimum of realism, just enough to create the illusion of actual life and make the reader believe in their fables. Hawthorne made many efforts to define his method for carrying out this intention. Most characteristic is his description of the ideal locale for his fictions:

A neutral territory, somewhere between the real world and fairy land, where the Actual and the Imaginary may meet, and each embue itself with the other, . . . a theatre, a little removed from the highway of ordinary travel, where the creatures of his brain may play their phantasmagorical antics, [with just] the faintest possible counterfeit of real life.

James, anxious to avoid what he felt was a major limitation in Hawthorne's "romances," sought his effects through technique rather than by mere choice of setting. He could only suggest how it worked through an elaborated conceit:

The balloon of experience is in fact of course tied to the earth, and under that necessity we swing, thanks to a rope of remarkable length, in the more or less commodious car of the imagination; but it is by that rope we know where we are, and from the moment that cable is cut we are at large and unrelated: we only swing apart from the globe—though remaining as exhilarated, naturally, as we like, especially when all goes well. The art of the romancer is, "for the fun of it," insidiously to cut the cable, cut it without our detecting him.

This was written as a preface to one of his early novels, *The American*. He felt, late in life, that the experience dealt with there had been a little too "liberated . . . from the conditions that we know usually attach to it." More precisely, he had cut the cable "too rashly" and so hurt the illusion of reality he had intended to create. Surveying now the long span of his career, he could indicate his gradual development of a more complex technique. First he mused on the difference between two opposite kinds of fiction: "By what art or mystery, what craft of selection, omission or commission, does a given picture of life appear to us to surround its theme, its figures and images, with the air of romance, while another picture close beside it may affect us as steeping the whole matter in the element of reality?" Instead of answering this question, he implied his own refusal to plump for either school by his definition of the ideal solution to this dilemma. The artist "of largest responding imagination before the human scene," like Balzac, "commits himself in both directions" at once.

In another late preface, to his very first novel (*Roderick Hudson*), he admitted that as a beginner he was "nestled, technically, in those days, and with yearning, in the great shadow of Balzac; his august example . . . towered for me over the scene." But James soon became aware "how easily his high practice might be delusive for my case." His own final development was as much away from Balzac as it was away from Hawthorne. Like the latter, it is true, he wanted to be freed from the necessity of a close and systematic representation of the actual world. But Hawthorne's concept of romance—as something that could be achieved by placing the scene in the far away, the long ago, or some strange corner of contemporary America—had led him into fantasy and allegory. Similarly his idea of evil, though an improvement over that of the Transcendentalists, suggested that he was too far removed from actual experience. These faults in his American predecessor James felt as deadly to what his own fictions were aimed at catching: the very quality of life in the modern world. So when he left for Europe in 1875, he was breaking from Hawthorne and the past in order to see what he could learn from the new French realists.

In Paris he could not only read the works of a brilliant group of living novelists but participate in their discussions of fictional theory. He still admired Balzac's colossal program to be the historian of an age—the most exhaustive documentation of human nature since Shakespeare, he admitted —but the dead end it led to was illustrated by his most radical young disciple. Zola's formula for the novel as a *tranche de vie* (slice of life) was a logical extension of the Balzacian method. But James had no difficulty in rejecting this as diametrically opposed to his own bent, though it became such a powerful influence over a whole generation of writers, he was still attacking it, as the "novel of saturation," at the close of his life.

Another disciple of Balzac was not so easily disposed of. Flaubert seemed in one sense a pioneer in the very kind of fiction he admired, what he was to champion to the end as the "novel of selection." There was much for the young American to learn from his doctrine of *le mot juste* and his dramatic compactness. More importantly, *Madame Bovary* proved his capacity for provoking serious thought while seemingly concerned only with the surface spectacle of life. James could not deny that this was a triumph for the school of realism, even while he felt that the book suffered from the same disease as other works of the French group. To him the French were superficial in spiritual insight, and they failed to write of people who were morally interesting. His turn against them, in the last analysis, was a matter of temperament as much as of disagreement about artistic method. He fell back with some comfort on the British author George Eliot, whose works he had read from the beginning, as proof that one could be a novelist and a moral philosopher at the same time. But she had disturbing faults as a craftsman, and James was already committed to technique as the path of his true development. Turgenev, the expatriate Russian novelist, proved the chief affirmative influence during this year in Paris. James mediated between the two extremes, combining the precision of the French with the humanity of Eliot.

I

James' first residence abroad for the purposes of his art, 1875-1876, brought to a head the really experimental period of his apprenticeship. By then he had learned what he could from his old and new masters as to method and theme, and he had completed his first successful novel, *The American*. It shows some influences of them all but chiefly that of Turgenev, an acute observer of life who was also a poet with sympathetic understanding of morally interesting characters. From him he had learned how to make the germ of his story not a plot but the development of a protagonist, in this instance one who though overwhelmed by external adversity is at the same time ennobled by it. This principle of development by unfolding awareness, culminating in self-knowledge, became a basic Jamesian method. But this novel was in no sense imitative, for he had also learned how to break from his models and strike out in his own way. Almost from the beginning he had glimpsed a theme that was to become central to much of his writing, the American character in relation to the mores of Europe. Though his predecessors had touched upon it from the time of Irving, no American author of fiction was so well qualified as Henry James, in temperament and experience, to bring out its full significance. Born to wealth, he had an international education that gave him the outlook of a cosmopolitan from an early age. He had already spent nearly ten years of his life in Europe, studying and traveling, when at the age of thirty-three he decided to make his permanent residence there. Of the dozen volumes of novels and stories published during his apprentice years, the great majority reflected this interest in the international theme. With *The American*, fruit of his Paris year, he first hit his stride and began to make a name for himself as a novelist of originality.

This is the story of an American businessman who, having retired with a fortune in middle life, goes to Europe to broaden his horizon and incidentally to pick the finest flower of French womanhood for his wife. The fictional mode James chose for embodying this leaned away from realism toward the romance, but he had not yet mastered this technique sufficiently to make it his own. The fault he noted in his later preface, that of cutting too rashly the cable anchoring him to reality, did not lead him into fantasy and allegory like Hawthorne, so much as into farce and melodrama. It is true that the comic spirit plays brightly enough over the novel as a whole, however, as reflected in the title and the names of the characters.

Christopher Newman is a kind of inverted Columbus, one of the nouveaux riches setting sail from America to discover the Old World. The natives he finds in that unknown land are the very opposite of savage Indians —aristocrats who are not only supersophisticated but decadent. They are typified by the hero's antagonists, the noble family of the lady he wants to marry, the Bellegardes. The name can be freely translated as "fine castle," *garde* being the inner fortress of their exclusiveness to which they have withdrawn. It is Newman who is the primitive, and his explorations in this highly civilized world provide the basis of much good comedy. But his mounting gaucheries as he makes more intimate contacts with such a refined society tend to burlesque, so that the reader finds it increasingly hard to take him seriously. Even more damaging to credibility is the author's resort to melodrama in order to contrast the evil of his European villains with the innocence of his American hero. This reaches its climax in the latter's discovery of a lurid murder in the secret past of the Bellegardes and

his noble decision not to use his weapon of exposure, because it would reduce him to their level of baseness. So the attempt at a tragic ending is
undermined by melodrama.

These technical flaws of overdoing, of cutting his romance loose from
its ties with a credible world, are partly a result of the misdirection of
theme. All of Newman's European "education" is used to illustrate the differences between two cultures, rather than the other way round, so that he
never really gets educated, never changes inside. He just becomes more and
more aware of the differences between France and America, and as the
various aspects meet his eye the total picture is filled out. Because of this
sociological emphasis the contrast is painted in strokes too broad to be
convincing: innocence and experience, naive simplicity and formal complexity, a new culture that is thin but moral set against an old one that is
rich in art and history but corrupt at heart. Since there is no real development such as to make possible any final self-recognition on Newman's part,
the reader's interest is always centered on the contrasts for their own sake.
And the accumulation of blacks and whites does tend to make all the characters figures in an allegory. Such strictures against a novel that is a good
one on many scores are justified only when judged by the high standards of
excellence to which James later brought his fictional treatment of the international theme.

This development began in a seemingly trivial way, his stories about the
American girl. But gradually he discovered the great opportunities offered
by this subject previously neglected in fiction. He found her many-sided,
with depths as well as surfaces—desires and repressions, curiosity and frankness, audacity and innocence—and in Europe all these qualities were
brought into high relief. In a series of short novels, culminating in the popular success of *Daisy Miller*, he explored her possibilities as an embodiment
of the international theme, but the focus was still sociological. His first artistic success came in *The Portrait of a Lady* with a shift of emphasis to
the "education" of his American heroine through the experience of Europe, the cultural contrast becoming merely the means to this end. This
meant turning from the argument of a thesis to the creation of characters,
the proper business of fiction. He now had a valid and highly original
theme, and needed only an adequate method for rendering it through art
rather than stating it by exposition.

Over the years he was to develop many effective techniques for this:
structure by dramatic scenes, manipulating the point of view, making full
use of the poetic resources of language, imagery, and symbolism. His
unique discovery was the method of "myth" for catching the total impact
of Europe on American character by weaving a fictional fabric of three
strands. Basic to all was the observed reality of place and people, recorded
with ever-greater precision as his own knowledge of Europe expanded.
Overlaying this and complicating the action were the various American

preconceptions of Europe, assigned to his characters with increasing subtlety of discrimination. In his critical commentary he always distinguished these two as Europe and "Europe," commenting in a letter as early as 1872: "It's a complex fate, being an American, and one of the responsibilities it entails is fighting against a superstitious valuation of Europe." Finally, there was James's own deliberately invented fable of Europe, which includes the other two and adds to the novel's representational powers the suggestiveness of poetry. *The Portrait of a Lady* marks the beginning of this achievement.

Isabel Archer, a young lady with a high potential for life, is literally launched on her career by the touch of a magic wand. She is rescued from a bare environment in Albany, New York, by a wealthy aunt who translates her to England, where she can be brought out into a world of richer opportunities. What might have been just a visit is prolonged indefinitely when a substantial portion of the Touchett fortune is settled on her so that, as her cousin Ralph puts it, she may "soar." Since she is extraordinarily attractive, and now well endowed in a material as well as a personal sense, one logical goal of her career would be a marriage equal to her possibilities. So her experience of Europe is partly structured around a series of courtships that take us well into the second half of the novel before reaching their climax, or anticlimax, in a decision to marry. But Isabel, as a young lady of intelligence and sensibility, has a broader view of her future. She wants not only marriage but education. She wants to absorb the beauty and knowledge that Europe has to offer: its art treasures, its storied past, its traditions, cities, and institutions, as well as its people and way of living. So another part of her experience consists of travel and study, as she seeks to understand a civilization that turns out to be far more dazzling than her fondest dreams.

As she makes her pilgrimage through England, France, and Italy all of this is presented with a masterly hand on the external level, for James's knowledge of the Old World was becoming increasingly better since his decision five years before to make it his permanent residence. The "great lighted scene" of Europe and its richly complex past are opened up to her eyes, through which readers also are enabled to see. As for the people, their manners and morals, he wisely limited himself to a minimum of European characters, doing only one at full length and that one an Englishman, her first suitor, Lord Warburton. James knew how hard it was for an American novelist, however cosmopolitan, to have a profound understanding of foreigners whose culture was as different from his own as their language. So Isabel gains experience of the Continent through her relations not with the French and Italians but with American expatriates who have lived abroad long enough to become almost indistinguishable from the natives of their adopted country. Madame Merle, for example, represents to her the combination of *femme du monde* and lady she feels could flower only in some such society as that of France. More importantly, Osmond, the suitor she finally marries, stands for that dedication to beauty and knowledge she associates with the genius of Italy. Even her impressions of life and character in England come largely through her relatives, the Touchetts, who have sunk their roots deep in that country. Yet all of these are transplanted Americans. They are, it is true, surrounded by minor figures—French, Italian, and British natives—who help to fill out her picture of Europe.

The great question is, "How much of all this does Isabel Archer really understand?" Since the focus of the novel is not sociological, it is not so much a question of what she learns about European civilization through these characters, but the other way round. How do her opinions of Europe influence her understanding of the people who form her intimate circle and shape her destiny? She and the other Americans all have attitudes and preconceptions about Europe that vary widely from one another and are clearly only approximations to the truth. For instance, the Old World is so foreign to all the values cherished by her American suitor, Goodwood, that he has no interest in understanding it and desires only to rescue her and bring her back home. Isabel's journalist friend, Miss Stackpole, finds Europe so backward and benighted that she brashly undertakes to bring it up to date and even reform it. Her husband, Gilbert Osmond, the most ostensibly Europeanized of them all, reflects its forms rather than its spirit, as she gradually comes to realize—the latter being better understood by her unassuming cousin Ralph Touchett. Isabel's own notions about Europe differ from all of these. She begins with high romantic expectations that color everything she sees and every person she meets. This precipitates most of her actions and leads to the painful complications of her life. Her final penetration to the realities beneath this idealized view constitutes her real education.

Because of Isabel's temperament and limited experience of the world, her native intelligence proves inadequate to her needs, supported though it is by a strong moral and aesthetic sense. Unable to discriminate between appearance and reality, she is actually the victim of events that happen to her even while she thinks she is making choices. In the sense that she is never really at the helm she is a passive rather than an active character, and James had the problem of how to make such a "weak" heroine the center of his novel. He solved this by treating all the others only in their relations to her—for she is endowed with great personal magnetism—and so avoided the danger of some stronger character stealing the show. But there was still the problem of how to make her the center of consciousness when there was so much she was unable to understand. He solved this by frankly "going outside," by offering insights into characters and events that are beyond her vision, even while keeping up the illusion that all is seen through her point of view.

There are many clues that enable the reader to see behind and through her partial or idealized understanding of the world around her. One of the most effective of these is an elaborate system of imagery—the objects used by her friends when characterizing one another in their conversations with Isabel, and occasionally symbols offered unobtrusively by the author himself. For example, her uncle is pictured as an old man contentedly drinking his tea (that is, what life has brewed for him) from "an unusually large cup, of a different pattern from the rest of the set and painted in brilliant colors." Madame Merle is compared to a rare and fine piece of porcelain, but with a crack in it. Her aunt is described as like one of the Medici in a fresco by Ghirlandaio; her newspaper friend, Miss Stackpole, appears to her cousin "as crisp and new and comprehensive as a first issue before the folding" and with "no misprints." Ralph, showing Isabel through his gallery, likens himself to the gentleman in a Watteau painting who is leaning against the statue of a nymph and playing his guitar to the ladies, "an ideal occupation." Her husband, on the other hand, is first shown with his latest water color, correct in technique but without warmth; at the end, making a faultless copy of an antique coin. Alert readers will be able to turn up a wealth of such suggestive images. Most of this is as available to Isabel as to them, but we wonder how much it reveals to her of the characters so symbolized.

The most elaborate series is applied to Isabel herself by friends as they try to characterize what she means to them, culminating in the scene where she appears to a young admirer, framed in the gilded doorway of her salon, as the very "picture of a gracious lady." But her devoted cousin knows this is a false portrait behind which she hides her suffering, the face of her true portrait being turned to the wall. On a larger scale are the images of four important houses: the bare but unpretentious Archer home back in Albany; the Touchett's fine old English country house, "Gardencourt"; Osmond's villa near Florence, like a miniature museum of the art and history of Italy; the grand Roman palace, "Rocanera," where the travesty of Isabel's married life is acted out. All are described in great detail, and two of them undergo considerable change in the developing perspective through which the heroine and the reader see them. They come to symbolize not only the characters who live in them and the events that take place there but the several stages of Isabel's education, thus forming the true structural pattern of the novel.

Three fourths the way through the book the real import of all she has been learning comes clear to her in a climactic scene, a long midnight vigil in which she reviews the high hopes and the tragic outcome of her life. It is in keeping with the novel's basic techniques that now at last understanding comes to her also through imagery, much of it being inversions of the same images she had failed to grasp the meaning of earlier. This great scene opens a door for the reader, too, into the novel's full significance. In his preface to *The Portrait of a Lady,* written a quarter century later, the old wizard of fictional skills complains that his early masterpiece is defective in proportioning, that he gave so much space to the beginning of her career he had to foreshorten mercilessly at the end. It is true that this novel lacks the architectonic symmetry of such late masterpieces as *The Ambassadors.* But it was in working his way out of this very dilemma that James hit upon the brilliant device of the midnight vigil, one short chapter in which the four years of Isabel's ordeal by marriage are evoked in a symbolic vision instead of having to be spelled out in discursive narrative. This not only brings his long story into dramatic focus, but justifies the freedom he allowed himself in elaborating her initiation into Europe during the first half of the book.

Recalling how he created *The Portrait,* Henry James said that, after conceiving the character of his heroine, he set her on her feet and asked himself, "What will she *do?*" The greater part of the novel, devoted to the unfolding before her eyes of all that England, France, and Italy seemed to offer during these early months, is given over to answering this question. But it is more in terms of what her European experience did to her (what *she* actually did being handled in flashbacks), and the last part is chiefly concerned with the full revelation to her of the meaning of this experience. In spite of the lack of emphasis on action she comes alive as few figures in fiction do, and she holds the center of the reader's interest, as well as of the other characters, by her freshness and magnetic charm. This answers the only other criticism that has been made of *The Portrait of a Lady,* raised by the author himself: the story is "unfinished," he admits, because he does not see the heroine through to the end of her situation. But by the conclusion of the novel the reader shares so completely Isabel's hard won self-knowledge that he knows what she will do because he knows what she is. She will go back to a life of duty, because her main purpose in acquiring an "education" has been to do some good in the world. So we can follow her future career in our imagination on beyond the last page. On this point James himself expressed the novelist's problem and its solution succinctly. "The *whole* of anything is never told; you can only take what groups together," he once said. "Really, universally, relations stop nowhere, and the exquisite problem of the artist is eternally but to draw, by a geometry of his own, the circle within which they shall happily appear to do so." This is achieved brilliantly in his portrait of Isabel Archer, whose education if not her life was brought full circle.

The Portrait of a Lady enjoyed the advantage of being the first major book that James wrote. It has the spontaneity that is possible only when an author lets himself go for the first time, unaware of his powers. In half-a-dozen later novels, and numerous shorter fictions, he equaled or surpassed this one in technical skill, though none of them could recapture its freshness. Always looming before him, with a challenge to match its excellence, was this early masterpiece. Yet this novel, published in 1881, was not only the culmination of fifteen years of dedicated apprenticeship to the art of fiction but the first promise of a great career to come.

II

It is a mistake to think of the international theme as being the whole of James—a widespread misconception—for it is absent from fully half of his fictions. This is particularly true of his middle period, when he turned aside to many other topics and even different kinds of writing. During the fifteen years following *The Portrait* a flood of fictions continued to come from his pen, of increasing subtlety of theme and complexity of handling. ("The Art of Fiction," 1884, shows his growing concern with critical theory too.) This was the period of his greatest experimentation in the novelette, and it ended with his attempt to write plays. During this time he also published four novels. The two best of them appeared in 1886, one laid entirely in America and the other in Europe, with no international cast of characters.

The Bostonians, a satire on New England reformers, is a return not only to his native country in subject matter but to his American master. In *The Blithedale Romance*, it is true, Hawthorne had been only mildly satirical of an earlier reform movement, the experiment in communal living at Brook Farm. But at the end of the century James found that the old high-minded radicalism of Boston had degenerated into grotesque comedy. The leading agitator for women's rights there, a bluestocking spinster, he astutely conceived as being motivated by hatred of the other sex—in a word, incipient Lesbianism. This is dramatized in her possessive sponsorship of a beautiful young girl with a prodigious gift for public speaking, Verena Tarrant. But the heroine is also, in a theatrical way, the very embodiment of feminine charm. As the opposition to this reform movement, and the unnatural friendship at its center, he chose a hero who was reactionary in social doctrine but at the same time chivalric toward women, a Southern gentleman named Basil Ransom. So the outward plot is an amusing tug of war for the hand of Verena between the two rivals—one a man, the other a woman. But James was also trying to write a social history in the Dickensian sense, which is a key to the novel's defective structure. For he became so engrossed with his hero's conservative principles for their own sake that he lost sight of him as a romantic champion of the sentiment of sex. The divided character of Ransom, as polemicist and as advocate of love and beauty, is part of the history of James's struggles with male characterizations.

In the earlier fictions there had been a temptation to divide them too neatly into categories, the rationalists and the men of imagination. The struggle continues into his middle period, but in the two most successful novels of the 1880's he solves the problem largely by a skillful use of point of view. In *The Portrait of a Lady* the cynical realist and the man of intuition are seen only through the consciousness of Isabel Archer. They are given a saving ambiguity by her romantic vision, which persists through half the book in seeing them in reverse, Osmond as the embodiment of art and Touchett as merely the invalid son of a successful banker. The final meaning of her pilgrimage from innocence to experience is spelled out in terms of her gradual recognition of their true nature.

The Princess Casamassima, published in the same year as *The Bostonians*, is an even more interesting treatment of a similar problem. For here the viewing consciousness, one of James's most convincing male characters, is literally split between two ways of life by his ambiguous heritage. The bastard son of an English lord and a French prostitute, Hyacinth Robinson is an abandoned waif drudging away as a bookbinder in the slums of London, alienated from any meaningful existence. He is excluded from one world by his illegitimacy and from the other by his tastes. Yet he is equally drawn to art as the chief glory of a hierarchical civilization and to the threatening revolution against that order. The logic of his depressed position makes him cast his lost with the latter. But since he has no capacity for ideologies, that potential half of him is gradually objectified in his alter ego, Paul Muniment, the chief London conspirator. Pre-eminently a man of imagination, Hyacinth has a brief flowering in art appreciation. But even this is snatched away from him by his economic and social situation, just as his actual tragedy is brought on by his entanglement in the anarchist movement. This exploration of the two poles of English life, James's fullest experiment in the manner of Balzac, is embodied in a highly original fictional mode—what he came to call the "fable." The fusion of sociology and fairy tale is entirely successful here, though it was not so in his American comedy, *The Bostonians*.

During his middle period James not only tried out new directions in the full-scale novel but made even more experiments in the long story or short novel, what he called "the beautiful and blest *nouvelle*." Ranging from about fifty to a hundred and fifty pages, it allowed space for considerable development and at the same time was short enough to demand compactness. This genre has not had many American practitioners, Melville being the main exception. But it offered a special challenge to James's talents, and he brought it to a degree of perfection that can be claimed for only a half dozen of his longer works. He had written several in his early period, and was to launch his major phase with a trial run of a few more. But during his middle years he produced the largest number of novelettes. It is by three of the best of these, dating from 1888 to 1898, that he is represented here. All of them deal with the problem of evil, varying degrees and kinds of it. As a writer of fiction James had been necessarily concerned with conduct, with morals as well as manners, but so far evil had not been the main theme of his novels. It is presented somewhat extensively in the aristocratic Bellegardes of *The American*, but their villainy seems contrived. Osmond in *The Portrait of a Lady* is a villain of greater complexity but still seen from the outside, and he serves chiefly as a foil to the good characters. It was not until the last great period that he placed evil at the center of full-scale novels, in the adulterous pair of *The Wings of a Dove* and *The Golden Bowl*, both of whom being principal characters show an inside view of evil at work in human lives sufficiently ambivalent to be convincing. Meantime, the novelette offered an opportunity for exploration of the theme.

Much of the evil in James's world is related to egotism in one form or the other. His bad and good characters can be separated into the categories of "exploiters" and "appreciators." The former is the person who consistently uses others for his own purposes, resorting to any thing that will aid his drive to self-aggrandizement, all the way from chicanery to ruthless force. The latter appreciates other people for their own worth, wants to enjoy them and help them fulfill themselves, and so expands his own realization of life's possibilities at the same time. The protagonist of *The Aspern Papers* is an exploiter of a special modern breed, one who invades the privacy of people's lives and uses it as grist for his own mill. It is significant that he is made a journalist, James's archetype of the man who has no qualms about prying. And since this also qualifies him as an astute observer and reporter it makes him an ideal narrator.

Because the story is concerned with ferreting out the lost letters of a handsome poet to his mistress, whose charms he celebrated in love lyrics, literary students will immediately see the parallel to Byron. This is clinched by setting the search in Venice, where the dashing romantic began his famous affair with the Countess Guiccioli (another of his mistresses having been the American Jane Clairemont). If this is to be all, and the poet is long dead, it promises to be just an exciting adventure that one could brand at worst as amoral. Even when the narrator-researcher confesses, "Hypocrisy, duplicity, . . . there's no baseness I wouldn't commit for Jeffrey Aspern's sake," one puts it down as part of the necessary ruthlessness of the historian in search of truth. The candor with which the hero admits these things throws one off guard at first. But the attentive reader who follows his reiterations of necessity as they are patterned with his deepening plunge into guile will begin to suspect that James is raising a moral issue. What is the relation of biography to art, of the private to the public aspects of an artist's career? Does the narrator genuinely love the poetry of Aspern, or is he hoping to win fame from an exposé of his life?

During the first half of the story his egotism takes chiefly the inoffensive form of pride in his ingenuity at playing an intricate game. Even when it becomes fully apparent that he must wrest the letters from the aging mistress against her will, this is mitigated by her proving a wily antagonist. She

is as unscrupulous in her desire to take advantage of him as he is to trick
her and get the precious letters. One follows their machinations as he
would watch a high form of sport. And since the game is one involving literary spoils, other interesting speculations are raised. Do the letters conceal
a sordid love affair behind the idealized poems? Is that "horrible green
shade" she wears over her eyes a mask to cover some evil aspect of her
that was incipiently there when she was the beloved young mistress? (Aspern was hardly one to idolize a saint.)

The truly evil aspect of the narrator emerges only in his relations with
the niece. Her involvement complicates not only the plot but the moral
problem. For all her naive trust and growing attachment to him, she must
be exploited as ruthlessly as the sarcastic and cunning old aunt. Even
though it is her innocence that keeps him from getting the letters in the
end, he is not comforted by her gift of Aspern's miniature. His last words
on the matter, years later, sum up his moral state: "When I look at it, I
can scarcely bear my loss—I mean of the precious papers." How Miss Tina
might bear her loss, what he had done to her, never penetrated his egotistic
shell. Yet he is not painted as a simple villain. There is sufficient ambivalence in his character to make him credible, as he wavers between self-
justification for his conduct and the lashings of conscience for going too
far. James also makes something of a comedy of the conflict between privacy and publicity by raising them to such extremes, the narrator as the epitome of the exploiting journalist, the two old ladies in their fantastic seclusion. But how is he other than a subtle modern embodiment of evil if he
has no qualms in sacrificing their lives to make his book?

In *The Pupil* evil goes underground, so to speak. That is, its manifestations are more in a way of being than a way of doing, its origins instinc-
tual rather than intellectual. This makes it even more horrible by suggesting that evil may be innate as well as contrived by man's ingenuity. But on
the surface the Moreens seem all kindness and confusion. At first the reader
feels more amusement than censure at their harum-scarum behavior. Even
when they fail to pay the tutor his salary, one may tend to see it as a result,
not of malice, but of the happy-go-lucky existence of people who simply
have never grown up. It is easy enough to see that they are vulgar beneath
their veneer of sophistication, that they are irresponsible, even unsavory
in their conduct. On the level of comedy they simply enact what their
name means: "moreen" is a sham fabric used for decorative purposes, em-
bossed on the surface but coarse stuff underneath. Only gradually does Pemberton himself come to the conclusion that they were "adventurers not
merely because they didn't pay their debts, because they lived on society,
but because their whole view of life, dim and confused and instinctive,
. . . was speculative and rapacious and mean." The reader becomes convinced of the correctness of this description as he sees them successively
revealed in their nakedness—without dignity, without integrity, even with-

out shame. One critic goes so far as to find them subconsciously motivated by "a great destructive force impelling them toward evil." His diagnosis of what makes people vulnerable to such depravity is couched in Jamesian language: "Where there is no light of imagination, no means of creative self-expression, life becomes a jungle in which blind animal impulses run their course." [1]

This is not an allegorical contest between devils and angels, however, and the characters are not lined up as pure blacks and whites. There is a comic pathos in the immorality of the Moreens, and the behavior of the forces of light has been called into question too by other critics. Did James want to suggest an abnormal attachment between tutor and pupil? Does Pemberton plant false hopes in Morgan's heart by planning a romantic escape from the family into a happy life of their own, then kill him in the end by refusing to take on the literal role of savior? Is the pupil offensively precocious in his feelings of superiority to his own parents; is the tutor just a prude in his puritanical revulsion against the Bohemianism of the Moreens? Instead of taking sides with one of these extreme interpretations, the reader will want to make his own. In any event, in addition to the entertainment provided by the antics of this family, and the compassion elicited by the two protagonists, *The Pupil* has enough ambiguity to provoke plenty of discussion as to its ultimate meaning. Even the title raises a question that is not easy to answer—"Who is the pupil?"—for in a way it is little Morgan who serves as Pemberton's tutor in their exploration of evil. In his preface the author says his method was that of "seeing 'through'—one thing through another . . . and still other things through *that*." One infers from this that no single character's view of the truth can be taken as final.

In these novelettes evil is represented on the level of manners and moral conduct. With *The Turn of the Screw* James took a deeper dive into the very nature of evil, almost in a theological sense, though not put in doctrinal terms. To do this without falling back on exposition, he needed a more complex form than the straight chronicle used in the other two. Instead of a discursive narrative spread out over several years, as in *The Pupil*, he tightened his span of action to a few months. Though he had previously used the protagonist as narrator to sharpen his focus in *The Aspern Papers*, he now took far more advantage of the retrospective view afforded by that device to achieve dramatic compactness. Still more effective, since he had a most remarkable story to tell, he objectified it by placing it in a frame, in fact, a triple frame. The author first removes himself in favor of a narrator, the "I" of the prologue. But that substitute merely introduces us to a circle of story tellers, one of whom, named Douglas, takes his turn. But he, instead of telling a story in his own right, reads one from an old manuscript. In the end what we get is the Governess's story, and even that was only

---

[1] See the entry under Walter Wright cited in Reading Suggestions. For the critics in the next paragraph, see *Seven Stories and Studies* (1961), ed. by Edward Stone.

written down by her years after the events it recounted had taken place.
All Douglas contributes is a testimonial to her character and a sketch of
her background. Brief as this is, it is of the utmost importance, since in
hearing a tale that is all but incredible one needs to know everything possible about the authority and trustworthiness of the teller.

Every word of these introductory pages must be weighed carefully. No
reader will miss the relevance of the setting in the opening sentence: each
of the stories that had held them "sufficiently breathless," around the fire,
was "gruesome, as, on Christmas eve in an old house, a strange tale should
essentially be." But only the alert will pay attention to the fact that the
particular ghost story comprising the final *Turn of the Screw* is not told
until four nights later, December 28. This happens to be the feast day com-
memorating the Slaughter of the Innocents. Though the Biblical analogy
is oblique, this too is an account of beautiful, almost angelic, children being destroyed by the forces of evil. (When the book was made into a play,
more than half a century afterwards, it was appropriately entitled "The
Innocents.") In his short prologue James has done much to provide an atmosphere that will make his readers accept the truth of an allegory of supernatural happenings. But he is careful to avoid the strict one-to-one correspondences expected in traditional allegories, opening out instead the
multiple meanings suggested by symbolism. At the drop of a word like evil
or ghosts one can expect controversy in a century of readers that have seen
violent fluctuations from orthodox belief to skepticism and back to a yearning after some viable, if secular, belief again. *The Turn of the Screw* has
raised a storm of controversy, and most of it has centered about the question, "Are the ghosts real?"

In an age of rationalism the answer is clearly "No," and there has been
a loud outcry against their existence led by an eminent critic, Edmund Wilson. (It is interesting to note that in the quarter century since his first pro-
nouncement he has changed his mind twice, in print.) If they are not real,
the explanation of these phenomena must be scientific: they are the hallucinations of a neurotic maiden lady, the Governess, who is suffering from
her suppressed love for the Master. The only further fuel needed to kindle
a modern fire is a strict Freudian reading. The opposition, led by another
fine critic, Robert Heilman, has asked a devastating question, "How then
does the housekeeper, a very matter-of-fact woman, identify the apparition
described by the Governess as a deceased former servant, Peter Quint,
whom she had never heard of?" Wilson's answer to this was that not only is
the "governess self-deceived but James is self-deceived about her." Then,
shifting back to his original position, he bolstered it by citing an article
suggesting that the Governess probably learned about Quint from village
gossip. (Anyone who wants to rewrite a great novel may do so: Ishmael went on another voyage, finally killed Moby-Dick, found Ahab in the
whale's belly—like Jonah—and the two of them returned to Nantucket and

became orthodox Calvinists.) The Freudian reading itself can be taken to any length. One can find impressive evidence, out of context, for a case of *pedophilia erotica* (erotic love for a child). The Governess persuades little Miles to call her "my dear," says his precocity makes him "as accessible" as an adult and that when left alone they are like "a shy young couple on their wedding journey," confesses in the end that he struck her as "a revelation of the possibilities of beautiful intercourse"—a loaded phrase.

Are the anti-Freudians equally out on a limb? There is plenty of evidence that the Governess is not neurotic, but does that mean the only alternative is to accept the ghosts as real? This has led to numerous interpretations of them as symbols, devices in a drama of salvation, and the like.[2] James certainly let himself go pretty far in the direction of allegory. The little girl is named Flora (flower) and the boy Miles (Latin for soldier). Thinking of them as the primal man and woman, one tends to see their world of Bly (Blythe?) as a kind of twilit Eden—their story begins in the lush fullness of early summer and ends in the blighted "fall." The housekeeper, who can see none of these superfine visitations, is named Mrs. Grose. The remote guardian of the children is called the Master and their present protecting angel simply the Governess, neither of them being otherwise named. But it would be unwise to push this suggestiveness further than the author did.

One can stop far short of reading the story as a religious allegory and still see everything as symbolic. For example, all may be interpreted as projections of the Governess's sensibility. She in one sense is the innocent, only twenty and from a sheltered background. Her translation from the parsonage to Bly seems like a fairy tale to her. She has a romantic view of life and a passionate love of youth, beauty, and goodness. The letter dismissing Miles from school, never specified, provides her first premonition of evil. Lacking any experience of what it is, she sees visions of what it may be. She knows that the "innocence" of all children will turn into the "experience" of adulthood, and the story is her drama of how this will work out for these two. Their youth will be replaced by old age, their beauty by ugliness, their goodness by evil—life by death. Both Flora and Miles and their corruptors can be thought of as embodiments of her apprehensions, and in a larger sense as faint symbols of the Christian belief in the dual nature of man.

The author himself dropped a pertinent hint in his Preface, written ten years later. He described his twofold problem as "the general proposition of our young woman's keeping crystalline her record of so many intense anomalies and obscurities—by which I don't of course mean her explanation of them, a different matter. . . . To knead [her] mystification thick, and yet strain the expression of it clear." Taking this as a clue, one critic

[2] Fifteen of the most interesting interpretations, including Wilson's and Heilman's, are collected in *A Casebook on the Turn of the Screw* (1960), ed. by Gerald Willen.

has made an interesting middle-of-the-road interpretation.[3] If the ghosts are explained away, he says, the story loses its horror; if the reader's uncertainty is clarified, it loses its mystery. Instead, James structured his novelette in a sequence of paired scenes so as to retain these very qualities. In the first of each pair the Governess represents an action, objectively and in detail, which results in horror; this scene is followed by another in which she gives her interpretation, subjective and challengeable, which produces mystification. Each group leads into a plan for coping with her problem that carries the narrative forward, all the way to the end where it stops abruptly with the presentation of Miles's ambiguous death. The best evidence of James's intentions may be found in the revisions he made when preparing the earlier text (here used) as part of the collected edition of his works. These alter the Governess's testimony from a report of things observed to one of things felt: "I perceived → I felt," "I now recollect → I now feel," "Mrs. Grose appeared to me → Mrs. Grose affected me," and so on. All his art is aimed at making readers accept her story as an honest and convincing record of her impressions. What really happened at Bly we will never know.

James was perfectly well aware of what he was about. The popular belief in spiritualism was at floodtide in the 1890's, and he was abreast of the most modern psychological theories about it. His brother William joined the Society for Psychical Research to combat it scientifically, becoming president in 1894. He prepared a "Census of Hallucinations" and wrote several papers for it, one of which the novelist read for the absent psychologist at a London meeting. The Archbishop of Canterbury, who provided the germ of his story as set down in the *Notebooks* for 1895, was also a member. James could have made his own ghost story as scientific as he wished, but he decided otherwise. "The mere modern 'psychical case,' washed clean of all queerness as by exposure to a flowing laboratory tap," he said in his preface, ". . . the new type clearly promised little, for the more it was respectably certified the less it seemed of a nature to rouse the dear old sacred terror."

Instead, he determined to write "a fairy-tale pure and simple, . . . an *amusette* to catch those not easily caught," whom he defined as the "disillusioned." Wanting to produce a drama of the potential terror lurking beneath the rational surface of life, he created his "prowling blighting presences" and "laid on them the dire duty of causing the situation to reek with the air of Evil." As an artist he knew that what is suggested has a far more powerful impact than what is specified. "Only make the reader's general vision of evil intense enough," he told himself, "and his own imagination . . . will supply him quite sufficiently with all the particulars." That his own vision was intense enough is amusingly put in the incident he re-

[3] See Donald Costello, "The Structure of *The Turn of the Screw*," *Modern Language Notes* (1959).

ported, when correcting the proofs of his own story in his own country house, that he was afraid to go upstairs to bed. Fifteen years later an English lady wrote him she had read *The Turn of the Screw* with mounting terror but without fully understanding what was happening. His reply placed the responsibility squarely on readers to make their own interpretation of the text: "My dear Mildred, no more do I. . . . As to understanding it, it just gleams and glooms."

III

The audience for Henry James's novels and tales had dropped to a minimum in the early nineties. When he turned his talents to the theater, he met with even more disastrous results. At the première of his one play to reach the stage, in January 1895, he was subjected to the mortifying experience of jeers and catcalls from the gallery when ill-advised friends called for the author at the end of a dismal performance. William James, in diagnosing his brother's failure as a playwright, warned him that he had drifted so far from the vital facts of human character he could not project dramatic tensions any longer. James was past fifty, his life seemed empty, and his career finished. The resolution with which he determined to begin all over again as a novelist was nothing short of heroic, and his rededication to art unique in literary history. He recorded it in his *Notebooks* during the weeks just following his fiasco in the theater:

I take up my *own* old pen again—the pen of all my old unforgettable efforts and sacred struggles. To myself—today—I need say no more. Large and full and high the future still opens. It is now indeed that I may do the work of my life. And I will. . . . I have my head, thank God, full of visions. One has never too many—one has never enough. Ah, just to let one's self go—at last: to surrender one's self to what through all the long years one has (quite heroically, I think) hoped for and waited for— . . . large and confident action—splendid and supreme creation.

In the ensuing months he filled his *Notebooks* with new plans and projects, including the germs of some of his greatest. But at first he held enthusiasm in check and took up his fictional pen as cautiously as if he were an apprentice, instead of the old master.

The first products of his major phase as an author were three remarkable novels that appeared between 1897 and 1899. In *The Spoils of Poynton* he took up a theme similar to the one used in *The Aspern Papers*, the devious intrigues and questionable conduct people can be led into by the desire to gain possession of valuable old treasures, but he made a technical triumph out of it by giving it the compactness of a drama. *What Maisie Knew* was a kind of sequel to *The Turn of the Screw*, the gradual discovery of evil in the adult world by a highly perceptive child, now extended to novel length. *The Awkward Age* was a study of morals and manners in a truly sophisticated society, as compared with the superficial one of *The Pupil*, but written "straight as a play," almost exclusively in dialogue. With these and other experiments he had not only got his hand in again but added many new techniques to an already well-stocked arsenal. He was now ready to let go. During the next five years he was working almost simultaneously on three full-scale novels, generally reckoned as the peak of his achievement. There are partisans to claim each as his very best. Certainly *The Wings of the Dove* is his one entirely satisfactory handling of passionate love between man and woman, as well as a powerful novel on many other scores. And *The Golden Bowl* is without peer as an example of his extraordinary virtuosity in maneuvering language and imagery. Out of an embarrassment of riches *The Ambassadors* is chosen here, since it marks the culmination of many themes and techniques previously discussed in this introduction.

All these late masterpieces return to the international contrast but with a notable difference, which can best be illustrated by the story of Lambert Strether. (There is an international cast of characters in two of the novelettes just discussed, but not an international theme.) The shift of emphasis from a sociological to a humanistic significance, first begun in *The Portrait of a Lady*, has been brought to fullest fruition by James's choice of a protagonist. For Strether can think and articulate, as well as see and feel, so that he makes a far more effective center of consciousness than Isabel Archer. The contrast between America and Europe is merely the metaphor that illustrates his education. His dawning awareness of the difference between what his life has been under American limitations and what it could have been under European freedoms and opportunities constitutes his growth in self-knowledge. The stages of his change are marked by his increasing ability to see, understand, and evaluate the civilization of Europe. And since he is a man of intelligence and sensitivity, its differences from America are presented with great subtlety, not lined up as good and bad.

For Strether is a man with two lives, one actual and the other potential, so that he appreciates the values of both worlds. The dramatic possibilities of the man divided against himself had led James to a number of experiments, notably in *The Bostonians* and *The Princess Casamassima*. But his real triumph in this kind came with *The Ambassadors*. The hero is not so much a man torn between two natures as one who develops from a false notion of himself to a full realization of his true nature. Until the age of fifty-five almost the whole of his life in America had been dictated by the conviction that he was a rational and practical man of business, the successful editor of a magazine. At that point his "ambassadorial" mission to Paris, for which he was chosen because of these supposed qualifications, gradually reveals to him that his basic trait is a heightened sensitivity to the promises of life, which he has buried by suppressing his imagination. Through a masterful handling of point of view there is unfolded to the reader layer by

layer an evaluation of this complex character that James, free at last of ambivalence himself, has firmly in control all the time.

Strether's role in the novel gives him exactly the right degree of involvement in the action, and detachment from it, to make him the ideal narrator. He is sent over by Mrs. Newsome, the wealthy patron of his magazine,
to fetch home her son Chad, whom she suspects of wasting his substance
in Paris—convinced he is in the clutches of some wicked French woman.
Strether is to observe all, then initiate the action of others. If he is successful in bringing Chad back to his duty as head of the family business, there
will be something in it for the ambassador too, the hand and fortune of
Mrs. Newsome. In this way he is quite personally involved in the outcome of the plot, removed though he is from taking any active part in it.
But the way in which Strether really becomes related to what goes on in
The Ambassadors is quite different from this and much more important. It
is rendered in terms of what he sees as an observer. Immediately upon his
arrival, the theme of Europe is sounded for him by his sight of an ancient
English town with intricate winding streets and unexpected vistas. He
senses that his official visit may also offer him something in the way of a
private adventure, extending the impressions of an all too brief visit there
as a young man long ago.

The development of Strether's personal adventure is strictly scenic, but
this is no travelogue. The scenes that bring him an understanding of his
own life are dramatically related to the outward plot. The germ of the novel
was an anecdote James heard about his fellow author Howells, who on being recalled to America from a visit to Paris in 1895 said to a compatriot:
"Oh, you are young, you are young—be glad of it: be glad of it and live.
Live all you can: it's a mistake not to." It was not until several years later
that he could begin writing his story, when he finally visualized the proper
setting for such a declaration: a charming old garden in the Faubourg St.
Germain, the ancient quarter of high society in Paris. The dramatic center
of the novel, both as a turning point in the plot and in the narrator's education, is Strether's similar declaration in just such a garden. Here he has
been dazzled by a vision of the world of fashion and art in the French capital, only to realize that the possibility for that kind of life had passed him
by. But it has been daily sustenance for Chad Newsome. He can only envy
the young man's attachment to Mme de Vionnet's daughter and wish that
his own fate had thrown him sooner in relation with the even more charming mother. As the many-faceted diamond of Paris is flashed before his
eyes, its brilliant surfaces suggesting hidden depths beneath, he sees simultaneously what he has missed and what the future holds for Chad. But the
garden scene is not a climax. It is a revelation of the possibilities of life
lived to the full.

Leading up to this center and building beyond it to ever-higher climaxes, James unveils scene after revealing scene. Two matching ones will illustrate the method. In his initiation into Paris Strether looks up at the façade of Chad's apartment in a neighborhood of quiet elegance and realizes how wrong have been the preconceptions of crude dissipation in some Bohemian garret. In such an atmosphere the young American can only be getting an education in the refinements of living. The narrator's own education reaches a high point later in the story when he dines alone with Mme de Vionnet at a Seine-side café, the light and color of an Impressionist painting *en plein air* suggesting the peak of French civilization at the end of the last century. Though scenes are multiplied, there is no end of variety.

For example, there are several reverse mirror images. Near the beginning, at a theater in London, Strether sees English society presented to him in the stalls and represented for him on the stage. As he looks from one to the other he wonders which is more real, the appearance or the actuality, and so knows his adventure is going to be interesting in its complexity. Near the end, when he thinks he has solved the complications of his Parisian puzzle, he takes an excursion into the French countryside to test it against the landscape by Lambinet he could not afford as a young man, in order to see if the former is "correct"—that is, properly picturesque. All day he insists on putting it into the gilded frame of memory, and is delighted to see that it fits. This leads immediately to the climactic scene of recognition. As a boat comes round the bend of the river he is confronted by a landscape with figures. This does not fit his picture of thirty-odd years ago or his romantic view of the present situation, which he has figured as anything but sordid. Yet he finds himself face to face with the evidence of adultery, Chad rowing while Mme de Vionnet sits in the stern under a pink parasol —American innocence in rendezvous with a French seductress almost old enough to be his mother.

As Strether's European experience opens out for him in picture after picture, marking the progressive stages of the plot and of his own education, there are no explicit comparisons with the drab scenes of his past in America. The emphasis being on his heightened sensitivity to the promises of life, all is cast in scenes of his new awareness of the opportunities Europe offers—or would have offered were it not too late for him now. The major weight of the international contrast is assigned to minor characters like the Pococks, Mrs. Newsome's daughter and son-in-law, who come out as substitute ambassadors when Strether turns in his portfolio. Their mission is carried out in the key of high comedy, bringing the remote provincial world of Woolett, Massachusetts, on stage sufficiently for purposes of comparison with no danger of its becoming the author's serious theme. There are no romantically overdone European aristocrats, no melodramatic subplots by which they trick the innocent Americans.

The narrator-hero, having resigned his mission, simply proceeds to complete his own education. The chief means for accomplishing this is by giving him a confidante, a sounding board against which he can evaluate his experiences. In Maria Gostrey, an intelligent American expatriate, James realized the full possibilities of this strategic device. She befriends Strether and would be glad, at the end, to offer him all the advantages of a married life in Europe. But if he cannot have what the world of Mme de Vionnet offers, he will be content with his awareness of what he has missed. So far from trying to drag Chad back home, he urges him not to be a fool. For the young man's sense of adventure, it turns out, was only a manifestation of the first flush of youth. Now, at one clear call from his mother, his sense of duty makes him renounce the life of golden opportunities for the gray routine of business success. Yet it was with him in mind, immediately following the introduction to Mme de Vionnet, that Strether had made his declaration for life—such a life as only Paris seemed to offer. So the outer plot and the inner theme answer each other as balanced opposites.

From the wreck of James's brief career as a playwright he had salvaged many things he could put to good use in his fictions. Not least of these was the over-all technique of what is meant by the theater term *mise en scène:* the total staging of a play, including setting, disposition of characters, arrangement of acts and scenes. *The Ambassadors* is not dramatically constructed in the sense of having a tightly knit plot wholly delivered by dialogue. It sacrifices compactness for the leisurely fullness appropriate to the outsized novel. But its structure is none the less scenic throughout. Everything is presented visually as in a kind of spectacle play. The great lighted scene of Europe becomes the stage on which is acted out the drama of possibilities offered to a man of imagination, as opposed to the limitations of a life lived by duty and logic. Strether was the perfect protagonist for this since he was a projection of the author's own potentialities. Each of the twelve books by which the novel is beautifully architectured renders a new level of his development in an unforgettable scene. If the three late masterpieces taken together are the peak of James's achievement, *The Ambassadors* by itself can be said to represent a culmination of all the major novelistic themes and techniques he had been mastering over a period of forty years.

CHARLES R. ANDERSON

A Note on the Text.   The text here followed for "The Aspern Papers" is that of the New York Edition (Charles Scribner's Sons, 1908), as a sample of James' revisions in his "later manner." For the others, the texts are those of the first editions, all published by The Macmillan Company simultaneously in London and New York: "The Pupil" in *The Lesson of the Master, etc.* (1892), "The Turn of the Screw" in *The Two Magics, etc.* (1898), and "The Art of Fiction" in *Partial Portraits* (1888).

THE ASPERN PAPERS

1

I HAD TAKEN Mrs. Prest into my confidence; without her in truth I should have made but little advance, for the fruitful idea in the whole business dropped from her friendly lips. It was she who found the short cut and loosed the Gordian knot. It is not supposed easy for women to rise to the large free view of anything, anything to be done; but they sometimes throw off a bold conception—such as a man wouldn't have risen to—with singular serenity. "Simply make them take you in on the footing of a lodger"—I don't think that unaided I should have risen to that. I was beating about the bush, trying to be ingenious, wondering by what combination or arts I might become an acquaintance, when she offered this happy suggestion that the way to become an acquaintance was first to become an intimate. Her actual knowledge of the Misses Bordereau was scarcely larger than mine, and indeed I had brought with me from England some definite facts that were new to her. Their name had been mixed up ages before with one of the greatest names of the century, and they now lived obscurely in Venice, lived on very small means, unvisited, unapproachable, in a sequestered and dilapidated old palace: this was the substance of my friend's impression of them. She herself had been established in Venice some fifteen years and had done a great deal of good there; but the circle of her benevolence had never embraced the two shy, mysterious and, as was somehow supposed, scarcely respectable Americans— they were believed to have lost in their long exile all national quality, besides being as their name implied of some remoter French affiliation—who asked no favours and desired no attention. In the early years of her residence she had made an attempt to see them, but this had been successful only as regards the little one, as Mrs. Prest called the niece; though in fact I afterwards found her the bigger of the two in inches. She had heard Miss Bordereau was ill and had a suspicion she was in want, and had gone to the house to offer aid, so that if there were suffering, American suffering in particular, she shouldn't have it on her conscience. The "little one" had received her in the great cold tarnished Venetian *sala*, the central hall of the house, paved with marble and roofed with dim cross-beams, and hadn't even asked her to sit down. This was all encouraging for me, who wished to sit so fast, and I remarked as much to Mrs. Prest. She replied, however, with profundity, "All, but there's all the difference: I went to confer a favour and you'll go to ask one. If they're proud you'll be on the right side." And she offered to show me their house to begin with—to row me thither in her gondola. I let her know I had already been to look at it half a dozen times; but I accepted her invitation, for it charmed me to hover about the place. I had made my way to it the day after my arrival in Venice—it had been described to me in advance by the friend in England to whom I owed definite information as to their possession of the papers—laying siege to it with my eyes while I considered my plan of campaign. Jeffrey Aspern had never been in it that I knew of, but some note of his voice seemed to abide there by a roundabout implication and in a "dying fall."

Mrs. Prest knew nothing about the papers, but was interested in my curiosity, as always in the joys and sorrows of her friends. As we went, however, in her gondola, gliding there under the sociable hood with the bright Venetian picture framed on either side by the moveable window, I saw how my eagerness amused her and that she found my interest in my possible spoil a fine case of monomania. "One would think you expected from it the answer to the riddle of the universe," she said; and I denied the impeachment only by replying that if I had to choose between that precious solution and a bundle of Jeffrey Aspern's letters I knew indeed which would appear to me the greater boon. She pretended to make light of his genius and I took no pains to defend him. One doesn't defend one's god: one's god is in himself a defence. Besides, to-day, after his long comparative obscuration, he hangs high in the heaven of our literature for all the world to see; he's a part of the light by which we walk. The most I said was that he was no doubt not a woman's poet: to which she rejoined aptly enough that he had been at least Miss Bordereau's. The strange thing had been for me to discover in England that she was still alive: it was as if I had been told Mrs. Siddons was, or Queen Caroline, or the famous Lady Hamilton, for it seemed to me that she belonged to a generation as extinct. "Why she must be tremendously old—at least a hundred," I had said; but on coming to consider dates I saw it not strictly involved that she should have far exceeded the common span. None the less she was of venerable age and her relations with Jeffrey Aspern had occurred in her early womanhood. "That's her excuse," said Mrs. Prest half sententiously and yet also somewhat as if she were ashamed of making a speech so little in the real tone of Venice. As if a woman needed an excuse for having loved the divine poet! He had been not only one of the most brilliant minds of his day—and in those years, when the century was young, there were, as every one knows, many—but one of the most genial men and one of the handsomest.

The niece, according to Mrs. Prest, was of minor antiquity, and the conjecture was risked that she was only a grand-niece. This was possible; I had nothing but my share in the very limited knowledge of my English fellow-worshipper John Cumnor, who had never seen the couple. The world, as I say, had recognised Jeffrey Aspern, but Cumnor and I had recognised him most. The multitude to-day flocked to his temple, but of that temple he and I regarded ourselves as the appointed ministers. We held, justly, as I think, that we had done more for his memory than any one else, and had done it simply by opening lights into his life. He had nothing to fear from us because he had nothing to fear from the truth, which alone at such a distance of time we could be interested in establishing. His early death had been the only dark spot, as it were, on his fame, unless the papers in Miss Bordereau's hands should perversely bring out others. There had been an impression about 1825 that he had "treated her badly," just as there had been an impression that he had "served," as the London populace says, several other ladies in the same masterful way. Each of these cases Cumnor and I had been able to investigate, and we had never failed to acquit him conscientiously of any grossness. I judged him perhaps more indulgently than my friend; certainly, at any rate, it appeared to me that no man could have walked straighter in the given circumstances. These had been almost always difficult and dangerous. Half the women of his time, to speak liberally, had flung themselves at his head, and while the fury raged—the more that it was very catching—accidents, some of them grave, had not failed to occur. He was not a woman's poet, as I had said to Mrs. Prest, in the modern phase of his reputation; but the situation had been different when the man's own voice was mingled with his song. That voice, by every testimony, was one of the most charming ever heard. "Orpheus and the Maenads!" had been of course my foreseen judgement when first I turned over his correspondence. Almost all the Maenads were unreasonable and many of them unbearable; it struck me that he had been kinder and more considerate than in his place—if I could imagine myself in any such box—I should have found the trick of.

It was certainly strange beyond all strangeness, and I shall not take up space with attempting to explain it, that whereas among all these other relations and in these other directions of research we had to deal with phantoms and dust, the mere echoes of echoes, the one living source of information that had lingered on into our time had been unheeded by us. Every one of Aspern's contemporaries had, according to our belief, passed away; we had not been able to look into a single pair of eyes into which his had looked or to feel a transmitted contact in any aged hand that his had touched. Most dead of all did poor Miss Bordereau appear, and yet she alone had survived. We exhausted in the course of months our wonder that we had not found her out sooner, and the substance of our explanation was that she had kept so quiet. The poor lady on the whole had had reason for doing so. But it was a revelation to us that self-effacement on such a scale had been possible in the latter half of the nineteenth century—the age of newspapers and telegrams and photographs and interviewers. She had taken no great trouble for it either—hadn't hidden herself away in an undiscoverable hole, had boldly settled down in a city of exhibition. The one apparent secret of her safety had been that Venice contained so many much greater curiosities. And then accident had somehow favoured her, as was shown for example in the fact that Mrs. Prest had never happened to name her to me, though I had spent three weeks in Venice—under her nose, as it were—five years before. My friend indeed had not named her much to any one; she appeared almost to have forgotten the fact of her continuance. Of course Mrs. Prest hadn't the nerves of an editor. It was meanwhile no explanation of the old woman's having eluded us to say that she lived abroad, for our researches had again and again taken us—not only by correspondence but by personal enquiry—to France, to Germany, to Italy, in which countries, not counting his important stay in England, so many of the too few years of Aspern's career had been spent. We were glad to think at least that in all our promulgations—some people now consider I believe that we have overdone them—we had only touched in passing and in the most discreet manner on Miss Bordereau's connexion. Oddly enough, even if we had had the material—and we had often wondered what could have become of it—this would have been the most difficult episode to handle.

The gondola stopped, the old palace was there; it was a house of the class which in Venice carries even in extreme dilapidation the dignified name. "How charming! It's gray and pink!" my companion exclaimed; and that is the most comprehensive description of it. It was not particularly old, only two or three centuries; and it had an air not so much of decay as of quiet discouragement, as if it had rather missed its career. But its wide front, with a stone balcony from end to end of the *piano nobile* or most important floor, was architectural enough, with the aid of various pilasters and arches; and the stucco with which in the intervals it had long ago been endued was rosy in the April afternoon. It overlooked a clean melancholy rather lonely canal, which had a narrow *riva* or convenient footway on either side. "I don't know why—there are no brick gables," said Mrs. Prest, "but this corner has seemed to me before more Dutch than Italian, more like Amsterdam than like Venice. It's eccentrically neat, for reasons of its own; and though you may pass on foot scarcely any one ever thinks of doing so. It's as negative—considering *where* it is—as a Protestant Sunday. Perhaps the people are afraid of the Misses Bordereau. I dare say they have the reputation of witches."

I forget what answer I made to this—I was given up to two other reflexions. The first of these was that if the old lady lived in such a big and imposing house she couldn't be in any sort of misery and therefore wouldn't be tempted by a chance to let a couple of rooms. I expressed this fear to Mrs. Prest, who gave me a very straight answer. "If she didn't live in a big house how could it be a question of her having rooms to spare? If she were not amply lodged you'd lack ground to approach her. Besides, a big house here, and especially in this *quartier perdu*,[1] proves nothing at all: it's perfectly consistent with a state of penury. Dilapidated old palazzi, if you'll go out of the way for them, are to be had for five shillings a year. And as for the people who live in them—no, until you've explored Venice socially as much as I have, you can form no idea of their domestic desolation. They live on nothing, for they've nothing to live on." The other idea that had come into my head was connected with a high blank wall which appeared to confine an expanse of ground on one side of the house. Blank I call it, but it was figured over with the patches that please a painter, repaired breaches, crumblings of

---

[1] A rundown section.

plaster, extrusions of brick that had turned pink with time; while a few thin trees, with the poles of certain rickety trellises, were visible over the top. The place was a garden and apparently attached to the house. I suddenly felt that so attached it gave me my pretext.

I sat looking out on all this with Mrs. Prest (it was covered with the golden glow of Venice) from the shade of our *felze*, and she asked me if I would go in then, while she waited for me, or come back another time. At first I couldn't decide—it was doubtless very weak of me. I wanted still to think I *might* get a footing, and was afraid to meet failure, for it would leave me, as I remarked to my companion, without another arrow for my bow. "Why not another?" she enquired as I sat there hesitating and thinking it over; and she wished to know why even now and before taking the trouble of becoming an inmate—which might be wretchedly uncomfortable after all, even if it succeeded—I hadn't the resource of simply offering them a sum of money down. In that way I might get what I wanted without bad nights.

"Dearest lady," I exclaimed, "excuse the impatience of my tone when I suggest that you must have fogotten the very fact—surely I communicated it to you—which threw me on your ingenuity. The old woman won't have her relics and tokens so much as spoken of; they're personal, delicate, intimate, and she hasn't the feelings of the day, God bless her! If I should sound that note first I should certainly spoil the game. I can arrive at my spoils only by putting her off her guard, and I can put her off her guard only by ingratiating diplomatic arts. Hypocrisy, duplicity are my only chance. I'm sorry for it, but there's no baseness I wouldn't commit for Jeffrey Aspern's sake. First I must take tea with her—then tackle the main job." And I told over what had happened to John Cumnor on his respectfully writing to her. No notice whatever had been taken of his first letter, and the second had been answered very sharply, in six lines, by the niece. "Miss Bordereau requested her to say that she couldn't imagine what he meant by troubling them. They had none of Mr. Aspern's 'literary remains,' and if they *had* had wouldn't have dreamed of showing them to any one on any account whatever. She couldn't imagine what he was talking about and begged he would let her alone." I certainly didn't want to be met that way.

"Well," said Mrs. Prest after a moment and all provokingly, "perhaps they really haven't anything. If they deny it flat how are you sure?"

"John Cumnor's sure, and it would take me long to tell you how his conviction, or his very strong presumption—strong enough to stand against the old lady's not unnatural fib—has built itself up. Besides, he makes much of the internal evidence of the niece's letter."

"The internal evidence?"

"Her calling him 'Mr. Aspern.'"

"I don't see what that proves."

"It proves familiarity, and familiarity implies the possession of mementoes, of tangible objects I can't tell you how that 'Mr.' affects me—how it bridges over the gulf of time and brings our hero near to me—nor what an edge it gives to my desire to see Juliana. You don't say 'Mr.' Shakespeare."

"Would I, any more, if I had a box full of his letters?"

"Yes, if he had been your lover and some one wanted them!" And I added that John Cumnor was so convinced, and so all the more convinced by Miss Bordereau's tone, that he would have come himself to Venice on the undertaking were it not for the obstacle of his having, for any confidence, to disprove his identity with the person who had written to them, which the old ladies would be sure to suspect in spite of dissimulation and a change of name. If they were to ask him point-blank if he were not their snubbed correspondent it would be too awkward for him to lie; whereas I was fortunately not tied in that way. I was a fresh hand—I could protest without lying.

"But you'll have to take a false name," said Mrs. Prest. "Juliana lives out of the world as much as it is possible to live, but she has none the less probably heard of Mr. Aspern's editors. She perhaps possesses what you've published."

"I've thought of that," I returned; and I drew out of my pocketbook a visiting card neatly engraved with a well-chosen *nom de guerre*.[2]

"You're very extravagant—it adds to your immorality. You might have done it in pencil or ink," said my companion.

"This looks more genuine."

"Certainly you've the courage of your curiosity. But it will be awkward about your letters; they won't come to you in that mask."

"My banker will take them in and I shall go every day to get them. It will give me a little walk."

"Shall you depend all on that?" asked Mrs. Prest. "Aren't you coming to see me?"

"Oh you'll have left Venice for the hot months long before there are any results. I'm prepared to roast all summer—as well as through the long hereafter perhaps you'll say! Meanwhile John Cumnor will bombard me with letters addressed, in my feigned name, to the care of the padrona."

"She'll recognise his hand," my companion suggested.

"On the envelope he can disguise it."

"Well, you're a precious pair! Doesn't it occur to you that even if you're able to say you're not Mr. Cumnor in person they may still suspect you of being his emissary?"

"Certainly, and I see only one way to parry that."

"And what may that be?"

I hesitated a moment. "To make love to the niece."

"Ah," cried my friend, "wait till you see her!"

2

"I must work the garden—I must work the garden," I said to myself five minutes later and while I waited, upstairs, in the long, dusky sala, where the bare scagliola floor gleamed vaguely in a chink of the closed shutters. The place was impressive, yet looked somehow cold and cautious. Mrs. Prest had floated away, giving me a rendezvous at the end of half an hour by some neighbouring water-steps; and I had been let into the house, after pulling the rusty bell-wire, by a small red-headed and white-faced maid-servant, who was

2 Battle—or fighting—name.

very young and not ugly and wore clicking pattens and a shawl in the fashion
of a hood. She had not contented herself with opening the door from above
by the usual arrangement of a creaking pulley, though she had looked down
at me first from an upper window, dropping the cautious challenge which in
Italy precedes the act of admission. I was irritated as a general thing by this
survival of mediaeval manners, though as so fond, if yet so special, an antiquarian I suppose I ought to have liked it; but, with my resolve to be genial
from the threshold at any price, I took my false card out of my pocket and
held it up to her, smiling as if it were a magic token. It had the effect of one
indeed, for it brought her, as I say, all the way down. I begged her to hand it
to her mistress, having first written on it in Italian the words: "Could you very
kindly see a gentleman, a travelling American, for a moment?" The little
maid wasn't hostile—even that was perhaps something gained. She coloured,
she smiled and looked both frightened and pleased. I could see that my arrival was a great affair, that visits in such a house were rare and that she was
a person who would have liked a bustling place. When she pushed forward
the heavy door behind me I felt my foot in the citadel and promised myself
ever so firmly to keep it there. She pattered across the damp stony lower hall
and I followed her up the high staircase—stonier still, as it seemed—without
an invitation. I think she had meant I should wait for her below, but such
was not my idea, and I took up my station in the sala. She flitted, at the far
end of it, into impenetrable regions, and I looked at the place with my heart
beating as I had known it to do in dentists' parlours. It had a gloomy grandeur,
but owed its character almost all to its noble shape and to the fine architectural doors, as high as those of grand frontages, which, leading into the
various rooms, repeated themselves on either side at intervals. They were
surmounted with old faded painted escutcheons, and here and there in the
spaces between them hung brown pictures, which I noted as speciously
bad, in battered and tarnished frames that were yet more desirable than the
canvases themselves. With the exception of several straw-bottomed chairs that
kept their backs to the wall the grand obscure vista contained little else to
minister to effect. It was evidently never used save as a passage, and scantly
even as that. I may add that by the time the door through which the maid-
servant had escaped opened again my eyes had grown used to the want of
light.

I hadn't meanwhile meant by my private ejaculation that I must myself
cultivate the soil of the tangled enclosure which lay beneath the windows, but
the lady who came toward me from the distance over the hard shining
floor might have supposed as much from the way in which, as I went rapidly
to meet her, I exclaimed, taking care to speak Italian: "The garden, the garden—do me the pleasure to tell me if it's yours!"

She stopped short, looking at me with wonder; and then, "Nothing here is
mine," she answered in English, coldly and sadly.

"Oh you're English; how delightful!" I ingenuously cried. "But surely the
garden belongs to the house?"

"Yes, but the house doesn't belong to me." She was a long lean pale person, habited apparently in a dull-coloured dressing-gown, and she spoke very
simply and mildly. She didn't ask me to sit down, any more than years be-

fore—if she were the niece—she had asked Mrs. Prest, and we stood face to face in the empty pompous hall.

"Well then, would you kindly tell me to whom I must address myself? I'm afraid you will think me horribly intrusive, but you know I *must* have a garden—upon my honour I must!"

Her face was not young, but it was candid; it was not fresh, but it was clear. She had large eyes which were not bright, and a great deal of hair which was not "dressed," and long fine hands which were—possibly—not clean. She clasped these members almost convulsively as, with a confused alarmed look, she broke out: "Oh, don't take it away from us; we like it ourselves!"

"You have the use of it then?"

"Oh yes. If it wasn't for that—!" And she gave a wan vague smile.

"Isn't it a luxury, precisely? That's why intending to be in Venice some weeks, possibly all summer, and having some literary work, some reading and writing to do, so that I must be quiet and yet if possible a great deal in the open air—that's why I've felt a garden to be really indispensable. I appeal to your own experience," I went on with as sociable a smile as I could risk. "Now can't I look at yours?"

"I don't know, I don't understand," the poor woman murmured, planted there and letting her weak wonder deal—helplessly enough, as I felt—with my strangeness.

"I mean only from one of those windows—such grand ones as you have here—if you'll let me open the shutters." And I walked toward the back of the house. When I had advanced halfway I stopped and waited as in the belief she would accompany me. I had been of necessity quite abrupt, but I strove at the same time to give her the impression of extreme courtesy. "I've looked at furnished rooms all over the place, and it seems impossible to find any with a garden attached. Naturally in a place like Venice gardens are rare. It's absurd if you like, for a man, but I can't live without flowers."

"There are none to speak of down there." She came nearer, as if, though she mistrusted me, I had drawn her by an invisible thread. I went on again, and she continued as she followed me: "We've a few, but they're very common. It costs too much to cultivate them; one has to have a man."

"Why shouldn't I be the man?" I asked. "I'll work without wages; or rather I'll put in a gardener. You shall have the sweetest flowers in Venice."

She protested against this with a small quaver of sound that might have been at the same time a gush of rapture for my free sketch. Then she gasped: "We don't know you—we don't know you."

"You know me as much as I know you, or rather much more, because you know my name. And if you're English I'm almost a countryman."

"We're not English," said my companion, watching me in practical submission while I threw open the shutters of one of the divisions of the wide high window.

"You speak the language so beautifully: might I ask what you are?" Seen from above the garden was in truth shabby, yet I felt at a glance that it had great capabilities. She made no rejoinder, she was so lost in her blankness and gentleness, and I exclaimed, "You don't mean to say you're also by chance American?"

"I don't know. We used to be."

"Used to be? Surely you haven't changed?"

"It's so many years ago. We don't seem to be anything now."

"So many years that you've been living here? Well, I don't wonder at that; it's a grand old house. I suppose you all use the garden," I went on, "but I assure you I shouldn't be in your way. I'd be very quiet and stay quite in one corner."

"We all use it?" she repeated after me vaguely, not coming close to the window but looking at my shoes. She appeared to think me capable of throwing her out.

"I mean all your family—as many as you are."

"There's only one other than me. She's very old. She never goes down."

I feel again my thrill at this close identification of Juliana; in spite of which, however, I kept my head. "Only one other in all this great house!" I feigned to be not only amazed but almost scandalized. "Dear lady, you must have space then to spare!"

"To spare?" she repeated—almost as for the rich unwonted joy to her of spoken words.

"Why you surely don't live (two quiet women—I see *you* are quiet, at any rate) in fifty rooms!" Then with a burst of hope and cheer I put the question straight: "Couldn't you for a good rent *let* me two or three? That would set me up!"

I had now struck the note that translated my purpose, and I needn't reproduce the whole of the tune I played. I ended by making my entertainer believe me an undesigning person, though of course I didn't even attempt to persuade her I was not an eccentric one. I repeated that I had studies to pursue; that I wanted quiet; that I delighted in a garden and had vainly sought one up and down the city; that I would undertake that before another month was over the dear old house should be smothered in flowers. I think it was the flowers that won my suit, for I afterwards found that Miss Tina —for such the name of this high tremulous spinster proved somewhat incongruously to be—had an insatiable appetite for them. When I speak of my suit as won I mean that before I left her she had promised me she would refer the question to her aunt. I invited information as to who her aunt might be and she answered "Why Miss Bordereau!" with an air of surprise, as if I might have been expected to know. There were contradictions like this in Miss Tina which, as I observed later, contributed to make her rather pleasingly incalculable and interesting. It was the study of the two ladies to live so that the world shouldn't talk of them or touch them, and yet they had never altogether accepted the idea that it didn't hear of them. In Miss Tina at any rate a grateful susceptibility to human contact had not died out, and contact of a limited order there would be if I should come to live in the house.

"We've never done anything of the sort; we've never had a lodger or any kind of inmate." So much as this she made a point of saying to me. "We're very poor, we live very badly—almost on nothing. The rooms are very bare —those you might take; they've nothing at all in them. I don't know how you'd sleep, how you'd eat."

"With your permission I could easily put in a bed and a few tables and chairs. *C'est la moindre des choses*[1] and the affair of an hour or two. I know a little man from whom I can hire for a trifle what I should so briefly want, what I should use; my gondolier can bring the things round in his boat. Of course in this great house you must have a second kitchen, and my servant who's a wonderfully handy fellow"—this personage was an evocation of the moment—"can easily cook me a chop there. My tastes and habits are of the simplest; I live on flowers!" And then I ventured to add that if they were very poor it was all the more reason they should let their rooms. They were bad economists—I had never heard of such a waste of material.

I saw in a moment my good lady had never before been spoken to in any such fashion—with a humorous firmness that didn't exclude sympathy, that was quite founded on it. She might easily have told me that my sympathy was impertinent, but this by good fortune didn't occur to her. I left her with the understanding that she would submit the question to her aunt and that I might come back the next day for their decision.

"The aunt will refuse; she'll think the whole proceeding very *louche!*"[2] Mrs. Prest declared shortly after this, when I had resumed my place in her gondola. She had put the idea into my head and now—so little are women to be counted on—she appeared to take a despondent view of it. Her pessimism provoked me and I pretended to have the best hopes; I went so far as to boast of a distinct prevision of success. Upon this Mrs. Prest broke out, "Oh I see what's in your head! You fancy you've made such an impression in five minutes that she's dying for you to come and can be depended on to bring the old one round. If you do get in you'll count it as a triumph."

I did count it as a triumph, but only for the commentator—in the last analysis—not for the man, who had not the tradition of personal conquest. When I went back on the morrow the little maid-servant conducted me straight through the long sala—it opened there as before in large perspective and was lighter now, which I thought a good omen—into the apartment from which the recipient of my former visit had emerged on that occasion. It was a spacious shabby parlour with a fine old painted ceiling under which a strange figure sat alone at one of the windows. They come back to me now almost with the palpitation they caused, the successive states marking my consciousness that as the door of the room closed behind me I was really face to face with the Juliana of some of Aspern's most exquisite and most re-nowned lyrics. I grew used to her afterwards, though never completely; but as she sat there before me my heart beat as fast as if the miracle of resurrec-tion had taken place for my benefit. Her presence seemed somehow to contain and express his own, and I felt nearer to him at that first moment of seeing her than I ever had been before or ever have been since. Yes, I remember my emotions in their order, even including a curious little tremor that took me when I saw the niece not to be there. With her, the day before, I had be-come sufficiently familiar, but it almost exceeded my courage—much as I had longed for the event—to be left alone with so terrible a relic as the aunt. She was too strange, too literally resurgent. Then came a check from the percep-tion that we weren't really face to face, inasmuch as she had over her eyes a

[1] It's a simple matter.
[2] Equivocal.

horrible green shade which served for her almost as a mask. I believed for the instant that she had put it on expressly, so that from underneath it she might take me all in without my getting at herself. At the same time it created a presumption of some ghastly death's head lurking behind it. The divine Juliana as a grinning skull—the vision hung there until it passed. Then it came to me that she *was* tremendously old—so old that death might take her at any moment, before I should have time to compass my end. The next thought was a correction to that; it lighted up the situation. She would die next week, she would die to-morrow—then I could pounce on her possessions and ransack her drawers. Meanwhile she sat there neither moving nor speaking. She was very small and shrunken, bent forward with her hands in her lap. She was dressed in black and her head was wrapped in a piece of old black lace which showed no hair.

My emotion keeping me silent she spoke first, and the remark she made was exactly the most unexpected.

3

"Our house is very far from the centre, but the little canal is very *comme il faut*." [1]

"It's the sweetest corner of Venice and I can imagine nothing more charming," I hastened to reply. The old lady's voice was very thin and weak, but it had an agreeable, cultivated murmur and there was wonder in the thought that that individual note had been in Jeffrey Aspern's ear.

"Please to sit down there. I hear very well," she said quietly, as if perhaps I had been shouting; and the chair she pointed to was at a certain distance. I took possession of it, assuring her I was perfectly aware of my intrusion and of my not having been properly introduced, and that I could but throw myself on her indulgence. Perhaps the other lady, the one I had had the honour of seeing the day before, would have explained to her about the garden. That was literally what had given me courage to take a step so unconventional. I had fallen in love at sight with the whole place—she herself was probably so used to it that she didn't know the impression it was capable of making on a stranger—and I had felt it really a case to risk something. Was her own kindness in receiving me a sign that I was not wholly out in my calculation? It would make me extremely happy to think so. I could give her my word of honour that I was a most respectable inoffensive person and that as a co-tenant of the palace, so to speak, they would be barely conscious of my existence. I would conform to any regulations, any restrictions, if they would only let me enjoy the garden. Moreover I should be delighted to give her references, guarantees; they would be of the very best, both in Venice and in England, as well as in America.

She listened to me in perfect stillness and I felt her look at me with great penetration, though I could see only the lower part of her bleached and shrivelled face. Independently of the refining process of old age it had a delicacy which once must have been great. She had been very fair, she had had a wonderful complexion. She was silent a little after I had ceased speak-

---

[1] Convenient (as needed).

ing; then she began: "If you're so fond of a garden why don't you go to *terra firma*,[2] where there are so many far better than this?"

"Oh it's the combination!" I answered, smiling; and then with rather a flight of fancy; "It's the idea of a garden in the middle of the sea."

"This isn't the middle of the sea; you can't so much as see the water."

I stared a moment, wondering if she wished to convict me of fraud. "Can't see the water? Why, dear madam, I can come up to the very gate in my boat."

She appeared inconsequent, for she said vaguely in reply to this: "Yes, if you've got a boat. I haven't any; it's many years since I have been in one of the *gondole*." She uttered these words as if they designed a curious far-away craft known to her only by hearsay.

"Let me assure you of the pleasure with which I would put mine at your service!" I returned. I had scarcely said this however before I became aware that the speech was in questionable taste and might also do me the injury of making me appear too eager, too possessed of a hidden motive. But the old woman remained impenetrable and her attitude worried me by suggesting that she had a fuller vision of me than I had of her. She gave me no thanks for my somewhat extravagant offer, but remarked that the lady I had seen the day before was her niece; she would presently come in. She had asked her to stay away a little on purpose—had had her reasons for seeing me first alone. She relapsed into silence and I turned over the fact of these unmentioned reasons and the question of what might come yet; also that of whether I might venture on some judicious remark in praise of her companion. I went so far as to say I should be delighted to see our absent friend again: she had been so very patient with me, considering how odd she must have thought me—a declaration which drew from Miss Bordereau another of her whimsical speeches.

"She has very good manners; I bred her up myself!" I was on the point of saying that that accounted for the easy grace of the niece, but I arrested myself in time, and the next moment the old woman went on: "I don't care who you may be—I don't want to know; it signifies very little to-day." This had all the air of being a formula of dismissal, as if her next words would be that I might take myself off now that she had had the amusement of looking on the face of such a monster of indiscretion. Therefore I was all the more surprised when she added in her soft venerable quaver: "You may have as many rooms as you like—if you'll pay me a good deal of money."

I hesitated but an instant, long enough to measure what she meant in particular by this condition. First it struck me that she must have really a large sum in her mind; then I reasoned quickly that her idea of a large sum would probably not correspond to my own. My deliberation, I think, was not so visible as to diminish the promptitude with which I replied: "I will pay with pleasure and of course in advance whatever you may think it proper to ask me."

"Well then, a thousand francs a month," she said instantly, while her baffling green shade continued to cover her attitude.

The figure, as they say, was startling and my logic had been at fault. The

2 Solid ground.

sum she had mentioned was, by the Venetian measure of such matters, exceedingly large; there was many an old palace in an out-of-the-way corner that I might on such terms have enjoyed the whole of by the year. But so far as my resources allowed I was prepared to spend money, and my decision was quickly taken. I would pay her with a smiling face what she asked, but in that case I would make it up by getting hold of my "spoils" for nothing. Moreover if she had asked five times as much I should have risen to the occasion, so odious would it have seemed to me to stand chaffering with Aspern's Juliana. It was queer enough to have a question of money with her at all. I assured her that her views perfectly met my own and that on the morrow I should have the pleasure of putting three months' rent into her hand. She received this announcement with apparent complacency and with no discoverable sense that after all it would become her to say that I ought to see the rooms first. This didn't occur to her, and indeed her serenity was mainly what I wanted. Our little agreement was just concluded when the door opened and the younger lady appeared on the threshold. As soon as Miss Bordereau saw her niece she cried out almost gaily: "He'll give three thousand—three thousand to-morrow!"

Miss Tina stood still, her patient eyes turning from one of us to the other; then she brought out, scarcely above her breath: "Do you mean francs?"

"Did you mean francs or dollars?" the old woman asked of me at this.

"I think francs were what you said," I sturdily smiled.

"That's very good," said Miss Tina, as if she had felt how overreaching her own question might have looked.

"What do *you* know? You're ignorant," Miss Bordereau remarked; not with acerbity but with a strange soft coldness.

"Yes, of money—certainly of money!" Miss Tina hastened to concede.

"I'm sure you've your own fine branches of knowledge," I took the liberty of saying genially. There was something painful to me, somehow, in the turn the conversation had taken, in the discussion of dollars and francs.

"She had a very good education when she was young. I looked into that myself," said Miss Bordereau. Then she added: "But she has learned nothing since."

"I have always been with *you*," Miss Tina rejoined very mildly, and of a certainty with no intention of an epigram.

"Yes, but for that—!" her aunt declared with more satirical force. She evidently meant that but for this her niece would never have got on at all; the point of the observation however being lost on Miss Tina, though she blushed at hearing her history revealed to a stranger. Miss Bordereau went on, addressing herself to me: "And what time will you come to-morrow with the money?"

"The sooner the better. If it suits you I'll come at noon."

"I am always here, but I have my hours," said the old woman as if her convenience were not to be taken for granted.

"You mean the times when you receive?"

"I never receive. But I'll see you at noon when you come with the money."

"Very good, I shall be punctual." To which I added: "May I shake hands with you on our contract?" I thought there ought to be some little form; it would make me really feel easier, for I was sure there would be no other.

Besides, though Miss Bordereau couldn't to-day be called personally attractive and there was something even in her wasted antiquity that bade one stand at one's distance, I felt an irresistible desire to hold in my own for a moment the hand Jeffrey Aspern had pressed.

For a minute she made no answer, and I saw that my proposal failed to meet with her approbation. She indulged in no movement of withdrawal, which I half expected; she only said coldly: "I belong to a time when that was not the custom."

I felt rather snubbed but I exclaimed good-humouredly to Miss Tina, "Oh you'll do as well!" I shook hands with her while she assented with a small flutter. "Yes, yes, to show it's all arranged!"

"Shall you bring the money in gold?" Miss Bordereau demanded as I was turning to the door.

I looked at her a moment. "Aren't you a little afraid, after all, of keeping such a sum as that in the house?" It was not that I was annoyed at her avidity, but was truly struck with the disparity between such a treasure and such scanty means of guarding it.

"Whom should I be afraid of if I'm not afraid of you?" she asked with her shrunken grimness.

"Ah well," I laughed, "I shall be in point of fact a protector and I'll bring gold if you prefer."

"Thank you," the old woman returned with dignity and with an inclination of her head which evidently signified my dismissal. I passed out of the room, thinking how hard it would be to circumvent her. As I stood in the sala again I saw that Miss Tina had followed me, and I supposed that as her aunt had neglected to suggest I should take a look at my quarters it was her purpose to repair the omission. But she made no such overture; she only stood there with a dim, though not a languid smile, and with an effect of irresponsible incompetent youth almost comically at variance with the faded facts of her person. She was not infirm, like her aunt, but she struck me as more deeply futile, because her inefficiency was inward, which was not the case with Miss Bordereau's. I waited to see if she would offer to show me the rest of the house but I didn't precipitate the question, inasmuch as my plan was from this moment to spend as much of my time as possible in her society. A minute indeed elapsed before I committed myself.

"I've had better fortune than I hoped. It was very kind of her to see me. Perhaps you said a good word for me."

"It was the idea of the money," said Miss Tina.

"And did you suggest that?"

"I told her you'd perhaps pay largely."

"What made you think that?"

"I told her I thought you were rich."

"And what put that into your head?"

"I don't know; the way you talked."

"Dear me, I must talk differently now," I returned. "I'm sorry to say it's not the case."

"Well," said Miss Tina, "I think that in Venice the *forestieri*[3] in general

3 Foreigners.

often give a great deal for something that after all isn't much." She appeared to make this remark with a comforting intention, to wish to remind me that if I had been extravagant I wasn't foolishly singular. We walked together along the sala, and as I took its magnificent measure I said that I was afraid it wouldn't form a part of my *quartiere*.[4] Were my rooms by chance to be among those that opened into it? "Not if you go above—to the second floor," she answered as if she had rather taken for granted I would know my proper place.

"And I infer that that's where your aunt would like me to be."

"She said your apartments ought to be very distinct."

"That certainly would be best." And I listened with respect while she told me that above I should be free to take whatever I might like; that there was another staircase, but only from the floor on which we stood, and that to pass from it to the garden-level or to come up to my lodging I should have in effect to cross the great hall. This was an immense point gained; I foresaw that it would constitute my whole leverage in my relations with the two ladies. When I asked Miss Tina how I was to manage at present to find my way up she replied with an access of that sociable shyness which constantly marked her manner:

"Perhaps you can't. I don't see—unless I should go with you." She evidently hadn't thought of this before.

We ascended to the upper floor and visited a long succession of empty rooms. The best of them looked over the garden; some of the others had above the opposite rough-tiled house-tops a view of the blue lagoon. They were all dusty and even a little disfigured with long neglect, but I saw that by spending a few hundred francs I should be able to make three or four of them habitable enough. My experiment was turning out costly, yet now that I had all but taken possession I ceased to allow this to trouble me. I mentioned to my companion a few of the things I should put in, but she replied rather more precipitately than usual that I might do exactly what I liked: she seemed to wish to notify me that the Misses Bordereau would take none but the most veiled interest in my proceedings. I guessed that her aunt had instructed her to adopt this tone, and I may as well say now that I came afterwards to distinguish perfectly (as I believed) between the speeches she made on her own responsibility and those the old woman imposed upon her. She took no notice of the unswept condition of the rooms and indulged neither in explanations nor in apologies. I said to myself that this was a sign Juliana and her niece—disenchanting idea!—were untidy persons with a low Italian standard; but I afterwards recognised that a lodger who had forced an entrance had no *locus standi* as a critic. We looked out of a good many windows, for there was nothing within the rooms to look at, and still I wanted to linger. I asked her what several different objects in the prospect might be, but in no case did she appear to know. She was evidently not familiar with the view—it was as if she had not looked at it for years—and I presently saw that she was too preoccupied with something else to pretend to care for it. Suddenly she said—the remark was not suggested:

[4] Apartment.

"I don't know whether it will make any difference to you, but the money is for me."

"The money—?"

"The money you're going to bring."

"Why you'll make me wish to stay here two or three years!" I spoke as benevolently as possible, though it had begun to act on my nerves that these women so associated with Aspern should so constantly bring the pecuniary question back.

"That would be very good for me," she answered almost gaily.

"You put me on my honour!"

She looked as if she failed to understand this, but went on: "She wants me to have more. She thinks she's going to die."

"Ah not soon I hope!" I cried with genuine feeling. I had perfectly considered the possibility of her destroying her documents on the day she should feel her end at hand. I believed that she would cling to them till then, and I was as convinced of her reading Aspern's letters over every night or at least pressing them to her withered lips. I would have given a good deal for some view of those solemnities. I asked Miss Tina if her venerable relative were seriously ill, and she replied that she was only very tired—she had lived so extraordinarily long. That was what she said herself—she wanted to die for a change. Besides, all her friends had been dead for ages; either they ought to have remained or she ought to have gone. That was another thing her aunt often said: she was not at all resigned—resigned, that is, to life.

"But people don't die when they like, do they?" Miss Tina inquired. I took the liberty of asking why, if there was actually enough money to maintain both of them, there would not be more than enough in case of her being left alone. She considered this difficult problem a moment and then said: "Oh well, you know, she takes care of me. She thinks that when I'm alone I shall be a great fool and shan't know how to manage."

"I should have supposed rather that you took care of *her*. I'm afraid she's very proud."

"Why, have you discovered that already?" Miss Tina cried with a dimness of glad surprise.

"I was shut up with her there for a considerable time and she struck me, she interested me extremely. It didn't take me long to make my discovery. She won't have much to say to me while I'm here."

"No, I don't think she will," my companion averred.

"Do you suppose she has some suspicion of me?"

Miss Tina's honest eyes gave me no sign I had touched a mark. "I shouldn't think so—letting you in after all so easily."

"You call it easily? She has covered her risk," I said. "But where is it one could take an advantage of her?"

"I oughtn't to tell you if I knew, ought I?" And Miss Tina added, before I had time to reply to this, smiling dolefully: "Do you think we've any weak points?"

"That's exactly what I'm asking. You'd only have to mention them for me to respect them religiously."

She looked at me hereupon with that air of timid but candid and even gratified curiosity with which she had confronted me from the first; after which she said: "There's nothing to tell. We're terribly quiet. I don't know how the days pass. We've no life."

"I wish I might think I should bring you a little."

"Oh we know what we want," she went on. "It's all right."

There were twenty things I desired to ask her: how in the world they did live; whether they had any friends or visitors, any relations in America or in other countries. But I judged such probings premature; I must leave it to a later chance. "Well, don't *you* be proud," I contented myself with saying. "Don't hide from me altogether."

"Oh I must stay with my aunt," she returned without looking at me. And at the same moment, abruptly, without any ceremony of parting, she quitted me and disappeared, leaving me to make my own way downstairs. I stayed a while longer, wandering about the bright desert—the sun was pouring in—of the old house, thinking the situation over on the spot. Not even the pattering little *serva* came to look after me, and I reflected that after all this treatment showed confidence.

4

Perhaps it did, but all the same, six weeks later, towards the middle of June, the moment when Mrs. Prest undertook her annual migration, I had made no measurable advance. I was obliged to confess to her that I had no results to speak of. My first step had been unexpectedly rapid, but there was no appearance it would be followed by a second. I was a thousand miles from taking tea with my hostesses—that privilege of which, as I reminded my good friend, we both had had a vision. She reproached me with lacking boldness and I answered that even to be bold you must have an opportunity: you may push on through a breach, but you can't batter down a dead wall. She returned that the breach I had already made was big enough to admit an army and accused me of wasting precious hours in whimpering in her salon when I ought to have been carrying on the struggle in the field. It is true that I went to see her very often—all on the theory that it would console me (I freely expressed my discouragement) for my want of success on my own premises. But I began to feel that it didn't console me to be perpetually chaffed for my scruples, especially since I was really so vigilant; and I was rather glad when my ironic friend closed her house for the summer. She had expected to gather amusement from the drama of my intercourse with the Misses Bordereau, and was disappointed that the intercourse, and consequently the drama, had not come off. "They'll lead you on to your ruin," she said before she left Venice. "They'll get all your money without showing you a scrap." I think I settled down to my business with more concentration after her departure.

It was a fact that up to that time I had not, save on a single brief occasion had even a moment's contact with my queer hostesses. The exception had occurred when I carried them according to my promise the terrible three thousand francs. Then I found Miss Tina awaiting me in the hall, and she took the money from my hand with a promptitude that prevented my seeing her aunt. The old lady had promised to receive me, yet apparently thought nothing of breaking that vow. The money was contained in a bag of chamois leather, of respectable dimensions, which my banker had given me, and Miss Tina had to make a big fist to receive it. This she did with extreme solemnity though I tried to treat the affair a little as a joke. It was in no jocular strain, yet it was with a clearness akin to a brightness that she enquired, weighing the money in her two palms: "Don't you think it's too much?" To which I replied that this would depend on the amount of pleasure I should get for it. Hereupon she turned away from me quickly, as she had done the day before, murmuring in a tone different from any she had used hitherto: "Oh pleasure, pleasure—there's no pleasure in this house!"

After that, for a long time, I never saw her, and I wondered the common chances of the day shouldn't have helped us to meet. It could only be evident that she was immensely on her guard against them; and in addition to this the house was so big that for each other we were lost in it. I used to look out for her hopefully as I crossed the sala in my comings and goings, but I was not rewarded with a glimpse of the tail of her dress. It was as if she never peeped out of her aunt's apartment. I used to wonder what she did there week after week and year after year. I had never met so stiff a policy of seclusion; it was more than keeping quiet—it was like hunted creatures feigning death. The two ladies appeared to have no visitors whatever and no sort of contact with the world. I judged at least that people couldn't have come to the house and that Miss Tina couldn't have gone out without my catching some view of it. I did what I disliked myself for doing—considering it but as once in a way: I questioned my servant about their habits and let him infer that I should be interested in any information he might glean. But he gleaned amazingly little for a knowing Venetian: it must be added that where there is a perpetual fast there are very few crumbs on the floor. His ability in other ways was sufficient, if not quite all I had attributed to him on the occasion of my first interview with Miss Tina. He had helped my gondolier to bring me round a boatload of furniture; and when these articles had been carried to the top of the palace and distributed according to our associated wisdom he organized my household with such dignity as answered to its being composed exclusively of himself. He made me in short as comfortable as I could be with my indifferent prospects. I should have been glad if he had fallen in love with Miss Bordereau's maid or, failing this, had taken her in aversion; either event might have brought about some catastrophe, and a catastrophe might have led to some parley. It was my idea that she would have been sociable, and I myself on various occasions saw her flit to and fro on domestic errands, so that I was sure she was accessible. But I tasted of no gossip from that fountain, and I afterwards learned that Pasquale's affections were fixed upon an object that made him heedless of other women. This was a young lady with a powdered face, a yellow cotton gown and much leisure, who used often to come to see him. She practised, at her convenience, the art of a stringer of beads—these ornaments are made in Venice to profusion; she had her pocket full of them and I used to find them on the floor of my apartment—and kept an eye on the possible rival in the house. It was not for me of course to make the domestics tattle, and I never said a word to Miss Bordereau's cook.

It struck me as a proof of the old woman's resolve to have nothing to do with me that she should never have sent me a receipt for my three months' rent. For some days I looked out for it and then, when I had given it up, wasted a good deal of time in wondering what her reason had been for neglecting so indispensable and familiar a form. At first I was tempted to send her a reminder; after which I put by the idea—against my judgement as to what was right in the particular case—on the general ground of wishing to keep quiet. If Miss Bordereau suspected me of ulterior aims she would suspect me less if I should be businesslike, and yet I consented not to be. It was possible she intended her omission as an impertinence, a visible irony, to show how she could overreach people who attempted to overreach her. On that hypothesis it was well to let her see that one didn't notice her little tricks. The real reading of the matter, I afterwards gathered, was simply the poor lady's desire to emphasise the fact that I was in the enjoyment of a favour as rigidly limited as it had been liberally bestowed. She had given me part of her house, but she wouldn't add to that so much as a morsel of paper with her name on it. Let me say that even at first this didn't make me too miserable, for the whole situation had the charm of its oddity. I foresaw that I should have a summer after my own literary heart, and the sense of playing with my opportunity was much greater after all than any sense of being played with. There could be no Venetian business without patience, and since I adored the place I was much more in the spirit of it for having laid in a large provision. That spirit kept me perpetual company and seemed to look out at me from the revived immortal face—in which all his genius shone—of the great poet who was my prompter. I had invoked him and he had come; he hovered before me half the time; it was as if his bright ghost had returned to earth to assure me he regarded the affair as his own no less than as mine and that we should see it fraternally and fondly to a conclusion. It was as if he had said: "Poor dear, be easy with her; she has some natural prejudices; only give her time. Strange as it may appear to you she was very attractive in 1820. Meanwhile aren't we in Venice together, and what better place is there for the meeting of dear friends? See how it glows with the advancing summer; how the sky and the sea and the rosy air and the marble of the palaces all shimmer and melt together." My eccentric private errand became a part of the general romance and the general glory—I felt even a mystic companionship, a moral fraternity with all those who in the past had been in the service of art. They had worked for beauty, for a devotion; and what else was I doing? That element was in everything that Jeffrey Aspern had written, and I was only bringing it to light.

I lingered in the sala when I went to and fro; I used to watch—as long as I thought decent—the door that led to Miss Bordereau's part of the house. A person observing me might have supposed I was trying to cast a spell on it or attempting some odd experiment in hypnotism. But I was only praying it might open or thinking what treasure probably lurked behind it. I hold it singular, as I look back, that I should never have doubted for a moment that the sacred relics were there; never have failed to know the joy of being beneath the same roof with them. After all they were under my hand—they had not escaped me yet; and they made my life continuous, in a fashion, with the illustrious life they had touched at the other end. I lost myself in this satisfaction to the point of assuming—in my quiet extravagance—that poor Miss Tina also went back, and still went back, as I used to phrase it. She did indeed, the gentle spinster, but not quite so far as Jeffrey Aspern, who was simple hearsay to her quite as he was to me. Only she had lived for years with Juliana, she had seen and handled all mementoes and—even though she was stupid—some esoteric knowledge had rubbed off on her. That was what the old woman represented—esoteric knowledge; and this was the idea with which my critical heart used to thrill. It literally beat faster often, of an evening when I had been out, as I stopped with my candle in the re-echoing hall on my way up to bed. It was as if at such a moment as that, in the stillness and after the long contradiction of the day, Miss Bordereau's secrets were in the air, the wonder of her survival more vivid. These were the acute impressions. I had them in another form, with more of a certain shade of reciprocity, during the hours I sat in the garden looking up over the top of my book at the closed windows of my hostess. In these windows no sign of life ever appeared; it was as if, for fear of my catching a glimpse of them, the two ladies passed their days in the dark. But this only emphasised their having matters to conceal; which was what I had wished to prove. Their motionless shutters became as expressive as eyes consciously closed, and I took comfort in the probability that, though invisible themselves, they kept me in view between the lashes.

I made a point of spending as much time as possible in the garden, to justify the picture I had originally given of my horticultural passion. And I not only spent time, but (hang it! as I said) spent precious money. As soon as I had got my rooms arranged and could give the question proper thought I surveyed the place with a clever expert and made terms for having it put in order. I was sorry to do this, for personally I liked it better as it was, with its weeds and its wild rich tangle, its sweet characteristic Venetian shabbiness. I had to be consistent, to keep my promise that I would smother the house in flowers. Moreover I clung to the fond fancy that by flowers I should make my way—I should succeed by big nosegays. I would batter the old women with lilies—I would bombard their citadel with roses. Their door would have to yield to the pressure when a mound of fragrance should be heaped against it. The place in truth had been brutally neglected. The Venetian capacity for dawdling is of the largest, and for a good many days unlimited litter was all my gardener had to show for his ministrations. There was a great digging of holes and carting about of earth, and after a while I grew so impatient that I had thoughts of sending for my "results" to the nearest stand. But I felt sure my friends would see through the chinks of their shutters where such tribute *couldn't* have been gathered, and might so make up their minds against my veracity. I possessed my soul and finally, though the delay was long, perceived some appearances of bloom. This encouraged me and I waited serenely enough till they multiplied. Meanwhile the real summer days arrived and began to pass, and as I look back upon them they seem to me almost the happiest of my life. I took more and more care to be in the garden whenever it was not too hot. I had an arbour arranged and a low table and an armchair put into it; and I carried out books and portfolios—I had always some business of writing in hand—and worked and waited and mused and hoped, while the golden hours elapsed and the plants drank in the light and the inscrutable old palace turned pale and then, as the day waned, began to recover and flush and my papers rustled in the wandering breeze of the Adriatic.

Considering how little satisfaction I got from it at first it is wonderful I shouldn't have grown more tired of trying to guess what mystic rites of ennui the Misses Bordereau celebrated in their darkened rooms; whether this had always been the tenor of their life and how in previous years they had escaped elbowing their neighbours. It was supposable they had then had other habits, forms and resources; that they must once have been young or at least middle-aged. There was no end to the questions it was possible to ask about them and no end to the answers it was not possible to frame. I had known many of my country-people in Europe and was familiar with the strange ways they were liable to take up there; but the Misses Bordereau formed altogether a new type of the American absentee. Indeed it was clear the American name had ceased to have any application to them—I had seen this in the ten minutes I spent in the old woman's room. You could never have said whence they came from the appearance of either of them; wherever it was they had long ago shed and unlearned all native marks and notes. There was nothing in them one recognised or fitted, and, putting the question of speech aside, they might have been Norwegians or Spaniards. Miss Bordereau, after all, had been in Europe nearly three-quarters of a century; it appeared by some verses addressed to her by Aspern on the occasion of his own second absence from America—verses of which Comnor and I had after infinite conjecture established solidly enough the date—that she was even then, as a girl of twenty, on the foreign side of the sea. There was a profession in the poem—I hope not just for the phrase—that he had come back for her sake. We had no real light on her circumstances at that moment, any more than we had upon her origin, which we believed to be of the sort usually spoken of as modest. Cumnor had a theory that she had been a governess in some family in which the poet visited and that, in consequence of her position, there was from the first something unavowed, or rather something quite clandestine, in their relations. I on the other hand had hatched a little romance according to which she was the daughter of an artist, a painter or a sculptor, who had left the Western world, when the century was fresh, to study in the ancient schools. It was essential to my hypothesis that this amiable man should have lost his wife, should have been poor and unsuccessful and should have had a second daughter of a disposition quite different from Juliana's. It was also indispensable that he should have been accompanied to Europe by these young ladies and should have established himself there for the remainder of a struggling saddened life. There was a further implication that Miss Bordereau had had in her youth a perverse and reckless, albeit a generous and fascinating character, and that she had braved some wondrous chances. By what passions had she been ravaged, by what adventures and sufferings had she been blanched, what store of memories had she laid away for the montonous future?

I asked myself these things as I sat spinning theories about her in my arbour and the bees droned in the flowers. It was incontestable that, whether for right or for wrong, most readers of certain of Aspern's poems (poems not as ambiguous as the sonnets—scarcely more divine, I think—of Shakespeare) had taken for granted that Juliana had not always adhered to the steep footway of renunciation. There hovered about her name a perfume of impenitent passion, an intimation that she had not been exactly as the respectable young person in general. Was this a sign that her singer had betrayed her, had given her away, as we say nowadays, to posterity? Certain it is that it would have been difficult to put one's finger on the passage in which her fair fame suffered injury. Moreover was not any fame fair enough that was so sure of duration and was associated with works immortal through their beauty? It was a part of my idea that the young lady had had a foreign lover—and say an unedifying tragical rupture—before her meeting with Jeffrey Aspern. She had lived with her father and sister in a queer old-fashioned expatriated artistic Bohemia of the days when the aesthetic was only the academic and the painters who knew the best models for *contadina* and *pifferaro*[1] wore peaked hats and long hair. It was a society less awake than the coteries of to-day—in its ignorance of the wonderful chances, the opportunities of the early bird, with which its path was strewn—to tatters of old stuff and fragments of old crockery; so that Miss Bordereau appeared not to have picked up or have inherited many objects of importance. There was no enviable *bric-à-brac*, with its provoking legend of cheapness, in the room in which I had seen her. Such a fact as that suggested bareness, but none the less it worked happily into the sentimental interest I had always taken in the early movements of my countrymen as visitors to Europe. When Americans went abroad in 1820 there was something romantic, almost heroic in it, as compared with the perpetual ferryings of the present hour, the hour at which photography and other conveniences have annihilated surprise. Miss Bordereau had sailed with her family on a tossing brig in the days of long voyages and sharp differences; she had had her emotions on the top of yellow diligences, passed the night at inns where she dreamed of travellers' tales, and was most struck, on reaching the Eternal City, with the elegance of Roman pearls and scarfs and mosaic brooches. There was something touching to me in all that, and my imagination frequently went back to the period. If Miss Bordereau carried it there of course Jeffrey Aspern had at other times done so with greater force. It was a much more important fact, if one was looking at his genius critically, that he had lived in the days before the general transfusion. It had happened to me to regret that he had known Europe at all; I should have liked to see what he would have written without that experience, by which he had incontestably been enriched. But as his fate had ruled otherwise I went with him—I tried to judge how the general old order would have struck him. It was not only there, however, I watched him; the relations he had entertained with the special new had even a livelier interest. His own country after all had had most of his life, and his muse, as they said at that time, was essentially American. That was originally what I had prized him for: that at a period when our native land was nude and crude and provincial, when the famous "atmosphere" it is supposed to lack was not even missed, when literature was lonely there and

---

[1] Peasant and piper.

art and form almost impossible, he had found means to live and write like
one of the first; to be free and general and not at all afraid; to feel, understand
and express everything.

5

I was seldom at home in the evening, for when I attempted to occupy myself in my apartments the lamplight brought in a swarm of noxious insects,
and it was too hot for closed windows. Accordingly I spent the late hours
either on the water—the moonlights of Venice are famous—or in the splendid
square which serves as a vast forecourt to the strange old church of Saint Mark.
I sat in front of Florian's café eating ices, listening to music, talking with acquaintances: the traveller will remember how the immense cluster of tables
and little chairs stretches like a promontory into the smooth lake of the Piazza.
The whole place, of a summer's evening, under the stars and with all the
lamps, all the voices and light footsteps on marble—the only sounds of the
immense arcade that encloses it—is an open-air saloon dedicated to cooling
drinks and to a still finer degustation, that of the splendid impressions received during the day. When I didn't prefer to keep mine to myself there was
always a stray tourist, disencumbered of his Bädeker, to discuss them with, or
some domesticated painter rejoicing in the return of the season of strong effects. The great basilica, with its low domes and bristling embroideries, the
mystery of its mosaic and sculpture, looked ghostly in the tempered gloom,
and the sea-breeze passed between the twin columns of the Piazzetta, the
lintels of a door no longer guarded, as gently as if a rich curtain swayed there.
I used sometimes on these occasions to think of the Misses Bordereau and of
the pity of their being shut up in apartments which in the Venetian July
even Venetian vastness couldn't relieve of some stuffiness. Their life seemed
miles away from the life of the Piazza, and no doubt it was really too late to
make the austere Juliana change her habits. But poor Miss Tina would have
enjoyed one of Florian's ices, I was sure; sometimes I even had thoughts of
carrying one home to her. Fortunately my patience bore fruit and I was not
obliged to do anything so ridiculous.

One evening about the middle of July I came in earlier than usual—I forgot what chance had led to this—and instead of going up to my quarters
made my way into the garden. The temperature was very high; it was such a
night as one would gladly have spent in the open air, and I was in no hurry to
go to bed. I had floated home in my gondola, listening to the slow splash of
the oar in the dark narrow canals, and now the only thought that occupied me
was that it would be good to recline at one's length in the fragrant darkness
on a garden bench. The odour of the canal was doubtless at the bottom of that
aspiration, and the breath of the garden, as I entered it, gave consistency to
my purpose. It was delicious—just such an air as must have trembled with
Romeo's vows when he stood among the thick flowers and raised his arms to
his mistress's balcony. I looked at the windows of the palace to see if by
chance the example of Verona—Verona being not far off—had been followed;
but everything was dim, as usual, and everything was still. Juliana might on
the summer nights of her youth have murmured down from open windows

at Jeffrey Aspern, but Miss Tina was not a poet's mistress any more than I was a poet. This however didn't prevent my gratification from being great as I became aware on reaching the end of the garden that my younger padrona was seated in one of the bowers. At first I made out but an indistinct figure, not in the least counting on such an overture from one of my hostesses; it even occurred to me that some enamoured maidservant had stolen in to keep a tryst with her sweetheart. I was going to turn away, not to frighten her, when the figure rose to its height and I recognised Miss Bordereau's niece. I must do myself the justice that I didn't wish to frighten her either, and much as I had longed for some such accident I should have been capable of retreating. It was as if I had laid a trap for her by coming home earlier than usual and by adding to that oddity my invasion of the garden. As she rose she spoke to me, and then I guessed that perhaps, secure in my almost inveterate absence, it was her nightly practice to take a lonely airing. There was no trap in truth, because I had had no suspicion. At first I took the words she uttered for an impatience of my arrival; but as she repeated them—I hadn't caught them clearly—I had the surprise of hearing her say: "Oh dear, I'm so glad you've come!" She and her aunt had in common the property of unexpected speeches. She came out of the arbour almost as if to throw herself in my arms.

I hasten to add that I escaped this ordeal and that she didn't even then shake hands with me. It was an ease to her to see me and presently she told me why—because she was nervous when out-of-doors at night alone. The plants and shrubs looked so strange in the dark, and there were all sorts of queer sounds—she couldn't tell what they were—like the noises of animals. She stood close to me, looking about her with an air of greater security but without any demonstration of interest in me as an individual. Then I felt how little nocturnal prowlings could have been her habit, and I was also reminded—I had been afflicted by the same in talking with her before I took possession—that it was impossible to allow too much for her simplicity.

"You speak as if you were lost in the backwoods," I cheeringly laughed. "How you manage to keep out of this charming place when you've only three steps to take to get into it is more than I've yet been able to discover. You hide away amazingly so long as I'm on the premises, I know; but I had a hope you peeped out a little at other times. You and your poor aunt are worse off than Carmelite nuns in their cells. Should you mind telling me how you exist without air, without exercise, without any sort of human contact? I don't see how you carry on the common business of life."

She looked at me as if I had spoken a strange tongue, and her answer was so little of one that I felt it make for irritation. "We go to bed very early—earlier than you'd believe." I was on the point of saying that this only deepened the mystery, but she gave me some relief by adding: "Before you came we weren't so private. But I've never been out at night."

"Never in these fragrant alleys, blooming here under your nose?"

"Ah," said Miss Tina, "they were never nice till now!" There was a finer sense in this and a flattering comparison, so that it seemed to me I had gained some advantage. As I might follow that further by establishing a good grievance I asked her why, since she thought my garden nice, she had never thanked me in any way for the flowers I had been sending up in such quantities for the previous three weeks. I had not been discouraged—there had been, as she would have observed, a daily armful; but I had been brought up in the common forms and a word of recognition now and then would have touched me in the right place.

"Why I didn't know they were for me!"

"They were for both of you. Why should I make a difference?"

Miss Tina reflected as if she might be thinking of a reason for that, but she failed to produce one. Instead of this she asked abruptly: "Why in the world do you want so much to know us?"

"I ought after all to make a difference," I replied. "That question's your aunt's; it isn't yours. You wouldn't ask it if you hadn't been put up to it."

"She didn't tell me to ask you," Miss Tina replied without confusion. She was indeed the oddest mixture of shyness and straightness.

"Well, she has often wondered about it herself and expressed her wonder to you. She has insisted on it, so that she has put the idea into your head that I'm insufferably pushing. Upon my word I think I've been very discreet. And how completely your aunt must have lost every tradition of sociability, to see anything out of the way in the idea that respectable intelligent people, living as we do under the same roof, should occasionally exchange a remark! What could be more natural? We are of the same country and have at least some of the same tastes, since, like you, I'm intensely fond of Venice."

My friend seemed incapable of grasping more than one clause in any proposition, and she now spoke quickly, eagerly, as if she were answering my whole speech: "I'm not in the least fond of Venice. I should like to go far away!"

"Has she always kept you back so?" I went on, to show her I could be as irrelevant as herself.

"She told me to come out to-night; she has told me very often," said Miss Tina. "It is I who wouldn't come. I don't like to leave her."

"Is she too weak, is she really failing?" I demanded, with more emotion, I think, than I meant to betray. I measured this by the way her eyes rested on me in the darkness. It embarrassed me a little, and to turn the matter off I continued genially: "Do let us sit down together comfortably somewhere— while you tell me all about her."

Miss Tina made no resistance to this. We found a bench less secluded, less confidential, as it were, than the one in the arbour; and we were still sitting there when I heard midnight ring out from those clear bells of Venice which vibrate with a solemnity of their own over the lagoon and hold the air so much more than the chimes of other places. We were together more than an hour and our interview gave, as it struck me, a great lift to my undertaking. Miss Tina accepted the situation without a protest; she had avoided me for three months, yet now she treated me almost as if these three months had made me an old friend. If I had chosen I might have gathered from this that though she had avoided me she had given a good deal of consideration to doing so. She paid no attention to the flight of time—never worried at my keeping her so long away from her aunt. She talked freely, answering questions and asking them and not even taking advantage of certain longish pauses by which they were naturally broken to say she thought she had better go in. It was

almost as if she were waiting for something—something I might say to her—
and intended to give me my opportunity. I was the more struck by this as she
told me how much less well her aunt had been for a good many days, and in a
way that was rather new. She was markedly weaker; at moments she showed no
strength at all; yet more than ever before she wished to be left alone. That was
why she had told her to come out—not even to remain in her own room,
which was alongside; she pronounced poor Miss Tina "a worry, a bore and a
source of aggravation." She sat still for hours together, as if for long sleep;
she had always done that, musing and dozing; but at such times formerly she
gave, in breaks, some small sign of life, of interest, liking her companion to
be near her with her work. This sad personage confided to me that at present her aunt was so motionless as to create the fear she was dead; moreover
she scarce ate or drank—one couldn't see what she lived on. The great thing
was that she still on most days got up; the serious job was to dress her, to wheel
her out of her bedroom. She clung to as many of her old habits as possible and
had always, little company as they had received for years, made a point of
sitting in the great parlour.

I scarce knew what to think of all this—of Miss Tina's sudden conversion
to sociability and of the strange fact that the more the old woman appeared to
decline to her end the less she should desire to be looked after. The story
hung indifferently together, and I even asked myself if it mightn't be a trap
laid for me, the result of a design to make me show my hand. I couldn't have
told why my companions (as they could only by courtesy be called) should
have this purpose—why they should try to trip up so lucrative a lodger. But
at any hazard I kept on my guard, so that Miss Tina shouldn't have occasion
again to ask me what I might really be "up to." Poor woman, before we
parted for the night my mind was at rest as to what *she* might be. She was up
to nothing at all.

She told me more about their affairs than I had hoped; there was no need
to be prying, for it evidently drew her out simply to feel me listen and care.
She ceased wondering why I *should,* and at last while describing the brilliant
life they had led years before, she almost chattered. It was Miss Tina who
judged it brilliant; she said that when they first came to live in Venice, years
and years back—I found her essentially vague about dates and the order in
which events had occurred—there was never a week they hadn't some visitor
or didn't make some pleasant *passeggio*[1] in the town. They had seen all the
curiosities; they had even been to the Lido in a boat—she spoke as if I might
think there was a way on foot; they had had a collation there, brought in three
baskets and spread out on the grass. I asked her what people they had
known and she said Oh very nice ones—the Cavaliere Bombicci and the Con-
tessa Altemura, with whom they had had a great friendship! Also English people—the Churtons and the Goldies and Mrs. Stock-Stock, whom they had
loved dearly; she was dead and gone, poor dear. That was the case with most of
their kind circle—this expression was Miss Tina's own; though a few were left,
which was a wonder considering how they had neglected them. She mentioned
the names of two or three Ventian old women; of a certain doctor, very

[1] Walk.

clever, who was so attentive—he came as a friend, he had really given up practice; of the *avvocato*[2] Pochintesta, who wrote beautiful poems and had addressed one to her aunt. These people came to see them without fail every year, usually at the *capo d'anno*,[3] and of old her aunt used to make them some little present—her aunt and she together: small things that she, Miss Tina, turned out with her own hand, paper lamp-shades, or mats for the decanters of wine at dinner, or those woollen things that in cold weather are worn on the wrists. The last few years there hadn't been many presents; she couldn't think what to make and her aunt had lost interest and never suggested. But the people came all the same; if the good Venetians liked you once they liked you for ever.

There was affecting matter enough in the good faith of this sketch of former social glories; the picnic at the Lido had remained vivid through the ages and poor Miss Tina evidently was of the impression that she had had a dashing youth. She had in fact had a glimpse of the Ventian world in its gossiping home-keeping parsimonious professional walks; for I noted for the first time how nearly she had acquired by contact the trick of the familiar soft-sounding almost infantile prattle of the place. I judged her to have imbibed this invertebrate dialect from the natural way the names of things and people—mostly purely local—rose to her lips. If she knew little of what they represented she knew still less of anything else. Her aunt had drawn in—the failure of interest in the table-mats and lamp-shades was a sign of that—and she hadn't been able to mingle in society or to entertain it alone; so that her range of reminiscence struck one as an old world altogether. Her tone, hadn't it been so decent, would have seemed to carry one back to the queer rococo Venice of Goldoni and Casanova. I found myself mistakenly think of her too as one of Jeffrey Aspern's contemporaries; this came from her having so little in common with my own. It was possible, I indeed reasoned, that she hadn't even heard of him; it might very well be that Juliana had forborne to lift for innocent eyes the veil that covered the temple of her glory. In this case she perhaps wouldn't know of the existence of the papers, and I welcomed that presumption—it made me feel more safe with her—till I remembered we had believed the letter of disavowal received by Cumnor to be in the handwriting of the niece. If it had been dictated to her she had of course to know what it was about; though the effect of it withal was to repudiate the idea of any connexion with the poet. I held it probable at all events that Miss Tina hadn't read a word of his poetry. Moreover if, with her companion, she had always escaped invasion and research, there was little occasion for her having got it into her head that people were "after" the letters. People had not been after them, for people hadn't heard of them. Cumnor's fruitless feeler would have been a solitary accident.

When midnight sounded Miss Tina got up; but she stopped at the door of the house only after she had wandered two or three times with me round the garden. "When shall I see you again?" I asked before she went in; to which she replied with promptness that she should like to come out the next

[2] Attorney.
[3] New Year's Day.

night. She added, however, that she shouldn't come—she was so far from doing everything she liked.

"You might do a few things *I* like," I quite sincerely sighed.

"Oh you—I don't believe you!" she murmured at this, facing me with her simple solemnity.

"Why don't you believe me?"

"Because I don't understand you."

"That's just the sort of occasion to have faith." I couldn't say more, though I should have liked to, as I saw I only mystified her; for I had no wish to have it on my conscience that I might pass for having made love to her. Nothing less should I have seemed to do had I continued to beg a lady to "believe in me" in an Italian garden on a midsummer night. There was some merit in my scruples, for Miss Tina lingered and lingered: I made out in her conviction that she shouldn't really soon come down again and the wish therefore to protract the present. She insisted too on making the talk between us personal to ourselves; and altogether her behaviour was such as would have been possible only to a perfectly artless and a considerably witless woman.

"I shall like the flowers better now that I know them also meant for me."

"How could you have doubted it? If you'll tell me the kind you like best I'll send a double lot."

"Oh I like them all best!" Then she went on familiarly: "Shall you study —shall you read and write—when you go up to your rooms?"

"I don't do that at night—at this season. The lamplight brings in the animals."

"You might have known that when you came."

"I did know it!"

"And in winter do you work at night?"

"I read a good deal, but I don't often write." She listened as if these details had a rare interest, and suddenly a temptation quite at odds with all the prudence I had been teaching myself glimmered at me in her plain mild face. Ah yes, she was safe and I could make her safer! It seemed to me from one moment to another that I couldn't wait longer—that I really must take a sounding. So I went on: "In general before I go to sleep (very often in bed; it's a bad habit, but I confess to it) I read some great poet. In nine cases out of ten it's a volume of Jeffrey Aspern."

I watched her well as I pronounced that name, but I saw nothing wonderful. Why should I indeed? Wasn't Jeffrey Aspern the property of the human race?

"Oh *we* read him—we *have* read him," she quietly replied.

"He's my poet of poets—I know him almost by heart."

For an instant Miss Tina hesitated; then her sociability was too much for her. "Oh by heart—that's nothing"; and, though dimly, she quite lighted. "My aunt used to know him—to know him"—she paused an instant and I wondered what she was going to say—"to know him as a visitor."

"As a visitor?" I guarded my tone.

"He used to call on her and take her out."

I continued to stare. "My dear lady, he died a hundred years ago!"

"Well," she said amusingly, "my aunt's a hundred and fifty."

"Mercy on us!" I cried; "why didn't you tell me before? I should like so to ask her about him."

"She wouldn't care for that—she wouldn't tell you," Miss Tina returned.

"I don't care what she cares for! She *must* tell me—it's not a chance to be lost."

"Oh you should have come twenty years ago. Then she still talked about him."

"And what did she say?" I eagerly asked.

"I don't know—that he liked her immensely."

"And she—didn't she like *him?*"

"She said he was a god." Miss Tina gave me this information flatly, without expression; her tone might have made it a piece of trivial gossip. But it stirred me deeply as she dropped the words into the summer night; their sound might have been the light rustle of an old unfolded love-letter.

"Fancy, fancy!" I murmured. And then, "Tell me this, please—has she got a portrait of him? They're distressingly rare."

"A portrait? I don't know," said Miss Tina; and now there was discomfiture in her face. "Well, good-night!" she added; and she turned into the house.

I accompanied her into the wide dusky stone-paved passage that corresponded on the ground floor with our grand sala. It opened at one end into the garden, at the other upon the canal, and was lighted now only by the small lamp always left for me to take up as I went to bed. An extinguished candle which Miss Tina apparently had brought down with her stood on the same table with it. "Good-night, good-night!" I replied, keeping beside her as she went to get her light. "Surely you'd know, shouldn't you, if she had one?"

"If she had what?" the poor lady asked, looking at me queerly over the flame of her candle.

"A portrait of the god. I don't know what I wouldn't give to see it."

"I don't know what she has got. She keeps her things locked up." And Miss Tina went away toward the staircase with the sense evidently of having said too much.

I let her go—I wished not to frighten her—and I contented myself with remarking that Miss Bordereau wouldn't have locked up such a glorious possession as that: a thing a person would be proud of and hang up in a prominent place on the parlour-wall. Therefore of course she hadn't any portrait. Miss Tina made no direct answer to this and, candle in hand, with her back to me, mounted two or three degrees. Then she stopped short and turned round, looking at me across the dusky space.

"Do you write—do you write?" There was a shake in her voice—she could scarcely bring it out.

"Do I write? Oh don't speak of my writing on the same day with Aspern's!"

"Do you write about *him*—do you pry into his life?"

"Ah that's your aunt's question; it can't be yours!" I said in a tone of slightly wounded sensibility.

"All the more reason then that you should answer it. Do you, please?"

I thought I had allowed for the falsehoods I should have to tell, but I found that in fact when it came to the point I hadn't. Besides, now that I had an opening there was a kind of relief in being frank. Lastly—it was perhaps fanciful, even fatuous—I guessed that Miss Tina personally wouldn't in the last resort be less my friend. So after a moment's hesitation I answered: "Yes, I've written about him and I'm looking for more material. In heaven's name have you got any?"

"*Santo Dio!*" [4] she exclaimed without heeding my question; and she hurried upstairs and out of sight. I might count upon her in the last resort, but for the present she was visibly alarmed. The proof of it was that she began to hide again, so that for a fortnight I kept missing her. I found my patience ebbing and after four or five days of this I told the gardener to stop the "floral tributes."

6

One afternoon, at last, however, as I came down from my quarters to go out, I found her in the sala: it was our first encounter on that ground since I had come to the house. She put on no air of being there by accident; there was an ignorance of such arts in her honest angular diffidence. That I might be quite sure she was waiting for me she mentioned it at once, but telling me with it that Miss Bordereau wished to see me: she would take me into the room at that moment if I had time. If I had been late for a love-tryst I would have stayed for this, and I quickly signified that I should be delighted to wait on my benefactress. "She wants to talk with you—to know you," Miss Tina said, smiling as if she herself appreciated that idea; and she led me to the door of her aunt's apartment. I stopped her a moment before she had opened it, looking at her with some curiosity. I told her that this was a great satisfaction to me and a great honour; but all the same I should like to ask what had made Miss Bordereau so markedly and suddenly change. It had been only the other day that she wouldn't suffer me near her. Miss Tina was not embarrassed by my question; she had as many little unexpected serenities, plausibilities almost, as if she told fibs, but the odd part of them was that they had on the contrary their source in her truthfulness. "Oh my aunt varies," she answered; "it's so terribly dull—I suppose she's tired."

"But you told me she wanted more and more to be alone."

Poor Miss Tina coloured as if she found me too pushing. "Well, if you don't believe she wants to see you, I haven't invented it! I think people often are capricious when they're very old."

"That's perfectly true. I only wanted to be clear as to whether you've repeated to her what I told you the other night."

"What you told me?"

"About Jeffrey Aspern—that I'm looking for materials."

"If I had told her do you think she'd have sent for you?"

"That's exactly what I want to know. If she wants to keep him to herself she might have sent for me to tell me so."

"She won't speak of him," said Miss Tina. Then as she opened the door she added in a lower tone: "I told her nothing."

[4] Holy God!

The old woman was sitting in the same place in which I had seen her last, in the same position, with the same mystifying bandage over her eyes. Her welcome was to turn her almost invisible face to me and show me that while she sat silent she saw me clearly. I made no motion to shake hands with her; I now felt too well that this was out of place for ever. It had been sufficiently enjoined on me that she was too sacred for trivial modernisms—too venerable to touch. There was something so grim in her aspect—it was partly the accident of her green shade—as I stood there to be measured, that I ceased on the spot to doubt her suspecting me, though I didn't in the least myself suspect that Miss Tina hadn't just spoken the truth. She hadn't betrayed me, but the old woman's brooding instinct had served her; she had turned me over and over in the long still hours and had guessed. The worst of it was that she looked terribly like an old woman who at a pinch would, even like Sardanapalus, burn her treasure. Miss Tina pushed a chair forward, saying to me: "This will be a good place for you to sit." As I took possession of it I asked after Miss Bordereau's health; expressed the hope that in spite of the very hot weather it was satisfactory. She answered that it was good enough—good enough; that it was a great thing to be alive.

"Oh as to that, it depends upon what you compare it with!" I returned with a laugh.

"I don't compare—I don't compare. If I did that I should have given everything up long ago."

I liked to take this for a subtle allusion to the rapture she had known in the society of Jeffrey Aspern—though it was true that such an allusion would have accorded ill with the wish I imputed to her to keep him buried in her soul. What it accorded with was my constant conviction that no human being had ever had a happier social gift than his, and what it seemed to convey was that nothing in the world was worth speaking of if one pretended to speak of that. But one didn't pretend! Miss Tina sat down beside her aunt, looking as if she had reason to believe some wonderful talk would come off between us.

"It's about the beautiful flowers," said the old lady; "you sent us so many —I ought to have thanked you for them before. But I don't write letters and I receive company but at long intervals."

She hadn't thanked me while the flowers continued to come, but she departed from her custom so far as to send for me as soon as she began to fear they wouldn't come any more. I noted this; I remembered what an acquisitive propensity she had shown when it was a question of extracting gold from me, and I privately rejoiced at the happy thought I had had in suspending my tribute. She had missed it and was willing to make a concession to bring it back. At the first sign of this concession I could only go to meet her. "I'm afraid you haven't had many, of late, but they shall begin again immediately —to-morrow, to-night."

"Oh do send us some to-night!" Miss Tina cried as if it were a great affair.

"What else should you do with them? It isn't a manly taste to make a bower of your room," the old woman remarked.

"I don't make a bower of my room, but I'm exceedingly fond of growing flowers, of watching their ways. There's nothing unmanly in that: it has been the amusement of philosophers, of statesmen in retirement; even I think of great captains."

"I suppose you know you can sell them—those you don't use," Miss Bordereau went on. "I dare say they wouldn't give you much for them; still, you could make a bargain."

"Oh I've never in my life made a bargain, as you ought pretty well to have gathered. My gardener disposes of them and I ask no questions."

"I'd ask a few, I can promise you!" said Miss Bordereau; and it was so I first heard the strange sound of her laugh, which was as if the faint "walking" ghost of her old-time tone had suddenly cut a caper. I couldn't get used to the idea that this vision of pecuniary profit was most what drew out the divine Juliana.

"Come into the garden yourself and pick them; come as often as you like; come every day. The flowers are all for you," I pursued, addressing Miss Tina and carrying off this veracious statement by treating it as an innocent joke. "I can't imagine why she doesn't come down," I added for Miss Bordereau's benefit.

"You must make her come; you must come up and fetch her," the old woman said to my stupefaction. "That odd thing you've made in the corner will do very well for her to sit in."

The allusion to the most elaborate of my shady coverts, a sketchy "summer-house," was irreverent; it confirmed the impression I had already received that there was a flicker of impertinence in Miss Bordereau's talk, a vague echo of the boldness or the archness of her adventurous youth and which had somehow automatically outlived passions and faculties. None the less I asked: "Wouldn't it be possible for you to come down there yourself? Wouldn't it do you good to sit there in the shade and the sweet air?"

"Oh, sir, when I move out of this it won't be to sit in the air, and I'm afraid that any that may be stirring around me won't be particularly sweet! It will be a very dark shade indeed. But that won't be just yet," Miss Bordereau continued cannily, as if to correct any hopes this free glance at the last receptacle of her mortality might lead me to entertain. "I've sat here many a day and have had enough of arbours in my time. But I'm not afraid to wait till I'm called."

Miss Tina had expected, as I felt, rare conversation, but perhaps she found it less gracious on her aunt's side—considering I had been sent for with a civil intention—than she had hoped. As to give the position a turn that would put our companion in a light more favourable she said to me: "Didn't I tell you the other night that she had sent me out? You see I can do what I like!"

"Do you pity her—do you teach her to pity herself?" Miss Bordereau demanded, before I had time to answer this appeal. "She has a much easier life than I had at her age."

"You must remember it has been quite open to me," I said, "to think you rather inhuman."

"Inhuman? That's what the poets used to call the women a hundred years ago. Don't try that; you won't do as well as they!" Juliana went on. "There's no more poetry in the world—that I know of at least. But I won't bandy words with you," she said, and I well remember the old-fashioned artificial sound she gave the speech. "You make me talk, talk, talk! It isn't good for me at all." I got up at this and told her I would take no more of her time; but she detained me to put a question, "Do you remember, the day I saw you about the rooms, that you offered us the use of your gondola?" And when I assented promptly, struck again with her disposition to make a "good thing" of my being there and wondering what she now had in her eye, she produced: "Why don't you take that girl out in it and show her the place?"

"Oh dear aunt, what do you want to do with me?" cried the "girl" with a piteous quaver. "I know all about the place!"

"Well then go with him and explain!" said Miss Bordereau, who gave an effect of cruelty to her implacable power of retort. This showed her as a sarcastic profane cynical old woman. "Haven't we heard that there have been all sorts of changes in all these years? You ought to see them, and at your age—I don't mean because you're so young—you ought to take the chances that come. You're old enough, my dear, and this gentleman won't hurt you. He'll show you the famous sunsets, if they still go on—*do* they go on? The sun set for me so long ago. But that's not a reason. Besides, I shall never miss you; you think you're too important. Take her to the Piazza; it used to be very pretty," Miss Bordereau continued, addressing herself to me. "What have they done with the funny old church? I hope it hasn't tumbled down. Let her look at the shops; she may take some money, she may buy what she likes."

Poor Miss Tina had got up, discountenanced and helpless, and as we stood there before her aunt it would certainly have struck a spectator of the scene that our venerable friend was making rare sport of us. Miss Tina protested in a confusion of exclamations and murmurs; but I lost no time in saying that if she would do me the honour to accept the hospitality of my boat I would engage she really shouldn't be bored. Or if she didn't want so much of my company, the boat itself, with the gondolier, was at her service; he was a capital oar and she might have every confidence. Miss Tina, without definitely answering this speech, looked away from me and out of the window, quite as if about to weep, and I remarked that once we had Miss Bordereau's approval we could easily come to an understanding. We would take an hour, whichever she liked, one of the very next days. As I made my obeisance to the old lady I asked her if she would kindly permit me to see her again.

For a moment she kept me; then she said: "Is it very necessary to your happiness?"

"It diverts me more than I can say."

"You're wonderfully civil. Don't you know it almost kills *me*?"

"How can I believe that when I see you more animated, more brilliant than when I came in?"

"That's very true, aunt," said Miss Tina. "I think it does you good."

"Isn't it touching, the solicitude we each have that the other shall enjoy herself?" sneered Miss Bordereau. "If you think me brilliant to-day you don't know what you are talking about; you've never seen an agreeable woman. What do you people know about good society?" she cried; but before I could tell her, "Don't try to pay me a compliment; I've been spoiled," she went on. "My door's shut, but you may sometimes knock."

With this she dismissed me and I left the room. The latch closed behind me, but Miss Tina, contrary to my hope, had remained within. I passed slowly across the hall and before taking my way downstairs waited a little. My hope was answered; after a minute my conductress followed me. "That's a delightful idea about the Piazza," I said. "When will you go—to-night, to-morrow?"

She had been disconcerted, as I have mentioned, but I had already perceived, and I was to observe again, that when Miss Tina was embarrassed she didn't—as most women would have in like case—turn away, floundering and hedging, but came closer, as it were, with a deprecating, a clinging appeal to be spared, to be protected. Her attitude was a constant prayer for aid and explanation, and yet no woman in the world could have been less of a comedian. From the moment you were kind to her she depended on you absolutely; her self-consciousness dropped and she took the greatest intimacy, the innocent intimacy that was all she could conceive, for granted. She didn't know, she now declared, what possessed her aunt, who had changed so quickly, who had got some idea. I replied that she must catch the idea and let me have it: we would go and take an ice together at Florian's and she should report while we listened to the band.

"Oh, it will take me a long time to be able to 'report'!" she said rather ruefully; and she could promise me this satisfaction neither for that night nor for the next. I was patient now, however, for I felt I had only to wait; and in fact at the end of the week, one lovely evening after dinner, she stepped into my gondola, to which in honour of the occasion I had attached a second oar.

We swept in the course of five minutes into the Grand Canal; whereupon she uttered a murmur of ecstasy as fresh as if she had been a tourist just arrived. She had forgotten the splendour of the great water-way on a clear summer evening, and how the sense of floating between marble palaces and reflected lights disposed the mind to freedom and ease. We floated long and far, and though my friend gave no high-pitched voice to her glee I was sure of her full surrender. She was more than pleased, she was transported; the whole thing was an immense liberation. The gondola moved with slow strokes, to give her time to enjoy it, and she listened to the plash of the oars, which grew louder and more musically liquid as we passed into narrow canals, as if it were a revelation of Venice. When I asked her how long it was since she had thus floated, she answered: "Oh I don't know; a long time—not since my aunt began to be ill." This was not the only show of her extreme vagueness about the previous years and the line marking off the period of Miss Bordereau's eminence. I was not at liberty to keep her out long, but we took a considerable giro[1] before going to the Piazza. I asked her no questions, holding off by design from her life at home and the things I wanted to know; I poured, rather, treasures of information about the objects before and around us into her ears, describing also Florence and Rome, discoursing on the charms and advantages of travel. She reclined, receptive, on the deep leather cushions, turned her eyes conscientiously to everything I noted and never mentioned to me till some

1 Turn, circuit.

time afterwards that she might be supposed to know Florence better than I, as she had lived there for years with her kinswoman. At last she said with the shy impatience of a child: "Are we not really going to the Piazza? That's what I want to see!" I immediately gave the order that we should go straight, after which we sat silent with the expectation of arrival. As some time still passed, however, she broke out of her own movement: "I've found out what's the matter with my aunt: she's afraid you'll go!"

I quite gasped. "What has put that into her head?"

"She has had an idea you've not been happy. That's why she is different now."

"You mean she wants to make me happier?"

"Well, she wants you not to go. She wants you to stay."

"I suppose you mean on account of the rent," I remarked candidly.

Miss Tina's candour but profited. "Yes, you know; so that I shall have more."

"How much does she want you to have?" I asked with all the gaiety I now felt. "She ought to fix the sum, so that I may stay till it's made up."

"Oh that wouldn't please me," said Miss Tina. "It would be unheard of, your taking that trouble."

"But suppose I should have my own reasons for staying in Venice?"

"Then it would be better for you to stay in some other house."

"And what would your aunt say to that?"

"She wouldn't like it at all. But I should think you'd do well to give up your reasons and go away altogether."

"Dear Miss Tina," I said, "it's not so easy to give up my reasons!"

She made no immediate answer to this, but after a moment broke out afresh: "I think I know what your reasons are!"

"I dare say, because the other night I almost told you how I wished you'd help me to make them good."

"I can't do that without being false to my aunt."

"What do you mean by being false to her?"

"Why she would never consent to what you want. She has been asked, she has been written to. It makes her fearfully angry."

"Then she *has* papers of value?" I precipitately cried.

"Oh she has everything!" sighed Miss Tina, with a curious weariness, a sudden lapse into gloom.

These words caused all my pulses to throb, for I regarded them as precious evidence. I felt them too deeply to speak, and in the interval the gondola approached the Piazzetta. After we had disembarked I asked my companion if she would rather walk round the square or go and sit before the great café; to which she replied that she would do whichever I liked best—I must only remember again how little time she had. I assured her there was plenty to do both, and we made the circuit of the long arcades. Her spirits revived at the sight of the bright shop-windows, and she lingered and stopped, admiring or disapproving of their contents, asking me what I thought of things, theorizing about prices. My attention wandered from her; her words of a while before "Oh she has everything!" echoed so in my consciousness. We sat down at last in the crowded circle at Florian's, finding an unoccupied table among those that were ranged in the square. It was a splendid night and all the world out-of-doors; Miss Tina couldn't have wished the elements more auspicious for her return to society. I saw she felt it all even more than she told, but her impressions were well-nigh too many for her. She had forgotten the attraction of the world and was learning that she had for the best years of her life been rather mercilessly cheated of it. This didn't make her angry; but as she took in the charming scene her face had, in spite of its smile of appreciation, the flush of a wounded surprise. She didn't speak, sunk in the sense of opportunities, for ever lost, that ought to have been easy; and this gave me a chance to say to her: "Did you mean a while ago that your aunt has a plan of keeping me on by admitting me occasionally to her presence?"

"She thinks it will make a difference with you if you sometimes see her. She wants you so much to stay that she's willing to make that concession."

"And what good does she consider I think it will do me to see her?"

"I don't know; it must be interesting," said Miss Tina simply. "You told her you found it so."

"So I did; but every one doesn't think that."

"No, of course not, or more people would try."

"Well, if she's capable of making that reflexion she's capable also of making this further one," I went on: "that I must have a particular reason for not doing as others do, in spite of the interest she offers—for not leaving her alone." Miss Tina looked as if she failed to grasp this rather complicated proposition; so I continued: "If you've not told her what I said to you the other night may she not at least have guessed it?"

"I don't know—she's very suspicious."

"But she hasn't been made so by indiscreet curiosity, by persecution?"

"No, no; it isn't that," said Miss Tina, turning on me a troubled face. "I don't know how to say it; it's on account of something—ages ago, before I was born—in her life."

"Something? What sort of thing?"—and I asked it as if I could have no idea.

"Oh she has never told me." And I was sure my friend spoke the truth.

Her extreme limpidity was almost provoking, and I felt for the moment that she would have been more satisfactory if she had been less ingenuous. "Do you suppose it's something to which Jeffrey Aspern's letters and papers —I mean the things in her possession—have reference?"

"I dare say it is!" my companion exclaimed as if this were a very happy suggestion. "I've never looked at any of those things."

"None of them? Then how do you know what they are?"

"I don't," said Miss Tina placidly. "I've never had them in my hands. But I've seen them when she has had them out."

"Does she have them out often?"

"Not now, but she used to. She's very fond of them."

"In spite of their being compromising?"

"Compromising?" Miss Tina repeated as if vague as to what that meant. I felt almost as one who corrupts the innocence of youth.

"I allude to their containing painful memories."

"Oh I don't think anything's painful."

"You mean there's nothing to affect her reputation?"

An odder look even than usual came at this into the face of Miss Border-eau's niece—a confession, it seemed, of helplessness, an appeal to me to deal fairly, generously with her. I had brought her to the Piazza, placed her among charming influences, paid her an attention she appreciated, and now I appeared to show it all as a bribe—a bribe to make her turn in some way against her aunt. She was of a yielding nature and capable of doing almost anything to please a person markedly kind to her; but the greatest kindness of all would be not to presume too much on this. It was strange enough, as I afterwards thought, that she had not the least air of resenting my want of consideration for her aunt's character, which would have been in the worst possible taste if anything less vital—from my point of view—had been at stake. I don't think she really measured it. "Do you mean she ever did something bad?" she asked in a moment.

"Heaven forbid I should say so, and it's none of my business. Besides, if she did," I agreeably put it, "that was in other ages, in another world. But why shouldn't she destroy her papers?"

"Oh she loves them too much."

"Even now, when she may be near her end?"

"Perhaps when she's sure of that she will."

"Well, Miss Tina," I said, "that's just what I should like you to prevent."

"How can I prevent it?"

"Couldn't you get them away from her?"

"And give them to you?"

This put the case, superficially, with sharp irony, but I was sure of her not intending that. "Oh I mean that you might let me see them and look them over. It isn't for myself, or that I should want them at any cost to any one else. It's simply that they would be of such immense interest to the public, such immeasurable importance as a contribution to Jeffrey Aspern's history."

She listened to me in her usual way, as if I abounded in matters she had never heard of, and I felt almost as base as the reporter of a newspaper who forces his way into a house of mourning. This was marked when she presently said: "There was a gentleman who some time ago wrote to her in very much those words. He also wanted her papers."

"And did she answer him?" I asked, rather ashamed of not having my friend's rectitude.

"Only when he had written two or three times. He made her very angry."

"And what did she say?"

"She said he was a devil," Miss Tina replied categorically.

"She used that expression in her letter?"

"Oh no; she said it to me. She made me write to him."

"And what did you say?"

"I told him there were no papers at all."

"Ah poor gentleman!" I groaned.

"I knew there were, but I wrote what she bade me."

"Of course you had to do that. But I hope I shan't pass for a devil."

"It will depend upon what you ask me to do for you," my companion smiled.

"Oh if there's a chance of *your* thinking so my affair's in a bad way! I shan't ask you to steal for me, nor even to fib—for you *can't* fib, unless on paper. But the principal thing is this—to prevent her destroying the papers."

"Why I've no control of her," said Miss Tina. "It's she who controls me."

"But she doesn't control her own arms and legs, does she? The way she would naturally destroy her letters would be to burn them. Now she can't burn them without fire, and she can't get fire unless you give it to her."

"I've always done everything she has asked," my poor friend pleaded. "Besides, there's Olimpia."

I was on the point of saying that Olimpia was probably corruptible, but I thought it best not to sound that note. So I simply put it that this frail creature might perhaps be managed.

"Every one can be managed by my aunt," said Miss Tina. And then she remembered that her holiday was over; she must go home.

I laid my hand on her arm, across the table, to stay her a moment. "What I want of you is a general promise to help me."

"Oh how *can* I, how *can* I?" she asked, wondering and troubled. She was half-surprised, half-frightened at my attaching that importance to her, at my calling on her for action.

"This is the main thing: to watch our friend carefully and warn me in time, before she commits that dreadful sacrilege."

"I can't watch her when she makes me go out."

"That's very true."

"And when you do too."

"Mercy on us—do you think she'll have done anything to-night?"

"I don't know. She's very cunning."

"Are you trying to frighten me?" I asked.

I felt this question sufficiently answered when my companion murmured in a musing, almost envious way: "Oh but she loves them—she loves them!"

This reflexion, repeated with such emphasis, gave me great comfort; but to obtain more of that balm I said: "If she shouldn't intend to destroy the objects we speak of before her death she'll probably have made some disposition by will."

"By will?"

"Hasn't she made a will for your benefit?"

"Ah she has so little to leave. That's why she likes money," said Miss Tina.

"Might I ask, since we're really talking things over, what you and she live on?"

"On some money that comes from America, from a gentleman—I think a lawyer—in New York. He sends it every quarter. It isn't much!"

"And won't she have disposed of that?"

My companion hesitated—I saw she was blushing. "I believe it's mine," she said; and the look and tone which accompanied these words betrayed so the absence of the habit of thinking of herself that I almost thought her charming. The next instant she added: "But she had in an *avvocato* here once, ever so long ago. And some people came and signed something."

"They were probably witnesses. And you weren't asked to sign? Well then," I argued, rapidly and hopefully, "it's because you're the legatee. She must have left all her documents to you!"

"If she has it's with very strict conditions," Miss Tina responded, rising quickly, while the movement gave the words a small character of decision. They seemed to imply that the bequest would be accompanied with a proviso that the articles bequeathed should remain concealed from every inquisitive eye, and that I was very much mistaken if I thought her the person to depart from an injunction so absolute.

"Oh of course you'll have to abide by the terms," I said; and she uttered nothing to mitigate the rigour of this conclusion. None the less, later on, just before we disembarked at her own door after a return which had taken place almost in silence, she said to me abruptly: "I'll do what I can to help you." I was grateful for this—it was very well so far as it went; but it didn't keep me from remembering that night in a worried waking hour that I now had her word for it to re-enforce my own impression that the old woman was full of craft.

7

The fear of what this side of her character might have led her to do made me nervous for days afterwards. I waited for an intimation from Miss Tina; I almost read it as her duty to keep me informed, to let me know definitely whether or no Miss Bordereau had sacrificed her treasures. But as she gave no sign I lost patience and determined to put the case to the very touch of my own senses. I sent late one afternoon to ask if I might pay the ladies a visit, and my servant came back with surprising news. Miss Bordereau could be approached without the least difficulty; she had been moved out into the sala and was sitting by the window that overlooked the garden. I descended and found this picture correct; the old lady had been wheeled forth into the world and had a certain air, which came mainly perhaps from some brighter element in her dress, of being prepared again to have converse with it. It had not yet, however, begun to flock about her; she was perfectly alone and, though the door leading to her own quarters stood open, I had at first no glimpse of Miss Tina. The window at which she sat had the afternoon shade and, one of the shutters having been pushed back, she could see the pleasant garden, where the summer sun had by this time dried up too many of the plants—she could see the yellow light and the long shadows.

"Have you come to tell me you'll take the rooms for six months more?" she asked as I approached her, startling me by something coarse in her cupidity almost as much as if she hadn't already given me a specimen of it. Juliana's desire to make our acquaintance lucrative had been, as I have sufficiently indicated, a false note in my image of the woman who had inspired a great poet with immortal lines; but I may say here definitely that I after all recognised large allowance to be made for her. It was I who had kindled the unholy flame; it was I who had put into her head that she had the means of making money. She appeared never to have thought of that; she had been living wastefully for years, in a house five times too big for her, on a footing that I could explain only by the presumption that, excessive as it was, the space she enjoyed cost her next to nothing and that, small as were her revenues, they left her, for Venice, an appreciable margin. I had descended on her one day and taught her to calculate, and my almost extravagant comedy on the subject of the garden had presented me irresistibly in the light of a victim. Like all persons who achieve the miracle of changing their point of view late in life, she had been intensely converted; she had seized my hint with a desperate tremulous clutch.

I invited myself to go and get one of the chairs that stood, at a distance, against the wall—she had given herself no concern as to whether I should sit or stand; and while I placed it near her I began gaily: "Oh dear madam, what an imagination you have, what an intellectual sweep! I'm a poor devil of a man of letters who lives from day to day. How can I take palaces by the year? My existence is precarious. I don't know whether six months hence I shall have bread to put in my mouth. I've treated myself for once; it has been an immense luxury. But when it comes to going on——!"

"Are your rooms too dear? If they are you can have more for the same money," Juliana responded. "We can arrange, we can *combinare*,[1] as they say here."

"Well yes, since you ask me, they're too dear, much too dear," I said. "Evidently you suppose me richer than I am."

She looked at me as from the mouth of her cave. "If you write books don't you sell them?"

"Do you mean don't people buy them? A little, a very little—not so much as I could wish. Writing books, unless one be a great genius—and even then! —is the last road to fortune. I think there's no more money to be made by good letters."

"Perhaps, you don't choose nice subjects. What do you write about?" Miss Bordereau implacably pursued.

"About the books of other people. I'm a critic, a commentator, an historian, in a small way." I wondered what she was coming to.

"And what other people now?"

"Oh better ones than myself: the great writers mainly—the great philosophers and poets of the past; those who are dead and gone and can't, poor darlings, speak for themselves."

"And what do you say about them?"

"I say they sometimes attached themselves to very clever women!" I replied as for pleasantness. I had measured, as I thought, my risk, but as my words fell upon the air they were to strike me as imprudent. However, I had launched them and I wasn't sorry, for perhaps after all the old woman would be willing to treat. It seemed tolerably obvious that she knew my secret; why therefore drag the process out? But she didn't take what I had said as a confession; she only asked:

"Do you think it's right to rake up the past?"

"I don't feel that I know what you mean by raking it up. How can we get at it unless we dig a little? The present has such a rough way of treading it down."

"Oh I like the past, but I don't like critics," my hostess declared with her hard complacency.

"Neither do I, but I like their discoveries."

[1] Make a change, come to terms.

"Aren't they mostly lies?"

"The lies are what they sometimes discover," I said, smiling at the quiet impertinence of this. "They often lay bare the truth."

"The truth is God's, it isn't man's; we had better leave it alone. Who can judge of it?—who can say?"

"We're terribly in the dark, I know," I admitted; "but if we give up trying what becomes of all the fine things? What becomes of the work I just mentioned, that of the great philosophers and poets? It's all vain words if there's nothing to measure it by."

"You talk as if you were a tailor," said Miss Bordereau whimsically; and then she added quickly and in a different manner: "This house is very fine; the proportions are magnificent. To-day I wanted to look at this part again. I made them bring me out here. When your man came just now to learn if I would see you I was on the point of sending for you to ask if you didn't mean to go on. I wanted to judge what I'm letting you have. This sala is very grand," she pursued like an auctioneer, moving a little, as I guessed, her invisible eyes. "I don't believe you often have lived in such a house, eh?"

"I can't often afford to!" I said.

"Well then how much will you give me for six months?"

I was on the point of exclaiming—and the air of excruciation in my face would have denoted a moral fact—"Don't, Juliana; for *his* sake, don't!" But I controlled myself and asked less passionately: "Why should I remain so long as that?"

"I thought you liked it," said Miss Bordereau with her shrivelled dignity.

"So I thought I should."

For a moment she said nothing more, and I left my own words to suggest to her what they might. I half-expected her to say, coldly enough, that if I had been disappointed we needn't continue the discussion, and this in spite of the fact that I believed her now to have in her mind—however it had come there—what would have told her that my disappointment was natural. But to my extreme surprise she ended by observing: "If you don't think we've treated you well enough perhaps we can discover some way of treating you better." This speech was somehow so incongruous that it made me laugh again, and I excused myself by saying that she talked as if I were a sulky boy pouting in the corner and having to be "brought round." I hadn't a grain of complaint to make; and could anything have exceeded Miss Tina's graciousness in accompanying me a few nights before to the Piazza? At this the old woman went on: "Well, you brought it on yourself!" And then in a different tone: "She's a very fine girl." I assented cordially to this proposition, and she expressed the hope that I did so not merely to be obliging, but that I really liked her. Meanwhile I wondered still more what Miss Bordereau was coming to. "Except for me, to-day," she said, "she hasn't a relation in the world." Did she by describing her niece as amiable and unencumbered wish to represent her as a *parti*?[2]

It was perfectly true that I couldn't afford to go on with my rooms at a fancy price and that I had already devoted to my undertaking almost all the

2 Eligible person.

hard cash I had set apart for it. My patience and my time were by no means exhausted, but I should be able to draw upon them only on a more usual Venetian basis. I was willing to pay the precious personage with whom my pecuniary dealings were such a discord twice as much as any other *padrona di casa*[3] would have asked, but I wasn't willing to pay her twenty times as much. I told her so plainly, and my plainness appeared to have some success, for she exclaimed: "Very good; you've done what I asked—you've made an offer!"

"Yes, but not for half a year. Only by the month."

"Oh I must think of that then." She seemed disappointed that I wouldn't tie myself to a period, and I guessed that she wished both to secure me and to discourage me; to say severely: "Do you dream that you can get off with less than six months? Do you dream that even by the end of that time you'll be appreciably nearer your victory?" What was most in my mind was that she had a fancy to play me the trick of making me engage myself when in fact she had sacrificed her treasure. There was a moment when my suspense on this point was so acute that I all but broke out with the question, and what kept it back was but an instinctive recoil—lest it should be a mistake—from the last violence of self-exposure. She was such a subtle old witch that one could never tell where one stood with her. You may imagine whether it cleared up the puzzle when, just after she had said she would think of my proposal and without any formal transition, she drew out of her pocket with an embarrassed hand a small object wrapped in crumpled white paper. She held it there a moment and then resumed: "Do you know much about curiosities?"

"About curiosities?"

"About antiquities, the old gimcracks that people pay so much for to-day. Do you know the kind of price they bring?"

I thought I saw what was coming, but I said ingenuously: "Do you want to buy something?"

"No, I want to sell. What would an amateur give me for that?" She unfolded the white paper and made a motion for me to take from her a small oval portrait. I possessed myself of it with fingers of which I could only hope that they didn't betray the intensity of their clutch, and she added: "I would part with it only for a good price."

At the first glance I recognized Jeffrey Aspern, and was well aware that I flushed with the act. As she was watching me however I had the consistency to exclaim: "What a striking face! Do tell me who it is."

"He's an old friend of mine, a very distinguished man in his day. He gave it me himself, but I'm afraid to mention his name, lest you never should have heard of him, critic and historian as you are. I know the world goes fast and one generation forgets another. He was all the fashion when I was young."

She was perhaps amazed at my assurance, but I was surprised at hers; at her having the energy, in her state of health and at her time of life, to wish to sport with me to that tune simply for her private entertainment—the humour to test me and practise on me and befool me. This at least was the interpretation that I put upon her production of the relic, for I couldn't

[3] House owner.

believe she really desired to sell it or cared for any information I might give her. What she wished was to dangle it before my eyes and put a prohibitive price on it. "The face comes back to me, it torments me," I said, turning the object this way and that and looking at it very critically. It was a careful but not a supreme work of art, larger than the ordinary miniature and representing a young man with a remarkably handsome face, in a high-collared green coat and a buff waistcoat. I felt in the little work a virtue of likeness and judged it to have been painted when the model was about twenty-five. There are, as all the world knows, three other portraits of the poet in existence, but none of so early a date as this elegant image. "I've never seen the original, clearly a man of a past age, but I've seen other reproductions of this face," I went on. "You expressed doubt of this generation's having heard of the gentleman, but he strikes me for all the world as a celebrity. Now who is he? I can't put my finger on him—I can't give him a label. Wasn't he a writer? Surely he's a poet." I was determined that it should be she, not I, who should first pronounce Jeffrey Aspern's name.

My resolution was taken in ignorance of Miss Bordereau's extremely resolute character, and her lips never formed in my hearing the syllables that meant so much for her. She neglected to answer my question, but raised her hand to take back the picture, using a gesture which though impotent was in a high degree peremptory. "It's only a person who should know for himself that would give me my price," she said with a certain dryness.

"Oh then you have a price?" I didn't restore the charming thing; not from any vindictive purpose, but because I instinctively clung to it. We looked at each other hard while I retained it.

"I know the least I would take. What it occurred to me to ask you about is the most I shall be able to get."

She made a movement, drawing herself together as if, in a spasm of dread at having lost her prize she had been impelled to the immense effort of rising to snatch it from me. I instantly placed it in her hand again, saying as I did so: "I should like to have it myself, but with your ideas it would be quite beyond my mark."

She turned the small oval plate over in her lap, with its face down, and I heard her catch her breath as after a strain or an escape. This however did not prevent her saying in a moment: "You'd buy a likeness of a person you don't know by an artist who has no reputation?"

"The artist may have no reputation, but that thing's wonderfully well painted," I replied, to give myself a reason.

"It's lucky you thought of saying that, because the painter was my father."

"That makes the picture indeed precious!" I returned with gaiety; and I may add that a part of my cheer came from this proof I had been right in my theory of Miss Bordereau's origin. Aspern had of course met the young lady on his going to her father's studio as a sitter. I observed to Miss Bordereau that if she would entrust me with her property for twenty-four hours I should be happy to take advice on it; but she made no other reply than to slip it in silence into her pocket. This convinced me still more that she had no sincere intention of selling it during her lifetime, though she may have desired to satisfy herself as to the sum her neice, should she leave it to her, might expect eventually to obtain for it. "Well, at any rate, I hope you won't offer it without giving me notice," I said as she remained irresponsive. "Remember me as a possible purchaser."

"I should want your money first!" she returned with unexpected rudeness; and then, as if she bethought herself that I might well complain of such a tone and wished to turn the matter off, asked abruptly what I talked about with her niece when I went out with her that way of an evening.

"You speak as if we had set up the habit," I replied. "Certainly I should be very glad if it were to become our pleasant custom. But in that case I should feel a still greater scruple at betraying a lady's confidence."

"Her confidence? Has my niece confidence?"

"Here she is—she can tell you herself," I said; for Miss Tina now appeared on the threshold of the old woman's parlour. "Have you confidence, Miss Tina? Your aunt wants very much to know."

"Not in her, not in her!" the younger lady declared, shaking her head with a dolefulness that was neither jocular nor affected. "I don't know what to do with her; she has fits of horrid imprudence. She's so easily tired—and yet she has begun to roam, to drag herself about the house." And she looked down at her yoke-fellow of long years with a vacancy of wonder, as if all their contact and custom hadn't made her perversities, on occasion, any more easy to follow.

"I know what I'm about. I'm not losing my mind. I dare say you'd like to think so," said Miss Bordereau with a crudity of cynicism.

"I don't suppose you came out here yourself. Miss Tina must have had to lend you a hand," I interposed for conciliation.

"Oh she insisted we should push her; and when she insists!" said Miss Tina, in the same tone of apprehension; as if there were no knowing what service she disapproved of her aunt might force her next to render.

"I've always got most things done I wanted, thank God! The people I've lived with have humoured me," the old woman continued, speaking out of the white ashes of her vanity.

I took it pleasantly up. "I suppose you mean they've obeyed you."

"Well, whatever it is—when they like one."

"It's just because I like you that I want to resist," said Miss Tina with a nervous laugh.

"Oh I suspect you'll bring Miss Bordereau upstairs next to pay me a visit," I went on; to which the old lady replied:

"Oh no; I can keep an eye on you from here!"

"You're very tired; you'll certainly be ill to-night!" cried Miss Tina.

"Nonsense, dear; I feel better at this moment than I've done for a month. To-morrow I shall come out again. I want to be where I can see this clever gentleman."

"Shouldn't you perhaps see me better in your sitting-room?" I asked.

"Don't you mean shouldn't you have a better chance at me?" she returned fixing me a moment with her green shade.

"Ah I haven't that anywhere! I look at you but don't see you."

"You agitate her dreadfully—and that's not good," said Miss Tina, giving me a reproachful deterrent headshake.

"I want to watch you—I want to watch you!" Miss Bordereau went on.

"Well then let us spend as much of our time together as possible—I don't care where. That will give you every facility."

"Oh I've seen you enough for to-day. I'm satisfied. Now I'll go home," Juliana said. Miss Tina laid her hands on the back of the wheeled chair and began to push, but I begged her to let me take her place. "Oh yes, you may move me this way—you shan't in any other!" the old woman cried as she felt herself propelled firmly and easily over the smooth hard floor. Before we reached the door of her own apartment she bade me stop, and she took a long last look up and down the noble sala. "Oh it's a prodigious house!" she murmured; after which I pushed her forward. When we had entered the parlour Miss Tina let me know she should now be able to manage, and at the same moment the little red-haired *donna* came to meet her mistress. Miss Tina's idea was evidently to get her aunt immediately back to bed. I confess that in spite of this urgency I was guilty of the indiscretion of lingering; it held me there to feel myself so close to the objects I coveted—which would be probably put away somewhere in the faded unsociable room. The place had indeed a bareness that suggested no hidden values; there were neither dusky nooks nor curtained corners, neither massive cabinets nor chests with iron bands. Moreover it was possible, it was perhaps even likely, that the old lady had consigned her relics to her bedroom, to some battered box that was shoved under the bed, to the drawer of some lame dressing-table, where they would be in the range of vision by the dim night-lamp. None the less I turned an eye on every article of furniture, on every conceivable cover for a hoard, and noticed that there were half a dozen things with drawers, and in particular a tall old secretary with brass ornaments of the style of the Empire —a receptacle somewhat infirm but still capable of keeping rare secrets. I don't know why this article so engaged me, small purpose as I had of breaking into it; but I stared at it so hard that Miss Tina noticed me and changed colour. Her doing this made me think I was right and that, wherever they might have been before, the Aspern papers at that moment languished behind the peevish little lock of the secretary. It was hard to turn my attention from the dull mahogany front when I reflected that a plain panel divided me from the goal of my hopes; but I gathered up my slightly scattered prudence and with an effort took leave of my hostess. To make the effort graceful I said to her that I should certainly bring her an opinion about the little picture.

"The little picture?" Miss Tina asked in surprise.

"What do *you* know about it, my dear?" the old woman demanded. "You needn't mind. I've fixed my price."

"And what may that be?"

"A thousand pounds."

"Oh Lord!" cried poor Miss Tina irrepressibly.

"Is that what she talks to you about?" said Miss Bordereau.

"Imagine your aunt's wanting to know!" I had to separate from my younger friend with only those words, though I should have liked immensely to add: "For heaven's sake meet me to-night in the garden!"

8

As it turned out the precaution had not been needed, for three hours later, just as I had finished my dinner, Miss Tina appeared, unannounced, in the open doorway of the room in which my simple repasts were served. I remember well that I felt no surprise at seeing her; which is not a proof of my not believing in her timidity. It was immense, but in a case in which there was a particular reason for boldness it never would have prevented her from running up to my floor. I saw that she was now quite full of a particular reason; it threw her forward—made her seize me, as I rose to meet her, by the arm.

"My aunt's very ill; I think she's dying!"

"Never in the world," I answered bitterly. "Don't you be afraid!"

"Do go for a doctor—do, do! Olimpia's gone for the one we always have, but she doesn't come back; I don't know what has happened to her. I told her that if he wasn't at home she was to follow him where he had gone; but apparently she's following him all over Venice. I don't know what to do —she looks so as if she were sinking."

"May I see her, may I judge?" I asked. "Of course I shall be delighted to bring some one; but hadn't we better send my man instead, so that I may stay with you?"

Miss Tina assented to this and I dispatched my servant for the best doctor in the neighbourhood. I hurried downstairs with her, and on the way she told me that an hour after I quitted them in the afternoon Miss Bordereau had had an attack of "oppression," a terrible difficulty in breathing. This had subsided, but had left her so exhausted that she didn't come up: she seemed all spent and gone. I repeated that she wasn't gone, that she wouldn't go yet; whereupon Miss Tina gave me a sharper sidelong glance than she had ever favoured me withal and said: "Really, what do you mean? I suppose you don't accuse her of making-believe!" I forget what reply I made to this, but I fear that in my heart I thought the old woman capable of any weird manoeuvre. Miss Tina wanted to know what I had done to her; her aunt had told her I had made her so angry. I declared I had done nothing whatever —I had been exceedingly careful; to which my companion rejoined that our friend had assured her she had had a scene with me—a scene that had upset her. I answered with some resentment that the scene had been of *her* making —that I couldn't think what she was angry with me for unless for not seeing my way to give a thousand pounds for the portrait of Jeffrey Aspern. "And did she show you that? Oh gracious—oh deary me!" groaned Miss Tina, who seemed to feel the situation pass out of her control and the elements of her fate thicken round her. I answered her I'd give anything to possess it, yet that I had no thousand pounds; but I stopped when we came to the door of Miss Bordereau's room. I had an immense curiosity to pass it, but I thought it my duty to represent to Miss Tina that if I made the invalid angry she ought perhaps to be spared the sight of me. "The sight of you? Do you think she can *see*?" my companion demanded, almost with indignation. I did think so but forbore to say it, and I softly followed my conductress.

I remember that what I said to her as I stood for a moment beside the old woman's bed was: "Does she never show you her eyes then? Have you never seen them?" Miss Bordereau had been divested of her green shade, but—it was not my fortune to behold Juliana in her nightcap—the upper half of her face was covered by the fall of a piece of dingy lacelike muslin, a sort of extemporised hood which, wound round her head, descended to the end of her nose, leaving nothing visible but her white withered cheeks and puckered mouth, closed tightly and, as it were, consciously. Miss Tina gave me a glance of surprise, evidently not seeing a reason for my impatience. "You mean she always wears something? She does it to preserve them."

"Because they're so fine?"

"Oh to-day, to-day!" And Miss Tina shook her head speaking very low. "But they used to be magnificent!"

"Yes indeed—we've Aspern's word for that." And as I looked again at the old woman's wrappings I could imagine her not having wished to allow any supposition that the great poet had overdone it. But I didn't waste my time in considering Juliana, in whom the appearance of respiration was so slight as to suggest that no human attention could ever help her more. I turned my eyes once more all over the room, rummaging with them the closets, the chests of drawers, the tables. Miss Tina at once noted their direction and read, I think, what was in them; but she didn't answer it, turning away restlessly, anxiously, so that I felt rebuked, with reason, for an appetite well-nigh indecent in the presence of our dying companion. All the same I took another view, endeavouring to pick out mentally the receptacle to try first, for a person who should wish to put his hand on Miss Bordereau's papers directly after her death. The place was a dire confusion; it looked like the dressing-room of an old actress. There were clothes hanging over chairs, odd-looking shabby bundles here and there, and various pasteboard boxes piled together, battered, bulging and discoloured, which might have been fifty years old. Miss Tina after a moment noticed the direction of my eyes again, and, as if she guessed how I judged such appearances—forgetting I had no business to judge them at all—said, perhaps to defend herself from the imputation of complicity in the disorder:

"She likes it this way; we can't move things. There are old bandboxes she has had most of her life." Then she added, half-taking pity on my real thought: "Those things were *there*." And she pointed to a small low trunk which stood under a sofa that just allowed room for it. It struck me as a queer superannuated coffer, of painted wood, with elaborate handles and shrivelled straps and with the colour—it had last been endued with a coat of light green—much rubbed off. It evidently had travelled with Juliana in the olden time—in the days of her adventures, which it had shared. It would have made a strange figure arriving at a modern hotel.

"*Were* there—they aren't now?" I asked, startled by Miss Tina's implication.

She was going to answer, but at that moment the doctor came in—the doctor whom the little maid had been sent to fetch and whom she had at last overtaken. My servant, going on his own errand, had met her with her companion in tow, and in the sociable Venetian spirit, retracing his steps with them, had also come up to the threshold of the padrona's room, where I saw him peep over the doctor's shoulder. I motioned him away the more instantly that the sight of his prying face reminded me how little I myself had to do there—an admonition confirmed by the sharp way the little doctor eyed me, his air of taking me for a rival who had the field before him. He was a short fat brisk gentleman who wore the tall hat of his profession and seemed to look at everything but his patient. He kept me still in range, as if it struck him I too should be better for a dose, so that I bowed to him and left him with the women, going down to smoke a cigar in the garden. I was nervous; I couldn't go further; I couldn't leave the place. I don't know exactly what I thought might happen, but I felt it important to be there. I wandered about the alleys—the warm night had come on—smoking cigar after cigar and studying the light in Miss Bordereau's windows. They were open now, I could see; the situation was different. Sometimes the light moved, but not quickly; it didn't suggest the hurry of a crisis. Was the old woman dying or was she already dead? Had the doctor said that there was nothing to be done at her tremendous age but to let her quietly pass away? or had he simply announced with a look a little more conventional that the end of the end had come? Were the other two women just going and coming over the offices that follow in such a case? It made me uneasy not to be nearer, as if I thought the doctor himself might carry away the papers with him. I bit my cigar hard while it assailed me again that perhaps there were now no papers to carry!

I wandered about an hour and more. I looked out for Miss Tina at one of the windows, having a vague idea that she might come there to give me some sign. Wouldn't she see the red tip of my cigar in the dark and feel sure I was hanging on to know what the doctor had said? I'm afraid it's proof of the grossness of my anxieties that I should have taken in some degree for granted at such an hour, in the mist of the greatest change that could fall on her, poor Miss Tina's having also a free mind for them. My servant came down and spoke to me; he knew nothing save that the doctor had gone after a visit of half an hour. If he had stayed half an hour then Miss Bordereau was still alive: it couldn't have taken so long to attest her decease. I sent the man out of the house; there were moments when the sense of his curiosity annoyed me, and this was one of them. *He* had been watching my cigar-tip from an upper window, if Miss Tina hadn't; he couldn't know what I was after and I couldn't tell him, though I suspected in him fantastic private theories about me which he thought fine and which, had I more exactly known them, I should have thought offensive.

I went upstairs at last, but I mounted no higher than the sala. The door of Miss Bordereau's apartment was open, showing from the parlour the dimness of a poor candle. I went toward it with a light tread, and at the same moment Miss Tina appeared and stood looking at me as I approached. "She's better, she's better," she said even before I had asked. "The doctor has given her something; she woke up, came back to life while he was there. He says there's no immediate danger."

"No immediate danger? Surely he thinks her condition serious!"

"Yes, because she had been excited. That affects her dreadfully."

"It will do so again then, because she works herself up. She did so this afternoon."

"Yes, she mustn't come out any more," said Miss Tina with one of her lapses into a deeper detachment.

"What's the use of making such a remark as that," I permitted myself to ask, "if you begin to rattle her about again the first time she bids you?"

"I won't—I won't do it any more."

"You must learn to resist her," I went on.

"Oh yes, I shall; I shall do so better if you tell me it's right."

"You mustn't do it for me—you must do it for yourself. It all comes back to you, if you're scared and upset."

"Well, I'm not upset now," said Miss Tina placidly enough. "She's very quiet."

"Is she conscious again—does she speak?"

"No, she doesn't speak, but she takes my hand. She holds it fast."

"Yes," I returned, "I can see what force she still has by the way she grabbed that picture this afternoon. But if she holds you fast how comes it that you're here?"

Miss Tina waited a little; though her face was in deep shadow—she had her back to the light in the parlour and I had put down my own candle far off, near the door of the sala—I though I saw her smile ingenuously. "I came on purpose—I had heard your step."

"Why I came on tiptoe, as soundlessly as possible."

"Well, I had heard you," said Miss Tina.

"And is your aunt alone now?"

"Oh no—Olimpia sits there."

On my side I debated. "Shall we then pass in there?" And I nodded at the parlour; I wanted more and more to be on the spot.

"We can't talk there—she'll hear us."

I was on the point of replying that in that case we'd sit silent, but I felt too much this wouldn't do, there was something I desired so immensely to ask her. Thus I hinted we might walk a little in the sala, keeping more at the other end, where we shouldn't disturb our friend. Miss Tina assented unconditionally; the doctor was coming again, she said, and she would be there to meet him at the door. We strolled through the fine superfluous hall, where on the marble floor—particularly as at first we said nothing—our footsteps were more audible than I had expected. When we reached the other end—the wide window, inveterately closed, connecting with the balcony that overhung the canal—I submitted that we had best remain there, as she would see the doctor arrive the sooner. I opened the window and we passed out on the balcony. The air of the canal seemed even heavier, hotter than that of the sala. The place was hushed and void; the quiet neighborhood had gone to sleep. A lamp, here and there, over the narrow black water, glimmered in double; the voice of a man going homeward singing, his jacket on his shoulder and his hat on his ear, came to us from a distance. This didn't prevent the scene from being very *comme il faut*, as Miss Bordereau had called it the first time I saw her. Presently a gondola passed along the canal with its slow rhythmical plash, and as we listened we watched it in silence. It didn't stop, it didn't carry the doctor; and after it had gone on I said to Miss Tina:

"And where are they now—the things that were in the trunk?"

"In the trunk?"

"That green box you pointed out to me in her room. You said her papers had been there; you seemed to mean she had transferred them."

"Oh yes; they're not in the trunk," said Miss Tina.

"May I ask if you've looked?"

"Yes, I've looked—for you."

"How for me, dear Miss Tina? Do you mean you'd have given them to me if you had found them?"—and I fairly trembled with the question.

She delayed to reply and I waited. Suddenly she broke out: "I don't know what I'd do—what I wouldn't!"

"Would you look again—somewhere else?"

She had spoken with a strange unexpected emotion, and she went on in the same tone: "I can't—I can't—while she lies there. It isn't decent."

"No, it isn't decent," I replied gravely. "Let the poor lady rest in peace." And the words, on my lips, were not hypocritical, for I felt reprimanded and shamed.

Miss Tina added in a moment, as if she had guessed this and were sorry for me, but at the same time wished to explain that I did push her, or at least harp on the chord, too much: "I can't deceive her that way. I can't deceive her—perhaps on her deathbed."

"Heaven forbid I should ask you, though I've been guilty myself!"

"You've been guilty?"

"I've sailed under false colours." I felt now I must make a clean breast of it, must tell her I had given her an invented name on account of my fear her aunt would have heard of me and so refuse to take me in. I explained this as well as that I had really been a party to the letter addressed them by John Cumnor months before.

She listened with great attention, almost in fact gaping for wonder, and when I had made my confession she said: "Then your real name—what is it?" She repeated it over twice when I had told her, accompanying it with the exclamation "Gracious, gracious!" Then she added: "I like your own best."

"So do I,"—and I felt my laugh rueful. "Ouf! it's a relief to get rid of the other."

"So it was a regular plot—a kind of conspiracy?"

"Oh a conspiracy—we were only two," I replied, leaving out of course Mrs. Prest.

She considered; I thought she was perhaps going to pronounce us very base. But this was not her way, and she remarked after a moment, as in candid impartial contemplation: "How much you must want them!"

"Oh I do, passionately!" I grinned, I fear to admit. And this chance made me go on, forgetting my compunction of a moment before. "How can she possibly have changed their place herself? How can she walk? How can she arrive at that sort of muscular exertion? How can she lift and carry things?"

"Oh when one wants and when one has so much will!" said Miss Tina as if she had thought over my question already herself and had simply had no choice but that answer—the idea that in the dead of night, or at some moment when the coast was clear, the old woman had been capable of a miraculous effort.

"Have you questioned Olimpia? Hasn't she helped her—hasn't she done it for her?" I asked; to which my friend replied promptly and positively that their servant had had nothing to do with the matter, though without admitting definitely that she had spoken to her. It was as if she were a little shy, a little ashamed now, of letting me see how much she had entered into my uneasiness and had me on her mind. Suddenly she said to me without any immediate relevance:

"I rather feel you a new person, you know, now that you've a new name."

"It isn't a new one; it's a very good old one, thank fortune!"

She looked at me a moment. "Well, I do like it better."

"Oh if you didn't I would almost go on with the other!"

"Would you really?"

I laughed again, but I returned for all answer: "Of course if she can rummage about that way she can perfectly have burnt them."

"You must wait—you must wait," Miss Tina mournfully moralised; and her tone ministered little to my patience, for it seemed after all to accept that wretched possibility. I would teach myself to wait, I declared nevertheless; because in the first place I couldn't do otherwise and in the second I had her promise, given me the other night, that she would help me.

"Of course if the papers are gone that's no use," she said; not as if she wished to recede, but only to be conscientious.

"Naturally. But if you could only find out!" I groaned, quivering again.

"I thought you promised you'd wait."

"Oh you mean wait for that?"

"For what then?"

"Ah, nothing," I answered rather foolishly, being ashamed to tell her what had been implied in my acceptance of delay—the idea that she would perhaps do more for me than merely find out.

I know not if she guessed this; at all events she seemed to bethink herself of some propriety of showing me more rigour. "I didn't promise to deceive, did I? I don't think I did."

"It doesn't much matter whether you did or not, for you couldn't!"

Nothing is more possible than that she wouldn't have contested this even hadn't she been diverted by our seeing the doctor's gondola shoot into the little canal and approach the house. I noted that he came as fast as if he believed our proprietress still in danger. We looked down at him while he disembarked and then went back into the sala to meet him. When he came up, however, I naturally left Miss Tina to go off with him alone, only asking her leave to come back later for news.

I went out of the house and walked far, as far as the Piazza, where my restlessness declined to quit me. I was unable to sit down; it was very late now though there were people still at the little tables in front of the cafés: I could but uneasily revolve, and I did so half a dozen times. The only comfort, none the less, was in my having told Miss Tina who I really was. At last I took my way home again, getting gradually and all but inextricably lost, as

I did whenever I went out in Venice: so that it was considerably past midnight when I reached my door. The sala, upstairs, was as dark as usual and my lamp as I crossed it found nothing satisfactory to show me. I was disappointed, for I had notified Miss Tina that I would come back for a report, and I thought she might have left a light there as a sign. The door of the ladies' apartment was closed; which seemed a hint that my faltering friend had gone to bed in impatience of waiting for me. I stood in the middle of the place, considering, hoping she would hear me and perhaps peep out, saying to myself too that she would never go to bed with her aunt in a state so critical; she would sit up and watch—she would be in a chair, in her dressing-gown. I went nearer the door; I stopped there and listened. I heard nothing at all and at last I tapped gently. No answer came and after another minute I turned the handle. There was no light in the room; this ought to have prevented my entrance, but it had no such effect. If I have frankly stated the importunities, the indelicacies, of which my desire to possess myself of Jeffrey Aspern's papers had made me capable I needn't shrink, it seems to me, from confessing this last indiscretion. I regard it as the worst thing I did, yet there were extenuating circumstances. I was deeply though doubtless not disinterestedly anxious for more news of Juliana, and Miss Tina had accepted from me, as it were, a rendezvous which it might have been a point of honour with me to keep. It may be objected that her leaving the place dark was a positive sign that she released me, and to this I can only reply that I wished not to be released.

The door to Miss Bordereau's room was open and I could see beyond it the faintness of a taper. There was no sound—my footstep caused no one to stir. I came further into the room; I lingered there lamp in hand. I wanted to give Miss Tina a chance to come to me if, as I couldn't doubt, she were still with her aunt. I made no noise to call her; I only waited to see if she wouldn't notice my light. She didn't, and I explained this—I found afterwards I was right—by the idea that she had fallen asleep. If she had fallen asleep her aunt was not on her mind, and my explanation ought to have led me to go out as I had come. I must repeat again that it didn't, for I found myself at the same moment given up to something else. I had no definite purpose, no bad intention, but felt myself held to the spot by an acute, though absurd, sense of opportunity. Opportunity for what I couldn't have said, inasmuch as it wasn't in my mind that I might proceed to thievery. Even had this tempted me I was confronted with the evident fact that Miss Bordereau didn't leave her secretary, her cupboard and the drawers of her tables gaping. I had no keys, no tools and no ambition to smash her furniture. None the less it came to me that I was now, perhaps alone, unmolested, at the hour of freedom and safety, nearer to the source of my hopes than I had ever been. I held up my lamp, let the light play on the different objects as if it could tell me something. Still there came no movement from the other room. If Miss Tina was sleeping she was sleeping sound. Was she doing so—generous creature—on purpose to leave me the field? Did she know I was there and was she just keeping quiet to see what I would do—what I *could* do? Yet might I, when it came to that? She herself knew even better than I how little.

I stopped in front of the secretary, gaping at it vainly and no doubt grotesquely; for what had it to say to me after all? In the first place it was locked, and in the second it almost surely contained nothing in which I was interested. Ten to one the papers had been destroyed, and even if they hadn't the keen old woman wouldn't have put them in such a place as that after removing them from the green trunk—wouldn't have transferred them, with the idea of their safety on her brain, from the better hiding-place to the worse. The secretary was more conspicuous, more exposed in a room in which she could no longer mount guard. It opened with a key, but there was a small brass handle, like a button as well; I saw this as I played my lamp over it. I did something more, for the climax of my crisis; I caught a glimpse of the possibility that Miss Tina wished me really to understand. If she didn't so wish me, if she wished me to keep away, why hadn't she locked the door of communication between the sitting-room and the sala? That would have been a definite sign that I was to leave them alone. If I didn't leave them alone she meant me to come for a purpose—a purpose now represented by the super-subtle inference that to oblige me she had unlocked the secretary. She hadn't left the key, but the lid would probably move if I touched the button. This possibility pressed me hard and I bent very close to judge. I didn't propose to do anything, not even—not in the least—to let down the lid; I only wanted to test my theory, to see if the cover *would* move. I touched the button with my hand—a mere touch would tell me; and as I did so—it is embarrassing for me to relate it—I looked over my shoulder. It was a chance, an instinct, for I had really heard nothing. I almost let my luminary drop and certainly I stepped back, straightening myself up at what I saw. Juliana stood there in her nightdress, by the doorway of her room, watching me; her hands were raised, she had lifted the everlasting curtain that covered half her face, and for the first, the last, the only time I beheld her extraordinary eyes. They glared at me; they were like the sudden drench, for a caught burglar, of a flood of gaslight; they made me horribly ashamed. I never shall forget her strange little bent white tottering figure, with its lifted head, her attitude, her expression; neither shall I forget the tone in which as I turned, looking at her, she hissed out passionately, furiously:

"Ah you publishing scoundrel!"

I can't now say what I stammered to excuse myself, to explain; but I went toward her to tell her I meant no harm. She waved me off with her old hands, retreating before me in horror; and the next thing I knew she had fallen back with a quick spasm, as if death had descended on her, into Miss Tina's arms.

9

I left Venice the next morning, directly on learning that my hostess had not succumbed, as I feared at the moment, to the shock I had given her—the shock I may also say she had given me. How in the world could I have supposed her capable of getting out of bed by herself? I failed to see Miss Tina before going; I only saw the *donna*,[1] whom I entrusted with a note for her younger mistress. In this note I mentioned that I should be absent but a few

---

[1] Maid.

days. I went to Treviso, to Bassano, to Castelfranco; I took walks and drives and looked at musty old churches with ill-lighted pictures; I spent hours seated smoking at the doors of cafés, where there were flies and yellow curtains, on the shady side of sleepy little squares. In spite of these pastimes, which were mechanical and perfunctory, I scantly enjoyed my travels: I had had to gulp down a bitter draught and couldn't get rid of the taste. It had been devilish awkward, as the young men say, to be found by Juliana in the dead of night examining the attachment of her bureau; and it had not been less so to have to believe for a good many hours after that it was highly probable I had killed her. My humiliation galled me, but I had to make the best of it, had, in writing to Miss Tina to minimise it, as well as account for the posture in which I had been discovered. As she gave me no word of answer I couldn't know what impression I made on her. It rankled for me that I had been called a publishing scoundrel, since certainly I did publish and no less certainly hadn't been very delicate. There was a moment when I stood convinced that the only way to purge my dishonour was to take myself straight away on the instant; to sacrifice my hopes and relieve the two poor women for ever of the oppression of my intercourse. Then I reflected that I had better try a short absence first, for I must already have had a sense (unexpressed and dim) that in disappearing completely it wouldn't be merely my own hopes I should condemn to extinction. It would perhaps answer if I kept dark long enough to give the elder lady time to believe herself rid of me. That she would wish to be rid of me after this—if I wasn't rid of her—was now not to be doubted: that midnight monstrosity would have cured her of the disposition to put up with my company for the sake of my dollars. I said to myself that after all I couldn't abandon Miss Tina, and I continued to say this even while I noted that she quite ignored my earnest request—I had given her two or three addresses, at little towns, *poste restante*[2]—for some sign of her actual state. I would have made my servant write me news but that he was unable to manage a pen. Couldn't I measure the scorn of Miss Tina's silence—little disdainful as she had ever been? Really the soreness pressed; yet if I had scruples about going back I had others about not doing so, and I wanted to put myself on a better footing. The end of it was that I did return to Venice on the twelfth day; and as my gondola gently bumped against our palace steps a fine palpitation of suspense showed me the violence my absence had done me.

I had faced about so abruptly that I hadn't even telegraphed to my servant. He was therefore not at the station to meet me, but he poked out his head from an upper window when I reached the house. "They have put her into earth, *quella vecchia*," [3] he said to me in the lower hall while he shouldered my valise; and he grinned and almost winked as if he knew I should be pleased with his news.

"She's dead!" I cried, giving him a very different look.

"So it appears, since they've buried her."

"It's all over then? When was the funeral?"

"The other yesterday. But a funeral you could scarcely call it, signore:

2 General Delivery.
3 That old lady.

roba da niente—un piccolo passeggio brutto of two gondolas. Poveretta!" [4] the man continued, referring apparently to Miss Tina. His conception of funerals was that they were mainly to amuse the living.

I wanted to know about Miss Tina, how she might be and generally where; but I asked him no more questions till we had got upstairs. Now that the fact had met me I took a bad view of it, especially of the idea that poor Miss Tina had had to manage by herself after the end. What did she know about arrangements, about the steps to take in such a case? Poveretta indeed! I could only hope the doctor had given her support and that she hadn't been neglected by the old friends of whom she had told me, the little band of the faithful whose fidelity consisted in coming to the house once a year. I elicited from my servant that two old ladies and an old gentleman had in fact rallied round Miss Tina and had supported her—they had come for her in a gondola of their own—during the journey to the cemetery, the little red-walled island of tombs which lies to the north of the town and on the way to Murano. It appeared from these signs that the Misses Bordereau were Catholics, a discovery I had never made, as the old woman couldn't go to church and her niece, so far as I perceived, either didn't, or went only to early mass in the parish before I was stirring. Certainly even the priests respected their seclusion; I had never caught the whisk of the curato's skirt. That evening, an hour later, I sent my servant down with five words on a card to ask if Miss Tina would see me for a few moments. She was not in the house, where he had sought her, he told me when he came back, but in the garden walking about to refresh herself and picking the flowers quite as if they belonged to her. He had found her there and she would be happy to see me.

I went down and passed half an hour with poor Miss Tina. She had always had a look of musty mourning, as if she were wearing out old robes of sorrow that wouldn't come to an end; and in this particular she made no different show. But she clearly had been crying, crying a great deal—simply, satisfyingly, refreshingly, with a primitive retarded sense of solitude and violence. But she had none of the airs or graces of grief, and I was almost surprised to see her stand there in the first dusk with her hands full of admirable roses and smile at me with reddened eyes. Her white face, in the frame of her mantilla, looked longer, leaner than usual. I hadn't doubted her being irreconcilably disgusted with me, her considering I ought to have been on the spot to advise her, to help her; and, though I believed there was no rancour in her composition and no great conviction of the importance of her affairs, I had prepared myself for a change in her manner, for some air of injury and estrangement, which should say to my conscience: "Well, you're a nice person to have professed things!" But historic truth compels me to declare that this poor lady's dull face ceased to be dull, almost ceased to be plain, as she turned it gladly to her late aunt's lodger. That touched him extremely and he thought it simplified his situation until he found it didn't. I was as kind to her that evening as I knew how to be, and I walked about the garden with her as long as seemed good. There was no explanation of any sort between us; I didn't ask her why she hadn't answered my letter. Still less did

[4] Nothing elaborate—an ugly little procession of two gondolas. Poor lady!

I repeat what I had said to her in that communication; if she chose to let me suppose she had forgotten the position in which Miss Bordereau had surprised me and the effect of the discovery on the old woman, I was quite willing to take it that way: I was grateful to her for not treating me as if I had killed her aunt.

We strolled and strolled, though really not much passed between us save the recognition of her bereavement, conveyed in my manner and in the expression she had of depending on me now, since I let her see I still took an interest in her. Miss Tina's was no breast for the pride or the pretence of independence; she didn't in the least suggest that she knew at present what would become of her. I forbore to press on that question, however, for I certainly was not prepared to say that I would take charge of her. I was cautious; not ignobly, I think, for I felt her knowledge of life to be so small that in her unsophisticated vision there would be no reason why—since I seemed to pity her—I shouldn't somehow look after her. She told me how her aunt had died, very peacefully at the last, and how everything had been done afterwards by the care of her good friends—fortunately, thanks to me, she said, smiling, there was money in the house. She repeated that when once the "nice" Italians like you they are your friends for life, and when we had gone into this she asked me about my *giro*, my impressions, my adventures, the places I had seen. I told her what I could, making it up partly, I'm afraid, as in my disconcerted state I had taken little in; and after she had heard me she exclaimed, quite as if she had forgotten her aunt and her sorrow, "Dear, dear, how much I should like to do such things—to take an amusing little journey!" It came over me for the moment that I ought to propose some enterprise, say I would accompany her anywhere she liked; and I remarked at any rate that a pleasant excursion—to give her a change—might be managed; we would think of it, talk it over. I spoke never a word of the Aspern documents, asked no question as to what she had ascertained or what had otherwise happened with regard to them before Juliana's death. It wasn't that I wasn't on pins and needles to know, but that I thought it more decent not to show greed again so soon after the catastrophe. I hoped she herself would say something, but she never glanced that way, and I thought this natural at the time. Later on, however, that night, it occurred to me that her silence was matter for suspicion; since if she had talked of my movements, of anything so detached as the Giorgione at Castelfranco, she might have alluded to what she could easily remember was in my mind. It was not to be supposed that the emotion produced by her aunt's death had blotted out the recollection that I was interested in that lady's relics, and I fidgeted afterwards as it came to me that her reticence might very possibly just mean that no relics survived. We separated in the garden—it was she who said she must go in; now that she was alone on the *piano nobile* I felt that (judged at any rate by Venetian ideas) I was on rather a different footing in regard to the invasion of it. As I shook hands with her for good-night I asked her if she had some general plan, had thought over what she had best do. "Oh yes, oh yes, but I haven't settled anything yet," she replied quite cheerfully. Was her cheerfulness explained by the impression that I would settle for her?

I was glad the next morning that we had neglected practical questions, as this gave me a pretext for seeing her again immediately. There was a practical enough question now to be touched on. I owed it to her to let her know formally that of course I didn't expect her to keep me on as a lodger, as also to show some interest in her own tenure, what she might have on her hands in the way of a lease. But I was not destined, as befell, to converse with her for more than an instant on either of these points. I sent her no message; I simply went down to the sala and walked to and fro there. I knew she would come out; she would promptly see me accessible. Somehow I preferred not to be shut up with her; gardens and big halls seemed better places to talk. It was a splendid morning, with something in the air that told of the waning of the long Venetian summer; a freshness from the sea that stirred the flowers in the garden and made a pleasant draught in the house, less shuttered and darkened now than when the old woman was alive. It was the beginning of autumn, of the end of the golden months. With this it was the end of my experiment—or would be in the course of half an hour, when I should really have learned that my dream had been reduced to ashes. After that there would be nothing left for me but to go to the station; for seriously—and as it struck me in the morning light—I couldn't linger there to act as guardian to a piece of middle-aged female helplessness. If she hadn't saved the papers wherein should I be indebted to her? I think I winced a little as I asked myself how much, if she *had* saved them, I should have to recognise and, as it were, reward such a courtesy. Mightn't that service after all saddle me with a guardianship? If this idea didn't make me more uncomfortable as I walked up and down it was because I was convinced I had nothing to look to. If the old woman hadn't destroyed everything before she pounced on me in the parlour she had done so the next day.

It took Miss Tina rather longer than I had expected to act on my calculation; but when at last she came out she looked at me without surprise. I mentioned I had been waiting for her and she asked why I hadn't let her know. I was glad a few hours later on that I had checked myself before remarking that a friendly intuition might have told her: it turned to comfort for me that I hadn't played even to that mild extent on her sensibility. What I did say was virtually the truth—that I was too nervous, since I expected her now to settle my fate.

"Your fate?" said Miss Tina, giving me a queer look; and as she spoke I noticed a rare change in her. Yes, she was other than she had been the evening before—less natural and less easy. She had been crying the day before and was not crying now, yet she struck me as less confident. It was as if something had happened to her during the night, or at least as if she had thought of something that troubled her—something in particular that affected her relations with me, made them more embarrassing and more complicated. Had she simply begun to feel that her aunt's not being there now altered my position?

"I mean about our papers. *Are* there any? You must know now."

"Yes, there are a great many; more than I supposed." I was struck with the way her voice trembled as she told me this.

"Do you mean you've got them in there—and that I may see them?"

"I don't think you can see them," said Miss Tina, with an extraordinary expression of entreaty in her eyes, as if the dearest hope she had in the world now was that I wouldn't take them from her. But how could she expect me to make such a sacrifice as that after all that had passed between us? What had I come back to Venice for but to see them, to take them? My joy at learning they were still in existence was such that if the poor woman had gone down on her knees to beseech me never to mention them again I would have treated the proceeding as a bad joke. "I've got them but I can't show them," she lamentably added.

"Not even to me? Ah Miss Tina!" I broke into a tone of infinite remonstrance and reproach.

She coloured and the tears came back to her eyes; I measured the anguish it cost her to take such a stand which a dreadful sense of duty had imposed on her. It made me quite sick to find myself confronted with that particular obstacle; all the more that it seemed to me I had been distinctly encouraged to leave it out of account. I quite held Miss Tina to have assured me that if she had no greater hindrance than that——! "You don't mean to say you made her a death-bed promise? It was precisely against your doing anything of that sort that I thought I was safe. Oh I would rather she had burnt the papers outright than have to reckon with such a treachery as that."

"No, it isn't a promise," said Miss Tina.

"Pray what is it then?"

She hung fire, but finally said: "She tried to burn them, but I prevented it. She had hid them in her bed."

"In her bed—?"

"Between the mattresses. That's where she put them when she took them out of the trunk. I can't understand how she did it, because Olimpia didn't help her. She tells me so and I believe her. My aunt only told her afterwards, so that she shouldn't undo the bed—anything but the sheets. So it was very badly made," added Miss Tina simply.

"I should think so! And how did she try to burn them?"

"She didn't try much; she was too weak those last days. But she told me —she charged me. Oh it was terrible! She couldn't speak after that night. She could only make signs."

"And what did you do?"

"I took them away. I locked them up."

"In the secretary?"

"Yes, in the secretary," said Miss Tina, reddening again.

"Did you tell her you'd burn them?"

"No, I didn't—on purpose."

"On purpose to gratify me?"

"Yes, only for that."

"And what good will you have done me if after all you won't show them?"

"Oh none. I know that—I know that," she dismally sounded.

"And did she believe you had destroyed them?"

"I don't know what she believed at the last. I couldn't tell—she was too far gone."

"Then if there was no promise and no assurance I can't see what ties you."

"Oh she hated it so—she hated it so! She was so jealous. But here's the portrait—you may have that," the poor woman announced, taking the little picture, wrapped up in the same manner in which her aunt had wrapped it, out of her pocket.

"I may have it—do you mean you give it to me?" I gasped as it passed into my hand.

"Oh yes."

"But it's worth money—a large sum."

"Well!" said Miss Tina, still with her strange look.

I didn't know what to make of it, for it could scarcely mean that she wanted to bargain like her aunt. She spoke as for making me a present. "I can't take it from you as a gift," I said, "and yet I can't afford to pay you for it according to the idea Miss Bordereau had of its value. She rated it at a thousand pounds."

"Couldn't we sell it?" my friend threw off.

"God forbid! I prefer the picture to the money."

"Well then keep it."

"You're very generous."

"So are you."

"I don't know why you should think so," I returned; and this was true enough, for the good creature appeared to have in her mind some rich reference that I didn't in the least seize.

"Well, you've made a great difference for me," she said.

I looked at Jeffrey Aspern's face in the little picture, partly in order not to look at that of my companion, which had begun to trouble me, even to frighten me a little—it had taken so very odd, so strained and unnatural a cast. I made no answer to this last declaration; I but privately consulted Jeffrey Aspern's delightful eyes with my own—they were so young and brilliant yet so wise and so deep; I asked him what on earth was the matter with Miss Tina. He seemed to smile at me with mild mockery; he might have been amused at my case. I had got into a pickle for him—as if he needed it! He was unsatisfactory for the only moment since I had known him. Nevertheless, now that I held the little picture in my hand I felt it would be a precious possession. "Is this a bribe to make me give up the papers?" I presently and all perversely asked. "Much as I value this, you know, if I were to be obliged to choose the papers are what I should prefer. Ah but ever so much!"

"How can you choose—how can you choose?" Miss Tina returned slowly and woefully.

"I see! Of course there's nothing to be said if you regard the interdiction that rules on you as quite insurmountable. In this case it must seem to you that to part with them would be an impiety of the worst kind, a simple sacrilege!"

She shook her head, only lost in the queerness of her case. "You'd understand if you had known her. I'm afraid," she quavered suddenly—"I'm afraid! She was terrible when she was angry."

"Yes, I saw something of that, that night. She was terrible. Then I saw her eyes. Lord, they were fine!"

"I see them—they stare at me in the dark!" said Miss Tina.

"You've grown nervous with all you've been through."

"Oh yes, very—very!"

"You mustn't mind; that will pass away," I said kindly. Then I added resignedly, for it really seemed to me that I must accept the situation: "Well, so it is, and it can't be helped. I must renounce." My friend, at this, with her eyes on me, gave a low soft moan, and I went on: "I only wish to goodness she had destroyed them; then there would be nothing more to say. And I can't understand why, with her ideas, she didn't."

"Oh she lived on them!" said Miss Tina.

"You can imagine whether that makes me want less to see them," I returned not quite so desperately. "But don't let me stand here as if I had it in my soul to tempt you to anything base. Naturally, you understand, I give up my rooms. I leave Venice immediately." And I took up my hat, which I had placed on a chair. We were still rather awkwardly on our feet in the middle of the sala. She had left the door of the apartments open behind her, but had not led me that way.

A strange spasm came into her face as she saw me take my hat. "Immediately—do you mean to-day?" The tone of the words was tragic—they were a cry of desolation.

"Oh no; not so long as I can be of the least service to you."

"Well, just a day or two more—just two or three days," she panted. Then controlling herself she added in another manner: "She wanted to say something to me—the last day—something very particular. But she couldn't."

"Something very particular?"

"Something more about the papers."

"And did you guess—have you any idea?"

"No, I've tried to think—but I don't know. I've thought all kinds of things."

"As for instance?"

"Well, that if you were a relation it would be different."

I wondered. "If I were a relation—?"

"If you weren't a stranger. Then it would be the same for you as for me. Anything that's mine would be yours, and you could do what you like. I shouldn't be able to prevent you—and you'd have no responsibility."

She brought out this droll explanation with a nervous rush and as if speaking words got by heart. They gave me an impression of a subtlety which at first I failed to follow. But after a moment her face helped me to see further, and then the queerest of light came to me. It was embarrassing, and I bent my head over Jeffrey Aspern's portrait. What an odd expression was in his face! "Get out of it as you can, my dear fellow!" I put the picture into the pocket of my coat and said to Miss Tina: "Yes, I'll sell it for you. I shan't get a thousand pounds by any means, but I shall get something good."

She looked at me through pitiful tears, but seemed to try to smile as she returned: "We can divide the money."

"No, no, it shall be all yours." Then I went on: "I think I know what your poor aunt wanted to say. She wanted to give directions that the papers should be buried with her."

Miss Tina appeared to weigh this suggestion; after which she answered with striking decision, "Oh no, she wouldn't have thought that safe!"

"It seems to me nothing could be safer."

"She had an idea that when people want to publish they're capable—!" And she paused, very red.

"Of violating a tomb? Mercy on us, what must she have thought of me!"

"She wasn't just, she wasn't generous!" my companion cried with sudden passion.

The light that had come into my mind a moment before spread further. "Ah don't say that, for we *are* a dreadful race." Then I pursued: "If she left a will that may give you some idea."

"I've found nothing of the sort—she destroyed it. She was very fond of me," Miss Tina added with an effect of extreme inconsequence. "She wanted me to be happy. And if any person should be kind to me—she wanted to speak of that."

I was almost awestricken by the astuteness with which the good lady found herself inspired, transparent astuteness as it was and stitching, as the phrase is, with white thread. "Depend upon it she didn't want to make any provision that would be agreeable to *me*."

"No, not to you, but quite to me. She knew I should like it if you could carry out your idea. Not because she cared for you, but because she did think of me," Miss Tina went on with her unexpected persuasive volubility. "You could see the things—you could use them." She stopped, seeing I grasped the sense of her conditional—stopped long enough for me to give some sign that I didn't give. She must have been conscious, however, that though my face showed the greatest embarrassment ever painted on a human countenance it was not set as a stone, it was also full of compassion. It was a comfort to me a long time afterwards to consider that she couldn't have seen in me the smallest symptom of disrespect. "I don't know what to do; I'm too tormented, I'm too ashamed!" she continued with vehemence. Then turning away from me and burying her face in her hands she burst into a flood of tears. If she didn't know what to do it may be imagined whether I knew better. I stood there dumb, matching her while her sobs resounded in the great empty hall. In a moment she was up at me again with her streaming eyes. "I'd give you everything, and she'd understand, where she is—she'd forgive me!"

"Ah Miss Tina—ah Miss Tina," I stammered for all reply. I didn't know what to do, as I say, but at a venture I made a wild vague movement in consequence of which I found myself at the door. I remember standing there and saying, "It wouldn't do, it wouldn't do!"—saying it pensively, awkwardly, grotesquely, while I looked away to the opposite end of the sala as at something very interesting. The next thing I remembered is that I was downstairs and out of the house. My gondola was there and my gondolier, reclining on the cushions, sprang up as soon as he saw me. I jumped in and to his usual "*Dove commanda?*" [5] replied, in a tone that made him stare: "Anywhere, anywhere; out into the lagoon!"

He rowed me away and I sat there prostrate, groaning softly to myself, my hat pulled over my brow. What in the name of the preposterous did she mean if she didn't mean to offer me her hand? That was the price—that was the price! And did she think I wanted it, poor deluded infatuated extravagant

[5] Where do you wish to go?

lady? My gondolier, behind me, must have seen my ears red as I wondered, motionless there under the fluttering *tenda* with my hidden face, noticing nothing as we passed—wondered whether her delusion, her infatuation had been my own reckless work. Did she think I had made love to her even to get the papers? I hadn't, I hadn't; I repeated that over to myself for an hour, for two hours, till I was wearied if not convinced. I don't know where, on the lagoon, my gondolier took me; we floated aimlessly and with slow rare strokes. At last I became conscious that we were near the Lido, far up, on the right hand, as you turn your back to Venice, and I made him put me ashore. I wanted to walk, to move, to shed some of my bewilderment. I crossed the narrow stip and got to the sea-beach—I took my way toward Malamocco. But presently I flung myself down again on the warm sand, in the breeze, on the coarse dry grass. It took it out of me to think I had been so much at fault, that I had unwittingly but none the less deplorably trifled. But I hadn't given her cause—distinctly I hadn't. I had said to Mrs. Prest that I would make love to her; but it had been a joke without consequences and I had never said it to my victim. I had been as kind as possible because I really liked her; but since when had that become a crime where a woman of such an age and such an appearance was concerned? I am far from remembering clearly the succession of events and feelings during this long day of confusion, which I spent entirely in wandering about, without going home, until late at night; it only comes back to me that there were moments when I pacified my conscience and others when I lashed it into pain. I didn't laugh all day—that I do recollect; the case, however it might have struck others, seemed to me so little amusing. I should have been better employed perhaps in taking in the comic side of it. At any rate, whether I had given cause or not, there was no doubt whatever that I couldn't pay the price. I couldn't accept the proposal. I couldn't, for a bundle of tattered papers, marry a ridiculous pathetic provincial old woman. It was a proof of how little she supposed the idea would come to me that she should have decided to suggest it herself in that practical argumentative heroic way—with the timidity, however, so much more striking than the boldness, that her reasons appeared to come first and her feelings afterward.

As the day went on I grew to wish I had never heard of Aspern's relics, and I cursed the extravagant curiosity that had put John Cumnor on the scent of them. We had more than enough material without them, and my predicament was the just punishment of that most fatal of human follies, our not having known when to stop. It was very well to say it was no predicament, that the way out was simple, that I had only to leave Venice by the first train in the morning, after addressing Miss Tina a note which should be placed in her hand as soon as I got clear of the house; for it was strong proof of my quandary that when I tried to make up the note to my taste in advance—I would put it on paper as soon as I got home, before going to bed—I couldn't think of anything but "How can I thank you for the rare confidence you've placed in me?" That would never do; it sounded exactly as if an acceptance were to follow. Of course I might get off without writing at all, but that would be brutal, and my idea was still to exclude brutal solutions. As my confusion cooled I lost myself in wonder at the importance I had attached to Juliana's crumpled scraps; the thought of them became odious to me and I was as vexed with the old witch for the superstition that had prevented her from destroying them as I was with myself for having already spent more money than I could afford in attempting to control their fate. I forget what I did, where I went after leaving the Lido, and at what hour or with what recovery of composure I made my way back to my boat. I only know that in the afternoon, when the air was aglow with the sunset, I was standing before the church of Saints John and Paul and looking up at the small square-jawed face of Bartolommeo Colleoni, the terrible *condottiere*[6] who sits so sturdily astride of his huge bronze horse on the high pedestal on which Venetian gratitude maintains him. The statue is incomparable, the finest of all mounted figures, unless that of Marcus Aurelius, who rides benignant before the Roman Capitol, be finer: but I was not thinking of that; I only found myself staring at the triumphant captain as if he had had an oracle on his lips. The western light shines into all his grimness at that hour and makes it wonderfully personal. But he continued to look far over my head, at the red immersion of another day—he had seen so many go down into the lagoon through the centuries—and if he were thinking of battles and stratagems they were of a different quality from any I had to tell him of. He couldn't direct me what to do, gaze up at him as I might. Was it before this or after that I wandered about for an hour in the small canals, to the continued stupefaction of my gondolier, who had never seen me so restless and yet so void of a purpose and could extract from me no order but "Go anywhere—everywhere—all over the place?" He reminded me that I had not lunched and expressed therefore respectfully the hope that I would dine earlier. He had had long periods of leisure during the day, when I had left the boat and rambled, so that I was not obliged to consider him, and I told him that till the morrow, for reasons, I should touch no meat. It was an effect of poor Miss Tina's proposal, not altogether auspicious, that I had quite lost my appetite. I don't know why it happened that on this occasion I was more than ever struck with that queer air of sociability, of cousinship and family life, which makes up half the expression of Venice. Without streets and vehicles, the uproar of wheels, the brutality of horses, and with its little winding ways where people crowd together, where voices sound as in the corridors of a house, where the human step circulates as if it skirted the angles of furniture and shoes never wear out, the place has the character of an immense collective apartment, in which Piazza San Marco is the most ornamented corner and palaces and churches, for the rest, play the part of great divans of repose, tables of entertainment, expanses of decoration. And somehow the splendid common domicile, familiar domestic and resonant, also resembles a theatre with its actors clicking over bridges and, in straggling processions, tripping along fondamentas. As you sit in your gondola the footways that in certain parts edge the canals assume to the eye the importance of a stage, meeting it at the same angle, and the Venetian figures, moving to and fro against the battered scenery of their little houses of comedy, strike you as members of an endless dramatic troupe.

I went to bed that night very tired and without being able to compose an address to Miss Tina. Was this failure the reason why I became conscious the

---

[6] Soldier of fortune.

next morning as soon as I awoke of a determination to see the poor lady again the first moment she would receive me? That had something to do with it, but what had still more was the fact that during my sleep the oddest revulsion had taken place in my spirit. I found myself aware of this almost as soon as I opened my eyes: it made me jump out of my bed with the movement of a man who remembers that he has left the house-door ajar on a candle burning under a shelf. Was I still in time to save my goods? That question was in my heart; for what had now come to pass was that in the unconscious cerebration of sleep I had swung back to a passionate appreciation of Juliana's treasure. The pieces composing it were now more precious than ever and a positive ferocity had come into my need to acquire them. The condition Miss Tina had attached to that act no longer appeared an obstacle worth thinking of, and for an hour this morning my repentant imagination brushed it aside. It was absurd I should be able to invent nothing; absurd to renounce so easily and turn away helpless from the idea that the only way to become possessed was to unite myself to her for life. I mightn't unite myself, yet I might still have what she had. I must add that by the time I sent down to ask if she would see me I had invented no alternative, though in fact I drew out my dressing in the interest of my wit. This failure was humiliating, yet what could the alternative be? Miss Tina sent back word I might come; and as I descended the stairs and crossed the sala to her door—this time she received me in her aunt's forlorn parlour—I hoped she wouldn't think my announcement was to be "favourable." She certainly would have understood my recoil of the day before.

As soon as I came into the room I saw that she had done so, but I also saw something which had not been in my forecast. Poor Miss Tina's sense of her failure had produced a rare alteration in her, but I had been too full of stratagems and spoils to think of that. Now I took it in; I can scarcely tell how it startled me. She stood in the middle of the room with a face of mildness bent upon me, and her look of forgiveness, of absolution, made her angelic. It beautified her; she was younger; she was not a ridiculous old woman. This trick of her expression, this magic of her spirit, transfigured her, and while I still noted it I heard a whisper somewhere in the depths of my conscience: "Why not, after all—why not?" It seemed to me I *could* pay the price. Still more distinctly however than the whisper I heard Miss Tina's own voice. I was so struck with the different effect she made on me that at first I wasn't clearly aware of what she was saying; then I recognised she had bade me good-bye—she said something about hoping I should be very happy.

"Good-bye—good-bye?" I repeated with an inflection interrogative and probably foolish.

I saw she didn't feel the interrogation, she only heard the words; she had strung herself up to accepting our separation and they fell upon her ear as a proof. "Are you going to-day?" she asked. "But it doesn't matter, for whenever you go I shall not see you again. I don't want to." And she smiled strangely, with an infinite gentleness. She had never doubted my having left her the day before in horror. How *could* she, since I hadn't come back before night to contradict, even as a simple form, even as an act of common humanity, such an idea? And now she had the force of soul—Miss Tina with force of soul was a new conception—to smile at me in her abjection.

"What shall you do—where shall you go?" I asked.

"Oh I don't know. I've done the great thing. I've destroyed the papers."

"Destroyed them?" I waited.

"Yes; what was I to keep them for? I burnt them last night, one by one, in the kitchen."

"One by one?" I coldly echoed it.

"It took a long time—there were so many." The room seemed to go round me as she said this and a real darkness for a moment descended on my eyes. When it passed, Miss Tina was there still, but the transfiguration was over and she had changed back to a plain dingy elderly person. It was in this character she spoke as she said "I can't stay with you longer, I can't"; and it was in this character she turned her back upon me, as I had turned mine upon her twenty-four hours before, and moved to the door of her room. Here she did what I hadn't done when I quitted her—she paused long enough to give me one look. I have never forgotten it and I sometimes still suffer from it, though it was not resentful. No, there was no resentment, nothing hard or vindictive in poor Miss Tina; for when, later, I sent her, as the price of the portrait of Jeffrey Aspern, a larger sum of money than I had hoped to be able to gather for her, writing to her that I had sold the picture, she kept it with thanks; she never sent it back. I wrote her that I had sold the picture, but I admitted to Mrs. Prest at the time—I met this other friend in London that autumn—that it hangs above my writing-table. When I look at it I can scarcely bear my loss—I mean of the precious papers.

1888

THE PUPIL

1

THE POOR YOUNG MAN hesitated and procrastinated: it cost him such an effort to broach the subject of terms, to speak of money to a person who spoke only of feelings and, as it were, of the aristocracy. Yet he was unwilling to take leave, treating his engagement as settled, without some more conventional glance in that direction than he could find an opening for in the manner of the large, affable lady who sat there drawing a pair of soiled *gants de Suède*[1] through a fat, jewelled hand and, at once pressing and gliding, repeated over

---

[1] Suede gloves.

and over everything but the thing he would have liked to hear. He would have liked to hear the figure of his salary; but just as he was nervously about to sound that note the little boy came back—the little boy Mrs. Moreen had sent out of the room to fetch her fan. He came back without the fan, only with the casual observation that he couldn't find it. As he dropped this cynical confession he looked straight and hard at the candidate for the honour of taking his education in hand. This personage reflected, somewhat grimly, that the first thing he should have to teach his little charge would be to appear to address himself to his mother when he spoke to her—especially not to make her such an improper answer as that.

When Mrs. Moreen bethought herself of this pretext for getting rid of their companion, Pemberton supposed it was precisely to approach the delicate subject of his remuneration. But it had been only to say some things about her son which it was better that a boy of eleven shouldn't catch. They were extravagantly to his advantage, save when she lowered her voice to sigh, tapping her left side familiarly: "And all overclouded by *this*, you know—all at the mercy of a weakness—!" Pemberton gathered that the weakness was in the region of the heart. He had known the poor child was not robust: this was the basis on which he had been invited to treat, through an English lady, an Oxford acquaintance, then at Nice, who happened to know both his needs and those of the amiable American family looking out for something really superior in the way of a resident tutor.

The young man's impression of his prospective pupil, who had first come into the room, as if to see for himself, as soon as Pemberton was admitted, was not quite the soft solicitation the visitor had taken for granted. Morgan Moreen was, somehow, sickly without being delicate, and that he looked intelligent (it is true Pemberton wouldn't have enjoyed his being stupid), only added to the suggestion that, as with his big mouth and big ears he really couldn't be called pretty, he might be unpleasant. Pemberton was modest—he was even timid; and the chance that his small scholar might prove cleverer than himself had quite figured, to his nervousness, among the dangers of an untried experiment. He reflected, however, that these were risks one had to run when one accepted a position, as it was called, in a private family; when as yet one's University honours had, pecuniarily speaking, remained barren. At any rate, when Mrs. Moreen got up as if to intimate that, since it was understood he would enter upon his duties within the week she would let him off now, he succeeded, in spite of the presence of the child, in squeezing out a phrase about the rate of payment. It was not the fault of the conscious smile which seemed a reference to the lady's expensive identity, if the allusion did not sound rather vulgar. This was exactly because she became still more gracious to reply: "Oh! I can assure you that all that will be quite regular."

Pemberton only wondered, while he took up his hat, what "all that" was to amount to—people had such different ideas. Mrs. Moreen's words, however, seemed to commit the family to a pledge definite enough to elicit from the child a strange little comment, in the shape of the mocking, foreign ejaculation, "Oh, là-là!"

Pemberton, in some confusion, glanced at him as he walked slowly to the window with his back turned, his hands in his pockets and the air in his elderly shoulders of a boy who didn't play. The young man wondered if he could teach him to play, though his mother had said it would never do and that this was why school was impossible. Mrs. Moreen exhibited no discomfiture; she only continued blandly: "Mr. Moreen will be delighted to meet your wishes. As I told you, he has been called to London for a week. As soon as he comes back you shall have it out with him."

This was so frank and friendly that the young man could only reply, laughing as his hostess laughed: "Oh! I don't imagine we shall have much of a battle."

"They'll give you anything you like," the boy remarked unexpectedly, returning from the window. "We don't mind what anything costs—we live awfully well."

"My darling, you're too quaint!" his mother exclaimed, putting out to caress him a practiced but ineffectual hand. He slipped out of it, but looked with intelligent, innocent eyes at Pemberton, who had already had time to notice that from one moment to the other his small satiric face seemed to change its time of life. At this moment it was infantine; yet it appeared also to be under the influence of curious intuitions and knowledges. Pemberton rather disliked precocity, and he was disappointed to find gleams of it in a disciple not yet in his teens. Nevertheless he divined on the spot that Morgan wouldn't prove a bore. He would prove on the contrary a kind of excitement. This idea held the young man, in spite of a certain repulsion.

"You pompous little person! We're not extravagant!" Mrs. Moreen gayly protested, making another unsuccessful attempt to draw the boy to her side. "You must know what to expect," she went on to Pemberton.

"The less you expect the better!" her companion interposed. "But we *are* people of fashion."

"Only so far as *you* make us so!" Mrs. Moreen mocked, tenderly. "Well, then, on Friday—don't tell me you're superstitious—and mind you don't fail us. Then you'll see us all. I'm so sorry the girls are out. I guess you'll like the girls. And, you know, I've another son, quite different from this one."

"He tries to imitate me," said Morgan to Pemberton.

"He tries? Why, he's twenty years old!" cried Mrs. Moreen.

"You're very witty," Pemberton remarked to the child—a proposition that his mother echoed with enthusiasm, declaring that Morgan's sallies were the delight of the house. The boy paid no heed to this; he only inquired abruptly of the visitor, who was surprised afterwards that he hadn't struck him as offensively forward: "Do you *want* very much to come?"

"Can you doubt it, after such a description of what I shall hear?" Pemberton replied. Yet he didn't want to come at all; he was coming because he had to go somewhere, thanks to the collapse of his fortune at the end of a year abroad, spent on the system of putting his tiny patrimony into a single full wave of experience. He had had his full wave, but he couldn't pay his hotel bill. Moreover, he had caught in the boy's eyes the glimpse of a far-off appeal.

"Well, I'll do the best I can for you," said Morgan; with which he turned away again. He passed out of one of the long windows; Pemberton saw him go and lean on the parapet of the terrace. He remained there while the young man took leave of his mother, who, on Pemberton's looking as if he expected a farewell from him, interposed with: "Leave him, leave him; he's so strange!" Pemberton suspected she was afraid of something he might say. "He's a genius—you'll love him," she added. "He's much the most interesting person in the family." And before he could invent some civility to oppose to this, she wound up with: "But we're all good, you know!"

"He's a genius—you'll love him!" were words that recurred to Pemberton before the Friday, suggesting, among other things, that geniuses were not invariably lovable. However, it was all the better if there was an element that would make tutorship absorbing: he had perhaps taken too much for granted that it would be dreary. As he left the villa after his interview, he looked up at the balcony and saw the child leaning over it. "We shall have great larks!" he called up.

Morgan hesitated a moment; then he answered, laughing: "By the time you come back I shall have thought of something witty!"

This made Pemberton say to himself: "After all he's rather nice."

2

On the Friday he saw them all, as Mrs. Moreen had promised, for her husband had come back and the girls and the other son were at home. Mr. Moreen had a white moustache, a confiding manner and, in his buttonhole, the ribbon of a foreign order—bestowed, as Pemberton eventually learned, for services. For what services he never clearly ascertained: this was a point— one of a large number—that Mr. Moreen's manner never confided. What it emphatically did confide was that he was a man of the world. Ulick, the first-born, was in visible training for the same profession—under the disadvantage as yet, however, of a buttonhole only feebly floral and a moustache with no pretensions to type. The girls had hair and figures and manners and small fat feet, but had never been out alone. As for Mrs. Moreen, Pemberton saw on a nearer view that her elegance was intermittent and her parts didn't always match. Her husband, as she had promised, met with enthusiasm Pemberton's ideas in regard to a salary. The young man had endeavoured to make them modest, and Mr. Moreen confided to him that *he* found them positively meagre. He further assured him that he aspired to be intimate with his children, to be their best friend, and that he was always looking out for them. That was what he went off for, to London and other places—to look out; and this vigilance was the theory of life, as well as the real occupation, of the whole family. They all looked out, for they were very frank on the subject of its being necessary. They desired it to be understood that they were earnest people, and also that their fortune, though quite adequate for earnest people, required the most careful administration. Mr. Moreen, as the parent bird, sought sustenance for the nest. Ulick found sustenance mainly at the club, where Pemberton guessed that it was usually served on green cloth. The girls used to do up their hair and their frocks themselves, and our young man felt appealed to to be glad, in regard to Morgan's education, that, though it must naturally be of the best, it didn't cost too much. After a little he *was* glad, forgetting at times his own needs in the interest inspired by the child's nature and education and the pleasure of making easy terms for him.

During the first weeks of their acquaintance Morgan had been as puzzling as a page in an unknown language—altogether different from the obvious little Anglo-Saxons who had misrepresented childhood to Pemberton. Indeed the whole mystic volume in which the boy had been bound demanded some practice in translation. To-day, after a considerable interval, there is something phantasmagoric, like a prismatic reflection or a serial novel, in Pemberton's memory of the queerness of the Moreens. If it were not for a few tangible tokens—a lock of Morgan's hair, cut by his own hand, and the half-dozen letters he got from him when they were separated—the whole episode and the figures peopling it would seem too inconsequent for anything but dreamland. The queerest thing about them was their success (as it appeared to him for a while at the time), for he had never seen a family so brilliantly equipped for failure. Wasn't it success to have kept him so hatefully long? Wasn't it success to have drawn him in that first morning at *déjeuner*,[1] the Friday he came—it was enough to *make* one superstitious—so that he utterly committed himself, and this not by calculation or a *mot d'ordre*,[2] but by a happy instinct which made them, like a band of gipsies, work so neatly together? They amused him as much as if they had really been a band of gipsies. He was still young and had not seen much of the world—his English years had been intensely usual; therefore the reversed conventions of the Moreens (for they had their standards), struck him as topsyturvy. He had encountered nothing like them at Oxford; still less had any such note been struck to his younger American ear during the four years at Yale in which he had richly supposed himself to be reacting against Puritanism. The reaction of the Moreens, at any rate, went ever so much further. He had thought himself very clever that first day in hitting them all off in his mind with the term "cosmopolite." Later, it seemed feeble and colourless enough—confessedly, helplessly provisional.

However, when he first applied it to them he had a degree of joy—for an instructor he was still empirical—as if from the apprehension that to live with them would really be to see life. Their sociable strangeness was an intimation of that—their chatter of tongues, their gaiety and good humour, their infinite dawdling (they were always getting themselves up, but it took forever, and Pemberton had once found Mr. Moreen shaving in the drawing-room), their French, their Italian and, in the spiced fluency, their cold, tough slices of American. They lived on macaroni and coffee (they had these articles prepared in perfection), but they knew recipes for a hundred other dishes. They overflowed with music and song, were always humming and catching each other up, and had a kind of professional acquaintance with continental cities. They talked of "good places" as if they had been strolling players. They had at Nice a villa, a carriage, a piano and a banjo, and they went to official parties. They were a perfect calendar of the "days" of their friends, which Pemberton knew them, when they were indisposed, to get out

[1] Late breakfast.
[2] Password.

of bed to go to, and which made the week larger than life when Mrs. Moreen talked of them with Paula and Amy. Their romantic initiations gave their new inmate at first an almost dazzling sense of culture. Mrs. Moreen had translated something, at some former period—an author whom it made Pemberton feel *borné*[3] never to have heard of. They could imitate Venetian and sing Neapolitan, and when they wanted to say something very particular they communicated with each other in an ingenious dialect of their own—a sort of spoken cipher, which Pemberton at first took for Volapuk, but which he learned to understand as he would not have understood Volapuk.

"It's the family language—Ultramoreen," Morgan explained to him drolly enough; but the boy rarely condescended to use it himself, though he attempted colloquial Latin as if he had been a little prelate.

Among all the "days" with which Mrs. Moreen's memory was taxed she managed to squeeze in one of her own, which her friends sometimes forgot. But the house derived a frequented air from the number of fine people who were freely named there and from several mysterious men with foreign titles and English clothes whom Morgan called the princes and who, on sofas with the girls, talked French very loud, as if to show they were saying nothing improper. Pemberton wondered how the princes could ever propose in that tone and so publicly: he took for granted cynically that this was what was desired of them. Then he acknowledged that even for the chance of such an advantage Mrs. Moreen would never allow Paula and Amy to receive alone. These young ladies were not at all timid, but it was just the safeguards that made them so graceful. It was a houseful of Bohemians who wanted tremendously to be Philistines.

In one respect, however, certainly, they achieved no rigour—they were wonderfully amiable and ecstatic about Morgan. It was a genuine tenderness, an artless admiration, equally strong in each. They even praised his beauty, which was small, and were rather afraid of him, as if they recognised that he was of a finer clay. They called him a little angel and a little prodigy and pitied his want of health effusively. Pemberton feared at first that their extravagance would make him hate the boy, but before this happened he had become extravagant himself. Later, when he had grown rather to hate the others, it was a bribe to patience for him that they were at any rate nice about Morgan, going on tiptoe if they fancied he was showing symptoms, and even giving up somebody's "day" to procure him a pleasure. But mixed with this was the oddest wish to make him independent, as if they felt that they were not good enough for him. They passed him over to Pemberton very much as if they wished to force a constructive adoption on the obliging bachelor and shirk altogether a responsibility. They were delighted when they perceived that Morgan liked his preceptor, and could think of no higher praise for the young man. It was strange how they contrived to reconcile the appearance, and indeed the essential fact, of adoring the child with their eagerness to wash their hands of him. Did they want to get rid of him before he should find them out? Pemberton was finding them out month by month. At any rate, the boy's relations turned their backs with exaggerated delicacy,

3 Insignificant.

as if to escape the charge of interfering. Seeing in time how little he had in common with them (it was by *them* he first observed it—they proclaimed it with complete humility), his preceptor was moved to speculate on the mysteries of transmission, the far jumps of heredity. Where his detachment from most of the things they represented had come from was more than an observer could say—it certainly had burrowed under two or three generations.

As for Pemberton's own estimate of his pupil, it was a good while before he got the point of view, so little had he been prepared for it by the smug young barbarians to whom the tradition of tutorship, as hitherto revealed to him, had been adjusted. Morgan was scrappy and surprising, deficient in many properties supposed common to the *genus* and abounding in others that were the portion only of the supernaturally clever. One day Pemberton made a great stride: it cleared up the question to perceive that Morgan *was* supernaturally clever and that, though the formula was temporarily meagre, this would be the only assumption on which one could successfully deal with him. He had the general quality of a child for whom life had not been simplified by school, a kind of homebred sensibility which might have been bad for himself but was charming for others, and a whole range of refinement and perception—little musical vibrations as taking as picked-up airs—begotten by wandering about Europe at the tail of his migratory tribe. This might not have been an education to recommend in advance, but its results with Morgan were as palpable as a fine texture. At the same time he had in his composition a sharp spice of stoicism, doubtless the fruit of having had to begin early to bear pain, which produced the impression of pluck and made it of less consequence that he might have been thought at school rather a polyglot little beast. Pemberton indeed quickly found himself rejoicing that school was out of the question: in any million of boys it was probably good for all but one, and Morgan was that millionth. It would have made him comparative and superior—it might have made him priggish. Pemberton would try to be school himself—a bigger seminary than five hundred grazing donkeys; so that, winning no prizes, the boy would remain unconscious and irresponsible and amusing—amusing, because, though life was already intense in his childish nature, freshness still made there a strong draught for jokes. It turned out that even in the still air of Morgan's various disabilities jokes flourished greatly. He was a pale, lean, acute, undeveloped little cosmopolite, who liked intellectual gymnastics and who, also, as regards the behaviour of mankind, had noticed more things than you might suppose, but who nevertheless had his proper playroom of superstitions, where he smashed a dozen toys a day.

3

At Nice once, towards evening, as the pair sat resting in the open air after a walk, looking over the sea at the pink western lights, Morgan said suddenly to his companion: "Do you like it—you know, being with us all in this intimate way?"

"My dear fellow, why should I stay if I didn't?"

"How do I know you will stay? I'm almost sure you won't, very long."

"I hope you don't mean to dismiss me," said Pemberton.

Morgan considered a moment, looking at the sunset. "I think if I did right I ought to."

"Well, I know I'm supposed to instruct you in virtue; but in that case don't do right."

"You're very young—fortunately," Morgan went on, turning to him again.

"Oh yes, compared with you!"

"Therefore, it won't matter so much if you do lose a lot of time."

"That's the way to look at it," said Pemberton accommodatingly.

They were silent a minute; after which the boy asked: "Do you like my father and mother very much?"

"Dear me, yes. They're charming people."

Morgan received this with another silence; then, unexpectedly, familiarly, but at the same time affectionately, he remarked: "You're a jolly old humbug!"

For a particular reason the words made Pemberton change colour. The boy noticed in an instant that he had turned red, whereupon he turned red himself and the pupil and the master exchanged a longish glance in which there was a consciousness of many more things than are usually touched upon, even tacitly, in such a relation. It produced for Pemberton an embarrassment; it raised, in a shadowy form, a question (this was the first glimpse of it), which was destined to play a singular and, as he imagined, owing to the altogether peculiar conditions, an unprecedented part in his intercourse with his little companion. Later, when he found himself talking with this small boy in a way in which few small boys could ever have been talked with, he thought of that clumsy moment on the bench at Nice as the dawn of an understanding that had broadened. What had added to the clumsiness then was that he thought it his duty to declare to Morgan that he might abuse him (Pemberton) as much as he liked, but must never abuse his parents. To this Morgan had the easy reply that he hadn't dreamed of abusing them; which appeared to be true: it put Pemberton in the wrong.

"Then why am I a humbug for saying I think them charming?" the young man asked, conscious of a certain rashness.

"Well—they're not *your* parents."

"They love you better than anything in the world—never forget that," said Pemberton.

"Is that why you like them so much?"

"They're very kind to me," Pemberton replied, evasively.

"You *are* a humbug!" laughed Morgan, passing an arm into his tutor's. He leaned against him, looking off at the sea again and swinging his long, thin legs.

"Don't kick my shins," said Pemberton, while he reflected: "Hang it, I can't complain of them to the child!"

"There's another reason, too," Morgan went on, keeping his legs still.

"Another reason for what?"

"Besides their not being your parents."

"I don't understand you," said Pemberton.

"Well, you will before long. All right!"

Pemberton did understand, fully, before long; but he made a fight
even with himself before he confessed it. He thought it the oddest thing to
have a struggle with the child about. He wondered he didn't detest the child
for launching him in such a struggle. But by the time it began the resource
of detesting the child was closed to him. Morgan was a special case, but to
know him was to accept him on his own odd terms. Pemberton had spent his
aversion to special cases before arriving at knowledge. When at last he did
arrive he felt that he was in an extreme predicament. Against every interest he
had attached himself. They would have to meet things together. Before they
went home that evening, at Nice, the boy had said, clinging to his arm:

"Well, at any rate you'll hang on to the last."

"To the last?"

"Till you're fairly beaten."

"*You* ought to be fairly beaten!" cried the young man, drawing him
closer.

4

A year after Pemberton had come to live with them Mr. and Mrs. Moreen
suddenly gave up the villa at Nice. Pemberton had got used to suddenness,
having seen it practiced on a considerable scale during two jerky little tours
—one in Switzerland the first summer, and the other late in the winter, when
they all ran down to Florence and then, at the end of ten days, liking it
much less than they had intended, straggled back in mysterious depression.
They had returned to Nice "for ever," as they said; but this didn't prevent
them from squeezing, one rainy, muggy May night, into a second-class rail-
way-carriage—you could never tell by which class they would travel—where
Pemberton helped them to stow away a wonderful collection of bundles and
bags. The explanation of this manoeuvre was that they had determined to
spend the summer "in some bracing place"; but in Paris they dropped into a
small furnished apartment—a fourth floor in a third-rate avenue, where there
was a smell on the staircase and the *portier* was hateful—and passed the next
four months in blank indigence.

The better part of this baffled sojourn was for the preceptor and his
pupil, who, visiting the Invalides and Notre Dame, the Conciergerie and all
the museums, took a hundred remunerative rambles. They learned to know
their Paris, which was useful, for they came back another year for a longer
stay, the general character of which in Pemberton's memory to-day mixes
pitiably and confusedly with that of the first. He sees Morgan's shabby
knickerbockers—the everlasting pair that didn't match his blouse and that
as he grew longer could only grow faded. He remembers the particular holes
in his three or four pair of coloured stockings.

Morgan was dear to his mother, but he never was better dressed than
was absolutely necessary—partly, no doubt, by his own fault, for he was as
indifferent to his appearance as a German philosopher. "My dear fellow, you
are coming to pieces," Pemberton would say to him in sceptical remonstrance;
to which the child would reply, looking at him serenely up and down: "My dear
fellow, so are you! I don't want to cast you in the shade." Pemberton could have

no rejoinder for this—the assertion so closely represented the fact. If however the deficiencies of his own wardrobe were a chapter by themselves he didn't like his little charge to look too poor. Later he used to say: "Well, if we are poor, why, after all, shouldn't we look it?" and he consoled himself with thinking there was something rather elderly and gentlemanly in Morgan's seediness—it differed from the untidiness of the urchin who plays and spoils his things. He could trace perfectly the degrees by which, in proportion as her little son confined himself to his tutor for society, Mrs. Moreen shrewdly forbore to renew his garments. She did nothing that didn't show, neglected him because he escaped notice, and then, as he illustrated this clever policy, discouraged at home his public appearances. Her position was logical enough—those members of her family who did show had to be showy.

During this period and several others Pemberton was quite aware of how he and his comrade might strike people; wandering languidly through the Jardin des Plantes as if they had nowhere to go, sitting, on the winter days, in the galleries of the Louvre, so splendidly ironical to the homeless, as if for the advantage of the *calorifère*.[1] They joked about it sometimes: it was the sort of joke that was perfectly within the boy's compass. They figured themselves as part of the vast, vague, hand-to-mouth multitude of the enormous city and pretended they were proud of their position in it—it showed them such a lot of life and made them conscious of a sort of democratic brotherhood. If Pemberton could not feel a sympathy in destitution with his small companion (for after all Morgan's fond parents would never have let him really suffer), the boy would at least feel it with him, so it came to the same thing. He used sometimes to wonder what people would think they were—fancy they were looked askance at, as if it might be a suspected case of kidnapping. Morgan wouldn't be taken for a young patrician with a preceptor—he wasn't smart enough; though he might pass for his companion's sickly little brother. Now and then he had a five-franc piece, and except once, when they bought a couple of lovely neckties, one of which he made Pemberton accept, they laid it out scientifically in old books. It was a great day, always spent on the quays, rummaging among the dusty boxes that garnish the parapets. These were occasions that helped them to live, for their books ran low very soon after the beginning of their acquaintance. Pemberton had a good many in England, but he was obliged to write to a friend and ask him kindly to get some fellow to give him something for them.

If the bracing climate was untasted that summer the young man had an idea that at the moment they were about to make a push the cup had been dashed from their lips by a movement of his own. It had been his first blow-out, as he called it, with his patrons; his first successful attempt (though there was little other success about it), to bring them to a consideration of his impossible position. As the ostensible eve of a costly journey the moment struck him as a good one to put in a signal protest—to present an ultimatum. Ridiculous as it sounded he had never yet been able to compass an uninterrupted private interview with the elder pair or with either of them singly. They were always flanked by their elder children, and poor Pemberton usually

[1] Heating.

had his own little charge at his side. He was conscious of its being a house in which the surface of one's delicacy got rather smudged; nevertheless he had kept the bloom of his scruple against announcing to Mr. and Mrs. Moreen with publicity that he couldn't go on longer without a little money. He was still simple enough to suppose Ulick and Paula and Amy might not know that since his arrival he had only had a hundred and forty francs; and he was magnanimous enough to wish not to compromise their parents in their eyes. Mr. Moreen now listened to him, as he listened to every one and to everything, like a man of the world, and seemed to appeal to him—though not of course too grossly—to try and be a little more of one himself. Pemberton recognised the importance of the character from the advantage it gave Mr. Moreen. He was not even confused, whereas poor Pemberton was more so than there was any reason for. Neither was he surprised—at least any more than a gentleman had to be who freely confessed himself a little shocked, though not, strictly, at Pemberton.

"We must go into this, mustn't we, dear?" he said to his wife. He assured his young friend that the matter should have his very best attention; and he melted into space as elusively as if, at the door, he were taking an inevitable but deprecatory precedence. When, the next moment, Pemberton found himself alone with Mrs. Moreen it was to hear her say: "I see, I see," stroking the roundness of her chin and looking as if she were only hesitating between a dozen easy remedies. If they didn't make their push Mr. Moreen could at least disappear for several days. During his absence his wife took up the subject again spontaneously, but her contribution to it was merely that she had thought all the while they were getting on so beautifully. Pemberton's reply to this revelation was that unless they immediately handed him a substantial sum he would leave them for ever. He knew she would wonder how he would get away, and for a moment expected her to inquire. She didn't, for which he was almost grateful to her, so little was he in a position to tell.

"You won't, you know you won't—you're too interested," she said. "You *are* interested, you know you are, you dear, kind man!" She laughed, with almost condemnatory archness, as if it were a reproach (but she wouldn't insist), while she flirted a soiled pocket-handkerchief at him.

Pemberton's mind was fully made up to quit the house the following week. This would give him time to get an answer to a letter he had despatched to England. If he did nothing of the sort—that is, if he stayed another year and then went away only for three months—it was not merely because before the answer to his letter came (most unsatisfactory when it did arrive), Mr. Moreen generously presented him—again with all the precautions of a man of the world—three hundred francs. He was exasperated to find that Mrs. Moreen was right, that he couldn't bear to leave the child. This stood out clearer for the very reason that, the night of his desperate appeal to his patrons, he had seen fully for the first time where he was. Wasn't it another proof of the success with which those patrons practiced their arts that they had managed to avert for so long the illuminating flash? It descended upon Pemberton with a luridity which perhaps would have struck a spectator as comically excessive, after he had returned to his little servile room, which looked into a close court where a bare, dirty opposite wall took, with the sound of shrill clatter, the reflection of lighted back-windows. He had simply given himself away to a band of adventurers. The idea, the word itself, had a sort of romantic horror for him—he had always lived on such safe lines. Later it assumed a more interesting, almost a soothing, sense: it pointed a moral, and Pemberton could enjoy a moral. The Moreens were adventurers not merely because they didn't pay their debts, because they lived on society, but because their whole view of life, dim and confused and instinctive, like that of clever colour-blind animals, was speculative and rapacious and mean. Oh! they were "respectable," and that only made them more *immondes*.[2] The young man's analysis of them put it at last very simply— they were adventurers because they were abject snobs. That was the completest account of them—it was the law of their being. Even when this truth became vivid to their ingenious inmate he remained unconscious of how much his mind had been prepared for it by the extraordinary little boy who had now become such a complication in his life. Much less could he then calculate on the information he was still to owe to the extraordinary little boy.

5

But it was during the ensuing time that the real problem came up— the problem of how far it was excusable to discuss the turpitude of parents with a child of twelve, of thirteen, of fourteen. Absolutely inexcusable and quite impossible it of course at first appeared; and indeed the question didn't press for a while after Pemberton had received his three hundred francs. They produced a sort of lull, a relief from the sharpest pressure. Pemberton frugally amended his wardrobe and even had a few francs in his pocket. He thought the Moreens looked at him as if he were almost too smart, as if they ought to take care not to spoil him. If Mr. Moreen hadn't been such a man of the world he would perhaps have said something to him about his neckties. But Mr. Moreen was always enough of a man of the world to let things pass—he had certainly shown that. It was singular how Pemberton guessed that Morgan, though saying nothing about it, knew something had happened. But three hundred francs, especially when one owed money, couldn't last for ever; and when they were gone—the boy knew when they were gone—Morgan did say something. The party had returned to Nice at the beginning of the winter, but not to the charming villa. They went to an hotel, where they stayed three months, and then they went to another hotel, explaining that they had left the first because they had waited and waited and couldn't get the rooms they wanted. These apartments, the rooms they wanted, were generally very splendid; but fortunately they never *could* get them—fortunately, I mean, for Pemberton, who reflected always that if they had got them there would have been still less for educational

2 Disgusting.

expenses. What Morgan said at last was said suddenly, irrelevantly, when the moment came, in the middle of a lesson, and consisted of the apparently unfeeling words: "You ought to *filer*, you know—you really ought."

Pemberton stared. He had learnt enough French slang from Morgan to know that to *filer* meant to go away. "Ah, my dear fellow, don't turn me off!"

Morgan pulled a Greek lexicon toward him (he used a Greek-German), to look out a word, instead of asking it of Pemberton. "You can't go on like this, you know."

"Like what, my boy?"

"You know they don't pay you up," said Morgan, blushing and turning his leaves.

"Don't pay me?" Pemberton stared again and feigned amazement. "What on earth put that into your head?"

"It has been there a long time," the boy replied, continuing his search.

Pemberton was silent, then he went on: "I say, what are you hunting for? They pay me beautifully."

"I'm hunting for the Greek for transparent fiction," Morgan dropped.

"Find that rather for gross impertinence, and disabuse your mind. What do I want of money?"

"Oh, that's another question!"

Pemberton hesitated—he was drawn in different ways. The severely correct thing would have been to tell the boy that such a matter was none of his business and bid him go on with his lines. But they were really too intimate for that; it was not the way he was in the habit of treating him; there had been no reason it should be. On the other hand Morgan had quite lighted on the truth—he really shouldn't be able to keep it up much longer; therefore why not let him know one's real motive for forsaking him? At the same time it wasn't decent to abuse to one's pupil the family of one's pupil; it was better to misrepresent than to do that. So in reply to Morgan's last exclamation he just declared, to dismiss the subject, that he had received several payments.

"I say—I say!" the boy ejaculated, laughing.

"That's all right," Pemberton insisted, "Give me your written rendering."

Morgan pushed a copybook across the table, and his companion began to read the page, but with something running in his head that made it no sense. Looking up after a minute or two he found the child's eyes fixed on him, and he saw something strange in them. Then Morgan said: "I'm not afraid of the reality."

"I haven't yet seen the thing that you *are* afraid of—I'll do you that justice!"

This came out with a jump (it was perfectly true), and evidently gave Morgan pleasure. "I've thought of it a long time," he presently resumed.

"Well, don't think of it any more."

The child appeared to comply, and they had a comfortable and even an amusing hour. They had a theory that they were very thorough, and yet they seemed always to be in the amusing part of lessons, the intervals between the tunnels, where there were waysides and views. Yet the morning was brought to a violent end by Morgan's suddenly leaning his arms on the table, burying his head in them and bursting into tears. Pemberton would have been startled at any rate; but he was doubly startled because, as it then occurred to him, it was the first time he had ever seen the boy cry. It was rather awful.

The next day, after much thought, he took a decision and, believing it to be just, immediately acted upon it. He cornered Mr. and Mrs. Moreen again and informed them that if, on the spot, they didn't pay him all they owed him, he would not only leave their house, but would tell Morgan exactly what had brought him to it.

"Oh, you *haven't* told him?" cried Mrs. Moreen, with a pacifying hand on her well-dressed bosom.

"Without warning you? For what do you take me?"

Mr. and Mrs. Moreen looked at each other, and Pemberton could see both that they were relieved and that there was a certain alarm in their relief. "My dear fellow," Mr. Moreen demanded, "what use *can* you have, leading the quiet life we all do, for such a lot of money?"—an inquiry to which Pemberton made no answer, occupied as he was in perceiving that what passed in the mind of his patrons was something like: "Oh, then, if we've felt that the child, dear little angel, has judged us and how he regards us, and we haven't been betrayed, he must have guessed—and, in short, it's *general!*" an idea that rather stirred up Mr. and Mrs. Moreen, as Pemberton had desired that it should. At the same time, if he had thought that his threat would do something towards bringing them round, he was disappointed to find that they had taken for granted (how little they appreciated his delicacy!) that he had already given them away to his pupil. There was a mystic uneasiness in their parental breasts, and that was the way they had accounted for it. None the less his threat did touch them; for if they had escaped it was only to meet a new danger. Mr. Moreen appealed to Pemberton, as usual, as a man of the world; but his wife had recourse, for the first time since the arrival of their inmate, to a fine *hauteur*, reminding him that a devoted mother, with her child, had arts that protected her against gross misrepresentation.

"I should misrepresent you grossly if I accused you of common honesty!" the young man replied; but as he closed the door behind him sharply, thinking he had not done himself much good, while Mr. Moreen lighted another cigarette, he heard Mrs. Moreen shout after him, more touchingly:

"Oh, you do, you *do*, put the knife to one's throat!"

The next morning, very early, she came to his room. He recognised her knock, but he had no hope that she brought him money; as to which he was wrong, for she had fifty francs in her hand. She squeezed forward in her dressing-gown, and he received her in his own, between his bath-tub and his bed. He had been tolerably schooled by this time to the "foreign ways" of his hosts. Mrs. Moreen was zealous, and when she was zealous she didn't care what she did; so she now sat down on his bed, his clothes being on the chairs, and, in her preoccupation, forgot, as she glanced round, to be ashamed of giving him such a nasty room. What Mrs. Moreen was zealous about on this occasion was to persuade him that in the first place she was very good-natured to bring him fifty francs, and, in the second, if he would only see it, he was really too absurd to expect to be *paid*. Wasn't he paid enough, without perpetual money—wasn't he paid by the comfortable, luxurious home that he enjoyed with them all, without a care, an anxiety, a solitary want? Wasn't he sure of his position, and wasn't that everything to a young man like him, quite unknown, with singularly little to show, the ground of whose exorbitant pretensions it was not easy to discover? Wasn't he paid, above all, by the delightful relation he had established with Morgan—quite ideal, as from master to pupil—and by the simple privilege of knowing and living with so amazingly gifted a child, than whom really—she meant literally what she said—there was no better company in Europe? Mrs. Moreen herself took to appealing to him as a man of the world; she said "Voyons, mon cher," and "My dear sir, look here now;" and urged him to be reasonable, putting it before him that it was really a chance for him. She spoke as if, according as he *should* be reasonable, he would prove himself worthy to be her son's tutor and of the extraordinary confidence they had placed in him.

After all, Pemberton reflected, it was only a difference of theory, and the theory didn't matter much. They had hitherto gone on that of remunerated, as now they would go on that of gratuitous, service; but why should they have so many words about it? Mrs. Moreen, however, continued to be convincing; sitting there with her fifty francs she talked and repeated, as women repeat, and bored and irritated him, while he leaned against the wall with his hands in the pockets of his wrapper, drawing it together round his legs and looking over the head of his visitor at the grey negations of his window. She wound up with saying: "You see I bring you a definite proposal."

"A definite proposal?"

"To make our relations regular, as it were—to put them on a comfortable footing."

"I see—it's a system," said Pemberton. "A kind of blackmail."

Mrs. Moreen bounded up, which was what the young man wanted.

"What do you mean by that?"

"You practice on one's fears—one's fears about the child if one should go away."

"And, pray, what would happen to him in that event?" demanded Mrs. Moreen, with majesty.

"Why, he'd be alone with *you*."

"And pray, with whom *should* a child be but with those whom he loves most?"

"If you think that, why don't you dismiss me?"

"Do you pretend that he loves you more than he loves *us*?" cried Mrs. Moreen.

"I think he ought to. I make sacrifices for him. Though I've heard of those *you* make, I don't see them."

Mrs. Moreen stared a moment; then, with emotion, she grasped Pemberton's hand. "*Will* you make it—the sacrifice?"

Pemberton burst out laughing. "I'll see—I'll do what I can—I'll stay a little longer. Your calculation is just—I *do* hate intensely to give him up; I'm fond of him and he interests me deeply, in spite of the inconvenience

I suffer. You know my situation perfectly; I haven't a penny in the world, and, occupied as I am with Morgan, I'm unable to earn money."

Mrs. Moreen tapped her undressed arm with her folded bank-note. "Can't you write articles? Can't you translate, as I do?"

"I don't know about translating; it's wretchedly paid."

"I am glad to earn what I can," said Mrs. Moreen virtuously, with her head high.

"You ought to tell me who you do it for." Pemberton paused a moment, and she said nothing; so he added: "I've tried to turn off some little sketches, but the magazines won't have them—they're declined with thanks."

"You see then you're not such a phoenix—to have such pretensions," smiled his interlocutress.

"I haven't time to do things properly," Pemberton went on. Then as it came over him that he was almost abjectly good-natured to give these explanations he added: "If I stay on longer it must be on one condition—that Morgan shall know distinctly on what footing I am."

Mrs. Moreen hesitated. "Surely you don't want to show off to a child?"

"To show *you* off, do you mean?"

Again Mrs. Moreen hesitated, but this time it was to produce a still finer flower. "And *you* talk of blackmail!"

"You can easily prevent it," said Pemberton.

"And *you* talk of practicing on fears," Mrs. Moreen continued.

"Yes, there's no doubt I'm a great scoundrel."

His visitor looked at him a moment—it was evident that she was sorely bothered. Then she thrust out her money at him. "Mr. Moreen desired me to give you this on account."

"I'm much obliged to Mr. Moreen; but we have no account."

"You won't take it?"

"That leaves me more free," said Pemberton.

"To poison my darling's mind?" groaned Mrs. Moreen.

"Oh, your darling's mind!" laughed the young man.

She fixed him a moment, and he thought she was going to break out tormentedly, pleadingly: "For God's sake, tell me what *is* in it!" But she checked this impulse—another was stronger. She pocketed the money—the crudity of the alternative was comical—and swept out of the room with the desperate concession: "You may tell him any horror you like!"

6

A couple of days after this, during which Pemberton had delayed to profit by Mrs. Moreen's permission to tell her son any horror, the two had been for a quarter of an hour walking together in silence when the boy became sociable again with the remark: "I'll tell you how I know it; I know it through Zénobie."

"Zénobie? Who in the world is *she?*"

"A nurse I used to have—ever so many years ago. A charming woman. I liked her awfully, and she liked me."

"There's no accounting for tastes. What is it you know through her?"

"Why, what their idea is. She went away because they didn't pay her. She did like me awfully, and she stayed two years. She told me all about it— that at last she could never get her wages. As soon as they saw how much she liked me they stopped giving her anything. They thought she'd stay for nothing, out of devotion. And she did stay ever so long—as long as she could. She was only a poor girl. She used to send money to her mother. At last she couldn't afford it any longer, and she went away in a fearful rage one night— I mean of course in a rage against *them*. She cried over me tremendously, she hugged me nearly to death. She told me all about it," Morgan repeated. "She told me it was their idea. So I guessed, ever so long ago, that they have had the same idea with you."

"Zénobie was very shrewd," said Pemberton. "And she made you so."

"Oh, that wasn't Zénobie; that was nature. And experience!" Morgan laughed.

"Well, Zénobie was a part of your experience."

"Certainly I was a part of hers, poor dear!" the boy exclaimed. "And I'm a part of yours."

"A very important part. But I don't see how you know that I've been treated like Zénobie."

"Do you take me for an idiot?" Morgan asked. "Haven't I been conscious of what we've been through together?"

"What we've been through?"

"Our privations—our dark days."

"Oh, our days have been bright enough."

Morgan went on in silence for a moment. Then he said: "My dear fellow, you're a hero!"

"Well, you're another!" Pemberton retorted.

"No, I'm not; but I'm not a baby. I won't stand it any longer. You must get some occupation that pays. I'm ashamed, I'm ashamed!" quavered the boy in a little passionate voice that was very touching to Pemberton.

"We ought to go off and live somewhere together," said the young man.

"I'll go like a shot if you'll take me."

"I'd get some work that would keep us both afloat," Pemberton continued.

"So would I. Why shouldn't I work? I ain't such a *crétin!*" [1]

"The difficulty is that your parents wouldn't hear of it," said Pemberton. "They would never part with you; they worship the ground you tread on. Don't you see the proof of it? They don't dislike me; they wish me no harm; they're very amiable people; but they're perfectly ready to treat me badly for your sake."

The silence in which Morgan received this graceful sophistry struck Pemberton somehow as expressive. After a moment Morgan repeated: "You *are* a hero!" Then he added: "They leave me with you altogether. You've all the responsibility. They put me off on you from morning till night. Why, then, should they object to my taking up with you completely? I'd help you."

[1] Idiot.

"They're not particularly keen about my being helped, and they delight in thinking of you as *theirs*. They're tremendously proud of you."

"I'm not proud of them. But you know *that*," Morgan returned.

"Except for the little matter we speak of they're charming people," said Pemberton, not taking up the imputation of lucidity, but wondering greatly at the child's own, and especially at this fresh reminder of something he had been conscious of from the first—the strangest thing in the boy's large little composition, a temper, a sensibility, even a sort of ideal, which made him privately resent the general quality of his kinsfolk. Morgan had in secret a small loftiness which begot an element of reflection, a domestic scorn not imperceptible to his companion (though they never had any talk about it), and absolutely anomalous in a juvenile nature, especially when one noted that it had not made this nature "old-fashioned," as the word is of children —quaint or wizened or offensive. It was as if he had been a little gentleman and had paid the penalty by discovering that he was the only such person in the family. This comparison didn't make him vain; but it could make him melancholy and a trifle austere. When Pemberton guessed at these young dimnesses he saw him serious and gallant, and was partly drawn on and partly checked, as if with a scruple, by the charm of attempting to sound the little cool shallows which were quickly growing deeper. When he tried to figure to himself the morning twilight of childhood, so as to deal with it safely, he perceived that it was never fixed, never arrested, that ignorance, at the instant one touched it, was already flushing faintly into knowledge, that there was nothing that at a given moment you could say a clever child didn't know. It seemed to him that *he* both knew too much to imagine Morgan's simplicity and too little to disembroil his tangle.

The boy paid no heed to his last remark; he only went on: "I should have spoken to them about their idea, as I call it, long ago, if I hadn't been sure what they would say."

"And what would they say?"

"Just what they said about what poor Zénobie told me—that it was a horrid, dreadful story, that they had paid her every penny they owed her."

"Well, perhaps they had," said Pemberton.

"Perhaps they've paid you!"

"Let us pretend they have, and *n'en parlons plus*." [2]

"They accused her of lying and cheating," Morgan insisted perversely. "That's why I don't want to speak to them."

"Lest they should accuse me, too?"

To this Morgan made no answer, and his companion, looking down at him (the boy turned his eyes, which had filled, away), saw that he couldn't have trusted himself to utter.

"You're right. Don't squeeze them," Pemberton pursued. "Except for that, they *are* charming people."

"Except for *their* lying and *their* cheating?"

"I say—I say!" cried Pemberton, imitating a little tone of the lad's which was itself an imitation.

[2] Don't let's speak of it any more.

"We must be frank, at the last; we *must* come to an understanding," said Morgan, with the importance of the small boy who lets himself think he is arranging great affairs—almost playing at shipwreck or at Indians. "I know all about everything," he added.

"I daresay your father has his reasons," Pemberton observed, too vaguely, as he was aware.

"For lying and cheating?"

"For saving and managing and turning his means to the best account. He has plenty to do with his money. You're an expensive family."

"Yes, I'm very expensive," Morgan rejoined, in a manner which made his preceptor burst out laughing.

"He's saving for *you*," said Pemberton. "They think of you in everything they do."

"He might save a little——" The boy paused. Pemberton waited to hear what. Then Morgan brought out oddly: "A little reputation."

"Oh, there's plenty of that. That's all right!"

"Enough of it for the people they know, no doubt. The people they know are awful."

"Do you mean the princes? We mustn't abuse the princes."

"Why not? They haven't married Paula—they haven't married Amy. They only clean out Ulick."

"You *do* know everything!" Pemberton exclaimed.

"No, I don't, after all. I don't know what they live on, or how they live, or *why* they live! What have they got and how did they get it? Are they rich, are they poor, or have they a *modeste aisance*? [3] Why are they always chiveying about—living one year like ambassadors and the next like paupers? Who are they, any way, and what are they? I've thought of all that— I've thought of a lot of things. They're so beastly worldly. That's what I hate most—oh, I've *seen* it! All they care about is to make an appearance and to pass for something or other. What do they want to pass for? What *do* they, Mr. Pemberton?"

"You pause for a reply," said Pemberton, treating the inquiry as a joke, yet wondering too, and greatly struck with the boy's intense, if imperfect, vision. "I haven't the least idea."

"And what good does it do? Haven't I seen the way people treat them— the 'nice' people, the ones they want to know? They'll take anything from them—they'll lie down and be trampled on. The nice ones hate that—they just sicken them. You're the only really nice person we know."

"Are you sure? They don't lie down for me!"

"Well, you shan't lie down for them. You've got to go—that's what you've got to do," said Morgan.

"And what will become of you?"

"Oh, I'm growing up. I shall get off before long. I'll see you later."

"You had better let me finish you," Pemberton urged, lending himself to the child's extraordinarily competent attitude.

Morgan stopped in their walk, looking up at him. He had to look up

---

[3] Moderate means.

much less than a couple of years before—he had grown, in his loose leanness, so long and high. "Finish me?" he echoed.

"There are such a lot of jolly things we can do together yet. I want to turn you out—I want you to do me credit."

Morgan continued to look at him. "To give you credit—do you mean?"

"My dear fellow, you're too clever to live."

"That's just what I'm afraid you think. No, no; it isn't fair—I can't endure it. We'll part next week. The sooner it's over the sooner to sleep."

"If I hear of anything—any other chance, I promise to go," said Pemberton.

Morgan consented to consider this. "But you'll be honest," he demanded; "you won't pretend you haven't heard?"

"I'm much more likely to pretend I have."

"But what can you hear of, this way, stuck in a hole with us? You ought to be on the spot, to go to England—you ought to go to America."

"One would think you were *my* tutor!" said Pemberton.

Morgan walked on, and after a moment he began again: "Well, now that you know that I know and that we look at the facts and keep nothing back —it's much more comfortable, isn't it?"

"My dear boy, it's so amusing, so interesting, that it surely will be quite impossible for me to forego such hours as these."

This made Morgan stop once more. "You *do* keep something back. Oh, you're not straight—*I* am!"

"Why am I not straight?"

"Oh, you've got your idea!"

"My idea?"

"Why, that I probably sha'n't live, and that you can stick it out till I'm removed."

"You *are* too clever to live!" Pemberton repeated.

"I call it a mean idea," Morgan pursued. "But I shall punish you by the way I hang on."

"Look out or I'll poison you!" Pemberton laughed.

"I'm stronger and better every year. Haven't you noticed that there hasn't been a doctor near me since you came?"

"*I'm* your doctor," said the young man, taking his arm and drawing him on again.

Morgan proceeded, and after a few steps he gave a sigh of mingled weariness and relief. "Ah, now that we look at the facts, it's all right!"

7

They looked at the facts a good deal after this; and one of the first consequences of their doing so was that Pemberton stuck it out, as it were, for the purpose. Morgan made the facts so vivid and so droll, and at the same time so bald and so ugly, that there was fascination in talking them over with him, just as there would have been heartlessness in leaving him alone with them. Now that they had such a number of perceptions in common it was useless for the pair to pretend that they didn't judge such people; but the very judgment, and the exchange of perceptions, created another tie. Morgan had never been so interesting as now that he himself was made plainer by the sidelight of these confidences. What came out in it most was the soreness of his characteristic pride. He had plenty of that, Pemberton felt—so much that it was perhaps well it should have had to take some early bruises. He would have liked his people to be gallant, and he had waked up too soon to the sense that they were perpetually swallowing humble-pie. His mother would consume any amount, and his father would consume even more than his mother. He had a theory that Ulick had wriggled out of an "affair" at Nice: there had once been a flurry at home, a regular panic, after which they all went to bed and took medicine, not to be accounted for on any other supposition. Morgan had a romantic imagination, fed by poetry and history, and he would have liked those who "bore his name" (as he used to say to Pemberton with the humour that made his sensitiveness manly), to have a proper spirit. But their one idea was to get in with people who didn't want them and to take snubs as if they were honourable scars. Why people didn't want them more he didn't know—that was people's own affair; after all they were not superficially repulsive—they were a hundred times cleverer than most of the dreary grandees, the "poor swells" they rushed about Europe to catch up with. "After all, they *are* amusing—they are!" Morgan used to say, with the wisdom of the ages. To which Pemberton always replied: "Amusing—the great Moreen troupe? Why, they're altogether delightful; and if it were not for the hitch that you and I (feeble performers!) make in the *ensemble*, they would carry everything before them."

What the boy couldn't get over was that this particular blight seemed, in a tradition of self-respect, so undeserved and so arbitrary. No doubt people had a right to take the line they liked; but why should *his* people have liked the line of pushing and toadying and lying and cheating? What had their forefathers—all decent folk, so far as he knew—done to them, or what had *he* done to them? Who had poisoned their blood with the fifth-rate social ideal, the fixed idea of making smart acquaintances and getting into the *monde chic*,[1] especially when it was foredoomed to failure and exposure? They showed so what they were after; that was what made the people they wanted not want *them*. And never a movement of dignity, never a throb of shame at looking each other in the face, never any independence or resentment or disgust. If his father or his brother would only knock some one down once or twice a year! Clever as they were they never guessed how they appeared. They were good-natured, yes—as good-natured as Jews at the doors of clothing-shops! But was that the model one wanted one's family to follow? Morgan had dim memories of an old grandfather, the maternal, in New York, whom he had been taken across the ocean to see, at the age of five: a gentleman with a high neckcloth and a good deal of pronunciation, who wore a dress-coat in the morning, which made one wonder what he wore in the evening, and had, or was supposed to have, "property" and something to do with the Bible Society. It couldn't have been but that *he* was a good type. Pemberton himself remembered Mrs. Clancy, a widowed sister of Mr. Moreen's, who was as irritating as a moral tale and had paid a fortnight's

[1] Fashionable world.

visit to the family at Nice shortly after he came to live with them. She was "pure and refined," as Amy said, over the banjo, and had the air of not knowing what they meant and of keeping something back. Pemberton judged that what she kept back was an approval of many of their ways; therefore it was to be supposed that she too was of a good type, and that Mr. and Mrs. Moreen and Ulick and Paula and Amy might easily have been better if they would.

But that they wouldn't was more and more perceptible from day to day. They continued to "chivey," as Morgan called it, and in due time became aware of a variety of reasons for proceeding to Venice. They mentioned a great many of them—they were always strikingly frank, and had the brightest friendly chatter, at the late foreign breakfast in especial, before the ladies had made up their faces, when they leaned their arms on the table, had something to follow the *demi-tasse*, and, in the heat of familiar discussion as to what they "really ought" to do, fell inevitably into the languages in which they could *tutoyer*.[2] Even Pemberton liked them, then; he could endure even Ulick when he heard him give his little flat voice for the "sweet sea-city." That was what made him have a sneaking kindness for them—that they were so out of the workaday world and kept him so out of it. The summer had waned when, with cries of ecstasy, they all passed out on the balcony that overhung the Grand Canal; the sunsets were splendid—the Dorringtons had arrived. The Dorringtons were the only reason they had not talked of at breakfast; but the reasons that they didn't talk of at breakfast always came out in the end. The Dorringtons, on the other hand, came out very little; or else, when they did, they stayed—as was natural—for hours, during which periods Mrs. Moreen and the girls sometimes called at their hotel (to see if they had returned) as many as three times running. The gondola was for the ladies; for in Venice too there were "days," which Mrs. Moreen knew in their order an hour after she arrived. She immediately took one herself, to which the Dorringtons never came, though on a certain occasion when Pemberton and his pupil were together at St. Mark's—where, taking the best walks they had ever had and haunting a hundred churches, they spent a great deal of time—they saw the old lord turn up with Mr. Moreen and Ulick, who showed him the dim basilica as if it belonged to them. Pemberton noted how much less, among its curiosities, Lord Dorrington carried himself as a man of the world; wondering too whether, for such services, his companions took a fee from him. The autumn, at any rate, waned, the Dorringtons departed, and Lord Verschoyle, the eldest son, had proposed neither for Amy nor for Paula.

One sad November day, while the wind roared round the old palace and the rain lashed the lagoon, Pemberton, for exercise and even somewhat for warmth (the Moreens were horribly frugal about fires—it was a cause of suffering to their inmate), walked up and down the big bare *sala* with his pupil. The scagliola floor was cold, the high battered casements shook in the storm, and the stately decay of the place was unrelieved by a particle of furniture. Pemberton's spirits were low, and it came over him that the fortune of the Moreens was now even lower. A blast of desolation, a prophecy of

[2] Use the intimate form of second person singular.

disaster and disgrace, seemed to draw through the comfortless hall. Mr. Moreen and Ulick were in the Piazza, looking out for something, strolling drearily, in mackintoshes, under the arcades; but still, in spite of mackintoshes, unmistakable men of the world. Paula and Amy were in bed—it might have been thought they were staying there to keep warm. Pemberton looked askance at the boy at his side, to see to what extent he was conscious of these portents. But Morgan, luckily for him, was now mainly conscious of growing taller and stronger and indeed of being in his fifteenth year. This fact was intensely interesting to him—it was the basis of a private theory (which, however, he had imparted to his tutor) that in a little while he should stand on his own feet. He considered that the situation would change—that, in short, he should be "finished," grown up, producible in the world of affairs and ready to prove himself of sterling ability. Sharply as he was capable, at times, of questioning his circumstances, there were happy hours when he was as superficial as a child; the proof of which was his fundamental assumption that he should presently go to Oxford, to Pemberton's college, and, aided and abetted by Pemberton, do the most wonderful things. It vexed Pemberton to see how little, in such a project, he took account of ways and means: on other matters he was so sceptical about them. Pemberton tried to imagine the Moreens at Oxford, and fortunately failed; yet unless they were to remove there as a family there would be no *modus vivendi* for Morgan. How could he live without an allowance, and where was the allowance to come from? He (Pemberton) might live on Morgan; but how could Morgan live on him? What was to become of him anyhow? Somehow, the fact that he was a big boy now, with better prospects of health, made the question of his future more difficult. So long as he was frail the consideration that he inspired seemed enough of an answer to it. But at the bottom of Pemberton's heart was the recognition of his probably being strong enough to live and not strong enough to thrive. He himself, at any rate, was in a period of natural, boyish rosiness about all this, so that the beating of the tempest seemed to him only the voice of life and the challenge of fate. He had on his shabby little overcoat, with the collar up, but he was enjoying his walk.

It was interrupted at last by the appearance of his mother at the end of the *sala*. She beckoned to Morgan to come to her, and while Pemberton saw him, complacent, pass down the long vista, over the damp false marble, he wondered what was in the air. Mrs. Moreen said a word to the boy and made him go into the room she had quitted. Then, having closed the door after him, she directed her steps swiftly to Pemberton. There *was* something in the air, but his wildest flight of fancy wouldn't have suggested what it proved to be. She signified that she had made a pretext to get Morgan out of the way, and then she inquired—without hesitation—if the young man could lend her sixty francs. While, before bursting into a laugh, he stared at her with surprise, she declared that she was awfully pressed for the money; she was desperate for it—it would save her life.

"Dear lady, *c'est trop fort!*" Pemberton laughed. "Where in the world do you suppose I should get sixty francs, *du train dont vous allez?*" [3]

"I thought you worked—wrote things; don't they pay you?"

[3] This is too much . . . , considering your behavior.

"Not a penny."

"Are you such a fool as to work for nothing?"

"You ought surely to know that."

Mrs. Moreen stared an instant, then she coloured a little. Pemberton saw she had quite forgotten the terms—if "terms" they could be called—that he had ended by accepting from herself; they had burdened her memory as little as her conscience. "Oh, yes, I see what you mean—you have been very nice about that; but why go back to it so often?" She had been perfectly urbane with him ever since the rough scene of explanation in his room, the morning he made her accept *his* "terms"—the necessity of his making his case known to Morgan. She had felt no resentment, after seeing that there was no danger of Morgan's taking the matter up with her. Indeed, attributing this immunity to the good taste of his influence with the boy, she had once said to Pemberton: "My dear fellow; it's an immense comfort you're a gentleman." She repeated this, in substance, now. "Of course you're a gentleman—that's a bother the less!" Pemberton reminded her that he had not "gone back" to anything; and she also repeated her prayer that, somewhere and somehow, he would find her sixty francs. He took the liberty of declaring that if he could find them it wouldn't be to lend them to *her*—as to which he consciously did himself injustice, knowing that if he had them he would certainly place them in her hand. He accused himself, at bottom and with some truth, of a fantastic, demoralised sympathy with her. If misery made strange bedfellows it also made strange sentiments. It was moreover a part of the demoralisation and of the general bad effect of living with such people that one had to make rough retorts, quite out of the tradition of good manners. "Morgan, Morgan, to what pass have I come for you?" he privately exclaimed, while Mrs. Moreen floated voluminously down the *sala* again, to liberate the boy; groaning, as she went, that everything was too odious.

Before the boy was liberated there came a thump at the door communicating with the staircase, followed by the apparition of a dripping youth who poked in his head. Pemberton recognised him as the bearer of a telegram and recognised the telegram as addressed to himself. Morgan came back as, after glancing at the signature (that of a friend in London), he was reading the words: "Found jolly job for you—engagement to coach opulent youth on own terms. Come immediately." The answer, happily, was paid, and the messenger waited. Morgan, who had drawn near, waited too, and looked hard at Pemberton; and Pemberton, after a moment, having met his look, handed him the telegram. It was really by wise looks (they knew each other so well), that, while the telegraph-boy, in his waterproof cape, made a great puddle on the floor, the thing was settled between them. Pemberton wrote the answer with a pencil against the frescoed wall, and the messenger departed. When he had gone Pemberton said to Morgan:

"I'll make a tremendous charge; I'll earn a lot of money in a short time, and we'll live on it."

"Well, I hope the opulent youth will be stupid—he probably will—" Morgan parenthesised, "and keep you a long time."

"Of course, the longer he keeps me the more we shall have for our old age."

"But suppose *they* don't pay you!" Morgan awfully suggested.

"Oh, there are not two such—!" Pemberton paused, he was on the point of using an invidious term. Instead of this he said "two such chances."

Morgan flushed—the tears came to his eyes. "*Dites toujours,*[4] two such rascally crews!" Then, in a different tone, he added: "Happy opulent youth!"

"Not if he's stupid!"

"Oh, they're happier then. But you can't have everything, can you?" the boy smiled.

Pemberton held him, his hands on his shoulders. "What will become of *you,* what will you do?" He thought of Mrs. Moreen, desperate for sixty francs.

"I shall turn into a man." And then, as if he recognised all the bearings of Pemberton's allusion: "I shall get on with them better when you're not here."

"Ah, don't say that—it sounds as if I set you against them!"

"You do—the sight of you. It's all right; you know what I mean. I shall be beautiful. I'll take their affairs in hand; I'll marry my sisters."

"You'll marry yourself!" joked Pemberton; as high, rather tense pleasantry would evidently be the right, or the safest, tone for their separation.

It was, however, not purely in this strain that Morgan suddenly asked: "But I say—how will you get to your jolly job? You'll have to telegraph to the opulent youth for money to come on."

Pemberton bethought himself. "They won't like that, will they?"

"Oh, look out for them!"

Then Pemberton brought out his remedy. "I'll go to the American Consul; I'll borrow some money of him—just for the few days, on the strength of the telegram."

Morgan was hilarious. "Show him the telegram—then stay and keep the money!"

Pemberton entered into the joke enough to reply that, for Morgan, he was really capable of that; but the boy, growing more serious, and to prove that he hadn't meant what he said, not only hurried him off to the Consulate (since he was to start that evening, as he had wired to his friend), but insisted on going with him. They splashed through the tortuous perforations and over the humpbacked bridges, and they passed through the Piazza, where they saw Mr. Moreen and Ulick go into a jeweller's shop. The Consul proved accommodating (Pemberton said it wasn't the letter, but Morgan's grand air), and on their way back they went into St. Mark's for a hushed ten minutes. Later they took up and kept up the fun of it to the very end; and it seemed to Pemberton a part of that fun that Mrs. Moreen, who was very angry when he had announced to her his intention, should charge him, grotesquely and vulgarly, and in reference to the loan she had vainly endeavoured to effect, with bolting lest they should "get something out" of him. On the other hand he had to do Mr. Moreen and Ulick the justice to recognise that when, on coming in, *they* heard the cruel news, they took it like perfect men of the world.

4 Speak frankly.

8

When Pemberton got at work with the opulent youth, who was to be taken in hand for Balliol, he found himself unable to say whether he was really an idiot or it was only, on his own part, the long association with an intensely living little mind that made him seem so. From Morgan he heard half-a-dozen times: the boy wrote charming young letters, a patchwork of tongues, with indulgent postscripts in the family Volapuk and, in little squares and rounds and crannies of the text, the drollest illustrations—letters that he was divided between the impulse to show his present disciple, as a kind of wasted incentive, and the sense of something in them that was profanable by publicity. The opulent youth went up, in due course, and failed to pass; but it seemed to add to the presumption that brilliancy was not expected of him all at once that his parents, condoning the lapse, which they good-naturedly treated as little as possible as if it were Pemberton's, should have sounded the rally again, begged the young coach to keep his pupil in hand another year.

The young coach was now in a position to lend Mrs. Moreen sixty francs, and he sent her a post-office order for that amount. In return for this favour he received a frantic, scribbled line from her: "Implore you to come back instantly—Morgan dreadfully ill." They were on the rebound, once more in Paris—often as Pemberton had seen them depressed he had never seen them crushed—and communication was therefore rapid. He wrote to the boy to ascertain the state of his health, but he received no answer to his letter. Accordingly he took an abrupt leave of the opulent youth and, crossing the Channel, alighted at the small hotel, in the quarter of the Champs Elysées, of which Mrs. Moreen had given him the address. A deep if dumb dissatisfaction with this lady and her companions bore him company: they couldn't be vulgarly honest, but they could live at hotels, in velvety *entresols*[1] amid a smell of burnt pastilles, in the most expensive city in Europe. When he had left them, in Venice, it was with an irrepressible suspicion that something was going to happen; but the only thing that had happened was that they succeeded in getting away. "How is he? where is he?" he asked of Mrs. Moreen; but before she could speak, these questions were answered by the pressure round his neck of a pair of arms, in shrunken sleeves, which were perfectly capable of an effusive young foreign squeeze.

"Dreadfully ill—I don't see it!" the young man cried. And then, to Morgan: "Why on earth didn't you relieve me? Why didn't you answer my letter?"

Mrs. Moreen declared that when she wrote he was very bad, and Pemberton learned at the same time from the boy that he had answered every letter he had received. This led to the demonstration that Pemberton's note had been intercepted. Mrs. Moreen was prepared to see the fact exposed, as Pemberton perceived, the moment he faced her, that she was prepared for a good many other things. She was prepared above all to maintain that she had acted from a sense of duty, that she was enchanted she had got him over, whatever they might say; and that it was useless of him to pretend that he

1 Lobbies.

didn't *know*, in all his bones, that his place at such a time was with Morgan. He had taken the boy away from them, and now he had no right to abandon him. He had created for himself the gravest responsibilities; he must at least abide by what he had done.

"Taken him away from you?" Pemberton exclaimed indignantly.

"Do it—do it, for pity's sake; that's just what I want. I can't stand *this*—and such scenes. They're treacherous!" These words broke from Morgan, who had intermitted his embrace, in a key which made Pemberton turn quickly to him, to see that he had suddenly seated himself, was breathing with evident difficulty and was very pale.

"*Now* do you say he's not ill—my precious pet?" shouted his mother, dropping on her knees before him with clasped hands, but touching him no more than if he had been a gilded idol. "It will pass—it's only for an instant; but don't say such dreadful things!"

"I'm all right—all right," Morgan panted to Pemberton, whom he sat looking up at with a strange smile, his hands resting on either side on the sofa.

"Now do you pretend I've been treacherous—that I've deceived?" Mrs. Moreen flashed at Pemberton as she got up.

"It isn't *he* says it, it's I!" the boy returned, apparently easier, but sinking back against the wall; while Pemberton, who had sat down beside him, taking his hand, bent over him.

"Darling child, one does what one can; there are so many things to consider," urged Mrs. Moreen. "It's his *place*—his only place. You see *you* think it is now."

"Take me away—take me away," Morgan went on, smiling to Pemberton from his white face.

"Where shall I take you, and how—oh, *how*, my boy?" the young man stammered, thinking of the rude way in which his friends in London held that, for his convenience, and without a pledge of instantaneous return, he had thrown them over; of the just resentment with which they would already have called in a successor, and of the little help as regarded finding fresh employment that resided for him in the flatness of his having failed to pass his pupil.

"Oh, we'll settle that. You used to talk about it," said Morgan. "If we can only go, all the rest's a detail."

"Talk about it as much as you like, but don't think you can attempt it. Mr. Moreen would never consent—it would be so precarious," Pemberton's hostess explained to him. Then to Morgan she explained: "It would destroy our peace, it would break our hearts. Now that he's back it will be all the same again. You'll have your life, your work and your freedom, and we'll all be happy as we used to be. You'll bloom and grow perfectly well, and we won't have any more silly experiments, will we? They're too absurd. It's Mr. Pemberton's place—every one in his place. You in yours, your papa in his, me in mine—*n'est-ce pas, chéri?* [2] We'll all forget how foolish we've been, and we'll have lovely times."

_____
[2] Isn't it so, dear?

She continued to talk and to surge vaguely about the little draped, stuffy *salon*, while Pemberton sat with the boy, whose colour gradually came back; and she mixed up her reasons, dropping that there were going to be changes, that the other children might scatter (who knew?—Paula had her ideas), and that then it might be fancied how much the poor old parent-birds would want the little nestling. Morgan looked at Pemberton, who wouldn't let him move; and Pemberton knew exactly how he felt at hearing himself called a little nestling. He admitted that he had had one or two bad days, but he protested afresh against the iniquity of his mother's having made them the ground of an appeal to poor Pemberton. Poor Pemberton could laugh now, apart from the comicality of Mrs. Moreen's producing so much philosophy for her defence (she seemed to shake it out of her agitated petticoats, which knocked over the light gilt chairs), so little did the sick boy strike him as qualified to repudiate any advantage.

He himself was in for it, at any rate. He should have Morgan on his hands again indefinitely; though indeed he saw the lad had a private theory to produce which would be intended to smooth this down. He was obliged to him for it in advance; but the suggested amendment didn't keep his heart from sinking a little, any more than it prevented him from accepting the prospect on the spot, with some confidence moreover that he would do so even better if he could have a little supper. Mrs. Moreen threw out more hints about the changes that were to be looked for, but she was such a mixture of smiles and shudders (she confessed she was very nervous), that he couldn't tell whether she were in high feather or only in hysterics. If the family were really at last going to pieces why shouldn't she recognise the necessity of pitching Morgan into some sort of lifeboat? This presumption was fostered by the fact that they were established in luxurious quarters in the capital of pleasure; that was exactly where they naturally *would* be established in view of going to pieces. Moreover didn't she mention that Mr. Moreen and the others were enjoying themselves at the opera with Mr. Granger, and wasn't *that* also precisely where one would look for them on the eve of a smash? Pemberton gathered that Mr. Granger was a rich, vacant American—a big bill with a flourishy heading and no items; so that one of Paula's "ideas" was probably that this time she had really done it, which was indeed an unprecedented blow to the general cohesion. And if the cohesion was to terminate what was to become of poor Pemberton? He felt quite enough bound up with them to figure, to his alarm, as a floating spar in case of a wreck.

It was Morgan who eventually asked if no supper had been ordered for him; sitting with him below, later, at the dim, delayed meal, in the presence of a great deal of corded green plush, a plate of ornamental biscuit and a langour marked on the part of the waiter. Mrs. Moreen had explained that they had been obliged to secure a room for the visitor out of the house; and Morgan's consolation (he offered it while Pemberton reflected on the nastiness of lukewarm sauces) proved to be, largely, that this circumstance would facilitate their escape. He talked of their escape (recurring to it often afterwards), as if they were making up a "boy's book" together. But he likewise expressed his sense that there was something in the air, that the Moreens couldn't keep it up much longer. In point of fact, as Pemberton was to see, they kept it up for five or six months. All the while, however, Morgan's contention was designed to cheer him. Mr. Moreen and Ulick, whom he had met the day after his return, accepted that return like perfect men of the world. If Paula and Amy treated it even with less formality an allowance was to be made for them, inasmuch as Mr. Granger had not come to the opera after all. He had only placed his box at their service, with a bouquet for each of the party; there was even one apiece, embittering the thought of his profusion, for Mr. Moreen and Ulick. "They're all like that," was Morgan's comment; "at the very last, just when we think we've got them fast, we're chucked!"

Morgan's comments, in these days, were more and more free; they even included a large recognition of the extraordinary tenderness with which he had been treated while Pemberton was away. Oh, yes, they couldn't do enough to be nice to him, to show him they had him on their mind and make up for his loss. That was just what made the whole thing so sad, and him so glad, after all, of Pemberton's return—he had to keep thinking of their affection less, had less sense of obligation. Pemberton laughed out at this last reason, and Morgan blushed and said: "You know what I mean." Pemberton knew perfectly what he meant; but there were a good many things it didn't make any clearer. This episode of his second sojourn in Paris stretched itself out wearily, with their resumed readings and wanderings and maunderings, their potterings on the quays, their hauntings of the museums, their occasional lingerings in the Palais Royal, when the first sharp weather came on and there was a comfort in warm emanations, before Chevet's wonderful succulent window. Morgan wanted to hear a great deal about the opulent youth—he took an immense interest in him. Some of the details of his opulence—Pemberton could spare him none of them—evidently intensified the boy's appreciation of all his friend had given up to come back to him; but in addition to the greater reciprocity established by such a renunciation he had always his little brooding theory, in which there was a frivolous gaiety too, that their long probation was drawing to a close. Morgan's conviction that the Moreens couldn't go on much longer kept pace with the unexpended impetus with which, from month to month, they did go on. Three weeks after Pemberton had rejoined them they went on to another hotel, a dingier one than the first; but Morgan rejoiced that his tutor had at least still not sacrificed the advantage of a room outside. He clung to the romantic utility of this when the day, or rather the night, should arrive for their escape.

For the first time, in this complicated connection, Pemberton felt sore and exasperated. It was, as he had said to Mrs. Moreen in Venice, *trop fort* —everything was *trop fort*. He could neither really throw off his blighting burden nor find in it the benefit of a pacified conscience or of a rewarded affection. He had spent all the money that he had earned in England, and he felt that his youth was going and that he was getting nothing back for it. It was all very well for Morgan to seem to consider that he would make up to him for all inconveniences by settling himself upon him permanently—there was an irritating flaw in such a view. He saw what the boy had in his mind; the conception that as his friend had had the generosity to come back to him he must show his gratitude by giving him his life. But the poor friend didn't desire the gift—what could he do with Morgan's life? Of course at the same time that Pemberton was irritated he remembered the reason, which was very honourable to Morgan and which consisted simply of the fact that he was perpetually making one forget that he was after all only a child. If one dealt with him on a different basis one's misadventures were one's own fault. So Pemberton waited in a queer confusion of yearning and alarm for the catastrophe which was held to hang over the house of Moreen, of which he certainly at moments felt the symptoms brush his cheek and as to which he wondered much in what form it would come.

Perhaps it would take the form of dispersal—a frightened *sauve qui peut*,[3] a scuttling into selfish corners. Certainly they were less elastic than of yore; they were evidently looking for something they didn't find. The Dorringtons hadn't reappeared, the princes had scattered; wasn't that the beginning of the end? Mrs. Moreen had lost her reckoning of the famous "days"; her social calendar was blurred—it had turned its face to the wall. Pemberton suspected that the great, the cruel, discomfiture had been the extraordinary behaviour of Mr. Granger, who seemed not to know what he wanted, or, what was much worse, what *they* wanted. He kept sending flowers, as if to bestrew the path of his retreat, which was never the path of return. Flowers were all very well, but—Pemberton could complete the proposition. It was now positively conspicuous that in the long run the Moreens were a failure; so that the young man was almost grateful the run had not been short. Mr. Moreen, indeed, was still occasionally able to get away on business, and, what was more surprising, he was also able to get back. Ulick had no club, but you could not have discovered it from his appearance, which was as much as ever that of a person looking at life from the window of such an institution; therefore Pemberton was doubly astonished at an answer he once heard him make to his mother, in the desperate tone of a man familiar with the worst privations. Her question Pemberton had not quite caught; it appeared to be an appeal for a suggestion as to whom they could get to take Amy. "Let the devil take her!" Ulick snapped; so that Pemberton could see that not only they had lost their amiability, but had ceased to believe in themselves. He could also see that if Mrs. Moreen was trying to get people to take her children she might be regarded as closing the hatches for the storm. But Morgan would be the last she would part with.

One winter afternoon—it was a Sunday—he and the boy walked far together in the Bois de Boulogne. The evening was so splendid, the cold lemon-coloured sunset so clear, the stream of carriages and pedestrians so amusing and the fascination of Paris so great, that they stayed out later than usual and became aware that they would have to hurry home to arrive in time for dinner. They hurried accordingly, arm-in-arm, good-humoured and hungry, agreeing that there was nothing like Paris after all and that after all, too, that had come and gone they were not yet sated with innocent pleasures. When they reached the hotel they found that, though scandalously late, they were in time for all the dinner they were likely to sit down to. Confusion reigned in the apartments of the Moreens (very shabby ones this time, but the best in the house), and before the interrupted service of the table (with

[3] Each man for himself.

objects displaced almost as if there had been a scuffle, and a great wine stain
from an overturned bottle), Pemberton could not blink the fact that there
had been a scene of proprietary mutiny. The storm had come—they were all
seeking refuge. The hatches were down—Paula and Amy were invisible (they
had never tried the most casual art upon Pemberton, but he felt that they
had enough of an eye to him not to wish to meet him as young ladies whose
frocks had been confiscated), and Ulick appeared to have jumped overboard.
In a word, the host and his staff had ceased to "go on" at the pace of their
guests, and the air of embarrassed detention, thanks to a pile of gaping trunks
in the passage, was strangely commingled with the air of indignant withdrawal.

When Morgan took in all this—and he took it in very quickly—he blushed
to the roots of his hair. He had walked, from his infancy, among difficulties
and dangers, but he had never seen a public exposure. Pemberton noticed, in
a second glance at him, that the tears had rushed into his eyes and that they
were tears of bitter shame. He wondered for an instant, for the boy's sake,
whether he might successfully pretend not to understand. Not successfully,
he felt, as Mr. and Mrs. Moreen, dinnerless by their extinguished hearth, rose
before him in their little dishonoured *salon*, considering apparently with much
intensity what lively capital would be next on their list. They were not
prostrate, but they were very pale, and Mrs. Moreen had evidently been crying.
Pemberton quickly learned however that her grief was not for the loss of her
dinner, much as she usually enjoyed it, but on account of a necessity much
more tragic. She lost no time in laying this necessity bare, in telling him
how the change had come, the bolt had fallen, and how they would all have to
turn themselves about. Therefore cruel as it was to them to part with their
darling she must look to him to carry a little further the influence he had so
fortunately acquired with the boy—to induce his young charge to follow him
into some modest retreat. They depended upon him, in a word, to take their
delightful child temporarily under his protection—it would leave Mr. Moreen
and herself so much more free to give the proper attention (too little, alas!
had been given), to the readjustment of their affairs.

"We trust you—we feel that we can," said Mrs. Moreen, slowly rubbing
her plump white hands and looking, with compunction, hard at Morgan,
whose chin, not to take liberties, her husband stroked with a tentative paternal
forefinger.

"Oh, yes; we feel that we can. We trust Mr. Pemberton fully, Morgan,"
Mr. Moreen conceded.

Pemberton wondered again if he might pretend not to understand; but
the idea was painfully complicated by the immediate perception that Morgan
had understood.

"Do you mean that he may take me to live with him—for ever and ever?"
cried the boy. "Away, away, anywhere he likes?"

"For ever and ever? *Comme vous-y-allez!*" [4] Mr. Moreen laughed indulgently. "For as long as Mr. Pemberton may be so good."

"We've struggled, we've suffered," his wife went on; "but you've made him
so your own that we've already been through the worst of the sacrifice."

---

[4] How you do go on!

Morgan had turned away from his father—he stood looking at Pemberton with a light in his face. His blush had died out, but something had come that was brighter and move vivid. He had a moment of boyish joy, scarcely mitigated by the reflection that, with this unexpected consecration of his hope—too sudden and too violent; the thing was a good deal less like a boy's book —the "escape" was left on their hands. The boyish joy was there for an instant, and Pemberton was almost frightened at the revelation of gratitude and affection that shone through his humiliation. When Morgan stammered "My dear fellow, what do you say to *that?*" he felt that he should say something enthusiastic. But he was still more frightened at something else that immediately followed and that made the lad sit down quickly on the nearest chair. He had turned very white and had raised his hand to his left side. They were all three looking at him, but Mrs. Moreen was the first to bound forward. "Ah, his darling little heart!" she broke out; and this time, on her knees before him and without respect for the idol, she caught him ardently in her arms. "You walked him too far, you hurried him too fast!" she tossed over her shoulder at Pemberton. The boy made no protest, and the next instant his mother, still holding him, sprang up with her face convulsed and with the terrified cry "Help, help! he's going, he's gone!" Pemberton saw, with equal horror, by Morgan's own stricken face, that he *was* gone. He pulled him half out of his mother's hands, and for a moment, while they held him together, they looked, in their dismay, into each other's eyes. "He couldn't stand it, with his infirmity," said Pemberton—"the shock, the whole scene, the violent emotion."

"But I thought he *wanted* to go to you!" wailed Mrs. Moreen.

"I *told* you he didn't, my dear," argued Mr. Moreen. He was trembling all over, and he was, in his way, as deeply affected as his wife. But, after the first, he took his bereavement like a man of the world.

1891

One of his 2 most famous and best short novels - the other is The Spoils of Poynton.

THE TURN OF THE SCREW (1898)

THE STORY HAD HELD us, round the fire, sufficiently breathless, but except the obvious remark that it was gruesome, as, on Christmas eve in an old house, a strange tale should essentially be, I remember no comment uttered till somebody happened to say that it was the only case he had met in which such a visitation had fallen on a child. The case, I may mention, was that of an apparition in just such an old house as had gathered us for the occasion—an appearance, of a dreadful kind, to a little boy sleeping in the room with his mother and waking her up in the terror of it; waking her not to dissipate

The sense of evil becoming more marked in James.

his dread and soothe him to sleep again, but to encounter also, herself, before she had succeeded in doing so, the same sight that had shaken him. It
was this observation that drew from Douglas—not immediately, but later in
the evening—a reply that had the interesting consequence to which I call attention. Someone else told a story not particularly effective, which I saw he
was not following. This I took for a sign that he had himself something to
produce and that we should only have to wait. We waited in fact till two
nights later; but that same evening, before we scattered, he brought out what
was in his mind.

"I quite agree—in regard to Griffin's ghost, or whatever it was—that its
appearing first to the little boy, at so tender an age, adds a particular touch.
But it's not the first occurrence of its charming kind that I know to have involved a child. If the child gives the effect another turn of the screw, what do
you say to *two* children—?"

"We say, of course," somebody exclaimed, "that they give two turns!
Also that we want to hear about them."

I can see Douglas there before the fire, to which he had got up to present
his back, looking down at his interlocutor with his hands in his pockets.
"Nobody but me, till now, has ever heard. It's quite too horrible." This, naturally, was declared by several voices to give the thing the utmost price, and
our friend, with quiet art, prepared his triumph by turning his eyes over the
rest of us and going on: "It's beyond everything. Nothing at all that I know
touches it."

"For sheer terror?" I remember asking.

He seemed to say it was not so simple as that; to be really at a loss how to
qualify it. He passed his hand over his eyes, made a little wincing grimace.
"For dreadful—dreadfulness!"

"Oh, how delicious!" cried one of the women.

He took no notice of her; he looked at me, but as if, instead of me, he
saw what he spoke of. "For general uncanny ugliness and horror and pain."

"Well then," I said, "just sit right down and begin."

He turned round to the fire, gave a kick to a log, watched it an instant.
Then as he faced us again: "I can't begin. I shall have to send to town."
There was a unanimous groan at this, and much reproach; after which, in
his preoccupied way, he explained. "The story's written. It's in a locked drawer
—it has not been out for years. I could write to my man and enclose the key;
he could send down the packet as he finds it." It was to me in particular that
he appeared to propound this—appeared almost to appeal for aid not to
hesitate. He had broken a thickness of ice, the formation of many a winter;
had had his reasons for a long silence. The others resented postponement,
but it was just his scruples that charmed me. I adjured him to write by the
first post and to agree with us for an early hearing; then I asked him if the
experience in question had been his own. To this his answer was prompt. "Oh,
thank God, no!"

"And is the record yours? You took the thing down?"

"Nothing but the impression. I took that *here*"—he tapped his heart.
"I've never lost it."

"Then your manuscript—?"

"Is in old, faded ink, and in the most beautiful hand." He hung fire again. "A woman's. She has been dead these twenty years. She sent me the pages in question before she died." They were all listening now, and of course there was somebody to be arch, or at any rate to draw the inference. But if he put the inference by without a smile it was also without irritation. "She was a most charming person, but she was ten years older than I. She was my sister's governess," he quietly said. "She was the most agreeable woman I've ever known in her position; she would have been worthy of any whatever. It was long ago, and this episode was long before. I was at Trinity, and I found her at home on my coming down the second summer. I was much there that year —it was a beautiful one; and we had, in her off-hours, some strolls and talks in the garden—talks in which she struck me as awfully clever and nice. Oh yes; don't grin: I liked her extremely and am glad to this day to think she liked me too. If she hadn't she wouldn't have told me. She had never told anyone. It wasn't simply that she said so, but that I knew she hadn't. I was sure; I could see. You'll easily judge why when you hear."

"Because the thing had been such a scare?"

He continued to fix me. "You'll easily judge," he repeated: "*you* will."

I fixed him too. "I see. She was in love."

He laughed for the first time. "You *are* acute. Yes, she was in love. That is, she had been. That came out—she couldn't tell her story without its coming out. I saw it, and she saw I saw it; but neither of us spoke of it. I remember the time and the place—the corner of the lawn, the shade of the great beeches and the long, hot summer afternoon. It wasn't a scene for a shudder; but oh—!" He quitted the fire and dropped back into his chair.

"You'll receive the packet Thursday morning?" I inquired.

"Probably not till the second post."

"Well then; after dinner—"

"You'll all meet me here?" He looked us round again. "Isn't anybody going?" It was almost the tone of hope.

"Everybody will stay!"

"*I* will—and *I* will!" cried the ladies whose departure had been fixed. Mrs. Griffin, however, expressed the need for a little more light. "Who was it she was in love with?"

"The story will tell," I took upon myself to reply.

"Oh, I can't wait for the story!"

"The story *won't* tell," said Douglas; "not in any literal, vulgar way."

"More's the pity, then. That's the only way I ever understand."

"Won't *you* tell, Douglas?" somebody else inquired.

He sprang to his feet again. "Yes—tomorrow. Now I must go to bed. Good-night." And quickly catching up a candlestick, he left us slightly bewildered. From our end of the great brown hall we heard his step on the stair; whereupon Mrs. Griffin spoke. "Well, if I don't know who she was in love with, I know who *he* was."

"She was ten years older," said her husband.

"*Raison de plus*—at that age! But it's rather nice, his long reticence."

"Forty years!" Griffin put in.

"With this outbreak at last."

"The outbreak," I returned, "will make a tremendous occasion of Thursday night"; and everyone so agreed with me that, in the light of it, we lost all attention for everything else. The last story, however incomplete and like the mere opening of a serial, had been told; we handshook and "candlestuck," as somebody said, and went to bed.

I knew the next day that a letter containing the key had, by the first post, gone off to his London apartments; but in spite of—or perhaps just on account of—the eventual diffusion of this knowledge we quite let him alone till after dinner, till such an hour of the evening, in fact, as might best accord with the kind of emotion on which our hopes were fixed. Then he became as communicative as we could desire and indeed gave us his best reason for being so. We had it from him again before the fire in the hall, as we had had our mild wonders of the previous night. It appeared that the narrative he had promised to read us really required for a proper intelligence a few words of prologue. Let me say here distinctly, to have done with it, that this narrative, from an exact transcript of my own made much later, is what I shall presently give. Poor Douglas, before his death—when it was in sight—committed to me the manuscript that reached him on the third of these days and that, on the same spot, with immense effect, he began to read to our hushed little circle on the night of the fourth. The departing ladies who had said they would stay didn't, of course, thank heaven, stay: they departed, in consequence of arrangements made, in a rage of curiosity, as they professed, produced by the touches with which he had already worked us up. But that only made his little final auditory more compact and select, kept it, round the hearth, subject to a common thrill.

The first of these touches conveyed that the written statement took up the tale at a point after it had, in a manner, begun. The fact to be in possession of was therefore that his old friend, the youngest of several daughters of a poor country parson, had, at the age of twenty, on taking service for the first time in the schoolroom, come up to London, in trepidation, to answer in person an advertisement that had already placed her in brief correspondence with the advertiser. This person proved, on her presenting herself, for judgment, at a house in Harley Street, that impressed her as vast and imposing—this prospective patron proved a gentleman, a bachelor in the prime of life, such a figure as had never risen, save in a dream or an old novel, before a fluttered, anxious girl out of a Hampshire vicarage. One could easily fix his type; it never, happily, dies out. He was handsome and bold and pleasant, off-hand and gay and kind. He struck her, inevitably, as gallant and splendid, but what took her most of all and gave her the courage she afterwards showed was that he put the whole thing to her as a kind of favour, an obligation he should gratefully incur. She conceived him as rich, but as fearfully extravagant—saw him all in a glow of high fashion, of good looks, of expensive habits, of charming ways with women. He had for his own town residence a big house filled with the spoils of travel and the trophies of the chase; but it was to his country home, an old family place in Essex, that he wished her immediately to proceed.

He had been left, by the death of their parents in India, guardian to a small nephew and a small niece, children of a younger, a military brother, whom he had lost two years before. These children were, by the strangest of chances for a man in his position,—a lone man without the right sort of experience or a grain of patience,—very heavily on his hands. It had all been a great worry and, on his own part doubtless, a series of blunders, but he immensely pitied the poor chicks and had done all he could: had in particular sent them down to his other house, the proper place for them being of course the country, and kept them there, from the first, with the best people he could find to look after them, parting even with his own servants to wait on them and going down himself, whenever he might, to see how they were doing. The awkward thing was that they had practically no other relations and that his own affairs took up all his time. He had put them in possession of Bly, which was healthy and secure, and had placed at the head of their little establishment—but below stairs only—an excellent woman, Mrs. Grose, whom he was sure his visitor would like and who had formerly been maid to his mother. She was now housekeeper and was also acting for the time as superintendent to the little girl, of whom, without children of her own, she was, by good luck, extremely fond. There were plenty of people to help, but of course the young lady who should go down as governess would be in supreme authority. She would also have, in holidays, to look after the small boy, who had been for a term at school—young as he was to be sent, but what else could be done?— and who, as the holidays were about to begin, would be back from one day to the other. There had been for the two children at first a young lady whom they had had the misfortune to lose. She had done for them quite beautifully —she was a most respectable person—till her death, the great awkwardness of which had, precisely, left no alternative but the school for little Miles. Mrs. Grose, since then, in the way of manners and things, had done as she could for Flora; and there were, further, a cook, a housemaid, a dairywoman, an old pony, an old groom, and an old gardener, all likewise thoroughly respectable.

So far had Douglas presented his picture when someone put a question. "And what did the former governess die of?—of so much respectability?"

Our friend's answer was prompt. "That will come out. I don't anticipate."

"Excuse me—I thought that was just what you *are* doing."

"In her successor's place," I suggested, "I should have wished to learn if the office brought with it—"

"Necessary danger to life?" Douglas completed my thought. "She did wish to learn, and she did learn. You shall hear tomorrow what she learnt. Meanwhile, of course, the prospect struck her as slightly grim. She was young, untried, nervous: it was a vision of serious duties and little company, of really great loneliness. She hesitated—took a couple of days to consult and consider. But the salary offered much exceeded her modest measure, and on a second interview she faced the music, she engaged." And Douglas, with this, made a pause that, for the benefit of the company, moved me to throw in—

"The moral of which was of course the seduction exercised by the splendid young man. She succumbed to it."

He got up and, as he had done the night before, went to the fire, gave a stir to a log with his foot, then stood a moment with his back to us. "She saw him only twice."

"Yes, but that's just the beauty of her passion."

A little to my surprise, on this, Douglas turned round to me. "It *was* the beauty of it. There were others," he went on, "who hadn't succumbed. He told her frankly all his difficulty—that for several applicants the conditions had been prohibitive. They were, somehow, simply afraid. It sounded dull—it sounded strange; and all the more so because of his main condition."

"Which was—?"

"That she should never trouble him—but never, never: neither appeal nor complain nor write about anything; only meet all questions herself, receive all moneys from his solicitor, take the whole thing over and let him alone. She promised to do this, and she mentioned to me that when, for a moment, disburdened, delighted, he held her hand, thanking her for the sacrifice, she already felt rewarded."

"But was that all her reward?" one of the ladies asked.

"She never saw him again."

"Oh!" said the lady; which, as our friend immediately left us again, was the only other word of importance contributed to the subject till, the next night, by the corner of the hearth, in the best chair, he opened the faded red cover of a thin old-fashioned gilt-edged album. The whole thing took indeed more nights than one, but on the first occasion the same lady put another question. "What is your title?"

"I haven't one."

"Oh, I have!" I said. But Douglas, without heeding me, had begun to read with a fine clearness that was like a rendering to the ear of the beauty of his author's hand.

1

I remember the whole beginning as a succession of flights and drops, a little see-saw of the right throbs and the wrong. After rising, in town, to meet his appeal, I had at all events a couple of very bad days—found myself doubtful again, felt indeed sure I had made a mistake. In this state of mind I spent the long hours of bumping, swinging coach that carried me to the stopping-place at which I was to be met by a vehicle from the house. This convenience, I was told, had been ordered, and I found, toward the close of the June afternoon, a commodious fly in waiting for me. Driving at that hour, on a lovely day, through a country to which the summer sweetness seemed to offer me a friendly welcome, my fortitude mounted afresh and, as we turned into the avenue, encountered a reprieve that was probably but a proof of the point to which it had sunk. I suppose I had expected, or had dreaded, something so melancholy that what greeted me was a good surprise. I remember as a most pleasant impression the broad, clear front, its open windows and fresh curtains and the pair of maids looking out; I remember the lawn and the bright flowers and the crunch of my wheels on the gravel and the clustered treetops over which the rooks circled and cawed in the golden sky. The scene had a greatness that made it a different affair from my own scant home, and there immediately appeared at the door, with a little girl in her hand, a civil person who dropped me as decent a curtsey as if I had been the mistress or a distinguished visitor. I had received in Harley Street a narrower notion of the place, and that, as I recalled it, made me think the proprietor still more of a gentleman, suggested that what I was to enjoy might be something beyond his promise.

I had no drop again till the next day, for I was carried triumphantly through the following hours by my introduction to the younger of my pupils. The little girl who accompanied Mrs. Grose appeared to me on the spot a creature so charming as to make it a great fortune to have to do with her. She was the most beautiful child I had ever seen, and I afterwards wondered that my employer had not told me more of her. I slept little that night—I was too much excited; and this astonished me too, I recollect, remained with me, adding to my sense of the liberality with which I was treated. The large, impressive room, one of the best in the house, the great state bed, as I al-most felt it, the full, figured draperies, the long glasses in which, for the first time, I could see myself from head to foot, all struck me—like the extraordi-nary charm of my small charge—as so many things thrown in. It was thrown in as well, from the first moment, that I should get on with Mrs. Grose in a relation over which, on my way, in the coach, I fear I had rather brooded. The only thing indeed that in this early outlook might have made me shrink again was the clear circumstance of her being so glad to see me. I perceived within half an hour that she was so glad—stout, simple, plain, clean, whole-some woman—as to be positively on her guard against showing it too much. I wondered even then a little why she should wish not to show it, and that, with reflection, with suspicion, might of course have made me uneasy.

But it was a comfort that there could be no uneasiness in a connection with anything so beatific as the radiant image of my little girl, the vision of whose angelic beauty had probably more than anything else to do with the restlessness that, before morning, made me several times rise and wander about my room to take in the whole picture and prospect; to watch, from my open window, the faint summer dawn, to look at such portions of the rest of the house as I could catch, and to listen, while, in the fading dusk, the first birds began to twitter, for the possible recurrence of a sound or two, less natural and not without, but within, that I had fancied I heard. There had been a moment when I believed I recognised, faint and far, the cry of a child; there had been another when I found myself just consciously starting as at the passage, before my door, of a light footstep. But these fancies were not marked enough not to be thrown off, and it is only in the light, or the gloom, I should rather say, of other and subsequent matters that they now come back to me. To watch, teach, "form" little Flora would too evidently be the making of a happy and useful life. It had been agreed between us downstairs that after this first occasion I should have her as a matter of course at night, her small white bed being already arranged, to that end, in my room. What I had under-taken was the whole care of her, and she had remained, just this last time, with Mrs. Grose only as an effect of our consideration for my inevitable strangeness and her natural timidity. In spite of this timidity—which the child herself, in the oddest way in the world, had been perfectly frank and brave about, allowing it, without a sign of uncomfortable consciousness, with the deep, sweet serenity indeed of one of Raphael's holy infants, to be dis-cussed, to be imputed to her and to determine us—I felt quite sure she would presently like me. It was part of what I already liked Mrs. Grose herself for, the pleasure I could see her feel in my admiration and wonder as I sat at supper with four tall candles and with my pupil, in a high chair and a bib, brightly facing me, between them, over bread and milk. There were naturally things that in Flora's presence could pass between us only as prodigious and gratified looks, obscure and roundabout allusions.

"And the little boy—does he look like her? Is he too so very remarkable?"

One wouldn't flatter a child. "Oh, Miss, *most* remarkable. If you think well of this one!"—and she stood there with a plate in her hand, beaming at our companion, who looked from one of us to the other with placid heavenly eyes that contained nothing to check us.

"Yes; if I do—?"

"You *will* be carried away by the little gentleman!"

"Well, that, I think, is what I came for—to be carried away. I'm afraid, however," I remember feeling the impulse to add, "I'm rather easily carried away. I was carried away in London!"

I can still see Mrs. Grose's broad face as she took this in. "In Harley Street?"

"In Harley Street."

"Well, Miss, you're not the first—and you won't be the last."

"Oh, I've no pretension," I could laugh, "to being the only one. My other pupil, at any rate, as I understand, comes back tomorrow?"

"Not tomorrow—Friday, Miss. He arrives, as you did, by the coach, under care of the guard, and is to be met by the same carriage."

I forthwith expressed that the proper as well as the pleasant and friendly thing would be therefore that on the arrival of the public conveyance I should be in waiting for him with his little sister; an idea in which Mrs. Grose concurred so heartily that I somehow took her manner as a kind of comforting pledge—never falsified, thank heaven!—that we should on every question be quite at one. Oh, she was glad I was there!

What I felt the next day was, I suppose, nothing that could be fairly called a reaction from the cheer of my arrival; it was probably at the most only a slight oppression produced by a fuller measure of the scale, as I walked round them, gazed up at them, took them in, of my new circumstances. They had, as it were, an extent and mass for which I had not been prepared and in the presence of which I found myself, freshly, a little scared as well as a little proud. Lessons, in this agitation, certainly suffered some delay; I reflected that my first duty was, by the gentlest arts I could contrive, to win the child into the sense of knowing me. I spent the day with her out of doors; I arranged with her, to her great satisfaction, that it should be she, she only, who might show me the place. She showed it step by step and room by room and secret by secret, with droll, delightful, childish talk about it and with the result, in half an hour, of our becoming immense friends. Young as she was, I was struck, throughout our little tour, with her confidence and courage with the way, in empty chambers and dull corridors, on crooked staircases that made me pause and even on the summit of an old machicolated square tower that made me dizzy, her morning music, her disposition to tell me so many more things than she asked, rang out and led me on. I have not seen Bly since the day I left it, and I dare say that to my older and more informed eyes it would now appear sufficiently contracted. But as my little conductress, with her hair of gold and her frock of blue, danced before me round corners and pattered down passages, I had the view of a castle of romance inhabited by a rosy sprite, such a place as would somehow, for diversion of the young idea, take all colour out of storybooks and fairy-tales. Wasn't it just a storybook over which I had fallen a-doze and a-dream? No; it was a big, ugly, antique, but convenient house, embodying a few features of a building still older, half re-placed and half utilised, in which I had the fancy of our being almost as lost as a handful of passengers in a great drifting ship. Well, I was, strangely, at the helm!

2

This came home to me when, two days later, I drove over with Flora to meet, as Mrs. Grose said, the little gentleman; and all the more for an inci-dent that, presenting itself the second evening, had deeply disconcerted me. The first day had been, on the whole, as I have expressed, reassuring; but I was to see it wind up in keen apprehension. The postbag, that evening,—it came late,—contained a letter for me, which, however, in the hand of my em-ployer, I found to be composed but of a few words enclosing another, ad-dressed to himself, with a seal still unbroken. "This, I recognise, is from the head-master, and the head-master's an awful bore. Read him, please; deal with him; but mind you don't report. Not a word. I'm off!" I broke the seal with a great effort—so great a one that I was a long time coming to it; took the unopened missive at last up to my room and only attacked it just before go-ing to bed. I had better have let it wait till morning, for it gave me a second sleepless night. With no counsel to take, the next day, I was full of distress; and it finally got so the better of me that I determined to open myself at least to Mrs. Grose.

"What does it mean? The child's dismissed his school."

She gave me a look that I remarked at the moment; then, visibly, with a quick blankness, seemed to try to take it back. "But aren't they all—?"

"Sent home—yes. But only for the holidays. Miles may never go back at all."

Consciously, under my attention, she reddened. "They won't take him?"

"They absolutely decline."

At this she raised her eyes, which she had turned from me; I saw them fill with good tears. "What has he done?"

I hesitated; then I judged best simply to hand her my letter—which, how-ever, had the effect of making her, without taking it, simply put her hands be-hind her. She shook her head sadly. "Such things are not for me, Miss."

My counsellor couldn't read! I winced at my mistake, which I attenu-ated as I could, and opened my letter again to repeat it to her; then, faltering in the act and folding it up once more, I put it back in my pocket. "Is he really *bad*?"

The tears were still in her eyes. "Do the gentlemen say so?"

"They go into no particulars. They simply express their regret that it should be impossible to keep him. That can have only one meaning." Mrs.

Grose listened with dumb emotion; she forebore to ask me what this meaning might be; so that, presently, to put the thing with some coherence and with the mere aid of her presence to my own mind, I went on: "That he's an injury to the others."

At this, with one of the quick turns of simple folk, she suddenly flamed up. "Master Miles! *him* an injury?"

There was such a flood of good faith in it that, though I had not yet seen the child, my very fears made me jump to the absurdity of the idea. I found myself, to meet my friend the better, offering it, on the spot, sarcastically. "To his poor little innocent mates!"

"It's too dreadful," cried Mrs. Grose, "to say such cruel things! Why, he's scarce ten years old."

"Yes, yes; it would be incredible."

She was evidently grateful for such a profession. "See him, Miss, first. *Then* believe it!" I felt forthwith a new impatience to see him; it was the beginning of a curiosity that, for all the next hours, was to deepen almost to pain. Mrs. Grose was aware, I could judge, of what she had produced in me, and she followed it up with assurance. "You might as well believe it of the little lady. Bless her," she added the next moment—"*look* at her!"

I turned and saw that Flora, whom, ten minutes before, I had established in the schoolroom with a sheet of white paper, a pencil, and a copy of nice "round O's," now presented herself to view at the open door. She expressed in her little way an extraordinary detachment from disagreeable duties, looking to me, however, with a great childish light that seemed to offer it as a mere result of the affection she had conceived for my person, which had rendered necessary that she should follow me. I needed nothing more than this to feel the full force of Mrs. Grose's comparison, and, catching my pupil in my arms, covered her with kisses in which there was a sob of atonement.

None the less, the rest of the day, I watched for further occasion to approach my colleague, especially as, toward evening, I began to fancy she rather sought to avoid me. I overtook her, I remember, on the staircase; we went down together, and at the bottom I detained her, holding her there with a hand on her arm. "I take what you said to me at noon as a declaration that *you've* never known him to be bad."

She threw back her head; she had clearly, by this time, and very honestly, adopted an attitude. "Oh, never known him—I don't pretend *that!*"

I was upset again. "Then you *have* known him—?"

"Yes indeed, Miss, thank God!"

On reflection I accepted this. "You mean that a boy who never is—?"

"Is no boy for *me!*"

I held her tighter. "You like them with the spirit to be naughty?" Then, keeping pace with her answer, "So do I!" I eagerly brought out. "But not to the degree to contaminate—"

"To contaminate?"—my big word left her at a loss. I explained it. "To corrupt."

She stared, taking my meaning in; but it produced in her an odd laugh. "Are you afraid he'll corrupt *you?*" She put the question with such a fine bold humour that, with a laugh, a little silly doubtless, to match her own, I gave way for the time to the apprehension of ridicule.

But the next day, as the hour for my drive approached, I cropped up in another place. "What was the lady who was here before?"

"The last governess? She was also young and pretty—almost as young and almost as pretty, Miss, even as you."

"Ah, then, I hope her youth and her beauty helped her!" I recollect throwing off. "He seems to like us young and pretty!"

"Oh, he *did*," Mrs. Grose assented: "it was the way he liked everyone!" She had no sooner spoken indeed than she caught herself up. "I mean that's *his* way—the master's."

I was struck. "But of whom did you speak first?"

She looked blank, but she coloured. "Why, of *him*."

"Of the master?"

"Of who else?"

There was so obviously no one else that the next moment I had lost my impression of her having accidentally said more than she meant; and I merely asked what I wanted to know. "Did *she* see anything in the boy—?"

"That wasn't right? She never told me."

I had a scruple, but I overcame it. "Was she careful—particular?"

Mrs. Grose appeared to try to be conscientious. "About some things—yes."

"But not about all?"

Again she considered. "Well, Miss—she's gone. I won't tell tales."

"I quite understand your feeling," I hastened to reply; but I thought it, after an instant, not opposed to this concession to pursue: "Did she die here?"

"No—she went off."

I don't know what there was in this brevity of Mrs. Grose's that struck me as ambiguous. "Went off to die?" Mrs. Grose looked straight out of the window, but I felt that, hypothetically, I had a right to know what young persons engaged for Bly were expected to do. "She was taken ill, you mean, and went home?"

"She was not taken ill, so far as appeared, in this house. She left it, at the end of the year, to go home, as she said, for a short holiday, to which the time she had put in had certainly given her a right. We had then a young woman— a nursemaid who had stayed on and who was a good girl and clever; and *she* took the children altogether for the interval. But our young lady never came back, and at the very moment I was expecting her I heard from the master that she was dead."

I turned this over. "But of what?"

"He never told me! But please, Miss," said Mrs. Grose, "I must get to my work."

3

Her thus turning her back on me was fortunately not, for my just preoccupations, a snub that could check the growth of our mutual esteem. We met, after I had brought home little Miles, more intimately than ever on the ground of my stupefaction, my general emotion: so monstrous was I then ready to pronounce it that such a child as had now been revealed to me should be under an interdict. I was a little late on the scene, and I felt, as he stood wistfully looking out for me before the door of the inn at which the coach had put him down, that I had seen him, on the instant, without and within, in the great glow of freshness, the same positive fragrance of purity, in which I had, from the first moment, seen his little sister. He was incredibly beautiful, and Mrs. Grose had put her finger on it; everything but a sort of passion of tenderness for him was swept away by his presence. What I then and there took him to my heart for was something divine that I have never found to the same degree in any child—his indescribable little air of knowing nothing in the world but love. It would have been impossible to carry a bad name with a greater sweetness of innocence, and by the time I had got back to Bly with him I remained merely bewildered—so far, that is, as I was not outraged—by the sense of the horrible letter locked up in my room, in a drawer. As soon as I could compass a private word with Mrs. Grose I declared to her that it was grotesque.

She promptly understood me. "You mean the cruel charge—?"

"It doesn't live an instant. My dear woman, *look* at him!"

She smiled at my pretension to have discovered his charm. "I assure you, Miss, I do nothing else! What will you say, then?" she immediately added.

"In answer to the letter?" I had made up my mind. "Nothing."

"And to his uncle?"

I was incisive. "Nothing."

"And to the boy himself?"

I was wonderful. "Nothing."

She gave with her apron a great wipe to her mouth. "Then I'll stand by you. We'll see it out."

"We'll see it out!" I ardently echoed, giving her my hand to make it a vow.

She held me there a moment, then whisked up her apron again with her detached hand. "Would you mind, Miss, if I used the freedom—"

"To kiss me? No!" I took the good creature in my arms and, after we had embraced like sisters, felt still more fortified and indignant.

This, at all events, was for the time: a time so full that, as I recall the way it went, it reminds me of all the art I now need to make it a little distinct. What I look back at with amazement is the situation I accepted. I had undertaken, with my companion, to see it out, and I was under a charm, apparently, that could smooth away the extent and the far and difficult connections of such an effort. I was lifted aloft on a great wave of infatuation and pity. I found it simple, in my ignorance, my confusion, and perhaps my conceit, to assume that I could deal with a boy whose education for the world was all on the point of beginning. I am unable even to remember at this day what proposal I framed for the end of his holidays and the resumption of his studies. Lessons with me, indeed, that charming summer, we all had a theory that he was to have; but I now feel that, for weeks, the lessons must have been rather my own. I learnt something—at first certainly—that had not been one of the teachings of my small, smothered life; learnt to be amused, and even amusing, and not to think for the morrow. It was the first time, in a manner, that I had known space and air and freedom, all the music of summer and all the mystery of nature. And then there was consideration—and consideration was sweet. Oh, it was a trap—not designed, but deep—to my imagination, to my delicacy, perhaps to my vanity; to whatever, in me, was most excitable. The best way to picture it all is to say that I was off my guard. They gave me so little trouble—they were of a gentleness so extraordinary. I used to speculate—but even this with a dim disconnectedness—as to how the rough future (for all futures are rough!) would handle them and might bruise them. They had the bloom of health and happiness; and yet, as if I had been in charge of a pair of little grandees, of princes of the blood, for whom everything, to be right, would have to be enclosed and protected, the only form that, in my fancy, the after-years could take for them was that of a romantic, a really royal extension of the garden and the park. It may be, of course, above all, that what suddenly broke into this gives the previous time a charm of stillness—that hush in which something gathers or crouches. The change was actually like the spring of a beast.

In the first weeks the days were long; they often, at their finest, gave me what I used to call my own hour, the hour when, for my pupils, tea-time and bed-time having come and gone, I had, before my final retirement, a small interval alone. Much as I liked my companions, this hour was the thing in the day I liked most; and I liked it best of all when, as the light faded—or rather, I should say, the day lingered and the last calls of the last birds sounded, in a flushed sky, from the old trees—I could take a turn into the grounds and enjoy, almost with a sense of property that amused and flattered me, the beauty and dignity of the place. It was a pleasure at these moments to feel myself tranquil and justified; doubtless, perhaps, also to reflect that by my discretion, my quiet good sense and general high propriety, I was giving pleasure—if he ever thought of it!—to the person to whose pressure I had responded. What I was doing was what he had earnestly hoped and directly asked of me, and that I *could*, after all, do it proved even a greater joy than I had expected. I dare say I fancied myself, in short, a remarkable young woman and took comfort in the faith that this would more publicly appear. Well, I needed to be remarkable to offer a front to the remarkable things that presently gave their first sign.

It was plump, one afternoon, in the middle of my very hour: the children were tucked away and I had come out for my stroll. One of the thoughts that, as I don't in the least shrink now from noting, used to be with me in these wanderings was that it would be as charming as a charming story suddenly to meet someone. Someone would appear there at the turn of a path and would stand before me and smile and approve. I didn't ask more than that—I only asked that he should *know*; and the only way to be sure he knew would be to see it, and the kind light of it, in his handsome face. That was exactly present to me—by which I mean the face was—when, on the first of these occasions, at the end of a long June day, I stopped short on emerging from one of the plantations and coming into view of the house. What arrested me on the spot —and with a shock much greater than any vision had allowed for—was the sense that my imagination had, in a flash, turned real. He did stand there!—

but high up, beyond the lawn and at the very top of the tower to which, on that first morning, little Flora had conducted me. This tower was one of a pair—square, incongruous, crenelated structures—that were distinguished, for some reason, though I could see little difference, as the new and the old. They flanked opposite ends of the house and were probably architectural absurdities, redeemed in a measure indeed by not being wholly disengaged nor of a height too pretentious, dating, in their gingerbread antiquity, from a romantic revival that was already a respectable past. I admired them, had fancies about them, for we could all profit in a degree, especially when they loomed through the dusk, by the grandeur of their actual battlements; yet it was not at such an elevation that the figure I had so often invoked seemed most in place.

It produced in me, this figure, in the clear twilight, I remember, two distinct gasps of emotion, which were, sharply, the shock of my first and that of my second surprise. My second was a violent perception of the mistake of my first: the man who met my eyes was not the person I had precipitately supposed. There came to me thus a bewilderment of vision of which, after these years, there is no living view that I can hope to give. An unknown man in a lonely place is a permitted object of fear to a young woman privately bred; and the figure that faced me was—a few more seconds assured me—as little anyone else I knew as it was the image that had been in my mind. I had not seen it in Harley Street—I had not seen it anywhere. The place, moreover, in the strangest way in the world, had, on the instant, and by the very fact of its appearance, become a solitude. To me at least, making my statement here with a deliberation with which I have never made it, the whole feeling of the moment returns. It was as if, while I took in—what I did take in—all the rest of the scene had been stricken with death. I can hear again, as I write, the intense hush in which the sounds of evening dropped. The rooks stopped cawing in the golden sky and the friendly hour lost, for the minute, all its voice. But there was no other change in nature, unless indeed it were a change that I saw with a stranger sharpness. The gold was still in the sky, the clearness in the air, and the man who looked at me over the battlements was as definite as a picture in a frame. That's how I thought, with extraordinary quickness, of each person that he might have been and that he was not. We were confronted across our distance quite long enough for me to ask myself with intensity who then he was and to feel, as an effect of my inability to say, a wonder that in a few instants more became intense.

The great question, or one of these, is, afterwards, I know, with regard to certain matters, the question of how long they have lasted. Well, this matter of mine, think what you will of it, lasted while I caught at a dozen possibilities, none of which made a difference for the better, that I could see, in there having been in the house—and for how long, above all?—a person of whom I was in ignorance. It lasted while I just bridled a little with the sense that my office demanded that there should be no such ignorance and no such person. It lasted while this visitant, at all events,—and there was a touch of the strange freedom, as I remember, in the sign of familiarity of his wearing no hat,—seemed to fix me, from his position, with just the question, just the scrutiny through the fading light, that his own presence provoked. We were too far apart to call to each other, but there was a moment at which, at shorter range, some challenge between us, breaking the hush, would have been the right result of our straight mutual stare. He was in one of the angles, the one away from the house, very erect, as it struck me, and with both hands on the ledge. So I saw him as I see the letters I form on this page; then, exactly, after a minute, as if to add to the spectacle, he slowly changed his place—passed, looking at me hard all the while, to the opposite corner of the platform. Yes, I had the sharpest sense that during this transit he never took his eyes from me, and I can see at this moment the way his hand, as he went, passed from one of the crenelations to the next. He stopped at the other corner, but less long, and even as he turned away still markedly fixed me. He turned away; that was all I knew.

4

It was not that I didn't wait, on this occasion, for more, for I was rooted as deeply as I was shaken. Was there a "secret" at Bly—a mystery of Udolpho or an insane, an unmentionable relative kept in unsuspected confinement? I can't say how long I turned it over, or how long, in a confusion of curiosity and dread, I remained where I had had my collision; I only recall that when I re-entered the house darkness had quite closed in. Agitation, in the interval, certainly had held me and driven me, for I must, in circling about the place, have walked three miles; but I was to be, later on, so much more overwhelmed that this mere dawn of alarm was a comparatively human chill. The most singular part of it in fact—singular as the rest had been—was the part I became, in the hall, aware of in meeting Mrs. Grose. This picture comes back to me in the general train—the impression, as I received it on my return, of the wide white panelled space, bright in the lamplight and with its portraits and red carpet, and of the good surprised look of my friend, which immediately told me she had missed me. It came to me straightway, under her contact, that, with plain heartiness, mere relieved anxiety at my appearance, she knew nothing whatever that could bear upon the incident I had there ready for her. I had not suspected in advance that her comfortable face would pull me up, and I somehow measured the importance of what I had seen by my thus finding myself hesitate to mention it. Scarce anything in the whole history seems to me so odd as this fact that my real beginning of fear was one, as I may say, with the instinct of sparing my companion. On the spot, accordingly, in the pleasant hall and with her eyes on me, I, for a reason that I couldn't then have phrased, achieved an inward revolution—offered a vague pretext for my lateness and, with the plea of the beauty of the night and of the heavy dew and wet feet, went as soon as possible to my room.

Here it was another affair; here, for many days after, it was a queer affair enough. There were hours, from day to day,—or at least there were moments, snatched even from clear duties,—when I had to shut myself up to think. It was not so much yet that I was more nervous than I could bear to be as that I was remarkably afraid of becoming so; for the truth I had now to turn over was, simply and clearly, the truth that I could arrive at no account whatever of the visitor with whom I had been so inexplicably and yet, as it seemed to me, so intimately concerned. It took little time to see that I could sound without forms of inquiry and without exciting remark any domestic complication. The shock I had suffered must have sharpened all my senses; I felt sure, at the end of three days and as the result of mere closer attention, that I had not been practised upon by the servants nor made the object of any "game." Of whatever it was that I knew nothing was known around me. There was but one sane inference: someone had taken a liberty rather gross. That was what, repeatedly, I dipped into my room and locked the door to say to myself. We had been, collectively, subject to an intrusion; some unscrupulous traveller, curious in old houses, had made his way in unobserved, enjoyed the prospect from the best point of view, and then stolen out as he came. If he had given me such a bold hard stare, that was but a part of his indiscretion. The good thing, after all, was that we should surely see no more of him.

This was not so good a thing, I admit, as not to leave me to judge that what, essentially, made nothing else much signify was simply my charming work. My charming work was just my life with Miles and Flora, and through nothing could I so like it as through feeling that I could throw myself into it in trouble. The attraction of my small charges was a constant joy, leading me to wonder afresh at the vanity of my original fears, the distaste I had begun by entertaining for the probable grey prose of my office. There was to be no grey prose, it appeared, and no long grind; so how could work not be charming that presented itself as daily beauty? It was all the romance of the nursery and the poetry of the schoolroom. I don't mean by this, of course, that we studied only fiction and verse; I mean I can express no otherwise the sort of interest my companions inspired. How can I describe that except by saying that instead of growing used to them—and it's a marvel for a governess: I call the sisterhood to witness!—I made constant fresh discoveries. There was one direction, assuredly, in which these discoveries stopped: deep obscurity continued to cover the region of the boy's conduct at school. It had been promptly given me, I have noted, to face that mystery without a pang. Perhaps even it would be nearer the truth to say that—without a word—he himself had cleared it up. He had made the whole charge absurd. My conclusion bloomed there with the real rose-flush of his innocence: he was only too fine and fair for the little horrid, unclean school-world, and he had paid a price for it. I reflected acutely that the sense of such differences, such superiorities of quality, always, on the part of the majority—which could include even stupid, sordid head-masters—turns infallibly to the vindictive.

Both the children had a gentleness (it was their only fault, and it never made Miles a muff) that kept them—how shall I express it?—almost impersonal and certainly quite unpunishable. They were like the cherubs of the anecdote, who had—morally, at any rate—nothing to whack! I remember feeling with Miles in especial as if he had had, as it were, no history. We expect of a small child a scant one, but there was in this beautiful little boy something extraordinarily sensitive, yet extraordinarily happy, that, more than in any creature of his age I have seen, struck me as beginning anew each day. He had never for a second suffered. I took this as a direct disproof of his having really been chastised. If he had been wicked he would have "caught" it, and I should have caught it by the rebound—I should have found the trace. I found nothing at all, and he was therefore angel. He never spoke of his school, never mentioned a comrade or a master; and I, for my part, was quite too much disgusted to allude to them. Of course I was under the spell, and the wonderful part is that, even at the time, I perfectly knew I was. But I gave myself up to it; it was an antidote to any pain, and I had more pains than one. I was in receipt in these days of disturbing letters from home, where things were not going well. But with my children, what things in the world mattered? That was the question I used to put to my scrappy retirements. I was dazzled by their loveliness.

There was a Sunday—to get on—when it rained with such force and for so many hours that there could be no procession to church; in consequence of which, as the day declined, I had arranged with Mrs. Grose that, should the evening show improvement, we would attend together the late service. The rain happily stopped, and I prepared for our walk, which, through the park and by the good road to the village, would be a matter of twenty minutes. Coming downstairs to meet my colleague in the hall, I remembered a pair of gloves that had required three stitches and that had received them—with a publicity perhaps not edifying—while I sat with the children at their tea, served on Sundays, by exception, in that cold, clean temple of mahogany and brass, the "grown-up" dining-room. The gloves had been dropped there, and I turned in to recover them. The day was grey enough, but the afternoon light still lingered, and it enabled me, on crossing the threshold, not only to recognise, on a chair near the wide window, then closed, the articles I wanted, but to become aware of a person on the other side of the window and looking straight in. One step into the room had sufficed; my vision was instantaneous; it was all there. The person looking straight in was the person who had already appeared to me. He appeared thus again with I won't say greater distinctness, for that was impossible, but with a nearness that represented a forward stride in our intercourse and made me, as I met him, catch my breath and turn cold. He was the same—he was the same, and seen, this time, as he had been seen before, from the waist up, the window, though the dining-room was on the ground-floor, not going down to the terrace on which he stood. His face was close to the glass, yet the effect of this better view was, strangely, only to show me how intense the former had been. He remained but a few seconds—long enough to convince me he also saw and recognised; but it was as if I had been looking at him for years and had known him always. Something, however, happened this time that had not happened before; his stare into my face, through the glass and across the room, was as deep and hard as then, but it quitted me for a moment during which I could still watch it, see it fix successively several other things. On the spot there came to me the added shock of a certitude that it was not for me he had come there. He had come for someone else.

The flash of this knowledge—for it was knowledge in the midst of dread—produced in me the most extraordinary effect, started, as I stood there, a sudden vibration of duty and courage. I say courage because I was beyond all doubt already far gone. I bounded straight out of the door again, reached that of the house, got, in an instant, upon the drive, and, passing along the terrace as fast as I could rush, turned a corner and came full in sight. But it was in sight of nothing now—my visitor had vanished. I stopped, I almost dropped, with the real relief of this; but I took in the whole scene—I gave him time to reappear. I call it time, but how long was it? I can't speak to the purpose to-day of the duration of these things. That kind of measure must have left me: they couldn't have lasted as they actually appeared to me to last. The terrace and the whole place, the lawn and the garden beyond it, all I could see of the park, were empty with a great emptiness. There were shrubberies and big trees, but I remember the clear assurance I felt that none of them concealed him. He was there or was not there: not there if I didn't see him. I got hold of this; then, instinctively, instead of returning as I had come, went to the window. It was confusedly present to me that I ought to place myself where he had stood. I did so; I applied my face to the pane and looked, as he had looked, into the room. As if, at this moment, to show me exactly what his range had been, Mrs. Grose, as I had done for himself just before, came in from the hall. With this I had the full image of a repetition of what had already occurred. She saw me as I had seen my own visitant; she pulled up short as I had done; I gave her something of the shock that I had received. She turned white, and this made me ask myself if I had blanched as much. She stared, in short, and retreated on just *my* lines, and I knew she had then passed out and come round to me and that I should presently meet her. I remained where I was, and while I waited I thought of more things than one. But there's only one I take space to mention. I wondered why *she* should be scared.

5

Oh, she let me know as soon as, round the corner of the house, she loomed again into view. "What in the name of goodness is the matter—?" She was now flushed and out of breath.

I said nothing till she came quite near. "With me?" I must have made a wonderful face. "Do I show it?"

"You're as white as a sheet. You look awful."

I considered; I could meet on this, without scruple, any innocence. My need to respect the bloom of Mrs. Grose's had dropped, without a rustle, from my shoulders, and if I wavered for the instant it was not with what I kept back. I put out my hand to her and she took it; I held her hard a little, liking to feel her close to me. There was a kind of support in the shy heave of her surprise. "You came for me for church, of course, but I can't go."

"Has anything happened?"

"Yes. You must know now. Did I look very queer?"

"Through this window? Dreadful!"

"Well," I said, "I've been frightened." Mrs. Grose's eyes expressed plainly that *she* had no wish to be, yet also that she knew too well her place not to be ready to share with me any marked inconvenience. Oh, it was quite settled that she *must* share! "Just what you saw from the dining-room a minute ago was the effect of that. What I saw—just before—was much worse."

Her hand tightened. "What was it?"

"An extraordinary man. Looking in."

"What extraordinary man?"

"I haven't the least idea."

Mrs. Grose gazed round us in vain. "Then where is he gone?"

"I know still less."

"Have you seen him before?"

"Yes—once. On the old tower."

She could only look at me harder. "Do you mean he's a stranger?"

"Oh, very much!"

"Yet you didn't tell me?"

"No—for reasons. But now that you've guessed—"

Mrs. Grose's round eyes encountered this charge. "Ah, I haven't guessed!" she said very simply. "How can I if *you* don't imagine?"

"I don't in the very least."

"You've seen him nowhere but on the tower?"

"And on this spot just now."

Mrs. Grose looked round again. "What was he doing on the tower?"

"Only standing there and looking down at me."

She thought a minute. "Was he a gentleman?"

I found I had no need to think. "No." She gazed in deeper wonder. "No."

"Then nobody about the place? Nobody from the village?"

"Nobody—nobody. I didn't tell you, but I made sure."

She breathed a vague relief: this was, oddly, so much to the good. It only went indeed a little way. "But if he isn't a gentleman—"

"What *is* he? He's a horror."

"A horror?"

"He's—God help me if I know *what* he is!"

Mrs. Grose looked round once more; she fixed her eyes on the duskier distance, then, pulling herself together, turned to me with abrupt inconsequence. "It's time we should be at church."

"Oh, I'm not fit for church!"

"Won't it do you good?"

"It won't do *them*—!" I nodded at the house.

"The children?"

"I can't leave them now."

"You're afraid—?"

I spoke boldly. "I'm afraid of *him*."

Mrs. Grose's large face showed me, at this, for the first time, the far-away faint glimmer of a consciousness more acute: I somehow made out in it the delayed dawn of an idea I myself had not given her and that was as yet quite obscure to me. It comes back to me that I thought instantly of this as something I could get from her; and I felt it to be connected with the desire she presently showed to know more. "When was it—on the tower?"

"About the middle of the month. At this same hour."

"Almost at dark?" said Mrs. Grose.

"Oh, no, not nearly. I saw him as I see you."

"Then how did he get in?"

"And how did he get out?" I laughed. "I had no opportunity to ask him! This evening, you see," I pursued, "he has not been able to get in."

"He only peeps?"

"I hope it will be confined to that!" She had now let go my hand; she turned away a little. I waited an instant; then I brought out: "Go to church. Good-bye. I must watch."

Slowly she faced me again. "Do you fear for them?"

We met in another long look. "Don't *you?*" Instead of answering she came nearer to the window and, for a minute, applied her face to the glass. "You see how he could see," I meanwhile went on.

She didn't move. "How long was he here?"

"Till I came out. I came to meet him."

Mrs. Grose at last turned round, and there was still more in her face. "I couldn't have come out."

"Neither could I!" I laughed again. "But I did come. I have my duty."

"So have I mine," she replied; after which she added: "What is he like?"

"I've been dying to tell you. But he's like nobody."

"Nobody?" she echoed.

"He has no hat." Then seeing in her face that she already, in this, with a deeper dismay, found a touch of picture, I quickly added stroke to stroke. "He has red hair, very red, close-curling, and a pale face, long in shape, with straight, good features and little, rather queer whiskers that are as red as his hair. His eyebrows are, somehow, darker; they look particularly arched and as if they might move a good deal. His eyes are sharp, strange—awfully; but I only know clearly that they're rather small and very fixed. His mouth's wide, and his lips are thin, and except for his little whiskers he's quite clean-shaven. He gives me a sort of sense of looking like an actor."

"An actor!" It was impossible to resemble one less, at least, than Mrs. Grose at that moment.

"I've never seen one, but so I suppose them. He's tall, active, erect," I continued, "but never—no, never!—a gentleman."

My companion's face had blanched as I went on; her round eyes started and her mild mouth gaped. "A gentleman?" she gasped, confounded, stupefied: "a gentleman *he?*"

"You know him then?"

She visibly tried to hold herself. "But he *is* handsome?"

I saw the way to help her. "Remarkably!"

"And dressed—?"

"In somebody's clothes. They're smart, but they're not his own."

She broke into a breathless affirmative groan. "They're the master's!"

I caught it up. "You *do* know him?"

She faltered but a second. "Quint!" she cried.

"Quint?"

"Peter Quint—his own man, his valet, when he was here!"

"When the master was?"

Gaping still, but meeting me, she pieced it all together. "He never wore his hat, but he did wear—well, there were waistcoats missed! They were both here—last year. Then the master went, and Quint was alone."

I followed, but halting a little. "Alone?"

"Alone with *us.*" Then, as from a deeper depth, "In charge," she added.

"And what became of him?"

She hung fire so long that I was still more mystified. "He went too," she brought out at last.

"Went where?"

Her expression, at this, became extraordinary. "God knows where! He died."

"Died?" I almost shrieked.

She seemed fairly to square herself, plant herself more firmly to utter the wonder of it. "Yes. Mr. Quint is dead."

<h1 style="text-align:center">6</h1>

It took of course more than that particular passage to place us together in presence of what we had now to live with as we could—my dreadful liability to impressions of the order so vividly exemplified, and my companion's knowledge, henceforth,—a knowledge half consternation and half compassion,—of that liability. There had been, this evening, after the revelation that left me, for an hour, so prostrate—there had been, for either of us, no attendance on any service but a little service of tears and vows, of prayers and promises, a climax to the series of mutual challenges and pledges that had straightway ensued on our retreating together to the schoolroom and shutting ourselves up there to have everything out. The result of our having everything out was simply to reduce our situation to the last rigour of its elements. She herself had seen nothing, not the shadow of a shadow, and nobody in the house but the governess was in the governess's plight; yet she accepted without directly impugning my sanity the truth as I gave it to her, and ended by showing me, on this ground, an awe-stricken tenderness, an expression of the sense of my more than questionable privilege, of which the very breath has remained with me as that of the sweetest of human charities.

What was settled between us, accordingly, that night, was that we thought we might bear things together; and I was not even sure that, in spite of her exemption, it was she who had the best of the burden. I knew at this hour, I think, as well as I knew later what I was capable of meeting to shelter my pupils; but it took me some time to be wholly sure of what my honest ally was prepared for to keep terms with so compromising a contract. I was queer company enough—quite as queer as the company I received; but as I trace over what we went through I see how much common ground we must have found in the one idea that, by good fortune, *could* steady us. It was the idea, the second movement, that led me straight out, as I may say, of the inner chamber of my dread. I could take the air in the court, at least, and there Mrs. Grose could join me. Perfectly can I recall now the particular way strength came to me before we separated for the night. We had gone over and over every feature of what I had seen.

"He was looking for someone else, you say—someone who was not you?"

"He was looking for little Miles." A portentous clearness now possessed me. "*That's* whom he was looking for."

"But how do you know?"

"I know, I know, I know!" My exaltation grew. "And *you* know, my dear!"

She didn't deny this, but I required, I felt, not even so much telling as that. She resumed in a moment, at any rate: "What if *he* should see him?"

"Little Miles? That's what he wants!"

She looked immensely scared again. "The child?"

"Heaven forbid! The man. He wants to appear to *them*." That he might was an awful conception, and yet, somehow, I could keep it at bay; which, morover, as we lingered there, was what I succeeded in practically proving. I had an absolute certainty that I could see again what I had already seen, but something within me said that by offering myself bravely as the sole subject of such experience, by accepting, by inviting, by surmounting it all, I should serve as an expiatory victim and guard the tranquillity of my companions. The children, in especial, I should thus fence about and absolutely save. I recall one of the last things I said that night to Mrs. Grose.

"It does strike me that my pupils have never mentioned—"

She looked at me hard as I musingly pulled up. "His having been here and the time they were with him?"

"The time they were with him, and his name, his presence, his history, in any way."

"Oh, the little lady doesn't remember. She never heard or knew."

"The circumstances of his death?" I thought with some intensity. "Perhaps not. But Miles would remember—Miles would know."

"Ah, don't try him!" broke from Mrs. Grose.

I returned her the look she had given me. "Don't be afraid." I continued to think. "It *is* rather odd."

"That he has never spoken of him?"

"Never by the least allusion. And you tell me they were 'great friends'?"

"Oh, it wasn't *him!*" Mrs. Grose with emphasis declared. "It was Quint's own fancy. To play with him, I mean—to spoil him." She paused a moment; then she added: "Quint was much too free."

This gave me, straight from my vision of his face—*such* a face—a sudden sickness of disgust. "Too free with *my* boy?"

"Too free with everyone!"

I forebore, for the moment, to analyse this description further than by the reflection that a part of it applied to several of the members of the household, of the half-dozen maids and men who were still of our small colony. But there was everything, for our apprehension, in the lucky fact that no discomfortable legend, no perturbation of scullions, had ever, within anyone's memory, attached to the kind old place. It had neither bad name nor ill fame, and Mrs. Grose, most apparently, only desired to cling to me and to quake in silence. I even put her, the very last thing of all, to the test. It was when, at midnight, she had her hand on the schoolroom door to take leave. "I have it from you then—for it's of great importance—that he was definitely and admittedly bad?"

"Oh, not admittedly. *I* knew it—but the master didn't."

"And you never told him?"

"Well, he didn't like tale-bearing—he hated complaints. He was terribly short with anything of that kind, and if people were all right to *him*—"

"He wouldn't be bothered with more?" This squared well enough with my impression of him: he was not a trouble-loving gentleman, nor so very particular perhaps about some of the company *he* kept. All the same, I pressed my interlocutress. "I promise you *I* would have told!"

She felt my discrimination. "I dare say I was wrong. But, really, I was afraid."

"Afraid of what?"

"Of things that man could do. Quint was so clever—he was so deep."

I took this in still more than, probably, I showed. "You weren't afraid of anything else? Not of his effect—?"

"His effect?" she repeated with a face of anguish and waiting while I faltered.

"On innocent little precious lives. They were in your charge."

"No, they were not in mine!" she roundly and distressfully returned. "The master believed in him and placed him here because he was supposed not to be well and the country air so good for him. So he had everything to say. Yes"—she let me have it—"even about *them*."

"Them—that creature?" I had to smother a kind of howl. "And you could bear it!"

"No. I couldn't—and I can't now!" And the poor woman burst into tears.

A rigid control, from the next day, was, as I have said, to follow them; yet how often and how passionately, for a week, we came back together to the subject! Much as we had discussed it that Sunday night, I was, in the immediate later hours in especial—for it may be imagined whether I slept—still haunted with the shadow of something she had not told me. I myself had kept back nothing, but there was a word Mrs. Grose had kept back. I was sure, moreover, by morning, that this was not from a failure of frankness, but because on every side there were fears. It seems to me indeed, in retrospect, that by the time the morrow's sun was high I had restlessly read into the facts before us almost all the meaning they were to receive from subsequent and more cruel occurrences. What they gave me above all was just the sinister figure of the living man—the dead one would keep awhile!—and of the months he had continuously passed at Bly, which, added up, made a formidable stretch. The limit of this evil time had arrived only when, on the dawn of a winter's morning, Peter Quint was found, by a labourer going to early work, stone dead on the road from the village: a catastrophe explained—superficially at least—by a visible wound to his head; such a wound as might have been produced—and as, on the final evidence, *had* been—by a fatal slip, in the dark and after leaving the public house, on the steepish icy slope, a wrong path, altogether, at the bottom of which he lay. The icy slope, the turn mistaken at night and in liquor, accounted for much—practically, in the end and after the inquest and boundless chatter, for everything; but there had been matters in his life—strange passages and perils, secret disorders, vices more than suspected—that would have accounted for a good deal more.

I scarce know how to put my story into words that shall be a credible picture of my state of mind; but I was in these days literally able to find a joy in the extraordinary flight of heroism the occasion demanded of me. I now saw that I had been asked for a service admirable and difficult; and there would be

a greatness in letting it be seen—oh, in the right quarter!—that I could succeed where many another girl might have failed. It was an immense help to
me—I confess I rather applaud myself as I look back!—that I saw my service
so strongly and so simply. I was there to protect and defend the little creatures
in the world the most bereaved and the most loveable, the appeal of whose
helplessness had suddenly become only too explicit, a deep, constant ache of
one's own committed heart. We were cut off, really, together; we were united
in our danger. They had nothing but me, and I—well, I had *them*. It was in
short a magnificent chance. This chance presented itself to me in an image
richly material. I was a screen—I was to stand before them. The more I saw,
the less they would. I began to watch them in a stifled suspense, a disguised
excitement that might well, had it continued too long, have turned to something like madness. What saved me, as I now see, was that it turned to
something else altogether. It didn't last as suspense—it was superseded by
horrible proofs. Proofs, I say, yes—from the moment I really took hold.

This moment dated from an afternoon hour that I happened to spend in
the grounds with the younger of my pupils alone. We had left Miles indoors,
on the red cushion of a deep window-seat; he had wished to finish a book,
and I had been glad to encourage a purpose so laudable in a young man whose
only defect was an occasional excess of the restless. His sister, on the contrary,
had been alert to come out, and I strolled with her half an hour, seeking the
shade, for the sun was still high and the day exceptionally warm. I was aware
afresh, with her, as we went, of how, like her brother, she contrived—it was
the charming thing in both children—to let me alone without appearing to
drop me and to accompany me without appearing to surround. They were
never importunate and yet never listless. My attention to them all really
went to seeing them amuse themselves immensely without me: this was a
spectacle they seemed actively to prepare and that engaged me as an active
admirer. I walked in a world of their invention—they had no occasion whatever to draw upon mine; so that my time was taken only with being, for them,
some remarkable person or thing that the game of the moment required and
that was merely, thinks to my superior, my exalted stamp, a happy and highly
distinguished sinecure. I forget what I was on the present occasion; I only
remember that I was something very important and very quiet and that Flora
was playing very hard. We were on the edge of the lake, and, as we had lately
begun geography, the lake was the Sea of Azof.

Suddenly, in these circumstances, I became aware that, on the other side
of the Sea of Azof, we had an interested spectator. The way this knowledge
gathered in me was the strangest thing in the world—the strangest, that is,
except the very much stranger in which it quickly merged itself. I had sat
down with a piece of work—for I was something or other that could sit—on
the old stone bench which overlooked the pond; and in this position I began to
take in with certitude, and yet without direct vision, the presence, at a distance, of a third person. The old trees, the thick shrubbery, made a great and
pleasant shade, but it was all suffused with the brightness of the hot, still hour.
There was no ambiguity in anything; none whatever, at least, in the conviction I from one moment to another found myself forming as to what I should
see straight before me and across the lake as a consequence of raising my eyes.

They were attached at this juncture to the stitching in which I was engaged, and I can feel once more the spasm of my effort not to move them till I should so have steadied myself as to be able to make up my mind what to do. There was an alien object in view—a figure whose right of presence I instantly, passionately questioned. I recollect counting over perfectly the possibilities, reminding myself that nothing was more natural, for instance, than the appearance of one of the men about the place, or even of a messenger, a postman or a tradesman's boy, from the village. That reminder had as little effect on my practical certitude as I was conscious—still even without looking—of its having upon the character and attitude of our visitor. Nothing was more natural than that these things should be the other things that they absolutely were not.

Of the positive identity of the apparition I would assure myself as soon as the small clock of my courage should have ticked out the right second; meanwhile, with an effort that was already sharp enough, I transferred my eyes straight to little Flora, who, at the moment, was about ten yards away. My heart had stood still for an instant with the wonder and terror of the question whether she too would see; and I held my breath while I waited for what a cry from her, what some sudden innocent sign either of interest or of alarm, would tell me. I waited, but nothing came; then, in the first place—and there is something more dire in this, I feel, than in anything I have to relate—I was determined by a sense that, within a minute, all sounds from her had previously dropped; and, in the second, by the circumstance that, also within the minute, she had, in her play, turned her back to the water. This was her attitude when I at last looked at her—looked with the confirmed conviction that we were still, together, under direct personal notice. She had picked up a small flat piece of wood, which happened to have in it a little hole that had evidently suggested to her the idea of sticking in another fragment that might figure as a mast and make the thing a boat. This second morsel, as I watched her, she was very markedly and intently attempting to tighten in its place. My apprehension of what she was doing sustained me so that after some seconds I felt I was ready for more. Then I again shifted my eyes—I faced what I had to face.

7

I got hold of Mrs. Grose as soon after this as I could; and I can give no intelligible account of how I fought out the interval. Yet I still hear myself cry as I fairly threw myself into her arms: "They *know*—it's too monstrous: they know, they know!"

"And what on earth—?" I felt her incredulity as she held me.

"Why, all that *we* know—and heaven knows what else besides!" Then, as she released me, I made it out to her, made it out perhaps only now with full coherency even to myself. "Two hours ago, in the garden"—I could scarce articulate—"Flora *saw!*"

Mrs. Grose took it as she might have taken a blow in the stomach. "She has told you?" she panted.

"Not a word—that's the horror. She kept it to herself! The child of eight, *that* child!" Unutterable still, for me, was the stupefaction of it.

Mrs. Grose, of course, could only gape the wider. "Then how do you know?"

"I was there—I saw with my eyes: saw that she was perfectly aware."

"Do you mean aware of *him?*"

"No—of *her.*" I was conscious as I spoke that I looked prodigious things, for I got the slow reflection of them in my companion's face. "Another person —this time; but a figure of quite as unmistakeable horror and evil: a woman in black, pale and dreadful—with such an air also, and such a face!—on the other side of the lake. I was there with the child—quiet for the hour; and in the midst of it she came."

"Came how—from where?"

"From where they come from! She just appeared and stood there—but not so near."

"And without coming nearer?"

"Oh, for the effect and the feeling, she might have been as close as you!"

My friend, with an odd impulse, fell back a step. "Was she someone you've never seen?"

"Yes. But someone the child has. Someone *you* have." Then, to show how I had thought it all out: "My predecessor—the one who died."

"Miss Jessel?"

"Miss Jessel. You don't believe me?" I pressed.

She turned right and left in her distress. "How can you be sure?"

This drew from me, in the state of my nerves, a flash of impatience. "Then ask Flora—*she's* sure!" But I had no sooner spoken than I caught myself up. "No, for God's sake, *don't!* She'll say she isn't—she'll lie!"

Mrs. Grose was not too bewildered instinctively to protest. "Ah, how *can* you?"

"Because I'm clear. Flora doesn't want me to know."

"It's only then to spare you."

"No, no—there are depths, depths! The more I go over it, the more I see in it, and the more I see in it the more I fear. I don't know what I *don't* see— what I *don't* fear!"

Mrs. Grose tried to keep up with me. "You mean you're afraid of seeing her again?"

"Oh, no; that's nothing—now!" Then I explained. "It's of *not* seeing her."

But my companion only looked wan. "I don't understand you."

"Why, it's that the child may keep it up—and that the child assurredly *will*—without my knowing it."

At the image of this possibility Mrs. Grose for a moment collapsed, yet presently to pull herself together again, as if from the positive force of the sense of what, should we yield an inch, there would really be to give way to. "Dear, dear—we must keep our heads! And after all, if she doesn't mind it—!" She even tried a grim joke. "Perhaps she likes it!"

"Likes *such* things—a scrap of an infant!"

"Isn't it just a proof of her blessed innocence?" my friend bravely inquired.

She brought me, for the instant, almost round. "Oh, we must clutch at *that*—we must cling to it! If it isn't a proof of what you say, it's a proof of— God knows what! For the woman's a horror of horrors."

Mrs. Grose, at this, fixed her eyes a minute on the ground; then at last raising them, "Tell me how you know," she said.

"Then you admit it's what she was?" I cried.

"Tell me how you know," my friend simply repeated.

"Know! By seeing her! By the way she looked."

"At you, do you mean—so wickedly?"

"Dear me, no—I could have borne that. She gave me never a glance. She only fixed the child."

Mrs. Grose tried to see it. "Fixed her?"

"Ah, with such awful eyes!"

She stared at mine as if they might really have resembled them. "Do you mean of dislike?"

"God help us, no. Of something much worse."

"Worse than dislike?"—this left her indeed at a loss.

"With a determination—indescribable. With a kind of fury of intention."

I made her turn pale. "Intention?"

"To get hold of her." Mrs. Grose—her eyes just lingering on mine—gave a shudder and walked to the window; and while she stood there looking out I completed my statement. "*That's* what Flora knows."

After a little she turned round. "The person was in black, you say?"

"In mourning—rather poor, almost shabby. But—yes—with extraordinary beauty." I now recognised to what I had at last, stroke by stroke, brought the victim of my confidence, for she quite visibly weighed this. "Oh, handsome—very, very," I insisted; "wonderfully handsome. But infamous."

She slowly came back to me. "Miss Jessel—*was* infamous." She once more took my hand in both her own, holding it as tight as if to fortify me against the increase of alarm I might draw from this disclosure. "They were both infamous," she finally said.

So, for a little, we faced it once more together; and I found absolutely a degree of help in seeing it now so straight. "I appreciate," I said, "the great decency of your not having hitherto spoken; but the time has certainly come to give me the whole thing." She appeared to assent to this, but still only in silence; seeing which I went on: "I must have it now. Of what did she die? Come, there was something between them."

"There was everything."

"In spite of the difference—?"

"Oh, of their rank, their condition"—she brought it woefully out. "*She* was a lady."

I turned it over; I again saw. "Yes—she was a lady."

"And he so dreadfully below," said Mrs. Grose.

I felt that I doubtless needn't press too hard, in such company, on the place of a servant in the scale; but there was nothing to prevent an acceptance of my companion's own measure of my predecessor's abasement. There was a way to deal with that, and I dealt; the more readily for my full vision—on the evidence—of our employer's late clever, good-looking "own" man; impudent, assured, spoiled, depraved. "The fellow was a hound."

Mrs. Grose considered as if it were perhaps a little a case for a sense of shades. "I've never seen one like him. He did what he wished."

"With *her?*"

"With them all."

It was as if now in my friend's own eyes Miss Jessel had again appeared. I seemed at any rate, for an instant, to see their evocation of her as distinctly as I had seen her by the pond; and I brought out with decision: "It must have been also what *she* wished!"

Mrs. Grose's face signified that it had been indeed, but she said at the same time: "Poor woman—she paid for it!"

"Then you do know what she died of?" I asked.

"No—I know nothing. I wanted not to know; I was glad enough I didn't; and I thanked heaven she was well out of this!"

"Yet you had, then, your idea—"

"Of her real reason for leaving? Oh, yes—as to that. She couldn't have stayed. Fancy it here—for a governess! And afterwards I imagined—and I still imagine. And what I imagine is dreadful."

"Not so dreadful as what *I* do," I replied; on which I must have shown her —as I was indeed but too conscious—a front of miserable defeat. It brought out again all her compassion for me, and at the renewed touch of her kindness my power to resist broke down. I burst, as I had, the other time, made her burst, into tears; she took me to her motherly breast, and my lamentation overflowed. "I don't do it!" I sobbed in despair; "I don't save or shield them. It's far worse than I dreamed—they're lost!"

8

What I had said to Mrs. Grose was true enough: there were in the matter I had put before her depths and possibilities that I lacked resolution to sound; so that when we met once more in the wonder of it we were of a common mind about the duty of resistance to extravagant fancies. We were to keep our heads if we should keep nothing else—difficult indeed as that might be in the face of what, in our prodigious experience, was least to be questioned. Late that night, while the house slept, we had another talk in my room, when she went all the way with me as to its being beyond doubt that I had seen exactly what I had seen. To hold her perfectly in the pinch of that, I found I had only to ask her how, if I had "made it up," I came to be able to give, of each of the persons appearing to me, a picture disclosing, to the last detail, their special marks—a portrait on the exhibition of which she had instantly recognised and named them. She wished, of course,—small blame to her!—to sink the whole subject; and I was quick to assure her that my own interest in it had now violently taken the form of a search for the way to escape from it. I encountered her on the ground of a probability that with recurrence—for recurrence we took for granted—I should get used to my danger, distinctly professing that my personal exposure had suddenly become the least of my discomforts. It was my new suspicion that was intolerable; and yet even to this complication the later hours of the day had brought a little ease.

On leaving her, after my first outbreak, I had of course returned to my pupils, associating the right remedy for my dismay with that sense of their charm which I had already found to be a thing I could positively cultivate and which had never failed me yet. I had simply, in other words, plunged afresh into Flora's special society and there become aware—it was almost a luxury!—that she could put her little conscious hand straight upon the spot that ached. She had looked at me in sweet speculation and then had accused me to my face of having "cried." I had supposed I had brushed away the ugly signs: but I could literally—for the time, at all events—rejoice, under this fathomless charity, that they had not entirely disappeared. To gaze into the depths of blue of the child's eyes and pronounce their loveliness a trick of premature cunning was to be guilty of a cynicism in preference to which I naturally preferred to abjure my judgment and, so far as might be, my agitation. I couldn't abjure for merely wanting to, but I could repeat to Mrs. Grose —as I did there, over and over, in the small hours—that with their voices in the air, their pressure on one's heart and their fragrant faces against one's cheek, everything fell to the ground but their incapacity and their beauty. It was a pity that, somehow, to settle this once for all, I had equally to re-enumerate the signs of subtlety that, in the afternoon, by the lake, had made a miracle of my show of self-possession. It was a pity to be obliged to re-investigate the certitude of the moment itself and repeat how it had come to me as a revelation that the inconceivable communion I then surprised was a matter, for either party, of habit. It was a pity that I should have had to quaver out again the reasons for my not having, in my delusion, so much as questioned that the little girl saw our visitant even as I actually saw Mrs. Grose herself, and that she wanted, by just so much as she did thus see, to make me suppose she didn't, and at the same time, without showing anything, arrive at a guess as to whether I myself did! It was a pity that I needed once more to describe the portentous little activity by which she sought to divert my attention—the perceptible increase of movement, the greater intensity of play, the singing, the gabbling of nonsense, and the invitation to romp.

Yet if I had not indulged, to prove there was nothing in it, in this review, I should have missed the two or three dim elements of comfort that still remained to me. I should not for instance have been able to asseverate to my friend that I was certain—which was so much to the good—that I at least had not betrayed myself. I should not have been prompted, by stress of need, by desperation of mind,—I scarce know what to call it,—to invoke such further aid to intelligence as might spring from pushing my colleague fairly to the wall. She had told me, bit by bit, under pressure, a great deal; but a small shifty spot on the wrong side of it all still sometimes brushed my brow like the wing of a bat; and I remember how on this occasion—for the sleeping house and the concentration alike of our danger and our watch seemed to help —I felt the importance of giving the last jerk to the curtain. "I don't believe anything so horrible," I recollect saying; "no, let us put it definitely, my dear, that I don't. But if I did, you know, there's a thing I should require now, just without sparing you the least bit more—oh, not a scrap, come!—to get out of you. What was it you had in mind when, in our distress, before Miles came back, over the letter from his school, you said, under my insistence, that you didn't pretend for him that he had not literally *ever* been 'bad'? He has *not* literally 'ever,' in these weeks that I myself have lived with him and so closely watched him; he has been an imperturbable little prodigy of delightful, loveable goodness. Therefore you might perfectly have made the claim for him if you had not, as it happened, seen an exception to take. What was your exception, and to what passage in your personal observation of him did you refer?"

It was a dreadfully austere inquiry, but levity was not our note, and, at any rate, before the grey dawn admonished us to separate I had got my answer. What my friend had had in mind proved to be immensely to the purpose. It was neither more nor less than the circumstance that for a period of several months Quint and the boy had been perpetually together. It was in fact the very appropriate truth that she had ventured to criticise the propriety, to hint at the incongruity, of so close an alliance, and even to go so far on the subject as a frank overture to Miss Jessel. Miss Jessel had, with a most strange manner, requested her to mind her business, and the good woman had, on this, directly approached little Miles. What she had said to him, since I pressed, was that *she* liked to see young gentlemen not forget their station.

I pressed again, of course, at this. "You reminded him that Quint was only a base menial?"

"As you might say! And it was his answer, for one thing, that was bad."

"And for another thing?" I waited. "He repeated your words to Quint?"

"No, not that. It's just what he *wouldn't!*" she could still impress upon me. "I was sure, at any rate," she added, "that he didn't. But he denied certain occasions."

"What occasions?"

"When they had been about together quite as if Quint were his tutor—and a very grand one—and Miss Jessel only for the little lady. When he had gone off with the fellow, I mean, and spent hours with him."

"He then prevaricated about it—he said he hadn't?" Her assent was clear enough to cause me to add in a moment: "I see. He lied."

"Oh!" Mrs. Grose mumbled. This was a suggestion that it didn't matter; which indeed she backed up by a further remark. "You see, after all, Miss Jessel didn't mind. She didn't forbid him."

I considered. "Did he put that to you as a justification?"

At this she dropped again. "No, he never spoke of it."

"Never mentioned her in connection with Quint?"

She saw, visibly flushing, where I was coming out. "Well, he didn't show anything. He denied," she repeated; "he denied."

Lord, how I pressed her now! "So that you could see he knew what was between the two wretches?"

"I don't know—I don't know!" the poor woman groaned.

"You do know, you dear thing," I replied; "only you haven't my dreadful boldness of mind, and you keep back, out of timidity and modesty and delicacy, even the impression that, in the past, when you had, without my aid, to flounder about in silence, most of all made you miserable. But I shall get it out of you yet! There was something in the boy that suggested to you," I continued, "that he covered and concealed their relation."

"Oh, he couldn't prevent—"

"Your learning the truth? I dare say! But, heavens," I fell, with vehe-

mence, a-thinking, "what it shows that they must, to that extent, have succeeded in making of him!"

"Ah, nothing that's not nice *now!*" Mrs. Grose lugubriously pleaded.

"I don't wonder you looked queer," I persisted, "when I mentioned to you
the letter from his school!"

"I doubt if I looked as queer as you!" she retorted with homely force.
"And if he was so bad then as that comes to, how is he such an angel now?"

"Yes, indeed—and if he was a fiend at school! How, how, how? Well," I
said in my torment, "you must put it to me again, but I shall not be able to tell
you for some days. Only, put it to me again!" I cried in a way that made my
friend stare. "There are directions in which I must not for the present let myself go." Meanwhile I returned to her first example—the one to which she had
just previously referred—of the boy's happy capacity for an occasional slip.
"If Quint—on your remonstrance at the time you speak of—was a base
menial, one of the things Miles said to you, I find myself guessing, was that
you were another." Again her admission was so adequate that I continued:
"And you forgave him that?"

"Wouldn't *you?*"

"Oh, yes!" And we exchanged there, in the stillness, a sound of the oddest
amusement. Then I went on: "At all events, while he was with the man—"

"Miss Flora was with the woman. It suited them all!"

It suited me too, I felt, only too well; by which I mean that it suited exactly the particularly deadly view I was in the very act of forbidding myself
to entertain. But I so far succeeded in checking the expression of this view that
I will throw, just here, no further light on it than may be offered by the mention of my final observation to Mrs. Grose. "His having lied and been impudent are, I confess, less engaging specimens than I had hoped to have from
you of the outbreak in him of the little natural man. Still," I mused, "they
must do, for they make me feel more than ever that I must watch."

It made me blush, the next minute, to see in my friend's face how much
more unreservedly she had forgiven him than her anecdote struck me as presenting to my own tenderness an occasion for doing. This came out when, at
the schoolroom door, she quitted me. "Surely you don't accuse *him*—"

"Of carrying on an intercourse that he conceals from me? Ah, remember
that, until further evidence, I now accuse nobody." Then, before shutting her
out to go, by another passage, to her own place, "I must just wait," I wound up.

9

I waited and waited, and the days, as they elapsed, took something from
my consternation. A very few of them, in fact, passing, in constant sight of
my pupils, without a fresh incident, sufficed to give to grievous fancies and
even to odious memories a kind of brush of the sponge. I have spoken of the
surrender to their extraordinary childish grace as a thing I could actively cultivate, and it may be imagined if I neglected now to address myself to this
source for whatever it would yield. Stranger than I can express, certainly, was
the effort to struggle against my new lights; it would doubtless have been how-

ever, a greater tension still had it not been so frequently successful. I used to wonder how my little charges could help guessing that I thought strange things about them; and the circumstance that these things only made them more interesting was not by itself a direct aid to keeping them in the dark. I trembled lest they should see that they *were* so immensely more interesting. Putting things at the worst, at all events, as in meditation I so often did, any clouding of their innocence could only be—blameless and foredoomed as they were —a reason the more for taking risks. There were moments when, by an irresistible impulse, I found myself catching them up and pressing them to my heart. As soon as I had done so I used to say to myself: "What will they think of that? Doesn't it betray too much?" It would have been easy to get into a sad, wild tangle about how much I might betray; but the real account, I feel, of the hours of peace that I could still enjoy was that the immediate charm of my companions was a beguilement still effective even under the shadow of the possibility that it was studied. For if it occurred to me that I might occasionally excite suspicion by the little outbreaks of my sharper passion for them, so too I remember wondering if I mightn't see a queerness in the traceable increase of their own demonstrations.

They were at this period extravagantly and preternaturally fond of me; which, after all, I could reflect, was no more than a graceful response in children perpetually bowed over and hugged. The homage of which they were so lavish succeeded, in truth, for my nerves, quite as well as if I never appeared to myself, as I may say, literally to catch them at a purpose in it. They had never, I think, wanted to do so many things for their poor protectress; I mean —though they got their lessons better and better, which was naturally what would please her most—in the way of diverting, entertaining, surprising her; reading her passages, telling her stories, acting her charades, pouncing out at her, in disguises, as animals and historical characters, and above all astonishing her by the "pieces" they had secretly got by heart and could interminably recite. I should never get to the bottom—were I to let myself go even now— of the prodigious private commentary, all under still more private correction, with which, in these days, I overscored their full hours. They had shown me from the first a facility for everything, a general faculty which, taking a fresh start, achieved remarkable flights. They got their little tasks as if they loved them and indulged, from the mere exuberance of the gift, in the most unimposed little miracles of memory. They not only popped out at me as tigers and as Romans, but as Shakespeareans, astronomers, and navigators. This was so singularly the case that it had presumably much to do with the fact as to which, at the present day, I am at a loss for a different explanation: I allude to my unnatural composure on the subject of another school for Miles. What I remember is that I was content not, for the time, to open the question, and that contentment must have sprung from the sense of his perpetually striking show of cleverness. He was too clever for a bad governess, for a parson's daughter, to spoil; and the strangest if not the brightest thread in the pensive embroidery I just spoke of was the impression I might have got, if I had dared to work it out, that he was under some influence operating in his small intellectual life as a tremendous incitement.

If it was easy to reflect, however, that such a boy could postpone school, it was at least as marked that for such a boy to have been "kicked out" by a school-master was a mystification without end. Let me add that in their company now—and I was careful almost never to be out of it—I could follow no scent very far. We lived in a cloud of music and love and success and private theatricals. The musical sense in each of the children was of the quickest, but the elder in especial had a marvellous knack of catching and repeating. The schoolroom piano broke into all gruesome fancies; and when that failed there were confabulations in corners, with a sequel of one of them going out in the highest spirits in order to "come in" as something new. I had had brothers myself, and it was no revelation to me that little girls could be slavish idolaters of little boys. What surpassed everything was that there was a little boy in the world who could have for the inferior age, sex, and intelligence so fine a consideration. They were extraordinarily at one, and to say that they never either quarrelled or complained is to make the note of praise coarse for their quality of sweetness. Sometimes, indeed, when I dropped into coarseness, I perhaps came across traces of little understandings between them by which one of them should keep me occupied while the other slipped away. There is a *naïf* side, I suppose, in all diplomacy; but if my pupils practised upon me, it was surely with the minimum of grossness. It was all in the other quarter that, after a lull, the grossness broke out.

I find that I really hang back; but I must take my plunge. In going on with the record of what was hideous at Bly, I not only challenge the most liberal faith—for which I little care; but—and this is another matter—I renew what I myself suffered, I again push my way through it to the end. There came suddenly an hour after which, as I look back, the affair seems to me to have been all pure suffering; but I have at least reached the heart of it, and the straightest road out is doubtless to advance. One evening—with nothing to lead up or to prepare it—I felt the cold touch of the impression that had breathed on me the night of my arrival and which, much lighter then, as I have mentioned, I should probably have made little of in memory had my subsequent sojourn been less agitated. I had not gone to bed; I sat reading by a couple of candles. There was a roomful of old books at Bly—last-century fiction, some of it, which, to the extent of a distinctly deprecated renown, but never to so much as that of a stray specimen, had reached the sequestered home and appealed to the unavowed curiosity of my youth. I remember that the book I had in my hand was Fielding's *Amelia*; also that I was wholly awake. I recall further both a general conviction that it was horribly late and a particular objection to looking at my watch. I figure, finally, that the white curtain draping, in the fashion of those days, the head of Flora's little bed, shrouded, as I had assured myself long before, the perfection of childish rest. I recollect in short that, though I was deeply interested in my author, I found myself, at the turn of a page and with his spell all scattered, looking straight up from him and hard at the door of my room. There was a moment during which I listened, reminded of the faint sense I had had, the first night, of there being something undefineably astir in the house, and noted the soft breath of the open casement just move the half-drawn blind. Then, with all the marks of a deliberation that must have seemed magnificent had there been anyone to admire it, I laid down my book, rose to my feet, and, taking a candle, went straight out of the room and, from the passage, on which my light made little impression, noiselessly closed and locked the door.

I can say now neither what determined nor what guided me, but I went straight along the lobby, holding my candle high, till I came within sight of the tall window that presided over the great turn of the staircase. At this point I precipitately found myself aware of three things. They were practically simultaneous, yet they had flashes of succession. My candle, under a bold flourish, went out, and I perceived, by the uncovered window, that the yielding dusk of earliest morning rendered it unnecessary. Without it, the next instant, I saw that there was someone on the stair. I speak of sequences, but I required no lapse of seconds to stiffen myself for a third encounter with Quint. The apparition had reached the landing halfway up and was therefore on the spot nearest the window, where at sight of me, it stopped short and fixed me exactly as it had fixed me from the tower and from the garden. He knew me as well as I knew him; and so, in the cold, faint twilight, with a glimmer in the high glass and another on the polish of the oak stair below, we faced each other in our common intensity. He was absolutely, on this occasion, a living, detestable, dangerous presence. But that was not the wonder of wonders; I reserve this distinction for quite another circumstance: the circumstance that dread had unmistakeably quitted me and that there was nothing in me there that didn't meet and measure him.

I had plenty of anguish after that extraordinary moment, but I had, thank God, no terror. And he knew I had not—I found myself at the end of an instant magnificently aware of this. I felt, in a fierce rigour of confidence, that if I stood my ground a minute I should cease—for the time, at least—to have him to reckon with; and during the minute, accordingly, the thing was as human and hideous as a real interview: hideous just because it *was* human, as human as to have met alone, in the small hours, in a sleeping house, some enemy, some adventurer, some criminal. It was the dead silence of our long gaze at such close quarters that gave the whole horror, huge as it was, its only note of the unnatural. If I had met a murderer in such a place and at such an hour, we still at least would have spoken. Something would have passed, in life, between us; if nothing had passed one of us would have moved. The moment was so prolonged that it would have taken but little more to make me doubt if even *I* were in life. I can't express what followed it save by saying that the silence itself—which was indeed in a manner an attestation of my strength—became the element into which I saw the figure disappear; in which I definitely saw it turn as I might have seen the low wretch to which it had once belonged turn on receipt of an order, and pass, with my eyes on the villainous back that no hunch could have more disfigured, straight down the staircase and into the darkness in which the next bend was lost.

10

I remained awhile at the top of the stair, but with the effect presently of understanding that when my visitor had gone, he had gone: then I returned to my room. The foremost thing I saw there by the light of the candle I had left burning was that Flora's little bed was empty; and on this I caught my breath with all the terror that, five minutes before, I had been able to re-sist. I dashed at the place in which I had left her lying and over which (for the small silk counterpane and the sheets were disarranged) the white curtains had been deceivingly pulled forward; then my step, to my unutterable relief, produced an answering sound: I perceived an agitation of the window-blind, and the child, ducking down, emerged rosily from the other side of it. She stood there in so much of her candour and so little of her nightgown, with her pink bare feet and the golden glow of her curls. She looked intensely grave, and I had never had such a sense of losing an advantage acquired (the thrill of which had just been so prodigious) as on my consciousness that she ad-dressed me with a reproach. "You naughty: where *have* you been?"—instead of challenging her own irregularity I found myself arraigned and explaining. She herself explained, for that matter, with the loveliest, eagerest simplicity. She had known suddenly, as she lay there, that I was out of the room, and had jumped up to see what had become of me. I had dropped, with the joy of her reappearance, back into my chair—feeling then, and then only, a little faint; and she had pattered straight over to me, thrown herself upon my knee, given her-self to be held with the flame of the candle full in the wonderful little face that was still flushed with sleep. I remember closing my eyes an instant, yield-ingly, consciously, as before the excess of something beautiful that shone out of the blue of her own. "You were looking for me out of the window?" I said. "You thought I might be walking in the grounds?"

"Well, you know, I thought someone was"—she never blanched as she smiled out that at me.

Oh, how I looked at her now! "And did you see anyone?"

"Ah, *no!*" she returned, almost with the full privilege of childish inconse-quence, resentfully, though with a long sweetness in her little drawl of the negative.

At that moment, in the state of my nerves, I absolutely believed she lied; and if I once more closed my eyes it was before the dazzle of the three or four possible ways in which I might take this up. One of these, for a moment, tempted me with such singular intensity that, to withstand it, I must have gripped my little girl with a spasm that, wonderfully she submitted to without a cry or a sign of fright. Why not break out at her on the spot and have it all over?—give it to her straight in her lovely little lighted face? "You see, you see, you *know* that you do and that you already quite suspect I believe it; therefore why not frankly confess it to me, so that we may at least live with it together and learn perhaps, in the strangeness of our fate, where we are and what it means?" This solicitation dropped, alas, as it came: if I could imme-diately have succumbed to it I might have spared myself—well you'll see what. Instead of succumbing I sprang again to my feet, looked at her bed, and took a helpless middle way. "Why did you pull the curtain over the place to make me think you were still there?"

Flora luminously considered; after which, with her little divine smile: "Because I don't like to frighten you!"

"But if I had, by your idea, gone out—?"

She absolutely declined to be puzzled; she turned her eyes to the flame of the candle as if the question were as irrelevant, or at any rate as impersonal,

as Mrs. Marcet or nine-times-nine. "Oh, but you know," she quite ade-
quately answered, "that you might come back, you dear, and that you *have!*"
And after a little, when she had got into bed, I had, for a long time, by
almost sitting on her to hold her hand, to prove that I recognised the pertinence of my return.

You may imagine the general complexion, from that moment, of my
nights. I repeatedly sat up till I didn't know when; I selected moments when
my room-mate unmistakeably slept, and, stealing out, took noiseless turns in
the passage and even pushed as far as to where I had last met Quint. But I never
met him there again; and I may as well say at once that I on no other occasion
saw him in the house. I just missed, on the staircase, on the other hand, a
different adventure. Looking down it from the top I once recognised the presence of a woman seated on one of the lower steps with her back presented to
me, her body half bowed and her head, in an attitude of woe, in her hands.
I had been there but an instant, however, when she vanished without looking
round at me. I knew, none the less, exactly what dreadful face she had to
show; and I wondered whether, if instead of being above I had been below,
I should have had, for going up, the same nerve I had lately shown Quint.
Well, there continued to be plenty of chance for nerve. On the eleventh
night after my latest encounter with that gentleman—they were all numbered
now—I had an alarm that perilously skirted it and that indeed, from the particular quality of its unexpectedness, proved quite my sharpest shock. It was
precisely the first night during this series that, weary with watching, I had felt
that I might again without laxity lay myself down at my old hour. I slept
immediately and, as I afterwards know, till about one o'clock; but when I
woke it was to sit straight up, as completely roused as if a hand had shook me.
I had left a light burning, but it was now out, and I felt an instant certainty that
Flora had extinguished it. This brought me to my feet and straight, in the
darkness, to her bed, which I found she had left. A glance at the window enlightened me further, and the striking of a match completed the picture.

The child had again got up—this time blowing out the taper, and had again,
for some purpose of observation or response, squeezed in behind the blind and
was peering out into the night. That she now saw—as she had not, I had
satisfied myself, the previous time—was proved to me by the fact that she was
disturbed neither by my re-illumination nor by the haste I made to get into
slippers and into a wrap. Hidden, protected, absorbed, she evidently rested
on the sill—the casement opened forward—and gave herself up. There was
a great still moon to help her, and this fact had counted in my quick decision.
She was face to face with the apparition we had met at the lake, and could
now communicate with it as she had not then been able to do. What I, on
my side, had to care for was, without disturbing her, to reach, from the corridor, some other window in the same quarter. I got to the door without her
hearing me; I got out of it, closed it and listened, from the other side, for some
sound from her. While I stood in the passage I had my eyes on her brother's
door, which was but ten steps off and which, indescribably, produced in
me a renewal of the strange impulse that I lately spoke of as my temptation.
What if I should go straight in and march to *his* window?—what if, by risk-

ing to his boyish bewilderment a revelation of my motive, I should throw across the rest of the mystery the long halter of my boldness?

This thought held me sufficiently to make me cross to his threshold and pause again. I preternaturally listened; I figured to myself what might portentously be; I wondered if his bed were also empty and he too were secretly at watch. It was a deep, soundless minute, at the end of which my impulse failed. He was quiet; he might be innocent; the risk was hideous; I turned away. There was a figure in the grounds—a figure prowling for a sight, the visitor with whom Flora was engaged; but it was not the visitor most concerned with my boy. I hesitated afresh, but on other grounds and only a few seconds; then I had made my choice. There were empty rooms at Bly, and it was only a question of choosing the right one. The right one suddenly presented itself to me as the lower one—though high above the gardens—in the solid corner of the house that I have spoken of as the old tower. This was a large, square chamber, arranged with some state as a bedroom, the extravagant size of which made it so inconvenient that it had not for years, though kept by Mrs. Grose in exemplary order, been occupied. I had often admired it and I knew my way about in it; I had only after just faltering at the first chill gloom of its disuse, to pass across it and unbolt as quietly as I could one of the shutters. Achieving this transit, I uncovered the glass without a sound and, applying my face to the pane, was able, the darkness without being much less than within, to see that I commanded the right direction. Then I saw something more. The moon made the night extraordinarily penetrable and showed me on the lawn a person, diminished by distance, who stood there motionless and as if fascinated, looking up to where I had appeared—looking, that is, not so much straight at me as at something that was apparently above me. There was clearly another person above me—there was a person on the tower; but the presence on the lawn was not in the least what I had conceived and had confidently hurried to meet. The presence on the lawn—I felt sick as I made it out—was poor little Miles himself.

11

It was not till late next day that I spoke to Mrs. Grose; the rigour with which I kept my pupils in sight making it often difficult to meet her privately, and the more as we each felt the importance of not provoking—on the part of the servants quite as much as on that of the children—any suspicion of a secret flurry or of a discussion of mysteries. I drew a great security in this particular from her mere smooth aspect. There was nothing in her fresh face to pass on to others my horrible confidences. She believed me, I was sure, absolutely: if she hadn't I don't know what would have become of me, for I couldn't have borne the business alone. But she was a magnificent monument to the blessing of a want of imagination, and if she could see in our little charges nothing but their beauty and amiability, their happiness and cleverness, she had no direct communication with the sources of my trouble. If they had been at all visibly blighted or battered, she would doubtless have grown, on tracing it back, haggard enough to match them; as matters stood, however, I could feel her, when she surveyed them, with her large white arms folded and the habit of serenity in all her look, thank the Lord's mercy that if they were ruined the pieces would still serve. Flights of fancy gave place, in her mind, to a steady fireside glow, and I had already begun to perceive how, with the development of the conviction that—as time went on without a public accident—our young things could, after all, look out for themselves, she addressed her greatest solicitude to the sad case presented by their instructress. That, for myself, was a sound simplification: I could engage that, to the world, my face should tell no tales, but it would have been, in the conditions, an immense added strain to find myself anxious about hers.

At the hour I now speak of she had joined me, under pressure, on the terrace, where, with the lapse of the season, the afternoon sun was now agreeable; and we sat there together while, before us, at a distance, but within call if we wished, the children strolled to and fro in one of their most manageable moods. They moved slowly, in unison, below us, over the lawn, the boy, as they went, reading aloud from a storybook and passing his arm round his sister to keep her quite in touch. Mrs. Grose watched them with positive placidity; then I caught the suppressed intellectual creak with which she conscientiously turned to take from me a view of the back of the tapestry. I had made her a receptacle of lurid things, but there was an odd recognition of my superiority—my accomplishments and my function—in her patience under my pain. She offered her mind to my disclosures as, had I wished to mix a witch's broth and proposed it with assurance, she would have held out a large clean saucepan. This had become thoroughly her attitude by the time that, in my recital of the events of the night, I reached the point of what Miles had said to me when, after seeing him, at such a monstrous hour, almost on the very spot where he happened now to be, I had gone down to bring him in; choosing then, at the window, with a concentrated need of not alarming the house, rather that method than a signal more resonant. I had left her meanwhile in little doubt of my small hope of representing with success even to her actual sympathy my sense of the real splendour of the little inspiration with which, after I had got him into the house, the boy met my final articulate challenge. As soon as I appeared in the moonlight on the terrace, he had come to me as straight as possible; on which I had taken his hand without a word and led him, through the dark spaces, up the staircase where Quint had so hungrily hovered for him, along the lobby where I had listened and trembled, and so to his forsaken room.

Not a sound, on the way, had passed between us, and I had wondered—oh, *how* I had wondered!—if he were groping about in his little mind for something plausible and not too grotesque. It would tax his invention, certainly, and I felt, this time, over his real embarrassment, a curious thrill of triumph. It was a sharp trap for the inscrutable! He couldn't play any longer at innocence; so how the deuce would he get out of it? There beat in me indeed, with the passionate throb of this question, an equal dumb appeal as to how the deuce *I* should. I was confronted at last, as never yet, with all the risk attached even now to sounding my own horrid note. I remember in fact that as we pushed into his little chamber, where the bed had not been slept in at all and the window, uncovered to the moonlight, made the place

so clear that there was no need of striking a match—I remember how I suddenly dropped, sank upon the edge of the bed from the force of the idea
that he must know how he really, as they say, "had" me. He could do
what he liked, with all his cleverness to help him, so long as I should continue to defer to the old tradition of the criminality of those caretakers of
the young who minister to superstitions and fears. He "had" me indeed, and
in a cleft stick; for who would ever absolve me, who would consent that I should
go unhung, if, by the faintest tremor of an overture, I were the first to introduce into our perfect intercourse an element so dire? No, no: it was useless to
attempt to convey to Mrs. Grose, just as it is scarcely less so to attempt to suggest here, how, in our short, stiff brush in the dark, he fairly shook me with
admiration. I was of course thoroughly kind and merciful; never, never yet
had I placed on his little shoulders hands of such tenderness as those with which,
while I rested against the bed, I held him there well under fire. I had no alternative but, in form at least, to put it to him.

"You must tell me now—and all the truth. What did you go out for?
What were you doing there?"

I can still see his wonderful smile, the whites of his beautiful eyes, and
the uncovering of his little teeth shine to me in the dusk. "If I tell you why,
will you understand?" My heart, at this, leaped into my mouth. *Would* he
tell me why? I found no sound on my lips to press it, and I was aware of replying only with a vague, repeated, grimacing nod. He was gentleness itself,
and while I wagged my head at him he stood there more than ever a little
fairy prince. It was his brightness indeed that gave a respite. Would it be
so great if he were really going to tell me? "Well," he said at last, "just exactly
in order that you should do this."

"Do what?"

"Think me—for a change—*bad!*" I shall never forget the sweetness and
gaiety with which he brought out the word, nor how, on top of it, he bent forward and kissed me. It was practically the end of everything. I met his kiss
and I had to make, while I folded him for a minute in my arms, the most
stupendous effort not to cry. He had given exactly the account of himself that
permitted least of my going behind it, and it was only with the effect of
confirming my acceptance of it that, as I presently glanced about the room,
I could say—

"Then you didn't undress at all?"

He fairly glittered in the gloom. "Not at all. I sat up and read."

"And when did you go down?"

"At midnight. When I'm bad I *am* bad!"

"I see, I see—it's charming. But how could you be sure I would know it?"

"Oh, I arranged that with Flora." His answers rang out with a readiness!
"She was to get up and look out."

"Which is what she did do." It was I who fell into the trap!

"So she disturbed you, and, to see what she was looking at, you also
looked—you saw."

"While you," I concurred, "caught your death in the night air!"

He literally bloomed so from this exploit that he could afford radiantly
to assent. "How otherwise should I have been bad enough?" he asked. Then,

after another embrace, the incident and our interview closed on my recognition of all the reserves of goodness that, for his joke, he had been able to draw upon.

12

The particular impression I had received proved in the morning light, I repeat, not quite successfully presentable to Mrs. Grose, though I reinforced it with the mention of still another remark that he had made before we separated. "It all lies in half-a-dozen words," I said to her, "words that really settle the matter. 'Think, you know, what I *might* do!' He threw that off to show me how good he is. He knows down to the ground what he 'might' do. That's what he gave them a taste of at school."

"Lord, you do change!" cried my friend.

"I don't change—I simply make it out. The four, depend upon it, perpetually meet. If on either of these last nights you had been with either child, you would clearly have understood. The more I've watched and waited the more I've felt that if there were nothing else to make it sure it would be made so by the systematic silence of each. *Never*, by a slip of the tongue, have they so much as alluded to either of their old friends, any more than Miles has alluded to his expulsion. Oh yes, we may sit here and look at them, and they may show off to us there to their fill; but even while they pretend to be lost in their fairy-tale they're steeped in their vision of the dead restored. He's not reading to her," I declared; "they're talking of *them*—they're talking horrors! I go on, I know, as if I were crazy; and it's a wonder I'm not. What I've seen would have made *you* so; but it has only made me more lucid, made me get hold of still other things."

My lucidity must have seemed awful, but the charming creatures who were victims of it, passing and repassing in their interlocked sweetness, gave my colleague something to hold on by; and I felt how tight she held as, without stirring in the breath of my passion, she covered them still with her eyes. "Of what other things have you got hold?"

"Why, of the very things that have delighted, fascinated, and yet, at bottom, as I now so strangely see, mystified and troubled me. Their more than earthly beauty, their absolutely unnatural goodness. It's a game," I went on; "it's a policy and a fraud!"

"On the part of little darlings—?"

"As yet mere lovely babies? Yes, mad as that seems!" The very act of bringing it out really helped me to trace it—follow it all up and piece it all together. "They haven't been good—they've only been absent. It has been easy to live with them, because they're simply leading a life of their own. They're not mine—they're not ours. They're his and they're hers!"

"Quint's and that woman's?"

"Quint's and that woman's. They want to get to them."

Oh, how, at this, poor Mrs. Grose appeared to study them! "But for what?"

"For the love of all the evil that, in those dreadful days, the pair put into them. And to ply them with that evil still, to keep up the work of demons, is what brings the others back."

"Laws!" said my friend under her breath. The exclamation was homely, but it revealed a real acceptance of my further proof of what, in the bad time— for there had been a worse even than this!—must have occurred. There could have been no such justification for me as the plain assent of her experience to whatever depth of depravity I found credible in our brace of scoundrels. It was in obvious submission of memory that she brought out after a moment: "They *were* rascals! But what can they now do?" she pursued.

"Do?" I echoed so loud that Miles and Flora, as they passed at their distance, paused an instant in their walk and looked at us. "Don't they do enough?" I demanded in a lower tone, while the children, having smiled and nodded and kissed hands to us, resumed their exhibition. We were held by it a minute; then I answered: "They can destroy them!" At this my companion did turn, but the inquiry she launched was a silent one, the effect of which was to make me more explicit. "They don't know, as yet, quite how— but they're trying hard. They're seen only across, as it were, and beyond—in strange places and on high places, the top of towers, the roof of houses, the outside of windows, the further edge of pools; but there's a deep design, on either side, to shorten the distance and overcome the obstacle; and the success of the tempters is only a question of time. They've only to keep to their suggestions of danger."

"For the children to come?"

"And perish in the attempt!" Mrs. Grose slowly got up, and I scupulously added: "Unless, of course, we can prevent!"

Standing there before me while I kept my seat, she visibly turned things over. "Their uncle must do the preventing. He must take them away."

"And who's to make him?"

She had been scanning the distance, but she now dropped on me a foolish face. "You, Miss."

"By writing to him that his house is poisoned and his little nephew and niece mad?"

"But if they *are*, Miss?"

"And if I am myself, you mean? That's charming news to be sent him by a governess whose prime undertaking was to give him no worry."

Mrs. Grose considered, following the children again. "Yes, he do hate worry. That was the great reason—"

"Why those fiends took him in so long? No doubt, though his indifference must have been awful. As I'm not a fiend, at any rate, I shouldn't take him in."

My companion, after an instant and for all answer, sat down again and grasped my arm. "Make him at any rate come to you."

I stared. "To *me*?" I had a sudden fear of what she might do. " 'Him'?"

"He ought to *be* here—he ought to help."

I quickly rose, and I think I must have shown her a queerer face than ever yet. "You see me asking him for a visit?" No, with her eyes on my face she evidently couldn't. Instead of it even—as a woman reads another—she could see what I myself saw: his derision, his amusement, his contempt for the break-down of my resignation at being left alone and for the fine machinery I had set in motion to attract his attention to my slighted charms. She didn't know—no one knew—how proud I had been to serve him and to stick to our terms; yet she none the less took the measure, I think, of the warning I now gave her. "If you should so lose your head as to appeal to him for me—"

She was really frightened. "Yes, Miss?"

"I would leave, on the spot, both him and you."

13

It was all very well to join them, but speaking to them proved quite as much as ever an effort beyond my strength—offered, in close quarters, difficulties as insurmountable as before. This situation continued a month, and with new aggravations and particular notes, the note above all, sharper and sharper, of the small ironic consciousness on the part of my pupils. It was not, I am as sure today as I was sure then, my mere infernal imagination: it was absolutely traceable that they were aware of my predicament and that this strange relation made, in a manner, for a long time, the air in which we moved. I don't mean that they had their tongues in their cheeks or did anything vulgar, for that was not one of their dangers: I do mean, on the other hand, that the element of the unnamed and untouched became, between us, greater than any other, and that so much avoidance could not have been so sucessfully effected without a great deal of tacit arrangement. It was as if, at moments, we were perpetually coming into sight of subjects before which we must stop short, turning suddenly out of alleys that we perceived to be blind, closing with a little bang that made us look at each other—for, like all bangs, it was something louder than we had intended—the doors we had indiscreetly opened. All roads lead to Rome, and there were times when it might have struck us that almost every branch of study or subject of conversation skirted forbidden ground. Forbidden ground was the question of the return of the dead in general and of whatever, in especial, might survive, in memory, of the friends little children had lost. There were days when I could have sworn that one of them had, with a small invisible nudge, said to the other: "She thinks she'll do it this time—but she *won't!*" To "do it" would have been to indulge for instance—and for once in a way—in some direct reference to the lady who had prepared them for my discipline. They had a delightful endless appetite for passages in my own history, to which I had again and again treated them; they were in possession of everything that had ever happened to me, had had, with every circumstance, the story of my smallest adventures and of those of my brothers and sisters and of the cat and the dog at home, as well as many particulars of the eccentric nature of my father, of the furniture and arrangement of our house, and of the conversation of the old women of our village. There were things enough, taking one with another, to chatter about, if one went very fast and knew by instinct when to go round. They pulled with an art of their own the strings of my invention and my memory; and nothing else perhaps, when I thought of such occasions afterwards, gave me so the suspicion of being watched from under cover. It was in any case over *my* life, *my* past, and *my* friends alone that we could take anything like our ease—a state of affairs that led them sometimes without the least pertinence to break out into sociable reminders. I was invited —with no visible connection—to repeat afresh Goody Gosling's celebrated *mot* or to confirm the details already supplied as to the cleverness of the vicarage pony.

It was partly at such junctures as these and partly at quite different ones that, with the turn my matters had how taken, my predicament, as I have called it, grew most sensible. The fact that the days passed for me without another encounter ought, it would have appeared, to have done something toward soothing my nerves. Since the light brush, that second night on the upper landing, of the presence of a woman at the foot of the stair, I had seen nothing, whether in or out of the house, that one had better not have seen. There was many a corner round which I expected to come upon Quint, and many a situation that, in a merely sinister way, would have favoured the appearance of Miss Jessel. The summer had turned, the summer had gone; the autumn had dropped upon Bly and had blown out half our lights. The place, with its grey sky and withered garlands, its bared spaces and scattered dead leaves, was like a theatre after the performance—all strewn with crumpled playbills. There were exactly states of the air, conditions of sound and of stillness, unspeakable impressions of the *kind* of ministering moment, that brought back to me, long enough to catch it, the feeling of the medium in which, that June evening out-of-doors, I had had my first sight of Quint, and in which, too, at those other instants, I had, after seeing him through the window, looked for him in vain in the circle of shrubbery. I recognised the signs, the portents—I recognised the moment, the spot. But they remained unaccompanied and empty, and I continued unmolested; if unmolested one could call a young woman whose sensibility had, in the most extraordinary fashion, not declined but deepened. I had said in my talk with Mrs. Grose on that horrid scene of Flora's by the lake—and had perplexed her by so saying —that it would from that moment distress me much more to loose my power than to keep it. I had then expressed what was vividly in my mind: the truth that, whether the children really saw or not—since, that is, it was not yet definitely proved—I greatly preferred, as a safeguard, the fulness of my own exposure. I was ready to know the very worst that was to be known. What I had then had an ugly glimpse of was that my eyes might be sealed just while theirs were most opened. Well, my eyes *were* sealed, it appeared, at present—a consummation for which it seemed blasphemous not to thank God. There was, alas, a difficulty about that: I would have thanked him with all my soul had I not had in a proportionate measure this conviction of the secret of my pupils.

How can I retrace today the strange steps of my obsession? There were times of our being together when I would have been ready to swear that, literally, in my presence, but with my direct sense of it closed, they had visitors who were known and were welcome. Then it was that, had I not been deterred by the very chance that such an injury might prove greater than the injury to be averted, my exultation would have broken out. "They're here, they're here, you little wretches," I would have cried, "and you can't deny it

now!" The little wretches denied it with all the added volume of their sociability and their tenderness, in just the crystal depths of which—like the flash of a
fish in a stream—the mockery of their advantage peeped up. The shock, in
truth, had sunk into me still deeper than I knew on the night when, looking
out to see either Quint or Miss Jessel under the stars, I had beheld the boy
over whose rest I watched and who had immediately brought in with him—
had straightway, there, turned it on me—the lovely upward look with which,
from the battlements above me, the hideous apparition of Quint had played.
If it was a question of a scare, my discovery on this occasion had scared me
more than any other, and it was in the condition of nerves produced by it that
I made my actual inductions. They harassed me so that sometimes, at odd
moments, I shut myself up audibly to rehearse—it was at once a fantastic
relief and a renewed despair—the manner in which I might come to the point.
I approached it from one side and the other while, in my room, I flung myself about, but I always broke down in the monstrous utterance of names. As
they died away on my lips, I said to myself that I should indeed help them to
represent something infamous, if by pronouncing them, I should violate as
rare a little case of instinctive delicacy as any schoolroom, probably, had ever
known. When I said to myself: "*They* have the manners to be silent, and
you, trusted as you are, the baseness to speak!" I felt myself crimson and I
covered my face with my hands. After these secret scenes I chattered more
than ever, going on volubly enough till one of our prodigious, palpable hushes
occurred—I can call them nothing else—the strange, dizzy lift or swim (I try
for terms!) into a stillness, a pause of all life, that had nothing to do with the
more or less noise that at the moment we might be engaged in making and
that I could hear through any deepened exhilaration or quickened recitation
or louder strum of the piano. Then it was that the others, the outsiders, were
there. Though they were not angels, they "passed," as the French say, causing
me, while they stayed, to tremble with the fear of their addressing to their
younger victims some yet more infernal message or more vivid image than
they had thought good enough for myself.

What it was most impossible to get rid of was the cruel idea that, whatever I had seen, Miles and Flora saw *more*—things terrible and unguessable
and that sprang from dreadful passages of intercourse in the past. Such things
naturally left on the surface, for the time, a chill which we vociferously denied
that we felt; and we had, all three, with repetition, got into such splendid
training that we went, each time, almost automatically, to mark the close of
the incident, through the very same movements. It was striking of the children,
at all events, to kiss me inveterately with a kind of wild irrelevance and never
to fail—one or the other—of the precious question that had helped us through
many a peril. "When do you think he *will* come? Don't you think we *ought* to
write?"—there was nothing like that inquiry, we found by experience, for
carrying off an awkwardness. "He" of course was their uncle in Harley Street;
and we lived in much profusion of theory that he might at any moment arrive
to mingle in our circle. It was impossible to have given less encouragement
than he had done to such a doctrine, but if we had not had the doctrine to
fall back upon we should have deprived each other of some of our finest

exhibitions. He never wrote to them—that may have been selfish, but it was a part of the flattery of his trust of me; for the way in which a man pays his highest tribute to a woman is apt to be but by the more festal celebration of one of the sacred laws of his comfort; and I held that I carried out the spirit of the pledge given not to appeal to him when I let my charges understand that their own letters were but charming literary exercises. They were too beautiful to be posted; I kept them myself; I have them all to this hour. This was a rule indeed which only added to the satiric effect of my being plied with the supposition that he might at any moment be among us. It was exactly as if my charges knew how almost more awkward than anything else that might be for me. There appears to me, moreover, as I look back, no note in all this more extraordinary than the mere fact that, in spite of my tension and of their triumph, I never lost patience with them. Adorable they must in truth have been, I now reflect, that I didn't in these days hate them! Would exasperation, however, if relief had longer been postponed, finally have betrayed me? It little matters, for relief arrived. I call it relief, though it was only the relief that a snap brings to a strain or the burst of a thunderstorm to a day of suffocation. It was at least change, and it came with a rush.

14

Walking to church a certain Sunday morning, I had little Miles at my side and his sister, in advance of us and at Mrs. Grose's, well in sight. It was a crisp, clear day, the first of its order for some time; the night had brought a touch of frost, and autumn air, bright and sharp, made the church-bells almost gay. It was an odd accident of thought that I should have happened at such a moment to be particularly and very gratefully struck with the obedience of my little charges. Why did they never resent my inexorable, my perpetual society? Something or other had brought nearer home to me that I had all but pinned the boy to my shawl and that, in the way our companions were marshalled before me, I might have appeared to provide against some danger of rebellion. I was like a gaoler with an eye to possible surprises and escapes. But all this belonged—I mean their magnificent little surrender—just to the special array of the facts that were most abysmal. Turned out for Sunday by his uncle's tailor, who had had a free hand and a notion of pretty waistcoats and of his grand little air, Miles's whole title to independence, the rights of his sex and situation, were so stamped upon him that if he had suddenly struck for freedom I should have had nothing to say. I was by the strangest of chances wondering how I should meet him when the revolution unmistakeably occurred. I call it a revolution because I now see how, with the word he spoke, the curtain rose on the last act of my dreadful drama and the catastrophe was precipitated. "Look here, my dear, you know," he charmingly said, "when in the world, please, am I going back to school?"

Transcribed here the speech sounds harmless enough, particularly as uttered in the sweet, high, casual pipe with which, at all interlocutors, but above all at his eternal governess, he threw off intonations as if he were tossing roses. There was something in them that always made one "catch," and I caught, at any rate, now so effectually that I stopped as short as if one of the trees of the park had fallen across the road. There was something new, on the spot, between us, and he was perfectly aware that I recognised it, though, to enable me to do so, he had no need to look a whit less candid and charming than usual. I could feel in him how he already, from my at first finding nothing to reply, perceived the advantage he had gained. I was so slow to find anything that he had plenty of time, after a minute, to continue with his suggestive but inconclusive smile: "You know, my dear, that for a fellow to be with a lady *always*—!" His "my dear" was constantly on his lips for me, and nothing could have expressed more the exact shade of the sentiment with which I desired to inspire my pupils than its fond familiarity. It was so respectfully easy.

But, oh, how I felt that at present I must pick my own phrases! I remember that, to gain time, I tried to laugh, and I seemed to see in the beautiful face with which he watched me how ugly and queer I looked. "And always with the same lady?" I returned.

He neither blenched nor winked. The whole thing was virtually out between us. "Ah, of course, she's a jolly, 'perfect' lady; but, after all, I'm a fellow, don't you see? that's—well, getting on."

I lingered there with him an instant ever so kindly. "Yes, you're getting on." Oh, but I felt helpless!

I have kept to this day the heartbreaking little idea of how he seemed to know that and to play with it. "And you can't say I've not been awfully good, can you?"

I laid my hand on his shoulder, for, though I felt how much better it would have been to walk on, I was not yet quite able. "No, I can't say that, Miles."

"Except just that one night, you know—!"

"That one night?" I couldn't look as straight as he.

"Why, when I went down—went out of the house."

"Oh, yes. But I forget what you did it for."

"You forget?"—he spoke with the sweet extravagance of childish reproach. "Why, it was to show you I could!"

"Oh, yes, you could."

"And I can again."

I felt that I might, perhaps, after all succeed in keeping my wits about me. "Certainly. But you won't."

"No, not *that* again. It was nothing."

"It was nothing," I said. "But we must go on."

He resumed our walk with me, passing his hand into my arm. "Then when *am* I going back?"

I wore, in turning it over, my most responsible air. "Were you very happy at school?"

He just considered. "Oh, I'm happy enough anywhere!"

"Well, then," I quavered, "if you're just as happy here—!"

"Ah, but that isn't everything! Of course *you* know a lot—"

"But you hint that you know almost as much?" I risked as he paused.

"Not half I want to!" Miles honestly professed. "But it isn't so much that."

"What is it, then?"

"Well—I want to see more life."

"I see; I see." We had arrived within sight of the church and of various persons, including several of the household of Bly, on their way to it and clustered about the door to see us go in. I quickened our step; I wanted to get there before the question between us opened up much further; I reflected hungrily that, for more than an hour, he would have to be silent; and I thought with envy of the comparative dusk of the pew and of the almost spiritual help of the hassock on which I might bend my knees. I seemed literally to be running a race with some confusion to which he was about to reduce me, but I felt that he had got in first when, before we had even entered the churchyard, he threw out—

"I want my own sort!"

It literally made me bound forward. "There are not many of your own sort, Miles!" I laughed. "Unless perhaps dear little Flora!"

"You really compare me to a baby girl?"

This found me singularly weak. "Don't you, then, *love* our sweet Flora?"

"If I didn't—and you too; if I didn't—!" he repeated as if retreating for a jump, yet leaving his thought so unfinished that, after we had come into the gate, another stop, which he imposed on me by the pressure of his arm, had become inevitable. Mrs. Grose and Flora had passed into the church, the other worshippers had followed, and we were, for the minute, alone among the old, thick graves. We had paused, on the path from the gate, by a low, oblong, table-like tomb.

"Yes. If you didn't—?"

He looked, while I waited, about at the graves. "Well, you know what!" But he didn't move, and he presently produced something that made me drop straight down on the stone slab, as if suddenly to rest. "Does my uncle think what *you* think?"

I markedly rested. "How do you know what I think?"

"Ah, well, of course I don't; for it strikes me you never tell me. But I mean does *he* know?"

"Know what, Miles?"

"Why, the way I'm going on."

I perceived quickly enough that I could make, to this inquiry, no answer that would not involve something of a sacrifice of my employer. Yet it appeared to me that we were all, at Bly, sufficiently sacrificed to make that venial. "I don't think your uncle much cares."

Miles, on this, stood looking at me. "Then don't you think he can be made to?"

"In what way?"

"Why, by his coming down."

"But who'll get him to come down?"

"*I* will!" the boy said with extraordinary brightness and emphasis. He gave me another look charged with that expression and then marched off alone into church.

15

The business was practically settled from the moment I never followed him. It was a pitiful surrender to agitation, but my being aware of this had somehow no power to restore me. I only sat there on my tomb and read into what my little friend had said to me the fulness of its meaning; by the time I had grasped the whole of which I had also embraced, for absence, the pretext that I was ashamed to offer my pupils and the rest of the congregation such an example of delay. What I said to myself above all was that Miles had got something out of me and that the proof of it, for him, would be just this awkward collapse. He had got out of me that there was something I was much afraid of and that he should probably be able to make use of my fear to gain, for his own purpose, more freedom. My fear was of having to deal with the intolerable question of the grounds of his dismissal from school, for that was really but the question of the horrors gathered behind. That his uncle should arrive to treat with me of these things was a solution that, strictly speaking, I ought now to have desired to bring on; but I could so little face the ugliness and the pain of it that I simply procrastinated and lived from hand to mouth. The boy, to my deep discomposure, was immensely in the right, was in a position to say to me: "Either you clear up with my guardian the mystery of this interruption of my studies, or you cease to expect me to lead with you a life that's so unnatural for a boy." What was so unnatural for the particular boy I was concerned with was this sudden revelation of a consciousness and a plan.

That was what really overcame me, what prevented my going in. I walked round the church, hesitating, hovering; I reflected that I had already, with him, hurt myself beyond repair. Therefore I could patch up nothing, and it was too extreme an effort to squeeze beside him into the pew: he would be so much more sure than ever to pass his arm into mine and make me sit there for an hour in close, silent contact which his commentary on our talk. For the first minute since his arrival I wanted to get away from him. As I paused beneath the high east window and listened to the sounds of worship, I was taken with an impulse that might master me, I felt, completely should I give it the least encouragement. I might easily put an end to my predicament by getting away altogether. Here was my chance; there was no one to stop me; I could give the whole thing up—turn my back and retreat. It was only a question of hurrying again, for a few preparations, to the house which the attendance at church of so many of the servants would practically have left unoccupied. No one, in short, could blame me if I should just drive desperately off. What was it to get away if I got away only till dinner? That would be in a couple of hours, at the end of which—I had the acute prevision—my little pupils would play at innocent wonder about my non-appearance in their train.

"What *did* you do, you naughty, bad thing? Why in the world, to worry us so—and take our thoughts off too, don't you know?—did you desert us at the very door?" I couldn't meet such questions nor, as they asked them, their false little lovely eyes; yet it was all so exactly what I should have to meet that, as the prospect grew sharp to me, I at last let myself go.

I got, so far as the immediate moment was concerned, away; I came straight out of the churchyard and, thinking hard, retraced my steps through the park. It seemed to me that by the time I reached the house I had made up my mind I would fly. The Sunday stillness both of the approaches and of the interior, in which I met no one, fairly excited me with a sense of opportunity. Were I to get off quickly, this way, I should get off without a scene, without a word. My quickness would have to be remarkable, however, and the question of a conveyance was the great one to settle. Tormented, in the hall, with difficulties and obstacles, I remember sinking down at the foot of the staircase—suddenly collapsing there on the lowest step and then, with a revulsion, recalling that it was exactly where more than a month before, in the darkness of night and just so bowed with evil things, I had seen the spectre of the most horrible of women. At this I was able to straighten myself; I went the rest of the way up; I made, in my bewilderment, for the schoolroom, where there were objects belonging to me that I should have to take. But I opened the door to find again, in a flash, my eyes unsealed. In the presence of what I saw I reeled straight back upon my resistance.

Seated at my own table in clear noonday light I saw a person whom, without my previous experience, I should have taken at the first blush for some housemaid who might have stayed at home to look after the place and who, availing herself of rare relief from observation and of the schoolroom table and my pens, ink, and paper, had applied herself to the considerable effort of a letter to her sweetheart. There was an effort in the way that, while her arms rested on the table, her hands with evident weariness supported her head; but at the moment I took this in I had already become aware that, in spite of my entrance, her attitude strangely persisted. Then it was—with the very act of its announcing itself—that her identity flared up in a change of posture. She rose, not as if she had heard me, but with an indescribable grand melancholy of indifference and detachment, and, within a dozen feet of me, stood there as my vile predecessor. Dishonoured and tragic, she was all before me; but even as I fixed and, for memory, secured it, the awful image passed away. Dark as midnight in her black dress, her haggard beauty and her unutterable woe, she had looked at me long enough to appear to say that her right to sit at my table was as good as mine to sit at hers. While these instants lasted indeed I had the extraordinary chill of a feeling that it was I who was the intruder. It was as a wild protest against it that, actually addressing her—"You terrible, miserable woman!"—I heard myself break into a sound that, by the open door, rang through the long passage and the empty house. She looked at me as if she heard me, but I had recovered myself and cleared the air. There was nothing in the room the next minute but the sunshine and a sense that I must stay.

16

I had so perfectly expected that the return of my pupils would be marked by a demonstration that I was freshly upset at having to take into account that they were dumb about my absence. Instead of gaily denouncing and caressing me, they made no allusion to my having failed them, and I was left, for the time, on perceiving that she too said nothing, to study Mrs. Grose's odd face. I did this to such purpose that I made sure they had in some way bribed her to silence; a silence that, however, I would engage to break down on the first private opportunity. This opportunity came before tea: I secured five minutes with her in the housekeeper's room, where, in the twilight, amid a smell of lately-baked bread, but with the place all swept and garnished, I found her sitting in pained placidity before the fire. So I see her still, so I see her best: facing the flame from her straight chair in the dusky, shining room, a large clean image of the "put away"—of drawers closed and locked and rest without a remedy.

"Oh, yes, they asked me to say nothing; and to please them—so long as they were there—of course I promised. But what had happened to you?"

"I only went with you for the walk," I said. "I had then to come back to meet a friend."

She showed her surprise. "A friend—you?"

"Oh, yes, I have a couple!" I laughed. "But did the children give you a reason?"

"For not alluding to your leaving us? Yes; they said you would like it better. Do you like it better?"

My face had made her rueful. "No, I like it worse!" But after an instant I added: "Did they say why I should like it better?"

"No; Master Miles only said, 'We must do nothing but what she likes'!"

"I wish indeed he would! And what did Flora say?"

"Miss Flora was too sweet. She said, 'Oh, of course, of course!'—and I said the same."

I thought a moment. "You were too sweet too—I can hear you all. But none the less, between Miles and me, it's now all out."

"All out?" My companion stared. "But what, Miss?"

"Everything. It doesn't matter. I've made up my mind. I came home, my dear," I went on, "for a talk with Miss Jessel."

I had by this time formed the habit of having Mrs. Grose literally well in hand in advance of my sounding that note; so that even now, as she bravely blinked under the signal of my word, I could keep her comparatively firm. "A talk! Do you mean she spoke?"

"It came to that. I found her, on my return, in the schoolroom."

"And what did she say?" I can hear the good woman still, and the candour of her stupefaction.

"That she suffers the torments—!"

It was this, of a truth, that made her, as she filled out my picture, gape. "Do you mean," she faltered, "—of the lost?"

"Of the lost. Of the damned. And that's why, to share them—" I faltered myself with the horror of it.

But my companion, with less imagination, kept me up. "To share them—?"

"She wants Flora." Mrs. Grose might, as I gave it to her, fairly have fallen away from me had I not been prepared. I still held her there, to show I was. "As I've told you, however, it doesn't matter."

"Because you've made up your mind? But to what?"

"To everything."

"And what do you call 'everything'?"

"Why, sending for their uncle."

"Oh, Miss, in pity do," my friend broke out.

"Ah, but I will, I *will!* I see it's the only way. What's 'out,' as I told you, with Miles is that if he thinks I'm afraid to—and has ideas of what he gains by that—he shall see he's mistaken. Yes, yes; his uncle shall have it here from me on the spot (and before the boy himself if necessary) that if I'm to be reproached with having done nothing again about more school—"

"Yes, Miss—" my companion pressed me.

"Well, there's that awful reason."

There were now clearly so many of these for my poor colleague that she was excusable for being vague. "But—a—which?"

"Why, the letter from his old place."

"You'll show it to the master?"

"I ought to have done so on the instant."

"Oh, no!" said Mrs. Grose with decision.

"I'll put it before him," I went on inexorably, "that I can't undertake to work the question on behalf of a child who has been expelled—"

"For we've never in the least known what!" Mrs. Grose declared.

"For wickedness. For what else—when he's so clever and beautiful and perfect? Is he stupid? Is he untidy? Is he infirm? Is he ill-natured? He's exquisite—so it can be only *that*; and that would open up the whole thing. After all," I said, "it's their uncle's fault. If he left here such people—!"

"He didn't really in the least know them. The fault's mine." She had turned quite pale.

"Well, you shan't suffer," I answered.

"The children shan't!" she emphatically returned.

I was silent awhile; we looked at each other. "Then what am I to tell him?"

"You needn't tell him anything. *I'll* tell him."

I measured this. "Do you mean you'll write—?" Remembering she couldn't, I caught myself up. "How do you communicate?"

"I tell the bailiff. *He* writes."

"And should you like him to write our story?"

My question had a sarcastic force that I had not fully intended, and it made her, after a moment, inconsequently break down. The tears were again in her eyes. "Ah, Miss, *you* write!"

"Well—tonight," I at last answered; and on this we separated.

17

I went so far, in the evening, as to make a beginning. The weather had changed back, a great wind was abroad, and beneath the lamp, in my room, with Flora at peace beside me, I sat for a long time before a blank sheet of paper and listened to the lash of the rain and the batter of the gusts. Finally I went out, taking a candle; I crossed the passage and listened a minute at Miles's door. What, under my endless obsession, I had been impelled to listen for was some betrayal of his not being at rest, and I presently caught one, but not in the form I had expected. His voice tinkled out. "I say, you there— come in." It was a gaiety in the gloom!

I went in with my light and found him, in bed, very wide awake, but very much at his ease. "Well, what are *you* up to?" he asked with a grace of sociability in which it occurred to me that Mrs. Grose, had she been present, might have looked in vain for proof that anything was "out."

I stood over him with my candle. "How did you know I was there?"

"Why, of course I heard you. Did you fancy you made no noise? You're like a troop of cavalry!" he beautifully laughed.

"Then you weren't asleep?"

"Not much! I lie awake and think."

I had put my candle, designedly, a short way off, and then, as he held out his friendly old hand to me, had sat down on the edge of his bed. "What is it," I asked, "that you think of?"

"What in the world, my dear, but *you?*"

"Ah, the pride I take in your appreciation doesn't insist on that! I had so far rather you slept."

"Well, I think also, you know, of this queer business of ours."

I marked the coolness of his firm little hand. "Of what queer business, Miles?"

"Why, the way you bring me up. And all the rest!"

I fairly held my breath a minute, and even from my glimmering taper there was light enough to show how he smiled up at me from his pillow. "What do you mean by all the rest?"

"Oh, you know, you know!"

I could say nothing for a minute, though I felt, as I held his hand and our eyes continued to meet, that my silence had all the air of admitting his charge and that nothing in the whole world of reality was perhaps at that moment so fabulous as our actual relation. "Certainly you shall go back to school," I said, "if it be that that troubles you. But not to the old place— we must find another, a better. How could I know it did trouble you, this question, when you never told me so, never spoke of it at all?" His clear, listening face, framed in its smooth whiteness, made him for the minute as appealing as some wistful patient in a children's hospital; and I would have given, as the resemblance came to me, all I possessed on earth really to be the nurse or the sister of charity who might have helped to cure him. Well, even as it was, I perhaps might help! "Do you know you've never said a word to me about your school—I mean the old one; never mentioned it in any way?"

He seemed to wonder; he smiled with the same loveliness. But he clearly gained time; he waited, he called for guidance. "Haven't I?" It wasn't for me to help him—it was for the thing I had met!

Something in his tone and the expression of his face, as I got this from him, set my heart aching with such a pang as it had never yet known; so unutterably touching was it to see his little brain puzzled and his little resources taxed to play, under the spell laid on him, a part of innocence and consistency. "No, never—from the hour you came back. You've never mentioned to me one of your masters, one of your comrades, nor the least little thing that ever happened to you at school. Never, little Miles—no, never—have you given me an inkling of anything that *may* have happened there. Therefore you can fancy how much I'm in the dark. Until you came out, that way, this morning, you had, since the first hour I saw you, scarce even made a reference to anything in your previous life. You seemed so perfectly to accept the present." It was extraordinary how my absolute conviction of his secret precocity (or whatever I might call the poison of an influence that I dared but half to phrase) made him, in spite of the faint breath of his inward trouble, appear as accessible as an older person—imposed him almost as an intellectual equal. "I thought you wanted to go on as you are."

It struck me that at this he just faintly coloured. He gave, at any rate, like a convalescent slightly fatigued, a languid shake of his head. "I don't—I don't. I want to get away."

"You're tired of Bly?"

"Oh, no, I like Bly."

"Well, then—?"

"Oh, *you* know what a boy wants!"

I felt that I didn't know so well as Miles, and I took temporary refuge. "You want to go to your uncle?"

Again, at this, with his sweet ironic face, he made a movement on the pillow. "Ah, you can't get off with that!"

I was silent a little, and it was I, now, I think, who changed colour. "My dear, I don't want to get off!"

"You can't, even if you do. You can't, you can't!"—he lay beautifully staring. "My uncle must come down, and you must completely settle things."

"If we do," I returned with some spirit, "you may be sure it will be to take you quite away."

"Well, don't you understand that that's exactly what I'm working for? You'll have to tell him—about the way you've let it all drop: you'll have to tell him a tremendous lot!"

The exultation with which he uttered this helped me somehow, for the instant, to meet him rather more. "And how much will *you*, Miles, have to tell him? There are things he'll ask you!"

He turned it over. "Very likely. But what things?"

"The things you've never told me. To make up his mind what to do with you. He can't send you back—"

"Oh, I don't want to go back!" he broke in. "I want a new field."

He said it with admirable serenity, with positive unimpeachable gaiety; and doubtless it was that very note that most evoked for me the poignancy, the unnatural childish tragedy, of his probable reappearance at the end of three months with all this bravado and still more dishonour. It overwhelmed me now that I should never be able to bear that, and it made me let myself go. I threw myself upon him and in the tenderness of my pity I embraced him. "Dear little Miles, dear little Miles—!"

My face was close to his, and he let me kiss him, simply taking it with indulgent good-humour. "Well, old lady?"

"Is there nothing—nothing at all that you want to tell me?"

He turned off a little, facing round toward the wall and holding up his hand to look at as one had seen sick children look. "I've told you—I told you this morning."

Oh, I was sorry for him! "That you just want me not to worry you?"

He looked round at me now, as if in recognition of my understanding him; then ever so gently, "To let me alone," he replied.

There was even a singular little dignity in it, something that made me release him, yet, when I had slowly risen, linger beside him. God knows I never wished to harass him, but I felt that merely, at this, to turn my back on him was to abandon or, to put it more truly, to lose him. "I've just begun a letter to your uncle," I said.

"Well, then, finish it!"

I waited a minute. "What happened before?"

He gazed up at me again. "Before what?"

"Before you came back. And before you went away."

For some time he was silent, but he continued to meet my eyes. "What happened?"

It made me, the sound of the words, in which it seemed to me that I caught for the very first time a small faint quaver of consenting consciousness —it made me drop on my knees beside the bed and seize once more the chance of possessing him. "Dear little Miles, dear little Miles, if you *knew* how I want to help you! It's only that, it's nothing but that, and I'd rather die than give you a pain or do you a wrong—I'd rather die than hurt a hair of you. Dear little Miles"—oh, I brought it out now even if I *should* go too far—"I just want you to help me to save you!" But I knew in a moment after this that I had gone too far. The answer to my appeal was instantaneous, but it came in the form of an extraordinary blast and chill, a gust of frozen air and a shake of the room as great as if, in the wild wind, the casement had crashed in. The boy gave a loud, high shriek, which, lost in the rest of the shock of sound, might have seemed, indistinctly, though I was so close to him, a note either of jubilation or of terror. I jumped to my feet again and was conscious of darkness. So for a moment we remained, while I stared about me and saw that the drawn curtains were unstirred and the window tight. "Why, the candle's out!" I then cried.

"It was I who blew it, dear!" said Miles.

18

The next day, after lessons, Mrs. Grose found a moment to say to me quietly: "Have you written, Miss?"

"Yes—I've written." But I didn't add—for the hour—that my letter, sealed and directed, was still in my pocket. There would be time enough to send it before the messenger should go to the village. Meanwhile there had been, on the part of my pupils, no more brilliant, more exemplary morning. It was exactly as if they had both had at heart to gloss over any recent little friction. They performed the dizziest feats of arithmetic, soaring quite out of *my* feeble range, and perpetrated, in higher spirits than ever, geographical and historical jokes. It was conspicuous of course in Miles in particular that he appeared to wish to show how easily he could let me down. This child, to my memory, really lives in a setting of beauty and misery that no words can translate; there was a distinction all his own in every impulse he revealed; never was a small natural creature, to the uninitiated eye all frankness and freedom, a more ingenious, a more extraordinary little gentleman. I had perpetually to guard against the wonder of contemplation into which my initiated view betrayed me; to check the irrelevant gaze and discouraged sigh in which I constantly both attacked and renounced the enigma of what such a little gentleman could have done that deserved a penalty. Say that, by the dark prodigy I knew, the imagination of all evil *had* been opened up to him: all the justice within me ached for the proof that it could ever have flowered into an act.

He had never, at any rate, been such a little gentleman as when, after our early dinner on this dreadful day, he came round to me and asked if I shouldn't like him, for half an hour, to play to me. David playing to Saul could never have shown a finer sense of the occasion. It was literally a charming exhibition of tact, of magnanimity, and quite tantamount to his saying outright: "The true knights we love to read about never push an advantage too far. I know what you mean now: you mean that—to be let alone yourself and not followed up—you'll cease to worry and spy upon me, won't keep me so close to you, will let me go and come. Well, I 'come,' you see—but I don't go! There'll be plenty of time for that. I do really delight in your society, and I only want to show you that I contended for a principle." It may be imagined whether I resisted this appeal or failed to accompany him again, hand in hand, to the schoolroom. He sat down at the old piano and played as he had never played, and if there are those who think he had better have been kicking a football I can only say that I wholly agree with them. For at the end of a time that under his influence I had quite ceased to measure I started up with a strange sense of having literally slept at my post. It was after luncheon, and by the schoolroom fire, and yet I hadn't really, in the least, slept: I had only done something much worse—I had forgotten. Where, all this time, was Flora? When I put the question to Miles he played on a minute before answering, and then could only say: "Why, my dear, how do I know?"—breaking moreover into a happy laugh which, immediately after, as if it were a vocal accompaniment, he prolonged into incoherent, extravagant song.

I went straight to my room, but his sister was not there; then, before going downstairs, I looked into several others. As she was nowhere about she would surely be with Mrs. Grose, whom, in the comfort of that theory, I accordingly proceeded in quest of. I found her where I had found her the evening before, but she met my quick challenge with blank, scared ignorance. She had only supposed that, after the repast, I had carried off both the children; as to which she was quite in her right, for it was the very first time I had allowed the little girl out of my sight without some special provision. Of course now indeed she might be with the maids, so that the immediate thing was to look for her without an air of alarm. This we promptly arranged between us; but when, ten minutes later and in pursuance of our arrangement, we met in the hall, it was only to report on either side that after guarded inquiries we had altogether failed to trace her. For a minute there, apart from observation, we exchanged mute alarms, and I could feel with what high interest my friend returned me all those I had from the first given her.

"She'll be above," she presently said—"in one of the rooms you haven't searched."

"No; she's at a distance." I had made up my mind. "She has gone out."

Mrs. Grose stared. "Without a hat?"

I naturally also looked volumes. "Isn't that woman always without one?"

"She's with *her?*"

"She's with *her!*" I declared. "We must find them."

My hand was on my friend's arm, but she failed for the moment, confronted with such an account of the matter, to respond to my pressure. She communed, on the contrary, on the spot, with her uneasiness. "And where's Master Miles?"

"Oh, *he's* with Quint. They're in the schoolroom."

"Lord, Miss!" My view, I was myself aware—and therefore I suppose my tone—had never yet reached so calm an assurance.

"The trick's played," I went on; "they've successfully worked their plan. He found the most divine little way to keep me quiet while she went off."

" 'Divine'?" Mrs. Grose bewilderedly echoed.

"Infernal, then!" I almost cheerfully rejoined. "He has provided for himself as well. But come!"

She had helplessly gloomed at the upper regions. "You leave him—?"

"So long with Quint? Yes—I don't mind that now."

She always ended, at these moments, by getting possession of my hand, and in this manner she could at present still stay me. But after gasping an instant at my sudden resignation, "Because of your letter?" she eagerly brought out.

I quickly, by way of answer, felt for my letter, drew it forth, held it up, and then, freeing myself, went and laid it on the great hall-table. "Luke will take it," I said as I came back. I reached the house-door and opened it; I was already on the steps.

My companion still demurred: the storm of the night and the early morning had dropped, but the afternoon was damp and grey. I came down to the drive while she stood in the doorway. "You go with nothing on?"

"What do I care when the child has nothing? I can't wait to dress," I cried, "and if you must do so, I leave you. Try meanwhile, yourself, upstairs."

"With *them?*" Oh, on this, the poor woman promptly joined me!

19

We went straight to the lake, as it was called at Bly, and I dare say rightly called, though I reflect that it may in fact have been a sheet of water less remarkable than it appeared to my untravelled eyes. My acquaintance with sheets of water was small, and the pool of Bly, at all events on the few occasions of my consenting, under the protection of my pupils, to affront its surface in the old flat-bottomed boat moored there for our use, had impressed me both with its extent and its agitation. The usual place of embarkation was half a mile from the house, but I had an intimate conviction that, wherever Flora might be, she was not near home. She had not given me the slip for any small adventure, and, since the day of the very great one that I had shared with her by the pond, I had been aware, in our walks, of the quarter to which she most inclined. This was why I had now given to Mrs. Grose's steps so marked a direction—a direction that made her, when she perceived it, oppose a resistance that showed me she was freshly mystified. "You're going to the water, Miss?—you think she's *in*—?"

"She may be, though the depth is, I believe, nowhere very great. But what I judge most likely is that she's on the spot from which, the other day, we saw together what I told you."

"When she pretended not to see—?"

"With that astounding self-possession! I've always been sure she wanted to go back alone. And now her brother has managed it for her."

Mrs. Grose still stood where she had stopped. "You suppose they really *talk* of them?"

I could meet this with a confidence! "They say things that, if we heard them, would simply appall us."

"And if she *is* there—?"

"Yes?"

"Then Miss Jessel is?"

"Beyond a doubt. You shall see."

"Oh, thank you!" my friend cried, planted so firm that, taking it in, I went straight on without her. By the time I reached the pool, however, she was close behind me, and I knew that, whatever, to her apprehension, might befall me, the exposure of my society struck her as her least danger. She exhaled a moan of relief as we at last came in sight of the greater part of the water without a sight of the child. There was no trace of Flora on that nearer side of the bank where my observation of her had been most startling, and none on the opposite edge, where, save for a margin of some twenty yards, a thick copse came down to the water. The pond, oblong in shape, had a width so scant compared to its length that, with its ends out of view, it might have been taken for a scant river. We looked at the empty expanse, and then I felt the suggestion of my friend's eyes. I knew what she meant and I replied with a negative headshake.

"No, no; wait! She has taken the boat."

My companion stared at the vacant mooring-place and then again across the lake. "Then where is it?"

"Our not seeing it is the strongest of proofs. She has used it to go over, and then has managed to hide it."

"All alone—that child?"

"She's not alone, and at such times she's not a child: she's an old, old woman." I scanned all the visible shore while Mrs. Grose took again, into the queer element I offered her, one of her plunges of submission; then I pointed out that the boat might perfectly be in a small refuge formed by one of the recesses of the pool, an indentation masked, for the hither side, by a projection of the bank and by a clump of trees growing close to the water.

"But if the boat's there, where on earth's *she?*" my colleague anxiously asked.

"That's exactly what we must learn." And I started to walk further.

"By going all the way around?"

"Certainly, far as it is. It will take us but ten minutes, but it's far enough to have made the child prefer not to walk. She went straight over."

"Laws!" cried my friend again; the chain of my logic was ever too much for her. It dragged her at my heels even now, and when we had got half-way round—a devious, tiresome process, on ground much broken and by a path choked with overgrowth—I paused to give her breath. I sustained her with a grateful arm, assuring her that she might hugely help me; and this started us afresh, so that in the course of but a few minutes more we reached a point from which we found the boat to be where I had supposed it. It had been intentionally left as much as possible out of sight and was tied to one of the stakes of a fence that came, just there, down to the brink and that had been an assistance to disembarking. I recognised, as I looked at the pair of short, thick oars, quite safely drawn up, the prodigious character of the feat for a little girl; but I had lived, by this time, too long among wonders and had panted to too many livelier measures. There was a gate in the fence, through which we passed, and that brought us, after a trifling interval, more into the open. Then, "There she is!" we both exclaimed at once.

Flora, a short way off, stood before us on the grass and smiled as if her performance was now complete. The next thing she did, however, was to stoop straight down and pluck—quite as if it were all she was there for—a big, ugly spray of withered fern. I instantly became sure she had just come out of the copse. She waited for us, not herself taking a step, and I was conscious of the rare solemnity with which we presently approached her. She smiled and smiled, and we met; but it was all done in a silence by this time flagrantly ominous. Mrs. Grose was the first to break the spell: she threw herself on her knees and, drawing the child to her breast, clasped in a long embrace the little tender, yielding body. While this dumb convulsion lasted I could only watch it—which I did the more intently when I saw Flora's face peep at me over our companion's shoulder. It was serious now—the flicker had left it; but it strengthened the pang with which I at that moment envied Mrs. Grose the simplicity of *her* relation. Still, all this while, nothing more passed between us save that Flora had let her foolish fern again drop to the ground. What she and I had virtually said to each other was that pretexts were useless now. When Mrs. Grose finally got up she kept the child's hand, so that the two were still before me; and the singular reticence of our communion was even more marked in the frank look she launched me. "I'll be hanged," it said, "if *I'll* speak!"

It was Flora who, gazing all over me in candid wonder, was the first. She was struck with our bareheaded aspect. "Why, where are your things?"

"Where yours are, my dear!" I promptly returned.

She had already got back her gaiety, and appeared to take this as an answer quite sufficient. "And where's Miles?" she went on.

There was something in the small valour of it that quite finished me: these three words from her were, in a flash like the glitter of a drawn blade, the jostle of the cup that my hand, for weeks and weeks, had held high and full to the brim and that now, even before speaking, I felt overflow in a deluge. "I'll tell you if you'll tell *me*—" I heard myself say, then heard the tremor in which it broke.

"Well, what?"

Mrs. Grose's suspense blazed at me, but it was too late now, and I brought the thing out handsomely. "Where, my pet, is Miss Jessel?"

20

Just as in the churchyard with Miles, the whole thing was upon us. Much as I had made of the fact that this name had never once, between us, been sounded, the quick, smitten glare with which the child's face now received it fairly likened my breach of the silence to the smash of a pane of glass. It added to the interposing cry, as if to stay the blow, that Mrs. Grose, at the same instant, uttered over my violence—the shriek of a creature scared, or rather wounded, which, in turn, within a few seconds, was completed by a gasp of my own. I seized my colleague's arm. "She's there, she's there!"

Miss Jessel stood before us on the opposite bank exactly as she had stood the other time, and I remember, strangely, as the first feeling now produced in me, my thrill of joy at having brought on a proof. She was there, and I was justified; she was there, and I was neither cruel nor mad. She was there for poor scared Mrs. Grose, but she was there most for Flora; and no moment of my monstrous time was perhaps so extraordinary as that in which I consciously threw out to her—with the sense that, pale and ravenous demon as she was, she would catch and understand it—an inarticulate message of gratitude. She rose erect on the spot my friend and I had lately quitted, and there was not, in all the long reach of her desire, an inch of her evil that fell short. This first vividness of vision and emotion were things of a few seconds, during which Mrs. Grose's dazed blink across to where I pointed struck me as a sovereign sign that she too at last saw, just as it carried my own eyes precipitately to the child. The revelation then of the manner in which Flora was affected startled me, in truth, far more than it would have done to find her also merely agitated, for direct dismay was of course not what I had expected. Prepared and on her guard as our pursuit had actually made her, she would repress every betrayal; and I was therefore shaken, on the spot, by my first glimpse of the particular one for which I had not allowed. To see her, without a convulsion of her small pink face, not even feign to glance in the direction of the prodigy I announced, but only, instead of that, turn at *me* an expression of hard, still gravity, an expression absolutely new and unprecedented and that appeared to read and accuse and judge me—this was a stroke that somehow converted the little girl herself into the very presence that could make me quail. I quailed even though my certitude that she thoroughly saw was never greater than at that instant, and in the immediate need to defend myself I called it passionately to witness. "She's there, you little unhappy thing—there, there, *there*, and you see her as well as you see me!" I had said shortly before to Mrs. Grose that she was not at these times a child, but an old, old woman, and that description of her could not have been more strikingly confirmed than in the way in which, for all answer to this, she simply showed me, without a concession, an admission, of her eyes, a countenance of deeper and deeper, of indeed suddenly quite fixed, reprobation. I was by this time—if I can put the whole thing at all together—more appalled at what I may properly call her manner than at anything else, though it was simultaneously with this that I became aware of having Mrs. Grose also, and very formidably, to reckon with. My elder companion, the next moment, at any rate, blotted out everything but her own flushed face and her loud, shocked protest, a burst of high disapproval. "What a dreadful turn, to be sure, Miss! Where on earth do you see anything?"

I could only grasp her more quickly yet, for even while she spoke the hideous plain presence stood undimmed and undaunted. It had already lasted a minute, and it lasted while I continued, seizing my colleague, quite thrusting her at it and presenting her to it, to insist with my pointing hand. "You don't see her exactly as *we* see?—you mean to say you don't now—*now*? She's as big as a blazing fire! Only look, dearest woman, *look*—!" She looked, even as I did, and gave me, with her deep groan of negation, repulsion, compassion—the mixture with her pity of her relief at her exemption—a sense, touching to me even then, that she would have backed me up if she could. I might well have needed that, for with this hard blow of the proof that her eyes were hopelessly sealed I felt my own situation horribly crumble, I felt —I saw—my livid predecessor press, from her position, on my defeat, and I was conscious, more than all, of what I should have from this instant to deal with in the astounding little attitude of Flora. Into this attitude Mrs. Grose immediately and violently entered, breaking, even while there pierced through my sense of ruin a prodigious private triumph, into breathless reassurance.

"She isn't there, little lady, and nobody's there—and you never see nothing, my sweet! How can poor Miss Jessel? when poor Miss Jessel's dead and buried? *We* know, don't we, love?"—and she appealed, blundering in, to the child. "It's all a mere mistake and a worry and a joke—and we'll go home as fast as we can!"

Our companion, on this, had responded with a strange, quick primness of propriety, and they were again, with Mrs. Grose on her feet, united, as it were, in pained opposition to me. Flora continued to fix me with her small mask of reprobation, and even at that minute I prayed God to forgive me for seeming to see that, as she stood there holding tight to our friend's dress, her incomparable childish beauty had suddenly failed, had quite vanished. I've said it already—she was literally, she was hideously, hard; she had turned common and almost ugly. "I don't know what you mean. I see nobody. I see nothing. I never *have*. I think you're cruel. I don't like you!" Then, after this deliverance, which might have been that of a vulgarly pert little girl in the street, she hugged Mrs. Grose more closely and buried in her skirts the dreadful little face. In this position she produced an almost furious wail. "Take me away, take me away—oh, take me away from *her*!"

"From *me*?" I panted.

"From you—from you!" she cried.

Even Mrs. Grose looked across at me dismayed, while I had nothing to do but communicate again with the figure that, on the opposite bank, without a movement, as rigidly still as if catching, beyond the interval, our voices, was as vividly there for my disaster as it was not there for my service. The wretched child had spoken exactly as if she had got from some outside source each of her stabbing little words, and I could therefore, in the full despair of all I had to accept, but sadly shake my head at her. "If I had ever doubted, all my doubt would at present have gone. I've been living with the miserable truth, and now it has only too much closed round me. Of course I've lost you: I've interfered, and you've seen—under *her* dictation"—with which I faced, over the pool again, our infernal witness—"the easy and perfect way to meet it. I've done my best, but I've lost you. Good-bye." For Mrs. Grose I had an imperative, an almost frantic "Go, go!" before which, in infinite distress, but mutely possessed of the little girl and clearly convinced, in spite of her blindness, that something awful had occurred and some collapse engulfed us, she retreated, by the way we had come, as fast as she could move.

Of what first happened when I was left alone I had no subsequent memory. I only knew that at the end of, I suppose, a quarter of an hour, an odorous dampness and roughness, chilling and piercing my trouble, had made me understand that I must have thrown myself, on my face, on the ground and given way to a wildness of grief. I must have lain there long and cried and sobbed, for when I raised my head the day was almost done. I got up and looked a moment, through the twilight, at the grey pool and its blank, haunted edge, and then I took, back to the house, my dreary and difficult course. When I reached the gate in the fence the boat, to my surprise, was gone, so that I had a fresh reflection to make on Flora's extraordinary command of the situation. She passed that night, by the most tacit, and I should add, were not the word so grotesque a false note, the happiest of arrangements, with Mrs. Grose. I saw neither of them on my return, but, on the other hand as by an ambiguous compensation, I saw a great deal of Miles. I saw—I can use no other phrase—so much of him that it was as if it were more than it had ever been. No evening I had passed at Bly had the portentous quality of this one; in spite of which—and in spite also of the deeper depths of consternation that had opened beneath my feet—there was literally, in the ebbing actual, an extraordinarily sweet sadness. On reaching the house I had never so much as looked for the boy; I had simply gone straight to my room to change what I was wearing and to take in, at a glance, much material testimony to Flora's rupture. Her little belongings had all been removed. When later, by the schoolroom fire, I was served with tea by the usual maid, I indulged, on the article of my other pupil, in no inquiry whatever. He had his freedom now—he might have it to the end! Well, he did have it; and it consisted—in part at least—of his coming in at about eight o'clock and sitting down with me in silence. On the removal of the tea-things I had blown out the candles and drawn my chair closer: I was conscious of a mortal coldness and felt as if I should never again be warm. So, when he appeared, I was sitting in the glow with my thoughts. He paused a moment by the door as if to look at me; then—as if to share them—came to the other side of the hearth and sank into a chair. We sat there in absolute stillness; yet he wanted, I felt, to be with me.

21

Before a new day, in my room, had fully broken, my eyes opened to Mrs. Grose, who had come to my bedside with worse news. Flora was so markedly feverish that an illness was perhaps at hand; she had passed a night of extreme unrest, a night agitated above all by fears that had for their subject not in the least her former, but wholly her present, governess. It was not against the possible re-entrance of Miss Jessel on the scene that she protested—it was conspicuously and passionately against mine. I was promptly on my feet of course, and with an immense deal to ask; the more that my friend had discernibly now girded her loins to meet me once more. This I felt as soon as I had put to her the question of her sense of the child's sincerity as against my own. "She persists in denying to you that she saw, or has ever seen, anything?"

My visitor's trouble, truly, was great. "Ah, Miss, it isn't a matter on which I can push her! Yet it isn't either, I must say, as if I much needed to. It has made her, every inch of her, quite old."

"Oh, I see her perfectly from here. She resents, for all the world like some high little personage, the imputation on her truthfulness and, as it were, her respectability. 'Miss Jessel indeed—*she!*' Ah, she's 'respectable,' the chit! The impression she gave me there yesterday was, I assure you, the very strangest of all; it was quite beyond any of the others. I *did* put my foot in it! She'll never speak to me again."

Hideous and obscure as it all was, it held Mrs. Grose briefly silent; then she granted my point with a frankness which, I made sure, had more behind it. "I think indeed, Miss, she never will. She do have a grand manner about it!"

"And that manner"—I summed it up—"is practically what's the matter with her now!"

Oh, that manner, I could see in my visitor's face, and not a little else besides! "She asks me every three minutes if I think you're coming in."

"I see—I see." I too, on my side, had so much more than worked it out. "Has she said to you since yesterday—except to repudiate her familiarity with anything so dreadful—a single other word about Miss Jessel?"

"Not one, Miss. And of course you know," my friend added, "I took it from her, by the lake, that, just then and there at least, there *was* nobody."

"Rather! And, naturally, you take it from her still."

"I don't contradict her. What else can I do?"

"Nothing in the world! You've the cleverest little person to deal with. They've made them—their two friends, I mean—still cleverer even then nature did; for it was wondrous material to play on! Flora has now her grievance, and she'll work it to the end."

"Yes, Miss; but to *what* end?"

"Why, that of dealing with me to her uncle. She'll make me out to him the lowest creature—!"

I winced at the fair show of the scene in Mrs. Grose's face; she looked for a minute as if she sharply saw them together. "And him who thinks so well of you!"

"He has an odd way—it comes over me now," I laughed, "—of proving it! But that doesn't matter. What Flora wants, of course, is to get rid of me."

My companion bravely concurred. "Never again to so much as look at you."

"So that what you've come to me now for," I asked, "is to speed me on my way?" Before she had time to reply, however, I had her in check. "I've a better idea—the result of my reflections. My going *would* seem the right thing, and on Sunday I was terribly near it. Yet that won't do. It's *you* who must go. You must take Flora."

My visitor, at this, did speculate. "But where in the world—?"

"Away from here. Away from *them*. Away, even most of all, now, from me. Straight to her uncle."

"Only to tell on you—?"

"No, not 'only'! To leave me, in addition, with my remedy."

She was still vague. "And what *is* your remedy?"

"Your loyalty, to begin with. And then Miles's."

She looked at me hard. "Do you think he—?"

"Won't if he has the chance, turn on me? Yes, I venture still to think it. At all events, I want to try. Get off with his sister as soon as possible and leave me with him alone." I was amazed, myself, at the spirit I had still in reserve, and therefore perhaps a trifle the more disconcerted at the way in which, in spite of this fine example of it, she hesitated. "There's one thing, of course," I went on: "they mustn't, before she goes, see each other for three seconds."

Then it came over me that, in spite of Flora's presumable sequestration from the instant of her return from the pool, it might already by too late. "Do you mean," I anxiously asked, "that they *have* met?"

At this she quite flushed. "Ah, Miss, I'm not such a fool as that! If I've been obliged to leave her three or four times, it has been each time with one of the maids, and at present, though she's alone, she's locked in safe. And yet—and yet!" There were too many things.

"And yet what?"

"Well, are you so sure of the little gentleman?"

"I'm not sure of anything but *you*. But I have, since last evening, a new hope. I think he wants to give me an opening. I do believe that—poor little exquisite wretch!—he wants to speak. Last evening, in the firelight and the silence, he sat with me for two hours as if it were just coming."

Mrs. Grose looked hard, through the window, at the grey, gathering day. "And did it come?"

"No, though I waited and waited, I confess it didn't, and it was without a breach of the silence or so much as a faint allusion to his sister's condition and absence that we at last kissed for good-night. All the same," I continued, "I can't, if her uncle sees her, consent to his seeing her brother without my having given the boy—and most of all because things have got so bad—a little more time."

My friend appeared on this ground more reluctant than I could quite understand. "What do you mean by more time?"

"Well, a day or two—really to bring it out. He'll then be on *my* side—of which you see the importance. If nothing comes, I shall only fail, and you will, at the worst, have helped me by doing, on your arrival in town, whatever you may have found possible." So I put it before her, but she continued for a little so inscrutably embarrassed that I came again to her aid. "Unless, indeed," I wound up, "you really want *not* to go."

I could see it, in her face, at last clear itself; she put out her hand to me as a pledge. "I'll go—I'll go. I'll go this morning."

I wanted to be very just. "If you *should* wish still to wait, I would engage she shouldn't see me."

"No, no: it's the place itself. She must leave it." She held me a moment with heavy eyes, then brought out the rest. "Your idea's the right one. I myself, Miss—"

"Well?"

"I can't stay."

The look she gave me with it made me jump at possibilities. "You mean that, since yesterday, you *have* seen—?"

She shook her head with dignity. "I've *heard*—!"

"Heard?"

"From that child—horrors! There!" she sighed with tragic relief. "On my honour, Miss, she says things—!" But at this evocation she broke down; she dropped, with a sudden sob, upon my sofa and, as I had seen her do before, gave way to all the grief of it.

It was quite in another manner that I, for my part, let myself go. "Oh, thank God!"

She sprang up again at this, drying her eyes with a groan. " 'Thank God'?"

"It so justifies me!"

"It does that, Miss!"

I couldn't have desired more emphasis, but I just hesitated. "She's so horrible?"

I saw my colleague scarce knew how to put it. "Really shocking."

"And about me?"

"About you, Miss—since you must have it. It's beyond everything, for a young lady; and I can't think wherever she must have picked up—"

"The appalling language she applied to me? I can, then!" I broke in with a laugh that was doubtless significant enough.

It only, in truth, left my friend still more grave. "Well, perhaps I ought to also—since I've heard some of it before! Yet I can't bear it," the poor woman went on while, with the same movement, she glanced, on my dressing-table, at the face of my watch. "But I must go back."

I kept her, however. "Ah, if you can't bear it—!"

"How can I stop with her, you mean? Why, just *for* that: to get her away. Far from this," she pursued, "far from *them*—"

"She may be different? she may be free?" I seized her almost with joy. "Then, in spite of yesterday, you *believe*—"

"In such doings?" Her simple description of them required, in the light of her expression, to be carried no further, and she gave me the whole thing as she had never done. "I believe."

Yes, it was a joy, and we were still shoulder to shoulder: if I might continue sure of that I should care but little what else happened. My support in the presence of disaster would be the same as it had been in my early need of confidence, and if my friend would answer for my honesty, I would answer for all the rest. On the point of taking leave of her, none the less, I was to some extent embarrassed. "There's one thing of course—it occurs to me—to remember. My letter, giving the alarm, will have reached town before you."

I now perceived still more how she had been beating about the bush and how weary at last it had made her. "Your letter won't have got there. Your letter never went."

"What then became of it?"

"Goodness knows! Master Miles—"

"Do you mean *he* took it?" I gasped.

She hung fire, but she overcame her reluctance, "I mean that I saw yesterday, when I came back with Miss Flora, that it wasn't where you had put it. Later in the evening I had the chance to question Luke, and he declared that he had neither noticed nor touched it." We could only exchange, on this, one of our deeper mutual soundings, and it was Mrs. Grose who first brought up the plumb with an almost elate "You see!"

"Yes, I see that if Miles took it instead he probably will have read it and destroyed it."

"And don't you see anything else?"

I faced her a moment with a sad smile. "It strikes me that by this time your eyes are open even wider than mine."

They proved to be so indeed, but she could still blush, almost, to show it. "I make out now what he must have done at school." And she gave, in her simple sharpness, an almost droll disillusioned nod. "He stole!"

I turned it over—I tried to be more judicial. "Well—perhaps."

She looked as if she found me unexpectedly calm. "He stole *letters!*"

She couldn't know my reasons for a calmness after all pretty shallow; so I showed them off as I might. "I hope then it was to more purpose than in this case! The note, at any rate, that I put on the table yesterday," I pursued, "will have given him so scant an advantage—for it contained only the bare demand for an interview—that he is already much ashamed of having gone so far for so little, and that what he had on his mind last evening was precisely the need of confession." I seemed to myself, for the instant, to have mastered it, to see it all. "Leave us, leave us"—I was already, at the door, hurrying her off. "I'll get it out of him. He'll meet me—he'll confess. If he confesses, he's saved. And if he's saved—"

"Then *you* are?" The dear woman kissed me on this, and I took her farewell. "I'll save you without him!" she cried as she went.

22

Yet it was when she had got off—and I missed her on the spot—that the great pinch really came. If I had counted on what it would give me to find myself alone with Miles, I speedily perceived, at least, that it would give me a measure. No hour of my stay in fact was so assailed with apprehensions as that of my coming down to learn that the carriage containing Mrs. Grose and my younger pupil had already rolled out of the gates. Now I *was*, I said to myself, face to face with the elements, and for much of the rest of the day, while I fought my weakness, I could consider that I had been supremely rash. It was a tighter place still than I had yet turned round in; all the more that, for the first time, I could see in the aspect of others a confused reflection of the crisis. What had happened naturally caused them all to stare; there was too little of the explained, throw out whatever we might, in the suddenness of my colleague's act. The maids and the men looked blank; the effect of which on my nerves was an aggravation until I saw the necessity of making it a positive aid. It was precisely, in short, by just clutching the helm that I avoided total wreck; and I dare say that, to bear up at all, I became, that morning, very grand and very dry. I welcomed the consciousness that I was charged with much to do, and I caused it to be known as well that, left thus to myself, I was quite remarkably firm. I wandered with that manner, for the next hour or two, all over the place and looked, I have no doubt, as if I were ready for any onset. So, for the benefit of whom it might concern, I paraded with a sick heart.

The person it appeared least to concern proved to be, till dinner, little Miles himself. My perambulations had given me meanwhile, no glimpse of him, but they had tended to make more public the change taking place in our relation as a consequence of his having at the piano, the day before, kept me, in Flora's interest, so beguiled and befooled. The stamp of publicity had of course been fully given by her confinement and departure, and the change itself was now ushered in by our non-observance of the regular custom of the schoolroom. He had already disappeared when, on my way down, I pushed open his door, and I learned below that he had breakfasted—in the presence of a couple of the maids—with Mrs. Grose and his sister. He had then gone out, as he said, for a stroll; than which nothing, I reflected, could better have expressed his frank view of the abrupt transformation of my office. What he would now permit this office to consist of was yet to be settled: there was a queer relief, at all events—I mean for myself in especial—in the renouncement of one pretension. If so much had sprung to the surface, I scarce put it too strongly in saying that what had perhaps sprung highest was the absurdity of our prolonging the fiction that I had anything more to teach him. It sufficiently stuck out that, by tacit little tricks in which even more than myself he carried out the care for my dignity, I had had to appeal to him to let me off straining to meet him on the ground of his true capacity. He had at any rate his freedom now; I was never to touch it again; as I had amply shown, moreover, when, on his joining me in the schoolroom the previous night, I had uttered, on the subject of the interval just concluded, neither challenge nor hint. I had too much, from this moment, my other ideas. Yet when he at last arrived the difficulty of applying them, the accumulations of my problem, were brought straight home to me by the beautiful little presence on which what had occurred had as yet, for the eye, dropped neither stain nor shadow.

To mark, for the house, the high state I cultivated I decreed that my meals with the boy should be served, as we called it, downstairs; so that I had been awaiting him in the ponderous pomp of the room outside of the window of which I had had from Mrs. Grose, that first scared Sunday, my flash of something it would scarce have done to call light. Here at present I felt afresh—for I had felt it again and again—how my equilibrium depended on the success of my rigid will, the will to shut my eyes as tight as possible to the truth that what I had to deal with was, revoltingly, against nature. I could only get on at all by taking "nature" into my confidence and my account, by treating my monstrous ordeal as a push in a direction unusual, of course, and unpleasant, but demanding, after all, for a fair front, only another turn of the screw of ordinary human virtue. No attempt, none the less, could well require more tact than just this attempt to supply, one's self, *all* the nature. How could I put even a little of that article into a suppression of reference to what had occurred? How, on the other hand, could I make a reference without a new plunge into the hideous obscure? Well, a sort of answer, after a time, had come to me, and it was so far confirmed as that I was met, incontestably, by the quickened vision of what was rare in my little companion. It was indeed as if he had found even now—as he had so often found at lessons—still some other delicate way to ease me off. Wasn't there light in the fact which, as we shared our solitude, broke out with a specious glitter it had never yet quite worn?—the fact that (opportunity aiding, precious opportunity which had now come) it would be preposterous, with a child so endowed, to forgo the help one might wrest from absolute intelligence? What had his intelligence been given him for but to save him? Mightn't one, to reach his mind, risk the stretch of an angular arm over his character? It was as if, when we were face to face in the dining-room, he had literally shown me the way. The roast mutton was on the table, and I had dispensed with attendance. Miles, before he sat down, stood a moment with his hands in his pockets and looked at the joint, on which he seemed on the point of passing some humorous judgment. But what he presently produced was: "I say, my dear, is she really very awfully ill?"

"Little Flora? Not so bad but that she'll presently be better. London will set her up. Bly had ceased to agree with her. Come here and take your mutton."

He alertly obeyed me, carried the plate carefully to his seat, and, when he was established, went on. "Did Bly disagree with her so terribly suddenly?"

"Not so suddenly as you might think. One had seen it coming on."

"Then why didn't you get her off before?"

"Before what?"

"Before she became too ill to travel."

I found myself prompt. "She's *not* too ill to travel: she only might have become so if she had stayed. This was just the moment to seize. The journey will dissipate the influence"—oh, I was grand!—"and carry it off."

"I see, I see"—Miles, for that matter, was grand too. He settled to his repast with the charming little "table manner" that, from the day of his arrival, had relieved me of all grossness of admonition. Whatever he had been driven from school for, it was not for ugly feeding. He was irreproachable, as always, today; but he was unmistakeably more conscious. He was discernibly trying to take for granted more things than he found, without assistance, quite easy; and he dropped into peaceful silence while he felt his situation. Our meal was of the briefest—mine a vain pretence, and I had the things immediately removed. While this was done Miles stood again with his hands in his little pockets and his back to me—stood and looked out of the wide window through which, that other day, I had seen what pulled me up. We continued silent while the maid was with us—as silent, it whimsically occurred to me, as some young couple who, on their wedding-journey, at the inn, feel shy in the presence of the waiter. He turned round only when the waiter had left us. "Well—so we're alone!"

23

"Oh, more or less." I fancy my smile was pale. "Not absolutely. We shouldn't like that!" I went on.

"No—I suppose we shouldn't. Of course we have the others."

"We have the others—we have indeed the others," I concurred.

"Yet even though we have them," he returned, still with his hands in his pockets and planted there in front of me, "they don't much count, do they?"

I made the best of it, but I felt wan. "It depends on what you call 'much'!"

"Yes"—with all accommodation—"everything depends!" On this, however, he faced to the window again and presently reached it with his vague, restless, cogitating step. He remained there awhile, with his forehead against the glass, in contemplation of the stupid shrubs I knew and the dull things of November. I had always my hypocrisy of "work," behind which, now, I gained the sofa. Steadying myself with it there as I had repeatedly done at those moments of torment that I have described as the moments of my knowing the children to be given to something from which I was barred, I sufficiently obeyed my habit of being prepared for the worst. But an extraordinary impression dropped on me as I extracted a meaning from the boy's embarrassed back—none other than the impression that I was not barred now. This inference grew in a few minutes to sharp intensity and seemed bound up with the direct perception that it was positively *he* who was. The frames and squares of the great window were a kind of image, for him, of a kind of failure. I felt that I saw him, at any rate, shut in or shut out. He was admirable, but not comfortable: I took it in with a throb of hope. Wasn't he looking, through the haunted pane, for something he couldn't see?—and wasn't it the first time in the whole business that he had known such a lapse? The first, the very first: I found it a splendid portent. It made him anxious, though he watched himself; he had been anxious all day and, even while in his usual sweet little manner he sat at table, had needed all his small strange genius to give it a gloss. When he at last turned round to meet me, it was almost as if this genius had succumbed. "Well, I think I'm glad Bly agrees with *me!*"

"You would certainly seem to have seen, these twenty-four hours, a good deal more of it than for some time before. I hope," I went on bravely, "that you've been enjoying yourself."

"Oh, yes, I've been ever so far; all round about—miles and miles away. I've never been so free."

He had really a manner of his own, and I could only try to keep up with him. "Well, do you like it?"

He stood there smiling; then at last he put into two words—"Do *you?*"—more discrimination than I had ever heard two words contain. Before I had time to deal with that, however, he continued as if with the sense that this was an impertinence to be softened. "Nothing could be more charming than the way you take it, for of course if we're alone together now it's you that are alone most. But I hope," he threw in, "you don't particularly mind!"

"Having to do with you?" I asked. "My dear child, how can I help minding? Though I've renounced all claim to your company,—you're so beyond me,—I at least greatly enjoy it. What else should I stay on for?"

He looked at me more directly, and the expression of his face, graver now, struck me as the most beautiful I had ever found in it. "You stay on just for *that*?"

"Certainly. I stay on as your friend and from the tremendous interest I take in you till something can be done for you that may be more worth your while. That needn't surprise you." My voice trembled so that I felt it impossible to suppress the shake. "Don't you remember how I told you, when I came and sat on your bed the night of the storm, that there was nothing in the world I wouldn't do for you?"

"Yes, yes!" He, on his side, more and more visibly nervous, had a tone to master; but he was so much more successful than I that, laughing out through his gravity, he could pretend we were pleasantly jesting. "Only that, I think, was to get me to do something for *you!*"

"It was partly to get you to do something," I conceded. "But, you know, you didn't do it."

"Oh, yes," he said with the brightest superficial eagerness, "you wanted me to tell you something."

"That's it. Out, straight out. What you have on your mind, you know."

"Ah, then, is *that* what you've stayed over for?"

He spoke with a gaiety through which I could still catch the finest little quiver of resentful passion; but I can't begin to express the effect upon me of an implication of surrender even so faint. It was as if what I had yearned for had come at last only to astonish me. "Well, yes—I may as well make a clean breast of it. It was precisely for that."

He waited so long that I supposed it for the purpose of repudiating the assumption on which my action had been founded; but what he finally said was: "Do you mean now—here?"

"There couldn't be a better place or time." He looked round him uneasily, and I had the rare—oh, the queer!—impression of the very first symptom I had seen in him of the approach of immediate fear. It was as if he were suddenly afraid of me—which struck me indeed as perhaps the best thing to make him. Yet in the very pang of the effort I felt it vain to try sternness, and I heard myself the next instant so gentle as to be almost grotesque. "You want so to go out again?"

"Awfully!" He smiled at me heroically, and the touching little bravery of it was enhanced by his actually flushing with pain. He had picked up his hat, which he had brought in, and stood twirling it in a way that gave me, even as I was just nearly reaching port, a perverse horror of what I was doing. To do it in *any* way was an act of violence, for what did it consist of but the obtrusion of the idea of grossness and guilt on a small helpless creature who had been for me a revelation of the possibilities of beautiful intercourse? Wasn't it base to create for a being so exquisite a mere alien awkwardness? I suppose I now read into our situation a clearness it couldn't have had at the time, for I seem to see our poor eyes already lighted with some spark of a prevision of the anguish that was to come. So we circled about, with terrors and scruples, like fighters not daring to close. But it was for each other we feared! That kept us a little longer suspended and unbruised. "I'll tell you everything," Miles said —"I mean I'll tell you anything you like. You'll stay on with me, and we shall both be all right and I *will* tell you—I *will*. But not now."

"Why not now?"

My insistence turned him from me and kept him once more at his window in a silence during which, between us, you might have heard a pin drop. Then he was before me again with the air of a person for whom, outside, someone who had frankly to be reckoned with was waiting. "I have to see Luke."

I had not yet reduced him to quite so vulgar a lie, and I felt proportionately ashamed. But, horrible as it was, his lies made up my truth. I achieved thoughtfully a few loops of my knitting. "Well, then, go to Luke, and I'll wait for what you promise. Only, in return for that, satisfy, before you leave me, one very much smaller request."

He looked as if he felt he had succeeded enough to be able still a little to bargain. "Very much smaller—?"

"Yes, a mere fraction of the whole. Tell me"—oh, my work preoccupied me, and I was off-hand!—"if, yesterday afternoon, from the table in the hall, you took, you know, my letter."

24

My sense of how he received this suffered for a minute from something that I can describe only as a fierce split of my attention—a stroke that at first, as I sprang straight up, reduced me to the mere blind movement of getting hold of him, drawing him close, and, while I just fell for support against the nearest piece of furniture, instinctively keeping him with his back to the window. The appearance was full upon us that I had already had to deal with here: Peter Quint had come into view like a sentinel before a prison. The next thing I saw was that, from outside, he had reached the window, and then I knew that, close to the glass and glaring in through it, he offered once more to the room his white face of damnation. It represents but grossly what took place within me at the sight to say that on the second my decision was made; yet I believe that no woman so overwhelmed ever in so short a time recovered her grasp of the *act*. It came to me in the very horror of the immediate presence that the act would be, seeing and facing what I saw and faced, to keep the boy himself unaware. The inspiration—I can call it by no other name— was that I felt how voluntarily, how transcendently, I *might*. It was like fighting with a demon for a human soul, and when I had fairly so appraised it I saw how the human soul—held out, in the tremor of my hands, at arm's length—had a perfect dew of sweat on a lovely childish forehead. The face that was close to mine was as white as the face against the glass, and out of it presently came a sound, not low nor weak, but as if from much further away, that I drank like a waft of fragrance.

"Yes—I took it."

At this, with a moan of joy, I enfolded, I drew him close; and while I held him to my breast, where I could feel in the sudden fever of his little body the tremendous pulse of his little heart, I kept my eyes on the thing at the window and saw it move and shift its posture. I have likened it to a sentinel, but its slow wheel, for a moment, was rather the prowl of a baffled beast. My present quickened courage, however, was such that, not too much to let it through, I had to shade, as it were, my flame. Meanwhile the glare of the face was again at the window, the scoundrel fixed as if to watch and wait. It was the very confidence that I might now defy him, as well as the positive certitude, by this time, of the child's unconsciousness, that made me go on. "What did you take it for?"

"To see what you said about me."

"You opened the letter?"

"I opened it."

My eyes were now, as I held him off a little again, on Miles's own face, in which the collapse of mockery showed me how complete was the ravage of uneasiness. What was prodigious was that at last, by my success, his sense was sealed and his communication stopped: he knew that he was in presence, but knew not of what, and knew still less that I also was and that I did know. And what did this strain of trouble matter when my eyes went back to the window only to see that the air was clear again and—by my personal triumph—the influence quenched? There was nothing there. I felt that the cause was mine and that I should surely get *all*. "And you found nothing!"—I let my elation out.

He gave the most mournful, thoughtful little headshake. "Nothing."

"Nothing, nothing!" I almost shouted in my joy.

"Nothing, nothing," he sadly repeated.

I kissed his forehead; it was drenched. "So what have you done with it?"

"I've burnt it."

"Burnt it?" It was now or never. "Is that what you did at school?"

Oh, what this brought up! "At school?"

"Did you take letters?—or other things?"

"Other things?" He appeared now to be thinking of something far off and that reached him only through the pressure of his anxiety. Yet it did reach him. "Did I *steal*?"

I felt myself redden to the roots of my hair as well as wonder if it were more strange to put to a gentleman such a question or to see him take it with allowances that gave the very distance of his fall in the world. "Was it for that you mightn't go back?"

The only thing he felt was rather a dreary little surprise. "Did you know I mightn't go back?"

"I know everything."

He gave me at this the longest and strangest look. "Everything?"

"Everything. Therefore *did* you—?" But I couldn't say it again.

Miles could, very simply. "No. I didn't steal."

My face must have shown him I believed him utterly; yet my hands—

but it was for pure tenderness—shook him as if to ask him why, if it was all for nothing, he had condemned me to months of torment. "What then did you do?"

He looked in vague pain all round the top of the room and drew his breath, two or three times over, as if with difficulty. He might have been standing at the bottom of the sea and raising his eyes to some faint green twilight. "Well—I said things."

"Only that?"

"They thought it was enough!"

"To turn you out for?"

Never, truly, had a person "turned out" shown so little to explain it as this little person! He appeared to weigh my question, but in a manner quite detached and almost helpless. "Well, I suppose I oughtn't."

"But to whom did you say them?"

He evidently tried to remember, but it dropped—he had lost it. "I don't know!"

He almost smiled at me in the desolation of his surrender, which was indeed practically, by this time, so complete that I ought to have left it there. But I was infatuated—I was blind with victory, though even then the very effect that was to have brought him so much nearer was already that of added separation. "Was it to everyone?" I asked.

"No; it was only to—" But he gave a sick little headshake. "I don't remember their names."

"Were they then so many?"

"No—only a few. Those I liked."

Those he liked? I seemed to float not into clearness, but into a darker obscure, and within a minute there had come to me out of my very pity the appalling alarm of his being perhaps innocent. It was for the instant confounding and bottomless, for if he *were* innocent, what then on earth was I? Paralysed, while it lasted, by the mere brush of the question, I let him go a little, so that, with a deep-drawn sigh, he turned away from me again; which, as he faced toward the clear window, I suffered, feeling that I had nothing now there to keep him from. "And did they repeat what you said?" I went on after a moment.

He was soon at some distance from me, still breathing hard and again with the air, though now without anger for it, of being confined against his will. Once more, as he had done before, he looked up at the dim day as if, of what had hitherto sustained him, nothing was left but an unspeakable anxiety. "Oh, yes," he nevertheless replied—"they must have repeated them. To those *they* liked," he added.

There was, somehow, less of it than I had expected; but I turned it over. "And these things came round—?"

"To the masters? Oh, yes!" he answered very simply. "But I didn't know they'd tell."

"The masters? They didn't—they've never told. That's why I ask you."

He turned to me again his little beautiful fevered face. "Yes, it was too bad."

"Too bad?"

"What I suppose I sometimes said. To write home."

I can't name the exquisite pathos of the contradiction given to such a speech by such a speaker; I only know that the next instant I heard myself throw off with homely force: "Stuff and nonsense!" But the next after that I must have sounded stern enough. "What were these things?"

My sternness was all for his judge, his executioner; yet it made him avert himself again, and that movement made *me*, with a single bound and an irrepressible cry, spring straight upon him. For there again, against the glass, as if to blight his confession and stay his answer, was the hideous author of our woe—the white face of damnation. I felt a sick swim at the drop of my victory and all the return of my battle, so that the wildness of my veritable leap only served as a great betrayal. I saw him, from the midst of my act, meet it with a divination, and on the perception that even now he only guessed, and that the window was still to his own eyes free, I let the impulse flame up to convert the climax of his dismay into the very proof of his liberation. "No more, no more, no more!" I shrieked, as I tried to press him against me, to my visitant.

"Is she *here*?" Miles panted as he caught with his sealed eyes the direction of my words. Then as his strange "she" staggered me and, with a gasp, I echoed it, "Miss Jessel, Miss Jessel!" he with a sudden fury gave me back.

I seized, stupefied, his supposition—some sequel to what we had done to Flora, but this made me only want to show him that it was better still than that. "It's not Miss Jessel! But it's at the window—straight before us. It's *there*—the coward horror, there for the last time!"

At this, after a second in which his head made the movement of a baffled dog's on a scent and then gave a frantic little shake for air and light, he was at me in a white rage, bewildered, glaring vainly over the place and missing wholly, though it now, to my sense, filled the room like the taste of poison, the wide, overwhelming presence. "It's *he*?"

I was so determined to have all my proof that I flashed into ice to challenge him. "Whom do you mean by 'he'?"

"Peter Quint—you devil!" His face gave again, round the room, its convulsed supplication. "*Where*?"

They are in my ears still, his supreme surrender of the name and his tribute to my devotion. "What does he matter now, my own?—what will he *ever* matter? *I* have you," I launched at the beast, "but he has lost you for ever!" Then, for the demonstration of my work, "There, *there*!" I said to Miles.

But he had already jerked straight round, stared, glared again, and seen but the quiet day. With the stroke of the loss I was so proud of he uttered the cry of a creature hurled over an abyss, and the grasp with which I recovered him might have been that of catching him in his fall. I caught him, yes, I held him—it may be imagined with what a passion; but at the end of a minute I began to feel what it truly was that I held. We were alone with the quiet day, and his little heart, dispossessed, had stopped.

1898

Henry James a most conscious artist—
Here are notes:
1. James a careful thinker about the nature & reality
2. the nature of art
3. and the relationship between the two.

THE ART OF FICTION

I SHOULD NOT have affixed so comprehensive a title to these few remarks, necessarily wanting in any completeness upon a subject the full consideration of which would carry us far, did I not seem to discover a pretext for my temerity in the interesting pamphlet lately published under this name by Mr. Walter Besant.[1] Mr. Besant's lecture at the Royal Institution—the original form of his pamphlet—appears to indicate that many persons are interested in the art of fiction, and are not indifferent to such remarks, as those who practise it may attempt to make about it. I am therefore anxious not to lose the benefit of this favourable association, and to edge in a few words under cover of the attention which Mr. Besant is sure to have excited. There is something very encouraging in his having put into form certain of his ideas on the mystery of story-telling.

It is a proof of life and curiosity—curiosity on the part of the brotherhood of novelists as well as on the part of their readers. Only a short time ago it might have been supposed that the English novel was not what the French call *discutable*. It had no air of having a theory, a conviction, a consciousness of itself behind it—of being the expression of an artistic faith, the result of choice and comparison. I do not say it was necessarily the worse for that: it would take much more courage than I possess to intimate that the form of the novel as Dickens and Thackeray (for instance) saw it had any taint of incompleteness. It was, however, *naïf* (if I may help myself out with another French word); and evidently if it be destined to suffer in any way for having lost its *naïveté* it has now an idea of making sure of the corresponding advantages. During the period I have alluded to there was a comfortable, good-humoured feeling abroad that a novel is a novel, as a pudding is a pudding, and that our only business with it could be to swallow it. But within a year or two, for some reason or other, there have been signs of returning animation—the era of discussion would appear to have been to a certain extent opened. Art lives upon discussion, upon experiment, upon curiosity, upon variety of attempt, upon the exchange of views and the comparison of standpoints; and there is a presumption that those times when no one has anything particular to say about it, and has no reason to give for practice or preference, though they may be times of honour, are not times of development—are times, possibly even, a little of dulness. The successful application of any art is a delightful spectacle, but the theory too is interesting; and though there is a great deal of the latter without the former I suspect there has never been a genuine success that has not had a latent core of conviction. Discussion, suggestion, formulation, these things are fertilising when they are frank and sincere. Mr. Besant has set an excellent example in say-

debatable
&

---

[1] A minor British novelist (1836-1901).

Belief: "Reality" as a story presents it, was twice translated, once through the author's experiencing of it, and again through the artistic representation of it. Both the initial impression and the execution were important.

ing what he thinks, for his part about the way in which fiction should be written, as well as about the way in which it should be published; for his view of the "art," carried on into an appendix, covers that too. Other labourers in the same field will doubtless take up the argument, they will give it the light of their experience, and the effect will surely be to make our interest in the novel a little more what it had for some time threatened to fail to be—a serious, active, inquiring interest under protection of which this delightful study may, in moments of confidence, venture to say a little more what it thinks of itself.

It must take itself seriously for the public to take it so. The old superstition about fiction being "wicked" has doubtless died out in England; but the spirit of it lingers in a certain oblique regard directed toward any story which does not more or less admit that it is only a joke. Even the most jocular novel feels in some degree the weight of the proscription that was formerly directed against literary levity: the jocularity does not always succeed in passing for orthodoxy. It is still expected, though perhaps people are ashamed to say it, that a production which is after all only a "make-believe" (for what else is a "story"?) shall be in some degree apologetic—shall renounce the pretension of attempting really to represent life. This, of course, any sensible, wide-awake story declines to do, for it quickly perceives that the tolerance granted to it on such a condition is only an attempt to stifle it disguised in the form of generosity. The old evangelical hostility to the novel, which was as explicit as it was narrow, and which regarded it as little less favourable to our immortal part than a stage-play, was in reality far less insulting. The only reason for the existence of a novel is that it does attempt to represent life. When it relinquishes this attempt, the same attempt that we see on the canvas of the painter, it will have arrived at a very strange pass. It is not expected of the picture that it will make itself humble in order to be forgiven; and the analogy between the art of the painter and the art of the novelist is, so far as I am able to see, complete. Their inspiration is the same, their process (allowing for the different quality of the vehicle), is the same, their success is the same. They may learn from each other, they may explain and sustain each other. Their cause is the same, and the honour of one is the honour of another. The Mahometans think a picture an unholy thing, but it is a long time since any Christian did, and it is therefore the more odd that in the Christian mind the traces (dissimulated though they may be) of a suspicion of the sister art should linger to this day. The only effectual way to lay it to rest is to emphasise the analogy to which I just alluded—to insist on the fact that as the picture is reality, so the novel is history. That is the only general description (which does it justice) that we may give of the novel. But history also is allowed to represent life; it is not, any more than painting, expected to apologise. The subject-matter of fiction is stored up likewise in documents and records, and if it will not give itself away, as they say in California, it must speak with assurance, with the tone of the historian. Certain accomplished novelists have a habit of giving themselves away which much often bring tears to the eyes of people who take their fiction seriously. I was lately struck, in reading over many pages of Anthony Trollope, with his want of discretion in this particular. In a degression, a parenthesis or an aside, he concedes to the reader that he and this trusting friend are only "making believe." He admits that the events he narrates have not really happened, and that he can give his narrative any turn the reader may like best. Such a betrayal of a sacred office seems to me, I confess, a terrible crime; it is what I mean by the attitude of apology, and it shocks me every whit as much in Trollope as it would have shocked me in Gibbon or Macaulay. It implies that the novelist is less occupied in looking for the truth (the truth, of course I mean, that he assumes, the premises that we must grant him, whatever they may be), than the historian, and in doing so it deprives him at a stroke of all his standing-room. To represent and illustrate the past, the actions of men, is the task of either writer, and the only difference that I can see is, in proportion as he succeeds, to the honour of the novelist, consisting as it does in his having more difficulty in collecting his evidence, which is so far from being purely literary. It seems to me to give him a great character, the fact that he has at once so much in common with the philosopher and the painter; this double analogy is a magnificent heritage.

It is of all this evidently that Mr. Besant is full when he insists upon the fact that fiction is one of the *fine* arts, deserving in its turn of all the honours and emoluments that have hitherto been reserved for the successful profession of music, poetry, painting, architecture. It is impossible to insist too much on so important a truth, and the place that Mr. Besant demands for the work of the novelist may be represented, a trifle less abstractly, by saying that he demands not only that it shall be reputed artistic, but that it shall be reputed very artistic indeed. It is excellent that he should have struck this note, for his doing so indicates that there was need of it, that his proposition may be to many people a novelty. One rubs one's eyes at the thought; but the rest of Mr. Besant's essay confirms the revelation. I suspect in truth that it would be possible to confirm it still further, and that one would not be far wrong in saying that in addition to the people to whom it has never occurred that a novel ought to be artistic, there are a great many others who, if this principle were urged upon them, would be filled with an indefinable mistrust. They would find it difficult to explain their repugnance, but it would operate strongly to put them on their guard. "Art," in our Protestant communities, where so many things have got so strangely twisted about, is supposed in certain circles to have some vaguely injurious effect upon those who make it an important consideration, who let it weigh in the balance. It is assumed to be opposed in some mysterious manner to morality, to amusement, to instruction. When it is embodied in the work of the painter (the sculptor is another affair!) you know what it is: it stands there before you, in the honesty of pink and green and a gilt frame; you can see the worst of it at a glance, and you can be on your guard. But when it is introduced into literature it becomes more insidious—there is danger of its hurting you before you know it. Literature should be either instructive or amusing, and there is in many minds an impression that these artistic preoccupations, the search for form, contribute to neither end, interfere indeed with both. They are too frivolous to be edifying, and too serious to be diverting; and they are moreover priggish and paradoxical and superfluous. That, I think, represents the manner in which the latent thought of many people who read novels as an exercise in skipping would explain itself if it were to become articulate. They would argue, of course, that a novel ought to be "good," but they would interpret this term in a fashion of their own, which indeed would vary considerably from one critic to another. One would say that being good means representing virtuous and aspiring characters, placed in prominent positions; another would say that it depends on a "happy ending," on a distribution at the last of prizes, pensions, husbands, wives, babies, millions, appended paragraphs, and cheerful remarks. Another still would say that it means being full of incident and movement, so that we shall wish to jump ahead, to see who was the mysterious stranger, and if the stolen will was ever found, and shall not be distracted from this pleasure by any tiresome analysis or "description." But they would all agree that the "artistic" idea would spoil some of their fun. One would hold it accountable for all the description, another would see it revealed in the absence of sympathy. Its hostility to a happy ending would be evident, and it might even in some cases render any ending at all impossible. The "ending" of a novel is, for many persons, like that of a good dinner, a course of dessert and ices, and the artist in fiction is regarded as a sort of meddlesome doctor who forbids agreeable aftertastes. It is therefore true that this conception of Mr. Besant's of the novel as a superior form encounters not only a negative but a positive indifference. It matters little that as a work of art it should really be as little or as much of its essence to supply happy endings, sympathetic characters, and an objective tone, as if it were a work of mechanics: the association of ideas, however incongruous, might easily be too much for it if an eloquent voice were not sometimes raised to call attention to the fact that it is at once as free and as serious a branch of literature as any other.

Certainly this might sometimes be doubted in presence of the enormous number of works of fiction that appeal to the credulity of our generation, for it might easily seem that there could be no great character in a commodity so quickly and easily produced. It must be admitted that good novels are much compromised by bad ones, and that the field at large suffers discredit from overcrowding. I think, however, that this injury is only superficial, and that the superabundance of written fiction proves nothing against the principle itself. It has been vulgarised, like all other kinds of literature, like everything else to-day, and it has proved more than some kinds accessible to vulgarisation. But there is as much difference as there ever was between a good novel and a bad one: the bad is swept with all the daubed canvases and spoiled marble into some unvisited limbo, or infinite rubbish-yard beneath the back-windows of the world, and the good subsists and emits its light and stimulates our desire for perfection. As I shall take the liberty of making but a single criticism of Mr. Besant, whose tone is so full of the love of his art, I may as well have done with it at once. He seems to me to mistake in attempting to say so definitely beforehand what sort of an affair the good novel will be. To indicate the danger of such an error as that has been the purpose of these few pages; to suggest that certain traditions on the subject, applied a priori, have already had much to answer for, and that the good health of an art which undertakes so immediately to reproduce life must demand that it be perfectly free. It lives upon exercise, and the very meaning of exercise is freedom. The only obligation to which in advance we may hold a novel, without incurring the accusation of being arbitrary, is that it be interesting. That general responsibility rests upon it, but it is the only one I can think of. The ways in which it is at liberty to accomplish this result (of interesting us) strike me as innumerable, and such as can only suffer from being marked out or fenced in by prescription. They are as various as the temperament of man, and they are successful in proportion as they reveal a particular mind, different from others. A novel is in its broadest definition a personal, a direct impression of life: that, to begin with, constitutes its value, which is greater or less according to the intensity of the impression. But there will be no intensity at all, and therefore no value, unless there is freedom to feel and say. The tracing of a line to be followed, of a tone to be taken, of a form to be filled out, is a limitation of that freedom and a suppression of the very thing that we are most curious about. The form, it seems to me, is to be appreciated after the fact: then the author's choice has been made, his standard has been indicated; then we can follow lines and directions and compare tones and resemblances. Then in a word we can enjoy one of the most charming of pleasures, we can estimate quality, we can apply the test of execution. The execution belongs to the author alone; it is what is most personal to him, and we measure him by that. The advantage, the luxury, as well as the torment and responsibility of the novelist, is that there is no limit to what he may attempt as an executant—no limit to his possible experiments, efforts, discoveries, successes. Here it is especially that he works, step by step, like his brother of the brush, of whom we may always say that he has painted his picture in a manner best known to himself. His manner is his secret, not necessarily a jealous one. He cannot disclose it as a general thing if he would; he would be at a loss to teach it to others. I say this with a due recollection of having insisted on the community of method of the artist who paints a picture and the artist who writes a novel. The painter *is* able to teach the rudiments of his practice, and it is possible, from the study of good work (granted the aptitude), both to learn how to paint and to learn how to write. Yet it remains true, without injury to the *rapprochement*, that the literary artist would be obliged to say to his pupil much more than the other, "Ah, well, you must do it as you can!" It is a question of degree, a matter of delicacy. If there are exact sciences, there are also exact arts, and the grammar of painting is so much more definite that it makes the difference.

I ought to add, however, that if Mr. Besant says at the beginning of his essay that the "laws of fiction may be laid down and taught with as much precision and exactness as the laws of harmony, perspective, and proportion," he mitigates what might appear to be an extravagance by applying his remark to "general" laws, and by expressing most of these rules in a manner with which it would certainly be unaccommodating to disagree. That the novelist must write from his experience, that his "characters must be real and such as might be met with in actual life"; that "a young lady brought up in a quiet country village should avoid descriptions of garrison life," and "a writer whose friends and personal experiences belong to the lower middle-class should carefully avoid introducing his characters into society"; that one should enter one's notes in a common-place book; that one's figures should be clear in outline; that making them clear by some trick of speech or of carriage is a bad method, and "describing them at length" is a worse one; that English Fiction should have a "conscious moral purpose"; that "it is almost impossible to estimate too highly the value of careful workmanship—that is, of style"; that "the most important point of all is the story," that "the story is every-thing": these are principles with most of which it is surely impossible not to sympathise. That remark about the lower middle-class writer and his knowing his place is perhaps rather chilling; but for the rest I should find it difficult to dissent from any one of these recommendations. At the same time, I should find it difficult positively to assent to them, with the exception, perhaps, of the injunction as to entering one's notes in a common-place book. They scarcely seem to me to have the quality that Mr. Besant attributes to the rules of the novelist—the "precision and exactness" of "the laws of har-mony, perspective, and proportion." They are suggestive, they are even in-spiring, but they are not exact, though they are doubtless as much so as the case admits of: which is a proof of that liberty of interpretation for which I just contended. For the value of these different injunctions—so beautiful and so vague—is wholly in the meaning one attaches to them. The characters, the situation, which strike one as real will be those that touch and interest one most, but the measure of reality is very difficult to fix. The reality of Don Quixote or of Mr. Micawber is a very delicate shade; it is a reality so coloured by the author's vision that, vivid as it may be, one would hesi-tate to propose it as a model: one would expose one's self to some very em-barrassing questions on the part of a pupil. It goes without saying that you will not write a good novel unless you possess the sense of reality; but it will be difficult to give you a recipe for calling that sense into being. Hu-manity is immense, and reality has a myriad forms; the most one can affirm is that some of the flowers of fiction have the odour of it, and others have not; as for telling you in advance how your nosegay should be composed, that is another affair. It is equally excellent and inconclusive to say that one must write from experience; to our supposititious aspirant such a declaration might savour of mockery. What kind of experience is intended, and where does it begin and end? Experience is never limited, and it is never complete; it is an immense sensibility, a kind of huge spider-web of the finest silken threads suspended in the chamber of consciousness, and catching every air-borne par-ticle in its tissue. It is the very atmosphere of the mind; and when the mind is imaginative—much more when it happens to be that of a man of genius—it takes to itself the faintest hints of life, it converts the very pulses of the air into revelations. The young lady living in a village has only to be a damsel upon whom nothing is lost to make it quite unfair (as it seems to me) to de-clare to her that she shall have nothing to say about the military. Greater miracles have been seen than that, imagination assisting, she should speak the truth about some of these gentlemen. I remember an English novelist,[2] a woman of genius, telling me that she was much commended for the im-pression she had managed to give in one of her tales of the nature and way of life of the French Protestant youth. She had been asked where she learned

Dickens'
David
Copperfield

[2] Thackeray's daughter, Lady Ritchie, wrote a novel (*The Story of Elizabeth*) that fits this description.

so much about this recondite being, she had been congratulated on her peculiar opportunities. These opportunities consisted in her having once, in Paris, as she ascended a staircase, passed an open door where, in the household of a *pasteur,* some of the young Protestants were seated at table round a finished meal. The glimpse made a picture; it lasted only a moment, but that moment was experience. She had got her direct personal impression, and she turned out her type. She knew what youth was, and what Protestantism; she also had the advantage of having seen what it was to be French, so that she converted these ideas into a concrete image and produced a reality. Above all, however, she was blessed with the faculty which when you give it an inch takes an ell, and which for the artist is a much greater source of strength than any accident of residence or of place in the social scale. The power to guess the unseen from the seen, to trace the implication of things, to judge the whole piece by the pattern, the condition of feeling life in general so completely that you are well on your way to knowing any particular corner of it —this cluster of gifts may almost be said to constitute experience, and they occur in country and in town, and in the most differing stages of education. If experience consists of impressions, it may be said that impressions *are* experience, just as (have we not seen it?) they are the very air we breathe. Therefore, if I should certainly say to a novice, "Write from experience and experience only," I should feel that this was rather a tantalising monition if I were not careful immediately to add, "Try to be one of the people on whom nothing is lost!"

I am far from intending by this to minimise the importance of exactness—of truth of detail. One can speak best from one's own taste, and I may therefore venture to say that the air of reality (solidity of specification) seems to me to be the supreme virtue of a novel—the merit on which all its other merits (including that conscious moral purpose of which Mr. Besant speaks) helplessly and submissively depend. If it be not there they are all as nothing, and if these be there, they owe their effect to the success with which the author has produced the illusion of life. The cultivation of this success, the study of this exquisite process, form, to my taste, the beginning and the end of the art of the novelist. They are his inspiration, his despair, his reward, his torment, his delight. It is here in very truth that he competes with life; it is here that he competes with his brother the painter in *his* attempt to render the look of things, the look that conveys their meaning, to catch the colour, the relief, the expression, the surface, the substance of the human spectacle. It is in regard to this that Mr. Besant is well inspired when he bids him take notes. He cannot possibly take too many, he cannot possibly take enough. All life solicits him, and to "render" the simplest surface, to produce the most momentary illusion, is a very complicated business. His case would be easier, and the rule would be more exact, if Mr. Besant had been able to tell him what notes to take. But this, I fear, he can never learn in any manual; it is the business of his life. He has to take a great many in order to select a few, he has to work them up as he can, and even the guides and philosophers who might have most to say to him must leave him alone when it comes to the application of precepts, as we leave the painter in communion with his palette. That his characters "must be clear in outline," as Mr. Besant says—he feels

[handwritten annotation: "A novel, in its broadest definition was a personal, a direct impression ∦ life"]

that down to his boots; but how he shall make them so is a secret between his good angel and himself. It would be absurdly simple if he could be taught that a great deal of "description" would make them so, or that on the contrary the absence of description and the cultivation of dialogue, or the absence of dialogue and the multiplication of "incident," would rescue him from his difficulties. Nothing, for instance, is more possible than that he be of a turn of mind for which this odd, literal opposition of description and dialogue, incident and description, has little meaning and light. People often talk of these things as if they had a kind of internecine distinctness, instead of melting into each other at every breath, and being intimately associated parts of one general effort of expression. I cannot imagine composition existing in a series of blocks, nor conceive, in any novel worth discussing at all, of a passage of description that is not in its intention narrative, a passage of dialogue that is not in its intention descriptive, a touch of truth of any sort that does not partake of the nature of incident, or an incident that derives its interest from any other source than the general and only source of the success of a work of art—that of being illustrative. A novel is a living thing, all one and continuous, like any other organism, and in proportion as it lives will it be found, I think, that in each of the parts there is something of each of the other parts. The critic who over the close texture of a finished work shall pretend to trace a geography of items will mark some frontiers as artificial, I fear, as any that have been known to history. There is an old-fashioned distinction between the novel of character and the novel of incident which must have cost many a smile to the intending fabulist who was keen about his work. It appears to me as little to the point as the equally celebrated distinction between the novel and the romance—to answer as little to any reality. There are bad novels and good novels, as there are bad pictures and good pictures; but that is the only distinction in which I see any meaning, and I can as little imagine speaking of a novel of character as I can imagine speaking of a picture of character. When one says picture one says of character, when one says novel one says of incident, and the terms may be transposed at will. What is character but the determination of incident? What is incident but the illustration of character? What is either a picture or a novel that is *not* of character? What else do we seek in it and find in it? It is an incident for a woman to stand up with her hand resting on a table and look out at you in a certain way; or if it be not an incident I think it will be hard to say what it is. At the same time it is an expression of character. If you say you don't see it (character in *that—allons donc!*), this is exactly what *[handwritten: Come now!]* the artist who has reasons of his own for thinking he *does* see it undertakes *[handwritten: (Nonsense)]* to show you. When a young man makes up his mind that he has not faith enough after all to enter the church as he intended, that is an incident, though you may not hurry to the end of the chapter to see whether perhaps he doesn't change once more. I do not say that these are extraordinary or startling incidents. I do not pretend to estimate the degree of interest proceeding from them, for this will depend upon the skill of the painter. It sounds almost puerile to say that some incidents are intrinsically much more important than others, and I need not take this precaution after having professed my sympathy for the major ones in remarking that the only classi-

fication of the novel that I can understand is into that which has life and
that which has it not.

The novel and the romance, the novel of incident and that of character—
these clumsy separations appear to me to have been made by critics and readers for their own convenience, and to help them out of some of their occasional queer predicaments, but to have little reality or interest for the producer,
from whose point of view it is of course that we are attempting to consider
the art of fiction. The case is the same with another shadowy category which
Mr. Besant apparently is disposed to set up—that of the "modern English
novel"; unless indeed it be that in this matter he has fallen into an accidental
confusion of standpoints. It is not quite clear whether he intends the remarks
in which he alludes to it to be didactic or historical. It is as difficult to suppose a person intending to write a modern English as to suppose him writing
an ancient English novel: that is a label which begs the question. One writes
the novel, one paints the picture, of one's language and of one's time,
and calling it modern English will not, alas! make the difficult task any easier.
No more, unfortunately, will calling this or that work of one's fellow-artist a
romance—unless it be, of course, simply for the pleasantness of the thing, as
for instance when Hawthorne gave this heading to his story of *Blithedale*.
The French, who have brought the theory of fiction to remarkable completeness, have but one name for the novel, and have not attempted smaller
things in it, that I can see, for that. I can think of no obligation to which the
"romancer" would not be held equally with the novelist; the standard of execution is equally high for each. Of course it is of execution that we are talking—that being the only point of a novel that is open to contention. This is
perhaps too often lost sight of, only to produce interminable confusions and
cross-purposes. We must grant the artist his subject, his idea, his *donnée*:
our criticism is applied only to what he makes of it. Naturally I do not mean
that we are bound to like it or find it interesting: in case we do not our course
is perfectly simple—to let it alone. We may believe that of a certain idea
even the most sincere novelist can make nothing at all, and the event may
perfectly justify our belief; but the failure will have been a failure to execute,
and it is in the execution that the fatal weakness is recorded. If we pretend
to respect the artist at all, we must allow him his freedom of choice, in the
face, in particular cases, of innumerable presumptions that the choice will
not fructify. Art derives a considerable part of its beneficial exercise from flying in the face of presumptions, and some of the most interesting experiments of which it is capable are hidden in the bosom of common things.
Gustave Flaubert has written a story about the devotion of a servant-girl to a
parrot, and the production, highly finished as it is, cannot on the whole be
called a success. We are perfectly free to find it flat, but I think it might
have been interesting; and I, for my part, am extremely glad he should have
written it; it is a contribution to our knowledge of what can be done—or
what cannot. Ivan Turgénieff has written a tale about a deaf and dumb serf
and a lap-dog, and the thing is touching, loving, a little masterpiece. He
struck the note of life where Gustave Flaubert missed it—he flew in the
face of a presumption and achieved a victory.[3]

---

[3] The stories referred to are Flaubert's *Un coeur simple* and Turgenev's *Mumu*.

Nothing, of course, will ever take the place of the good old fashion of "liking" a work of art or not liking it: the most improved criticism will not abolish that primitive, that ultimate test. I mention this to guard myself from the accusation of intimating that the idea, the subject, of a novel or a picture, does not matter. It matters, to my sense, in the highest degree, and if I might put up a prayer it would be that artists should select none but the richest. Some, as I have already hastened to admit, are much more remunerative than others, and it would be a world happily arranged in which persons intending to treat them should be exempt from confusions and mistakes. This fortunate condition will arrive only, I fear, on the same day that critics become purged from error. Meanwhile, I repeat, we do not judge the artist with fairness unless we say to him, "Oh, I grant you your starting-point, because if I did not I should seem to prescribe to you, and heaven forbid I should take that responsibility. If I pretend to tell you what you must not take, you will call upon me to tell you then what you must take; in which case I shall be prettily caught. Moreover, it isn't till I have accepted your data that I can begin to measure you. I have the standard, the pitch; I have no right to tamper with your flute and then criticise your music. Of course I may not care for your idea at all; I may think it silly, or stale, or unclean; in which case I wash my hands of you altogether. I may content myself with believing that you will not have succeeded in being interesting, but I shall, of course, not attempt to demonstrate it, and you will be as indifferent to me as I am to you. I needn't remind you that there are all sorts of tastes: who can know it better? Some people, for excellent reasons, don't like to read about carpenters; others, for reasons even better, don't like to read about courtesans. Many object to Americans. Others (I believe they are mainly editors and publishers) won't look at Italians. Some readers don't like quiet subjects; others don't like bustling ones. Some enjoy a complete illusion, others the consciousness of large concessions. They choose their novels accordingly, and if they don't care about your idea they won't, *a fortiori*, care about your treatment."

So that it comes back very quickly, as I have said, to the liking: in spite of M. Zola, who reasons less powerfully than he represents, and who will not reconcile himself to this absoluteness of taste, thinking that there are certain things that people ought to like, and that they can be made to like. I am quite at a loss to imagine anything (at any rate in this matter of fiction) that people *ought* to like or to dislike. Selection will be sure to take care of itself, for it has a constant motive behind it. That motive is simply experience. As people feel life, so they will feel the art that is most closely related to it. This closeness of relation is what we should never forget in talking of the effort of the novel. Many people speak of it as a factitious, artificial form, a product of ingenuity, the business of which is to alter and arrange the things that surround us, to translate them into conventional, traditional moulds. This, however, is a view of the matter which carries us but a very short way, condemns the art to an eternal repetition of a few familiar *clichés*, cuts short its development, and leads us straight up to a dead wall. Catching the very note and trick, the strange irregular rhythm of life, that is the attempt whose strenuous force keeps Fiction upon her feet. In proportion as in what she offers us we see life *without* rearrangement do we feel that we are touching the truth; in proportion as we see it *with* rearrangement do we feel that we are being put off with a substitute, a compromise and convention. It is not uncommon to hear an extraordinary assurance of remark in regard to this matter of rearranging, which is often spoken of as if it were the last word of art. Mr. Besant seems to me in danger of falling into the great error with his rather unguarded talk about "selection." Art is essentially selection, but it is a selection whose main care is to be typical, to be inclusive. For many people art means rose-coloured window-panes, and selection means picking a bouquet for Mrs. Grundy. They will tell you glibly that artistic considerations have nothing to do with the disagreeable, with the ugly; they will rattle off shallow commonplaces about the province of art and the limits of art till you are moved to some wonder in return as to the province and the limits of ignorance. It appears to me that no one can ever have made a seriously artistic attempt without becoming conscious of an immense increase—a kind of revelation—of freedom. One perceives in that case—by the light of a heavenly ray—that the province of art is all life, all feeling, all observation, all vision. As Mr. Besant so justly intimates, it is all experience. That is a sufficient answer to those who maintain that it must not touch the sad things of life, who stick into its divine unconscious bosom little prohibitory inscriptions on the end of sticks, such as we see in public gardens—"It is forbidden to walk on the grass; it is forbidden to touch the flowers; it is not allowed to introduce dogs or to remain after dark; it is requested to keep to the right." The young aspirant in the line of fiction whom we continue to imagine will do nothing without taste, for in that case his freedom would be of little use to him; but the first advantage of his taste will be to reveal to him the absurdity of the little sticks and tickets. If he have taste, I must add, of course he will have ingenuity, and my disrespectful reference to that quality just now was not meant to imply that it is useless in fiction. But it is only a secondary aid; the first is a capacity for receiving straight impressions.

Mr. Besant has some remarks on the question of "the story" which I shall not attempt to criticise, though they seem to me to contain a singular ambiguity, because I do not think I understand them. I cannot see what is meant by talking as if there were a part of a novel which is the story and part of it which for mystical reasons is not—unless indeed the distinction be made in a sense in which it is difficult to suppose that any one should attempt to convey anything. "The story," if it represents anything, represents the subject, the idea, the *donnée* of the novel; and there is surely no "school" —Mr. Besant speaks of a school—which urges that a novel should be all treatment and no subject. There must assuredly be something to treat; every school is intimately conscious of that. This sense of the story being the idea, the starting-point, of the novel, is the only one that I see in which it can be spoken of as something different from its organic whole; and since in proportion as the work is successful the idea permeates and penetrates it, informs and animates it, so that every word and every punctuation-point contribute directly to the expression, in that proportion do we lose our sense of the story being a blade which may be drawn more or less out of its sheath. The story and the novel, the idea and the form, are the needle and thread, and I never heard of a guild of tailors who recommended the use of the thread without the needle, or the needle without the thread. Mr. Besant is not the only critic who may be observed to have spoken as if there were certain things in life which constitute stories, and certain others which do not. I find the same odd implication in an entertaining article in the *Pall Mall Gazette*, devoted, as it happens, to Mr. Besant's lecture. "The story is the thing!" says this graceful writer, as if with a tone of opposition to some other idea. I should think it was, as every painter who, as the time for "sending in" his picture looms in the distance, finds himself still in quest of a subject—as every belated artist not fixed about his theme will heartily agree. There are some subjects which speak to us and others which do not, but he would be a clever man who should undertake to give a rule—an index expurgatorius—by which the story and the no-story should be known apart. It is impossible (to me at least) to imagine any such rule which shall not be altogether arbitrary. The writer in the *Pall Mall* opposes the delightful (as I suppose) novel of *Margot la Balafrée* to certain tales in which "Bostonian nymphs" appear to have "rejected English dukes for psychological reasons." I am not acquainted with the romance just designated, and can scarcely forgive the *Pall Mall* critic for not mentioning the name of the author,[4] but the title appears to refer to a lady who may have received a scar in some heroic adventure. I am inconsolable at not being acquainted with this episode, but am utterly at a loss to see why it is a story when the rejection (or acceptance) of a duke is not, and why a reason, psychological or other, is not a subject when a cicatrix is. They are all particles of the multitudinous life with which the novel deals, and surely no dogma which pretends to make it lawful to touch the one and unlawful to touch the other will stand for a moment on its feet. It is the special picture that must stand or fall, according as it seem to possess truth or to lack it. Mr. Besant does not, to my sense, light up the subject by intimating that a story must, under penalty of not being a story, consist of "adventures." Why of adventures more than of green spectacles? He mentions a category of impossible things, and among them he places "fiction without adventure." Why without adventure, more than without matrimony, or celibacy, or parturition, or cholera, or hydropathy, or Jansenism? This seems to me to bring the novel back to the hapless little *rôle* of being an artificial, ingenious thing—bring it down from its large, free character of an immense and exquisite correspondence with life. And what *is* adventure, when it comes to that, and by what sign is the listening pupil to recognise it? It is an adventure—an immense one—for me to write this little article; and for a Bostonian nymph to reject an English duke is an adventure only less stirring, I should say, than for an English duke to be rejected by a Bostonian nymph. I see dramas within dramas in that, and innumerable points of view. A psychological reason is, to my imagination, an object adorably pictorial; to catch the tint of its complexion—I feel as if that idea might inspire one to Titianesque efforts. There are few things more exciting to me, in short, than a psychological reason, and yet, I protest, the novel seems to me the most magnificent form of art. I have just been reading, at the same time, the delightful story of *Treasure Island*, by Mr. Robert

---

[4] James's own novelette, *An International Episode* (1879), fits this description.

Louis Stevenson and, in a manner less consecutive, the last tale from M.
Edmond de Goncourt, which is entitled *Chérie*. One of these works treats of
murders, mysteries, islands of dreadful renown, hairbreadth escapes, miraculous coincidences and buried doubloons. The other treats of a little French
girl who lived in a fine house in Paris, and died of wounded sensibility because no one would marry her. I call *Treasure Island* delightful, because it
appears to me to have succeeded wonderfully in what it attempts; and I venture to bestow no epithet upon *Chérie*, which strikes me as having failed deplorably in what it attempts—that is in tracing the development of the
moral consciousness of a child. But one of these productions strikes me as exactly as much of a novel as the other, and as having a "story" quite as
much. The moral consciousness of a child is as much a part of life as the
islands of the Spanish Main, and the one sort of geography seems to me to
have those "surprises" of which Mr. Besant speaks quite as much as the
other. For myself (since it comes back in the last resort, as I say, to the
preference of the individual), the picture of the child's experience has the advantage that I can at successive steps (an immense luxury, near to the "sensual pleasure" of which Mr. Besant's critic in the *Pall Mall* speaks) say
Yes or No, as it may be, to what the artist puts before me. I have been a child
in fact, but I have been on a quest for a buried treasure only in supposition, and it is a simple accident that with M. de Goncourt I should have
for the most part to say No. With George Eliot, when she painted that
country with a far other intelligence, I always said Yes.

    The most interesting part of Mr. Besant's lecture is unfortunately the
briefest passage—his very cursory allusion to the "conscious moral purpose" of
the novel. Here again it is not very clear whether he be recording a fact or
laying down a principle; it is a great pity that in the latter case he should
not have developed his idea. This branch of the subject is of immense importance, and Mr. Besant's few words point to considerations of the widest
reach, not to be lightly disposed of. He will have treated the art of fiction
but superficially who is not prepared to go every inch of the way that these
considerations will carry him. It is for this reason that at the beginning of
these remarks I was careful to notify the reader that my reflections on so
large a theme have no pretension to be exhaustive. Like Mr. Besant, I have
left the question of the morality of the novel till the last, and at the last I find
I have used up my space. It is a question surrounded with difficulties, as
witness the very first that meets us, in the form of a definite question, on the
threshold. Vagueness, in such a discussion, is fatal, and what is the meaning
of your morality and your conscious moral purpose? Will you not define
your terms and explain how (a novel being a picture) a picture can be
either moral or immoral? You wish to paint a moral picture or carve a
moral statue: will you not tell us how you would set about it? We are discussing the Art of Fiction; questions of art are questions (in the widest
sense) of execution; questions of morality are quite another affair, and will
you not let us see how it is that you find it so easy to mix them up? These
things are so clear to Mr. Besant that he has deduced from them a law which
he sees embodied in English Fiction, and which is "a truly admirable thing
and a great cause for congratulation." It is a great cause for congratulation

indeed when such thorny problems become as smooth as silk. I may add
that in so far as Mr. Besant perceives that in point of fact English Fiction
has addressed itself preponderantly to these delicate questions he will appear
to many people to have made a vain discovery. They will have been positively struck, on the contrary, with the moral timidity of the usual English
novelist; with his (or with her) aversion to face the difficulties with which on
every side the treatment of reality bristles. He is apt to be extremely shy
(whereas the picture that Mr. Besant draws is a picture of boldness), and the
sign of his work, for the most part, is a cautious silence on certain subjects. In the English novel (by which of course I mean the American as well),
more than in any other, there is a traditional difference between that which
people know and that which they agree to admit that they know, that which
they see and that which they speak of, that which they feel to be a part of life
and that which they allow to enter into literature. There is the great difference, in short, between what they talk of in conversation and what they talk
of in print. The essence of moral energy is to survey the whole field, and I
should directly reverse Mr. Besant's remark and say not that the English
novel has a purpose, but that it has a diffidence. To what degree a purpose
in a work of art is a source of corruption I shall not attempt to inquire; the
one that seems to me least dangerous is the purpose of making a perfect work.
As for our novel, I may say lastly on this score that as we find it in England
to-day it strikes me as addressed in a large degree to "young people," and
that this in itself constitutes a presumption that it will be rather shy. There
are certain things which it is generally agreed not to discuss, not even to mention, before young people. That is very well, but the absence of discussion is
not a symptom of the moral passion. The purpose of the English novel—
"a truly admirable thing, and a great cause for congratulation"—strikes me
therefore as rather negative.

There is one point at which the moral sense and the artistic sense lie very
near together; that is in the light of the very obvious truth that the deepest
quality of a work of art will always be the quality of the mind of the producer. In proportion as that intelligence is fine will the novel, the picture, the statue partake of the substance of beauty and truth. To be consti-
tuted of such elements is, to my vision, to have purpose enough. No good
novel will ever proceed from a superficial mind; that seems to me an axiom
which, for the artist in fiction, will cover all needful moral ground: if the
youthful aspirant take it to heart it will illuminate for him many of the mysteries of "purpose." There are many other useful things that might be
said to him, but I have come to the end of my article, and can only touch
them as I pass. The critic in the *Pall Mall Gazette*, whom I have already
quoted, draws attention to the danger, in speaking of the art of fiction, of
generalising. The danger that he has in mind is rather, I imagine, that of par-
ticularising, for there are some comprehensive remarks which, in addition
to those embodied in Mr. Besant's suggestive lecture, might without fear of
misleading him be addressed to the ingenuous student. I should remind him
first of the magnificence of the form that is open to him, which offers to
sight so few restrictions and such innumerable opportunities. The other arts,
in comparison, appear confined and hampered; the various conditions under

which they are exercised are so rigid and definite. But the only condition that I can think of attaching to the composition of the novel is, as I have already said, that it be sincere. This freedom is a splendid privilege, and the first lesson of the young novelist is to learn to be worthy of it. "Enjoy it as it deserves," I should say to him; "take possession of it, explore it to its utmost extent, publish it, rejoice in it. All life belongs to you, and do not listen either to those who would shut you up into corners of it and tell you that it is only here and there that art inhabits, or to those who would persuade you that this heavenly messenger wings her way outside of life altogether, breathing a superfine air, and turning away her head from the truth of things. There is no impression of life, no manner of seeing it and feeling it, to which the plan of the novelist may not offer a place; you have only to remember that talents so dissimilar as those of Alexandre Dumas and Jane Austen, Charles Dickens and Gustave Flaubert have worked in this field with equal glory. Do not think too much about optimism and pessimism; try and catch the colour of life itself. In France to-day we see a prodigious effort (that of Emile Zola, to whose solid and serious work no explorer of the capacity of the novel can allude without respect), we see an extraordinary effort vitiated by a spirit of pessimism on a narrow basis. M. Zola is magnificent, but he strikes an English reader as ignorant; he has an air of working in the dark; if he had as much light as energy, his results would be of the highest value. As for the aberrations of a shallow optimism, the ground (of English fiction especially) is strewn with their brittle particles as with broken glass. If you must indulge in conclusions, let them have the taste of a wide knowledge. Remember that your first duty is to be as complete as possible—to make as perfect a work. Be generous and delicate and pursue the prize."

1884

Reading Suggestions

The most complete edition of James's fiction is the one edited by Percy Lubbock for Macmillan, *The Novels and Stories of Henry James* (London, 1921-1923) in thirty-five volmes. The more widely used "New York Edition," *The Novels and Tales of Henry James* (1907-1909, 1917—now being reprinted), in twenty-six volumes, excludes eight of the novels and one volume of stories. For both these editions James revised the text of his earlier works to bring them in line with his later manner. A large number of his fictions, long and short, are now being issued in paperbacks. Besides fiction James wrote some thirty volumes of miscellaneous prose, much of which is out of print, though some of the more important works have been made available recently. Among these are *Henry James: Autobiography* (1956), edited by F. J. Dupee, comprising the three volumes first published in 1913-1917; *The Complete Plays of Henry James* (1949), edited by Leon Edel; and *The Art of Travel* (1958), edited by Morton Zabel, being selections from several travel books dating from 1875 to 1909. James's important critical writings have not fared so well. Six volumes of them were published by the author during his lifetime, but all are out of print. Though there have been numerous recent reprintings of his criticism, they are either overlapping selections from these key volumes or previously uncollected minor essays on painting and the theater as well as literature. Out of this confusion the best single volume of selections is *The Art of Fiction* (1948), edited by Morris Roberts. To this should be added *The Art of the Novel* (1935), edited by R. P. Blackmur, a collection of all the critical prefaces James wrote late in life describing the creation of his fictions. A companion volume, *The Notebooks of Henry James* (1947), edited by Matthiessen and Murdock, contains the genesis of his tales and novels from 1880 on. These three books are indispensable to any serious study of Henry James.

The largest collection of his correspondence now available is *The Letters of Henry James* (1920), two volumes, edited by Percy Lubbock. A convenient volume of *Selected Letters* (1955) was edited by Leon Edel, who has under way several additional volumes from the manuscripts of more than 1500 letters by James at Harvard. F. O. Matthiessen's *The James Family* (1947) is a voluminous collection of extracts from the published writings, letters, diaries, and other documents of Henry, William, and other members of this extraordinary family of minds. The long-felt need for a full-scale biography of James is being supplied by Leon Edel. Three volumes have already appeared: *The Untried Years* (1953), *The Conquest of London* (1962), and *The Middle Years* (1962), bringing the story down to 1895; the fourth and final volume is now in preparation. This is the definitive life, though it is more concerned with a psychological analysis of the author than with a literary study of his works. (Edel and Laurence's A *Bibliography of Henry James* [1957] is the standard listing of all his works.)

There have been more than fifty critical books devoted to Henry James, mostly in the last few decades, so that only a highly selective list can be given here. Of the earlier studies, Morris Roberts's *Henry James's Criticism* (1929) is the best analysis of his principles as a literary critic; and J. W. Beach's *The Method of Henry James* (1918), the pioneer study of his theory and practice as a novelist, is still one of the best. It was reprinted in 1955 with the addition of a hundred-page introduction evaluating much of the James criticism down to that date. A comprehensive summary of the whole body of criticism of his novels, in articles as well as books, can be found in Oscar Cargill's *The Novels of Henry James* (1961). The most helpful introductory book is F. W. Dupee's *Henry James* (1951), a skillful blend of biography and criticism surveying the whole career of James, within the limits of the American Men of Letters series. Of the studies covering the entire body of his writings, but from a single point of view, two are outstanding: H. T. McCarthy's *Henry James* (1958) attempts a synthesis of all the major aspects of his aesthetics; Christof Wegelin's *The Image of Europe in Henry James* (1958) is an original study of his major theme. Of the more special studies, two must suffice: W. R. Poirier's *The Comic Sense of Henry James* (1960) offers a close reading of six early novels; F. O. Matthiessen's *Henry James, the Major Phase* (1944) does the same for the last three great ones.

No American author has been more elaborately subjected to criticism than James, and the articles on him now run into the hundreds. In *The Question of Henry James* (1945) F. W. Dupee has collected twenty-five key essays, from Howells to Auden, concluding with a full listing of others. This selection should be supplemented by R. E. Spiller's James bibliography in *Eight American Authors* (1956), edited by Floyd Stovall. Special James numbers have been published by the *Kenyon Review* (Autumn 1943) and *Modern Fiction Studies* (Spring 1957). The best articles devoted to James's novels are summarized in Cargill's volume, mentioned above. For the fiction included in this anthology: A *Casebook of the Turn of the Screw* (1960), edited by Gerald Willen, reprints fifteen interpretations of this controversial book; and *Henry James: Seven Stories and Studies* (1961), edited by Edward Stone, contains seven on *The Pupil.*

Biography

In environment and educational opportunities favorable to an author's career, no American has been so fortunate as Henry James. When his father inherited a fortune, unlike the typical man of wealth, he turned aside from making more money and devoted his life to experience and understanding, in the most cultivated sense of those terms. More important, he made the same freedom available to his whole family. It is not surprising then that out of a household of lively children two of them grew up to be distinguished, the novelist and his older brother William, the philosopher and psychologist. Young Henry enjoyed the first fruits of these advantages during a boyhood in New York City, where he was born on April 15, 1843, in a fine old town house on Washington Square. Here he was encouraged to absorb the world through every avenue of sensibility and intelligence, and was educated more by observation and the guidance of tutors than by formal schooling. Then his father, wanting the family to know several different civilizations and approaches to life, took them all to Europe. There James spent four years of his adolescence studying, in school and out, at London, Geneva, and especially Paris.

On their return to America he passed his young manhood in New England, first at Newport, then Cambridge. At the former he and his brother studied painting with John LaFarge, the artist whose friendship was to mean so much to Henry Adams too. At the latter they both entered Harvard, William in the scientific school, Henry in law. (A back injury had prevented the younger son from serving in the Civil War.) By the age of twenty-one the future novelist had determined on his career. During the next five years he devoted himself to the cause of literature in America, publishing a steady stream of stories and critical essays, chiefly in magazines edited by friends of his father. Acquaintance with these men—Lowell, James T. Fields, E. L. Godkin—was influential. Still more so was his reading of the French novelists, of George Eliot, and above all Hawthorne. The last, whose death came as a shock the very year he began his career, had at least proved to him that an American could be an artist. But Hawthorne raised the question whether Europe might not offer a better place of residence for the writer of fiction.

In his youth James had been exposed to the culture of the Old World, more recently to the best in the new. Now in 1869 he began a long period of search for the vantage point from which he could best see the world as a novelist. On his first adult journey to Europe he discovered Italy. Then, back in Cambridge for two years, he began his lifelong friendship with the young author and editor Howells, who as champion of the new realism strengthened his confidence in the future of American literature. To Europe again in 1872, this time for nearly three years—England, France, and Italy—with the unexpected conclusion that though he loved Italy best it would serve least well for his residence as an artist. After a winter in New York, he decided to give Paris a serious testing out. He lived and wrote there for a full year, 1875-1876, in intimate contact with the new school of realists and naturalists from whom he learned much, especially Flaubert and Turgenev. At the end of that time he made his decision, settled in London, and spent the remaining forty years of his life as an author in England, though with many excursions on the continent.

By the age of thirty-four James had published (in addition to enough uncollected stories and essays to fill half-a-dozen posthumous volumes) one book of travel sketches, another of short fictions, and three novels. With the last of these, *The American* (1877), he made his first bid for recognition as a serious author, primarily as the explorer of the international theme. It was a theme rich in possibilities, and no one was better qualified than he to exploit it, as his prolific writings of the next few years testified. Then came two critical volumes on his masters, the French authors and Hawthorne, spanning the Atlantic. And there were seven books of fiction, ranging from short stories through the novelette to a large two-volume novel, mostly dealing with the contrast between American innocence and European experience. One, *Daisy Miller,* was his nearest approach to a popular success. But it was *The Portrait of a Lady* (1881), with its much subtler handling of the international theme, that brought his early period to a high culmination and pointed the way to his final achievement. It was at this time, on a visit back to America, that James declared: "I have made my choice. . . . My choice is the old world. . . . My work lies there." But he was aware of the responsibilities this entailed for the novelist: "The burden is necessarily greater for an American—for he *must* deal, more or less, even if only by implication, with Europe; whereas no European is obliged to deal in the least with America"—adding prophetically, "as yet."

The next ten years were equally prolific. James not only published four more volumes of essays and nine books of fiction but also reprinted some earlier works and issued through his London publisher a collected edition of his stories and novels down to 1883. His audience had always been limited, if ardent, and this deluge apparently flooded his market. For near the end of this decade he was to complain that the demand for his productions had been reduced to zero. This was not because of a decline in excellence, though he was perhaps tempted to write too much. (Contrary to popular opinion, based on his family's money, James supported himself with his pen down to the age of fifty.) It was instead his exaggerated comment on the strangely hostile criticism of his last two novels. One of them, *The Princess Casamassima,* ranks with his half-dozen widely recognized masterpieces, but it was ahead of its time—the story of an abortive proletarian revolution. James was not discouraged in spite of the poor reception of two fine novels. He continued his bold experiments until the mid-nineties, when he made a disastrous attempt to write plays. This indeed brought him to the verge of despair. He was past fifty and his career seemed at an end, but he staged the most remarkable comeback in literary annals.

With renewed dedication to technique, as the artist's victorious weapon, he began to apply the dramatic methods he had learned from the theater, forging a new kind of fiction "straight as a play." He was also eager to learn what the best of the younger novelists, like Conrad, had to teach. At first he confined himself to modest efforts—stories, then novelettes, then short novels, including some of his finest. (The three included in this anthology date from 1888 to 1898.) By the turn of the century he felt himself ready. He had moved from London to an old country house in Sussex, and in this peaceful retreat came his final flowering. In rapid succession he wrote and published three full-scale novels, reckoned by many critics among the best in the English language: *The Wings of the Dove* (1902), *The Ambassadors* (1903), and *The Golden Bowl* (1904). In these he returned to the international contrast, which had gradually dropped out of his fiction during the middle years. Now he turned it from a sociological to a humanistic theme of the highest significance. It was a triumph almost without parallel.

On a visit back to his native country, the first in twenty years, his achievement was celebrated by his American publisher with the launching of a handsome "New York Edition" of his collected novels and tales. For this he wrote a remarkable series of critical prefaces, and undertook the unusual task of revising his earlier fictions to bring them in line with his later manner. James's declining years were spent writing his autobiography and publishing some charming travel books and the last fruits of his criticism. His had been a life quiet as to external event but intense in its devotion to art in all its forms, above all to literature. When he decided to become a British citizen in 1915, as a formal protest against his country's aloofness to World War I, this in no way altered the fact that he remained until his death in 1916 indisputably an American novelist, one of our most distinguished.

Revolted against   1. Social conditions
2. traditional
codes of
morality
3. literary formalities

From this came his uncompromising
realistic writings.

STEPHEN CRANE ✦

1871-1900

Crane was one of the first
to portray horror of war.

He has been called "the
chatterton of Am. Lit."

Crane, rather more subtle as a poet, was sometimes less labored in his handling of symbolism, but much of it came into his work — usually in the form of images seen through the eyes and interpreted by the minds of his characters. Such images both pictured and interpreted details.

Crane — probably most intuitive artist of the period — thoughts and feelings of characters were important

Introduction

In a passage that he later eliminated from *The Red Badge of Courage*, Stephen Crane wrote, "It was always clear to Fleming that he was entirely different from other men, that he had been cast in a unique mold." In certain moods at least, Crane liked to think of himself in this way: as a single, naked self confronting experience with few weapons except ardor and determinations. "I began the battle of life," he said, "with no talent, no equipment, but with an ardent admiration and desire." Of course, as Crane himself recognized in other moods, this statement was quite inaccurate. He had talent, a talent so extraordinary that William Dean Howells saw him as springing into life, not naked, but "fully armed." We may sum up his talent as a vivid apprehension of consciousness or mood, together with an ironic perception of the incompatibility between this consciousness and objective reality. He also had "equipment," though it was rather ordinary, middle-class, and threadbare, consisting chiefly of a conventional reaction against convention.

The most obvious and most important convention that Crane lived by, wrote about, and derided was the success story. This is the familiar story of the provincial young man who breaks loose from the limitations of his birth and rearing and goes to the big city to seek his fortune. He is usually gifted with physical charm, some intelligence, and a driving ambition, qualities that enable him to enter society and make his way upward by adapting its code to his ends. A well-known pattern in European fiction of the nineteenth century, it was more readily applicable, as everyone knew or thought he knew, to the fluid social and economic structure of American life, especially after Benjamin Franklin's *Autobiography* had shown the way.

Like most conventions, this one has always provoked parody or counterstatement, which in its turn becomes conventional. In fiction, the antitype of the successful young man is the story of the outcast, the runaway, the sensitive young man. Unlike the youth who is initiated into society and

215

rises to fame and fortune, the protagonist of these stories remains an outsider. His story is concerned with a series of retreats from involvement, his search for identity frustrated by the crassness or cruelty of the world, his refusal to conform, and deficiencies in his own character. One thinks of Melville's ship-jumping questers, Sherwood Anderson's adolescents, Thomas Wolfe's Eugene Gant, and J. D. Salinger's Holden Caulfield.

Crane's life tended to oscillate between these two patterns. Somewhat sickly as a child, the youngest of fourteen children, he was rather precocious and impressed his classmates as being "different." At college—he spent one semester at Lafayette and one at Syracuse—he rebelled against the "cut-and-dried curriculum," dressed unconventionally, and smoked incessantly. As a young reporter, he had a way of neglecting names and addresses in favor of describing how things struck him, and his honest, ironic reporting of a workers' parade in Asbury Park cost him his job. Between 1892 and 1893 he eked out a living as a free-lance writer in New York, living a Bohemian existence and absorbing what he called his "artistic education on the Bowery." His first novel, *Maggie*, was turned down by publishers, and when he borrowed money to print it privately in 1893 under the pseudonym of "Johnston Smith," it did not sell.

This record of nonconformity and financial failure can be balanced by a list of achievements that come uncomfortably close to the standard success story, just as the sensitivity and irresponsibility in his character were balanced by a driving will. Although he was only five feet six inches tall and never weighed more than one hundred and twenty, he became a baseball star in school and college and excelled in sandlot football. Despite his idiosyncrasies, he was quite popular with his classmates and even joined a fraternity in college. (How many other serious American writers have belonged to a fraternity?) After enduring poverty and the disappointment of *Maggie's* cold reception, he became a best-selling novelist and a celebrity with the publication of *The Red Badge of Courage* in 1895. His reaction to fame was characteristically and conventionally double-edged. To a friend he wrote candidly, "You ought to see the effect of such things upon my family. Aint they swelled up though! . . . It's great. I am no longer a black sheep but a star." But to an editor he confessed that "somehow I am not as happy as I was in the uncertain, happy-go-lucky newspaper writing days. I used to dream continually of success then. Now that I have achieved it in some measure it seems like mere flimsy paper."

Success, then, proved to be attractive as a dream but tissue-thin as a reality. On a deeper level, Crane sought the equivalent of religious salvation, influenced by his family heritage even as he rebelled against it. His father was a gentle Methodist minister who believed in the innocence of all men and preached against the vices that stained it: alcohol, tobacco, novels, and baseball, all of them duly cultivated by his son. His mother was an apocalyptic Methodist, whose faith was more fervid and imprecatory than her husband's. Still Stephen remembered her as being "more of a Christian than a Methodist," partly because she had courageously defied her pious friends by temporarily sheltering an unwed mother in her home. He grew up, therefore, in a household dominated by sermons, Bible reading, and evangelical tracts, and although his early enjoyment of prayer meetings "cooled off" by the time he was an adolescent, Biblical phrasing remained an important feature of his style.

Crane's rebellion against the religion of his mother and her family is most evident in his volume of poems entitled *The Black Riders* (1895). The omnipotent God may rule the universe, but it is a "rudderless" world, "going ridiculous voyages." Crane hated dogma of any kind, and the doctrine he found in Exodus 20:5: ". . . The sins of the fathers shall be visited upon the heads of the children," inspired this bitter reaction:

> Well, then, I hate thee, unrighteous picture;
> Wicked image, I hate thee;
> So, strike with Thy vengeance
> The heads of those little men
> Who come blindly
> It will be a brave thing.
>
> *Black Riders*, XII

Elsewhere in the same volume he described God as "blustering" and "Stamping across the sky/ With loud swagger."

If "God is cold," the college curriculum dry, and the myth of success thin, what remains as a source of strength? As some of his other poems indicate, Crane was not merely iconoclastic. To the brutally unjust God who rules the universe, indifferent to man's fate, he opposed a God of compassion:

> Withal there is One whom I fear;
> I fear to see grief upon that face.

> *   *   *

> Ah sooner would I die
> Than see tears in those eyes of my soul.

This God is more victim than master; He is the sacrificial redeemer, identified with man chiefly by his suffering:

> The wounded make gestures like Thy Son's . . . .

The line suggests both the major theme and the drastically narrow limits of Crane's fiction. Because there are no longer any universal truths to which man can appeal, he is best defined by the emotions of courage and cowardice, the virtue and vice of the self-sufficient individual. Like many of his contemporaries, Crane substituted a physical trial for the spiritual conversion preached by his ancestors. Only after a man has been through a crisis, an extreme test of bravery and endurance, can we judge his stature. Yet to pass through such an ordeal is to be one of the wounded, physically or psychically; man then shares the dignity and sacredness of the redemptive God—but he is, after all, maimed for life.

In preferring sports to books, the strenuous life to religion and middle-class comfort, Crane was characteristic of his time, the era of Theodore Roosevelt, Walter Camp, and Frederic Remington. Lacking the high culture of Henry James and the folklore of Mark Twain, he found in athletics a civilized ferocity and the ideal of masculine solidarity. "Culture in it's [sic] true sense, I take it," Crane wrote to a friend, "is a comprehension of the man at one's shoulder. It has nothing to do with an adoration for effete jugs and old kettles." In the same letter Crane went on to associate the effete and genteel with the East, and masculine vigor with the West. "Damn the East! I fell in love with the straight out-and-out, sometimes hideous, often braggart westerners because I thought them to be the truer men. . . . When they are born, they take one big gulp of wind and then they live." Yet even in this praise of the westerner we note the severe qualifications. The eastern man of fashion is usually civilized but effete; the westerner vigorous but full of wind, swollen with defensive pride.

Crane's reaction against his heritage thus left him with a set of conflicting attitudes. The son of a gentle minister, he sought war and violence all his life. A product of the middle class, he seemed, as one contemporary observed, able to breathe only "in the slums or among aristocrats." An easterner who spent most of his life in New Jersey, New York, and England, he yearned to buy a ranch in Texas. These contradictions were resolved only in his role as a writer who found in them one of his major resources— an ironic vision of the disparities between the self and the world. Yet even here we find a last bitter contradiction. The writer who affirmed as "the only thing worth while" an absolute "personal honesty," that is, a fidelity to his vision, managed to crank out a considerable quantity of sentimental trash in the desperate hope that it would sell. Again, however, he was characteristically without illusions. "I . . . do not say that I am honest. I merely say that I am as nearly honest as weak mental machinery will allow."

I

Since Crane's explicit literary creed was fragmentary and deceptively simple, we need to supplement it by reference to his best creative work. All of his comments add up to the fact that he identified himself with the "realists," specifically with the former westerners William Dean Howells and Hamlin Garland. Thus he became involved in what he called the "beautiful war between those who say that art is man's substitute for nature and we are most successful in art when we approach the nearest to nature and truth," and those editors and critics who maintain that fiction should be respectable and idealistic. Crane maintained that "the nearer a writer gets to life the greater he becomes as an artist." But these remarks have little value unless we go on to ask what he meant when he said "I try to give my readers a slice out of life." What aspects of life does he put in? What does he leave out? How does he get "nearer" to "Nature" and "truth?" Crane's "realism" is not Howells' "realism," though their generalizations about art often sound identical.

Unlike Howells, Crane was not concerned with the normal or probable aspects of middle-class American life. He chose instead extreme or abnormal situations, charged with violence, latent or actual: two men burying a friend during combat, a Negro ostracized from a small town after he rescued a small boy from a fire, four castaways at sea in an open boat, brawling and murder in Nebraska, the seduction, prostitution, and suicide of a Bowery girl, a war correspondent seeking combat and running from it in Greece, a drunken Texan shooting up a town. Although these stories use a wide variety of locales and differ somewhat in technique, they have in common a view of the human condition that is outlined in one of Crane's wry poems:

> A man said to the universe:
> "Sir, I exist!"
> "However," replied the universe,
> "The fact has not created in me
> A sense of obligation."

In Crane's fiction about all that a man can affirm is that he exists. His heroes are displaced, like the Swede who finds himself a stranger in Ft. Romper, Nebraska ("The Blue Hotel") and the correspondent who is lost at sea ("The Open Boat"); or they are at war; or they discover that the previously familiar environment has become alien and hostile ("The Monster"; *Maggie*). Thrust suddenly into the role of strangers, they usually try to order their present experience by familiar, often romantic conventions. The Swede has derived his notions of the Wild West from reading dime novels, Henry Fleming's ideas about war come from books and newspapers, in his emergency the correspondent recalls a poem, memorized in childhood, about a soldier dying in Algiers. More often than not, ironically enough, these apparently false or meaningless stereotypes turn out finally to have a measure of truth. The Swede *does* get killed, the correspondent identifies with the soldier in the poem, Henry Fleming does become a hero.

"I know what the professors say, that a fellow can't comprehend a condition that he has never experienced," Crane wrote, "and I argued that many times with the Professor." He also argued it many times with himself. The conclusion that emerges from his fiction is that ideas inherited from others may be true, but that their truth is not known until they have been experienced in action and suffering. Thus Crane himself would not rest until he had tested his imagined account of war in *The Red Badge of Courage* under combat conditions in Greece and found it to be "all right." He was able to transfer emotion from one kind of crisis to another; hence his argument with the professor. But he was always keenly aware of the gap between vivid personal experience and the inevitably limited and abstracted account of that experience. " 'To get at the real thing!' " he has a correspondent exclaim in "War Memories." " 'It seems impossible! It is because war is neither magnificent nor squalid; it is simply life, and an expression of life can always evade us. We can never tell life, one to another, although sometimes we think we can.' "

In his effort to express life, Crane strove to represent as fully as possible the elements of discontinuity and chaos. The short, fragmentary paragraphs that came naturally to him from his journalistic training worked to create this effect, as did the absence of authorial commentary. "Preaching is fatal to art in literature," he said, and certainly it would have been fatal to his art. For him there are no universally valid truths, no single, intelligible system; there are only individual centers of experience, vivid, agonized, and plural.

Unfortunately, the individual is not dependable either. At odds with his environment, man also wars with himself. "I perceived," said Crane soon after his first success, "that the fight was not going to be with the world but with myself." Like the universe, the self is not obligated to be friendly or rational. Its puzzling destructive qualities are suggested in another of Crane's brief, paradoxical poems:

> A man feared that he might find an assassin:
> Another that he might find a victim.
> One was more wise than the other.

Although the poem is too bare and artless to permit much analysis, Crane's fiction would suggest that both of these men fear self-discovery. Once a man rebels against conventional norms, he tends to regard himself in all his naked uniqueness as either assassin or victim, swollen with murderous pride or deflated to infinitesimal minuteness. As one critic put it, Crane's heroes are "pretentious and scared." The Swede in "The Blue Hotel" first falsely imagines himself as the potential victim of the Wild West; then, aided by alcohol, he becomes a kind of assassin, thumping "the soul" out of one man and attacking another; finally the result is that he becomes a real victim, a corpse alone in the saloon, its eyes fixed upon the cash register.

In a world dominated by violence—the slums, a raging sea, the blizzard-swept Middle West, the battlefield being its appropriate scenes—human relations, as Crane sees them, naturally reduce themselves to the level of assassin and victim. (Crane broadens the term "assassin" to mean any assailant.) The situation is complicated by two facts. First, man's situation and his attitude toward it are not necessarily identical. Crane's ironic vision forces us to distinguish between men who sentimentally imagine themselves as victims and those who have really been wounded. Second, more often than not, a man is both assassin and victim, conspiring to turn the destructive aspects of his rebelliousness against himself. Thus the Bowery bum in "An Experiment in Misery," known throughout the story as "the assassin," is the victim of his own cowardice, his willingness to be knocked flat.

Cowardice is the vice that murders the self; courage, as we have said, is the virtue that defines and creates it. Yet what Crane's anatomy of these two primary emotions adds up to finally is that they are irrational and thus the self is unintelligible. The heroism of Collins in "A Mystery of Heroism" is nearly as meaningless as the cowardice of the Bowery bum. The same man may be a coward on one occasion, a hero on another, and the shift seems to depend more on circumstance than on growth of character or will. Only the heroic act retains its dignity; the motive preceding it and the interpretation following it are usually stupid or distorted.

Acts of heroism in Crane's fiction are usually rewarded by self-sacrifice: Billie the oiler in "The Open Boat" rows heroically and is the only one of the four to drown; Henry Johnson saves a boy from a fire and becomes "The Monster"; old Henry Fleming in "The Veteran" rushes into a burning barn to save some colts and immolates himself. If man defines himself by acts of courage and these acts result in death or mutilation, what hope is there? Crane's answer is bleak. We are reminded of George Orwell's image in 1984: "If you want a picture of the future, imagine a boot stomping on a human face—forever." In Crane's fiction the terrible vulnerability of man is chillingly captured in the image of the upturned face. Crane's readers are haunted by the memory of Henry Johnson, lying unconscious on his back, the fiery acid dripping slowly onto his face, and by the corpse in Chapter VII of *The Red Badge of Courage*. ("Over the gray skin of the face ran little ants. One was trundling some sort of bundle along the upper lip.") We tend, therefore, to sympathize with Grierson in "The Price of the Harness," who, after watching his friend Nolan die, says, "Cover his face," or with the anguished Timothy Lean in "The Upturned Face," who, after partially burying a friend, cries out irritably to the adjutant: "Good God, why didn't you turn him somehow when you put him in?"

For Crane, then, life is war, its basic principles being external force, internal vividness, and incongruity everywhere between them. Thus the labels that best describe his art are naturalism, impressionism, and irony. Insofar as he envisions society and nature as assailing man, he is a naturalist; insofar as he candidly records the naked emotions and random sensations of consciousness, he is an impressionist; and insofar as he recognizes that motive and act, object and subject, self and world have come unglued, he finds his inevitable fictional form in irony.

II

The Red Badge of Courage was published first in condensed serial form in the Philadelphia Press in December 1894, and then in full-length book form in 1895. Although some flaws, particularly in the last chapter, prevent it from being as perfect artistically as "The Open Boat," it remains the central work in Crane's canon, the major example of his ironic vision. War offered him the necessary simplification, the desirable detachment from ordinary social texture that he needed if as an extremely young man he were to write a convincing novel. It also contained the basic dualism upon which his ironic sense could play. For Henry Fleming (and, to some extent, for Crane) war provided everything that ought to bring out the heroic in man: imaginativeness, courage, endurance, independence. Yet military discipline, routine, the harnessed destructive forces of technology, and the chaos of battle seemed to make for the very opposite: a man became merely a machine, trapped in a moving box, or an irrational beast, bent on assassinating his fellows.

As a structural principle in fiction, irony builds upon this basic dualism by developing a parody of the heroic element as it is embodied in romance and myth. By applying popular and romantic conventions to realistic material, it reveals where they unexpectedly fit and where they burst apart. If read with sufficient carelessness, The Red Badge resembles a bad movie, the sentimental military version of the success story. (As we would expect, Hollywood was alert to this possibility and made the movie.) The young man fresh from the farm enlists in the army, frets about whether he will be a coward or a hero, fights briefly and then runs. Ashamed and confused, he wanders around until he witnesses the agonizing death of his buddy. Determined to redeem himself, he roars back into action, leading a charge and carrying the flag. Crane said that he learned about the emotions of combat from playing football. Seen from the romantic perspective, there is a resemblance between Crane's hero and the injured left halfback who comes off the bench in the last minute of play and scores the winning touchdown. One is also reminded of Scott Fitzgerald's later vision of "the romantic Buzz Law . . . kicking from behind his own goal line with a bloody bandage round his head."

During World War I, Arthur Guy Empey, author of Over the Top, must have read the book this way. It "sends a warm glow through the heart of the reader," he wrote in his introduction to The Red Badge in 1917, "makes him want to carry the Stars and Stripes into the thick of the enemy, to be up and at them, and makes him feel proud that he also belongs to Uncle Sam, and that he also has a flag to carry in this War, our War, our Flag. If he does not feel this way, he is not a red-blooded man—he is a worm." Apparently ignoring Crane's descriptions of chaos and corpses, Empey went on to remark that the book would make "a wonderful recruiting film." On the other hand, a veteran of the Civil War, General A. C. Mc-Clurg, considered the book a vicious satire directed against patriotism. "There is no evidence of drill, none of discipline," he said in a natural reaction to a work where all generals, to Henry Fleming at least, are "stupids" and "idiots."

It is easy to chuckle at McClurg's wounded pride and Empey's flag waving. Both veterans were obviously naive in their misreading of the book. Yet their misinterpretations point to the basic problem faced by the most sympathetic and discerning readers. Crane uses, and at times seems to believe in, traditional ideas of war-induced maturation, while at the same time he undermines them. And these ideas are not limited to the sentimental failure-success formula we have just outlined. It is possible, by emphasizing certain aspects of the book and ignoring others, to read *The Red Badge* as a semireligious quest for salvation, an initiation story in which the youth ventures forth like the mythic hero of old and encounters the red monster War. According to this reading, Henry's growth follows the traditional pattern of withdrawal and return. His redemption is brought about by the death of Jim Conklin, the tall soldier, whose wounds, stature, and initials indicate that he is a Christ figure. His death has a mysterious ritualistic quality; he resembles "the devotee of a mad religion, blood-sucking, muscle-wrenching, bone-crushing." Having witnessed his friend's weird dance of death, Henry receives a wound at the hands of a retreating Union soldier, is guided by a cheery man back to his regiment, and rejoins his friend Wilson. In the loud soldier now become humble, he sees another example to guide him. The next day the two of them fight bravely, and after the battle is over we are told that Henry "had been to touch the great death and found that, after all, it was but the great death. He was a man." The suggestion is that Henry has discovered his identity by merging with the group, that he is now a permanent member of the "mysterious fraternity born of the smoke and danger of death" that he had briefly known before he ran from battle.

No one will deny that the quest for manhood is an important part of *The Red Badge of Courage*. But Crane spends much effort in denying what seems superficially to be affirmed; the plot, the characterization, and the point of view effectively demolish the interpretation we have just summarized. Consider, for example, Henry Fleming's motives and behavior after he witnesses Jim Conklin's death. Our sentimental expectations are that he will be outraged by his friend's death, feel the full force of his own guilt, return to his regiment, confess his cowardice to his friends, and then go into battle determined to redeem himself. But this is not what happens.

The outrage occurs, but it is brief and self-centered. Henry does not seek his regiment and gird himself for revenge; instead, he deserts the badly wounded tattered soldier and wanders around in a fog, rationalizing his flight, dreaming of heroism, dreading his reception if he were to return to his unit. Only as a result of circumstance—being clubbed on the head and being led by the cheery man—does he rejoin the outfit. Has the death of Conklin affected him? Certainly not; he lies to Wilson about being shot, forgets all about Conklin's death until the next day when he remembers the packet the formerly loud soldier had entrusted to him. Crane unrelentingly records the youth's self-delusion in Chapter XV: "He had performed his mistakes in the dark, so he was still a man. . . . He had license to be pompous and veteranlike." Clearly, the redemptive value of Conklin's so-called sacrificial death will not stand up under scrutiny.

The final value of masculine solidarity, when tested by the action, is more debatable. The "subtle battle brotherhood" supports Henry when he first encounters enemy fire, but it crumbles when the enemy charges again. Henry follows others when he turns "like a proverbial chicken" and deserts. In a book that supposedly affirms the virtue of masculine fellowship, Crane has included a large number of incidents that diminish our faith in Fleming's comrades. The contacts among Union soldiers are notably abrasive, beginning at the very start of the book with the quarrel between Conklin and Wilson. During the regiment's march into battle "a man fell down, and as he reached for his rifle a comrade, unseeing, trod upon his hand. He of the injured fingers swore bitterly and aloud. A low, tittering laugh went among his fellows." It is a very minor incident, of course, but Crane keeps reminding us of this man, Bill Smithers, who goes to the hospital with three "crunched" fingers. " 'Th' dern doctor wanted t'amputate 'm.' " The harsh collisions between Union soldiers reach their climax when Henry receives his wound in an encounter that is more vivid and personal than any of his rather vague brushes with the enemy. In the concluding chapters the intramural strife diminishes again to the sort of chronic scuffling that occurred in the beginning.

One reason why Crane selected these incidents is, of course, simply verisimilitude. Armies have always produced a number of their own casualties, just as they have always required men to be bored, to hurry up and wait, to advance and retreat. Crane's "slice out of life" in The Red Badge, though primarily a slice of consciousness, contains an impressive leaven of solid, specified detail: the way a canteen bobs on a running soldier's hip, the low voices of the men playing cards at night, the grumbled complaint of "sore feet an' damned short rations." So it is difficult, if not impossible, to determine the author's final attitude toward the fraternity of veterans in this book. We know that he later affirmed the reality of brotherhood earned in a crisis in "The Open Boat," and that he was downright sentimental in praising the regular army in Wounds in the Rain (1900). But in The Red

Badge, the tone of the last chapter is ambiguous. Judging from manuscript passages that Crane excluded from the published version of this chapter, he made some effort to tone down the acidity of his original attitude toward Henry's comrades. In the manuscript, for instance, he had reduced Wilson's moral stature somewhat by having him recall that he had intended to get some water for the wounded Jimmie Rogers. " 'I clean forgot what I —say, has anybody seen Jimmie Rogers?' " The answer of the men is definitive: " 'Seen him? No! He's dead.' "

Our difficulty in confirming intrinsic values in *The Red Badge* leads us back to Crane's main point: in war, which is his metaphor for life, meaning has been replaced by incoherence, events occur in succession but not in cause-and-effect sequence, rational analysis is irrelevant, and moral responses do not occur. The value of comradeship is automatically undermined by the fact that full characterization of Fleming's close friends would have been alien to Crane's vision of the war world. The characters have no past; we are told that Henry had known Jim Conklin since childhood, but the two men are related only as they react to the central question: "How does a man act under combat conditions?" And the bareness of their relation typifies the lack of dramatic interaction among the other characters. These nearly anonymous men are distinguished chiefly by their movements and by a single characteristic: fat, tall, tattered, loud, cheery. Henry is struck by the fact that he never saw the cheery man's face, but the other characters' faces are not described either. Crane's camera moves close up for the dead man's face with the ants crawling over it; the living men in the book, though their voices convince us that they are near at hand, tend to be seen at a murky distance.

How things are seen—or seen, heard, and felt—here, as all perceptive readers have noticed, lies the secret of *The Red Badge,* the reason why it seems a perpetually modern book. Seen from the outside, Henry Fleming in the concluding chapters would have resembled "the romantic Buzz Law." But we see from the inside, and with our intimate knowledge of Henry's distorted vision and vacillating moods, we are not deluded by his delusions (except, perhaps, in the final chapter). Crane may well have chosen to limit the point of view because he knew the Civil War only at second hand, from talking with veterans and from reading books like Wilbur F. Hinman's *Corporal Si Klegg and His "Pard."* But like all great artists he made a virtue out of his limitations. By restricting the point of view to Henry Fleming's consciousness yet permitting us to see beyond it, he found the inevitable form for expressing his image of irrational man in an indifferent world. In his published interview with Howells, Crane quoted with evident approval the older novelist's definition of the novel as a "perspective." "The novel, in its real meaning, adjusts proportions." Crane adjusts proportions in *The Red Badge* first by showing us how Henry Fleming, an individual deliberately cut off from tradition and society (his mother, the regiment), reacts to the threat of large external forces by alternating between inflation and deflation. By simply recording his extravagances, Crane cuts him down to normal size. The youth sees himself as a savior: "Perhaps the general, unable to comprehend chaos, might call upon him for information. And he would tell him." Or he sees himself as a victim: "It occurred to him that he had never wished to come to the war. He had not enlisted of his free will. He had been dragged by the merciless government. And now they were taking him out to be slaughtered." Henry's self-estimate obviously does not tally with external conditions. The piercing corrective usually comes in fragments of conversation, like the tattered man's query, " 'where yeh hit?' " or the general's contemptuous characterization of the regiment as "mud diggers."

Furthermore, by presenting the youth's consciousness in all of its uneven flow, Crane flattens out the distinction between the magnificent and the trivial. Henry's cowardice and his heroism are given no more space or emphasis than his aimless wandering. His actions are embedded in a stream of colorful, spotty detail, so that it would be difficult to say where the climax of the book occurs. Precise timing and precise spatial location, essential in any successful military operation, are notably absent. Henry is usually unaware of landmarks and the passage of time, and his state of confusion becomes part of Crane's general leveling process. From a military point of view, Henry and his regiment do not seem to get anywhere.

All serious war novels attempt to shape in artistic form the most violent and chaotic of human experiences. There are two broad categories within the genre of war fiction: books that attempt to give order to these experiences by showing how characters mature during war or how they operate in a larger context of political ideas and war aims; and books like Vance Bourjaily's *The End of My Life* and Joseph Heller's *Catch-22* that make little or no effort to rationalize war. Most of the novels written after the two world wars fall into the second category. *The Red Badge of Courage* ushers the modern war novel into being, though it does so somewhat uneasily. Crane completely ignores war aims and political ideas, but he is finally ambiguous about war as an initiation ritual. Total rejection of war's values presumably demands a fable in which the hero is either sterile, aimless, deserting, or dead at the end. Crane uses the fable of initiation, undermines it with great gusto, but in the final chapter imposes a conclusion that seems to support it. The book reflects the divided convictions of its author. War maims and kills people, kills them blindly, irrationally; it ought to be debunked. And yet the completely pacifistic war novel does not give the whole picture either. The tall soldier who gives his life without whining about the human condition deserves our respect and reverence even though, like Henry Fleming, we quickly forget him.

ROY MALE

A Note on the Text. The text of *The Red Badge of Courage* reprinted here is that of the first issue of the first edition, published by D. Appleton and Company in 1895. Obvious typographical errors have been silently corrected, but grammatical errors have been allowed to stand. The complete manuscript, now part of the Barrett Collection at the University of Virginia, contains passages deleted by Crane before printing as well as some passages not canceled but nevertheless omitted from the first printed edition. Robert W. Stallman, editor, in *Stephen Crane: An Omnibus* (New York: Alfred A. Knopf, Inc., 1952) discusses the textual problems; he has restored twenty-six of these omitted passages in brackets in the text. Though they have interest for the specialist, in every instance the omission of these passages was an improvement. Since Crane thought *The Red Badge* was too long, he may have authorized editorial omission of the passages, or he may have omitted them from the typescript made for the printer. At any rate, because he made no revisions of the book during the five years between its publication and his death, we may assume that he approved the text of the first edition.

[handwritten annotation: Here the hero discovers naturalistic truths on the blood-drenched field of battle]

THE RED BADGE OF COURAGE

1

THE COLD PASSED reluctantly from the earth, and the retiring fogs revealed an army stretched out on the hills, resting. As the landscape changed from brown to green, the army awakened, and began to tremble with eagerness at the noise of rumors. It cast its eyes upon the roads, which were growing from long troughs of liquid mud to proper thoroughfares. A river, amber-tinted in the shadow of its banks, purled at the army's feet; and at night, when the stream had become of a sorrowful blackness, one could see across it the red, eyelike gleam of hostile camp-fires set in the low brows of distant hills.

Once a certain tall soldier developed virtues and went resolutely to wash a shirt. He came flying back from a brook waving his garment bannerlike. He was swelled with a tale he had heard from a reliable friend, who had heard it from a truthful cavalryman, who had heard it from his trustworthy brother, one of the orderlies at division headquarters. He adopted the important air of a herald in red and gold.

"We're goin' t' move t' morrah—sure," he said pompously to a group in the company street. "We're goin' 'way up the river, cut across, an' come around in behint 'em."

To his attentive audience he drew a loud and elaborate plan of a very brilliant campaign. When he had finished, the blue-clothed men scattered into small arguing groups between the rows of squat brown huts. A negro teamster who had been dancing upon a cracker box with the hilarious encouragement of twoscore soldiers was deserted. He sat mournfully down. Smoke drifted lazily from a multitude of quaint chimneys.

"It's a lie! that's all it is—a thunderin' lie!" said another private loudly. His smooth face was flushed, and his hands were thrust sulkily into his trousers' pockets. He took the matter as an affront to him. "I don't believe the derned old army's ever going to move. We're set. I've got ready to move eight times in the last two weeks, and we ain't moved yet."

The tall soldier felt called upon to defend the truth of a rumor he himself had introduced. He and the loud one came near to fighting over it.

A corporal began to swear before the assemblage. He had just put a costly board floor in his house, he said. During the early spring he had refrained from adding extensively to the comfort of his environment because he had felt that the army might start on the march at any moment. Of late, however, he had been impressed that they were in a sort of eternal camp.

Many of the men engaged in a spirited debate. One outlined in a peculiarly lucid manner all the plans of the commanding general. He was opposed by men who advocated that there were other plans of campaign. They clamored at each other, numbers making futile bids for the popular attention. Meanwhile, the soldier who had fetched the rumor bustled about with much importance. He was continually assailed by questions.

"What's up, Jim?"

"Th' army's goin' t' move."

"Ah, what yeh talkin' about? How yeh know it is?"

"Well, yeh kin b'lieve me er not, jest as yeh like. I don't care a hang."

There was much food for thought in the manner in which he replied. He came near to convincing them by disdaining to produce proofs. They grew much excited over it.

There was a youthful private who listened with eager ears to the words of the tall soldier and to the varied comments of his comrades. After receiving a fill of discussions concerning marches and attacks, he went to his hut and crawled through an intricate hole that served it as a door. He wished to be alone with some new thoughts that had lately come to him.

He lay down on a wide bunk that stretched across the end of the room. In the other end, cracker boxes were made to serve as furniture. They were grouped about the fireplace. A picture from an illustrated weekly was upon the log walls, and three rifles were paralleled on pegs. Equipment hung on handy projections, and some tin dishes lay upon a small pile of firewood. A folded tent was serving as a room. The sunlight, without, beating upon it, made it glow a light yellow shade. A small window shot an oblique square of whiter light upon the cluttered floor. The smoke from the fire at times neglected the clay chimney and wreathed into the room, and this flimsy chimney of clay and sticks made endless threats to set ablaze the whole establishment.

The youth was in a little trance of astonishment. So they were at last going to fight. On the morrow, perhaps, there would be a battle, and he would be in it. For a time he was obliged to labor to make himself believe. He could not accept with assurance an omen that he was about to mingle in one of those great affairs of the earth.

He had, of course, dreamed of battles all his life—of vague and bloody conflicts that had thrilled him with their sweep and fire. In visions he had seen himself in many struggles. He had imagined peoples secure in the shadow of his eagle-eyed prowess. But awake he had regarded battles as crimson blotches on the pages of the past. He had put them as things of the bygone with his thought-images of heavy crowns and high castles. There was a portion of the world's history which he had regarded as the time of wars, but it, he thought, had been long gone over the horizon and had disappeared forever.

From his home his youthful eyes had looked upon the war in his own country with distrust. It must be some sort of a play affair. He had long despaired of witnessing a Greeklike struggle. Such would be no more, he had said. Men were better, or more timid. Secular and religious education had effaced the throat-grappling instinct, or else firm finance held in check the passions.

He had burned several times to enlist. Tales of great movements shook the land. They might not be distinctly Homeric, but there seemed to be much glory in them. He had read of marches, sieges, conflicts, and he had longed to see it all. His busy mind had drawn for him large pictures extravagant in color, lurid with breathless deeds.

But his mother had discouraged him. She had affected to look with some contempt upon the quality of his war ardor and patriotism. She could calmly seat herself and with no apparent difficulty give him many hundreds of reasons why he was of vastly more importance on the farm than on the field of battle. She had had certain ways of expression that told him that her statements on the subject came from a deep conviction. Moreover, on her side, was his belief that her ethical motive in the argument was impregnable.

At last, however, he had made firm rebellion against this yellow light thrown upon the color of his ambitions. The newspapers, the gossip of the village, his own picturings, had aroused him to an uncheckable degree. They were in truth fighting finely down there. Almost every day the newspapers printed accounts of a decisive victory.

One night, as he lay in bed, the winds had carried to him the clangoring of the church bell as some enthusiast jerked the rope frantically to tell the twisted news of a great battle. This voice of the people rejoicing in the night had made him shiver in a prolonged ecstasy of excitement. Later, he had gone down to his mother's room and had spoken thus: "Ma, I'm going to enlist."

"Henry, don't you be a fool," his mother had replied. She had then covered her face with the quilt. There was an end to the matter for that night.

Nevertheless, the next morning he had gone to a town that was near his mother's farm and had enlisted in a company that was forming there. When he had returned home his mother was milking the brindle cow. Four others stood waiting. "Ma, I've enlisted," he had said to her diffidently. There was a short silence. "The Lord's will be done, Henry," she had finally replied, and had then continued to milk the brindle cow.

When he had stood in the doorway with his soldier's clothes on his back, and with the light of excitement and expectancy in his eyes almost defeating the glow of regret for the home bonds, he had seen two tears leaving their trails on his mother's scarred cheeks.

Still, she had disappointed him by saying nothing whatever about returning with his shield or on it. He had privately primed himself for a beautiful scene. He had prepared certain sentences which he thought could be used with touching effect. But her words destroyed his plans. She had doggedly peeled potatoes and addressed him as follows: "You watch out, Henry, an' take good care of yerself in this here fighting business—you watch out, an' take good care of yerself. Don't go a-thinkin' you can lick the hull rebel army at the start, because yeh can't. Yer jest one little feller amongst a hull lot of others, and yeh've got to keep quiet an' do what they tell yeh. I know how you are, Henry.

"I've knet yeh eight pair of socks, Henry, and I've put in all yer best shirts, because I want my boy to be jest as warm and comf'able as anybody in the army. Whenever they get holes in 'em, I want yeh to send 'em right-away back to me, so's I kin dern 'em.

"An' allus be careful an' choose yer comp'ny. There's lots of bad men in the army, Henry. The army makes 'em wild, and they like nothing better than the job of leading off a young feller like you, as ain't never been away from home much and has allus had a mother, an' a-learning 'em to drink and swear. Keep clear of them folks, Henry. I don't want yeh to ever do anything, Henry, that yeh would be 'shamed to let me know about. Jest think as if I was a-watchin' yeh. If yeh keep that in yer mind allus, I guess yeh'll come out about right.

"Yeh must allus remember yer father, too, child, an' remember he never drunk a drop of licker in his life, and seldom swore a cross oath.

"I don't know what else to tell yeh, Henry, excepting that yeh must never do no shirking, child, on my account. If so be a time comes when yeh have to be kilt or do a mean thing, why, Henry, don't think of anything 'cept what's right, because there's many a woman has to bear up 'ginst sech things these times, and the Lord 'll take keer of us all.

"Don't forgit about the socks and the shirts, child; and I've put a cup of blackberry jam with yer bundle, because I know yeh like it above all things. Good-by, Henry. Watch out, and be a good boy."

He had, of course, been impatient under the ordeal of this speech. It had not been quite what he expected, and he had borne it with an air of irritation. He departed feeling vague relief.

Still, when he had looked back from the gate, he had seen his mother kneeling among the potato parings. Her brown face, upraised, was stained with tears, and her spare form was quivering. He bowed his head and went on, feeling suddenly ashamed of his purposes.

From his home he had gone to the seminary to bid adieu to many school-mates. They had thronged about him with wonder and admiration. He had felt the gulf now between them and had swelled with calm pride. He and some of his fellows who had donned blue were quite overwhelmed with privileges for all of one afternoon, and it had been a very delicious thing. They had strutted.

A certain light-haired girl had made vivacious fun at his martial spirit, but there was another and darker girl whom he had gazed at steadfastly, and he thought she grew demure and sad at sight of his blue and brass. As he had walked down the path between the rows of oaks, he had turned his head and detected her at a window watching his departure. As he perceived her, she had immediately begun to stare up through the high tree branches at the sky. He had seen a good deal of flurry and haste in her movement as she changed her attitude. He often thought of it.

On the way to Washington his spirit had soared. The regiment was fed and caressed at station after station until the youth had believed that he must be a hero. There was a lavish expenditure of bread and cold meats, coffee, and pickles and cheese. As he basked in the smiles of the girls and was patted and complimented by the old men, he had felt growing within him the strength to do mighty deeds of arms.

After complicated journeyings with many pauses, there had come months of monotonous life in a camp. He had had the belief that real war was a series of death struggles with small time in between for sleep and meals; but since his regiment had come to the field the army had done little but sit still and try to keep warm.

He was brought then gradually back to his old ideas. Greeklike struggles would be no more. Men were better, or more timid. Secular and religious education had effaced the throat-grappling instinct, or else firm finance held in check the passions.

He had grown to regard himself merely as a part of a vast blue demonstration. His province was to look out, as far as he could, for his personal comfort. For recreation he could twiddle his thumbs and speculate on the thoughts which must agitate the minds of the generals. Also, he was drilled and drilled and reviewed, and drilled and drilled and reviewed.

The only foes he had seen were some pickets along the river bank. They were a sun-tanned, philosophical lot, who sometimes shot reflectively at the blue pickets. When reproached for this afterward, they usually expressed sorrow, and swore by their gods that the guns had exploded without their permission. The youth, on guard duty one night, conversed across the stream with one of them. He was a slightly ragged man, who spat skillfully between his shoes and possessed a great fund of bland and infantile assurance. The youth liked him personally.

"Yank," the other had informed him, "yer a right dum good feller." This sentiment, floating to him upon the still air, had made him temporarily regret war.

Various veterans had told him tales. Some talked of gray, bewhiskered hordes who were advancing with relentless curses and chewing tobacco with unspeakable valor; tremendous bodies of fierce soldiery who were sweeping along like the Huns. Others spoke of tattered and eternally hungry men who fired despondent powders. "They'll charge through hell's fire an' brimstone t' git a holt on a haversack, an' sech stomachs ain't a-lastin' long," he was told. From the stories, the youth imagined the red, live bones sticking out through slits in the faded uniforms.

Still, he could not put a whole faith in veterans' tales, for recruits were their prey. They talked much of smoke, fire, and blood, but he could not tell how much might be lies. They persistently yelled "Fresh fish!" at him, and were in no wise to be trusted.

However, he perceived now that it did not greatly matter what kind of soldiers he was going to fight, so long as they fought, which fact no one disputed. There was a more serious problem. He lay in his bunk pondering upon it. He tried to mathematically prove to himself that he would not run from a battle.

Previously he had never felt obliged to wrestle too seriously with this question. In his life he had taken certain things for granted, never challenging his belief in ultimate success, and bothering little about means and roads. But here he was confronted with a thing of moment. It had suddenly appeared to him that perhaps in a battle he might run. He was forced to admit that as far as war was concerned he knew nothing of himself.

A sufficient time before he would have allowed the problem to kick its heels at the outer portals of his mind, but now he felt compelled to give serious attention to it.

A little panic-fear grew in his mind. As his imagination went forward to a fight, he saw hideous possibilities. He contemplated the lurking menaces of the future, and failed in an effort to see himself standing stoutly in the midst of them. He recalled his visions of broken-bladed glory, but in the shadow of the impending tumult he suspected them to be impossible pictures.

He sprang from the bunk and began to pace nervously to and fro. "Good Lord, what's th' matter with me?" he said aloud.

He felt that in this crisis his laws of life were useless. Whatever he had learned of himself was here of no avail. He was an unknown quantity. He saw that he would again be obliged to experiment as he had in early youth. He must accumulate information of himself, and meanwhile he resolved to remain close upon his guard lest those qualities of which he knew nothing should everlastingly disgrace him. "Good Lord!" he repeated in dismay.

After a time the tall soldier slid dexterously through the hole. The loud private followed. They were wrangling.

"That's all right," said the tall soldier as he entered. He waved his hand expressively. "You can believe me or not, jest as you like. All you got to do is to sit down and wait as quiet as you can. Then pretty soon you'll find out I was right."

His comrade grunted stubbornly. For a moment he seemed to be searching for a formidable reply. Finally he said: "Well, you don't know everything in the world, do you?"

"Didn't say I knew everything in the world," retorted the other sharply. He began to stow various articles snugly into his knapsack.

The youth, pausing in his nervous walk, looked down at the busy figure. "Going to be a battle, sure, is there, Jim?" he asked.

"Of course there is," replied the tall soldier. "Of course there is. You jest wait 'til to-morrow, and you'll see one of the biggest battles ever was. You jest wait."

"Thunder!" said the youth.

"Oh, you'll see fighting this time, my boy, what'll be regular out-and-out fighting," added the tall soldier, with the air of a man who is about to exhibit a battle for the benefit of his friends.

"Huh!" said the loud one from a corner.

"Well," remarked the youth, "like as not this story'll turn out jest like them others did."

"Not much it won't," replied the tall soldier, exasperated. "Not much it won't. Didn't the cavalry all start this morning?" He glared about him. No one denied his statement. "The cavalry started this morning," he continued. "They say there ain't hardly any cavalry left in camp. They're going to Richmond, or some place, while we fight all the Johnnies. It's some dodge like that. The regiment's got orders, too. A feller what seen 'em go to headquarters told me a little while ago. And they're raising blazes all over camp—anybody can see that."

"Shucks!" said the loud one.

The youth remained silent for a time. At last he spoke to the tall soldier. "Jim!"

"What?"

"How do you think the reg'ment 'll do?"

"Oh, they'll fight all right, I guess, after they once get into it," said the other with cold judgment. He made a fine use of the third person. "There's been heaps of fun poked at 'em because they're new, of course, and all that; but they'll fight all right, I guess."

"Think any of the boys 'll run?" persisted the youth.

"Oh, there may be a few of 'em run, but there's them kind in every regiment, 'specially when they first goes under fire," said the other in a tolerant way. "Of course it might happen that the hull kit-and-boodle might start and run, if some big fighting came first-off, and then again they might stay and fight like fun. But you can't bet on nothing. Of course they ain't never been under fire yet, and it ain't likely they'll lick the hull rebel army all-to-oncet the first time; but I think they'll fight better than some, if worse than others. That's the way I figger. They call the reg'ment 'Fresh fish' and everything; but the boys come of good stock, and most of 'em 'll fight like sin after they oncet git shootin'," he added, with a mighty emphasis on the last four words.

"Oh, you think you know——" began the loud soldier with scorn.

The other turned savagely upon him. They had a rapid altercation, in which they fastened upon each other various strange epithets.

The youth at last interrupted them. "Did you ever think you might run yourself, Jim?" he asked. On concluding the sentence he laughed as if he had meant to aim a joke. The loud soldier also giggled.

The tall private waved his hand. "Well," said he profoundly, "I've thought it might get too hot for Jim Conklin in some of them scrimmages, and if a whole lot of boys started and run, why, I s'pose I'd start and run. And if I once started to run, I'd run like the devil, and no mistake. But if everybody was a-standing and a-fighting, why, I'd stand and fight. Be jiminey, I would. I'll bet on it."

"Huh!" said the loud one.

The youth of this tale felt gratitude for these words of his comrade. He had feared that all of the untried men possessed a great and correct confidence. He now was in a measure reassured.

2

The next morning the youth discovered that his tall comrade had been the fast-flying messenger of a mistake. There was much scoffing at the latter by those who had yesterday been firm adherents of his views, and there was even a little sneering by men who had never believed the rumor. The tall one fought with a man from Chatfield Corners and beat him severely.

The youth felt, however, that his problem was in no wise lifted from him. There was, on the contrary, an irritating prolongation. The tale had created in him a great concern for himself. Now, with the newborn question in his mind, he was compelled to sink back into his old place as part of a blue demonstration.

For days he made ceaseless calculations, but they were all wondrously unsatisfactory. He found that he could establish nothing. He finally concluded that the only way to prove himself was to go into the blaze, and then figuratively to watch his legs to discover their merits and faults. He reluctantly admitted that he could not sit still and with a mental slate and pencil derive an answer. To gain it, he must have blaze, blood, and danger, even as a chemist requires this, that, and the other. So he fretted for an opportunity.

Meanwhile he continually tried to measure himself by his comrades. The tall soldier, for one, gave him some assurance. This man's serene unconcern dealt him a measure of confidence, for he had known him since childhood, and from his intimate knowledge he did not see how he could be capable of anything that was beyond him, the youth. Still, he thought that his comrade might be mistaken about himself. Or, on the other hand, he might be a man heretofore doomed to peace and obscurity, but, in reality, made to shine in war.

The youth would have liked to have discovered another who suspected himself. A sympathetic comparison of mental notes would have been a joy to him.

He occasionally tried to fathom a comrade with seductive sentences. He looked about to find men in the proper mood. All attempts failed to bring forth any statement which looked in any way like a confession to those doubts which he privately acknowledged in himself. He was afraid to make an open declaration of his concern, because he dreaded to place some unscrupulous confidant upon the high plane of the unconfessed from which elevation he could be derided.

In regard to his companions his mind wavered between two opinions, according to his mood. Sometimes he inclined to believing them all heroes. In fact, he usually admitted in secret the superior development of the higher qualities in others. He could conceive of men going very insignificantly about the world bearing a load of courage unseen, and although he had known many of his comrades through boyhood, he began to fear that his judgment of them had been blind. Then, in other moments, he flouted these theories, and assured himself that his fellows were all privately wondering and quaking.

His emotions made him feel strange in the presence of men who talked excitedly of a prospective battle as of a drama they were about to witness, with nothing but eagerness and curiosity apparent in their faces. It was often that he suspected them to be liars.

He did not pass such thoughts without severe condemnation of himself. He dinned reproaches at times. He was convicted by himself of many shameful crimes against the gods of traditions.

In his great anxiety his heart was continually clamoring at what he considered the intolerable slowness of the generals. They seemed content to perch tranquilly on the river bank, and leave him bowed down by the weight of a great problem. He wanted it settled forthwith. He could not long bear such a load, he said. Sometimes his anger at the commanders reached an acute stage, and he grumbled about the camp like a veteran.

One morning, however, he found himself in the ranks of his prepared regiment. The men were whispering speculations and recounting the old rumors. In the gloom before the break of the day their uniforms glowed a deep purple hue. From across the river the red eyes were still peering. In the eastern sky there was a yellow patch like a rug laid for the feet of the coming sun; and against it, black and patternlike, loomed the gigantic figure of the colonel on a gigantic horse.

From off in the darkness came the trampling of feet. The youth could occasionally see dark shadows that moved like monsters. The regiment stood at rest for what seemed a long time. The youth grew impatient. It was unendurable the way these affairs were managed. He wondered how long they were to be kept waiting.

As he looked all about him and pondered upon the mystic gloom, he began to believe that at any moment the ominous distance might be aflare, and the rolling crashes of an engagement come to his ears. Staring once at the red eyes across the river, he conceived them to be growing larger, as the orbs of a row of dragons advancing. He turned toward the colonel and saw him lift his gigantic arm and calmly stroke his mustache.

At last he heard from along the road at the foot of the hill the clatter of a horse's galloping hoofs. It must be the coming of orders. He bent forward, scarce breathing. The exciting clickety-click, as it grew louder and louder, seemed to be beating upon his soul. Presently a horseman with jangling equipment drew rein before the colonel of the regiment. The two held a short, sharp-worded conversation. The men in the foremost ranks craned their necks.

As the horseman wheeled his animal and galloped away he turned to shout over his shoulder, "Don't forget that box of cigars!" The colonel mumbled in reply. The youth wondered what a box of cigars had to do with war.

A moment later the regiment went swinging off into the darkness. It was now like one of those moving monsters wending with many feet. The air was heavy, and cold with dew. A mass of wet grass, marched upon, rustled like silk.

There was an occasional flash and glimmer of steel from the backs of all these huge crawling reptiles. From the road came creakings and grumblings as some surly guns were dragged away.

The men stumbled along still muttering speculations. There was a subdued debate. Once a man fell down, and as he reached for his rifle a comrade, unseeing, trod upon his hand. He of the injured fingers swore bitterly and aloud. A low, tittering laugh went among his fellows.

Presently they passed into a roadway and marched forward with easy strides. A dark regiment moved before them, and from behind also came the tinkle of equipments on the bodies of marching men.

The rushing yellow of the developing day went on behind their backs. When the sunrays at last struck full and mellowingly upon the earth, the youth saw that the landscape was streaked with two long, thin, black columns which disappeared on the brow of a hill in front and rearward vanished in a wood. They were like two serpents crawling from the cavern of the night.

The river was not in view. The tall soldier burst into praises of what he thought to be his powers of perception.

Some of the tall one's companions cried with emphasis that they, too, had evolved the same thing, and they congratulated themselves upon it. But there were others who said that the tall one's plan was not the true one at all. They persisted with other theories. There was a vigorous discussion.

The youth took no part in them. As he walked along in careless line he was engaged with his own eternal debate. He could not hinder himself from dwelling upon it. He was despondent and sullen, and threw shifting glances about him. He looked ahead, often expecting to hear from the advance the rattle of firing.

But the long serpents crawled slowly from hill to hill without bluster of smoke. A dun-colored cloud of dust floated away to the right. The sky overhead was of a fairy blue.

The youth studied the faces of his companions, ever on the watch to detect kindred emotions. He suffered disappointment. Some ardor of the air which was causing the veteran commands to move with glee—almost with song— had infected the new regiment. The men began to speak of victory as of a thing they knew. Also, the tall soldier received his vindication. They were certainly going to come around in behind the enemy. They expressed commiseration for that part of the enemy which had been left upon the river bank, felicitating themselves upon being a part of a blasting host.

The youth, considering himself as separated from the others, was saddened by the blithe and merry speeches that went from rank to rank. The company wags all made their best endeavors. The regiment tramped to the tune of laughter.

The blatant soldier often convulsed whole files by his biting sarcasms aimed at the tall one.

And it was not long before all the men seemed to forget their mission. Whole brigades grinned in unison, and regiments laughed.

A rather fat soldier attempted to pilfer a horse from a dooryard. He planned to load his knapsack upon it. He was escaping with his prize when a young girl rushed from the house and grabbed the animal's mane. There followed a wrangle. The young girl, with pink cheeks and shining eyes, stood like a dauntless statue.

The observant regiment, standing at rest in the roadway, whooped at once, and entered whole-souled upon the side of the maiden. The men became so engrossed in this affair that they entirely ceased to remember their own large war. They jeered the piratical private, and called attention to various defects in his personal appearance; and they were wildly enthusiastic in support of the young girl.

To her, from some distance, came bold advice. "Hit him with a stick."

There were crows and catcalls showered upon him when he retreated without the horse. The regiment rejoiced at his downfall. Loud and vociferous congratulations were showered upon the maiden, who stood panting and regarding the troops with defiance.

At nightfall the column broke into regimental pieces, and the fragments went into the fields to camp. Tents sprang up like strange plants. Campfires, like red, peculiar blossoms, dotted the night.

The youth kept from intercourse with his companions as much as circumstances would allow him. In the evening he wandered a few paces into the gloom. From this little distance the many fires, with the black forms of men passing to and fro before the crimson rays, made weird and satanic effects.

He lay down in the grass. The blades pressed tenderly against his cheek. The moon had been lighted and was hung in a treetop. The liquid stillness of the night enveloping him made him feel vast pity for himself. There was a caress in the soft winds; and the whole mood of the darkness, he thought, was one of sympathy for himself in his distress.

He wished, without reserve, that he was at home again making the endless rounds from the house to the barn, from the barn to the fields, from the fields to the barn, from the barn to the house. He remembered he had often cursed the brindle cow and her mates, and had sometimes flung milking stools. But, from his present point of view, there was a halo of happiness about each of their heads, and he would have sacrificed all the brass buttons on the continent to have been enabled to return to them. He told himself that he was not formed for a soldier. And he mused seriously upon the radical differences between himself and those men who were dodging implike around the fires.

As he mused thus he heard the rustle of grass, and, upon turning his head, discovered the loud soldier. He called out, "Oh, Wilson!"

The latter approached and looked down. "Why, hello, Henry; is it you? What you doing here?"

"Oh, thinking," said the youth.

The other sat down and carefully lighted his pipe. "You're getting blue, my boy. You're looking thundering peeked. What the dickens is wrong with you?"

"Oh, nothing," said the youth.

The loud soldier launched them into the subject of the anticipated fight. "Oh, we've got 'em now!" As he spoke his boyish face was wreathed in a gleeful smile, and his voice had an exultant ring. "We've got 'em now. At last, by the eternal thunders, we'll lick 'em good!"

"If the truth was known," he added, more soberly, "*they've* licked *us* about every clip up to now; but this time—this time—we'll lick 'em good!"

"I thought you was objecting to this march a little while ago," said the youth coldly.

"Oh, it wasn't that," explained the other. "I don't mind marching, if there's going to be fighting at the end of it. What I hate is this getting moved here and moved there, with no good coming of it, as far as I can see, excepting sore feet and damned short rations."

"Well, Jim Conklin says we'll get a plenty of fighting this time."

"He's right for once, I guess, though I can't see how it come. This time we're in for a big battle, and we've got the best end of it, certain sure. Gee rod! how we will thump 'em!"

He arose and began to pace to and fro excitedly. The thrill of this enthusiasm made him walk with an elastic step. He was sprightly, vigorous, fiery in his belief in success. He looked into the future with clear, proud eye, and he swore with the air of an old soldier.

The youth watched him for a moment in silence. When he finally spoke his voice was as bitter as dregs. "Oh, you're going to do great things, I s'pose!"

The loud soldier blew a thoughtful cloud of smoke from his pipe. "Oh, I don't know," he remarked with dignity; "I don't know. I s'pose I'll do as well as the rest. I'm going to try like thunder." He evidently complimented himself upon the modesty of this statement.

"How do you know you won't run when the time comes?" asked the youth.

"Run?" said the loud one; "run?—of course not!" He laughed.

"Well," continued the youth, "lots of good-a-'nough men have thought they was going to do great things before the fight, but when the time come they skedaddled."

"Oh, that's all true, I s'pose," replied the other; "but I'm not going to skedaddle. The man that bets on my running will lose his money, that's all." He nodded confidently.

"Oh, shucks!" said the youth. "You ain't the bravest man in the world, are you?"

"No, I ain't," exclaimed the loud soldier indignantly; "and I didn't say I was the bravest man in the world, either. I said I was going to do my share of fighting—that's what I said. And I am, too. Who are you, anyhow? You talk as if you thought you was Napoleon Bonaparte." He glared at the youth for a moment, and then strode away.

The youth called in a savage voice after his comrade: "Well, you needn't git mad about it!" But the other continued on his way and made no reply.

He felt alone in space when his injured comrade had disappeared. His failure to discover any mite of resemblance in their viewpoints made him more miserable than before. No one seemed to be wrestling with such a terrific personal problem. He was a mental outcast.

He went slowly to his tent and stretched himself on a blanket by the side of the snoring tall soldier. In the darkness he saw visions of a thousand-tongued fear that would babble at his back and cause him to flee, while others were going coolly about their country's business. He admitted that he would not be able to cope with this monster. He felt that every nerve in his body would be an ear to hear the voices, while other men would remain stolid and deaf.

And as he sweated with the pain of these thoughts, he could hear low, serene sentences. "I'll bid five." "Make it six." "Seven." "Seven goes."

He stared at the red, shivering reflection of a fire on the white wall of his tent until, exhausted and ill from the monotony of his suffering, he fell asleep.

3

When another night came the columns, changed to purple streaks, filed across two pontoon bridges. A glaring fire wine-tinted the waters of the river. Its rays, shining upon the moving masses of troops, brought forth here and there sudden gleams of silver or gold. Upon the other shore a dark and mysterious range of hills was curved against the sky. The insect voices of the night sang solemnly.

After this crossing the youth assured himself that at any moment they might be suddenly and fearfully assaulted from the caves of the lowering woods. He kept his eyes watchfully upon the darkness.

But his regiment went unmolested to a camping place, and its soldiers slept the brave sleep of wearied men. In the morning they were routed out with early energy, and hustled along a narrow road that led deep into the forest.

It was during this rapid march that the regiment lost many of the marks of a new command.

The men had begun to count the miles upon their fingers, and they grew tired. "Sore feet an' damned short rations, that's all," said the loud soldier. There was perspiration and grumblings. After a time they began to shed their knapsacks. Some tossed them unconcernedly down; others hid them carefully, asserting their plans to return for them at some convenient time. Men extricated themselves from thick shirts. Presently few carried anything but their necessary clothing, blankets, haversacks, canteens, and arms and ammunition. "You can now eat and shoot," said the tall soldier to the youth. "That's all you want to do."

There was sudden change from the ponderous infantry of theory to the light and speedy infantry of practice. The regiment, relieved of a burden, received a new impetus. But there was much loss of valuable knapsacks, and, on the whole, very good shirts.

But the regiment was not yet veteranlike in appearance. Veteran regiments in the army were likely to be very small aggregations of men. Once, when the command had first come to the field, some perambulating veterans, noting the length of their column, had accosted them thus: "Hey, fellers, what brigade is that?" And when the men had replied that they formed a regiment and not a brigade, the older soldiers had laughed, and said, "O Gawd!"

Also, there was too great a similarity in the hats. The hats of a regiment should properly represent the history of headgear for a period of years. And, moreover, there were no letters of faded gold speaking from the colors. They were new and beautiful, and the color bearer habitually oiled the pole.

Presently the army again sat down to think. The odor of the peaceful pines was in the men's nostrils. The sound of monotonous axe blows rang through the forest, and the insects, nodding upon their perches, crooned like old women. The youth returned to his theory of a blue demonstration.

One gray dawn, however, he was kicked in the leg by the tall soldier, and then, before he was entirely awake, he found himself running down a wood road in the midst of men who were panting from the first effects of speed. His canteen banged rhythmically upon his thigh, and his haversack bobbed softly. His musket bounced a trifle from his shoulder at each stride and made his cap feel uncertain upon his head.

He could hear the men whisper jerky sentences: "Say—what's all this—about?" "What th' thunder—we—skedaddlin' this way fer?" "Billie—keep off m' feet. Yeh run—like a cow." And the loud soldier's shrill voice could be heard: "What th' devil they in sich a hurry for?"

The youth thought the damp fog of early morning moved from the rush of a great body of troops. From the distance came a sudden spatter of firing.

He was bewildered. As he ran with his comrades he strenuously tried to think, but all he knew was that if he fell down those coming behind would tread upon him. All his faculties seemed to be needed to guide him over and past obstructions. He felt carried along by a mob.

The sun spread disclosing rays, and, one by one, regiments burst into view like armed men just born of the earth. The youth perceived that the time had come. He was about to be measured. For a moment he felt in the face of his great trial like a babe, and the flesh over his heart seemed very thin. He seized time to look about him calculatingly.

But he instantly saw that it would be impossible for him to escape from the regiment. It inclosed him. And there were iron laws of tradition and law on four sides. He was in a moving box.

As he perceived this fact it occurred to him that he had never wished to come to the war. He had not enlisted of his free will. He had been dragged by the merciless government. And now they were taking him out to be slaughtered.

The regiment slid down a bank and wallowed across a little stream. The mournful current moved slowly on, and from the water, shaded black, some white bubble eyes looked at the men.

As they climbed the hill on the farther side artillery began to boom. Here the youth forgot many things as he felt a sudden impulse of curiosity. He scrambled up the bank with a speed that could not be exceeded by a bloodthirsty man.

He expected a battle scene.

There were some little fields girted and squeezed by a forest. Spread over the grass and in among the tree trunks, he could see knots and waving lines of skirmishers who were running hither and thither and firing at the landscape, A dark battle line lay upon a sunstruck clearing that gleamed orange color. A flag fluttered.

Other regiments floundered up the bank. The brigade was formed in line of battle, and after a pause started slowly through the woods in the rear of the receding skirmishers, who were continually melting into the scene to appear again farther on. They were always busy as bees, deeply absorbed in their little combats.

The youth tried to observe everything. He did not use care to avoid trees and branches, and his forgotten feet were constantly knocking against stones or getting entangled in briers. He was aware that these battalions with their commotions were woven red and startling into the gentle fabric of softened greens and browns. It looked to be a wrong place for a battle field.

The skirmishers in advance fascinated him. Their shots into thickets and at distant and prominent trees spoke to him of tragedies—hidden, mysterious, solemn.

Once the line encountered the body of a dead soldier. He lay upon his back staring at the sky. He was dressed in an awkward suit of yellowish brown. The youth could see that the soles of his shoes had been worn to the thinness of writing paper, and from a great rent in one the dead foot projected piteously. And it was as if fate had betrayed the soldier. In death it exposed to his enemies that poverty which in life he had perhaps concealed from his friends.

The ranks opened covertly to avoid the corpse. The invulnerable dead man forced a way for himself. The youth looked keenly at the ashen face. The wind raised the tawny beard. It moved as if a hand were stroking it. He vaguely desired to walk around and around the body and stare; the impulse of the living to try to read in dead eyes the answer to the Question.

During the march the ardor which the youth had acquired when out of view of the field rapidly faded to nothing. His curiosity was quite easily satisfied. If an intense scene had caught him with its wild swing as he came to the top of the bank, he might have gone roaring on. This advance upon Nature was too calm. He had opportunity to reflect. He had time in which to wonder about himself and to attempt to probe his sensations.

Absurd ideas took hold upon him. He thought that he did not relish the landscape. It threatened him. A coldness swept over his back, and it is true that his trousers felt to him that they were no fit for his legs at all.

A house standing placidly in distant fields had to him an ominous look. The shadows of the woods were formidable. He was certain that in this vista there lurked fierce-eyed hosts. The swift thought came to him that the generals did not know what they were about. It was all a trap. Suddenly those close forests would bristle with rifle barrels. Ironlike brigades would appear in the rear. They were all going to be sacrificed. The generals were stupids. The enemy would presently swallow the whole command. He glared about him, expecting to see the stealthy approach of his death.

He thought that he must break from the ranks and harangue his comrades. They must not all be killed like pigs; and he was sure it would come to pass unless they were informed of these dangers. The generals were idiots to send them marching into a regular pen. There was but one pair of eyes in the corps. He would step forth and make a speech. Shrill and passionate words came to his lips.

The line, broken into moving fragments by the ground, went calmly on through fields and woods. The youth looked at the men nearest him, and saw, for the most part, expressions of deep interest, as if they were investigating something that had fascinated them. One or two stepped with overvaliant airs as if they were already plunged into war. Others walked as upon thin ice. The greater part of the untested men appeared quiet and absorbed. They were going to look at war, the red animal—war, the blood-swollen god. And they were deeply engrossed in this march.

As he looked the youth gripped his outcry at his throat. He saw that even if the men were tottering with fear they would laugh at his warning. They would jeer him, and, if practicable, pelt him with missiles. Admitting that he might be wrong, a frenzied declamation of the kind would turn him into a worm.

He assumed, then, the demeanor of one who knows that he is doomed alone to unwritten responsibilities. He lagged, with tragic glances at the sky.

He was surprised presently by the young lieutenant of his company, who began heartily to beat him with a sword, calling out in a loud and insolent voice: "Come, young man, get up into ranks there. No skulking 'll do here." He mended his pace with suitable haste. And he hated the lieutenant, who had no appreciation of fine minds. He was a mere brute.

After a time the brigade was halted in the cathedral light of a forest. The busy skirmishers were still popping. Through the aisles of the wood could be seen the floating smoke from their rifles. Sometimes it went up in little balls, white and compact.

During this halt many men in the regiment began erecting tiny hills in front of them. They used stones, sticks, earth, and anything they thought might turn a bullet. Some built comparatively large ones, while others seemed content with little ones.

This procedure caused a discussion among the men. Some wished to fight like duelists, believing it to be correct to stand erect and be, from their feet to their foreheads, a mark. They said they scorned the devices of the cautious. But the others scoffed in reply, and pointed to the veterans on the flanks who were digging at the ground like terriers. In a short time there was quite a barricade along the regimental fronts. Directly, however, they were ordered to withdraw from that place.

This astounded the youth. He forgot his stewing over the advance movement. "Well, then, what did they march us out here for?" he demanded of the tall soldier. The latter with calm faith began a heavy explanation, although he had been compelled to leave a little protection of stones and dirt to which he had devoted much care and skill.

When the regiment was aligned in another position each man's regard for his safety caused another line of small intrenchments. They ate their noon meal behind a third one. They were moved from this one also. They were marched from place to place with apparent aimlessness.

The youth had been taught that a man became another thing in a battle. He saw his salvation in such a change. Hence this waiting was an ordeal to him. He was in a fever of impatience. He considered that there was denoted a lack of purpose on the part of the generals. He began to complain to the tall soldier. "I can't stand this much longer," he cried. "I don't see what good it does to make us wear out our legs for nothin'." He wished to return to camp, knowing that this affair was a blue demonstration; or else to go into battle and discover that he had been a fool in his doubts, and was, in truth, a man of traditional courage. The strain of present circumstances he felt to be intolerable.

The philosophical tall soldier measured a sandwich of cracker and pork and swallowed it in a nonchalant manner. "Oh, I suppose we must go reconnoitering around the country jest to keep 'em from getting too close, or to develop 'em, or something."

"Huh!" said the loud soldier.

"Well," cried the youth, still fidgeting, "I'd rather do anything most than go tramping 'round the country all day doing no good to nobody and jest tiring ourselves out."

"So would I," said the loud soldier. "It ain't right. I tell you if anybody with any sense was a-runnin' this army it——"

"Oh, shut up!" roared the tall private. "You little fool. You little damn' cuss. You ain't had that there coat and them pants on for six months, and yet you talk as if——"

"Well, I wanta do some fighting anyway," interrupted the other. "I didn't come here to walk. I could 'ave walked to home—'round an' 'round the barn, if I jest wanted to walk."

The tall one, red-faced, swallowed another sandwich as if taking poison in despair.

But gradually, as he chewed, his face became again quiet and contented. He could not rage in fierce argument in the presence of such sandwiches. During his meals he always wore an air of blissful contemplation of the food he had swallowed. His spirit seemed then to be communing with the viands.

He accepted new environment and circumstance with great coolness, eating from his haversack at every opportunity. On the march he went along with the stride of a hunter, objecting to neither gait nor distance. And he had not raised his voice when he had been ordered away from three little protective piles of earth and stone, each of which had been an engineering feat worthy of being made sacred to the name of his grandmother.

In the afternoon the regiment went out over the same ground it had taken in the morning. The landscape then ceased to threaten the youth. He had been close to it and become familiar with it.

When, however, they began to pass into a new region, his old fears of stupidity and incompetence reassailed him, but this time he doggedly let them babble. He was occupied with his problem, and in his desperation he concluded that the stupidity did not greatly matter.

Once he thought he had concluded that it would be better to get killed directly and end his troubles. Regarding death thus out of the corner of his eye, he conceived it to be nothing but rest, and he was filled with a momentary astonishment that he should have made an extraordinary commotion over the mere matter of getting killed. He would die; he would go to some place where he would be understood. It was useless to expect appreciation of his profound and fine senses from such men as the lieutenant. He must look to the grave for comprehension.

The skirmish fire increased to a long clattering sound. With it was mingled far-away cheering. A battery spoke.

Directly the youth would see the skirmishers running. They were pursued by the sound of musketry fire. After a time the hot, dangerous flashes of the rifles were visible. Smoke clouds went slowly and insolently across the fields like observant phantoms. The din became crescendo, like the roar of an on-coming train.

A brigade ahead of them and on the right went into action with a rending roar. It was as if it had exploded. And thereafter it lay stretched in the distance behind a long gray wall, that one was obliged to look twice at to make sure that it was smoke.

The youth, forgetting his neat plan of getting killed, gazed spellbound. His eyes grew wide and busy with the action of the scene. His mouth was a little ways open.

Of a sudden he felt a heavy and sad hand laid upon his shoulder. Awakening from his trance of observation he turned and beheld the loud soldier.

"It's my first and last battle, old boy," said the latter, with intense gloom. He was quite pale and his girlish lip was trembling.

"Eh?" murmured the youth in great astonishment.

"It's my first and last battle, old boy," continued the loud soldier. "Something tells me——"

"What?"

"I'm a gone coon this first time and—and I w-want you to take these here things—to—my—folks." He ended in a quavering sob of pity for himself. He handed the youth a little packet done up in a yellow envelope.

"Why, what the devil——" began the youth again.

But the other gave him a glance as from the depths of a tomb, and raised his limp hand in a prophetic manner and turned away.

4

The brigade was halted in the fringe of a grove. The men crouched among the trees and pointed their restless guns out at the fields. They tried to look beyond the smoke.

Out of this haze they could see running men. Some shouted information and gestured as they hurried.

The men of the new regiment watched and listened eagerly, while their tongues ran on in gossip of the battle. They mouthed rumors that had flown like birds out of the unknown.

"They say Perry has been driven in with big loss."

"Yes, Carrott went t' th' hospital. He said he was sick. That smart lieutenant is commanding 'G' Company. Th' boys say they won't be under Carrott no more if they all have t' desert. They allus knew he was a——"

"Hannises' batt'ry is took."

"It ain't either. I saw Hannises' batt'ry off on th' left not more'n fifteen minutes ago."

"Well——"

"Th' general, he ses he is goin' t' take th' hull command of th' 304th when we go inteh action, an' then he ses we'll do sech fightin' as never another one reg'ment done."

"They say we're catchin' it over on th' left. They say th' enemy driv' our line inteh a devil of a swamp an' took Hannises' batt'ry."

"No sech thing. Hannises' batt'ry was 'long here 'bout a minute ago."

"That young Hasbrouck, he makes a good off'cer. He ain't afraid 'a nothin'."

"I met one of th' 148th Maine boys an' he ses his brigade fit th' hull rebel army fer four hours over on th' turnpike road an' killed about five thousand of 'em. He ses one more sech fight as that an' th' war 'll be over."

"Bill wasn't scared either. No, sir! It wasn't that. Bill ain't a-gittin' scared easy. He was jest mad, that's what he was. When that feller trod on his hand, he up an' sed that he was willin' t' give his hand t' his country, but he be dumbed if he was goin' t' have every dumb bushwhacker in th' kentry walkin' 'round on it. Se he went t' th' hospital disregardless of th' fight. Three fingers was crunched. Th' dern doctor wanted t' amputate 'em, an' Bill, he raised a heluva row, I hear. He's a funny feller."

The din in front swelled to a tremendous chorus. The youth and his fellows were frozen to silence. They could see a flag that tossed in the smoke angrily. Near it were the blurred and agitated forms of troops. There came a turbulent stream of men across the fields. A battery changing position at a frantic gallop scattered the stragglers right and left.

A shell screaming like a storm banshee went over the huddled heads of the reserves. It landed in the grove, and exploding redly flung the brown earth. There was a little shower of pine needles.

Bullets began to whistle among the branches and nip at the trees. Twigs and leaves came sailing down. It was as if a thousand axes, wee and invisible, were being wielded. Many of the men were constantly dodging and ducking their heads.

The lieutenant of the youth's company was shot in the hand. He began to swear so wondrously that a nervous laugh went along the regimental line. The officer's profanity sounded conventional. It relieved the tightened senses of the new men. It was if he had hit his fingers with a tack hammer at home.

He held the wounded member carefully away from his side so that the blood would not drip upon his trousers.

The captain of the company, tucking his sword under his arm, produced a handkerchief and began to bind with it the lieutenant's wound. And they disputed as to how the binding should be done.

The battle flag in the distance jerked about madly. It seemed to be struggling to free itself from an agony. The billowing smoke was filled with horizontal flashes.

Men running swiftly emerged from it. They grew in numbers until it was seen that the whole command was fleeing. The flag suddenly sank down as if dying. Its motion as it fell was a gesture of despair.

Wild yells came from behind the walls of smoke. A sketch in gray and red dissolved into a moblike body of men who galloped like wild horses.

The veteran regiments on the right and left of the 304th immediately began to jeer. With the passionate song of the bullets and the banshee shrieks of shells were mingled loud catcalls and bits of facetious advice concerning places of safety.

But the new regiment was breathless with horror. "Gawd! Saunders's got crushed!" whispered the man at the youth's elbow. They shrank back and crouched as if compelled to await a flood.

The youth shot a swift glance along the blue ranks of the regiment. The profiles were motionless, carven; and afterward he remembered that the color sergeant was standing with his legs apart, as if he expected to be pushed to the ground.

The following throng went whirling around the flank. Here and there were officers carried along on the stream like exasperated chips. They were striking about them with their swords and with their left fists, punching every head they could reach. They cursed like highwaymen.

A mounted officer displayed the furious anger of a spoiled child. He raged with his head, his arms, and his legs.

Another, the commander of the brigade, was galloping about bawling. His hat was gone and his clothes were awry. He resembled a man who has come from bed to go to a fire. The hoofs of his horse often threatened the heads of the running men, but they scampered with singular fortune. In this rush they were apparently all deaf and blind. They heeded not the largest and longest of the oaths that were thrown at them from all directions.

Frequently over this tumult could be heard the grim jokes of the critical veterans; but the retreating men apparently were not even conscious of the presence of an audience.

The battle reflection that shone for an instant in the faces on the mad current made the youth feel that forceful hands from heaven would not have been able to have held him in place if he could have got intelligent control of his legs.

There was an appalling imprint upon these faces. The struggle in the smoke had pictured an exaggeration of itself on the bleached cheeks and in the eyes wild with one desire.

The sight of this stampede exerted a floodlike force that seemed able to drag sticks and stones and men from the ground. They of the reserves had to hold on. They grew pale and firm, and red and quaking.

The youth achieved one little thought in the midst of this chaos. The composite monster which had caused the other troops to flee had not then appeared. He resolved to get a view of it, and then, he thought he might very likely run better than the best of them.

5

There were moments of waiting. The youth thought of the village street at home before the arrival of the circus parade on a day in the spring. He remembered how he had stood, a small, thrillful boy, prepared to follow the dingy lady upon the white horse, or the band in its faded chariot. He saw the yellow road, the lines of expectant people, and the sober houses. He particularly remembered an old fellow who used to sit upon a cracker box in front of the store and feign to despise such exhibitions. A thousand details of color and form surged in his mind. The old fellow upon the cracker box appeared in middle prominence.

Some one cried, "Here they come!"

There was rustling and muttering among the men. They displayed a fever-ish desire to have every possible cartridge ready to their hands. The boxes were pulled around into various positions, and adjusted with great care. It was as if seven hundred new bonnets were being tried on.

The tall soldier, having prepared his rifle, produced a red handkerchief of some kind. He was engaged in knitting it about his throat with exquisite at-tention to its position, when the cry was repeated up and down the line in a muffled roar of sound.

"Here they come! Here they come!" Gun locks clicked.

Across the smoke-infested fields came a brown swarm of running men who were giving shrill yells. They came on, stooping and swinging their rifles at all angles. A flag, tilted forward, sped near the front.

As he caught sight of them the youth was momentarily startled by a thought that perhaps his gun was not loaded. He stood trying to rally his fal-tering intellect so that he might recollect the moment when he had loaded, but he could not.

A hatless general pulled his dripping horse to a stand near the colonel of the 304th. He shook his fist in the other's face. "You've got to hold 'em back!" he shouted, savagely; "you've got to hold 'em back!"

In his agitation the colonel began to stammer. "A-all r-right, General, all right, by Gawd! We-we'll do our—we-we'll d-d-do—do our best, General." The general made a passionate gesture and galloped away. The colonel, per-chance to relieve his feelings, began to scold like a wet parrot. The youth, turning swiftly to make sure that the rear was unmolested, saw the commander regarding his men in a highly resentful manner, as if he regretted above ev-erything his association with them.

The man at the youth's elbow was mumbling, as if to himself: "Oh, we're in for it now! oh, we're in for it now!"

The captain of the company had been pacing excitedly to and fro in the rear. He coaxed in schoolmistress fashion, as to a congregation of boys with primers. His talk was an endless repetition. "Reserve your fire, boys—don't shoot till I tell you—save your fire—wait till they get close up—don't be damned fools——"

Perspiration streamed down the youth's face, which was soiled like that of a weeping urchin. He frequently, with a nervous movement, wiped his eyes with his coat sleeve. His mouth was still a little ways open.

He got the one glance at the foe-swarming field in front of him, and in-stantly ceased to debate the question of his piece being loaded. Before he was ready to begin—before he had announced to himself that he was about to fight—he threw the obedient, well-balanced rifle into position and fired a first wild shot. Directly he was working at his weapon like an automatic affair.

He suddenly lost concern for himself, and forgot to look at a menacing fate. He became not a man but a member. He felt that something of which he was a part—a regiment, an army, a cause, or a country—was in a crisis. He was welded into a common personality which was dominated by a single de-sire. For some moments he could not flee no more than a little finger can com-mit a revolution from a hand.

If he had thought the regiment was about to be annihilated perhaps he could have amputated himself from it. But its noise gave him assurance. The regiment was like a firework that, once ignited, proceeds superior to circumstances until its blazing vitality fades. It wheezed and banged with a mighty power. He pictured the ground before it as strewn with the discomfited.

There was a consciousness always of the presence of his comrades about him. He felt the subtle battle brotherhood more potent even than the cause for which they were fighting. It was a mysterious fraternity born of the smoke and danger of death.

He was at a task. He was like a carpenter who has made many boxes, making still another box, only there was furious haste in his movements. He, in his thought, was careering off in other places, even as the carpenter who as he works whistles and thinks of his friend or his enemy, his home or a saloon. And these jolted dreams were never perfect to him afterward, but remained a mass of blurred shapes.

Presently he began to feel the effects of the war atmosphere—a blistering sweat, a sensation that his eyeballs were about to crack like hot stones. A burning roar filled his ears.

Following this came a red rage. He developed the acute exasperation of a pestered animal, a well-meaning cow worried by dogs. He had a mad feeling against his rifle, which could only be used against one life at a time. He wished to rush forward and strangle with his fingers. He craved a power that would enable him to make a world-sweeping gesture and brush all back. His impotency appeared to him, and made his rage into that of a driven beast.

Buried in the smoke of many rifles his anger was directed not so much against the men whom he knew were rushing toward him as against the swirling battle phantoms which were choking him, stuffing their smoke robes down his parched throat. He fought frantically for respite for his senses, for air, as a babe being smothered attacks the deadly blankets.

There was a blare of heated rage mingled with a certain expression of intentness on all faces. Many of the men were making low-toned noises with their mouths, and these subdued cheers, snarls, imprecations, prayers, made a wild, barbaric song that went as an undercurrent of sound, strange and chant-like with the resounding chords of the war march. The man at the youth's elbow was babbling. In it there was something soft and tender like the monologue of a babe. The tall soldier was swearing in a loud voice. From his lips came a black procession of curious oaths. Of a sudden another broke out in a querulous way like a man who has mislaid his hat. "Well, why don't they support us? Why don't they send supports? Do they think——"

The youth in his battle sleep heard this as one who dozes hears.

There was a singular absence of heroic poses. The men bending and surging in their haste and rage were in every impossible attitude. The steel ramrods clanked and clanged with incessant din as the men pounded them furiously into the hot rifle barrels. The flaps of the cartridge boxes were all unfastened, and bobbed idiotically with each movement. The rifles, once loaded, were jerked to the shoulder and fired without apparent aim into the smoke or at one of the blurred and shifting forms which upon the field before the regiment had been growing larger and larger like puppets under a magician's hand.

The officers, at their intervals, rearward, neglected to stand in picturesque attitudes. They were bobbing to and fro roaring directions and encouragements. The dimensions of their howls were extraordinary. They expended their lungs with prodigal wills. And often they nearly stood upon their heads in their anxiety to observe the enemy on the other side of the tumbling smoke.

The lieutenant of the youth's company had encountered a soldier who had fled screaming at the first volley of his comrades. Behind the lines these two were acting a little isolated scene. The man was blubbering and staring with sheeplike eyes at the lieutenant, who had seized him by the collar and was pommeling him. He drove him back into the ranks with many blows. The soldier went mechanically, dully, with his animal-like eyes upon the officer. Perhaps there was to him a divinity expressed in the voice of the other—stern, hard, with no reflection of fear in it. He tried to reload his gun, but his shaking hands prevented. The lieutenant was obliged to assist him.

The men dropped here and there like bundles. The captain of the youth's company had been killed in an early part of the action. His body lay stretched out in the position of a tired man resting, but upon his face there was an astonished and sorrowful look, as if he thought some friend had done him an ill turn. The babbling man was grazed by a shot that made the blood stream widely down his face. He clapped both hands to his head. "Oh!" he said, and ran. Another grunted suddenly as if he had been struck by a club in the stomach. He sat down and gazed ruefully. In his eyes there was mute, indefinite reproach. Farther up the line a man, standing behind a tree, had had his knee joint splintered by a ball. Immediately he had dropped his rifle and gripped the tree with both arms. And there he remained, clinging desperately and crying for assistance that he might withdraw his hold upon the tree.

At last an exultant yell went along the quivering line. The firing dwindled from an uproar to a last vindictive popping. As the smoke slowly eddied away, the youth saw that the charge had been repulsed. The enemy were scattered into reluctant groups. He saw a man climb to the top of the fence, straddle the rail, and fire a parting shot. The waves had receded, leaving bits of dark *débris* upon the ground.

Some in the regiment began to whoop frenziedly. Many were silent. Apparently they were trying to contemplate themselves.

After the fever had left his veins, the youth thought that at last he was going to suffocate. He became aware of the foul atmosphere in which he had been struggling. He was grimy and dripping like a laborer in a foundry. He grasped his canteen and took a long swallow of the warmed water.

A sentence with variations went up and down the line. "Well, we've helt 'em back. We've helt 'em back; derned if we haven't." The men said it blissfully, leering at each other with dirty smiles.

The youth turned to look behind him and off to the right and off to the left. He experienced the joy of a man who at last finds leisure in which to look about him.

Under foot there were a few ghastly forms motionless. They lay twisted in fantastic contortions. Arms were bent and heads were turned in incredible ways. It seemed that the dead men must have fallen from some great height to get into such positions. They looked to be dumped out upon the ground from the sky.

From a position in the rear of the grove a battery was throwing shells over it. The flash of the guns startled the youth at first. He thought they were aimed directly at him. Through the trees he watched the black figures of the gunners as they worked swiftly and intently. Their labor seemed a complicated thing. He wondered how they could remember its formula in the midst of confusion.

The guns squatted in a row like savage chiefs. They argued with abrupt violence. It was a grim pow-wow. Their busy servants ran hither and thither.

A small procession of wounded men were going wearily toward the rear. It was a flow of blood from the torn body of the brigade.

To the right and to left were the dark lines of other troops. Far in front he thought he could see lighter masses protruding in points from the forest. They were suggestive of unnumbered thousands.

Once he saw a tiny battery go dashing along the line of the horizon. The tiny riders were beating the tiny horses.

From a sloping hill came the sound of cheerings and clashes. Smoke welled slowly through the leaves.

Batteries were speaking with thunderous oratorical effort. Here and there were flags, the red in the stripes dominating. They splashed bits of warm color upon the dark lines of troops.

The youth felt the old thrill at the sight of the emblem. They were like beautiful birds strangely undaunted in a storm.

As he listened to the din from the hillside, to a deep pulsating thunder that came from afar to the left, and to the lesser clamors which came from many directions, it occurred to him that they were fighting, too, over there, and over there, and over there. Heretofore he had supposed that all the battle was directly under his nose.

As he gazed around him the youth felt a flash of astonishment at the blue, pure sky and the sun gleamings on the trees and fields. It was surprising that Nature had gone tranquilly on with her golden process in the midst of so much devilment.

6

The youth awakened slowly. He came gradually back to a position from which he could regard himself. For moments he had been scrutinizing his person in a dazed way as if he had never before seen himself. Then he picked up his cap from the ground. He wriggled in his jacket to make a more comfortable fit, and kneeling relaced his shoe. He thoughtfully mopped his reeking features.

So it was all over at last! The supreme trial had been passed. The red, formidable difficulties of war had been vanquished.

He went into an ecstasy of self-satisfaction. He had the most delightful sensations of his life. Standing as if apart from himself, he viewed that last scene. He perceived that the man who had fought thus was magnificent.

He felt that he was a fine fellow. He saw himself even with those ideals which he had considered as far beyond him. He smiled in deep gratification.

Upon his fellows he beamed tenderness and good will. "Gee! ain't it hot, hey?" he said affably to a man who was polishing his streaming face with his coat sleeves.

"You bet!" said the other, grinning sociably. "I never seen sech dumb hotness." He sprawled out luxuriously on the ground. "Gee, yes! An' I hope we don't have no more fightin' till a week from Monday."

There were some handshakings and deep speeches with men whose features were familiar, but with whom the youth now felt the bonds of tied hearts. He helped a cursing comrade to bind up a wound of the shin.

But, of a sudden, cries of amazement broke out along the ranks of the new regiment. "Here they come ag'in! Here they come ag'in!" The man who had sprawled upon the ground started up and said, "Gosh!"

The youth turned quick eyes upon the field. He discerned forms begin to swell in masses out of a distant wood. He again saw the tilted flag speeding forward.

The shells, which had ceased to trouble the regiment for a time, came swirling again, and exploded in the grass or among the leaves of the trees. They looked to be strange war flowers bursting into fierce bloom.

The men groaned. The luster faded from their eyes. Their smudged countenances now expressed a profound dejection. They moved their stiffened bodies slowly, and watched in sullen mood the frantic approach of the enemy. The slaves toiling in the temple of this god began to feel rebellion at his harsh tasks.

They fretted and complained each to each. "Oh, say, this is too much of a good thing! Why can't somebody send us supports?"

"We ain't never goin' to stand this second banging. I didn't come here to fight the hull damn' rebel army."

There was one who raised a doleful cry. "I wish Bill Smithers had trod on my hand, insteader me treddin' on his'n." The sore joints of the regiment creaked as it painfully floundered into position to repulse.

The youth stared. Surely, he thought, this impossible thing was not about to happen. He waited as if he expected the enemy to suddenly stop, apologize, and retire bowing. It was all a mistake.

But the firing began somewhere on the regimental line and ripped along in both directions. The level sheets of flame developed great clouds of smoke that tumbled and tossed in the mild wind near the ground for a moment, and then rolled through the ranks as through a gate. The clouds were tinged an earthlike yellow in the sunrays and in the shadow were a sorry blue. The flag was sometimes eaten and lost in this mass of vapor, but more often it projected, sun-touched, resplendent.

Into the youth's eyes there came a look that one can see in the orbs of a jaded horse. His neck was quivering with nervous weakness and the muscles of his arms felt numb and bloodless. His hands, too, seemed large and awkward as if he was wearing invisible mittens. And there was a great uncertainty about his knee joints.

The words that comrades had uttered previous to the firing began to recur to him. "Oh, say, this is too much of a good thing! What do they take us for—

why don't they send supports? I didn't come here to fight the hull damned rebel army."

He began to exaggerate the endurance, the skill, and the valor of those who were coming. Himself reeling from exhaustion, he was astonished beyond measure at such persistency. They must be machines of steel. It was very gloomy struggling against such affairs, wound up perhaps to fight until sundown.

He slowly lifted his rifle and catching a glimpse of the thick-spread field he blazed at a cantering cluster. He stopped then and began to peer as best he could through the smoke. He caught changing views of the ground covered with men who were all running like pursued imps, and yelling.

To the youth it was an onslaught of redoubtable dragons. He became like the man who lost his legs at the approach of the red and green monster. He waited in a sort of a horrified, listening attitude. He seemed to shut his eyes and wait to be gobbled.

A man near him who up to this time had been working feverishly at his rifle suddenly stopped and ran with howls. A lad whose face had borne an expression of exalted courage, the majesty of him who dares give his life, was, at an instant, smitten abject. He blanched like one who has come to the edge of a cliff at midnight and is suddenly made aware. There was a revelation. He, too, threw down his gun and fled. There was no shame in his face. He ran like a rabbit.

Others began to scamper away through the smoke. The youth turned his head, shaken from his trance by this movement as if the regiment was leaving him behind. He saw the few fleeting forms.

He yelled then with fright and swung about. For a moment, in the great clamor, he was like a proverbial chicken. He lost the direction of safety. Destruction threatened him from all points.

Directly he began to speed toward the rear in great leaps. His rifle and cap were gone. His unbuttoned coat bulged in the wind. The flap of his cartridge box bobbed wildly, and his canteen, by its slender cord, swung out behind. On his face was all the horror of those things which he imagined.

The lieutenant sprang forward bawling. The youth saw his features wrathfully red, and saw him make a dab with his sword. His one thought of the incident was that the lieutenant was a peculiar creature to feel interested in such matters upon this occasion.

He ran like a blind man. Two or three times he fell down. Once he knocked his shoulder so heavily against a tree that he went headlong.

Since he had turned his back upon the fight his fears had been wondrously magnified. Death about to thrust him between the shoulder blades was far more dreadful than death about to smite him between the eyes. When he thought of it later, he conceived the impression that it is better to view the appalling than to be merely within hearing. The noises of the battle were like stones; he believed himself liable to be crushed.

As he ran on he mingled with others. He dimly saw men on his right and on his left, and he heard footsteps behind him. He thought that all the regiment was fleeing, pursued by these ominous crashes.

In his flight the sound of these following footsteps gave him his one meager relief. He felt vaguely that death must make a first choice of the men who were nearest; the initial morsels for the dragons would be then those who were following him. So he displayed the zeal of an insane sprinter in his purpose to keep them in the rear. There was a race.

As he, leading, went across a little field, he found himself in a region of shells. They hurtled over his head with long wild screams. As he listened he imagined them to have rows of cruel teeth that grinned at him. Once one lit before him and the livid lightning of the explosion effectually barred the way in his chosen direction. He groveled on the ground and then springing up went careering off through some bushes.

He experienced a thrill of amazement when he came within view of a battery in action. The men there seemed to be in conventional moods, altogether unaware of the impending annihilation. The battery was disputing with a distant antagonist and the gunners were wrapped in admiration of their shooting. They were continually bending in coaxing postures over the guns. They seemed to be patting them on the back and encouraging them with words. The guns, stolid and undaunted, spoke with dogged valor.

The precise gunners were coolly enthusiastic. They lifted their eyes every chance to the smoke-wreathed hillock from whence the hostile battery addressed them. The youth pitied them as he ran. Methodical idiots! Machinelike fools! The refined joy of planting shells in the midst of the other battery's formation would appear a little thing when the infantry came swooping out of the woods.

The face of a youthful rider, who was jerking his frantic horse with an abandon of temper he might display in a placid barnyard, was impressed deeply upon his mind. He knew that he looked upon a man who would presently be dead.

Too, he felt a pity for the guns, standing, six good comrades, in a bold row.

He saw a brigade going to the relief of its pestered fellows. He scrambled upon a wee hill and watched it sweeping finely, keeping formation in difficult places. The blue of the line was crusted with steel color, and the brilliant flags projected. Officers were shouting.

This sight also filled him with wonder. The brigade was hurrying briskly to be gulped into the infernal mouths of the war god. What manner of men were they, anyhow? Ah, it was some wondrous breed! Or else they didn't comprehend—the fools.

A furious order caused commotion in the artillery. An officer on a bounding horse made maniacal motions with his arms. The teams went swinging up from the rear, the guns were whirled about, and the battery scampered away. The cannon with their noses poked slantingly at the ground grunted and grumbled like stout men, brave but with objections to hurry.

The youth went on, moderating his pace since he had left the place of noises.

Later he came upon a general of division seated upon a horse that pricked its ears in an interested way at the battle. There was a great gleaming of yellow and patent leather about the saddle and bridle. The quiet man astride looked mouse-colored upon such a splendid charger.

A jingling staff was galloping hither and thither. Sometimes the general was surrounded by horsemen and at other times he was quite alone. He looked to be much harassed. He had the appearance of a business man whose market is swinging up and down.

The youth went slinking around this spot. He went as near as he dared trying to overhear words. Perhaps the general, unable to comprehend chaos, might call upon him for information. And he could tell him. He knew all concerning it. Of a surety the force was in a fix, and any fool could see that if they did not retreat while they had opportunity—why——

He felt that he would like to thrash the general, or at least approach and tell him in plain words exactly what he thought him to be. It was criminal to stay calmly in one spot and make no effort to stay destruction. He loitered in a fever of eagerness for the division commander to apply to him.

As he warily moved about, he heard the general call out irritably: "Tompkins, go over an' see Taylor, an' tell him not t' be in such an all-fired hurry; tell him t' halt his brigade in th' edge of th' woods; tell him t' detach a reg'-ment—say I think th' center 'll break if we don't help it out some; tell him t' hurry up."

A slim youth on a fine chestnut horse caught these swift words from the mouth of his superior. He made his horse bound into a gallop almost from a walk in his haste to go upon his mission. There was a cloud of dust.

A moment later the youth saw the general bounce excitedly in his saddle.

"Yes, by heavens, they have!" The officer leaned forward. His face was aflame with excitement. "Yes, by heavens, they 've held 'im! They 've held 'im!"

He began to blithely roar at his staff: "We 'll wallop 'im now. We 'll wallop 'im now. We 've got 'em sure." He turned suddenly upon an aid: "Here—you—Jones—quick—ride after Tompkins—see Taylor—tell him t' go in—everlastingly—like blazes—anything."

As another officer sped his horse after the first messenger, the general beamed upon the earth like a sun. In his eyes was a desire to chant a paean. He kept repeating, "They 've held 'em, by heavens!"

His excitement made his horse plunge, and he merrily kicked and swore at it. He held a little carnival of joy on horseback.

7

The youth cringed as if discovered in a crime. By heavens, they had won after all! The imbecile line had remained and become victors. He could hear cheering.

He lifted himself upon his toes and looked in the direction of the fight. A yellow fog lay wallowing on the treetops. From beneath it came the clatter of musketry. Hoarse cries told of an advance.

He turned away amazed and angry. He felt that he had been wronged.

He had fled, he told himself, because annihilation approached. He had done a good part in saving himself, who was a little piece of the army. He had considered the time, he said, to be one in which it was the duty of every little piece to rescue itself if possible. Later the officers could fit the little pieces together again, and make a battle front. If none of the little pieces were wise enough to save themselves from the flurry of death at such a time, why, then, where would be the army? It was all plain that he had proceeded according to very correct and commendable rules. His actions had been sagacious things. They had been full of strategy. They were the work of a master's legs.

Thoughts of his comrades came to him. The brittle blue line had withstood the blows and won. He grew bitter over it. It seemed that the blind ignorance and stupidity of those little pieces had betrayed him. He had been overturned and crushed by their lack of sense in holding the position, when intelligent deliberation would have convinced them that it was impossible. He, the enlightened man who looks afar in the dark, had fled because of his superior perceptions and knowledge. He felt a great anger against his comrades. He knew it could be proved that they had been fools.

He wondered what they would remark when later he appeared in camp. His mind heard howls of derision. Their density would not enable them to understand his sharper point of view.

He began to pity himself acutely. He was ill used. He was trodden beneath the feet of an iron injustice. He had proceeded with wisdom and from the most righteous motives under heaven's blue only to be frustrated by hateful circumstances.

A dull, animal-like rebellion against his fellows, war in the abstract, and fate grew within him. He shambled along with bowed head, his brain in a tumult of agony and despair. When he looked loweringly up, quivering at each sound, his eyes had the expression of those of a criminal who thinks his guilt and his punishment great, and knows that he can find no words.

He went from the fields into a thick woods, as if resolved to bury himself. He wished to get out of hearing of the crackling shots which were to him like voices.

The ground was cluttered with vines and bushes, and the trees grew close and spread out like bouquets. He was obliged to force his way with much noise. The creepers, catching against his legs, cried out harshly as their sprays were torn from the barks of trees. The swishing saplings tried to make known his presence to the world. He could not conciliate the forest. As he made his way, it was always calling out protestations. When he separated embraces of trees and vines the disturbed foliages waved their arms and turned their face leaves toward him. He dreaded lest these noisy motions and cries should bring men to look at him. So he went far, seeking dark and intricate places.

After a time the sound of musketry grew faint and the cannon boomed in the distance. The sun, suddenly apparent, blazed among the trees. The insects were making rhythmical noises. They seemed to be grinding their teeth in unison. A woodpecker stuck his impudent head around the side of a tree. A bird flew on lighthearted wing.

Off was the rumble of death. It seemed now that Nature had no ears.

This landscape gave him assurance. A fair field holding life. It was the religion of peace. It would die if its timid eyes were compelled to see blood. He conceived Nature to be a woman with a deep aversion to tragedy.

He threw a pine cone at a jovial squirrel, and he ran with chattering fear.

High in a treetop he stopped, and, poking his head cautiously from behind a branch, looked down with an air of trepidation.

The youth felt triumphant at this exhibition. There was the law, he said. Nature had given him a sign. The squirrel, immediately upon recognizing danger, had taken to his legs without ado. He did not stand stolidly baring his furry belly to the missile, and die with an upward glance at the sympathetic heavens. On the contrary, he had fled as fast as his legs could carry him; and he was but an ordinary squirrel, too—doubtless no philosopher of his race. The youth wended, feeling that Nature was of his mind. She reenforced his argument with proofs that lived where the sun shone.

Once he found himself almost into a swamp. He was obliged to walk upon bog tufts and watch his feet to keep from the oily mire. Pausing at one time to look about him he saw, out at some black water, a small animal pounce in and emerge directly with a gleaming fish.

The youth went again into the deep thickets. The brushed branches made a noise that drowned the sounds of cannon. He walked on, going from obscurity into promises of a greater obscurity.

At length he reached a place where the high, arching boughs made a chapel. He softly pushed the green doors aside and entered. Pine needles were a gentle brown carpet. There was a religious half light.

Near the threshold he stopped, horror-stricken at the sight of a thing.

He was being looked at by a dead man who was seated with his back against a columnlike tree. The corpse was dressed in a uniform that once had been blue, but was now faded to a melancholy shade of green. The eyes, staring at the youth, had changed to the dull hue to be seen on the side of a dead fish. The mouth was open. Its red had changed to an appalling yellow. Over the gray skin of the face ran little ants. One was trundling some sort of a bundle along the upper lip.

The youth gave a shriek as he confronted the thing. He was for moments turned to stone before it. He remained staring into the liquid-looking eyes. The dead man and the living man exchanged a long look. Then the youth cautiously put one hand behind him and brought it against a tree. Leaning upon this he retreated, step by step, with his face still toward the thing. He feared that if he turned his back the body might spring up and stealthily pursue him.

The branches, pushing against him, threatened to throw him over upon it. His unguided feet, too, caught aggravatingly in brambles; and with it all he received a subtle suggestion to touch the corpse. As he thought of his hand upon it he shuddered profoundly.

At last he burst the bonds which had fastened him to the spot and fled, unheeding the underbrush. He was pursued by a sight of the black ants swarming greedily upon the gray face and venturing horribly near to the eyes.

After a time he paused, and, breathless and panting, listened. He imagined some strange voice would come from the dead throat and squawk after him in horrible menaces.

The trees about the portal of the chapel moved soughingly in a soft wind. A sad silence was upon the little guarding edifice.

8

The trees began softly to sing a hymn of twilight. The sun sank until slanted bronze rays struck the forest. There was a lull in the noises of insects as if they had bowed their beaks and were making a devotional pause. There was silence save for the chanted chorus of the trees.

Then, upon this stillness, there suddenly broke a tremendous clangor of sounds. A crimson roar came from the distance.

The youth stopped. He was transfixed by this terrific medley of all noises. It was as if worlds were being rended. There was the ripping sound of musketry and the breaking crash of the artillery.

His mind flew in all directions. He conceived the two armies to be at each other panther fashion. He listened for a time. Then he began to run in the direction of the battle. He saw that it was an ironical thing for him to be running thus toward that which he had been at such pains to avoid. But he said, in substance, to himself that if the earth and the moon were about to clash, many persons would doubtless plan to get upon the roofs to witness the collision.

As he ran, he became aware that the forest had stopped its music, as if at last becoming capable of hearing the foreign sounds. The trees hushed and stood motionless. Everything seemed to be listening to the crackle and clatter and ear-shaking thunder. The chorus pealed over the still earth.

It suddenly occurred to the youth that the fight in which he had been was, after all, but perfunctory popping. In the hearing of this present din he was doubtful if he had seen real battle scenes. This uproar explained a celestial battle; it was tumbling hordes a-struggle in the air.

Reflecting, he saw a sort of a humor in the point of view of himself and his fellows during the late encounter. They had taken themselves and the enemy very seriously and had imagined that they were deciding the war. Individuals must have supposed that they were cutting the letters of their names deep into everlasting tablets of brass, or enshrining their reputations forever in the hearts of their countrymen, while, as to fact, the affair would appear in printed reports under a meek and immaterial title. But he saw that it was good, else, he said, in battle every one would surely run save forlorn hopes and their ilk.

He went rapidly on. He wished to come to the edge of the forest that he might peer out.

As he hastened, there passed through his mind pictures of stupendous conflicts. His accumulated thought upon such subjects was used to form scenes. The noise was as the voice of an eloquent being, describing.

Sometimes the brambles formed chains and tried to hold him back. Trees, confronting him, stretched out their arms and forbade him to pass. After its previous hostility this new resistance of the forest filled him with a fine bitterness. It seemed that Nature could not be quite ready to kill him.

But he obstinately took roundabout ways, and presently he was where he could see long gray walls of vapor where lay battle lines. The voices of cannon shook him. The musketry sounded in long irregular surges that played havoc with his ears. He stood regardant for a moment. His eyes had an awestruck expression. He gawked in the direction of the fight.

Presently he proceeded again on his forward way. The battle was like the grinding of an immense and terrible machine to him. Its complexities and powers, its grim processes, fascinated him. He must go close and see it produce corpses.

He came to a fence and clambered over it. On the far side, the ground was littered with clothes and guns. A newspaper, folded up, lay in the dirt. A dead soldier was stretched with his face hidden in his arm. Farther off there was a group of four or five corpses keeping mournful company. A hot sun had blazed upon the spot.

In this place the youth felt that he was an invader. This forgotten part of the battle ground was owned by the dead men, and he hurried, in the vague apprehension that one of the swollen forms would rise and tell him to begone.

He came finally to a road from which he could see in the distance dark and agitated bodies of troops, smoke-fringed. In the lane was a blood-stained crowd streaming to the rear. The wounded men were cursing, groaning, and wailing. In the air, always, was a mighty swell of sound that it seemed could sway the earth. With the courageous words of the artillery and the spiteful sentences of the musketry mingled red cheers. And from this region of noises came the steady current of the maimed.

One of the wounded men had a shoeful of blood. He hopped like a schoolboy in a game. He was laughing hysterically.

One was swearing that he had been shot in the arm through the commanding general's mismanagement of the army. One was marching with an air imitative of some sublime drum major. Upon his features was an unholy mixture of merriment and agony. As he marched he sang a bit of doggerel in a high and quavering voice:

> "Sing a song 'a vic'try,
> A pocketful 'a bullets,
> Five an' twenty dead men
> Baked in a—pie."

Parts of the procession limped and staggered to this tune.

Another had the gray seal of death already upon his face. His lips were curled in hard lines and his teeth were clinched. His hands were bloody from where he had pressed them upon his wound. He seemed to be awaiting the moment when he should pitch headlong. He stalked like the specter of a soldier, his eyes burning with the power of a stare into the unknown.

There were some who proceeded sullenly, full of anger at their wounds, and ready to turn upon anything as an obscure cause.

An officer was carried along by two privates. He was peevish. "Don't joggle so, Johnson, yeh fool," he cried. "Think m' leg is made of iron? If yeh can't carry me decent, put me down an' let some one else do it."

He bellowed at the tottering crowd who blocked the quick march of his bearers. "Say, make way there, can't yeh? Make way, dickens take it all."

They sulkily parted and went to the roadsides. As he was carried past they made pert remarks to him. When he raged in reply and threatened them, they told him to be damned.

The shoulder of one of the tramping bearers knocked heavily against the spectral soldier who was staring into the unknown.

The youth joined this crowd and marched along with it. The torn bodies expressed the awful machinery in which the men had been entangled.

Orderlies and couriers occasionally broke through the throng in the road-way, scattering wounded men right and left, galloping on followed by howls. The melancholy march was continually disturbed by the messengers, and sometimes by bustling batteries that came swinging and thumping down upon them, the officers shouting orders to clear the way.

There was a tattered man, fouled with dust, blood and powder stain from hair to shoes, who trudged quietly at the youth's side. He was listening with eagerness and much humility to the lurid descriptions of a bearded sergeant. His lean features wore an expression of awe and admiration. He was like a listener in a country store to wondrous tales told among the sugar barrels. He eyed the story-teller with unspeakable wonder. His mouth was agape in yokel fashion.

The sergeant, taking note of this, gave pause to his elaborate history while he administered a sardonic comment. "Be keerful, honey, you'll be a-ketchin' flies," he said.

The tattered man shrank back abashed.

After a time he began to sidle near to the youth, and in a different way try to make him a friend. His voice was gentle as a girl's voice and his eyes were pleading. The youth saw with surprise that the soldier had two wounds, one in the head, bound with a blood-soaked rag, and the other in the arm, making that member dangle like a broken bough.

After they had walked together for some time the tattered man mustered sufficient courage to speak. "Was pretty good fight, wa'n't it?" he timidly said. The youth, deep in thought, glanced up at the bloody and grim figure with its lamblike eyes. "What?"

"Was pretty good fight, wa'n't it?"

"Yes," said the youth shortly. He quickened his pace.

But the other hobbled industriously after him. There was an air of apology in his manner, but he evidently thought that he needed only to talk for a time, and the youth would perceive that he was a good fellow.

"Was pretty good fight, wa'n't it?" he began in a small voice, and then he achieved the fortitude to continue. "Dern me if I ever see fellers fight so. Laws, how they did fight! I knowed th' boys 'd like when they onct got square at it. Th' boys ain't had no fair chanct up t' now, but this time they showed what they was. I knowed it 'd turn out this way. Yeh can't lick them boys. No, sir! They 're fighters, they be."

He breathed a deep breath of humble admiration. He had looked at the youth for encouragement several times. He received none, but gradually he seemed to get absorbed in his subject.

"I was talkin' 'cross pickets with a boy from Georgie, onct, an' that boy, he ses, 'Your fellers 'll all run like hell when they onct hearn a gun,' he ses.

'Mebbe they will,' I ses, 'but I don't b'lieve none of it,' I ses; 'an' b'jiminey,' I ses back t' 'um, 'mebbe your fellers 'll all run like hell when they onct hearn a gun,' I ses. He larfed. Well, they didn't run t' day, did they, hey? No, sir! They fit, an' fit, an' fit."

His homely face was suffused with a light of love for the army which was to him all things beautiful and powerful.

After a time he turned to the youth. "Where yeh hit, ol' boy?" he asked in a brotherly tone.

The youth felt instant panic at this question, although at first its full import was not borne in upon him.

"What?" he asked.

"Where yeh hit?" repeated the tattered man.

"Why," began the youth, "I—I—that is—why—I——"

He turned away suddenly and slid through the crowd. His brow was heavily flushed, and his fingers were picking nervously at one of his buttons. He bent his head and fastened his eyes studiously upon the button as if it were a little problem.

The tattered man looked after him in astonishment.

9

The youth fell back in the procession until the tattered soldier was not in sight. Then he started to walk on with the others.

But he was amid wounds. The mob of men was bleeding. Because of the tattered soldier's question he now felt that his shame could be viewed. He was continually casting sidelong glances to see if the men were contemplating the letters of guilt he felt burned into his brow.

At times he regarded the wounded soldiers in an envious way. He conceived persons with torn bodies to be peculiarly happy. He wished that he, too, had a wound, a red badge of courage.

The spectral soldier was at his side like a stalking reproach. The man's eyes were still fixed in a stare into the unknown. His gray, appalling face had attracted attention in the crowd, and men, slowing to his dreary pace, were walking with him. They were discussing his plight, questioning him and giving him advice. In a dogged way he repelled them, signing to them to go on and leave him alone. The shadows of his face were deepening and his tight lips seemed holding in check the moan of great despair. There could be seen a certain stiffness in the movements of his body, as if he were taking infinite care not to arouse the passion of his wounds. As he went on, he seemed always looking for a place, like one who goes to choose a grave.

Something in the gesture of the man as he waved the bloody and pitying soldiers away made the youth start as if bitten. He yelled in horror. Tottering forward he laid a quivering hand upon the man's arm. As the latter slowly turned his waxlike features toward him, the youth screamed:

"Gawd! Jim Conklin!"

The tall soldier made a little commonplace smile. "Hello, Henry," he said.

The youth swayed on his legs and glared strangely. He stuttered and stammered. "Oh, Jim—oh, Jim—oh, Jim——"

The tall soldier held out his gory hand. There was a curious red and black combination of new blood and old blood upon it. "Where yeh been, Henry?" he asked. He continued in a monotonous voice, "I thought mebbe yeh got keeled over. There's been thunder t' pay t'-day. I was worryin' about it a good deal."

The youth still lamented. "Oh, Jim—oh, Jim—oh, Jim——"

"Yeh know," said the tall soldier, "I was out there." He made a careful gesture. "An', Lord, what a circus! An', b'jiminey, I got shot—I got shot. Yes, b'jiminey, I got shot." He reiterated this fact in a bewildered way, as if he did not know how it came about.

The youth put forth anxious arms to assist him, but the tall soldier went firmly on as if propelled. Since the youth's arrival as a guardian for his friend, the other wounded men had ceased to display much interest. They occupied themselves again in dragging their own tragedies toward the rear.

Suddenly, as the two friends marched on, the tall soldier seemed to be overcome by a terror. His face turned to a semblance of gray paste. He clutched the youth's arm and looked all about him, as if dreading to be overheard. Then he began to speak in a shaking whisper:

"I tell yeh what I'm 'fraid of, Henry—I'll tell yeh what I'm 'fraid of. I'm 'fraid I'll fall down an' then yeh know—them damned artillery wagons —they like as not 'll run over me. That's what I'm 'fraid of——"

The youth cried out to him hysterically: "I'll take care of yeh, Jim! I'll take care of yeh! I swear t' Gawd I will!"

"Sure—will yeh, Henry?" the tall soldier beseeched.

"Yes—yes—I tell yeh—I'll take care of yeh, Jim!" protested the youth. He could not speak accurately because of the gulpings in his throat.

But the tall soldier continued to beg in a lowly way. He now hung babelike to the youth's arm. His eyes rolled in the wildness of his terror. "I was allus a good friend t' yeh, wa'n't I, Henry? I've allus been a pretty good feller, ain't I? An' it ain't much t' ask, is it? Jes t' pull me along outer th' road? I'd do it fer you, wouldn't I, Henry?"

He paused in piteous anxiety to await his friend's reply.

The youth had reached an anguish where the sobs scorched him. He strove to express his loyalty, but he could only make fantastic gestures.

However, the tall soldier seemed suddenly to forget all those fears. He became again the grim, stalking specter of a soldier. He went stonily forward. The youth wished his friend to lean upon him, but the other always shook his head and strangely protested. "No—no—no—leave me be—leave me be——"

His look was fixed again upon the unknown. He moved with mysterious purpose, and all of the youth's offers he brushed aside. "No—no—leave me be —leave me be——"

The youth had to follow.

Presently the latter heard a voice talking softly near his shoulders. Turning he saw that it belonged to the tattered soldier. "Ye 'd better take 'im outa th' road, pardner. There 's a batt'ry comin' helitywhoop down th' road an' he 'll git runned over. He 's a goner anyhow in about five minutes—yeh kin see that. Ye 'd better take 'im outa th' road. Where th' blazes does he git his stren'th from?"

"Lord knows!" cried the youth. He was shaking his hands helplessly.

He ran forward presently and grasped the tall soldier by the arm. "Jim! Jim!" he coaxed, "come with me."

The tall soldier weakly tried to wrench himself free. "Huh," he said vacantly. He stared at the youth for a moment. At last he spoke as if dimly comprehending. "Oh! Inteh th' fields? Oh!"

He started blindly through the grass.

The youth turned once to look at the lashing riders and jouncing guns of the battery. He was startled from this view by a shrill outcry from the tattered man.

"Gawd! He's runnin'!"

Turning his head swiftly, the youth saw his friend running in a staggering and stumbling way toward a little clump of bushes. His heart seemed to wrench itself almost free from his body at this sight. He made a noise of pain. He and the tattered man began a pursuit. There was a singular race.

When he overtook the tall soldier he began to plead with all the words he could find. "Jim—Jim—what are you doing—what makes you do this way— you 'll hurt yerself."

The same purpose was in the tall soldier's face. He protested in a dulled way, keeping his eyes fastened on the mystic place of his intentions. "No— no—don't tech me—leave me be—leave me be——"

The youth, aghast and filled with wonder at the tall soldier, began quaveringly to question him. "Where yeh goin', Jim? What you thinking about? Where you going? Tell me, won't you, Jim?"

The tall soldier faced about as upon relentless pursuers. In his eyes there was a great appeal. "Leave me be, can't yeh? Leave me be fer a minnit."

The youth recoiled. "Why, Jim," he said, in a dazed way, "what's the matter with you?"

The tall soldier turned and, lurching dangerously, went on. The youth and the tattered soldier followed, sneaking as if whipped, feeling unable to face the stricken man if he should again confront them. They began to have thoughts of a solemn ceremony. There was something ritelike in these movements of the doomed soldier. And there was a resemblance in him to a devotee of a mad religion, blood-sucking, muscle-wrenching, bone-crushing. They were awed and afraid. They hung back lest he have at command a dreadful weapon.

At last, they saw him stop and stand motionless. Hastening up, they perceived that his face wore an expression telling that he had at last found the place for which he had struggled. His spare figure was erect; his bloody hands were quietly at his side. He was waiting with patience for something that he had come to meet. He was at the rendezvous. They paused and stood, expectant.

There was a silence.

Finally, the chest of the doomed soldier began to heave with a strained motion. It increased in violence until it was as if an animal was within and was kicking and tumbling furiously to be free.

This spectacle of gradual strangulation made the youth writhe, and once as his friend rolled his eyes, he saw something in them that made him sink wailing to the ground. He raised his voice in a last supreme call.

"Jim—Jim—Jim——"

The tall soldier opened his lips and spoke. He made a gesture. "Leave me be—don't tech me—leave me be——"

There was another silence while he waited.

Suddenly, his form stiffened and straightened. Then it was shaken by a prolonged ague. He stared into space. To the two watchers there was a curious and profound dignity in the firm lines of his awful face.

He was invaded by a creeping strangeness that slowly enveloped him. For a moment the tremor of his legs caused him to dance a sort of hideous hornpipe. His arms beat wildly about his head in expression of implike enthusiasm.

His tall figure stretched itself to its full height. There was a slight rending sound. Then it began to swing forward, slow and straight, in the manner of a falling tree. A swift muscular contortion made the left shoulder strike the ground first.

The body seemed to bounce a little way from the earth. "God!" said the tattered soldier.

The youth had watched, spellbound, this ceremony at the place of meeting. His face had been twisted into an expression of every agony he had imagined for his friend.

He now sprang to his feet and, going closer, gazed upon the pastelike face. The mouth was open and the teeth showed in a laugh.

As the flap of the blue jacket fell away from the body, he could see that the side looked as if it had been chewed by wolves.

The youth turned, with sudden, livid rage, toward the battlefield. He shook his fist. He seemed about to deliver a philippic.

"Hell——"

The red sun was pasted in the sky like a wafer.

10

The tattered man stood musing.

"Well, he was reg'lar jim-dandy fer nerve, wa'n't he," said he finally in a little awestruck voice. "A reg'lar jim-dandy." He thoughtfully poked one of the docile hands with his foot. "I wonner where he got 'is stren'th from? I never seen a man do like that before. It was a funny thing. Well, he was a reg'lar jim-dandy."

The youth desired to screech out his grief. He was stabbed, but his tongue lay dead in the tomb of his mouth. He threw himself again upon the ground and began to brood.

The tattered man stood musing.

"Look-a-here, pardner," he said, after a time. He regarded the corpse as he spoke. "He 's up an' gone, ain't 'e, an' we might as well begin t' look out fer ol' number one. This here thing is all over. He 's up an' gone, ain't 'e? An' he 's all right here. Nobody won't bother 'im. An' I must say I ain't enjoying any great health m'self these days."

The youth, awakened by the tattered soldier's tone, looked quickly up. He saw that he was swinging uncertainly on his legs and that his face had turned to a shade of blue.

"Good Lord!" he cried, "you ain't goin' t'—not you, too."

The tattered man waved his hand. "Nary die," he said. "All I want is some pea soup an' a good bed. Some pea soup," he repeated dreamfully.

The youth arose from the ground. "I wonder where he came from. I left him over there." He pointed. "And now I find 'im here. And he was coming from over there, too." He indicated a new direction. They both turned toward the body as if to ask of it a question.

"Well," at length spoke the tattered man, "there ain't no use in our stayin' here an' tryin' t' ask him anything."

The youth nodded an assent wearily. They both turned to gaze for a moment at the corpse.

The youth murmured something.

"Well, he was a jim-dandy, wa'n't 'e?" said the tattered man as if in response.

They turned their backs upon it and started away. For a time they stole softly, treading with their toes. It remained laughing there in the grass.

"I'm commencin' t' feel pretty bad," said the tattered man, suddenly breaking one of his little silences. "I'm commencin' t' feel pretty damn' bad."

The youth groaned. "O Lord!" He wondered if he was to be the tortured witness of another grim encounter.

But his companion waved his hand reassuringly. "Oh, I'm not goin' t' die yit! There too much dependin' on me fer me t' die yit. No, sir! Nary die! I *can't!* Ye'd oughta see th' swad a' chil'ren I've got, an' all like that."

The youth glancing at his companion could see by the shadow of a smile that he was making some kind of fun.

As they plodded on the tattered soldier continued to talk. "Besides, if I died, I wouldn't die th' way that feller did. That was th' funniest thing. I'd jest flop down, I would. I never seen a feller die th' way that feller did.

"Yeh know Tom Jamison, he lives next door t' me up home. He's a nice feller, he is, an' we was allus good friends. Smart, too. Smart as a steel trap. Well, when we was a-fightin' this afternoon, all-of-a-sudden he begin t' rip up an' cuss an' beller at me. 'Yer shot, yeh blamed infernal!'—he swear horrible—he ses t' me. I put up m' hand t' m' head an' when I looked at m' fingers, I seen, sure 'nough, I was shot. I give a holler an' began t' run, but b'fore I could git away another one hit me in th' arm an' whirl' me clean 'round. I got skeared when they was all ashootin' b'hind me an' I run t' beat all, but I cotch it pretty bad. I've an idee I'd a' been fightin' yit, if t'was n't fer Tom Jamison."

Then he made a calm announcement: "There's two of 'em—little ones—but they 're beginnin' t' have fun with me now. I don't b'lieve I kin walk much furder."

They went slowly on in silence. "Yeh look pretty peek-ed yerself," said the tattered man at last. "I bet yeh 've got a worser one than yeh think. Ye'd better take keer of yer hurt. It don't do t' let sech things go. It might be inside mostly, an' them plays thunder. Where is it located?" But he continued his harangue without waiting for a reply. "I see 'a feller git hit plum in th' head when my reg'ment was a-standin' at ease once. An' everybody yelled out to 'im: Hurt, John? Are yeh hurt much? 'No,' ses he. He looked kinder surprised, an' he went on tellin' 'em how he felt. He sed he didn't feel nothin'. But, by dad, th' first thing that feller knowed he was dead. Yes, he was dead—stone dead. So, yeh wanta watch out. Yeh might have some queer kind 'a hurt yerself. Yeh can't never tell. Where is your'n located?"

The youth had been wriggling since the introduction of this topic. He now gave a cry of exasperation and made a furious motion with his hand. "Oh, don't bother me!" he said. He was enraged against the tattered man, and could have strangled him. His companions seemed ever to play intolerable parts. They were ever upraising the ghost of shame on the stick of their curiosity. He turned toward the tattered man as one at bay. "Now, don't bother me," he repeated with desperate menace.

"Well, Lord knows I don't wanta bother anybody," said the other. There was a little accent of despair in his voice as he replied, "Lord knows I 've gota 'nough m' own t' tend to."

The youth, who had been holding a bitter debate with himself and casting glances of hatred and contempt at the tattered man, here spoke in a hard voice. "Good-by," he said.

The tattered man looked at him in gaping amazement. "Why—why, pardner, where yeh goin'?" he asked unsteadily. The youth looking at him, could see that he, too, like that other one, was beginning to act dumb and animal-like. His thoughts seemed to be floundering about in his head. "Now—now—look—a—here, you Tom Jamison—now—I won't have this—this here won't do. Where—where yeh goin'?"

The youth pointed vaguely. "Over there," he replied.

"Well, now look—a—here—now," said the tattered man, rambling on in idiot fashion. His head was hanging forward and his words were slurred. "This thing won't do, now, Tom Jamison. It won't do. I know yeh, yeh pigheaded devil. Yeh wanta go trompin' off with a bad hurt. It ain't right—now— Tom Jamison—it ain't. Yeh wanta leave me take keer of yeh, Tom Jamison. It ain't—right—it ain't—fer yeh t' go—trompin' off—with a bad hurt—it ain't—ain't—ain't right—it ain't."

In reply the youth climbed a fence and started away. He could hear the tattered man bleating plaintively.

Once he faced about angrily. "What?"

"Look—a—here, now, Tom Jamison—now—it ain't——"

The youth went on. Turning at a distance he saw the tattered man wandering about helplessly in the field.

He now thought that he wished he was dead. He believed that he envied those men whose bodies lay strewn over the grass of the fields and on the fallen leaves of the forest.

The simple questions of the tattered man had been knife thrusts to him. They asserted a society that probes pitilessly at secrets until all is apparent. His late companion's chance persistency made him feel that he could not keep his crime concealed in his bosom. It was sure to be brought plain by one of those arrows which cloud the air and are constantly pricking, discovering, proclaiming those things which are willed to be forever hidden. He admitted that he could not defend himself against this agency. It was not within the power of vigilance.

11

He became aware that the furnace roar of the battle was growing louder. Great brown clouds had floated to the still heights of air before him. The noise, too, was approaching. The woods filtered men and the fields became dotted.

As he rounded a hillock, he perceived that the roadway was now a crying mass of wagons, teams, and men. From the heaving tangle issued exhortations, commands, imprecations. Fear was sweeping it all along. The cracking whips bit and horses plunged and tugged. The white-topped wagons strained and stumbled in their exertions like fat sheep.

The youth felt comforted in a measure by this sight. They were all retreating. Perhaps, then, he was not so bad after all. He seated himself and watched the terror-stricken wagons. They fled like soft, ungainly animals. All the roarers and lashers served to help him to magnify the dangers and horrors of the engagement that he might try to prove to himself that the thing with which men could charge him was in truth a symmetrical act. There was an amount of pleasure to him in watching the wild march of this vindication.

Presently the calm head of a forward-going column of infantry appeared in the road. It came swiftly on. Avoiding the obstructions gave it the sinuous movement of a serpent. The men at the head butted mules with their musket stocks. They prodded teamsters indifferent to all howls. The men forced their way through parts of the dense mass by strength. The blunt head of the column pushed. The raving teamsters swore many strange oaths.

The commands to make way had the ring of a great importance in them. The men were going forward to the heart of the din. They were to confront the eager rush of the enemy. They felt the pride of their onward movement when the remainder of the army seemed trying to dribble down this road. They tumbled teams about with a fine feeling that it was no matter so long as their column got to the front in time. This importance made their faces grave and stern. And the backs of the officers were very rigid.

As the youth looked at them the black weight of his woe returned to him. He felt that he was regarding a procession of chosen beings. The separation was as great to him as if they had marched with weapons of flame and banners of sunlight. He could never be like them. He could have wept in his longings.

He searched about in his mind for an adequate malediction for the indefinite cause, the thing upon which men turn the words of final blame. It—whatever it was—was responsible for him, he said. There lay the fault.

The haste of the column to reach the battle seemed to the forlorn young man to be something much finer than stout fighting. Heroes, he thought, could find excuses in that long seething lane. They could retire with perfect self-respect and make excuses to the stars.

He wondered what those men had eaten that they could be in such haste to force their way to grim chances of death. As he watched his envy grew until he thought that he wished to change lives with one of them. He would have liked to have used a tremendous force, he said, throw off himself and become a better. Swift pictures of himself, apart, yet in himself, came to him—a blue desperate figure leading lurid charges with one knee forward and a broken blade high—a blue, determined figure standing before a crimson and steel assault, getting calmly killed on a high place before the eyes of all. He thought of the magnificent pathos of his dead body.

These thoughts uplifted him. He felt the quiver of war desire. In his ears, he heard the ring of victory. He knew the frenzy of a rapid successful charge. The music of the trampling feet, the sharp voices, the clanking arms of the column near him made him soar on the red wings of war. For a few moments he was sublime.

He thought that he was about to start for the front. Indeed, he saw a picture of himself, dust-stained, haggard, panting, flying to the front at the proper moment to seize and throttle the dark, leering witch of calamity.

Then the difficulties of the thing began to drag at him. He hesitated, balancing awkwardly on one foot.

He had no rifle; he could not fight with his hands, said he resentfully to his plan. Well, rifles could be had for the picking. They were extraordinarily profuse.

Also, he continued, it would be a miracle if he found his regiment. Well, he could fight with any regiment.

He started forward slowly. He stepped as if he expected to tread upon some explosive thing. Doubts and he were struggling.

He would truly be a worm if any of his comrades should see him returning thus, the marks of his flight upon him. There was a reply that the intent fighters did not care for what happened rearward saving that no hostile bayonets appeared there. In the battle-blur his face would, in a way be hidden, like the face of a cowled man.

But then he said that his tireless fate would bring forth, when the strife lulled for a moment, a man to ask of him an explanation. In imagination he felt the scrutiny of his companions as he painfully labored through some lies.

Eventually, his courage expended itself upon these objections. The debates drained him of his fire.

He was not cast down by this defeat of his plan, for, upon studying the affair carefully, he could not but admit that the objections were very formidable.

Furthermore, various ailments had begun to cry out. In their presence he could not persist in flying high with the wings of war, they rendered it almost impossible for him to see himself in a heroic light. He tumbled headlong.

He discovered that he had a scorching thirst. His face was so dry and grimy that he thought he could feel his skin crackle. Each bone of his body had an ache in it, and seemingly threatened to break with each movement. His feet were like two sores. Also, his body was calling for food. It was more powerful than a direct hunger. There was a dull, weight-like feeling in his stomach, and, when he tried to walk, his head swayed and he tottered. He could not see with distinctness. Small patches of green mist floated before his vision.

While he had been tossed by many emotions, he had not been aware of ailments. Now they beset him and made clamor. As he was at last compelled to pay attention to them, his capacity for self-hate was multiplied. In despair, he declared that he was not like those others. He now conceded it to be impossible that he should ever become a hero. He was a craven loon. Those pictures of glory were piteous things. He groaned from his heart and went staggering off.

A certain mothlike quality within him kept him in the vicinity of the battle. He had a great desire to see, and to get news. He wished to know who was winning.

He told himself that, despite his unprecedented suffering, he had never lost his greed for a victory, yet, he said, in a half-apologetic manner to his conscience, he could not but know that a defeat for the army this time might mean many favorable things for him. The blows of the enemy would splinter regiments into fragments. Thus, many men of courage, he considered, would be obliged to desert the colors and scurry like chickens. He would appear as one of them. They would be sullen brothers in distress, and he could then easily believe he had not run any farther or faster than they. And if he himself could believe in his virtuous perfection, he conceived that there would be small trouble in convincing all others.

He said, as if in excuse for this hope, that previously the army had encountered great defeats and in a few months had shaken off all blood and tradition of them, emerging as bright and valiant as a new one; thrusting out of sight the memory of disaster, and appearing with the valor and confidence of unconquered legions. The shrilling voices of the people at home would pipe dismally for a time, but various generals were usually compelled to listen to these ditties. He of course felt no compunctions for proposing a general as a sacrifice. He could not tell who the chosen for the barbs might be, so he could center no direct sympathy upon him. The people were afar and he did not conceive public opinion to be accurate at long range. It was quite probable they would hit the wrong man who, after he had recovered from his amazement would perhaps spend the rest of his days in writing replies to the songs of his alleged failure. It would be very unfortunate, no doubt, but in this case a general was of no consequence to the youth.

In a defeat there would be a roundabout vindication of himself. He thought it would prove, in a manner, that he had fled early because of his superior powers of perception. A serious prophet upon predicting a flood should be the first man to climb a tree. This would demonstrate that he was indeed a seer.

A moral vindication was regarded by the youth as a very important thing. Without salve, he could not, he thought, wear the sore badge of his dishonor through life. With his heart continually assuring him that he was despicable, he could not exist without making it, through his actions, apparent to all men.

If the army had gone gloriously on he would be lost. If the din meant that now his army's flags were tilted forward he was a condemned wretch. He would be compelled to doom himself to isolation. If the men were advancing, their indifferent feet were trampling upon his chances for a successful life.

As these thoughts went rapidly through his mind, he turned upon them and tried to thrust them away. He denounced himself as a villain. He said that he was the most unutterably selfish man in existence. His mind pictured the soldiers who would place their defiant bodies before the spear of the yelling battle fiend, and as he saw their dripping corpses on an imagined field, he said that he was their murderer.

Again he thought that he wished he was dead. He believed that he envied a corpse. Thinking of the slain, he achieved a great contempt for some of them, as if they were guilty for thus becoming lifeless. They might have been killed by lucky chances, he said, before they had had opportunities to flee or before they had been really tested. Yet they would receive laurels from tradition. He cried out bitterly that their crowns were stolen and their robes of glorious memories were shams. However, he still said that it was a great pity he was not as they.

A defeat of the army had suggested itself to him as a means of escape from the consequences of his fall. He considered, now, however, that it was useless to think of such a possibility. His education had been that success for that mighty blue machine was certain; that it would make victories as a contrivance turns out buttons. He presently discarded all his speculations in the other direction. He returned to the creed of soldiers.

When he perceived again that it was not possible for the army to be defeated, he tried to bethink him of a fine tale which he could take back to his regiment, and with it turn the expected shafts of derision.

But, as he mortally feared these shafts, it became impossible for him to invent a tale he felt he could trust. He experimented with many schemes, but threw them aside one by one as flimsy. He was quick to see vulnerable places in them all.

Furthermore, he was much afraid that some arrow of scorn might lay him mentally low before he could raise his protecting tale.

He imagined the whole regiment saying: "Where's Henry Fleming? He run, didn't 'e? Oh, my!" He recalled various persons who would be quite sure to leave him no peace about it. They would doubtless question him with sneers, and laugh at his stammering hesitation. In the next engagement they would try to keep watch of him to discover when he would run.

Wherever he went in camp, he would encounter insolent and lingeringly cruel stares. As he imagined himself passing near a crowd of comrades, he could hear some one say, "There he goes!"

Then, as if the heads were moved by one muscle, all the faces were turned toward him with wide, derisive grins. He seemed to hear some one make a humorous remark in a low tone. At it the others all crowed and cackled. He was a slang phrase.

12

The column that had butted stoutly at the obstacles in the roadway was barely out of the youth's sight before he saw dark waves of men come sweeping out of the woods and down through the fields. He knew at once that the steel fibers had been washed from their hearts. They were bursting from their coats and their equipments as from entanglements. They charged down upon him like terrified buffaloes.

Behind them blue smoke curled and clouded above the treetops, and through the thickets he could sometimes see a distant pink glare. The voices of the cannon were clamoring in interminable chorus.

The youth was horror-stricken. He stared in agony and amazement. He forgot that he was engaged in combating the universe. He threw aside his mental pamphlets on the philosophy of the retreated and rules for the guidance of the damned.

The fight was lost. The dragons were coming with invincible strides. The army, helpless in the matted thickets and blinded by the overhanging night, was going to be swallowed. War, the red animal, war, the blood-swollen god, would have bloated fill.

Within him something bade to cry out. He had the impulse to make a rallying speech, to sing a battle hymn, but he could only get his tongue to call into the air: "Why—why—what—what 's th' matter?"

Soon he was in the midst of them. They were leaping and scampering all about him. Their blanched faces shone in the dusk. They seemed, for the most part, to be very burly men. The youth turned from one to another of them as they galloped along. His incoherent questions were lost. They were heedless of his appeals. They did not seem to see him.

They sometimes gabbled insanely. One huge man was asking of the sky: "Say, where de plank road? Where de plank road!" It was as if he had lost a child. He wept in his pain and dismay.

Presently, men were running hither and thither in all ways. The artillery booming, forward, rearward, and on the flanks made jumble of ideas of direction. Landmarks had vanished into the gathered gloom. The youth began to imagine that he had got into the center of the tremendous quarrel, and he could perceive no way out of it. From the mouths of the fleeing men came a thousand wild questions, but no one made answers.

The youth, after rushing about and throwing interrogations at the heedless bands of retreating infantry, finally clutched a man by the arm. They swung around face to face.

"Why—why——" stammered the youth struggling with his balking tongue.

The man screamed: "Let go me! Let go me!" His face was livid and his eyes were rolling uncontrolled. He was heaving and panting. He still grasped his rifle, perhaps having forgotten to release his hold upon it. He tugged frantically, and the youth being compelled to lean forward was dragged several paces.

"Let go me! Let go me!"

"Why—why——" stuttered the youth.

"Well, then!" bawled the man in a lurid rage. He adroitly and fiercely swung his rifle. It crushed upon the youth's head. The man ran on.

The youth's fingers had turned to paste upon the other's arm. The energy was smitten from his muscles. He saw the flaming wings of lightning flash before his vision. There was a deafening rumble of thunder within his head.

Suddenly his legs seemed to die. He sank writhing to the ground. He tried to arise. In his efforts against the numbing pain he was like a man wrestling with a creature of the air.

There was a sinister struggle.

Sometimes he would achieve a position half erect, battle with the air for a moment, and then fall again, grabbing at the grass. His face was of a clammy pallor. Deep groans were wrenched from him.

At last, with a twisting movement, he got upon his hands and knees, and from thence, like a babe trying to walk, to his feet. Pressing his hands to his temples he went lurching over the grass.

He fought an intense battle with his body. His dulled senses wished him to swoon and he opposed them stubbornly, his mind portraying unknown dangers and mutilations if he should fall upon the field. He went tall soldier fashion. He imagined secluded spots where he could fall and be unmolested. To search for one he strove against the tide of his pain.

Once he put his hand to the top of his head and timidly touched the wound. The scratching pain of the contact made him draw a long breath through his clinched teeth. His fingers were dabbled with blood. He regarded them with a fixed stare.

Around him he could hear the grumble of jolted cannon as the scurrying horses were lashed toward the front. Once, a young officer on a besplashed charger nearly ran him down. He turned and watched the mass of guns, men, and horses sweeping in a wide curve toward a gap in a fence. The officer was making excited motions with a gauntleted hand. The guns followed the teams with an air of unwillingness, of being dragged by the heels.

Some officers of the scattered infantry were cursing and railing like fishwives. Their scolding voices could be heard above the din. Into the unspeakable jumble in the roadway rode a squadron of cavalry. The faded yellow of their facings shone bravely. There was a mighty altercation.

The artillery were assembling as if for a conference.

The blue haze of evening was upon the field. The lines of forest were long purple shadows. One cloud lay along the western sky partly smothering the red.

As the youth left the scene behind him, he heard the guns suddenly roar out. He imagined them shaking in black rage. They belched and howled like brass devils guarding a gate. The soft air was filled with the tremendous remonstrance. With it came the shattering peal of opposing infantry. Turning to look behind him, he could see sheets of orange light illumine the shadowy distance. There were subtle and sudden lightnings in the far air. At times he thought he could see heaving masses of men.

He hurried on in the dusk. The day had faded until he could barely distinguish place for his feet. The purple darkness was filled with men who lectured and jabbered. Sometimes he could see them gesticulating against the blue and somber sky. There seemed to be a great ruck of men and munitions spread about in the forest and in the fields.

The little narrow roadway now lay lifeless. There were overturned wagons like sun-dried bowlders. The bed of the former torrent was choked with the bodies of horses and splintered parts of war machines.

It had come to pass that his wound pained him but little. He was afraid to move rapidly, however, for a dread of disturbing it. He held his head very still and took many precautions against stumbling. He was filled with anxiety, and his face was pinched and drawn in anticipation of the pain of any sudden mistake of his feet in the gloom.

His thoughts, as he walked, fixed intently upon his hurt. There was a cool, liquid feeling about it and he imagined blood moving slowly down under his hair. His head seemed swollen to a size that made him think his neck to be inadequate.

The new silence of his wound made much worriment. The little blistering voices of pain that had called out from his scalp were, he thought, definite in their expression of danger. By then he believed that he could measure his plight. But when they remained ominously silent he became frightened and imagined terrible fingers that clutched into his brain.

Amid it he began to reflect upon various incidents and conditions of the past. He bethought him of certain meals his mother had cooked at home, in which those dishes of which he was particularly fond had occupied prominent positions. He saw the spread table. The pine walls of the kitchen were glowing in the warm light from the stove. Too, he remembered how he and his companions used to go from the schoolhouse to the bank of a shaded pool. He saw his clothes in disorderly array upon the grass of the bank. He felt the swash of the fragrant water upon his body. The leaves of the overhanging maple rustled with melody in the wind of youthful summer.

He was overcome presently by a dragging weariness. His head hung forward and his shoulders were stooped as if he were bearing a great bundle. His feet shuffled along the ground.

He held continuous arguments as to whether he should lie down and sleep at some near spot, or force himself on until he reached a certain haven. He often tried to dismiss the question, but his body persisted in rebellion and his senses nagged at him like pampered babies.

At last he heard a cheery voice near his shoulder: "Yeh seem t' be in a pretty bad way, boy?"

The youth did not look up, but he assented with thick tongue. "Uh!"

The owner of the cheery voice took him firmly by the arm. "Well," he said, with a round laugh, "I'm goin' your way. Th' hull gang is goin' your way. An' I guess I kin give yeh a lift." They began to walk like a drunken man and his friend.

As they went along, the man questioned the youth and assisted him with the replies like one manipulating the mind of a child. Sometimes he interjected anecdotes. "What reg'ment do yeh b'long teh? Eh? What 's that? Th' 304th N' York? Why, what corps is that in? Oh, it is? Why, I thought they wasn't engaged t'-day—they 're 'way over in th' center. Oh, they was, eh? Well, pretty nearly everybody got their share 'a fightin' t'-day. By dad, I give myself up fer dead any number 'a times. There was shootin' here an' shootin' there, an' hollerin' here an' hollerin' there, in th' damn' darkness, until I couldn't tell t' save m' soul which side I was on. Sometimes I thought I was sure 'nough from Ohier, an' other times I could 'a swore I was from th' bitter end of Florida. It was th' most mixed up dern thing I ever see. An' these here hull woods is a reg'lar mess. It 'll be a miracle if we find our reg'ments t'-night. Pretty soon, though, we 'll meet a-plenty of guards an' provost-guards, an' one thing an' another. Ho! there they go with an off'cer, I guess. Look at his hand a-draggin'. He 's got all th' war he wants, I bet. He won't be talkin' so big about his reputation an' all when they go t' sawin' off his leg. Poor feller! My brother 's got whiskers jest like that. How did yeh git 'way over here, anyhow? Your reg'ment is a long way from here, ain't it? Well, I guess we can find it. Yeh know there was a boy killed in my comp'ny t'-day that I thought th' world an' all of. Jack was a nice feller: By ginger, it hurt like thunder t' see ol' Jack jest git knocked flat. We was a-standin' purty peaceable fer a spell, 'though there was men runnin' ev'ry way all 'round us, an' while we was a-standin' like that, 'long come a big fat feller. He began t' peck at Jack's elbow, an' he ses: 'Say, where 's th' road t' th' river? An' Jack, he never paid no attention, an' th' feller kept on a-peckin' at his elbow an' sayin': 'Say, where 's th' road t' th' river?' Jack was a-lookin' ahead all th' time tryin' t' see th' Johnnies comin' through th' woods, an' he never paid no attention t' this big fat feller fer a long time, but at last he turned 'round an' he says: 'Ah, go t' hell an' find th' road t' th' river!' An' jest then a shot slapped him bang on th' side th' head. He was a sergeant, too. Them was his last words. Thunder, I wish we was sure 'a findin' our reg'ments t'-night. It 's goin' be long huntin'. But I guess we kin do it."

In the search which followed, the man of the cheery voice seemed to the youth to possess a wand of a magic kind. He threaded the mazes of the tangled forest with a strange fortune. In encounters with guards and patrols he displayed the keenness of a detective and the valor of a gamin. Obstacles fell before him and became of assistance. The youth, with his chin still on his breast, stood woodenly by while his companion beat ways and means out of sullen things.

The forest seemed a vast hive of men buzzing about in frantic circles, but the cheery man conducted the youth without mistakes, until at last he began to chuckle with glee and self-satisfaction. "Ah, there yeh are! See that fire?"

The youth nodded stupidly.

"Well, there 's where your reg'ment is. An' now, good-by, ol' boy, good luck t' yeh."

A warm and strong hand clasped the youth's languid fingers for an instant, and then he heard a cheerful and audacious whistling as the man strode away. As he who had so befriended him was thus passing out of his life, it suddenly occurred to the youth that he had not once seen his face.

13

The youth went slowly toward the fire indicated by his departed friend. As he reeled, he bethought him of the welcome his comrades would give him. He had a conviction that he would soon feel in his sore heart the barbed missiles of ridicule. He had no strength to invent a tale; he would be a soft target.

He made vague plans to go off into the deeper darkness and hide, but they were all destroyed by the voices of exhaustion and pain from his body. His ailments, clamoring, forced him to seek the place of food and rest, at whatever cost.

He swung unsteadily toward the fire. He could see the forms of men throwing black shadows in the red light, and as he went nearer it became known to him in some way that the ground was strewn with sleeping men.

Of a sudden he confronted a black and monstrous figure. A rifle barrel caught some glinting beams. "Halt! halt!" He was dismayed for a moment, but he presently thought that he recognized the nervous voice. As he stood tottering before the rifle barrel, he called out: "Why, hello, Wilson, you— you here?"

The rifle was lowered to a position of caution and the loud soldier came slowly forward. He peered into the youth's face. "That you, Henry?"

"Yes, it's—it's me."

"Well, well, ol' boy," said the other, "by ginger, I'm glad t' see yeh! I give yeh up fer a goner. I thought yeh was dead sure enough." There was husky emotion in his voice.

The youth found that now he could barely stand upon his feet. There was a sudden sinking of his forces. He thought he must hasten to produce his tale to protect him from the missiles already at the lips of his redoubtable comrades. So, staggering before the loud soldier, he began: "Yes, yes. I've— I've had an awful time. I've been all over. Way over on th' right. Ter'ble fightin' over there. I had an awful time. I got separated from th' reg'ment. Over on th' right, I got shot. In th' head. I never see sech fightin'. Awful time. I don't see how I could a' got separated from th' reg'ment. I got shot, too."

His friend had stepped forward quickly. "What? Got shot? Why didn't yeh say so first? Poor ol' boy, we must—hol' on a minnit; what am I doin'. I'll call Simpson."

Another figure at that moment loomed in the gloom. They could see that it was the corporal. "Who yeh talkin' to, Wilson?" he demanded. His voice was anger-toned. "Who yeh talkin' to? Yeh th' derndest sentinel—why— hello, Henry, you here? Why, I thought you was dead four hours ago! Great Jerusalem, they keep turnin' up every ten minutes or so! We thought we'd lost forty-two men by straight count, but if they keep on a-comin' this way, we'll git th' comp'ny all back by mornin' yit. Where was yeh?"

"Over on th' right. I got separated"—began the youth with considerable glibness.

But his friend had interrupted hastily. "Yes, an' he got shot in th' head an' he's in a fix, an' we must see t' him right away." He rested his rifle in the hollow of his left arm and his right around the youth's shoulder.

"Gee, it must hurt like thunder!" he said.

The youth leaned heavily upon his friend. "Yes, it hurts—hurts a good deal," he replied. There was a faltering in his voice.

"Oh," said the corporal. He linked his arm in the youth's and drew him forward. "Come on, Henry. I'll take keer 'a yeh."

As they went on together the loud private called out after them: "Put 'im t' sleep in my blanket, Simpson. An'—hol' on a minnit—here's my canteen. It's full 'a coffee. Look at his head by th' fire an' see how it looks. Maybe it's a pretty bad un. When I git relieved in a couple 'a minnits, I'll be over an' see t' him."

The youth's senses were so deadened that his friend's voice sounded from afar and he could scarcely feel the pressure of the corporal's arm. He submitted passively to the latter's directing strength. His head was in the old manner hanging forward upon his breast. His knees wobbled.

The corporal led him into the glare of the fire. "Now, Henry," he said, "let's have look at yer ol' head."

The youth sat down obediently and the corporal, laying aside his rifle, began to fumble in the bushy hair of his comrade. He was obliged to turn the other's head so that the full flush of the fire light would beam upon it. He puckered his mouth with a critical air. He drew back his lips and whistled through his teeth when his fingers came in contact with the splashed blood and the rare wound.

"Ah, here we are!" he said. He awkwardly made further investigations. "Jest as I thought," he added, presently. "Yeh've been grazed by a ball. It's raised a queer lump jest as if some feller had lammed yeh on th' head with a club. It stopped a-bleedin' long time ago. Th' most about it is that in th' mornin' yeh'll feel that a number ten hat wouldn't fit yeh. An' your head'll be all het up an' feel as dry as burnt pork. An' yeh may git a lot 'a other sicknesses, too, by mornin'. Yeh can't never tell. Still, I don't much think so. It's jest a damn' good belt on th' head, an' nothin' more. Now, you jest sit here an' don't move, while I go rout out th' relief. Then I'll send Wilson t' take keer 'a yeh."

The corporal went away. The youth remained on the ground like a parcel. He stared with a vacant look into the fire.

After a time he aroused, for some part, and the things about him began to take form. He saw that the ground in the deep shadows was cluttered with men, sprawling in every conceivable posture. Glancing narrowly into the more distant darkness, he caught occasional glimpses of visages that loomed pallid and ghostly, lit with a phosphorescent glow. These faces expressed in their lines the deep stupor of the tired soldiers. They made them appear like men drunk with wine. This bit of forest might have appeared to an ethereal wanderer as a scene of the result of some frightful debauch.

On the other side of the fire the youth observed an officer asleep, seated bolt upright, with his back against a tree. There was something perilous in his position. Badgered by dreams, perhaps, he swayed with little bounces and starts, like an old, toddy-stricken grandfather in a chimney corner. Dust and stains were upon his face. His lower jaw hung down as if lacking strength to assume its normal position. He was the picture of an exhausted soldier after a feast of war.

He had evidently gone to sleep with his sword in his arms. These two had slumbered in an embrace, but the weapon had been allowed in time to fall unheeded to the ground. The grass-mounted hilt lay in contact with some parts of the fire.

Within the gleam of rose and orange light from the burning sticks were other soldiers, snoring and heaving, or lying deathlike in slumber. A few pairs of legs were stuck forth, rigid and straight. The shoes displayed the mud or dust of marches and bits of rounded trousers, protruding from the blankets, showed rents and tears from hurried pitchings through the dense brambles.

The fire crackled musically. From it swelled light smoke. Overhead the foliage moved softly. The leaves, with their faces turned toward the blaze, were colored shifting hues of silver, often edged with red. Far off to the right, through a window in the forest could be seen a handful of stars lying, like glittering pebbles, on the black level of the night.

Occasionally, in this low-arched hall, a soldier would arouse and turn his body to a new position, the experience of his sleep having taught him of uneven and objectionable places upon the ground under him. Or, perhaps, he would lift himself to a sitting posture, blink at the fire for an unintelligent moment, throw a swift glance at his prostrate companion, and then cuddle down again with a grunt of sleepy content.

The youth sat in a forlorn heap until his friend the loud young soldier came, swinging two canteens by their light strings. "Well, now, Henry, ol' boy," said the latter, "we'll have yeh fixed up in jest about a minnit."

He had the bustling ways of an amateur nurse. He fussed around the fire and stirred the sticks to brilliant exertions. He made his patient drink largely from the canteen that contained the coffee. It was to the youth a delicious draught. He tilted his head afar back and held the canteen long to his lips. The cool mixture went caressingly down his blistered throat. Having finished, he sighed with comfortable delight.

The loud young soldier watched his comrade with an air of satisfaction. He later produced an extensive handkerchief from his pocket. He folded it into a manner of bandage and soused water from the other canteen upon the middle of it. This crude arrangement he bound over the youth's head, tying the ends in a queer knot at the back of the neck.

"There," he said, moving off and surveying his deed, "yeh look like th' devil, but I bet yeh feel better."

The youth contemplated his friend with grateful eyes. Upon his aching and swelling head the cold cloth was like a tender woman's hand.

"Yeh don't holler ner say nothin'," remarked his friend approvingly. "I know I'm a blacksmith at takin' keer 'a sick folks, an' yeh never squeaked. Yer a good un, Henry. Most 'a men would a' been in th' hospital long ago. A shot in th' head ain't foolin' business."

The youth made no reply, but began to fumble with the buttons of his jacket.

"Well, come, now," continued his friend, "come on. I must put yeh t' bed an' see that yeh git a good night's rest."

The other got carefully erect, and the loud young soldier led him among the sleeping forms lying in groups and rows. Presently he stooped and picked up his blankets. He spread the rubber one upon the ground and placed the woolen one about the youth's shoulders.

"There now," he said, "lie down an' git some sleep."

The youth, with his manner of doglike obedience, got carefully down like a crone stooping. He stretched out with a murmur of relief and comfort. The ground felt like the softest couch.

But of a sudden he ejaculated: "Hol' on a minnit! Where you goin' t' sleep?"

His friend waved his hand impatiently. "Right down there by yeh."

"Well, but hol' on a minnit," continued the youth. "What yeh goin' t' sleep in? I've got your———"

The loud young soldier snarled: "Shet up an' go on t' sleep. Don't be makin' a damn' fool 'a yerself," he said severely.

After the reproof the youth said no more. An exquisite drowsiness had spread through him. The warm comfort of the blanket enveloped him and made a gentle languor. His head fell forward on his crooked arm and his weighted lids went softly down over his eyes. Hearing a splatter of musketry from the distance, he wondered indifferently if those men sometimes slept. He gave a long sigh, snuggled down into his blanket, and in a moment was like his comrades.

14

When the youth awoke it seemed to him that he had been asleep for a thousand years, and he felt sure that he opened his eyes upon an unexpected world. Gray mists were slowly shifting before the first efforts of the sun rays. An impending splendor could be seen in the eastern sky. An icy dew had chilled his face, and immediately upon arousing he curled farther down into his blanket. He stared for a while at the leaves overhead, moving in a heraldic wind of the day.

The distance was splintering and blaring with the noise of fighting. There was in the sound an expression of deadly persistency, as if it had not begun and was not to cease.

About him were the rows and groups of men that he had dimly seen the previous night. They were getting a last draught of sleep before the awakening. The gaunt, careworn features and dusty figures were made plain by this quaint light at the dawning, but it dressed the skin of the men in corpselike hues and made the tangled limbs appear pulseless and dead. The youth started up with a little cry when his eyes first swept over this motionless mass of men, thick-spread upon the ground, pallid, and in strange postures. His disordered mind interpreted the hall of the forest as a charnel place. He believed for an instant that he was in the house of the dead, and he did not dare to move lest these corpses start up, squalling and squawking. In a second, however, he achieved his proper mind. He swore a complicated oath at himself. He saw that this somber picture was not a fact of the present, but a mere prophecy.

He heard then the noise of a fire crackling briskly in the cold air, and, turning his head, he saw his friend pottering busily about a small blaze. A few other figures moved in the fog, and he heard the hard cracking of axe blows.

Suddenly there was a hollow rumble of drums. A distant bugle sang faintly. Similar sounds, varying in strength, came from near and far over the forest. The bugles called to each other like brazen gamecocks. The near thunder of the regimental drums rolled.

The body of men in the woods rustled. There was a general uplifting of heads. A murmuring of voices broke upon the air. In it there was much bass of grumbling oaths. Strange gods were addressed in condemnation of the early hours necessary to correct war. An officer's peremptory tenor rang out and quickened the stiffened movement of the men. The tangled limbs unraveled. The corpse-hued faces were hidden behind fists that twisted slowly in the eye sockets.

The youth sat up and gave vent to an enormous yawn. "Thunder!" he remarked petulantly. He rubbed his eyes, and then putting up his hand felt carefully of the bandage over his wound. His friend, perceiving him to be awake, came from the fire. "Well, Henry, ol' man, how do yeh feel this mornin'?" he demanded.

The youth yawned again. Then he puckered his mouth to a little pucker. His head, in truth, felt precisely like a melon, and there was an unpleasant sensation at his stomach.

"Oh, Lord, I feel pretty bad," he said.

"Thunder!" exclaimed the other. "I hoped ye'd feel all right this mornin'. Let's see th' bandage—I guess it's slipped." He began to tinker at the wound in rather a clumsy way until the youth exploded.

"Gosh-dern it!" he said in sharp irritation; "you're the hangdest man I ever saw! You wear muffs on your hands. Why in good thunderation can't you be more easy? I'd rather you'd stand off an' throw guns at it. Now, go slow, an' don't act as if you was nailing down carpet."

He glared with insolent command at his friend, but the latter answered soothingly. "Well, well, come now, an' git some grub," he said. "Then, maybe, yeh'll feel better."

At the fireside the loud young soldier watched over his comrade's wants with tenderness and care. He was very busy marshaling the little black vagabonds of tin cups and pouring into them the streaming, iron colored mixture from a small and sooty tin pail. He had some fresh meat, which he roasted hurriedly upon a stick. He sat down then and contemplated the youth's appetite with glee.

The youth took note of a remarkable change in his comrade since those days of camp life upon the river bank. He seemed no more to be continually regarding the proportions of his personal prowess. He was not furious at small words that pricked his conceits. He was no more a loud young soldier. There was about him now a fine reliance. He showed a quiet belief in his purposes and his abilities. And this inward confidence evidently enabled him to be indifferent to little words of other men aimed at him.

The youth reflected. He had been used to regarding his comrade as a blatant child with an audacity grown from his inexperience, thoughtless, headstrong, jealous, and filled with a tinsel courage. A swaggering babe accustomed to strut in his own dooryard. The youth wondered where had been born these new eyes; when his comrade had made the great discovery that there were many men who would refuse to be subjected by him. Apparently, the other had now climbed a peak of wisdom from which he could perceive himself as a very wee thing. And the youth saw that ever after it would be easier to live in his friend's neighborhood.

His comrade balanced his ebony coffee-cup on his knee. "Well Henry," he said, "what d'yeh think th' chances are? D'yeh think we'll wallop 'em?"

The youth considered for a moment. "Day-b'fore-yesterday," he finally replied, with boldness, "you would 'a' bet you'd lick the hull kit-an'-boodle all by yourself."

His friend looked a trifle amazed. "Would I?" he asked. He pondered. "Well, perhaps I would," he decided at last. He stared humbly at the fire.

The youth was quite disconcerted at this surprising reception of his remarks. "Oh, no, you wouldn't either," he said, hastily trying to retrace.

But the other made a deprecating gesture. "Oh, yeh needn't mind, Henry," he said. "I believe I was a pretty big fool in those days." He spoke as after a lapse of years.

There was a little pause.

"All th' officers say we've got th' rebs in a pretty tight box," said the friend, clearing his throat in a commonplace way. "They all seem t' think we've got 'em jest where we want 'em."

"I don't know about that," the youth replied. "What I seen over on th' right makes me think it was th' other way about. From where I was, it looked as if we was gettin' a good poundin' yestirday."

"D'yeh think so?" inquired the friend. "I thought we handled 'em pretty rough yestirday."

"Not a bit," said the youth. "Why, lord, man, you didn't see nothing of the fight. Why!" Then a sudden thought came to him. "Oh! Jim Conklin's dead."

His friend started. "What? Is he? Jim Conklin?"

The youth spoke slowly. "Yes. He's dead. Shot in th' side."

"Yeh don't say so. Jim Conklin . . . poor cuss!"

All about them were other small fires surrounded by men with their little black utensils. From one of these near came sudden sharp voices in a row. It appeared that two light-footed soldiers had been teasing a huge, bearded man, causing him to spill coffee upon his blue knees. The man had gone into a rage and had sworn comprehensively. Stung by his language, his tormentors had immediately bristled at him with a great show of resenting unjust oaths. Possibly there was going to be a fight.

The friend arose and went over to them, making pacific motions with his arms. "Oh, here, now, boys, what's th' use?" he said. "We'll be at th' rebs in less'n an hour. What's th' good fightin' 'mong ourselves?"

One of the light-footed soldiers turned upon him red-faced and violent. "Yeh needn't come around here with yer preachin'. I s'pose yeh don't approve 'a fightin' since Charley Morgan licked yeh; but I don't see what business this here is 'a yours or anybody else."

"Well, it ain't," said the friend mildly. "Still I hate t' see——"

There was a tangled argument.

"Well, he——," said the two, indicating their opponent with accusative forefingers.

The huge soldier was quite purple with rage. He pointed at the two soldiers with his great hand, extended clawlike. "Well, they——"

But during this argumentative time the desire to deal blows seemed to pass, although they said much to each other. Finally the friend returned to his old seat. In a short while the three antagonists could be seen together in an amiable bunch.

"Jimmie Rogers ses I'll have t' fight him after th' battle t'-day," announced the friend as he again seated himself. "He ses he don't allow no interferin' in his business. I hate t' see th' boys fightin' 'mong themselves."

The youth laughed. "Yer changed a good bit. Yeh ain't at all like yeh was. I remember when you an' that Irish feller——" He stopped and laughed again.

"No, I didn't use t' be that way," said his friend thoughtfully. "That's true 'nough."

"Well, I didn't mean——" began the youth.

The friend made another deprecatory gesture. "Oh, yeh needn't mind, Henry."

There was another little pause.

"Th' reg'ment lost over half th' men yestirday," remarked the friend eventually. "I thought a course they was all dead, but, laws, they kep' a-comin' back last night until it seems, after all, we didn't lose but a few. They'd been scattered allover, wanderin' around in th' woods, fightin' with other reg'ments, an' everything. Jest like you done."

"So?" said the youth.

15

The regiment was standing at order arms at the side of a lane, waiting for the command to march, when suddenly the youth remembered the little packet enwrapped in a faded yellow envelope which the loud young soldier with lugubrious words had intrusted to him. It made him start. He uttered an exclamation and turned toward his comrade.

"Wilson!"

"What?"

His friend, at his side in the ranks, was thoughtfully staring down the road. From some cause his expression was at that moment very meek. The youth, regarding him with sidelong glances, felt impelled to change his purpose. "Oh, nothing," he said.

His friend turned his head in some surprise, "Why, what was yeh goin' t' say?"

"Oh, nothing," repeated the youth.

He resolved not to deal the little blow. It was sufficient that the fact made him glad. It was not necessary to knock his friend on the head with the misguided packet.

He had been possessed of much fear of his friend, for he saw how easily questionings could make holes in his feelings. Lately, he had assured himself that the altered comrade would not tantalize him with a persistent curiosity, but he felt certain that during the first period of leisure his friend would ask him to relate his adventures of the previous day.

He now rejoiced in the possession of a small weapon with which he could prostrate his comrade at the first signs of a cross-examination. He was master. It would now be he who could laugh and shoot the shafts of derision.

The friend had, in a weak hour, spoken with sobs of his own death. He had delivered a melancholy oration previous to his funeral, and had doubtless in the packet of letters, presented various keepsakes to relatives. But he had not died, and thus he had delivered himself into the hands of the youth.

The latter felt immensely superior to his friend, but he inclined to condescension. He adopted toward him an air of patronizing good humor.

His self-pride was now entirely restored. In the shade of its flourishing growth he stood with braced and self-confident legs, and since nothing could now be discovered he did not shrink from an encounter with the eyes of judges, and allowed no thoughts of his own to keep him from an attitude of manfulness. He had performed his mistakes in the dark, so he was still a man.

Indeed, when he remembered his fortunes of yesterday, and looked at them from a distance he began to see something fine there. He had license to be pompous and veteranlike.

His panting agonies of the past he put out of his sight.

In the present, he declared to himself that it was only the doomed and the damned who roared with sincerity at circumstance. Few but they ever did it. A man with a full stomach and the respect of his fellows had no business to scold about anything that he might think to be wrong in the ways of the universe, or even with the ways of society. Let the unfortunates rail; the others may play marbles.

He did not give a great deal of thought to these battles that lay directly before him. It was not essential that he should plan his ways in regard to them. He had been taught that many obligations of a life were easily avoided. The lessons of yesterday had been that retribution was a laggard and blind. With these facts before him he did not deem it necessary that he should become feverish over the possibilities of the ensuing twenty-four hours. He could leave much to chance. Besides, a faith in himself had secretly blossomed. There was a little flower of confidence growing within him. He was now a man of experience. He had been out among the dragons, he said, and he assured himself that they were not so hideous as he had imagined them. Also, they were inaccurate; they did not sting with precision. A stout heart often defied, and defying, escaped.

And, furthermore, how could they kill him who was the chosen of gods and doomed to greatness?

He remembered how some of the men had run from the battle. As he recalled their terror-struck faces he felt a scorn for them. They had surely been more fleet and more wild than was absolutely necessary. They were weak mortals. As for himself, he had fled with discretion and dignity.

He was roused from this reverie by his friend, who, having hitched about nervously and blinked at the trees for a time, suddenly coughed in an introductory way, and spoke.

"Fleming!"

"What?"

The friend put his hand up to his mouth and coughed again. He fidgeted in his jacket.

"Well," he gulped, at last, "I guess yeh might as well give me back them letters." Dark, prickling blood had flushed into his cheeks and brow.

"All right, Wilson," said the youth. He loosened two buttons of his coat, thrust in his hand, and brought forth the packet. As he extended it to his friend the latter's face was turned from him.

He had been slow in the act of producing the packet because during it he had been trying to invent a remarkable comment upon the affair. He could conjure nothing of sufficient point. He was compelled to allow his friend to escape unmolested with his packet. And for this he took unto himself considerable credit. It was a generous thing.

His friend at his side seemed suffering great shame. As he contemplated him, the youth felt his heart grow more strong and stout. He had never been compelled to blush in such manner for his acts; he was an individual of extraordinary virtues.

He reflected, with condescending pity: "Too bad! Too bad! The poor devil, it makes him feel tough!"

After this incident, and as he reviewed the battle pictures he had seen, he felt quite competent to return home and make the hearts of the people glow with stories of war. He could see himself in a room of warm tints telling tales to listeners. He could exhibit laurels. They were insignificant; still, in a district where laurels were infrequent, they might shine.

He saw his gaping audience picturing him as the central figure in blazing scenes. And he imagined the consternation and the ejaculations of his mother and the young lady at the seminary as they drank his recitals. Their vague feminine formula for beloved ones doing brave deeds on the field of battle without risk of life would be destroyed.

16

A sputtering of musketry was always to be heard. Later, the cannon had entered the dispute. In the fog-filled air their voices made a thudding sound. The reverberations were continued. This part of the world led a strange, battleful existence.

The youth's regiment was marched to relieve a command that had lain long in some damp trenches. The men took positions behind a curving line of rifle pits that had been turned up, like a large furrow, along the line of woods. Before them was a level stretch, peopled with short, deformed stumps. From the woods beyond came the dull popping of the skirmishers and pickets, firing in the fog. From the right came the noise of a terrific fracas.

The men cuddled behind the small embankment and sat in easy attitudes awaiting their turn. Many had their backs to the firing. The youth's friend lay down, buried his face in his arms, and almost instantly, it seemed, he was in a deep sleep.

The youth leaned his breast against the brown dirt and peered over at the woods and up and down the line. Curtains of trees interfered with his ways of vision. He could see the low line of trenches but for a short distance. A few idle flags were perched on the dirt hills. Behind them were rows of dark bodies with a few heads sticking curiously over the top.

Always the noise of skirmishers came from the woods on the front and left, and the din on the right had grown to frightful proportions. The guns were roaring without an instant's pause for breath. It seemed that the cannon had come from all parts and were engaged in a stupendous wrangle. It became impossible to make a sentence heard.

The youth wished to launch a joke—a quotation from newspapers. He desired to say, "All quiet on the Rappahannock," but the guns refused to permit even a comment upon their uproar. He never successfully concluded the sentence. But at last the guns stopped, and among the men in the rifle pits rumors again flew, like birds, but they were now for the most part black creatures who flapped their wings drearily near to the ground and refused to rise on any wings of hope. The men's faces grew doleful from the interpreting of omens. Tales of hesitation and uncertainty on the part of those high in place and responsibility came to their ears. Stories of disaster were borne into their minds with many proofs. This din of musketry on the right, growing like a released genie of sound, expressed and emphasized the army's plight.

The men were disheartened and began to mutter. They made gestures expressive of the sentence: "Ah, what more can we do?" And it could always be seen that they were bewildered by the alleged news and could not fully comprehend a defeat.

Before the gray mists had been totally obliterated by the sun rays, the regiment was marching in a spread column that was retiring carefully through the woods. The disordered, hurrying lines of the enemy could sometimes be seen down through the groves and little fields. They were yelling, shrill and exultant.

At this sight the youth forgot many personal matters and became greatly enraged. He exploded in loud sentences. "B'jiminey, we're generaled by a lot 'a lunkheads."

"More than one feller has said that t'-day," observed a man.

His friend, recently aroused, was still very drowsy. He looked behind him until his mind took in the meaning of the movement. Then he sighed. "Oh, well, I s'pose we got licked," he remarked sadly.

The youth had a thought that it would not be handsome for him to freely condemn other men. He made an attempt to restrain himself, but the words upon his tongue were too bitter. He presently began a long and intricate denunciation of the commander of the forces.

"Mebbe, it wa'n't all his fault—not all together. He did th' best he knowed. It's our luck t' git licked often," said his friend in a weary tone. He was trudging along with stooped shoulders and shifting eyes like a man who has been caned and kicked.

"Well, don't we fight like the devil? Don't we do all that men can?" demanded the youth loudly.

He was secretly dumfounded at this sentiment when it came from his lips. For a moment his face lost its valor and he looked guiltily about him. But no one questioned his right to deal in such words, and presently he recovered his air of courage. He went on to repeat a statement he had heard going from group to group at the camp that morning. "The brigadier said he never saw a new reg'ment fight the way we fought yestirday, didn't he? And we didn't do better than many another reg'ment, did we? Well, then, you can't say it's th' army's fault, can you?"

In his reply, the friend's voice was stern, " 'A course not," he said. "No man dare say we don't fight like th' devil. No man will ever dare say it. Th' boys fight like hell-roosters. But still—still, we don't have no luck."

"Well, then, if we fight like the devil an' don't ever whip, it must be the general's fault," said the youth grandly and decisively. "And I don't see any sense in fighting and fighting and fighting, yet always losing through some derned old lunkhead of a general."

A sarcastic man who was tramping at the youth's side, then spoke lazily. "Mebbe, yeh think yeh fit th' hull battle yestirday, Fleming," he remarked.

The speech pierced the youth. Inwardly he was reduced to an abject pulp by these chance words. His legs quaked privately. He cast a frightened glance at the sarcastic man.

"Why, no," he hastened to say in a conciliating voice, "I don't think I fought the whole battle yesterday."

But the other seemed innocent of any deeper meaning. Apparently, he had no information. It was merely his habit. "Oh!" he replied in the same tone of calm derision.

The youth, nevertheless, felt a threat. His mind shrank from going near to the danger, and thereafter he was silent. The significance of the sarcastic man's words took from him all loud moods that would make him appear prominent. He became suddenly a modest person.

There was low-toned talk among the troops. The officers were impatient and snappy, their countenances clouded with the tales of misfortune. The troops, sifting through the forest, were sullen. In the youth's company once a man's laugh rang out. A dozen soldiers turned their faces quickly toward him and frowned with vague displeasure.

The noise of firing dogged their footsteps. Sometimes, it seemed to be driven a little way, but it always returned again with increased insolence. The men muttered and cursed, throwing black looks in its direction.

In a clear space the troops were at last halted. Regiments and brigades, broken and detached through their encounters with thickets, grew together again and lines were faced toward the pursuing bark of the enemy's infantry.

This noise, following like the yellings of eager, metallic hounds, increased to a loud and joyous burst, and then, as the sun went serenely up the sky, throwing illuminating rays into the gloomy thickets, it broke forth into prolonged pealings. The woods began to crackle as if afire.

"Whoop-a-dadee," said a man, "here we are! Everybody fightin'. Blood an' destruction."

"I was willin' t' bet they'd attack as soon as th' sun got fairly up," savagely asserted the lieutenant who commanded the youth's company. He jerked without mercy at his little mustache. He strode to and fro with dark dignity in the rear of his men, who were lying down behind whatever protection they had collected.

A battery had trundled into position in the rear and was thoughtfully shelling the distance. The regiment, unmolested as yet, awaited the moment when the gray shadows of the woods before them should be slashed by the lines of flame. There was much growling and swearing.

"Good Gawd," the youth grumbled, "we're always being chased around like rats! It makes me sick. Nobody seems to know where we go or why we go. We just get fired around from pillar to post and get licked here and get licked there, and nobody knows what it's done for. It makes a man feel like a damn' kitten in a bag. Now, I'd like to know what the eternal thunders we was marched into these woods for anyhow, unless it was to give the rebs a regular pot shot at us. We came in here and got our legs all tangled up in these cussed briers, and then we begin to fight and the rebs had an easy time of it. Don't tell me it's just luck! I know better. It's this derned old——"

The friend seemed jaded, but he interrupted his comrade with a voice of calm confidence. "It'll turn out all right in th' end," he said.

"Oh, the devil it will! You always talk like a dog-hanged parson. Don't tell me! I know——"

At this time there was an interposition by the savage-minded lieutenant, who was obliged to vent some of his inward dissatisfaction upon his men. "You boys shut right up! There no need 'a your wastin' your breath in long-winded arguments about this an' that an' th' other. You've been jawin' like a lot 'a old hens. All you've got t' do is to fight, an' you'll get plenty 'a that t' do in about ten minutes. Less talkin' an' more fightin' is what's best for you, boys. I never saw sech gabbing jackasses."

He paused, ready to pounce upon any man who might have the temerity to reply. No words being said, he resumed his dignified pacing.

"There's too much chin music an' too little fightin' in this war, anyhow," he said to them, turning his head for a final remark.

The day had grown more white, until the sun shed his full radiance upon the thronged forest. A sort of a gust of battle came sweeping toward that part of the line where lay the youth's regiment. The front shifted a trifle to meet it squarely. There was a wait. In this part of the field there passed slowly the intense moments that precede the tempest.

A single rifle flashed in a thicket before the regiment. In an instant it was joined by many others. There was a mighty song of clashes and crashes that went sweeping through the woods. The guns in the rear, aroused and enraged by shells that had been thrown burr-like at them, suddenly involved themselves in a hideous altercation with another band of guns. The battle roar settled to a rolling thunder, which was a single, long explosion.

In the regiment there was a peculiar kind of hesitation denoted in the attitudes of the men. They were worn, exhausted, having slept but little and labored much. They rolled their eyes toward the advancing battle as they stood awaiting the shock. Some shrank and flinched. They stood as men tied to stakes.

17

This advance of the enemy had seemed to the youth like a ruthless hunting. He began to fume with rage and exasperation. He beat his foot upon the ground, and scowled with hate at the swirling smoke that was approaching

like a phantom flood. There was a maddening quality in this seeming resolution of the foe to give him no rest, to give him no time to sit down and
think. Yesterday he had fought and had fled rapidly. There had been many
adventures. For to-day he felt that he had earned opportunities for contem-
plative repose. He could have enjoyed portraying to uninitiated listeners
various scenes at which he had been a witness or ably discussing the processes
of war with other proved men. Too it was important that he should have
time for physical recuperation. He was sore and stiff from his experiences.
He had received his fill of all exertions, and he wished to rest.

But those other men seemed never to grow weary; they were fighting with
their old speed. He had a wild hate for the relentless foe. Yesterday, when
he had imagined the universe to be against him, he had hated it, little gods
and big gods; to-day he hated the army of the foe with the same great hatred.
He was not going to be badgered of his life, like a kitten chased by boys, he
said. It was not well to drive men into final corners; at those moments they
could all develop teeth and claws.

He leaned and spoke into his friend's ear. He menaced the words with a
gesture. "If they keep on chasing us, by Gawd, they'd better watch out.
Can't stand *too* much."

The friend twisted his head and made a calm reply. "If they keep on
a-chasin' us they'll drive us all inteh th' river."

The youth cried out savagely at this statement. He crouched behind a
little tree, with his eyes burning hatefully and his teeth set in a cur-like
snarl. The awkward bandage was still about his head, and upon it, over his
wound, there was a spot of dry blood. His hair was wondrously tousled, and
some straggling, moving locks hung over the cloth of the bandage down
toward his forehead. His jacket and shirt were open at the throat, and exposed his young bronzed neck. There could be seen spasmodic gulpings at
his throat.

His fingers twined nervously about his rifle. He wished that it was an
engine of annihilating power. He felt that he and his companions were being
taunted and derided from sincere convictions that they were poor and puny.
His knowledge of his inability to take vengeance for it made his rage into a
dark and stormy specter, that possessed him and made him dream of abomina-
ble cruelties. The tormentors were flies sucking insolently at his blood, and
he thought that he would have given his life for a revenge of seeing their
faces in pitiful plights.

The winds of battle had swept all about the regiment, until the one rifle,
instantly followed by others, flashed in its front. A moment later the regiment roared forth its sudden and valiant retort. A dense wall of smoke settled slowly down. It was furiously slit and slashed by the knifelike fire from the
rifles.

To the youth the fighters resembled animals tossed for a death struggle
into a dark pit. There was a sensation that he and his fellows, at bay, were
pushing back, always pushing fierce onslaughts of creatures who were slippery. Their beams of crimson seemed to get no purchase upon the bodies of
their foes; the latter seemed to evade them with ease, and come through,
between, around, and about with unopposed skill.

When, in a dream, it occurred to the youth that his rifle was an impotent stick, he lost sense of everything but his hate, his desire to smash into pulp the glittering smile of victory which he could feel upon the faces of his enemies.

The blue smoke-swallowed line curled and writhed like a snake stepped upon. It swung its ends to and fro in an agony of fear and rage.

The youth was not conscious that he was erect upon his feet. He did not know the direction of the ground. Indeed, once he even lost the habit of balance and fell heavily. He was up again immediately. One thought went through the chaos of his brain at the time. He wondered if he had fallen because he had been shot. But the suspicion flew away at once. He did not think more of it.

He had taken up a first position behind the little tree, with a direct determination to hold it against the world. He had not deemed it possible that his army could that day succeed, and from this he felt the ability to fight harder. But the throng had surged in all ways, until he lost directions and locations, save that he knew where lay the enemy.

The flames bit him, and the hot smoke broiled his skin. His rifle barrel grew so hot that ordinarily he could not have borne it upon his palms; but he kept on stuffing cartridges into it, and pounding them with his clanking, bending ramrod. If he aimed at some changing form through the smoke, he pulled his trigger with a fierce grunt, as if he were dealing a blow of the fist with all his strength.

When the enemy seemed falling back before him and his fellows, he went instantly forward, like a dog who, seeing his foes lagging, turns and insists upon being pursued. And when he was compelled to retire again, he did it slowly, sullenly, taking steps of wrathful despair.

Once he, in his intent hate, was almost alone, and was firing, when all those near him ceased. He was so engrossed in his occupation that he was not aware of a lull.

He was recalled by a hoarse laugh and a sentence that came to his ears in a voice of contempt and amazement. "Yeh infernal fool, don't yeh know enough t' quit when there ain't anything t' shoot at? Good Gawd!"

He turned then and, pausing with his rifle thrown half into position, looked at the blue line of his comrades. During this moment of leisure they seemed all to be engaged in staring with astonishment at him. They had become spectators. Turning to the front again he saw, under the lifted smoke, a deserted ground.

He looked bewildered for a moment. Then there appeared upon the glazed vacancy of his eyes a diamond point of intelligence. "Oh," he said, comprehending.

He returned to his comrades and threw himself upon the ground. He sprawled like a man who had been thrashed. His flesh seemed strangely on fire, and the sounds of the battle continued in his ears. He groped blindly for his canteen.

The lieutenant was crowing. He seemed drunk with fighting. He called out to the youth: "By heavens, if I had ten thousand wild cats like you I could tear th' stomach outa this war in less'n a week!" He puffed out his chest with large dignity as he said it.

Some of the men muttered and looked at the youth in awe-struck ways.

It was plain that as he had gone on loading and firing and cursing without the proper intermission, they had found time to regard him. And they now looked upon him as a war devil.

The friend came staggering to him. There was some fright and dismay in his voice. "Are yeh all right, Fleming? Do yeh feel all right? There ain't nothin' th' matter with yeh, Henry, is there?"

"No," said the youth with difficulty. His throat seemed full of knobs and burs.

These incidents made the youth ponder. It was revealed to him that he had been a barbarian, a beast. He had fought like a pagan who defends his religion. Regarding it, he saw that it was fine, wild, and, in some ways, easy. He had been a tremendous figure, no doubt. By this struggle he had overcome obstacles which he had admitted to be mountains. They had fallen like paper peaks, and he was now what he called a hero. And he had not been aware of the process. He had slept and, awakening, found himself a knight.

He lay and basked in the occasional stares of his comrades. Their faces were varied in degrees of blackness from the burned powder. Some were utterly smudged. They were reeking with perspiration, and their breaths came hard and wheezing. And from these soiled expanses they peered at him.

"Hot work! Hot work!" cried the lieutenant deliriously. He walked up and down, restless and eager. Sometimes his voice could be heard in a wild, incomprehensible laugh.

When he had a particularly profound thought upon the science of war he always unconsciously addressed himself to the youth.

There was some grim rejoicing by the men. "By thunder, I bet this army'll never see another new reg'ment like us!"

"You bet!"

"A dog, a woman, an' a walnut tree,
Th' more yeh beat 'em, th' better they be!

That's like us."

"Lost a piler men, they did. If an' ol' woman swep' up th' woods she'd git a dustpanful."

"Yes, an' if she'll come around ag'in in'bout an' hour she'll git a pile more."

The forest still bore its burden of clamor. From off under the trees came the rolling clatter of the musketry. Each distant thicket seemed a strange porcupine with quills of flame. A cloud of dark smoke, as from smoldering ruins, went up toward the sun now bright and gay in the blue, enameled sky.

18

The ragged line had respite for some minutes, but during its pause the struggle in the forest became magnified until the trees seemed to quiver from the firing and the ground to shake from the rushing of the men. The voices of the cannon were mingled in a long and interminable row. It seemed difficult to live in such an atmosphere. The chests of the men strained for a bit of freshness, and their throats craved water.

There was one shot through the body, who raised a cry of bitter lamentation when came this lull. Perhaps he had been calling out during the fighting also, but at that time no one had heard him. But now the men turned at the woeful complaints of him upon the ground.

"Who is it? Who is it?"

"It's Jimmie Rogers. Jimmie Rogers."

When their eyes first encountered him there was a sudden halt, as if they feared to go near. He was thrashing about in the grass, twisting his shuddering body into many strange postures. He was screaming loudly. This instant's hesitation seemed to fill him with a tremendous, fantastic contempt, and he damned them in shrieked sentences.

The youth's friend had a geographical illusion concerning a stream, and he obtained permission to go for some water. Immediately canteens were showered upon him. "Fill mine, will yeh?" "Bring me some, too." "And me, too." He departed, ladened. The youth went with his friend, feeling a desire to throw his heated body onto the stream and, soaking there, drink quarts.

They made a hurried search for the supposed stream, but did not find it. "No water here," said the youth. They turned without delay and began to retrace their steps.

From their position as they again faced toward the place of the fighting, they could of course comprehend a greater amount of the battle than when their visions had been blurred by the hurling smoke of the line. They could see dark stretches winding along the land, and on one cleared space there was a row of guns making gray clouds, which were filled with large flashes of orange-colored flame. Over some foliage they could see the roof of a house. One window, glowing a deep murder red, shone squarely through the leaves. From the edifice a tall leaning tower of smoke went far into the sky.

Looking over their own troops, they saw mixed masses slowly getting into regular form. The sunlight made twinkling points of the bright steel. To the rear there was a glimpse of a distant roadway as it curved over a slope. It was crowded with retreating infantry. From all the interwoven forest arose the smoke and bluster of the battle. The air was always occupied by a blaring.

Near where they stood shells were flip-flapping and hooting. Occasional bullets buzzed in the air and spanged into tree trunks. Wounded men and other stragglers were slinking through the woods.

Looking down an aisle of the grove, the youth and his companion saw a jangling general and his staff almost ride upon a wounded man, who was crawling on his hands and knees. The general reined strongly at his charger's opened and foamy mouth and guided it with dexterous horsemanship past the man. The latter scrambled in wild and torturing haste. His strength evidently failed him as he reached a place of safety. One of his arms suddenly weakened, and he fell, sliding over upon his back. He lay stretched out, breathing gently.

A moment later the small, creaking cavalcade was directly in front of the two soldiers. Another officer, riding with the skillful abandon of a cowboy, galloped his horse to a position directly before the general. The two unnoticed foot soldiers made a little show of going on, but they lingered near in the desire to overhear the conversation. Perhaps, they thought, some great inner historical things would be said.

The general, whom the boys knew as the commander of their division, looked at the other officer and spoke coolly, as if he were criticising his clothes. "Th' enemy's formin' over there for another charge," he said. "It'll be directed against Whiterside, an' I fear they'll break through there unless we work like thunder t' stop them."

The other swore at his restive horse, and then cleared his throat. He made a gesture toward his cap. "It'll be hell t' pay stoppin' them," he said shortly.

"I presume so," remarked the general. Then he began to talk rapidly and in a lower tone. He frequently illustrated his words with a pointing finger. The two infantrymen could hear nothing until finally he asked: "What troops can you spare?"

The officer who rode like a cowboy reflected for an instant. "Well," he said, "I had to order in th' 12th to help th' 76th, an' I haven't really got any. But there's th' 304th. They fight like a lot 'a mule drivers. I can spare them best of any."

The youth and his friend exchanged glances of astonishment.

The general spoke sharply. "Get 'em ready, then. I'll watch developments from here, an' send you word when t' start them. It'll happen in five minutes."

As the other officer tossed his fingers toward his cap and wheeling his horse, started away, the general called out to him in a sober voice: "I don't believe many of your mule drivers will get back."

The other shouted something in reply. He smiled.

With scared faces, the youth and his companion hurried back to the line.

These happenings had occupied an incredibly short time, yet the youth felt that in them he had been made aged. New eyes were given to him. And the most startling thing was to learn suddenly that he was very insignificant. The officer spoke of the regiment as if he referred to a broom. Some part of the woods needed sweeping, perhaps, and he merely indicated a broom in a tone properly indifferent to its fate. It was war, no doubt, but it appeared strange.

As the two boys approached the line, the lieutenant perceived them and swelled with wrath. "Fleming—Wilson—how long does it take yeh to git water, anyhow—where yeh been to."

But his oration ceased as he saw their eyes, which were large with great tales. "We're goin' t' charge—we're goin' t' charge!" cried the youth's friend, hastening with his news.

"Charge?" said the lieutenant. "Charge? Well, b'Gawd! Now, this is real fightin'." Over his soiled countenance there went a boastful smile. "Charge? Well, b'Gawd!"

A little group of soldiers surrounded the two youths. "Are we, sure 'nough? Well, I'll be derned! Charge? What fer? What at? Wilson, you're lyin'."

"I hope to die," said the youth, pitching his tones to the key of angry remonstrance. "Sure as shooting, I tell you."

And his friend spoke in re-enforcement. "Not by a blame sight, he ain't lyin'. We heard 'em talkin'."

They caught sight of two mounted figures a short distance from them. One was the colonel of the regiment and the other was the officer who had received orders from the commander of the division. They were gesticulating at each other. The soldier, pointing at them, interpreted the scene.

One man had a final objection: "How could yeh hear 'em talkin'?" But the men, for a large part, nodded, admitting that previously the two friends had spoken truth.

They settled back into reposeful attitudes with airs of having accepted the matter. And they mused upon it, with a hundred varieties of expression. It was an engrossing thing to think about. Many tightened their belts carefully and hitched at their trousers.

A moment later the officers began to bustle among the men, pushing them into a more compact mass and into a better alignment. They chased those that straggled and fumed at a few men who seemed to show by their attitudes that they had decided to remain at that spot. They were like critical shepherds struggling with sheep.

Presently, the regiment seemed to draw itself up and heave a deep breath. None of the men's faces were mirrors of large thoughts. The soldiers were bended and stooped like sprinters before a signal. Many pairs of glinting eyes peered from the grimy faces toward the curtains of the deeper woods. They seemed to be engaged in deep calculations of time and distance.

They were surrounded by the noises of the monstrous altercation between the two armies. The world was fully interested in other matters. Apparently, the regiment had its small affair to itself.

The youth, turning, shot a quick, inquiring glance at his friend. The latter returned to him the same manner of look. They were the only ones who possessed an inner knowledge. "Mule drivers—hell t' pay—don't believe many will get back." It was an ironical secret. Still, they saw no hesitation in each other's faces, and they nodded a mute and unprotesting assent when a shaggy man near them said in a meek voice: "We'll git swallowed."

19

The youth stared at the land in front of him. Its foliages now seemed to veil powers and horrors. He was unaware of the machinery of orders that started the charge, although from the corners of his eyes he saw an officer, who looked like a boy a-horseback, come galloping, waving his hat. Suddenly he felt a straining and heaving among the men. The line fell slowly forward like a toppling wall, and, with a convulsive gasp that was intended for a cheer, the regiment began its journey. The youth was pushed and jostled for a moment before he understood the movement at all, but directly he lunged ahead and began to run.

He fixed his eye upon a distant and prominent clump of trees where he had concluded the enemy were to be met, and he ran toward it as toward a goal. He had believed throughout that it was a mere question of getting over an unpleasant matter as quickly as possible, and he ran desperately, as if pursued for a murder. His face was drawn hard and tight with the stress of his endeavor. His eyes were fixed in a lurid glare. And with his soiled and disordered dress, his red and inflamed features surmounted by the dingy rag with its spot of blood, his wildly swinging rifle and banging accouterments, he looked to be an insane soldier.

As the regiment swung from its position out into a cleared space the woods and thickets before it awakened. Yellow flames leaped toward it from many directions. The forest made a tremendous objection.

The line lurched straight for a moment. Then the right wing swung forward; it in turn was surpassed by the left. Afterward the center careered to the front until the regiment was a wedge-shaped mass, but an instant later the opposition of the bushes, trees, and uneven places on the ground split the command and scattered it into detached clusters.

The youth, light-footed, was unconsciously in advance. His eyes still kept note of the clump of trees. From all places near it the clannish yell of the enemy could be heard. The little flames of rifles leaped from it. The song of the bullets was in the air and shells snarled among the treetops. One tumbled directly into the middle of a hurrying group and exploded in crimson fury. There was an instant's spectacle of a man, almost over it, throwing up his hands to shield his eyes.

Other men, punched by bullets, fell in grotesque agonies. The regiment left a coherent trail of bodies.

They had passed into a clearer atmosphere. There was an effect like a revelation in the new appearance of the landscape. Some men working madly at a battery were plain to them, and the opposing infantry's lines were defined by the gray walls and fringes of smoke.

It seemed to the youth that he saw everything. Each blade of the green grass was bold and clear. He thought that he was aware of every change in the thin, transparent vapor that floated idly in sheets. The brown or gray trunks of the trees showed each roughness of their surfaces. And the men of the regiment, with their starting eyes and sweating faces, running madly, or falling, as if thrown headlong, to queer, heaped-up corpses—all were comprehended. His mind took a mechanical but firm impression, so that afterward everything was pictured and explained to him, save why he himself was there.

But there was a frenzy made from this furious rush. The men, pitching forward insanely, had burst into cheerings, moblike and barbaric, but tuned in strange keys that can arouse the dullard and the stoic. It made a mad enthusiasm that, it seemed, would be incapable of checking itself before granite and brass. There was the delirium that encounters despair and death, and is heedless and blind to the odds. It is a temporary but sublime absence of selfishness. And because it was of this order was the reason, perhaps, why the youth wondered, afterward, what reasons he could have had for being there.

Presently the straining pace ate up the energies of the men. As if by agreement, the leaders began to slacken their speed. The volleys directed against them had had a seeming windlike effect. The regiment snorted and blew. Among some stolid trees it began to falter and hesitate. The men, staring intently, began to wait for some of the distant walls of smoke to move and disclose to them the scene. Since much of their strength and their breath had vanished, they returned to caution. They were become men again.

The youth had a vague belief that he had run miles, and he thought, in a way, that he was now in some new and unknown land.

The moment the regiment ceased its advance the protesting splutter of musketry became a steadied roar. Long and accurate fringes of smoke spread out. From the top of a small hill came level belchings of yellow flame that caused an inhuman whistling in the air.

The men, halted, had opportunity to see some of their comrades dropping with moans and shrieks. A few lay under foot, still or wailing. And now for an instant the men stood, their rifles slack in their hands, and watched the regiment dwindle. They appeared dazed and stupid. This spectacle seemed to paralyze them, overcome them with a fatal fascination. They stared woodenly at the sights, and, lowering their eyes, looked from face to face. It was a strange pause, and a strange silence.

Then, above the sounds of the outside commotion, arose the roar of the lieutenant. He strode suddenly forth, his infantile features black with rage.

"Come on, yeh fools!" he bellowed. "Come on! Yeh can't stay here. Yeh must come on." He said more, but much of it could not be understood.

He started rapidly forward, with his head turned toward the men. "Come on," he was shouting. The men stared with blank and yokel-like eyes at him. He was obliged to halt and retrace his steps. He stood then with his back to the enemy and delivered gigantic curses into the faces of the men. His body vibrated from the weight and force of his imprecations. And he could string oaths with the facility of a maiden who strings beads.

The friend of the youth aroused. Lurching suddenly forward and dropping to his knees, he fired an angry shot at the persistent woods. This action awakened the men. They huddled no more like sheep. They seemed suddenly to bethink them of their weapons, and at once commenced firing. Belabored by their officers, they began to move forward. The regiment, involved like a cart involved in mud and muddle, started unevenly with many jolts and jerks. The men stopped now every few paces to fire and load, and in this manner moved slowly on from trees to trees.

The flaming opposition in their front grew with their advance until it seemed that all forward ways were barred by the thin leaping tongues, and off to the right an ominous demonstration could sometimes be dimly discerned. The smoke lately generated was in confusing clouds that made it difficult for the regiment to proceed with intelligence. As he passed through each curling mass the youth wondered what would confront him on the farther side.

The command went painfully forward until an open space interposed between them and the lurid lines. Here, crouching and cowering behind some trees, the men clung with desperation, as if threatened by a wave. They looked wild-eyed, and as if amazed at this furious disturbance they had stirred. In the storm there was an ironical expression of their importance. The faces of the men, too, showed a lack of a certain feeling of responsibility for being there. It was as if they had been driven. It was the dominant animal failing to remember in the supreme moments the forceful causes of various superficial qualities. The whole affair seemed incomprehensible to many of them.

As they halted thus the lieutenant again began to bellow profanely. Regardless of the vindictive threats of the bullets, he went about coaxing, berating, and bedamning. His lips, that were habitually in a soft and childlike curve, were now writhed into unholy contortions. He swore by all possible deities.

Once he grabbed the youth by the arm. "Come on, yeh lunkhead!" he roared. "Come on! We'll all git killed if we stay here. We've on'y got t' go across that lot. An' then"—the remainder of his idea disappeared in a blue haze of curses.

The youth stretched forth his arm. "Cross there?" His mouth was puckered in doubt and awe.

"Certainly. Jest 'cross th' lot! We can't stay here," screamed the lieutenant. He poked his face close to the youth and waved his bandaged hand. "Come on!" Presently he grappled with him as if for a wrestling bout. It was as if he planned to drag the youth by the ear on to the assault.

The private felt a sudden unspeakable indignation against his officer. He wrenched fiercely and shook him off.

"Come on yerself, then," he yelled. There was a bitter challenge in his voice.

They galloped together down the regimental front. The friend scrambled after them. In front of the colors the three men began to bawl: "Come on! come on!" They danced and gyrated like tortured savages.

The flag, obedient to these appeals, bended its glittering form and swept toward them. The men wavered in indecision for a moment, and then with a long, wailful cry the dilapidated regiment surged forward and began its new journey.

Over the field went the scurrying mass. It was a handful of men splattered into the faces of the enemy. Toward it instantly sprang the yellow tongues. A vast quantity of blue smoke hung before them. A mighty banging made ears valueless.

The youth ran like a madman to reach the woods before a bullet could discover him. He ducked his head low, like a football player. In his haste his eyes almost closed, and the scene was a wild blur. Pulsating saliva stood at the corners of his mouth.

Within him, as he hurled himself forward, was born a love, a despairing fondness for this flag which was near him. It was a creation of beauty and invulnerability. It was a goddess, radiant, that bended its form with an imperious gesture to him. It was a woman, red and white, hating and loving, that called him with the voice of his hopes. Because no harm could come to it he endowed it with power. He kept near, as if it could be a saver of lives, and an imploring cry went from his mind.

In the mad scramble he was aware that the color sergeant flinched suddenly, as if struck by a bludgeon. He faltered, and then became motionless, save for his quivering knees.

He made a spring and a clutch at the pole. At the same instant his friend grabbed it from the other side. They jerked at it, stout and furious, but the color sergeant was dead, and the corpse would not relinquish its trust. For a moment there was a grim encounter. The dead man, swinging with bended back, seemed to be obstinately tugging, in ludicrous and awful ways, for the possession of the flag.

It was past in an instant of time. They wrenched the flag furiously from the dead man, and, as they turned again, the corpse swayed forward with bowed head. One arm swung high, and the curved hand fell with heavy protest on the friend's unheeding shoulder.

20

When the two youths turned with the flag they saw that much of the regiment had crumbled away, and the dejected remnant was coming slowly back. The men, having hurled themselves in projectile fashion, had presently expended their forces. They slowly retreated, with their faces still toward the spluttering woods, and their hot rifles still replying to the din. Several officers were giving orders, their voices keyed to screams.

"Where in hell yeh goin'?" the lieutenant was asking in a sarcastic howl. And a red-bearded officer, whose voice of triple brass could plainly be heard, was commanding: "Shoot into 'em! Shoot into 'em, Gawd damn their souls!" There was a *melée* of screeches, in which the men were ordered to do conflicting and impossible things.

The youth and his friend had a small scuffle over the flag. "Give it t' me!" "No, let me keep it!" Each felt satisfied with the other's possession of it, but each felt bound to declare, by an offer to carry the emblem, his willingness to further risk himself. The youth roughly pushed his friend away.

The regiment fell back to the stolid trees. There it halted for a moment to blaze at some dark forms that had begun to steal upon its track. Presently it resumed its march again, curving among the tree trunks. By the time the depleted regiment had again reached the first open space they were receiving a fast and merciless fire. There seemed to be mobs all about them.

The greater part of the men, discouraged, their spirits worn by the turmoil, acted as if stunned. They accepted the pelting of the bullets with bowed and weary heads. It was of no purpose to strive against walls. It was of no use to batter themselves against granite. And from this consciousness that they had attempted to conquer an unconquerable thing there seemed to arise a feeling that they had been betrayed. They glowered with bent brows, but dangerously, upon some of the officers, more particularly upon the red-bearded one with the voice of triple brass.

However, the rear of the regiment was fringed with men, who continued to shoot irritably at the advancing foes. They seemed resolved to make every trouble. The youthful lieutenant was perhaps the last man in the disordered mass. His forgotten back was toward the enemy. He had been shot in the arm. It hung straight and rigid. Occasionally he would cease to remember it, and be about to emphasize an oath with a sweeping gesture. The multiplied pain caused him to swear with incredible power.

The youth went along with slipping, uncertain feet. He kept watchful eyes rearward. A scowl of mortification and rage was upon his face. He had thought of a fine revenge upon the officer who had referred to him and his fellows as mule drivers. But he saw that it could not come to pass. His dreams had collapsed when the mule drivers, dwindling rapidly, had wavered and hesitated on the little clearing, and then had recoiled. And now the retreat of the mule drivers was a march of shame to him.

A dagger-pointed gaze from without his blackened face was held toward the enemy, but his greater hatred was riveted upon the man, who, not knowing him, had called him a mule driver.

When he knew that he and his comrades had failed to do anything in successful ways that might bring the little pangs of a kind of remorse upon the officer, the youth allowed the rage of the baffled to possess him. This cold officer upon a monument, who dropped epithets unconcernedly down, would be finer as a dead man, he thought. So grievous did he think it that he could never possess the secret right to taunt truly in answer.

He had pictured red letters of curious revenge. "We *are* mule drivers, are we?" And now he was compelled to throw them away.

He presently wrapped his heart in the cloak of his pride and kept the flag erect. He harangued his fellows, pushing against their chests with his free hand. To those he knew well he made frantic appeals, beseeching them by name. Between him and the lieutenant, scolding and near to losing his mind with rage, there was felt a subtle fellowship and equality. They supported each other in all manner of hoarse, howling protests.

But the regiment was a machine run down. The two men babbled at a forceless thing. The soldiers who had heart to go slowly were continually shaken in their resolves by a knowledge that comrades were slipping with speed back to the lines. It was difficult to think of reputations when others were thinking of skins. Wounded men were left crying on this black journey.

The smoke fringes and flames blustered always. The youth, peering once through a sudden rift in a cloud, saw a brown mass of troops, interwoven and magnified until they appeared to be thousands. A fierce-hued flag flashed before his vision.

Immediately, as if the uplifting of the smoke had been prearranged, the discovered troops burst into a rasping yell, and a hundred flames jetted toward the retreating band. A rolling gray cloud again interposed as the regiment doggedly replied. The youth had to depend again upon his misused ears, which were trembling and buzzing from the *melée* of musketry and yells.

The way seemed eternal. In the clouded haze men became panicstricken with the thought that the regiment had lost its path, and was proceeding in a perilous direction. Once the men who headed the wild procession turned and came pushing back against their comrades, screaming that they were being fired upon from points which they had considered to be toward their own lines. At this cry a hysterical fear and dismay beset the troops. A soldier, who heretofore had been ambitious to make the regiment into a wise little band that would proceed calmly amid the huge-appearing difficulties, suddenly sank down and buried his face in his arms with an air of bowing to a doom. From another a shrill lamentation rang out filled with profane allusions to a general. Men ran hither and thither, seeking with their eyes roads of escape. With serene regularity, as if controlled by a schedule, bullets buffed into men.

The youth walked stolidly into the midst of the mob, and with his flag in his hands took a stand as if he expected an attempt to push him to the ground. He unconsciously assumed the attitude of the color bearer in the fight of the preceding day. He passed over his brow a hand that trembled. His breath did not come freely. He was choking during this small wait for the crisis.

His friend came to him. "Well, Henry, I guess this is good-by—John."

"Oh, shut up, you damned fool!" replied the youth, and he would not look at the other.

The officers labored like politicians to beat the mass into a proper circle to face the menaces. The ground was uneven and torn. The men curled into depressions and fitted themselves snugly behind whatever would frustrate a bullet.

The youth noted with vague surprise that the lieutenant was standing mutely with his legs far apart and his sword held in the manner of a cane. The youth wondered what had happened to his vocal organs that he no more cursed.

There was something curious in this little intent pause of the lieutenant. He was like a babe which, having wept its fill, raises its eyes and fixes upon a distant joy. He was engrossed in this contemplation, and the soft under lip quivered from self-whispered words.

Some lazy and ignorant smoke curled slowly. The men, hiding from the bullets, waited anxiously for it to lift and disclose the plight of the regiment.

The silent ranks were suddenly thrilled by the eager voice of the youthful lieutenant bawling out: "Here they come! Right onto us, b'Gawd!" His further words were lost in a roar of wicked thunder from the men's rifles.

The youth's eyes had instantly turned in the direction indicated by the awakened and agitated lieutenant, and he had seen the haze of treachery disclosing a body of soldiers of the enemy. They were so near that he could see their features. There was a recognition as he looked at the types of faces. Also he perceived with dim amazement that their uniforms were rather gay in effect, being light gray, accented with a brilliant-hued facing. Too, the clothes seemed new.

These troops had apparently been going forward with caution, their rifles held in readiness, when the youthful lieutenant had discovered them and their movement had been interrupted by the volley from the blue regiment. From the moment's glimpse, it was derived that they had been unaware of the proximity of their dark-suited foes or had mistaken the direction. Almost instantly they were shut utterly from the youth's sight by the smoke from the energetic rifles of his companions. He strained his vision to learn the accomplishment of the volley, but the smoke hung before him.

The two bodies of troops exchanged blows in the manner of a pair of boxers. The fast angry firings went back and forth. The men in blue were intent with the despair of their circumstances and they seized upon the revenge to be had at close range. Their thunder swelled loud and valiant. Their curving front bristled with flashes and the place resounded with the clangor of their ramrods. The youth ducked and dodged for a time and achieved a few unsatisfactory views of the enemy. There appeared to be many of them and they were replying swiftly. They seemed moving toward the blue regiment, step by step. He seated himself gloomily on the ground with his flag between his knees.

As he noted the vicious, wolflike temper of his comrades he had a sweet thought that if the enemy was about to swallow the regimental broom as a large prisoner, it could at least have the consolation of going down with bristles forward.

But the blows of the antagonist began to grow more weak. Fewer bullets ripped the air, and finally, when the men slackened to learn of the fight, they could see only dark, floating smoke. The regiment lay still and gazed. Presently some chance whim came to the pestering blur, and it began to coil heavily away. The men saw a ground vacant of fighters. It would have been an empty stage if it were not for a few corpses that lay thrown and twisted into fantastic shapes upon the sward.

At sight of this tableau, many of the men in blue sprang from behind their covers and made an ungainly dance of joy. Their eyes burned and a hoarse cheer of elation broke from their dry lips.

It had begun to seem to them that events were trying to prove that they were impotent. These little battles had evidently endeavored to demonstrate that the men could not fight well. When on the verge of submission to these opinions, the small duel had showed them that the proportions were not impossible, and by it they had revenged themselves upon their misgivings and upon the foe.

The impetus of enthusiasm was theirs again. They gazed about them with looks of uplifted pride, feeling new trust in the grim, always confident weapons in their hands. And they were men.

21

Presently they knew that no firing threatened them. All ways seemed once more opened to them. The dusty blue lines of their friends were disclosed a short distance away. In the distance there were many colossal noises, but in all this part of the field there was a sudden stillness.

They perceived that they were free. The depleted band drew a long breath of relief and gathered itself into a bunch to complete its trip.

In this last length of journey the men began to show strange emotions. They hurried with nervous fear. Some who had been dark and unfaltering in the grimmest moments now could not conceal an anxiety that made them frantic. It was perhaps that they dreaded to be killed in insignificant ways after the times for proper military deaths had passed. Or, perhaps, they thought it would be too ironical to get killed at the portals of safety. With backward looks of perturbation, they hastened.

As they approached their own lines there was some sarcasm exhibited on the part of a gaunt and bronzed regiment that lay resting in the shade of trees. Questions were wafted to them.

"Where th' hell yeh been?"

"What yeh comin' back fer?"

"Why didn't yeh stay there?"

"Was it warm out there, sonny?"

"Goin' home now, boys?"

One shouted in taunting mimicry: "Oh, mother, come quick an' look at th' sojers!"

There was no reply from the bruised and battered regiment, save that one man made broadcast challenges to fist fights and the red-bearded officer walked rather near and glared in great swashbuckler style at a tall captain in the other regiment. But the lieutenant suppressed the man who wished to fist fight, and the tall captain, flushing at the little fanfare of the red-bearded one, was obliged to look intently at some trees.

The youth's tender flesh was deeply stung by these remarks. From under his creased brows he glowered with hate at the mockers. He meditated upon a few revenges. Still, many in the regiment hung their heads in criminal fashion, so that it came to pass that the men trudged with sudden heaviness, as if they bore upon their bended shoulders the coffin of their honor. And the youthful lieutenant, recollecting himself, began to mutter softly in black curses.

They turned when they arrived at their old position to regard the ground over which they had charged.

The youth in this contemplation was smitten with a large astonishment. He discovered that the distances, as compared with the brilliant measurings of his mind, were trivial and ridiculous. The stolid trees, where much had taken place, seemed incredibly near. The time, too, now that he reflected, he saw to have been short. He wondered at the number of emotions and events that had been crowded into such little spaces. Elfin thoughts must have exaggerated and enlarged everything, he said.

It seemed, then, that there was bitter justice in the speeches of the gaunt and bronzed veterans. He veiled a glance of disdain at his fellows who strewed the ground, choking with dust, red from perspiration, misty-eyed, disheveled.

They were gulping at their canteens, fierce to wring every mite of water from them, and they polished at their swollen and watery features with coat sleeves and bunches of grass.

However, to the youth there was a considerable joy in musing upon his performance during the charge. He had had very little time previously in which to appreciate himself, so that there was now much satisfaction in quietly thinking of his actions. He recalled bits of color that in the flurry had stamped themselves unawares upon his engaged senses.

As the regiment lay heaving from its hot exertions the officer who had named them as mule drivers came galloping along the line. He had lost his cap. His tousled hair streamed wildly, and his face was dark with vexation and wrath. His temper was displayed with more clearness by the way in which he managed his horse. He jerked and wrenched savagely at his bridle, stopping the hard-breathing animal with a furious pull near the colonel of the regiment. He immediately exploded in reproaches which came unbidden to the ears of the men. They were suddenly alert, being always curious about black words between officers.

"Oh, thunder, MacChesnay, what an awful bull you made of this thing!"

began the officer. He attempted low tones, but his indignation caused certain of the men to learn the sense of his words. "What an awful mess you made! Good Lord, man, you stopped about a hundred feet this side of a very pretty success! If your men had gone a hundred feet farther you would have made a great charge, but as it is—what a lot of mud diggers you've got anyway!"

The men, listening with bated breath, now turned their curious eyes upon the colonel. They had a ragamuffin interest in this affair.

The colonel was seen to straighten his form and put one hand forth in oratorical fashion. He wore an injured air; it was as if a deacon had been accused of stealing. The men were wiggling in an ecstasy of excitement.

But of a sudden the colonel's manner changed from that of a deacon to that of a Frenchman. He shrugged his shoulders. "Oh, well, general, we went as far as we could," he said calmly.

"As far as you could? Did you, b'Gawd?" snorted the other. "Well, that wasn't very far, was it?" he added, with a glance of cold contempt into the other's eyes. "Not very far, I think. You were intended to make a diversion in favor of Whiterside. How well you succeeded your own ears can now tell you." He wheeled his horse and rode stiffly away.

The colonel, bidden to hear the jarring noises of an engagement in the woods to the left, broke out in vague damnations.

The lieutenant, who had listened with an air of impotent rage to the interview, spoke suddenly in firm and undaunted tones. "I don't care what a man is—whether he is a general or what—if he says th' boys didn't put up a good fight out there he's a damned fool."

"Lieutenant," began the colonel, severely, "this is my own affair, and I'll trouble you——"

The lieutenant made an obedient gesture. "All right, colonel, all right," he said. He sat down with an air of being content with himself.

The news that the regiment had been reproached went along the line. For a time the men were bewildered by it. "Good thunder!" they ejaculated, staring at the vanishing form of the general. They conceived it to be a huge mistake.

Presently, however, they began to believe that in truth their efforts had been called light. The youth could see this conviction weigh upon the entire regiment until the men were liked cuffed and cursed animals, but withal rebellious.

The friend, with a grievance in his eye, went to the youth. "I wonder what he does want," he said. "He must think we went out there an' played marbles! I never see sech a man!"

The youth developed a tranquil philosophy for these moments of irritation. "Oh, well," he rejoined, "he probably didn't see nothing of it at all and got mad as blazes, and concluded we were a lot of sheep, just because we didn't do what he wanted done. It's a pity old Grandpa Henderson got killed yesterday—he'd have known that we did our best and fought good. It's just our awful luck, that's what."

"I should say so," replied the friend. He seemed to be deeply wounded at an injustice. "I should say we did have awful luck! There's no fun in fightin' fer people when everything yeh do—no matter what—ain't done right. I have a notion t' stay behind next time an' let 'em take their ol' charge an' go t' th' devil with it.''

The youth spoke soothingly to his comrade. "Well, we both did good. I'd like to see the fool what'd say we both didn't do as good as we could!"

"Of course we did," declared the friend stoutly. "An' I'd break th' feller's neck if he was as big as a church. But we're all right, anyhow, for I heard one feller say that we two fit th' best in th' reg'ment, an' they had a great argument 'bout it. Another feller, 'a course, he had t' up an' say it was a lie—he seen all what was goin' on an' he never seen us from th' beginnin' t' th' end. An' a lot more struck in an' ses it wasn't a lie—we did fight like thunder, an' they give us quite a send-off. But this is what I can't stand—these everlastin' ol' soldiers, titterin' an' laughin', an' then that general, he's crazy."

The youth exclaimed with sudden exasperation: "He's a lunkhead! He makes me mad. I wish he'd come along next time. We'd show 'im what——"

He ceased because several men had come hurrying up. Their faces expressed a bringing of great news.

"O Flem, yeh jest oughta heard!" cried one, eagerly.

"Heard what?" said the youth.

"Yeh jest oughta heard!" repeated the other, and he arranged himself to tell his tidings. The others made an excited circle. "Well, sir, th' colonel met your lieutenant right by us—it was damnedest thing I ever heard—an' he ses: 'Ahem! ahem!' he ses. 'Mr. Hasbrouck!' he ses, 'by th' way, who was that lad what carried th' flag?' he ses. There, Flemin', what d' yeh think 'a that? 'Who was th' lad what carried th' flag?' he ses, an' th' lieutenant, he speaks up right away: 'That's Flemin', an' he's a jimhickey,' he ses, right away. What? I say he did. 'A jimhickey,' he ses—those 'r words. He did, too. I say he did. If you kin tell this story better than I kin, go ahead an' tell it. Well, then, keep yer mouth shet. Th' lieutenant, he ses: 'He's a jimhickey,' an' th' colonel, he ses: 'Ahem! ahem! he is, indeed a very good man t' have, ahem! He kep' th' flag 'way t' th' front. I saw 'im. He's a good un,' ses th' colonel. 'You bet,' ses th' lieutenant, 'he an' a feller named Wilson was at th' head 'a th' charge, an' howlin' like Indians all th' time,' he ses. 'Head 'a th' charge all th' time,' he ses. 'A feller named Wilson,' he ses. There, Wilson, m'boy, put that in a letter an' send it hum t' yer mother, hay? 'A feller named Wilson,' he ses. An' the colonel, he ses: 'Were they, indeed? Ahem! ahem! My sakes!' he ses. 'At th' head 'a th' reg'ment?' he ses. 'They were,' ses th' lieutenant. 'My sakes!' ses th' colonel. He ses: 'Well, well, well,' he ses, 'those two babies?' 'They were,' ses th' lieutenant. 'Well, well,' ses th' colonel, 'they deserve t' be major generals,' he ses. 'They deserve t' be major-generals.'"

The youth and his friend had said: "Huh!" "Yer lyin', Thompson." "Oh, go t' blazes!" "He never sed it." "Oh, what a lie!" "Huh!" But despite these youthful scoffings and embarrassments, they knew that their faces were deeply flushing from thrills of pleasure. They exchanged a secret glance of joy and congratulation.

They speedily forgot many things. The past held no pictures of error and disappointment. They were very happy, and their hearts swelled with grateful affection for the colonel and the youthful lieutenant.

22

When the woods again began to pour forth the dark-hued masses of the enemy the youth felt serene self-confidence. He smiled briefly when he saw men dodge and duck at the long screechings of shells that were thrown in giant handfuls over them. He stood, erect and tranquil, watching the attack begin against a part of the line that made a blue curve along the side of an adjacent hill. His vision being unmolested by smoke from the rifles of his companions, he had opportunities to see parts of the hard fight. It was a relief to perceive at last from whence came some of these noises which had been roared into his ears.

Off a short way he saw two regiments fighting a little separate battle with two other regiments. It was in a cleared space, wearing a set-apart look. They were blazing as if upon a wager, giving and taking tremendous blows. The firings were incredibly fierce and rapid. These intent regiments apparently were oblivious of all larger purposes of war, and were slugging each other as if at a matched game.

In another direction he saw a magnificent brigade going with the evident intention of driving the enemy from a wood. They passed in out of sight and presently there was a most awe-inspiring racket in the wood. The noise was unspeakable. Having stirred this prodigious uproar, and, apparently, finding it too prodigious, the brigade, after a little time, came marching airily out again with its fine formation in nowise disturbed. There were no traces of speed in its movements. The brigade was jaunty and seemed to point a proud thumb at the yelling wood.

On a slope to the left there was a long row of guns, gruff and maddened, denouncing the enemy, who, down through the woods, were forming for another attack in the pitiless monotony of conflicts. The round red discharges from the guns made a crimson flare and a high, thick smoke. Occasional glimpses could be caught of groups of the toiling artillerymen. In the rear of this row of guns stood a house, calm and white, amid bursting shells. A congregation of horses, tied to a long railing, were tugging frenziedly at their bridles. Men were running hither and thither.

The detached battle between the four regiments lasted for some time. There chanced to be no interference, and they settled their dispute by themselves. They struck savagely and powerfully at each other for a period of minutes, and then the lighter-hued regiments faltered and drew back, leaving the dark-blue lines shouting. The youth could see the two flags shaking with laughter amid the smoke remnants.

Presently there was a stillness, pregnant with meaning. The blue lines shifted and changed a trifle and stared expectantly at the silent woods and fields before them. The hush was solemn and churchlike, save for a distant battery that, evidently unable to remain quiet, sent a faint rolling thunder over the ground. It irritated, like the noises of unimpressed boys. The men imagined that it would prevent their perched ears from hearing the first words of the new battle.

Of a sudden the guns on the slope roared out a message of warning. A spluttering sound had begun in the woods. It swelled with amazing speed to a profound clamor that involved the earth in noises. The splitting crashes swept along the lines until an interminable roar was developed. To those in the midst of it it became a din fitted to the universe. It was the whirring and thumping of gigantic machinery, complications among the smaller stars. The youth's ears were filled up. They were incapable of hearing more.

On an incline over which a road wound he saw wild and desperate rushes of men perpetually backward and forward in riotous surges. These parts of the opposing armies were two long waves that pitched upon each other madly at dictated points. To and fro they swelled. Sometimes, one side by its yells and cheers would proclaim decisive blows, but a moment later the other side would be all yells and cheers. Once the youth saw a spray of light forms go in hound-like leaps toward the wavering blue lines. There was much howling, and presently it went away with a vast mouthful of prisoners. Again, he saw a blue wave dash with such thunderous force against a gray obstruction that it seemed to clear the earth of it and leave nothing but trampled sod. And always in their swift and deadly rushes to and fro the men screamed and yelled like maniacs.

Particular pieces of fence or secure positions behind collections of trees were wrangled over, as gold thrones or pearl bedsteads. There were desperate lunges at these chosen spots seemingly every instant, and most of them were bandied like light toys between the contending forces. The youth could not tell from the battle flags flying like crimson foam in many directions which color of cloth was winning.

His emaciated regiment bustled forth with undiminished fierceness when its time came. When assaulted again by bullets, the men burst out in a barbaric cry of rage and pain. They bent their heads in aims of intent hatred behind the projected hammers of their guns. Their ramrods clanged loud with fury as their eager arms pounded the cartridges into the rifle barrels. The front of the regiment was a smoke-wall penetrated by the flashing points of yellow and red.

Wallowing in the fight, they were in an astonishingly short time re-smudged. They surpassed in stain and dirt all their previous appearances. Moving to and fro with strained exertion, jabbering the while, they were, with their swaying bodies, black faces, and glowing eyes, like strange and ugly fiends jigging heavily in the smoke.

The lieutenant, returning from a tour after a bandage, produced from a hidden receptacle of his mind new and portentous oaths suited to the emergency. Strings of expletives he swung lashlike over the backs of his men, and it was evident that his previous efforts had in nowise impaired his resources.

The youth, still the bearer of the colors, did not feel his idleness. He was deeply absorbed as a spectator. The crash and swing of the great drama made him lean forward, intent-eyed, his face working in small contortions. Sometimes he prattled, words coming unconsciously from him in grotesque exclamations. He did not know that he breathed; that the flag hung silently over him, so absorbed was he.

A formidable line of the enemy came within dangerous range. They could be seen plainly—tall, gaunt men with excited faces running with long strides toward a wandering fence.

At sight of this danger the men suddenly ceased their cursing monotone. There was an instant of strained silence before they threw up their rifles and fired a plumping volley at the foes. There had been no order given; the men, upon recognizing the menace, had immediately let drive their flock of bullets without waiting for word of command.

But the enemy were quick to gain the protection of the wandering line of fence. They slid down behind it with remarkable celerity, and from this position they began briskly to slice up the blue men.

These latter braced their energies for a great struggle. Often, white clinched teeth shone from the dusky faces. Many heads surged to and fro, floating upon a pale sea of smoke. Those behind the fence frequently shouted and yelped in taunts and gibelike cries, but the regiment maintained a stressed silence. Perhaps, at this new assault the men recalled the fact they had been named mud diggers, and it made their situation thrice bitter. They were breathlessly intent upon keeping the ground and thrusting away the rejoicing body of the enemy. They fought swiftly and with a despairing savageness denoted in their expressions.

The youth had resolved not to budge whatever should happen. Some arrows of scorn that had buried themselves in his heart had generated strange and unspeakable hatred. It was clear to him that his final and absolute revenge was to be achieved by his dead body lying, torn and gluttering, upon the field. This was to be a poignant retaliation upon the officer who had said "mule drivers," and later "mud diggers," for in all the wild graspings of his mind for a unit responsible for his sufferings and commotions he always seized upon the man who had dubbed him wrongly. And it was his idea, vaguely formulated, that his corpse would be for those eyes a great and salt reproach.

The regiment bled extravagantly. Grunting bundles of blue began to drop. The orderly sergeant of the youth's company was shot through the cheeks. Its supports being injured, his jaw hung afar down, disclosing in the wide cavern of his mouth a pulsing mass of blood and teeth. And with it all he made attempts to cry out. In his endeavor there was a dreadful earnestness, as if he conceived that one great shriek would make him well.

The youth saw him presently go rearward. His strength seemed in nowise impaired. He ran swiftly, casting wild glances for succor.

Others fell down about the feet of their companions. Some of the wounded crawled out and away, but many lay still, their bodies twisted into impossible shapes.

The youth looked once for his friend. He saw a vehement young man, powder-smeared and frowzled, whom he knew to be him. The lieutenant, also, was unscathed in his position at the rear. He had continued to curse, but it was now with the air of a man who was using his last box of oaths.

For the fire of the regiment had begun to wane and drip. The robust voice, that had come strangely from the thin ranks, was growing rapidly weak.

23

The colonel came running along back of the line. There were other officers following him. "We must charge 'm!" they shouted. "We must charge 'em!" they cried with resentful voices, as if anticipating a rebellion against this plan by the men.

The youth, upon hearing the shouts, began to study the distance between him and the enemy. He made vague calculations. He saw that to be firm soldiers they must go forward. It would be death to stay in the present place, and with all the circumstances to go backward would exalt too many others. Their hope was to push the galling foes away from the fence.

He expected that his companions, weary and stiffened, would have to be driven to this assault, but as he turned toward them he perceived with a certain surprise that they were giving quick and unqualified expressions of assent. There was an ominous, clanging overture to the charge when the shafts of the bayonets rattled upon the rifle barrels. At the yelled words of command the soldiers sprang forward in eager leaps. There was new and unexpected force in the movement of the regiment. A knowledge of its faded and jaded condition made the charge appear like a paroxysm, a display of the strength that comes before a final feebleness. The men scampered in insane fever of haste, racing as if to achieve a sudden success before an exhilarating fluid should leave them. It was a blind and despairing rush by the collection of men in dusty and tattered blue, over a green sward and under a sapphire sky, toward a fence, dimly outlined in smoke, from behind which spluttered the fierce rifles of enemies.

The youth kept the bright colors to the front. He was waving his free arm in furious circles, the while shrieking mad calls and appeals, urging on those that did not need to be urged, for it seemed that the mob of blue men hurling themselves on the dangerous group of rifles were again grown suddenly wild with an enthusiasm of unselfishness. From the many firings starting toward them, it looked as if they would merely succeed in making a great sprinkling of corpses on the grass between their former position and the fence. But they were in a state of frenzy, perhaps because of forgotten vanities, and it made an exhibition of sublime recklessness. There was no obvious questioning, nor figurings, nor diagrams. There was, apparently, no considered loopholes. It appeared that the swift wings of their desires would have shattered against the iron gates of the impossible.

He himself felt the daring spirit of a savage, religion-mad. He was capable of profound sacrifices, a tremendous death. He had no time for dissections, but he knew that he thought of the bullets only as things that could prevent him from reaching the place of his endeavor. There were subtle flashings of joy within him that thus should be his mind.

He strained all his strength. His eyesight was shaken and dazzled by the tension of thought and muscle. He did not see anything excepting the mist of smoke gashed by the little knives of fire, but he knew that in it lay the aged fence of a vanished farmer protecting the snuggled bodies of the gray men.

As he ran a thought of the shock of contact gleamed in his mind. He expected a great concussion when the two bodies of troops crashed together. This became a part of his wild battle madness. He could feel the onward swing of the regiment about him and he conceived of a thunderous, crushing blow that would prostrate the resistance and spread consternation and amazement for miles. The flying regiment was going to have a catapultian effect. This dream made him run faster among his comrades, who were giving vent to hoarse and frantic cheers.

But presently he could see that many of the men in gray did not intend to abide the blow. The smoke, rolling, disclosed men who ran, their faces still turned. These grew to a crowd, who retired stubbornly. Individuals wheeled frequently to send a bullet at the blue wave.

But at one part of the line there was a grim and obdurate group that made no movement. They were settled firmly down behind posts and rails. A flag, ruffled and fierce, waved over them and their rifles dinned fiercely.

The blue whirl of men got very near, until it seemed that in truth there would be a close and frightful scuffle. There was an expressed disdain in the opposition of the little group, that changed the meaning of the cheers of the men in blue. They became yells of wrath, directed, personal. The cries of the two parties were now in sound an interchange of scathing insults.

They in blue showed their teeth; their eyes shone all white. They launched themselves as at the throats of those who stood resisting. The space between dwindled to an insignificant distance.

The youth had centered the gaze of his soul upon that other flag. Its possession would be high pride. It would express bloody minglings, near blows. He had a gigantic hatred for those who made great difficulties and complications. They caused it to be as a craved treasure of mythology, hung amid tasks and contrivances of danger.

He plunged like a mad horse at it. He was resolved it should not escape if wild blows and darings of blows could seize it. His own emblem, quivering and aflare, was winging toward the other. It seemed there would shortly be an encounter of strange beaks and claws, as of eagles.

The swirling body of blue men came to a sudden halt at close and disastrous range and roared a swift volley. The group in gray was split and broken by this fire, but its riddled body still fought. The men in blue yelled again and rushed in upon it.

The youth, in his leapings, saw, as through a mist, a picture of four or five men stretched upon the ground or writhing upon their knees with bowed heads as if they had been stricken by bolts from the sky. Tottering among them was the rival color bearer, who the youth saw had been bitten vitally by the bullets of the last formidable volley. He perceived this man fighting a last struggle, the struggle of one whose legs are grasped by demons. It was a ghastly battle. Over his face was the bleach of death, but set upon it were the dark and hard lines of desperate purpose. With this terrible grin of resolution he hugged his precious flag to him and was stumbling and staggering in his design to go the way that led to safety for it.

But his wounds always made it seem that his feet were retarded, held, and he fought a grim fight, as with invisible ghouls fastened greedily upon his limbs. Those in advance of the scampering blue men, howling cheers, leaped at the fence. The despair of the lost was in his eyes as he glanced back at them.

The youth's friend went over the obstruction in a tumbling heap and sprang at the flag as a panther at prey. He pulled at it and, wrenching it free, swung up its red brilliancy with a mad cry of exultation even as the color bearer, gasping, lurched over in a final throe and, stiffening convulsively, turned his dead face to the ground. There was much blood upon the grass blades.

At the place of success there began more wild clamorings of cheers. The men gesticulated and bellowed in an ecstasy. When they spoke it was as if they considered their listener to be a mile away. What hats and caps were left to them they often slung high in the air.

At one part of the line four men had been swooped upon, and they now sat as prisoners. Some blue men were about them in an eager and curious circle. The soldiers had trapped strange birds, and there was an examination. A flurry of fast questions was in the air.

One of the prisoners was nursing a superficial wound in the foot. He cuddled it, baby-wise, but he looked up from it often to curse with an astonishing utter abandon straight at the noses of his captors. He consigned them to red regions; he called upon the pestilential wrath of strange gods. And with it all he was singularly free from recognition of the finer points of the conduct of prisoners of war. It was as if a clumsy clod had trod upon his toe and he conceived it to be his privilege, his duty, to use deep, resentful oaths.

Another, who was a boy in years, took his plight with great calmness and apparent good nature. He conversed with the men in blue, studying their faces with his bright and keen eyes. They spoke of battles and conditions. There was an acute interest in all their faces during this exchange of view points. It seemed a great satisfaction to hear voices from where all had been darkness and speculation.

The third captive sat with a morose countenance. He preserved a stoical and cold attitude. To all advances he made one reply without variation, "Ah, go t' hell!"

The last of the four was always silent and, for the most part, kept his face turned in unmolested directions. From the views the youth received he seemed to be in a state of absolute dejection. Shame was upon him, and with it profound regret that he was, perhaps, no more to be counted in the ranks of his fellows. The youth could detect no expression that would allow him to believe that the other was giving a thought to his narrowed future, the pictured dungeons, perhaps, and starvations and brutalities, liable to the imagination. All to be seen was shame for captivity and regret for the right to antagonize.

After the men had celebrated sufficiently they settled down behind the old rail fence, on the opposite side to the one from which their foes had been driven. A few shot perfunctorily at distant marks.

There was some long grass. The youth nestled in it and rested, making a convenient rail support the flag. His friend, jubilant and glorified, holding his treasure with vanity, came to him there. They sat side by side and congratulated each other.

24

The roarings that had stretched in a long line of sound across the face of the forest began to grow intermittent and weaker. The stentorian speeches of the artillery continued in some distant encounter, but the crashes of the musketry had almost ceased. The youth and his friend of a sudden looked up, feeling a deadened form of distress at the waning of these noises, which had become a part of life. They could see changes going on among the troops. There were marchings this way and that. A battery wheeled leisurely. On the crest of a small hill was the thick gleam of many departing muskets.

The youth arose. "Well, what now, I wonder?" he said. By his tone he seemed to be preparing to resent some new monstrosity in the way of dins and smashes. He shaded his eyes with his grimy hand and gazed over the field.

His friend also arose and stared. "I bet we're goin' t' git along out of this an' back over th' river," said he.

"Well, I swan!" said the youth.

They waited, watching. Within a little while the regiment received orders to retrace its way. The men got up grunting from the grass, regretting the soft repose. They jerked their stiffened legs, and stretched their arms over their heads. One man swore as he rubbed his eyes. They all groaned "O Lord!" They had as many objections to this change as they would have had to a proposal for a new battle.

They trampled slowly back over the field across which they had run in a mad scamper.

The regiment marched until it had joined its fellows. The reformed brigade, in column, aimed through a wood at the road. Directly they were in a mass of dust-covered troops, and were trudging along in a way parallel to the enemy's lines as these had been defined by the previous turmoil.

They passed within view of a stolid white house, and saw in front of it groups of their comrades lying in wait beneath a neat breastwork. A row of guns were booming at a distant enemy. Shells thrown in reply were raising clouds of dust and splinters. Horsemen dashed along the line of intrenchments.

At this point of its march the division curved away from the field and went winding off in the direction of the river. When the significance of this movement had impressed itself upon the youth he turned his head and looked over his shoulder toward the trampled and *débris*-strewed ground. He breathed a breath of new satisfaction. He finally nudged his friend. "Well, it's all over," he said to him.

His friend gazed backward. "B'Gawd, it is," he assented. They mused.

For a time the youth was obliged to reflect in a puzzled and uncertain way. His mind was undergoing a subtle change. It took moments for it to cast off its battleful ways and resume its accustomed course of thought. Gradually his brain emerged from the clogged clouds, and at last he was enabled to more closely comprehend himself and circumstance.

He understood then that the existence of shot and counter-shot was in the past. He had dwelt in a land of strange, squalling upheavals and had come forth. He had been where there was red of blood and black of passion, and he was escaped. His first thoughts were given to rejoicings at this fact.

Later he began to study his deeds, his failures, and his achievements. Thus, fresh from scenes where many of his usual machines of reflection had been idle, from where he had proceeded sheeplike, he struggled to marshal all his acts.

At last they marched before him clearly. From this present viewpoint he was enabled to look upon them in spectator fashion and to criticise them with some correctness, for his new condition had already defeated certain sympathies.

Regarding his procession of memory he felt gleeful and unregretting, for in it his public deeds were paraded in great and shining prominence. Those performances which had been witnessed by his fellows marched now in wide purple and gold, having various deflections. They went gayly with music. It was pleasure to watch these things. He spent delightful minutes viewing the gilded images of memory.

He saw that he was good. He recalled with a thrill of joy the respectful comments of his fellows upon his conduct.

Nevertheless, the ghost of his flight from the first engagement appeared to him and danced. There were small shoutings in his brain about these matters. For a moment he blushed, and the light of his soul flickered with shame.

A specter of reproach came to him. There loomed the dogging memory of the tattered soldier—he who, gored by bullets and faint for blood, had fretted concerning an imagined wound in another; he who had loaned his last of strength and intellect for the tall soldier; he who, blind with weariness and pain, had been deserted in the field.

For an instant a wretched chill of sweat was upon him at the thought that he might be detected in the thing. As he stood persistently before his vision, he gave vent to a cry of sharp irritation and agony.

His friend turned. "What's the matter, Henry?" he demanded. The youth's reply was an outburst of crimson oaths.

As he marched along the little branch-hung roadway among his prattling companions this vision of cruelty brooded over him. It clung near him always and darkened his view of these deeds in purple and gold. Whichever way his thoughts turned they were followed by the somber phantom of the desertion in the fields. He looked stealthily at his companions, feeling sure that they must discern in his face evidences of this pursuit. But they were plodding in ragged array, discussing with quick tongues the accomplishments of the late battle.

"Oh, if a man should come up an' ask me, I'd say we got a dum good lickin'."

"Lickin'—in yer eye! We ain't licked, sonny. We're goin' down here always, swing aroun', and' come in behint 'em."

"Oh, hush, with your comin' in behint 'em. I've seen all 'a that I wanta. Don't tell me about comin' in behint——"

"Bill Smithers, he ses he'd rather been in ten hundred battles than been in that heluva hospital. He ses they got shootin' in the nighttime, an' shells dropped plum among 'em in th' hospital. He ses sech hollerin' he never see."

"Hasbrouck? He's th' best off'cer in this here reg'ment. He's a whale."

"Didn't I tell yeh we'd come aroun' in behint 'em? Didn't I tell yeh so? We——"

"Oh, shet yer mouth!"

For a time this pursuing recollection of the tattered man took all elation from the youth's veins. He saw his vivid error, and he was afraid that it would stand before him all his life. He took no share in the chatter of his comrades, nor did he look at them or know them, save when he felt sudden suspicion that they were seeing his thoughts and scrutinizing each detail of the scene with the tattered soldier.

Yet gradually he mustered force to put the sin at a distance. And at last his eyes seemed to open to some new ways. He found that he could look back upon the brass and bombast of his earlier gospels and see them truly. He was gleeful when he discovered that he now despised them.

With this conviction came a store of assurance. He felt a quiet manhood, nonassertive but of sturdy and strong blood. He knew that he would no more quail before his guides wherever they should point. He had been to touch the great death, and found that, after all, it was but the great death. He was a man.

So it came to pass that as he trudged from the place of blood and wrath his soul changed. He came from hot plowshares to prospects of clover tranquilly, and it was as if hot plowshares were not. Scars faded as flowers.

It rained. The procession of weary soldiers became a bedraggled train, despondent and muttering, marching with churning effort in a trough of liquid brown mud under a low, wretched sky. Yet the youth smiled, for he saw that the world was a world for him, though many discovered it to be made of oaths and walking sticks. He had rid himself of the red sickness of battle. The sultry nightmare was in the past. He had been an animal blistered and sweating in the heat and pain of war. He turned now with a lover's thirst to images of tranquil skies, fresh meadows, cool brooks—an existence of soft and eternal peace.

Over the river a golden ray of sun came through the hosts of leaden rain clouds.

Theme topic: The Role of the "Loud One" 1895
in The Red Badge of Courage

Reading Suggestions

Students interested in Stephen Crane will find that the artistry of his best short stories equals that of *The Red Badge of Courage*. The stories are readily available in inexpensive editions edited with excellent introductions by William M. Gibson (1950), Daniel G. Hoffman (1957), and Richard Chase (1960). A wider selection, though it omits "The Monster," is found in *Stephen Crane: An Omnibus* (1952). All of the above except the Hoffman edition include Crane's first novel, *Maggie*. The standard and only collected edition of Crane is *The Work of Stephen Crane*, edited by Wilson Follett, twelve volumes (1925-1927), which includes interesting introductions by writers like Sherwood Anderson, Willa Cather, Joseph Hergesheimer, Amy Lowell, and H. L. Mencken.

One might think that an accurate biography of Crane would be relatively easy to write, since he died young and was a well-known figure after 1895. But he has proved to be a baffling subject, partly because private owners of important documents have refused to make them public and partly because Crane's personality was enigmatic. Only two full-length biographies exist. The first, Thomas Beer's *Stephen Crane* (1923), is a lively impressionistic study of Crane and his times, full of anecdote and imaginative surmise. It cannot be trusted for exact information about dates and the sequence of events, and yet it is still probably the best place to start if one wants to know more about Crane. John W. Berryman's *Stephen Crane* (1950) corrects some of Beer's mistakes and is a spirited, illuminating, crotchety book in its own right. Berryman's chapter "The Color of This Soul" is a brilliant example of Freudian analysis as used by a poet to interpret another poet's psyche. Somewhat overingenious, perhaps, it is nevertheless quite persuasive. Those who decry this kind of probing have not been able to supplant it with any convincing account of Crane's sensibility. But a number of documents has been opened to public use since Berryman's book was written, so that it cannot be considered a definitive biography.

An excellent way to supplement these two biographies is to consult *Stephen Crane: Letters* (1960), edited by Robert W. Stallman and Lillian Gilkes. Miss Gilkes's brilliant biography of Crane's "wife," *Cora Crane* (1960), is a triumph of detective work which reveals among other things the depth of Crane's reluctance to return to England from Havana in 1898. Also helpful in correcting and filling out the portrait of Crane are the reminiscences written by one of his artist friends, Corwin K. Linson, *My Stephen Crane* (1958) edited by Edwin H. Cady and Professor Cady's *Stephen Crane* (1962).

Almost all the important criticism of Crane's work appeared either before 1925 or after 1950. The early criticism from 1896 through 1900 contained some extraordinarily penetrating essays by George Wyndham, Edward Garnett, and H. G. Wells, all of them now available in somewhat abridged form in *The Red Badge of Courage* (1962), edited by Scully Bradley, Richmond C. Beatty, and E. Hudson Long. Wells, in particular, spotted the essence of Crane's art when he referred to his "enormous repudiations. Was ever a man before who wrote of battles so abundantly as he has done and never had a word . . . of the purpose and justification of the war? . . . It is as if the racial thought and tradition had been razed from his mind . . . he is the first expression of the opening mind of a new period." Joseph Conrad's preface to an edition of *The Red Badge* in 1925 brought to an end the important criticism of Crane by his contemporaries, most of them creative writers.

Then in 1950, with the publication of Berryman's biography and Gibson's anthology, a period of more intensive and academic criticism began. It was spearheaded by Robert W. Stallman's essay on *The Red Badge of Courage* in his edition of that book in 1951 and in *Omnibus* in 1952. Professor Stallman interpreted Jim Conklin as a Christ-figure and Fleming's growth as a religious redemption. Since that time interpretations of *The Red Badge* have divided loosely into two groups: those maintaining that the book reveals some kind of initiation ritual, and those maintaining that Henry's failure to change essentially is an ironic commentary on such a ritual. The most important essays in the first group are by Maxwell Geismar, John E. Hart, James T. Cox, and Eric Solomon; the most convincing in the second group are by Philip Rahv, Stanley B. Greenfield, Norman Friedman, and Charles C. Walcutt. Although all these articles shed some light on the book, an unfortunate result of the controversy has been a good deal of redundancy and quibbling over images like the "red sun . . . pasted in the sky like a wafer." More recently, essays by James B. Colvert and Max Westbrook have attempted to reconcile the two main lines of interpretation.

One of the most important recent books is Daniel G. Hoffman's *The Poetry of Stephen Crane* (1957). It elucidates Crane's poetry by examining his "enormous repudiations," his religious heritage, and his sensibility, so that the value of Hoffman's book extends to the fiction as well as the poetry. Two other important essays are Marcus Cunliffe's, "Stephen Crane and the American Background of *Maggie*," and George W. Johnson's, "Stephen Crane's Metaphor of Decorum," in *Publications of the Modern Language Association* (June 1963). The location of the other essays mentioned here, as well as a host of other materials, may be found by consulting the check list in the Stephen Crane issue of *Modern Fiction Studies*, V (Autumn 1959) compiled by Maurice Beebe and Thomas A. Gullason, or the bibliography in Edwin Cady's volume mentioned above.

Biography

Stephen Crane always described his life as a battle, "a sincere, desperate, lonely battle," and one way to see it in something like his perspective is to identify the warring elements. As he surveyed his own ancestry, he noted that it was composed chiefly of fighters and ministers. The fighters were a few generations back on his father's side. The first Stephen Crane had arrived in America in 1635; the third one (for whom the author was named) signed The Declaration of Independence and contributed three sons to active and meritorious fighting in the Revolution. On his mother's side everyone seemed to have become a Methodist clergyman, including Stephen's uncle, who was a bishop in that church.

Born in Newark, New Jersey, on November 1, 1871, Crane was the fourteenth child of a Methodist minister, the Reverend Jonathan Townley Crane, and Mary Helen Peck Crane. His father, a Princeton graduate with what his son described as "a great, fine, simple mind," died when the boy was eight, and his mother, who was also well educated, supported the family by writing for Methodist periodicals. Although Crane's boyhood was quite happy, as a youth he rebelled against the Methodist tradition and joyfully cultivated the vices that this father had preached against. His rebellion against authority and dogma extended to his teachers at school, who found him a "difficult" student. After attending public school at Asbury Park from 1882 to 1888, the Pennington Seminary and the Hudson River Academy at Claverack, New York, from 1888 to 1890, he spent a semester at Lafayette and a semester at Syracuse in 1890. There he belonged to the Delta Upsilon fraternity and distinguished himself in baseball but not in the classroom. "Not that I disliked books," he wrote later, "but the cut-and-dried curriculum of the college did not appeal to me. Humanity was a more interesting study." With his study of humanity that spring, Crane managed to make an "A" in English literature and to write what was probably the first draft of *Maggie: A Girl of the Streets*.

His war with formal education at an end, Crane became a reporter, working for his brother's news agency in Asbury Park until August 1892, when he wrote an account of a workers' parade there with his usual honesty and irony. The resultant political scandal ruined his brother's agency and forced Crane to become a free-lance writer in New York, with genteel editors and prudent publishers as his targets and poverty-ridden artists as his friends. He had *Maggie* printed at his own expense under the pseudonym of "Johnston Smith" early in 1893, but the booksellers refused it and the public ignored it. Crane gave away about one hundred copies to his friends, including Hamlin Garland, who was much impressed by Crane's work and introduced it to Howell and other editors. Having borrowed thirty dollars to have the manuscript of *The Red Badge of Courage* typed, Crane finally sold it in shortened form to McClure's syndicate for publication in New York and Philadelphia papers late in 1894. When the longer version appeared in book form in 1895 and was enthusiastically greeted by British reviewers, Crane's reputation was made. "The two years of fighting have been well spent," he wrote. "They [the editors] used to call me 'that terrible young radical,' but now they are beginning to hem and haw and smile—those very old coons who used to adopt a condescending air toward me."

Having conquered the editors at the age of twenty-four, Crane became aware that "the fight was not going to be with the world but with myself." His irrational, self-destructive tendencies were not limited to sloppy personal habits and incessant smoking despite a wracking cough. Like most rebels, he quickly and intensely sympathized with victims, both animal and human. By publicly defending some prostitutes in New York in 1896, he incurred the wrath and persecution of the police force. And his love affairs included some quixotic commitments to older women of dubious reputation. In November 1896, while waiting in Jacksonville, Florida, for passage to Cuba where he was to report the rebellion for a news syndicate, Crane met Cora Taylor, colorful proprietress of a brothel called the Hotel de Dream. Twice unhappily married, she was separated but not divorced from her second husband. After Crane was shipwrecked at sea in the episode he later described in "The Open Boat," she took care of him. When he went to Greece to report the Greco-Turkish War, she followed him in the role of "the first woman war correspondent," and after the war ended in May 1897, she lived with him as his "wife" in England. Here he wrote some of his best short stories, including "The Monster," "The Bride Comes to Yellow Sky," "The Blue Hotel," and "Death and the Child." His friends included Joseph Conrad, Henry James, and a host of uninvited guests who exhausted Crane's nervous and financial resources.

From the pressures of domesticity, mounting household expenses, and unwelcome convivial guests, Crane escaped again to war, this time the Spanish-American War. More or less trapped in his role as a star correspondent, he deliberately exposed himself to enemy fire, contracted malaria to go with his active tuberculosis, and exhausted himself trying to help the combat soldiers. At the end of the war he dropped out of sight in Havana, apparently reluctant to return to England. Reported as "missing" in the papers, he continued to send stories, poetry, and war pieces to his agent in New York, together with urgent appeals that they be quickly sold. Cora finally raised some money in England and got Crane to return. They moved into a ruined manor house called Brede Place, where Crane spent all but the last few days of his life, desperately cranking out potboilers while he spat blood. He died on June 5, 1900, at the age of twenty-eight—not at home but as a stranger in Badenweiler in the Bavarian Alps. Cora had taken him to a sanitarium there in one last drastic effort to save him.

Mark Twain's *The Gilded Age* exposed political corruption in the national capital where votes were bought and sold. Henry Adams' *Democracy* (1880) turned a censorious eye similar political phenomena. However, Adams remained a ~~good~~ fascinated observer and refused to surrender his belief in democracy despite ~~the~~ its current evil manifestations.

HENRY ADAMS

1838-1918

Remember that Adams was not interested in the richness of contemporary Europe so much as in the richness of its medieval past.

His "dynamic theory of history" — by which he might explain the modern world and perhaps predict its future course, Adams centered his interest in 12th century France and in the Cathedral of Chartres as the epitome of that time and place.

His entire life a process of education and a quest of values. Results: a failure as he saw it. Lived in an acquisitive period of Am. society and could not adjust.

Philosophy: "that the laws which govern animated beings will be ultimately found to be at bottom the same with those which rule inanimate nature."

Adams writes in the 3rd person instead of using the pronoun I. This was his attempt at objectivity

Introduction

Quest for form is the keynote of Adams' whole career as a writer. Because he had many things to say he experimented with many forms, always searching for the one that would embody the meaning he was trying to express in a particular work. But in spite of the variety of his writings there is one purpose underlying them all: to discover the meaning of history and man's place in it, or at least to chart its direction, since motion might be its only meaning and history itself might be something quite different from what it was traditionally supposed to be. His heritage as an Adams placed him at the center of his own country's history. His wide travel and study in Europe, later extended to the Orient, broadened his scope to a world view.

Naturally enough, then, he began as a professional historian, though hardly an orthodox one, first on the faculty at Harvard (1870-1877), afterward as an independent researcher and author of a dozen volumes that still occupy a prominent place in the American canon. This impressive achievement, to which he devoted twenty years of his prime, tended during his lifetime to put him in a category quite outside the bounds of a literary anthology. But his last two works, by which he set greatest store, are of a different sort entirely. They raise the question whether history was his real goal or merely one of several means toward a more ambitious end. These books, reaching a wide audience only after his death, have tended during the twentieth century to bring Adams into the fold of American literature as a major author, though there is still considerable uncertainty as to why he should be so classified. A brief survey of his whole shelf is essential to an understanding of the two volumes that form the capstone of his career.

One of the most striking things about Adams' historical writings is how closely related they are to his own family's role in American history, how personal they are compared to works like Prescott's *Conquest of Peru* and Motley's *Rise of the Dutch Republic*, at least in terms of the subjects chosen. His *magnum opus*, the nine-volume *History of the United States* (1891), is focused on the administrations of Jefferson and Madison, the interregnum of Virginia Democrats between the presidencies of two Adams Federalists from Massachusetts. John had tried to set the conservative tone for the new republic, and John Quincy had tried in vain to restore it before the liberal tendencies of Andrew Jackson swept away all the old foundations. Their descendant, feeling that these first decades of the nineteenth century were crucial to American history, sought to discover their meaning by a detailed chronicle of events. This was the newest and most approved method, following the "scientific" historian Ranke. But Adams was never satisfied with it because he was coming to think that history should be an art as well as a science, and he could not find any unified form in mere sequence. His central theme in the *History* is the inability of man to shape his own life or control the forces outside himself. Things happen because they must.

As offshoots from this major effort he turned to biographies, as a kind of test of Carlyle's theory of heroes, to see if the meaning of history could be found in the lives of great men. It is interesting that his chosen subjects were Albert Gallatin (1879), a staunch Adams man though serving as a cabinet member under the opposition, and John Randolph (1882), the temptuous antagonist of both John and John Quincy. Two others rounded out his efforts in biography, the unfinished or lost life of Aaron Burr and the late one on Cabot Lodge (1911), again enemies and friends of the Adams family. In the relation of man to his times he failed once more to find a form that would reveal the meanings he sought. Then his work as a historian was brought to an end with an exotic footnote, *Memoirs of Arii Tamai E* (1893), a search for the great theme of modern history in capsule form by placing in juxtaposition the international exploitation of Tahiti and reminiscences he recorded painstakingly from the last island queen. But his writing career was far from over.

If history could not be given significance by making it into a science, perhaps art could be made the vehicle of ideas. During the period of his laborious researches Adams threw off two novels, *Democracy* (1880) and *Esther* (1884), dealing with issues of the first importance: the corruption of government by business and the beginnings of religious skepticism as a result of scientific discoveries. Somewhat later he even tried his hand at poetry, notably his "Prayer to the Virgin at Chartres." But his writings in these genres give him no status in the realm of literature, for they are the work of a competent amateur rather than an inspired artist. Having other things to say that called for exposition, even argument, Adams also wrote a large number of essays, enough to fill a volume during his lifetime and two posthumous ones. But it is not as a essayist that he takes rank today as a literary author.

That claim, and it is a growing one, rests exclusively on two works written in his old age, *The Education of Henry Adams* (1907) and *Mont-Saint-Michel and Chartres* (1904). Both are highly personal books, one taking the form of autobiography and the other that of a summer tour in France with his niece. One of their most striking features is that both are aimed at discovering the meaning of history, his perennial theme. If he could not find it in chronological sequence or the lives of other men, in ideological fiction or polemical essays, maybe he could find it in the story of his own life, if seen imaginatively and aesthetically. Their other striking feature is the emphasis on form in both prefaces. If he could find the right forms he could at last express what he had to say.

Though the *Education* was written second and as a sequel to *Chartres*, it is the best one to begin with for several reasons. It takes up the story of America's past where Adams' formal histories leave off and brings it right down into the twentieth century. It appeals more directly to modern readers, as a consequence, having an impact as dramatic and timely today as when first issued. It fits more closely with an American literary tradition, one that includes Franklin's *Autobiography*, Thoreau's *Walden*, and Mark Twain's *Life on the Mississippi*. But it is more successful as a piece of literature than the first of these three books, more ambitious and significant in scope than the other two. It is the classic example in America of the full-scale autobiography shaped by the creative imagination into a work of art.

I

Henry Adams launched his *Education* in its posthumous edition with two prefaces. One he wrote for his editor, H. C. Lodge, to sign, when the book was published six months after his death in 1918. The other is the acknowledged author's preface to the privately printed edition, dated February 16, 1907. Both are crucial to an understanding of the book's method and meaning. In the first he defines his purpose: to treat man as a force, which can be measured only by "motion from a fixed point." This leads to his concept of how the two books are linked, by suggesting as a subtitle for *Chartres* "A Study of Thirteenth-Century Unity" and for the *Education* "A Study of Twentieth-Century Multiplicity." With the aid of these two "points of relation," he said, he could project his lines forward and backward indefinitely. But the second book proved more difficult to write than the first.

The major problem posed by the *Education* was "the usual one of literary form." There are many statements in the letters to support this prefatory aside. To William James he wrote, "As for the volume, it interests me chiefly as a literary experiment, hitherto, as far as I know, never tried or never successful. Your brother Harry [Henry James the novelist] tries such experiments in literary art daily, and would know instantly what I mean." To a young painter he said:

Between artists, or people trying to be artists, the sole interest is that of form. Whether one builds a house, or paints a picture, or tells a story, our point of vision regards only the form—not the matter. [The *Education* has] not been done in order to teach others, but to educate myself in the possibilities of literary form. The arrangement, the construction, the composition, the art of climax are our only serious study. . . . The Confessions of St. Augustine [was] my literary model.

This point is followed up in a second letter to James:

Did you ever read the Confessions of St. Augustine, or of Cardinal de Retz, or of Rousseau, or of Benvenuto Cellini, or even of my dear Gibbon? Of them all, I think St. Augustine alone has an idea of literary form—a notion of writing a story with an end and object, not for the sake of the object, but the form, like a romance. I have worked ten years to satisfy myself that the thing cannot be done today. The world does not furnish the contrasts or the emotion.

In his preface Adams made explicit the differing problems facing the modern author and his classic model: "St. Augustine, like a great artist, had worked from multiplicity to unity, while he, like a small one, had to reverse the method and work back from unity to multiplicity. The scheme became unmanageable as he approached his end." But there is always irony or ambiguity in Adams' references to his life and writings as "failures." The failure here referred to is clearly that of literary form. His revolutionary "dynamic theory of history" simply could not be rendered dramatically through his own life story, so that in the last three chapters the chosen device of autobiography broke down into something like expository essays.

Yet in spite of his protestations that the *Education* remained "unfinished," Adams did not forbid its publication after his death, and during his life he himself had printed a small edition for private circulation. The author's preface to this is chiefly concerned with the use of autobiography as a literary form. Of the two models there mentioned, Franklin is singled out as the only American guide but is dismissed as being only a model of "self-teaching," not for "high education." Rousseau's *Confessions* is played with at some length but only to set it up as a monumental warning against the ego: "Since his time, and largely thanks to him, the Ego has steadily tended to efface itself, and for purposes of model, to become a manikin on which the toilet of education is to be draped in order to show the fit or misfit of the clothes."

Those who have pondered the two prefaces will certainly not expect the book they introduce to be a straightforward personal narrative of Henry Adams or a mere surface picture of the nineteenth-century world he lived in, much as they may serve for its outward subject matter. In the passage just quoted, the verbal play alone should alert readers to the possibility that in the following pages imagery and structure may have as much to do with meaning as facts and ideas or historical events and persons. The author of these prefaces is clearly one who uses language like a poet. Perhaps his purpose was not to record his life and times as a factual story, but to compose a book that would suggest larger meanings. Two passages from Adams' letters confirm this. To the novelist James he wrote punningly of the *Education*, "The volume is a mere shield of protection in the grave. I advise you to take your own life in the same way, in order to prevent biographers from taking it in theirs." To the psychologist James he added, "With this I send you the volume. . . . I feel that Sargent squirms in the portrait. I am not there." This cryptic reference to a contemporary portrait painter, whose work he thought mannered and either idealized or distorted, implies that his own work is so far from a self-portrait that the real Henry Adams is conspicuous by his absence.

The *Education* may be thought of, therefore, as a fiction that uses autobiography as a mere starting point. The first problem in escaping from the limitations of such a literary device is how to achieve the proper distance from one's materials, how to arrive at meanings that are objective and universal while taking full advantage of the drama afforded by a narrative of personal experiences during a crucial period in history. Adams' strategy for this, in the preface, is to make a play on the "Clothes Philosophy" that forms the center of *Sartor Resartus*, though without naming this influential book of the early nineteenth century. In it language was described as the clothing of thought, and body as the clothing of soul, the universe itself being but "the living garment of God." For the transcendental Carlyle clothes were mere appearances covering the true Reality, the one thing worth studying. Adams reverses this, saying that, for him, "The object of study is the garment, not the figure. . . . The tailor's object, in this volume, is to fit young men, in universities or elsewhere, to be men of the world, equipped for any emergency; and the garment offered to them is meant to show the faults of the patchwork fitted on their fathers."

Thus the persona Henry Adams, who is written about in the third person as the subject of the *Education*, has been reduced to a tailor's dummy, even to the mannequin used by window dressers and artists. He is reduced still further by a final meaning of the term "manikin": a little man or dwarf. Such is the shrunken status of Everyman in the modern world. Nineteenth-century discoveries in geology, astronomy, and biology had pushed the history of the earth back from thousands to millions of years, located it as a mere speck on the periphery of the Galaxy, and assigned man only a relative superiority over other animals—all of which destroyed the myth of a special creation and of man, fashioned in God's image, as lord of all creatures. A similar thing had been happening in the changing concepts of the human world brought about by the trend toward collectivism in society and the new theories of behavioral psychology, which turned man into a pawn moved by external and internal forces beyond his control.

In the drift from a humanistic to a deterministic view of himself modern man had indeed become a manikin, so that Adams' emphasis is shifted from autobiography to history. Even in this he allows himself an artist's freedom, saying that the tailor can adapt the clothes as well as the model "to his patron's wants," that is, to the reading public he is trying to reach. And since in this elaborate conceit language is the "clothing of thought," literary form rather than content is once again emphasized as the key to meaning. Having achieved complete detachment from his materials, Adams can now select and maneuver them at will. The facts of his own life and of the historical period through which he lived can be used or omitted, heightened or played down, reshaped in any way dictated by his artistic purpose. And having freed himself from the literal Henry Adams, his task is to create a persona to take his place: "The manikin, therefore, has the same value as any other geometrical figure of three or more dimensions, which is used for the study of relation. For that purpose it cannot be spared; . . . it must have the air of reality; it must be taken for real; must be treated as though it had life." Such is the animated puppet that is moved through the experiences of a long and complex education.

One of the advantages of using autobiography as a literary device is that the narrator who is telling his own story has already lived through all the experiences down to the last page before he begins to write the first one. Because of this he can render the meaning of his life by the form and expression he chooses to give it. In general, the two chief masks in the book are (a) the subject Henry Adams, who is passed off as a manikin for easy display, and (b) the narrator Henry Adams, who is the objective author commenting on his whole past career. But the former becomes an endless variety of personae as (b) tries to reconstruct (a) at the several stages of his education: as child, student, diplomatic secretary, historian, consultant to statesmen, commentator on modern man and his civilization. This continues right on down to the time when the aging subject merges with the narrator, the dispassionate old man seeking to make his autobiography yield the greater truth of his education.

In the shifting perspectives of the book the narrator's role is complicated still further by the several "voices" through which he can speak. Is it the historian who is proving the muddleheadedness of British politicians during the Civil War, or the scientific determinist who has taken the stance that history is chaos rather than sequence? Is it the postgraduate student or the later historian-turned-artist who finds the chief value of his foreign education in the discovery of Reubens and Beethoven? It is crucial to decide which voice of Henry Adams is speaking at any given point. It is equally important to remember that not only the objective narrator but each changing subject-persona is a pose, none of them corresponding exactly to the factual Henry Adams at any stage. They are a series of masks assumed under the shifting mask of the speaker. Thus the whole narrative is removed from the mode of strict autobiography and becomes a fictive account in the best and deepest sense of that term.

In addition to the various voices of the narrator there are other ways in which the style is modulated, notably the shift from that of a detached intellectual to that of one emotionally involved. The bulk of the book is written in the former style: factual for the narrative parts, dry and sharp in the commentary. This gives a tone of authority to the whole. The vignettes are detailed, the portraits clearly etched, the chronicle straightforward, the conclusions faced unflinchingly. Readers are aware that many things have been left out, of necessity, and that the opinions are controlled by a personal value system. But here is a writer, they are convinced, who can record his own life truthfully and evaluate it without self-inflation or apology. The book gains in dependability even from the one way in which it seems to depart from the truth—Adams' tendency to be much too hard on himself. His unique heritage is played down by understatement, his personal abilities and accomplishments undercut by constant deflation. Everyone knows, on the contrary, that his position as an Adams was unrivaled in nineteenth-century America, and the book itself is evidence of his high intelligence and extraordinary learning.

This mode of negation is not the result of an absurd modesty. In his letters as well as his books Adams assumed the roles of arrogance and humility at will. Admitting his error in a political prediction once, he declared, "Hitherto in my life I have always been right; it is other people who are wrong." Yet ten days later, in obvious reference to both *Chartres* and the *Education,* he could say:

Vanity is a danger I can hardly fear now; on the contrary, self-deprecation has always been my vice, and morbid self-contempt my moral weakness, as it was in that of the 12th-century mystics, which is the bond of sympathy between us; but we each recoup ourselves by feeling a calm, unruffled, instinctive, unfathomed skepticism about the existence of a world at all. . . . There are but two schools; one turns the world onto me; the other turns me onto the world; the result is the same. The so-called me is a very, very small and foolish puppy-dog, but it is all that exists, and it tries all its life to get a little bigger by enlarging its energies.

Even in the letters it is the author rather than the person who is writing.

In the *Education* this mode of negation is a conscious strategy that pervades the whole book. All the chief personages are treated with the same irony, all the main events viewed with the same skepticism. The drift to collectivism is accepted as inevitable, the individual as overwhelmed by the forces of determinism—not just Adams alone. The "personal failure" theme, therefore, is not a reflection of any failure in his own life but is used to dramatize his pessimism over the loss of values in the modern world, the impending failure of civilization itself. It is a literary device used deliberately for reader-irritation, to keep raising the question: "What does this pessimist with impossibly high standards really want?" By the end of the book it is clear what he wants: to expose relentlessly the fraudulent aspects of modern society and to shock man into awareness of his plight, so he can meet his doom with self-respect and even try to control it with confidence and intelligent purpose. Instead, "the menagerie is chewing its tail in religious silence," Adams concludes, while the universe either runs down or explodes.

The ground tone of the book is set by this objective analysis of his life and times. It is for this reason that the subjective passages stand out with such dramatic effect. They are few and brief, but they always come at crucial stages in his career. As each one occurs it is dismissed as accidental education, or "education only sensual." At the time, the persona is blind to any value it may have in fitting him for his world. But the wary reader soon becomes aware, as the author has been all along, that until Adams can bridge the gap between intellect and emotion he will not have any education at all. Those who take the book as literal autobiography can be easily misled into concluding that the author was simply a cold intellectual, even a sour old man, who occasionally gave vent to extravagant feelings. But the literary student will recognize these as contrasting styles deliberately played against each other for strategic purposes. The subjective episodes, all but submerged under the objective surface, provide a measure for one of the book's most important meanings: that modern man's dependence on fact and reason has been largely responsible for the fragmentation of his world. He has lost the capacity to feel—the capacity for war and worship, for love and art—that brought unity out of multiplicity in the medieval world of *Chartres*.

Equally important is the clue to Adams' method of dramatizing his autobiography offered by these subjective passages. Two of them are available in the following selections for readers to analyze. The first occurs when, as a young man, he visits Antwerp Cathedral on the way to graduate studies in Berlin (Chapter 5). Prostrating himself before Reubens' "Descent from the Cross," he tries to use this painting as a doorway into the lost religion of the Middle Ages. There is no biographical evidence that he ever had such an emotional experience. But there is ample evidence in the text of the *Education* to show how this highly subjective episode fills out a major theme of the book: the disappearance of religion in the modern world. The second comes at the age of thirty-two, when he witnesses the death of his sister in the terrible convulsions of lockjaw (Chapter 19). His personal grief and shock are played up to the full as the dramatic cause of his abandoning orthodox attitudes toward God and nature, leading him to embrace the modern belief in scientific determinism. But this reorientation is conspicuously absent from the letters of 1870, which record the actual experience with clinical detachment.

This particular subjective episode also shows why Adams rejected some of his autobiographical materials and used others. His grief and shock over personal loss could have been illustrated far more dramatically by the death of his wife in 1885, without need of literary heightening. After thirteen years of happy marriage, Marian Adams, suffering from melancholia, took her own life. Her husband's was broken in fragments, and he only found some degree of wholeness again after years of wandering and searching for peace. Yet this entire segment of his mature career—all the happiness and the pain (not to mention his great achievement as a historian)—is omitted from the *Education*. Chapter 20 ends just before his marriage in 1872; Chapter 21 takes up the narrative again under the title "Twenty Years After (1892)," with no comment on the hiatus. As an artist he chose to by-pass the tragic end of his marriage and transfer its powerful emotional impact to a previous event, the death of his sister, on which it was easier to gain perspective. Besides, the chief literary use he wanted to make of his confrontation with violent and meaningless death was that chaos rather than sequence is the law of nature, even as he intended to prove it is the law of history. It was more strategic to fix this turning point in his thinking by a dramatic episode of 1870, just prior to his assuming the role of professional historian, rather than by his wife's suicide in 1885, long after he had begun applying his "scientific" theory of anarchic forces in nature to the historical process. These are some of the ways by which Adams transformed his autobiography into a work of art and gave it meanings far transcending the personal. Interested students can discover many others for themselves and find out how they work to achieve the literary form the author was seeking.

II

A number of patterns mesh together to give the *Education* its over-all structure. Most obvious of these is the story line, which creates the effect of a chronicle from childhood to old age. But this autobiographical pattern, at most a surface device, is breached more often than the casual reader may notice. Many chapters, scattered throughout the book, drop the personal narrative for broader topics—international diplomacy in London during the Civil War, the breakdown of American government and society during Reconstruction, the impact of new discoveries in science and inventions such as the dynamo, and so on. The last three chapters abandon the story line altogether, with the frank admission that he can formulate his radical theory of history only by shifting to the essay form. Autobiography is by-passed even more by the omission of many significant matters, as a check with the actual record will show. Virtually nothing is told about Adams' affectionate relation with family and kin, or his intimate and wide-ranging friendships—except for the public life of previous Adamses and the careers in politics and science of two close friends, Hay and King. In sum, he left out all the subjective parts of his life, all the emotional and humanizing aspects, unless he could fit them into the design of his "education." The most notable omission is of the entire account of his marriage and its anguished aftermath, as shown above. This skipping of the whole period of his prime, from age thirty-four to fifty-four, breaks the book into two parts, even as his wife's death had broken his life.

Adams once described the *Education* as a centipede that crawls twenty chapters downhill, then fifteen chapters up a little "for the view." This whimsy is the clue to a patterning much more important than the autobiographical one, as far as structure is related to meaning. The first part is his search during youth and early maturity for a career in the world appropriate to his heritage. The second, after a gap of twenty years, is the retired historian's quest to understand the breakdown of his world into multiplicity. In the one he defines his aim as being "to control power in some form." For the other, he sees the need of redefining his goal: "to react with vigor and economy . . . and by choice" to the forces that are turning an ordered world into chaos. Most of the personal narrative comes in the first part, most of the commentary in the second. There, having given up action, he can turn to theory and try to draw conclusions from the meaning of his life. The relation between action and theory establishes the relation of the two parts. As might be expected, all the subjective episodes are in part one, since feelings are the result of personal experience. Part two is almost wholly objective, limited to facts and ideas, as he turns himself into a representative manikin of the collapsing modern world.

This balancing of modes in the over-all structure is repeated on a smaller scale in the arrangement of the first twenty chapters, which follow the chronological order fairly closely. Chapters 1 through 6 make a distinct unit, dealing with the years of his formal education from grammar school in Boston through post-graduate studies in Berlin. The failure of this attempt to prepare himself to be one of the "men of the world, equipped for any emergency" is dramatized by "Treason," in which the America of his heritage is rent asunder by the violence of Civil War. Thus Chapter 7 forms a link with the next group, eight chapters dealing with his experiences in England as Secretary to the American Minister, in which he is educated by public affairs as a spectator. There the multiplication of forces beyond man's control, in politics and economics as well as war, suggests the impending breakdown of all Western civilization. At the end of his English residence he tries to convert himself into a Darwinist, applying the principles of biological evolution to society, in a desperate attempt to find a new faith in order and unity that will replace the lost one of religion. So the last of these chapters, "Darwinism," leads into the final group of five, centering around the Washington years when he becomes a reformer and writes essays on current events. But this evangelism is short lived. The weakness and drift under President Grant strike him as "evolution in reverse," and social Darwinism is soon rejected as a practical program for hastening ultimate perfection. The railroad conspiracy and the gold scandal show that corruption is widespread. The outbreak of the Franco-Prussian War extends this chaos in society to the international scene, and the death of his sister in the same year suggests that anarchy is the law of nature too. As his ordered world falls into fragments he withdraws to a professorship at Harvard. His "failure" there is that of one expected to teach history as meaningful sequence when he is convinced it is essentially "incoherent and immoral."

The chronicle of his early life thus divides itself naturally into three sections: his formal schooling, his education by public affairs as a spectator, and his experiences as a participant who fails to find his proper role. But this structure by outward events is far less important to meaning than the dramatic juxtaposition of subjective and objective experiences, whereby the rare emotional passages achieve their effect by being sounded against the hard factual narrative that gives the book its tone. The first and third sections gain their special significance through experiences that appeal to feeling only, as previously indicated. His formal education reaches its climax not in university studies but in the discovery of painting and religion at Antwerp Cathedral, symbolizing medieval unity, and in the discovery of Beethoven in a Berlin beer garden, when a "prison-wall that barred his senses on one great side of life suddenly fell." Shortly afterward in Rome, as he meditates on the decline of classical and medieval culture, based on art and emotion, he can only ask the agonized question "Why?"

In the long middle section there are no such strong subjective passages, since it is devoted to analyzing problems in society and government, as he tries to fit himself for a traditional Adams role in the world. There are incidental experiences in England that raise the unsolved issue of unity again, as in the meeting with Swinburne, when he envies the fusion of mind and sensibility achieved by the poet; or that reveal his internal conflicts, as when his mind tries to embrace evolution as a "new form of religious hope" though his instinct rejects it because he can only perceive time as motion and change. But on the whole these chapters are concerned with ideas and facts, and as such they form the objective core of part one.

The third section returns to the use of climactic emotional experiences for achieving meaning. Just as intellect fails to find any vestiges of an ordered world left in post Civil War America, so on the death of his sister the previous coherence of his personal life is ruptured by the "insanity of force" that is nature. Ignorant of the value of "education only sensual," the persona requires twenty more years of experience before he is able to "restore the finite to its place." The very next scene, the last subjective moment in the book, suggests a possible way for doing this. An enthusiastic new friendship with the geologist King, begun in the Rocky Mountains of Colorado, gives promise that somehow the outward beauty and the inner chaos of nature can be reconciled, that by a synthesis of science and aesthetics man may impose unity on his experience. On this hopeful note the first part of the *Education* comes to an end.

The persona has now been established as a manikin for the study of relations—between feeling and intellect, unity and multiplicity, the past religious phase of history and the present mechanical one. The last fifteen chapters, in which he crawls back uphill for the view, are unrelieved by any dramatic emotional episodes. They continue the objective narrative that was the staple of part one also, but with much less emphasis on personal experiences, in order to display the social and scientific forces that move the manikin through the modern world. On the surface they seem like a proliferation of illustrations of multiplicity. But as he learns to incorporate sensual experience in his total education, he is able to work out the new theory of history that concludes the book. This conclusion is far from being a victory over the anarchic forces of society and nature. Man cannot hope to control them, or even to stop the drift toward multiplicity. But he can set himself the task of understanding them so he can unify his own experience, if only by expressing it in a work of art based on a new theory of history. This would be the intelligent use of doom, as one critic has phrased it. "Unity is vision," Adams said flatly, and by implication reality is—and always has been—complex and chaotic. The only question is, "Can modern man impose his vision of order on the chaos of the world as effectively as medieval man did?"

Part two of the *Education* is structured most effectively by the full development of two patterns: the manipulation of time, and the creation of images to symbolize the phases of history. Both had been used in part one, though sparingly. From the beginning Adams extends his life span over three centuries, pretending that though he lived in the nineteenth century he was educated for the eighteenth and so unfitted for the twentieth. By an ingenious trick of telescoping time all three are made to exist simultaneously. The eighteenth century came to an end in 1848, he declares theatrically, when ex-President Adams collapsed on the floor of Congress. And since this was the very date of Marx's *Manifesto* and the outbreak of revolutions all over Europe, the same year ushered in the twentieth century. Thus the nineteenth, which comprises virtually the whole education of the persona, vanishes before it fairly begins.

This time-game is proved "scientifically" in the book's penultimate chapter by applying the "Law of Acceleration" to history. The religious phase had dragged itself out over so many millennia, refusing to admit its own decline and death, that the mechanical phase burst on the scene fully formed—long prepared for by the admission of reason into St. Thomas' theology, which made way for Newton and applied science. This squeeze play reduces the nineteenth century to a mere point in time between the two great phases of history. Of course it could be argued that the grandfather, last embodiment of the great family tradition, did die in 1848 and Adams was simply reporting that fact. But a more historically precise date for the end of the Federalist era would have been 1829, when John Quincy was defeated by the new Jacksonian democracy, or even 1801, when John Adams was defeated by Jefferson. It was simply more appropriate for the author's literary purposes to choose the date in mid-century and so bring the demise of the eighteenth into dramatic juxtaposition with the rise of Communist theory and the drift toward twentieth-century collectivism.

These three centuries, lumped together to form the modern world of the persona, are expanded as well as collapsed at will. Adams refers to Quincy, where he began his nineteenth-century boyhood, as not only "colonial" but "troglodytic." At the age of thirty, meditating on the fossilized *pteraspis* recently found near Wenlock Abbey, he accepts this shark out of the Silurian age as his first ancestor. In his prime, with the discovery of anarchic force as the true reality behind the appearance of order, he does not hesitate to project his lines forward and predict the exact year in the twentieth century when the world will blow up or grind to a halt.

Another use to which he puts this maneuverable time scheme is in linking his two books as sequels. The ratio of change, so slow throughout most of recorded history, is now accelerating at such a dizzy speed he can bring the medieval and modern periods together. The three-century unit of the *Education* is paralleled by the three chosen for *Chartres*. During the eleventh, twelfth, and thirteenth centuries the religious power that had given unity to civilization for so long reached its highest expression, then began to show signs of breaking down. In the nineteenth century the persona Henry Adams is watching this process work itself out in the fragmentation of the modern world even as he clings to the illusion of an ordered one he has inherited. In Chapter 25, "The Dynamo and the Virgin," as his education enters the twentieth century, he tentatively brings the two poles of history together, in more than the title. The love of Mary he traces back as a sexual force to Venus, even to Eve. Then with the decline of Mariolatry, he blasphemously offers up a scientific prayer to the dynamo. In a later chapter, "Vis Nova" (The New Power), he adds a comic footnote in the episode where he visits the shrines of the Virgin in an automobile.

To make concrete his dramatic handling of time, Adams creates a number of striking symbols. Most effective is his violent yoking of the central symbols of Christianity with two drawn from modern technology. The Cross to which Christ was nailed had brought salvation, so elevating the worth of all men and uniting them in the brotherhood of love. It is a constant in the religious world of *Chartres*, almost nonexistent in the secular one of the *Education*. But it does appear twice, with telling effect: in the

experience at Antwerp Cathedral as a young man and in that of the old
man at the Paris Exposition, where it is described as "a revelation of mysterious energy" now largely lost to man. In bold contrast to the Cross he
sets up the railroad, running all through the nineteenth century, that nails
man to its crossties and brings death to the individual. As it comes into full
power during the decades after the Civil War, it emerges as a symbol of
the new industrial energies drawing all human movement to itself in a
novel kind of unity, yet one that offers, paradoxically, only the anonymity
of a collective society. It represents the victory of Boston over Quincy, of a
mechanistic civilization over a traditional humanistic one.

The second pair is his most daring conjunction of symbols. So furiously
is the law of acceleration operating that the mechanical phase of history is
hardly established before it is replaced by the "supersensual" one, railroads
by dynamos and radium, which dramatically reveal the progressive degradation of energy and the instability of matter itself. Having failed to find any
meaningful sequence in history or society—"while the mere sequence of
time was artificial, and the sequence of thought was chaos"—Adams turns
at last to study the sequence of force. But by 1900 he finds "his historical
neck broken" by energies that are anarchical and totally unsuspected, giving history a new phase by rupturing the unity of natural force. He knows
he can never understand this until he can learn to relate the power of the
dynamo in the twentieth century to that of the Virgin in the twelfth. "He
made up his mind to venture it; he would risk translating rays into faith."

The only common value he can find to measure the difference between
faith and force is their attraction on his own mind, as representative of the
mind of other men. He knows that electricity could no more have built
Chartres Cathedral than worship of the Virgin could have led to the invention of the dynamo. "The force of the Virgin was still felt at Lourdes,
and seemed to be as potent as X-rays; but in America neither Venus nor
Virgin ever had value as force," though modern man's blind obedience to
scientific power suggests the terms of a new worship. Perhaps a parallel is
possible, and the dynamo can be shown to be a "moral force" much as
early Christians felt the Cross. Thus he sets the terms of his "scientific" experiment. If he could show that Cross and railroad, Virgin and dynamo, are
all symbols of power worshiped by man—differing from each other only
because they are the expressions of different epochs—he might be able to
show that history does have sequence. If love of the Virgin, symbolizing
medieval religion even more powerfully than the crucified Christ does, had
led to a new synthesis in the theology of St. Thomas, then understanding
modern force might lead to a synthetic theory of history couched in scientific terms and so acceptable to modern man. First, by using the feeling self
as a center to measure the forces of Virgin and dynamo, representing two
poles of history, he might be able to give meaning and unity to his own experience. Then this private synthesis could be extended to a public one.

The search for a new dynamic theory of history is the goal of part two of the *Education*.

Chapters 21-35 divide themselves into three sections, the three phases of his search.[1] In the first five, the decline of art symbolizes the change that has come over Adams' inherited world and his isolation from the new industrial one that has replaced it. His education as an Adams fitted him for the eighteenth century rather than the twentieth, his temperament for art rather than science. Yet, because the persona has been part of the very historical process causing his alienation from the modern world, he is peculiarly qualified to analyze it. And he does achieve some sense of personal unity as he learns to fuse feeling with intellect, solving the problem that had proved a barrier to his earlier education in part one. Though the succeeding chapters record the drift to multiplicity in differing areas—government, science, his personal life, and so on—they are united by a common concern: to achieve the artist's vision of order and impose it on the disorder of the contemporary world. Searching for peace (after the death of his wife), Adams begins his far-flung travels. First he goes to the Orient where he discovers the ancient past, then to the South Seas and primitive art. The meeting with the painter La Farge, who goes with him on these trips, is crucial. From him he learns that the aesthetic sense is another way of knowing, opposite to reason, and this enables him to discard the idea that sensual education is valueless. Then comes his exploration of the cathedrals in Normandy, where his study of medieval art gives him "a new sense of history," a conviction that it can be understood intuitively as well as intellectually.

Meantime he has been striving to keep abreast of the modern world—the chaos of politics and economics in Washington, the dynamos first glimpsed in Chicago. By the time of the Paris Exposition in 1900, when he can fathom the meaning of these new machines representing the anarchic forces released by science, he is ready to write his climactic chapter "The Dynamo and the Virgin." Believing with Bergson that the intuition must find the goals for the mind to analyze, he first allows himself to feel the relations between these two symbols of power, then uses his intellect to measure the degree of their attraction on men and their influence on history. Just how significant the role of feeling is in establishing the book's meaning he made explicit in a letter several years after its publication:

I like best Bergson's frank surrender to the superiority of Instinct over Intellect. You know how I have preached that principle, and how I have studied the facts of it. In fact I wrote once a whole volume—called my *Education*— . . . in order to recall how Education may be shown to consist in following the intuitions of instinct.

[1] The following analysis of the structure of part two of the *Education* is indebted to the study by Conder listed in Reading Suggestions.

But the book's chosen method dictates a rational, even scientific, "demonstration" of his conclusions, though they have been arrived at intuitively. This requires him to undertake a new kind of education. Convinced that "the alternative to art was arithmetic," he plunges into statistics to chart the present and the immediate future.

Chapter 26, "Twilight," is a transitional one in which he tries to relate the pattern of his personal experiences to the whole movement of contemporary history. The next six chapters form the second group, setting forth the views of the Conservative Christian Anarchist, a fictive role he creates for himself as one who perceives order and chaos simultaneously everywhere. In the first three he sees the impending conflict between Imperial Russia and the West as one between inertia and acceleration, unity and multiplicity, but every effort to fuse these contradictory forces breaks down. The Russo-Japanese War, in which the new scientific forces are being applied to instruments of destruction, actually raises the question of the survival of civilization. In the second three chapters he tries to work this out "scientifically." All the forces making for unity are discussed in "Vis Inertiae," all the forces of chaos in "Vis Nova," with an attempted resolution in "The Grammar of Science." But each chapter reaches the same conclusion: it is a "toss-up between anarchy and order." So long as man could face the chaos of reality and still impose on it his vision of an ordered world— religious in the Middle Ages, political in the founding of the American Republic—he could achieve at least the illusion of unity. But even his capacity for creating illusions may be lost in the flood of new forces overwhelming him now. This first of the twentieth-century world wars, coming right on the heels of Adams' vision of the dynamo and radium in 1900, seems a direct application to human society of the anarchy being unleashed by scientific discovery. Chapters 27-32 are his attempt to resolve the conflict between man's fading dream of unity and the fact of multiplicity made vivid by science.

The final section of the *Education* is a triad of chapters in which the retired historian makes a last heroic effort to come to terms with the chaos of the modern world. Having felt the power of the Virgin and the dynamo as personal experience, he extends them from private to public history by making them into symbols of unity and multiplicity, so as to prophesy the future as well as understand the past. It is in these three concluding chapters that Adams says his literary form failed him, the chosen device of autobiography having to be replaced by expository essays. As he wrote to Barrett Wendell, a professor of literature at Harvard, "I found that a narrative style was so incompatible with a didactic or scientific style, that I had to write a long supplementary chapter [actually three] to explain in scientific terms what I could not put into narration without ruining the narrative." The main outlines of this synthesis can be pondered by students in the last selection from the *Education*, "A Dynamic Theory of History." The next chapter, "A Law of Acceleration," presents elaborate statistics from the history of science to substantiate his theory; and the process by which power is increasing in a geometrical ratio is imaged as a comet ready to explode. In the final chapter the reader is told he must begin his education where Henry Adams' leave off, in the age of supersensual chaos.

Several passages from the letters will throw light on this complex argument and furnish evidence that its real method is literary rather than scientific, its purpose moral rather than historical. Just as the *Education* was being brought to its conclusion, Adams sounded his stoical note of hope in the face of impending doom:

> What is the end of doubling up our steam and electric power every five years to infinity if we don't increase thought power? As I see it, the society of today shows no more thought power than in our youth, though it showed precious little then. To me the whole lesson lies in this experiment. Can our society double up its mind-capacity? It must do it or die; and I see no reason why it may not widen its consciousness of complex conditions far enough to escape wreck; but it must hurry. Our power is always running ahead of our mind.

And even during the composition of *Chartres*, several years earlier, he was already projecting the dilemma that would be posed at the end of the *Education*:

> I apprehend for the next hundred years an ultimate, colossal, cosmic collapse; but not on any of our old lines. My belief is that science is to wreck us, and that we are like monkeys monkeying with a loaded shell; we don't in the least know or care where our practically infinite energies come from or will bring us to. . . . It is mathematically certain to me that another thirty years of energy-development at the rate of the last century, must reach an *impasse*.
>
> This is, however, a line of ideas wholly new, and very repugnant to our contemporaries, . . . I owe it to my having always had a weakness for science mixed with metaphysics. I am a dilution of Lord Kelvin and St. Thomas Aquinas.

Aquinas' philosophy makes the final chapter of the *Chartres*. Kelvin's Second Law of Thermodynamics brings the *Education* to its conclusion. A third letter, written just after he had completed one book and was beginning the other, makes it clear how the two books were linked in his mind:

> I am trying to work out a formula of anarchism; the law of expansion from unity, simplicity, morality, to multiplicity, contradiction, police. . . . The assumption of unity which was the mark of human thought in the middle-ages has yielded very slowly to the proofs of complexity. The stupor of science before radium is proof of it.

Chartres and the *Education* were planned and executed as sequels. Only by reading them as such can the student grasp their full significance.

III

The best approach to Adams' intentions and methods in *Mont-Saint-Michel and Chartres* can likewise be picked up from comments in his correspondence. To a medieval historian, H. O. Taylor, he wrote (with a copy of the book):

I have no object but a superficial one, as far as history is concerned. To me, accuracy is relative. I care very little whether my details are exact, if only my *ensemble* is in scale. You need to be thorough in your study and accurate in your statements. Your middle ages exist for their own sake, not for ours. To me, who stand in gaping wonder before this preposterous spectacle of thought, [the conceptions of modern scientific philosophers,] . . . the middle-ages present a picture that has somehow to be brought into relation with ourselves.

Here Adams explicitly disclaimed the role of historian, just as in the letters quoted previously he denied that he was writing autobiography in his *Education*. His purpose in the *Chartres*, he said, was to create a structure—"a picture" of the past—that would help man to reorient his thinking today. Some five years later he commented to A. S. Cook, another medievalist:

I wanted to show the intensity of the vital energy of a given time, and of course that intensity had to be stated in its two highest terms—religion and art. As our society stands, this way of presenting a subject can be felt only by a small number of persons . . . . the one-in-a-thousand of born artists and poets.

To Taylor again, in a letter near the end of his life, he made a statement that clarifies his use of religion as one of the two main themes in his book:

Logically the religious solution is inadmissible—pure hypothesis. It discards reason. I do not object to it on that account: as a working energy I prefer instinct to reason; but as you put it, the Augustinian adjustment seems to be only the Stoic, with a supernatural or hypothetical supplement nailed to it by violence. The religionists preached it, and called it Faith.

His real purpose was to grasp medieval unity through the vision of an artist, the historian's view being inadequate and the religious one lost to modern man.

Adams' bantering complaints about the dwindling audience today— especially for books on art, poetry, and religion—reflect his deep concern over the alienation of the artist in the modern world. But he played the game with zest. Both of his novels were published anonymously, the second one even "suppressed," as an experiment with the reading public to see if an unadvertised book would sell. His last two works, which he considered his greatest achievement, were issued only in limited editions for private circulation. And his pessimism about the plight of the serious author prompted him to mockery in his comments on them. To an English friend he wrote, "I hardly think my *Education* is fit for any public." As for *Chartres*, he declared to William James, "The last three chapters are alone worth reading, and of course are never read." It was of this book ("the only book I ever wrote that was worth writing") that he said jocularly at the time of its first publication, "I deny that it is a book; it is only a running chatter with my nieces and those of us who love old art." Then he added with comic exaggeration, "It was meant only for . . . women, [since] men no longer read at all"—meaning that their reading is confined to the factual and scientific.

These frivolous remarks were addressed to one of those bright young women who formed a coterie around him in his old age, one of the "nieces in wish" to whom he dedicates his pages in the preface to *Chartres*. There he gives free play to his banter about the shrunken relation of author to reader, saying the only one possible now is between an uncle and his niece. "Nieces have been known to read in early youth, and in some cases may have read their uncles." But this is to be a book in the guise of a tour to the cathedrals of Normandy. "For convenience of travel in France," he adds, "the nieces shall count as one only. . . . One niece is much more likely than two to listen. One niece is also more likely than two to carry a kodak and take interest in it." But even with a captive audience of one there are limitations: "One cannot assume, even in a niece, too emotional a nature, but one may assume a kodak." This little fiction establishes the point of view for the whole book. In talking about religion and art today, he implies, one is limited to addressing a feminine sensibility; and the camera suggests the value of pictures to stimulate the emotional response if it should need bolstering. Narrator and niece are summer tourists and so need not take anything too seriously—architecture, theology, history. They may come back simply with a feeling or a picture, but the garrulous uncle reserves the right to slip in some comments on its meaning. The last words in the preface are "the uncle talks:" . . . All that follows is what he says, certainly the most rewarding "running chatter" a niece ever listened to.

Chartres adopts the mode of a travel-guide-book as a literary device in much the same way that the *Education* uses autobiography. The fictional sightseeing trip through the cathedral country of France furnishes at most a mechanical structure. Even this outward form is abandoned midway, the tour proper coming to an end with Chapter 10. The second half of the book is a tour of medieval civilization—its history, poetry, religion, and philosophy—rather than of architectural shrines. So it is a travel book in two ways far transcending a mere guide for tourists. It is an imaginative journey across the *"pons seclorum,* the bridge of ages, between us and our ancestors," into the emotional and intellectual world of the Middle Ages, as Adams says in the opening chapter. It is also an attempted pilgrimage,

he says near the end, across the *"Pons Sanctorum*—over which only children
and saints can pass"—though he undertakes it as a pilgrim of art, not of
faith. In part one the stones of architecture are used to build a foundation
on which the drama of medieval civilization can be acted out in part two,
as a recent critic has pointed out.[2] The architecture provides a vocabulary
which becomes metaphor later on. The tour in space becomes a journey
in time. The shift from tourist geography to poetic history marks the shift of
interest from the two famous shrines of the title to the whole of French
medieval culture.

The first part of the book is divided into two distinct sections. Chapters 1-4 are focused on the eleventh century and are concerned with action,
the church and state militant. This was the period of the early crusades and
the conquest of England. With the zeal of converts the Normans boldly
asserted their new faith in the one and only God, not the Trinity or the
Virgin. They symbolized the Christian soldier's union with Him in the fortress abbey at Mont-Saint-Michel. The last of these chapters forms an architectural transition from Romanesque to Gothic, and a geographical transit
from Normandy to the Île de France. The second section, Chapter 5-10, is
centered on the twelfth century and concerned with feeling, worship of the
Virgin as symbolized by the great era of cathedral building that culminated
at Chartres. As intercessor, Mary harmonized man's acts with God's will,
thus bringing unity out of multiplicity. The two sections differ in that one
approaches God directly, the other through love of the Virgin; one expresses its faith in acts, the other in art. But they are more like each other
than what follows, since both are simple assertions of unity needing no rational proof.

This alternation between masculine and feminine emphases is reversed
in the second part, which likewise divides itself into two sections. Chapters 11-13 are devoted to women and the dominant role they played in the
history, poetry, and miracles of the period. These recreate medieval society
as reflected in literature and legend. Mary is still a constant referent, but
as her power declines she tends to be analyzed as a human and sexual force
rather than a divine one. This prepares for the breakdown of intuitive faith
in the thirteenth century, the focus of Chapters 14-16. This final section is
concerned with reason and the reassertion of unity through the doctrine of
the Trinity. The scholastic philosophers did not assume God but tried to
prove Him, notably in the *Summa Theologiae* of St. Thomas Aquinas. Yet
the conclusion they sought was but the starting point of the eleventh and
twelfth centuries. In part one the narrator tries to adopt the medieval viewpoint of feeling and faith. In part two he shifts to the rational analysis of a
modern commentator. But both perspectives are present throughout,

[2] See Levenson in Reading Suggestions. This study and Conder's have proved helpful
at several points in the following analysis.

though the presumed unity achieved by act, intuition, and reason in the Middle Ages can be understood by the narrator only aesthetically.

Such is the substantive "argument" of this difficult book. But far more complex patternings enrich its structure and meaning. For Adams said of *Chartres*, in the same letter defining his intent and method in the *Education*, that it too had "not been done in order to teach others, but to educate myself in the possibilities of literary form"—his sole interest being, once again, not the matter, but the style, the structure, and the art of climax. Of the many literary devices employed, one of his most effective is the maneuvering of time. As in the *Education*, *Chartres* also spans three centuries, but each has a differing conception of unity, so that the Middle Ages tend to become a period of motion and flux like any other. To create the illusion of unity artistically (the religious unity of Christian belief being hard for modern man to grasp) he constantly telescopes time, each section of the book displaying all three centuries.

For example, though the solid masculine foundations that make the abbey church distinctive are eleventh-century, its glorious Merveille dates from the twelfth, and its crowning cloister from the thirteenth. Adams insists on the harmony of all three, saying that the "restrained strength of the Romanesque married to the graceful imagination of the Gothic" makes an ideal union. So he can assert dogmatically, "The whole Mount kept the grand style; it expressed the unity of Church and State, God and Man, Peace and War, Life and Death, Good and Bad; it solved the whole problem of the universe. . . . God reconciles all. The world is an evident, obvious, sacred harmony." But further additions to Mont-Saint-Michel were made in the fifteenth century that shattered this harmony, Adams admits, and the only way he can preserve his fiction of unity is to say the Middle Ages had ended long before that date. He makes his point by a prophecy of impending disunity as extravagant as his previous claim of unity had been: "Not till two centuries afterwards did the Mount take on the modern expression of war as a discord in God's providence. . . . [The châtelet] jars on the religion of the place; it forebodes wars of religion; dissolution of society; loss of unity; the end of the world."

Similarly, in the last section, the resort to reason that undermined the unity of a religion based on faith is focused on the great work of Aquinas in the mid-thirteenth century. Yet this tendency is shown to have been under way for a long time, dating back at least to the end of the eleventh when Abélard launched his attack on orthodox theology, using the new weapon of scientific logic. It is true he was defeated ultimately by Bernard, the champion of intuition, and there was a short-lived transition (1140-1200) during which the French mystics tried to reconcile reason and emotion as a dual way to God. Yet it was Abélard's insistence on proving unity that re-emerged more than a century later in Thomism. Thus the forces of disunity were actually at work all during the twelfth century, fixed by Adams as the high point of medieval unity. This glorious period of the Transition, dominated by worship of the Virgin, forms the vital center of his book and provides its artistic unity. Yet it is shown as only an unstable equilibrium of the components of the eleventh century's unquestioning belief and the inroads of rational doubt in the thirteenth. Medieval unity he finally admits was a vision, not a fact. But it was this continuing effort to impose order on chaos, and the faith that it could be done, which distinguished the world of *Chartres* from that of the *Education*.

A far more subtle time strategy is the pervasive ambiguity in Adams' treatment of youth and age, the present world of the tour and the past as embodied in the shrines being visited. The key to the first ten chapters, where he tries to translate himself from modern fact and reason to medieval feeling, is given in a paradox: "The man who wanders into the twelfth century is lost, unless he can grow prematurely young." The contrast is set up in the preface by the fictive tourists themselves, the old uncle and the young niece. This device is most prominent at the beginning of Chapters 1 and 6 and at the conclusion of Chapter 10. It is exactly as these crucial points that the ambiguity of old and young is most emphatic. In the first two (the entrance to the Mount and to Chartres Cathedral) the imaginative act by which the narrator seeks to recover the vision of youth in the Middle Ages is rendered by invoking the famous "Ode: Intimations of Immortality." In the third (just before the tour proper ends) the full effect of the literary parallel is revealed: through it Adams' entrance into medieval religious art is made possible. By becoming a child again—following both Wordsworth and the Biblical prescript for entering the kingdom of heaven—he can at last experience Chartres in its glory. A detailed study of the analogy will prove rewarding.

This ambiguous play back and forth from age to youth is part of the over-all strategy of shifting between objective and subjective modes. The predominance of one over the other is reversed in *Chartres* from what it was in the *Education*. There the style was mainly dry, hard, and sharp because the persona was exploring the unknown, pitting his intellect against the hopeless multiplicity of the modern world. Here the style is mainly warm and lyrical, giving a sense of re-exploring the familiar to recover a lost unity, the beauty of art if not religion in the Middle Ages. Though the narrator pretends at times to concern himself with historical and architectural facts, and so manages to slip in a great many documentary details, he quickly discounts them as of no interest to mere tourists—just as he had dismissed the subjective episodes in the other book as accidental education. Subjectivity is pervasive in the first half of *Chartres*, especially at every crucial point, with the uncle insisting on an emotional response in himself and in his niece. As niece fuses with uncle, so the reader fuses with both. At the outset he declares his purpose is "to catch not a fact but a feeling." And by the end of part one of the tour there is a flat statement that feeling must prevail:

We have set out to go from Mont-Saint-Michel to Chartres, . . . trying to get, on the way, not technical knowledge; not accurate information; not correct views either on history, art, or religion; not anything that can possibly be useful or instructive; but only a sense of what those centuries had to say, and a sympathy with their ways of saying it.

Then he carefully disavows any devotional intent: "We are not now seeking religion. . . . We are only trying to feel Gothic art."

In the next five chapters, however, as the appeal to emotion is emphasized, the tour is rendered increasingly in religious terms for dramatic effect. By the device of growing prematurely young and learning to feel again, uncle and niece are transformed in gradual stages from modern tourists into medieval pilgrims. Surrounded by the full glory of Chartres Cathedral in "The Court of the Queen of Heaven" (Chapter 10), their identification with the "crowd of kneeling worshippers" becomes complete, and a twelfth-century sacrament is enacted in the present tense. As they lift their eyes "after the miracle of the mass," they see a vision far above the high altar: "There is heaven! and Mary looks down from it, into her church, where she sees us on our knees, and knows each one of us by name. There she actually is—not in symbol or in fancy, but in person." This vision should not be taken as spiritual autobiography, of course. This event took place in Adams' study, not in church. It was created for the sake of its function in the book: a means of access into the medieval world of art and feeling. Even so, the recovery is only transient. As he slips back into the role of twentieth-century tourist, the narrator comments on his "experience" in the past tense:

It was very childlike, very foolish, very beautiful, and very true—as art, at least; . . . when we rise from our knees now, we have finished our pilgrimage. We have done with Chartres. For seven hundred years Chartres has seen pilgrims, coming and going more or less like us, and will perhaps see them for another seven hundred years; but we shall see it no more, and can safely leave the Virgin in her majesty, . . . looking down from a deserted heaven, into an empty church, on a dead faith.

The literary brilliance of this fictive scene consists in the blasphemous shock of dropping the narrator's spiritual progress at its climactic moment. Thereafter the personal story becomes secondary. But the vision has enabled the twentieth-century tourist to see beyond architectural surfaces and so to understand the drama that was acted out between the eleventh and thirteenth centuries.

This is the substance of the second part of *Chartres*. There the mode of presentation changes radically, as Levenson has demonstrated. The action of moving from one architectural shrine to another, which gave the structure to part one, was no longer possible when he turned to exploring the monuments of literature and philosophy, to show how religion permeated medieval society and held it together in a unity. Similarly the narrator's role shifts, and the speaking uncle subsides into a choric figure commenting on the human actors as they perform their parts on the stage of the medieval imagination. It was easier to make their actions dramatic when they were drawn from actual history, as in Chapter 11. This one, "The Three Queens," serves the additional purpose of linking the two halves of the book, as the narrator points out, by "the coincidence that while the Virgin was miraculously using the power of spiritual love to elevate and purify the people, Eleanor and her daughters were using the power of earthly love to discipline and refine the courts." Even when the characters were drawn from fiction and legend he could let them speak from texts that were inherently dramatic, as in the next two chapters showing the dominance of women in secular poetry and the Virgin's pervasive influence in popular accounts of her miracles. But the philosophic texts that were his only documents for the last triad of chapters offered meager possibilities, Levenson continues, and more ingenious tactics were necessary to dramatize his conclusion. For the conflict of reason and intuition, he does not hesitate to invent an imaginary debate between Abélard and his opponents. For the final scholastic synthesis, he avoids a formal analysis of Aquinas' writings and interprets them instead as an elaborate metaphor: a Church Intellectual that paralleled the design of the Church Architectural. And by showing its builder in the process of creating his philosophic edifice, he makes a heroic effort to translate theology into drama.

As the talking uncle becomes more and more a commentator on the main action of medieval history in part two, he becomes less and less aware of his listening niece. But the narrator-auditor device is picked up again in the last chapter to round out the tour. There, in comparing the *Summa Theologiae* to a Gothic cathedral, he declares that the equilibrium of each structure is precarious, showing "the visible effort to throw off a visible strain":

Faith alone supports it, and if Faith fails, Heaven is lost. . . . The delight of its aspirations is flung up to the sky. The pathos of its self-distrust and anguish of doubt is buried in the earth as its last secret. You can read out of it whatever pleases your youth and confidence; to me, this is all.

So the book ends with the uncle resuming his proper role as the rational old man, but not without a challenge to his niece, and all who are young enough, to find if they can a new faith that will unify their world.

If historians rebuke Adams because his concept of medieval unity does not fit the facts, scientists and theologians balk even more at his proposition that St. Thomas' introduction of reason into religion paved the way for

Newton and modern multiplicity. It is argued outright in "The Virgin and the Dynamo," urged suggestively in *Chartres*. Both the *Summa* and the late Gothic cathedral, he says in the latter, were "excessively modern, scientific, and technical"; yet the result was "an art marked by singular unity, which endured and served its purpose until man changed his attitude toward the universe." The medieval vision of unity reached its peak and began its decline simultaneously in the rationalism of the thirteenth century. "From that time, the universe has steadily become more complex and less reducible to a central control."

Adams was clearly more interested in his art than in his argument. For despite his complaint that the literary form of *Chartres* (like that of the *Education*) fails toward the end, as the fictional device of the tour gives way to three essays on the scholastic synthesis from Abélard to Aquinas, he was never more artful than in these final chapters. Under the pretense of expounding theology, he creates in them a drama of the debates illustrating the movement from instinct to reason during the Middle Ages, an ideological counterpart of the architectural metaphor of the transition from Romanesque to Gothic. So they complete the artistic unity of his tour of the French cathedrals, forming a capstone to the structure of *Chartres*. At the same time they provide the link with his next book. The pilgrim, again turned tourist, continues his journey beyond the last page right back into the modern world of doubt and loss, and we next hear him speaking as the persona of the *Education*. In a letter to another and greater creator of fictions, Henry James, he made explicit this relation between the two books:

> I note for your exclusive use the intent of the literary artist—*c'est moi!* —to make this volume a completion and mathematical conclusion from the previous volume about the Thirteenth Century,—the three concluding chapters of this being only a working out to Q.E.D. of the three concluding chapters of that.

It is when they are read thus, as sequels, that *Mont-Saint-Michel and Chartres* and *The Education of Henry Adams* seem most fully what they are— created works of art.

CHARLES R. ANDERSON

A Note on the Text.   The text here followed for the chapters from the two books is that of the first published editions: *The Education of Henry Adams* (Boston: Houghton Mifflin Company, 1918) and *Mont-Saint-Michel and Chartres* (Boston: Houghton Mifflin Company, 1913)—sponsored by the Massachusetts Historical Society and the American Institute of Architects, respectively. The text for Letters 1, 2, and 4 is taken from H. D. Cater, editor, *Henry Adams and His Friends* (Boston: Houghton

Ed. is perhaps the best statement in our literature of the background of our present problems.

Mifflin Company, 1947), pages 558-560, 644-646, and 769-770; for Letter 3: W. C. Ford, editor, *Letters of Henry Adams, 1892-1918* (Boston: Houghton Mifflin Company, 1938), page 546.

An account of Adams's continuously baffled search for some up-to-date, unified meaning or faith, comparable to that which had motivated medieval worshipers.

THE EDUCATION OF HENRY ADAMS[1]

1. *Quincy* (1838-1848)

Note use of 3rd person — emphasizes his "playful" objectivity

UNDER THE SHADOW of Boston State House, turning its back on the house of John Hancock, the little passage called Hancock Avenue runs, or ran, from Beacon Street, skirting the State House grounds, to Mount Vernon Street, on the summit of Beacon Hill; and there, in the third house below Mount Vernon Place, February 16, 1838, a child was born, and christened later by his uncle, the minister of the First Church after the tenets of Boston Unitarianism, as Henry Brooks Adams.

Had he been born in Jerusalem under the shadow of the Temple and circumcised in the Synagogue by his uncle the high priest, under the name of Israel Cohen, he would scarcely have been more distinctly branded, and not much more heavily handicapped in the races of the coming century, in running for such stakes as the century was to offer; but, on the other hand, the ordinary traveller, who does not enter the field of racing, finds advantage in being, so to speak, ticketed through life, with the safeguards of an old, established traffic. Safeguards are often irksome, but sometimes convenient, and if one needs them at all, one is apt to need them badly. A hundred years earlier, such safeguards as his would have secured any young man's success; and although in 1838 their value was not very great compared with what they would have had in 1738, yet the mere accident of starting a twentieth-century career from a nest of associations so colonial—so troglodytic—as the First Church, the Boston State House, Beacon Hill, John Hancock and John Adams, Mount Vernon Street and Quincy, all crowding on ten pounds of unconscious babyhood, was so queer as to offer a subject of curious speculation to the baby long after he had witnessed the solution. What could become of such a child of the seventeenth and eighteenth centuries, when he should wake up to find himself required to play the game of the twentieth? Had he been consulted, would he have cared to play the game at all, holding such cards as he held, and suspecting that the game was to be one of which neither he nor any one else back to the beginning of time knew the rules or the risks or the stakes?

From *The Education of Henry Adams*, by Henry Brooks Adams. Copyright 1946 by Charles F. Adams. Reprinted with the permission of Houghton Mifflin Company.

[1] Since the chronicle of events in this book provides an outward structure, narrative links have been inserted in brackets, in italic, between the selections.

Style: quiet, reserved, cynical

Subtlety and sureness down to the minutest detail make the bk. a masterpiece

Conclusion he believes " chaos was the law of nature; order was the dream of man."

THE EDUCATION OF HENRY ADAMS 343

He was not consulted and was not responsible, but had he been taken into the confidence of his parents, he would certainly have told them to change nothing as far as concerned him. He would have been astounded by his own luck. Probably no child, born in the year, held better cards than he. Whether life was an honest game of chance, or whether the cards were marked and forced, he could not refuse to play his excellent hand. He could never make the usual plea of irresponsibility. He accepted the situation as though he had been a party to it, and under the same circumstances would do it again, the more readily for knowing the exact values. To his life as a whole he was a consenting, contracting party and partner from the moment he was born to the moment he died. Only with that understanding—as a consciously assenting member in full partnership with the society of his age—had his education an interest to himself or to others.

As it happened, he never got to the point of playing the game at all; he lost himself in the study of it, watching the errors of the players; but this is the only interest in the story, which otherwise has no moral and little incident. A story of education—seventy years of it—the practical value remains to the end in doubt, like other values about which men have disputed since the birth of Cain and Abel; but the practical value of the universe has never been stated in dollars. Although every one cannot be a Gargantua-Napoleon-Bismarck and walk off with the great bells of Notre Dame, every one must bear his own universe, and most persons are moderately interested in learning how their neighbors have managed to carry theirs.

This problem of education, started in 1838, went on for three years, while the baby grew, like other babies, unconsciously, as a vegetable, the outside world working as it never had worked before, to get his new universe ready for him. Often in old age he puzzled over the question whether, on the doctrine of chances, he was at liberty to accept himself or his world as an accident. No such accident had ever happened before in human experience. For him, alone, the old universe was thrown into the ash-heap and a new one created. He and his eighteenth-century, troglodytic Boston were suddenly cut apart—separated forever—in act if not in sentiment, by the opening of the Boston and Albany Railroad; the appearance of the first Cunard steamers in the bay; and the telegraphic messages which carried from Baltimore to Washington the news that Henry Clay and James K. Polk were nominated for the Presidency. This was in May, 1844; he was six years old; his new world was ready for use, and only fragments of the old met his eyes.

Of all this that was being done to complicate his education, he knew only the color of yellow. He first found himself sitting on a yellow kitchen floor in strong sunlight. He was three years old when he took this earliest step in education; a lesson of color. The second followed soon; a lesson of taste. On December 3, 1841, he developed scarlet fever. For several days he was as good as dead, reviving only under the careful nursing of his family. When he began to recover strength, about January 1, 1842, his hunger must have been stronger than any other pleasure or pain, for while in after life he retained not the faintest recollection of his illness, he remembered quite clearly his aunt entering the sick-room bearing in her hand a saucer with a baked apple.

The order of impressions retained by memory might naturally be that of color and taste, although one would rather suppose that the sense of pain would be first to educate. In fact, the third recollection of the child was that of discomfort. The moment he could be removed, he was bundled up in blankets and carried from the little house in Hancock Avenue to a larger one which his parents were to occupy for the rest of their lives in the neighboring Mount Vernon Street. The season was midwinter, January 10, 1842, and he never forgot his acute distress for want of air under his blankets, or the noises of moving furniture.

As a means of variation from a normal type, sickness in childhood ought to have a certain value not to be classed under any fitness or unfitness of natural selection; and especially scarlet fever affected boys seriously, both physically and in character, though they might through life puzzle themselves to decide whether it had fitted or unfitted them for success; but this fever of Henry Adams took greater and greater importance in his eyes, from the point of view of education, the longer he lived. At first, the effect was physical. He fell behind his brothers two or three inches in height, and proportionally in bone and weight. His character and processes of mind seemed to share in this fining-down process of scale. He was not good in a fight, and his nerves were more delicate than boys' nerves ought to be. He exaggerated these weaknesses as he grew older. The habit of doubt; of distrusting his own judgment and of totally rejecting the judgment of the world; the tendency to regard every question as open; the hesitation to act except as a choice of evils; the shirking of responsibility; the love of line, form, quality; the horror of ennui; the passion for companionship and the antipathy to society—all these are well-known qualities of New England character in no way peculiar to individuals but in this instance they seemed to be stimulated by the fever, and Henry Adams could never make up his mind whether, on the whole, the change of character was morbid or healthy, good or bad for his purpose. His brothers were the type; he was the variation.

As far as the boy knew, the sickness did not affect him at all, and he grew up in excellent health, bodily and mental, taking life as it was given; accepting its local standards without a difficulty, and enjoying much of it as keenly as any other boy of his age. He seemed to himself quite normal, and his companions seemed always to think him so. Whatever was peculiar about him was education, not character, and came to him, directly and indirectly, as the result of that eighteenth-century inheritance which he took with his name.

The atmosphere of education in which he lived was colonial, revolutionary, almost Cromwellian, as though he were steeped, from his greatest grandmother's birth, in the odor of political crime. Resistance to something was the law of New England nature; the boy looked out on the world with the instinct of resistance; for numberless generations his predecessors had viewed the world chiefly as a thing to be reformed, filled with evil forces to be abolished, and they saw no reason to suppose that they had wholly succeeded in the abolition; the duty was unchanged. That duty implied not only resistance to evil, but hatred of it. Boys naturally look on all force as an enemy, and generally find it so, but the New Englander, whether boy or man, in his long struggle with a stingy or hostile universe, had learned also to love the pleasure of hating; his joys were few.

Politics, as a practice, whatever its professions, had always been the systematic organization of hatreds, and Massachusetts politics had been as harsh
as the climate. The chief charm of New England was harshness of contrasts
and extremes of sensibility—a cold that froze the blood, and a heat that
boiled it—so that the pleasure of hating—one's self if no better victim offered
—was not its rarest amusement; but the charm was a true and natural child of
the soil, not a cultivated weed of the ancients. The violence of the contrast
was real and made the strongest motive of education. The double exterior
nature gave life its relative values. Winter and summer, cold and heat, town
and country, force and freedom, marked two modes of life and thought, balanced like lobes of the brain. Town was winter confinement, school, rule, discipline; straight, gloomy streets, piled with six feet of snow in the middle;
frosts that made the snow sing under wheels or runners; thaws when the
streets became dangerous to cross; society of uncles, aunts, and cousins who
expected children to behave themselves, and who were not always gratified;
above all else, winter represented the desire to escape and go free. Town was
restraint, law, unity. Country, only seven miles away, was liberty, diversity,
outlawry, the endless delight of mere sense impressions given by nature for
nothing, and breathed by boys without knowing it.

Boys are wild animals, rich in the treasures of sense, but the New England
boy had a wider range of emotions than boys of more equable climates. He
felt his nature crudely, as it was meant. To the boy Henry Adams, summer
was drunken. Among senses, smell was the strongest—smell of hot pine-woods
and sweet-fern in the scorching summer noon; of new-mown hay; of ploughed
earth; of box hedges; of peaches, lilacs, syringas; of stables, barns, cow-yards;
of salt water and low tide on the marshes; nothing came amiss. Next to smell
came taste, and the children knew the taste of everything they saw or touched,
from pennyroyal and flagroot to the shell of a pignut and the letters of a
spelling-book—the taste of A-B, AB, suddenly revived on the boy's tongue
sixty years afterwards. Light, line, and color as sensual pleasures, came later
and were as crude as the rest. The New England light is glare, and the atmosphere harshens color. The boy was a full man before he ever knew what was
meant by atmosphere; his idea of pleasure in light was the blaze of a New
England sun. His idea of color was a peony, with the dew of early morning on
its petals. The intense blue of the sea, as he saw it a mile or two away, from
the Quincy hills; the cumuli in a June afternoon sky; the strong reds and
greens and purples of colored prints and children's picture-books, as the American colors then ran; these were ideals. The opposites or antipathies, were the
cold grays of November evenings, and the thick, muddy thaws of Boston winter. With such standards, the Bostonian could not but develop a double nature. Life was a double thing. After a January blizzard, the boy who could
look with pleasure into the violent snow-glare of the cold white sunshine, with
its intense light and shade, scarcely knew what was meant by tone. He could
reach it only by education.

Winter and summer, then, were two hostile lives, and bred two separate
natures. Winter was always the effort to live; summer was tropical license.
Whether the children rolled in the grass, or waded in the brook, or swam in
the salt ocean, or sailed in the bay, or fished for smelts in the creeks, or netted

minnows in the salt-marshes, or took to the pine-woods and the granite quarries, or chased muskrats and hunted snapping-turtles in the swamps, or mushrooms or nuts on the autumn hills, summer and country were always sensual living, while winter was always compulsory learning. Summer was the multiplicity of nature; winter was school.

The bearing of the two seasons on the education of Henry Adams was no fancy; it was the most decisive force he ever knew; it ran through life, and made the division between its perplexing, warring, irreconcilable problems, irreducible opposites, with growing emphasis to the last year of study. From earliest childhood the boy was accustomed to feel that, for him, life was double. Winter and summer, town and country, law and liberty, were hostile, and the man who pretended they were not, was in his eyes a schoolmaster— that is, a man employed to tell lies to little boys. Though Quincy was but two hours' walk from Beacon Hill, it belonged in a different world. For two hundred years, every Adams, from father to son, had lived within sight of State Street,[2] and sometimes had lived in it, yet none had ever taken kindly to the town, or been taken kindly by it. The boy inherited his double nature. He knew as yet nothing about his great-grandfather, who had died a dozen years before his own birth: he took for granted that any great-grandfather of his must have always been good, and his enemies wicked; but he divined his great-grandfather's character from his own. Never for a moment did he connect the two ideas of Boston and John Adams; they were separate and antagonistic; the idea of John Adams went with Quincy. He knew his grandfather John Quincy Adams only as an old man of seventy-five or eighty who was friendly and gentle with him, but except that he heard his grandfather always called "the President," and his grandmother "the Madam," he had no reason to suppose that his Adams grandfather differed in character from his Brooks grandfather who was equally kind and benevolent. He liked the Adams side best, but for no other reason than that it reminded him of the country, the summer, and the absence of restraint. Yet he felt also that Quincy was in a way inferior to Boston, and that socially Boston looked down on Quincy. The reason was clear enough even to a five-year old child. Quincy had no Boston style. Little enough style had either; a simpler manner of life and thought could hardly exist, short of cave-dwelling. The flint-and-steel with which his grandfather Adams used to light his own fires in the early morning was still on the mantelpiece of his study. The idea of a livery or even a dress for servants, or of an evening toilette, was next to blasphemy. Bathrooms, water-supplies, lighting, heating, and the whole array of domestic comforts, were unknown at Quincy. Boston had already a bathroom, a water-supply, a furnace, and gas. The superiority of Boston was evident, but a child liked it no better for that.

The magnificence of his grandfather Brooks's[3] house in Pearl Street or South Street has long ago disappeared, but perhaps his country house at Med-

[2] The financial center of Boston, symbol to Adams of the conservative branch of the Federalist party with whom his ancestors had always been at odds, and later in the nineteenth century a symbol of the commercial-industrial forces in America opposed to the humanistic values of Quincy.

[3] Peter Chardon Brooks on his death in 1849 left an estate valued at two million dollars, the largest in Boston. Adams' mother was one of his heirs.

ford may still remain to show what impressed the mind of a boy in 1845 with the idea of city splendor. The President's place at Quincy was the larger and older and far the more interesting of the two; but a boy felt at once its inferiority in fashion. It showed plainly enough its want of wealth. It smacked of colonial age, but not of Boston style or plush curtains. To the end of his life he never quite overcame the prejudice thus drawn in with his childish breath. He never could compel himself to care for nineteenth-century style. He was never able to adopt it, any more than his father or grandfather or great-grandfather had done. Not that he felt it as particularly hostile, for he reconciled himself to much that was worse; but because, for some remote reason, he was born an eighteenth-century child. The old house at Quincy was eighteenth century. What style it had was in its Queen Anne mahogany panels and its Louis Seize chairs and sofas. The panels belonged to an old colonial Vassall who built the house; the furniture had been brought back from Paris in 1789 or 1801 or 1817, along with porcelain and books and much else of old diplomatic remnants; and neither of the two eighteenth-century styles—neither English Queen Anne nor French Louis Seize—was comfortable for a boy, or for any one else. The dark mahogany had been painted white to suit daily life in winter gloom. Nothing seemed to favor, for a child's objects, the older forms. On the contrary, most boys, as well as grown-up people, preferred the new, with good reason, and the child felt himself distinctly at a disadvantage for the taste.

Nor had personal preference any share in his bias. The Brooks grandfather was as amiable and as sympathetic as the Adams grandfather. Both were born in 1767, and both died in 1848. Both were kind to children, and both belonged rather to the eighteenth than to the nineteenth centuries. The child knew no difference between them except that one was associated with winter and the other with summer; one with Boston, the other with Quincy. Even with Medford, the association was hardly easier. Once as a very young boy he was taken to pass a few days with his grandfather Brooks under charge of his aunt, but became so violently homesick that within twenty-four hours he was brought back in disgrace. Yet he could not remember ever being seriously homesick again.

The attachment to Quincy was not altogether sentimental or wholly sympathetic. Quincy was not a bed of thornless roses. Even there the curse of Cain set its mark. There as elsewhere a cruel universe combined to crush a child. As though three or four vigorous brothers and sisters, with the best will, were not enough to crush any child, every one else conspired towards an education which he hated. From cradle to grave this problem of running order through chaos, direction through space, discipline through freedom, unity through multiplicity, has always been, and must always be, the task of education, as it is the moral of religion, philosophy, science, art, politics, and economy; but a boy's will is his life, and he dies when it is broken, as the colt dies in harness, taking a new nature in becoming tame. Rarely has the boy felt kindly towards his tamers. Between him and his master has always been war. Henry Adams never knew a boy of his generation to like a master, and the task of remaining on friendly terms with one's own family, in such a relation, was never easy.

All the more singular it seemed afterwards to him that his first serious contact with the President should have been a struggle of will, in which the old man almost necessarily defeated the boy, but instead of leaving, as usual in such defeats, a lifelong sting, left rather an impression of as fair treatment as could be expected from a natural enemy. The boy met seldom with such restraint. He could not have been much more than six years old at the time— seven at the utmost—and his mother had taken him to Quincy for a long stay with the President during the summer. What became of the rest of the family he quite forgot; but he distinctly remembered standing at the house door one summer morning in a passionate outburst of rebellion against going to school. Naturally his mother was the immediate victim of his rage; that is what mothers are for, and boys also; but in this case the boy had his mother at unfair disadvantage, for she was a guest, and had no means of enforcing obedience. Henry showed a certain tactical ability by refusing to start, and he met all efforts at compulsion by successful, though too vehement protest. He was in fair way to win, and was holding his own, with sufficient energy, at the bottom of the long staircase which led up to the door of the President's library, when the door opened, and the old man slowly came down. Putting on his hat, he took the boy's hand without a word, and walked with him, paralyzed by awe, up the road to the town. After the first moments of consternation at this interference in a domestic dispute, the boy reflected that an old gentleman close on eighty would never trouble himself to walk near a mile on a hot summer morning over a shadeless road to take a boy to school, and that it would be strange if a lad imbued with the passion of freedom could not find a corner to dodge around, somewhere before reaching the school door. Then and always, the boy insisted that this reasoning justified his apparent submission; but the old man did not stop, and the boy saw all his strategical points turned, one after another, until he found himself seated inside the school, and obviously the centre of curious if not malevolent criticism. Not till then did the President release his hand and depart.

The point was that this act, contrary to the inalienable rights of boys, and nullifying the social compact, ought to have made him dislike his grandfather for life. He could not recall that it had this effect even for a moment. With a certain maturity of mind, the child must have recognized that the President, though a tool of tyranny, had done his disreputable work with a certain intelligence. He had shown no temper, no irritation, no personal feeling, and had made no display of force. Above all, he had held his tongue. During their long walk he had said nothing; he had uttered no syllable of revolting cant about the duty of obedience and the wickedness of resistance to law; he had shown no concern in the matter; hardly even a consciousness of the boy's existence. Probably his mind at that moment was actually troubling itself little about his grandson's iniquities, and much about the iniquities of President Polk, but the boy could scarcely at that age feel the whole satisfaction of thinking that President Polk was to be the vicarious victim of his own sins, and he gave his grandfather credit for intelligent silence. For this forbearance he felt instinctive respect. He admitted force as a form of right; he admitted even temper, under protest; but the seeds of a moral education would at that moment have fallen on the stoniest soil in Quincy, which is, as every one knows, the stoniest glacial and tidal drift known in any Puritan land.

Neither party to this momentary disagreement can have felt rancor, for during these three or four summers the old President's relations with the boy were friendly and almost intimate. Whether his older brothers and sisters were still more favored he failed to remember, but he was himself admitted to a sort of familiarity which, when in his turn he had reached old age, rather shocked him, for it must have sometimes tried the President's patience. He hung about the library; handled the books; deranged the papers; ransacked the drawers; searched the old purses and pocket-books for foreign coins; drew the sword-cane; snapped the travelling-pistols; upset everything in the corners, and penetrated the President's dressing-closet where a row of tumblers, inverted on the shelf, covered caterpillars which were supposed to become moths or butterflies, but never did. The Madam bore with fortitude the loss of the tumblers which her husband purloined for these hatcheries; but she made protest when he carried off her best cut-glass bowls to plant with acorns or peachstones that he might see the roots grow, but which, she said, he commonly forgot like the caterpillars.

At that time the President rode the hobby of tree-culture, and some fine old trees should still remain to witness it, unless they have been improved off the ground; but his was a restless mind, and although he took his hobbies seriously and would have been annoyed had his grandchild asked whether he was bored like an English duke, he probably cared more for the processes than for the results, so that his grandson was saddened by the sight and smell of peaches and pears, the best of their kind, which he brought up from the garden to rot on his shelves for seed. With the inherited virtues of his Puritan ancestors, the little boy Henry conscientiously brought up to him in his study the finest peaches he found in the garden, and ate only the less perfect. Naturally he ate more by way of compensation, but the act showed that he bore no grudge. As for his grandfather, it is even possible that he may have felt a certain self-reproach for his temporary rôle of schoolmaster—seeing that his own career did not offer proof of the worldly advantages of docile obedience—for there still exists somewhere a little volume of critically edited Nursery Rhymes with the boy's name in full written in the President's trembling hand on the fly-leaf. Of course there was also the Bible, given to each child at birth, with the proper inscription in the President's hand on the fly-leaf; while their grandfather Brooks supplied the silver mugs.

So many Bibles and silver mugs had to be supplied, that a new house, or cottage, was built to hold them. It was "on the hill," five minutes' walk above "the old house," with a far view eastward over Quincy Bay, and northward over Boston. Till his twelfth year, the child passed his summers there, and his pleasures of childhood mostly centred in it. Of education he had as yet little to complain. Country schools were not very serious. Nothing stuck to the mind except home impressions, and the sharpest were those of kindred children; but as influences that warped a mind, none compared with the mere effect of the back of the President's bald head, as he sat in his pew on Sundays, in line with that of President Quincy,[4] who, though some ten years younger, seemed to children about the same age. Before railways entered the New England town, every parish church showed half-a-dozen of these leading

[4] Josiah Quincy, President of Harvard from 1829 to 1845.

citizens, with gray hair, who sat on the main aisle in the best pews, and had sat there, or in some equivalent dignity, since the time of St. Augustine, if not since the glacial epoch. It was unusual for boys to sit behind a President grandfather, and to read over his head the tablet in memory of a President great-grandfather, who had "pledged his life, his fortune, and his sacred honor" to secure the independence of his country and so forth; but boys naturally supposed, without much reasoning, that other boys had the equivalent of President grandfathers, and that churches would always go on, with the bald-headed leading citizens on the main aisle, and presidents or their equivalents on the walls. The Irish gardener once said to the child: "You'll be thinkin' you'll be President too!" The casuality of the remark made so strong an impression on his mind that he never forgot it. He could not remember ever to have thought on the subject; to him, that there should be a doubt of his being President was a new idea. What had been would continue to be. He doubted neither about Presidents nor about Churches, and no one suggested at that time a doubt whether a system of society which had lasted since Adam would outlast one Adams more.

The Madam was a little more remote than the President, but more decorative. She stayed much in her own room with the Dutch tiles, looking out on her garden with the box walks, and seemed a fragile creature to a boy who sometimes brought her a note or a message, and took distinct pleasure in looking at her delicate face under what seemed to him very becoming caps. He liked her refined figure; her gentle voice and manner; her vague effect of not belonging there, but to Washington or to Europe, like her furniture, and writing-desk with little glass doors above and little eighteenth-century volumes in old binding, labelled "Peregrine Pickle" or "Tom Jones" or "Hannah More." Try as she might, the Madam could never be Bostonian, and it was her cross in life, but to the boy it was her charm. Even at that age, he felt drawn to it. The Madam's life had been in truth far from Boston. She was born in London in 1775, daughter of Joshua Johnson, an American merchant, brother of Governor Thomas Johnson of Maryland; and Catherine Nuth, of an English family in London. Driven from England by the Revolutionary War, Joshua Johnson took his family to Nantes, where they remained till the peace. The girl Louisa Catherine was nearly ten years old when brought back to London, and her sense of nationality must have been confused; but the influence of the Johnsons and the services of Joshua obtained for him from President Washington the appointment of Consul in London on the organization of the Government in 1790. In 1794 President Washington appointed John Quincy Adams Minister to The Hague. He was twenty-seven years old when he returned to London, and found the Consul's house a very agreeable haunt. Louisa was then twenty.

At that time, and long afterwards, the Consul's house, far more than the Minister's, was the centre of contact for travelling Americans, either official or other. The Legation was a shifting point, between 1785 and 1815; but the Consulate, far down in the City, near the Tower, was convenient and inviting; so inviting that it proved fatal to young Adams. Louisa was charming, like a Romney portrait, but among her many charms that of being a New England woman was not one. The defect was serious. Her future mother-in-law, Abigail, a famous New England woman whose authority over her turbulent husband, the second President, was hardly so great as that which she exercised over her son, the sixth to be, was troubled by the fear that Louisa might not be made of stuff stern enough, or brought up in conditions severe enough, to suit a New England climate, or to make an efficient wife for her paragon son, and Abigail was right on that point, as on most others where sound judgment was involved; but sound judgment is sometimes a source of weakness rather than of force, and John Quincy already had reason to think that his mother held sound judgments on the subject of daughters-in-law which human nature, since the fall of Eve, made Adams helpless to realize. Being three thousand miles away from his mother, and equally far in love, he married Louisa in London, July 26, 1797, and took her to Berlin to be the head of the United States Legation. During three or four exciting years, the young bride lived in Berlin; whether she was happy or not, whether she was content or not, whether she was socially successful or not, her descendants did not surely know; but in any case she could by no chance have become educated there for a life in Quincy or Boston. In 1801 the overthrow of the Federalist Party[5] drove her and her husband to America, and she became at last a member of the Quincy household, but by that time her children needed all her attention, and she remained there with occasional winters in Boston and Washington, till 1809. Her husband was made Senator in 1803, and in 1809 was appointed Minister to Russia. She went with him to St. Petersburg, taking her baby, Charles Francis, born in 1807; but broken-hearted at having to leave her two older boys behind. The life at St. Petersburg was hardly gay for her; they were far too poor to shine in that extravagant society; but she survived it, though her little girl baby did not, and in the winter of 1814-15, alone with the boy of seven years old, crossed Europe from St. Petersburg to Paris, in her travelling-carriage, passing through the armies, and reaching Paris in the *Cent Jours* after Napoleon's return from Elba. Her husband next went to England as Minister, and she was for two years at the Court of the Regent. In 1817 her husband came home to be Secretary of State, and she lived for eight years in F Street, doing her work of entertainer for President Monroe's administration. Next she lived four miserable years in the White House. When that chapter was closed in 1829, she had earned the right to be tired and delicate, but she still had fifteen years to serve as wife of a Member of the House, after her husband went back to Congress in 1833. Then it was that the little Henry, her grandson, first remembered her, from 1843 to 1848, sitting in her panelled room, at breakfast, with her heavy silver teapot and sugar-bowl and cream-jug, which still exist somewhere as an heirloom of the modern safety-vault. By that time she was seventy years old or more, and thoroughly weary of being beaten about a stormy world. To the boy she seemed singularly peaceful, a vision of silver gray, presiding over her old President and her Queen Anne mahogany; an exotic, like her Sèvres china; an object of deference to every one, and of great affection to her son Charles; but hardly more Bostonian than she had been fifty years before, on her wedding-day, in the shadow of the Tower of London.

Such a figure was even less fitted than that of her old husband, the Presi-

[5] By the election of Thomas Jefferson to the presidency and the rise of his democratic ("Republican") party.

dent, to impress on a boy's mind, the standards of the coming century. She was Louis Seize, like the furniture. The boy knew nothing of her interior life, which had been, as the venerable Abigail, long since at peace, foresaw, one of severe stress and little pure satisfaction. He never dreamed that from her might come some of those doubts and self-questionings, those hesitations, those rebellions against law and discipline, which marked more than one of her descendants; but he might even then have felt some vague instinctive suspicion that he was to inherit from her the seeds of the primal sin, the fall from grace, the curse of Abel, that he was not of pure New England stock, but half exotic. As a child of Quincy he was not a true Bostonian, but even as a child of Quincy he inherited a quarter taint of Maryland blood. Charles Francis, half Marylander by birth, had hardly seen Boston till he was ten years old, when his parents left him there at school in 1817, and he never forgot the experience. He was to be nearly as old as his mother had been in 1845, before he quite accepted Boston, or Boston quite accepted him.

A boy who began his education in these surroundings, with physical strength inferior to that of his brothers, and with a certain delicacy of mind and bone, ought rightly to have felt at home in the eighteenth century and should, in proper self-respect, have rebelled against the standards of the nineteenth. The atmosphere of his first ten years must have been very like that of his grandfather at the same age, from 1767 till 1776, barring the battle of Bunker Hill, and even as late as 1846, the battle of Bunker Hill remained actual. The tone of Boston society was colonial. The true Bostonian always knelt in self-abasement before the majesty of English standards; far from concealing it as a weakness, he was proud of it as his strength. The eighteenth century ruled society long after 1850. Perhaps the boy began to shake it off rather earlier than most of his mates.

Indeed this prehistoric stage of education ended rather abruptly with his tenth year. One winter morning he was conscious of a certain confusion in the house in Mount Vernon Street, and gathered, from such words as he could catch, that the President, who happened to be then staying there, on his way to Washington, had fallen and hurt himself. Then he heard the word paralysis. After that day he came to associate the word with the figure of his grandfather, in a tall-backed, invalid armchair, on one side of the spare bedroom fireplace, and one of his old friends, Dr. Parkman or P. P. F. Degrand, on the other side, both dozing.

The end of this first, or ancestral and Revolutionary, chapter came on February 21, 1848—and the month of February brought life and death as a family habit—when the eighteenth century, as an actual and living companion, vanished. If the scene on the floor of the House, when the old President fell, struck the still simple-minded American public with a sensation unusually dramatic, its effect on a ten-year-old boy, whose boy-life was fading away with the life of his grandfather, could not be slight. One had to pay for Revolutionary patriots; grandfathers and grandmothers; Presidents; diplomats; Queen Anne mahogany and Louis Seize chairs, as well as for Stuart portraits. Such things warp young life. Americans commonly believed that they ruined it, and perhaps the practical common-sense of the American mind judged right. Many a boy might be ruined by much less than the emotions of the

funeral service in the Quincy church, with its surroundings of national respect and family pride. By another dramatic chance it happened that the
clergyman of the parish, Dr. Lunt, was an unusual pulpit orator, the ideal of
a somewhat austere intellectual type, such as the school of Buckminster and
Channing inherited from the old Congregational clergy. His extraordinarily refined appearance, his dignity of manner, his deeply cadenced voice, his remarkable English and his fine appreciation, gave to the funeral service a character that left an overwhelming impression on the boy's mind. He was to see
many great functions—funerals and festivals—in after-life, till his only
thought was to see no more, but he never again witnessed anything nearly so
impressive to him as the last services at Quincy over the body of one President and the ashes of another.

The effect of the Quincy service was deepened by the official ceremony
which afterwards took place in Faneuil Hall, when the boy was taken to hear
his uncle, Edward Everett, deliver a Eulogy. Like all Mr. Everett's orations,
it was an admirable piece of oratory, such as only an admirable orator and
scholar could create; too good for a ten-year-old boy to appreciate at its value;
but already the boy knew that the dead President could not be in it, and had
even learned why he would have been out of place there; for knowledge was
beginning to come fast. The shadow of the War of 1812 still hung over State
Street; the shadow of the Civil War to come had already begun to darken
Faneuil Hall. No rhetoric could have reconciled Mr. Everett's audience to
his subject. How could he say there, to an assemblage of Bostonians in the
heart of mercantile Boston, that the only distinctive mark of all the Adamses,
since old Sam Adams's father a hundred and fifty years before, had been their
inherited quarrel with State Street, which had again and again broken out into
riot, bloodshed, personal feuds, foreign and civil war, wholesale banishments
and confiscations, until the history of Florence was hardly more turbulent than
that of Boston? How could he whisper the word Hartford Convention[6] before
the men who had made it? What would have been said had he suggested the
chance of Secession and Civil War?

Thus already, at ten years old, the boy found himself standing face to face
with a dilemma that might have puzzled an early Christian. What was he?—
where was he going? Even then he felt that something was wrong, but he concluded that it must be Boston. Quincy had always been right, for Quincy represented a moral principle—the principle of resistance to Boston. His Adams
ancestors must have been right, since they were always hostile to State Street.
If State Street was wrong, Quincy must be right! Turn the dilemma as he
pleased, he still came back on the eighteenth century and the law of Resistance; of Truth; of Duty, and of Freedom. He was a ten-year-old priest and
politician. He could under no circumstances have guessed what the next fifty
years had in store, and no one could teach him; but sometimes, in his old age,
he wondered—and could never decide—whether the most clear and certain
knowledge would have helped him. Supposing he had seen a New York stock-
list of 1900, and had studied the statistics of railways, telegraphs, coal, and
steel—would he have quitted his eighteenth-century, his ancestral prejudices,

[6] A secret Federalist meeting in 1814 threatening resistance to President Madison
for continuing to prosecute the war against England.

his abstract ideals, his semi-clerical training, and the rest, in order to perform an expiatory pilgrimage to State Street, and ask for the fatted calf of his grandfather Brooks and a clerkship in the Suffolk Bank?

Sixty years afterwards he was still unable to make up his mind. Each course had its advantages, but the material advantages, looking back, seemed to lie wholly in State Street.

[*In the same year that his grandfather ex-President Adams died, his father Charles Francis Adams was nominated for Vice-President by the new antislavery or Free Soil Party. He was not elected, but young Adams learned much about politics from the discussions of liberal Republicans at his home. The next year, 1849, his family inherited wealth on the death of his Brooks grandfather, the richest man in Boston. A trip to Washington in 1850 gave him his first impressions of the South, in contrast to New England. During the decade 1848-1858 Adams continued his education at Boston schools and Harvard College, followed by postgraduate studies at the University of Berlin.*]

5. Berlin (1858-1859)

A fourth child has the strength of his weakness. Being of no great value, he may throw himself away if he likes, and never be missed. Charles Francis Adams, the father, felt no love for Europe, which, as he and all the world agreed, unfitted Americans for America. A captious critic might have replied that all the success he or his father or his grandfather achieved was chiefly due to the field that Europe gave them, and it was more than likely that without the help of Europe they would have all remained local politicians or lawyers, like their neighbors, to the end. Strictly followed, the rule would have obliged them never to quit Quincy; and, in fact, so much more timid are parents for their children than for themselves, that Mr. and Mrs. Adams would have been content to see their children remain forever in Mount Vernon Street, unexposed to the temptations of Europe, could they have relied on the moral influences of Boston itself. Although the parents little knew what took place under their eyes, even the mothers saw enough to make them uneasy. Perhaps their dread of vice, haunting past and present, worried them less than their dread of daughters-in-law or sons-in-law who might not fit into the somewhat narrow quarters of home. On all sides were risks. Every year some young person alarmed the parental heart even in Boston, and although the temptations of Europe were irresistible, removal from the temptations of Boston might be imperative. The boy Henry wanted to go to Europe; he seemed well behaved, when any one was looking at him; he observed conventions, when he could not escape them; he was never quarrelsome, towards a superior; his morals were apparently good, and his moral principles, if he had any, were not known to be bad. Above all, he was timid and showed a certain sense of self-respect, when in public view. What he was at heart, no one could say; least of all himself; but he was probably human, and no worse than some others. Therefore, when he presented to an exceedingly indulgent father and mother his request to begin at a German university the study of the Civil Law—although neither he nor they knew what the Civil Law was, or any reason for his studying it—the parents dutifully consented, and walked with him down to the railway-station at Quincy to bid him good-bye, with a smile which he almost thought a tear.

Whether the boy deserved such indulgence, or was worth it, he knew no more than they, or than a professor at Harvard College; but whether worthy or not, he began his third or fourth attempt at education in November, 1858, by sailing on the steamer Persia. . . .

[Adams first stopped in England for a brief visit before proceeding to Antwerp, Belgium, and then to his destination, Berlin. Professor Lowell of Harvard had urged him to continue his studies at the university there.]

Education went backward. Adams, still a boy, could not guess how intensely intimate this London grime was to become to him as a man, but he could still less conceive himself returning to it fifty years afterwards, noting at each turn how the great city grew smaller as it doubled in size; cheaper as it quadrupled its wealth; less imperial as its empire widened; less dignified as it tried to be civil. He liked it best when he hated it. Education began at the end, or perhaps would end at the beginning. Thus far it had remained in the eighteenth century, and the next step took it back to the sixteenth. He crossed to Antwerp. As the Baron Osy steamed up the Scheldt in the morning mists, a travelling band on deck began to play, and groups of peasants, working along the fields, dropped their tools to join in dancing. Ostade and Teniers were as much alive as they ever were, and even the Duke of Alva was still at home. The thirteenth-century cathedral [1] towered above a sixteenth-century mass of tiled roofs, ending abruptly in walls and a landscape that had not changed. The taste of the town was thick, rich, ripe, like a sweet wine; it was mediæval, so that Rubens seemed modern; it was one of the strongest and fullest flavors that ever touched the young man's palate; but he might as well have drunk out his excitement in old Malmsey, for all the education he got from it. Even in art, one can hardly begin with Antwerp Cathedral and the Descent from the Cross. He merely got drunk on his emotions, and had then to get sober as he best could. He was terribly sober when he saw Antwerp half a century afterwards. One lesson he did learn without suspecting that he must immediately lose it. He felt his middle ages and the sixteenth century alive. He was young enough, and the towns were dirty enough—unimproved, unrestored, untouristed—to retain the sense of reality. As a taste or a smell, it was education, especially because it lasted barely ten years longer; but it was education only sensual. He never dreamed of trying to educate himself to the Descent from the Cross. He was only too happy to feel himself kneeling at the foot of the Cross; he learned only to loathe the sordid necessity of getting up again, and going about his stupid business.

This was one of the foreseen dangers of Europe, but it vanished rapidly enough to reassure the most anxious of parents. Dropped into Berlin one morning without guide or direction, the young man in search of education

---

[1] Actually a church, not begun until the mid-fourteenth century, and not finished until the sixteenth. The "Descent from the Cross," mentioned below, was one of three paintings for the church made by Rubens about a hundred years after its completion.

floundered in a mere mess of misunderstandings. He could never recall what
he expected to find, but whatever he expected, it had no relation with what
it turned out to be. A student at twenty takes easily to anything, even to Berlin,
and he would have accepted the thirteenth century pure and simple since his
guides assured him that this was his right path; but a week's experience left
him dazed and dull. Faith held out, but the paths grew dim. Berlin astonished
him, but he had no lack of friends to show him all the amusement it had to
offer. Within a day or two he was running about with the rest to beer-cellars
and music-halls and dance-rooms, smoking bad tobacco, drinking poor beer,
and eating sauerkraut and sausages as though he knew no better. This was
easy. One can always descend the social ladder. The trouble came when he
asked for the education he was promised. His friends took him to be registered
as a student of the university; they selected his professors and courses; they
showed him where to buy the Institutes of Gaius and several German works on
the Civil Law in numerous volumes; and they led him to his first lecture.

His first lecture was his last. The young man was not very quick, and he
had almost religious respect for his guides and advisers; but he needed no
more than one hour to satisfy him that he had made another failure in education, and this time a fatal one. That the language would require at least
three months' hard work before he could touch the Law was an annoying
discovery; but the shock that upset him was the discovery of the university itself. He had thought Harvard College a torpid school, but it was instinct with
life compared with all that he could see of the University of Berlin. The German students were strange animals, but their professors were beyond pay. The
mental attitude of the university was not of an American world. What sort of
instruction prevailed in other branches, or in science, Adams had no occasion
to ask, but in the Civil Law he found only the lecture system in its deadliest
form as it flourished in the thirteenth century. The professor mumbled his
comments; the students made, or seemed to make, notes; they could have
learned from books or discussion in a day more than they could learn from
him in a month, but they must pay his fees, follow his course, and be his
scholars, if they wanted a degree. To an American the result was worthless. He
could make no use of the Civil Law without some previous notion of the
Common Law; but the student who knew enough of the Common Law to
understand what he wanted, had only to read the Pandects or the commentators at his ease in America, and be his own professor. Neither the
method nor the matter nor the manner could profit an American education.

This discovery seemed to shock none of the students. They went to the
lectures, made notes, and read textbooks, but never pretended to take their
professor seriously. They were much more serious in reading Heine. They
knew no more than Heine what good they were getting, beyond the Berlin
accent—which was bad; and the beer—which was not to compare with Munich; and the dancing—which was better at Vienna. They enjoyed the beer
and music, but they refused to be responsible for the education. Anyway, as
they defended themselves, they were learning the language. . . .

Before the month of April arrived, the experiment of German education
had reached this point. Nothing was left of it except the ghost of the Civil
Law shut up in the darkest of closets, never to gibber again before any one

who could repeat the story. The derisive Jew laughter of Heine ran through
the university and everything else in Berlin. Of course, when one is twenty
years old, life is bound to be full, if only of Berlin beer, although German
student life was on the whole the thinnest of beer, as an American looked on
it, but though nothing except small fragments remained of the education that
had been so promising—or promised—this is only what most often happens in
life, when by-products turn out to be more valuable than staples. The German university and German law were failures; German society, in an American sense, did not exist, or if it existed, never showed itself to an American;
the German theatre, on the other hand, was excellent, and German opera,
with the ballet, was almost worth a journey to Berlin; but the curious and perplexing result of the total failure of German education was that the student's
only clear gain—his single step to a higher life—came from time wasted;
studies neglected; vices indulged; education reversed;—it came from the despised beer-garden and music-hall; and it was accidental, unintended, unforeseen.

When his companions insisted on passing two or three afternoons in the
week at music-halls, drinking beer, smoking German tobacco, and looking at
fat German women knitting, while an orchestra played dull music, Adams
went with them for the sake of the company, but with no pretence of enjoyment; and when Mr. Apthorp gently protested that he exaggerated his indifference, for of course he enjoyed Beethoven, Adams replied simply that he
loathed Beethoven; and felt a slight surprise when Mr. Apthorp and the others
laughed as though they thought it humor. He saw no humor in it. He supposed that, except musicians, every one thought Beethoven a bore, as every one
except mathematicians thought mathematics a bore. Sitting thus at his beer-
table, mentally impassive, he was one day surprised to notice that his mind followed the movement of a Sinfonie. He could not have been more astonished
had he suddenly read a new language. Among the marvels of education, this
was the most marvellous. A prison-wall that barred his senses on one great side
of life, suddenly fell, of its own accord, without so much as his knowing when
it happened. Amid the fumes of coarse tobacco and poor beer, surrounded
by the commonest of German Haus-frauen, a new sense burst out like a flower
in his life, so superior to the old senses, so bewildering, so astonished at its own
existence, that he could not credit it, and watched it as something apart,
accidental, and not to be trusted. He slowly came to admit that Beethoven
had partly become intelligible to him, but he was the more inclined to think
that Beethoven must be much overrated as a musician, to be so easily followed. This could not be called education, for he had never so much as listened to the music. He had been thinking of other things. Mere mechanical
repetition of certain sounds had stuck to his unconscious mind. Beethoven
might have this power, but not Wagner, or at all events not the Wagner later
than "Tannhäuser." Near forty years passed before he reached the "Götter-
dämmerung."

One might talk of the revival of an atrophied sense—the mechanical reaction of a sleeping consciousness—but no other sense awoke. His sense of line
and color remained as dull as ever, and as far as ever below the level of an artist.
His metaphysical sense did not spring into life, so that his mind could leap

the bars of German expression into sympathy with the idealities of Kant and Hegel. Although he insisted that his faith in German thought and literature was exalted, he failed to approach German thought, and he shed never a tear of emotion over the pages of Goethe and Schiller. When his father rashly ventured from time to time to write him a word of common sense, the young man would listen to no sense at all, but insisted that Berlin was the best of educations in the best of Germanies; yet, when, at last, April came, and some genius suggested a tramp in Thüringen, his heart sang like a bird; he realized what a nightmare he had suffered, and he made up his mind that, wherever else he might, in the infinities of space and time, seek for education, it should not be again in Berlin.

[After another year and a half in Europe, devoted to independent study and travel, Adams returned home. He spent the year 1860-1861 in Washington as secretary to his father, then a member of Congress. When Charles Francis Adams was appointed United States Minister to the Court of St. James, his son accompanied him, again in the capacity of private secretary. During the whole of the Civil War and for three years thereafter he lived in England. His position at the center of international diplomacy gave him a wide acquaintance with leaders in British government and society. He also made many personal friends, including distinguished men in science, literature, and art. In 1868 he returned to Washington as an observer and free lance writer, contributing numerous essays on politics, current events, and history to newspapers and magazines. In the summer of 1870 he went to England for a vacation.]

19. Chaos (1870)

* * *

He had been some weeks in London when he received a telegram from his brother-in-law at the Bagni di Lucca telling him that his sister had been thrown from a cab and injured, and that he had better come on. He started that night, and reached the Bagni di Lucca on the second day. Tetanus had already set in.

The last lesson—the sum and term of education—began then. He had passed through thirty years of rather varied experience without having once felt the shell of custom broken. He had never seen Nature—only her surface —the sugar-coating that she shows to youth. Flung suddenly in his face, with the harsh brutality of chance, the terror of the blow stayed by him thenceforth for life, until repetition made it more than the will could struggle with; more than he could call on himself to bear. He found his sister, a woman of forty, as gay and brilliant in the terrors of lockjaw as she had been in the careless fun of 1859, lying in bed in consequence of a miserable cab-accident that had bruised her foot. Hour by hour the muscles grew rigid, while the mind remained bright, until after ten days of fiendish torture she died in convulsions.

One had heard and read a great deal about death, and even seen a little of it, and knew by heart the thousand commonplaces of religion and poetry which seemed to deaden one's senses and veil the horror. Society being immortal, could put on immortality at will. Adams being mortal, felt only the mortality. Death took features altogether new to him, in these rich and sensuous surroundings. Nature enjoyed it, played with it, the horror added to her charm, she liked the torture, and smothered her victim with caresses. Never had one seen her so winning. The hot Italian summer brooded outside, over the market-place and the picturesque peasants, and, in the singular color of the Tuscan atmosphere, the hills and vineyards of the Apennines seemed bursting with mid-summer blood. The sick-room itself glowed with the Italian joy of life; friends filled it; no harsh northern lights pierced the soft shadows; even the dying woman shared the sense of the Italian summer, the soft, velvet air, the humor, the courage, the sensual fulness of Nature and man. She faced death, as women mostly do, bravely and even gaily, racked slowly to unconsciousness, but yielding only to violence, as a soldier sabred in battle. For many thousands of years, on these hills and plains, Nature had gone on sabring men and women with the same air of sensual pleasure.

Impressions like these are not reasoned or catalogued in the mind; they are felt as part of violent emotion; and the mind that feels them is a different one from that which reasons; it is thought of a different power and a different person. The first serious consciousness of Nature's gesture—her attitude towards life—took form then as a phantasm, a nightmare, an insanity of force. For the first time, the stage-scenery of the senses collapsed; the human mind felt itself stripped naked, vibrating in a void of shapeless energies, with resistless mass, colliding, crushing, wasting, and destroying what these same energies had created and labored from eternity to perfect. Society became fantastic, a vision of pantomime with a mechanical motion; and its so-called thought merged in the mere sense of life, and pleasure in the sense. The usual anodynes of social medicine became evident artifice. Stoicism was perhaps the best; religion was the most human; but the idea that any personal deity could find pleasure or profit in torturing a poor woman, by accident, with a fiendish cruelty known to man only in perverted and insane temperaments, could not be held for a moment. For pure blasphemy, it made pure atheism a comfort. God might be, as the Church said, a Substance, but He could not be a Person.

With nerves strained for the first time beyond their power of tension, he slowly travelled northwards with his friends, and stopped for a few days at Ouchy to recover his balance in a new world; for the fantastic mystery of coincidences had made the world, which he thought real, mimic and reproduce the distorted nightmare of his personal horror. He did not yet know it, and he was twenty years in finding it out; but he had need of all the beauty of the Lake below and of the Alps above, to restore the finite to its place. For the first time in his life, Mont Blanc for a moment looked to him what it was—a chaos of anarchic and purposeless forces—and he needed days of repose to see it clothe itself again with the illusions of his senses, the white purity of its snows, the splendor of its light, and the infinity of its heavenly peace. Nature was kind; Lake Geneva was beautiful beyond itself, and the Alps put on charms real as terrors; but man became chaotic, and before the illusions of Nature were wholly restored, the illusions of Europe suddenly vanished, leaving a new world to learn.

On July 4, all Europe had been in peace; on July 14, Europe was in full chaos of war.[1] One felt helpless and ingorant, but one might have been king or kaiser without feeling stronger to deal with the chaos. Mr. Gladstone was as much astounded as Adams; the Emperor Napoleon was nearly as stupefied as either, and Bismarck himself hardly knew how he did it. As education, the outbreak of the war was wholly lost on a man dealing with death hand-to-hand, who could not throw it aside to look at it across the Rhine. Only when he got up to Paris, he began to feel the approach of catastrophe. Providence set up no *affiches* to announce the tragedy. Under one's eyes France cut herself adrift, and floated off, on an unknown stream, towards a less known ocean. Standing on the curb of the Boulevard, one could see as much as though one stood by the side of the Emperor or in command of an army corps. The effect was lurid. The public seemed to look on the war, as it had looked on the wars of Louis XIV and Francis I, as a branch of decorative art. The French, like true artists, always regarded war as one of the fine arts. Louis XIV practised it; Napoleon I perfected it; and Napoleon III had till then pursued it in the same spirit with singular success. In Paris, in July, 1870, the war was brought out like an opera of Meyerbeer. . . .

[*While visiting a friend in England, before returning home, Adams received an invitation from President Eliot of Harvard to become an assistant professor in the Department of History and editor of the* North American Review. *He sailed for America in September, still undecided whether to accept the post.*]

Henry knew the university well enough to know that the department of history was controlled by one of the most astute and ideal administrators in the world—Professor Gurney—and that it was Gurney who had established the new professorship, and had cast his net over Adams to carry the double load of mediæval history and the *Review.* He could see no relation whatever between himself and a professorship. He sought education; he did not sell it. He knew no history; he knew only a few historians; his ignorance was mischievous because it was literary, accidental, indifferent. On the other hand he knew Gurney, and felt much influenced by his advice. One cannot take one's self quite seriously in such matters; it could not much affect the sum of solar energies whether one went on dancing with girls in Washington, or began talking to boys at Cambridge. The good people who thought it did matter had a sort of right to guide. One could not reject their advice; still less disregard their wishes.

The sum of the matter was that Henry went out to Cambridge and had a few words with President Eliot which seemed to him almost as American as the talk about diplomacy with his father ten years before. "But, Mr. President," urged Adams, "I know nothing about Mediæval History." With the courteous manner and bland smile so familiar for the next generation of Americans, Mr. Eliot mildly but firmly replied, "If you will point out to me any

[1] The outbreak of the Franco-Prussian War, 1870-1871.

one who knows more, Mr. Adams, I will appoint him." The answer was neither logical nor convincing, but Adams could not meet it without over-stepping his privileges. He could not say that, under the circumstances, the appointment of any professor at all seemed to him unnecessary.

So, at twenty-four hours' notice, he broke his life in halves again in order to begin a new education, on lines he had not chosen, in subjects for which he cared less than nothing; in a place he did not love, and before a future which repelled. . . .

20. Failure (1871)

[Adams joined the faculty at Harvard in the fall of 1870.]

* * *

Not that his ignorance troubled him! He knew enough to be ignorant. His course had led him through oceans of ignorance; he had tumbled from one ocean into another till he had learned to swim; but even to him education was a serious thing. A parent gives life, but as parent, gives no more. A mur-derer takes life, but his deed stops there. A teacher affects eternity; he can never tell where his influence stops. A teacher is expected to teach truth, and may perhaps flatter himself that he does so, if he stops with the alphabet or the multiplication table, as a mother teaches truth by making her child eat with a spoon; but morals are quite another truth and philosophy is more complex still. A teacher must either treat history as a catalogue, a record, a romance, or as an evolution; and whether he affirms or denies evolution, he falls into all the burning faggots of the pit. He makes of his scholars either priests or atheists, plutocrats or socialists, judges or anarchists, almost in spite of himself. In essence incoherent and immoral, history had either to be taught as such—or falsified.

Adams wanted to do neither. He had no theory of evolution to teach, and could not make the facts fit one. He had no fancy for telling agreeable tales to amuse sluggish-minded boys, in order to publish them afterwards as lectures. He could still less compel his students to learn the Anglo-Saxon Chronicle and the Venerable Bede by heart. He saw no relation whatever be-tween his students and the Middle Ages unless it were the Church, and there the ground was particularly dangerous. He knew better than though he were a professional historian that the man who should solve the riddle of the Middle Ages and bring them into the line of evolution from past to present, would be a greater man than Lamarck or Linnaeus; but history had nowhere broken down so pitiably, or avowed itself so hopelessly bankrupt, as there. Since Gib-bon, the spectacle was almost a scandal. History had lost even the sense of shame. It was a hundred years behind the experimental sciences. For all seri-ous purpose, it was less instructive than Walter Scott and Alexandre Dumas.

All this was without offence to Sir Henry Maine, Tylor, McLennan, Buckle, Auguste Comte,[1] and the various philosophers who, from time to

[1] Of these nineteenth-century historians and philosophers only Comte had any ap-preciable influence on Adams.

time, stirred the scandal, and made it more scandalous. No doubt, a teacher might make some use of these writers on their theories; but Adams could fit them into no theory of his own. The college expected him to pass at least half his time in teaching the boys a few elementary dates and relations, that they might not be a disgrace to the university. This was formal; and he could frankly tell the boys that, provided they passed their examinations, they might get their facts where they liked, and use the teacher only for questions. The only privilege a student had that was worth his claiming, was that of talking to the professor, and the professor was bound to encourage it. His only difficulty on that side was to get them to talk at all. He had to devise schemes to find what they were thinking about, and induce them to risk criticism from their fellows. Any large body of students stifles the student. No man can instruct more than a half-a-dozen students at once. The whole problem of education is one of its cost in money.

The lecture system to classes of hundreds, which was very much that of the twelfth century, suited Adams not at all. Barred from philosophy and bored by facts, he wanted to teach his students something not wholly useless. The number of students whose minds were of an order above the average was, in his experience, barely one in ten; the rest could not be much stimulated by any inducements a teacher could suggest. All were respectable, and in seven years of contact, Adams never had cause to complain of one; but nine minds in ten take polish passively, like a hard surface; only the tenth sensibly reacts.

Adams thought that, as no one seemed to care what he did, he would try to cultivate this tenth mind, though necessarily at the expense of the other nine. He frankly acted on the rule that a teacher, who knew nothing of his subject, should not pretend to teach his scholars what he did not know, but should join them in trying to find the best way of learning it. The rather pretentious name of historical method was sometimes given to this process of instruction, but the name smacked of German pedagogy, and a young professor who respected neither history nor method, and whose sole object of interest was his students' minds, fell into trouble enough without adding to it a German parentage.

The task was doomed to failure for a reason which he could not control. Nothing is easier than to teach historical method, but, when learned, it has little use. History is a tangled skein that one may take up at any point, and break when one has unravelled enough; but complexity precedes evolution. The *Pteraspis*[2] grins horribly from the closed entrance. One may not begin at the beginning, and one has but the loosest relative truths to follow up. Adams found himself obliged to force his material into some shape to which a method could be applied. He could think only of law as subject; the Law School as end; and he took, as victims of his experiment, half-a-dozen highly intelligent young men who seemed willing to work. The course began with the beginning, as far as the books showed a beginning in primitive man, and came down through the Salic Franks to the Norman English. Since no textbooks existed, the professor refused to profess, knowing no more than his students, and the students read what they pleased and compared their results.

[2] A recently discovered fossilized shark from the Silurian age, discussed at some length by Adams in Chapter 15, "Darwinism" (omitted), as evidence against evolution.

As pedagogy, nothing could be more triumphant. The boys worked like rabbits, and dug holes all over the field of archaic society; no difficulty stopped them; unknown languages yielded before their attack, and customary law became familiar as the police court; undoubtedly they learned, after a fashion, to chase an idea, like a hare, through as dense a thicket of obscure facts as they were likely to meet at the bar; but their teacher knew from his own experience that his wonderful method led nowhere and they would have to exert themselves to get rid of it in the Law School even more than they exerted themselves to acquire it in the college. Their science had no system, and could have none, since its subject was merely antiquarian. Try as hard as he might, the professor could not make it actual.

What was the use of training an active mind to waste its energy? The experiments might in time train Adams as a professor, but this result was still less to his taste. He wanted to help the boys to a career, but not one of his many devices to stimulate the intellectual reaction of the student's mind satisfied either him or the students. For himself he was clear that the fault lay in the system, which could lead only to inertia. Such little knowledge of himself as he possessed warranted him in affirming that his mind required conflict, competition, contradiction even more than that of the student. He too wanted a rank-list to set his name upon. His reform of the system would have begun in the lecture-room at his own desk. He would have seated a rival assistant professor opposite him, whose business should be strictly limited to expressing opposite views. Nothing short of this would ever interest either the professor or the student; but of all university freaks, no irregularity shocked the intellectual atmsphere so much as contradiction or competition between teachers. In that respect the thirteenth-century university system was worth the whole teaching of the modern school.

All his pretty efforts to create conflicts of thought among his students failed for want of system. None met the needs of instruction. In spite of President Eliot's reforms and his steady, generous, liberal support, the system remained costly, clumsy and futile. The university—as far as it was represented by Henry Adams—produced at great waste of time and money results not worth reaching.

He made use of his lost two years of German schooling to inflict their results on his students, and by a happy chance he was in the full tide of fashion. The Germans were crowning their new emperor at Versailles, and surrounding his head with a halo of Pepins and Merwigs, Othos and Barbarossas. James Bryce had even discovered the Holy Roman Empire. Germany was never so powerful, and the Assistant Professor of History had nothing else as his stock in trade. He imposed Germany on his scholars with a heavy hand. He was rejoiced; but he sometimes doubted whether they should be grateful. On the whole, he was content neither with what he had taught nor with the way he had taught it. The seven years he passed in teaching seemed to him lost.

The uses of adversity are beyond measure strange. As a professor, he regarded himself as a failure. Without false modesty he thought he knew what he meant. He had tried a great many experiments, and wholly succeeded in none. He had succumbed to the weight of the system. He had accomplished nothing that he tried to do. He regarded the system as wrong; more mischievous to the teachers than to the students; fallacious from the beginning to end. He quitted the university at last, in 1877, with a feeling, that, if it had not been for the invariable courtesy and kindness shown by every one in it, from the President to the injured students, he should be sore at his failure. . . .

[*The period of Adams' prime, 1872-1892, is omitted from the Education. This included most of his years at Harvard, his whole career as an independent research historian, his married life in Washington, and his grief over the suicide of his wife in 1885. In the following decade and a half came his far-flung travels, as he searched for peace and a new meaning for his life. The Education takes up the story again in Chapter 21, "Twenty Years After (1892)." He first saw the newly invented dynamo at the Chicago Exposition of 1893, then at the Great Exposition in Paris seven years later.*]

25. The Dynamo and the Virgin (1900)

Until the Great Exposition of 1900 closed its doors in November, Adams haunted it, aching to absorb knowledge, and helpless to find it. He would have liked to know how much of it could have been grasped by the best-informed man in the world. While he was thus meditating chaos, Langley came by, and showed it to him. At Langley's behest, the Exhibition dropped its superfluous rags and stripped itself to the skin, for Langley knew what to study, and why, and how; while Adams might as well have stood outside in the night, staring at the Milky Way. Yet Langley said nothing new, and taught nothing that one might not have learned from Lord Bacon, three hundred years before; but though one should have known the "Advancement of Science" [1] as well as one knew the "Comedy of Errors," the literary knowledge counted for nothing until some teacher should show how to apply it. Bacon took a vast deal of trouble in teaching King James I and his subjects, American or other, towards the year 1620, that true science was the development or economy of forces; yet an elderly American in 1900 knew neither the formula nor the forces; or even so much as to say to himself that his historical business in the Exposition concerned only the economies or developments of force since 1893, when he began the study at Chicago.

Nothing in education is so astonishing as the amount of ignorance it accumulates in the form of inert facts. Adams had looked at most of the accumulations of art in the storehouses called Art Museums; yet he did not know how to look at the art exhibits of 1900. He had studied Karl Marx and his doctrines of history with profound attention, yet he could not apply them at Paris. Langley, with the ease of a great master of experiment, threw out of the field every exhibit that did not reveal a new application of force, and naturally threw out, to begin with, almost the whole art exhibit. Equally, he ignored almost the whole industrial exhibit. He led his pupil directly to the

---

[1] Presumably *The Advancement of Learning* (1605); Bacon's *Novum Organum* was published in 1620. Langley, mentioned above, was a pioneer in the invention of the airplane; Daimler, below, of the automobile.

1893 — year of World's Columbian Exposition at Chicago.

Gottlieb Daimler (1834-1900) the discoverer of impt. improvements in the gasoline engine.

forces. His chief interest was in new motors to make his airship feasible, and he taught Adams the astonishing complexities of the new Daimler motor, and of the automobile, which, since 1893, had become a nightmare at a hundred kilometres an hour, almost as destructive as the electric tram which was only ten years older; and threatening to become as terrible as the locomotive steam-engine itself, which was almost exactly Adams's own age.

Then he showed his scholar the great hall of dynamos, and explained how little he knew about electricity or force of any kind, even of his own special sun, which spouted heat in inconceivable volume, but which, as far as he knew, might spout less or more, at any time, for all the certainty he felt in it. To him, the dynamo itself was but an ingenious channel for conveying somewhere the heat latent in a few tons of poor coal hidden in a dirty engine-house carefully kept out of sight; but to Adams the dynamo became a symbol of infinity. As he grew accustomed to the great gallery of machines, he began to feel the forty-foot dynamos as a moral force, much as the early Christians felt the Cross. The planet itself seemed less impressive, in its old-fashioned, deliberate, annual or daily revolution, than this huge wheel, revolving within arm's-length at some vertiginous speed, and barely murmuring—scarcely humming an audible warning to stand a hair's-breadth further for respect of power—while it would not wake the baby lying close against its frame. Before the end, one began to pray to it; inherited instinct taught the natural expression of man before silent and infinite force. Among the thousand symbols of ultimate energy, the dynamo was not so human as some, but it was the most expressive.

Yet the dynamo, next to the steam-engine, was the most familiar of exhibits. For Adams's objects its value lay chiefly in its occult mechanism. Between the dynamo in the gallery of machines and the engine-house outside, the break of continuity amounted to abysmal fracture for a historian's objects. No more relation could he discover between the steam and the electric current than between the Cross and the cathedral. The forces were interchangeable if not reversible, but he could see only an absolute *fiat* in electricity as in faith. Langley could not help him. Indeed, Langley seemed to be worried by the same trouble, for he constantly repeated that the new forces were anarchical, and especially that he was not responsible for the new rays, that were little short of parricidal in their wicked spirit towards science. His own rays, with which he had doubled the solar spectrum, were altogether harmless and beneficent; but Radium[2] denied its God—or, what was to Langley the same thing, denied the truths of his Science. The force was wholly new.

A historian who asked only to learn enough to be as futile as Langley or Kelvin, made rapid progress under this teaching, and mixed himself up in the tangle of ideas until he achieved a sort of Paradise of ignorance vastly consoling to his fatigued senses. He wrapped himself in vibrations and rays

[2] The discovery of radium in 1898 upset science by showing the disintegration of what had been thought to be an "element."

Of the scientists in the next paragraph, Kelvin formulated the Second Law of Thermodynamics (the "degradation" of energy) that greatly influenced Adams's thinking; the inventions of Marconi and Branly harnessed radio waves for use in wireless telegraphy.

Wm. Thomson (Kelvin) (1824-1907) British mathematician & physicist. authority on molecular dynamics

Edward Branly (1846-1940)
French physicist. Branly's coherer
was useful in detecting electric waves.

which were new, and he would have hugged Marconi and Branly had he met them, as he hugged the dynamo; while he lost his arithmetic in trying to figure out the equation between the discoveries and the economies of force. The economies, like the discoveries, were absolute, supersensual, occult; incapable of expression in horse-power. What mathematical equivalent could he suggest as the value of a Branly coherer? Frozen air, or the electric furnace, had some scale of measurement, no doubt, if somebody could invent a thermometer adequate to the purpose; but X-rays had played no part whatever in man's consciousness, and the atom itself had figured only as a fiction of thought. In these seven years man had translated himself into a new universe which had no common scale of measurement with the old. He had entered a supersensual world, in which he could measure nothing except by chance collisions of movements imperceptible to his senses, perhaps even imperceptible to his own instruments, but perceptible to each other, and so to some known ray at the end of the scale. Langley seemed prepared for anything, even for an indeterminable number of universes interfused—physics stark mad in metaphysics.

Historians undertake to arrange sequences,—called stories, or histories—assuming in silence a relation of cause and effect. These assumptions, hidden in the depths of dusty libraries, have been astounding, but commonly unconscious and childlike; so much so, that if any captious critic were to drag them to light, historians would probably reply, with one voice, that they had never supposed themselves required to know what they were talking about. Adams, for one, had toiled in vain to find out what he meant. He had even published a dozen volumes of American history for no other purpose than to satisfy himself whether, by the severest process of stating, with the least possible comment, such facts as seemed sure, in such order as seemed rigorously consequent, he could fix for a familiar moment a necessary sequence of human movement. The result had satisfied him as little as at Harvard College. Where he saw sequence, other men saw something quite different, and no one saw the same unit of measure. He cared little about his experiments and less about his statesmen, who seemed to him quite as ignorant as himself and, as a rule, no more honest; but he insisted on a relation of sequence, and if he could not reach it by one method, he would try as many methods as science knew. Satisfied that the sequence of men led to nothing and that the sequence of their society could lead no further, while the mere sequence of time was artificial, and the sequence of thought was chaos, he turned at last to the sequence of force; and thus it happened that, after ten years' pursuit, he found himself lying in the Gallery of Machines at the Great Exposition of 1900, his historical neck broken by the sudden irruption of forces totally new.

Galileo Galilei
1564-
1642
It.
astronomer.

Since no one else showed much concern, an elderly person without other cares had no need to betray alarm. The year 1900 was not the first to upset schoolmasters. Copernicus and Galileo had broken many professorial necks about 1600; Columbus had stood the world on its head towards 1500; but the nearest approach to the revolution of 1900 was that of 310, when Constantine set up the Cross. The rays that Langley disowned, as well as those which he fathered, were occult, supersensual, irrational; they were a revelation of mysterious energy like that of the Cross; they were what, in

Nikolaus Copernicus (1473-1543) - Polish new
astronomer who had revolutionized thought
concerning the mechanics of the universe.

terms of mediaeval science, were called immediate modes of the divine substance.

The historian was thus reduced to his last resources. Clearly if he was bound to reduce all these forces to a common value, this common value could have no measure but that of their attraction on his own mind. He must treat them as they had been felt; as convertible, reversible, interchangeable attractions on thought. He made up his mind to venture it; he would risk translating rays into faith. Such a reversible process would vastly amuse a chemist, but the chemist could not deny that he, or some of his fellow physicists, could feel the force of both. When Adams was a boy in Boston, the best chemist in the place had probably never heard of Venus except by way of scandal, or of the Virgin except as idolatry; neither had he heard of dynamos or automobiles or radium; yet his mind was ready to feel the force of all, though the rays were unborn and the women were dead.

Here opened another totally new education, which promised to be by far the most hazardous of all. The knife-edge along which he must crawl, like Sir Lancelot in the twelfth century, divided two kingdoms of force which had nothing in common but attraction. They were as different as a magnet is from gravitation, supposing one knew what a magnet was, or gravitation, or love. The force of the Virgin was still felt at Lourdes, and seemed to be as potent as X-rays; but in America neither Venus nor Virgin ever had value as force—at most as sentiment. No American had ever been truly afraid of either.

This problem in dynamics gravely perplexed an American historian. The Woman had once been supreme; in France she still seemed potent, not merely as a sentiment, but as a force. Why was she unknown in America? For evidently America was ashamed of her, and she was ashamed of herself, otherwise they would not have strewn fig-leaves so profusely all over her. When she was a true force, she was ignorant of fig-leaves, but the monthly-magazine-made American female had not a feature that would have been recognized by Adam. The trait was notorious, and often humorous, but any one brought up among Puritans knew that sex was sin. In any previous age, sex was strength. Neither art nor beauty was needed. Every one, even among Puritans, knew that neither Diana of the Ephesians nor any of the Oriental goddesses was worshipped for her beauty. She was goddess because of her force; she was the animated dynamo; she was reproduction—the greatest and most mysterious of all energies; all she needed was to be fecund. Singularly enough, not one of Adams's many schools of education had ever drawn his attention to the opening lines of Lucretius, though they were perhaps the finest in all Latin literature, where the poet invoked Venus exactly as Dante invoked the Virgin:—

"Quae quoniam rerum naturam sola gubernas." [3]

The Venus of Epicurean philosophy survived in the Virgin of the Schools:—

[3] "Since thou alone governest the nature of things" (from De Rerum Natura, i, 21).
The passage from Dante, immediately following, may be translated: "Lady, so great art thou and of such worth that, if one would have grace and has not recourse to thee, his longing would fly without wings."

"Donna, sei tanto grande, e tanto vali,
Che qual vuol grazia, e a te non ricorre,
Sua disianza vuol volar senz' ali."

All this was to American thought as though it had never existed. The true American knew something of the facts, but nothing of the feelings; he read the letter, but he never felt the law. Before this historical chasm, a mind like that of Adams felt itself helpless; he turned from the Virgin to the Dynamo as though he were a Branly coherer. On one side, at the Louvre and at Chartres, as he knew by the record of work actually done and still before his eyes, was the highest energy ever known to man, the creator of four-fifths of his noblest art, exercising vastly more attraction over the human mind than all the steam-engines and dynamos ever dreamed of; and yet this energy was unknown to the American mind. An American Virgin would never dare command; an American Venus would never dare exist.

The question, which to any plain American of the nineteenth century seemed as remote as it did to Adams, drew him almost violently to study, once it was posed; and on this point Langleys were as useless as though they were Herbert Spencers or dynamos. The idea survived only as art. There one turned as naturally as though the artist were himself a woman. Adams began to ponder, asking himself whether he knew of any American artist who had ever insisted on the power of sex, as every classic had always done; but he could think only of Walt Whitman; Bret Harte, as far as the magazines would let him venture; and one or two painters, for the flesh-tones. All the rest had used sex for sentiment, never for force; to them, Eve was a tender flower, and Herodias an unfeminine horror. American art, like the American language and American education, was as far as possible sexless. Society regarded this victory over sex as its greatest triumph, and the historian readily admitted it, since the moral issue, for the moment, did not concern one who was studying the relations of unmoral force. He cared nothing for the sex of the dynamo until he could measure its energy.

Vaguely seeking a clue, he wandered through the art exhibit, and, in his stroll, stopped almost every day before St. Gaudens's General Sherman, which had been given the central post of honor. St. Gaudens[4] himself was in Paris, putting on the work his usual interminable last touches, and listening to the usual contradictory suggestions of brother sculptors. Of all the American artists who gave to American art whatever life it breathed in the seventies, St. Gaudens was perhaps the most sympathetic, but certainly the most inarticulate. General Grant or Don Cameron had scarcely less instinct of rhetoric than he. All the others—the Hunts, Richardson, John La Farge, Stanford White—were exuberant; only St. Gaudens could never discuss or dilate on an emotion, or suggest artistic arguments for giving to his work the forms that he felt. He never laid down the law, or affected the despot, or became brutalized like Whistler by the brutalities of his world. He required no incense; he was no egoist; his simplicity of thought was excessive; he could not imitate, or give any form but his own to the creations of his hand. No one

[4] The American sculptor employed by Adams for the monument in Rock Creek Cemetery, Washington, memorializing his wife. Of the American architects and painters mentioned in the following sentences, La Farge strongly influenced Adams.

[handwritten top margin: Richard Hunt (1827-1895) an architect / Wm. Morris Hunt (1824-1879) a painter]

felt more strongly than he the strength of other men, but the idea that they could affect him never stirred an image in his mind.

This summer his health was poor and his spirits were low. For such a temper, Adams was not the best companion, since his own gaiety was not *folle*; but he risked going now and then to the studio on Mont Parnasse to draw him out for a stroll in the Bois de Boulogne, or dinner as pleased his moods, and in return St. Gaudens sometimes let Adams go about in his company. *[handwritten: mad or extravagant]*

Once St. Gaudens took him down to Amiens, with a party of Frenchmen, to see the cathedral. Not until they found themselves actually studying the sculpture of the western portal, did it dawn on Adams's mind that, for his purposes, St. Gaudens on that spot had more interest to him than the cathedral itself. Great men before great monuments express great truths, provided they are not taken too solemnly. Adams never tired of quoting the supreme phrase of his idol Gibbon, before the Gothic cathedrals: "I darted a contemptuous look on the stately monuments of superstition." Even in the footnotes of his history, Gibbon had never inserted a bit of humor more human than this, and one would have paid largely for a photograph of the fat little historian, on the background of Notre Dame of Amiens, trying to persuade his readers—perhaps himself—that he was darting a contemptuous look on the stately monument, for which he felt in fact the respect which every man of his vast study and active mind always feels before objects worthy of it; but besides the humor, one felt also the relation. Gibbon ignored the Virgin, because in 1789 religious monuments were out of fashion. In 1900 his remark sounded fresh and simple as the green fields to ears that had heard a hundred years of other remarks, mostly no more fresh and certainly less simple. Without malice, one might find it more instructive than a whole lecture of Ruskin. One sees what one brings, and at that moment Gibbon brought the French Revolution. Ruskin brought reaction against the Revolution. St. Gaudens had passed beyond all. He liked the stately monuments much more than he liked Gibbon or Ruskin; he loved their dignity; their unity; their scale; their lines; their lights and shadows; their decorative sculpture; but he was even less conscious than they of the force that created it all—the Virgin, the Woman—by whose genius "the stately monuments of superstition" were built, through which she was expressed. He would have seen more meaning in Isis with the cow's horns, at Edfoo, who expressed the same thought. The art remained, but the energy was lost even upon the artist.

Yet in mind and person St. Gaudens was a survival of the 1500; he bore the stamp of the Renaissance, and should have carried an image of the Virgin round his neck, or stuck in his hat, like Louis XI. In mere time he was a lost soul that had strayed by chance into the twentieth century, and forgotten where it came from. He writhed and cursed at his ignorance, much as Adams did at his own, but in the opposite sense. St. Gaudens was a child of Benvenuto Cellini, smothered in an American cradle. Adams was a quintessence of Boston, devoured by curiosity to think like Benvenuto. St. Gaudens's art was starved from birth, and Adams's instinct was blighted from babyhood. Each had but half of a nature, and when they came together before the Virgin of Amiens they ought both to have felt in her the force that made them

[handwritten right margin: James M. Whistler (1834-1903) sharp-tongued Am. artist who lived in Europe.]

[handwritten right margin: Edward Gibbon (1737-1794) Eng. historian and skeptic]

[handwritten right margin: John Ruskin (1819-1900) Eng. art critic]

[handwritten right margin: Egyptian goddess fertility]

[handwritten right margin: 1423-1483 King of France.]

[handwritten right margin: Benvenuto Cellini (1500-1571) Italian goldsmith, notable.]

[handwritten bottom margin: Henry H. Richardson (1838-1886) an architect. / John La Farge (1835-1910) painter & sculptor / Stanford White (1853-1906) an architect]

Site of temple which contains statue of
Aphrodite, masterpiece by Greek sculptor Praxiteles
370   HENRY ADAMS

one; but it was not so. To Adams she became more than ever a channel of force; to St. Gaudens she remained as before a channel of taste.

For a symbol of power, St. Gaudens instinctively preferred the horse, as was plain in his horse and Victory of the Sherman monument. Doubtless Sherman also felt it so. The attitude was so American that, for at least forty years, Adams had never realized that any other could be in sound taste. How many years had he taken to admit a notion of what Michael Angelo and Rubens were driving at? He could not say; but he knew that only since 1895 had he begun to feel the Virgin or Venus as force, and not everywhere even so. At Chartres—perhaps at Lourdes—possibly at Cnidos if one could still find there the divinely naked Aphrodite of Praxiteles—but otherwise one must look for force to the goddesses of Indian mythology. The idea died out long ago in the German and English stock. St. Gaudens at Amiens was hardly less sensitive to the force of the female energy than Matthew Arnold at the Grande Chartreuse.[5] Neither of them felt goddesses as power—only as reflected emotion, human expression, beauty, purity, taste, scarcely even as sympathy. They felt a railway train as power; yet they, and all other artists, constantly complained that the power embodied in a railway train could never be embodied in art. All the steam in the world could not, like the Virgin, build Chartres.

Yet in mechanics, whatever the mechanicians might think, both energies acted as interchangeable forces on man, and by action on man all known force may be measured. Indeed, few men of science measured force in any other way. After once admitting that a straight line was the shortest distance between two points, no serious mathematician cared to deny anything that suited his convenience, and rejected no symbol, unproved or unproveable, that helped him to accomplish work. The symbol was force, as a compass needle or a triangle was force, as the mechanist might prove by losing it, and nothing could be gained by ignoring their value. Symbol or energy, the Virgin had acted as the greatest force the Western world ever felt, and had drawn man's activities to herself more strongly than any other power, natural or supernatural, had ever done; the historian's business was to follow the track of the energy; to find where it came from and where it went to; its complex source and shifting channels; its values, equivalents, conversions. It could scarcely be more complex than radium; it could hardly be deflected, diverted, polarized, absorbed more perplexingly than other radiant matter. Adams knew nothing about any of them, but as a mathematical problem of influence on human progress, though all were occult, all reacted on his mind, and he rather inclined to think the Virgin easiest to handle.

The pursuit turned out to be long and tortuous, leading at last into the vast forests of scholastic science. From Zeno to Descartes, hand in hand with Thomas Aquinas, Montaigne, and Pascal, one stumbled as stupidly as though one were still a German student of 1860. Only with the instinct of despair

[5] Arnold's "Stanzas from the Grande Chartreuse," a favorite of Adams, contains two lines that could serve as an epigraph to the *Education*:

> Wandering between two worlds, one dead
> The other powerless to be born.

could one force one's self into this old thicket of ignorance after having been repulsed at a score of entrances more promising and more popular. Thus far, no path had led anywhere, unless perhaps to an exceedingly modest living. Forty-five years of study had proved to be quite futile for the pursuit of power; one controlled no more force in 1900 than in 1850, although the amount of force controlled by society had enormously increased. The secret of education still hid itself somewhere behind ignorance, and one fumbled over it as feebly as ever. In such labyrinths, the staff is a force almost more necessary than the legs; the pen becomes a sort of blind-man's dog, to keep him from falling into the gutters. The pen works for itself, and acts like a hand, modelling the plastic material over and over again to the form that suits it best. The form is never arbitrary, but is a sort of growth like crystal-lization, as any artist knows too well; for often the pencil or pen runs into side-paths and shapelessness, loses its relations, stops or is bogged. Then it has to return on its trail, and recover, if it can, its line of force. The result of a year's work depends more on what is struck out than on what is left in; on the sequence of the main lines of thought, than on their play or variety. Com-pelled once more to lean heavily on this support, Adams covered more thou-sands of pages with figures as formal as though they were algebra, labori-ously striking out, altering, burning, experimenting, until the year had ex-pired, the Exposition had long been closed, and winter drawing to its end, before he sailed from Cherbourg, on January 19, 1901, for home.

[At some time around the turn of the century Adams' plans had begun to take shape for a study of thirteenth-century unity. It was completed and pri-vately printed in 1904, under the title Mont-Saint-Michel and Chartres. Mean-time he had conceived the Education as its sequel, a study of twentieth-century multiplicity, the climactic chapter of which follows.]

33. A Dynamic Theory of History (1904)

A dynamic theory, like most theories, begins by begging the question: it defines Progress as the development and economy of Forces. Further, it de-fines force as anything that does, or helps to do work. Man is a force; so is the sun; so is a mathematical point, though without dimensions or known ex-istence.

Man commonly begs the question again by taking for granted that he cap-tures the forces. A dynamic theory, assigning attractive force to opposing bodies in proportion to the law of mass, takes for granted that the forces of nature capture man. The sum of force attracts; the feeble atom or molecule called man is attracted; he suffers education or growth; he is the sum of the forces that attract him; his body and his thought are alike their product; the movement of the forces controls the progress of his mind, since he can know nothing but the motions which impinge on his senses, whose sum makes education.

For convenience as an image, the theory may liken man to a spider in its web, watching for chance prey. Forces of nature dance like flies before the net, and the spider pounces on them when it can; but it makes many fatal mis-

Pascal, Blaise (1623-1662) Fr. mathematician and philosopher.

takes, though its theory of force is sound. The spider-mind acquires a faculty of memory, and, with it, a singular skill of analysis and synthesis, taking apart and putting together in different relations the meshes of its trap. Man had in the beginning no power of analysis or synthesis approaching that of the spider, or even of the honey-bee; but he had acute sensibility to the higher forces. Fire taught him secrets that no other animal could learn; running water probably taught him even more, especially in his first lessons of mechanics; the animals helped to educate him, trusting themselves into his hands merely for the sake of their food, and carrying his burdens or supplying his clothing; the grasses and grains were academies of study. With little or no effort on his part, all these forces formed his thought, induced his action, and even shaped his figure.

Long before history began, his education was complete, for the record could not have been started until he had been taught to record. The universe that had formed him took shape in his mind as a reflection of his own unity, containing all forces except himself. Either separately, or in groups, or as a whole, these forces never ceased to act on him, enlarging his mind as they enlarged the surface foliage of a vegetable, and the mind needed only to respond, as the forests did, to these attractions. Susceptibility to the highest forces is the highest genius; selection between them is the highest science; their mass is the highest educator. Man always made, and still makes, grotesque blunders in selecting and measuring forces, taken at random from the heap, but he never made a mistake in the value he set on the whole, which he symbolized as unity and worshipped as God. To this day, his attitude towards it has never changed, though science can no longer give to force a name.

Man's function as a force of nature was to assimilate other forces as he assimilated food. He called it the love of power. He felt his own feebleness, and he sought for an ass or a camel, a bow or a sling, to widen his range of power, as he sought a fetish or a planet in the world beyond. He cared little to know its immediate use, but he could afford to throw nothing away which he could conceive to have possible value in this or any other existence. He waited for the object to teach him its use, or want of use, and the process was slow. He may have gone on for hundreds of thousands of years, waiting for Nature to tell him her secrets; and, to his rivals among the monkeys, Nature has taught no more than at their start; but certain lines of force were capable of acting on individual apes, and mechanically selecting types of race or sources of variation. The individual that responded or reacted to lines of new force then was possibly the same individual that reacts on it now, and his conception of the unity seems never to have changed in spite of the increasing diversity of forces; but the theory of variation is an affair of other science than history, and matters nothing to dynamics. The individual or the race would be educated on the same lines of illusion, which, according to Arthur Balfour, had not essentially varied down to the year 1900.[1]

To the highest attractive energy, man gave the name of divine, and for its control he invented the science called Religion, a word which meant, and

[1] In 1904 Balfour delivered his presidential address "On the Future of Science" to the British Association, expressing an attitude that parallels that of Adams on the illusory nature of nineteenth-century scientific assumptions.

still means, cultivation of occult force whether in detail or mass. Unable to define Force as a unity, man symbolized it and pursued it, both in himself, and in the infinite, as philosophy and theology; the mind is itself the subtlest of all known forces, and its self-introspection necessarily created a science which had the singular value of lifting his education, at the start, to the finest, subtlest, and broadest training both in analysis and synthesis, so that, if language is a test, he must have reached his highest powers early in his history; while the mere motive remained as simple an appetite for power as the tribal greed which led him to trap an elephant. Hunger, whether for food or for the infinite, sets in motion multiplicity and infinity of thought, and the sure hope of gaining a share of infinite power in eternal life would lift most minds to effort.

He had reached this completeness five thousand years ago, and added nothing to his stock of known forces for a very long time. The mass of nature exercised on him so feeble an attraction that one can scarcely account for his apparent motion. Only a historian of very exceptional knowledge would venture to say at what date between 3000 B.C. and 1000 A.D., the momentum of Europe was greatest; but such progress as the world made consisted in economies of energy rather than in its development; it was proved in mathematics, measured by names like Archimedes, Aristarchus, Ptolemy, and Euclid; or in Civil Law, measured by a number of names which Adams had begun life by failing to learn; or in coinage, which was most beautiful near its beginning, and most barbarous at its close; or it was shown in roads, or the size of ships, or harbors; or by the use of metals, instruments, and writing; all of them economies of force, sometimes more forceful than the forces they helped; but the roads were still travelled by the horse, the ass, the camel, or the slave; the ships were still propelled by sails or oars; the lever, the spring, and the screw bounded the region of applied mechanics. Even the metals were old.

Much the same thing could be said of religious or supernatural forces. Down to the year 300 of the Christian era they were little changed, and in spite of Plato and the sceptics were more apparently chaotic than ever. The experience of three thousand years had educated society to feel the vastness of Nature, and the infinity of her resources of power, but even this increase of attraction had not yet caused economies in its methods of pursuit.

There the Western world stood till the year A.D. 305, when the Emperor Diocletian abdicated; and there it was that Adams broke down on the steps of Ara Coeli, his path blocked by the scandalous failure of civilization at the moment it had achieved complete success. In the year 305 the empire had solved the problems of Europe more completely than they have ever been solved since. The Pax Romana, the Civil Law, and Free Trade should, in four hundred years, have put Europe far in advance of the point reached by modern society in the four hundred years since 1500, when conditions were less simple.

The efforts to explain, or explain away, this scandal had been incessant, but none suited Adams unless it were the economic theory of adverse exchanges and exhaustion of minerals; but nations are not ruined beyond a certain point by adverse exchanges, and Rome had by no means exhausted her resources. On the contrary, the empire developed resources and energies quite astounding. No other four hundred years of history before A.D. 1800 knew anything like it; and although some of these developments, like the Civil Law, the roads, aqueducts, and harbors, were rather economies than force, yet in northwestern Europe alone the empire had developed three energies—France, England, and Germany—competent to master the world. The trouble seemed rather to be that the empire developed too much energy, and too fast.

A dynamic law requires that two masses—nature and man—must go on, reacting upon each other, without stop, as the sun and a comet react on each other, and that any appearance of stoppage is illusive. The theory seems to exact excess, rather than deficiency, of action and reaction to account for the dissolution of the Roman Empire, which should, as a problem of mechanics, have been torn to pieces by acceleration. If the student means to try the experiment of framing a dynamic law, he must assign values to the forces of attraction that caused the trouble; and in this case he has them in plain evidence. With the relentless logic that stamped Roman thought, the empire, which had established unity on earth, could not help establishing unity in heaven. It was induced by its dynamic necessities to economize the gods.

The Church has never ceased to protest against the charge that Christianity ruined the empire, and, with its usual force, has pointed out that its reforms alone saved the State. Any dynamic theory gladly admits it. All it asks is to find and follow the force that attracts. The Church points out this force in the Cross, and history needs only to follow it. The empire loudly asserted its motive. Good taste forbids saying that Constantine the Great speculated as audaciously as a modern stock-broker on values of which he knew at the utmost only the volume; or that he merged all uncertain forces into a single trust, which he enormously over-capitalized, and forced on the market; but this is the substance of what Constantine himself said in his Edict of Milan in the year 313, which admitted Christianity into the Trust of State Religions. Regarded as an Act of Congress, it ruins: "We have resolved to grant to Christians as well as all others the liberty to practise the religion they prefer, in order that whatever exists of divinity or celestial power may help and favor us and all who are under our government." The empire pursued power—not merely spiritual but physical—in the sense in which Constantine issued his army order the year before, at the battle of the Milvian Bridge: *In hoc signo vinces!* [2] using the Cross as a train of artillery, which, to his mind, it was. Society accepted it in the same character. Eighty years afterwards, Theodosius marched against his rival Eugene with the Cross for physical champion; and Eugene raised the image of Hercules to fight for the pagans; while society on both sides looked on, as though it were a boxing-match, to decide a final test of force between the divine powers. The Church was powerless to raise the ideal. What is now known as religion affected the mind of old society but little. The laity, the people, the million, almost to a man, bet on the gods as they bet on a horse.

No doubt the Church did all it could to purify the process, but society was almost wholly pagan in its point of view, and was drawn to the Cross because, in its system of physics, the Cross had absorbed all the old occult or

bridge over Tiber where Maxentius was drowned

2 "In this sign conquer!"

THE EDUCATION OF HENRY ADAMS 375

fetish-power. The symbol represented the sum of nature—the Energy of modern science—and society believed it to be as real as X-rays; perhaps it was! The emperors used it like gunpowder in politics; the physicians used it like rays in medicine; the dying clung to it as the quintessence of force, to protect them from the forces of evil on their road to the next life.

Throughout these four centuries the empire knew that religion disturbed economy, for even the cost of heathen incense affected the exchanges; but no one could afford to buy or construct a costly and complicated machine when he could hire an occult force at trifling expense. Fetish-power was cheap and satisfactory, down to a certain point. Turgot and Auguste Comte long ago fixed this stage of economy as a necessary phase of social education, and historians seem now to accept it as the only gain yet made towards scientific history. Great numbers of educated people—perhaps a majority—cling to the method still, and practise it more or less strictly; but, until quite recently, no other was known. The only occult power at man's disposal was fetish. Against it, no mechanical force could compete except within narrow limits.

Outside of occult or fetish-power, the Roman world was incredibly poor. It knew but one productive energy resembling a modern machine—the slave. No artificial force of serious value was applied to production or transportation, and when society developed itself so rapidly in political and social lines, it had no other means of keeping its economy on the same level than to extend its slave-system and its fetish-system to the utmost.

The result might have been stated in a mathematical formula as early as the time of Archimedes, six hundred years before Rome fell. The economic needs of a violently centralizing society forced the empire to enlarge its slave-system until the slave-system consumed itself and the empire too, leaving society no resource but further enlargement of its religious system in order to compensate for the losses and horrors of the failure. For a vicious circle, its mathematical completeness approached perfection. The dynamic law of attraction and reaction needed only a Newton to fix it in algebraic form.

At last, in 410, Alaric sacked Rome, and the slave-ridden, agricultural, uncommercial Western Empire—the poorer and less Christianized half—went to pieces. Society, though terribly shocked by the horrors of Alaric's storm, felt still more deeply the disappointment in its new power, the Cross, which had failed to protect its Church. The outcry against the Cross became so loud among Christians that its literary champion, Bishop Augustine of Hippo—a town between Algiers and Tunis—was led to write a famous treatise[3] in defence of the Cross, familiar still to every scholar, in which he defended feebly the mechanical value of the symbol—arguing only that pagan symbols equally failed—but insisted on its spiritual value in the *Civitas Dei* which had taken the place of the *Civitas Romae* in human interest. "Granted that we have lost all we had! Have we lost faith? Have we lost piety? Have we lost the wealth of the inner man who is rich before God? These are the wealth of Christians!" The *Civitas Dei*, in its turn, became the sum of attraction for the Western world, though it also showed the same weakness in me-

---

[3] *De Civitate Dei* (The City of God). St. Augustine's other famous work, *The Confessions*, was cited by Adams as his model in the preface to his *Education*, as pointed out in the Introduction (p. 320, above).

chanics that had wrecked the *Civitas Romae*. St. Augustine and his people perished at Hippo towards 430, leaving society in appearance dull to new attraction.

Yet the attraction remained constant. The delight of experimenting on occult force of every kind is such as to absorb all the free thought of the human race. The gods did their work; history has no quarrel with them; they led, educated, enlarged the mind; taught knowledge; betrayed ignorance, stimulated effort. So little is known about the mind—whether social, racial, sexual or heritable; whether material or spiritual; whether animal, vegetable or mineral—that history is inclined to avoid it altogether; but nothing forbids one to admit, for convenience, that it may assimilate food like the body, storing new force and growing, like a forest, with the storage. The brain has not yet revealed its mysterious mechanism of gray matter. Never has Nature offered it so violent a stimulant as when she opened to it the possibility of sharing infinite power in eternal life, and it might well need a thousand years of prolonged and intense experiment to prove the value of the motive. During these so-called Middle Ages, the Western mind reacted in many forms, on many sides, expressing its motives in modes, such as Romanesque and Gothic architecture, glass windows and mosaic walls, sculpture and poetry, war and love, which still affect some people as the noblest work of man, so that, even to-day, great masses of idle and ignorant tourists travel from far countries to look at Ravenna and San Marco, Palermo and Pisa, Assisi, Cordova, Chartres, with vague notions about the force that created them, but with a certain surprise that a social mind of such singular energy and unity should still lurk in their shadows.

The tourist more rarely visits Constantinople or studies the architecture of Sancta Sofia, but when he does, he is distinctly conscious of forces not quite the same. Justinian has not the simplicity of Charlemagne. The Eastern Empire showed an activity and variety of forces that classical Europe had never possessed. The navy of Nicephoras Phocas[4] in the tenth century would have annihilated in half an hour any navy that Carthage or Athens or Rome ever set afloat. The dynamic scheme began by asserting rather recklessly that between the Pyramids (B.C. 3000), and the Cross (A.D. 300), no new force affected Western progress, and antiquarians may easily dispute the fact; but in any case the motive influence, old or new, which raised both Pyramids and Cross was the same attraction of power in a future life that raised the dome of Sancta Sofia and the Cathedral at Amiens, however much it was altered, enlarged, or removed to distance in space. Therefore, no single event has more puzzled historians than the sudden, unexplained appearance of at least two new natural forces of the highest educational value in mechanics, for the first time within record of history. Literally, these two forces seemed to drop from the sky at the precise moment when the Cross on one side and the Crescent on the other, proclaimed the complete triumph of the *Civitas Dei*. Had the Manichean doctrine of Good and Evil as rival deities been orthodox, it would alone have accounted for this simultaneous victory of hostile powers.

Of the compass, as a step towards demonstration of the dynamic law, one

---

4 Emperor of the Eastern Roman Empire (*d.* 969).

may confidently say that it proved, better than any other force, the widening scope of the mind, since it widened immensely the range of contact between nature and thought. The compass educated. This must prove itself as needing no proof.

Of Greek fire and gunpowder, the same thing cannot certainly be said, for they have the air of accidents due to the attraction of religious motives. They belong to the spiritual world; or to the doubtful ground of Magic which lay between Good and Evil. They were chemical forces, mostly explosive, which acted and still act as the most violent educators ever known to man, but they were justly feared as diabolic, and whatever insolence man may have risked towards the milder teachers of his infancy, he was an abject pupil towards explosives. The Sieur de Joinville left a record of the energy with which the relatively harmless Greek fire educated and enlarged the French mind in a single night in the year 1249, when the crusaders were trying to advance on Cairo. The good king St. Louis and all his staff dropped on their knees at every fiery flame that flew by, praying—"God have pity on us!" and never had man more reason to call on his gods than they, for the battle of religion between Christian and Saracen was trifling compared with that of education between gunpowder and the Cross.

The fiction that society educated itself, or aimed at a conscious purpose, was upset by the compass and gunpowder which dragged and drove Europe at will through frightful bogs of learning. At first, the apparent lag for want of volume in the new energies lasted one or two centuries, which closed the great epochs of emotion by the Gothic cathedrals and scholastic theology. The moment had Greek beauty and more than Greek unity, but it was brief; and for another century or two, Western society seemed to float in space without apparent motion. Yet the attractive mass of nature's energy continued to attract. and education became more rapid than ever before. Society began to resist, but the individual showed greater and greater insistence, without realizing what he was doing. When the Crescent drove the Cross in ignominy from Constantinople in 1453, Gutenberg and Fust were printing their first Bible at Mainz under the impression that they were helping the Cross. When Columbus discovered the West Indies in 1492, the Church looked on it as a victory of the Cross. When Luther and Calvin upset Europe half a century later, they were trying, like St. Augustine, to substitute the *Civitas Dei* for the *Civitas Romae*. When the Puritans set out for New England in 1620, they too were looking to found a *Civitas Dei* in State Street; and when Bunyan made his Pilgrimage in 1678, he repeated St. Jerome.[5] Even when, after centuries of license, the Church reformed its discipline, and, to prove it, burned Giordano Bruno in 1600, besides condemning Galileo in 1630—as science goes on repeating to us every day—it condemned anarchists, not atheists. None of the astronomers were irreligious men; all of them made a point of magnifying God through his works; a form of science which did their religion no credit. Neither Galileo nor Kepler, neither Spinoza nor Descartes, neither Leibnitz nor

[5] The ironies in this compact sentence should not be overlooked. During the nineteenth century the commercial interest of New England, symbolized by State Street, superseded the influence of the Puritan clergy; Bunyan's *Pilgrim's Progress* (1678), like St. Jerome's Latin translation of the Bible in the fourth century, revolutionized established religion.

Newton, any more than Constantine the Great—if so much—doubted Unity. The utmost range of their heresies reached only its personality.

This persistence of thought-inertia is the leading idea of modern history. Except as reflected in himself, man has no reason for assuming unity in the universe, or an ultimate substance, or a prime-motor. The *a priori* insistence on this unity ended by fatiguing the more active—or reactive— minds; and Lord Bacon tried to stop it. He urged society to lay aside the idea of evolving the universe from a thought, and to try evolving thought from the universe. The mind should observe and register forces—take them apart and put them together—without assuming unity at all. "Nature, to be commanded, must be obeyed." "The imagination must be given not wings but weights." As Galileo reversed the action of earth and sun, Bacon reversed the relation of thought to force. The mind was thenceforth to follow the movement of matter, and unity must be left to shift for itself.

The revolution in attitude seemed voluntary, but in fact was as mechanical as the fall of a feather. Man created nothing. After 1500, the speed of progress so rapidly surpassed man's gait as to alarm every one, as though it were the acceleration of a falling body which the dynamic theory takes it to be. Lord Bacon was as much astonished by it as the Church was, and with reason. Suddenly society felt itself dragged into situations altogether new and anarchic—situations which it could not affect, but which painfully affected it. Instinct taught it that the universe in its thought must be in danger when its reflection lost itself in space. The danger was all the greater because men of science covered it with "larger synthesis," and poets called the undevout astronomer mad. Society knew better. Yet the telescope held it rigidly standing on its head; the microscope revealed a universe that defied the senses; gunpowder killed whole races that lagged behind; the compass coerced the most imbruted mariner to act on the impossible idea that the earth was round; the press drenched Europe with anarchism. Europe saw itself, violently resisting, wrenched into false positions, drawn along new lines as a fish that is caught on a hook; but unable to understand by what force it was controlled. The resistance was often bloody, sometimes humorous, always constant. Its contortions in the eighteenth century are best studied in the wit of Voltaire, but all history and all philosophy from Montaigne and Pascal to Schopenhauer and Nietzsche deal with nothing else; and still, throughout it all, the Baconian law held good; thought did not evolve nature, but nature evolved thought. Not one considerable man of science dared face the stream of thought; and the whole number of those who acted, like Franklin, as electric conductors of the new forces from nature to man, down to the year 1800, did not exceed a few score, confined to a few towns in western Europe. Asia refused to be touched by the stream, and America, except for Franklin, stood outside.

Very slowly the accretion of these new forces, chemical and mechanical, grew in volume until they acquired sufficient mass to take the place of the old religious science, substituting their attraction for the attractions of the *Civitas Dei*, but the process remained the same. Nature, not mind, did the work that the sun does on the planets. Man depended more and more absolutely on forces other than his own, and on instruments which superseded his senses. Bacon foretold it: "Neither the naked hand nor the understanding, left to itself, can effect much. It is by instruments and helps that the work is done." Once done, the mind resumed its illusion, and society forgot its impotence; but no one better than Bacon knew its tricks, and for his true followers science always meant self-restraint, obedience, sensitiveness to impulse from without. "Non fingendum aut excogitandum sed inveniendum quid Natura faciat aut ferat." [6]

The success of this method staggers belief, and even to-day can be treated by history only as a miracle of growth, like the sports of nature. Evidently a new variety of mind had appeared. Certain men merely held out their hands—like Newton, watched an apple; like Franklin, flew a kite; like Watt, played with a tea-kettle—and great forces of nature stuck to them as though she were playing ball. Governments did almost nothing but resist. Even gunpowder and ordnance, the great weapon of government, showed little development between 1400 and 1800. Society was hostile or indifferent, as Priestley and Jenner, and even Fulton, with reason complained in the most advanced societies in the world, while its resistance became acute wherever the Church held control; until all mankind seemed to draw itself out in a long series of groups, dragged on by an attractive power in advance, which even the leaders obeyed without understanding, as the planets obeyed gravity, or the trees obeyed heat and light.

The influx of new force was nearly spontaneous. The reaction of mind on the mass of nature seemed not greater than that of a comet on the sun; and had the spontaneous influx of force stopped in Europe, society must have stood still, or gone backward, as in Asia or Africa. Then only economies of process would have counted as new force, and society would have been better pleased; for the idea that new force must be in itself a good is only an animal or vegetable instinct. As Nature developed her hidden energies, they tended to become destructive. Thought itself became tortured, suffering reluctantly, impatiently, painfully, the coercion of new method. Easy thought had always been movement of inertia, and mostly mere sentiment; but even the processes of mathematics measured feebly the needs of force.

The stupendous acceleration after 1800 ended in 1900 with the appearance of the new class of supersensual forces, before which the man of science stood at first as bewildered and helpless, as in the fourth century, a priest of Isis before the Cross of Christ.

This, then, or something like this, would be a dynamic formula of history. Any schoolboy knows enough to object at once that it is the oldest and most universal of all theories. Church and State, theology and philosophy, have always preached it, differing only in the allotment of energy between nature and man. Whether the attractive energy has been called God or Nature, the mechanism has been always the same, and history is not obliged to decide whether the Ultimate tends to a purpose or not, or whether ultimate energy is one or many. Every one admits that the will is a free force, habitually decided by motives. No one denies that motives exist adequate to decide the will; even though it may not always be conscious of them. Science has proved that forces, sensible and occult, physical and metaphysical, simple and

[6] "One must not imagine or invent but find out what nature does and makes manifest."

complex, surround, traverse, vibrate, rotate, repel, attract, without stop; that man's senses are conscious of few, and only in a partial degree; but that, from the beginning of organic existence his consciousness has been induced, expanded, trained in the lines of his sensitiveness; and that the rise of his faculties from a lower power to a higher, or from a narrower to a wider field, may be due to the function of assimilating and storing outside force or forces. There is nothing unscientific in the idea that, beyond the lines of force felt by the senses, the universe may be—as it has always been—either a supersensuous chaos or a divine unity, which irresistibly attracts, and is either life or death to penetrate. Thus far, religion, philosophy, and science seem to go hand in hand. The schools begin their vital battle only there. In the earlier stages of progress, the forces to be assimilated were simple and easy to absorb, but, as the mind of man enlarged its range, it enlarged the field of complexity, and must continue to do so, even into chaos, until the reservoirs of sensuous or supersensuous energies are exhausted, or cease to affect him, or until he succumbs to their excess.

For past history, this way of grouping its sequences may answer for a chart of relations, although any serious student would need to invent another, to compare or correct its errors; but past history is only a value of relation to the future, and this value is wholly one of convenience, which can be tested only by experiment. Any law of movement must include, to make it a convenience, some mechanical formula of acceleration.

[*Chapter 34, "A Law of Acceleration," presents elaborate statistics from the history of science to substantiate his dynamic theory of history. The next and final chapter, "Nunc Age (1905)," applies it to his own life.*]

1907

MONT-SAINT-MICHEL
AND CHARTRES[1]

1. *Saint Michiel de la Mer del Peril*[2]

THE ARCHANGEL loved heights. Standing on the summit of the tower that crowned his church, wings upspread, sword uplifted, the devil crawling be-

From *Mont-Saint-Michel and Chartres*, by Henry Brooks Adams. Reprinted with the permission of Houghton Mifflin Company.

[1] Since there is no important use of narrative to provide structure in this book, the only needed links between the selections are thematic ones, which may be found in the Introduction, pages 334 *ff.*, above. Also, since history in the conventional sense is only tangential to Adams's purposes, proper names are not identified unless essential to an understanding of those purposes, which might be obscured by over-annotation.

[2] "Saint Michael of the Sea of Peril." In the opening paragraph Adams turns the phrase around to read "in Peril of the Sea."

[handwritten: At Chartres he found the perfect symbol of unity. Built for Virgin who influenced all men of all degrees.]

MONT-SAINT-MICHEL AND CHARTRES 381

[handwritten right margin: Virgin greatest force! He was! energizing, controlling, comforting, beautifying]

neath, and the cock, symbol of eternal vigilance, perched on his mailed foot, Saint Michael held a place of his own in heaven and on earth which seems, in the eleventh century, to leave hardly room for the Virgin of the Crypt at Chartres, still less for the Beau Christ of the thirteenth century at Amiens. The Archangel stands for Church and State, and both militant. He is the conqueror of Satan, the mightiest of all created spirits, the nearest to God. His place was where the danger was greatest; therefore you find him here. For the same reason he was, while the pagan danger lasted, the patron saint of France. So the Normans, when they were converted to Christianity, put themselves under his powerful protection. So he stood for centuries on his Mount in Peril of the Sea, watching across the tremor of the immense ocean—*immensi tremor oceani*—as Louis XI, inspired for once to poetry, inscribed on the collar of the Order of Saint Michael which he created. So soldiers, nobles, and monarchs went on pilgrimage to his shrine; so the common people followed, and still follow, like ourselves.

The church stands high on the summit of this granite rock, and on its west front is the platform, to which the tourist ought first to climb. From the edge of this platform, the eye plunges down, two hundred and thirty-five feet, to the wide sands or the wider ocean, as the tides recede or advance, under an infinite sky, over a restless sea, which even we tourists can understand and feel without books or guides; but when we turn from the western view, and look at the church door, thirty or forty yards from the parapet where we stand, one needs to be eight centuries old to know what this mass of encrusted architecture meant to its builders, and even then one must still learn to feel it. The man who wanders into the twelfth century is lost, unless he can grow prematurely young.

One can do it, as one can play with children. Wordsworth,[3] whose practical sense equalled his intuitive genius, carefully limited us to "a season of calm weather," which is certainly best; but granting a fair frame of mind, one can still "have sight of that immortal sea" which brought us hither from the twelfth century; one can even travel thither and see the children sporting on the shore. Our sense is partially atrophied from disuse, but it is still alive, at least in old people, who alone, as a class, have the time to be young.

One needs only to be old enough in order to be as young as one will. From the top of this Abbey Church one looks across the bay to Avranches, and towards Coutances and the Cotentin—the *Constantinus pagus* [province of Constantine]—whose shore, facing us, recalls the coast of New Eng-

[3] "Ode: Intimations of Immortality," lines 165-171; also 67-68:

> Hence in a season of calm weather
> Though inland far we be,
> Our Souls have sight of that immortal sea
> Which brought us hither,
> Can in a moment travel thither,
> And see the Children sport upon the shore,
> And hear the mighty waters rolling evermore.

* * *

> Shades of the prison-house begin to close
> Upon the growing Boy.

land. The relation between the granite of one coast and that of the other
may be fanciful, but the relation between the people who live on each is as
hard and practical a fact as the granite itself. When one enters the church,
one notes first the four great triumphal piers or columns, at the intersection
of the nave and transepts, and on looking into M. Corroyer's architectural
study which is the chief source of all one's acquaintance with the Mount,
one learns that these piers were constructed in 1058. Four out of five American tourists will instantly recall the only date of mediaeval history they
ever knew, the date of the Norman Conquest. Eight years after these piers
were built, in 1066, Duke William of Normandy raised an army of forty
thousand men in these parts, and in northern France, whom he took to
England, where they mostly stayed. For a hundred and fifty years, until 1204,
Normandy and England were united; the Norman peasant went freely to
England with his lord, spiritual or temporal; the Norman woman, a very capable person, followed her husband or her parents; Normans held nearly all
the English fiefs; filled the English Church; crowded the English Court; created the English law; and we know that French was still currently spoken in
England as late as 1400, or thereabouts, "After the scole of Stratford atte
bowe." [4] The aristocratic Norman names still survive in part, and if we look
up their origin here we shall generally find them in villages so remote and insignificant that their place can hardly be found on any ordinary map; but the
common people had no surnames, and cannot be traced, although for every
noble whose name or blood survived in England or in Normandy, we must
reckon hundreds of peasants. Since the generation which followed William to
England in 1066, we can reckon twenty-eight or thirty from father to son,
and, if you care to figure up the sum, you will find that you had about two
hundred and fifty million arithmetical ancestors living in the middle of the
eleventh century. The whole population of England and northern France
may then have numbered five million, but if it were fifty it would not much
affect the certainty that, if you have any English blood at all, you have also
Norman. If we could go back and live again in all our two hundred and fifty
million arithmetical ancestors of the eleventh century, we should find ourselves doing many surprising things, but among the rest we should pretty
certainly be ploughing most of the fields of the Cotentin and Calvados; going
to mass in every parish church in Normandy; rendering military service to
every lord, spiritual or temporal, in all this region; and helping to build the
Abbey Church at Mont-Saint-Michel. From the roof of the Cathedral of
Coutances over yonder, one may look away over the hills and woods, the
farms and fields of Normandy, and so familiar, so homelike are they, one
can almost take oath that in this, or the other, or in all, one knew life once
and has never so fully known it since.

   Never so fully known it since! For we of the eleventh century, hard-
headed, close-fisted, grasping, shrewd, as we were, and as Normans are still
said to be, stood more fully in the centre of the world's movement than our
English descendants ever did. We were a part, and a great part, of the
Church, of France, and of Europe. The Leos and Gregories of the tenth and

----

[4] The reference is to the Anglicized French spoken by Chaucer's Prioress, "For
Frenssh of Parys was to hire unknowe" (see *Canterbury Tales*, Prologue, lines 125-126).

eleventh centuries leaned on us in their great struggle for reform. Our Duke
Richard-Sans-Peur, in 966, turned the old canons out of the Mount in order to
bring here the highest influence of the time, the Benedictine monks of Monte
Cassino. Richard II, grandfather of William the Conqueror, began this Abbey
Church in 1020, and helped Abbot Hildebert to build it. When William the
Conqueror in 1066 set out to conquer England, Pope Alexander II stood be-
hind him and blessed his banner. From that moment our Norman Dukes cast
the Kings of France into the shade. Our activity was not limited to northern
Europe, or even confined by Anjou and Gascony. When we stop at Coutances,
we will drive out to Hauteville to see where Tancred came from, whose sons
Robert and Roger were conquering Naples and Sicily at the time when the
Abbey Church was building on the Mount. Normans were everywhere in
1066, and everywhere in the lead of their age. We were a serious race. If you
want other proof of it, besides our record in war and in politics, you have only
to look at our art. Religious art is the measure of human depth and sincerity; any triviality, any weakness cries aloud. If this church on the Mount is
not proof enough of Norman character, we will stop at Coutances for a wider
view. Then we will go to Caen and Bayeux. From there, it would almost be
worth our while to leap at once to Palermo. It was in the year 1131 or thereabouts that Roger began the Cathedral at Cefalu and the Chapel Royal at
Palermo; it was about the year 1174 that his grandson William began the
Cathedral of Monreale. No art—either Greek or Byzantine, Italian or Arab—
has ever created two religious types so beautiful, so serious, so impressive,
and yet so different, as Mont-Saint-Michel watching over its northern ocean,
and Monreale, looking down over its forests of orange and lemon, on Palermo and the Sicilian seas.

Down nearly to the end of the twelfth century the Norman was fairly
master of the world in architecture as in arms, although the thirteenth century belonged to France, and we must look for its glories on the Seine and
Marne and Loire; but for the present we are in the eleventh century—tenants
of the Duke or of the Church or of small feudal lords who take their names
from the neighbourhood—Beaumont, Carteret, Gréville, Percy, Pierpont—
who, at the Duke's bidding, will each call out his tenants, perhaps ten men-at-
arms with their attendants, to fight in Brittany, or in the Vexin toward Paris,
or on the great campaign for the conquest of England which is to come within
ten years,—the greatest military effort that has been made in western Europe
since Charlemagne and Roland were defeated at Roncesvalles three hundred
years ago. For the moment, we are helping to quarry granite for the Abbey
Church, and to haul it to the Mount, or load it on our boat. We never fail to
make our annual pilgrimage to the Mount on the Archangel's Day, October 16. We expect to be called out for a new campaign which Duke William
threatens against Brittany, and we hear stories that Harold the Saxon, the
powerful Earl of Wessex in England, is a guest, or, as some say, a prisoner or
a hostage, at the Duke's Court, and will go with us on the campaign. The year
is 1058.

All this time we have been standing on the *parvis*, looking out over the
sea and sands which are as good eleventh-century landscape as they ever
were; or turning at times towards the church door which is the *pons seclorum*,

the bridge of ages, between us and our ancestors. Now that we have made an attempt, such as it is, to get our minds into a condition to cross the bridge without breaking down in the effort, we enter the church and stand face to face with eleventh-century architecture; a ground-plan which dates from 1020; a central tower, or its piers, dating from 1058; and a church completed in 1135. France can offer few buildings of this importance equally old, with dates so exact. Perhaps the closest parallel to Mont-Saint-Michel is Saint-Benoît-sur-Loire, above Orléans, which seems to have been a shrine almost as popular as the Mount, at the same time. Chartres was also a famous shrine, but of the Virgin, and the west porch of Chartres, which is to be our peculiar pilgrimage, was a hundred years later than the ground-plan of Mont-Saint-Michel, although Chartres porch is the usual starting-point of northern French art. Queen Matilda's Abbaye-aux-Dames, now the Church of the Trinity, at Caen, dates from 1066. Saint Sernin at Toulouse, the porch of the Abbey Church at Moissac, Notre-Dame-du-Port at Clermont, the Abbey Church at Vézelay, are all said to be twelfth-century. Even San Marco at Venice was new in 1020.

Yet in 1020 Norman art was already too ambitious. Certainly nine hundred years leave their traces on granite as well as on other material, but the granite of Abbot Hildebert would have stood securely enough, if the Abbot had not asked too much from it. Perhaps he asked too much from the Archangel, for the thought of the Archangel's superiority was clearly the inspiration of his plan. The apex of the granite rock rose like a sugar-loaf two hundred and forty feet (73.6 metres) above mean sea-level. Instead of cutting the summit away to give his church a secure rock foundation, which would have sacrificed about thirty feet of height, the Abbot took the apex of the rock for his level, and on all sides built out foundations of masonry to support the walls of his church. The apex of the rock is the floor of the *croisée*, the intersection of nave and transept. On this solid foundation the Abbot rested the chief weight of the church, which was the central tower, supported by the four great piers which still stand; but from the croisée in the centre westward to the parapet of the platform, the Abbot filled the whole space with masonry, and his successors built out still farther, until some two hundred feet of stonework ends now in a perpendicular wall of eighty feet or more. In this space are several ranges of chambers, but the structure might perhaps have proved strong enough to support the light Romanesque front which was usual in the eleventh century, had not fashions in architecture changed in the great epoch of building, a hundred and fifty years later, when Abbot Robert de Torigny thought proper to reconstruct the west front, and build out two towers on its flanks. The towers were no doubt beautiful, if one may judge from the towers of Bayeux and Coutances, but their weight broke down the vaulting beneath, and one of them fell in 1300. In 1618 the whole façade began to give way, and in 1776 not only the façade but also three of the seven spans of the nave were pulled down. Of Abbot Hildebert's nave, only four arches remain.

Still, the overmastering strength of the eleventh century is stamped on a great scale here, not only in the four spans of the nave, and in the transepts, but chiefly in the triumphal columns of the croisée. No one is likely to forget what Norman architecture was, who takes the trouble to pass once through this fragment of its earliest bloom. The dimensions are not great, though greater than safe construction warranted. Abbot Hildebert's whole church did not exceed two hundred and thirty feet in length in the interior, and the span of the triumphal arch was only about twenty-three feet, if the books can be trusted. The nave of the Abbaye-aux-Dames appears to have about the same width, and probably neither of them was meant to be vaulted. The roof was of timber, and about sixty-three feet high at its apex. Compared with the great churches of the thirteenth century, this building is modest, but its size is not what matters to us. Its style is the starting-point of all our future travels. Here is your first eleventh-century church! How does it affect you?

Serious and simple to excess! is it not? Young people rarely enjoy it. They prefer the Gothic, even as you see it here, looking at us from the choir, through the great Norman arch. No doubt they are right, since they are young: but men and women who have lived long and are tired,—who want rest,—who have done with aspirations and ambition—whose life has been a broken arch, —feel this repose and self-restraint as they feel nothing else. The quiet strength of these curved lines, the solid support of these heavy columns, the moderate proportions, even the modified lights, the absence of display, of effort, of self-consciousness, satisfy them as no other art does. They come back to it to rest, after a long circle of pilgrimage—the cradle of rest from which their ancestors started. Even here they find the repose none too deep.

Indeed, when you look longer at it, you begin to doubt whether there is any repose in it at all,—whether it is not the most unreposeful thought ever put into architectural form. Perched on the extreme point of this abrupt rock, the Church Militant with its aspirant Archangel stands high above the world, and seems to threaten heaven itself. The idea is the stronger and more restless because the Church of Saint Michael is surrounded and protected by the world and the society over which it rises, as Duke William rested on his barons and their men. Neither the Saint nor the Duke was troubled by doubts about his mission. Church and State, Soul and Body, God and Man, are all one at Mont-Saint-Michel, and the business of all is to fight, each in his own way, or to stand guard for each other. Neither Church nor State is intellectual, or learned, or even strict in dogma. Here we do not feel the Trinity at all; the Virgin but little; Christ hardly more; we feel only the Archangel and the Unity of God. We have little logic here, and simple faith, but we have energy. We cannot do many things which are done in the centre of civilization, at Byzantium, but we can fight, and we can build a church. No doubt we think first of the church, and next of our temporal lord; only in the last instance do we think of our private affairs, and our private affairs sometimes suffer for it; but we reckon the affairs of Church and State to be ours, too, and we carry this idea very far. Our church on the Mount is ambitious, restless, striving for effect; our conquest of England, with which the Duke is infatuated, is more ambitious still; but all this is a trifle to the outburst which is coming in the next generation; and Saint Michael on his Mount expresses it all.

Taking architecture as an expression of energy, we can some day compare Mont-Saint-Michel with Beauvais, and draw from the comparison whatever

moral suits our frame of mind; but you should first note that here, in the
eleventh century, the Church, however simple-minded or unschooled, was
not cheap. Its self-respect is worth noticing, because it was short-lived in its
art. Mont-Saint-Michel, throughout, even up to the delicate and intricate
stonework of its cloisters, is built of granite. The crypts and substructures
are as well constructed as the surfaces most exposed to view. When we get
to Chartres, which is largely a twelfth-century work, you will see that the
cathedral there, too, is superbly built, of the hardest and heaviest stone
within reach, which has nowhere settled or given way; while, beneath, you
will find a crypt that rivals the church above. The thirteenth century did not
build so. The great cathedrals after 1200 show economy, and sometimes
worse. The world grew cheap, as worlds must.

You may like it all the better for being less serious, less heroic, less militant, and more what the French call *bourgeois,* just as you may like the style
of Louis XV better than that of Louis XIV—Madame du Barry better than
Madame de Montespan—for taste is free, and all styles are good which amuse;
but since we are now beginning with the earliest, in order to step down
gracefully to the stage, whatever it is, where you prefer to stop, we must try
to understand a little of the kind of energy which Norman art expressed,
or would have expressed if it had thought in our modes. The only word
which describes the Norman style is the French word *naïf.* Littré says that
naïf comes from *natif,* as *vulgar* comes from *vulgus,* as though native traits
must be simple, and commonness must be vulgar. Both these derivative
meanings were strange to the eleventh century. Naïveté was simply natural
and vulgarity was merely coarse. Norman naïveté was not different in kind
from the naïveté of Burgundy or Gascony or Lombardy, but it was slightly
different in expression, as you will see when you travel south. Here at
Mont-Saint-Michel we have only a mutilated trunk of an eleventh-century
church to judge by. We have not even a façade, and shall have to stop at
some Norman village—at Thaon or Ouistreham—to find a west front
which might suit the Abbey here, but wherever we find it we shall find something a little more serious, more military, and more practical than you will
meet in other Romanesque work, farther south. So, too, the central tower or
lantern—the most striking feature of Norman churches—has fallen here
at Mont-Saint-Michel, and we shall have to replace it from Cérisy-la-Forêt,
and Lessay, and Falaise. We shall find much to say about the value of
the lantern on a Norman church, and the singular power it expresses.
We shall have still more to say of the towers which flank the west front of
Norman churches, but these are mostly twelfth-century, and will lead us
far beyond Coutances and Bayeux, from *flèche*[5] to *flèche,* till we come to
the flèche of all flèches, at Chartres.

We shall have a whole chapter of study, too, over the eleventh-century
apse, but here at Mont-Saint-Michel, Abbot Hildebert's choir went the way of
his nave and tower. He built out even more boldly to the east than to the
west, and although the choir stood for some four hundred years, which is a
sufficient life for most architecture, the foundations gave way at last, and it

---

5 "Spire" (literally "arrow").

fell in 1421, in the midst of the English wars, and remained a ruin until 1450. Then it was rebuilt, a monument of the last days of the Gothic, so that now, standing at the western door, you can look down the church, and see the two limits of mediaeval architecture married together,—the earliest Norman and the latest French. Through the Romanesque arches of 1058, you look into the exuberant choir of latest Gothic, finished in 1521. Although the two structures are some five hundred years apart, they live pleasantly together. The Gothic died gracefully in France. The choir is charming, —far more charming than the nave, as the beautiful woman is more charming than the elderly man. One need not quarrel about styles of beauty, as long as the man and woman are evidently satisfied and love and admire each other still, with all the solidity of faith to hold them up; but, at least, one cannot help seeing, as one looks from the older to the younger style, that whatever the woman's sixteenth-century charm may be, it is not the man's eleventh-century trait of naïveté;—far from it! The simple, serious, silent dignity and energy of the eleventh century have gone. Something more complicated stands in their place; graceful, self-conscious, rhetorical, and beautiful as perfect rhetoric, with its clearness, light, and line, and the wealth of tracery that verges on the florid.

The crypt of the same period, beneath, is almost finer still, and even in seriousness stands up boldly by the side of the Romanesque; but we have no time to run off into the sixteenth century: we have still to learn the alphabet of art in France. One must live deep into the eleventh century in order to understand the twelfth, and even after passing years in the twelfth, we shall find the thirteenth in many ways a world of its own, with a beauty not always inherited, and sometimes not bequeathed. At the Mount we can go no farther into the eleventh as far as concerns architecture. We shall have to follow the Romanesque to Caen and so up the Seine to the Île de France, and across to the Loire and the Rhone, far to the South where its home lay. All the other eleventh-century work has been destoyed here or built over, except at one point, on the level of the splendid crypt we just turned from, called the Gros Piliers,[6] beneath the choir.

There, according to M. Corroyer, in a corner between great constructions of the twelfth century and the vast Merveille of the thirteenth, the old refectory of the eleventh was left as a passage from one group of buildings to the other. Below it is the kitchen of Hildebert. Above, on the level of the church, was the dormitory. These eleventh-century abbatial buildings faced north and west, and are close to the present parvis, opposite the last arch of the nave. The lower levels of Hildebert's plan served as supports or buttresses to the church above, and must therefore be older than the nave; probably older than the triumphal piers of 1058.

Hildebert planned them in 1020, and died after carrying his plans out so far that they could be completed by Abbot Ralph de Beaumont, who was especially selected by Duke William in 1048, "more for his high birth than for his merits." Ralph de Beaumont died in 1060, and was succeeded by Abbot

---

[6] "Large Pillars." The Merveille, mentioned in the next paragraph (and described at length in Chapter 3, omitted), is a vast pile of superimposed buildings with a façade 230 by 180 feet.

Ranulph, an especial favourite of Duchess Matilda, and held in high esteem by Duke William. The list of names shows how much social importance was attributed to the place. The Abbot's duties included that of entertainment on a great scale. The Mount was one of the most famous shrines of northern Europe. We are free to take for granted that all the great people of Normandy slept at the Mount and, supposing M. Corroyer to be right, that they dined in this room, between 1050, when the building must have been in use, down to 1122 when the new abbatial quarters were built.

How far the monastic rules restricted social habits is a matter for antiquaries to settle if they can, and how far those rules were observed in the case of great secular princes; but the eleventh century was not very strict, and the rule of the Benedictines was always mild, until the Cistercians and Saint Bernard stiffened its discipline toward 1120. Even then the Church showed strong leanings toward secular poetry and popular tastes. The drama belonged to it almost exclusively, and the Mysteries and Miracle plays which were acted under its patronage often contained nothing of religion except the miracle. The greatest poem of the eleventh century was the "Chanson de Roland," and of that the Church took a sort of possession. At Chartres we shall find Charlemagne and Roland dear to the Virgin, and at about the same time, as far away as at Assisi in the Perugian country, Saint Francis himself—the nearest approach the Western world ever made to an Oriental incarnation of the divine essence—loved the French *romans*, and typified himself in the "Chanson de Roland." With Mont-Saint-Michel, the "Chanson de Roland" is almost one. The "Chanson" is in poetry what the Mount is in architecture. Without the "Chanson," one cannot approach the feeling which the eleventh century built into the Archangel's church. Probably there was never a day, certainly never a week, during several centuries, when portions of the "Chanson" were not sung, or recited, at the Mount, and if there was one room where it was most at home, this one, supposing it to be the old refectory, claims to be the place.

6. The Virgin of Chartres

We must take ten minutes to accustom our eyes to the light, and we had better use them to seek the reason why we come to Chartres rather than to Rheims or Amiens or Bourges, for the cathedral that fills our ideal. The truth is, there are several reasons; there generally are, for doing the things we like; and after you have studied Chartres to the ground, and got your reasons settled, you will never find an antiquarian to agree with you; the architects will probably listen to you with contempt; and even these excellent priests, whose kindness is great, whose patience is heavenly, and whose good opinion you would so gladly gain, will turn from you with pain, if not with horror. The Gothic is singular in this; one seems easily at home in the Renaissance; one is not too strange in the Byzantine; as for the Roman, it is ourselves; and we could walk blindfolded through every chink and cranny of the Greek mind; all these styles seem modern, when we come close to them; but the Gothic gets away. No two men think alike about it, and no woman agrees with either man. The Church itself never agreed about it, and the architects agree even less than the priests. To most minds it casts too many shadows; it wraps itself in mystery; and when people talk of mystery, they commonly mean fear. To others, the Gothic seems hoary with age and decrepitude, and its shadows mean death. What is curious to watch is the fanatical conviction of the Gothic enthusiast, to whom the twelfth century means exuberant youth, the eternal child of Wordsworth, over whom its immortality broods like the day; it is so simple and yet so complicated; it sees so much and so little; it loves so many toys and cares for so few necessities; its youth is so young, its age so old, and its youthful yearning for old thought is so disconcerting, like the mysterious senility of the baby that

> Deaf and silent, reads the eternal deep
> Haunted forever by the eternal mind.[1]

One need not take it more seriously than one takes the baby itself. Our amusement is to play with it, and to catch its meaning in its smile; and whatever Chartres may be now, when young it was a smile. To the Church, no doubt, its cathedral here has a fixed and administrative meaning, which is the same as that of every other bishop's seat and with which we have nothing whatever to do. To us, it is a child's fancy; a toyhouse to please the Queen of Heaven,—to please her so much that she would be happy in it,—to charm her till she smiled.

The Queen Mother was as majestic as you like; she was absolute; she could be stern; she was not above being angry; but she was still a woman, who loved grace, beauty, ornament—her toilette, robes, jewels;—who considered the arrangements of her palace with attention, and liked both light and colour; who kept a keen eye on her Court, and exacted prompt and willing obedience from king and archbishops as well as from beggars and drunken priests. She protected her friends and punished her enemies. She required space, beyond what was known in the Courts of kings, because she was liable at all times to have ten thousand people begging her for favours—mostly inconsistent with law—and deaf to refusal. She was extremely sensitive to neglect, to disagreeable impressions, to want of intelligence in her surroundings. She was the greatest artist, as she was the greatest philosopher and musician and theologist, that ever lived on earth, except her Son, Who, at Chartres, is still an Infant under her guardianship. Her taste was infallible; her sentence eternally final. This church was built for her in this spirit of simple-minded, practical, utilitarian faith,—in this singleness of thought, exactly as a little girl sets up a doll-house for her favourite blonde doll. Unless you can go back to your dolls, you are out of place here. If you

---

[1] Wordsworth, "Ode: Intimations of Immortality," lines 112-113. The lines immediately preceding and following this quotation (108-111, 114) read:

> Thou, whose exterior semblance doth belie
> Thy Soul's immensity;
> Thou best Philosopher, who yet dost keep
> Thy heritage, thou Eye among the blind,

> * * *

> Mighty Prophet! Seer blest!

can go back to them, and get rid for one small hour of the weight of custom, you shall see Chartres in glory.

The palaces of earthly queens were hovels compared with these palaces of the Queen of Heaven at Chartres, Paris, Laon, Noyon, Rheims, Amiens, Rouen, Bayeux, Coutances—a list that might be stretched into a volume. The nearest approach we have made to a palace was the Merveille at Mont-Saint-Michel, but no Queen had a palace equal to that. The Merveille was built, or designed, about the year 1200; toward the year 1500, Louis XI built a great castle at Loches in Touraine, and there Queen Anne de Bretagne had apartments which still exist, and which we will visit. At Blois you shall see the residence which served for Catherine de Medicis till her death in 1589. Anne de Bretagne was trebly queen, and Catherine de Medicis took her standard of comfort from the luxury of Florence. At Versailles you can see the apartments which the queens of the Bourbon line occupied through their century of magnificence. All put together, and then trebled in importance, could not rival the splendour of any single cathedral dedicated to Queen Mary in the thirteenth century; and of them all, Chartres was built to be peculiarly and exceptionally her delight.

One has grown so used to this sort of loose comparison, this reckless waste of words, that one no longer adopts an idea unless it is driven in with hammers of statistics and columns of figures. With the irritating demand for literal exactness and perfectly straight lines which lights up every truly American eye, you will certainly ask when this exaltation of Mary began, and unless you get the dates, you will doubt the facts. It is your own fault if they are tiresome; you might easily read them all in the "Iconographie de la Sainte Vierge," [2] by M. Rohault de Fleury, published in 1878. You can start at Byzantium with the Empress Helena in 326, or with the Council of Ephesus in 431. You will find the Virgin acting as the patron saint of Constantinople and of the Imperial residence, under as many names as Artemis or Aphrodite had borne. As Godmother ($\Theta\epsilon o\mu\eta\tau\eta\rho$), Deipara ($\Theta\epsilon o\tau o\kappa o\varsigma$),[3] Pathfinder ('$O\delta\eta\gamma\eta\tau\rho\iota a$), she was the chief favourite of the Eastern Empire, and her picture was carried at the head of every procession and hung on the wall of every hut and hovel, as it is still wherever the Greek Church goes. In the year 610, when Heraclius sailed from Carthage to dethrone Phocas at Constantinople, his ships carried the image of the Virgin at their mastheads. In 1143, just before the flèche on the Chartres clocher was begun, the Basileus John Comnenus died, and so devoted was he to the Virgin that, on a triumphal entry into Constantinople, he put the image of the Mother of God in his chariot, while he himself walked. In the Western Church the Virgin had always been highly honoured, but it was not until the crusades that she began to overshadow the Trinity itself. Then her miracles became more frequent and her shrines more frequented, so that Chartres, soon after 1100, was rich enough to build its western portal with Byzantine splendour. A proof of the new outburst can be read in the story of Citeaux. For us, Citeaux means Saint Bernard, who joined the Order in 1112,

[2] "Iconography [Study of Images] of the Holy Virgin." Maurice de Fleury was one of two chief historians of French architecture cited by Adams, Viollet-le-Duc being the other (see Chapter 16, below).

[3] Latin (and Greek) for "God-bearer."

and in 1115 founded his Abbey of Clairvaux in the territory of Troyes. In him, the religious emotion of the half-century between the first and second crusades (1095-1145) centred as in no one else. He was a French precursor of Saint Francis of Assisi who lived a century later. If we were to plunge into the story of Citeaux and Saint Bernard we should never escape, for Saint Bernard incarnates what we are trying to understand, and his mind is further from us than the architecture. You would lose hold of everything actual, if you could comprehend in its contradictions the strange mixture of passion and caution, the austerity, the self-abandonment, the vehemence, the restraint, the love, the hate, the miracles, and the scepticism of Saint Bernard. The Cistercian Order, which was founded in 1098, from the first put all its churches under the special protection of the Virgin, and Saint Bernard in his time was regarded as the apple of the Virgin's eye. Tradition as old as the twelfth century, which long afterwards gave to Murillo the subject of a famous painting, told that once, when he was reciting before her statue the "Ave Maris Stella," and came to the words, "Monstra te esse Matrem," [4] the image, pressing its breast, dropped on the lips of her servant three drops of the milk which had nourished the Saviour. The same miracle, in various forms, was told of many other persons, both saints and sinners; but it made so much impression on the mind of the age that, in the fourteenth century, Dante, seeking in Paradise for some official introduction to the foot of the Throne, found no intercessor with the Queen of Heaven more potent than Saint Bernard. You can still read Bernard's hymns to the Virgin, and even his sermons, if you like. To him she was the great mediator. In the eyes of a culpable humanity, Christ was too sublime, too terrible, too just, but not even the weakest human frailty could fear to approach his Mother. Her attribute was humility; her love and pity were infinite. "Let him deny your mercy who can say that he has ever asked it in vain."

Saint Bernard was emotional and to a certain degree mystical, like Adam de Saint-Victor, whose hymns were equally famous, but the emotional saints and mystical poets were not by any means allowed to establish exclusive rights to the Virgin's favour. Abélard was as devoted as they were, and wrote hymns as well. Philosophy claimed her, and Albert the Great, the head of scholasticism, the teacher of Thomas Aquinas, decided in her favour the question: "Whether the Blessed Virgin possessed perfectly the seven liberal arts." The Church at Chartres had decided it a hundred years before by putting the seven liberal arts next her throne, with Aristotle himself to witness; but Albertus gave the reason: "I hold that she did, for it is written, 'Wisdom has built herself a house, and has sculptured seven columns.' That house is the blessed Virgin; the seven columns are the seven liberal arts. Mary, therefore, had perfect mastery of science." Naturally she had also perfect mastery of economics, and most of her great churches were built in economic centres. The guilds were, if possible, more devoted to her than the monks; the bourgeoisie of Paris, Rouen, Amiens, Laon, spent money by millions to gain her favour. Most surprising of all, the great military class was perhaps the most vociferous. Of all inappropriate haunts for the gentle, courteous, pitying Mary, a field of

[4] "Hail, Star of the Sea . . . show us that thou art our mother."

battle seems to be the worst, if not distinctly blasphemous; yet the greatest French warriors insisted on her leading them into battle, and in the actual mêlée when men were killing each other, on every battlefield in Europe, for at least five hundred years, Mary was present, leading both sides. The battle-cry of the famous Constable du Guesclin was "Notre-Dame-Guesclin"; "Notre-Dame-Coucy" was the cry of the great Sires de Coucy; "Notre-Dame-Auxerre"; "Notre-Dame-Sancerre"; "Notre-Dame-Hainault"; "Notre-Dame-Gueldres"; "Notre-Dame-Bourbon"; "Notre-Dame-Bearn";—all well-known battle-cries. The King's own battle at one time cried, "Notre-Dame-Saint-Denis-Montjoie"; the Dukes of Burgundy cried, "Notre-Dame-Bourgogne"; and even the soldiers of the Pope were said to cry, "Notre-Dame-Saint-Pierre."

The measure of this devotion, which proves to any religious American mind, beyond possible cavil, its serious and practical reality, is the money it cost. According to statistics, in the single century between 1170 and 1270, the French built eighty cathedrals and nearly five hundred churches of the cathedral class, which would have cost, according to an estimate made in 1840, more than five thousand millions to replace. Five thousand million francs is a thousand million dollars, and this covered only the great churches of a single century. The same scale of expenditure had been going on since the year 1000, and almost every parish in France had rebuilt its church in stone; to this day France is strewn with the ruins of this architecture, and yet the still preserved churches of the eleventh and twelfth centuries, among the churches that belong to the Romanesque and Transition period, are numbered by hundreds until they reach well into the thousands. The share of this capital which was —if one may use a commercial figure—invested in the Virgin cannot be fixed, any more than the total sum given to religious objects between 1000 and 1300; but in a spiritual and artistic sense, it was almost the whole, and expressed an intensity of conviction never again reached by any passion, whether of religion, of loyalty, of patriotism, or of wealth; perhaps never even paralleled by any single economic effort except in war. Nearly every great church of the twelfth and thirteenth centuries belonged to Mary, until in France one asks for the church of Notre Dame as though it meant cathedral; but, not satisfied with this, she contracted the habit of requiring in all churches a chapel of her own, called in English the "Lady Chapel," which was apt to be as large as the church but was always meant to be handsomer; and there, behind the high altar, in her own private apartment, Mary sat, receiving her innumerable suppliants, and ready at any moment to step up upon the high altar itself to support the tottering authority of the local saint.

Expenditure like this rests invariably on an economic idea. Just as the French of the nineteenth century invested their surplus capital in a railway system in the belief that they would make money by it in this life, in the thirteenth they trusted their money to the Queen of Heaven because of their belief in her power to repay it with interest in the life to come. The investment was based on the power of Mary as Queen rather than on any orthodox Church conception of the Virgin's legitimate station. Papal Rome never greatly loved Byzantine empresses or French queens. The Virgin of Chartres was never wholly sympathetic to the Roman Curia. To this day the Church writers—like the Abbé Bulteau or M. Rohault de Fleury—are singularly shy of the true Virgin of majesty, whether at Chartres or at Byzantium or wherever she is seen. The fathers Martin and Cahier at Bourges alone felt her true value. Had the Church controlled her, the Virgin would perhaps have remained prostrate at the foot of the Cross. Dragged by a Byzantine Court, backed by popular insistence and impelled by overpowering self-interest, the Church accepted the Virgin throned and crowned, seated by Christ, the Judge throned and crowned; but even this did not wholly satisfy the French of the thirteenth century who seemed bent on absorbing Christ in His Mother, and making the Mother the Church, and Christ the Symbol.

The Church had crowned and enthroned her almost from the beginning, and could not have dethroned her if it would. In all Christian art—sculpture or mosaic, painting or poetry—the Virgin's rank was expressly asserted. Saint Bernard, like John Comnenus, and probably at the same time (1120-40), chanted hymns to the Virgin as Queen:

O salutaris Virgo Stella Maris Generans prolem, Aequitatis solem,	O saviour Virgin, Star of Sea, Who bore for child the Son of Justice.

Lucis auctorem, Retinens pudorem,
    Suscipe laudem!
	The source of Light, Virgin always
	    Hear our praise!

Celi Regina Per quam medicina Datur aegrotis, Gratia devotis,	Queen of Heaven who have given Medicine to the sick, Grace to the devout,

Gaudium moestis, Mundo lux coelestis,
    Spesque salutis;
	Joy to the sad, Heaven's light to the world
	    And hope of salvation;

Aula regalis, Virgo specialis,
Posce medelam Nobis et tutelam,
Suscipe vota, Precibusque cuncta
    Pelle molesta!
	Court royal, Virgin typical,
	Grant us cure and guard,
	Accept our vows, and by prayers
	    Drive all griefs away!

As the lyrical poet of the twelfth century, Adam de Saint-Victor seems to have held rank higher if possible than that of Saint Bernard, and his hymns on the Virgin are certainly quite as emphatic an assertion of her majesty:

Imperatix supernorum!
Superatrix infernorum!
Eligenda via coeli,
Retinenda spe fideli,
Separatos a te longe
Revocatos ad te junge
    Tuorum collegio!
	Empress of the highest,
	Mistress over the lowest,
	Chosen path of Heaven,
	Held fast by faithful hope,
	Those separated from you far,
	Recalled to you, unite
	    In your fold!

To delight in the childish jingle of the mediaeval Latin is a sign of a futile mind, no doubt, and I beg pardon of you and of the Church for wasting your precious summer day on poetry which was regarded as mystical in its age and which now sounds like a nursery rhyme; but a verse or two of Adam's hymn on the Assumption of the Virgin completes the record of her rank, and goes to complete also the documentary proof of her majesty at Chartres:

Salve, Mater Salvatoris!
Vas electum! Vas honoris!
   Vas coelestis Gratiae!
Ab aeterno Vas provisum!
Vas insigne! Vas excisum
   Manu sapientiae!

Salve, Mater pietatis,
Et totius Trinitatis
Nobile Triclinium!
Verbi tamen incarnati

Speciale majestati

   Praeparans hospitium!

O Maria! Stella maris!
Dignitate singularis,
Super omnes ordinaris
   Ordines coelestium!
In supermo sita poli
Nos commenda tuae proli,
Ne terrores sive doli
   Nos supplantent hostium!

Mother of our Saviour, hail!
Chosen vessel! Sacred Grail!
   Font of celestial grace!
From eternity forethought!
By the hand of Wisdom wrought!
   Precious, faultless Vase!

Hail, Mother of Divinity!
Hail, Temple of the Trinity!
   Home of the Triune God!
In whom the Incarnate Word
   had birth,
The King! to whom you gave on
   earth
Imperial abode.

Oh, Maria! Constellation!
Inspiration! Elevation!
Rule and Law and Ordination
   Of the angels' host!
Highest height of God's Creation,
Pray your Son's commiseration,
Lest, by fear or fraud, salvation
   For our souls be lost!

Constantly—one might better say at once, officially, she was addressed in
these terms of supreme majesty: "Imperatrix supernorum!" "Coeli Regina!"
"Aula regalis!" [5] but the twelfth century seemed determined to carry the idea
out to its logical conclusion in defiance of dogma. Not only was the Son absorbed in the Mother, or represented as under her guardianship, but the Father
fared no better, and the Holy Ghost followed. The poets regarded the Virgin
as the "Templum Trinitatis"; "totius Trinitatis nobile Triclinium." [6] She
was the refectory of the Trinity—the "Triclinium"—because the refectory
was the largest room and contained the whole of the members, and was divided in three parts by two rows of columns. She was the "Templum Trinitatis," the Church itself, with its triple aisle. The Trinity was absorbed in her.

This is a delicate subject in the Church, and you must feel it with delicacy,
without brutally insisting on its necessary contradictions. All theology and all
philosophy are full of contradictions quite as flagrant and far less sympathetic.
This particular variety of religious faith is simply human, and has made its
appearance in one form or another in nearly all religions; but though the
twelfth century carried it to an extreme, and at Chartres you see it in its most
charming expression, we have got always to make allowances for what was
going on beneath the surface in men's minds, consciously or unconsciously,
and for the latent scepticism which lurks behind all faith. The Church itself
never quite accepted the full claims of what was called Mariolatry. One may
be sure, too, that the bourgeois capitalist and the student of the schools, each
from his own point of view, watched the Virgin with anxious interest. The

5 "Empress of the Highest," "Queen of Heaven," "Royal Power."

6 "Temple of the Trinity," "Noble Refectory [dining room] of the whole Trinity."

bourgeois had put an enormous share of his capital into what was in fact an economical speculation, not unlike the South Sea Scheme, or the railway system of our own time; except that in one case the energy was devoted to shortening the road to Heaven; in the other, to shortening the road to Paris; but no serious schoolman could have felt entirely convinced that God would enter into a business partnership with man, to establish a sort of joint-stock society for altering the operation of divine and universal laws. The bourgois cared little for the philosophical doubt if the economical result proved to be good, but he watched this result with his usual practical sagacity, and required an experience of only about three generations (1200-1300) to satisfy himself that relics were not certain in their effects; that the Saints were not always able or willing to help; that Mary herself could not certainly be bought or bribed; that prayer without money seemed to be quite as efficacious as prayer with money; and that neither the road to Heaven nor Heaven itself had been made surer or brought nearer by an investment of capital which amounted to the best part of the wealth of France. Economically speaking, he became satisfied that his enormous money-investment had proved to be an almost total loss, and the reaction on his mind was as violent as the emotion. For three hundred years it prostrated France. The efforts of the bourgeoisie and the peasantry to recover their property, so far as it was recoverable, have lasted to the present day and we had best take care not to get mixed in those passions.

If you are to get the full enjoyment of Chartres, you must, for the time, believe in Mary as Bernard and Adam did, and feel her presence as the architects did, in every stone they placed, and every touch they chiselled. You must try first to rid your mind of the traditional idea that the Gothic is an intentional expression of religious gloom. The necessity for light was the motive of the Gothic architects. They needed light and always more light, until they sacrificed safety and common sense in trying to get it. They converted their walls into windows, raised their vaults, diminished their piers, until their churches could no longer stand. You will see the limits at Beauvais; at Chartres we have not got so far, but even here, in places where the Virgin wanted it—as above the high altar—the architect has taken all the light there was to take. For the same reason, fenestration became the most important part of the Gothic architect's work, and at Chartres was uncommonly interesting because the architect was obliged to design a new system, which should at the same time satisfy the laws of construction and the taste and imagination of Mary. No doubt the first command of the Queen of Heaven was for light, but the second, at least equally imperative, was for colour. Any earthly queen, even though she were not Byzantine in taste, loved colour; and the truest of queens —the only true Queen of Queens—had richer and finer taste in colour than the queens of fifty earthly kingdoms, as you will see when we come to the immense effort to gratify her in the glass of her windows. Illusion for illusion— granting for the moment that Mary was an illusion—the Virgin Mother in this instance repaid to her worshippers a larger return for their money than the capitalist has ever been able to get, at least in this world, from any other illusion of wealth which he has tried to make a source of pleasure and profit.

The next point on which Mary evidently insisted was the arrangement for her private apartments, the apse, as distinguished from her throne-room, the choir; both being quite distinct from the hall, or reception-room of the public, which was the nave with its enlargement in the transepts. This arrangement marks the distinction between churches built as shrines for deity and churches built as halls of worship for the public. The difference is chiefly in the apse, and the apse of Chartres is the most interesting of all apses from this point of view.

The Virgin required chiefly these three things, or, if you like, these four: space, light, convenience; and colour decoration to unite and harmonize the whole. This concerns the interior; on the exterior she required statuary, and the only complete system of decorative sculpture that existed seems to belong to her churches: Paris, Rheims, Amiens, and Chartres. Mary required all this magnificence at Chartres for herself alone, not for the public. As far as one can see into the spirit of the builders, Chartres was exclusively intended for the Virgin, as the Temple of Abydos was intended for Osiris. The wants of man, beyond a mere roof-cover, and perhaps space to some degree, enter to no very great extent into the problem of Chartres. Man came to render homage or to ask favours. The Queen received him in her palace, where she alone was at home, and alone gave commands.

The artist's second thought was to exclude from his work everything that could displease Mary; and since Mary differed from living queens only in infinitely greater majesty and refinement, the artist could admit only what pleased the actual taste of the great ladies who dictated taste at the Courts of France and England, which surrounded the little Court of the Counts of Chartres. What they were—these women of the twelfth and thirteenth centuries—we shall have to see or seek in other directions; but Chartres is perhaps the most magnificent and permanent monument they left of their taste, and we can begin here with learning certain things which they were not.

In the first place, they were not in the least vague, dreamy, or mystical in a modern sense;—far from it! They seemed anxious only to throw the mysteries into a blaze of light; not so much physical, perhaps,—since they, like all women, liked moderate shadow for their toilettes—but luminous in the sense of faith. There is nothing about Chartres that you would think mystical, who know your Lohengrin, Siegfried, and Parsifal. If you care to make a study of the whole literature of the subject, read M. Mâle's "Art Religieux du XIIIe Siècle en France," and use it for a guide-book. Here you need only note how symbolic and how simple the sculpture is, on the portals and porches. Even what seems a grotesque or an abstract idea is no more than the simplest child's personification. On the walls you may have noticed the *Ane qui vielle*,—the ass playing the lyre; and on all the old churches you can see "bestiaries," as they were called, of fabulous animals, symbolic or not; but the symbolism is as simple as the realism of the oxen at Laon. It gave play to the artist in his effort for variety of decoration, and it amused the people,—probably the Virgin also was not above being amused;—now and then it seems about to suggest what you would call an esoteric meaning, that is to say, a meaning which each one of us can consider private property reserved for our own amusement, and from which the public is excluded; yet, in truth, in the Virgin's churches the public is never excluded, but invited. The Virgin even had the additional charm to the public that she was popularly supposed to have no very marked fancy for priests as such; she was a queen, a woman, and a mother, functions, all, which priests could not perform. Accordingly, she seems to have had little taste for mysteries of any sort, and even the symbols that seem most mysterious were clear to every old peasant-woman in her church. The most pleasing and promising of them all is the woman's figure you saw on the front of the cathedral in Paris; her eyes bandaged; her head bent down; her crown falling; without cloak or royal robe; holding in her hand a guidon or banner with its staff broken in more than one place. On the opposite pier stands another woman, with royal mantle, erect and commanding. The symbol is so graceful that one is quite eager to know its meaning; but every child in the Middle Ages would have instantly told you that the woman with the falling crown meant only the Jewish Synagogue, as the one with the royal robe meant the Church of Christ.

Another matter for which the female taste seemed not much to care was theology in the metaphysical sense. Mary troubled herself little about theology except when she retired into the south transept with Pierre de Dreux.[7] Even there one finds little said about the Trinity, always the most metaphysical subtlety of the Church. Indeed, you might find much amusement here in searching the cathedral for any distinct expression at all of the Trinity as a dogma recognized by Mary. One cannot take seriously the idea that the three doors, the three portals, and the three aisles express the Trinity, because, in the first place, there was no rule about it; churches might have what portals and aisles they pleased; both Paris and Bourges have five; the doors themselves are not allotted to the three members of the Trinity, nor are the portals; while another more serious objection is that the side doors and aisles are not of equal importance with the central, but mere adjuncts and dependencies, so that the architect who had misled the ignorant public into accepting so black a heresy would have deserved the stake, and would probably have gone to it. Even this suggestion of trinity is wanting in the transepts, which have only one aisle, and in the choir, which has five, as well as five or seven chapels, and, as far as an ignorant mind can penetrate, no triplets whatever. Occasionally, no doubt, you will discover in some sculpture or window, a symbol of the Trinity, but this discovery itself amounts to an admission of its absence as a controlling idea, for the ordinary worshipper must have been at least as blind as we are, and to him, as to us, it would have seemed a wholly subordinate detail. Even if the Trinity, too, is anywhere expressed, you will hardly find here an attempt to explain its metaphysical meaning—not even a mystic triangle.

The church is wholly given up to the Mother and the Son. The Father seldom appears; the Holy Ghost still more rarely. At least, this is the impression made on an ordinary visitor who has no motive to be orthodox; and it must have been the same with the thirteenth-century worshipper who came here with his mind absorbed in the perfections of Mary. Chartres represents,

[7] The south transept and porch, dedicated to Christ, was built by this powerful duke; those on the north, dedicated to the Virgin, were built by Queen Blanche. In Chapter 10 (pp. 403 ff., below) Adams ascribes this difference of emphasis more to the political feud between them than to any clash in their theological beliefs.

not the Trinity, but the identity of the Mother and Son. The Son represents the Trinity, which is thus absorbed in the Mother. The idea is not orthodox, but this is no affair of ours. The Church watches over its own.

The Virgin's wants and tastes, positive and negative, ought now to be clear enough to enable you to feel the artist's sincerity in trying to satisfy them; but first you have still to convince yourselves of the people's sincerity in employing the artists. This point is the easiest of all, for the evidence is express. In the year 1145 when the old flèche was begun,—the year before Saint Bernard preached the second crusade at Vézelay—Abbot Haimon, of Saint-Pierre-sur-Dives in Normandy, wrote to the monks of Tutbury Abbey in England a famous letter to tell of the great work which the Virgin was doing in France and which began at the Church of Chartres. "Hujus sacrae institutionis ritus apud Carnotensem ecclesiam est inchoatus." [8] From Chartres it had spread through Normandy, where it produced among other things the beautiful spire which we saw at Saint-Pierre-sur-Dives. "Postremo per totam fere Normanniam longe lateque convaluit ac loca per singula Matri misericordiae dicata praecipue occupavit." The movement affected especially the places devoted to Mary, but ran through all Normandy, far and wide. Of all Mary's miracles, the best attested, next to the preservation of her church, is the building of it; not so much because it surprises us as because it surprised even more the people of the time and the men who were its instruments. Such deep popular movements are always surprising, and at Chartres the miracle seems to have occurred three times, coinciding more or less with the dates of the crusades, and taking the organization of a crusade, as Archbishop Hugo of Rouen described it in a letter to Bishop Thierry of Amiens. The most interesting part of this letter is the evident astonishment of the writer, who might be talking to us today, so modern is he:

The inhabitants of Chartres have combined to aid in the construction of their church by transporting the materials; our Lord has rewarded their humble zeal by miracles which have roused the Normans to imitate the piety of their neighbours. . . . Since then the faithful of our diocese and of other neighbouring regions have formed associations for the same object; they admit no one into their company unless he has been to confession, has renounced enmities and revenges, and has reconciled himself with his enemies. That done, they elect a chief, under whose direction they conduct their waggons in silence and with humility.

The quarries at Berchères-l'Evêque are about five miles from Chartres. The stone is excessively hard, and was cut in blocks of considerable size, as you can see for yourselves; blocks which required great effort to transport and lay in place. The work was done with feverish rapidity, as it still shows, but it is the solidest building of the age, and without a sign of weakness yet. The Abbot told, with more surprise than pride, of the spirit which was built into the cathedral with the stone:

[8] "The observance of this holy custom is only just begun among the congregation at Chartres." The Latin quotation two sentences below is freely translated by Adams in the next sentence.

Who has ever seen!—Who has ever heard tell, in times past, that powerful princes of the world, that men brought up in honour and in wealth, that nobles, men and women, have bent their proud and haughty necks to the harness of carts, and that, like beasts of burden, they have dragged to the abode of Christ these waggons, loaded with wines, grains, oil, stone, wood, and all that is necessary for the wants of life, or for the construction of the church? But while they draw these burdens, there is one thing admirable to observe; it is that often when a thousand persons and more are attached to the chariots,—so great is the difficulty,—yet they march in such silence that not a murmur is heard, and truly if one did not see the thing with one's eyes, one might believe that among such a multitude there was hardly a person present. When they halt on the road, nothing is heard but the confession of sins, and pure and suppliant prayer to God to obtain pardon. At the voice of the priests who exhort their hearts to peace, they forget all hatred, discord is thrown far aside, debts are remitted, the unity of hearts is established.

But if any one is so far advanced in evil as to be unwilling to pardon an offender, or if he rejects the counsel of the priest who has piously advised him, his offering is instantly thrown from the wagon as impure, and he himself ignominiously and shamefully excluded from the society of the holy. There one sees the priests who preside over each chariot exhort every one to penitence, to confession of faults, to the resolution of better life! There one sees old people, young people, little children, calling on the Lord with a suppliant voice, and uttering to Him, from the depth of the heart, sobs and sighs with words of glory and praise! After the people, warned by the sound of trumpets and the sight of banners, have resumed their road, the march is made with such ease that no obstacle can retard it. . . . When they have reached the church they arrange the wagons about it like a spiritual camp, and during the whole night they celebrate the watch by hymns and canticles. On each waggon they light tapers and lamps; they place there the infirm and sick, and bring them the precious relics of the Saints for their relief. Afterwards the priests and clerics close the ceremony by processions which the people follow with devout heart, imploring the clemency of the Lord and of his Blessed Mother for the recovery of the sick.

Of course, the Virgin was actually and constantly present during all this labour, and gave her assistance to it, but you would get no light on the architecture from listening to an account of her miracles, nor do they heighten the effect of popular faith. Without the conviction of her personal presence, men would not have been inspired; but, to us, it is rather the inspiration of the art which proves the Virgin's presence, and we can better see the conviction of it in the work than in the words. Every day, as the work went on, the Virgin was present, directing the architects, and it is in this direction that we are going to study, if you have now got a realizing sense of what it meant. Without this sense, the church is dead. Most persons of a deeply religious nature would tell you emphatically that nine churches out of ten actually were dead-born, after the thirteenth century, and that church architecture became a pure matter of mechanism and mathematics; but that is a question for you to decide when you come to it; and the pleasure consists not in seeing the death, but in feeling the life.

Now let us look about!

10. The Court of the Queen of Heaven

All artists love the sanctuary of the Christian Church, and all tourists love the rest. The reason becomes clear as one leaves the choir, and goes back to the broad, open hall of the nave. The choir was not made for the pilgrim but for the deity, and is as old as Adam, or perhaps older; at all events old enough to have existed in complete artistic and theological form, with the whole mystery of the Trinity, the Mother and Child, and even the Cross, thousands of years before Christ was born; but the Christian Church not only took the sanctuary in hand, and gave it a new form, more beautiful and much more refined than the Romans or Greeks or Egyptians had ever imagined, but it also added the idea of the nave and transepts, and developed it into imperial splendour. The pilgrim-tourist feels at home in the nave because it was built for him; the artist loves the sanctuary because he built it for God.

Chartres was intended to hold ten thousand people easily, or fifteen thousand when crowded, and the decoration of this great space, though not a wholly new problem, had to be treated in a new way. Sancta Sofia[1] was built by the Emperor Justinian, with all the resources of the Empire, in a single violent effort, in six years, and was decorated throughout with mosaics on a general scheme, with the unity that Empire and Church could give, when they acted together. The Norman Kings of Sicily, the richest princes of the twelfth century, were able to carry out a complete work of the most costly kind, in a single sustained effort from beginning to end, according to a given plan. Chartres was a local shrine, in an agricultural province, not even a part of the royal domain, and its cathedral was the work of society, without much more tie than the Virgin gave it. Socially Chartres, as far as its stone-work goes, seems to have been mostly rural; its decoration, in the porches and transepts, is royal and feudal; in the nave and choir it is chiefly bourgeois. The want of unity is much less surprising than the unity, but it is still evident, especially in the glass. The mosaics of Monreale begin and end; they are a series; they connection is artistic and theological at once; they have unity. The windows of Chartres have no sequence, and their charm is in variety, in individuality, and sometimes even in downright hostility to each other, reflecting the picturesque society that gave them. They have, too, the charm that the world has made no attempt to popularize them for its modern uses, so that, except for the useful little guide-book of the Abbé Clerval, one can see no clue to the legendary chaos; one has it to one's self, without much fear of being trampled upon by critics or Jew dealers in works of art; any Chartres beggar-woman can still pass a summer's day here, and never once be mortified by ignorance of things that every dealer in bric-à-brac is supposed to know.

Yet the artists seem to have begun even here with some idea of sequence,

---

[1] The great Byzantine cathedral built at Constantinople in the sixth century. The Norman cathedral built at Palermo in the twelfth century, mentioned in the next sentence, is Monreale. The architectural unity, made possible by royal wealth, is contrasted with the special kind of unity claimed by Adams for Chartres, whose construction had to be extended over several centuries because it was financed by society as a whole.

for the first window in the north aisle, next the new tower, tells the story of
Noah; but the next plunges into the local history of Chartres, and is devoted
to Saint Lubin, a bishop of this diocese who died in or about the year 556, and
was, for some reason, selected by the Wine-Merchants to represent them, as
their interesting medallions show. Then follow three amusing subjects, charmingly treated: Saint Eustace, whose story has been told; Joseph and his breth-
ren; and Saint Nicholas, the most popular saint of the thirteenth century,
both in the Greek and in the Roman Churches. The sixth and last window
on the north aisle of the nave is the New Alliance.

Opposite these, in the south aisle, the series begins next the tower with
John the Evangelist, followed by Saint Mary Magdalen, given by the Water-
Carriers. The third, the Good Samaritan, given by the Shoemakers, has a rival
at Sens which critics think even better. The fourth is the Death, Assumption,
and Coronation of the Virgin. Then comes the fifteenth-century Chapel of
Vendôme, to compare the early and later glass. The sixth is, or was, devoted to
the Virgin's Miracles at Chartres; but only one complete subject remains.

These windows light the two aisles of the nave and decorate the lower walls
of the church with a mass of colour and variety of line still practically intact in
spite of much injury; but the windows of the transepts on the same level have
almost disappeared, except the Prodigal Son and a border to what was once a
Saint Lawrence, on the north; and, on the south, part of a window to Saint
Apollinaris of Ravenna, with an interesting hierarchy of angels above: sera-
phim and cherubim with six wings, red and blue; Dominations; Powers; Prin-
cipalities; all, except Thrones.

All this seems to be simple enough, at least to the people for whom the
nave was built, and to whom the windows were meant to speak. There is nothing esoteric here; nothing but what might have suited the great hall of a great
palace. There is no difference in taste between the Virgin in the choir, and
the Water-Carriers by the doorway. Blanche, the young Queen, liked the same
colours, legends, and lines that her Grocers and Bakers liked. All equally loved
the Virgin. There was not even a social difference. In the choir, Thibaut, the
Count of Chartres, immediate lord of the province, let himself be put in a
dark corner next the Belle-Verrière,[2] and left the Bakers to display their
wealth in the most serious spot in the church, the central window of the central chapel, while in the nave and transepts all the lower windows that bear
signatures were given by trades, as though that part of the church were
abandoned to the commons. One might suppose that the feudal aristocracy
would have fortified itself in the clerestory and upper windows, but even there
the bourgeoisie invaded them, and you can see, with a glass, the Pastrycooks
and Turners looking across at the Weavers and Curriers and Money-Changers,
and the "Men of Tours." Beneath the throne of the Mother of God, there
was no distinction of gifts; and above it the distinction favoured the com-
monalty. Of the seven immense windows above and around the high altar,
which are designed as one composition, none was given by a prince or a noble.
The Drapers, the Butchers, the Bakers, the Bankers are charged with the highest duties attached to the Virgin's service. Apparently neither Saint Louis, nor

2 "The fine, or great, stained-glass window."

his father Louis VIII, nor his mother Blanche, nor his uncle Philippe
Hurepel, nor his cousin Saint Ferdinand of Castile, nor his other cousin Pierre
de Dreux, nor the Duchess Alix of Brittany, cared whether their portraits or
armorial shields were thrust out of sight into corners by Pastrycooks and Teamsters, or took a whole wall of the church to themselves. The only relation that
connects them is their common relation to the Virgin, but that is emphatic,
and dominates the whole.

It dominates us, too, if we reflect on it, even after seven hundred years that
its meaning has faded. When one looks up to this display of splendour in the
clerestory, and asks what was in the minds of the people who joined to produce, with such immense effort and at such self-sacrifice, this astonishing effect,
the question seems to answer itself like an echo. With only half of an atrophied imagination, in a happy mood we could still see the nave and transepts
filled with ten thousand people on their knees, and the Virgin, crowned and
robed, seating herself on the embroidered cushion that covered her imperial
throne; sparkling with gems; bearing in her right hand the sceptre, and in her
lap the infant King; but, in the act of seating herself, we should see her pause a
moment to look down with love and sympathy on us,—her people—,who pack
the enormous hall, and throng far out beyond the open portals; while, an
instant later, she glances up to see that her great lords, spiritual and temporal, the advisers of her judgment, the supports of her authority, the agents of
her will, shall be in place; robed, mitred, armed; bearing the symbols of her
authority and their office; on horseback, lance in hand; all of them ready at
a sign to carry out a sentence of judgment or an errand of mercy; to touch
with the sceptre or to strike with the sword; and never err.

There they still stand! unchanged, unfaded, as alive and complete as when
they represented the real world, and the people below were the unreal and
ephemeral pageant! Then the reality was the Queen of Heaven on her throne
in the sanctuary, and her court in the glass; not the queens or princes who
were prostrating themselves, with the crowd, at her feet. These people knew
the Virgin as well as they knew their own mothers; every jewel in her crown,
every stitch of gold-embroidery in her many robes; every colour; every fold; every
expression on the perfectly familiar features of her grave, imperial face;
every care that lurked in the silent sadness of her power; repeated over and
over again, in stone, glass, ivory, enamel, wood; in every room, at the head of
every bed, hanging on every neck, standing at every street-corner, the Virgin
was as familiar to every one of them as the sun or the seasons; far more familiar than their own earthly queen or countess, although these were no
strangers in their daily life; familiar from the earliest childhood to the last
agony; in every joy and every sorrow and every danger; in every act and almost
in every thought of life, the Virgin was present with a reality that never belonged to her Son or to the Trinity, and hardly to any earthly being, prelate,
king, or kaiser; her daily life was as real to them as their own loyalty which
brought to her the best they had to offer as the return for her boundless sympathy; but while they knew the Virgin as though she were one of themselves,
and because she had been one of themselves, they were not so familiar with all
the officers of her court at Chartres; and pilgrims from abroad, like us, must
always have looked with curious interest at the pageant.

Far down the nave, next the western towers, the rank began with saints, prophets, and martyrs, of all ages and countries; local, like Saint Lubin; national, like Saint Martin of Tours and Saint Hilary of Poitiers; popular like Saint Nicholas; militant like Saint George; without order; symbols like Abraham and Isaac; the Virgin herself, holding on her lap the Seven Gifts of the Holy Ghost; Christ with the Alpha and Omega; Moses and Saint Augustine; Saint Peter; Saint Mary the Egyptian; Saint Jerome; a whole throne-room of heavenly powers, repeating, within, the pageant carved on the porches and on the portals without. From the croisée in the centre, where the crowd is most dense, one sees the whole almost better than Mary sees it from her high altar, for there all the great rose windows flash in turn, and the three twelfth-century lancets glow on the western sun. When the eyes of the throng are directed to the north, the Rose of France strikes them almost with a physical shock of colour, and, from the south, the Rose of Dreux challenges the Rose of France.

Every one knows that there is war between the two! The thirteenth century has few secrets. There are no outsiders. We are one family as we are one Church. Every man and woman here, from Mary on her throne to the beggar on the porch, knows that Pierre de Dreux detests Blanche of Castile, and that their two windows carry on war across the very heart of the cathedral. Both unite only in asking help from Mary; but Blanche is a woman, alone in the world with young children to protect, and most women incline strongly to suspect that Mary will never desert her. Pierre, with all his masculine strength, is no courtier. He wants to rule by force. He carries the assertion of his sex into the very presence of the Queen of Heaven.

The year happens to be 1230, when the roses may be supposed just finished and showing their whole splendour for the first time. Queen Blanche is forty-three years old, and her son Louis is fifteen. Blanche is a widow these four years, and Pierre a widower since 1221. Both are regents and guardians for their heirs. They have necessarily carried their disputes before Mary. Queen Blanche claims for her son, who is to be Saint Louis, the place of honour at Mary's right hand; she has taken possession of the north porch outside, and of the north transept within, and has filled the windows with glass, as she is filling the porch with statuary. Above is the huge rose; below are five long windows; and all proclaim the homage that France renders to the Queen of Heaven.

The Rose of France shows in its centre the Virgin in her majesty, seated, crowned, holding the sceptre with her right hand, while her left supports the infant Christ-King on her knees; which shows that she, too, is acting as regent for her Son. Round her, in a circle, are twelve medallions; four containing doves; four six-winged angels or Thrones; four angels of a lower order, but all symbolizing the gifts and endowments of the Queen of Heaven. Outside these are twelve more medallions with the Kings of Judah, and a third circle contains the twelve lesser prophets. So Mary sits, hedged in by all the divinity that graces earthly or heavenly kings; while between the two outer circles are twelve quatrefoils bearing on a blue ground the golden lilies of France; and in each angle below the rose are four openings, showing alternately the lilies of Louis and the castles of Blanche. We who are below, the common people, understand that France claims to protect and defend the Virgin of Chartres, as her chief vassal, and that this ostentatious profusion of lilies and castles is intended not in honour of France, but as a demonstration of loyalty to Notre Dame, and an assertion of her rights as Queen Regent of Heaven against all comers, but particularly against Pierre, the rebel, who has the audacity to assert rival rights in the opposite transept.

Beneath the rose are five long windows, very unlike the twelfth-century pendants to the western rose. These five windows blaze with red, and their splendour throws the Virgin above quite into the background. The artists, who felt that the twelfth-century glass was too fine and too delicate for the new scale of the church, have not only enlarged their scale and coarsened their design, but have coarsened their colour-scheme also, discarding blue in order to crush us under the earthly majesty of red. These windows, too, bear the stamp and seal of Blanche's Spanish temper as energetically as though they bore her portrait. The great central figure, the tallest and most commanding in the whole church, is not the Virgin, but her mother Saint Anne, standing erect on the trumeau of the door beneath, and holding the infant Mary on her left arm. She wears no royal crown, but bears a flowered sceptre. The only other difference between Mary and her mother, that seems intended to strike attention, is that Mary sits, while her mother stands; but as though to proclaim still more distinctly that France supports the royal and divine pretensions of Saint Anne, Queen Blanche has put beneath the figure a great shield blazoned with the golden lilies on an azure ground.

With singular insistence on this motive, Saint Anne has at either hand a royal court of her own, marked as her own by containing only figures from the Old Testament. Standing next on her right is Solomon, her Prime Minister, bringing wisdom in worldly counsel, and trampling on human folly. Beyond Wisdom stands Law, figured by Aaron with the Book, trampling on the lawless Pharaoh. Opposite them, on Saint Anne's left, is David, the energy of State, trampling on a Saul suggesting suspicions of a Saul de Dreux; while last, Melchisedec who is Faith, tramples on a disobedient Nebuchadnezzar Mauclerc.

How can we, the common people, help seeing all this and much more, when we know that Pierre de Dreux has been for years in constant strife with the Crown and the Church? He is very valiant and lion-hearted;—so say the chroniclers, priests though they are;—very skilful and experienced in war whether by land or sea; very adroit, with more sense than any other great lord in France; but restless, factious, and regardless of his word. Brave and bold as the day; full of courtesy and "largesse"; but very hard on the clergy; a good Christian but a bad churchman! Certainly the first man of his time, says Michelet! "I have never found any that sought to do me more ill than he," says Blanche, and Joinville gives her very words; indeed, this year, 1230, she has summoned our own Bishop of Chartres among others to Paris in a court of peers, where Pierre has been found guilty of treason and deposed. War still continues, but Pierre must make submission. Blanche has beaten him in politics and in the field! Let us look round and see how he fares in theology and art!

There is his rose—so beautiful that Blanche may well think it seeks to do hers ill! As colour, judge for yourselves whether it holds its own against the flaming self-assertion of the opposite wall! As subject, it asserts flat defiance of the monarchy of Queen Blanche. In the central circle, Christ as King is seated on a royal throne, both arms raised, one holding the golden cup of eternal priesthood, the other, blessing the world. Two great flambeaux burn beside Him. The four Apocalyptic figures surround and worship Him; and in the concentric circles round the central medallion are the angels and the kings in a blaze of colour, symbolizing the New Jerusalem.

All the force of the Apocalypse is there, and so is some of the weakness of theology, for, in the five great windows below, Pierre shows his training in the schools. Four of these windows represent what is called, for want of a better name, the New Alliance; the dependence of the New Testament on the Old; but Pierre's choice in symbols was as masculine as that of Blanche was feminine. In each of the four windows, a gigantic Evangelist strides the shoulders of a colossal Prophet. Saint John rides on Ezekiel; Saint Mark bestrides Daniel; Saint Matthew is on the shoulders of Isaiah; Saint Luke is carried by Jeremiah. The effect verges on the grotesque. The balance of Christ's Church seems uncertain. The Evangelists clutch the Prophets by the hair, and while the synagogue stands firm, the Church looks small, feeble, and vacillating. The new dispensation has not the air of mastery either physical or intellectual; the old gives it all the support it has, and, in the absence of Saint Paul, both old and new seem little concerned with the sympathies of Frenchmen. The synagogue is stronger than the Church, but even the Church is Jew.

That Pierre could ever have meant this is not to be dreamed; but when the true scholar gets thoroughly to work, his logic is remorseless, his art is implacable, and his sense of humour is blighted. In the rose above, Pierre had asserted the exclusive authority of Christ in the New Jerusalem, and his scheme required him to show how the Church rested on the Evangelists below, who in their turn had no visible support except what the Prophets gave them. Yet the artist may have had a reason for weakening the Evangelists, because there remained the Virgin! One dares no more than hint at a motive so disrespectful to the Evangelists; but it is certainly true that, in the central window, immediately beneath the Christ, and His chief support, with the four staggering Evangelists and Prophets on either hand, the Virgin stands, and betrays no sign of weakness.

The compliment is singularly masculine; a kind of twelfth-century flattery that might have softened the anger of Blanche herself, if the Virgin had been her own; but the Virgin of Dreux is not the Virgin of France. No doubt she still wears her royal crown, and her head is circled with the halo; her right hand still holds the flowered sceptre, and her left the infant Christ, but she stands, and Christ is King. Note, too, that she stands directly opposite to her mother Saint Anne in the Rose of France, so as to place her one stage lower than the Virgin of France in the hierarchy. She is the Saint Anne of France, and shows it. "She is no longer," says the official Monograph, "that majestic queen who was seated on a throne, with her feet on the stool of honour; the personages have become less imposing and the heads show the decadence." She is the Virgin of Theology; she has her rights, and no more; but she is not the Virgin of Chartres.

She, too, stands on an altar or pedestal, on which hangs a shield bearing the ermines, an exact counterpart of the royal shield beneath Saint Anne. In this excessive display of armorial bearings—for the two roses above are crowded with them—one likes to think that these great princes had in their minds not so much the thought of their own importance—which is a modern sort of religion—as the thought of their devotion to Mary. The assertion of power and attachment by one is met by the assertion of equal devotion by the other, and while both loudly proclaim their homage to the Virgin, each glares defiance across the church. Pierre meant the Queen of Heaven to know that, in case of need, her left hand was as good as her right, and truer; that the ermines were as well able to defend her as the lilies, and that Brittany would fight her battles as bravely as France. Whether his meaning carried with it more devotion to the Virgin or more defiance to France depends a little on the date of the windows, but, as a mere point of history, every one must allow that Pierre's promise of allegiance was kept more faithfully by Brittany than that of Blanche and Saint Louis has been kept by France.

The date seems to be fixed by the windows themselves. Beneath the Prophets kneel Pierre and his wife Alix, while their two children, Yolande and Jean, stand. Alix died in 1221. Jean was born in 1217. Yolande was affianced in marriage in 1227, while a child, and given to Queen Blanche to be brought up as the future wife of her younger son John, then in his eighth year. When John died, Yolande was contracted to Thibaut of Champagne in 1231, and Blanche is said to have written to Thibaut in consequence: "Sire Thibauld of Champagne, I have heard that you have covenanted and promised to take to wife the daughter of Count Perron of Brittany. Wherefore I charge you, if you do not wish to lose whatever you possess in the kingdom of France, not to do it. If you hold dear or love aught in the said kingdom, do it not." Whether Blanche wrote in these words or not, she certainly prevented the marriage, and Yolande remained single until 1238 when she married the Comte de la Marche, who was, by the way, almost as bitter an enemy of Blanche as Pierre had been; but by that time both Blanche and Pierre had ceased to be regents. Yolande's figure in the window is that of a girl, perhaps twelve or fourteen years old; Jean is younger, certainly not more than eight or ten years of age; and the appearance of the two children shows that the window itself should date between 1225 and 1230, the year when Pierre de Dreux was condemned because he had renounced his homage to King Louis, declared war on him, and invited the King of England into France. As already told, Philippe Hurepel de Boulogne, the Comte de la Marche, Enguerrand de Couci,—nearly all the great nobles,—had been leagued with Pierre de Dreux since Blanche's regency began in 1226.

That these transept windows harmonize at all, is due to the Virgin, not to the donors. At the time they were designed, supposing it to be during Blanche's regency (1226-36), the passions of these donors brought France to momentary ruin, and the Virgin in Blanche's Rose de France, as she looked across the church, could not see a single friend of Blanche. What is more curious, she saw enemies in plenty, and in full readiness for battle. We have seen in the centre of the small rose in the north transept, Philippe Hurepel still waiting her orders; across the nave, in another small rose of the south transept, sits Pierre de Dreux on his horse. The upper windows on the side walls of the choir are very interesting but impossible to see, even with the best glasses, from the floor of the church. Their sequence and dates have already been discussed; but their feeling is shown by the character of the Virgin, who in French territory, next the north transept, is still the Virgin of France, but in Pierre's territory, next the Rose de Dreux, becomes again the Virgin of Dreux, who is absorbed in the Child,—not the Child absorbed in her, —and accordingly the window shows the chequers and ermines.

The figures, like the stone figures outside, are the earliest of French art, before any school of painting fairly existed. Among them, one can see no friend of Blanche. Indeed, outside of her own immediate family and the Church, Blanche had no friend of much importance except the famous Thibaut of Champagne, the single member of the royal family who took her side and suffered for her sake, and who, as far as books tell, has no window or memorial here. One might suppose that Thibaut, who loved both Blanche and the Virgin, would have claimed a place, and perhaps he did; but one seeks him in vain. If Blanche had friends here, they are gone. Pierre de Dreux, lance in hand, openly defies her, and it was not on her brother-in-law Philippe Hurepel that she could depend for defence.

This is the court pageant of the Virgin that shows itself to the people who are kneeling at high mass. We, the public, whoever we are—Chartrain, Breton, Norman, Angevin, Frenchman, Percherain, or what not,—know our local politics as intimately as our lords do, or even better, for our imaginations are active, and we do not love Blanche of Castile. We know how to read the passions that fill the church. From the north transept Blanche flames out on us in splendid reds and flings her Spanish castles in our face. From the south transept Pierre retorts with a brutal energy which shows itself in the Prophets who serve as battle-chargers and in the Evangelists who serve as knights,— mounted warriors of faith,—whose great eyes follow us across the church and defy Saint Anne and her French shield opposite. Pierre was not effeminate; Blanche was fairly masculine. Between them, as a matter of sex, we can see little to choose; and, in any case, it is a family quarrel; they are all cousins; they are all equals on earth, and none means to submit to any superior except the Virgin and her Son in heaven. The Virgin is not afraid. She has seen many troubles worse than this; she knows how to manage perverse children, and if necessary she will shut them up in a darker room than ever their mothers kept open for them in this world. One has only to look at the Virgin to see!

There she is, of course, looking down on us from the great window above the high altar, where we never forget her presence! Is there a thought of disturbance there? Around the curve of the choir are seven great windows, without roses, filling the whole semicircle and the whole vault, forty-seven feet high, and meant to dominate the nave as far as the western portal, so that we may never forget how Mary fills her church without being disturbed by quarrels, and may understand why Saint Ferdinand and Saint Louis creep out of our sight, close by the Virgin's side, far up above brawls; and why France and Brittany hide their ugly or their splendid passions at the end of the transepts, out of sight of the high altar where Mary is to sit in state as Queen with the young King on her lap. In an instant she will come, but we have a moment still to look about at the last great decoration of her palace, and see how the artists have arranged it.

Since the building of Sancta Sofia, no artist has had such a chance. No

doubt, Rheims and Amiens and Bourges and Beauvais, which are now building, may be even finer, but none of them is yet finished, and all must take
their ideas from here. One would like, before looking at it, to think over the
problem, as though it were new, and so choose the scheme that would suit us
best if the decoration were to be done for the first time. The architecture is
fixed; we have to do only with the colour of this mass of seven huge windows,
forty-seven feet high, in the clerestory, round the curve of the choir, which
close the vista of the church as viewed from the entrance. This vista is about
three hundred and thirty feet long. The windows rise about a hundred feet.
How ought this vast space to be filled? Should the perpendicular upward leap
of the architecture be followed and accented by a perpendicular leap of colour? The decorators of the fifteenth and sixteenth centuries seem to have
thought so, and made perpendicular architectural drawings in yellow that simulated gold, and lines that ran with the general lines of the building. Many
fifteenth-century windows seem to be made up of florid Gothic details rising
in stages to the vault. No doubt critics complained, and still complain, that
the monotony of this scheme, and its cheapness of intelligence, were objections; but at least the effect was light, decorative, and safe. The artist could
not go far wrong and was still at liberty to do beautiful work, as can be seen
in any number of churches scattered broadcast over Europe and swarming in
Paris and France. On the other hand, might not the artist disregard the architecture and fill the space with a climax of colour? Could he not unite the
Roses of France and Dreux above the high altar in an overpowering outburst
of purples and reds? The seventeenth century might have preferred to mass
clouds and colours, and Michael Angelo, in the sixteenth, might have known
how to do it. What we want is not the feeling of the artist so much as the
feeling of Chartres. What shall it be—the jewelled brilliancy of the western
windows, or the fierce self-assertion of Pierre Mauclerc, or the royal splendour
of Queen Blanche, or the feminine grace and decorative refinement of the
Charlemagne and Santiago windows in the apse?

Never again in art was so splendid a problem offered, either before or
since, for the artist of Chartres solved it, as he did the whole matter of fenestration, and later artists could only offer variations on his work. You will see
them at Bourges and Tours and in scores of thirteenth and fourteenth and
fifteenth and sixteenth century churches and windows, and perhaps in some
of the twentieth century,—all of them interesting and some of them beautiful,
—and far be it from us, mean and ignorant pilgrims of art, to condemn any
intelligent effort to vary or improve the effect; but we have set out to seek the
feeling, and while we think of art in relation to ourselves, the sermon of
Chartres, from beginning to end, teaches and preaches and insists and reiterates and hammers into our torpid minds the moral that the art of the Virgin
was not that of her artists but her own. We inevitably think of our tastes;
they thought instinctively of hers.

In the transepts, Queen Blanche and Duke Perron, in legal possession of
their territory, showed that they were thinking of each other as well as of the
Virgin, and claimed loudly that they ought each to be first in the Virgin's favour; and they stand there in place, as the thirteenth century felt them. Subject to their fealty to Mary, the transepts belonged to them, and if Blanche

did not, like Pierre, assert herself and her son on the Virgin's window, perhaps she thought the Virgin would resent Pierre's boldness the more by contrast with her own good taste. So far as is known, nowhere does Blanche appear
in person at Chartres; she felt herself too near the Virgin to obtrude a useless
image, or she was too deeply religious to ask anything for herself. A queen who
was to have two children sainted, to intercede for her at Mary's throne, stood
in a solitude almost as unique as that of Mary, and might ignore the raw brutalities of a man-at-arms; but neither she nor Pierre has carried the quarrel
into Mary's presence, nor has the Virgin condescended even to seem conscious
of their temper. This is the theme of the artist—the purity, the beauty, the
grace, and the infinite loftiness of Mary's nature, among the things of earth, and
above the clamour of kings.

Therefore, when we, and the crushed crowd of kneeling worshippers around
us, lift our eyes at last after the miracle of the mass, we see, far above the high
altar, high over all the agitation of prayer, the passion of politics, the anguish
of suffering, the terrors of sin, only the figure of the Virgin in majesty, looking down on her people, crowned, throned, glorified, with the infant Christ on
her knees. She does not assert herself; probably she intends to be felt rather
than feared. Compared with the Greek Virgin, as you see her, for example,
at Torcello, the Chartres Virgin is retiring and hardly important enough for
the place. She is not exaggerated either in scale, drawing, or colour. She shows
not a sign of self-consciousness, not an effort for brilliancy, not a trace of stage
effect—hardly even a thought of herself, except that she is at home, among
her own people, where she is loved and known as well as she knows them. The
seven great windows are one composition; and it is plain that the artist, had he
been ordered to make an exhibition of power, could have overwhelmed us
with a storm of purple, red, yellows, or given us a Virgin of Passion who would
have torn the vault asunder; his ability is never in doubt, and if he has kept
true to the spirit of the western portal and the twelfth century, it is because the
Virgin of Chartres was the Virgin of Grace, and ordered him to paint her so.
One shudders to think how a single false note—a suggestion of meanness, in
this climax of line and colour—would bring the whole fabric down in ruins
on the eighteenth-century meanness of the choir below; and one notes, almost
bashfully, the expedients of the artists to quiet their effects. So the lines of the
seven windows are built up, to avoid the horizontal, and yet not exaggerate
the vertical. The architect counts here for more than the colourist; but the
colour, when you study it, suggests the same restraint. Three great windows on
the Virgin's right, balanced by three more on her left, show the prophets and
precursors of her Son; all architecturally support and exalt the Virgin, in her
celestial atmosphere of blue, shot with red, calm in the certainty of heaven.
Any one who is prematurely curious to see the difference in treatment between different centuries should go down to the church of Saint Pierre in
the lower town, and study there the methods of the Renaissance. Then we can
come back to study again the ways of the thirteenth century. The Virgin will
wait; she will not be angry; she knows her power; we all come back to her in the
end.

Or the Renaissance, if one prefers, can wait equally well, while one kneels
with the thirteenth century, and feels the little one still can feel of what it felt.

Technically these apsidal windows have not received much notice; the books rarely speak of them; travellers seldom look at them; and their height is such that even with the best glass, the quality of the work is beyond our power to judge. We see, and the artists meant that we should see, only the great lines, the colour, and the Virgin. The mass of suppliants before the choir look up to the light, clear blues and reds of this great space, and feel there the celestial peace and beauty of Mary's nature and abode. There is heaven! and Mary looks down from it, into her church, where she sees us on our knees, and knows each one of us by name. There she actually is—not in symbol or in fancy, but in person, descending on her errands of mercy and listening to each one of us, as her miracles prove, or satisfying our prayers merely by her presence which calms our excitement as that of a mother calms her child. She is there as Queen, not merely as intercessor, and her power is such that to her the difference between us earthly beings is nothing. Her quiet, masculine strength enchants us most. Pierre Mauclerc and Philippe Hurepel and their men-at-arms are afraid of her, and the Bishop himself is never quite at his ease in her presence; but to peasants, and beggars, and people in trouble, this sense of her power and calm is better than active sympathy. People who suffer beyond the formulas of expression—who are crushed into silence, and beyond pain—want no display of emotion—no bleeding heart—no weeping at the foot of the Cross—no hysterics—no phrases! They want to see God, and to know that He is watching over His own. How many women are there, in this mass of thirteenth-century suppliants, who have lost children? Probably nearly all, for the death rate is very high in the conditions of mediaeval life. There are thousands of such women here, for it is precisely this class who come most; and probably every one of them has looked up to Mary in her great window, and has felt actual certainty, as though she saw with her own eyes—there, in heaven, while she looked—her own lost baby playing with the Christ-Child at the Virgin's knee, as much at home as the saints, and much more at home than the kings. Before rising from her knees, every one of these women will have bent down and kissed the stone pavement in gratitude for Mary's mercy. The earth, she says, is a sorry place, and the best of it is bad enough, no doubt, even for Queen Blanche and the Duchess Alix who has had to leave her children here alone; but there above is Mary in heaven who sees and hears me as I see her, and who keeps my little boy till I come; so I can wait with patience, more or less! Saints and prophets and martyrs are all very well, and Christ is very sublime and just, but Mary *knows!*

It was very childlike, very foolish, very beautiful, and very true,—as art, at least: so true that everything else shades off into vulgarity, as you see the Persephone of a Syracusan coin shade off into the vulgarity of a Roman emperor; as though the heaven that lies about us in our infancy[3] too quickly takes colours that are not so much sober as sordid, and would be welcome if no

[3] The final allusion to Wordsworth's "Intimations of Immortality." Lines 64-68 read:
> But trailing clouds of glory do we come
> From God, who is our home:
> Heaven lies about us in our infancy!
> Shades of the prison-house begin to close
> Upon the growing Boy.

worse than that. Vulgarity, too, has feeling, and its expression in art has truth and even pathos, but we shall have time enough in our lives for that, and all the more because, when we rise from our knees now, we have finished our pilgrimage. We have done with Chartres. For seven hundred years Chartres has seen pilgrims, coming and going more or less like us, and will perhaps see them for another seven hundred years; but we shall see it no more, and can safely leave the Virgin in her majesty, with her three great prophets on either hand, as calm and confident in their own strength and in God's providence as they were when Saint Louis was born, but looking down from a deserted heaven, into an empty church, on a dead faith.

16. Saint Thomas Aquinas

Long before Saint Francis's death, in 1226, the French mystics had exhausted their energies and the siècle had taken new heart. Society could not remain forever balancing between thought and act. A few gifted natures could absorb themselves in the absolute, but the rest lived for the day, and needed shelter and safety. So the Church bent again to its task, and bade the Spaniard Dominic arm new levies with the best weapons of science, and flaunt the name of Aristotle on the Church banners along with that of Saint Augustine. The year 1215, which happened to be the date of Magna Charta and other easily fixed events, like the birth of Saint Louis, may serve to mark the triumph of the schools. The pointed arch revelled at Rheims and the Gothic architects reached perfection at Amiens just as Francis died at Assisi and Thomas was born at Aquino. The Franciscan Order itself was swept with the stream that Francis tried to dam, and the great Franciscan schoolman, Alexander Hales, in 1222, four years before the death of Francis, joined the order and began lecturing as though Francis himself had lived only to teach scholastic philosophy.

The rival Dominican champion, Albertus Magnus, began his career a little later, in 1228. Born of the noble Swabian family of Bollstadt, in 1193, he drifted, like other schoolmen, to Paris, and the Rue Maître Albert, opposite Notre Dame, still records his fame as a teacher there. Thence he passed to a school established by the order at Cologne, where he was lecturing with great authority in 1243 when the general superior of the order brought up from Italy a young man of the highest promise to be trained as his assistant.

Thomas, the new pupil, was born under the shadow of Monte Cassino in 1226 or 1227. His father, the Count of Aquino, claimed descent from the imperial line of Swabia; his mother, from the Norman princes of Sicily; so that in him the two most energetic strains in Europe met. His social rank was royal, and the order set the highest value on it. He took the vows in 1243, and went north at once to help Albertus at Cologne. In 1245, the order sent Albertus back to Paris, and Thomas with him. There he remained till 1248 when he was ordered to Cologne as assistant lecturer, and only four years afterwards, at twenty-five years old, he was made full professor at Paris. His industry and activity never rested till his death in 1274, not yet fifty years old, when he bequeathed to the Church a mass of manuscript that tourists will never know enough to estimate except by weight. His complete works, repeatedly printed, fill between twenty and thirty quarto volumes. For so famous a doctor, this is almost meagre. Unfortunately his greatest work, the "Summa Theologiae," is unfinished—like Beauvais Cathedral.

Perhaps Thomas's success was partly due to his memory which is said to have been phenomenal; for, in an age when cyclopaedias were unknown, a cyclopaedic memory must have counted for half the battle in these scholastic disputes where authority could be met only by authority; but in this case, memory was supported by mind. Outwardly Thomas was heavy and slow in manner, if it is true that his companions called him "the big dumb ox of Sicily"; and in fashionable or court circles he did not enjoy reputation for acute sense of humour. Saint Louis's household offers a picture not wholly clerical, least of all among the King's brothers and sons; and perhaps the dinner-table was not much more used then than now to abrupt interjections of theology into the talk about hunting and hounds; but however it happened, Thomas one day surprised the company by solemnly announcing—"I have a decisive argument against the Manicheans!" No wit or humour could be more to the point—between two saints that were to be—than a decisive argument against enemies of Christ, and one greatly regrets that the rest of the conversation was not reported, unless, indeed, it is somewhere in the twenty-eight quarto volumes; but it probably lacked humour for courtiers.

The twenty-eight quarto volumes must be closed books for us. None but Dominicans have a right to interpret them. No Franciscan—or even Jesuit—understands Saint Thomas exactly or explains him with authority. For summer tourists to handle these intricate problems in a theological spirit would be altogether absurd; but, for us, these great theologians were also architects who undertook to build a Church Intellectual, corresponding bit by bit to the Church Administrative, both expressing—and expressed by—the Church Architectural. Alexander Hales, Albert the Great, Thomas Aquinas, Duns Scotus, and the rest, were artists; and if Saint Thomas happens to stand at their head as type, it is not because we choose him or understand him better than his rivals, but because his order chose him rather than his master Albert, to impose as authority on the Church; and because Pope John XXII canonized him on the ground that his decisions were miracles; and because the Council of Trent placed his "Summa" among the sacred books on their table; and because Innocent VI said that his doctrine alone was sure; and finally, because Leo XIII very lately made a point of declaring that, on the wings of Saint Thomas's genius, human reason has reached the most sublime height it can probably ever attain.

Although the Franciscans, and, later, the Jesuits, have not always shown as much admiration as the Dominicans for the genius of Saint Thomas, and the mystics have never shown any admiration whatever for the philosophy of the schools, the authority of Leo XIII is final, at least on one point and the only one that concerns us. Saint Thomas is still alive and overshadows as many schools as he ever did; at all events, as many as the Church maintains. He has outlived Descartes and Leibnitz and a dozen other schools of philosophy more or less serious in their day. He has mostly outlived Hume, Voltaire, and the militant sceptics. His method is typical and classic; his sentences, when interpreted by the Church, seem, even to an untrained mind, intelligible and consistent; his Church Intellectual remains practically unchanged, and, like the Cathedral of Beauvais, erect, although the storms of six or seven centuries have prostrated, over and over again, every other social or political or juristic shelter. Compared with it, all modern systems are complex and chaotic, crowded with self-contradictions, anomalies, impracticable functions and outworn inheritances; but beyond all their practical shortcomings is their fragmentary character. An economic civilization troubles itself about the universe much as a hive of honey-bees troubles about the ocean, only as a region to be avoided. The hive of Saint Thomas sheltered God and man, mind and matter, the universe and the atom, the one and the multiple, within the walls of an harmonious home.

Theologians, like architects, were supposed to receive their Church complete in all its lines; they were modern judges who interpreted the law, but never invented it. Saint Thomas merely selected between disputed opinions, but he allowed himself to wander very far afield, indeed, in search of opinions to dispute. The field embraced all that existed, or might have existed, or could never exist. The immense structure rested on Aristotle and Saint Augustine at the last, but as a work of art it stood alone, like Rheims or Amiens Cathedral, as though it had no antecedents. Then, although, like Rheims, its style was never meant to suit modern housekeeping and is ill-seen by the École des Beaux Arts, it reveals itself in its great mass and intelligence as a work of extraordinary genius; a system as admirably proportioned as any cathedral and as complete; a success not universal either in art or science.

Saint Thomas's architecture, like any other work of art, is best studied by itself as though he created it outright; otherwise a tourist would never get beyond its threshold. Beginning with the foundation which is God and God's active presence in His Church, Thomas next built God into the walls and towers of His Church, in the Trinity and its creation of mind and matter in time and space; then finally he filled the Church by uniting mind and matter in man, or man's soul, giving to humanity a free will that rose, like the flèche, to heaven. The foundation—the structure—the congregation—are enough for students of art; his ideas of law, ethics, and politics; his vocabulary, his syllogisms, his arrangement are, like the drawings of Villard de Honnecourt's sketch-book, curious but not vital. After the eleventh-century Romanesque Church of Saint Michael came the twelfth-century Transition Church of the Virgin, and all merged and ended at last in the thirteenth-century Gothic Cathedral of the Trinity. One wants to see the end.

The foundation of the Christian Church should be—as the simple deist might suppose—always the same, but Saint Thomas knew better. His foundation was Norman, not French; it spoke the practical architect who knew the mathematics of his art, and who saw that the foundation laid by Saint Bernard, Saint Victor, Saint Francis, the whole mystical, semi-mystical, Cartesian, Spinozan foundation, past or future, could not bear the weight of the structure to be put on it. Thomas began by sweeping the ground clear of them. God must be a concrete thing, not a human thought. God must be proved by the senses like any other concrete thing; "nihil est in intellectu quin prius fuerit in sensu";[1] even if Aristotle had not affirmed the law, Thomas would have discovered it. He admitted at once that God could not be taken for granted.

The admission, as every boy-student of the Latin Quarter knew, was exceedingly bold and dangerous. The greatest logicians commonly shrank from proving unity by multiplicity. Thomas was one of the greatest logicians that ever lived; the question had always been at the bottom of theology; he deliberately challenged what every one knew to be an extreme peril. If his foundation failed, his Church fell. Many critics have thought that he saw dangers four hundred years ahead. The time came, about 1650-1700, when Descartes, deserting Saint Thomas, started afresh with the idea of God as a concept, and at once found himself charged with a deity that contained the universe; nor did the Cartesians—until Spinoza made it clear—seem able or willing to see that the Church could not accept this deity because the Church required a God who caused the universe. The two deities destroyed each other. One was passive; the other active. Thomas warned Descartes of a logical quicksand which must necessarily swallow up any Church, and which Spinoza explored to the bottom. Thomas said truly that every true cause must be proved as a cause, not merely as a sequence; otherwise they must end in a universal energy or substance without causality—a source.

Whatever God might be to others, to His Church he could not be a sequence or a source. That point had been admitted by William of Champeaux, and made the division between Christians and infidels. On the other hand, if God must be proved as a true cause in order to warrant the Church or the State in requiring men to worship Him as Creator, the student became the more curious—if a churchman, the more anxious—to be assured that Thomas succeeded in his proof, especially since he did not satisfy Descartes and still less Pascal. That the mystics should be dissatisfied was natural enough, since they were committed to the contrary view, but that Decartes should desert was a serious blow which threw the French Church into consternation from which it never quite recovered.

"I see motion," said Thomas: "I infer a motor!" This reasoning, which may be fifty thousand years old, is as strong as ever it was; stronger than some more modern inferences of science; but the average mechanic stated it differently. "I see motion," he admitted: "I infer energy. I see motion everywhere; I infer energy everywhere." Saint Thomas barred this door to materialism by adding: "I see motion; I cannot infer an infinite series of motors: I can only infer, somewhere at the end of the series, an intelligent, fixed motor." The average modern mechanic might not dissent but would certainly hesitate. "No doubt!" he might say; "we can conduct our works as well on that as on any other theory, or as we could on no theory at all; but, if you offer it as proof, we can only say that we have not yet reduced all motion to one source or all energies to one law, much less to one act of creation, although we have tried our best." The result of some centuries of experiment tended to raise rather than silence doubt, although, even in his own day, Thomas would have been scandalized beyond the resources of his Latin had Saint Bonaventure met him at Saint Louis's dinner-table and complimented him, in the King's hear-

---

[1] "Nothing is in the understanding that was not first in the senses."

ing, on having proved, beyond all Franciscan cavils, that the Church Intellectual had necessarily but one first cause and creator—himself.

The Church Intellectual, like the Church Architectural, implied not one architect, but myriads, and not one fixed, intelligent architect at the end of the series, but a vanishing vista without a beginning at any definite moment; and if Thomas pressed his argument, the twentieth-century mechanic who should attend his conférences at the Sorbonne would be apt to say so. "What is the use of trying to argue me into it? Your inference may be sound logic, but is not proof. Actually we know less about it than you did. All we know is the thing we handle, and we cannot handle your fixed, intelligent prime motor. To your old ideas of form we have added what we call force, and we are rather further than ever from reducing the complex to unity. In fact, if you are aiming to convince me, I will tell you flatly that I know only the multiple, and have no use for unity at all."

In the thirteenth century men did not depend so much as now on actual experiment, but the nominalist said in effect the same thing. Unity to him was a pure concept, and any one who thought it real would believe that a triangle was alive and could walk on its legs. Without proving unity, philosophers saw no way to prove God. They could only fall back on an attempt to prove that the concept of unity proved itself, and this phantasm drove the Cartesians to drop Thomas's argument and assert that "the mere fact of having within us the idea of a thing more perfect than ourselves, proves the real existence of that thing." Four hundred years earlier Saint Thomas had replied in advance that Descartes wanted to prove altogether too much, and Spinoza showed mathematically that Saint Thomas had been in the right. The finest religious mind of the time—Pascal—admitted it and gave up the struggle, like the mystics of Saint-Victor.

Thus some of the greatest priests and professors of the Church, including Duns Scotus himself, seemed not wholly satisfied that Thomas's proof was complete, but most of them admitted that it was the safest among possible foundations, and that it showed, as architecture, the Norman temper of courage and caution. The Norman was ready to run great risks, but he would rather grasp too little than too much; he narrowed the spacing of his piers rather than spread them too wide for safe vaulting. Between Norman blood and Breton blood was a singular gap, as Renan and every other Breton has delighted to point out. Both Abélard and Descartes were Breton. The Breton seized more than he could hold; the Norman took less than he would have liked.

God, then, is proved. What the schools called form, what science calls energy, and what the intermediate period called the evidence of design, made the foundation of Saint Thomas's cathedral. God is an intelligent, fixed prime motor—not a concept, or proved by concepts;—a concrete fact, proved by the senses of sight and touch. On the foundation Thomas built. The walls and vaults of his Church were more complex than the foundation; especially the towers were troublesome. Dogma, the vital purpose of the Church, required support. The most weighty dogma, the central tower of the Norman cathedral, was the Trinity, and between the Breton solution which was too heavy, and the French solution which was too light, the Norman Thomas found a way. Remembering how vehemently the French Church, under Saint Bernard, had protected the Trinity from all interference whatever, one turns anxiously to see what Thomas said about it; and unless one misunderstands him—as is very likely, indeed, to be the case, since no one may even profess to understand the Trinity,—Thomas treated it as simply as he could. "God, being conscious of Himself, thinks Himself; his thought is Himself, his own reflection in the Verb—the so-called Son." "Est in Deo intelligere seipsum Verbum Dei quasi Deus intellectus." [2] The idea was not new, and as ideas went it was hardly a mystery; but the next step was naïf:—God, as a double consciousness, loves Himself, and realizes Himself in the Holy Ghost. The third side of the triangle is love or grace.

Many theologians have found fault with this treatment of the subject, which seemed open to every objection that had been made to Abélard, Gilbert de la Porée, or a thousand other logicians. They commonly asked why Thomas stopped the Deity's self-realizations at love, or inside the triangle, since these realizations were real, not symbolic, and the square was at least as real as any other combination of line. Thomas replied that knowledge and will —the Verb and the Holy Ghost—were alone essential. The reply did not suit every one, even among doctors, but since Saint Thomas rested on this simple assertion, it is no concern of ours to argue the theology. Only as art, one can afford to say that the form is more architectural than religious; it would surely have been suspicious to Saint Bernard. Mystery there was none, and logic little. The concept of the Holy Ghost was childlike; for a pupil of Aristotle it was inadmissible, since it led to nothing and helped no step toward the universe.

Admitting, if necessary, the criticism, Thomas need not admit the blame, if blame there were. Every theologian was obliged to stop the pursuit of logic by force, before it dragged him into paganism and pantheism. Theology begins with the universal—God—who must be a reality, not a symbol; but it is forced to limit the process of God's realizations somewhere, or the priest soon becomes a worshipper of God in sticks and stones. Theologists had commonly chosen, from time immemorial, to stop at the Trinity; within the triangle they were wholly realist; but they could not admit that God went on to realize Himself in the square and circle, or that the third member of the Trinity contained multiplicity, because the Trinity was a restless weight on the Church piers, which, like the central tower, constantly tended to fall, and needed to be lightened. Thomas gave it the lightest form possible, and there fixed it.

Then came his great tour-de-force, the vaulting of his broad nave; and, if ignorance is allowed an opinion, even a lost soul may admire the grand simplicity of Thomas's scheme. He swept away the horizontal lines altogether, leaving them barely as a part of decoration. The whole weight of his arches fell, as in the latest Gothic, where the eye sees nothing to break the sheer spring of the nervures, from the rosette on the keystone a hundred feet above down to the church floor. In Thomas's creation nothing intervened between God and his world; secondary causes became ornaments; only two forces, God and man, stood in the Church.

The chapter of Creation is so serious, and Thomas's creation, like every

---

[2] Adams makes a very free rendering of this in the preceding sentence.

other, is open to so much debate, that no student can allow another to explain it; and certainly no man whatever, either saint or sceptic, can ever yet have understood Creation aright unless divinely inspired; but whatever Thomas's theory was as he meant it, he seems to be understood as holding that every created individual—animal, vegetable, or mineral—was a special, divine act. Whatever has form is created, and whatever is created takes form directly from the will of God, which is also his act. The intermediate universals—the secondary causes—vanish as causes; they are, at most, sequences or relations; all merge in one universal act of will; instantaneous, infinite, eternal.

Saint Thomas saw God, much as Milton saw him, resplendent in

> That glorious form, that light unsufferable,
> And that far-beaming blaze of Majesty,
> Wherewith he wont, at Heaven's high council-table,
> To sit the midst of Trinal Unity;[3]

except that, in Thomas's thought, the council-table was a work-table, because God did not take counsel; He was an act. The Trinity was an infinite possibility of will; nothing within but

> The baby image of the giant mass
> Of things to come at large.

Neither time nor space, neither matter nor mind, not even force existed, nor could any intelligence conceive how, even though they should exist, they could be united in the lowest association. A crystal was as miraculous as Socrates. Only abstract force, or what the schoolmen called form, existed undeveloped from eternity, like the abstract line in mathematics.

Fifty or a hundred years before Saint Thomas settled the Church dogma, a monk of Citeaux or some other abbey, a certain Alain of Lille, had written a Latin poem, as abstruse an allegory as the best, which had the merit of painting the scene of man's creation as far as concerned the mechanical process much as Thomas seems to have seen it. . . . Alain conceded to the weakness of human thought, that God was working in time and space, or rather on His throne in heaven, when nature, proposing to create a new and improved man, sent Reason and Prudence up to ask Him for a soul to fit the new body. Having passed through various adventures and much scholastic instruction, the messenger Prudence arrived, after having dropped her dangerous friend Reason by the way. The request was respectfully presented to God, and favourably received. God promised the soul, and at once sent His servant Noys—Thought—to the storehouse of ideas, to choose it:

Ipse Deus rem prosequitur, producit in actum	God Himself pursues the task, and sets in act
Quod pepigit. Vocat ergo Noym quae praepaert illi	What He promised. So he calls Noys to seek
Numinis exemplar, humanae mentis Idaeam,	A copy of His will, Idea of the human mind,

[3] Milton's "On the Morning of Christs Nativity," ll. 8-11. The quotation immediately following is from Shakespeare's *Troilus and Cressida*, I. 3, line 343.

Ad cujus formam formetur spiritus omni	To whose form the spirit should be shaped,
Munere virtutum dives, qui, nube caducae	Rich in every virtue, which, veiled in garb
Carnis odumbratus veletur corporis umbra.	Of frail flesh, is to be hidden in a shade of body,
Tunc Noys ad regis praceptum singula rerum	Then Noys, at the King's order, turning one by one
Vestigans exempla, novam perquirit Idaeam.	Each sample, seeks the new Idea.
Inter tot species, speciem vix invenit illam	Among so many images she hardly finds that
Quam petit; offertur tandem quaesita petenti.	Which she seeks; at last the sought one appears.
Hanc formam Noys ipsa Deo praesentat ut ejus	This form Noys herself brings to God for Him
Formet ad exemplar animam. Tunc ille sigillum	To form a soul to its pattern. He takes the seal,
Sumit, ad ipsius formae vestigia formam	And gives form to the soul after the model
Dans animae, vultum qualem deposcit Idaea	Of the form itself, stamping on the sample
Imprimit exemplo; totas usurpat imago	The figure such as the Idea requires. The seal
Exemplaris opes, loquiturque figura sigillum.	Covers the whole field, and the impression expresses the stamp.

The translation is probably full of mistakes; indeed, one is permitted to doubt whether Alain himself accurately understood the process; but in substance he meant that God contained a storehouse of ideas, and stamped each creation with one of these forms. The poets used a variety of figures to help out their logic, but that of the potter and his pot was one of the most common. Omar Khayyám was using it at the same time with Alain of Lille, but with a difference: for his pot seems to have been matter alone, and his soul was the wine it received from God; while Alain's soul seems to have been the form and not the contents of the pot.

The figure matters little. In any case God's act was the union of mind with matter by the same act or will which created both. No intermediate cause or condition intervened; no secondary influence had anything whatever to do with the result. Time had nothing to do with it. Every individual that has existed or shall exist was created by the same instantaneous act, for all time. "When the question regards the universal agent who produces beings *and* time, we cannot consider him as acting *now* and *before*, according to the succession of time." God emanated time, force, matter, mind, as He might emanate gravitation, not as a part of His substance but as an energy of His will, and maintains them in their activity by the same act, not by a new one. Every individual is a part of the direct act; not a secondary outcome. The soul has no father or mother. Of all errors one of the most serious is to suppose that the soul descends by generation. "Having life and action of its own, it subsists without the body; . . . it must therefore be produced directly, and since it is not a material substance, it cannot be produced by way of generation; it must necessarily be created by God. Consequently to suppose that the intelligence [or intelligent soul] is the effect of generation is to suppose that it is not a pure and simple substance, but corruptible like the body. It is therefore heresy to say that this soul is transmitted by generation." What is true of the soul should be true of all other form, since no form is a material substance. The utmost possible relation between any two individuals is that God may have used the same stamp or mould for a series of creations, and especially for the less spiritual: "God is the first model for all things. One may also say that, among His creatures some serve as types or models for others because there are some which are made in the image of others"; but generation means sequence, not cause. The only true cause is God. Creation is His sole act, in which no second cause can share. "Creation is more perfect and loftier than generation, because it aims at producing the whole substance of the being, though it starts from absolute nothing."

Thomas Aquinas, when he pleased, was singularly lucid, and on this point he was particularly positive. The architect insisted on the controlling idea of his structure. The Church was God, and its lines excluded interference. God and the Church embraced all the converging lines of the universe, and the universe showed none but lines that converged. Between God and man, nothing whatever intervened. The individual was a compound of form, or soul, and matter; but both were always created together, by the same act, out of nothing. "Simpliciter fatendum est animas simul cum corporibus creari et infundi." [4] It must be distinctly understood that souls were not created before bodies, but that they were created at the same time as the bodies they animate. Nothing whatever preceded this union of two substances which did not exist: "Creatio est productio alicujus rei secundum suam totam substantiam, nullo praesupposito, quod sit vel increatum vel ab aliquo creatum." Language can go no further in exclusion of every possible preceding, secondary, or subsequent cause, "Productio universalis entis a Deo non est motus nec mutatio, sed est quaedam simplex emanatio." The whole universe is, so to speak, a simple emanation from God.

The famous junction, then, is made!—that celebrated fusion of the universal with the individual, of unity with multiplicity, of God and nature, which had broken the neck of every philosophy ever invented; which had ruined William of Champeaux and was to ruin Descartes; this evolution of the finite from the infinite was accomplished. The supreme triumph was as easily effected by Thomas Aquinas as it was to be again effected, four hundred years later, by Spinoza. He had merely to assert the fact: "It is so! it cannot be otherwise!" "For the thousandth and hundred-thousandth time;— what is the use of discussing this prime motor, this Spinozan substance, any longer? We know it is there!" that—as Professor Haeckel very justly repeats for the millionth time—is enough.

One point, however, remained undetermined. The Prime Motor and His action stood fixed, and no one wished to disturb Him; but this was not the point that had disturbed William of Champeaux. Abélard's question still

---

[4] The general meanings of this quotation from Aquinas and the two at the end of the paragraph are freely rendered by Adams in the sentences immediately preceding or following the Latin.

remained to be answered. How did Socrates differ from Plato—Judas from John—Thomas Aquinas from Professor Haeckel? Were they, in fact two, or one? What made an individual? What was God's centimetre measure? The abstract form or soul which existed as a possibility in God, from all time— was it one or many? To the Church, this issue overshadowed all else, for, if humanity was one and not multiple, the Church, which dealt only with individuals, was lost. To the schools, also, the issue was vital, for, if the soul or form was already multiple from the first, unity was lost; the ultimate substance and prime motor itself became multiple; the whole issue was reopened.

To the consternation of the Church, and even of his own order, Thomas, following closely his masters, Albert and Aristotle, asserted that the soul was measured by matter. "Division occurs in substances in ratio of quantity, as Aristotle says in his 'Physics.' And so dimensional quantity is a principle of individuation." The soul is a fluid absorbed by matter in proportion to the absorptive power of the matter. The soul is an energy existing in matter proportionately to the dimensional quantity of the matter. The soul is a wine, greater or less in quantity according to the size of the cup. In our report of the great debate[5] of 1110, between Champeaux and Abélard, we have seen William persistently tempting Abélard to fall into this admission that matter made the man;—that the universal equilateral triangle became an individual if it were shaped in metal, the matter giving it reality which mere form could not give; and Abélard evading the issue as though his life depended on it. In fact, had Abélard dared to follow Aristotle into what looked like an admission that Socrates and Plato were identical as form and differed only in weight, his life might have been the forfeit. How Saint Thomas escaped is a question closely connected with the same inquiry about Saint Francis of Assisi. A Church which embraced, with equal sympathy, and within a hundred years, the Virgin, Saint Bernard, William of Champeaux and the School of Saint-Victor, Peter the Venerable, Saint Francis of Assisi, Saint Dominic, Saint Thomas Aquinas, and Saint Bonaventure, was more liberal than any modern State can afford to be. Radical contradictions the State may perhaps tolerate, though hardly, but never embrace or profess. Such elasticity long ago vanished from human thought.

Yet only Dominicans believe that the Church adopted this law of individualization, or even assented to it. If M. Jourdain is right, Thomas was quickly obliged to give it another form: that, though all souls belonged to the same species, they differed in their aptitudes for uniting with particular bodies. "This soul is commensurate with this body, and not with that other one." The idea is double; for either the souls individualized themselves, and Thomas abandoned his doctrine of their instantaneous creation, with the bodies, out of nothing; or God individualized them in the act of creation, and matter had nothing to do with it. The difficulty is no concern of ours, but the great scholars who took upon themselves to explain it made it worse, until at last one gathers only that Saint Thomas held one of three views: either the soul of humanity was individualized by God, or it individualized itself, or it was divided by ratio of quantity, that is, by matter. This amounts to saying that

<hr/>

[5] This debate, a fiction invented by Adams, forms the dramatic center of Chapter 14 (omitted).

one knows nothing about it, which we knew before and may admit with calmness; but Thomas Aquinas was not so happily placed, between the Church and the schools. Humanity had a form common to itself, which made it what it was. By some means this form was associated with matter; in fact, matter was only known as associated with form. If, then, God, by an instantaneous act, created matter and gave it form according to the dimensions of the matter, innocent ignorance might infer that there was, in the act of God, one world-soul and one world-matter, which He united in different proportions to make men and things. Such a doctrine was fatal to the Church. No greater heresy could be charged against the worst Arab or Jew, and Thomas was so well aware of his danger that he recoiled from it with a vehemence not at all in keeping with his supposed phlegm. With feverish eagerness to get clear of such companions, he denied and denounced, in all companies, in season and out of season, the idea that intellect was one and the same for all men, differing only with the quantity of matter it accompanied. He challenged the adherent of such a doctrine to battle; "let him take the pen if he dares!" No one dared, seeing that even Jews enjoyed a share of common sense and had seen some of their friends burn at the stake not very long before for such opinions, not even openly maintained; while uneducated people, who are perhaps incapable of receiving intellect at all, but for whose instruction and salvation the great work of Saint Thomas and his scholars must chiefly exist, cannot do battle because they cannot understand Thomas's doctrine of matter and form which to them seems frank pantheism.

So it appeared to Duns Scotus also, if one may assert in the Doctor Subtilis[6] any opinion without qualification. Duns began his career only about 1300, after Thomas's death, and stands, therefore, beyond our horizon; but he is still the pride of the Franciscan Order and stands second in authority to the great Dominican alone. In denying Thomas's doctrine that matter individualizes mind, Duns laid himself open to the worse charge of investing matter with a certain embryonic, independent, shadowy soul of its own. Scot's system, compared with that of Thomas, tended toward liberty. Scot held that the excess of power in Thomas's prime motor neutralized the power of his secondary causes, so that these appeared altogether superfluous. This is a point that ought to be left to the Church to decide, but there can be no harm in quoting, on the other hand, the authority of some of Scot's critics within the Church, who have thought that his doctrine tended to deify matter and to keep open the road to Spinoza. Narrow and dangerous was the border-line always between pantheism and materialism, and the chief interest of the schools was in finding fault with each other's paths.

The opinions in themselves need not disturb us, although the question is as open to dispute as ever it was and perhaps as much disputed; but the turn of Thomas's mind is worth study. A century or two later, his passion to be reasonable, scientific, architectural would have brought him within range of the Inquisition. Francis of Assisi was not more archaic and cave-dweller than Thomas of Aquino was modern and scientific. In his effort to be logical he forced his Deity to be as logical as himself, which hardly suited Omnipotence.

[6] "The Subtle Doctor" was a nickname for Duns Scotus, famous for his ingenious theological arguments.

He hewed the Church dogmas into shape as though they were rough stones. About no dogma could mankind feel interest more acute than about that of immortality, which seemed to be the single point vitally necessary for any Church to prove and define as clearly as light itself. Thomas trimmed down the soul to half its legitimate claims as an immortal being by insisting that God created it from nothing in the same act or will by which He created the body and united the two in time and space. The soul existed as form for the body, and had no previous existence. Logic seemed to require that when the body died and dissolved, after the union which had lasted, at most, only an instant or two of eternity, the soul, which fitted that body and no other, should dissolve with it. In that case the Church dissolved, too, since it had no reason for existence except the soul. Thomas met the difficulty by suggesting that the body's form might take permanence from the matter to which it gave form. That matter should individualize mind was itself a violent wrench of logic, but that it should also give permanence—the one quality it did not possess—to this individual mind seemed to many learned doctors a scandal. Perhaps Thomas meant to leave the responsibility on the Church, where it belonged as a matter not of logic but of revealed truth. At all events, this treatment of mind and matter brought him into trouble which few modern logicians would suspect.

The human soul having become a person by contact with matter, and having gained eternal personality by the momentary union, was finished, and remains to this day for practical purposes unchanged; but the angels and devils, a world of realities then more real than man, were never united with matter, and therefore could not be persons. Thomas admitted and insisted that the angels, being immaterial,—neither clothed in matter, nor stamped on it, nor mixed with it,—were universals; that is, each was a species in himself, a class, or perhaps what would be now called an energy, with no other individuality than he gave himself.

The idea seems to modern science reasonable enough. Science has to deal, for example, with scores of chemical energies which it knows little about except that they always seem to be constant to the same conditions; but every one knows that in the particular relation of mind to matter the battle is as furious as ever. The soul has always refused to live in peace with the body. The angels, too, were always in rebellion. They insisted on personality, and the devils even more obstinately than the angels. The dispute was—and is —far from trifling. Mind would rather ignore matter altogether. In the thirteenth century mind did, indeed, admit that matter was something,—which it quite refuses to admit in the twentieth,—but treated it as a nuisance to be abated. To the pure in spirit one argued in vain that spirit must compromise; that nature compromised; that God compromised; that man himself was nothing but a somewhat clumsy compromise. No argument served. Mind insisted on absolute despotism. Schoolmen as well as mystics would not believe that matter was what it seemed,—if, indeed, it existed;—unsubstantial, shifty, shadowy; changing with incredible swiftness into dust, gas, flame; vanishing in mysterious lines of force into space beyond hope of recovery; whirled about in eternity and infinity by that mind, form, energy, or thought which guides and rules and tyrannizes and is the universe. The Church wanted to be pure spirit; she regarded matter with antipathy as something foul, to be held at arms' length lest it should stain and corrupt the soul; the most she would willingly admit was that mind and matter might travel side by side, like a double-headed comet, on parallel lines that never met, with a pre-established harmony that existed only in the prime motor.

Thomas and his master Albert were almost alone in imposing on the Church the compromise so necessary for its equilibrium. The balance of matter against mind was the same necessity in the Church Intellectual as the balance of trusts in the arch of the Gothic cathedral. Nowhere did Thomas show his architectural obstinacy quite so plainly as in thus taking matter under his protection. Nothing would induce him to compromise with the angels. He insisted on keeping man wholly apart, as a complex of energies in which matter shared equally with mind. The Church must rest firmly on both. The angels differed from other beings below them precisely because they were immaterial and impersonal. Such rigid logic outraged the spiritual Church. Perhaps Thomas's sudden death in 1274 alone saved him from the fate of Abélard, but it did not save his doctrine. Two years afterwards, in 1276, the French and English churches combined to condemn it. Étienne Tempier, Bishop of Paris, presided over the French Synod; Robert Kilwardeby, of the Dominican Order, Archbishop of Canterbury, presided over the Council at Oxford. The synods were composed of schoolmen as well as churchmen, and seem to have been the result of a serious struggle for power between the Dominican and Franciscan Orders. Apparently the Church compromised between them by condemning the errors of both. Some of these errors, springing from Alexander Hales and his Franciscan schools, were in effect the foundation of another Church. Some were expressly charged against Brother Thomas. "Contra fratrem Thomam" the councils forbade teaching that—"quia intelligentiae non habent materiam, Deus non potest plures ejusdem speciei facere; et quod materia non est in angelis"; further, the councils struck at the vital centre of Thomas's system,—"quod Deus non potest individua multiplicare sub una specie sine materia"; and again in its broadest form,—"quod formae non accipiunt divisionem nisi secundam materiam." [7] These condemnations made a great stir. Old Albertus Magnus, who was the real victim of attack, fought for himself and for Thomas. After a long and earnest effort, the Thomists rooted out opposition in the order, and carried their campaign to Rome. After fifty years of struggle, by use of every method known in Church politics, the Dominican Order, in 1323, caused John XXII to canonize Thomas and in effect affirm his doctrine.

The story shows how modern, how heterodox, how material, how altogether new and revolutionary the system of Saint Thomas seemed at first even in the schools; but that was the affair of the Church and a matter of pure theology. We study only his art. Step by step, stone by stone, we see him build his church-building like a stone mason, "with the care that the twelfth-century architects put into" their work, as Viollet-le-Duc saw some similar architect at Rouen, building the tower of Saint-Romain: "He has thrown over his work the grace and finesse, the study of detail, the sobriety in projections, the per-

---

[7] In summing up the teachings of Aquinas, two paragraphs above ("The human soul . . . himself"), Adams gives a free rendering of these charges delivered in Latin by the Church Council "Contra fratem Thomam" (against brother Thomas).

fect harmony," which belongs to his school, and yet he was rigidly structural
and Norman. The foundation showed it; the elevation, which is God, developed it; the vaulting, with its balance of thrusts in mind and matter, proved
it; but he had still the hardest task in art, to model man.

The cathedral, then, is built, and God is built into it, but, thus far, God
is there alone, filling it all, and maintains the equilibrium by balancing
created matter separately against created mind. The proportions of the building are superb; nothing so lofty, so large in treatment, so true in scale, so
eloquent of multiplicity in unity, has ever been conceived elsewhere; but it
was the virtue or the fault of superb structures like Bourges and Amiens
and the Church universal that they seemed to need man more than man
needed them; they were made for crowds, for thousands and tens of thousands of human beings; for the whole human race, on its knees, hungry
for pardon and love. Chartres needed no crowd, for it was meant as a palace
of the Virgin, and the Virgin filled it wholly; but the Trinity made their
church for no other purpose than to accommodate man, and made man for
no other purpose than to fill their church; if man failed to fill it, the church
and the Trinity seemed equally failures. Empty, Bourges and Beauvais are
cold; hardly as religious as a wayside cross; and yet, even empty, they are
perhaps more religious than when filled with cattle and machines. Saint
Thomas needed to fill his Church with real men, and although he had created his own God for that special purpose, the task was, as every boy knew by
heart, the most difficult that Omnipotence had dealt with.

God, as Descartes justly said, we know! but what is man? The schools
answered: Man is a rational animal! So was apparently a dog, or a bee, or a
beaver, none of which seemed to need churches. Modern science, with infinite effort, has discovered and announced that man is a bewildering complex
of energies, which helps little to explain his relations with the ultimate substance or energy or prime motor whose existence both science and schoolmen
admit; which science studies in laboratories and religion worships in churches.
The man whom God created to fill his Church, must be an energy independent of God; otherwise God filled his own Church with his own energy.
Thus far, the God of Saint Thomas was alone in His Church. The beings He
had created out of nothing—Omar's pipkins of clay and shape—stood against
the walls, waiting to receive the wine of life, a life of their own. Of that life,
energy, will, or wine,—whatever the poets or professors called it,—God was
the only cause, as He was also the immediate cause, and support. Thomas
was emphatic on that point. God is the cause of energy as the sun is the cause
of colour: "prout sol dicitur causa manifestationis coloris." [8] He not only
gives forms to his pipkins, or energies to his agents, but He also maintains
those forms in being: "dat formas creaturis agentibus et eas tenet in esse." He
acts directly, not through secondary causes, on everything and every one: "Deus
in omnibus intime operatur." If, for an instant, God's action, which is also
His will, were to stop, the universe would not merely fall to pieces, but would
vanish, and must then be created anew from nothing: "Quia non habet
radicem in aere, statim cessat lumen, cessante actione solis. Sic autem se habet
omnis creatura ad Deum sicut aer ad solem illuminantem." God radiates en-

---

[8] Adams's translation is given in the first half of the sentence.

ergy as the sun radiates light, and "the whole fabric nature would return to nothing" if that radiation ceased even for an instant. Everything is created by one instantaneous, eternal, universal act of will, and by the same act is maintained in being.

Where, then,—in what mysterious cave outside of creation,—could man, and his free will, and his private world of responsibilities and duties, lie hidden? Unless man was a free agent in a world of his own beyond constraint, the Church was a fraud, and it helped little to add that the State was another. If God was the sole and immediate cause and support of everything in His creation, God was also the cause of its defects, and could not—being Justice and Goodness in essence—hold man responsible for His own omissions. Still less could the State or Church do it in His name.

Whatever truth lies in the charge that the schools discussed futile questions by faulty methods, one cannot decently deny that in this case the question was practical and the method vital. Theist or atheist, monist or anarchist must all admit that society and science are equally interested with theology in deciding whether the universe is one or many, a harmony or a discord. The Church and State asserted that it was a harmony, and that they were its representatives. They say so still. Their claim led to singular but unavoidable conclusions, with which society has struggled for seven hundred years, and is still struggling.

Freedom could not exist in nature, or even in God, after the single, unalterable act or will which created. The only possible free will was that of God before the act. Abélard with his rigid logic averred that God had no freedom; being Himself whatever is most perfect, He produced necessarily the most perfect possible world. Nothing seemed more logical, but if God acted necessarily, His world must also be of necessity the only possible product of His act, and the Church became an impertinence, since man proved only fatuity by attempting to interfere. Thomas dared not disturb the foundations of the Church, and therefore began by laying down the law that God— previous to His act—could choose, and had chosen, whatever scheme of creation He pleased, and that the harmony of the actual scheme proved His perfections. Thus he saved God's free will.

This philosophical apse would have closed the lines and finished the plan of his church-choir had the universe not shown some divergencies or discords needing to be explained. The student of the Latin Quarter was then harder to convince than now that God was Infinite Love and His world a perfect harmony, when perfect love and harmony showed them, even in the Latin Quarter, and still more in revealed truth, a picture of suffering, sorrow, and death; plague, pestilence, and famine; inundations, droughts, and frosts; catastrophes world-wide and accidents in corners; cruelty, perversity, stupidity, uncertainty, insanity; virtue begetting vice; vice working for good; happiness without sense, selfishness without gain, misery without cause, and horrors undefined. The students in public dared not ask, as Voltaire did, "avec son hideux sourire," [9] whether the Lisbon earthquake was the final proof of God's infinite goodness, but in private they used the *argumentum ad personam*

---

[9] "With his hideous smile." The Latin phrase immediately following means: "argument against a divine person."

divinam freely enough, and when the Church told them that evil did not exist, the ribalds laughed.

Saint Augustine certainly tempted Satan when he fastened the Church to this doctrine that evil is only the privation of good, an *amissio boni;*[10] and that good alone exists. The point was infinitely troublesome. Good was order, law, unity. Evil was disorder, anarchy, multiplicity. Which was truth? The Church had committed itself to the dogma that order and unity were the ultimate truth, and that the anarchist should be burned. She could do nothing else, and society supported her—still supports her; yet the Church, who was wiser than the State, had always seen that Saint Augustine dealt with only half the question. She knew that evil might be an excess of good as well as absence of it; that good leads to evil, evil to good; and that, as Pascal says, "three degrees of polar elevation upset all jurisprudence; a meridian decides truth; fundamental laws change; rights have epochs. Pleasing Justice! bounded by a river or a mountain! truths on this side the Pyrenees! errors beyond!" Thomas conceded that God Himself, with the best intentions, might be the source of evil, and pleaded only that his action might in the end work benefits. He could offer no proof of it, but he could assume as probable a plan of good which became the more perfect for the very reason that it allowed great liberty in detail.

One hardly feels Saint Thomas here in all his force. He offers suggestion rather than proof;—apology—the weaker because of obvious effort to apologize—rather than defence, for Infinite Goodness, Justice, and Power; scoffers might add that he invented a new proof *ab defectu,* or argument for proving the perfection of a machine by the number of its imperfections; but at all events, society has never done better by way of proving its right to enforce morals or unity of opinion. Unless it asserts law, it can only assert force. Rigid theology went much further. In God's providence, man was as nothing. With a proper sense of duty, every solar system should be content to suffer, if thereby the efficiency of the Milky Way were improved. Such theology shocked Saint Thomas, who never wholly abandoned man in order to exalt God. He persistently brought God and man together, and if he erred, the Church rightly pardons him because he erred on the human side. Whenever the path lay through the valley of despair he called God to his aid, as though he felt the moral obligation of the Creator to help His creation.

At best the vision of God, sitting forever at His work-table, willing the existence of mankind exactly as it is, while conscious that, among these myriad arbitrary creations of His will, hardly one in a million could escape temporary misery or eternal damnation, was not the best possible background for a Church, as the Virgin and the Saviour frankly admitted by taking the foreground; but the Church was not responsible for it. Mankind could not admit an anarchical—a dual or a multiple—universe. The world was there, staring them in the face, with all its chaotic conditions, and society insisted on its unity in self-defence. Society still insists on treating it as unity, though no longer affecting logic. Society insists on its free will, although free will has never been explained to the satisfaction of any but those who much wish to

---

[10] Adams gives the phrase first in English, then in Latin. In the next paragraph *ab defectu* is freely rendered in the words immediately following.

be satisfied, and although the words in any common sense implied not unity but duality in creation. The Church had nothing to do with inventing this riddle—the oldest that fretted mankind. Apart from all theological interferences—fall of Adam or fault of Eve, Atonement, Justification, or Redemption—either the universe was one, or it was two, or it was many; either energy was one, seen only in powers of itself, or it was several; either God was harmony, or He was discord. With practical unanimity, mankind rejected the dual or multiple scheme; it insisted on unity. Thomas took the question as it was given him. The unity was full of defects; he did not deny them; but he claimed that they might be incidents, and that the admitted unity might even prove their beneficence. Granting this enormous concession, he still needed a means of bringing into the system one element which vehemently refused to be brought: that is, Man himself, who insisted that the universe was a unit, but that he was a universe; that energy was one, but that he was another energy; that God was omnipotent, but that man was free. The contradiction had always existed, exists still, and always must exist, unless man either admits that he is a machine, or agrees that anarchy and chaos are the habit of nature, and law and order its accident. The agreement may become possible, but it was not possible in the thirteenth century nor is it now. Saint Thomas's settlement could not be a simple one or final, except for practical use, but it served, and it holds good still.

No one ever seriously affirmed the literal freedom of will. Absolute liberty is absence of restraint; responsibility is restraint; therefore, the ideally free individual is responsible only to himself. This principle is the philosophical foundation of anarchism, and, for anything that science has yet proved, may be the philosophical foundation of the universe; but it is fatal to all society and is especially hostile to the State. Perhaps the Church of the thirteenth century might have found a way to use even this principle for a good purpose; certainly, the influence of Saint Bernard was sufficiently unsocial and that of Saint Francis was sufficiently unselfish to conciliate even anarchists of the militant class; but Saint Thomas was working for the Church and the State, not for the salvation of souls, and his chief object was to repress anarchy. The theory of absolute free will never entered his mind, more than the theory of material free will would enter the mind of an architect. The Church gave him no warrant for discussing the subject in such a sense. In fact, the Church never admitted free will, or used the word when it could be avoided. In Latin, the term used was "liberum arbitrium,"—free choice— and in French to this day it remains in strictness "libre arbitre" still. From Saint Augustine downwards the Church was never so unscientific as to admit of liberty beyond the faculty of choosing between paths, some leading through the Church and some not, but all leading to the next world; as a criminal might be allowed the liberty of choosing between the guillotine and the gallows, without infringing on the supremacy of the judge.

Thomas started from that point, already far from theoretic freedom. "We are masters of our acts," he began, "in the sense that we can choose such and such a thing; now, we have not to choose our end, but the means that relate to it, as Aristotle says." Unfortunately, even this trenchant amputation of man's free energies would not accord with fact or with logic. Experience proved that man's power of choice in action was very far from absolute, and logic seemed to require that every choice should have some predetermining cause which decided the will to act. Science affirmed that choice was not free, —could not be free,—without abandoning the unity of force and the foundation of law. Society insisted that its choice must be left free, whatever became of science or unity. Saint Thomas was required to illustrate the theory of "liberum arbitrium" by choosing a path through these difficulties, where path there was obviously none.

Thomas's method for treating this problem was sure to be as scientific as the vaulting of a Gothic arch. Indeed, one follows it most easily by translating his school-vocabulary into modern technical terms. With very slight straining of equivalents, Thomas might now be written thus:

By the term God, is meant a prime motor which supplies all energy to the universe, and acts directly on man as well as on all other creatures, moving him as a mechanical motor might do; but man, being specially provided with an organism more complex than the organisms of other creatures, enjoys an exceptional capacity for reflex action,—a power of reflection,—which enables him within certain limits to choose between paths; and this singular capacity is called free choice or free will. Of course, the reflection is not choice, and though a man's mind reflected as perfectly as the facets of a light-house lantern, it would never reach a choice without an energy which impels it to act.

Now let us read Saint Thomas:

Some kind of an agent is required to determine one's choice; that agent is reflection. Man reflects, then, in order to learn what choice to make between the two acts which offer themselves. But reflection is, in its turn, a faculty of doing opposite things, for we can reflect or not reflect; and we are no further forward than before. One cannot carry back this process infinitely, for in that case one would never decide. The fixed point is not in man, since we meet in him, as a being apart by himself, only the alternative faculties; we must, therefore, recur to the intervention of an exterior agent who shall impress on our will a movement capable of putting an end to its hesitations: That exterior agent is nothing else than God!

The scheme seems to differ little, and unwillingly, from a system of dynamics as modern as the dynamo. Even in the prime motor, from the moment of action, freedom of will vanished. Creation was not successive; it was one instantaneous thought and act, identical with the will, and was complete and unchangeable from end to end, including time as one of its functions. Thomas was as clear as possible on that point: "Supposing God wills anything in effect; He cannot will not to will it, because His will cannot change." He wills that some things shall be contingent and others necessary, but He wills in the same act that the contingency shall be necessary. "They are contingent because God has willed them to be so, and with this object has subjected them to causes which are so." In the same way He wills that His creation shall develop itself in time and space and sequence, but He creates these conditions as well as the events. He creates the whole, in one act, complete, unchangeable, and it is then unfolded like a rolling panorama, with its predetermined contingencies.

Man's free choice—liberum arbitrium—falls easily into place as a predetermined contingency. God is the first cause, and acts in all secondary causes directly; but while He acts mechanically on the rest of creation,—as far as is known,—He acts freely at one point, and this free action remains free as far as it extends on that line. Man's freedom derives from this source, but it is simply apparent, as far as he is a cause; it is a reflex action determined by a new agency of the first cause.

However abstruse these ideas may once have sounded, they are far from seeming difficult in comparison with modern theories of energy. Indeed, measured by that standard, the only striking feature of Saint Thomas's motor is its simplicity. Thomas's prime motor was very powerful, and its lines of energy were infinite. Among these infinite lines, a certain group ran to the human race, and, as long as the conduction was perfect, each man acted mechanically. In cases where the current, for any reason, was for a moment checked, —that is to say, produced the effect of hesitation or reflection in the mind,— the current accumulated until it acquired power to leap the obstacle. As Saint Thomas expressed it, the Prime Motor, Who was nothing else than God, intervened to decide the channel of the current. The only difference between man and a vegetable was the reflex action of the complicated mirror which was called mind, and the mark of mind was reflective absorption or choice. The apparent freedom was an illusion arising from the extreme delicacy of the machine, but the motive power was in fact the same—that of God.

This exclusion of what men commonly called freedom was carried still further in the process of explaining dogma. Supposing the conduction to be insufficient for a given purpose; a purpose which shall require perfect conduction? Under ordinary circumstances, in ninety-nine cases out of a hundred, the conductor will be burned out, so to speak; condemned, and thrown away. This is the case with most human beings. Yet there are cases where the conductor is capable of receiving an increase of energy from the prime motor, which enables it to attain the object aimed at. In dogma, this store of reserved energy is technically called Grace. In the strict, theological sense of the word, as it is used by Saint Thomas, the exact, literal meaning of Grace is "a motion which the Prime Motor, as a supernatural cause, produces in the soul, perfecting free will." It is a reserved energy, which comes to aid and reinforce the normal energy of the battery.

To religious minds this scientific inversion of solemn truths seems, and is, sacrilege; but Thomas's numerous critics in the Church have always brought precisely this charge against his doctrine, and are doing so still. They insist that he has reduced God to a mechanism and man to a passive conductor of force. He has left, they say, nothing but God in the universe. The terrible word which annihilates all other philosophical systems against which it is hurled, has been hurled freely against his for six hundred years and more, without visibly affecting the Church; and yet its propriety seems, to the vulgar, beyond reasonable cavil. To Father de Régnon, of the extremely learned and intelligent Society of Jesus, the difference between pantheism and Thomism reduces itself to this: "Pantheism, starting from the notion of an infinite substance which is the plenitude of being, concludes that there can exist no other beings than the being; no other realities than the absolute reality. Thomism, starting from the efficacy of the first cause, tends to reduce more and more the efficacy of second causes, and to replace it by a passivity which receives without producing, which is determined without de-termining." To students of architecture, who know equally little about pan-theism and about Thomism,—or, indeed, for that matter, about architecture, too,—the quality that rouses most surprise in Thomism is its astonishingly scientific method. The Franciscans and the Jesuits call it pantheism, but sci-ence, too, is pantheism, or has till very recently been wholly pantheistic. Avowedly science has aimed at nothing but the reduction of multiplicity to unity, and has excommunicated, as though it were itself a Church, any one who doubted or disputed its object, its method, or its results. The effort is as evident and quite as laborious in modern science, starting as it does from multiplicity, as in Thomas Aquinas, who started from unity; and it is neces-sarily less successful, for its true aims, as far as it is science and not disguised religion, were equally attained by reaching infinite complexity; but the as-sertion or assumption of ultimate unity has characterized the Law of Energy as emphatically as it has characterized the definition of God in theology. If it is a reproach to Saint Thomas, it is equally a reproach to Clerk-Maxwell. In truth, it is what men most admire in both—the power of broad and lofty generalization.

Under any conceivable system the process of getting God and man under the same roof—of bringing two independent energies under the same con-trol—required a painful effort, as science has much cause to know. No doubt, many good Christians and some heretics have been shocked at the tour de force by which they felt themselves suddenly seized, bound hand and foot, attached to each other, and dragged into the Church, without con-sent or consultation. To religious mystics, whose scepticism concerned chiefly themselves and their own existence, Saint Thomas's man seemed hardly worth herding, at so much expense and trouble, into a Church where he was not eager to go. True religion felt the nearness of God without caring to see the mechanism. Mystics like Saint Bernard, Saint Francis, Saint Bonaventure, or Pascal had a right to make this objection, since they got into the Church, so to speak, by breaking through the windows; but society at large accepted and retains Saint Thomas's man much as Saint Thomas delivered him to the Government; a two-sided being, free or unfree, responsible or irresponsible, an energy or a victim of energy, moved by choice or moved by compulsion, as the interests of society seemed for the moment to need. Certainly Saint Thomas lavished no excess of liberty on the man he created, but still he was more generous than the State has ever been. Saint Thomas asked little from man, and gave much; even as much freedom of will as the State gave or now gives; he added immortality hereafter and eternal happiness under reasonable restraints; his God watched over man's temporal welfare far more anxiously than the State has ever done, and assigned him space in the Church which he never can have in the galleries of Parliament or Congress; more than all this, Saint Thomas and his God placed man in the centre of the universe, and made the sun and the stars for his uses. No statute law ever did as much for man, and no social reform ever will try to do it; yet man bitterly com-plained that he had not his rights, and even in the Church is still complain-ing, because Saint Thomas set a limit, more or less vague, to what the man was obstinate in calling his freedom of will.

Thus Saint Thomas completed his work, keeping his converging lines clear and pure throughout, and bringing them together, unbroken, in the curves that gave unity to his plan. His sense of scale and proportion was that of the great architects of his age. One might go on studying it for a lifetime. He showed no more hesitation in keeping his Deity in scale than in adjusting man to it. Strange as it sounds, although man thought himself hardly treated in respect to freedom, yet, if freedom meant superiority, man was in action much the superior of God, Whose freedom suffered, from Saint Thomas, under restraints that man never would have tolerated. Saint Thomas did not allow God even an undetermined will; He was pure Act, and as such He could not change. Man alone was allowed, in act, to change direction. What was more curious still, man might absolutely prove his freedom by refusing to move at all; if he did not like his life he could stop it, and habitually did so, or ac- quiesced in its being done for him; while God could not commit suicide or even cease for a single instant His continuous action. If man had the singu- lar fancy of making himself absurd,—a taste confined to himself but attested by evidence exceedingly strong,—he could be as absurd as he liked; but God could not be absurd. Saint Thomas did not allow the Deity the right to con- tradict Himself, which is one of man's chief pleasures. While man enjoyed what was, for his purposes, an unlimited freedom to be wicked,—a privilege which, as both Church and State bitterly complained and still complain, he has outrageously abused,—God was Goodness, and could be nothing else. While man moved about his relatively spacious prison with a certain degree of ease, God, being everywhere, could not move. In one respect, at least, man's free- dom seemed to be not relative but absolute, for his thought was an energy paying no regard to space or time or order or object or sense; but God's thought was His act and will at once; speaking correctly, God could not think; He is. Saint Thomas would not, or could not, admit that God was Ne- cessity, as Abélard seems to have held, but he refused to tolerate the idea of a divine maniac, free from moral obligation to himself. The atmosphere of Saint Louis surrounds the God of Saint Thomas, and its pure ether shuts out the corruption and pollution to come,—the Valois and Bourbons, the Occams and Hobbes's, the Tudors and the Medicis, of an enlightened Europe.

The theology turns always into art at the last, and ends in aspiration. The spire justifies the church. In Saint Thomas's Church, man's free will was the aspiration to God, and he treated it as the architects of Chartres and Laon had treated their famous flèches. The square foundation-tower, the expression of God's power in act,—His Creation,—rose to the level of the Church façade as a part of the normal unity of God's energy; and then, suddenly, without show of effort, without break, without logical violence, became a many- sided, voluntary, vanishing human soul, and neither Villard de Honnecourt nor Duns Scotus could distinguish where God's power ends and man's free will begins. All they saw was the soul vanishing into the skies. How it was done, one does not care to ask; in a result so exquisite, one has not the heart to find fault with "adresse." [11]

About Saint Thomas's theology we need not greatly disturb ourselves; it

---

[11] "Skill," a term applied to the architect's craftsmanship.

can matter now not much, whether he put more pantheism than the law
allowed or more materialism than Duns Scotus approved—or less of either—
into his universe, since the Church is still on the spot, responsible for its own
doctrines; but his architecture is another matter. So scientific and structural
a method was never an accident or the property of a single mind even with
Aristotle to prompt it. Neither his Church nor the architect's church was
a sketch, but a completely studied structure. Every relation of parts, every disturbance of equilibrium, every detail of construction was treated with infinite
labour, as the result of two hundred years of experiment and discussion
among thousands of men whose minds and whose instincts were acute, and
who discussed little else. Science and art were one. Thomas Aquinas would
probably have built a better cathedral at Beauvais than the actual architect
who planned it; but it is quite likely that the architect might have saved
Thomas some of his errors, as pointed out by the Councils of 1276. Both
were great artists; perhaps in their professions, the greatest that ever lived;
and both must have been great students beyond their practice. Both were
subject to constant criticism from men and bodies of men whose minds
were as acute and whose learning was as great as their own. If the Archbishop
of Canterbury and the Bishop of Paris condemned Thomas, the Bernardines
had, for nearly two hundred years, condemned Beauvais in advance. Both the
"Summa Theologiae" and Beauvais Cathedral were excessively modern, scientific, and technical, marking the extreme points reached by Europe on the
lines of scholastic science. This is all we need to know. If we like, we can
go on to study, inch by inch, the slow decline of the art. The essence of it—
the despotic central idea—was that of organic unity both in the thought and
the building. From that time, the universe has steadily become more complex
and less reducible to a central control. With as much obstinacy as though it
were human, it has insisted on expanding its parts; with as much elusiveness
as though it were feminine, it has evaded the attempt to impose on it a
single will. Modern science, like modern art, tends, in practice, to drop the
dogma of organic unity. Some of the mediaeval habit of mind survives, but
even that is said to be yielding before the daily evidence of increasing and
extending complexity. The fault, then, was not in man, if he no longer
looked at science or art as an organic whole or as the expression of unity.
Unity turned itself into complexity, multiplicity, variety, and even contradiction. All experience, human and divine, assured man in the thirteenth
century that the lines of the universe converged. How was he to know that
these lines ran in every conceivable and inconceivable direction, and that at
least half of them seemed to diverge from any imaginable centre of unity!
Dimly conscious that his Trinity required in logic a fourth dimension, how
was the schoolman to supply it, when even the mathematician of today can
only infer its necessity? Naturally man tended to lose his sense of scale and
relation. A straight line, or a combination of straight lines, may have still a
sort of artistic unity, but what can be done in art with a series of negative
symbols? Even if the negative were continuous, the artist might express at
least a negation; but supposing that Omar's kinetic analogy of the ball and the
players[12] turned out to be a scientific formula!—supposing that the highest

[12] See the *Rubáiyát of Omar Khayyám*, LXII (translated by Edward Fitzgerald).

scientific authority, in order to obtain any unity at all, had to resort to the Middle Ages for an imaginary demon to sort his atoms!—how could art deal with such problems, and what wonder that art lost unity with philosophy and science! Art had to be confused in order to express confusion; but perhaps it was truest, so.

Some future summer, when you are older, and when I have left, like Omar, only the empty glass of my scholasticism for you to turn down, you can amuse yourself by going on with the story after the death of Saint Louis, Saint Thomas, and William of Lorris, and after the failure of Beauvais. The pathetic interest of the drama deepens with every new expression, but at least you can learn from it that your parents in the nineteenth century were not to blame for losing the sense of unity in art. As early as the fourteenth century, signs of unsteadiness appeared, and, before the eighteenth century, unity became only a reminiscence. The old habit of centralizing a strain at one point, and then dividing and subdividing it, and distributing it on visble lines of support to a visible foundation, disappeared in architecture soon after 1500, but lingered in theology two centuries longer, and even, in very old-fashioned communities, far down to our own time; but its values were forgotten, and it survived chiefly as a stock jest against the clergy. The passage between the two epochs is as beautiful as the Slave of Michael Angelo; but, to feel its beauty, you should see it from above, as it came from its radiant source. Truth, indeed, may not exist; science avers it to be only a relation; but what men took for truth stares one everywhere in the eye and begs for sympathy. The architects of the twelfth and thirteenth centuries took the Church and the universe for truths, and tried to express them in a structure which should be final. Knowing by an enormous experience precisely where the strains were to come, they enlarged their scale to the utmost point of material endurance, lightening the load and distributing the burden until the gutters and gargoyles that seem mere ornament, and the grotesques that seem rude absurdities, all do work either for the arch or for the eye; and every inch of material, up and down, from crypt to vault, from man to God, from the universe to the atom, had its task, giving support where support was needed, or weight where concentration was felt, but always with the condition of showing conspicuously to the eye the great lines which led to unity and the curves which controlled divergence; so that, from the cross on the flèche and the keystone of the vault, down through the ribbed nervures, the columns, the windows, to the foundation of the flying buttresses far beyond the walls, one idea controlled every line; and this is true of Saint Thomas's Church as it is of Amiens Cathedral. The method was the same for both, and the result was an art marked by singular unity, which endured and served its purpose until man changed his attitude toward the universe. The trouble was not in the art or the method or the structure, but in the universe itself which presented different aspects as man moved. Granted a Church, Saint Thomas's Church was the most expressive that man has made, and the great Gothic cathedrals were its most complete expression.

Perhaps the best proof of it is their apparent instability. Of all the elaborate symbolism which has been suggested for the Gothic cathedral, the most vital and most perfect may be that the slender nervure, the springing motion of the broken arch, the leap downwards of the flying buttress,—the visible effort to throw off a visible strain,—never let us forget that Faith alone supports it, and that, if Faith fails, Heaven is lost. The equilibrium is visibly delicate beyond the line of safety; danger lurks in every stone. The peril of the heavy tower, of the restless vault, of the vagrant buttress; the uncertainty of logic, the inequalities of the syllogism, the irregularities of the mental mirror,—all these haunting nightmares of the Church are expressed as strongly by the Gothic cathedral as though it had been the cry of human suffering, and as no emotion had ever been expressed before or is likely to find expression again. The delight of its aspirations is flung up to the sky. The pathos of its self-distrust and anguish of doubt is buried in the earth as its last secret. You can read out of it whatever else pleases your youth and confidence; to me, this is all.

1904

LETTERS

1

[H. O. Taylor (1856-1941), a medieval historian, had been a student of Adams' at Harvard. Of the scientists mentioned in the third paragraph, the first four were eminent contemporaries of Adams, the others famous innovators of the seventeenth and eighteenth centuries. Professor Robinson, referred to in the next paragraph, was a young American historian.]

TO HENRY OSBORN TAYLOR

1603 H Street
[Washington, D.C.]
17 Jan. 1905

My dear Taylor

Many thanks for your letter and its literary references. I imagine you are almost the only man in America who are competent to supply them to me, and I shall use them with proper care.

My own interest in the subject is scientific to such an extent that my play with it is awkward, like a kitten in walnuts. I am trying to work out the formula of anarchism; the law of expansion from unity, simplicity, morality, to multiplicity, contradiction, police. I have done it scientifically, by formulating the

This and the following letter, to Barrett Wendell, are from *Henry Adams and His Friends*, edited by H. D. Cater. Copyright 1947 by H. D. Cater. Reprinted with the permission of Houghton Mifflin Company.

ratio of development in energy, as in explosives, or chemical energies. I can see it in the development of steampower, and in the various economies of conveyance. Radium thus far is the term for these mechanical ratios. The ratio for thought is not so easy to fix. I can get a time-ratio only in philosophy. The assumption of unity which was the mark of human thought in the middle-ages has yielded very slowly to the proofs of complexity. The stupor of science before radium is a proof of it. Yet it is quite sure, according to my score of ratios and curves, that, at the accelerated rate of progression shown since 1600, it will not need another century or half century to tip thought upside down. Law, in that case, would disappear as theory or *à priori* principle, and give place to force. Morality would become police. Explosives would reach cosmic violence. Disintegration would overcome integration.

This was the point that leads me back to the twelfth century as the fixed element of the equation. From the relative unity of twelfth-century conceptions of the Prime Motor, I can work down pretty safely to Karl Pearsen's [Pearson's] Grammar of Science or Wallace's Man's Place in Nature, or to Mack [Mach] and Ostwald and the other Germans of today. By intercalating Descartes, Newton, Dalton and a few others, I can even make almost a time ratio. This is where my middle-ages will work out.

I tell you this in order that you may explain to Prof. Robinson why the volume is not offered to the public. It is what it professes to be, and I do not propose to invite attention to it by offering it to anyone except personal friends. You can lend him your copy, and if, on looking it over, he seriously wants the volume, I will with the greatest pleasure send him one, but I do not want him to treat it as anything but what it is,—a sketch-study intended for my own and my nieces' amusement.

Your work is of a totally different kind. I have no object but a superficial one, as far as history is concerned. To me, accuracy is relative. I care very little whether my details are exact, if only my *ensemble* is in scale. You need to be thorough in your study and accurate in your statements. Your middle-ages exist for their own sake, not for ours. To me, who stand in gaping wonder before this preposterous spectacle of thought, and who can see nothing in all nature so iconoclastic, miraculous and anarchistic as Shakespeare, the middle-ages present a picture that has somehow to be brought into relation with ourselves. To you, there is no difficulty in transferring ourselves into the middle-ages. You require serious and complete study, and careful attention to details. Our two paths run in a manner parallel in reverse directions, but I can run and jump along mine, while you must employ a powerful engine to drag your load. I am glad to know that your engine is powerful enough.

Time is very short, but at any rate our middle-ages are long, and the rest matters little to us now. What I most want is an intelligent man of science, a thing I shall never find.

Ever Yrs.

Henry Adams

2

✤ [Barrett Wendell (1855-1921), author and professor of English, had taken a
history course from Adams at Harvard. Of the other writers mentioned in this
letter, all can be found in standard reference works except William of Lorris, thirteenth-
century poet and author of the *Roman de la Rose*.]

TO BARRETT WENDELL

1603 H Street
[Washington, D.C.]
12 March, 1909

My dear Wendell

A letter, so kind as yours, calls for immediate acknowledgment. I am
amused to find myself at last in a little atmosphere of criticism. . . . I am
glad of it, because we are smothered in this American vacuum, and gasp
for intelligent attack. . . .

My dispute, or rather my defense against self-criticism, is that our failures are really not due to ourselves alone. Society has a great share in it.
When I read St. Augustine's *Confessions*, or Rousseau's, I feel certain that
their faults, as literary artists, are worse than mine. We have all three undertaken to do what cannot be successfully done—mix narrative and didactic
purpose and style. The charm of the effort is not in winning the game but in
playing it. We all enjoy the failure. St. Augustine's narrative subsides at last
into the dry sands of metaphysical theology. Rousseau's narrative fails wholly
in didactic result; it subsides into still less artistic egoism. And I found that a
narrative style was so incompatible with a didactic or scientific style, that I
had to write a long supplementary chapter to explain in scientific terms
what I could not put into narration without ruining the narrative. The game
was singularly simple in that sense, but never played out successfully by any
artist however great. Even allegory, as in Bunyan, remains only a relative
success. The *Roman de la Rose* (the first part) is the best popular triumph
ever won.

Yet I contend that the failure would be proportional (other things being
equal) to the atmosphere, or setting. With St. Augustine's background, or
Benvenuto [Cellini]'s, or Saint-Simon's the failure would be less perceptible
than mine. Do what we please, the *tour-de-force* of writing drama with what is
essentially undramatic, must always be unpleasantly evident. It is artistically
violent in Bunyan, and only less so in William of Lorris because it is there disguised in verse; but both these great writers had the advantage of a dramatic
mise-en-scène which I denied to myself. I feel sure that the want of action is
not the difficulty. The *Roman de la Rose* has no action, and St. Augustine
but little. The huge mass of military writers (except Froissart) who have nothing but action, have very rarely succeeded as artists. The modern novel may be
full of action, or devoid of it; both schemes may succeed.

My conclusion is that we need far more art than ever to accomplish a
much smaller artistic effect. This is to say, we are unduly handicapped. We
are forced to write science because our purpose is scientific, and cannot be

rendered by narrative. To us, who do not propose to instruct, but only to amuse, and whose own amusement is in the game rather than in the stakes, the highest scientific or didactic success is failure. To gain it, we must throw up our hand. My experiment of trying to find the exact point of equilibrium where the two motives would be held in contact was bound to be a failure, but was very amusing to carry out; and I still maintain that, if I could have had a dramatic setting like St. Augustine or Benvenuto or even Fanny Burney, I could have made it a success.

Of course, I make no question about pure narrative which is an art by itself, and does not concern me more than pure science.

At bottom, the problem is common to us all, which is my excuse for proposing it in the *Education* and in *Mont St. Michel.* The last three chapters of each make one didactic work in disguise.

Ever Yrs

Henry Adams

3

[A. S. Cook (1853-1927) was a professor of Anglo-Saxon language and literature. See the Introduction, page 331 above, for further comment on the relation of Adams' ideas about instinct to those of Bergson, mentioned at the end of this letter.]

TO ALBERT STANBURROUGH COOK

Paris, 6 August, 1910

* * *

Perhaps I should explain that, for more than thirty years since I left Harvard Collge, I have regarded myself as *emeritus,*—a normal-school instructor,—a teacher of teachers,—whose business was to help active teachers in doing their work; but not to load them with objections or instructions. For that reason I have not even published my books, of late. Since 1890, all my books have been sent about privately, as suggestions to teachers. They have to filter into the class-room, or quietly go to waste. Naturally the one or the other result comes out indifferently to me, since I have nothing to gain in either case.

The *Chartres* volume was the second in the series, and intended to fix the starting-point, since I could not get enough material to illustrate primitive society, or the society of the seventh century B.C., as I would have liked. I wanted to show the intensity of the vital energy of a given time, and of course that intensity had to be stated in its two highest terms—religion and art. As our society stands, this way of presenting a subject can be felt only by a small number of persons. My idea is that world outside—the so-called modern world—can only pervert and degrade the conceptions of the primi-

The letter to Albert Stanburrough Cook is from *Letters of Henry Adams,* edited W. C. Ford. Copyright 1938 by W. C. Ford. Reprinted with the permission of Houghton Mifflin Company.

tive instinct of art and feeling, and that our only chance is to accept the limited number of survivors—the one-in-a-thousand of born artists and poets —and to intensify the energy of feeling within that radiant centre. In other words, I am a creature of our poor old Calvinistic, St. Augustinian fathers, and am not afraid to carry out my logic to the rigorous end of regarding our present society, its ideals and purposes, as dregs and fragments of some primitive, essential instinct now nearly lost. If you are curious to see the theory stated as official instruction, you have only to look over Bergson's *Evolution Créatrice* (pp. 288, 289). The tendencies of thought in Europe seem to me very strongly that way.

You see, therefore, why I should be not merely indifferent [to], but positively repellent of, a popular following. It means to me a crowd of summer-tourists, vulgarising every thought known to artists. In act, it is the Oberammergau Passion-play as now run for Cook's tourists.

4

[H. C. Lodge (1850-1924), Senator and author, had been a student and protégé of Adams at Harvard. He was president of the Massachusetts Historical Society from 1915 to 1924 and supervised its edition of the *Education* in 1918—the first actual publication of the book.]

TO HENRY CABOT LODGE

1603 H Street
[Washington, D.C.]
1 March, 1915

My dear Cabot

I send you herewith a sealed packet containing a copy of my *Education* corrected and prepared for publication. Should the question arise at any future time, I wish that you, on behalf of the Historical Society, would take charge of the matter, and see that the volume is printed as I leave it.

With this view, I have written a so-called Editor's Preface, which you have read, and which I have taken the liberty, subject to your assent, to stamp with you initials.

Also, may I beg that you will bar the introduction of all illustrations of any sort. You know that I do not consider illustrations as my work, or having part in any correct rendering of my ideas. Least of all do I wish portraits. I have always tried to follow the rule of making the reader think only of the text, and I do not want to abandon it here.

Pray bear in mind that the publication itself as well as the manner of it is left at your discretion. The volume has now been ten years in existence, and I have never thought its publication likely to benefit anyone at any special moment, but I will not undertake to control your judgment, after my own disappearance.

The letter to Henry Cabot Lodge is from *Henry Adams and His Friends*, edited by H. C. Cater. Copyright 1947 by H. C. Cater. Reprinted with the permission of Houghton Mifflin Company.

I might add that, if the Society should ever care to resume, on my behalf, the publication of the *Chartres*, it might follow the same rule, besides
correcting some of the rather annoying misprints.

I am very truly

Henry Adams

Reading Suggestions

There is no collected edition of the writings of Henry Adams, but this is
less of a handicap to the literary student than to the historian. The former's
interest is centered on two books, *Chartres* and the *Education*, both of which
are in print. Supplementary to these are the novels and essays listed in the
biographical sketch below. The rest of Adams' works, comprising two thirds of
his output, belong to history rather than to literature. Much of Adams' correspondence, however, is of great importance to students of *Chartres* and the
Education. Of the six volumes of letters published since his death the most
rewarding are *Henry Adams and His Friends* (1947), edited by H. D. Cater,
and *Letters of Henry Adams, 1892-1918* (1938), edited by W. C. Ford. A
convenient volume of *Selected Letters of Henry Adams* (1951) was edited by
Newton Arvin.

Because of the intricate relations between Adams' life and his literary
works, a detailed and reliable biography such as that by Ernest Samuels is an
indispensable tool. Two parts of it have appeared: *The Young Henry Adams*
(1948) and *Henry Adams, the Middle Years* (1958); the third and final
volume is now in preparation.

Several critical studies have appeared in recent years, more concerned with
Adams as historian and thinker than as literary artist. In the first category,
William Jordy's *Henry Adams: Scientific Historian* (1952) is a sharp analysis
of his use of theories borrowed from science to structure and give meaning
to the *Education.* In the second category, Max Baym's *The French Education
of Henry Adams* (1951) is an interesting account of Adams' lifelong study
of French authors, historians, and philosophers—though it tends to overem-
phasize this influence. The two most valuable books for students of literature
deal with both the literary and intellectual aspects of the subject. George
Hochfield's *Henry Adams: An Introduction and Interpretation* (1962) is probably the best monograph for beginners. The fullest and finest of all is Jacob
Levenson's *The Mind and Art of Henry Adams* (1957), a full-scale critical
study with excellent chapters on *Chartres* and the *Education.* A forthcoming
study by John Conder, focused on these two books as Adams' experiments in
literary form, will make a significant addition to the criticisms already published.

Of the numerous essays on Adams only a few can be cited here. The best
treatment of him as a historian is the one by H. S. Commager, collected in the
Marcus W. Jernegan Essays in American Historiography (1937), edited by
W. T. Hutchinson. The chapter by R. S. Spiller in *Literary History of the
United States* (1948) is a sane and balanced introductory essay on Adams as a
literary man. The chapter on him by Yvor Winters in *The Anatomy of Nonsense*
(1943) presents a challenging thesis on the influence of Puritanism. A seminal
article on the *Education* by R. P. Blackmur was included in his volume, *The
Lion and the Honeycomb* (1955), and a valuable one on *Chartres*, "The Har-

mony of True Liberalism," was published by him in the *Sewanee Review* (Winter 1952). A further study by Jacob Levenson relating Adams' ideas to those of the Enlightenment, Transcendentalism, pragmatism, and science may be found in *Studies in American Culture* (1959), edited by Kwiat and Turpie. Gene Koretz has investigated an important literary parallel in "Augustine's *Confessions* and *The Education of Henry Adams*," in *Comparative Literature* (Summer 1960). For a study of intention and method in the *Education* see Gerrit Roelofs, "Henry Adams: Pessimism and the Intelligent Use of Doom," *English Literary History* (Spring 1950).

Biography

In a number of his writings Henry Adams drew on the facts of his own life, but changed them to suit his literary purposes. Readers, therefore, need a hard core of biography against which to check these seemingly autobiographical works: the relation of the person to the persona in the *Education* and *Chartres*, the suggestive parallels with his own life in the two novels, the ironical self-references in his letters, even in conversation. One of his many private jokes about himself was that he had been an average young man. This was classic understatement for the life that began when Henry Brooks Adams was born in Boston on February 16, 1838. His heritage was unique in American annals: descendant of two Presidents of the early Republic, and son of Charles Francis Adams, who had a distinguished public career in the mid-nineteenth century. To be an Adams was to make history rather than to observe and comment on it. The family tradition bore heavily on young Adams and inhibited his own development for many years. He was over thirty before he struck out on the path that suited his particular talents, the profession of authorship.

His boyhood was divided between Boston and the country home at near-by Quincy, where he enjoyed the freedom of rural life and sports to balance the winter discipline of school. His formal education led quite naturally to Harvard. At college he was a bookish student with a flair for literary expression and foreign languages. His complaint in the *Education* about Harvard's conservatism in such subjects as economics was justifiable, but there were some distinguished faculty members in science and letters. One of his most influential teachers was Agassiz, the noted critic of Darwin. The other was Lowell, who persuaded him to continue his education at the University of Berlin. For two years, 1858–1860, Adams studied and traveled in Europe. He learned little from the lectures in civil law, but much about Western civilization, past and present. When he returned at the age of twenty-two, to serve as assistant to Congressman Adams in Washington, he was a remarkably well-educated young man.

With the outbreak of the Civil War his father was appointed Ambassador to England, and the son went along as private secretary, remaining there from 1861 to 1868. These years broadened his education in many ways. The family had entrée as a matter of course into the top circles of English society and intellectual life, and Henry Adams took full advantage of his opportunities. London was first of all a school of practical politics at this time of crisis, bringing him acquaintance with the leading statesmen of the day. Far more important for his ultimate education were his excursions into art, literature, and science. He met authors like Swinburne and became an intimate of Lyell, Darwin's champion. Rich and varied as these experiences were, they still had not provided any independent career for young Adams. But even during the busy English years he had begun to try a line of his own, publishing essays on historical and economic problems in American periodicals. After his duties to his father in London were over, he spent two years in Washington consolidating his reputation as a vigorous new writer.

Then, in 1870, came the real turning point in his life. He was offered an assistant professorship in history at Harvard, combined with the editorship of the *North American Review*, and he accepted the dual post. His reluctance at withdrawing from public life was overcome by the challenge to make a profession out of what had been only a side interest, the study and writing of history. The main purpose for which he was brought there, teaching, he declared was a failure. Actually his success was striking. He revolutionized the methods of instruction, especially by introducing the German seminar for graduate students. All this whetted his appetite for research, convinced him of the need to formulate a new historiography, and led him to revamp his ideas about the meaning of education. Adams's seven years at Harvard paved the way for his career as an author.

He resigned in 1877, weary of teaching and eager to make himself into a professional historian. Having married in 1872 a Boston heiress and intellectual, Marian Hooper, he now established himself in a Washington mansion near the White House. There the couple presided over a brilliant salon that included distinguished foreign visitors, leaders in government like John Hay, prominent figures in science and art like Clarence King, William and Henry James, St. Gaudens and La Farge. From this vantage point Adams could keep an eye on the present state of the nation even as he began his serious research into its past, having abandoned medieval for American history. In a series of biographies he tested out the new German scientific method of writing history. Then the availability of Jefferson's and Madison's papers made it possible for him to write a precise and detailed history from original sources, focusing on the opposition administrations between those of John and John Quincy Adams. This monumental labor, a nine volume *History of the United States*, absorbed most of his energies for fifteen years, finally appearing in 1891.

Other events of moment occurred during the same period. Long before, in a letter to his brother just after graduating from Harvard, he had posed the question of his future career: "Could I write a history, do you think, or a novel, or anything that would be likely to make it worth while for me to try?" In the midst of his biographical and historical work he published two novels, *Democracy* (1880) and *Esther* (1884), the latter with a heroine modeled closely on Marian Adams. Then in 1885 fate struck in the suicide of his wife. The next year Adams went on a trip to Japan, the beginning of wanderings that continued for the next two decades. There was a long visit in the South Seas, followed by a tour around the world, explorations of the Far West from Canada to Mexico, and journeyings in Europe from Scandinavia to the Near East. After 1895 France and the Gothic cathedrals drew him most.

These travels in space were matched by others in time, especially back into the Middle Ages. Gradually there was shaping up the twin project that occupied his old age and crowned his career as a writer: his search for unity in the Christian civilization of the thirteenth century, his analysis of its breakdown into multiplicity in the twentieth. *Mont-Saint-Michel and Chartres* was privately issued in 1904 and published in 1913; *The Education of Henry Adams* in 1907, then in the posthumous edition of 1918. These last two books have some thematic relations to his novels and some ideological connections with his historical writings, but they were essentially new departures. It is solely on them that Adams' high rank in American literature depends. During his declining years he wrote several key essays supplementary to the *Education*, collected after his death in *The Degradation of the Democratic Dogma*. Except for occasional trips to Europe, he passed his days in Washington surrounded by a circle of younger admirers, the intimate friends of his prime having all died. The unrelenting pursuit of his education continued until paralysis slowed him down. The first stroke came in 1912. The last came in 1918, shortly after his eightieth birthday and shortly before the cataclysm of World War I came to an end. The brightest intellectual light in America had gone out, and with it one of the keenest sensibilities and most remarkable talents in our literary annals.

O'Neill, the outstanding dramatist of the interwar period. He was a highly experimental author. Shifted from realistic play writing Beyond the Horizon (1920) and Anna Christie (1921) to expressionistic writing as The Emperor

EUGENE O'NEILL ❖ Jones
1888-1953
(1920) and

Sometimes called a Primitivist

The Hairy Ape (1922)

Know the Kinds of theatres:

1. The Greek Theater
2. The Medieval
3. The Elizabethan
4. The Theatre of modern Realism.

Types of Drama
1. Allegory
2. Burlesque
3. Comedy
4. Drama or drama
5. Entertainment
6. Expressionism
7. Farce
8. History Play
9. Melodrama
10. Mime
11. Miracle play
12. Morality play
13. Mystery
14. Naturalism
15. Problem play
16. Realism
17. Symbolism
18. Tragedy
19. Tragicomedy

Supp. 740+
Character + Conflict
by Kernan

Critical Terms:
1. Anticlimax
2. Aside
3. Atmosphere
4. Bathos
5. Catastrophe
6. Catharsis
7. Chorus
8. Climax
9. Comic Relief
10. Contrast
11. Conventions
12. Dénouement
13. Deus Ex Machina
14. Dramatis Personae
15. Episodic Plot
16. Exposition
17. Fable
18. Falling action
19. Foreshadowing
20. Imagery
21. Irony
22. Obligatory Scene
23. Pathos
24. Personification
25. Point of attack
26. Probability
28. Recognition

Introduction

The career of Eugene O'Neill was one long rebellion, conducted on more than one front. First, it was a rebellion against his father, James O'Neill, a famous and successful actor in the tradition of nineteenth-century melodrama. Second, by a natural extension perhaps, the rebellion was against the melodramatic tradition itself. James O'Neill was for many years the owner, manager, producer, and principal player in *The Count of Monte Cristo*, a prize example of the kind of sentimentality that made the tradition popular. Its tinsel heroics were very good box office, netting in some years as much as $40,000. However, when Eugene O'Neill began to write plays, in 1912 or 1913, he deliberately departed as far as possible from the popular clichés. He read Greek drama and German philosophy—particularly Friedrich Nietzsche's *The Birth of Tragedy* and *Thus Spake Zarathustra*—and the modern experimental works of the Swedish playwright August Strindberg and the German Frank Wedekind.

In many ways the rebellion was extremely successful. Though he never quite broke away from his father, or even from the use of melodramatic effects, O'Neill did break through the old sentimentalism into a new dramatic tradition, which he did more than any other American to establish. He was not, however, working alone, but was part of a general movement, the literary renaissance which is usually dated in the 1920's but which began with the early work of Edwin Arlington Robinson, or with that of the so-called "naturalist" writers of fiction, or with the late novels of Henry James, or with Mark Twain's *Huckleberry Finn*, or with some other phenomenon, depending on the interest or the taste or the point of view of the literary historian. Within the American drama there had been serious efforts at reform, the most notable product being probably William Vaughn Moody's *The Great Divide*, first produced in 1906. If Moody had not died in 1910, at the age of forty-one, he might have done much more. Other playwrights of the 1910's and 1920's, such as Percy MacKaye, Sidney How-

445

ard, Elmer Rice, George Kelly, and Paul Green, helped bring a new vigor, a great variety of new techniques, a new honesty, which sometimes expressed itself in a new harshness, and a new opportunity for anyone with sufficient ability to do original, substantial work. New playwrights, actors, directors, and stage designers have continued to spring up, and to do good work, to the present time. Arthur Miller, Tennessee Williams, and many other playwrights today are indebted to O'Neill and the modern movement in the theater which he did so much to foster.

O'Neill himself was a member of the "lost generation" before it got lost; that is, before World War I came along to catalyze and concentrate the feelings of rebellion that had been gathering for a quarter century or more. Born in the same year as T. S. Eliot, he shared Eliot's sense of a Waste Land quality in modern life and culture, a curse of sterility that demanded some new birth of spiritual and physical creative power if life and culture were to go on. *Desire under the Elms* accordingly takes its historical place with such works as Eliot's *The Waste Land,* Fitzgerald's *The Great Gatsby,* Hemingway's *The Sun Also Rises,* and Faulkner's *The Sound and the Fury,* all of which deal in various ways with the cultural crisis of the time. Therefore we may say that *Desire under the Elms* is an intensely American work in spite of European influences on O'Neill, and that it is intensely a work of the 1920's, though its events are supposed to occur in 1850 and 1851. Its theme concerns the things that made the "lost generation" writers fear the approaching downfall of modern civilization: stupidity, narrow-mindedness, greed, conformity, hypocrisy, moral, religious, and cultural intolerance, crudeness of feeling, and materialistic shortsightedness. Like many other works of the 1920's, *Desire under the Elms* is full of savage ridicule directed against the commercial virtues in terms of which old Ephraim Cabot, his sons Simeon and Peter, and his new wife Abbie rationalize their various selfish desires. Like many of his fellow authors, O'Neill does little, at least on the surface, to offset the pessimistic implications of the way these destructive desires end by ruining the lives of his characters.

Perhaps the most important external factor in making O'Neill's career as a dramatist successful, both commercially and artistically, was the rapid development, at the time he was getting started, of an American experimental theater. O'Neill was exposed to this movement, at least in theory, during a term with Professor George Pierce Baker in the famous 47 Workshop at Harvard, in 1914-1915. A more practical exposure led to a fertile collaboration when, in 1916, he encountered the Provincetown Players. The year before, this group of summer colonists from New York had converted an old fishing wharf into a playhouse. O'Neill, visiting a friend who had a shack on Cape Cod, was invited to read some manuscript to the group. By that time he had written a good many plays, and some of them had been published, at his father's expense, in 1914. But he had never had one produced on any stage. *Bound East for Cardiff*, one of his first full-length dramas, based on his experience as a sailor, was read to the members, who immediately adopted O'Neill and staged the play. "Then," Susan Glaspell, one of those present, wrote later, "we knew what we were for." From that time until 1934, when O'Neill's first period of activity in the theater ended, his association with the Provincetown group continued, while they established themselves as theatrical producers in New York and developed the Playwright's Theatre and the Theatre Guild. They put on most of his plays, including the most ambitiously conceived ones, *Strange Interlude* and *Mourning Becomes Electra*; some of the least successful, such as *Marco Millions*, *Dynamo*, and *Days without End*; and some of the best, including *The Emperor Jones*, *The Hairy Ape*, and *Ah, Wilderness!* *Desire under the Elms* was first produced by the Provincetown Playhouse, Inc., at the Greenwich Village Theatre, on November 11, 1924.

I

Because *Desire under the Elms* is a serious play, and because it ends in a catastrophe, most critics regard it as a tragedy, at least by intention. Others, however, are unwilling to apply that term either to *Desire under the Elms* or to any other modern drama. Modern men, they say, no longer have the personal stature, the individual dignity, to be tragic heroes. Or, we are too deterministic to believe in human free will. Or, we are too much interested in novelty to pay attention any more to the absolute values and eternal truths on which the tragic attitude is based. Or, the mass market which James O'Neill exploited with *The Count of Monte Cristo*, and which television advertisers now exploit with the same kind of thing and worse, will not support the degree of serious art that tragedy demands.

O'Neill himself, at the time he was working on *Desire under the Elms*, and for years after its appearance, was troubled by such questions and problems. In an interview published in 1922, when *The Hairy Ape* had brought him his first fame and wide publicity, he was asked what his "creed" or "philosophy" was. "I suppose," he said, "it is the idea I try to put into all my plays. People talk of the 'tragedy' in them, and call it 'sordid,' 'depressing,' 'pessimistic'—the words usually applied to anything of a tragic nature. But tragedy, I think, has the meaning the Greeks gave it. To them it brought exaltation, an urge toward life and ever more life." This idea probably came to O'Neill more from Germany than from Greece. In *The Birth of Tragedy* Nietzsche had emphasized the mythic and symbolic aspects of Greek drama, which he associated with a "Dionysian" quality of energetic life, "the eternal life behind all phenomena, and in spite of all annihilation." This eternal life, this life beyond life, is what O'Neill seems always to be aiming at, rather than a realistic or naturalistic account of life in the material world.

In the interview he went on to say,

Explain

> The point is that life in itself is nothing. It is the *dream* that keeps us fighting, willing—living! . . . A man wills his own defeat when he pursues the unattainable. But his struggle is his success! He is an example of the spiritual significance which life attains when it aims high enough, when the individual fights all the hostile forces within and without himself to achieve a future of nobler values. . . . He may be a failure in our materialistic sense. . . . Yet isn't he the most inspiring of all successes?

The literary naturalists of the late nineteenth and early twentieth centuries, notably Stephen Crane, Frank Norris, and Theodore Dreiser, were equally concerned with "the urge toward life," with "the hostile forces within and without" the individual, and with the effort to transcend the contradiction they felt between human personality on the one hand and an alien, indifferent, or hostile material world on the other. Their work, like that of O'Neill, was called "sordid," "depressing," and "pessimistic." They too had a tendency, in the dilemma posed by the choice between an idealism that was dead and a materialism that had never been alive, to escape into the fantasy of "the dream" or "the unattainable." They too really hated the mechanistic philosophy, although they were intellectually convinced that it embodied the truth.

The difference between these writers and O'Neill lies partly in the fact that O'Neill, coming somewhat later, was a little more clearly aware of his position. He called himself, on one occasion, "a dynamist of the drama," and his emphasis is more on symbolism than on realism. He tried to explain this point in a note on Strindberg which he wrote for a Provincetown Players production of *The Spook Sonata* in 1924:

> . . . it is only by means of some form of "supernaturalism" that we may express in the theater what we comprehend intuitively of that self-obsession which is the particular discount we moderns have to pay for the loan of life. The old "naturalism"—or "realism" . . . —no longer applies. It represents our fathers' daring aspirations toward self-recognition by holding the family kodak up to ill-nature. But to us their old audacity is *blague*, we have taken too many snapshots of each other in every graceless position. We have endured too much from the banality of surfaces.

O'Neill hoped, by the use of more or less expressionistic symbolism, to pierce beyond "the banality of surfaces" in order to communicate, as directly, dynamically, and powerfully as possible, "the urge toward life."

What he meant by "life" becomes a little clearer in a letter he wrote to Arthur Hobson Quinn in the fall of 1926, calling himself "a most confirmed mystic" because, as he said,

I'm always, always trying to interpret Life in terms of lives, never just lives in terms of character. I'm always acutely conscious of the Force behind—(Fate, God, our biological past creating our present, whatever one calls it—Mystery certainly)—and of the one eternal tragedy of Man in his glorious, self-destructive struggle to make the Force express him instead of being, as an animal is, an infinitesimal incident in its expression.

O'Neill was not, of course, a mystic in any proper sense of the word. A better term for him would perhaps be "romantic idealist." His capitalized "Life" is not essentially different from the principle of life that pervades the universe and the individual in the philosophy of Coleridge, Carlyle, and Emerson; only his attitude toward it is different. They tend to find their freedom in a harmony with the universal living force or principle; O'Neill seeks freedom in rebellion against it, or in an attempt, which he feels is hopeless, to dominate it. The early romantics cooperate with "Life"; O'Neill, like many others of his era, is in desperate conflict with it. Nevertheless, his work is an intense celebration of life, both in individuals and in the world. Old Ephraim Cabot in *Desire under the Elms*, for all his puritanical repression of himself and others, and for all his piously flavored hypocrisy about sex, is a magnificent embodiment of both the love of life and the conflict with it which lend so much of the force and point to O'Neill's dramatic situations.

The "tragic" transfiguration of O'Neill's heroes would therefore seem to lie somewhere in the relation between the individual life and the universal life, as the romantic transfiguration does in *Leaves of Grass* or *Walden* or *Moby Dick*. O'Neill makes a fairly clear suggestion in such plays as *The Fountain, Marco Millions*, and *Lazarus Laughed* that the death of the hero, or of the individual human being, is not the end of life but only one of many transformations through which life goes. The same point seems to be suggested also, less clearly but more dramatically, in *The Hairy Ape*, where Yank's desire to "belong" is, according to the final stage direction, "perhaps" fulfilled in death. In *Desire under the Elms* the reconciliation of Eben and Abbie, under the shadow of death, seems to hint at a comparable solution. It is the life beyond this life, or the universal life to which these individual lives belong and against which they hopelessly rebel, that O'Neill tries to express. At the same time, there is the feeling, as in the earlier romantic literature, that in death the individual, instead of being destroyed—or going as an individual to heaven, hell, or purgatory—is reabsorbed into the universal life from which, as Whitman puts it, he has been separated by the identity of his body. The logic of this formula seems to fit O'Neill's purpose. The individual, having been separated from the universal life at birth, struggles throughout this life to impose his own identity, his own will, on the universe. He fails, and he dies; that is, he is reabsorbed by the larger life. His struggle is the fate of humanity, and it brings out, according to O'Neill in his letter to Quinn, a "transfiguring nobility," even "in seemingly the most ignoble, debased lives." It must be admitted, however, that O'Neill never made these ideas very clear.

If this is tragedy, it is clearly a different sort from that of either the Greeks or the Elizabethans; it does not describe the downfall of an illustrious man, or illuminate an ideal perfection of human character, or define the limits of the human condition, or even consist of a beginning, middle, and end. What it does is to convey the sense of a vitally dynamic process in which, through an indefinitely continuing cycle of struggle, defeat, and death, individual lives are expanded into the universal life, so that, as O'Neill somewhat cryptically says, the apparent self-destruction of the hero is really his triumph. Whether we call it tragedy or whether, as may be more advisable, we merely call it serious modern drama, it is capable of impressive dramatic effects, as O'Neill proved in *Desire under the Elms* and a number of his other plays.

II

Drama, however, is not made of logic or metaphysics alone. The playwright as thinker must give way to the playwright as artist, operating on the experience of the playwright as a man, in order to do the work. In some sense, every play is a translation, into a form and into language that the public can understand and appreciate, of the author's inner life, its quality, its meaning, and its value. In O'Neill's work there is much of himself and of his personal feeling—so much, in fact, that a rather crucial test of his artistry is the degree to which he succeeds in distilling from himself the kind of work that can be said to have a general or public aesthetic value.

Some of his late plays are openly autobiographical; and one of these in particular, *Long Day's Journey into Night*, may help us to see what *Desire under the Elms* means, in terms of the personal qualities of life that went into it. The Tyrone family in *Long Day's Journey into Night* corresponds very closely to the O'Neill family as it was in 1912, just before Eugene went to a sanatorium for tuberculosis and became a playwright. James Tyrone matches James O'Neill; Jamie Tyrone matches Eugene's older brother, also called Jamie; Mary Cavan Tyrone matches his mother, Ella Quinlan O'Neill; and Edmund Tyrone matches Eugene himself, the first name being that of another older brother who died as a baby and whose counterpart in the play is named Eugene. It is said that Eugene in real life was conceived in order to replace this dead brother; and it is also said that Mrs. O'Neill's drug addiction, painfully dramatized in the play, resulted from her use of pain-relieving medication after Eugene's birth. Edmund, in the play, feels that he is being condemned to death by his father's miserly decision to send him to a state sanatorium instead of a privately run hospital. It is as though the author were saying he is not sure who he is, himself or his dead brother; if he is himself (though he bears his dead brother's name) he is responsible for the destruction of his mother. He suspects that his parents never wanted him for his own sake; and now, whoever he is, he has a fatal disease, and his father wants him to die. All this is in spite of his being twenty-four years old at the time, and, we might fairly point out, in spite of O'Neill's being fifty-three when he finished the play.

Philip Weissman, a psychoanalytical critic, has suggested that the conscious autobiography of *Long Day's Journey into Night* is paralleled by unconscious autobiography in *Desire under the Elms*. A typical pattern in the plays and in the life of O'Neill, Weissman observes, is compounded of resentment toward the father, dependence on the mother, ambivalence toward any woman who might be suitable as wife or lover, and rejection of children. The biographical facts are that O'Neill was married three times, had children by his first two wives, and deserted these two families in a most irresponsible fashion. His emotional immaturity is further emphasized by the fact that, especially as a young man, he was excruciatingly shy in company, preferring to be with outcasts, alcoholics, and criminals rather than more normal people, and the fact that he rather insisted on being an outcast himself and was, at least periodically, a compulsive heavy drinker.

The autobiographical element in *Desire under the Elms* may or may not be entirely unconscious, but the parallels to O'Neill's own life are certainly there. Eben, the young protagonist, is unreasonably antagonistic to his father, unduly dependent on his mother, and shockingly ambivalent toward Abbie and her son. Although he is twenty-five, he behaves like a boy, with a boy's lack of moral sophistication, a boy's innocence or ignorance of healthy, adult, responsible sexual feeling and behavior. His inability to accept responsibility for his own feelings and actions as rapidly as he should is what causes most of the trouble in the play and the catastrophe at the end. The focus is on the problem of individual growth. The situation demands that Eben develop a mature attitude in the several dimensions indicated by his relations to his father, his half-brothers, his dead mother, his new stepmother, and the farm, which seems to represent nature, the natural world, or the universe.

To some extent, though awkwardly and at best equivocally, he succeeds. He gets his half-brothers out of the way by exploiting their greed for gold. He takes his father's and his half-brothers' place with the prostitute Min. He gains the love of his stepmother, Abbie, and brings her over to his side in his struggle to gain control of the farm. He becomes a father. But he fails to move, or to grow, fast enough to keep up with changes in the situation; specifically, he fails to achieve a true appreciation of Abbie's love for him, or a true understanding of the crime she commits to prove it, in time to save her. The measure of his failure is taken by old Ephraim when he learns that the baby is dead and that Eben has gone for the Sheriff, and says to Abbie, "Ye'd ought t' loved me. I'm a man. If ye'd loved me, I'd never

told no Sheriff on ye no matter what ye did, if they was t' brile me alive!"
But the measure of failure becomes the measure of a kind of desperate success when, in the midst of the catastrophe his shortcomings have brought
about, Eben realizes his mistakes and accepts his share of the responsibility
by confessing his complicity in the death of the child. Even Ephraim, who
in some respects plays Ahab to Eben's Ishmael, is somewhat impressed.
"Purty good," he says, "—fur yew!"

In real life, the failure of a young man to grow up fast enough to handle
his responsibilities is likely to be not only pathetic but ridiculous. O'Neill's
own experience, as reported in recent biographical studies, was on occasion both. But, by the alchemy of art, the ugliest horrors of life often become the best materials with which to dramatize the highest values. *Desire
under the Elms*, however directly based on O'Neill's experience, has a universal theme. We all live in a changing world; we all develop somehow; and
we all sometimes feel we are not moving fast enough. Events press hard
and outrun us, we fall behind; sometimes castastrophes destroy us; always, sooner or later, death catches up. When this truth of universal experience comes home to us in dramatic fiction as if we were ourselves the suffering hero, it is not ridiculous but extremely serious and meaningful. We
realize that life is valuable to the degree that we are aware of death, and
growth is valued to the degree that it meets resistance and failure. These
values are most real to us when we see them put to an ultimate test, when
we see the destruction of a potentially good man by forces or inertias too
great for him to overcome, in somewhat the same way materials are tested
in a laboratory by being loaded beyond their breaking point. Eben has a
potential for growth, for responsible moral action, for the kind of manhood
that Ephraim impressively though imperfectly illustrates. This potential
reaches its highest point at precisely the moment of greatest opposition,
misfortune, and failure. Some ultimate test, issuing in some kind of affirmation, has always been characteristic of tragedy. It is no less characteristic of,
and necessary to, the serious modern drama we are dealing with, whether
or not we call it tragedy.

Many intelligent critics feel that O'Neill has not succeeded in making
the impression he must have intended. For example, Bonamy Dobrée,
writing in 1937, maintained that "All the people in *Desire under the Elms*
are half-witted; the drama deals entirely with the play of brute instinct, as
though this, without its interplay with something implying different values,
were of any interest whatever." Such criticism—and there has been a good
deal of it—badly misses the point O'Neill meant to make. He meant to
show brute lust becoming human love, and love itself transformed, in the
end, into something higher. Doubtless he would concede that Eben's intelligence is weak in the beginning, but he could still maintain that it is developed and spiritualized through the kind of suffering that begets under-

standing until—albeit too late for practical happiness—it becomes almost purely ideal in at least the intention of the final self-sacrifice. The development, though it is fatally too slow, is logically, morally, and aesthetically sound.

III

One reason for O'Neill's frequent failure in getting his point across is undoubtedly a weakness in his style as a writer, about which Dobrée and many other critics have complained. His language is generally awkward and often more obscure than it needs to be. When he tries especially hard to be "poetic," as in *Lazarus Laughed*, *The Fountain*, and several other plays, the result is sometimes so bad that it is practically impossible to stage. He seems unable, in either these or his more "realistic" plays, such as *Desire under the Elms*, to combine apparent simplicity with real depth and subtlety, as Mark Twain does in *Huckleberry Finn*, or as Hemingway does in most of his fiction. The subtlety, the symbolism, the poetry—the reaching by some means beyond the ordinary bounds of human speech—is very much needed in O'Neill's plays because their conception is so essentially poetic. As Joseph Wood Krutch remarks, "We do not wish that *Ghosts* or *Major Barbara* were in verse, but we do wish that the author of *Desire under the Elms* or *Mourning Becomes Electra* could find the words which would not be out of place and, for which, indeed, we find ourselves longing almost with exasperation." But instead of good poetry (which of course need not be written in verse) we too often get the kind of speech Eben makes about Min, the prostitute: "She's like t'night, she's soft 'n' wa'm, her eyes kin wink like a star, her mouth's wa'm, her arms're wa'm, she smells like a wa'm plowed field, she's purty. . . ." The poetic intention is only too obvious, and so is the poetic technique; so, unfortunately, is the failure of the language. It is full of feeling and energy, but its rhythms lack the grace and cogency needed to convey the inner sense of the speaker's personality.

In spite of these and other defects, *Desire under the Elms* is an impressively successful play; and it is more successful, as it should be, on the stage than in the study. One of the more obvious of O'Neill's virtues and one of the most important, which this play exemplifies, is his talent for the purely dramatic effect. His plays are "good theater," even sometimes when they have little else to recommend them. There are in *Desire under the Elms*, for example, some excellent visual effects, to which O'Neill gives careful attention. The elms bending over the roof of the house, the stone wall in front, and the rooms into which the audience is allowed to see, through walls that become transparent to reveal the action inside, all contribute to the total impression the author wants to make. These devices are not intended primarily to generate an illusion of objective reality, but rather to provide an appropriate emotional atmosphere or setting for the action.

The text itself is equally "good theater" in the competence and economy of its exposition, the balance of scene against scene, the working-up of the climax, and the dramatic relations among the characters. The beginning and ending of each scene are cogently calculated, and the curtain lines, though sometimes melodramatic, are always strong. Accompanying sound effects are managed with similar care, from the clanging of Eben's bell at the opening, through the brothers' singing and shouting at old Ephraim, to the noisy party with which Ephraim celebrates the birth of the baby. O'Neill, the son of a highly competent actor, the intimate associate of the expert directors and stage designers in the Provincetown group, grew up and lived in the theater, and he probably mastered its techniques more fully than any other American playwright.

The speeches and the acting directions, as well as the setting, are liberally larded with symbolism, which may seem heavy-handed in a close reading but which is not so obtrusive on the stage. The "desire" of the title is developed in many contexts, and in considerable depth. Eben's desire to control and own the farm, the brothers' desire for gold, Abbie's desire for a home, Ephraim's desire for a son, and Eben's confused desire for maternal and sexual love combine to complicate the central desire for Eben's manhood and to embody in all the characters and their mutual relations an overwhelming desire for life itself, with all its confusions, pains, and agonies, and all its exaltations. Ephraim especially, with his affinity for the cows, his passion for the land, and his ability to "make corn sprout out o' stones," exemplifies the power of life, inhibited though it is in him by religious fanaticism and restrictive pride of ownership.

In spite of sordid conditions, in spite of animal associations, in spite of earthy obstructions, in spite of human error, weakness, and evil, the power of life goes moiling and surging through the play, destroying and creating, suffering and triumphing. The pain and the wonder of it fascinate O'Neill, and he puts the pain, the wonder, and the fascination into the play as few other playwrights do. *Desire under the Elms* may be in some sense a failure, as O'Neill himself might be the first to say; it may not be a tragedy; it may not be sufficiently poetic; it certainly deals with some ugly people, who do some shocking things. Nevertheless it succeeds in doing what few plays ever do or ever have done. It embodies life.

R. P. ADAMS

A Note on the Text. The text of *Desire under the Elms* is that of *The Complete Works of Eugene O'Neill* (New York: Boni & Liveright, 1924), with the exception that the capitalization and punctuation of the stage directions have been modernized slightly.

DESIRE
UNDER
THE ELMS

Dealing with the culture crisis of the time.

Naturalism found here,

CHARACTERS

EPHRAIM CABOT

SIMEON
PETER } His sons
EBEN

Theme: Greed —
Lust — hate — love

ABBIE PUTNAM

Young Girl, Two Farmers, The Fiddler, A Sheriff, and other folk from the neighboring farms

The action of the entire play takes place in, and immediately outside of, the Cabot farmhouse in New England, in the year 1850. The south end of the house faces front to a stone wall with a wooden gate at center opening on a country road. The house is in good condition but in need of paint. Its walls are a sickly grayish, the green of the shutters faded. Two enormous elms are on each side of the house. They bend their trailing branches down over the roof. They appear to protect and at the same time subdue. There is a sinister maternity in their aspect, a crushing, jealous absorption. They have developed from their intimate contact with the life of man in the house an appalling humaneness. They brood oppressively over the house. They are like exhausted women resting their sagging breasts and hands and hair on its roof, and when it rains their tears trickle down monotonously and rot on the shingles.

There is a path running from the gate around the right corner of the house to the front door. A narrow porch is on this side. The end wall facing us has two windows in its upper story, two larger ones on the floor below. The two upper are those of the father's bedroom and that of the brothers. On the left, ground floor, is the kitchen—on the right, the parlor, the shades of which are always drawn down.

PART I

SCENE ONE

(Exterior of the Farmhouse. It is sunset of a day at the beginning of summer in the year 1850. There is no wind and everything is still. The sky above *the roof is suffused with deep colors, the green of the elms glows, but the house is in shadow, seeming pale and washed out by contrast.*

A door opens and EBEN CABOT *comes to the end of the porch and stands looking down the road to the right. He has a large bell in his hand and this he swings mechanically, awakening a deafening clangor. Then he puts his hands on his hips and stares up at the sky. He sighs with a puzzled awe and blurts out with halting appreciation.*)

EBEN   God! Purty! (*His eyes fall and he stares about him frowningly. He is twenty-five, tall and sinewy. His face is well-formed, good-looking, but its expression is resentful and defensive. His defiant, dark eyes remind one of a wild animal's in captivity. Each day is a cage in which he finds himself trapped but inwardly unsubdued. There is a fierce repressed vitality about him. He has black hair, mustache, a thin curly trace of beard. He is dressed in rough farm clothes.*

He spits on the ground with intense disgust, turns and goes back into the house.

SIMEON *and* PETER *come in from their work in the fields. They are tall men, much older than their half-brother,* [SIMEON *is thirty-nine and* PETER *thirty-seven*], *built on a squarer, simpler model, fleshier in body, more bovine and homelier in face, shrewder and more practical. Their shoulders stoop a bit from years of farm work. They clump heavily along in their clumsy thick-soled boots caked with earth. Their clothes, their faces, hands, bare arms and throats are earth-stained. They smell of earth. They stand together for a moment in front of the house and, as if with the one impulse, stare dumbly up at the sky, leaning on their hoes. Their faces have a compressed, unresigned expression. As they look upward, this softens.*)

SIMEON   (*grudgingly*)   Purty.

PETER   Ay-eh.

SIMEON   (*suddenly*)   Eighteen year ago.

PETER   What?

SIMEON   Jenn. My woman. She died.

PETER   I'd fergot.

SIMEON   I rec'lect—now an' agin. Makes it lonesome. She'd hair long's a hoss's tail—an' yaller like gold!

PETER   Waal—she's gone. (*this with indifferent finality—then after a pause*) They's gold in the West, Sim.

SIMEON   (*still under the influence of sunset—vaguely*)   In the sky?

PETER   Waal—in a manner o' speakin'—thar's the promise. (*growing excited*) Gold in the sky—in the west—Golden Gate—Californi-a!—Goldest West!—fields o' gold! [1]

SIMEON   (*excited in his turn*)   Fortunes layin' just atop o' the ground waitin' t' be picked! Solomon's mines, they says! (*For a moment they continue looking up at the sky—then their eyes drop.*)

---

[1] Gold was discovered in California, on land belonging to John A. Sutter, on the Sacramento River, in 1848.

PETER (*with sardonic bitterness*) Here—it's stones atop o' the ground—stones atop o' stones—makin' stone walls—year atop o' year—him 'n' yew 'n' me 'n' then Eben—makin' stone walls fur him to fence us in!

SIMEON We've wuked. Give our strength. Give our years. Plowed 'em under in the ground,—(*he stamps rebelliously*)—rottin'—makin' soil for his crops! (*a pause*) Waal—the farm pays good for hereabouts.

PETER If we plowed in Californi-a, they'd be lumps o' gold in the furrow—!

SIMEON Californi-a's t'other side o' earth, a'most. We got t' calc'late—

PETER (*after a pause*) 'Twould be hard fur me, too, to give up what we've 'arned here by our sweat—(*a pause.* EBEN *sticks his head out of the dining room window, listening.*)

SIMEON Ay-eh. (*a pause*) Mebbe—he'll die soon.

PETER (*doubtfully*) Mebbe.

SIMEON Mebbe—fur all we knows—he's dead now.

PETER Ye'd need proof—

SIMEON He's been gone two months—with no word.

PETER Left us in the fields an evenin' like this. Hitched up an' druv off into the West. That's plum onnateral. He hain't never been off this farm 'ceptin' t' the village in thirty year or more, not since he married Eben's maw. (*a pause—shrewdly*) I calc'late we might git him declared crazy by the court.

SIMEON He skinned 'em too slick. He got the best o' all on 'em. They'd never b'lieve him crazy. (*a pause*) We got t' wait—till he's under ground.

EBEN (*with a sardonic chuckle*) Honor thy father! (*They turn, startled, and stare at him. He grins, then scowls.*) I pray he's died. (*They stare at him. He continues matter of factly*) Supper's ready.

SIMEON *and* PETER (*together*) Ay-eh.

EBEN (*gazing up at the sky*) Sun's downin' purty.

SIMEON *and* PETER (*together*) Ay-eh. They's gold in the West.

EBEN Ay-eh. (*pointing*) Yonder atop o' the hill pasture, ye mean?

SIMEON *and* PETER (*together*) In Californi-a!

EBEN Hunh? (*Stares at them indifferently for a second, then drawls*) Waal —supper's gittin' cold. (*He turns back into kitchen.*)

SIMEON (*startled—smacks his lips*) I air hungry!

PETER (*sniffing*) I smells bacon!

SIMEON (*with hungry appreciation*) Bacon's good!

PETER (*in same tone*) Bacon's bacon! (*They turn, shouldering each other, their bodies bumping and rubbing together as they hurry clumsily to their food, like two friendly oxen toward their evening meal. They disappear around the right corner of house and can be heard entering the door.*)

(*Curtain*)

(The color fades from the sky. Twilight begins. The interior of the kitchen is now visible. A pine table is at center, a cook-stove in the right rear corner, four rough wooden chairs, a tallow candle on the table. In the middle of the rear wall is fastened a big advertising poster with a ship in full sail and the word "California" in big letters. Kitchen utensils hang from nails. Everything is neat and in order but the atmosphere is of a men's camp kitchen rather than that of a home.

Places for three are laid. EBEN *takes boiled potatoes and bacon from the stove and puts them on the table, also a loaf of bread and a crock of water.* SIMEON *and* PETER *shoulder in, slump down in their chairs without a word.* EBEN *joins them. The three eat in silence for a moment, the two elder as naturally unrestrained as beasts of the field,* EBEN *picking at his food without appetite, glancing at them with a tolerant dislike.)*

SIMEON   *(suddenly turns to* EBEN*)*   Looky here! Ye'd oughtn't t' said that, Eben.

PETER   'Twa'n't righteous.

EBEN   What?

SIMEON   Ye prayed he'd died.

EBEN   Waal—don't yew pray it? *(a pause)*

PETER   He's our Paw.

EBEN   *(violently)*   Not mine!

SIMEON   *(dryly)*   Ye'd not let no one else say that about yer Maw! Ha! *(He gives one abrupt sardonic guffaw.* PETER *grins.)*

EBEN   *(very pale)*   I meant—I hain't his'n—I hain't like him—he hain't me—

PETER   He's our Paw.

EBEN   *(intensely)*   I'm Maw—every drop o' blood! *(A pause. They stare at him with indifferent curiosity.)*

PETER   *(reminiscently)*   She was good t' Sim 'n' me. A good stepmaw's scurse.

SIMEON   She was good t' everyone.

EBEN   *(greatly moved, gets to his feet and makes an awkward bow to each of them—stammering)*   I be thankful t'ye. I'm her—her heir. *(He sits down in confusion.)*

PETER   *(after a pause—judicially)*   She was good even t' him.

EBEN   *(fiercely)*   An' fur thanks he killed her!

SIMEON   *(after a pause)*   Noone never kills nobody. It's allus somethin'. That's the murderer.

EBEN   Didn't he slave Maw t' death?

PETER   He's slaved himself t' death. He's slaved Sim 'n' me 'n' yew t' death —on'y none o' us hain't died—yit.

SIMEON   It's somethin'—drivin' him—t' drive us!

EBEN (*vengefully*) Waal—I hold him t' jedgment! (*then scornfully*) Some-thin'! What's somethin'?

SIMEON Dunno.

EBEN (*sardonically*) What's drivin' yew to Californi-a, mebbe? (*They look at him in surprise.*) Oh, I've heerd ye! (*then, after a pause*) But ye'll never go t' the gold fields!

PETER (*assertively*) Mebbe!

EBEN Whar'll ye git the money?

PETER We kin walk. It's an a'mighty ways—Californi-a—but if yew was t' put all the steps we've walked on this farm end t' end we'd be in the moon!

EBEN The Injuns'll skulp ye on the plains.

SIMEON (*with grim humor*) We'll mebbe make 'em pay a hair fur a hair!

EBEN (*decisively*) But t'ain't that. Ye won't never go because ye'll wait here fur yer share o' the farm, thinkin' allus he'll die soon.

SIMEON (*after a pause*) We've a right.

PETER Two-thirds belongs t' us.

EBEN (*jumping to his feet*) Ye've no right! She wa'n't yewr Maw! It was her farm! Didn't he steal it from her? She's dead. It's my farm.

SIMEON (*sardonically*) Tell that t' Paw—when he comes! I'll bet ye a dol-lar he'll laugh—fur once in his life. Ha! (*He laughs himself in one single mirthless bark.*)

PETER (*amused in turn, echoes his brother*) Ha!

SIMEON (*after a pause*) What've ye got held agin us, Eben? Year arter year it's skulked in yer eye—somethin'.

PETER Ay-eh.

EBEN Ay-eh. They's somethin'. (*sudden exploding*) Why didn't ye never stand between him 'n' my maw when he was slavin' her to her grave—t' pay her back fur the kindness she done t' yew? (*There is a long pause. They stare at him in surprise.*)

SIMEON Waal—the stock'd got t' be watered.

PETER 'R they was woodin' t' do.

SIMEON 'R plowin'.

PETER 'R hayin'.

SIMEON 'R spreadin' manure.

PETER 'R weedin'.

SIMEON 'R prunin'.

PETER 'R milkin'.

EBEN (*breaking in harshly*) An' makin' walls—stone atop o' stone—makin' walls till yer heart's a stone ye heft up out o' the way o' growth onto a stone wall t' wall in yer heart!

SIMEON (*matter-of-factly*) We never had no time t' meddle.

PETER (*to* EBEN) Yew was fifteen afore yer Maw died—an' big fur yer age. Why didn't ye never do nothin'?

EBEN (*harshly*) They was chores t' do, wa'n't they? (*a pause—then slowly*) It was on'y arter she died I come to think o' it. Me cookin'—doin' her work —that made me know her, suffer her sufferin'—she'd come back t' help— come back t' bile potatoes—come back t' fry bacon—come back t' bake biscuits—come back all cramped up t' shake the fire, an' carry ashes, her eyes weepin' an' bloody with smoke an' cinders same's they used t' be. She still comes back—stands by the stove thar in the evenin'—she can't find it nateral sleepin' an' restin' in peace. She can't git used t' bein' free—even in her grave.

SIMEON She never complained none.

EBEN She'd got too tired. She'd got too used t' bein' too tired. That was what he done. (*with vengeful passion*) An' soon'r later, I'll meddle. I'll say the thin's I didn't say then t' him! I'll yell 'em at the top o' my lungs. I'll see t' it my Maw gits some rest an' sleep in her grave! (*He sits down again, relapsing into a brooding silence. They look at him with a queer indifferent curiosity.*)

PETER (*after a pause*) Whar in tarnation d'ye s'pose he went, Sim?

SIMEON Dunno. He druv off in the buggy, all spick an' span, with the mare all breshed an' shiny, druv off clackin' his tongue an' wavin' his whip. I remember it right well. I was finishin' plowin', it was spring an' May an' sunset, an' gold in the West, an' he druv off into it. I yells "Whar ye goin', Paw?" an' he hauls up by the stone wall a jiffy. His old snake's eyes was glitterin' in the sun like he'd been drinkin' a jugful an' he says with a mule's grin: "Don't ye run away till I come back!"

PETER Wonder if he knowed we was wantin' fur Californi-a?

SIMEON Mebbe. I didn't say nothin' and he says, lookin' kinder queer an' sick: "I been hearin' the hens cluckin' an' the roosters crowin' all the durn day. I been listenin' t' the cows lowin' an' everythin' else kickin' up till I can't stand it no more. It's spring an' I'm feelin' damned," he says. "Damned like an old bare hickory tree fit on'y fur burnin'," he says. An' then I calc'late I must've looked a mite hopeful, fur he adds real spry and vicious: "But don't git no fool idee I'm dead. I've sworn t' live a hundred an' I'll do it, if on'y t' spite yer sinful greed! An' now I'm ridin' out t' learn God's message t' me in the spring, like the prophets done. An' yew git back t' yer plowin'," he says. An' he druv off singin' a hymn. I thought he was drunk—'r I'd stopped him goin'.

EBEN (*scornfully*) No, ye wouldn't! Ye're scared o' him. He's stronger— inside—than both o' ye put together!

PETER (*sardonically*) An' yew—be yew Samson?

EBEN I'm gittin' stronger. I kin feel it growin' in me—growin' an' growin' —till it'll bust out—! (*He gets up and puts on his coat and a hat. They watch him, gradually breaking into grins. EBEN avoids their eyes sheepishly.*) I'm goin' out fur a spell—up the road.

PETER T' the village?

SIMEON T' see Minnie?

EBEN (*defiantly*) Ay-eh!

PETER *(jeeringly)* The Scarlet Woman!

SIMEON Lust—that's what's growin' in ye!

EBEN Waal—she's purty!

PETER She's been purty fur twenty year!

SIMEON A new coat o' paint'll make a heifer out of forty.

EBEN She hain't forty!

PETER If she hain't, she's teeterin' on the edge.

EBEN *(desperately)* What d'yew know—

PETER All they is . . . Sim knew her—an' then me arter—

SIMEON An' Paw kin tell yew somethin' too! He was fust!

EBEN D'ye mean t' say he . . . ?

SIMEON *(with a grin)* Ay-eh! We air his heirs in everythin'!

EBEN *(intensely)* That's more to it! That grows on it! It'll bust soon! *(then violently)* I'll go smash my fist in her face! *(He pulls open the door in rear violently.)*

SIMEON *(with a wink at* PETER—*drawlingly)* Mebbe—but the night's wa'm—purty—by the time ye git thar mebbe ye'll kiss her instead!

PETER Sart'n he will! *(They both roar with coarse laughter.* EBEN *rushes out and slams the door—then the outside front door—comes around the corner of the house and stands still by the gate, staring up at the sky.)*

SIMEON *(looking after him)* Like his Paw.

PETER Dead spit an' image!

SIMEON Dog'll eat dog!

PETER Ay-eh. *(pause—with yearning)* Mebbe a year from now we'll be in Californi-a.

SIMEON Ay-eh *(a pause. Both yawn.)* Let's git t'bed. *(He blows out the candle. They go out door in rear.* EBEN *stretches his arms up to the sky—rebelliously.)*

EBEN Waal—thar's a star, an' somewhar's they's him, an' here's me, an' thar's Min up the road—in the same night. What if I does kiss her? She's like t'night, she's soft 'n' wa'm, her eyes kin wink like a star, her mouth's wa'm, her arms're wa'm, she smells like a wa'm plowed field, she's purty . . . Ay-eh! By God A'mighty she's purty, an' I don't give a damn how many sins she's sinned afore mine or who she's sinned 'em with, my sin's as purty as any one on 'em! *(He strides off down the road to the left.)*

SCENE THREE

(It is the pitch darkness just before dawn, EBEN *comes in from the left and goes around to the porch, feeling his way, chuckling bitterly and cursing half-aloud to himself.)*

EBEN The cussed old miser! *(He can be heard going in the front door.*

There is a pause as he goes upstairs, then a loud knock on the bedroom door of the brothers.) Wake up!

SIMEON   (*startedly*)   Who's thar?

EBEN   (*pushing open the door and coming in, a lighted candle in his hand. The bedroom of the brothers is revealed. Its ceiling is the sloping roof. They can stand upright only close to the center dividing wall of the upstairs.* SIMEON *and* PETER *are in a double bed, front.* EBEN'S *cot is to the rear.* EBEN *has a mixture of silly grin and vicious scowl on his face.*)   I be!

PETER   (*angrily*)   What in hell'sfire . . . ?

EBEN   I got news fur ye! Ha! (*He gives one abrupt sardonic guffaw.*)

SIMEON   (*angrily*)   Couldn't ye hold it 'til we'd got our sleep?

EBEN   It's nigh sunup. (*then explosively*)   He's gone an' married agen!

SIMEON *and* PETER   (*explosively*)   Paw?

EBEN   Got himself hitched to a female 'bout thirty-five—an' purty, they says . . .

SIMEON   (*aghast*)   It's a durn lie!

PETER   Who says?

SIMEON   They been stringin' ye!

EBEN   Think I'm a dunce, do ye? The hull village says. The preacher from New Dover, he brung the news—told it t'our preacher—New Dover, that's whar the old loon got himself hitched—that's whar the woman lived—

PETER   (*no longer doubting—stunned*)   Waal . . . !

SIMEON   (*the same*)   Waal . . . !

EBEN   (*sitting down on a bed—with vicious hatred*)   Ain't he a devil out o' hell? It's jest t' spite us—the damned old mule!

PETER   (*after a pause*)   Everythin'll go t' her now.

SIMEON   Ay-eh. (*a pause—dully*)   Waal—if it's done—

PETER   It's done us. (*pause—then persuasively*)   They's gold in the fields o' Californi-a, Sim. No good a-stayin' here now.

SIMEON   Jest what I was a-thinkin'. (*then with decision*)   S'well fust's last! Let's light out and git this mornin'.

PETER   Suits me.

EBEN   Ye must like walkin'.

SIMEON   (*sardonically*)   If ye'd grow wings on us we'd fly thar!

EBEN   Ye'd like ridin' better—on a boat, wouldn't ye? (*fumbles in his pocket and takes out a crumpled sheet of foolscap*)   Waal, if ye sign this ye kin ride on a boat. I've had it writ out an' ready in case ye'd ever go. It says fur three hundred dollars t' each ye agree yewr shares o' the farm is sold t' me. (*They look suspiciously at the paper. A pause.*)

SIMEON   (*wonderingly*)   But if he's hitched agen—

PETER   An' whar'd yew git that sum o' money, anyways?

EBEN   (*cunningly*)   I know whar it's hid. I been waitin'—Maw told me.

She knew whar it lay fur years, but she was waitin' . . . It's her'n—the money he hoarded from her farm an' hid from Maw. It's my money by rights now.

PETER Whar's it hid?

EBEN (*cunningly*) Whar yew won't never find it without me. Maw spied on him—'r she'd never knowed. (*A pause. They look at him suspiciously, and he at them.*) Waal, is it fa'r trade?

SIMEON Dunno.

PETER Dunno.

SIMEON (*looking at window*) Sky's grayin'.

PETER Ye better start the fire, Eben.

SIMEON An' fix some vittles.

EBEN Ay-eh. (*then with a forced jocular heartiness*) I'll git ye a good one. If ye're startin' t' hoof it t' Californi-a ye'll need somethin' that'll stick t' yer ribs. (*He turns to the door, adding meaningly*) But ye kin ride on a boat if ye'll swap. (*He stops at the door and pauses. They stare at him.*)

SIMEON (*suspiciously*) Whar was ye all night?

EBEN (*defiantly*) Up t' Min's. (*then slowly*) Walkin' thar, fust I felt 's if I'd kiss her; then I got a-thinkin' o' what ye'd said o' him an' her an' I says, I'll bust her nose fur that! Then I got t' the village an' heerd the news an' I got madder'n hell an' run all the way t' Min's not knowin' what I'd do— (*He pauses—then sheepishly but more defiantly*) Waal—when I seen her, I didn't hit her—nor I didn't kiss her nuther—I begun t' beller like a calf an' cuss at the same time, I was so durn mad—an' she got scared—an' I jest grabbed holt an' tuk her! (*proudly*) Yes, sirree! I tuk her. She may've been his'n—an' your'n, too—but she's mine now!

SIMEON (*dryly*) In love, air yew?

EBEN (*with lofty scorn*) Love! I don't take no stock in sech slop!

PETER (*winking at* SIMEON) Mebbe Eben's aimin' t' marry, too.

SIMEON Min'd make a true faithful he'pmeet! (*They snicker.*)

EBEN What do I care fur her—'ceptin' she's round an' wa'm? The p'int is she was his'n—an' now she belongs t' me! (*He goes to the door—then turns—rebelliously.*) An' Min hain't sech a bad un. They's worse'n Min in the world, I'll bet ye! Wait'll we see this cow the Old Man's hitched t'! She'll beat Min, I got a notion! (*He starts to go out.*)

SIMEON (*suddenly*) Mebbe ye'll try t' make her your'n, too?

PETER Ha! (*He gives a sardonic laugh of relish at this idea.*)

EBEN (*spitting with disgust*) Her—here—sleepin' with him—stealin' my Maw's farm! I'd as soon pet a skunk 'r kiss a snake! (*He goes out. The two stare after him suspiciously. A pause. They listen to his steps receding.*)

PETER He's startin' the fire.

SIMEON I'd like t' ride t' Californi-a—but—

PETER Min might o' put some scheme in his head.

SIMEON Mebbe it's all a lie 'bout Paw marryin'. We'd best wait an' see the bride.

PETER An' don't sign nothin' till we does—

SIMEON Nor till we've tested it's good money! (*then with a grin*) But if Paw's hitched we'd be sellin' Eben somethin' we'd never git nohow!

PETER We'll wait an' see. (*then with sudden vindictive anger*) An' till he comes, let's yew 'n' me not wuk a lick, let Eben tend to thin's if he's a mind t', let's us jest sleep an' eat an' drink likker, an' let the hull damned farm go t' blazes!

SIMEON (*excitedly*) By God, we've 'arned a rest! We'll play rich fur a change. I hain't a-going to stir outa bed till breakfast's ready.

PETER An' on the table!

SIMEON (*after a pause—thoughtfully*) What d' ye calc'late she'll be like —our new Maw? Like Eben thinks?

PETER More'n likely.

SIMEON (*vindictively*) Waal—I hope she's a she-devil that'll make him wish he was dead an' livin' in the pit o' hell fur comfort!

PETER (*fervently*) Amen!

SIMEON (*imitating his father's voice*) "I'm ridin out t' learn God's message t' me in the spring like the prophets done," he says. I'll bet right then an' thar he knew plumb well he was goin' whorin', the stinkin' old hypocrite!

SCENE FOUR

(*Same as Scene Two—shows the interior of the kitchen with a lighted candle on table. It is gray dawn outside.* SIMEON *and* PETER *are just finishing their breakfast.* EBEN *sits before his plate of untouched food, brooding frowningly.*)

PETER (*glancing at him rather irritably*) Lookin' glum don't help none.

SIMEON (*sarcastically*) Sorrowin' over his lust o' the flesh!

PETER (*with a grin*) Was she yer fust?

EBEN (*angrily*) None o' yer business. (*a pause*) I was thinkin' o' him. I got a notion he's gittin' near—I kin feel him comin' on like yew kin feel malaria chill afore it takes ye.

PETER It's too early yet.

SIMEON Dunno. He'd like t' catch us nappin'—jest t' have somethin' t' hoss us 'round over.

PETER (*mechanically gets to his feet.* SIMEON *does the same.*) Waal— let's git t' wuk. (*They both plod mechanically toward the door before they realize. Then they stop short.*)

SIMEON (*grinning*) Ye're a cussed fool, Pete—and I be wuss! Let him see we hain't wukin'! We don't give a durn!

PETER (*as they go back to the table*) Not a damned durn! It'll serve t' show him we're done with him. (*They sit down again.* EBEN *stares from one to the other with surprise.*)

SIMEON   (*grins at him*)   We're aimin' t' start bein' lilies o' the field.

PETER   Nary a toil 'r spin 'r lick o' wuk do we put in!

SIMEON   Ye're sole owner—till he comes—that's what ye wanted. Waal, ye got t' be sole hand, too.

PETER   The cows air bellerin'. Ye better hustle at the milkin'.

EBEN   (*with excited joy*)   Ye mean ye'll sign the paper?

SIMEON   (*dryly*)   Mebbe.

PETER   Mebbe.

SIMEON   We're considerin'. (*peremptorily*) Ye better git t' wuk.

EBEN   (*with queer excitement*)   It's Maw's farm agen! It's my farm! Them's my cows! I'll milk my durn fingers off fur cows o' mine! (*He goes out door in rear, they stare after him indifferently.*)

SIMEON   Like his Paw.

PETER   Dead spit 'n' image!

SIMEON   Waal—let dog eat dog! (*EBEN comes out of front door and around the corner of the house. The sky is beginning to grow flushed with sunrise. EBEN stops by the gate and stares around him with glowing, possessive eyes. He takes in the whole farm with his embracing glance of desire.*)

EBEN   It's purty! It's damned purty! It's mine! (*He suddenly throws his head back boldly and glares with hard, defiant eyes at the sky.*) Mine, d'ye hear? Mine! (*He turns and walks quickly off left, rear, toward the barn. The two brothers light their pipes.*)

SIMEON   (*putting his muddy boots up on the table, tilting back his chair, and puffing defiantly*) Waal—this air solid comfort—fur once.

PETER   Ay-eh. (*He follows suit. A pause. Unconsciously they both sigh.*)

SIMEON   (*suddenly*)   He never was much o' a hand at milkin', Eben wa'n't.

PETER   (*with a snort*)   His hands air like hoofs! (*a pause*)

SIMEON   Reach down the jug thar! Let's take a swaller. I'm feelin' kind o' low.

PETER   Good idee! (*He does so—gets two glasses—they pour out drinks of whisky.*) Here's t' the gold in Californi-a!

SIMEON   An' luck t' find it! (*They drink—puff resolutely—sigh—take their feet down from the table.*)

PETER   Likker don't pear t' sot right.

SIMEON   We hain't used t' it this early. (*A pause. They become very restless.*)

PETER   Gittin' close in this kitchen.

SIMEON   (*with immense relief*)   Let's git a breath o' air. (*They arise briskly and go out rear—appear around house and stop by the gate. They stare up at the sky with a numbed appreciation.*)

PETER   Purty!

SIMEON   Ay-eh. Gold's t' the East now.

PETER   Sun's startin' with us fur the Golden West.

SIMEON   (*staring around the farm, his compressed face tightened, unable to conceal his emotion*)   Waal—it's our last mornin'—mebbe.

PETER   (*the same*)   Ay-eh.

SIMEON   (*stamps his foot on the earth and addresses it desperately*)   Waal —ye've thirty year o' me buried in ye—spread out over ye—blood an' bone an' sweat—rotted away—fertilizin' ye—richin' yer soul—prime manure, by God, that's what I been t' ye!

PETER   Ay-eh! An' me!

SIMEON   An' yew, Peter. (*He sighs—then spits.*) Waal—no use'n cryin' over spilt milk.

PETER   They's gold in the West—an' freedom, mebbe. We been slaves t' stone walls here.

SIMEON   (*defiantly*)   We hain't nobody's slaves from this out—nor no thin's slaves nuther. (*a pause—restlessly*) Speakin' o' milk, wonder how Eben's managin'?

PETER   I s'pose he's managin'.

SIMEON   Mebbe we'd ought t' help—this once.

PETER   Mebbe. The cows knows us.

SIMEON   An' likes us. They don't know him much.

PETER   An' the hosses, an' pigs, an' chickens. They don't know him much.

SIMEON   They knows us like brothers—an' likes us! (*proudly*) Hain't we raised 'em t' be fust-rate, number one prize stock?

PETER   We hain't—not no more.

SIMEON   (*dully*)   I was fergittin'. (*then resignedly*) Waal, let's go help Eben a spell an' git waked up.

PETER   Suits me. (*They are starting off down left, rear, for the barn when* EBEN *appears from there hurrying toward them, his face excited.*)

EBEN   (*breathlessly*)   Waal—har they be! The old mule an' the bride! I seen 'em from the barn down below at the turnin'.

PETER   How could ye tell that far?

EBEN   Hain't I as far-sight as he's near-sight? Don't I know the mare 'n' buggy, an' two people settin' in it? Who else . . . ? An' I tell ye I kin feel 'em a-comin', too! (*He squirms as if he had the itch.*)

PETER   (*beginning to be angry*)   Waal—let him do his own unhitchin'!

SIMEON   (*angry in his turn*)   Let's hustle in an' git our bundles an' be a-goin' as he's a-comin'. I don't want never t' step inside the door agen arter he's back. (*They both start back around the corner of the house.* EBEN *follows them.*)

EBEN   (*anxiously*)   Will ye sign it afore ye go?

PETER   Let's see the color o' the old skinflint's money an' we'll sign. (*They disappear left. The two brothers clump upstairs to get their bundles.* EBEN *appears in the kitchen, runs to window, peers out, comes back and pulls up a strip of flooring in under stove, takes out a canvas bag and puts it on table, then sets the floorboard back in place. The two brothers appear a moment after. They carry old carpet bags.*)

EBEN (*puts his hand on bag guardingly*) Have ye signed?

SIMEON (*shows paper in his hand*) Ay-eh. (*greedily*) Be that the money?

EBEN (*opens bag and pours out pile of twenty-dollar gold pieces*) Twenty-dollar pieces—thirty on 'em. Count 'em. (PETER *does so, arranging them in stacks of five, biting one or two to test them.*)

PETER Six hundred. (*He puts them in bag and puts it inside his shirt carefully.*)

SIMEON (*handing paper to* EBEN) Har ye be.

EBEN (*after a glance, folds it carefully and hides it under his shirt—gratefully*) Thank yew.

PETER Thank yew fur the ride.

SIMEON We'll send ye a lump o' gold fur Christmas. (*a pause.* EBEN *stares at them and they at him.*)

PETER (*awkwardly*) Waal—we're a-goin'.

SIMEON Comin' out t' the yard?

EBEN No. I'm waitin' in here a spell. (*another silence. The brothers edge awkwardly to door in rear—then turn and stand.*)

SIMEON Waal—good-by.

PETER Good-by.

EBEN Good-by. (*They go out. He sits down at the table, faces the stove and pulls out the paper. He looks from it to the stove. His face, lighted up by the shaft of sunlight from the window, has an expression of trance. His lips move. The two brothers come out to the gate.*)

PETER (*looking off toward barn*) Thar he be—unhitchin'.

SIMEON (*with a chuckle*) I'll bet ye he's riled!

PETER An' thar she be.

SIMEON Let's wait 'n' see what our new Maw looks like.

PETER (*with a grin*) An' give him our partin' cuss!

SIMEON (*grinning*) I feel like raisin' fun. I feel light in my head an' feet.

PETER Me, too. I feel like laffin' till I'd split up the middle.

SIMEON Reckon it's the likker?

PETER No. My feet feel itchin' t' walk an' walk—an' jump high over thin's —an'. . . .

SIMEON Dance? (*a pause*)

PETER (*puzzled*) It's plumb onnateral.

SIMEON (*a light coming over his face*) I calc'late it's 'cause school's out. It's holiday. Fur once we're free!

PETER (*dazedly*) Free?

SIMEON The halter's broke—the harness is busted—the fence bars is down— the stone walls air crumblin' an' tumblin'! We'll be kickin' up an' tearin' away down the road!

PETER   (*drawing a deep breath—oratorically*)   Anybody that wants this stinkin' old rock-pile of a farm kin hev it. 'Tain't our'n, no sirree!

SIMEON   (*takes the gate off its hinges and puts it under his arm*)   We harby 'bolishes shet gates an' open gates, an' all gates, by thunder!

PETER   We'll take it with us fur luck an' let 'er sail free down some river.

SIMEON   (*as a sound of voices comes from left, rear*)   Har they comes! (*The two brothers congeal into two stiff, grim-visaged statues.* EPHRAIM CABOT *and* ABBIE PUTNAM *come in.* CABOT *is seventy-five, tall and gaunt, with great, wiry, concentrated power, but stoop-shouldered from toil. His face is as hard as if it were hewn out of a boulder, yet there is a weakness in it, a petty pride in its own narrow strength. His eyes are small, close together, and extremely near-sighted, blinking continually in the effort to focus on objects, their stare having a straining, ingrowing quality. He is dressed in his dismal black Sunday suit.* ABBIE *is thirty-five, buxom, full of vitality. Her round face is pretty but marred by its rather gross sensuality. There is strength and obstinacy in her jaw, a hard determination in her eyes, and about her whole personality the same unsettled, untamed, desperate quality which is so apparent in* EBEN.)

CABOT   (*as they enter—a queer strangled emotion in his dry cracking voice*) Har we be t' hum, Abbie.

ABBIE   (*with lust for the word*)   Hum? (*Her eyes gloating on the house without seeming to see the two stiff figures at the gate*) It's purty—purty! I can't b'lieve it's r'ally mine.

CABOT   (*sharply*)   Yewr'n? Mine! (*He stares at her penetratingly. She stares back. He adds relentingly*) Our'n—mebbe! It was lonesome too long. I was growin' old in the Spring. A hum's got t' hev a woman.

ABBIE   (*her voice taking possession*)   A woman's got t' hev a hum!

CABOT   (*nodding uncertainly*)   Ay-eh. (*then irritably*) Whar be they? Ain't thar nobody about—'r wukin'—r' nothin'?

ABBIE   (*sees the brothers. She returns their stare of cold appraising contempt with interest—slowly*)   Thar's two men loafin' at the gate an' starin' at me like a couple o' strayed hogs.

CABOT   (*straining his eyes*)   I kin see 'em—but I can't make out. . . .

SIMEON   It's Simeon.

PETER   It's Peter.

CABOT   (*exploding*)   Why hain't ye wukin'?

SIMEON   (*dryly*)   We're waitin' t' welcome ye hum—yew an' the bride!

CABOT   (*confusedly*)   Huh? Waal—this be yer new Maw, boys. (*She stares at them and they at her.*)

SIMEON   (*turns away and spits contemptuously*)   I see her!

PETER   (*spits also*)   An' I see her!

ABBIE   (*with the conqueror's conscious superiority*)   I'll go in an' look at *my* house. (*She goes slowly around to porch.*)

SIMEON   (*with a snort*)   Her house!

PETER (*calls after her*) Ye'll find Eben inside. Ye better not tell him it's *yewr* house.

ABBIE (*mouthing the name*) Eben. (*then quietly*) I'll tell Eben.

CABOT (*with a contemptuous sneer*) Ye needn't heed Eben. Eben's a dumb fool—like his Maw—soft an' simple!

SIMEON (*with his sardonic burst of laughter*) Ha! Eben's a chip o' yew— spit 'n' image—hard 'n' bitter's a hickory tree! Dog'll eat dog. He'll eat ye yet, old man!

CABOT (*commandingly*) Ye git t' wuk!

SIMEON (*as* ABBIE *disappears in house—winks at* PETER *and says tauntingly*) So that thar's our new Maw, be it? Whar in hell did ye dig her up? (*He and* PETER *laugh.*)

PETER Ha! Ye'd better turn her in the pen with the other sows. (*They laugh uproariously, slapping their thighs.*)

CABOT (*so amazed at their effrontery that he stutters in confusion*) Simeon! Peter! What's come over ye? Air ye drunk?

SIMEON We're free, old man—free o' yew an' the hull damned farm! (*They grow more and more hilarious and excited.*)

PETER An' we're startin' out fur the gold fields o' Californi-a!

SIMEON Ye kin take this place an' burn it!

PETER An' bury it—fur all we cares!

SIMEON We're free, old man! (*He cuts a caper.*)

PETER Free! (*He gives a kick in the air.*)

SIMEON (*in a frenzy*) Whoop!

PETER Whoop! (*They do an absurd Indian war dance about the old man who is petrified between rage and the fear that they are insane.*)

SIMEON We're free as Injuns! Lucky we don't sculp ye!

PETER An' burn yer barn an' kill the stock!

SIMEON An' rape yer new woman! Whoop! (*He and* PETER *stop their dance, holding their sides, rocking with wild laughter.*)

CABOT (*edging away*) Lust fur gold—fur the sinful, easy gold o' Californi-a! It's made ye mad!

SIMEON (*tauntingly*) Wouldn't ye like us to send ye back some sinful gold, ye old sinner?

PETER They's gold besides what's in Californi-a! (*He retreats back beyond the vision of the old man and takes the bag of money and flaunts it in the air above his head, laughing.*)

SIMEON And sinfuller, too!

PETER We'll be voyagin' on the sea! Whoop! (*He leaps up and down.*)

SIMEON Livin' free! Whoop! (*He leaps in turn.*)

CABOT (*suddenly roaring with rage*) My cuss on ye!

SIMEON Take our'n in trade fur it! Whoop!

CABOT   I'll hev ye both chained up in the asylum!

PETER   Ye old skinflint! Good-by!

SIMEON   Ye old blood sucker! Good-by!

CABOT   Go afore I . . . !

PETER   Whoop! (*He picks a stone from the road.* SIMEON *does the same.*)

SIMEON   Maw'll be in the parlor.

PETER   Ay-eh! One! Two!

CABOT   (*frightened*)   What air ye . . . ?

PETER   Three! (*They both throw, the stones hitting the parlow window with a crash of glass, tearing the shade.*)

SIMEON   Whoop!

PETER   Whoop!

CABOT   (*in a fury now, rushing toward them*)   If I kin lay hands on ye—I'll break yer bones fur ye! (*But they beat a capering retreat before him,* SIMEON *with the gate still under his arm.* CABOT *comes back, panting with impotent rage. Their voices as they go off take up the song of the gold-seekers to the old tune of "Oh, Susannah!"*)

> "I jumped aboard the Liza ship,
> And traveled on the sea,
> And every time I thought of home
> I wished it wasn't me!
> Oh! Californi-a,
> That's the land fur me!
> I'm off to Californi-a!
> With my wash bowl on my knee."

(*In the meantime, the window of the upper bedroom on right is raised and* ABBIE *sticks her head out. She looks down at* CABOT—*with a sigh of relief.*)

ABBIE   Waal—that's the last o' them two, hain't it? (*He doesn't answer. Then in possessive tones*) This here's a nice bedroom, Ephraim. It's a r'al nice bed. Is it my room, Ephraim?

CABOT   (*grimly—without looking up*)   Our'n! (*She cannot control a grimace of aversion and pulls back her head slowly and shuts the window. A sudden horrible thought seems to enter* CABOT's *head.*) They been up to somethin'! Mebbe—mebbe they've pizened the stock—'r somethin'! (*He almost runs off down toward the barn. A moment later the kitchen door is slowly pushed open and* ABBIE *enters. For a moment she stands looking at* EBEN. *He does not notice her at first. Her eyes take him in penetratingly with a calculating appraisal of his strength as against hers. But under this her desire is dimly awakened by his youth and good looks. Suddenly he becomes conscious of her presence and looks up. Their eyes meet. He leaps to his feet, glowering at her speechlessly.*)

ABBIE   (*in her most seductive tones which she uses all through this scene*) Be you—Eben? I'm Abbie— (*She laughs.*) I mean, I'm yer new Maw.

EBEN   (*viciously*)   No, damn ye!

ABBIE (*as if she hadn't heard—with a queer smile*) Yer Paw's spoke a lot o' yew. . . .

EBEN Ha!

ABBIE Ye mustn't mind him. He's an old man. (*a long pause. They stare at each other.*) I don't want t' pretend playin' Maw t' ye, Eben. (*admiringly*) Ye're too big an' too strong fur that. I want t' be frens with ye. Mebbe with me fur a fren ye'd find ye'd like livin' here better. I kin make it easy fur ye with him, mebbe. (*with a scornful sense of power*) I calc'late I kin git him t' do most anythin' fur me.

EBEN (*with bitter scorn*) Ha! (*They stare again,* EBEN *obscurely moved, physically attracted to her—in forced stilted tones*) Yew kin go t' the devil!

ABBIE (*calmly*) If cussin' me does ye good, cuss all ye've a mind t'. I'm all prepared t' have ye agin me—at fust. I don't blame ye nuther. I'd feel the same at any stranger comin' t' take my Maw's place. (*He shudders. She is watching him carefully.*) Yew must've cared a lot fur yewr Maw, didn't ye? My Maw died afore I'd growed. I don't remember her none. (*a pause*) But yew won't hate me long, Eben. I'm not the wust in the world—an' yew an' me've got a lot in common. I kin tell that by lookin' at ye. Waal—I've had a hard life, too—oceans o' trouble an' nuthin' but wuk fur reward. I was a orphan early an' had t' wuk fur others in other folks' hums. Then I married an' he turned out a drunken spreer an' so he had to wuk fur others an' me too agen in other folks' hums, an' the baby died, an' my husband got sick an' died too, an' I was glad sayin' now I'm free fur once, on'y I diskivered right away all I was free fur was t' wuk agen in other folks' hums, doin' other folks' wuk till I'd most give up hope o' ever doin' my own wuk in my own hum, an' then your Paw come. . . . (CABOT *appears returning from the barn. He comes to the gate and looks down the road the brothers have gone. A faint strain of their retreating voices is heard: "Oh, Californi-a! That's the place for me." He stands glowering, his fist clenched, his face grim with rage.*)

EBEN (*fighting against his growing attraction and sympathy—harshly*) An' bought yew—like a harlot! (*She is stung and flushes angrily. She has been sincerely moved by the recital of her troubles. He adds furiously*) An' the price he's payin' ye—this farm—was my Maw's, damn ye!—an' mine now!

ABBIE (*with a cool laugh of confidence*) Yewr'n? We'll see 'bout that! (*then strongly*) Waal—what if I did need a hum? What else'd I marry an old man like him fur?

EBEN (*maliciously*) I'll tell him ye said that!

ABBIE (*smiling*) I'll say ye're lyin' a-purpose—an' he'll drive ye off the place!

EBEN Ye devil!

ABBIE (*defying him*) This be my farm—this be my hum—this be my kitchen—!

EBEN (*furiously, as if he were going to attack her*) Shut up, damn ye!

ABBIE (*walks up to him—a queer coarse expression of desire in her face and body—slowly*) An' upstairs—that be my bedroom—an' my bed! (*He stares into her eyes, terribly confused and torn. She adds softly*) I hain't bad nor mean—'ceptin' fur an enemy—but I got t' fight fur what's due me out o' life, if I ever 'spect t' git it. (*then putting her hand on his arm—seductively*) Let's yew 'n' me be frens, Eben.

EBEN (*stupidly—as if hypnotized*) Ay-eh. (*then furiously flinging off her arm*) No, ye durned old witch! I hate ye! (*He rushes out the door.*)

ABBIE (*looks after him smiling satisfiedly—then half to herself, mouthing the word*) Eben's nice. (*She looks at the table, proudly.*) I'll wash up *my* dishes now. (EBEN *appears outside, slamming the door behind him. He comes around corner, stops on seeing his father, and stands staring at him with hate.*)

CABOT (*raising his arms to heaven in the fury he can no longer control*) Lord God o' Hosts, smite the undutiful sons with Thy wust cuss!

EBEN (*breaking in violently*) Yew 'n' yewr God! Allus cussin' folks—allus naggin' 'em!

CABOT (*oblivious to him—summoningly*) God o' the old! God o' the lonesome!

EBEN (*mockingly*) Naggin' His sheep t' sin! T' hell with yewr God! (CABOT *turns. He and* EBEN *glower at each other.*)

CABOT (*harshly*) So it's yew. I might've knowed it. (*shaking his finger threateningly at him*) Blasphemin' fool! (*then quickly*) Why hain't ye t' wuk?

EBEN Why hain't yew? They've went. I can't wuk it all alone.

CABOT (*contemptuously*) Nor noways! I'm wuth ten o' ye yit, old's I be! Ye'll never be more'n half a man! (*then, matter-of-factly*) Waal—let's git t' the barn. (*They go. A last faint note of the "Californi-a" song is heard from the distance.* ABBIE *is washing her dishes.*)

(*The Curtain Falls*)

PART II

SCENE ONE

(*The exterior of the farmhouse, as in Part One—a hot Sunday afternoon two months later.* ABBIE, *dressed in her best, is discovered sitting in a rocker at the end of the porch. She rocks listlessly, enervated by the heat, staring in front of her with bored, half-closed eyes.*

EBEN *sticks his head out of his bedroom window. He looks around furtively and tries to see—or hear—if anyone is on the porch, but although he has been careful to make no noise, Abbie has sensed his movement. She stops rocking, her face grows animated and eager, she waits attentively.* EBEN *seems to feel her presence, he scowls back his thoughts of her and spits with exaggerated disdain—then withdraws back into the room.* ABBIE *waits, holding her breath as she listens with passionate eagerness for every sound within the house.*

EBEN *comes out. Their eyes meet. His falter, he is confused, he turns *away and slams the door resentfully. At this gesture,* ABBIE *laughs tantalizingly, amused but at the same time piqued and irritated. He scowls, strides off the porch to the path and starts to walk past her to the road with a grand swagger of ignoring her existence. He is dressed in his store suit, spruced up, his face shines from soap and water.* ABBIE *leans forward on her chair, her eyes hard and angry now, and, as he passes her, gives a sneering, taunting chuckle.*)

EBEN (*stung—turns on her furiously*) What air yew cacklin' 'bout?

ABBIE (*triumphant*) Yew!

EBEN What about me?

ABBIE Ye look all slicked up like a prize bull.

EBEN (*with a sneer*) Waal—ye hain't so durned purty yerself, be ye? (*They stare into each other's eyes, his held by hers in spite of himself, hers glowingly possessive. Their physical attraction becomes a palpable force quivering in the hot air.*)

ABBIE (*softly*) Ye don't mean that, Eben. Ye may think ye mean it, mebbe, but ye don't. Ye can't. It's agin nature, Eben. Ye been fightin' yer nature ever since the day I come—tryin' t' tell yerself I hain't purty t'ye. (*She laughs a low humid laugh without taking her eyes from his. A pause—her body squirms desirously—she murmurs languorously*) Hain't the sun strong an' hot? Ye kin feel it burnin' into the earth—Nature—makin' thin's grow— bigger 'n' bigger—burnin' inside ye—makin' ye want t' grow—into somethin' else—till ye're jined with it—an' it's your'n—but it owns ye, too—an' makes ye grow bigger—like a tree—like them elums— (*She laughs again softly, holding his eyes. He takes a step toward her, compelled against his will.*) Nature'll beat ye, Eben. Ye might's well own up t' it fust 's last.

EBEN (*trying to break from her spell—confusedly*) If Paw'd hear ye goin' on. . . . (*resentfully*) But ye've made such a damned idjit out o' the old devil. . . . (ABBIE *laughs.*)

ABBIE Waal—hain't it easier fur yew with him changed softer?

EBEN (*defiantly*) No. I'm fightin' him—fightin' yew—fightin' fur Maw's rights t'her hum! (*This breaks her spell for him. He glowers at her.*) An' I'm onto ye. Ye hain't foolin' me a mite. Ye're aimin' t' swaller up everythin' an' make it your'n. Waal, you'll find I'm a heap sight bigger hunk nor yew kin chew! (*He turns from her with a sneer.*)

ABBIE (*trying to regain her ascendancy—seductively*) Eben!

EBEN Leave me be! (*He starts to walk away.*)

ABBIE (*more commandingly*) Eben!

EBEN (*stops—resentfully*) What d'ye want?

ABBIE (*trying to conceal a growing excitement*) Whar air ye goin'?

EBEN (*with malicious nonchalance*) Oh—up the road a spell.

ABBIE T' the village?

EBEN (*airily*) Mebbe.

ABBIE (*excitedly*) T' see that Min, I s'pose?

EBEN   Mebbe.

ABBIE   (*weakly*)   What d'ye want t' waste time on her fur?

EBEN   (*revenging himself now—grinning at her*)   Ye can't beat Nature, didn't ye say? (*He laughs and again starts to walk away.*)

ABBIE   (*bursting out*)   An ugly old hake!

EBEN   (*with a tantalizing sneer*)   She's purtier'n yew be!

ABBIE   That every wuthless drunk in the country has. . . .

EBEN   (*tauntingly*)   Mebbe—but she's better'n yew. She owns up fa'r 'n' squar' t' her doin's.

ABBIE   (*furiously*)   Don't ye dare compare. . . .

EBEN   She don't go sneakin' an' stealin'—what's mine.

ABBIE   (*savagely seizing on his weak point*)   Your'n? Yew mean—my farm?

EBEN   I mean the farm yew sold yerself fur like any other old whore—my farm!

ABBIE   (*stung—fiercely*)   Ye'll never live t' see the day when even a stinkin' weed on it'll belong t' ye! (*then in a scream*) Git out o' my sight! Go on t' yer slut—disgracin' yer Paw 'n' me! I'll git yer Paw t' horsewhip ye off the place if I want t'! Ye're only livin' here 'cause I tolerate ye! Git along! I hate the sight o' ye! (*She stops, panting and glaring at him.*)

EBEN   (*returning her glance in kind*)   An' I hate the sight o' yew! (*He turns and strides off up the road. She follows his retreating figure with concentrated hate. Old* CABOT *appears coming up from the barn. The hard, grim expression of his face has changed. He seems in some queer way softened, mellowed. His eyes have taken on a strange, incongruous dreamy quality. Yet there is no hint of physical weakness about him—rather he looks more robust and younger.* ABBIE *sees him and turns away quickly with unconcealed aversion. He comes slowly up to her.*)

CABOT   (*mildly*)   War yew an' Eben quarrelin' agin?

ABBIE   (*shortly*)   No.

CABOT   Ye was talkin' a'mighty loud. . . . (*He sits down on the edge of porch.*)

ABBIE   (*snappishly*)   If ye heered us they hain't no need askin' questions.

CABOT   I didn't hear what ye said.

ABBIE   (*relieved*)   Waal—it wa'n't nothin' t' speak on.

CABOT   (*after a pause*)   Eben's queer.

ABBIE   (*bitterly*)   He's the dead spit 'n' image o' yew!

CABOT   (*queerly interested*)   D'ye think so, Abbie? (*after a pause, ruminatingly*) Me 'n' Eben's allus fit 'n' fit. I never could b'ar him noways. He's so thunderin' soft—like his Maw.

ABBIE   (*scornfully*)   Ay-eh! 'Bout as soft as yew be!

CABOT   (*as if he hadn't heard*)   Mebbe I been too hard on him.

ABBIE   (*jeeringly*)   Waal—ye're gettin' soft now—soft as slop! That's what Eben was sayin'.

CABOT (*his face instantly grim and ominous*) Eben was sayin'? Waal, he'd best not do nothin' t' try me 'r he'll soon diskiver. . . . (*a pause. She keeps her face turned away. His gradually softens. He stares up at the sky.*) Purty, hain't it?

ABBIE (*crossly*) I don't see nothin' purty.

CABOT The sky. Feels like a wa'm field up thar.

ABBIE (*sarcastically*) Air yew aimin' t' buy up over the farm too? (*She snickers contemptuously.*)

CABOT (*strangely*) I'd like t' own my place up thar. (*a pause*) I'm gittin' old, Abbie, I'm gittin' ripe on the bough. (*a pause. She stares at him mystified. He goes on*) It's allus lonesome cold in the house—even when it's bilin' hot outside. Hain't yew noticed?

ABBIE No.

CABOT It's wa'm down t' the barn—nice smellin' an' warm—with the cows. (*a pause*) Cows is queer.

ABBIE Like yew?

CABOT Like Eben. (*a pause*) I'm gittin' t' feel resigned t' Eben—jest as I got t' feel 'bout his Maw. I'm gittin' t' learn to b'ar his softness—jest like her'n. I calc'late I c'd a'most take t' him—if he wa'n't sech a dumb fool! (*a pause*) I s'pose it's old age a-creepin' in my bones.

ABBIE (*indifferently*) Waal—ye hain't dead yet.

CABOT (*roused*) No, I hain't, yew bet—not by a hell of a sight—I'm sound 'n' tough as hickory! (*then moodily*) But arter three score and ten the Lord warns ye t' prepare. (*a pause*) That's why Eben's come in my head. Now that his cussed sinful brothers is gone their path t' hell, they's no one left but Eben.

ABBIE (*resentfully*) They's me, hain't they? (*agitatedly*) What's all this sudden likin' ye tuk to Eben? Why don't ye say nothin' 'bout me? Hain't I yer lawful wife?

CABOT (*simply*) Ay-eh. Ye be. (*A pause—he stares at her desirously—his eyes grow avid—then with a sudden movement he seizes her hands and squeezes them, declaiming in a queer camp meeting preacher's tempo*) Yew air my Rose o' Sharon! Behold, yew air fair; yer eyes air doves; yer lips air like scarlet; yer two breasts air like two fawns; yer navel be like a round goblet; yer belly be like a heap o' wheat. . . . (*He covers her hand with kisses. She does not seem to notice. She stares before her with hard angry eyes.*)

ABBIE (*jerking her hands away—harshly*) So ye're plannin' t' leave the farm t' Eben, air ye?

CABOT (*dazedly*) Leave . . . ? (*then with resentful obstinacy*) I hain't a-givin' it t' no one!

ABBIE (*remorselessly*) Ye can't take it with ye.

CABOT (*thinks a moment—then reluctantly*) No, I calc'late not. (*after a pause—with a strange passion*) But if I could, I would, by the Etarnal! 'R if I could, in my dyin' hour, I'd set it afire an' watch it burn—this house an' every ear o' corn an' every tree down t' the last blade o' hay! I'd sit an' know it was all a-dying with me an' noone else'd ever own what was mine, what I'd made out o' nothin' with my own sweat 'n' blood! (*A pause—then he adds with a queer affection*) 'Ceptin' the cows. Them I'd turn free.

ABBIE (*harshly*) An' me?

CABOT (*with a queer smile*) Ye'd be turned free, too.

ABBIE (*furiously*) So that's the thanks I git fur marryin' ye—t' have ye change kind to Eben who hates ye, an' talk o' turnin' me out in the road.

CABOT (*hastily*) Abbie! Ye know I wa'n't. . . .

ABBIE (*vengefully*) Just let me tell ye a thing or two 'bout Eben. Whar's he gone? T' see that harlot, Min! I tried fur t' stop him. Disgracin' yew an' me—on the Sabbath, too!

CABOT (*rather guiltily*) He's a sinner—nateral-born. It's lust eatin' his heart.

ABBIE (*enraged beyond endurance—wildly vindictive*) An' his lust fur me! Kin ye find excuses fur that?

CABOT (*stares at her—after a dead pause*) Lust—fur yew?

ABBIE (*defiantly*) He was tryin' t' make love t' me—when ye heerd us quarrelin'.

CABOT (*stares at her. Then a terrible expression of rage comes over his face—he springs to his feet shaking all over.*) By the A'mighty God—I'll end him!

ABBIE (*frightened now for* EBEN) No! Don't ye!

CABOT (*violently*) I'll git the shotgun an' blow his soft brains t' the top o' them elums!

ABBIE (*throwing her arms around him*) No, Ephraim!

CABOT (*pushing her away violently*) I will, by God!

ABBIE (*in a quieting tone*) Listen, Ephraim. 'Twa'n't nothin' bad—on'y a boy's foolin'—'twa'n't meant serious—jest jokin' an' teasin'. . . .

CABOT Then why did ye say—lust?

ABBIE It must hev sounded wusser'n I meant. An' I was mad at thinkin'—ye'd leave him the farm.

CABOT (*quieter but still grim and cruel*) Waal then, I'll horsewhip him off the place if that much'll content ye.

ABBIE (*reaching out and taking his hand*) No. Don't think o' me! Ye mustn't drive him off. 'Tain't sensible. Who'll ye get to help ye on the farm? They's noone hereabouts.

CABOT (*considers this—then nodding his appreciation*) Ye got a head on ye. (*then irritably*) Waal, let him stay. (*He sits down on the edge of the porch. She sits beside him. He murmurs contemptuously*) I oughtn't t' git riled so—at that 'ere fool calf. (*a pause*) But har's the p'int. What son o' mine'll keep on here t' the farm—when the Lord does call me? Simeon an' Peter air gone t' hell—an' Eben's follerin' 'em—

ABBIE They's me.

CABOT   Ye're on'y a woman.

ABBIE   I'm yewr wife.

CABOT   That hain't me. A son is me—my blood—mine. Mine ought t' git mine. An' then it's still mine—even though I be six foot under. D'ye see?

ABBIE   (*giving him a look of hatred*) Ay-eh. I see. (*She becomes very thoughtful, her face growing shrewd, her eyes studying* CABOT *craftily.*)

CABOT   I'm gittin' old—ripe on the bough. (*then with a sudden forced reassurance*) Not but what I hain't a hard nut t' crack even yet—an' fur many a year t' come! By the Etarnal, I kin break most o' the young fellers' backs at any kind o' work any day o' the year!

ABBIE   (*suddenly*) Mebbe the Lord'll give *us* a son.

CABOT   (*turns and stares at her eagerly*) Ye mean—a son—t' me 'n' yew?

ABBIE   (*with a cajoling smile*) Ye're a strong man yet, hain't ye? 'Tain't noways impossible, be it? We know that. Why d'ye stare so? Hain't ye never thought o' that afore? I been thinkin' o' it all along. Ay-eh—an' I been prayin' it'd happen, too.

CABOT   (*his face growing full of joyous pride and a sort of religious ecstasy*) Ye been prayin', Abbie?—fur a son?—t' us?

ABBIE   Ay-eh. (*with a grim resolution*) I want a son now.

CABOT   (*excitedly clutching both of her hands in his*) It'd be the blessin' o' God, Abbie—the blessin' o' God A'mighty on me—in my old age—in my lonesomeness! They hain't nothin' I wouldn't do fur ye then, Abbie. Ye'd hev on'y t' ask it—anythin' ye'd a mind t'!

ABBIE   (*interrupting*) Would ye will the farm t' me then—t' me an' it . . . ?

CABOT   (*vehemently*) I'd do anythin' ye axed, I tell ye! I swar it! May I be everlastin' damned t' hell if I wouldn't! (*He sinks to his knees pulling her down with him. He trembles all over with the fervor of his hopes.*) Pray t' the Lord agin, Abbie. It's the Sabbath! I'll jine ye! Two prayers air better nor one. "An' God hearkened unto Rachel"! An' God hearkened unto Abbie! Pray Abbie! Pray fur him to hearken! (*He bows his head, mumbling. She pretends to do likewise but gives him a side glance of scorn and triumph.*)

SCENE TWO

(*About eight in the evening. The interior of the two bedrooms on the top floor is shown—*EBEN *is sitting on the side of his bed in the room on the left. On account of the heat he has taken off everything but his undershirt and pants. His feet are bare. He faces front, brooding moodily, his chin propped on his hands, a desperate expression on his face.*

In the other room CABOT *and* ABBIE *are sitting side by side on the edge of their bed, an old four-poster with feather mattress. He is in his night shirt, she in her nightdress. He is still in the queer, excited mood into which the notion of a son has thrown him. Both rooms are lighted dimly and flickeringly by tallow candles.*)

CABOT   The farm needs a son.

ABBIE   I need a son.

CABOT   Ay-eh. Sometimes ye air the farm an' sometimes the farm be yew. That's why I clove t' ye in my lonesomeness. (*A pause. He pounds his knee with his fist.*) Me an' the farm has got t' beget a son!

ABBIE   Ye'd best go t' sleep. Ye're gittin' thin's all mixed.

CABOT   (*with an impatient gesture*)   No, I hain't. My mind's clear's a well. Ye don't know me, that's it. (*He stares hopelessly at the floor.*)

ABBIE   (*indifferently*)   Mebbe. (*In the next room* EBEN *gets up and paces up and down distractedly.* ABBIE *hears him. Her eyes fasten on the intervening wall with concentrated attention.* EBEN *stops and stares. Their hot glances seem to meet through the wall. Unconsciously he stretches out his arms for her and she half rises. Then aware, he mutters a curse at himself and flings himself face downward on the bed, his clenched fists above his head, his face buried in the pillow.* ABBIE *relaxes with a faint sigh but her eyes remain fixed on the wall, she listens with all her attention for some movement from* EBEN.)

CABOT   (*suddenly raises his head and looks at her—scornfully*)   Will ye ever know me—'r will any man 'r woman? (*shaking his head*) No. I calc'late 't wa'n't t' be. (*He turns away.* ABBIE *looks at the wall. Then, evidently unable to keep silent about his thoughts, without looking at his wife, he puts out his hand and clutches her knee. She starts violently, looks at him, sees he is not watching her, concentrates again on the wall and pays no attention to what he says.*) Listen, Abbie. When I come here fifty odd year ago—I was jest twenty an' the strongest an' hardest ye ever seen—ten times as strong an' fifty times as hard as Eben. Waal—this place was nothin' but fields o' stones. Folks laughed when I tuk it. They couldn't know what I knowed. When ye kin make corn sprout out o' stones, God's livin' in yew! They wa'n't strong enuf fur that! They reckoned God was easy. They laughed. They don't laugh no more. Some died hereabouts. Some went West an' died. They're all under ground—fur follerin' arter an easy God. God hain't easy. (*He shakes his head slowly.*) An' I growed hard. Folks kept allus sayin' he's a hard man like 'twas sinful t' be hard, so's at last I said back at 'em: Waal then, by thunder, ye'll git me hard an' see how ye like it! (*then suddenly*) But I give in t' weakness once. 'Twas arter I'd been here two year. I got weak—despairful —they was so many stones. They was a party leavin', givin' up, goin' West. I jined 'em. We tracked on 'n' on. We come t' broad medders, plains, whar the soil was black an' rich as gold. Nary a stone. Easy. Ye'd on'y to plow an' sow an' then set an' smoke yer pipe an' watch thin's grow. I could o' been a rich man—but somethin' in me fit me an' fit me—the voice o' God sayin': "This hain't wuth nothin' t' Me. Git ye back t' hum!" I got afeerd o' that voice an' I lit out back t' hum here, leavin' my claim an' crops t' whoever'd a mind t' take 'em. Ay-eh. I actoolly give up what was rightful mine! God's hard, not easy! God's in the stones! Build my church on a rock—out o' stones an' I'll be in them! That's what He meant t' Peter! (*He sighs heavily —a pause.*) Stones. I picked 'em up an' piled 'em into walls. Ye kin read the years o' my life in them walls, every day a hefted stone, climbin' over the hills up and down, fencing in the fields that was mine, whar I'd made thin's grow out o' nothin'—like the will o' God, like the servant o' His hand. It wa'nt easy. It was hard an' He made me hard fur it. (*He pauses.*) All the time I kept gittin' lonesomer. I tuk a wife. She bore Simeon an' Peter. She was a good woman. She wuked hard. We was married twenty year. She never knowed me. She helped but she never knowed what she was helpin'. I was allus lonesome. She died. After that it wa'n't so lonesome fur a spell. (*a pause*) I lost count o' the years. I had no time t' fool away countin' 'em. Sim an' Peter helped. The farm growed. It was all mine! When I thought o' that I didn't feel lonesome. (*a pause*) But ye can't hitch yer mind t' one thin' day an' night. I tuk another wife—Eben's Maw. Her folks was contestin' me at law over my deeds t' the farm—my farm! That's why Eben keeps a-talkin' his fool talk o' this bein' his Maw's farm. She bore Eben. She was purty— but soft. She tried t' be hard. She couldn't. She never knowed me nor nothin'. It was lonesomer 'n hell with her. After a matter o' sixteen odd years, she died. (*a pause*) I lived with the boys. They hated me 'cause I was hard. I hated them 'cause they was soft. They coveted the farm without knowin' what it meant. It made me bitter 'n wormwood. It aged me—them coveting what I'd made fur mine. Then this Spring the call come—the voice o' God cryin' in my wilderness, in my lonesomeness—t' go out an' seek an' find! (*turning to her with strange passion*) I sought ye an' I found ye! Yew air my Rose o' Sharon! Yer eyes air like. . . . (*She has turned a blank face, resentful eyes to his. He stares at her for a moment—then harshly*) Air ye any the wiser fur all I've told ye?

ABBIE (*confusedly*) Mebbe.

CABOT (*pushing her away from him—angrily*) Ye don't know nothin'—nor never will. If ye don't hev a son t' redeem ye . . . . (*this in a tone of cold threat*)

ABBIE (*resentfully*) I've prayed, hain't I?

CABOT (*bitterly*) Pray agin—fur understandin'!

ABBIE (*a veiled threat in her tone*) Ye'll have a son out o' me, I promise ye.

CABOT How can ye promise?

ABBIE I got second-sight, mebbe. I kin foretell. (*She gives a queer smile.*)

CABOT I believe ye have. Ye give me the chills sometimes. (*He shivers.*) It's cold in this house. It's oneasy. They's thin's pokin' about in the dark—in the corners. (*He pulls on his trousers, tucking in his night shirt, and pulls on his boots.*)

ABBIE (*surprised*) Whar air ye goin'?

CABOT (*queerly*) Down whar it's restful—whar it's warm—down t' the barn. (*bitterly*) I kin talk t' the cows. They know. They know the farm an' me. They'll give me peace. (*He turns to go out the door.*)

ABBIE (*a bit frightenedly*) Air ye ailin' tonight, Ephraim?

CABOT Growin'. Growin' ripe on the bough. (*He turns and goes, his boots clumping down the stairs.* EBEN *sits up with a start, listening.* ABBIE *is conscious of his movement and stares at the wall.* CABOT *comes out of the house around the corner and stands by the gate, blinking at the sky. He stretches up his hands in a tortured gesture.)* God A'mighty, call from the dark! (*He listens as if expecting an answer. Then his arms drop, he shakes his head and plods off toward the barn.* EBEN *and* ABBIE *stare at each other through the wall.* EBEN *sighs heavily and* ABBIE *echoes it. Both become terribly nervous, uneasy. Finally* ABBIE *gets up and listens, her ear to the wall. He acts as if he saw every move she was making, he becomes resolutely still. She seems driven into a decision—goes out the door in rear determinedly. His eyes follow her. Then as the door of his room is opened softly, he turns away, waits in an attitude of strained fixity.* ABBIE *stands for a second staring at him, her eyes burning with desire. Then with a little cry she runs over and throws her arms about his neck, she pulls his head back and covers his mouth with kisses. At first, he submits dumbly; then he puts his arms about her neck and returns her kisses but finally, suddenly aware of his hatred, he hurls her away from him, springing to his feet. They stand speechless and breathless, panting like two animals.)*

ABBIE   (*at last—painfully*) Ye shouldn't, Eben—ye shouldn't—I'd make ye happy!

EBEN   (*harshly*) I don't want t' be happy—from yew!

ABBIE   (*helplessly*) Ye do, Eben! Ye do! Why d'ye lie?

EBEN   (*viciously*) I don't take t'ye, I tell ye! I hate the sight o' ye!

ABBIE   (*with an uncertain troubled laugh*) Waal, I kissed ye anyways—an' ye kissed back—yer lips was burnin'—ye can't lie 'bout that! (*intensely*) If ye don't care, why did ye kiss me back—why was yer lips burnin'?

EBEN   (*wiping his mouth*) It was like pizen on 'em (*then tauntingly*) When I kissed ye back, mebbe I thought 'twas someone else.

ABBIE   (*wildly*) Min?

EBEN   Mebbe.

ABBIE   (*torturedly*) Did ye go t' see her? Did ye r'ally go? I thought ye mightn't. Is that why ye throwed me off jest now?

EBEN   (*sneeringly*) What if it be?

ABBIE   (*raging*) Then ye're a dog, Eben Cabot!

EBEN   (*threateningly*) Ye can't talk that way t' me!

ABBIE   (*with a shrill laugh*) Can't I? Did ye think I was in love with ye —a weak thin' like yew? Not much! I on'y wanted ye fur a purpose o' my own—an' I'll hev ye fur it yet 'cause I'm stronger'n yew be!

EBEN   (*resentfully*) I knowed well it was on'y part o' yer plan t' swaller everythin'!

ABBIE   (*tauntingly*) Mebbe!

EBEN   (*furious*) Git out o' my room!

ABBIE   This air my room an' ye're on'y hired help!

EBEN   (*threateningly*) Git out afore I murder ye!

ABBIE   (*quite confident now*) I hain't a mite afeerd. Ye want me, don't ye? Yes, ye do! An' yer Paw's son'll never kill what he wants! Look at yer eyes! They's lust fur me in 'em, burnin' 'em up! Look at yer lips now! They're tremblin' an' longin' t' kiss me, an' yer teeth t' bite! (*He is watching her now with a horrible fascination. She laughs a crazy triumphant laugh.*) I'm a-goin' t' make all o' this hum my hum! They's one room hain't mine yet, but it's a-goin' to' be tonight. I'm a-goin down now an' light up! (*She makes him a mocking bow.*) Won't ye come courtin' me in the best parlor, Mister Cabot?

EBEN (*staring at her—horribly confused—dully*) Don't ye dare! It hain't been opened since Maw died an' was laid out thar! Don't ye . . . . (*But her eyes are fixed on his so burningly that his will seems to wither before hers. He stands swaying toward her helplessly.*)

ABBIE (*holding his eyes and putting all her will into her words as she backs out the door*) I'll expect ye afore long, Eben.

EBEN (*stares after her for a while, walking toward the door. A light appears in the parlor window. He murmurs*) In the parlor? (*This seems to arouse connotations for he comes back and puts on his white shirt, collar, half ties the tie mechanically, puts on coat, takes his hat, stands barefooted looking about him in bewilderment, mutters wonderingly*) Maw! Whar air yew? (*then goes slowly toward the door in rear*)

SCENE THREE

(*A few minutes later. The interior of the parlor is shown. A grim, repressed room like a tomb in which the family has been interred alive. ABBIE sits on the edge of the horsehair sofa. She has lighted all the candles and the room is revealed in all its preserved ugliness. A change has come over the woman. She looks awed and frightened now, ready to run away.*

The door is opened and EBEN appears. His face wears an expression of obsessed confusion. He stands staring at her, his arms hanging disjointedly from his shoulders, his feet bare, his hat in his hand.)

ABBIE (*after a pause—with a nervous, formal politeness*) Won't ye set?

EBEN (*dully*) Ay-eh. (*Mechanically he places his hat carefully on the floor near the door and sits stiffly beside her on the edge of the sofa. A pause. They both remain rigid, looking straight ahead with eyes full of fear.*)

ABBIE When I fust come in—in the dark—they seemed somethin' here.

EBEN (*simply*) Maw.

ABBIE I kin still feel—somethin'. . . .

EBEN It's Maw.

ABBIE At fust I was feered o' it. I wanted t' yell an' run. Now—since yew come—seems like it's growin' soft an' kind t' me. (*addressing the air— queerly*) Thank yew.

EBEN Maw allus loved me.

ABBIE Mebbe it knows I love yew too. Mebbe that makes it kind t' me.

EBEN (*dully*) I dunno. I should think she'd hate ye.

ABBIE (*with certainty*) No. I kin feel it don't—not no more.

EBEN   Hate ye fur stealin' her place—here in her hum—settin' in her parlor whar she was laid. . . . (*He suddenly stops, staring stupidly before him.*)

ABBIE   What is it, Eben?

EBEN   (*in a whisper*)   Seems like Maw didn't want me t' remind ye.

ABBIE   (*excitedly*)   I knowed, Eben! It's kind t' me! It don't b'ar me no grudges fur what I never knowed an' couldn't help!

EBEN   Maw b'ars him a grudge.

ABBIE   Waal, so does all o' us.

EBEN   Ay-eh. (*with passion*) I does, by God!

ABBIE   (*taking one of his hands in hers and patting it*)   Thar! Don't git riled thinkin' o' him. Think o' yer Maw who's kind t' us. Tell me about yer Maw, Eben.

EBEN   They hain't nothin' much— She was kind. She was good.

ABBIE   (*putting one arm over his shoulder. He does not seem to notice— passionately*)   I'll be kind an' good t' ye!

EBEN   Sometimes she used t' sing fur me.

ABBIE   I'll sing fur ye!

EBEN   This was her hum. This was her farm.

ABBIE   This is my hum! This is my farm!

EBEN   He married her t' steal 'em. She was soft an' easy. He couldn't 'preciate her.

ABBIE   He can't 'preciate me!

EBEN   He murdered her with his hardness.

ABBIE   He's murderin' me!

EBEN   She died. (*a pause*) Sometimes she used to sing fur me. (*He bursts into a fit of sobbing.*)

ABBIE   (*both her arms around him—with wild passion*)   I'll sing fur ye! I'll die fur ye! (*In spite of her overwhelming desire for him, there is a sincere maternal love in her manner and voice—a horribly frank mixture of lust and mother love.*) Don't cry, Eben! I'll take yer Maw's place! I'll be everythin' she was t' ye! Let me kiss ye, Eben! (*She pulls his head around. He makes a bewildered pretense of resistance. She is tender.*) Don't be afeered! I'll kiss ye pure, Eben—same 's if I was a Maw t' ye—an' ye kin kiss me back 's if yew was my son—my boy—sayin' good-night t' me! Kiss me, Eben. (*They kiss in restrained fashion. Then suddenly wild passion overcomes her. She kisses him lustfully again and again and he flings his arms about her and returns her kisses. Suddenly, as in the bedroom, he frees himself from her violently and springs to his feet. He is trembling all over, in a strange state of terror.* ABBIE *strains her arms toward him with fierce pleading.*) Don't ye leave me, Eben! Can't ye see it hain't enuf—lovin' ye like a Maw—can't ye see it's got t' be that an' more—much more—a hundred times more—fur me t' be happy—fur yew t' be happy?

EBEN   (*to the presence he feels in the room*)   Maw! Maw! What d'ye want? What air ye tellin' me?

ABBIE   She's tellin' ye t' love me. She knows I love ye an' I'll be good t' ye. Can't ye feel it? Don't ye know? She's tellin' ye t' love me, Eben!

EBEN   Ay-eh. I feel—mebbe she—but—I can't figger out—why—when ye've stole her place—here in her hum—in the parlor whar she was. . . .

ABBIE   (*fiercely*)   She knows I love ye!

EBEN   (*his face suddenly lighting up with a fierce, triumphant grin*)   I see it! I sees why. It's her vengeance on him—so's she kin rest quiet in her grave!

ABBIE   (*wildly*)   Vengeance o' God on the hull o' us! What d'we give a durn? I love ye, Eben! God knows I love ye! (*She stretches out her arms for him.*)

EBEN   (*throws himself on his knees beside the sofa and grabs her in his arms —releasing all his pent-up passion*)   An' I love yew, Abbie!—now I kin say it! I been dyin' fur want o' ye—every hour—since ye come! I love ye! (*Their lips meet in a fierce, bruising kiss.*)

SCENE FOUR

(*Exterior of the farmhouse. It is just dawn. The front door at right is opened and* EBEN *comes out and walks around to the gate. He is dressed in his working clothes. He seems changed. His face wears a bold and confident expression, he is grinning to himself with evident satisfaction. As he gets near the gate, the window of the parlor is heard opening and the shutters are flung back and* ABBIE *sticks her head out. Her hair tumbles over her shoulders in disarray, her face is flushed, she looks at* EBEN *with tender, languorous eyes and calls softly.*)

ABBIE   Eben. (*as he turns—playfully*) Jest one more kiss afore ye go. I'm goin' to miss ye fearful all day.

EBEN   An' me yew, ye kin bet! (*He goes to her. They kiss several times. He draws away, laughingly.*) Thar. That's enuf, hain't it? Ye won't hev none left fur next time.

ABBIE   I got a million o' 'em left fur yew! (*then a bit anxiously*) D'ye r'ally love me, Eben?

EBEN   (*emphatically*)   I like ye better'n any gal I ever knowed! That's gospel!

ABBIE   Likin' hain't lovin'.

EBEN   Waal then—I love ye. Now air yew satisfied?

ABBIE   Ay-eh, I be. (*She smiles at him adoringly.*)

EBEN   I better git t' the barn. The old critter's liable t' suspicion an' come sneakin' up.

ABBIE   (*with a confident laugh*)   Let him! I kin allus pull the wool over his eyes. I'm goin' t' leave the shutters open and let in the sun 'n' air. This room's been dead long enuf. Now it's goin' t' be my room!

EBEN   (*frowning*)   Ay-eh.

ABBIE   (*hastily*)   I meant—our room.

EBEN   Ay-eh.

ABBIE   We made it our'n last night, didn't we? We give it life—our lovin' did. (*a pause*)

EBEN   (*with a strange look*)   Maw's gone back t' her grave. She kin sleep now.

ABBIE   May she rest in peace! (*then tenderly rebuking*) Ye oughtn't t' talk o' sad thin's—this mornin'.

EBEN   It jest come up in my mind o' itself.

ABBIE   Don't let it. (*He doesn't answer. She yawns.*) Waal, I'm a-goin' t' steal a wink o' sleep. I'll tell the Old Man I hain't feelin' pert. Let him git his own vittles.

EBEN   I see him comin' from the barn. Ye better look smart an' git upstairs.

ABBIE   Ay-eh. Good-by. Don't fergit me. (*She throws him a kiss. He grins— then squares his shoulders and awaits his father confidently.* CABOT *walks slowly up from the left, staring up at the sky with a vague face.*)

EBEN   (*jovially*)   Mornin', Paw. Star-gazin' in daylight?

CABOT   Purty, hain't it?

EBEN   (*looking around him possessively*)   It's a durned purty farm.

CABOT   I mean the sky.

EBEN   (*grinning*)   How d'ye know? Them eyes o' your'n can't see that fur. (*This tickles his humor and he slaps his thigh and laughs.*) Ho-ho! That's a good un!

CABOT   (*grimly sarcastic*)   Ye're feelin' right chipper, hain't ye? Whar'd ye steal the likker?

EBEN   (*good-naturedly*)   'Tain't likker. Jest life. (*suddenly holding out his hand—soberly*) Yew 'n' me is quits. Let's shake hands.

CABOT   (*suspiciously*)   What's come over ye?

EBEN   Then don't. Mebbe it's jest as well. (*a moment's pause*) What's come over me? (*queerly*) Didn't ye feel her passin'—goin' back t' her grave?

CABOT   (*dully*)   Who?

EBEN   Maw. She kin rest now an' sleep content. She's quits with ye.

CABOT   (*confusedly*)   I rested. I slept good—down with the cows. They know how t' sleep. They're teachin' me.

EBEN   (*suddenly jovial again*)   Good fur the cows! Waal—ye better git t' work.

CABOT   (*grimly amused*)   Air yew bossin' me, ye calf?

EBEN   (*beginning to laugh*)   Ay-eh! I'm bossin' yew! Ha-ha-ha! see how ye like it! Ha-ha-ha! I'm the prize rooster o' this roost. Ha-ha-ha! (*He goes off toward the barn laughing.*)

CABOT   (*looks after him with scornful pity*)   Soft-headed. Like his Maw. Dead spit 'n' image. No hope in him! (*He spits with contemptuous disgust.*) A born fool! (*then matter-of-factly*) Waal—I'm gittin' peckish. (*He goes toward door.*)

(*The Curtain Falls*)

PART III

SCENE ONE

(A *night in late spring the following year. The kitchen and the two bed-rooms upstairs are shown. The two bedrooms are dimly lighted by a tallow candle in each.* EBEN *is sitting on the side of the bed in his room, his chin propped on his fists, his face a study of the struggle he is making to understand his conflicting emotions. The noisy laughter and music from below where a kitchen dance is in progress annoy and distract him. He scowls at the floor.*

In the next room a cradle stands beside the double bed.

In the kitchen all is festivity. The stove has been taken down to give more room to the dancers. The chairs, with wooden benches added, have been pushed back against the walls. On these are seated, squeezed in tight against one another, farmers and their wives and their young folks of both sexes from the neighboring farms. They are all chattering and laughing loudly. They evidently have some secret joke in common. There is no end of winking, of nudging, of meaning nods of the head toward CABOT *who, in a state of extreme hilarious excitement increased by the amount he has drunk, is standing near the rear door where there is a small keg of whisky and serving drinks to all the men. In the left corner, front, dividing the attention with her husband,* ABBIE *is sitting in a rocking chair, a shawl wrapped about her shoulders. She is very pale, her face is thin and drawn, her eyes are fixed anxiously on the open door in rear as if waiting for someone.*

The musician is tuning up his fiddle, seated in the far right corner. He is a lanky young fellow with a long, weak face. His pale eyes blink incessantly and he grins about him slyly with a greedy malice.)

ABBIE   (*suddenly turning to a young girl on her right*)   Whar's Eben?

YOUNG GIRL   (*eying her scornfully*)   I dunno, Mrs. Cabot. I hain't seen Eben in ages. (*meaningly*) Seems like he's spent most o' his time t' hum since yew come.

ABBIE   (*vaguely*)   I tuk his Maw's place.

YOUNG GIRL   Ay-eh. So I've heerd. (*She turns away to retail this bit of gossip to her mother sitting next to her.* ABBIE *turns to her left to a big stoutish middle-aged man whose flushed face and staring eyes show the amount of "likker" he has consumed.*)

ABBIE   Ye hain't seen Eben, hev ye?

MAN   No, I hain't. (*Then he adds with a wink*) If yew hain't, who would?

ABBIE   He's the best dancer in the county. He'd ought t' come an' dance.

MAN   (*with a wink*)   Mebbe he's doin' the dutiful an' walkin' the kid t' sleep. It's a boy, hain't it?

ABBIE   (*nodding vaguely*)   Ay-eh—born two weeks back—purty's a pic-ter . . .

MAN   They all is—t' their Maws. (*then in a whisper with a nudge and a leer*) Listen, Abbie—if ye ever git tired o' Eben, remember me! Don't fergit now! (*He looks at her uncomprehending face for a second—then grunts disgustedly*) Waal—guess I'll likker again. (*He goes over and joins* CABOT *who is arguing noisily with an old farmer over cows. They all drink.*)

ABBIE (*this time appealing to nobody in particular*) Wonder what Eben's a-doin'? (*Her remark is repeated down the line with many a guffaw and titter until it reaches the fiddler. He fastens his blinking eyes on* ABBIE.)

FIDDLER (*raising his voice*) Bet I kin tell ye, Abbie, what Eben's doin'! He's down t' the church offerin' up prayers o' thanksgivin'. (*They all titter expectantly.*)

MAN What fur? (*another titter.*)

FIDDLER 'Cause unto him a—(*he hesitates just long enough*) brother is born! (*a roar of laughter. They all look from* ABBIE *to* CABOT. *She is oblivious, staring at the door.* CABOT, *although he hasn't heard the words, is irritated by the laughter and steps forward, glaring about him. There is an immediate silence.*)

CABOT What're ye all bleatin' about—like a flock o' goats? Why don't ye dance, damn ye? I axed ye here t' dance—t' eat, drink an' be merry—an' thar ye set cacklin' like a lot o' wet hens with the pip! Ye've swilled my likker an' guzzled my vittles like hogs, hain't ye? Then dance fur me, can't ye? That's fa'r an' squar', hain't it? (*A grumble of resentment goes around but they are all evidently in too much awe of him to express it openly.*)

FIDDLER (*slyly*) We're waitin' fur Eben. (*a suppressed laugh*)

CABOT (*with a fierce exultation*) T'hell with Eben! Eben's done fur now! I got a new son! (*his mood switching with drunken suddenness*) But ye needn't t' laugh at Eben, none o' ye! He's my blood, if he be a dumb fool. He's better nor any o' yew! He kin do a day's work a'most up t' what I kin—an' that'd put any o' yew pore critters t' shame!

FIDDLER An' he kin do a good night's work, too! (*a roar of laughter*)

CABOT Laugh, ye damn fools! Ye're right jist the same, Fiddler. He kin work day an' night too, like I kin, if need be!

OLD FARMER (*from behind the keg where he is weaving drunkenly back and forth—with great simplicity*) They hain't many t' touch ye, Ephraim—a son at seventy-six. That's a hard man fur ye! I be on'y sixty-eight an' I couldn't do it. (*a roar of laughter in which* CABOT *joins uproariously.*)

CABOT (*slapping him on the back*) I'm sorry fur ye, Hi. I'd never suspicion sech weakness from a boy like yew!

OLD FARMER An' I never reckoned yew had it in ye nuther, Ephraim. (*There is another laugh.*)

CABOT (*suddenly grim*) I got a lot in me—a hell of a lot—folks don't know on. (*turning to the* FIDDLER) Fiddle 'er up, durn ye! Give 'em somethin' t' dance t'! What air ye, an ornament? Hain't this a celebration? Then grease yer elbow an' go it!

FIDDLER (*seizes a drink which the* OLD FARMER *holds out to him and downs it*) Here goes! (*He starts to fiddle "Lady of the Lake." Four young fellows and four girls form in two lines and dance a square dance. The* FIDDLER *shouts directions for the different movements, keeping his words in the rhythm of the music and interspersing them with jocular personal remarks to the dancers themselves. The people seated along the walls stamp their feet and clap their hands in unison.* CABOT *is especially active in this respect. Only* ABBIE *remains apathetic, staring at the door as if she were alone in a silent room.*)

FIDDLER Swing your partner t' the right! That's it, Jim! Give her a b'ar hug! Her Maw hain't lookin'. (*laughter*) Change partners! That suits ye, don't it, Essie, now ye got Reub afore ye? Look at her redden up, will ye! Waal, life is short an' so's love, as the feller says. (*laughter*)

CABOT (*excitedly, stamping his foot*) Go it, boys! Go it, gals!

FIDDLER (*with a wink at the others*) Ye're the spryest seventy-six ever I sees, Ephraim! Now if ye'd on'y good eye-sight . . ! (*suppressed laughter. He gives* CABOT *no chance to retort but roars*) Promenade! Ye're walkin' like a bride down the aisle, Sarah! Waal, while they's life they's allus hope, I've heerd tell. Swing your partner to the left! Gosh A'mighty, look at Johnny Cook high-steppin'! They hain't goin' t' be much strength left fur howin' in the corn lot t'morrow. (*laughter*)

CABOT Go it! Go it! (*Then suddenly, unable to restrain himself any longer, he prances into the midst of the dancers, scattering them, waving his arms about wildly.*) Ye're all hoofs! Git out o' my road! Give me room! I'll show ye dancin'. Ye're all too soft! (*He pushes them roughly away. They crowd back toward the walls, muttering, looking at him resentfully.*)

FIDDLER (*jeeringly*) Go it, Ephraim! Go it! (*He starts "Pop Goes the Weasel," increasing the tempo with every verse until at the end he is fiddling crazily as fast as he can go.*)

CABOT (*starts to dance, which he does very well and with tremendous vigor. Then he begins to improvise, cuts incredibly grotesque capers, leaping up and cracking his heels together, prancing around in a circle with body bent in an Indian war dance, then suddenly straightening up and kicking as high as he can with both legs. He is like a monkey on a string. And all the while he intersperses his antics with shouts and derisive comments.*) Whoop! Here's dancin' fur ye! Whoop! See that! Seventy-six, if I'm a day! Hard as iron yet! Beatin' the young 'uns like I allus done! Look at me! I'd invite ye t' dance on my hundredth birthday on'y ye'll all be dead by then. Ye're a sickly generation! Yer hearts air pink, not red! Yer veins is full o' mud an' water! I be the on'y man in the county! Whoop! See that! I'm a Injun! I've killed Injuns in the West afore ye was born—an' skulped 'em too! They's a arrer wound on my backside I c'd show ye! The hull tribe chased me. I outrun 'em all— with the arrer stuck in me! An' I tuk vengeance on 'em. Ten eyes fur an eye, that was my motter! Whoop! Look at me! I kin kick the ceilin' off the room! Whoop!

FIDDLER (*stops playing—exhaustedly*) God A'mighty, I got enuf. Ye got the devil's strength in ye.

CABOT (*delightedly*) Did I beat yew, too? Wa'al, ye played smart. Hev a swig. (*He pours whisky for himself and* FIDDLER. *They drink. The others*

watch CABOT *silently with cold, hostile eyes. There is a dead pause. The* FID-
DLER *rests.* CABOT *leans against the keg, panting, glaring around him confusedly. In the room above,* EBEN *gets to his feet and tiptoes out the door in
rear, appearing a moment later in the other bedroom. He moves silently, even
frightenedly, toward the cradle and stands there looking down at the baby.
His face is as vague as his reactions are confused, but there is a trace of tenderness, of interested discovery. At the same moment that he reaches the cradle,*
ABBIE *seems to sense something. She gets up weakly and goes to* CABOT.)

ABBIE   I'm goin' up t' the baby.

CABOT   (*with real solicitation*)   Air ye able fur the stairs? D'ye want me t'
help ye, Abbie?

ABBIE   No. I'm able. I'll be down agin soon.

CABOT   Don't ye git wore out! He needs ye, remember—our son does! (*He
grins affectionately, patting her on the back. She shrinks from his touch.*)

ABBIE   (*dully*)   Don't—tech me. I'm goin'—up. (*She goes.* CABOT *looks
after her. A whisper goes around the room.* CABOT *turns. It ceases. He wipes
his forehead streaming with sweat. He is breathing pantingly.*)

CABOT   I'm a-goin' out t' git fresh air. I'm feelin' a mite dizzy. Fiddle up
thar! Dance, all o' ye! Here's likker fur them as wants it. Enjoy yerselves. I'll
be back. (*He goes, closing the door behind him.*)

FIDDLER   (*sarcastically*)   Don't hurry none on our account! (*a suppressed
laugh. He imitates* ABBIE.) Whar's Eben? (*more laughter*)

A WOMAN   (*loudly*)   What's happened in this house is plain as the nose on
yer face! (ABBIE *appears in the doorway upstairs and stands looking in surprise
and adoration at* EBEN *who does not see her.*)

A MAN   Ssshh! He's li'ble t' be listenin' at the door. That'd be like him.
(*Their voices die to an intensive whispering. Their faces are concentrated on
this gossip. A noise as of dead leaves in the wind comes from the room.*
CABOT *has come out from the porch and stands by the gate, leaning on it,
staring at the sky blinkingly.* ABBIE *comes across the room silently.* EBEN *does
not notice her until quite near.*)

EBEN   (*starting*)   Abbie!

ABBIE   Ssshh! (*She throws her arms around him. They kiss—then bend over
the cradle together*) Ain't he purty?—dead spit'n' image o' yew!

EBEN   (*pleased*)   Air he? I can't tell none.

ABBIE   E-zactly like!

EBEN   (*frowningly*)   I don't like this. I don't like lettin' on what's mine's
his'n. I been doin' that all my life. I'm gittin' t' the end o' b'arin' it!

ABBIE   (*putting her finger on his lips*)   We're doin' the best we kin. We got
t' wait. Somethin's bound t' happen. (*She puts her arms around him.*) I got
t' go back.

EBEN   I'm goin' out. I can't b'ar it with the fiddle playin' an' the laughin'.

ABBIE   Don't git feelin' low. I love ye, Eben. Kiss me. (*He kisses her. They
remain in each other's arms.*)

CABOT (*at the gate, confusedly*) Even the music can't drive it out—somethin'. Ye kin feel it droppin' off the elums, climbin' up the roof, sneakin' down the chimney, pokin' in the corners . . . They's no peace in houses, they's no rest livin' with folks. Somethin's always livin' with ye. (*with a deep sigh*) I'll go t' the barn an' rest a spell. (*He goes wearily toward the barn.*)

FIDDLER (*tuning up*) Let's celebrate the old skunk gittin' fooled! We kin have some fun now he's went. (*He starts to fiddle "Turkey in the Straw." There is real merriment now. The young folks get up to dance.*)

SCENE TWO

(*A half hour later—Exterior—*EBEN *is standing by the gate looking up at the sky, an expression of dumb pain bewildered by itself on his face.* CABOT *appears, returning from the barn, walking wearily, his eyes on the ground. He sees* EBEN *and his whole mood immediately changes. He becomes excited, a cruel, triumphant grin comes to his lips, he strides up and slaps* EBEN *on the back. From within comes the whining of the fiddle and the noise of stamping feet and laughing voices.*)

CABOT So har ye be!

EBEN (*startled, stares at him with hatred for a moment—then dully*) Ay-eh.

CABOT (*surveying him jeeringly*) Why hain't ye been in t' dance? They was all axin fur ye.

EBEN Let 'em ax!

CABOT They's a hull passel o' purty gals. . .

EBEN T' hell with 'em!

CABOT Ye'd ought t' be marryin' one o' 'em soon.

EBEN I hain't marryin' no one.

CABOT Ye might 'arn a share o' a farm that way.

EBEN (*with a sneer*) Like yew did, ye mean? I hain't that kind.

CABOT (*stung*) Ye lie! 'Twas yer Maw's folks aimed t' steal my farm from me.

EBEN Other folks don't say so. (*after a pause—defiantly*) An' I got a farm, anyways!

CABOT (*derisively*) Whar?

EBEN (*stamps a foot on the ground*) Har!

CABOT (*throws his head back and laughs coarsely*) Ho-ho! Ye hev, hev ye? Waal, that's a good un!

EBEN (*controlling himself—grimly*) Ye'll see!

CABOT (*stares at him suspiciously, trying to make him out—a pause—then with scornful confidence*) Ay-eh. I'll see. So'll ye. It's ye that's blind—blind as a mole underground. (EBEN *suddenly laughs, one short sardonic bark:* "Ha." *A pause.* CABOT *peers at him with renewed suspicion.*) What air ye hawin' 'bout? (EBEN *turns away without answering.* CABOT *grows angry.*) God

A'mighty, yew air a dumb dunce! They's nothin' in that thick skull o' your'n but noise—like a empty keg it be! (EBEN *doesn't seem to hear.* CABOT's *rage grows.*) Yewr farm! God A'mighty! If ye wa'n't a born donkey ye'd know ye'll never own stick nor stone on it, specially now arter him bein' born. It's his'n, I tell ye—his'n arter I die—but I'll live a hundred jest t' fool ye all—an' he'll be growed then—yewr age a'most! (EBEN *laughs again his sardonic "Ha." This drives* CABOT *into a fury.*) Ha? Ye think ye kin git 'round that someways, do ye? Waal, it'll be her'n, too—Abbie's—ye won't git 'round her—she knows yer tricks—she'll be too much fur ye—she wants the farm her'n—she was afeerd o' ye—she told me ye was sneakin' 'round tryin' t' make love t' her t' git her on yer side . . . ye . . . ye mad fool, ye! (*He raises his clenched fists threateningly.*)

EBEN   (*is confronting him choking with rage*)   Ye lie, ye old skunk! Abbie never said no sech thing!

CABOT   (*suddenly triumphant when he sees how shaken* EBEN *is*)   She did. An' I says, I'll blow his brains t' the top o' them elums—an' she says no, that hain't sense, who'll ye git t' help ye on the farm in his place—an' then she says yew'n me ought t' have a son—I know we kin, she says—an' I says, if we do, ye kin have anythin' I've got ye've a mind t'. An' she says, I wants Eben cut off so's this farm'll be mine when ye die! (*with terrible gloating*) An' that's what's happened, hain't it? An' the farm's her'n! An' the dust o' the road—that's you'rn! Ha! Now who's hawin'?

EBEN   (*has been listening, petrified with grief and rage—suddenly laughs wildly and brokenly*)   Ha-ha-ha! So that's her sneakin' game—all along!— like I suspicioned at fust—t' swaller it all—an' me, too . . . ! (*madly*) I'll murder her! (*He springs toward the porch but* CABOT *is quicker and gets in between.*)

CABOT   No, ye don't!

EBEN   Git out o' my road! (*He tries to throw* CABOT *aside. They grapple in what becomes immediately a murderous struggle. The old man's concentrated strength is too much for* EBEN. CABOT *gets one hand on his throat and presses him back across the stone wall. At the same moment,* ABBIE *comes out on the porch. With a stifled cry she runs toward them.*)

ABBIE   Eben! Ephraim! (*She tugs at the hand on* EBEN's *throat*) Let go, Ephraim! Ye're chokin' him!

CABOT   (*removes his hand and flings* EBEN *sideways full length on the grass, gasping and choking. With a cry,* ABBIE *kneels beside him, trying to take his head on her lap, but he pushes her away.* CABOT *stands looking down with fierce triumph.*) Ye needn't t've fret, Abbie, I wa'n't aimin' t' kill him. He hain't wuth hangin' fur—not by a hell of a sight! (*more and more triumphantly*) Seventy-six an' him not thirty yit—an' look whar he be fur thinkin' his Paw was easy! No, by God, I hain't easy! An' him upstairs, I'll raise him t' be like me! (*He turns to leave them.*) I'm goin' in an' dance!—sing an' celebrate! (*He walks to the porch—then turns with a great grin.*) I don't calc'-late it's left in him, but if he gits pesky, Abbie, ye jest sing out. I'll come a-runnin' an' by the Etarnal, I'll put him across my knee an' birch him! Ha-

ha-ha! (*He goes into the house laughing. A moment later his loud "whoop" is heard.*)

ABBIE (*tenderly*) Eben. Air ye hurt? (*She tries to kiss him but he pushes her violently away and struggles to a sitting position.*)

EBEN (*gaspingly*) T'hell—with ye!

ABBIE (*not believing her ears*) It's me, Eben—Abbie—don't ye know me?

EBEN (*glowering at her with hatred*) Ay-eh—I know ye—now! (*He suddenly breaks down, sobbing weakly.*)

ABBIE (*fearfully*) Eben—what's happened t' ye—why did ye look at me 's if ye hated me?

EBEN (*violently, between sobs and gasps*) I do hate ye! Ye're a whore —a damn trickin' whore!

ABBIE (*shrinking back horrified*) Eben! Ye don't know what ye're sayin'!

EBEN (*scrambling to his feet and following her—accusingly*) Ye're nothin' but a stinkin' passel o' lies! Ye've been lyin' t' me every word ye spoke, day an' night, since we fust—done it. Ye've kept sayin' ye loved me. . . .

ABBIE (*frantically*) I do love ye! (*She takes his hand but he flings hers away.*)

EBEN (*unheeding*) Ye've made a fool o' me—a sick, dumb fool—a-purpose! Ye've been on'y playin' yer sneakin', stealin' game all along—gittin' me t' lie with ye so's ye'd hev a son he'd think was his'n, an' makin' him promise he'd give ye the farm and let me eat dust, if ye did git him a son! (*staring at her with anguished, bewildered eyes*) They must be a devil livin' in ye! 'Tain't human t' be as bad as that be!

ABBIE (*stunned—dully*) He told yew . . . ?

EBEN Hain't it true? It hain't no good in yew lyin'. . . .

ABBIE (*pleadingly*) Eben, listen—ye must listen—it was long ago—afore we done nothin'—yew was scornin' me—goin' t' see Min—when I was lovin' ye—an' I said it t' him t' git vengeance on ye!

EBEN (*unheedingly—with tortured passion*) I wish ye was dead! I wish I was dead along with ye afore this come! (*ragingly*) But I'll git my vengeance too! I'll pray Maw t' come back t' help me—t' put her cuss on yew an' him!

ABBIE (*brokenly*) Don't ye, Eben! Don't ye! (*She throws herself on her knees before him, weeping.*) I didn't mean t' do bad t'ye! Fergive me, won't ye?

EBEN (*not seeming to hear her—fiercely*) I'll git squar' with the old skunk —an' yew! I'll tell him the truth 'bout the son he's so proud o'! Then I'll leave ye here t' pizen each other—with Maw comin' out o' her grave at nights —an' I'll go t' the gold fields o' Californi-a whar Sim an' Peter be. . . .

ABBIE (*terrified*) Ye won't—leave me? Ye can't!

EBEN (*with fierce determination*) I'm a-goin', I tell ye! I'll git rich thar an' come back an' fight him fur the farm he stole—an' I'll kick ye both out in the road—t' beg an' sleep in the woods—an' yer son along with ye—t' starve an' die! (*He is hysterical at the end.*)

ABBIE   (*with a shudder—humbly*)   He's yewr son, too, Eben.

EBEN   (*torturedly*)   I wish he never was born! I wish he'd die this minit! I wish I'd never sot eyes on him! It's him—yew havin' him—a-purpose t' steal —that's changed everythin'!

ABBIE   (*gently*)   Did ye believe I loved ye—afore he come?

EBEN   Ay-eh—like a dumb ox!

ABBIE   An' ye don't believe no more?

EBEN   B'lieve a lyin' thief! Ha!

ABBIE   (*shudders—then humbly*)   An did ye really love me afore?

EBEN   (*brokenly*)   Ay-eh—an' ye was trickin' me!

ABBIE   An' ye don't love me now!

EBEN   (*violently*)   I hate ye, I tell ye!

ABBIE   An' ye're truly goin' West—goin' t' leave me—all account o' him being born?

EBEN   I'm a-goin' in the mornin'—or may God strike me t' hell!

ABBIE   (*after a pause—with a dreadful cold intensity—slowly*)   If that's what his comin's done t' me—killin' yewr love—takin' yew away—my on'y joy—the on'y joy I ever knowed—like heaven t' me—purtier'n heaven—then I hate him, too, even if I be his Maw!

EBEN   (*bitterly*)   Lies! Ye love him! He'll steal the farm fur ye! (*brokenly*) But 'tain't the farm so much—not no more—it's yew foolin' me—gittin' me t' love ye—lyin' yew loved me—jest t' git a son t' steal . . . !

ABBIE   (*distractedly*)   He won't steal! I'd kill him fust! I do love ye! I'll prove t' ye . . . !

EBEN   (*harshly*)   'Tain't no use lyin' no more. I'm deaf t' ye! (*He turns away.*) I hain't seein' ye agen. Good-by!

ABBIE   (*pale with anguish*)   Hain't ye even goin' t' kiss me—not once—arter all we loved . . . ?

EBEN   (*in a hard voice*)   I hain't wantin' t' kiss ye never again! I'm wantin' t' forgit I ever sot eyes on ye!

ABBIE   Eben!—ye mustn't—wait a spell—I want t' tell ye. . . .

EBEN   I'm a-goin' in t' git drunk. I'm a-goin' t' dance.

ABBIE   (*clinging to his arm—with passionate earnestness*)   If I could make it —'s if he'd never come up between us—if I could prove t' ye he wa'n't schemin' t' steal from ye—so's everythin' could be jest the same with us, lovin' each other jest the same, kissin' an' happy the same's we've been happy afore he come—if I could do it—ye'd love me agen, wouldn't ye? Ye'd kiss me again? Ye wouldn't never leave me, would ye?

EBEN   (*moved*)   I calc'late not. (*then shaking her hand off his arm—with a bitter smile*) But ye hain't God, be ye?

ABBIE   (*exultantly*)   Remember ye've promised! (*then with strange intensity*) Mebbe I kin take back one thin' God does!

EBEN   (*peering at her*)   Ye're gittin' cracked, hain't ye? (*then going towards door*) I'm a-goin' t' dance.

ABBIE (*calls after him intensely*) I'll prove t' ye! I'll prove I love ye better'n. . . . (*He goes in the door, not seeming to hear. She remains standing
where she is, looking after him—then she finishes desperately*) Better'n
anythin' else in the world!

SCENE THREE

(JUST *before dawn in the morning—shows the kitchen and* CABOT's *bedroom. In the kitchen, by the light of a tallow candle on the table,* EBEN *is sitting, his chin propped on his hands, his drawn face blank and expressionless.
His carpetbag is on the floor beside him. In the bedroom, dimly lighted by a
small whale-oil lamp,* CABOT *lies asleep.* ABBIE *is bending over the cradle,
listening, her face full of terror yet with an undercurrent of desperate
triumph. Suddenly, she breaks down and sobs, appears about to throw herself on her knees beside the cradle; but the old man turns restlessly, groaning
in his sleep, and she controls herself, and shrinking away from the cradle with
a gesture of horror, backs swiftly toward the door in rear and goes out. A moment later she comes into the kitchen and, running to* EBEN, *flings her arms
about his neck and kisses him wildly. He hardens himself, he remains un-
moved and cold, he keeps his eyes straight ahead.*)

ABBIE (*hysterically*) I done it, Eben! I told ye I'd do it! I've proved I
love ye—better'n everythin'—so's ye can't never doubt me no more!

EBEN (*dully*) Whatever ye done, it hain't no good now.

ABBIE (*wildly*) Don't ye say that! Kiss me, Eben, won't ye? I need ye t'
kiss me arter what I done! I need ye t' say ye love me!

EBEN (*kisses her without emotion—dully*) That's fur good-by. I'm a-goin'
soon.

ABBIE No! No! Ye won't go—not now!

EBEN (*going on with his own thoughts*) I been a-thinkin'—an' I hain't
goin' t' tell Paw nothin'. I'll leave Maw t' take vengeance on ye. If I told him,
the old skunk'd jest be stinkin' mean enuf to take it out on that baby. (*his voice
showing emotion in spite of him*) An' I don't want nothin' bad t' happen t'
him. He hain't t' blame fur yew. (*He adds with a certain queer pride*) An'
he looks like me! An' by God, he's mine! An' some day I'll be a-comin' back
an' . . . !

ABBIE (*too absorbed in her own thoughts to listen to him—pleadingly*)
They's no cause fur ye t' go now—they's no sense—it's all the same's it was
—they's nothin' come b'tween us now—arter what I done!

EBEN (*something in her voice arouses him. He stares at her a bit frightenedly.*) Ye look mad, Abbie. What did ye do?

ABBIE I—I killed him, Eben.

EBEN (*amazed*) Ye killed him?

ABBIE (*dully*) Ay-eh.

EBEN (*recovering from his astonishment—savagely*) An' serves him right!

But we got t' do somethin' quick t' make it look s'if the old skunk'd killed himself when he was drunk. We kin prove by 'em all how drunk he got. . . .

ABBIE (*wildly*) No! No! Not him! (*laughing distractedly*) But that's what I ought t' done, hain't it? I oughter killed him instead! Why didn't ye tell me?

EBEN (*appalled*) Instead? What d'ye mean?

ABBIE Not him.

EBEN (*his face grown ghastly*) Not—not that baby!

ABBIE (*dully*) Ay-eh!

EBEN (*falls to his knees as if he'd been struck—his voice trembling with horror*) Oh, God A'mighty! A'mighty God! Maw, whar was ye, why didn't ye stop her?

ABBIE (*simply*) She went back t' her grave that night we fust done it, remember? I hain't felt her about since. (*A pause.* EBEN *hides his head in his hands, trembling all over as if he had the ague. She goes on dully*) I left the piller over his little face. Then he killed himself. He stopped breathin'. (*She begins to weep softly.*)

EBEN (*rage beginning to mingle with grief*) He looked like me. He was mine, damn ye!

ABBIE (*slowly and brokenly*) I didn't want t' do it. I hated myself fur doin' it. I loved him. He was so purty—dead spit 'n' image o' yew. But I loved yew more—an' yew was goin' away—far off whar I'd never see ye agen, never kiss ye, never feel ye pressed agin me agen—an' ye said ye hated me fur havin' him—ye said ye hated him an' wished he was dead—ye said if it hadn't been fur him comin' it'd be the same's afore between us.

EBEN (*unable to endure this, springs to his feet in a fury, threatening her, his twitching fingers seeming to reach out for her throat*) Ye lie! I never said —I never dreamed ye'd—I'd cut off my head afore I'd hurt his finger!

ABBIE (*piteously, sinking on her knees*) Eben, don't ye look at me like that—hatin' me—not after what I done fur ye—fur us—so's we could be happy agen—

EBEN (*furiously now*) Shut up, or I'll kill ye! I see yer game now—the same old sneakin' trick—ye're aimin' t' blame me fur the murder ye done!

ABBIE (*moaning—putting her hands over her ears*) Don't ye, Eben! Don't ye! (*She grasps his legs.*)

EBEN (*his mood suddenly changing to horror, shrinks away from her*) Don't ye tech me! Ye're pizen! How could ye—t' murder a pore little critter — Ye must've swapped yer soul t' hell! (*sudden raging*) Ha! I kin see why ye done it! Not the lies ye jest told—but 'cause ye wanted t' steal agen— steal the last thin' ye'd left me—my part o' him—no, the hull o' him—ye saw he looked like me—ye knowed he was all mine—an' ye couldn't b'ar it —I know ye! Ye killed him fur bein' mine! (*All this has driven him almost insane. He makes a rush past her for the door—then turns—shaking both fists at her, violently.*) But I'll take vengeance now! I'll git the Sheriff! I'll tell him everythin'! Then I'll sing "I'm off to Californi-a!" an' go—gold —Golden Gate—gold sun—fields o' gold in the West! (*This last he half*

shouts, half croons incoherently, suddenly breaking off passionately)
a-goin' fur the Sheriff t' come an' git ye! I want ye tuk away, locked up from
me! I can't stand t' luk at ye! Murderer an' thief 'r not, ye still tempt me!
I'll give ye up t' the Sheriff! (*He turns and runs out, around the corner of
house, panting and sobbing, and breaks into a swerving sprint down the road.*)

ABBIE (*struggling to her feet, runs to the door, calling after him*) I love
ye, Eben! I love ye! (*She stops at the door weakly, swaying, about to fall.*) I
don't care what ye do—if ye'll on'y love me agen—if ye'll on'y love me! (*She
falls limply to the floor in a faint.*)

SCENE FOUR

(*About an hour later. Same as Scene Three. Shows the kitchen and
CABOT's bedroom. It is after dawn. The sky is brilliant with the sunrise. In the
kitchen, ABBIE sits at the table, her body limp and exhausted, her head bowed
down over her arms, her face hidden. Upstairs, CABOT is still asleep but
awakens with a start. He looks toward the window and gives a snort of surprise and irritation—throws back the covers and begins hurriedly pulling on
his clothes. Without looking behind him, he begins talking to ABBIE whom
he supposes beside him.*)

CABOT Thunder 'n' lightnin', Abbie! I hain't slept this late in fifty year!
Looks 's if the sun was full riz a'most. Must've been the dancin' an' likker.
Must be gittin' old. I hope Eben's t'wuk. Ye might've tuk the trouble t' rouse
me, Abbie. (*He turns—sees no one there—surprised*) Waal—whar air she?
Gittin' vittles, I calc'late. (*He tiptoes to the cradle and peers down—proudly*)
Mornin', sonny. Purty's a picter! Sleepin' sound. He don't beller all night
like most o' 'em. (*He goes quietly out the door in rear—a few moments later
enters kitchen—sees ABBIE—with satisfaction*) So thar ye be. Ye got any vittles
cooked?

ABBIE (*without moving*) No.

CABOT (*coming to her, almost sympathetically*) Ye feelin' sick?

ABBIE No.

CABOT (*pats her on shoulder. She shudders.*) Ye'd best lie down a spell.
(*half jocularly*) Yer son'll be needin' ye soon. He'd ought t' wake up with a
gnashin' appetite, the sound way he's sleepin'.

ABBIE (*shudders—then in a dead voice*) He ain't never goin' to wake up.

CABOT (*jokingly*) Takes after me this mornin'. I ain't slept so late in . . . .

ABBIE He's dead.

CABOT (*stares at her—bewilderedly*) What . . . .

ABBIE I killed him.

CABOT (*stepping back from her—aghast*) Air ye drunk—'r crazy—'r . . . !

ABBIE (*suddenly lifts her head and turns on him—wildly*) I killed him, I
tell ye! I smothered him. Go up an' see if ye don't b'lieve me! (*CABOT stares
at her a second, then bolts out the rear door, can be heard bounding up the
stairs, and rushes into the bedroom and over to the cradle. ABBIE has sunk

...er former position. CABOT *puts his hand down on the body ... ...pression of fear and horror comes over his face.*)

...nking away—tremblingly) God A'mighty! God A'mighty. (*He ... out the door—in a short while returns to the kitchen—comes to ... the stunned expression still on his face—hoarsely*) Why did ye do it? ...y? (*As she doesn't answer, he grabs her violently by the shoulder and ...nakes her.*) I ax ye why ye done it! Ye'd better tell me 'r . . . !

ABBIE (*gives him a furious push which sends him staggering back and springs to her feet—with wild rage and hatred*) Don't ye dare tech me! What right hev ye t' question me 'bout him? He wa'n't yewr son! Think I'd have a son by yew? I'd die fust! I hate the sight o' ye an' allus did! It's yew I should've murdered, if I'd had good sense! I hate ye! I love Eben. I did from the fust. An' he was Eben's son—mine an' Eben's—not your'n!

CABOT (*stands looking at her dazedly—a pause—finding his words with an effort—dully*) That was it—what I felt—pokin' round the corners—while ye lied—holdin' yerself from me—sayin' ye'd a'ready conceived— (*He lapses into crushed silence—then with a strange emotion*) He's dead, sart'n. I felt his heart. Pore little critter! (*He blinks back one tear, wiping his sleeve across his nose.*)

ABBIE (*hysterically*) Don't ye! Don't ye! (*She sobs unrestrainedly.*)

CABOT (*with a concentrated effort that stiffens his body into a rigid line and hardens his face into a stony mask—through his teeth to himself*) I got t' be—like a stone—a rock o' jedgment! (*A pause. He gets complete control over himself—harshly*) If he was Eben's, I be glad he air gone! An' mebbe I suspicioned it all along. I felt they was somethin' onnateral—somewhars— the house got so lonesome—an' cold—drivin' me down t' the barn—t' the beasts o' the field. . . . Ay-eh. I must've suspicioned—somethin'. Ye didn't fool me—not altogether, leastways—I'm too old a bird—growin' ripe on the bough. . . . (*He becomes aware he is wandering, straightens again, looks at* ABBIE *with a cruel grin.*) So ye'd liked t' hev murdered me 'stead o' him, would ye? Waal, I'll live to a hundred! I'll live t' see ye hung! I'll deliver ye up t' the jedgment o' God an' the law! I'll git the Sheriff now. (*starts for the door*)

ABBIE (*dully*) Ye needn't. Eben's gone fur him.

CABOT (*amazed*) Eben—gone fur the Sheriff?

ABBIE Ay-eh.

CABOT T' inform agen ye?

ABBIE Ay-eh.

CABOT (*considers this—a pause—then in a hard voice*) Waal, I'm thankful fur him savin' me the trouble. I'll git t' wuk. (*He goes to the door—then turns—in a voice full of strange emotion*) He'd ought t' been my son, Abbie. Ye'd ought t' loved me. I'm a man. If ye'd loved me, I'd never told no Sheriff on ye no matter what ye did, if they was t' brile me alive!

ABBIE (*defensively*) They's more to it nor yew know, makes him tell.

CABOT (*dryly*) Fur yewr sake, I hope they be. (*He goes out—comes around to the gate—stares up at the sky. His control relaxes. For a moment he is old and weary. He murmurs despairingly)* God A'mighty, I be lonesomer'n ever! *(He hears running footsteps from the left, immediately is himself again.* EBEN *runs in, panting exhaustedly, wild-eyed and mad looking. He lurches through the gate.* CABOT *grabs him by the shoulder.* EBEN *stares at him dumbly.)* Did ye tell the Sheriff?

EBEN   *(nodding stupidly)*   Ay-eh.

CABOT   *(gives him a push away that sends him sprawling—laughing with withering contempt)*   Good fur ye! A prime chip o' yer Maw ye be! *(He goes toward the barn, laughing harshly.* EBEN *scrambles to his feet. Suddenly* CABOT *turns—grimly threatening.)* Git off this farm when the Sheriff takes her—or, by God, he'll have t' come back an' git me fur murder, too! *(He stalks off.* EBEN *does not appear to have heard him. He runs to the door and comes into the kitchen.* ABBIE *looks up with a cry of anguished joy.* EBEN *stumbles over and throws himself on his knees beside her—sobbing brokenly.)*

EBEN   Fergive me!

ABBIE   *(happily)*   Eben! *(She kisses him and pulls his head over against her breast.)*

EBEN   I love ye! Fergive me!

ABBIE   *(ecstatically)*   I'd fergive ye all the sins in hell fur sayin' that! *(She kisses his head, pressing it to her with a fierce passion of possession.)*

EBEN   *(brokenly)*   But I told the Sheriff. He's comin' fur ye!

ABBIE   I kin b'ar what happens t' me—now!

EBEN   I woke him up. I told him. He says, wait 'til I git dressed. I was waiting. I got to thinkin' o' yew. I got to thinkin' how I'd loved ye. It hurt like somethin' was bustin' in my chest an' head. I got t' cryin'. I knowed sudden I loved ye yet, an' allus would love ye!

ABBIE   *(caressing his hair—tenderly)*   My boy, hain't ye?

EBEN   I begun t' run back. I cut across the fields an' through the woods. I thought ye might have time t' run away—with me—an' . . . .

ABBIE   *(shaking her head)*   I got t' take my punishment—t' pay fur my sin.

EBEN   Then I want t' share it with ye.

ABBIE   Ye didn't do nothin'.

EBEN   I put it in yer head. I wisht he was dead! I as much as urged ye t' do it!

ABBIE   No. It was me alone!

EBEN   I'm as guilty as yew be! He was the child o' our sin.

ABBIE   *(lifting her head as if defying God)*   I don't repent that sin! I hain't askin' God t' fergive that!

EBEN   Nor me—but it led up t' the other—an' the murder ye did, ye did 'count o' me—an' it's my murder, too, I'll tell the Sheriff—an' if ye deny it, I'll say we planned it t'gether—an' they'll all b'lieve me, fur they suspicion everythin' we've done, an' it'll seem likely an' true to 'em. An' it is true— way down. I did help ye—somehow.

ABBIE   (*laying her head on his—sobbing*)   No! I don't want yew t' suffer!

EBEN   I got t' pay fur my part o' the sin! An' I'd suffer wuss leavin' ye, goin' West, thinkin' o' ye day an' night, bein' out when yew was in—(*Lowering his voice*)—'r bein' alive when yew was dead. (*a pause*) I want t' share with ye, Abbie—prison 'r death 'r hell 'r anythin'! (*He looks into her eyes and forces a trembling smile.*) If I'm sharin' with ye, I won't feel lonesome, leastways.

ABBIE   (*weakly*)   Eben! I won't let ye! I can't let ye!

EBEN   (*kissing her—tenderly*)   Ye can't he'p yerself. I got ye beat fur once!

ABBIE   (*forcing a smile—adoringly*)   I hain't beat—s'long's I got ye!

EBEN   (*hears the sound of feet outside*)   Ssshh! Listen! They've come t' take us!

ABBIE   No, it's him. Don't give him no chance to fight ye, Eben. Don't say nothin'—no matter what he says. An' I won't, neither. (*It is* CABOT. *He comes up from the barn in a great state of excitement and strides into the house and then into the kitchen.* EBEN *is kneeling beside* ABBIE, *his arm around her, hers around him. They stare straight ahead.*)

CABOT   (*stares at them, his face hard. A long pause—vindictively*)   Ye make a slick pair o' murderin' turtle doves! Ye'd ought t' be both hung on the same limb an' left thar t' swing in the breeze an' rot—a warnin' t' old fools like me t' b'ar their lonesomeness alone—an' fur young fools like ye t' hobble their lust. (*a pause. The excitement returns to his face, his eyes snap, he looks a bit crazy.*) I couldn't work today. I couldn't take no interest. T' hell with the farm! I'm leavin' it! I've turned the cows an' other stock loose! I've druv 'em into the woods whar they kin be free! By freein' 'em, I'm freein' myself! I'm quittin' here today! I'll set fire t' house an' barn an' watch 'em burn, an' I'll leave yer Maw t' haunt the ashes, an' I'll will the fields back t' God, so that nothin' human kin never touch 'em! I'll be a-goin' to Californi-a—t' jine Simeon an' Peter—true sons o' mine if they be dumb fools—an' the Cabots'll find Solomon's Mines t'gether! (*He suddenly cuts a mad caper.*) Whoop! What was the song they sung? "Oh, Californi-a! That's the land fur me." (*He sings this— then gets on his knees by the floorboard under which the money was hid.*) An' I'll sail thar on one o' the finest clippers I kin find! I've got the money! Pity ye didn't know whar this was hidden so's ye could steal . . . . (*He has pulled up the board. He stares—feels—stares again. A pause of dead silence. He slowly turns, slumping into a sitting position on the floor, his eyes like those of a dead fish, his face the sickly green of an attack of nausea. He swallows painfully several times—forces a weak smile at last.*) So—ye did steal it!

EBEN   (*emotionlessly*)   I swapped it t' Sim an' Peter fur their share o' the farm—t' pay their passage t' Californi-a.

CABOT   (*with one sardonic*)   Ha! (*He begins to recover. Gets slowly to his feet—strangely*)   I calc'late God give it to 'em—not yew! God's hard, not easy! Mebbe they's easy gold in the West but it hain't God's gold. It hain't fur me. I kin hear His voice warnin' me agen t' be hard an' stay on my farm. I kin see his hand usin' Eben t' steal t' keep me from weakness. I kin feel I be **in** the palm o' His hand, His fingers guidin' me. (*A pause—then he mutters* *sadly*) It's a-goin' t' be lonesomer now than ever it war afore—an' I'm gittin' old, Lord—ripe on the bough. . . . (*then stiffening*) Waal—what d'ye want? God's lonesome, hain't He? God's hard an' lonesome! (*a pause. The Sheriff with two men comes up the road from the left. They move cautiously to the door. The Sheriff knocks on it with the butt of his pistol.*)

SHERIFF   Open in the name o' the law! (*They start.*)

CABOT   They've come fur ye. (*He goes to the rear door.*) Come in, Jim! (*The three men enter.* CABOT *meets them in doorway.*) Jest a minit, Jim. I got 'em safe here. (*The Sheriff nods. He and his companions remain in the doorway.*)

EBEN   (*suddenly calls*)   I lied this mornin,' Jim. I helped her to do it. Ye kin take me, too.

ABBIE   (*brokenly*)   No!

CABOT   Take 'em both. (*He comes forward—stares at* EBEN *with a trace of grudging admiration.*) Purty good—fur yew! Waal, I got t' round up the stock. Good-by.

EBEN   Good-by.

ABBIE   Good-by. (CABOT *turns and strides past the men—comes out and around the corner of the house, his shoulders squared, his face stony, and stalks grimly toward the barn. In the meantime the Sheriff and men have come into the room.*)

SHERIFF   (*embarrassedly*)   Waal—we'd best start.

ABBIE   Wait. (*turns to* EBEN) I love ye, Eben.

EBEN   I love ye, Abbie. (*They kiss. The three men grin and shuffle embarrassedly.* EBEN *takes* ABBIE'S *hand. They go out the door in rear, the men following, and come from the house, walking hand in hand to the gate.* EBEN *stops there and points to the sunrise sky.*) Sun's a-rizin'. Purty, hain't it?

ABBIE   Ay-eh. (*They both stand for a moment looking up raptly in attitudes strangely aloof and devout.*)

SHERIFF   (*looking around at the farm enviously—to his companion*)   It's a jim-dandy farm, no denyin'. Wished I owned it!

(*The Curtain Falls*)

1924

Reading Suggestions

Some of O'Neill's early one-act plays, especially those which draw on his experience as a sailor, are among his most interesting works: *Bound East for Cardiff, In the Zone, The Long Voyage Home,* and *Moon of the Caribbees.* Among the better full-length plays of a later period are *Anna Christie, The Emperor Jones, The Hairy Ape,* and his only comedy, *Ah, Wilderness!* His longest and most ambitious plays are *Strange Interlude* and *Mourning Becomes Electra.*

There is no complete edition; the most voluminous collection is *The Plays of Eugene O'Neill* (1934-1935), in twelve volumes. Other works are *Lost*

Plays of Eugene O'Neill, edited by Lawrence Gellert (1950); *The Iceman Cometh* (1946); *A Moon for the Misbegotten* (1952); *Long Day's Journey into Night* (1956); *A Touch of the Poet* (1957); and *Hughie* (1959).

The most recent and most detailed biography is Crosswell Bowen, *The Curse of the Misbegotten* (1959). Barrett H. Clark, *Eugene O'Neill: The Man and His Plays*, revised edition (1947), is still valuable. An excellent shorter study is Hamilton Basso, "The Tragic Sense," *New Yorker* (February 28, March 6, 13, 1948). A very illuminating interview is reported in Mary B. Mullett, "The Extraordinary Story of Eugene O' Neill," *American Magazine* (November 1922).

The most recent and valuable book of criticism is Doris V. Falk, *Eugene O'Neill and the Tragic Tension* (1958). Edwin A. Engel, *The Haunted Heroes of Eugene O'Neill* (1953) is also useful. Notable shorter criticisms are Bonamy Dobrée, "The Plays of Eugene O'Neill," *Southern Review* (Winter 1937); Frederic I. Carpenter, "The Romantic Tragedy of Eugene O'Neill," *American Literature and the Dream* (1955); Philip Weissman, "Conscious and Unconscious Autobiographical Dramas of Eugene O'Neill," *Journal of the American Psychoanalytic Association* (July 1957); Roger Asselineau, "Mourning Becomes Electra as a Tragedy," *Modern Drama* (December 1958); and three essays by Joseph Wood Krutch: "The Tragic Fallacy," *The Modern Temper* (1956); "Tragedy: Eugene O'Neill," *The American Drama since 1918* (1938); and "O'Neill's Tragic Sense," *American Scholar* (Summer 1947).

Biography

Eugene O'Neill was born in New York City, October 16, 1888. He got his education touring with his father's acting company, attending Catholic boarding schools, Betts Academy, and Princeton (where he did not quite complete his freshman year); later by working as a common sailor and living as a common derelict in Buenos Aires and New York, working as a reporter on the New London, Connecticut, *Telegraph*, reading and writing plays during a six-months' confinement in a tuberculosis sanatorium, and attending Professor George Pierce Baker's playwriting class, the 47 Workshop, at Harvard during the 1914-1915 term.

His professional career had begun, rather tentatively, with the publication, at his father's expense, of five one-act plays in the summer of 1914. It was not until 1916 that he met the Provincetown Players, who produced *Bound East for Cardiff* and *Thirst* that summer and many of O'Neill's best plays thereafter. From that point on, his success grew, first in critical esteem and before long in popularity: in 1920 *Beyond the Horizon* was produced in New York, ran for 111 performances, grossed $117,071, and paid O'Neill $7,600; in 1922 his royalties were running about $850 a week. Some of his most successful plays in this period were *The Emperor Jones* (1920), *Anna Christie* (1921), *The Hairy Ape* (1922), *Desire under the Elms* and *The Great God Brown* (1924), *Strange Interlude* (1928), *Mourning Becomes Electra* (1931), and *Ah, Wilderness!* (1933). There were also some less successful plays and several failures, one of which was *Days without End* (1934), the last play of O'Neill's to be newly produced for twelve years.

O'Neill had not stopped writing; he was working on a cycle of eleven plays tracing the history of an American family from the eighteenth century to the present. This work, however, was increasingly hampered by the fact that

O'Neill had Parkinson's disease, one symptom of which is a progressively more severe palsy. The cycle was never finished, and only one play belonging to it has been produced: *A Touch of the Poet,* posthumously, in 1958. Two other new plays were produced in O'Neill's lifetime: *The Iceman Cometh* (1946) and *A Moon for the Misbegotten* (1947). O'Neill died in 1953, and one other play, *Long Day's Journey into Night,* was produced posthumously in 1956.

O'Neill was much less successful in his personal than in his professional career. He was first married to Kathleen Jenkins, in 1909, without the consent of her parents or of his own. The results were that he was bundled off on an unfruitful gold-hunting expedition to Honduras; a son, Eugene Jr., was born in 1910; and the parents were divorced in 1912. In the fall of 1917 O'Neill met Agnes Boulton, a short-story writer; he took her to Provincetown for the winter, and married her in the spring. His second son, Shane, was born in 1919, his daughter Oona in 1925. In 1928 O'Neill went to Europe with Carlotta Monterey, deserting Agnes and the children; he divorced Agnes in 1929, and married Carlotta. His son Shane became a drug addict during World War II. In 1943 his daughter Oona, eighteen, married Charles Chaplin, who was just a year younger than her father. O'Neill severed all relations with her; however, the marriage turned out very well. In 1950 Eugene O'Neill, Jr., who had been a brilliant classical scholar at Yale, committed suicide. When O'Neill died, he left his estate to Carlotta, and specifically cut off both Shane and Oona.

The errors and misfortunes of his life may be reflected in some of the darker aspects of his work; they serve, at any rate, to present a dark background for the public recognition represented by his award of three Pulitzer prizes, the first in 1920, an honorary degree from Yale in 1926, and the Nobel prize in 1936.

Poets of belief and skepticism:
1. Robinson, Edwin Arlington (1869-1935)
2. Frost, Robert (1875-1963)
3. Lindsay, Vachel (1879-1931)
4. Jeffers, Robinson, (1887-
5. Sandburg, Carl (1878-
6. Eliot, Thomas Stearns (1888-
7. Tate, Allen (1899-

Robinson: attitude toward life
is calm, rather gloomy.
He did not use free verse, yet
his dialogues are like ordinary speech.
His poems show a sympathy and
understanding of human nature.
His long Arthurian poems all
end gloomily, after long passages
of beauty. His short poems
are character sketches.

Robinson protégé of President
Theodore Roosevelt. He was not
concerned with social problems,
but he was interested in
portraying characters that he knew
during his days of poverty.

EDWIN ARLINGTON

Poet of belief
and skepticism

ROBINSON ✦

1869-1935

His poetry reveals a restless,
uncertain, but persistent search for
moral values.

Technically, he is very precise.

Terribly interested in the Middle Ages.

With Henry Adams, Robinson recoiled
from the collapse of 19th century
idealism his undying faith in humanity and,
thus, fortified in made out to meet
the dragon of modern
scientific determinism.

Accepted tragedy & life without
complaint. Perhaps had self in mind:
"Where was he going, this man
   against the sky?
You know not, nor do I."

ROBINSON

Sources & Materials:
Heir to the idealism & Emerson
and the skepticism & Dickinson,
Robinson looked about him in
his native Gardiner, Maine,
and learned to write and find
poetry in the lives & his
fellow townsmen.

His Tilbury Town anticipated by
many years Winesburg, Ohio & dint
Sherwood Anderson, and there Gopher -to most
Prairie, Minnesota & Sinclair
Lewis, as capsules of most
human experience.

Introduction

In his introduction to Robinson's posthumous *King Jasper*, Robert Frost characterized Robinson as a poet who, in the midst of poetic revolt, "stayed content with the old-fashioned way to be new." Frost admired the restraint that never let grief "go further than it could in play," and in this relation between sadness and humor he discovered the supreme quality of Robinson's style. "If it is with outer seriousness, it must be with inner humor. If it is with outer humor, it must be with inner seriousness. Neither one alone without the other . . . will do."

Neither Frost nor Robinson owed his art to the poetic renascence that made such a stir and created so many unsubstantial reputations (largely through Harriet Monroe's establishing the magazine *Poetry* in 1912 and Ezra Pound's genius for espousing movements). But the Imagists, especially the flamboyant Amy Lowell, accepted Robinson as a pioneer of the new poetry, as indeed he had been, in his rejection of a stock "poetic" language, for almost twenty lonely years while poetry was at its nadir. In a country that abandoned the artist to a terrifying isolation, there was no finer example than Robinson of dedication to art. In 1916 one of the Imagists, John Gould Fletcher, observed that Robinson's "lonely integrity in defeat" was "utterly alien to most Americans."

Henry Adams had remarked that ever since the youth of Emerson the feeling for religion and poetry had vanished in the American male, so that the poet had "no choice but to appeal to the woman." In Gardiner, Maine, where Robinson grew up, and in his own family, he might study not only the indifference and hostility to art and intellect but also the failure that overtook all sorts and conditions of men, including those who had smugly put their trust in material success. His father, who opposed higher education as impractical, lost a considerable fortune in the panic of 1893. After this financial collapse, the business-minded son, Herman, took to drink, developed tuberculosis, and died alone in a public ward of the Boston City Hospital. Meanwhile, the intellectually brilliant son, Horace Dean, sacrificing a career in medical research to a country practice, had died a victim of morphine and liquor. Small wonder that Edwin, of whom it was asked what he intended to do, adopted an ironic attitude toward the national obsession with mere external success and became the laureate of failure in one psychological portrait after another, like that of Bewick Finzer, in whose brain "something crumbled" "when his half million went."

In his recognition of failure and suffering Robinson was as naturalistic as a Zola might wish; but Robinson's naturalism was accompanied by a "desperate hope," in Hyatt Waggoner's phrase, that the mechanistic world view of the late nineteenth century did not rule out the claims of idealistic philosophy and poetry. As a poet, Robinson accepted the romantic affirmations of Wordsworth, Carlyle, and Emerson, although their doctrinal apparatus had attenuated in him to a mere stubborn faith, expressed in "Credo":

> I know the far-sent message of the years,
> I feel the coming glory of the Light!

In 1915, at the height of his powers, he attacked mechanistic naturalism in "The Man against the Sky," a poem that he regarded as one of his two best, the other being the character portrayal, "Rembrandt to Rembrandt." Both illustrate his dual interests: belief in a cosmic purpose—the "Light," as he called it—and integrity of character despite suffering and defeat. For Robinson outward success often hid inner failure, as with Flammonde, the man "from God knows where," with a "small satanic sort of kink" in his brain, and Richard Cory, who went home "one calm summer night" and "put a bullet through his head." Alternately, outward failure could mask inner triumph, as with Rembrandt. Robinson always informs his subject with humor, pity, irony, and a sense of wonder—a commiserating and complex view best exemplified in some of the poems of medium length written during his early and middle period. Taking his own ordeal into account, it should not come as a surprise that Robinson discovered integrity, the quality he most admired, in the artistic career.

The early sonnets (1896–1902) provide adequate light on the emergence of Robinson's art. They are all finished products, for in his apprentice years Robinson was a close student of form, especially the medieval French verse forms, the ballade, villanelle, and triolet; titles like "Ballade by the Fire," "Ballade of Broken Flutes," and "Villanelle of Change" occur, and the famous "The House on the Hill" is also a villanelle. After his early period he dropped these strict forms, for the most part, but the mastery he had achieved through them he incorporated in such lyrics as "For a Dead Lady" and "Eros Turannos." He never abandoned the Italian sonnet, however, and he became one of the chief exponents of that form in

His quiet rebellion gave to Am. poetry an idiom that was in the native grain, and his leadership in the new movement was immediately around.

English, skillfully molding it to his own purposes of dramatic situation or characterization.

In these early sonnets one is struck by the names of those to whom, apparently, he is drawn by sympathy: George Crabbe, the realistic poet of rural poverty at the beginning of the century; Thomas Hood, a generation later, the poet of comic and ironic pity; Zola, another generation later, the implacable realist in fiction; and finally Erasmus, the great Dutch humanist and religious reformer of the early sixteenth century. One perceives that the common denominator among these personalities of such varying capabilities and fame is the appeal that their forthright honesty made to Robinson. This direct appeal, however, as in "Zola," does not permit Robinson to rise above the prose level of angry statement against a "squeamish and emasculate" public. The mechanically contrived paradox that God's heart is human and man's divine scarcely achieves the poetic transmutation.

"Cliff Klingenhagen" begins to operate on a higher level of humorous and ironic ambiguity. Cliff Klingenhagen, who belongs to the honest lineage of Robinson's intellectual heroes, has the speaker in to dinner and afterward fills two glasses, one with wormwood, the other with wine; drinking the wormwood, he offers the wine to his guest, who at the close of the sonnet, wonders a long time when he will be as happy as Cliff Klingenhagen. The paradox is obvious; yet it provides the kind of puzzle that Robinson was to employ with increasing mastery of implication. It compels the reader to ponder the image of Klingenhagen drinking wormwood; in such a gesture lies the deeper mystery or paradox of the poem as of life—the inexplicable happiness resulting from a stoic regard for the human condition. This sonnet begins to reverberate with questions and meanings, as the one on Zola does not.

But "The Clerks" makes an even greater advance upon "Zola," though written at about the same time, for it goes the whole way toward metaphor. The poem humorously rebukes those who can see only the sublimity of poetry (or the glamour of royal descent) and fail to acknowledge, therefore, the dull work that goes into the making of greatness. They do not realize that poets and kings are "clerks of Time," "dry-goods" clerks measuring off calico, gingham, and muslin in such a Yankee general store as, evidently, Robinson had revisited after an interval. With a mild surprise he had noted the same old clerks, "a shop-worn brotherhood." This occasion Robinson imaginatively transmuted with a wry humor, as he took the dry-goods clerks to typify the poetic genius of all time. In rejecting the sentimental view that it must be marvelously sublime to be a poet, he ironically substituted the alternate view that it is rather tedious after all, since the stuff of poetry is "the same dull webs of discontent" piled toweringly high on the shelves. But in the most offhand manner, Robinson intensified the irony by remarking that, in spite of their "ancient air," the clerks were "just as good" "as in the days they dreamed of," and in this laconic observation paid his respects to the human qualities that endure.

I

"Luke Havergal," "Isaac and Archibald," "For a Dead Lady," "Eros Turannos," and "Rembrandt to Rembrandt" extend our perception of Robinson's development from the 1890's to his full maturity in the early 1920's. One or another of these poems will illustrate Robinson's treatment of romantic themes, his classical sense of form, or his penetrating character portrayal.

"Luke Havergal" gains by being considered a companion piece to "The Book of Annandale," for "Luke Havergal" is an impressionistic mood study, in thirty-two lines, of a dead universe, and "The Book of Annandale" is a similarly impressionistic study, with almost no narrative in more than five hundred lines, of the theme of death and rebirth. Because "Luke Havergal" has had the benefit of close critical attention, it need not be examined minutely here. In a poem that depends on atmosphere for its effect, with a narrative scarcely even implied, the symbolical notation obviously becomes important. Luke has lost his beloved, so one must suppose, and a voice comes "out of a grave" to tell him to go to the western gate (a symbol for death), and there, in faith and trust, he is to listen for her call. There is a contrast between dark and the west, on the one hand, and on the other, dawn and eastern skies, but only for the purpose, evidently, of denying the light; the impression, altogether, is that of a dead universe without meaning. "God slays Himself with every leaf that flies," and the darkness of the universe is matched by "the fiery night that's in your eyes." Both the cosmic and the personal situations dictate suicide, because "the dark [cosmic death] will end the dark [personal loss], if anything." To reenforce the vision of gloom, Luke is told in the last stanza that the words uttered by the leaves are dead and that he will not "feel them as they fall."

If the poem, as Robinson confessed, is "a piece of deliberate degeneration," Luke must be regarded as a hallucinated neurotic who projects his own voice from the grave out of a hope for reunion with his beloved, a hope that is aborted by the melancholy realities of a dead universe. And here is the cruel dilemma for Luke, who believes, presumably, in a love beyond the grave and, at the same time, lives in a universe without meaning. The third stanza presents this confused, vague neurotic state with its two contradictory reasons for suicide simultaneously entertained. In a dead world (lines 17–20) love can have no meaning, and suicide is to be contemplated solely on universal grounds; suicide, indeed, for personal reasons would blind "you to the way that you must go" toward utter annihilation, since, presumably a lover's death would unite him with his beloved and would therefore, in some sense, be an affirmation of life antagonistic to the universal death. In lines 21–24 this lover's reason for suicide is presented, yet scarcely in language precise enough to differentiate it from the other, because in a dead cosmos words cannot render meanings, only vague moods. With a poem like "Luke Havergal," however, one must exercise caution, and since there are other interpretations, whichever a reader chooses, he must realize that the symbolic rendition of a neurotic mood transcends any precise meaning, and that in spite of all the critical disagreement "Luke Havergal" remains a lyric masterpiece of its kind.

By contrast, "The Book of Annandale" is something of a failure, though worth exploring for its interesting manipulation of romantic themes. As in "Luke Havergal," the narrative is impressionistically vague. The story suggests the growth of love between George Annandale, whose wife has just died, and Damaris, who five years earlier had lost a husband to whom she had promised lasting faithfulness. The poem stresses the growth of personality and of consciousness, a groping toward freedom, rebirth out of death. The book that Annandale had been writing, without quite understanding it, becomes the symbol of dynamic growth, of unconscious motivation, and of the ultimate union of Annandale and Damaris, whose face it was that had intruded upon his drowsed awareness. Significantly, Damaris is capable of seeing the Light, and she reacts vigorously to the words of Annandale's book, for they embody what "had for long been variously at work in her." Like "Luke Havergal," this poem has an autumnal setting, but in the contrast between death in the one poem and renewed life in the other, perhaps the most telling symbolic device is words—dead words in the first poem, living and eternal words in the second.

By itself "Luke Havergal" (1896) might appear to be only the chance product of a neurotic romanticism that flourished hectically in the 1890's. But it is more proper to regard it as an early statement in Robinson's developing view embracing the questions of personality, consciousness, and man's relation to the cosmos in terms of the choice between suicide and life and between a mechanistic and therefore dead universe and a living and purposive universe. "The Book of Annandale" (1902) is an affirmative response to the negations in "Luke Havergal," and "The Man against the Sky" (1916) is a repudiation of a mechanistic universe. In Robinson's weighing of all these questions across a span of twenty years one cannot fail to see in the background, whatever other literary and philosophical influences there were, the presence of one book—Carlyle's *Sartor Resartus*, which had a lasting influence on Robinson.

"For a Dead Lady" and "Eros Turannos" are Robinson's best lyrics, and they are among the best in the language; but they may be dealt with briefly, since Louis Coxe and Richard Adams have analyzed them expertly, and the reader will want to consult their essays. Yet several matters may be stressed here.

In "For a Dead Lady" the shift from the terms of Greek myth in the second stanza to the terms of mechanistic law in the third is managed so easily that a reader, impressed by the beautiful elegiac tone, may not be aware of the shift. But when he becomes aware he will grant the rightness of it, especially when the poem ends on a note of skepticism that universalizes human experience from the Greek to the modern: we do not know what "inexorable cause" makes such "vicious" reaping. When man confronts the discrepancy between human beauty and values and the cruel waste of nature he experiences what has been called the cosmic chill; and "For a Dead Lady" is an aesthetic record of that temperature.

The situation in "Eros Turannos" may be readily inferred. The woman has a worthless husband, but she would rather endure him than live alone, and she is indifferent to the gossip of the town. The poem suggests that the man is a social parasite, "allured" solely by the tradition that she represents. As the domestic tragedy unfolds, the perceptive reader discerns that, in a very real sense, the man matters not at all, for the denouement pictures a woman in the throes of a passion that the mythic-minded Greek understood. Hers has been a high, supra-human fate to strive with a god, and, as the significant title indicates, the god has prevailed. Both "For a Dead Lady" and "Eros Turannos" have the large abstract quality of myth, a poise and serenity that Robinson derived from his practice of French forms and his interest in Greek tragedy.

II

"Isaac and Archibald" (1902) and "Rembrandt to Rembrandt" (1921) are Robinson's highest achievements. The Rembrandt poem is distinctly superior to the favorite anthology piece, "Ben Jonson Entertains a Man from Stratford" (1916). And "The Man Against the Sky," however human its protest against a mechanistic universe, remains flat prose statement; "Isaac and Archibald," on the contrary, is a happy fusion of all the elements likely to ensure long life to a score of Robinson's poems. "Isaac and Archibald" is, moreover, at the center of his most deeply felt mythic enterprise, the creation of Tilbury Town, an imaginary New England community, undoubtedly inspired by Gardiner. In poem after poem it provided the background for wry destinies, false successes, real failures and tragedies, and it anticipated by many years the mythic communities of Edgar Lee Masters, Sherwood Anderson, and Sinclair Lewis. More than half of the selections that follow are Tilbury Town poems, as well as "Bewick Finzer," "Richard Cory," "The House on the Hill," "Flammonde," and others that are not included. In such poems Robinson delineated human destiny in the large, abstract, and typifying manner of all myth, rendering each particular life with the awareness of timeless significance.

In the narrative setting of a walk that a boy takes from Tilbury Town with one old man to visit another in the country, "Isaac and Archibald" unfolds a rich thematic and symbolical pattern as well as a complex arrangement of points of view. The boy sees Isaac and Archibald humorously and imaginatively, and they see him both as a recipient of their worried confidences about each other and also as a young innocent to be initiated into the lessons of experience. These points of view are bound together in the note of piety struck by the mature man who once was that boy and who now reminisces: "I may have laughed at them," "but I must have honored them."

Isaac himself is pious, thanking God for good things like water, at the pump during the hot walk, and cider, later in Archibald's cellar. When he confides in the boy he expatiates on the difference between the boy's innocence and a grown man's experience, and he keeps his talk on this personal level by asking the boy to remember him and the moment. In contrast to Archibald, "with one hand on his back" and limping with "his huge-headed cane," Isaac is a vigorous old man, striding in the sun on the five-mile walk, "like something out of Homer—powerful and awful"; and as the narrative progresses, the boy identifies him with Ulysses.

The boy decides, however, that Archibald "had no heroics" and that "his white beard was too long/ And too straight down to be like things in Homer." If Isaac is Homeric he is also, therefore, simple; but Archibald is philosophical, and he does not ask the boy to remember him, but "the light behind the stars." All creatures (and even "the weed there at your feet") are "children of the sun," and Archibald, who is now "in the shadow," exhorts the boy to "live to see clearly" and the light will come to him. Then when his time comes "to say it," he is to say it. Both Isaac's and Archibald's talks give a sense of invocation, the one at the human level, the other at the philosophical. One of the finest touches in emblematic characterization remains to be mentioned: in a poem that is always gently humorous, Isaac, in his "commendable unrest," is identified with "a thing so nervous as an ant," and Archibald, in his "sepulchral" cellar, is identified with the cricket that "feeds on darkness." The triumph is that in a poem so colloquially Yankee and so philosophically Greek, Robinson should have introduced, so easily and without a jar, a motif reminiscent of Aesop.

The boy has Wordsworthian intuitions, and it is his ready submission to the romantic influences of nature, "the mightiness of the white sun," that breeds fancy and myth. At twilight he returns home, and in his dreams that night Isaac and Archibald become angels playing cards; in this manner the poem moves through a day that allegorically marks the passage of time, the transition from light to dark, from life to death. Here we reach the heart of the thematic development of the poem; if all things flow, what stay is there against time? Only in the imagination of the boy and the pious memory of the grown man can time be arrested in a timeless present:

> The present and the future and the past,
> Isaac and Archibald, the burning bush,
> The Trojans and the walls of Jericho,
> Were beautifully fused . . . .

Light imagery in the poem is impressive, as we have already noted, and in this key passage, which in the references to Troy and Jericho stresses the passage of time, there is likewise a culmination of light imagery in the example of the burning bush, a symbol of the immanence of divinity in the universe. The final commentary on such an altogether satisfactory poem ought to be that Robinson emphasizes here as elsewhere a sense of human values, the passing down from one generation to the next of the durable qualities of the human spirit; and this is no less intimated in the fusion of Yankee, Greek, and Hebraic elements than in explicit philosophical statements.

III

The impressiveness of "Rembrandt to Rembrandt" is enhanced by the knowledge of Rembrandt's life and work that a reader brings to the poem. Rembrandt's rise to eminence had been swift, and superficially it appeared that he had amassed great wealth. In 1639, then only thirty-three, he purchased a large house in Amsterdam, which was a great financial burden and contributed to his bankruptcy in 1656. In his earlier years, up to the 1640's, he was an extroverted Dutchman with no less a materialistic bent than others had. At the same time he indulged extravagant and imaginative tastes, and at auctions he bought not only paintings and curiosities but also unusual clothing. Many self-portraits show him in splendid costumes; but often enough, unless a formal portrait was commissioned, he appareled his subjects in the same manner.

In 1642 Rembrandt was commissioned to do a large portrait of the Civic Guard, or Shooting Company, of Captain Frans Banning Cocq; this is the picture referred to in lines 18–23 of Robinson's poem. Portraits of guilds and corporations were frequently commissioned, and artists like Frans Hals and van der Helst gave their subjects their money's worth, depicting them in full light so that they could be readily identified in the throng. Rembrandt's portraits of this kind are not merely groups of faces, however; they stress dramatic moments with the intensest human or psychological interest, as may be seen in his early "Anatomy Lesson of Dr. Nicolaes Tulp" (1632) and his late "The Syndics" (1662). The portrait of the Civic Guard, as one authority describes it, shows a burgher company issuing from a huge portal for a parade or shooting match; Rembrandt has caught them in motion before their captain commands a formation, and has therefore subordinated the individual portrait to a dynamic group action. For this reason many of the Civic Guard were displeased, but the legend that this picture was responsible for his loss of patronage is an exaggeration; and insofar as Robinson accepts the legend his portrayal of Rembrandt is defective on the score of historical fact.

Wisely, however, and characteristically, Robinson seized upon Rembrandt's artistic growth and integrity as his theme, and he saw Rembrandt's decline chiefly from that point of view. The portrait of the Civic Guard is a significant symptom of an artistic fulfillment that led consciously to Rembrandt's withdrawal from competition for public favor. Robinson concentrates upon an introspective moment as Rembrandt confronts a self-portrait of 1645 and anticipates his artistic loneliness in "the cold wash of Holland scorn." He tells himself that he must not expect Holland to understand his departure from the external realism of portraiture and still life for the penetrating study of human nature. But if the extrovert of the successful years has become the introvert of failure, we should let Jakob Rosenberg remind us that Rembrandt's nature swung from one extreme to the other, that "the sensuous and the spiritual Rembrandt are two component parts of one vital personality."

Robinson portrays a Rembrandt who faces his tragedy with unsparing insight. It is good, Rembrandt muses, that his wife Saskia has died, for had she survived she might not be able to endure the change in his fortunes. But Rembrandt is just as unsentimental in his view of himself. One of his demons cynically suggests that he pander to the popular taste, "Why not paint herrings, Rembrandt?" A wiser spirit, however, counsels a stoic indifference to circumstance, and a pursuit of art "as Apollo sees it." If with Saskia there is no sentimentality, so here there are no false heroics, for if Rembrandt's appraisal of his genius is egotistically high, there is an unflinching grandeur of purpose in his resolve.

The poem is dominated by Rembrandt's chiaroscuro, the "golden shadow," which is also Robinson's. From the start Rembrandt is aware of impending shadows in his life, and at the end of the poem he remarks that if he sighs for "wayside shouting" he may as well end it all in a ditch and "forget [his] darkness in the dark." But a powerful shaft of light falls athwart the dark expanse of the poem, as in so many of Rembrandt's pictures, not least the portrait of the Civic Guard. The light is the golden flood of inspiration that Rembrandt by implication compares to the sun itself (lines 179–186). No other subject provided Robinson with such an opportunity to apply his favorite metaphor so variously, and the conjunction of two such compatible artistic temperaments as those of Rembrandt and Robinson is one of the happiest in the history of the fructifying influence of one art upon another. In the long perspective of Robinson's development many of his most significant poems of the early and middle period receive their fulfillment in this poem. Finally, we should be taking an inadequate measure of "Rembrandt to Rembrandt" if we did not acknowl-

edge that it is also, very much, in its portrayal of ethical and artistic ideals,
"Robinson to Robinson." *Worth remembering that he*

is the man who achieved the greatest

of an essential martyrdom for his faith CARL F. STRAUCH

in the inescapable need of life in the spirit and in

A Note on the Text. The text of the poems is that of *The Children of*
the Night (Boston: R. C. Badger and Company, 1897), *The Town down*
the River (New York: Charles Scribner's Sons, 1910), or *Collected Poems*
(New York: The Macmillan Company, 1921, 1927, etc.). The reader
should consult the notes of acknowledgment to ascertain the text and
present copyright holder for each poem. The date of first book publication
is given at the end of each poem.

Technically he is very precise
He is a portrait painter giving
us an entire
gallery of memorable
figures.

CREDO

["Credo" represents Robinson's early quest for a philosophy. During his stay at
Harvard as a special student (1891-1893), Robinson met George Burnham, a
law student interested in Oriental philosophy, who told him that the word "divine" had
its origin in the Sanskrit word meaning "light."]

> I cannot find my way: there is no star
> In all the shrouded heavens anywhere;
> And there is not a whisper in the air
> Of any living voice but one so far
> That I can hear it only as a bar   5
> Of lost, imperial music, played when fair
> And angel fingers wove, and unaware,
> Dead leaves to garlands where no roses are.
>
> No, there is not a glimmer, nor a call,
> For one that welcomes, welcomes when he fears,   10
> The black and awful chaos of the night;
> For through it all,—above, beyond it all,—
> I know the far-sent message of the years,
> I feel the coming glory of the Light!

                                             1896

"Credo," and the following seven poems ("Zola," "The Clerks," "George Crabbe,"
"Thomas Hood," "Cliff Klingenhagen," "The Pity of the Leaves," and "The Tavern")
are reprinted with the permission of Charles Scribner's Sons from *The Children of the
Night* by Edwin Arlington Robinson (1897).

His prose reveals a restless uncertain,
but persistent search for moral values.

THE CLERKS   517

ZOLA

[In a letter, dated February 19, 1896, to Harry De Forest Smith, Robinson said that he had visited Jones (first name unknown), a new Gardiner acquaintance, who defended Zola "for the truth and sincerity that lies at the bottom of his nastiness." More than a year later, in another letter to Smith, April 4, 1897, and after "Zola" had appeared in print, Robinson said that he was reading Zola's *L'Assommoir*. Many years later, writing to Mrs. Laura E. Richards, June 19, 1929, Robinson had a lapse of memory: "When I wrote that rather pinfeatherish Zola sonnet I had read only *L'Assommoir*, and I have read only one of his books since then."]

Because he puts the compromising chart
Of hell before your eyes, you are afraid;
Because he counts the price that you have paid
For innocence, and counts it from the start,
You loathe him. But he sees the human heart   5
Of God meanwhile, and in God's hand has weighed
Your squeamish and emasculate crusade
Against the grim dominion of his art.

Never until we conquer the uncouth
Connivings of our shamed indifference   10
(We call it Christian faith!) are we to scan
The racked and shrieking hideousness of Truth
To find, in hate's polluted self-defence
Throbbing, the pulse, the divine heart of man.

1896

THE CLERKS

["The Clerks" was first printed in the *Boston Evening Transcript*, June 4, 1896. In a letter of July 11, 1917, to L. N. Chase, a professor of English, Robinson recalled that he had spent a month tinkering with this sonnet.]

I did not think that I should find them there
When I came back again; but there they stood,
As in the days they dreamed of when young blood
Was in their cheeks and women called them fair.
Be sure, they met me with an ancient air,—   5
And yes, there was a shop-worn brotherhood
About them; but the men were just as good,
And just as human as they ever were.

And you that ache so much to be sublime,
And you that feed yourselves with your descent,   10

What comes of all your visions and your fears?
Poets and kings are but the clerks of Time,
Tiering the same dull webs of discontent,
Clipping the same sad alnage¹ of the years.

1896

GEORGE CRABBE

[George Crabbe (1754-1832), whose realistic poetry, like *The Village* (1783) and *The Borough* (1810), attracted Robinson, had rebelled against the effete pastoralism of late eighteenth-century British verse just as, a hundred years later, Robinson rejected the empty verse of his own late-Victorian background.]

Give him the darkest inch your shelf allows,
Hide him in lonely garrets, if you will,—
But his hard, human pulse is throbbing still
With the sure strength that fearless truth endows.
In spite of all fine science disavows,   5
Of his plain excellence and stubborn skill
There yet remains what fashion cannot kill,
Though years have thinned the laurel from his brows.

Whether or not we read him, we can feel
From time to time the vigor of his name   10
Against us like a finger for the shame
And emptiness of what our souls reveal
In books that are as altars where we kneel
To consecrate the flicker, not the flame.²

1896

THOMAS HOOD

[In a letter to Smith, December 8, 1891, Robinson disclosed that the *Harvard Monthly* had just rejected this sonnet; and it did not appear until February 1896, when *The Globe*, a New York quarterly, printed it.]

The man who cloaked his bitterness within
This winding-sheet of puns and pleasantries,
God never gave to look with common eyes
Upon a world of anguish and of sin:

¹ The measurement of cloth by the ell, a measure, varying from country to country, now little used.

² Robinson may well have borrowed the imagery of the altar and the flame from Henry James' "The Lesson of the Master," which, as he said in a letter to Smith, February 7, 1896, he had just read.

His brother was the branded man of Lynn;[1]   5
And there are woven with his jollities
The nameless and eternal tragedies
That render hope and hopelessness akin.

We laugh, and crown him; but anon we feel
A still chord sorrow-swept,—a weird unrest;   10
And thin dim shadows home to midnight steal,
As if the very ghost of mirth were dead—
As if the joys of time to dreams had fled,
Or sailed away with Ines to the West.[2]

1896

CLIFF KLINGENHAGEN

Cliff Klingenhagen had me in to dine
With him one day; and after soup and meat,
And all the other things there were to eat,
Cliff took two glasses and filled one with wine
And one with wormwood. Then, without a sign   5
For me to choose at all, he took the draught
Of bitterness himself, and lightly quaffed
It off, and said the other one was mine.

And when I asked him what the deuce he meant
By doing that, he only looked at me   10
And grinned, and said it was a way of his.
And though I know the fellow, I have spent
Long time a-wondering when I shall be
As happy as Cliff Klingenhagen is.

1897

THE PITY OF THE LEAVES

[This sonnet was first printed in *The Critic* for November 21, 1896.]

Vengeful across the cold November moors,
Loud with ancestral shame there came the bleak

[1] The "branded man of Lynn" is a reference to Hood's "The Dream of Eugene Aram" and Hood's note on the poem. Aram, confessing that he had dreamed of murdering a man, had actually done so and was, in Hood's prose comment, marked with "the brand of Cain." In this kind of allusion Robinson is acknowledging Hood's universal sympathy for all unfortunates.

[2] The reference is to Hood's "Fair Ines," in which the beautiful girl romantically sails "into the West" with her lover and leaves saddened admirers behind on the shore.

Sad wind that shrieked, and answered with a shriek,
Reverberant through lonely corridors.
The old man heard it; and he heard, perforce,   5
Words out of lips that were no more to speak—
Words of the past that shook the old man's cheek
Like dead, remembered footsteps on old floors.

And then there were the leaves that plagued him so!
The brown, thin leaves that on the stones outside   10
Skipped with a freezing whisper. Now and then
They stopped, and stayed there—just to let him know
How dead they were; but if the old man cried,
They fluttered off like withered souls of men.

                                                              1897

THE TAVERN

Whenever I go by there nowadays
And look at the rank weeds and the strange grass,
The torn blue curtains and the broken glass,
I seem to be afraid of the old place;
And something stiffens up and down my face,   5
For all the world as if I saw the ghost
Of old Ham Amory, the murdered host,
With his dead eyes turned on me all aglaze.

The Tavern has a story, but no man
Can tell us what it is. We only know   10
That once long after midnight, years ago,
A stranger galloped up from Tilbury Town,
Who brushed, and scared, and all but overran
That skirt-crazed reprobate, John Evereldown.

                                                              1897

ERASMUS

[In a letter to Daniel Gregory Mason, May 18, 1900, Robinson said that he was "trying to do something" with his sonnet on Erasmus, most likely a reference to his effort to have it printed. Its first appearance was in the *Harvard Monthly* for December 1900.]

When he protested, not too solemnly,
That for a world's achieving maintenance

The crust of overdone divinity
Lacked aliment, they called it recreance;
And when he chose through his own glass to scan   5
Sick Europe, and reduced, unyieldingly,
The monk within the cassock to the man
Within the monk, they called it heresy.

And when he made so perilously bold
As to be scattered forth in black and white,   10
Good fathers looked askance at him and rolled
Their inward eyes in anguish and affright;
There were some of them did shake at what was told,
And they shook best who knew that he was right.

1902

JOHN EVERELDOWN could not revisit the lure of women.

[Both this poem and "Luke Havergal" (following), as well as the fictional
Tilbury Town, are first mentioned in a letter to Smith, December 14, 1895. The
name of the town is derived from the tilbury, a smart two-wheeled open carriage. Apparently, Evereldown was a composite of two local characters.]

"Where are you going to-night, to-night,—
    Where are you going, John Evereldown?
There's never the sign of a star in sight,
    Nor a lamp that's nearer than Tilbury Town.
Why do you stare as a dead man might?   5
Where are you pointing away from the light?
And where are you going to-night, to-night,—
    Where are you going, John Evereldown?"

"Right through the forest, where none can see,
    There's where I'm going, to Tilbury Town.   10
The men are asleep,—or awake, may be,—
    But the women are calling John Evereldown.
Ever and ever they call for me,
And while they call can a man be free?
So right through the forest, where none can see,   15
    There's where I'm going, to Tilbury Town."

"But why are you going so late, so late,—
    Why are you going, John Evereldown?
Though the road be smooth and the path be straight,
    There are two long leagues to Tilbury Town.   20

"John Evereldown" and the following poem, "Luke Havergal," are reprinted with the
permission of Charles Scribner's Sons from *The Children of the Night* by Edwin Arlington Robinson (1897).

Come in by the fire, old man, and wait!
Why do you chatter out there by the gate?
And why are you going so late, so late,—
    Why are you going, John Evereldown?"

"I follow the women wherever they call,—   25
    That's why I'm going to Tilbury Town.
God knows if I pray to be done with it all,
    But God is no friend to John Evereldown.
So the clouds may come and the rain may fall,
The shadows may creep and the dead men crawl,   30
But I follow the women wherever they call,
    And that's why I'm going to Tilbury Town."

1896

LUKE HAVERGAL

[handwritten: ruined life could only "go t. the Western gate"]

[handwritten left margin: a companion piece t. "Richard Cory"]

[In the letter to Smith referred to above, Robinson described "Luke Havergal"
as a "piece of deliberate degeneration." During the summer, as indicated in an
earlier letter to Smith, June 9, 1895, he had been reading Max Nordau's *Degeneration*
(first American edition, 1895), which pointed to symbolism and naturalism in literature and impressionism in painting as evidence of a decline in civilization. On October
6, writing again to Smith, Robinson said, "I like the red leaves. Red leaves makes me
think of *Degeneration* . . ."; Adams surmises that this may be a reference to Nordau's
claim that " 'degenerates' take a special pleasure in the color red because it is 'dynamog-
enous,' or 'force-producing.' " Robinson's use of Nordau must not be interpreted as
approval of his strictures upon contemporary literature and art.]

[handwritten left margin: Havergal, bereaved and in blinding despair, hears a voice out of a grave that bids him relinquish renewal of the past.]

Go to the western gate, Luke Havergal,—
There where the vines cling crimson on the wall,—
And in the twilight wait for what will come.
The wind will moan, the leaves will whisper some—
Whisper of her, and strike you as they fall;   5
But go, and if you trust her she will call.
Go to the western gate, Luke Havergal—
Luke Havergal.

No, there is not a dawn in eastern skies   *[handwritten: past]*
To rift the fiery night that's in your eyes;   10
But there, where western glooms are gathering,   *[handwritten: faith]*
The dark will end the dark, if anything: *[handwritten: darkness]*
God slays Himself with every leaf that flies,
And hell is more than half of paradise.
No, there is not a dawn in eastern skies—   15
In eastern skies.

Out of a grave I come to tell you this,—
Out of a grave I come to quench the kiss

[handwritten bottom: The bitter truth which must be known before faith is possible — before she will call. (life after death)]

That flames upon your forehead with a glow
That blinds you to the way that you must go.   20
Yes, there is yet one way to where she is,—
Bitter, but one that faith can never miss.
Out of a grave I come to tell you this—
To tell you this.

There is the western gate, Luke Havergal,   25
There are the crimson leaves upon the wall.
Go,—for the winds are tearing them away,—
Nor think to riddle the dead words they say,
Nor any more to feel them as they fall;
But go! and if you trust her she will call.   30
There is the western gate, Luke Havergal—
Luke Havergal.

1896

THE BOOK OF ANNANDALE

[Robinson started "The Book of Annandale" on January 13, 1898 (see his letter
of that date to Smith), wrote steadily on it into the spring, dropped it for a
while, and finished it two years later.]

I

Partly to think, more to be left alone,
George Annandale said something to his friends—
A word or two, brusque, but yet smoothed enough
To suit their funeral gaze—and went upstairs;
And there, in the one room that he could call   5
His own, he found a sort of meaningless
Annoyance in the mute familiar things
That filled it; for the grate's monotonous gleam
Was not the gleam that he had known before,
The books were not the books that used to be,   10
The place was not the place. There was a lack
Of something; and the certitude of death
Itself, as with a furtive questioning,
Hovered, and he could not yet understand.
He knew that she was gone—there was no need   15
Of any argued proof to tell him that,
For they had buried her that afternoon,
Under the leaves and snow; and still there was
A doubt, a pitiless doubt, a plunging doubt,
That struck him, and upstartled when it struck,   20
The vision, the old thought in him. There was

A lack, and one that wrenched him; but it was
Not that—not that. There was a present sense
Of something indeterminably near—
The soul-clutch of a prescient emptiness   25
That would not be foreboding. And if not,
What then?—or was it anything at all?
Yes, it was something—it was everything—
But what was everything? or anything?

Tired of time, bewildered, he sat down;   30
But in his chair he kept on wondering
That he should feel so desolately strange
And yet—for all he knew that he had lost
More of the world than most men ever win—
So curiously calm. And he was left   35
Unanswered and unsatisfied: there came
No clearer meaning to him than had come
Before; the old abstraction was the best
That he could find, the farthest he could go;
To that was no beginning and no end—   40
No end that he could reach. So he must learn
To live the surest and the largest life
Attainable in him, would he divine
The meaning of the dream and of the words
That he had written, without knowing why,   45
On sheets that he had bound up like a book
And covered with red leather. There it was—
There in his desk, the record he had made,
The spiritual plaything of his life:
There were the words no eyes had ever seen   50
Save his; there were the words that were not made
For glory or for gold. The pretty wife
Whom he had loved and lost had not so much
As heard of them. They were not made for her.
His love had been so much the life of her,   55
And hers had been so much the life of him,
That any wayward phrasing on his part
Would have had no moment. Neither had lived enough
To know the book, albeit one of them
Had grown enough to write it. There it was,   60
However, though he knew not why it was:
There was the book, but it was not for her,
For she was dead. And yet, there was the book

Thus would his fancy circle out and out,
And out and in again, till he would make   65
As if with a large freedom to crush down
Those under-thoughts. He covered with his hands
His tired eyes, and waited: he could hear—

Or partly feel and hear, mechanically—
The sound of talk, with now and then the steps   70
And skirts of some one scudding on the stairs,
Forgetful of the nerveless funeral feet
That she had brought with her; and more than once
There came to him a call as of a voice—
A voice of love returning—but not hers.   75
Whose he knew not, nor dreamed; nor did he know,
Nor did he dream, in his blurred loneliness
Of thought, what all the rest might think of him.

For it had come at last, and she was gone
With all the vanished women of old time,—   80
And she was never coming back again.
Yes, they had buried her that afternoon,
Under the frozen leaves and the cold earth,
Under the leaves and snow. The flickering week,
The sharp and certain day, and the long drowse   85
Were over, and the man was left alone.
He knew the loss—therefore it puzzled him
That he should sit so long there as he did,
And bring the whole thing back—the love, the trust,
The pallor, the poor face, and the faint way   90
She last had looked at him—and yet not weep,
Or even choose to look about the room
To see how sad it was; and once or twice
He winked and pinched his eyes against the flame
And hoped there might be tears. But hope was all,   95
And all to him was nothing: he was lost.
And yet he was not lost: he was astray—
Out of his life and in another life;
And in the stillness of this other life
He wondered and he drowsed. He wondered when   100
It was, and wondered if it ever was
On earth that he had known the other face—
The searching face, the eloquent, strange face—
That with a sightless beauty looked at him
And with a speechless promise uttered words   105
That were not the world's words, or any kind
That he had known before. What was it, then?
What was it held him—fascinated him?
Why should he not be human? He could sigh,
And he could even groan,—but what of that?   110
There was no grief left in him. Was he glad?

Yet how could he be glad, or reconciled,
Or anything but wretched and undone?
How could he be so frigid and inert—
So like a man with water in his veins   115

Where blood had been a little while before?
How could he sit shut in there like a snail?
What ailed him? What was on him? Was he glad?
Over and over again the question came,
Unanswered and unchanged,—and there he was.   120
But what in heaven's name did it all mean?
If he had lived as other men had lived,
If home had ever shown itself to be
The counterfeit that others had called home,
Then to this undivined resource of his   125
There were some key; but now . . . Philosophy?
Yes, he could reason in a kind of way
That he was glad for Miriam's release—
Much as he might be glad to see his friends
Laid out around him with their grave-clothes on,   130
And this life done for them; but something else
There was that foundered reason, overwhelmed it,
And with a chilled, intuitive rebuff
Beat back the self-cajoling sophistries
That his half-tutored thought would half-project.   135

What was it, then? Had he become transformed
And hardened through long watches and long grief
Into a loveless, feelingless dead thing
That brooded like a man, breathed like a man,—
Did everything but ache? And was a day   140
To come some time when feeling should return
Forever to drive off that other face—
The lineless, indistinguishable face—
That once had thrilled itself between his own
And hers there on the pillow,—and again   145
Between him and the coffin-lid had flashed
Like fate before it closed,—and at the last
Had come, as it should seem, to stay with him,
Bidden or not? He were a stranger then,
Foredrowsed awhile by some deceiving draught   150
Of poppied anguish, to the covert grief
And the stark loneliness that waited him,
And for the time were cursedly endowed
With a dull trust that shammed indifference
To knowing there would be no touch again   155
Of her small hand on his, no silencing
Of her quick lips on his, no feminine
Completeness and love-fragrance in the house,
No sound of some one singing any more,
No smoothing of slow fingers on his hair,   160
No shimmer of pink slippers on brown tiles.

But there was nothing, nothing, in all that:
He had not fooled himself so much as that;
He might be dreaming or he might be sick,
But not like that. There was no place for fear,   165
No reason for remorse. There was the book
That he had made, though. . . . It might be the book,
Perhaps he might find something in the book;
But no, there could be nothing there at all—
He knew it word for word; but what it meant—   170
He was not sure that he had written it
For what it meant; and he was not quite sure
That he had written it;—more likely it
Was all a paper ghost. . . . But the dead wife
Was real: he knew all that, for he had been   175
To see them bury her; and he had seen
The flowers and the snow and the stripped limbs
Of trees; and he had heard the preacher pray;
And he was back again, and he was glad.
Was he a brute? No, he was not a brute: 180
He was a man—like any other man:
He had loved and married his wife Miriam,
They had lived a little while in paradise
And she was gone; and that was all of it.

But no, not all of it—not all of it: 185
There was the book again; something in that
Pursued him, overpowered him, put out
The futile strength of all his whys and wheres,
And left him unintelligibly numb—
Too numb to care for anything but rest.   190
It must have been a curious kind of book
That he had made it: it was a drowsy book
At any rate. The very thought of it
Was like the taste of some impossible drink—
A taste that had no taste, but for all that   195
Had mixed with it a strange thought-cordial,
So potent that it somehow killed in him
The ultimate need of doubting any more—
Of asking any more. Did he but live
The life that he must live, there were no more   200
To seek.—The rest of it was on the way.

Still there was nothing, nothing, in all this—
Nothing that he cared now to reconcile
With reason or with sorrow. All he knew
For certain was that he was tired out: 205
His flesh was heavy and his blood beat small;
Something supreme had been wrenched out of him

As if to make vague room for something else.
He had been through too much. Yes, he would stay
There where he was and rest.—And there he stayed;   210
The daylight became twilight, and he stayed;
The flame and the face faded, and he slept.
And they had buried her that afternoon,
Under the tight-screwed lid of a long box,
Under the earth, under the leaves and snow.   215

                              I I

Look where she would, feed conscience how she might,
There was but one way now for Damaris—
One straight way that was hers, hers to defend,
At hand, imperious. But the nearness of it,
The flesh-bewildering simplicity,   220
And the plain strangeness of it, thrilled again
That wretched little quivering single string
Which yielded not, but held her to the place
Where now for five triumphant years had slept
The flameless dust of Argan.—He was gone,   225
The good man she had married long ago;
And she had lived, and living she had learned,
And surely there was nothing to regret:
Much happiness had been for each of them,
And they had been like lovers to the last: 230
And after that, and long, long after that,
Her tears had washed out more of widowed grief
Than smiles had ever told of other joy.—
But could she, looking back, find anything
That should return to her in the new time,   235
And with relentless magic uncreate
This temple of new love where she had thrown
Dead sorrow on the altar of new life?
Only one thing, only one thread was left;
When she broke that, when reason snapped it off,   240
And once for all, baffled, the grave let go
The trivial hideous hold it had on her,—
Then she were free, free to be what she would,
Free to be what she was.—And yet she stayed,
Leashed, as it were, and with a cobweb strand,   245
Close to a tombstone—maybe to starve there.

But why to starve? And why stay there at all?
Why not make one good leap and then be done
Forever and at once with Argan's ghost
And all such outworn churchyard servitude?   250
For it was Argan's ghost that held the string,
And her sick fancy that held Argan's ghost—
Held it and pitied it. She laughed, almost,

There for the moment; but her strained eyes filled
With tears, and she was angry for those tears—   255
Angry at first, then proud, then sorry for them.
So she grew calm; and after a vain chase
For thoughts more vain, she questioned of herself
What measure of primeval doubts and fears
Were still to be gone through that she might win   260
Persuasion of her strength and of herself
To be what she could see that she must be,
No matter where the ghost was.—And the more
She lived, the more she came to recognize
That something out of her thrilled ignorance   265
Was luminously, proudly being born,
And thereby proving, thought by forward thought,
The prowess of its image; and she learned
At length to look right on to the long days
Before her without fearing. She could watch   270
The coming course of them as if they were
No more than birds, that slowly, silently,
And irretrievably should wing themselves
Uncounted out of sight. And when he came
Again, she might be free—she would be free.   275
Else, when he looked at her she must look down,
Defeated, and malignly dispossessed
Of what was hers to prove and in the proving
Wisely to consecrate. And if the plague
Of that perverse defeat should come to be—   280
If at that sickening end she were to find
Herself to be the same poor prisoner
That he had found at first—then she must lose
All sight and sound of him, she must abjure
All possible thought of him; for he would go   285
So far and for so long from her that love—
Yes, even a love like his, exiled enough,
Might for another's touch be born again—
Born to be lost and starved for and not found;
Or, at the next, the second wretchedest,   290
It might go mutely flickering down and out,
And on some incomplete and piteous day,
Some perilous day to come, she might at last
Learn, with a noxious freedom, what it is
To be at peace with ghosts. Then were the blow   295
Thrice deadlier than any kind of death
Could ever be: to know that she had won
The truth too late—there were the dregs indeed
Of wisdom, and of love the final thrust
Unmerciful; and there where now did lie   300
So plain before her the straight radiance
Of what was her appointed way to take,

Were only the bleak ruts of an old road
That stretched ahead and faded and lay far
Through deserts of unconscionable years.   305

But vampire thoughts like these confessed the doubt
That love denied; and once, if never again,
They should be turned away. They might come back—
More craftily, perchance, they might come back—
And with a spirit-thirst insatiable   310
Finish the strength of her; but now, to-day
She would have none of them. She knew that love
Was true, that he was true, that she was true;
And should a death-bed snare that she had made
So long ago be stretched inexorably   315
Through all her life, only to be unspun
With her last breathing? And were bats and threads,
Accursedly devised with watered gules,
To be Love's heraldry? What were it worth
To live and to find out that life were life   320
But for an unrequited incubus
Of outlawed shame that would not be thrown down
Till she had thrown down fear and overcome
The woman that was yet so much of her
That she might yet go mad? What were it worth   325
To live, to linger, and to be condemned
In her submission to a common thought
That clogged itself and made of its first faith
Its last impediment? What augured it,
Now in this quick beginning of new life,   330
To clutch the sunlight and be feeling back,
Back with a scared fantastic fearfulness,
To touch, not knowing why, the vexed-up ghost
Of what was gone?

                         Yes, there was Argan's face,
Pallid and pinched and ruinously marked   335
With big pathetic bones; there were his eyes,
Quiet and large, fixed wistfully on hers;
And there, close-pressed again within her own,
Quivered his cold thin fingers. And, ah! yes,
There were the words, those dying words again,   340
And hers that answered when she promised him.
Promised him? . . . yes. And had she known the truth
Of what she felt that he should ask her that,
And had she known the love that was to be,
God knew that she could not have told him then.   345
But then she knew it not, nor thought of it;
There was no need of it; nor was there need
Of any problematical support

Whereto to cling while she convinced herself
That love's intuitive utility,   350
Inexorably merciful, had proved
That what was human was unpermanent
And what was flesh was ashes. She had told
Him then that she would love no other man,
That there was not another man on earth   355
Whom she could ever love, or who could make
So much as a love thought go through her brain;
And he had smiled. And just before he died
His lips had made as if to say something—
Something that passed unwhispered with his breath,   360
Out of her reach, out of all quest of it.
And then, could she have known enough to know
The meaning of her grief, the folly of it,
The faithlessness and the proud anguish of it,
There might be now no threads to punish her,   365
No vampire thoughts to suck the coward blood,
The life, the very soul of her.

                                            Yes, Yes,
They might come back. . . . But why should they come back?
Why was it she had suffered? Why had she
Struggled and grown these years to demonstrate   370
That close without those hovering clouds of gloom
And through them here and there forever gleamed
The Light itself, the life, the love, the glory,
Which was of its own radiance good proof
That all the rest was darkness and blind sight?   375
And who was *she?* The woman she had known—
The woman she had petted and called "I"—
The woman she had pitied, and at last
Commiserated for the most abject
And persecuted of all womankind,—   380
Could it be she that had sought out the way
To measure and thereby to quench in her
The woman's fear—the fear of her not fearing?
A nervous little laugh that lost itself,
Like logic in a dream, fluttered her thoughts   385
An instant there that ever she should ask
What she might then have told so easily—
So easily that Annandale had frowned,
Had he been given wholly to be told
The truth of what had never been before   390
So passionately, so inevitably
Confessed

                    For she could see from where she sat
The sheets that he had bound up like a book
And covered with red leather; and her eyes

Could see between the pages of the book,   395
Though her eyes, like them, were closed. And she could read
As well as if she had them in her hand,
What he had written on them long ago,—
Six years ago, when he was waiting for her.
She might as well have said that she could see   400
The man himself, as once he would have looked
Had she been there to watch him while he wrote
Those words, and all for her. . . . For her whose face
Had flashed itself, prophetic and unseen,
But not unspirited, between the life   405
That would have been without her and the life
That he had gathered up like frozen roots
Out of a grave-clod lying at his feet,
Unconsciously, and as unconsciously
Transplanted and revived. He did not know   410
The kind of life that he had found, nor did
He doubt, not knowing it; but well he knew
That it was life—new life, and that the old
Might then with unimprisoned wings go free,
Onward and all along to its own light,   415
Through the appointed shadow.

                                While she gazed
Upon it there she felt within herself
The growing of a newer consciousness—
The pride of something fairer than her first
Outclamoring of interdicted thought   420
Had ever quite foretold; and all at once
There quivered and requivered through her flesh,
Like music, like the sound of an old song,
Triumphant, love-remembered murmurings
Of what for passion's innocence had been   425
Too mightily, too perilously hers,
Ever to be reclaimed and realized
Until to-day. To-day she could throw off
The burden that had held her down so long,
And she could stand upright, and she could see   430
The way to take, with eyes that had in them
No gleam but of the spirit. Day or night,
No matter; she could see what was to see—
All that had been till now shut out from her,
The service, the fulfillment, and the truth,   435
And thus the cruel wiseness of it all.

So Damaris, more like than anything
To one long prisoned in a twilight cave
With hovering bats for all companionship,
And after time set free to fight the sun,   440

Laughed out, so glad she was to recognize
The test of what had been, through all her folly,
The courage of her conscience; for she knew,
Now on a late-flushed autumn afternoon
That else had been too bodeful of dead things   445
To be endured with aught but the same old
Inert, self-contradicted martyrdom
Which she had known so long, that she could look
Right forward through the years, nor any more
Shrink with a cringing prescience to behold   450
The glitter of dead summer on the grass,
Or the brown-glimmered crimson of still trees
Across the intervale where flashed along,
Black-silvered, the cold river. She had found,
As if by some transcendent freakishness   455
Of reason, the glad life that she had sought
Where naught but obvious clouds could ever be—
Clouds to put out the sunlight from her eyes,
And to put out the love-light from her soul.
But they were gone—now they were all gone;   460
And with a whimsied pathos, like the mist
Of grief that clings to new-found happiness
Hard wrought, she might have pity for the small
Defeated quest of them that brushed her sight
Like flying lint—lint that had once been thread. . . .   465

Yes, like an anodyne, the voice of him,
There were the words that he had made for her,
For her alone. The more she thought of them
The more she lived them, and the more she knew
The life-grip and the pulse of warm strength in them.   470
They were the first and last of words to her,
And there was in them a far questioning
That had for long been variously at work,
Divinely and elusively at work,
With her, and with the grave that had been hers;   475
They were eternal words, and they diffused
A flame of meaning that men's lexicons
Had never kindled; they were choral words
That harmonized with love's enduring chords
Like wisdom with release; triumphant words   480
That rang like elemental orisons
Through ages out of ages; words that fed
Love's hunger in the spirit; words that smote;
Thrilled words that echoed, and barbed words that clung:—
And every one of them was like a friend   485
Whose obstinate fidelity, well tried,
Had found at last and irresistibly

The way to her close conscience, and thereby
Revealed the unsubstantial Nemesis
That she had clutched and shuddered at so long;   490
And every one of them was like a real
And ringing voice, clear toned and absolute,
But of a love-subdued authority
That uttered thrice the plain significance
Of what had else been generously vague   495
And indolently true. It may have been
The triumph and the magic of the soul,
Unspeakably revealed, that finally
Had reconciled the grim probationing
Of Wisdom with unalterable faith,   500
But she could feel—not knowing what it was,
For the sheer freedom of it—a new joy
That humanized the latent wizardry
Of his prophetic voice and put for it
The man within the music.

                                        So it came   505
To pass, like many a long-compelled emprise
That with its first accomplishment almost
Annihilates its own severity,
That she could find, whenever she might look,
The certified achievement of a love   510
That had endured, self-guarded and supreme,
To the glad end of all that wavering;
And she could see that now the flickering world
Of autumn was awake with sudden bloom,
New-born, perforce, of a slow bourgeoning.   515
And she had found what more than half had been
The grave-deluded, flesh-bewildered fear
Which men and women struggle to call faith,
To be the paid progression to an end
Whereat she knew the foresight and the strength   520
To glorify the gift of what was hers,
To vindicate the truth of what she was.
And had it come to her so suddenly?
There was a pity and a weariness
In asking that, and a great needlessness;   525
For now there were no wretched quivering strings
That held her to the churchyard any more:
There were no thoughts that flapped themselves like bats
Around her any more. The shield of love
Was clean, and she had paid enough to learn   530
How it had always been so. And the truth,
Like silence after some far victory,
Had come to her, and she had found it out

As if it were a vision, a thing born
So suddenly!—just as a flower is born, 535
Or as a world is born—so suddenly.

1902

AUNT IMOGEN

❖ [In May 1898, returning to Gardiner from New York, Robinson was unsuccessful in a proposal of marriage. This poem, originally with the title "The Old Maid," is the direct and immediate literary result, for Robinson transfers to a woman the feelings of accommodation he himself had to develop toward the single life. The poem is autobiographical also in the welcome that the children give Aunt Imogen. Two years later Robinson revised the poem and gave it the present title. It is possible that the name "Imogen" was suggested to Robinson by Shakespeare's *Measure for Measure*, which had had a powerful effect upon him (see his letter to Smith, March 4, 1894).]

Aunt Imogen was coming, and therefore
The children—Jane, Sylvester, and Young George—
Were eyes and ears; for there was only one
Aunt Imogen to them in the whole world,
And she was in it only for four weeks 5
In fifty-two. But those great bites of time
Made all September a Queen's Festival;
And they would strive, informally, to make
The most of them.—The mother understood,
And wisely stepped away. Aunt Imogen 10
Was there for only one month in the year,
While she, the mother,—she was always there;
And that was what made all the difference.
She knew it must be so, for Jane had once
Expounded it to her so learnedly 15
That she had looked away from the child's eyes
And thought; and she had thought of many things.

There was a demonstration every time
Aunt Imogen appeared, and there was more
Than one this time. And she was at a loss 20
Just how to name the meaning of it all:
It puzzled her to think that she could be
So much to any crazy thing alive—
Even to her sister's little savages
Who knew no better than to be themselves; 25
But in the midst of her glad wonderment
She found herself besieged and overcome

By two tight arms and one tumultuous head,
And therewith half bewildered and half pained
By the joy she felt and by the sudden love   30
That proved itself in childhood's honest noise.
Jane, by the wings of sex, had reached her first;
And while she strangled her, approvingly,
Sylvester thumped his drum and Young George howled.
But finally, when all was rectified,   35
And she had stilled the clamor of Young George
By giving him a long ride on her shoulders,
They went together into the old room
That looked across the fields; and Imogen
Gazed out with a girl's gladness in her eyes,   40
Happy to know that she was back once more
Where there were those who knew her, and at last
Had gloriously got away again
From cabs and clattered asphalt for a while;
And there she sat and talked and looked and laughed   45
And made the mother and the children laugh.
Aunt Imogen made everybody laugh.

There was the feminine paradox—that she
Who had so little sunshine for herself
Should have so much for others. How it was   50
That she could make, and feel for making it,
So much of joy for them, and all along
Be covering, like a scar, and while she smiled,
That hungering incompleteness and regret—
That passionate ache for something of her own,   55
For something of herself—she never knew.
She knew that she could seem to make them all
Believe there was no other part of her
Than her persistent happiness; but the why
And how she did not know. Still none of them   60
Could have a thought that she was living down—
Almost as if regret were criminal,
So proud it was and yet so profitless—
The penance of a dream, and that was good.
Her sister Jane—the mother of little Jane,   65
Sylvester, and Young George—might make herself
Believe she knew, for she—well, she was Jane.

Young George, however, did not yield himself
To nourish the false hunger of a ghost
That made no good return. He saw too much: 70
The accumulated wisdom of his years
Had so conclusively made plain to him
The permanent profusion of a world
Where everybody might have everything

To do, and almost everything to eat,   75
That he was jubilantly satisfied
And all unthwarted by adversity.
Young George knew things. The world, he had found out,
Was a good place, and life was a good game—
Particularly when Aunt Imogen   80
Was in it. And one day it came to pass—
One rainy day when she was holding him
And rocking him—that he, in his own right,
Took it upon himself to tell her so;
And something in his way of telling it—   85
The language, or the tone, or something else—
Gripped like insidious fingers on her throat,
And then went foraging as if to make
A plaything of her heart. Such undeserved
And unsophisticated confidence   90
Went mercilessly home; and had she sat
Before a looking glass, the deeps of it
Could not have shown more clearly to her then
Than one thought-mirrored little glimpse had shown,
The pang that wrenched her face and filled her eyes   95
With anguish and intolerable mist.
The blow that she had vaguely thrust aside
Like fright so many times had found her now:
Clean-thrust and final it had come to her
From a child's lips at last, as it had come   100
Never before, and as it might be felt
Never again. Some grief, like some delight,
Stings hard but once: to custom after that
The rapture or the pain submits itself,
And we are wiser than we were before.   105
And Imogen was wiser; though at first
Her dream-defeating wisdom was indeed
A thankless heritage: there was no sweet,
No bitter now; nor was there anything
To make a daily meaning for her life—   110
Till truth, like Harlequin, leapt out somehow
From ambush and threw sudden savor to it—
But the blank taste of time. There were no dreams,
No phantoms in her future any more:
One clinching revelation of what was,   115
One by-flash of irrevocable chance,
Had acridly but honestly foretold
The mystical fulfillment of a life
That might have once . . . But that was all gone by:
There was no need of reaching back for that: 120
The triumph was not hers: there was no love
Save borrowed love: there was no might have been.

But there was yet Young George—and he had gone
Conveniently to sleep, like a good boy;
And there was yet Sylvester with his drum,   125
And there was frowzle-headed little Jane;
And there was Jane the sister, and the mother,—
Her sister, and the mother of them all.
They were not hers, not even one of them:
She was not born to be so much as that,   130
For she was born to be Aunt Imogen.
Now she could see the truth and look at it;
Now she could make stars out where once had palled
A future's emptiness; now she could share
With others—ah, the others!—to the end   135
The largess of a woman who could smile;
Now it was hers to dance the folly down,
And all the murmuring; now it was hers
To be Aunt Imogen.—So, when Young George
Woke up and blinked at her with his big eyes,   140
And smiled to see the way she blinked at him,
'T was only in old concord with the stars
That she took hold of him and held him close,
Close to herself, and crushed him till he laughed.

1902

ISAAC AND ARCHIBALD

[This poem was inspired by two elderly friends, each of whom confided in Robinson his conviction that the other was crazy. The poem was finished in January
or early February 1901 and, together with "The Book of Annandale," sent off to
be typed during April.]

Isaac and Archibald were two old men.
I knew them, and I may have laughed at them
A little; but I must have honored them
For they were old, and they were good to me.

I do not think of either of them now,   5
Without remembering, infallibly,
A journey that I made one afternoon
With Isaac to find out what Archibald
Was doing with his oats. It was high time
Those oats were cut, said Isaac; and he feared   10
That Archibald—well, he could never feel
Quite sure of Archibald. Accordingly
The good old man invited me—that is,
Permitted me—to go along with him;
And I, with a small boy's adhesiveness   15

To competent old age, got up and went.
I do not know that I cared overmuch
For Archibald's or anybody's oats,
But Archibald was quite another thing,
And Isaac yet another; and the world   20
Was wide, and there was gladness everywhere.
We walked together down the River Road
With all the warmth and wonder of the land
Around us, and the wayside flash of leaves,—
And Isaac said the day was glorious;   25
But somewhere at the end of the first mile
I found that I was figuring to find
How long those ancient legs of his would keep
The pace that he had set for them. The sun
Was hot, and I was ready to sweat blood;   30
But Isaac, for aught I could make of him,
Was cool to his hat-band. So I said then
With a dry gasp of affable despair,
Something about the scorching days we have
In August without knowing it sometimes;   35
But Isaac said the day was like a dream,
And praised the Lord, and talked about the breeze.
I made a fair confession of the breeze,
And crowded casually on his thought
The nearness of a profitable nook   40
That I could see. First I was half inclined
To caution him that he was growing old,
But something that was not compassion soon
Made plain the folly of all subterfuge.
Isaac was old, but not so old as that.   45

So I proposed, without an overture,
That we be seated in the shade a while,
And Isaac made no murmur. Soon the talk
Was turned on Archibald, and I began
To feel some premonitions of a kind   50
That only childhood knows; for the old man
Had looked at me and clutched me with his eye,
And asked if I had ever noticed things.
I told him that I could not think of them,
And I knew then, by the frown that left his face   55
Unsatisfied, that I had injured him.
"My good young friend," he said, "you cannot feel
What I have seen so long. You have the eyes—
Oh, yes—but you have not the other things:
The sight within that never will deceive,   60
You do not know—you have no right to know;
The twilight warning of experience,

The singular idea of loneliness,—
These are not yours. But they have long been mine,
And they have shown me now for seven years   65
That Archibald is changing. It is not
So much that he should come to his last hand,
And leave the game, and go the old way down;
But I have known him in and out so long,
And I have seen so much of good in him   70
That other men have shared and have not seen,
And I have gone so far through thick and thin,
Through cold and fire with him, that now it brings
To this old heart of mine an ache that you
Have not yet lived enough to know about.   75
But even unto you, and your boy's faith,
Your freedom, and your untried confidence,
A time will come to find out what it means
To know that you are losing what was yours,
To know that you are being left behind;   80
And then the long contempt of innocence—
God bless you, boy!—don't think the worse of it
Because an old man chatters in the shade—
Will all be like a story you have read
In childhood and remembered for the pictures.   85
And when the best friend of your life goes down,
When first you know in him the slackening
That comes, and coming always tells the end,—
Now in a common word that would have passed
Uncaught from any other lips than his,   90
Now in some trivial act of every day,
Done as he might have done it all along
But for a twinging little difference
That nips you like a squirrel's teeth—oh, yes,
Then you will understand it well enough.   95
But oftener it comes in other ways;
It comes without your knowing when it comes;
You know that he is changing, and you know
That he is going—just as I know now
That Archibald is going, and that I   100
Am staying. . . . Look at me, my boy,
And when the time shall come for you to see
That I must follow after him, try then
To think of me, to bring me back again,
Just as I was to-day. Think of the place   105
Where we are sitting now, and think of me—
Think of old Isaac as you knew him then,
When you set out with him in August once
To see old Archibald."—The words come back
Almost as Isaac must have uttered them,   110

And there comes with them a dry memory
Of something in my throat that would not move.

If you had asked me then to tell just why
I made so much of Isaac and the things
He said, I should have gone far for an answer; 115
For I knew it was not sorrow that I felt,
Whatever I may have wished it, or tried then
To make myself believe. My mouth was full
Of words, and they would have been comforting
To Isaac, spite of my twelve years, I think; 120
But there was not in me the willingness
To speak them out. Therefore I watched the ground;
And I was wondering what made the Lord
Create a thing so nervous as an ant,
When Isaac, with commendable unrest, 125
Ordained that we should take the road again—
For it was yet three miles to Archibald's,
And one to the first pump. I felt relieved
All over when the old man told me that;
I felt that he had stilled a fear of mine 130
That those extremities of heat and cold
Which he had long gone through with Archibald
Had made the man impervious to both;
But Isaac had a desert somewhere in him,
And at the pump he thanked God for all things 135
That He had put on earth for men to drink,
And he drank well,—so well that I proposed
That we go slowly lest I learn too soon
The bitterness of being left behind,
And all those other things. That was a joke 140
To Isaac, and it pleased him very much;
And that pleased me—for I was twelve years old.

At the end of an hour's walking after that
The cottage of old Archibald appeared.
Little and white and high on a smooth round hill 145
It stood, with hackmatacks and apple-trees
Before it, and a big barn-roof beyond;
And over the place—trees, house, fields and all—
Hovered an air of still simplicity
And a fragrance of old summers—the old style 150
That lives the while it passes. I dare say
That I was lightly conscious of all this
When Isaac, of a sudden, stopped himself,
And for the long first quarter of a minute
Gazed with incredulous eyes, forgetful quite 155
Of breezes and of me and of all else
Under the scorching sun but a smooth-cut field,

Faint yellow in the distance. I was young,
But there were a few things that I could see,
And this was one of them.—"Well, well!" said he;   160
And "Archibald will be surprised, I think,"
Said I. But all my childhood subtlety
Was lost on Isaac, for he strode along
Like something out of Homer—powerful
And awful on the wayside, so I thought.   165
Also I thought how good it was to be
So near the end of my short-legged endeavor
To keep the pace with Isaac for five miles.

Hardly had we turned in from the main road
When Archibald, with one hand on his back   170
And the other clutching his huge-headed cane,
Came limping down to meet us.—"Well! well! well!"
Said he; and then he looked at my red face,
All streaked with dust and sweat, and shook my hand,
And said it must have been a right smart walk   175
That we had had that day from Tilbury Town.—
"Magnificent," said Isaac; and he told
About the beautiful west wind there was
Which cooled and clarified the atmosphere.
"You must have made it with your legs, I guess,"   180
Said Archibald; and Isaac humored him
With one of those infrequent smiles of his
Which he kept in reserve, apparently,
For Archibald alone. "But why," said he,
"Should Providence have cider in the world   185
If not for such an afternoon as this?"
And Archibald, with a soft light in his eyes,
Replied that if he chose to go down cellar,
There he would find eight barrels—one of which
Was newly tapped, he said, and to his taste   190
An honor to the fruit. Isaac approved
Most heartily of that, and guided us
Forthwith, as if his venerable feet
Were measuring the turf in his own door-yard,
Straight to the open rollway. Down we went,   195
Out of the fiery sunshine to the gloom,
Grateful and half sepulchral, where we found
The barrels, like eight potent sentinels,
Close ranged along the wall. From one of them
A bright pine spile stuck out alluringly,   200
And on the black flat stone, just under it,
Glimmered a late-spilled proof that Archibald
Had spoken from unfeigned experience.
There was a fluted antique water-glass

Close by, and in it, prisoned, or at rest, 205
There was a cricket, of the brown soft sort
That feeds on darkness. Isaac turned him out,
And touched him with his thumb to make him jump,
And then composedly pulled out the plug
With such a practised hand that scarce a drop 210
Did even touch his fingers. Then he drank
And smacked his lips with a slow patronage
And looked along the line of barrels there
With a pride that may have been forgetfulness
That they were Archibald's and not his own. 215
"I never twist a spigot nowadays,"
He said, and raised the glass up to the light,
"But I thank God for orchards." And that glass
Was filled repeatedly for the same hand
Before I thought it worth while to discern 220
Again that I was young, and that old age,
With all his woes, had some advantages.

"Now, Archibald," said Isaac, when we stood
Outside again, "I have it in my mind
That I shall take a sort of little walk— 225
To stretch my legs and see what you are doing.
You stay and rest your back and tell the boy
A story: Tell him all about the time
In Stafford's cabin forty years ago,
When four of us were snowed up for ten days 230
With only one dried haddock. Tell him all
About it, and be wary of your back.
Now I will go along."—I looked up then
At Archibald, and as I looked I saw
Just how his nostrils widened once or twice 235
And then grew narrow. I can hear to-day
The way the old man chuckled to himself—
Not wholesomely, not wholly to convince
Another of his mirth,—as I can hear
The lonely sigh that followed.—But at length 240
He said: "The orchard now's the place for us;
We may find something like an apple there,
And we shall have the shade, at any rate."
So there we went and there we laid ourselves
Where the sun could not reach us; and I champed 245
A dozen of worm-blighted astrakhans
While Archibald said nothing—merely told
The tale of Stafford's cabin, which was good,
Though "master chilly"—after his own phrase—
Even for a day like that. But other thoughts 250
Were moving in his mind, imperative,

And writhing to be spoken: I could see
The glimmer of them in a glance or two,
Cautious, or else unconscious, that he gave
Over his shoulder: . . . "Stafford and the rest—   255
But that's an old song now, and Archibald
And Isaac are old men. Remember, boy,
That we are old. Whatever we have gained,
Or lost, or thrown away, we are old men.
You look before you and we look behind,   260
And we are playing life out in the shadow—
But that's not all of it. The sunshine lights
A good road yet before us if we look,
And we are doing that when least we know it;
For both of us are children of the sun,   265
Like you, and like the weed there at your feet.
The shadow calls us, and it frightens us—
We think; but there's a light behind the stars
And we old fellows who have dared to live,
We see it—and we see the other things,   270
The other things . . . Yes, I have seen it come
These eight years, and these ten years, and I know
Now that it cannot be for very long
That Isaac will be Isaac. You have seen—
Young as you are, you must have seen the strange   275
Uncomfortable habit of the man?
He'll take my nerves and tie them in a knot
Sometimes, and that's not Isaac. I know that—
And I know what it is: I get it here
A little, in my knees, and Isaac—here."   280
The old man shook his head regretfully
And laid his knuckles three times on his forehead.
"That's what it is: Isaac is not quite right.
You see it, but you don't know what it means:
The thousand little differences—no,   285
You do not know them, and it's well you don't;
You'll know them soon enough—God bless you, boy!—
You'll know them, but not all of them—not all.
So think of them as little as you can:
There's nothing in them for you, or for me—   290
But I am old and I must think of them;
I'm in the shadow, but I don't forget
The light, my boy,—the light behind the stars.
Remember that: remember that I said it;
And when the time that you think far away   295
Shall come for you to say it—say it, boy;
Let there be no confusion or distrust
In you, no snarling of a life half lived,
Nor any cursing over broken things

That your complaint has been the ruin of.   300
Live to see clearly and the light will come
To you, and as you need it.—But there, there,
I'm going it again, as Isaac says,
And I'll stop now before you go to sleep.—
Only be sure that you growl cautiously,   305
And always where the shadow may not reach you."

Never shall I forget, long as I live,
The quaint thin crack in Archibald's old voice,
The lonely twinkle in his little eyes,
Or the way it made me feel to be with him.   310
I know I lay and looked for a long time
Down through the orchard and across the road,
Across the river and the sun-scorched hills
That ceased in a blue forest, where the world
Ceased with it. Now and then my fancy caught   315
A flying glimpse of a good life beyond—
Something of ships and sunlight, streets and singing,
Troy falling, and the ages coming back,
And ages coming forward: Archibald
And Isaac were good fellows in old clothes,   320
And Agamemnon was a friend of mine;
Ulysses coming home again to shoot
With bows and feathered arrows made another,
And all was as it should be. I was young.

So I lay dreaming of what things I would,   325
Calm and incorrigibly satisfied
With apples and romance and ignorance,
And the still smoke from Archibald's clay pipe.
There was a stillness over everything,
As if the spirit of heat had laid its hand   330
Upon the world and hushed it; and I felt
Within the mightiness of the white sun
That smote the land around us and wrought out
A fragrance from the trees, a vital warmth
And fullness for the time that was to come,   335
And a glory for the world beyond the forest.
The present and the future and the past,
Isaac and Archibald, the burning bush,
The Trojans and the walls of Jericho,
Were beautifully fused; and all went well   340
Till Archibald began to fret for Isaac
And said it was a master day for sunstroke.
That was enough to make a mummy smile,
I thought; and I remained hilarious,
In face of all precedence and respect,   345
Till Isaac (who had come to us unheard)

Found he had no tobacco, looked at me
Peculiarly, and asked of Archibald
What ailed the boy to make him chirrup so.
From that he told us what a blessed world   350
The Lord had given us.—"But, Archibald,"
He added, with a sweet severity
That made me think of peach-skins and goose-flesh,
"I'm half afraid you cut those oats of yours
A day or two before they were well set."   355
"They were set well enough," said Archibald,—
And I remarked the process of his nose
Before the words came out. "But never mind
Your neighbor's oats: you stay here in the shade
And rest yourself while I go find the cards.   360
We'll have a little game of seven-up
And let the boy keep count."—"We'll have the game,
Assuredly," said Isaac; "and I think
That I will have a drop of cider, also."

They marched away together towards the house   365
And left me to my childish ruminations
Upon the ways of men. I followed them
Down cellar with my fancy, and then left them
For a fairer vision of all things at once
That was anon to be destroyed again   370
By the sound of voices and of heavy feet—
One of the sounds of life that I remember,
Though I forget so many that rang first
As if they were thrown down to me from Sinai.

So I remember, even to this day,   375
Just how they sounded, how they placed themselves,
And how the game went on while I made marks
And crossed them out, and meanwhile made some Trojans.
Likewise I made Ulysses, after Isaac,
And a little after Flaxman. Archibald   380
Was injured when he found himself left out,
But he had no heroics, and I said so:
I told him that his white beard was too long
And too straight down to be like things in Homer.
"Quite so," said Isaac.—"Low," said Archibald;   385
And he threw down a deuce with a deep grin
That showed his yellow teeth and made me happy.
So they played on till a bell rang from the door,
And Archibald said, "Supper."—After that
The old men smoked while I sat watching them   390
And wondered with all comfort what might come
To me, and what might never come to me;
And when the time came for the long walk home

With Isaac in the twilight, I could see
The forest and the sunset and the sky-line, 395
No matter where it was that I was looking:
The flame beyond the boundary, the music,
The foam and the white ships, and two old men
Were things that would not leave me.—And that night
There came to me a dream—a shining one, 400
With two old angels in it. They had wings,
And they were sitting where a silver light
Suffused them, face to face. The wings of one
Began to palpitate as I approached,
But I was yet unseen when a dry voice 405
Cried thinly, with unpatronizing triumph,
"I've got you, Isaac; high, low, jack, and the game."

Isaac and Archibald have gone their way
To the silence of the loved and well-forgotten.
I knew them, and I may have laughed at them; 410
But there's a laughing that has honor in it,
And I have no regret for light words now.
Rather I think sometimes they may have made
Their sport of me;—but they would not do that,
They were too old for that. They were old men, 415
And I may laugh at them because I knew them.

1. In what spirit is M.C. 1902 presented?
Note how his name is repeated at
beginning of each stanza.

MINIVER CHEEVY — *frustrated dreamer*

[This poem was first printed in *Scribner's Magazine* for March 1907. Robinson is lightly satirizing himself.]

out of sympathy with modern life

Miniver Cheevy, child of scorn,
    Grew lean while he assailed the seasons;
He wept that he was ever born,
    And he had reasons.

Miniver loved the days of old 5
    When swords were bright and steeds were prancing;
The vision of a warrior bold
    Would set him dancing.

Miniver sighed for what was not,
    And dreamed, and rested from his labors; 10
He dreamed of Thebes and Camelot,
    And Priam's neighbors.

"Miniver Cheevy" (Copyright 1907 Charles Scribner's Sons; renewal copyright 1935).

Thebes: ancient Greece — famous city
Camelot: city of King Arthur
Priam: King of Troy during time Greece besieged it

In some ways a Comic poem.

Miniver mourned the ripe renown
   That made so many a name so fragrant;
He mourned Romance, now on the town,
   And Art, a vagrant.   15

glittered when he walked.

Miniver loved the Medici,   *family ∮ 16th – 17th*
   Albeit he had never seen one;   *centuries – Florence*
He would have sinned incessantly   *Italy*
   Could he have been one.   20

Miniver cursed the commonplace
   And eyed a khaki suit with loathing;
He missed the mediaeval grace
   Of iron clothing.

Miniver scorned the gold he sought,   25
   But sore annoyed was he without it;
Miniver thought, and thought, and thought,
   And thought about it.

The final note of failure

Miniver Cheevy, born too late,
   Scratched his head and kept on thinking;   30
Miniver coughed, and called it fate,
   And kept on drinking.

1910

FOR A DEAD LADY

[This poem was first printed in *Scribner's Magazine* for September 1909.]

No more with overflowing light
Shall fill the eyes that now are faded,
Nor shall another's fringe with night
Their woman-hidden world as they did.
No more shall quiver down the days   5
The flowing wonder of her ways,
Whereof no language may requite
The shifting and the many-shaded.

The grace, divine, definitive,
Clings only as a faint forestalling;   10
The laugh that love could not forgive
Is hushed, and answers to no calling;

The forehead and the little ears
Have gone where Saturn keeps the years;
The breast where roses could not live   15
Has done with rising and with falling.

The beauty, shattered by the laws
That have creation in their keeping,
No longer trembles at applause,
Or over children that are sleeping;   20
And we who delve in beauty's lore
Know all that we have known before
Of what inexorable cause
Makes Time so vicious in his reaping.

1910

EROS TURANNOS

[This poem was written during the summer of 1913 and first printed in *Poetry* for March 1914.]

She fears him, and will always ask
    What fated her to choose him;
She meets in his engaging mask
    All reasons to refuse him;
But what she meets and what she fears   5
Are less than are the downward years,
Drawn slowly to the foamless weirs
    Of age, were she to lose him.

Between a blurred sagacity
    That once had power to sound him,   10
And Love, that will not let him be
    The Judas that she found him,
Her pride assuages her almost,
As if it were alone the cost.—
He sees that he will not be lost,   15
    And waits and looks around him.

A sense of ocean and old trees
    Envelops and allures him;
Tradition, touching all he sees,
    Beguiles and reassures him;   20
And all her doubts of what he says
Are dimmed with what she knows of days—

Till even prejudice delays
   And fades, and she secures him.

The falling leaf inaugurates   25
   The reign of her confusion;
The pounding wave reverberates
   The dirge of her illusion;
And home, where passion lived and died,
Becomes a place where she can hide,   30
While all the town and harbor side
   Vibrate with her seclusion.

We tell you, tapping on our brows,
   The story as it should be,—
As if the story of a house   35
   Were told, or ever could be;
We'll have no kindly veil between
Her visions and those we have seen,—
As if we guessed what hers have been,
   Or what they are or would be.   40

Meanwhile we do no harm; for they
   That with a god have striven,
Not hearing much of what we say,
   Take what the god has given;
Though like waves breaking it may be,   45
Or like a changed familiar tree,
Or like a stairway to the sea
   Where down the blind are driven.

1916

THE DARK HILLS

Dark hills at evening in the west,
Where sunset hovers like a sound
Of golden horns that sang to rest
Old bones of warriors under ground,
Far now from all the bannered ways   5
Where flash the legions of the sun,
You fade—as if the last of days
Were fading, and all wars were done.

1920

In a sense poem suggest the loneliness of N.E. (rural) In a larger sense the loneliness of old age anywhere.

MR. FLOOD'S PARTY *one of the best of his short pieces*

✦ [This poem was first printed in the *Nation* for November 24, 1920. It was inspired by Robinson's recollection of Harry De Forest Smith's father's "story of a Maine eccentric who used to propose and drink toasts to himself." [1]]

Tilbury Town portraits.

Old Eben Flood, climbing alone one night
Over the hill between the town below
And the forsaken upland hermitage
That held as much as he should ever know
On earth again of home, paused warily.
The road was his with not a native near;
And Eben, having leisure, said aloud,
For no man else in Tilbury Town to hear:

The party consists of one person.

Mr. Flood's contemporaries are dead. The younger generation unfriendly

"Well, Mr. Flood, we have the harvest moon
Again, and we may not have many more;
The bird is on the wing, the poet says,[2]
And you and I have said it here before.
Drink to the bird." He raised up to the light
The jug that he had gone so far to fill,
And answered huskily: "Well, Mr. Flood,
Since you propose it, I believe I will."

Reduced to the misfortune of drinking alone

Alone, as if enduring to the end
A valiant armor of scarred hopes outworn,
He stood there in the middle of the road
Like Roland's ghost winding a silent horn.[3]
Below him, in the town among the trees,
Where friends of other days had honored him,
A phantom salutation of the dead
Rang thinly till old Eben's eyes were dim.

The only similarity between Mr. Flood and Roland is that each fought a losing battle alone and went down in defeat at last

Then, as a mother lays her sleeping child
Down tenderly, fearing it may awake,
He set the jug down slowly at his feet
With trembling care, knowing that most things break;
And only when assured that on firm earth

[1] Emery Neff, *Edwin Arlington Robinson*, p. 198.

[2] A reference to Omar Khayyam's *Rubaiyat*, translated by Edward Fitzgerald.

[3] Most interpretations favor *The Song of Roland* as a reference, but Browning's "Childe Roland to the Dark Tower Came" has also been proposed; certainly, Browning's narrative is psychologically closer to Robinson's than is the medieval epic.

It stood, as the uncertain lives of men   30
Assuredly did not, he paced away,
And with his hand extended paused again:

"Well, Mr. Flood, we have not met like this
In a long time; and many a change has come
To both of us, I fear, since last it was   35
We had a drop together. Welcome home!"
Convivially returning with himself,
Again he raised the jug up to the light;
And with an acquiescent quaver said:
"Well, Mr. Flood, if you insist, I might.   40

"Only a very little, Mr. Flood—
For auld lang syne. No more, sir; that will do."
So, for the time, apparently it did,
And Eben evidently thought so too;
For soon amid the silver loneliness   45
Of night he lifted up his voice and sang,
Secure, with only two moons listening,
Until the whole harmonious landscape rang—

"For auld lang syne." The weary throat gave out,
The last word wavered; and the song being done,   50
He raised again the jug regretfully
And shook his head, and was again alone.
There was not much that was ahead of him,
And there was nothing in the town below—
Where strangers would have shut the many doors   55
That many friends had opened long ago.

                                             1921

LOST ANCHORS

[This poem was first printed in the Nation for February 2, 1921.]

Like a dry fish flung inland far from shore,
There lived a sailor, warped and ocean-browned,
Who told of an old vessel, harbor-drowned
And out of mind a century before,
Where divers, on descending to explore   5
A legend that had lived its way around
The world of ships, in the dark hulk had found
Anchors, which had been seized and seen no more.

Improving a dry leisure to invest
Their misadventure with a manifest   10

Analogy that he may read who runs,
The sailor made it old as ocean grass—
Telling of much that once had come to pass
With him, whose mother should have had no sons.

1921

MANY ARE CALLED

[This poem was first printed in the *New Republic* for November 3, 1920.]

The Lord Apollo, who has never died,
Still holds alone his immemorial reign,
Supreme in an impregnable domain
That with his magic he has fortified;
And though melodious multitudes have tried
In ecstasy, in anguish, and in vain,
With invocation sacred and profane
To lure him, even the loudest are outside.

Only at unconjectured intervals,
By will of him on whom no man may gaze,   10
By word of him whose law no man has read,
A questing light may rift the sullen walls,
To cling where mostly its infrequent rays
Fall golden on the patience of the dead.

1921

THE SHEAVES

[This poem was first printed in the *Literary Review of the New York Evening Post* for December 15, 1923.]

Where long the shadows of the wind had rolled,
Green wheat was yielding to the change assigned;
And as by some vast magic undivined
The world was turning slowly into gold.
Like nothing that was ever bought or sold   5
It waited there, the body and the mind;
And with a mighty meaning of a kind
That tells the more the more it is not told.

So in a land where all days are not fair,
Fair days went on till on another day   10
A thousand golden sheaves were lying there,
Shining and still, but not for long to stay—
As if a thousand girls with golden hair
Might rise from where they slept and go away.

1925

REMBRANDT TO REMBRANDT

(Amsterdam, 1645)

[This poem was written in midsummer 1920.]

And there you are again, now as you are.
Observe yourself as you discern yourself
In your discredited ascendency;
Without your velvet or your feathers now,
Commend your new condition to your fate,   5
And your conviction to the sieves of time.
Meanwhile appraise yourself, Rembrandt van Ryn,
Now as you are—formerly more or less
Distinguished in the civil scenery,
And once a painter. There you are again,   10
Where you may see that you have on your shoulders
No lovelier burden for an ornament
Than one man's head that's yours. Praise be to God
That you have that; for you are like enough
To need it now, my friend, and from now on;   15
For there are shadows and obscurities
Immediate or impending on your view,
That may be worse than you have ever painted
For the bewildered and unhappy scorn
Of injured Hollanders in Amsterdam   20
Who cannot find their fifty florins' worth
Of Holland face where you have hidden it
In your new golden shadow that excites them,[1]
Or see that when the Lord made color and light
He made not one thing only, or believe   25
That shadows are not nothing. Saskia said,[2]

Handwritten left margin: of all the values of human experience, the one which Robinson never seriously challenged are those connected with the creative triumphs of art.

Handwritten right margin: Here Robinson defends the artist who has refused to compromise with commercialism and has persisted in respecting the integrity which he describes as "your particular consistency in your particular folly."

[1] Rembrandt's painting of the Civic Guard (1642) has been popularly and mistakenly known since the end of the eighteenth century as "The Night Watch" because of its deep shadows, which were, however, layers of varnish and dirt. After World War II the picture was cleaned, and the magnificent chiaroscuro was revealed.

[2] Saskia van Uylenburgh, whom Rembrandt married in 1634.

Before she died, how they would swear at you,
And in commiseration at themselves.
She laughed a little, too, to think of them—
And then at me. . . . That was before she died.   30

And I could wonder, as I look at you,
There as I have you now, there as you are,
Or nearly so as any skill of mine
Has ever caught you in a bilious mirror,—
Yes, I could wonder long, and with a reason,   35
If all but everything achievable
In me were not achieved and lost already,
Like a fool's gold. But you there in the glass,
And you there on the canvas, have a sort
Of solemn doubt about it; and that's well   40
For Rembrandt and for Titus.³ All that's left
Of all that was is here; and all that's here
Is one man who remembers, and one child
Beginning to forget. One, two, and three,
The others died, and then—then Saskia died;   45
And then, so men believe, the painter died.
So men believe. So it all comes at once.
And here's a fellow painting in the dark,—
A loon who cannot see that he is dead
Before God lets him die. He paints away   50
At the impossible, so Holland has it,
For venom or for spite, or for defection,
Or else for God knows what. Well, if God knows,
And Rembrandt knows, it matters not so much
What Holland knows or cares. If Holland wants   55
Its heads all in a row, and all alike,
There's Franz to do them and to do them well—⁴
Rat-catchers, archers, or apothecaries,
And one as like a rabbit as another.
Value received, and every Dutchman happy.   60
All's one to Franz, and to the rest of them,—
Their ways being theirs, are theirs.—But you, my friend,
If I have made you something as you are,
Will need those jaws and eyes and all the fight
And fire that's in them, and a little more,   65
To take you on and the world after you;
For now you fare alone, without the fashion
To sing you back and fling a flower or two
At your accusing feet. Poor Saskia saw
This coming that has come, and with a guile   70

³ Titus, Rembrandt's son by Saskia, was born in 1641.
⁴ Frans Hals (1580?–1666), who did many group portraits of the kind derisively referred to in the next line.

Of kindliness that covered half her doubts
Would give me gold, and laugh . . . before she died.

And if I see the road that you are going,
You that are not so jaunty as aforetime,
God knows if she were not appointed well   75
To die. She might have wearied of it all
Before the worst was over, or begun.
A woman waiting on a man's avouch
Of the invisible, may not wait always
Without a word betweenwhiles, or a dash   80
Of poison on his faith. Yes, even she.
She might have come to see at last with others,
And then to say with others, who say more,
That you are groping on a phantom trail
Determining a dusky way to nowhere;   85
That errors unconfessed and obstinate
Have teemed and cankered in you for so long
That even your eyes are sick, and you see light
Only because you dare not see the dark
That is around you and ahead of you.   90
She might have come, by ruinous estimation
Of old applause and outworn vanities,
To clothe you over in a shroud of dreams,
And so be nearer to the counterfeit
Of her invention than aware of yours.   95
She might, as well as any, by this time,
Unwillingly and eagerly have bitten . .
Another devil's-apple of unrest,
And so, by some attendant artifice
Or other, might anon have had you sharing   100
A taste that would have tainted everything,
And so had been for two, instead of one,
The taste of death in life—which is the food
Of art that has betrayed itself alive
And is a food of hell. She might have heard   105
Unhappily the temporary noise
Of louder names than yours, and on frail urns
That hardly will ensure a dwelling-place
For even the dust that may be left of them,
She might, and angrily, as like as not,   110
Look soon to find your name, not finding it.
She might, like many another born for joy
And for sufficient fulness of the hour,
Go famishing by now, and in the eyes
Of pitying friends and dwindling satellites   115
Be told of no uncertain dereliction
Touching the cold offence of my decline.

And even if this were so, and she were here
Again to make a fact of all my fancy,
How should I ask of her to see with me   120
Through night where many a time I seem in vain
To seek for new assurance of a gleam
That comes at last, and then, so it appears,
Only for you and me—and a few more,
Perchance, albeit their faces are not many   125
Among the ruins that are now around us.
That was a fall, my friend, we had together—
Or rather it was my house, mine alone,
That fell, leaving you safe. Be glad for that.
There's life in you that shall outlive my clay   130
That's for a time alive and will in time
Be nothing—but not yet. You that are there
Where I have painted you are safe enough,
Though I see dragons. Verily, that was a fall—
A dislocating fall, a blinding fall,   135
A fall indeed. But there are no bones broken;
And even the teeth and eyes that I make out
Among the shadows, intermittently,
Show not so firm in their accoutrement
Of terror-laden unreality   140
As you in your neglect of their performance,—
Though for their season we must humor them
For what they are: devils undoubtedly,
But not so parlous and implacable
In their undoing of poor human triumph   145
As easy fashion—or brief novelty
That ails even while it grows, and like sick fruit
Falls down anon to an indifferent earth
To break with inward rot. I say all this,
And I concede, in honor of your silence,   150
A waste of innocent facility
In tints of other colors than are mine.
I cannot paint with words, but there's a time
For most of us when words are all we have
To serve our stricken souls. And here you say,   155
"Be careful, or you may commit your soul
Soon to the very devil of your denial."
I might have wagered on you to say that,
Knowing that I believe in you too surely
To spoil you with a kick or paint you over.   160

No, my good friend, Mynheer Rembrandt van Ryn—
Sometime a personage in Amsterdam,
But now not much—I shall not give myself
To be the sport of any dragon-spawn

Of Holland, or elsewhere. Holland was hell   165
Not long ago, and there were dragons then
More to be fought than any of these we see
That we may foster now. They are not real,
But not for that the less to be regarded;
For there are slimy tyrants born of nothing   170
That harden slowly into seeming life
And have the strength of madness. I confess,
Accordingly, the wisdom of your care
That I look out for them. Whether I would
Or not, I must; and here we are as one   175
With our necessity. For though you loom
A little harsh in your respect of time
And circumstance, and of ordained eclipse,
We know together of a golden flood
That with its overflow shall drown away   180
The dikes that held it; and we know thereby
That in its rising light there lives a fire
No devils that are lodging here in Holland
Shall put out wholly, or much agitate,
Except in unofficial preparation   185
They put out first the sun. It's well enough
To think of them; wherefore I thank you, sir,
Alike for your remembrance and attention.

But there are demons that are longer-lived
Than doubts that have a brief and evil term   190
To congregate among the futile shards
And architraves of eminent collapse.
They are a many-favored family,
All told, with not a misbegotten dwarf
Among the rest that I can love so little   195
As one occult abortion in especial
Who perches on a picture (when it's done)
And says, "What of it, Rembrandt, if you do?"
This incubus would seem to be a sort
Of chorus, indicating, for our good,   200
The silence of the few friends that are left:
"What of it, Rembrandt, even if you know?"
It says again; "and you don't know for certain.
What if in fifty or a hundred years
They find you out? You may have gone meanwhile   205
So greatly to the dogs that you'll not care
Much what they find. If this be all you are—
This unaccountable aspiring insect—
You'll sleep as easy in oblivion
As any sacred monk or parricide;   210
And if, as you conceive, you are eternal,
Your soul may laugh, remembering (if a soul

Remembers) your befrenzied aspiration
To smear with certain ochres and some oil
A few more perishable ells of cloth,   215
And once or twice, to square your vanity,
Prove it was you alone that should achieve
A mortal eye—that may, no less, tomorrow
Show an immortal reason why today
Men see no more. And what's a mortal eye   220
More than a mortal herring, who has eyes
As well as you? Why not paint herrings, Rembrandt?
Or if not herrings, why not a split beef? 5
Perceive it only in its unalloyed
Integrity, and you may find in it   225
A beautified accomplishment no less
Indigenous than one that appertains
To gentlemen and ladies eating it.
The same God planned and made you, beef and human;
And one, but for His whim, might be the other."   230

That's how he says it, Rembrandt, if you listen;
He says it, and he goes. And then, sometimes,
There comes another spirit in his place—
One with a more engaging argument,
And with a softer note for saying truth   235
Not soft. Whether it be the truth or not,
I name it so; for there's a string in me
Somewhere that answers—which is natural,
Since I am but a living instrument
Played on by powers that are invisible.   240
"You might go faster, if not quite so far,"
He says, "if in your vexed economy
There lived a faculty for saying yes
And meaning no, and then for doing neither;
But since Apollo sees it otherwise,   245
Your Dutchmen, who are swearing at you still
For your pernicious filching of their florins,
May likely curse you down their generation,
Not having understood there was no malice
Or grinning evil in a golden shadow   250
That shall outshine their slight identities
And hold their faces when their names are nothing.
But this, as you discern, or should by now
Surmise, for you is neither here nor there:
You made your picture as your demon willed it;   255
That's about all of that. Now make as many

---

5 Still life, here referred to derisively, was brought to a high point of achievement in seventeenth-century Holland. The demon, who is speaking, taunts Rembrandt with the implicit reminder that he had painted in this genre. As late as 1655 Rembrandt did "The Slaughtered Ox."

As may be to be made,—for so you will,
Whatever the toll may be, and hold your light
So that you see, without so much to blind you
As even the cobweb-flash of a misgiving,   260
Assured and certain that if you see right
Others will have to see—albeit their seeing
Shall irk them out of their serenity
For such a time as umbrage may require.
But there are many reptiles in the night   265
That now is coming on, and they are hungry;
And there's a Rembrandt to be satisfied
Who never will be, howsoever much
He be assured of an ascendency
That has not yet a shadow's worth of sound   270
Where Holland has its ears. And what of that?
Have you the weary leisure or sick wit
That breeds of its indifference a false envy
That is the vermin on accomplishment?
Are you inaugurating your new service   275
With fasting for a food you would not eat?
You are the servant, Rembrandt, not the master,—
But you are not assigned with other slaves
That in their freedom are the most in fear.
One of the few that are so fortunate   280
As to be told their task and to be given
A skill to do it with a tool too keen
For timid safety, bow your elected head
Under the stars tonight, and whip your devils
Each to his nest in hell. Forget your days,   285
And so forgive the years that may not be
So many as to be more than you may need
For your particular consistency
In your peculiar folly. You are counting
Some fewer years than forty at your heels;   290
And they have not pursued your gait so fast
As your oblivion—which has beaten them,
And rides now on your neck like an old man
With iron shins and fingers. Let him ride
(You haven't so much to say now about that),   295
And in a proper season let him run.
You may be dead then, even as you may now
Anticipate some other mortal strokes
Attending your felicity; and for that,
Oblivion heretofore has done some running   300
Away from graves, and will do more of it."

That's how it is your wiser spirit speaks,
Rembrandt. If you believe him, why complain?

If not, why paint? And why, in any event,
Look back for the old joy and the old roses,   305
Or the old fame? They are all gone together,
And Saskia with them; and with her left out,
They would avail no more now than one strand
Of Samson's hair wound round his little finger
Before the temple fell. Nor more are you   310
In any sudden danger to forget
That in Apollo's house there are no clocks
Or calendars to say for you in time
How far you are away from Amsterdam,
Or that the one same law that bids you see   315
Where now you see alone forbids in turn
Your light from Holland eyes till Holland ears
Are told of it; for that way, my good fellow,
Is one way more to death. If at the first
Of your long turning, which may still be longer   320
Than even your faith has measured it, you sigh
For distant welcome that may not be seen,
Or wayside shouting that will not be heard,
You may as well accommodate your greatness
To the convenience of an easy ditch,   325
And, anchored there with all your widowed gold,[6]
Forget your darkness in the dark, and hear
No longer the cold wash of Holland scorn.

1921

Reading Suggestions

The *Collected Poems* of Edwin Arlington Robinson, first printed in 1921, has been reprinted several times, the first complete edition being that of 1937. The long psychological narratives are now, for the most part, unreadable, but *Merlin* (1917), *Lancelot* (1920), and *Tristram* (1927) are well worth reading. *Selected Letters of Edwin Arlington Robinson*, with an introduction by Robinson's friend, Ridgely Torrence, appeared in 1940, and in 1947 *Untriangulated Stars: Letters of Edwin Arlington Robinson to Harry De Forest Smith*, edited by Denham Sutcliffe. In 1936 Charles Beecher Hogan published *A Bibliography of Edwin Arlington Robinson.*

Hermann Hagedorn has written the standard biography, *Edwin Arlington Robinson* (1938), but Emery Neff's *Edwin Arlington Robinson* (1948) contains new material and attempts a critical evaluation, probably too flattering. Interpretive studies of book length are Charles Cestre's *An Introduction to Ed-*

[6] Saskia was an heiress and willed Rembrandt her considerable inheritance, which, apparently, he never realized because of lawsuits. Here at the end of the poem, in the juxtaposition of Saskia's gold and the darkness of his life, there is a telling and ironic contrast to the "golden shadow" of his art, which transcends the fortunes of human existence.

win Arlington Robinson (1930), R. P. T. Coffin's New Poetry of New England: Frost and Robinson (1938), Yvor Winters' Edwin Arlington Robinson (1946), Edwin S. Barnard's Edwin Arlington Robinson: A Critical Study (1952), and Edwin S. Fussell's Edwin Arlington Robinson: The Literary Background of a Traditional Poet (1954). Estelle Kaplan's Philosophy in the Poetry of Edwin Arlington Robinson (1940) concentrates largely on the long psychological narratives.

Helpful monographs and articles are Floyd Stovall's "The Optimism behind Robinson's Tragedies." American Literature (March 1938); Frederic I. Carpenter's "Tristram the Transcendent," New England Quarterly (September 1938); Louis O. Coxe's "Edwin Arlington Robinson: The Lost Tradition," Sewanee Review (Spring 1954), and his Edwin Arlington Robinson (1962) in the series of the University of Minnesota Pamphlets; Robert D. Stevick's "Robinson and William James," University of Kansas City Review (Summer 1959); Richard P. Adams' "The Failure of Edwin Arlington Robinson," Tulane Studies in English (1961); and Charles T. Davis' "Image Patterns in the Poetry of E. A. Robinson," College English (March 1961).

Biography

Edwin Arlington Robinson was born in the village of Head Tide, Maine, on December 22, 1869, where his father had a prosperous business in grain and lumber. In 1870 the family moved to the neighboring town of Gardiner. Here Edwin attended high school, showing a strong inclination toward literature. Soon he came under the influence of Dr. Alanson Tucker Schumann, a homeopathic physician and eccentric, who had a passion for poetry and who introduced him to a small literary circle in the town. Exceedingly shy and sensitive, Edwin also confided in a few high school friends, particularly Harry De Forest Smith, who went on to Bowdoin and subsequently became a Professor of Greek at Amherst.

When Edwin had to go to Boston for treatment of a diseased ear, his father, though he had never intended that the son should go to college, permitted him to attend Harvard as a special student. The two years in Cambridge (1891-1893) were of decisive importance in opening up the world of knowledge and culture for him. In 1896, after unsuccessful efforts at writing short stories, he brought out his first book of poems, The Torrent and the Night Before, with the self-conscious flourish, "This book is dedicated to any man, woman, or critic who will cut the edges of it—I have done the top." In the following year he published The Children of the Night, made up of poems from the previous volume together with new ones.

Convinced that provincial, commercial Gardiner was no environment for a poet, he moved to New York to try his luck with writing poetry and starving. For many years he led a precarious existence, yielding occasionally to the despair of liquor; but his own stubborn faith in poetry as a vocation and the aid of friends who provided food and shelter saw him through the dark years. The periodicals would not accept his poems, and his third volume, Captain Craig (1902), appeared only after the most discouraging delays and only with the financial guarantee of two friends. In 1903, in a brave effort to earn his way, he became a time checker in a subway being built, but the following year, upon its completion, he was laid off; and, of course, during this period he wrote no poetry.

Meanwhile Kermit Roosevelt, a student at Groton, had been introduced to *The Children of the Night*, which he admired, and in turn he introduced his father, Theodore Roosevelt, President of the United States, to the book. Our most literary President liked it immensely and said so in an article in the *Outlook* (1905). The practical upshot was a job for Robinson in the New York Custom House, and with this security and leisure he wrote enough poems for another book, *The Town down the River* (1910).

In 1911 Hermann Hagedorn introduced him to the MacDowell Colony at Peterborough, New Hampshire, established by the widow of the composer, Edward MacDowell, as a retreat where artists and writers might work. At first skeptical, Robinson fell in love with the place and returned every summer thereafter; and as the years passed he became the revered Senior Citizen of the Colony. He still needed financial support, however, and in 1916 a group of friends established a fund upon which he might draw for the next four years.

Though he maintained a high level of achievement in *The Man against the Sky*, published in 1916, Robinson had to wait until the 1920's to come into his own. The *Collected Poems* (1921), representing twenty-five years of work, convinced a large number of readers and critics that Robinson's position at the head of American poetry could no longer be denied. The book won the Pulitzer Prize, as did two subsequent volumes—*The Man Who Died Twice* (1924) and *Tristram* (1927). The latter, a Literary Guild selection, sold 75,000 copies in the first year. From 1929 on he published one long narrative poem a year, but these did little to enhance or damage a reputation that was secure in any event. He died of cancer in New York on April 6, 1935, *King Jasper* being published posthumously.

Decided to be a poet
when he studied Virgil in high school.

Frost has remained untouched
by contemporary fads and styles
in poetry. Nothing of the
"experimental" in his technique,
no influence of Pound, Eliot,
or the modern avant-garde
schools of poetry. Reason
for this is that his literary
attitudes formed prior to
avant-garde movements —
another is that he has an
instinctive distrust of literary
exhibitionism, of poets
who contrive to be deliberately
obscure in order to be original.

Frost is best remembered as an
intellectual aristocrat.
I desire the best and greatest poet
of New England people and countryside.

ROBERT FROST ✤
a sturdy individualist 1874-1963

He is a realistic lover of
nature.

When asked what had influenced
him most in life he replied,
"When 12 yrs. old worked in
a shoe shop and carried nails
in mouth — neither swollowed
or inhaled!"

See: Robert Frost An Introduction by
Greenberg and Hepburn

as Frost deals with characterist

"Brecke" is an example of his
conversation pieces.

Introduction

The most striking thing about Frost is the distinctive voice that sounds through his poetry. His is not just another of the many efforts since Wordsworth's day to restore the living language to verse. He does that too, using the words and idioms of everyday speech rather than of literary convention. This method is characteristic of most modern poets, even writers as opposite to him as Eliot and Stevens, but Frost differs radically from the dominant school in both technique and goal. His concern with voice tones comes from an orientation and leads to a poetic structure entirely different from theirs. Both began with an emphasis on colloquial language, as well as on sharp visual images, but their divergence was marked from that point on. Frost retained the surface logic of speech in the present tense because he wanted to render his meanings, symbolically or dramatically, in the immediate scene. The Symbolists abandoned it because they wanted to let their images range through time and take on the associated meanings of a long historical tradition. In a word, because of a fundamental disagreement about the nature of meaning in poetry they developed opposite techniques.

The difference between the two kinds of poetry has long been recognized, but some curious results have flowed from a failure to see the reasons for it. Frost has won a wide following with the general reader; Eliot has long been the center of a powerful critical élite. The opposing camps have treated this divergence as irreconcilable, and their hostility has been so extreme as to leave the impression one cannot admire both kinds of poetry. Frost's very popularity has been held against him on the grounds that it comes from his lacking the complexity of thought and form central to the best modern verse—the irony, paradox, tension, bold metaphor, learned symbolism, and myth. The opposite charge, that Eliot and the dominant school are too complex and obscure, need not concern the serious student since much great literature is too difficult to interest the general public. But Frost deserves to be rescued from the misapprehension of certain prominent critics, for he has been attacked as well as admired for the wrong reasons, the controversy frequently centering on lesser poems. His best poetry offers all the challenge, both in idea and art, that modern readers demand. His simplicity is only apparent, an easy surface beneath which lurk disturbing ambiguities and questionings. Neither his speaking voice nor his regional settings are for the sake of picturesqueness, but are the deliberate devices of a special poetic mode. His old-fashioned rural posture has been adopted as a point of view for seeing the modern world in a new light.

I

The surest way into the heart of Frost's major achievement is through understanding his use of pastoral, as set forth in a recent study.[1] One of the oldest modes in Western poetry, pastoralism flowered again during the English Renascence until its decay in the eighteenth century. Traditionalist though he may be, Frost was not one to attach himself to an outworn convention. Dropping all the artificial machinery of pastoral—shepherds and pipes, country dances and lovers' laments—he retained only the fundamental form, that is, the perspective, and gave it new life with the local details of his own countryside. Theocritus had discovered in his Sicilian boyhood a frame for viewing the teeming city life of Alexandria in the third century B.C. Similarly, Frost, during his English residence, discovered that remote rural New England could serve as a novel Arcadia, and when he adopted the point of view of the farmer as his poetic mask he came into his own as an artist.

A newly published letter, written in the crucial summer of 1913 between his first and second volumes, makes this explicit. "In 'Mowing,'" he said of his best lyric in A Boy's Will, "I come so near what I long to get that I almost despair of coming nearer." What he needed was not just a subject matter but a poetic structure. Then, referring to the radically new poems he was shaping up for North of Boston, he added: "I had some character strokes I had to get in somewhere and I chose a sort of eclogue form for them. Rather I dropped into that form. And I dropped to an everyday level of diction that even Wordsworth kept above. . . . The language is appropriate to the virtues I celebrate." Early commentators noticed this new direction. His English publisher wanted to call the volume embodying it Yankee Eclogues. Ezra Pound reviewed it under the rubric "American Georgics," and Amy Lowell called these poems "true pastorals of the hill country." All this has been so lost sight of over the years it needs to be pointed out again today just how North of Boston marks the beginning of Frost's distinctive achievement.

The pastoral mode gave him the setting, events, and characters of New

---

[1] John Lynen, The Pastoral Art of Robert Frost (1960). The next few pages are indebted to this work, which is basic to any reading of Frost's poetry.

England farm life, quite obviously, but this is an overworked point. More significantly, it furnished the characteristic design for his best poems—the speaking voice, imagery, and structure—though only a few of them are actually written in this genre. Its real purpose is not to praise the country at the expense of the city, as being closer to reality, free of social evils, and wise in its simplicity. This would be sentimental and irrelevant to modern experience, since both the poet and his audience today are unavoidably urban. Instead, it provides a contrast showing the complexity of relations between the two worlds and the values they stand for. By creating a myth of his unique and isolated world, the pastoralist transforms it into a symbolic one. This gives him a new perspective for implicit commentary on its differences from the one we actually live in, as well as the human realities basic to both. Frost's symbolism in these poems does not work primarily through allusion, metaphor, and allegory. Instead, it emerges from the analogies inherent in the very framework of his special vision, a sustained series of contrasts that open out from the rural microcosm to the great world beyond.

"The Pasture," consistently printed as an epigraph to his collections, is a clue to the kind of poetry he wrote during the first half of his career. Its "Come away" is not a call to action, urging a return to the agrarian life, but an invitation to participate in this world enough to know it as a touchstone. Its values are rendered by the poet, not didactically, but in images, and the reader who is ignorant of their meaning must be initiated. Spring and cow raise the analogy of water faucet and the carton of milk he buys at the chain store. But he must be reminded of the beauty and knowledge that go with the practical task of providing the necessities of life on a farm. What one sees in cleaning the pasture spring, what one learns from the process of calving and milking, not to mention the charm of this innocent idyll—all this modern man has lost in his striving for efficiency. The urban world that poet and reader bring with them by implication, superior as it is in many ways, furnishes a background against which the rural world stands out sharply. And because the analogy is implied, not stated, the meanings that open out are generalized, suggesting the limitations as well as the values of both ways of life.

So with the central image in "Mending Wall." By telling a simple anecdote from rural life, presenting two conflicting points of view, it raises all the questions involved in erecting any man-made barrier. To limit it to only one of these would falsify the poem's meaning. The same is true of his best pastorals. The buzz saw and amputated hand in "Out, Out—" (with its title from the famous soliloquy in *Macbeth*) symbolize the one piece of machinery most essential to rural life in tragic conflict with the human instrument that is a source both of livelihood and of the creative power for becoming an effective man in that world. Again, in "An Old Man's Winter Night," the lamp and the moon suggest the reason and imaginative awareness by which man tries to give order and meaning to his life, so he can "keep" not only a farm but a whole countryside. Such symbols may be broad, but they are not indefinite. Lacking the precision characteristic of those in Eliot's poetry, they are not arrows moving from images to specific ideas but vistas that open out on whole classes of experience, as Professor Lynen points out. What is definite is the direction of vision, seeing the urban world from the perspective of the rural.

Unlike most regional writers, Frost does not present New England as it really is, but a stylized portrayal in words of its essence. It is strictly limited to the rural areas north of Boston, omitting the industrial cities and prosperous farms, the Brahmins and the Irish immigrants. By a disciplined art of selection it is still further reduced to those few local traits significant for his pastoralism. The landscape includes orchard, farm, and mountain, trees and flowers, brook and spring, buck, spider, moth, and bird. Though much is excluded this makes a small familiar scene for action and, more importantly, a frame for the poet's imagination. There is a limited set of man-made objects: stone walls, cellar and barn, woodpile and axe, grindstone and ladder and well, gravel roads and old houses. Many details are suppressed, but the precision with which a few are etched gives a vivid impression of farm life, and every sketch of a particular locale conjures up the region as a whole. The actors on this scene are restricted to special kinds of characters. There are hired hands and an aging farmer, young lovers and a rustic philosopher, isolated couples, a lonely wife, a conservative widow, and a witch. If all were listed they would suggest quite a range, until one remembered how many are left out.

Like all myth makers, his method is symbolic. Yet Frost's success is proved by the fact that he has been widely accepted as a realist, his pastoral version being taken for New England itself. The description seems so true the surface reader overlooks the symbolism. He willingly suspends his disbelief that New England is rural even while he knows it is largely urban. The industrial world Frost omits is standardized and lacking in coherence. The regional world he portrays in poem after poem is stable and unified, yet bristling with human differences. What is important is the art by which imaginative symbols are presented as if they were literal facts. In creating such a world all depends on the poet's skill in selecting. There are two controlling principles: to relate the characters to the land, and the whole region to the value system of those who share this way of life. The long pastoral "New Hampshire" is a comic account of how he changed the locale to suit his mythic purposes, and so best illustrates the basic function and design of pastoralism in his poetry.

Setting alone would never have created this special vision. It is dramatized by his famous "Yankee manner," a deliberately contrived idiom for presenting his rural scene, characters, and action. Much has been said about

Frost's distinctive voice tones, but it is misleading to think of them as simply transcribed from the people in some particular upcountry region. The poet himself has given a more likely clue: "Hard to trace my origins. First thought I heard the voice from the printed page in Virgilian eclogue and Hamlet." And the explicit denial: "My sounds are not dialect; just accent." He has made many attempts to define his intentions and his method. One must write not only with his eye on the object but "with the ear on the speaking voice," and then arrange his words in a sequence so as "to control the intonations and the pauses" of the reader. "The living part of a poem is the intonation entangled somehow in the syntax, idiom, and meaning of a sentence," he has said, "fastened to the page for the ear of the imagination." He has even been so extravagant as to claim that since "every meaning has a particular sound-posture" he can listen to a conversation beyond closed doors, when the words are inaudible, and still catch its meaning in "the sound of sense." But all this is not a matter of pure technique, to extend the practice of Shakespeare and the theory of Wordsworth by recapturing the living language in poetry. Frost's chief purpose has been to further his pastoralism by creating a generalized vernacular suited to his mythical region without being so uniquely of New England as to be unreadable by outsiders, as in Lowell's "Bigelow Papers." It is not just a picturesque way of speaking but a style symbolic of a mode of thinking. It not only dramatizes the character but also defines the attitudes of a whole society.

This function of style is neatly illustrated in "The Code," where the Yankee manner is subject as well as medium. The title, by its double meaning, stands for both a code of behavior and the code for expressing it. The two must be inseparable if the Yankee laborer is to keep his high concept of self-respect in regard to his work from being compromised. More interesting is the function of the voice in "The Grindstone," for it dramatizes a more complexly conceived character. The speaker here has gone back in memory to a boyhood experience, and as he tries to articulate it he begins to view it symbolically. So the poet can hint at its meanings in just the right way, the symbols themselves growing naturally out of the process of perception and expression. The stone becomes an analogue of the earth, as Frost has confirmed in a letter, "an image of the naughty world," adding: "You know Herschel had a grindstone theory [of the shape] of the universe." [2] The symbolism extends to the grinders too, the old man and the boy. The former, like the stone turning in a circle, has never gotten "anywhere." But the speaker has. He has progressed from youth to maturity. As a man, moving through linear time, he is also subject to death at the sweep of Father Time's scythe. These meanings are suggested by the symbolism, then rendered by the manner of speaking, which dramatizes the

[2] Quoted in Lynen, p. 91.

character, his values, and his mode of thinking. Hence the central importance of the speaker, who presents the poem as the exploration of a trivial incident for hidden meanings.

II

This kind of poetry clearly had possibilities for further development There was a tendency to drama in the very nature of Frost's pastoral vision, which offered him not only characters and rudimentary action but a theater, a very real rural scene and society, bound together by a clearly defined set of values. It was just a step, then, from his lyrics and narratives to his great dramatic poems. When his "Yankee speaker" was placed in a sufficiently intense situation, he turned naturally into a monologist. When there were two, monologue became dialogue. Some twenty of the longer poems are essentially dramatic, though judged strictly as to form only a few can be so classified because most are inclosed within a narrative frame. The true test, according to Professor Lynen, is that the main concern should be to portray action, "action felt to be happening in the present." The range of these poems is wide, beginning with the most relaxed conversational pieces like "The Grindstone" and "The Ax-Helve," which record a reminiscence or a past anecdote. A middle stage is the narrative whose brief present action merely provides the frame for a story of past events, and the monologist a viewpoint for understanding it. Such a poem is "The Black Cottage" and "The Code" itself. The highest level is reached in the dramas fully unfolded before the reader's eyes, where action is all and the speech is impassioned.

Frost's dramatic dialogues are like one-act plays. "The Death of the Hired Man" and "Home Burial," the two included here, can be read as complementary pieces on the theme of sympathy. The action of both consists in the struggle for understanding between a woman of feeling and her practical husband, and is carried out exclusively through their exchanges. In each the focus is off stage—on the hired man who comes "home" to die and on the first-born child lying in the family graveyard— but each of these characters is made vivid by a symbol arising naturally from the setting: the moon and cloud in one, the burial ground framed by the stair window in the other. From this point on they diverge widely by a reversal of the roles of sympathy, leading to quiet resolution in the former and the mounting intensity of a threatened break in the latter. The dramatic monologues are limited to psychological action that takes place entirely within the character speaking, except for flashbacks, since the others are present only as audience. The result may be self-recognition, as in "The Witch of Coös" (Coös being the name of a county in New Hampshire). At a moment of crisis she faces the truth of her own past and tells a spine-chiller of her pretended witchcraft, as a cover for feelings of sexual guilt, that has been called the best thing of its kind since Chaucer. Or the out-come may hover painfully between self-revelation and self-realization, as in Frost's most appalling drama.

"A Servant to Servants" is the attempted unburdening of a pent-up hill wife that runs nearly two hundred lines without pause for response. The occasion for this breathless monologue is set by some strangers who have come to thank her for permission to camp on her land, and who out of gratitude and courtesy must listen, passive and spellbound. Their presence is acknowledged only in the opening and closing lines that frame her com-pulsive account of herself. The upcountry vernacular is handled flawlessly as realism. More importantly, her flat intoning voice is the key to her real trouble, a failure of the capacity to feel and communicate. Yet the steady flood of her self-diagnosis suggests countless rehearsals, until it has lost its horror for her and much of its meaning. These are symptoms of a mind verging on collapse.

This fear too is finally confessed, indirectly, in the story of her uncle's madness. It gives the poem its dramatic center, drawing together the ran-dom associations flung out by her monologue. Locked upstairs in a cage, "Like a beast's stall," her father's brother was kept, stripping himself naked in his violence and shouting obscenities. Her identification with this uncle —"It's time I took my turn upstairs in jail"—shows the desperation of her plight. The root of it is suggested by the poem's title, which refers to the biblical account of Noah's drunkenness, when his son Ham saw his naked-ness. The punishment for this violation of decency was curiously visited on the next generation: "Cursed be Canaan; a servant of servants shall he be" (Genesis 9:21–25). Like the grandson who did not see Noah naked, so the niece who never saw her uncle has become "A Servant to Servants." Like the uncle, she too is imprisoned in her own house without communion. Whatever traumatic experience in the past may have fixed her mind in an attraction-repulsion to nudity is not revealed. Instead, the poem's drama lies in the pathetic dignity with which she strives for realization as well as reve-lation of her plight. When the strangers, anxious to be freed of entrapment in her monologue, say they are afraid that they are "keeping" her from her work, she faces its utmost implication: "I need to *be* kept." The double meaning, emphasized by italics, delivers the full import of the poem in one stroke.

All of these poems develop out of Frost's pastoralism and are controlled by it—in setting, personae, action, voice tone, and value system. The pas-toral and dramatic veins run parallel in his poetry, reaching their highest achievement in *North of Boston* and *New Hampshire,* and remain domi-nant until mid-career. The later volumes show a shift of interest. Drama fades back into pure narrative or turns aside into satire of contemporary is-sues. Far more important are the short poems with a bent toward metaphys-ical wit. Finest of all his later work are the lyrics that come back again to nature, but in a new way, as will be seen. Even when he apparently returns to the form of drama his purpose is really philosophical, to dramatize an idea. The one example included here is "West-Running Brook," the title poem in a pivotal volume published in 1928. The setting could be New England, but the focus is not rural, and the Yankee speaker has been replaced by a sophisticated young couple. Instead of dramatic dialogue, there is conversational banter to explore several sides of an idea. This play of oppositions in the lovers' argument, suggesting that their harmony is somehow attained by reconciling contraries, matches the very belief they finally arrive at. It is the idea that life in man as well as in nature originates in an instinctive resistance to the pull of death, like the wave in this brook with its backward thrust against the current and toward its source. This poem is neither pastoral in perspective nor dramatic in expression.

III

Pastoralism may open the main door into Frost's house of poetry, but it does not unlock all the rooms. Nor does it exhaust all the possibilities of even those poems that seem most in the tradition, as a close look at form and figure in two important ones will show. For example, there is the false notion that his use of imagery is sparse and tame in comparison with poets like Eliot, that he limits himself instead to a kind of natural symbolism springing from the analogies of pastoral (for example, "winter" equals "death"). All this is refuted by the poet himself, who says, "Every poem is a new metaphor inside or it is nothing." Imagery of all sorts—allusion, simile, metaphor, symbol, myth—functions significantly in his best work by reason of the very economy with which it is employed.

"The Ax-Helve," an anecdote about a Canadian woodsman who makes his own axe-handles, is on the surface a simple pastoral narrative. But the poem is actually an intricate structure of images framed by a pair of similes. The first one describes the store-bought handle, where straight-grained wood and machine design are at cross purposes, as being "Like the two strokes across a dollar sign." This is an ingenious piece of wit directed against the profit motive, with a sidelong allusion to the proverb: "For the love of money is the root of all evil" (I Timothy 6:10)—just what one would expect from the rural-urban contrast. But even here the one word used for the proper shape of any axe-helve, "serpentine," prepares for the surprise simile at the conclusion. There the craftsman, displaying his own creation for the narrator's admiration, sets it on end "Erect . . . as when the snake stood up for evil in the Garden."

The shock of this figure sends the reader again to the Bible for his clue, then back through the poem for submerged meanings. How is the hand-made helve, as well as the commercial one, a symbol of evil? In the Eden myth the evil taught by the serpent was knowledge, the very subject these two have been discussing during the carving—that is, man's capacity to understand and hence his skill to do. God's resentment at Adam's knowledge of good and evil is clearly stated in Genesis 3:22: "the man is become as one of us," godlike because a potential creator. Baptiste has made an axe, the narrator a poem. They are most in harmony over their theory of creativity, as rendered in a metaphor buried at the center of the poem: the lines of a good helve are "native to the grain" before the knife expresses them. This is Frost's theory of organic form accommodated to convention by the artist's skill, proving that "The Ax-Helve" is a poem about the making of poems. It takes its meaning as well as its shape from the startling serpentine images that underlie the innocent pastoral surface.

The notion is equally untenable that Frost has cut himself off from the richest resources of modern verse by his adherence to traditional forms. He is at odds with the main line followed by the Symbolists, it is true. But he is well aware of the issues and is a bolder experimenter than has been realized. Poetic form, he holds, is experience shaped by pressures from within and from without: "He who knows not both knows neither." Writing in free verse he has likened to playing tennis with the net down, adding that there is "a better wildness of logic than of inconsequence." He likes the challenge of conventional meters, stanzas, and forms because they afford endless opportunities for novelty through the poet's skill in exploiting them to render his unique vision. But for him form and meaning are inseparable. Knowledge comes to the poet in the "wild free ways of wit and art," but only when subjected to the dual discipline of a steadying theme and a steadying verse pattern. The problem is how to achieve an original tune "in such a straightness as meter." The "figure a poem makes" is an accommodation between the organic form native to the grain of a chosen subject and the traditional form the poet commits himself to.

Frost has given an exaggerated account of the role played by formal techniques in the creation of one of his best known lyrics, "Stopping by Woods on a Snowy Evening." With the first line he had set up a four-beat pattern, but he adds, "I'm not terribly committed there. I can do a great many things." But the second line, in the same meter and rhymed, seemed like a commitment to couplets. With one more rhyming pair "I'd be in for it. I'd have to have couplets all the way"; but so far "I was dancing still. I was free. Then I committed a stanza." The pattern was a quatrain, rhymed *aaba*, but this left the third line still uncommitted. By picking up its end sound for the rhyming lines of the next stanza, and so on to the end, he had an interlocking scheme as intricate as one of the early Italian forms. But his very success had its drawback: "How was I going to get out of that stanza?" He solved the problem of his endless chain link by rhyming all four lines of the final stanza, with the last two lines identical. It was a magnificent stroke, and no mere verse acrobatics but the poem's greatest achievement of meaning. The repeated last line, "And miles to go before I sleep," emphasizes the natural symbolism that turns an unspecified errand with sleep at the end into the journey of life and the final rest of death. By the perfect marriage of pastoral subject to sophisticated verse form, he has illustrated his own witty definition of how a poem is created. (See "The Figure a Poem Makes," pages 624-626.)

The capacity to perform with freedom in spite of strict controls Frost calls "moving easy in harness." Once, in "Acquainted with the Night," he put himself in double reins, only to come in at the finish with a new style suited to the ambiguity of his thought. He begins with terza rima, Dante's interlocking triplets, as to rhyme scheme; then divides his poem into the two components of a sonnet, with event and comment; and ends in a fourteenth line that circles back to repeat the first, but with a new meaning from the variation in stress. The fusion of these two traditional forms suggests an extended meditation, broken off as futile, then deftly rounded into a single idea. After gazing fearlessly into the abyss of the infinite, he can only report that man's finite clock is "neither wrong nor right."

Again, his most original astronomical poem adapts the short lyric line of Herrick to the conditions of twentieth-century thought. On the page it takes the shape of a telescope pointed up to heaven. Its title, "I Will Sing You One-O," identical with that of an old crusader's song in praise of the One-and-Only God, is an ironic reference to the diminished hold of Christian revelation on men's minds. Instead, he sends his thoughts up toward the "cosmic motes" in a kind of scientific prayer, and the relation he discovers between finite and infinite time is rendered by a metaphysical image that invokes the dictum of Sir James Jeans: "We cannot move a finger without disturbing all the stars." This is not the comfortable Deism of Newton's mechanistic universe, but the more precarious harmony of modern astrophysics. Both are city poems, in which the perspective of science replaces that of the rural world.

Frost's reworkings of the old forms is one of his greatest claims to originality. But in order to transmute them he needed the discipline necessary for moving easy in harness. A number of his lesser poems are expert renderings of the heroic couplet, ballad, formal quatrain, and the more complex stanzas favored by Romantic poets. The sonnet pure and simple he could execute with consummate skill, as in "The Silken Tent," which is a witty conceit for the complexities of the sonnet itself. But it is the strictness of such traditional forms that "has driven so many to free verse," as Frost realizes. The sonneteer, for example, must face the problem "whether he will outlast or last out the fourteen lines—have to cramp or stretch to come out even." Like Hopkins, Frost has maneuvered its formal limitations to find a new freedom. "For Once, Then, Something," is such a deviationist sonnet, yet it encompasses a theme that Eliot or Stevens would have found valid.

The greatest freedom Frost ever allowed himself was in blank verse without any of the shackles of stanza or rhyme. Here, his departures from strict iambic pentameter, the one formal element retained, go as far as Shakespeare's latest experiments and anticipate the relaxed verse approximations of Eliot's plays. Though he believed that formal meter was the discipline most essential to poetry, he knew that language keeps breaking loose from all attempts to order it, and he wanted to preserve this freedom even as he brought it to form. His characteristic rhythms are produced by a tug of war between the absolute demands of meter and the flexible patterns of speech, with an edge of victory to the latter. "The possibilities of tune from the dramatic tones of meaning struck across the rigidity of a limited meter are endless," Frost has theorized, and this is borne out in his pastorals, dialogues, and monologues. The human voice in all its living modulations is what one chiefly hears in those "talk-poems," as he calls them, loosening to the breaking point the strict metrical requirements.

This has been discussed earlier in connection with his creation of the "Yankee manner" in terms of idiom, tune, inflection, and so on. But it is also a matter of vocabulary, sense as well as sound, the simple words of rural people having a special relation to rhythm and meaning. For one thing, most monosyllables can either take or leave off accent ("Whose woods these are I think I know"), thus allowing for great flexibility in making the speech go with or against the formally imposed meter. They predominate in the poems of his early and middle periods; in such a typical one as "Stopping by Woods," for example, there are 89 monosyllables in a total count of 109 words. Again, the speech of New England yeomen, limited though it is to a basic vocabulary, gains color and variety from their vigorous tone of saying, as he learned from Emerson's praise of it in "Monadnock." "He came pretty near making me an anti-vocabularian," Frost says, but this should not be taken to mean that he cut himself off from the full resources of the English language. He stylized it to rural talk for the pastorals and dramas, and retained this living tone modulated to different needs in other and later poems, but he himself is a word monger of the most sophisticated sort.

Emerson also first set him thinking about how to revitalize language in general: " 'Cut these sentences and they bleed,' he says. . . . he had me there, I never got over that." The extent of this influence is suggested by Frost's own formulation late in life of what the poet must learn about the meanings of words, in context as well as in usage: "Form in language is such a disjected lot of old broken pieces it seems almost as non-existent as the spirit till the two embrace in the sky. They are not to be thought of as encountering in rivalry but in creation." In most of the techniques for renewing poetic language—puns, playing with magnitudes, abrupt shifts from one level of discourse to another, levying on root meanings—Frost is in the main stream of experimenters since Baudelaire. These characteristics become more prominent the further he moves away from pastoral, though the skill was developed early, as in "Fire and Ice." The meaning there may be embodied in the two bold metaphors, but what gives them their intensity is the clipped style of the commentary, the jagged short lines, the clever rhymes, the language of wit and surprise for rendering a serious theme. This line of development reaches its furthest verbal and metaphorical experimentation in such a late poem as "Design," which demands close reading.[3]

IV

In his later work Frost has opened up many "further ranges" beyond his regional world. It is notable that the best of these poems involve a return to nature, but with a difference. They depart widely from the pastoral tradition, which used nature only as a setting or to define the point of view of the rural characters. Now he confronts it directly as a means of exploring the human condition, what man can discover of ultimate truth at least about himself if not about the alien natural world. This is the new theme of the poems referred to above in terms of his new directions in technique. They move toward a metaphysical use of language instead of the idiom of the Yankee voice. They use a mode of wit and precision in place of the relaxed forms of pastoral and dramatic monologue. If the earlier ones are "talk-poems," as Frost defined them, the later can be described as "gaze-poems," a term appropriate to both mode and meaning. For example, in "Desert Places" one can watch him fix his telescope on the vast reaches of interstellar space, only to conclude that he can find an equally terrifying loneliness within. In "Neither Out Far Nor In Deep" he follows the gaze of all men out to sea, but can report only an emptiness incommensurable with human need.

These later poems of Frost, notably such cryptic ones as "Design" and "All Revelation," challenge the reader's utmost powers of analysis and understanding. They also make effective answer to any charge that he is a belated Victorian who has evaded the real problems of the modern predicament. Fine as these poems are, however, overemphasis on them in an attempt to make him into a fashionable neometaphysical poet tends to distract attention from his unique achievement as a pastoralist. Moreover, they are a new departure in manner rather than theme, for he has been gazing out far and in deep all along. Actually, half of the ones just mentioned as outside the pastoral tradition date from the 1920's.

Frost has added an even further dimension to his achievement by returning in several late poems to his early manner, yet employing it with signal success to confront the most existential aspects of the human condition today. "The Most of It" is pastoral in setting, subject, and techniques, but it makes a very modern figure of the will braving alien entanglements (to use his definition in "The Constant Symbol"). In "Two Look at Two," a

[3] See Jarrell's explication listed in Reading Suggestions.

companion poem written twenty years before in the same regional mode, a pair of young lovers had found communion with a doe and buck on a mountain slope just beyond the last outpost of civilization. Now a solitary older man faces nature in an even wilder situation and cries out for some answer other than a mocking echo of his own voice. But there is no meaningful response of "counter-love," as before. Instead, silence—then the crashing of a great buck on the shore, symbolizing nature in all its remoteness from human need. He can admire the magnificence of this vision, but the only meaning it can offer is its utter indifference to him. Having discovered the limitations of any human relation with the natural world, however, he can face himself in the loneliness and heroism of his isolation.

"Beech," another of Frost's later poems, returns to the basic symbol of man-made barriers but with a long metaphysical leap beyond the limited meanings of "Mending Wall." Like the earlier poem, this one is pastoral in perspective, for only in that setting can man fence off the familiar world of farm from the uncharted wilderness that lies beyond. The "imaginary line" the poet runs gives him "proof of being not unbounded," the double negative suggesting the device of understatement that characterizes the Yankee manner. But in style as well as thought this poem is significantly modern; for the same conceptual symbol that marks out man's area of ownership imprisons him in it, and at the same time changes his relation to nature (the beech has been "deeply wounded" by the surveyor's mark). He has lost the innocence of Eden and become trapped in such abstract ideas as property. This is one sense in which the beech has been "impressed as Witness Tree." But the capitals make this also a submerged reference to the tree on which Christ was nailed. So it becomes a novel conceit for man's idea that he may be a creature capable of salvation. Such a religious interpretation is supported by the short appended poem. It recounts the biblical incident of Zaccheus, who "because he was of little stature" thought it was necessary to see God visibly in order to be redeemed (Luke 19:2–8). That the central Christian symbol should be invoked so indirectly by Frost in "Beech" is simply a sign of his diminished capacity for orthodox belief and his need to create new symbols. His witness trees are his poems, that erect barriers against the surrounding "dark and doubt" of the modern world by staking out the area of his faith in man, rather than in Christ.

The most significant poem in Frost's later volumes, "Directive," executes another return to an early and pervasive symbol. Just as he himself has placed "The Pasture" as an epigraph to his collected poems, one would like to print as a coda this pastoral written thirty-five years later. The former uses a spring as the source of beauty and well-being in the rural world, the latter a brook as the source of living waters from which sick modern man may drink and be whole again. It marks the end of his search for new symbols to replace the discarded ones of traditional religion. The title suggests a command rather than an invitation to return to the pastoral world. But that world is now so admittedly lost in the past it can be arrived at only in the imagination, and the goal finally reached is just a vision, made grasp-able by a private ritual. The conditions laid down for rediscovery of the source of life, "if you're lost enough to find yourself," echo Christ's instruc-tions for losing the worldly life in order to find the spiritual (Matthew 10: 39). The route is difficult, as is the Christian way, and the pilgrimage is properly to a humble spot, though once the "source" of living waters. Here the pilgrim is invited to renew his spirit by drinking from a broken goblet "like the Grail," hidden so the wrong people cannot find it, "So can't get saved, as Saint Mark says."

These referents make a theological interpretation of the whole poem inevitable. The last allusion may be to the dictum: "He that believeth and is baptized shall be saved; he that believeth not shall be damned"; or to the less-known one: "Unto you it is given to know the mystery of the kingdom of God" but not unto those who "may see, and not perceive, . . . may hear, and not understand" (Mark 16: 16; 4: 11–12). But neither doctrine is to be taken as literally applicable. Although Frost's theme is clearly the lost and saved conditions, all the references to traditional religion (which the reader should work out in detail) are muted and slanted to an unorthodox conclusion. The self-administered communion at the end, "Drink and be whole again beyond confusion," is only a poetic sacrament. The goblet, broken as a traditional religious form, is restored in the perfect form of a poem that serves at least as a momentary stay against the spiritual confu-sion of the modern world—his definition of "The Figure a Poem Makes."

A private vision of private wholeness, integrity gained by self-reliant courage, is all man can have, according to Frost, but it is enough. It can best be achieved by him through the mode of pastoralism. That this is a poetic strategy and not escapism is made doubly clear by this poem. In "Directive" the tone and the perspective are still pastoral, but the setting is existential and the symbols metaphysical. There is no real commitment to formal religion in any of Frost's writings; yet his best poems can be described as ventures of the spirit into matter. His humanism, broadly speaking, comes out of the long tradition running from Emerson to William James, but it has taken a distinctively new direction. And since he is a poet he has found it in a new formulation of language, not of religion or philosophy. "All the fun's in how you say a thing," he once lightly phrased the key to his whole performance. The play of the mind in the right play of words brings the idea to its perfect form.

CHARLES R. ANDERSON

A Note on the Text.   The text followed here for both the poems and the essay is that of *Complete Poems of Robert Frost* (New York: Holt, Rine-hart and Winston, Inc., 1949). The date following each poem is that of its first publication in book form.

✤

THE PASTURE

I'm going out to clean the pasture spring;
I'll only stop to rake the leaves away
(And wait to watch the water clear, I may):
I sha'n't be gone long.—You come too.

I'm going out to fetch the little calf   5
That's standing by the mother. It's so young,
It totters when she licks it with her tongue.
I sha'n't be gone long.—You come too.

1914

MOWING

Frost said he wrote this poem about 1900. The year he settled on a farm near Derry, N. H.

There was never a sound beside the wood but one,
And that was my long scythe whispering to the ground.
What was it it whispered? I knew not well myself;
Perhaps it was something about the heat of the sun,
Something, perhaps, about the lack of sound—
And that was why it whispered and did not speak.
It was no dream of the gift of idle hours,
Or easy gold at the hand of fay or elf:
Anything more than the truth would have seemed too weak *Here he touches upon the relation of labor to "the truth", "the fact"*
To the earnest love that laid the swale in rows,   10
Not without feeble-pointed spikes of flowers
(Pale orchises), and scared a bright green snake.
The fact is the sweetest dream that labor knows.
My long scythe whispered and left the hay to make.

1913

MENDING WALL

Here we see two elements— and opposed forces.

Something there is that doesn't love a wall, *theme*
That sends the frozen-ground-swell under it, *Pun*
And spills the upper-boulders in the sun;
And makes gaps even two can pass abreast.
The work of hunters is another thing: 5
I have come after them and made repair
Where they have left not one stone on a stone,
But they would have the rabbit out of hiding,
To please the yelping dogs. The gaps I mean,
No one has seen them made or heard them made   10
But at spring mending-time we find them there.
I let my neighbor know beyond the hill;
And on a day we meet to walk the line
And set the wall between us once again.
We keep the wall between us as we go.   15
To each the boulders that have fallen to each.
And some are loaves and some so nearly balls
We have to use a spell to make them balance:
'Stay where you are until our backs are turned!'
We wear our fingers rough with handling them.   20
Oh, just another kind of out-door game,
One on a side. It comes to little more:
There where it is we do not need the wall:
He is all pine and I am apple orchard.
My apple trees will never get across   25
And eat the cones under his pines, I tell him.
He only says, 'Good fences make good neighbors.' *theme*
Spring is the mischief in me, and I wonder
If I could put a notion in his head: *up the poem*
'*Why* do they make good neighbors? Isn't it   30
Where there are cows? But here there are no cows.
Before I built a wall I'd ask to know
What I was walling in or walling out,
And to whom I was like to give offence.
Something there is that doesn't love a wall,   35
That wants it down.' I could say 'Elves' to him,
But it's not elves exactly, and I'd rather
He said it for himself. I see him there
Bringing a stone grasped firmly by the top
In each hand, like an old-stone savage armed.   40
He moves in darkness as it seems to me,
Not of woods only and the shade of trees.
He will not go behind his father's saying,

Not too smart

[handwritten marginalia: "form of dialogue"]

And he likes having thought of it so well
He says again, 'Good fences make good neighbors.'   45

[handwritten marginalia: "Not too smart"]

1914

[handwritten marginalia: "one of the first poems of our time."]

THE DEATH OF THE HIRED MAN

[handwritten marginalia: "An expert on loading hay who came to farms when work was scarce."]

Mary sat musing on the lamp-flame at the table
Waiting for Warren. When she heard his step,
She ran on tip-toe down the darkened passage
To meet him in the doorway with the news
And put him on his guard. 'Silas is back.'   5
She pushed him outward with her through the door
And shut it after her. 'Be kind,' she said.
She took the market things from Warren's arms
And set them on the porch, then drew him down
To sit beside her on the wooden steps.   10

[handwritten marginalia: "Imp't" with double underline]

'When was I ever anything but kind to him?
But I'll not have the fellow back,' he said.
'I told him so last haying, didn't I?
If he left then, I said, that ended it.
What good is he? Who else will harbor him   15
At his age for the little he can do?
What help he is there's no depending on.
Off he goes always when I need him most.
He thinks he ought to earn a little pay,
Enough at least to buy tobacco with,   20
So he won't have to beg and be beholden,
"All right," I say, "I can't afford to pay
Any fixed wages, though I wish I could."
"Someone else can." "Then someone else will have to."
I shouldn't mind his bettering himself   25
If that was what it was. You can be certain,
When he begins like that, there's someone at him
Trying to coax him off with pocket-money,—
In haying time, when any help is scarce.
In winter he comes back to us. I'm done.'   30

[handwritten marginalia: "Subtle analysis of male and female's attitude toward justice and mercy."]

[handwritten marginalia: "Warren is outwardly antagonistic toward Silas, an unreliable worker."]

'Sh! not so loud: he'll hear you,' Mary said.

'I want him to: he'll have to soon or late.'

[handwritten marginalia: "Mary, emotions closer to the surface, begs him to forgive Silas."]

'He's worn out. He's asleep beside the stove.
When I came up from Rowe's I found him here,
Huddled against the barn-door fast asleep,   35

[handwritten marginalia: "When Warren discovers him dead, we know that he cares as much for Silas as does Mary."]

A miserable sight, and frightening, too—
You needn't smile—I didn't recognise him—
I wasn't looking for him—and he's changed.
Wait till you see.'

             'Where did you say he'd been?'   40

'He didn't say. I dragged him to the house,
And gave him tea and tried to make him smoke.
I tried to make him talk about his travels.
Nothing would do: he just kept nodding off.'

'What did he say? Did he say anything?'   45

'But little.'

             'Anything? Mary, confess
He said he'd come to ditch the meadow for me.'

'Warren!'

           'But did he? I just want to know.'   50

'Of course he did. What would you have him say?
Surely you wouldn't grudge the poor old man
Some humble way to save his self-respect.
He added, if you realy care to know,
He meant to clear the upper pasture, too.   55
That sounds like something you have heard before?
Warren, I wish you could have heard the way
He jumbled everything. I stopped to look
Two or three times—he made me feel so queer—
To see if he was talking in his sleep.   60
He ran on Harold Wilson—you remember—
The boy you had in haying four years since.
He's finished school, and teaching in his college.
Silas declares you'll have to get him back.
He says they two will make a team for work: 65
Between them they will lay this farm as smooth!
The way he mixed that in with other things.
He thinks young Wilson a likely lad, though daft
On education—you know how they fought
All through July under the blazing sun,   70
Silas up on the cart to build the load,
Harold along beside to pitch it on.'

'Yes, I took care to keep well out of earshot.'

'Well, those days trouble Silas like a dream.
You wouldn't think they would. How some things linger!   75
Harold's young college boy's assurance piqued him.
After so many years he still keeps finding
Good arguments he sees he might have used.

I sympathize. I know just how it feels
To think of the right thing to say too late.   80
Harold's associated in his mind with Latin.
He asked me what I thought of Harold's saying
He studied Latin like the violin
Because he liked it—that an argument!
He said he couldn't make the boy believe   85
He could find water with a hazel prong—
Which showed how much good school had ever done him
He wanted to go over that. But most of all
He thinks if he could have another chance
To teach him how to build a load of hay—   90

'I know, that's Silas' one accomplishment.
He bundles every forkful in its place,
And tags and numbers it for future reference,
So he can find and easily dislodge it
In the unloading. Silas does that well.   95
He takes it out in bunches like big birds' nests.
You never see him standing on the hay
He's trying to lift, straining to lift himself.'

'He thinks if he could teach him that, he'd be
Some good perhaps to someone in the world.   100
He hates to see a boy the fool of books.
Poor Silas, so concerned for other folk,
And nothing to look backward to with pride,
And nothing to look forward to with hope,
So now and never any different.'   105

Part of a moon was falling down the west,
Dragging the whole sky with it to the hills.
Its light poured softly in her lap. She saw it
And spread her apron to it. She put out her hand
Among the harp-like morning-glory strings   110
Taut with the dew from garden bed to eaves,
As if she played unheard some tenderness
That wrought on him beside her in the night.
'Warren,' she said, 'he has come home to die:
You needn't be afraid he'll leave you this time.'   115

'Home,' he mocked gently.

                        'Yes, what else but home?

It all depends on what you mean by home.
Of course he's nothing to us, any more
Than was the hound that came a stranger to us   120
Out of the woods, worn out upon the trail.'

simile

'Home is the place where, when you have to go there,
They have to take you in.'

       'I should have called it
Something you somehow haven't to deserve.'   125

Warren leaned out and took a step or two,
Picked up a little stick, and brought it back
And broke it in his hand and tossed it by.
'Silas has better claim on us you think
Than on his brother? Thirteen little miles   130
As the road winds would bring him to his door.
Silas has walked that far no doubt to-day.
Why didn't he go there? His brother's rich,
A somebody—director in the bank.'

'He never told us that.'   135

      'We know it though.'

'I think his brother ought to help, of course.
I'll see to that if there is need. He ought of right
To take him in, and might be willing to—
He may be better than appearances.   140
But have some pity on Silas. Do you think
If he had any pride in claiming kin
Or anything he looked for from his brother,
He'd keep so still about him all this time?'

'I wonder what's between them.   145

       'I can tell you.
Silas is what he is—we wouldn't mind him—
But just the kind that kinsfolk can't abide.
He never did a thing so very bad.
He don't know why he isn't quite as good   150
As anybody. Worthless though he is,
He won't be made ashamed to please his brother.'

'I can't think Si ever hurt anyone.'

'No, but he hurt my heart the way he lay
And rolled his head on that sharp-edged chairback.   155
He wouldn't let me put him on the lounge.
You must go in and see what you can do.
I made the bed up for him there to-night.
You'll be surprised at him—how much he's broken.
His working days are done; I'm sure of it.'   160

'I'd not be in a hurry to say that.'

'I haven't been. Go, look, see for yourself.
But, Warren, please remember how it is:

He's come to help you ditch the meadow.
He has a plan. You musn't laugh at him.   165
He may not speak of it, and then he may.
I'll sit and see if that small sailing cloud
Will hit or miss the moon.'

          It hit the moon.
Then there were three there, making a dim row,   170
The moon, the little silver cloud, and she.

Warren returned—too soon, it seemed to her,
Slipped to her side, caught up her hand and waited.

'Warren?' she questioned.

          'Dead,' was all he answered.   175

          1914

HOME BURIAL

He saw her from the bottom of the stairs
Before she saw him. She was starting down,
Looking back over her shoulder at some fear.
She took a doubtful step and then undid it
To raise herself and look again. He spoke   5
Advancing toward her. 'What is it you see
From up there always—for I want to know.'
She turned and sank upon her skirts at that,
And her face changed from terrified to dull.
He said to gain time: 'What is it you see,'   10
Mounting until she cowered under him.
'I will find out now—you must tell me, dear.'
She, in her place, refused him any help
With the least stiffening of her neck and silence.
She let him look, sure that he wouldn't see,   15
Blind creature; and a while he didn't see.
But at last he murmured, 'Oh,' and again, 'Oh.'

'What is it—what?' she said.

          'Just that I see.'

'You don't,' she challenged. 'Tell me what it is.'   20

'The wonder is I didn't see at once.
I never noticed it from here before.
I must be wonted to it—that's the reason.
The little graveyard where my people are!
So small the window frames the whole of it.   25

Not so much larger than a bedroom, is it?
There are three stones of slate and one of marble,
Broad-shouldered little slabs there in the sunlight
On the sidehill. We haven't to mind *those*.
But I understand: it is not the stones,   30
But the child's mound—'

       'Don't, don't, don't, don't,' she cried.

She withdrew shrinking from beneath his arm
That rested on the banister, and slid downstairs;
And turned on him with such a daunting look,   35
He said twice over before he knew himself:
'Can't a man speak of his own child he's lost?'

'Not you! Oh, where's my hat? Oh, I don't need it!
I must get out of here. I must get air.
I don't know rightly whether any man can.'   40

'Amy! Don't go to someone else this time.
Listen to me. I won't come down the stairs.'
He sat and fixed his chin between his fists.
'There's something I should like to ask you, dear.'

'You don't know how to ask it.   45

               'Help me, then.'

Her fingers moved the latch for all reply.

'My words are nearly always an offence.
I don't know how to speak of anything
So as to please you. But I might be taught   50
I should suppose. I can't say I see how.
A man must partly give up being a man
With women-folk. We could have some arrangement
By which I'd bind myself to keep hands off
Anything special you're a-mind to name.   55
Though I don't like such things 'twixt those that love
Two that don't love can't live together without them.
But two that do can't live together with them.'
She moved the latch a little. 'Don't—don't go.
Don't carry it to someone else this time.   60
Tell me about it if it's something human.
Let me into your grief. I'm not so much
Unlike other folks as your standing there
Apart would make me out. Give me my chance.
I do think, though, you overdo it a little.   65
What was it brought you up to think it the thing
To take your mother-loss of a first child

So inconsolably—in the face of love.
You'd think his memory might be satisfied—'

'There you go sneering now!'   70

                              'I'm not, I'm not!
You make me angry. I'll come down to you.
God, what a woman! And it's come to this,
A man can't speak of his own child that's dead.'

'You can't because you don't know how to speak.   75
If you had any feelings, you that dug
With your own hand—how could you?—his little grave;
I saw you from that very window there,
Making the gravel leap and leap in air,
Leap up, like that, like that, and land so lightly   80
And roll back down the mound beside the hole.
I thought, Who is that man? I didn't know you.
And I crept down the stairs and up the stairs
To look again, and still your spade kept lifting.
Then you came in. I heard your rumbling voice   85
Out in the kitchen, and I don't know why,
But I went near to see with my own eyes.
You could sit there with the stains on your shoes
Of the fresh earth from your own baby's grave
And talk about your everyday concerns.   90
You had stood the spade up against the wall
Outside there in the entry, for I saw it.'

'I shall laugh the worst laugh I ever laughed.
I'm cursed. God, if I don't believe I'm cursed.'

'I can repeat the very words you were saying.   95
"Three foggy mornings and one rainy day
Will rot the best birch fence a man can build."
Think of it, talk like that at such a time!
What had how long it takes a birch to rot
To do with what was in the darkened parlor.   100
You *couldn't* care! The nearest friends can go
With anyone to death, comes so far short
They might as well not try to go at all.
No, from the time when one is sick to death,
One is alone, and he dies more alone.   105
Friends make pretence of following to the grave,
But before one is in it, their minds are turned
And making the best of their way back to life
And living people, and things they understand.
But the world's evil. I won't have grief so   110
If I can change it. Oh, I won't, I won't!'

'There, you have said it all and you feel better.
You won't go now. You're crying. Close the door.
The heart's gone out of it: why keep it up.
Amy! There's someone coming down the road!'   115

'*You*—oh, you think the talk is all. I must go—
Somewhere out of this house. How can I make you—'

'If—you—do!' She was opening the door wider.
'Where do you mean to go? First tell me that.
I'll follow and bring you back by force. I *will!*—'   120

1914

◁   THE BLACK COTTAGE

Note the
positive,
tight-lipped
old lady.

We chanced in passing by that afternoon
To catch it in a sort of special picture
Among tar-banded ancient cherry trees,
Set well back from the road in rank lodged grass,
The little cottage we were speaking of,   5
A front with just a door between two windows,
Fresh painted by the shower a velvet black.
We paused, the minister and I, to look.
He made as if to hold it at arm's length
Or put the leaves aside that framed it in.   10
'Pretty,' he said. 'Come in. No one will care.'
The path was a vague parting in the grass
That led us to a weathered window-sill.
We pressed our faces to the pane. 'You see,' he said,
'Everything's as she left it when she died.   15
Her sons won't sell the house or the things in it.
They say they mean to come and summer here
Where they were boys. They haven't come this year.
They live so far away—one is out west—
It will be hard for them to keep their word.   20
Anyway they won't have the place disturbed.'
A buttoned hair-cloth lounge spread scrolling arms
Under a crayon portrait on the wall,

daguerro'o tip

Done sadly from an old daguerreotype.
'That was the father as he went to war.   25
She always, when she talked about the war,
Sooner or later came and leaned, half knelt
Against the lounge beside it, though I doubt
If such unlifelike lines kept power to stir
Anything in her after all the years.   30
He fell at Gettysburg or Fredericksburg,
I ought to know—it makes a difference which:

Fredericksburg wasn't Gettysburg, of course.
But what I'm getting to is how forsaken
A little cottage this has always seemed;   35
Since she went more than ever, but before—
I don't mean altogether by the lives
That had gone out of it, the father first,
Then the two sons, till she was left alone.
(Nothing could draw her after those two sons.   40
She valued the considerate neglect
She had at some cost taught them after years.)
I mean by the world's having passed it by—
As we almost got by this afternoon.
It always seems to me a sort of mark   45
To measure how far fifty years have brought us.
Why not sit down if you are in no haste?
These doorsteps seldom have a visitor.
The warping boards pull out their own old nails
With none to tread and put them in their place.   50
She had her own idea of things, the old lady.
And she liked talk. She had seen Garrison
And Whittier, and had her story of them.
One wasn't long in learning that she thought
Whatever else the Civil War was for,   55
It wasn't just to keep the States together,
Nor just to free the slaves, though it did both.
She wouldn't have believed those ends enough
To have given outright for them all she gave.
Her giving somehow touched the principle   60
That all men are created free and equal.
And to hear her quaint phrases—so removed
From the world's view today of all those things.
That's a hard mystery of Jefferson's.
What did he mean? Of course the easy way   65
Is to decide it simply isn't true.
It may not be. I heard a fellow say so.
But never mind, the Welshman got it planted
Where it will trouble us a thousand years.
Each age will have to reconsider it.   70
You couldn't tell her what the West was saying,
And what the South to her serene belief.
She had some art of hearing and yet not
Hearing the latter wisdom of the world.
White was the only race she ever knew.   75
Black she had scarcely seen, and yellow never.
But how could they be made so very unlike
By the same hand working in the same stuff?
She had supposed the war decided that.
What are you going to do with such a person?   80

Strange how such innocence gets its own way.
I should be surprised if in this world
It were the force that would at last prevail.
Do you know but for her there was a time   85
When to please younger members of the church,
Or rather say non-members in the church,
Whom we all have to think of nowadays,
I would have changed the Creed a very little?
Not that she ever had to ask me not to;
It never got so far as that; but the bare thought   90
Of her old tremulous bonnet in the pew,
And of her half asleep was too much for me.
Why, I might wake her up and startle her.
It was the words "descended into Hades"
That seemed too pagan to our liberal youth.   95
You know they suffered from a general onslaught.
And well, if they weren't true why keep right on
Saying them like the heathen? We could drop them.
Only—there was the bonnet in the pew.
Such a phrase couldn't have meant much to her.   100
But suppose she had missed it from the Creed
As a child misses the unsaid Good-night,
And falls asleep with heartache—how should I feel?
I'm just as glad she made me keep hands off,
For, dear me, why abandon a belief   105
Merely because it ceases to be true.
Cling to it long enough, and not a doubt
It will turn true again, for so it goes.
Most of the change we think we see in life
Is due to truths being in and out of favor.   110
As I sit here, and oftentimes, I wish
I could be monarch of a desert land
I could devote and dedicate forever
To the truths we keep coming back and back to.
So desert it would have to be, so walled   115
By mountain ranges half in summer snow,
No one would covet it or think it worth
The pains of conquering to force change on.
Scattered oases where men dwelt, but mostly   120
Sand dunes held loosely in tamarisk
Blown over and over themselves in idleness.
Sand grains should sugar in the natal dew
The babe born to the desert, the sand storm
Retard mid-waste my cowering caravans—   125
There are bees in this wall.' He struck the clapboards,
Fierce heads looked out; small bodies pivoted.
We rose to go. Sunset blazed on the windows.

1914

A SERVANT TO SERVANTS

I didn't make you know how glad I was
To have you come and camp here on our land.
I promised myself to get down some day
And see the way you lived, but I don't know!
With a houseful of hungry men to feed   5
I guess you'd find. . . . It seems to me
I can't express my feelings any more
Than I can raise my voice or want to lift
My hand (oh, I can lift it when I have to).
Did ever you feel so? I hope you never.   10
It's got so I don't even know for sure
Whether I *am* glad, sorry, or anything.
There's nothing but a voice-like left inside
That seems to tell me how I ought to feel,
And would feel if I wasn't all gone wrong.   15
You take the lake. I look and look at it.
I see it's a fair, pretty sheet of water.
I stand and make myself repeat out loud
The advantages it has, so long and narrow,
Like a deep piece of some old running river   20
Cut short off at both ends. It lies five miles
Straight away through the mountain notch
From the sink window where I wash the plates,
And all our storms come up toward the house,
Drawing the slow waves whiter and whiter and whiter.   25
It took my mind off doughnuts and soda biscuit
To step outdoors and take the water dazzle
A sunny morning, or take the rising wind
About my face and body and through my wrapper,
When a storm threatened from the Dragon's Den,   30
And a cold chill shivered across the lake.
I see it's a fair, pretty sheet of water,
Our Willoughby! How did you hear of it?
I expect, though, everyone's heard of it.
In a book about ferns? Listen to that!   35
You let things more like feathers regulate
Your going and coming. And you like it here?
I can see how you might. But I don't know!
It would be different if more people came,
For then there would be business. As it is,   40
The cottages Len built, sometimes we rent them,
Sometimes we don't. We've a good piece of shore
That ought to be worth something, and may yet.
But I don't count on it as much as Len.
He looks on the bright side of everything,   45

cooks for hired hands - she does not even know the names of hired men.

Campers interested in ferns - contrast with husbands.

Len is a hard working Puritan

Including me. He thinks I'll be all right
With doctoring. But it's not medicine—
Lowe is the only doctor's dared to say so—
It's rest I want—there, I have said it out—
From cooking meals for hungry hired men   50
And washing dishes after them—from doing
Things over and over that just won't stay done.
By good rights I ought not to have so much
Put on me, but there seems no other way.
Len says one steady pull more ought to do it.   55
He says the best way out is always through.
And I agree to that, or in so far
As that I can see no way out but through—
Leastways for me—and then they'll be convinced.
It's not that Len don't want the best for me.   60
It was his plan our moving over in
Beside the lake from where that day I showed you
We used to live—ten miles from anywhere.
We didn't change without some sacrifice,
But Len went at it to make up the loss.   65
His work's a man's, of course, from sun to sun,
But he works when he works as hard as I do—
Though there's small profit in comparisons.
(Women and men will make them all the same.)
But work ain't all. Len undertakes too much.   70
He's into everything in town. This year
It's highways, and he's got too many men
Around him to look after that make waste.
They take advantage of him shamefully,
And proud, too, of themselves for doing so.   75
We have four here to board, great good-for-nothings,
Sprawling about the kitchen with their talk
While I fry their bacon. Much they care!
No more put out in what they do or say
Than if I wasn't in the room at all.   80
Coming and going all the time, they are:
I don't learn what their names are, let alone
Their characters, or whether they are safe
To have inside the house with doors unlocked.
I'm not afraid of them, though, if they're not   85
Afraid of me. There's two can play at that.
I have my fancies: it runs in the family.
My father's brother wasn't right. They kept him
Locked up for years back there at the old farm.
I've been away once—yes, I've been away.   90
The State Asylum. I was prejudiced;
I wouldn't have sent anyone of mine there;
You know the old idea—the only asylum

Was the poorhouse, and those who could afford, 95
Rather than send their folks to such a place,
Kept them at home; and it does seem more human.
But it's not so: the place is the asylum.
There they have every means proper to do with,
And you aren't darkening other people's lives— 100
Worse than no good to them, and they no good
To you in your condition; you can't know
Affection or the want of it in that state.
I've heard too much of the old-fashioned way.
My father's brother, he went mad quite young. 105
Some thought he had been bitten by a dog,
Because his violence took on the form
Of carrying his pillow in his teeth;
But it's more likely he was crossed in love,
Or so the story goes. It was some girl. 110
Anyway all he talked about was love.
They soon saw he would do someone a mischief
If he wa'n't kept strict watch of, and it ended
In father's building him a sort of cage,
Or room within a room, of hickory poles, 115
Like stanchions in the barn, from floor to ceiling,—
A narrow passage all the way around.
Anything they put in for furniture
He'd tear to pieces, even a bed to lie on.
So they made the place comfortable with straw, 120
Like a beast's stall, to ease their consciences.
Of course they had to feed him without dishes.
They tried to keep him clothed, but he paraded
With his clothes on his arm—all of his clothes.
Cruel—it sounds. I 'spose they did the best 125
They knew. And just when he was at the height,
Father and mother married, and mother came,
A bride, to help take care of such a creature,
And accommodate her young life to his.
That was what marrying father meant to her. 130
She had to lie and hear love things made dreadful
By his shouts in the night. He'd shout and shout
Until the strength was shouted out of him,
And his voice died down slowly from exhaustion.
He'd pull his bars apart like bow and bowstring, 135
And let them go and make them twang until
His hands had worn them smooth as any oxbow.
And then he'd crow as if he thought that child's play
The only fun he had. I've heard them say, though,
They found a way to put a stop to it. 140
He was before my time—I never saw him;
But the pen stayed exactly as it was

There in the upper chamber in the ell,
A sort of catch-all full of attic clutter.
I often think of the smooth hickory bars.
It got so I would say—you know, half fooling—   145
'It's time I took my turn upstairs in jail'—
Just as you will till it becomes a habit.
No wonder I was glad to get away.
Mind you, I waited till Len said the word.
I didn't want the blame if things went wrong.   150
I was glad though, no end, when we moved out,
And I looked to be happy, and I was,
As I said, for a while—but I don't know!
Somehow the change wore out like a prescription.
And there's more to it than just window-views   155
And living by a lake. I'm past such help—
Unless Len took the notion, which he won't,
And I won't ask him—it's not sure enough.
I s'pose I've got to go the road I'm going:
Other folks have to, and why shouldn't I?   160
I almost think if I could do like you,
Drop everything and live out on the ground—
But it might be, come night, I shouldn't like it,
Or a long rain. I should soon get enough,
And be glad of a good roof overhead.   165
I've lain awake thinking of you, I'll warrant,
More than you have yourself, some of these nights.
The wonder was the tents weren't snatched away
From over you as you lay in your beds.
I haven't courage for a risk like that.   170
Bless you, of course, you're keeping me from work,
But the thing of it is, I need to *be* kept.
There's work enough to do—there's always that;
But behind's behind. The worst that you can do
Is set me back a little more behind.   175
I sha'n't catch up in this world, anyway.
I'd *rather* you'd not go unless you must.

1914

THE CODE

There were three in the meadow by the brook
Gathering up windrows, piling cocks of hay,
With an eye always lifted toward the west
Where an irregular sun-bordered cloud
Darkly advanced with a perpetual dagger   5
Flickering across its bosom. Suddenly

One helper, thrusting pitchfork in the ground,
Marched himself off the field and home. One stayed.
The town-bred farmer failed to understand.

'What is there wrong?'

       'Something you just now said.'   10

'What did I say?'

     'About our taking pains.'

'To cock the hay?—because it's going to shower?
I said that more than half an hour ago.   15
I said it to myself as much as you.'

'You didn't know. But James is one big fool.
He thought you meant to find fault with his work.
That's what the average farmer would have meant.
James would take time, of course, to chew it over 20
Before he acted: he's just got round to act.'

'He is a fool if that's the way he takes me.'

'Don't let it bother you. You've found out something
The hand that knows his business won't be told
To do work better or faster—those two things. 25
I'm as particular as anyone:
Most likely I'd have served you just the same.
But I know you don't understand our ways.
You were just talking what was in your mind,
What was in all our minds, and you weren't hinting. 30
Tell you a story of what happened once:
I was up here in Salem at a man's
Named Sanders with a gang of four or five
Doing the haying. No one liked the boss.
He was one of the kind sports call a spider, 35
All wiry arms and legs that spread out wavy
From a humped body nigh as big's a biscuit
But work! that man could work, especially
If by so doing he could get more work
Out of his hired help. I'm not denying 40
He was hard on himself. I couldn't find
That he kept any hours—not for himself.
Daylight and lantern-light were one to him:
I've heard him pounding in the barn all night.
But what he liked was someone to encourage. 45
Them that he couldn't lead he'd get behind
And drive, the way you can, you know, in mowing—
Keep at their heels and threaten to mow their legs off

I'd seen about enough of his bulling tricks
(We call that bulling). I'd been watching him.   50
So when he paired off with me in the hayfield
To load the load, thinks I, Look out for trouble.
I built the load and topped it off; old Sanders
Combed it down with a rake and says, "O.K."
Everything went well till we reached the barn   55
With a big jag to empty in a bay.
You understand that meant the easy job
For the man up on top of throwing *down*
The hay and rolling it off wholesale,
Where on a mow it would have been slow lifting.   60
You wouldn't think a fellow'd need much urging
Under those circumstances, would you now?
But the old fool seizes his fork in both hands,
And looking up bewhiskered out of the pit,
Shouts like an army captain, "Let her come!"   65
Thinks I, D'ye mean it? "What was that you said?"
I asked out loud, so's there'd be no mistake,
"Did you say, Let her come?" "Yes, let her come."
He said it over, but he said it softer.
Never you say a thing like that to a man,   70
Not if he values what he is. God, I'd as soon
Murdered him as left out his middle name.
I'd built the load and knew right where to find it.
Two or three forkfuls I picked lightly round for
Like meditating, and then I just dug in   75
And dumped the rackful on him in ten lots.
I looked over the side once in the dust
And caught sight of him treading-water-like,
Keeping his head above. "Damn ye," I says,
"That gets ye!" He squeaked like a squeezed rat.   80
That was the last I saw or heard of him.
I cleaned the rack and drove out to cool off.
As I sat mopping hayseed from my neck,
And sort of waiting to be asked about it,
One of the boys sings out, "Where's the old man?"   85
"I left him in the barn under the hay.
If ye want him, ye can go and dig him out."
They realized from the way I swobbed my neck
More than was needed something must be up.
They headed for the barn; I stayed where I was.   90
They told me afterward. First they forked hay,
A lot of it, out into the barn floor.
Nothing! They listened for him. Not a rustle.
I guess they thought I'd spiked him in the temple
Before I buried him, or I couldn't have managed.   95
They excavated more. "Go keep his wife

Out of the barn." Someone looked in a window,
And curse me if he wasn't in the kitchen
Slumped way down in a chair, with both his feet
Against the stove, the hottest day that summer   100
He looked so clean disgusted from behind
There was no one that dared to stir him up,
Or let him know that he was being looked at.
Apparently I hadn't buried him
(I may have knocked him down); but my just trying   105
To bury him had hurt his dignity.
He had gone to the house so's not to meet me.
He kept away from us all afternoon.
We tended to his hay. We saw him out
After a while picking peas in his garden: 110
He couldn't keep away from doing something.'

'Weren't you relieved to find he wasn't dead?'

No! and yet I don't know—it's hard to say.
I went about to kill him fair enough.'

'You took an awkward way. Did he discharge you?'   115

'Discharge me? No! He knew I did just right.'

AFTER APPLE-PICKING

My long two-pointed ladder's sticking through a tree
Toward heaven still,
And there's a barrel that I didn't fill
Beside it, and there may be two or three
Apples I didn't pick upon some bough.   5
But I am done with apple-picking now.
Essence of winter sleep is on the night,
The scent of apples: I am drowsing off.
I cannot rub the strangeness from my sight
I got from looking through a pane of glass   10
I skimmed this morning from the drinking trough
And held against the world of hoary grass.
It melted, and I let it fall and break.
But I was well
Upon my way to sleep before it fell,   15
And I could tell
What form my dreaming was about to take.
Magnified apples appear and disappear,
Stem end and blossom end,

And every fleck of russet showing clear.
My instep arch not only keeps the ache,
It keeps the pressure of a ladder-round.
I feel the ladder sway as the boughs bend.   20
And I keep hearing from the cellar bin
The rumbling sound   25
Of load on load of apples coming in.
For I have had too much
Of apple-picking: I am overtired
Of the great harvest I myself desired.
There were ten thousand thousand fruit to touch,   30
Cherish in hand, lift down, and not let fall.
For all
That struck the earth,
No matter if not bruised or spiked with stubble,
Went surely to the cider-apple heap   35
As of no worth.
One can see what will trouble
This sleep of mine, whatever sleep it is.
Were he not gone,
The woodchuck could say whether it's like his   40
Long sleep, as I describe its coming on,
Or just some human sleep.

1914

THE WOODPILE

Out walking in the frozen swamp one gray day,
I paused and said, 'I will turn back from here.
No, I will go on farther—and we shall see.'
The hard snow held me, save where now and then
One foot went through. The view was all in lines   5
Straight up and down of tall slim trees
Too much alike to mark or name a place by
So as to say for certain I was here
Or somewhere else: I was just far from home.
A small bird flew before me. He was careful   10
To put a tree between us when he lighted,
And say no word to tell me who he was
Who was so foolish as to think what *he* thought.
He thought that I was after him for a feather—
The white one in his tail; like one who takes   15
Everything said as personal to himself.
One flight out sideways would have undeceived him.
And then there was a pile of wood for which
I forgot him and let his little fear
Carry him off the way I might have gone,   20

*The moon for his fatigue: his own
demanding standards. This led him to
reject any creation
of inferior
quality*

Without so much as wishing him good-night.
He went behind it to make his last stand.
It was a cord of maple, cut and split
And piled—and measured, four by four by eight.
And not another like it could I see.   25
No runner tracks in this year's snow looped near it.
And it was older sure than this year's cutting,
Or even last year's or the year's before.
The wood was grey and the bark warping off it
And the pile somewhat sunken. Clematis   30
Had wound strings round and round it like a bundle
What held it though on one side was a tree
Still growing, and on one a stake and prop,
These latter about to fall. I thought that only
Someone who lived in turning to fresh tasks   35
Could so forget his handiwork on which
He spent himself, the labor of his axe,
And leave it there far from a useful fireplace
To warm the frozen swamp as best it could
With the slow smokeless burning of decay.   40

1914

AN OLD MAN'S WINTER NIGHT

All out of doors looked darkly in at him
Through the thin frost, almost in separate stars,
That gathers on the pane in empty rooms.
What kept his eyes from giving back the gaze
Was the lamp tilted near them in his hand.   5
What kept him from remembering the need
That brought him to that creaking room was age.
He stood with barrels round him—at a loss.
And having scared the cellar under him
In clomping there, he scared it once again   10
In clomping off;—and scared the outer night,
Which has its sounds, familiar, like the roar
Of trees and crack of branches, common things,
But nothing so like beating on a box.
A light he was to no one but himself   15
Where now he sat concerned with he knew what,
A quiet light, and then not even that.
He consigned to the moon, such as she was,
So late-arising, to the broken moon
As better than the sun in any case   20
For such a charge, his snow upon the roof,
His icicles along the wall to keep;
And slept. The log that shifted with a jolt

Once in the stove, disturbed him and he shifted,
And eased his heavy breathing, but still slept.   25
One aged man—one man—can't keep a house,
A farm, a countryside, or if he can,
It's thus he does it of a winter night.

                                                                      1916

OUT, OUT—

The buzz-saw snarled and rattled in the yard
And made dust and dropped stove-length sticks of wood,
Sweet-scented stuff when the breeze drew across it.
And from there those that lifted eyes could count
Five mountain ranges one behind the other   5
Under the sunset far into Vermont.
And the saw snarled and rattled, snarled and rattled,
As it ran light, or had to bear a load.
And nothing happened: day was all but done.
Call it a day, I wish they might have said   10
To please the boy by giving him the half hour
That a boy counts so much when saved from work.
His sister stood beside them in her apron
To tell them 'Supper.' At the word, the saw,
As if to prove saws knew what supper meant,   15
Leaped out at the boy's hand, or seemed to leap—
He must have given the hand. However it was,
Neither refused the meeting. But the hand!
The boy's first outcry was a rueful laugh,
As he swung toward them holding up the hand   20
Half in appeal, but half as if to keep
The life from spilling. Then the boy saw all—
Since he was old enough to know, big boy
Doing a man's work, though a child at heart—
He saw all spoiled. 'Don't let him cut my hand off—   25
The doctor, when he comes. Don't let him, sister!'
So. But the hand was gone already.
The doctor put him in the dark of ether.
He lay and puffed his lips out with his breath.
And then—the watcher at his pulse took fright.   30
No one believed. They listened at his heart.
Little—less—nothing!—and that ended it.
No more to build on there. And they, since they
Were not the one dead, turned to their affairs.

                                                                      1916

THE AX-HELVE

I've known ere now an interfering branch
Of alder catch my lifted axe behind me.
But that was in the woods, to hold my hand
From striking at another alder's roots,
And that was, as I say, an alder branch. 5
This was a man, Baptiste, who stole one day
Behind me on the snow in my own yard
Where I was working at the chopping-block,
And cutting nothing not cut down already.
He caught my axe expertly on the rise, 10
When all my strength put forth was in his favor,
Held it a moment where it was, to calm me,
Then took it from me—and I let him take it.
I didn't know him well enough to know
What it was all about. There might be something 15
He had in mind to say to a bad neighbor
He might prefer to say to him disarmed.
But all he had to tell me in French-English
Was what he thought of—not me, but my axe;
Me only as I took my axe to heart. 20
It was the bad axe-helve some one had sold me—
'Made on machine,' he said, ploughing the grain
With a thick thumbnail to show how it ran
Across the handle's long drawn serpentine,
Like the two strokes across a dollar sign. 25
'You give her one good crack, she's snap raght off.
Den where's your hax-ead flying t'rough de hair?'
Admitted; and yet, what was that to him?

'Come on my house and I put you one in
What's las' awhile—good hick'ry what's grow crooked, 30
De second growt' I cut myself—tough, tough!'

Something to sell? That wasn't how it sounded.

'Den when you say you come? It's cost you nothing.
Tonaght?'

       As well tonight as any night. 35

Beyond an over-warmth of kitchen stove
My welcome differed from no other welcome.
Baptiste knew best why I was where I was.
So long as he would leave enough unsaid,
I shouldn't mind his being overjoyed 40
(If overjoyed he was) at having got me

Where I must judge if what he knew about an axe
That not everybody else knew was to count
For nothing in the measure of a neighbor.
Hard if, though cast away for life with Yankees,   45
A Frenchman couldn't get his human rating!

Mrs. Baptiste came in and rocked a chair
That had as many motions as the world:
One back and forward, in and out of shadow,
That got her nowhere; one more gradual,   50
Sideways, that would have run her on the stove
In time, had she not realized her danger
And caught herself up bodily, chair and all,
And set herself back where she started from.
'She ain't spick too much Henglish—dat's too bad.'   55

I was afraid, in brightening first on me,
Then on Baptiste, as if she understood
What passed between us, she was only feigning.
Baptiste was anxious for her; but no more
Than for himself, so placed he couldn't hope   60
To keep his bargain of the morning with me
In time to keep me from suspecting him
Of really never having meant to keep it.

Needlessly soon he had his axe-helves out,
A quiverful to choose from, since he wished me   65
To have the best he had, or had to spare—
Not for me to ask which, when what he took
Had beauties he had to point me out at length
To insure their not being wasted on me.
He liked to have it slender as a whipstock,   70
Free from the least knot, equal to the strain
Of bending like a sword across the knee.
He showed me that the lines of a good helve
Were native to the grain before the knife
Expressed them, and its curves were no false curves   75
Put on it from without. And there its strength lay
For the hard work. He chafed its long white body
From end to end with his rough hand shut round it.
He tried it at the eye-hole in the axe-head.
'Hahn, hahn,' he mused, 'don't need much taking down.'   80
Baptiste knew how to make a short job long
For love of it, and yet not waste time either.

Do you know, what we talked about was knowledge?
Baptiste on his defence about the children
He kept from school, or did his best to keep—   85
Whatever school and children and our doubts
Of laid-on education had to do

With the curves of his axe-helves and his having
Used these unscrupulously to bring me
To see for once the inside of his house.   90
Was I desired in friendship, partly as some one
To leave it to, whether the right to hold
Such doubts of education should depend
Upon the education of those who held them?

But now he brushed the shavings from his knee   95
And stood the axe there on its horse's hoof,
Erect, but not without its waves, as when
The snake stood up for evil in the Garden,—
Top-heavy with a heaviness his short,
Thick hand made light of, steel-blue chin drawn down   100
And in a little—a French touch in that.
Baptiste drew back and squinted at it, pleased;
'See how she's cock her head!'

1923

THE GRINDSTONE

Having a wheel and four legs of its own
Has never availed the cumbersome grindstone
To get it anywhere that I can see.
These hands have helped it go, and even race;
Not all the motion, though, they ever lent,   5
Not all the miles it may have thought it went,
Have got it one step from the starting place.
It stands beside the same old apple tree.
The shadow of the apple tree is thin
Upon it now, its feet are fast in snow   10
All other farm machinery's gone in,
And some of it on no more legs and wheel
Than the grindstone can boast to stand or go.
(I'm thinking chiefly of the wheelbarrow.)
For months it hasn't known the taste of steel,   15
Washed down with rusty water in a tin.
But standing outdoors hungry, in the cold,
Except in towns at night, is not a sin.
And, anyway, its standing in the yard
Under a ruinous live apple tree   20
Has nothing any more to do with me,
Except that I remember how of old
One summer day, all day I drove it hard,
And someone mounted on it rode it hard,
And he and I between us ground a blade.   25

I gave it the preliminary spin,
And poured on water (tears it might have been);
And when it almost gayly jumped and flowed,
A Father-Time-like man got on and rode,
Armed with a scythe and spectacles that glowed.   30
He turned on will-power to increase the load
And slow me down—and I abruptly slowed,
Like coming to a sudden railroad station.
I changed from hand to hand in desperation.
I wondered what machine of ages gone   35
This represented an improvement on.
For all I knew it may have sharpened spears
And arrowheads itself. Much use for years
Had gradually worn it an oblate
Spheroid that kicked and struggled in its gait,   40
Appearing to return me hate for hate;
(But I forgive it now as easily
As any other boyhood enemy
Whose pride has failed to get him anywhere).
I wondered who it was the man thought ground—   45
The one who held the wheel back or the one
Who gave his life to keep it going round?
I wondered if he really thought it fair
For him to have the say when we were done.
Such were the bitter thoughts to which I turned.   50

Not for myself was I so much concerned.
Oh no!—although, of course, I could have found
A better way to pass the afternoon
Than grinding discord out of a grindstone,
And beating insects at their gritty tune.   55
Nor was I for the man so much concerned.
Once when the grindstone almost jumped its bearing
It looked as if he might be badly thrown
And wounded on his blade. So far from caring,
I laughed inside, and only cranked the faster,   60
(It ran as if it wasn't greased but glued);
I'd welcome any moderate disaster
That might be calculated to postpone
What evidently nothing could conclude.
The thing that made me more and more afraid   65
Was that we'd ground it sharp and hadn't known.
And now were only wasting precious blade.
And when he raised it dripping once and tried
The creepy edge of it with wary touch,
And viewed it over his glasses funny-eyed,   70
Only disinterestedly to decide
It needed a turn more, I could have cried

Wasn't there danger of a turn too much?
Mightn't we make it worse instead of better?
I was for leaving something to the whetter.   75
What if it wasn't all it should be? I'd
Be satisfied if he'd be satisfied.

                                                    1923

THE WITCH OF COÖS

I stayed the night for shelter at a farm
Behind the mountain, with a mother and son,
Two old-believers. They did all the talking.

MOTHER. Folks think a witch who has familiar spirits
She could call up to pass a winter evening,   •   5
But won't, should be burned at the stake or something.
Summoning spirits isn't 'Button, button,
Who's got the button,' I would have them know.

SON. Mother can make a common table rear
And kick with two legs like an army mule.   10

MOTHER. And when I've done it, what good have I done?
Rather than tip a table for you, let me
Tell you what Ralle the Sioux Control once told me.
He said the dead had souls, but when I asked him
How could that be—I thought the dead were souls,   15
He broke my trance. Don't that make you suspicious
That there's something the dead are keeping back?
Yes, there's something the dead are keeping back.

SON. You wouldn't want to tell him what we have
Up attic, mother?   20

MOTHER. Bones—a skeleton.

SON. But the headboard of mother's bed is pushed
Against the attic door: the door is nailed.
It's harmless. Mother hears it in the night
Halting perplexed behind the barrier   25
Of door and headboard. Where it wants to get
Is back into the cellar where it came from.

MOTHER. We'll never let them, will we, son! We'll never!

SON. It left the cellar forty years ago
And carried itself like a pile of dishes
Up one flight from the cellar to the kitchen,   30
Another from the kitchen to the bedroom,

Another from the bedroom to the attic,
Right past both father and mother, and neither stopped it.
Father had gone upstairs; mother was downstairs.
I was a baby: I don't know where I was.   35

MOTHER. The only fault my husband found with me—
I went to sleep before I went to bed,
Especially in winter when the bed
Might just as well be ice and the clothes snow.
The night the bones came up the cellar-stairs   40
Toffile had gone to bed alone and left me,
But left an open door to cool the room off
So as to sort of turn me out of it.
I was just coming to myself enough
To wonder where the cold was coming from,   45
When I heard Toffile upstairs in the bedroom
And thought I heard him downstairs in the cellar.
The board we had laid down to walk dry-shod on
When there was water in the cellar in spring
Struck the hard cellar bottom. And then someone   50
Began the stairs, two footsteps for each step,
The way a man with one leg and a crutch,
Or a little child, comes up. It wasn't Toffile:
It wasn't anyone who could be there.
The bulkhead double-doors were double-locked   55
And swollen tight and buried under snow.
The cellar windows were banked up with sawdust
And swollen tight and buried under snow.
It was the bones. I knew them—and good reason.
My first impulse was to get to the knob   60
And hold the door. But the bones didn't try
The door; they halted helpless on the landing,
Waiting for things to happen in their favor.
The faintest restless rustling ran all through them.
I never could have done the thing I did   65
If the wish hadn't been too strong in me
To see how they were mounted for this walk.
I had a vision of them put together
Not like a man, but like a chandelier.
So suddenly I flung the door wide on him.   70
A moment he stood balancing with emotion,
And all but lost himself. (A tongue of fire
Flashed out and licked along his upper teeth.
Smoke rolled inside the sockets of his eyes.)
Then he came at me with one hand outstretched,   75
The way he did in life once; but this time
I struck the hand off brittle on the floor,
And fell back from him on the floor myself.

The finger-pieces slid in all directions.
(Where did I see one of those pieces lately? 80
Hand me my button-box—it must be there.)
I sat up on the floor and shouted, 'Toffile,
It's coming up to you.' It had its choice
Of the door to the cellar or the hall.
It took the hall door for the novelty, 85
And set off briskly for so slow a thing,
Still going every which way in the joints, though,
So that it looked like lightning or a scribble,
From the slap I had just now given its hand.
I listened till it almost climbed the stairs 90
From the hall to the only finished bedroom,
Before I got up to do anything;
Then ran and shouted, 'Shut the bedroom door,
Toffile, for my sake!' 'Company?' he said,
'Don't make me get up; I'm too warm in bed.' 95
So lying forward weakly on the handrail
I pushed myself upstairs, and in the light
(The kitchen had been dark) I had to own
I could see nothing. 'Toffile, I don't see it.
It's with us in the room though. It's the bones.' 100
'What bones?' 'The cellar bones—out of the grave.'
That made him throw his bare legs out of bed
And sit up by me and take hold of me.
I wanted to put out the light and see
If I could see it, or else mow the room, 105
With our arms at the level of our knees,
And bring the chalk-pile down. 'I'll tell you what—
It's looking for another door to try.
The uncommonly deep snow has made him think
Of his old song, *The Wild Colonial Boy*, 110
He always used to sing along the tote-road.
He's after an open door to get out-doors.
Let's trap him with an open door up attic.'
Toffile agreed to that, and sure enough,
Almost the moment he was given an opening, 115
The steps began to climb the attic stairs.
I heard them. Toffile didn't seem to hear them.
'Quick!' I slammed to the door and held the knob
'Toffile, get nails.' I made him nail the door shut
And push the headboard of the bed against it 120
Then we asked was there anything
Up attic that we'd ever want again.
The attic was less to us than the cellar.
If the bones liked the attic, let them have it.
Let them stay in the attic. When they sometimes 125
Come down the stairs at night and stand perplexed

Behind the door and headboard of the bed,
Brushing their chalky skull with chalky fingers,
With sounds like the dry rattling of a shutter,
That's what I sit up in the dark to say—   130
To no one any more since Toffile died.
Let them stay in the attic since they went there.
I promised Toffile to be cruel to them
For helping them be cruel once to him.

SON. We think they had a grave down in the cellar.   135

MOTHER. We know they had a grave down in the cellar.

SON. We never could find out whose bones they were.

MOTHER. Yes, we could too, son. Tell the truth for once
They were a man's his father killed for me.
I mean a man he killed instead of me.   140
The least I could do was to help dig their grave.
We were about it one night in the cellar.
Son knows the story: but 'twas not for him
To tell the truth, suppose the time had come.
Son looks surprised to see me end a lie   145
We'd kept all these years between ourselves
So as to have it ready for outsiders.
But tonight I don't care enough to lie—
I don't remember why I ever cared.
Toffile, if he were here, I don't believe   150
Could tell you why he ever cared himself. . . .

She hadn't found the finger-bone she wanted
Among the buttons poured out in her lap.
I verified the name next morning: Toffile.
The rural letter-box said Toffile Lajway.   155

                                                              1923

FIRE AND ICE

Some say the world will end in fire,
Some say in ice.
From what I've tasted of desire
I hold with those who favor fire.
But if it had to perish twice,   5
I think I know enough of hate
To say that for destruction ice
Is also great
And would suffice.

                                                              1923

FOR ONCE, THEN, SOMETHING

Others taunt me with having knelt at well-curbs
Always wrong to the light, so never seeing
Deeper down in the well than where the water
Gives me back in a shining surface picture
Me myself in the summer heaven godlike   5
Looking out of a wreath of fern and cloud puffs.
Once, when trying with chin against a well-curb,
I discerned, as I thought, beyond the picture,
Through the picture, a something white, uncertain,
Something more of the depths—and then I lost it.   10
Water came to rebuke the too clear water.
One drop fell from a fern, and lo, a ripple
Shook whatever it was lay there at bottom,
Blurred it, blotted it out. What was that whiteness?
Truth? A pebble of quartz? For once, then, something.   15

1923

I WILL SING YOU ONE-O

It was long I lay
Awake that night
Wishing the tower
Would name the hour
And tell me whether   5
To call it day
(Though not yet light)
And give up sleep.
The snow fell deep
With the hiss of spray;   10
Two winds would meet,
One down one street,
One down another,
And fight in a smother
Of dust and feather.   15
I could not say,
But feared the cold
Had checked the pace
Of the tower clock
By tying together   20
Its hands of gold
Before its face.

Then came one knock!
A note unruffled
Of earthly weather,   25
Though strange and muffled
The tower said, 'One!'
And then a steeple.
They spoke to themselves
And such few people   30
As winds might rouse
From sleeping warm
(But not unhouse).
They left the storm
That struck *en masse*   35
My window glass
Like a beaded fur.
In that grave One
They spoke of the sun
And moon and stars,   40
Saturn and Mars
And Jupiter.
Still more unfettered,
They left the named
And spoke of the lettered,   45
The sigmas and taus
Of constellations.
They filled their throats
With the furthest bodies
To which man sends his   50
Speculation,
Beyond which God is;
The cosmic motes
Of yawning lenses.
Their solemn peals   55
Were not their own:
They spoke for the clock
With whose vast wheels
Theirs interlock.
In that grave word   60
Uttered alone
The utmost star
Trembled and stirred,
Though set so far
Its whirling frenzies   65
Appear like standing
In one self station.
It has not ranged,
And save for the wonder
Of once expanding   70

To be a nova,
It has not changed
To the eye of man
On planets over
Around and under   75
It in creation
Since man began
To drag down man
And nation nation.

1923

NOTHING GOLD CAN STAY

Nature's first green is gold,
Her hardest hue to hold.
Her early leaf's a flower;
But only so an hour.
Then leaf subsides to leaf.   5
So Eden sank to grief,
So dawn goes down to day.
Nothing gold can stay.

" 1923

One of his best lyrics short

one of his "untroubled" poems.

STOPPING BY WOODS ON A
SNOWY EVENING

Practical people, like the practical little horse, might think it queer to stop at the words on a dark, snowy evening. The reason is given in line 4.

Frost said that the poem contained "all I ever know".

Whose woods these are I think I know
His house is in the village though;
He will not see me stopping here
To watch his woods fill up with snow. ← *in line 4.*

My little horse must think it queer   5
To stop without a farmhouse near
Between the woods and frozen lake
The darkest evening of the year.

The lure of "the terrible that attracts and repulse." as I. a. ben puts it.

He gives his harness bells a shake
To ask if there is some mistake.
The only other sound's the sweep
Of easy wind and downy flake.   10

The woods are lovely, dark and deep.
But I have promises to keep,

Richly imaginative and symbolic

It perhaps involves: nature, beauty, duty, action, time, death.

And miles to go before I sleep,   15
And miles to go before I sleep.

                          1923

TO EARTHWARD

Love at the lips was touch
As sweet as I could bear;
And once that seemed too much;
I lived on air

That crossed me from sweet things,   5
The flow of—was it musk
From hidden grapevine springs
Down hill at dusk?

I had the swirl and ache
From sprays of honeysuckle   10
That when they're gathered shake
Dew on the knuckle.

I craved strong sweets, but those
Seemed strong when I was young;
The petal of the rose   15
It was that stung.

Now no joy but lacks salt
That is not dashed with pain
And weariness and fault;
I crave the stain   20

Of tears, the aftermark
Of almost too much love,
The sweet of bitter bark
And burning clove.

When stiff and sore and scarred   25
I take away my hand
From leaning on it hard
In grass and sand,

The hurt is not enough:
I long for weight and strength   30
To feel the earth as rough
To all my length.

                          1923

TWO LOOK AT TWO

Love and forgetting might have carried them
A little further up the mountain side
With night so near, but not much further up.
They must have halted soon in any case
With thoughts of the path back, how rough it was 5
With rock and washout, and unsafe in darkness;
When they were halted by a tumbled wall
With barbed-wire binding. They stood facing this,
Spending what onward impulse they still had
In one last look the way they must not go, 10
On up the failing path, where, if a stone
Or earthslide moved at night, it moved itself;
No footstep moved it. 'This is all,' they sighed,
'Good-night to woods.' But not so; there was more.
A doe from round a spruce stood looking at them 15
Across the wall, as near the wall as they.
She saw them in their field, they her in hers.
The difficulty of seeing what stood still,
Like some up-ended boulder split in two,
Was in her clouded eyes: they saw no fear there. 20
She seemed to think that two thus they were safe.
Then, as if they were something that, though strange,
She could not trouble her mind with too long,
She sighed and passed unscared along the wall.
'This, then, is all. What more is there to ask?' 25
But no, not yet. A snort to bid them wait.
A buck from round the spruce stood looking at them
Across the wall as near the wall as they.
This was an antlered buck of lusty nostril,
Not the same doe come back into her place. 30
He viewed them quizzically with jerks of head,
As if to ask, 'Why don't you make some motion?
Or give some sign of life? Because you can't.
I doubt if you're as living as you look.'
Thus till he had them almost feeling dared 35
To stretch a proffering hand—and a spell-breaking.
Then he too passed unscared along the wall.
Two had seen two, whichever side you spoke from.
'This must be all.' It was all. Still they stood,
A great wave from it going over them, 40
As if the earth in one unlooked-for favor
Had made them certain earth returned their love.

1923

ACQUAINTED WITH THE NIGHT

I have been one acquainted with the night.
I have walked out in the rain—and back in rain.
I have outwalked the furthest city light.

I have looked down the saddest city lane.
I have passed by the watchman on his beat   5
And dropped my eyes, unwilling to explain.

I have stood still and stopped the sound of feet
When far away an interrupted cry
Came over houses from another street,

But not to call me back or say good-by;   10
And further still at an unearthly height,
One luminary clock against the sky

Proclaimed the time was neither wrong nor right
I have been one acquainted with the night.

1928

WEST-RUNNING BROOK

'Fred, where is north?'

         'North? North is there, my love.
The brook runs west.'

        'West-running Brook then call it.'
(West-running Brook men call it to this day.)   5
'What does it think it's doing running west
When all the other country brooks flow east
To reach the ocean? It must be the brook
Can trust itself to go by contraries
The way I can with you—and you with me—   10
Because we're—we're—I don't know what we are.
What are we?'

        'Young or new?'

        'We must be something.
We've said we two. Let's change that to we three.   15
As you and I are married to each other,
We'll both be married to the brook. We'll build
Our bridge across it, and the bridge shall be
Our arm thrown over it asleep beside it.

Idea we get an expression X Frost's social attitude, or rather his steadfast and sometimes eccentric individualism.

Look, look, it's waving to us with a wave   20
To let us know it hears me.'

                 'Why, my dear,
That wave's been standing off this jut of shore—'
(The black stream, catching on a sunken rock,
Flung backward on itself in one white wave,
And the white water rode the black forever,
Not gaining but not losing, like a bird
White feathers from the struggle of whose breast
Flecked the dark stream and flecked the darker pool
Below the point, and were at last driven wrinkled   30
In a white scarf against the far shore alders.)
'That wave's been standing off this jut of shore
Ever since rivers, I was going to say,
Were made in heaven. It wasn't waved to us.'

'It wasn't, yet it was. If not to you   35
It was to me—in an annunciation.'

'Oh, if you take it off to lady-land,
As't were the country of the Amazons
We men must see you to the confines of   40
And leave you there, ourselves forbid to enter,
It is your brook! I have no more to say.'

'Yes, you have, too. Go on. You thought of something,'

'Speaking of contraries, see how the brook
In that white wave runs counter to itself.
It is from that in water we were from   45
Long, long before we were from any creature.
Here we, in our impatience of the steps,
Get back to the beginning of beginnings,
The stream of everything that runs away.
Some say existence like a Pirouot
And Pirouette, forever in one place,   50
Stands still and dances, but it runs away,
It seriously, sadly, runs away
To fill the abyss' void with emptiness.
It flows beside us in this water brook,
But it flows over us. It flows between us   55
To separate us for a panic moment.
It flows between us, over us, and *with* us.
And it is time, strength, tone, light, life and love—
And even substance lapsing unsubstantial;   60
The universal cataract of death
That spends to nothingness—and unresisted,
Save by some strange resistance in itself,
Not just a swerving, but a throwing back,

Then:

The poem describes a N. Eng. brook which runs west whereas normal brooks run east to the Atlantic.

The analogy X the levels is 'that X their own defiance X society and civil conventions'

Struggle upstream

As if regret were in it and were sacred.   65
It had this throwing backward on itself
So that the fall of most of it is always
Raising a little, sending up a little.
Our life runs down in sending up the clock
The brook runs down in sending up our life.   70
The run runs down in sending up the brook.
And there is something sending up the sun.
It is this backward motion toward the source,
Against the stream, that most we see ourselves in,
The tribute of the current to the source.   75
It is from this in nature we are from.
It is most us.'

                    'Today will be the day
        You said so.'

                    'No, today will be the day   80
        You said the brook was called West-running Brook.'

    'Today will be the day of what we both said.'

                                                    1928

DESERT PLACES

Snow falling and night falling fast, oh fast
In a field I looked into going past,
And the ground almost covered smooth in snow,
But a few weeds and stubble showing last.

The woods around it have it—it is theirs.   5
All animals are smothered in their lairs.
I am too absent-spirited to count;
The loneliness includes me unawares.

And lonely as it is that loneliness
Will be more lonely ere it will be less—   10
A blanker whiteness of benighted snow
With no expression, nothing to express.

They cannot scare me with their empty spaces
Between stars—on stars where no human race is.
I have it in me so much nearer home   15
To scare myself with my own desert places.

                                                    1934

DESIGN

I found a dimpled spider, fat and white,
On a white heal-all, holding up a moth
Like a white piece of rigid satin cloth—
Assorted characters of death and blight
Mixed ready to begin the morning right,   5
Like the ingredients of a witches' broth—
A snow-drop spider, a flower like froth,
And dead wings carried like a paper kite.

What had that flower to do with being white,
The wayside blue and innocent heal-all?   10
What brought the kindred spider to that height,
Then steered the white moth thither in the night?
What but design of darkness to appall?—
If design govern in a thing so small.

                                   1936

NOTE: That the effect of this poem depends on its language and imagery is proved by comparison with an early version, written twenty-five years before:

A dented spider like a snow drop white
On a white Heal-all, holding up a moth
Like a white piece of lifeless satin cloth—
Saw ever curious eye so strange a sight?—
Portent in little, assorted death and blight
Like the ingredients of a witches' broth?—
The beady spider, the flower like a froth,
And the moth carried like a paper kite.

What had that flower to do with being white,
The blue prunella every child's delight.
What brought the kindred spider to that height?
(Make we no thesis of the miller's plight.)
What but design of darkness and of night?
Design, design! Do I use the word aright?

NEITHER OUT FAR NOR IN DEEP

The people along the sand
All turn and look one way.
They turn their back on the land.
They look at the sea all day.

As long as it takes to pass   5
A ship keeps raising its hull;
The wetter ground like glass
Reflects a standing gull.

The land may vary more;
But wherever the truth may be—   10
The water comes ashore,
And the people look at the sea.

They cannot look out far.
They cannot look in deep.
But when was that ever a bar   15
To any watch they keep?

1934

THE SILKEN TENT

She is as in a field a silken tent
At midday when a sunny summer breeze
Has dried the dew and all its ropes relent,
So that in guys it gently sways at ease,
And its supporting central cedar pole,   5
That is its pinnacle to heavenward
And signifies the sureness of the soul,
Seems to owe naught to any single cord,
But strictly held by none, is loosely bound
By countless silken ties of love and thought   10
To everything on earth the compass round,
And only by one's going slightly taut
In the capriciousness of summer air
Is of the slightest bondage made aware.

1939

ALL REVELATION

A head thrusts in as for the view,
But where it is it thrusts in from
Or what it is it thrusts into
By that Cyb'laean avenue,
And what can of its coming come,   5

And whither it will be withdrawn,
And what take hence or leave behind,
These things the mind has pondered on
A moment and still asking gone.
Strange apparition of the mind!   10

But the impervious geode
Was entered, and its inner crust
Of crystals with a ray cathode
At every point and facet glowed
In answer to the mental thrust.   15

Eyes seeking the response of eyes
Bring out the stars, bring out the flowers,
Thus concentrating earth and skies
So none need be afraid of size.
All revelation has been ours.   20

1942

THE MOST OF IT

He thought he kept the universe alone;
For all the voice in answer he could wake
Was but the mocking echo of his own
From some tree-hidden cliff across the lake.
Some morning from the boulder-broken beach   5
He would cry out on life, that what it wants
Is not its own love back in copy speech,
But counter-love, original response.
And nothing ever came of what he cried
Unless it was the embodiment that crashed   10
In the cliff's talus on the other side,
And then in the far distant water splashed,
But after a time allowed for it to swim,
Instead of proving human when it neared
And someone else additional to him,   15
As a great buck it powerfully appeared,
Pushing the crumpled water up ahead,
And landed pouring like a waterfall,
And stumbled through the rocks with horny tread,
And forced the underbrush—and that was all.   20

1942

BEECH

Where my imaginary line
Bends square in woods, an iron spine
And pile of real rocks have been founded.
And off this corner in the wild,
Where these are driven in and piled,   5

One tree, by being deeply wounded,
Has been impressed as Witness Tree
And made commit to memory
My proof of being not unbounded.
Thus truth's established and borne out,   10
Though circumstanced with dark and doubt—
Though by a world of doubt surrounded.

The Moodie Forester

1942

SYCAMORE

Zaccheus he
Did climb the tree
Our Lord to see.

The New England Primer

1942

DIRECTIVE

Back out of all this now too much for us,
Back in a time made simple by the loss
Of detail, burned, dissolved, and broken off
Like graveyard marble sculpture in the weather,
There is a house that is no more a house   5
Upon a farm that is no more a farm
And in a town that is no more a town.
The road there, if you'll let a guide direct you
Who only has at heart your getting lost,
May seem as if it should have been a quarry—   10
Great monolithic knees the former town
Long since gave up pretense of keeping covered.
And there's a story in a book about it:
Besides the wear of iron wagon wheels
The ledges show lines ruled southeast northwest,   15
The chisel work of an enormous Glacier
That braced his feet against the Arctic Pole.
You must not mind a certain coolness from him
Still said to haunt this side of Panther Mountain.
Nor need you mind the serial ordeal   20
Of being watched from forty cellar holes
As if by eye pairs out of forty firkins.

As for the woods' excitement over you
That sends light rustle rushes to their leaves,
Charge that to upstart inexperience.   25
Where were they all not twenty years ago?
They think too much of having shaded out
A few old pecker-fretted apple trees.
Make yourself up a cheering song of how
Someone's road home from work this once was,   30
Who may be just ahead of you on foot
Or creaking with a buggy load of grain.
The height of the adventure is the height
Of country where two village cultures faded
Into each other. Both of them are lost.   35
And if you're lost enough to find yourself
By now, pull in your ladder road behind you
And put a sign up CLOSED to all but me.
Then make yourself at home. The only field
Now left's no bigger than a harness gall.   40
First there's the children's house of make believe,
Some shattered dishes underneath a pine,
The playthings in the playhouse of the children.
Weep for what little things could make them glad.
Then for the house that is no more a house,   45
But only a belilaced cellar hole,
Now slowly closing like a dent in dough.
This was no playhouse but a house in earnest.
Your destination and your destiny's
A brook that was the water of the house,   50
Cold as a spring as yet so near its source,
Too lofty and original to rage.
(We know the valley streams that when aroused
Will leave their tatters hung on barb and thorn.)
I have kept hidden in the instep arch   55
Of an old cedar at the waterside
A broken drinking goblet like the Grail
Under a spell so the wrong ones can't find it,
So can't get saved, as Saint Mark says they mustn't.
(I stole the goblet from the children's playhouse.) 60
Here are your waters and your watering place.
Drink and be whole again beyond confusion.

1947

THE FIGURE A POEM MAKES

ABSTRACTION IS AN old story with the philosophers, but it has been like a new toy in the hands of the artists of our day. Why can't we have any one quality of poetry we choose by itself? We can have in thought. Then it will go hard if we can't in practice. Our lives for it.

Granted no one but a humanist much cares how sound a poem is if it is only *a* sound. The sound is the gold in the ore. Then we will have the sound out alone and dispense with the inessential. We do till we make the discovery that the object in writing poetry is to make all poems sound as different as possible from each other, and the resources for that of vowels, consonants, punctuation, syntax, words, sentences, meter are not enough. We need the help of context—meaning—subject matter. That is the greatest help towards variety. All that can be done with words is soon told. So also with meters—particularly in our language where there are virtually but two, strict iambic and loose iambic. The ancients with many were still poor if they depended on meters for all tune. It is painful to watch our sprung-rhythmists straining at the point of omitting one short from a foot for relief from monotony. The possibilities for tune from the dramatic tones of meaning struck across the rigidity of a limited meter are endless. And we are back in poetry as merely one more art of having something to say, sound or unsound. Probably better if sound, because deeper and from wider experience.

Then there is this wildness whereof it is spoken. Granted again that it has an equal claim with sound to being a poem's better half. If it is a wild tune, it is a poem. Our problem then is, as modern abstractionists, to have the wildness pure; to be wild with nothing to be wild about. We bring up as aberrationists, giving way to undirected associations and kicking ourselves from one chance suggestion to another in all directions as of a hot afternoon in the life of a grass-hopper. Theme alone can steady us down. Just as the first mystery was how a poem could have a tune in such a straightness as meter, so the second mystery is how a poem can have wildness and at the same time a subject that shall be fulfilled.

It should be of the pleasure of a poem itself to tell how it can. The figure a poem makes. It begins in delight and ends in wisdom. The figure is the same as for love. No one can really hold that the ecstasy should be static and stand still in one place. It begins in delight, it inclines to the impulse, it assumes direction with the first line laid down, it runs a course of lucky events, and ends in a clarification of life—not necessarily a great clarification, such as sects and cults are founded on, but in a momentary stay against confusion. It has denouement. It has an outcome that though unforeseen was predestined from the first image of the original mood—and indeed from the very mood. It is but a trick poem and no poem at all if the best of it was thought of first and saved for the last. It finds its own name as it goes and discovers the best waiting for it in some final phrase at once wise and sad—the happy-sad blend of the drinking song.

No tears in the writer, no tears in the reader. No surprise for the writer, no surprise for the reader. For me the initial delight is in the surprise of remembering something I didn't know I knew. I am in a place, in a situation, as if I had materialized from cloud or risen out of the ground. There is a glad recognition of the long lost and the rest follows. Step by step the wonder of unexpected supply keeps growing. The impressions most useful to my purpose seem always those I was unaware of and so made no note of at the time when taken, and the conclusion is come to that like giants we are always hurling experience ahead of us to pave the future with against the day when we may want to strike a line of purpose across it for somewhere. The line will have the more charm for not being mechanically straight. We enjoy the straight crookedness of a good walking stick. Modern instruments of precision are being used to make things crooked as if by eye and hand in the old days.

I tell how there may be a better wildness of logic than of inconsequence. But the logic is backward, in retrospect, after the act. It must be more felt than seen ahead like prophecy. It must be a revelation, or a series of revelations, as much for the poet as for the reader. For it to be that there must have been the greatest freedom of the material to move about in it and to establish relations in it regardless of time and space, previous relation, and everything but affinity. We prate of freedom. We call our schools free because we are not free to stay away from them till we are sixteen years of age. I have given up my democratic prejudices and now willingly set the lower classes free to be completely taken care of by the upper classes. Political freedom is nothing to me. I bestow it right and left. All I would keep for myself is the freedom of my material—the condition of body and mind now and then to summons aptly from the vast chaos of all I have lived through.

Scholars and artists thrown together are often annoyed at the puzzle of where they differ. Both work from knowledge; but I suspect they differ most importantly in the way their knowledge is come by. Scholars get theirs with conscientious thoroughness along projected lines of logic; poets theirs cavalierly and as it happens in and out of books. They stick to nothing deliberately, but let what will stick to them like burrs where they walk in the fields. No acquirement is on assignment, or even self-assignment. Knowledge of the second kind is much more available in the wild free ways of wit and art. A schoolboy may be defined as one who can tell you what he knows in the order in which he learned it. The artist must value himself as he snatches a thing from some previous order in time and space into a new order with not so much as a ligature clinging to it of the old place where it was organic.

More than once I should have lost my soul to radicalism if it had been the originality it was mistaken for by its young converts. Originality and initiative are what I ask for my country. For myself the originality need be no more than the freshness of a poem run in the way I have described: from delight to wisdom. The figure is the same as for love. Like a piece of ice on a hot stove the poem must ride on its own melting. A poem may be worked over once it is in being, but may not be worried into being. Its most precious quality will remain its having run itself and carried away the poet with it. Read it a hundred times: it will forever keep its freshness as a

metal keeps its fragrance. It can never lose its sense of a meaning that once
unfolded by surprise as it went.

1949

Reading Suggestions

There are a number of "further ranges" in Frost's poetry, including some
anthology favorites, that have been omitted here because they did not measure
up to his best. There are lyrics like "The Road Not Taken," purely humorous
poems like "Brown's Descent," other long dramatic narratives like "In the
Home Stretch" and "The Housekeeper," the even longer comic-pastoral "New
Hampshire." Then there are poems that have been the focus of controversy:
lyric-narratives of a whimsical sort, all too often ending with overt didacticism,
admired by Frost's friends and scorned by his detractors ("Birches" and "Wild
Grapes"); satires on philosophy, science, industrialism, and sociology, enjoyed
by gay-minded humanists but rejected by the serious-minded as anti-intellectual
("The Bear," "The White-Tailed Hornet," "The Egg and the Machine,"
"Two Tramps in Mud-Time"). Finally, there are the two late volumes in a new
key, *A Masque of Reason* and *A Masque of Mercy*.

Interested readers will find these and many more in *The Complete Poems
of Robert Frost* (1949)—a collection of all ten volumes published by the poet
during his lifetime, prefaced by his essay, "The Figure a Poem Makes." A generous selection from the first seven of these volumes is conveniently available
in the Modern Library edition of *The Poems of Robert Frost*, prefaced by his
essay, "The Constant Symbol." (See *Robert Frost: A Bibliography* [1937], by
W. B. S. Clymer and C. R. Green; and *The Intervals of Robert Frost: A Critical Bibliography* [1947], by Louis and Esther Mertins.)

The fullest biography is Elizabeth Sergeant's *Robert Frost: The Trial by
Existence* (1960); a labor of love, it is without documentation and without
critical pretensions. (The official biography is now in preparation by Professor
Lawrence Thompson.) The best book of criticism is John Lynen's *The Pastoral
Art of Robert Frost* (1960); in addition to detailed analyses of more than
twenty-five poems, it opens up a new way of understanding Frost's major
achievement. Another sensitive reading is Reuben Brower's *The Poetry of Robert
Frost: Constellations of Intention* (1963). Lawrence Thompson's *Fire and Ice*
(1942) is a more general commentary on "The Art and Thought of Robert
Frost"; more helpful on individual poems is his pamphlet in the University of
Minnesota series on American writers, No. 2 (1959). Of the half dozen
books on Frost, mostly partisan, two may be mentioned (one pro and one con):
Reginald Cook's *The Dimensions of Robert Frost* (1959) contains records of
conversations with Frost; George Nitchie's *Human Values in the Poetry of Robert Frost* (1960) attacks him for the limitations of his ideas.

There are three collections of articles about Frost, one early and two late—
Recognition of Robert Frost (1937), edited by Richard Thornton, and *Robert
Frost: An Introduction* (1961), edited by R. A. Greenberg and J. G. Hepburn
—and *Robert Frost: A Collection of Critical Essays* (1962), edited with an introduction by James M. Cox. The first two are concerned chiefly with the personality of the poet and the controversy over his worth. The best general critical
essays on Frost's poetry (in addition to those in the last-named volume), are
James Cox, "Robert Frost and the Edge of the Clearing," *Virginia Quarterly*

(Winter 1959); Randall Jarrell, in *Poetry and the Age* (1953); Roy Pearce, "Frost's Momentary Stay," *Kenyon Review* (Spring 1961); Hyatt Waggoner, "The Humanistic Idealism of Robert Frost," *American Literature* (November 1941); Charles Anderson, "Form and Figure in the Poetry of Frost," *Saturday Review* (February 23, 1963).

Biography

Rural New England, particularly the region of small mountain farms in southern New Hampshire and Vermont, is closely connected in the popular mind with Frost's life as well as with his poetry. But this relation needs to be defined, for he was most certainly not a farmer-turned-poet. It was not until after the age of twenty-five that he lived in the now famous "North of Boston" world, and even then only off and on. He had a city boyhood in San Francisco, where he was born on March 26, 1874. At the age of eleven, on the death of his father, he was taken by his Scottish mother back to the paternal home of the Frosts in Lawrence, Massachusetts. For the next fifteen years this small industrial city was the center of his life. Graduating from the local high school in 1892, he entered Dartmouth but left after two months, then drifted through various jobs as teacher, millworker, and reporter. In 1897, married and needing security, he went to Harvard to prepare for a career in college teaching. But after two years he again abandoned formal education and finally, in 1900, settled on a farm in Derry, New Hampshire, bought for him by his grandfather, where he hoped to solve the question of his future. During all these years of early maturity his one desire had been to write poetry, and his problem was to find a means of support that would allow him the requisite freedom. "I kept farm, so to speak for nearly ten years, but less as a farmer than as a fugitive from the world," he has said. "I went away to save myself and fix myself before I measured my strength against all creation." But he soon failed at farming and had to turn to schoolteaching to make ends meet, first at the Derry Academy, then at the normal school in Plymouth.

In 1912 Frost made a decision that proved the turning point in his life. For twenty years he had besieged editors with his poems but only a handful were accepted. Now, deciding to stake all on art, he sold the farm and moved with his growing family to England, where he could be poor and write poetry, as he put it, "without further scandal." During his residence there his talents flowered and he came into his own. After forty years of obscurity he won recognition, then fame, with the publication in London of his first two volumes, *A Boy's Will* (1913) and *North of Boston* (1914). England brought him two great gifts, literary friendship and perspective. In London he met Ezra Pound and his circle, including such diverse figures as Amy Lowell and Yeats, but he refused to be drawn into Imagism or other modern movements. Instead, he found his best friends among the "Georgians," a minor English group whose direction was more congenial to his own. Living in the English countryside as the companion of poets who were writing from that vantage point, he rediscovered rural New England as the focus for a new kind of pastoral poetry, and so discovered his poetic self. His second book marked the beginning of his distinctive achievement, and when it was reprinted in America on his return in 1915 his reputation was made on both sides of the Atlantic.

He at once settled on a farm near Franconia, New Hampshire, but in less than two years he was drawn back to the more sophisticated atmosphere of a college town, taking a post in the English Department at Amherst. At about this time he summed up his first forty-three years as follows: "25 years in cities, 9 in villages, 9 on farms"—and the pattern remained about the same through the rest of his life. Thus, he was poet-in-residence or faculty member at Amherst, Michigan, Harvard, and elsewhere; founder and teacher for many summers at the Bread Loaf School of English; lecturer in cities and at universities all over the country—but constantly returning to various farms that he owned in Vermont, during vacations and longer periods, for renewal of the spirit. There are interesting paradoxes in this long career. His projected role as farmer-poet is a fictive one, yet it corresponds to the deepest inward impulses of his poetic self. The college diploma that he did not earn was replaced many times over by honorary degrees from universities, including Harvard and Yale, Oxford and Cambridge; also his long running battle with formal education was matched by an equally long attachment to academic communities. During the first half of his life he was a neglected and unknown poet, but the second half was enriched with fame and honors, four times Pulitzer Prize winner and the recipient of many medals and awards—a popularity, ironically and unjustly, that has hurt his reputation with serious critics.

Few poets have been as successful as Frost in bringing their life and career into harmony. During the first ten years after his return to America he consolidated and extended his achievement as a pastoralist with *Mountain Interval* (1916) and *New Hampshire* (1923). His fifth volume, *West-Running Brook* (1928), showed a turn toward philosophical poetry that was later continued in *A Further Range* (1936), *A Witness Tree* (1942), and *Steeple Bush* (1947), with experiments in satire and metaphysical wit. Though not an intellectual, Frost was always deeply involved in ideas. He once taught psychology and philosophy as well as literature, and he was studying at Harvard when the conflict between religious idealism and scientific determinism engaged the minds of a distinguished group on that faculty. This area was not as fruitful for his poetry as pastoralism, however, and he never again measured up to the consistent high level of *North of Boston*, but the later volumes reveal not so much a decline as a change of direction in his poetic energies. *A Masque of Reason* and *A Masque of Mercy*, published after he was seventy, are remarkable achievements. The *Complete Poems*, issued on his seventy-fifth birthday, showed continuing powers. A final gathering of lighter pieces, *In the Clearing*, was issued shortly before his death on January 20, 1963. The celebration of his eighty-fifth birthday at a dinner in New York, with resolutions from the United States Senate, was the culmination of a public recognition such as has been extended to no other living American writer.

Sister Carrie caused a flurry
when it came out in 1900.

THEODORE DREISER ✦

Books condemned as   **1871-1945**
immoral.

He lacks sense of humor.

His prose is pedestrian (plebeian
or common people)

His method of piling up of
detail makes for dull reading.

often gives us pictures of
weak and disintegrating
personalities

The story is the portrayal
of a young man's tragic
attempt to make a place
for himself in a world
whose demands he was incapable
of meeting.
The resolution shows Clyde
Griffiths' crime was the result
of environmental factors over
which his weak nature
had little control, and that
society, with its aggressive
materialism, was at the bar
of judgment along with the
criminal — a powerful
fictional appraisal of
fundamental modern dilemmas.

Dreiser, unlike some of the French naturalists, had a good deal of contempt for niceties of style.

Introduction

An American Tragedy, published in 1925 when its author was fifty-four years old, was the climax of Theodore Dreiser's career. Though he lived for twenty more years and published eight more books, none of these showed a serious modification of his characteristic preoccupations, or added substantially to his reputation, or altered the judgments that critics had formed about him from his previous work. Only two were novels, and both of these had been begun many years before *An American Tragedy* was even conceived. *The Bulwark* (1946), though many critics took it as an indication that Dreiser had passed through his time of groping and had arrived in his last years at a faith that was almost Quaker, can hardly be interpreted in that way, for *The Bulwark* had been started as early as 1914 or 1915, and its ethical hero Solon Barnes was evidently intended as a counterportrait to balance the Nietzschean Frank Cowperwood of *The Financier* (1912) and *The Titan* (1914). Dreiser's final novel was *The Stoic* (1947), which completed the Cowperwood trilogy. In no sense new fictional business, it had been in preparation over a period of thirty years.

That is to say, not only was *An American Tragedy* Dreiser's climactic novel; it was his last real burst of creation if we except the brief flurry just before his death when he completed the manuscripts of *The Bulwark* and *The Stoic*. What happened after 1925 was mainly a sweeping-up of chips and shavings. When Dreiser and his friends expected the Nobel Prize in 1930, the year it was awarded to Sinclair Lewis, they expected it on the strength of *An American Tragedy*. For this novel represented its author's profoundest feeling about American life, his developed understanding of the dialogue between desire and restriction, his considered judgment about conventional right and wrong, his lifelong sympathy for "the sensitive and seeking individual in his pitiful struggle with nature—with his enormous urges and his pathetic equipment."

This sympathy was one possible response to what his experience, his reading, and the climate of his times had taught him: that life was "a fierce, grim struggle in which no quarter was either given or taken, and in which all men laid traps, lied, squandered, erred through illusion. . . ." Superior "chemisms" permitted the strong to survive and succeed, but they were no more praiseworthy for their success, or responsible for their ruthlessness, than the weak were for their weakness. The view of life as a jungle was common among the newspapermen of Chicago, St. Louis, and Pittsburgh with whom Dreiser spent his most formative years. It was explicit in Herbert Spencer's *First Principles*, which Dreiser testified "blew [him] to bits" when he read it in the Carnegie Library in Pittsburgh. It was suggested by all the ugliness and venality that the young police reporter encountered. It had been blown into the air and disseminated like thistle seeds by the novels of Zola and by such works of American naturalism as Stephen Crane's *Maggie: A Girl of the Streets* (1893) and Frank Norris' *McTeague* (1899). It does not really matter whether or not Dreiser had read these books (during his formative years he seems to have been reading mainly Balzac and du Maurier instead). What matters is that as America grew from rural to urban and from agricultural to industrial, acquiring on the way unprecedented problems of immigration, unemployment, slums, and social injustice, Dreiser turned with it: poor boy, city boy, child of the urban jungle, heir to the ideas of his time as he would have been heir to certain endemic children's diseases.

Half-educated as he was, he was incapable of discriminating among ideas or of judging accurately the sterile mechanism he learned from Spencer. Coming from America's underside, the son of an immigrant and hence cut off from any abiding tradition, he had nothing in common with the genteel realism of Henry James, Edith Wharton, and William Dean Howells; characteristically, he thought Howells "uninformed." With Crane he shared the vision of the city as the symbolic jungle world, with Norris a fascinated interest in man's animal nature. His novels are full of animal imagery, as Stuart Pratt Sherman long ago pointed out: a scene in *Sister Carrie* is interrupted to permit the insertion of a quotation about Siberian wolves who eat their hurt fellows; in *The Financier*, Frank Cowperwood and Aileen "run together like two leopards"; in the same novel, an aquarium battle between a lobster and a squid is used as a paradigm of the law of life. But aside from these standard trappings of naturalism, Dreiser is *sui generis*. Clumsy, ardent, hating and envying wealth, a defender of the underdog even while he felt in himself the capacities for success and power, ignorant of the traditions of thought and literature that had formed his country but aware as few have been of the literal truths of its mean streets, he was like no writer of his time. His very limitations gave him an awkward but powerful originality, and let him see what others overlooked or had been taught to ignore.

Seeing the world made up of victims and victimizers, and feeling in himself not only the scars of poverty and weakness but the ambition to wreak his will on life, Dreiser divided his early books between the defeated and the ruthless. In *Sister Carrie* (1900), his heroine falls and rises without conscious willing. Her rise is not inhibited by a double fall from sexual purity; the same blind chance that carries her to success on the stage carries her companion Hurstwood downward to beggary and suicide. Dreiser's second heroine, the soft and yielding Jennie Gerhardt, the most appealing of all Dreiser's women, gives all and gains nothing, victimized by forces she cannot even understand, much less control. And as with the victims, so with the victimizers. Frank Cowperwood of *The Financier* (1912) and *The Titan* (1914) is a powerful tycoon, Eugene Witla of *The "Genius"* (1915) is an artist. Both are men of power and ambition, dangerous to rivals and to women, and both unquestionably mirror modified images of Dreiser's own flaming ambition and sexuality. Neither is to be blamed, we are told over and over, for living according to his nature. As far back as *Sister Carrie*, Dreiser had written that "on the tiger, no responsibility rests."

But forceful though these characters are, they do not wedge themselves into our sympathy. In the end, it was with the defeated that Dreiser allied himself, and he could never quite reconcile in his own nature the things that led him away from them. As he wrote in *A Book about Myself* (1922),

Later in life I began to suspect that a gross favoritism in regard to certain things at least was being practiced in my behalf. I was never without friends, never without someone to do me a good turn at a critical moment, never without love and the sacrifices of beauty on the part of someone in my behalf, never without a certain amount of applause and repute. Was I worthy of it?

It is not, ultimately, for his Nietzschean predators that we keep returning to Dreiser's novels, but for the unlucky ones, the weak ones, the pitiful chips swept on by the blind forces of life. Dreiser came back to the weak ones in *An American Tragedy*, and made out of the unprepossessing and unappealing figure of Clyde Griffiths the strongest demonstration of his pitying view of human weakness. In 1925 he was as thoroughgoing a naturalist as he had been in 1900, and as awkwardly lonely a figure in the literary scene. *An American Tragedy* had no closer resemblance to characteristic novels of the mid-twenties—say, to *The Great Gatsby* or *The Sun Also Rises*—than *Sister Carrie* had had to James's *The Ambassadors* or Wharton's *The House of Mirth*. Dreiser remained stubbornly himself, and though he learned to avoid some of the worst mannerisms of the earlier books—the interpolated essays of *Sister Carrie*, the mechanically alternating chapters of high finance and seduction that had marked *The Titan*—neither his method nor his philosophical position nor his interest in the incompetent, the botched, and the defeated had much changed.

To Louise Campbell, who was preparing the manuscript of *An Ameri-*

can Tragedy for the press, Dreiser wrote in January 1925, "This book will be a terrible thing." That was his judgment, as it had been his intention. The novel begins in desire and proceeds inexorably through frustration and temptation to crime—or at least the intention of crime—and punishment. After its publication Dreiser was very specific, in a number of letters and interviews, about why he had created a protagonist "painfully hampered by poverty" and "tempted by love and material comfort, as well as a foolish dream of social superiority."

Part One of my book was . . . devoted to setting forth such social miseries as might naturally depress, inhibit, and frustrate, and therefore exaggerate, the emotions and desires of a very sensitive and almost sensually exotic boy most poorly equipped for the great life struggle which confronts all youth.

Part Two . . . was planned to show how such a temperament might fortuitously be brought face to face with a more fortunate world which would intensify all his deepest desires of luxury and love, and show how, in the usual unequal contest between poverty and ignorance and desire and the world's great toys, he might . . . through no real willing of his own find himself defeated and even charged with murder. . . .

Part Three . . . was planned to show how such an inhibited, weak temperament, once in the hands of his dreams and later the law, might be . . . forced by an ignorant, conventional, and revengeful background of rural souls who would, in their turn, by reason of their lacks and social and religious inhibitions and beliefs, be the last to understand. . . .

Dreiser felt that America, by teaching respect for money and what money would buy, taught many a poor boy to dream of getting them by marriage with a rich girl. But often such a boy, presented with an opportunity to realize the American dream of something for nothing, found himself already encumbered with a girl of his own station who resisted being put aside; and sometimes his desperate efforts to rid himself of her led him all the way to murder. Dreiser saw this situation "as one which was produced by the very society that condemned the outcome," and he deliberately set out to write a novel that would be an exemplum of this "typical" American tragedy. After a search through the records of at least fifteen such murders, he found the crime and the trial—Parts Two and Three of the novel—in the case of Chester Gillette, who was prosecuted, convicted, and executed for the murder of Grace Brown in Herkimer County, New York, in 1906. He found the case so ready-made to his purposes that he carried from it into his novel many personalities and details, including parts of the prosecutor's speech, literal newspaper reports, most of the details of the crime itself, and some of the pathetic letters of Grace Brown.

Some have protested the method as too documentary, an attempt to make facts serve as truths. But the documentary look is deceptive. Even when he worked closest to the facts, Dreiser was bending, emphasizing, suppressing, altering in small but significant ways so that the Gillette case, almost a perfect illustration of his thesis in the first place, should become an absolutely perfect one. It has been said of Dreiser, and he claimed for himself, that he was a ruthlessly "honest" reporter of life as it is. But he was a novelist, however reportorial his method, and the truths that a novel reflects are sure to be the novelist's personal truths, conditioned and limited by his personal vision and experience. All we may legitimately demand of a novelist is that he present with all honesty his own personal vision; there is no such thing as a documentary novel, if by documentary we mean that based entirely on unselected and verifiable facts. Truth may never be verified,—an explanation of why facts are so often used to back it up in an *appearance* of proof. Dreiser selected the Gillette case because it demonstrated his thesis, and where its demonstration was weak he altered the facts, as when he blurred the crime itself into an ambiguous half accident. Then, still following the dictates of his thesis and the inescapable processes of creation, he deliberately rigged, in Part One, the sort of background and character that would make Parts Two and Three inevitable.

And the further he got from his documentation the better he wrote. For though the crime and punishment of Clyde Griffiths were closely modeled on those of Chester Gillette, Clyde's desires, frustrations, dreams, and weaknesses, all the motivating and conditioning circumstances of the character, were remembered from Dreiser's deprived youth, and have an authenticity that is beyond documentation. Dreiser could imagine and invent Clyde's secret and selfish emotional life with terrible power, because dreams and desires and shames very like these had once scalded his own insides. He could comprehend a Clyde Griffiths totally because he knew that but for the grace of God and the luck of talent he could have been one. Part One was a triumphant addition to the documentary and representative Gillette case, for it permitted Dreiser to add much of his desiring and suffering self to a boy who might otherwise have remained cardboard. In Part One Dreiser fully exposed Clyde's character—which is to say, he prefabricated his fate.

Let us forget, then, H. L. Mencken's suggestion that the reader should concentrate on the crime and the trial, and leave Part One to be read by his clergyman. There was never more wrongheaded advice given about any novel; for though Part Three is as essential to the total novel as either of the other two sections, it is the section most open to the charge of over-documentation, and is even somewhat tedious to read. In it, Dreiser sums up his case against the society which punishes Clyde for accepting the values it has taught him; this is where he is most expository, where he draws or implies large philosophical conclusions with which we cannot always agree. But in Part Two, in which Clyde winds himself more and more inextricably in the net of his own character, and especially in Part One, where that character is first exposed, Dreiser cannot be argued with. This is where he most feels, and it is in his feelings that he is a great novelist. As F. O. Matthiessen says, he is a gifted primitive, with a primitive's weaknesses and a primitive's strengths. He sometimes judges wrong, he often expresses himself clumsily, he is full of inconsistencies and vulgarities, he roils his books with not always necessary intrusions of his own insistent presence. But he rarely "feels" wrong, especially when he is dealing with one of those weak and longing people who have in them a good part of himself—who have fallen, to use his own phrase, into the hands of their dreams.

Preliminary as it is, and part of a larger whole, Part One is a fictional entity. It has its own internal curve of desire, temptation, guilt, and ruin. Though Dreiser's novelistic skill is often disparaged or denied, mainly because he had a bad ear and wrote clumsy prose, the structural cunning of *An American Tragedy* is impressive, and nowhere more so than in the opening section. What must serve as an entry into larger themes and a larger action is itself a prefiguring of the whole action and a short harsh statement of those themes. Traits of character that we are to know in excruciating detail for hundreds of pages are unmistakably sketched in twenty. Actions that seem self-contained are later revealed to have been suggestive forecasts. Symbols that will loom ominously as the novel grinds on are present, and already ominous, here.

The method, though powerful, is not subtle. Dreiser never learned any of the technical finesse that more sophisticated contemporaries brought to their writing. He never employed limited or oblique points of view, he knew nothing of the tricks of irony and ambiguity that could be played through narrative masks, it never occurred to him that there was any way to tell a story except chronologically, with heavy accumulations of brute detail for verisimilitude and frequent intrusions of the author for the instruction and guidance of the reader. These authorial intrusions, which he learned from Balzac and which he thought a special elegance, had led him, in *Sister Carrie* and other works, into frequent bathos. But here, however old-fashioned it seems in a novel published in 1925, the method is neither so clumsy nor so ineffective as it looks. If it is obvious, it is by the same token never ambiguous or obscure, and nothing does more to "lift the obvious into the inexplicable," as Mencken put it, than Dreiser's own brooding presence as commentator. The result of the omniscient approach is a mighty singleness, a massive consistency, like the movement of a great stone rolling down a hill. We are seldom simply shown anything; we are both shown and told. As James T. Farrell pointed out, Dreiser's dialogue is illustrative; it is less a means of carrying the action forward than a means of preparing for, or fulfilling, or corroborating action. In the same way, the means of characterization are nearly as often expository as dramatic.

Thus Clyde, introduced as an unwilling participant while his family raises "its collective voice against the vast skepticism and apathy of life" in a Kansas City street, reveals by his actions and in his thoughts how the whole scene shames him. But we hear the authorial voice too: we are told that Clyde is "plainly pagan rather than religious," and that his mind is "responsive to phases of beauty and pleasure" that do not touch his parents. Similarly, Dreiser breaks in even more bluntly on page 16 to inform us that "the truth about Esta was that in spite of her guarded upbringing . . . she was just a sensuous, weak girl." When Clyde is dazzled by the glittering and irresistible vulgarity of the Green-Davidson Hotel, of all possible influences "perhaps the most dangerous for him, considering his temperament," Dreiser must make absolutely sure that we comprehend his error: "For his ideas of luxury were in the main so extreme and mistaken and gauche—mere wanderings of a repressed and unsatisfied fancy."

There is no point in multiplying instances. This is a novel which steers us all the way. We are asked, not to judge for ourselves, but to accept the author's prejudgment, and this insistence, like the careful selection and prefabrication of the action to fit a thesis, contradicts the view of Dreiser as an "honest" reporter who set down everything just as it happened. He is making it happen, he is stacking the deck; but what appears a flaw in the "objectivity" of the novel is a clear and splendid strength if we consider it structurally. From the opening scene to the wreck which destroys Clyde's dream of pleasure and self-indulgence, Part One is a machine in which every action is geared into every other; the clumsy stylist and fumbling philosopher reveals himself a magnificent engineer. Whether one can derive from the career of Clyde Griffiths the essential meaning of the universe or the law of American society is debatable; but there is no doubt that we know Clyde as we know few people in life, and that his every feeling, every motive, every act, is part of a most persuasive inevitability. Even the usual faults of style are less marked here than in much of Dreiser's work. He does not let himself be tempted into elephantine elegancies, and mannerisms such as the use of participles instead of verbs, irritatingly common in Parts Two and Three, are missing or infrequent in Part One.

The first scene may be taken to illustrate the essential rightness of the whole section. It is right atmospherically, right in terms of character, right in the signposts it erects to be comprehended later, right in its early statement of the contrasting symbols of constriction and space that will operate throughout the novel.

Clyde's craving nature, combined with the poverty and piety of his family, will be his downfall; we have the germ of it all by the third page. The opportunity which will destroy him will come through a rich uncle in Lycurgus, New York; the uncle appears in Clyde's vague dreams on page 13. Esta, betrayed by a vain and sensuous nature that is frankly analogous to Clyde's, will fall; we see her vanity in the opening scene when she tries to win the curious or indifferent street audience with her reedy voice and her pitiful rag of charm. Esta's own fall will be paralleled by the plight of the woman abandoned by her lover at the Green-Davidson, and both the abandoned woman and Esta will announce the theme that will be fully developed in the story of Roberta Alden in Part Two. In Esta's shame, her one support is her warm and troubled mother; much later, when Clyde is being tried for his life, his mother will be the one person in all the world on whom he can depend for unquestioning love and help. All through his short career, Clyde will weakly evade responsibilities and try to lie his way out of corners; we see him at it early, lying to his mother about his earnings and his activities, giving only a pittance for the help of the family or of Esta, spending lavishly on himself or on the gold-digging Hortense. Yet with all this careful plotting, Dreiser manages to escape the appearance of manipulation. These people seem to us simply to be acting in character. Character itself, in its struggle with social pressures, is the force that drives them and the fate toward which they move.

Dreiser is not usually thought of as a symbolist, and surely his method is almost laboriously dependent on naturalistic detail. Yet in *An American Tragedy* at least one element—his treatment of space—is too symbolically appropriate to be accidental. Throughout the novel we have the sense of walls pressing in, being broken out briefly into sun and freedom and pleasure, pressing in again. Yearning human faces look out from the imprisonment of their lives—Esta's and Roberta's from their shabby rooms, Clyde's from his cell. Clyde's story begins under the high constricting walls of the city and ends in the death house. His family, who at the end of the first chapter walk up their narrow side street (symbolically narrow, symbolically off the main ways) to the "yellow unprepossessing door" they have labeled "The Door of Hope," walk at the novel's end through just such another yellow unprepossessing door toward just such another "hope."

Whenever Clyde seems to have within his grasp the satisfaction of his desires, the scene opens out; when he is frustrated, it closes in again. The whorehouse to which his companions lead him is on no narrow side street, but on a wide and lively one in which, despite the lack of lights, "there was a sense of vivid, radiant life." The brief time of pleasure with Hortense and the bellboys is set in the spacious world of the Green-Davidson, Frissell's, and the Wigwam; it ends with the borrowed Packard piled against a dead end while dazed boys and girls struggle to escape from the entangling bodies of their companions.

In Part Two, also, Clyde alternates between confinement and escape, oscillating between the "shrinking room" in the collar factory's basement and the open countryside where he and Roberta play out their courtship. From the beginning, we are made to feel that openness and freedom are dangerous to one of Clyde's temperament. They are associated in the first half of the novel with temptations he is incompetent to resist, and they become all the more dangerous as he is taken into the ample and luxurious world of Sondra Finchley. The space and openness toward which he yearns turn into a horror of exposure as he hurries with his suitcase down the forest road, escaping from the bittern-haunted lake where Roberta has drowned, or as he hides in the woods within earshot of the laughter of his rich friends while the law hunts him down.

All the long painful development of Part Two is implicit in Clyde's character and in his response to the circumstances of Part One. He will evade his responsibilities toward Roberta as he evades them toward his mother and Esta. He will be bewitched by the beauty of Sondra Finchley as he is bewitched by the cheap charms of Hortense. He will yearn toward the careless ease of the elite of Lycurgus as he yearns toward the vulgar glitter of the Green-Davidson. His effort to make sure of wealth and status, to shake the clinging Roberta and cross over into another social class, is foreshadowed by his effort to repudiate the shabbiness of his family and to trade its shameful piety for the looser morality of pleasure.

Through all of this, Dreiser's sympathy is with the tempted one, for he felt that a man is responsible neither for the temptations the world puts in his path nor for the weak nature heredity may have handed him. Nevertheless, he does not give us this novel as an instrument of, or an incitation to, social reform; he seems rather to assume that social injustices and inequalities are as inescapable as fate. His response is simply pity—pity for the creature of circumstances who can escape neither his nature nor his upbringing. For him, as for Hippolyte Taine, virtue and vice, good and evil, right and wrong, seem to have been products of the social mixture, as predictable as vitriol or sugar might be from a chemical mixture. And his identification with Clyde Griffiths was so strong that he grew furious when the movie version turned Clyde into a mere drugstore cowboy. Dreiser had suffered too much through and with this boy to have him cheapened.

Nevertheless, even so broad a pity as Dreiser's was not absolute; even so determined a belief that to understand all was to forgive all broke down on occasion. As he was selective in the characters and incidents that would demonstrate his vision of American life, so he was selective about the characters for whom he asked sympathy, and the nonmoralistic approach which he attempted reveals itself as imperfect, perhaps impossible.

For the fact is that in this novel, as in the novels which preceded it, he cannot help disliking or blaming certain characters, and adopting toward them the tone of personal judgment that he scrupulously rejects in his treatment of Clyde—in his treatment, for that matter, of any of the weak and victimized people of his fictional world or of any of the predators, such as Frank Cowperwood and Eugene Witla, who victimize them. Some of the unsympathetic characters are curiously suggestive. It is clear, for instance, that Dreiser actively dislikes Hortense, though she is guilty of no more than selfishness, for which Dreiser refuses to blame Clyde, and unchastity, a sin in which Dreiser did not believe. He dislikes her because she makes life a hell for the dangling and infatuated Clyde, who has so much of Dreiser in him. Even with Roberta Alden, in Part Two, Dreiser adopts a somewhat querulous tone once she begins to be difficult; it is as if a clinging and desperate woman made him nervous. (Another woman with demands, the first Mrs. Hurstwood in *Sister Carrie*, he had treated contemptuously, and still another, Aileen in *The Titan*, he had turned into a virago.) Some of the male characters of *An American Tragedy* are likewise prejudged; we can feel the contempt or the animus behind creations such as Clyde's ineffectual father, his cold cousin Gilbert, and the ambitious district attorney. In the end, we are left with the impression that Dreiser's sympathy and pity were almost unlimited for people who failed as Dreiser himself might have failed, who were tempted as Dreiser himself might have been tempted, or who were ruthless in ways that Dreiser himself might have condoned, but that he was altogether less charitable to types he personally disliked or feared. And this perception must ultimately affect our judgment of his celebrated compassion, for if we pity only people like ourselves we are neither godlike nor objective nor detached, but perilously close to self-pity.

The fault, happily, is not fatal, but only a demonstration that a novelist is a moralist in spite of himself, and that as a moral reflector he will surely be personal and may be flawed. What matters much more is that the people whom Dreiser did select for our understanding and pity are consistent and totally persuasive. Clyde Griffiths is a boy we know, and care about, and are troubled by, even though Dreiser is scrupulous to point out everything weak and venal in his nature. When Clyde first feels "the wonder of girls at first range" during his short job at the soda fountain, he represents one sort of adolescent longing. When he stares into the Green-Davidson's marble and palms and feels he is looking into the Gates of Paradise, the sympathy of his creator transforms those tawdry public rooms into something magical. When Clyde adopts the "eager, ingratiating smile of the boy who wants to get on"; when he assures himself that he will "make more money. A lot of it to spend on himself"; when, after lying to his mother, he suffers "a pang of commingled self-commiseration and self-contempt"; and when, in the middle of his desire for Hortense, he senses in her "a disturbing vitality which he might not be able to match," he speaks to us with the voice of our own uneasy memories and our own shames.

He is as real a boy, however contemptible to a rigid moralist, as ever appeared on the pages of an American book. Dreiser did him so thoroughly in Part One that he might almost have ended the novel with him fleeing desperate and winded from the wreckage of the Packard, for by that time the course of his life is already plain. The character which is his fate has been made clear, and so have the consequences, to others and himself, of his "pitiful struggle with nature, with his enormous urges and his pathetic equipment." What is more, we have been made to care. We cannot dismiss him as a cheap drugstore cowboy or a poor boy on the make, for we have been implicated in him, his weakness calls on us for the charity of our own complicity in humanity. Whether Dreiser's view of life was adequate or not, whether his somewhat rigid mechanism was a fit paradigm of the world, whether his compassion reached out to everyone or only to those most like himself, the creation of one Clyde Griffiths is achievement enough. The true Dreiser is not the philosopher who pretends to know the bleak answers to the riddles of the universe; he is the suffering and imperfect mortal who, as he admitted himself, had learned nothing and understood nothing in his passage through life, but passed as he came, confused and dismayed.

WALLACE STEGNER

A Note on the Text. The text here followed is that of the first edition of Theodore Dreiser's *An American Tragedy* (New York: Boni & Liveright, 1925), Volume I, Book 1.

That a young man can grow up in America with no higher ideals than those of a Clyde Griffith, there is a national disgrace if not a national tragedy. Therefore, the word "tragedy" cannot be used in the classical sense.

Dreiser was unable to believe totally in either positivism or transcendentalism. He was a life-long skeptic who found it difficult to believe in anything for very long. (Theory of Universe) Note

[He conceived the universe to operate on the theory that virtue is punished and vice rewarded with no apparent moral foundation.]

Dreiser worked out what he felt
to be a characteristic Am. fate
and built An Am. Tragedy on the
extensive study of real murder trials —

✤ ✤ ✤

transporting them bodily from real to
make-belief — it incorporates many
details of Chester Gillette, who was
convicted and executed for the murder of
what recent blc.   his girl in upstate
pub. on real   New York in 1906.
murder In Cold Blood
        Capote

AN AMERICAN TRAGEDY

This weakest quality is his style.
                    Made into a ‾

✤ ✤ ✤ Movie: A Place
                    in the sun   montgom.
Here is seen a blend of clift, Shelly
of the fictional and the documentary.
                                    Taylor

Remember that fiction demands
a ventriloquist. The fictional
author can make himself invisible
either by being a camera or by
burying himself in the subjective
consciousness of one of his characters.

N/b

Based on court records, & an
actual trial,
Clyde's tragic flaw: an attempt
to rise in society regardless of the cost.

Few novelists respond to human
beings as sensitively as he does.

Dreiser tries to present
not only the ~~courtroom~~ Court room but
also what goes on outside of it too.

"Getting ahead" the only religion Clyde knows
"Portico" ~~Practice~~ the only satisfying activity
the light of the ideal is refracted
only through a woman's eyes.
He cannot be expected to tie
himself to a pregnant shopgirl
who has now lost all the charm
she ever had for him, at the
moment when his affair with
the beautiful, wealthy, and socially
prominent Sondra Finchly is
making such unexpected progress.

Clyde did not drown Roberta
at Big Bittern, was it
conscience or lack of nerve
that blocked him? It was as
accident + he lowest wished her
dead.

Dreiser worked out what he felt
to be a characteristic Am. fate
and built An Am. Tragedy on the
extensive study of real murder trials —

✦ ✦ ✦

transporting them bodily from real to
make-belief — it incorporates many
details of Chester Gillette, who was
convicted and executed for the murder of
his girl in upstate
New York in 1906.

what recent blk.
pub. on real
murder In Cold Blood
Capote

AN AMERICAN TRAGEDY

Its weakest quality is his style.

✦ ✦ ✦

Made into a
Movie: A Place
in the sun

Montgomery
Clift, Shelly
Winters, Eliz.
Taylor

Here is seen a blend of
of the fictional and the documentary.

Remember that fiction demands
a ventriloquist. The fictional
author can make himself invisible
either by being a camera or by
burying himself in the subjective
consciousness of one of his characters.

n/6

Based on court records, & an
actual trial,
Clyde's tragic flaw: an attempt
to rise in society regardless of the cost.

Few novelists respond to human beings as sensitively as he does.

Dreiser tries to present not only the Court room (Courtroom) but also what goes on outside of it too.

"Getting ahead" the only religion Clyde knew. "Practice" "Poetics" the only satisfying activity. The light of the ideal is refracted only through a woman's eyes. He cannot be expected to tie himself to a pregnant shopgirl who has now lost all the charm she ever had for him, at the moment when his affair with the beautiful, wealthy, and socially prominent Sondra Finchy is making such unexpected progress.

Clyde did not drown Roberta at Big Bittern, was it conscience or lack of nerve that blocked him? It was an accident + he never wished her dead.

The evangelist-mother and the Rev. McMillan clergyman are as moving in their simple goodness as they can be in any novel written by a devout believer

Book One

1

This novel helped pave the way for public acceptance of frank and hard-hitting novels of the twenties.

Dusk—of a summer night.

And the tall walls of the commercial heart of an American city of perhaps 400,000 inhabitants—such walls as in time may linger as a mere fable.

And up the broad street, now comparatively hushed, a little band of six,—a man of about fifty, short, stout, with bushy hair protruding from under a round black felt hat, a most unimportant-looking person, who carried a small portable organ such as is customarily used by street preachers and singers. And with him a woman perhaps five years his junior, taller, not so broad, but solid of frame and vigorous, very plain in face and dress, and yet not homely, leading with one hand a small boy of seven and in the other carrying a Bible and several hymn books. With these three, but walking independently behind, was a girl of fifteen, a boy of twelve and another girl of nine, all following obediently, but not too enthusiastically, in the wake of the others.

It was hot, yet with a sweet languor about it all.

Crossing at right angles the great thoroughfare on which they walked, was a second canyon-like way, threaded by throngs and vehicles and various lines of cars which clanged their bells and made such progress as they might amid swiftly moving streams of traffic. Yet the little group seemed unconscious of anything save a set purpose to make its way between the contending lines of traffic and pedestrians which flowed by them.

Having reached an intersection this side of the second principal thoroughfare—really just an alley between two tall structures—now quite bare of life of any kind, the man put down the organ, which the woman immediately opened, setting up a music rack upon which she placed a wide flat hymn book. Then handing the Bible to the man, she fell back in line with him, while the twelve-year-old boy put down a small camp-stool in front of the organ. The man—the father, as he chanced to be—looked about him with seeming wide-eyed assurance, and announced, without appearing to care whether he had any auditors or not:

"We will first sing a hymn of praise, so that any who may wish to acknowledge the Lord may join us. Will you oblige, Hester?"

At this the eldest girl, who until now had attempted to appear as unconscious and unaffected as possible, bestowed her rather slim and as yet undeveloped figure upon the camp chair and turned the leaves of the hymn book, pumping the organ while her mother observed:

"I should think it might be nice to sing twenty-seven to-night—'How Sweet the Balm of Jesus' Love.'"

Ida turned to study of physics and chemistry in an effort to widen his scientific background.

By this time various homeward-bound individuals of diverse grades and walks of life, noticing the small group disposing itself in this fashion, hesitated for a moment to eye them askance or paused to ascertain the character of their work. This hesitancy, construed by the man apparently to constitute attention, however mobile, was seized upon by him and he began addressing them as though they were specifically here to hear him.

"Let us all sing twenty-seven, then—'How Sweet the Balm of Jesus' Love.' "

At this the young girl began to interpret the melody upon the organ, emitting a thin though correct strain, at the same time joining her rather high soprano with that of her mother, together with the rather dubious baritone of the father. The other children piped weakly along, the boy and girl having taken hymn books from the small pile stacked upon the organ. As they sang, this nondescript and indifferent street audience gazed, held by the peculiarity of such an unimportant-looking family publicly raising its collective voice against the vast skepticism and apathy of life. Some were interested or moved sympathetically by the rather tame and inadequate figure of the girl at the organ, others by the impractical and materially inefficient texture of the father, whose weak blue eyes and rather flabby but poorly-clothed figure bespoke more of failure than anything else. Of the group the mother alone stood out as having that force and determination which, however blind or erroneous, makes for self-preservation, if not success in life. She, more than any of the others, stood up with an ignorant, yet somehow respectable air of conviction. If you had watched her, her hymn book dropped to her side, her glance directed straight before her into space, you would have said: "Well, here is one who, whatever her defects, probably does what she believes as nearly as possible." A kind of hard, fighting faith in the wisdom and mercy of that definite overruling and watchful power which she proclaimed, was written in her every feature and gesture.

> "The love of Jesus saves me whole,
> The love of God my steps control,"

she sang resonantly, if slightly nasally, between the towering walls of the adjacent buildings.

The boy moved restlessly from one foot to the other, keeping his eyes down, and for the most part only half singing. A tall and as yet slight figure, surmounted by an interesting head and face—white skin, dark hair—he seemed more keenly observant and decidedly more sensitive than most of the others—appeared indeed to resent and even to suffer from the position in which he found himself. Plainly pagan rather than religious, life interested him, although as yet he was not fully aware of this. All that could be truly said of him now was that there was no definite appeal in all this for him. He was too young, his mind much too responsive to phases of beauty and pleasure which had little, if anything, to do with the remote and cloudy romance which swayed the minds of his mother and father.

Indeed the home life of which this boy found himself a part and the various contacts, material and psychic, which thus far had been his, did not tend to convince him of the reality and force of all that his mother and father seemed so certainly to believe and say. Rather, they seemed more or

Asa— healer or physician

less troubled in their lives, at least materially. His father was always reading the Bible and speaking in meeting at different places, especially in the "mission," which he and his mother conducted not so far from this corner. At the same time, as he understood it, they collected money from various interested or charitably inclined business men here and there who appeared to believe in such philanthropic work. Yet the family was always "hard up," never very well clothed, and deprived of many comforts and pleasures which seemed common enough to others. And his father and mother were constantly proclaiming the love and mercy and care of God for him and for all. Plainly there was something wrong somewhere. He could not get it all straight, but still he could not help respecting his mother, a woman whose force and earnestness, as well as her sweetness, appealed to him. Despite much mission work and family cares, she managed to be fairly cheerful, or at least sustaining, often declaring most emphatically "God will provide" or "God will show the way," especially in times of too great stress about food or clothes. Yet apparently, in spite of this, as he and all the other children could see, God did not show any very clear way, even though there was always an extreme necessity for His favorable intervention in their affairs.

To-night, walking up the great street with his sisters and brother, he wished that they need not do this any more, or at least that he need not be a part of it. Other boys did not do such things, and besides, somehow it seemed shabby and even degrading. On more than one occasion, before he had been taken on the street in this fashion, other boys had called to him and made fun of his father, because he was always publicly emphasizing his religious beliefs or convictions. Thus in one neighborhood in which they had lived, when he was but a child of seven, his father, having always preluded every conversation with "Praise the Lord," he heard boys call "Here comes old Praise-the-Lord Griffiths." Or they would call out after him "Hey, you're the fellow whose sister plays the organ. Is there anything else she can play?"

"What does he always want to go around saying, 'Praise the Lord' for? Other people don't do it."

It was that old mass yearning for a likeness in all things that troubled them, and him. Neither his father nor his mother was like other people, because they were always making so much of religion, and now at last they were making a business of it.

On this night in this great street with its cars and crowds and tall buildings, he felt ashamed, dragged out of normal life, to be made a show and jest of. The handsome automobiles that sped by, the loitering pedestrians moving off to what interests and comforts he could only surmise; the gay pairs of young people, laughing and jesting and the "kids" staring, all troubled him with a sense of something different, better, more beautiful than his, or rather their life.

And now units of this vagrom and unstable street throng, which was forever shifting and changing about them, seemed to sense the psychologic error of all this in so far as these children were concerned, for they would nudge one another, the more sophisticated and indifferent lifting an eyebrow and smiling contemptuously, the more sympathetic or experienced commenting on the useless presence of these children.

"I see these people around here nearly every night now—two or three times a week, anyhow," this from a young clerk who had just met his girl and was escorting her toward a restaurant. "They're just working some religious dodge or other, I guess."

"That oldest boy don't wanta be here. He feels outa place, I can see that. It ain't right to make a kid like that come out unless he wants to. He can't understand all this stuff, anyhow." This from an idler and loafer of about forty, one of those odd hangers-on about the commercial heart of a city, addressing a pausing and seemingly amiable stranger.

"Yeh, I guess that's so," the other assented, taking in the peculiar cast of the boy's head and face. In view of the uneasy and self-conscious expression upon the face whenever it was lifted, one might have intelligently suggested that it was a little unkind as well as idle to thus publicly force upon a temperament as yet unfitted to absorb their import, religious and psychic services best suited to reflective temperaments of maturer years.

Yet so it was.

As for the remainder of the family, both the youngest girl and boy were too small to really understand much of what it was all about or to care. The eldest girl at the organ appeared not so much to mind, as to enjoy the attention and comment her presence and singing evoked, for more than once, not only strangers, but her mother and father, had assured her that she had an appealing and compelling voice, which was only partially true. It was not a good voice. They did not really understand music. Physically, she was of a pale, emasculate and unimportant structure, with no real mental force or depth, and was easily made to feel that this was an excellent field in which to distinguish herself and attract a little attention. As for the parents, they were determined upon spiritualizing the world as much as possible, and, once the hymn was concluded, the father launched into one of those hackneyed descriptions of the delights of a release, via self-realization of the mercy of God and the love of Christ and the will of God toward sinners, from the burdensome cares of an evil conscience.

"All men are sinners in the light of the Lord," he declared. "Unless they repent, unless they accept Christ, His love and forgiveness of them, they can never know the happiness of being spiritually whole and clean. Oh, my friends! If you could but know the peace and content that comes with the knowledge, the inward understanding, that Christ lived and died for you and that He walks with you every day and hour, by light and by dark, at dawn and at dusk, to keep and strengthen you for the tasks and cares of the world that are ever before you. Oh, the snares and pitfalls that beset us all! And then the soothing realization that Christ is ever with us, to counsel, to aid, to hearten, to bind up our wounds and make us whole! Oh, the peace, the satisfaction, the comfort, the glory of that!"

"Amen!" asseverated his wife, and the daughter, Hester, or Esta, as she was called by the family, moved by the need of as much public support as possible for all of them—echoed it after her.

Clyde, the eldest boy, and the two younger children merely gazed at the ground, or occasionally at their father, with a feeling that possibly it was all true and important, yet somehow not as significant or inviting as some of the other things which life held. They heard so much of this, and to their young and eager minds life was made for something more than street and mission hall protestations of this sort.

Finally, after a second hymn and an address by Mrs. Griffiths, during which she took occasion to refer to the mission work jointly conducted by them in a near-by street, and their services to the cause of Christ in general, a third hymn was indulged in, and then some tracts describing the mission rescue work being distributed, such voluntary gifts as were forthcoming were taken up by Asa—the father. The small organ was closed, the camp chair folded up and given to Clyde, the Bible and hymn books picked up by Mrs. Griffiths, and with the organ supported by a leather strap passed over the shoulder of Griffiths, senior, the missionward march was taken up.

During all this time Clyde was saying to himself that he did not wish to do this any more, that he and his parents looked foolish and less than normal —"cheap" was the word he would have used if he could have brought himself to express his full measure of resentment at being compelled to participate in this way—and that he would not do it any more if he could help. What good did it do them to have him along? His life should not be like this. Other boys did not have to do as he did. He meditated now more determinedly than ever a rebellion by which he would rid himself of the need of going out in this way. Let his elder sister go if she chose; she liked it. His younger sister and brother might be too young to care. But he—

"They seemed a little more attentive than usual to-night, I thought," commented Griffiths to his wife as they walked along, the seductive quality of the summer evening air softening him into a more generous interpretation of the customary indifferent spirit of the passer-by.

"Yes; twenty-seven took tracts to-night as against eighteen on Thursday."

"The love of Christ must eventually prevail," comforted the father, as much to hearten himself as his wife. "The pleasures and cares of the world hold a very great many, but when sorrow overtakes them, then some of these seeds will take root."

"I am sure of it. That is the thought which always keeps me up. Sorrow and the weight of sin eventually bring some of them to see the error of their way."

They now entered into the narrow side street from which they had emerged, and walking as many as a dozen doors from the corner, entered the door of a yellow single-story wooden building, the large window and the two glass panes in the central door of which had been painted a gray-white. Across both windows and the smaller panels in the double door had been painted: "The Door of Hope. Bethel Independent Mission. Meetings Every Wednesday and Saturday night, 8 to 10. Sundays at 11, 3 and 8. Everybody Welcome." Under this legend on each window were printed the words: "God is Love," and below this again, in smaller type: "How Long Since You Wrote to Mother?"

The small company entered the yellow unprepossessing door and disappeared.

2

THAT SUCH A family, thus cursorily presented, might have a different and somewhat peculiar history could well be anticipated, and it would be true. Indeed, this one presented one of those anomalies of psychic and social reflex and motivation such as would tax the skill of not only the psychologist but the chemist and physicist as well, to unravel. To begin with, Asa Griffiths, the father, was one of those poorly integrated and correlated organisms, the product of an environment and a religious theory, but with no guiding or mental insight of his own, yet sensitive and therefore highly emotional, and without any practical sense whatsoever. Indeed it would be hard to make clear just how life appealed to him, or what the true hue of his emotional responses was. On the other hand, as has been indicated, his wife was of a firmer texture but with scarcely any truer or more practical insight into anything.

The history of this man and his wife is of no particular interest here save as it affected their boy of twelve, Clyde Griffiths. This youth, aside from a certain emotionalism and exotic sense of romance which characterized him, and which he took more from his father than from his mother, brought a more vivid and intelligent imagination to things, and was constantly thinking of how he might better himself, if he had a chance; places to which he might go, things he might see, and how differently he might live, if only this, that and the other thing were true. The principal thing that troubled Clyde up to his fifteenth year, and for long after in retrospect, was that the calling or profession of his parents was the shabby thing that it appeared to be in the eyes of others. For so often throughout his youth in different cities in which his parents had conducted a mission or spoken on the streets—Grand Rapids, Detroit, Milwaukee, Chicago, lastly Kansas City—it had been obvious that people, at least the boys and girls he encountered, looked down upon him and his brothers and sisters for being the children of such parents. On several occasions, and much against the mood of his parents, who never countenanced such exhibitions of temper, he had stopped to fight with one or another of these boys. But always, beaten or victorious, he had been made conscious of the fact that the work his parents did was not satisfactory to others,—shabby, trivial. And always he was thinking of what he would do, once he reached the place where he could get away.

For Clyde's parents had proved impractical in the matter of the future of their children. They did not understand the importance or the essential necessity for some form of practical or professional training for each and every one of their young ones. Instead, being wrapped up in the notion of evangelizing the world, they had neglected to keep their children in school in any one place. They had moved here and there, sometimes in the very midst of an advantageous school season, because of a larger and better religious field in which to work. And there were times when, the work proving highly unprofitable and Asa being unable to make much money at the two things he most understood—gardening and canvassing for one invention or another—they were quite without sufficient food or decent clothes, and the children could not go to school. In the face of such situations as these, whatever the children might think, Asa and his wife remained as optimistic as ever, or they insisted to themselves that they were, and had unwavering faith in the Lord and His intention to provide.

The combination home and mission which this family occupied was dreary enough in most of its phases to discourage the average youth or girl of any spirit. It consisted in its entirety of one long store floor in an old and decidedly colorless and inartistic wooden building which was situated in that part of Kansas City which lies north of Independence Boulevard and west of Troost Avenue, the exact street or place being called Bickel, a very short thoroughfare opening off Missouri Avenue, a somewhat more lengthy but no less nondescript highway. And the entire neighborhood in which it stood was very faintly and yet not agreeably redolent of a commercial life which had long since moved farther south, if not west. It was some five blocks from the spot on which twice a week the open air meetings of these religious enthusiasts and proselytizers were held.

And it was the ground floor of this building, looking out into Bickel Street at the front and some dreary back yards of equally dreary frame houses, which was divided at the front into a hall forty by twenty-five feet in size, in which had been placed some sixty collapsible wood chairs, a lectern, a map of Palestine or the Holy Land, and for wall decorations some twenty-five printed but unframed mottoes which read, in part:

WINE IS A MOCKER, STRONG DRINK IS RAGING AND WHOSOEVER IS DECEIVED THEREBY IS NOT WISE.

TAKE HOLD OF SHIELD AND BUCKLER, AND STAND UP FOR MINE HELP. PSALMS 35:2.

AND YE, MY FLOCK, THE FLOCK OF MY PASTURE, *are men*, AND I AM YOUR GOD, SAITH THE LORD GOD. EZEKIEL 34:31.

O GOD, THOU KNOWEST MY FOOLISHNESS, AND MY SINS ARE NOT HID FROM THEE. PSALMS 69:5.

IF YE HAVE FAITH AS A GRAIN OF MUSTARD SEED, YE SHALL SAY UNTO THIS MOUNTAIN, REMOVE HENCE TO YONDER PLACE; AND IT SHALL MOVE; AND NOTHING SHALL BE IMPOSSIBLE UNTO YOU. MATTHEW 17:20.

FOR THE DAY OF THE LORD IS NEAR. OBADIAH 15.

FOR THERE SHALL BE NO REWARD TO THE EVIL MAN. PROVERBS 24:20.

LOOK, THEN, NOT UPON THE WINE WHEN IT IS RED: IT BITETH LIKE A SERPENT, AND STINGETH LIKE AN ADDER. PROVERBS 23:31, 32.

These mighty adjurations were as silver and gold plates set in a wall of dross.

The rear forty feet of this very commonplace floor was intricately and yet neatly divided into three small bedrooms, a living room which overlooked the backyard and wooden fences of yards no better than those at the back; also, a combination kitchen and dining room exactly ten feet square, and a store room for mission tracts, hymnals, boxes, trunks and whatever else of non-

immediate use, but of assumed value, which the family owned. This particular
small room lay immediately to the rear of the mission hall itself, and into it
before or after speaking or at such times as a conference seemed important,
both Mr. and Mrs. Griffiths were wont to retire—also at times to meditate
or pray.

How often had Clyde and his sisters and younger brother seen his
mother or father, or both, in conference with some derelict or semi-
repentant soul who had come for advice or aid, most usually for aid. And
here at times, when his mother's and father's financial difficulties were greatest, they were to be found thinking, or as Asa Griffiths was wont helplessly
to say at times, "praying their way out," a rather ineffectual way, as Clyde
began to think later.

And the whole neighborhood was so dreary and run-down that he hated
the thought of living in it, let alone being part of a work that required
constant appeals for aid, as well as constant prayer and thanksgiving to sustain it.

Moth

Mrs. Elvira Griffiths before she had married Asa had been nothing but an
ignorant farm girl, brought up without much thought of religion of any kind.
But having fallen in love with him, she had become inoculated with the virus
of Evangelism and proselytizing which dominated him, and had followed him
gladly and enthusiastically in all of his ventures and through all of his vagaries.
Being rather flattered by the knowledge that she could speak and sing, her
ability to sway and persuade and control people with the "word of God," as
she saw it, she had become more or less pleased with herself on this account
and so persuaded to continue.

Occasionally a small band of people followed the preachers to their mission, or learning of its existence through their street work, appeared there later
—those odd and mentally disturbed or distrait souls who are to be found in
every place. And it had been Clyde's compulsory duty throughout the years
when he could not act for himself to be in attendance at these various meet-

*type of
People
who came
to mission*

ings. And always he had been more irritated than favorably influenced by the
types of men and women who came here—mostly men—down-and-out laborers, loafers, drunkards, wastrels, the botched and helpless who seemed to drift
in, because they had no other place to go. And they were always testifying as
to how God or Christ or Divine Grace had rescued them from this or that
predicament—never how they had rescued any one else. And always his father and mother were saying "Amen" and "Glory to God," and singing
hymns and afterward taking up a collection for the legitimate expenses of the
hall—collections which, as he surmised, were little enough—barely enough to
keep the various missions they had conducted in existence.

The one thing that really interested him in connection with his parents
was the existence somewhere in the east—in a small city called Lycurgus, near
Utica he understood—of an uncle, a brother of his father's, who was plainly

uncle

different from all this. That uncle—Samuel Griffiths by name—was rich. In
one way and another, from casual remarks dropped by his parents, Clyde had
heard references to certain things this particular uncle might do for a person,
if he but would; references to the fact that he was a shrewd, hard business
man; that he had a great house and a large factory in Lycurgus for the manu-

facture of collars and shirts, which employed not less than three hundred people; that he had a son who must be about Clyde's age, and several daughters, two at least, all of whom must be, as Clyde imagined, living in luxury in Lycurgus. News of all this had apparently been brought west in some way by people who knew Asa and his father and brother. As Clyde pictured this uncle, he must be a kind of Croesus, living in ease and luxury there in the east, while here in the west—Kansas City—he and his parents and his brother and sisters were living in the same wretched and hum-drum, hand-to-mouth state that had always characterized their lives.

But for this—apart from anything he might do for himself, as he early began to see—there was no remedy. For at fifteen, and even a little earlier, Clyde began to understand that his education, as well as his sisters' and brother's, had been sadly neglected. And it would be rather hard for him to overcome this handicap, seeing that other boys and girls with more money and better homes were being trained for special kinds of work. How was one to get a start under such circumstances? Already when, at the age of thirteen, fourteen and fifteen, he began looking in the papers, which, being too worldly, had never been admitted to his home, he found that mostly skilled help was wanted, or boys to learn trades in which at the moment he was not very much interested. For true to the standard of the American youth, or the general American attitude toward life, he felt himself above the type of labor which was purely manual. What! Run a machine, lay bricks, learn to be a carpenter, or a plasterer, or a plumber, when boys no better than himself were clerks and druggists' assistants and bookkeepers and assistants in banks and real estate offices and such! Wasn't it menial, as miserable as the life he had thus far been leading, to wear old clothes and get up so early in the morning and do all the commonplace things such people had to do?

For Clyde was as vain and proud as he was poor. He was one of those interesting individuals who looked upon himself as a thing apart—never quite wholly and indissolubly merged with the family of which he was a member, and never with any profound obligations to those who had been responsible for his coming into the world. On the contrary, he was inclined to study his parents, not too sharply or bitterly, but with a very fair grasp of their qualities and capabilities. And yet, with so much judgment in that direction, he was never quite able—at least not until he had reached his sixteenth year—to formulate any policy in regard to himself, and then only in a rather fumbling and tentative way.

Incidentally by that time the sex lure or appeal had begun to manifest itself and he was already intensely interested and troubled by the beauty of the opposite sex, its attractions for him and his attraction for it. And, naturally and coincidentally, the matter of his clothes and his physical appearance had begun to trouble him not a little—how he looked and how other boys looked. It was painful to him now to think that his clothes were not right; that he was not as handsome as he might be, not as interesting. What a wretched thing it was to be born poor and not to have any one to do anything for you and not to be able to do so very much for yourself!

Casual examination of himself in mirrors whenever he found them tended rather to assure him that he was not so bad-looking—a straight, well-cut nose, high white forehead, wavy, glossy, black hair, eyes that were black and rather melancholy at times. And yet the fact that his family was the unhappy thing that it was, that he had never had any real friends, and could not have any, as he saw it, because of the work and connection of his parents, was now tending more and more to induce a kind of mental depression or melancholia which promised not so well for his future. It served to make him rebellious and hence lethargic at times. Because of his parents, and in spite of his looks, which were really agreeable and more appealing than most, he was inclined to misinterpret the interested looks which were cast at him occasionally by young girls in very different walks of life from him—the contemptuous and yet rather inviting way in which they looked to see if he were interested or disinterested, brave or cowardly.

And yet, before he had ever earned any money at all, he had always told himself that if only he had a better collar, a nicer shirt, finer shoes, a good suit, a swell overcoat like some boys had! Oh, the fine clothes, the handsome homes, the watches, rings, pins that some boys sported; the dandies many youths of his years already were! Some parents of boys of his years actually gave them cars of their own to ride in. They were to be seen upon the principal streets of Kansas City flitting to and fro like flies. And pretty girls with them. And he had nothing. And he never had had.

And yet the world was so full of so many things to do—so many people were so happy and so successful. What was he to do? Which way to turn? What one thing to take up and master—something that would get him somewhere. He could not say. He did not know exactly. And these peculiar parents were in no way sufficiently equipped to advise him.

3

ONE OF THE things that served to darken Clyde's mood just about the time when he was seeking some practical solution for himself, to say nothing of its profoundly disheartening effect on the Griffiths family as a whole, was the fact that his sister Esta, in whom he took no little interest (although they really had very little in common), ran away from home with an actor who happened to be playing in Kansas City and who took a passing fancy for her.

The truth in regard to Esta was that in spite of her guarded up-bringing, and the seeming religious and moral fervor which at times appeared to characterize her, she was just a sensuous, weak girl who did not by any means know yet what she thought. Despite the atmosphere in which she moved, essentially she was not of it. Like the large majority of those who profess and daily repeat the dogmas and creeds of the world, she had come into her practices and imagined attitude so insensibly from her earliest childhood on, that up to this time, and even later, she did not know the meaning of it all. For the necessity of thought had been obviated by advice and law, or "revealed" truth, and so long as other theories or situations and impulses of an external, or even internal, character did not arise to clash with these, she was safe enough. Once they did, however, it was a foregone conclusion that her religious notions, not being grounded on any conviction or temperamental bias of her own, were not likely to withstand the shock. So that all the while, and not un- like her brother Clyde, her thoughts as well as her emotions were wandering here and there—to love, to comfort—to things which in the main had little, if anything, to do with any self-abnegating and self-immolating religious theory. Within her was a chemism of dreams which somehow counteracted all they had to say.

Yet she had neither Clyde's force, nor, on the other hand, his resistance. She was in the main a drifter, with a vague yearning toward pretty dresses, hats, shoes, ribbons and the like, and superimposed above this, the religious theory or notion that she should not be. There were the long bright streets of a morning and afternoon after school or of an evening. The charm of certain girls swinging along together, arms locked, secrets a-whispering, or that of boys, clownish, yet revealing through their bounding ridiculous animality the force and meaning of that chemistry and urge toward mating which lies back of all youthful thought and action. And in herself, as from time to time she ob- served lovers or flirtation-seekers who lingered at street corners or about door- ways, and who looked at her in a longing and seeking way, there was a stirring, a nerve plasm palpitation that spoke loudly for all the seemingly material things of life, not for the thin pleasantries of heaven.

And the glances drilled her like an invisible ray, for she was pleasing to look at and was growing more attractive hourly. And the moods in others awakened responsive moods in her, those rearranging chemisms upon which all the morality or immorality of the world is based.

And then one day, as she was coming home from school, a youth of that plausible variety known as "masher" engaged her in conversation, largely be- cause of a look and a mood which seemed to invite it. And there was little to stay her, for she was essentially yielding, if not amorous. Yet so great had been her home drilling as to the need of modesty, circumspection, purity and the like, that on this occasion at least there was no danger of any immediate lapse. Only this attack once made, others followed, were accepted, or not so quickly fled from, and by degrees, these served to break down that wall of reserve which her home training had served to erect. She became secretive and hid her ways from her parents.

Youths occasionally walked and talked with her in spite of herself. They demolished that excessive shyness which had been hers, and which had served to put others aside for a time at least. She wished for other contacts—dreamed of some bright, gay, wonderful love of some kind, with some one.

Finally, after a slow but vigorous internal growth of mood and desire, there came this actor, one of those vain, handsome, animal personalities, all clothes and airs, but no morals (no taste, no courtesy or real tenderness even), but of compelling magnetism, who was able within the space of one brief week and a few meetings to completely befuddle and enmesh her so that she was really his to do with as he wished. And the truth was that he scarcely cared for her at all. To him, dull as he was, she was just another girl—fairly pretty, obviously sensuous and inexperienced, a silly who could be taken by a few soft words— a show of seemingly sincere affection, talk of the opportunity of a broader, freer life on the road, in other great cities, as his wife.

And yet his words were those of a lover who would be true forever. All she had to do, as he explained to her, was to come away with him and be his bride, at once—now. Delay was so vain when two such as they had met. There was difficulty about marriage here, which he could not explain—it related to friends—but in St. Louis he had a preacher friend who would wed them. She was to have new and better clothes than she had ever known, delicious adventures, love. She would travel with him and see the great world. She would never need to trouble more about anything save him; and while it was truth to her—the verbal surety of a genuine passion—to him it was the most ancient and serviceable type of blarney, often used before and often successful.

In a single week then, at odd hours, morning, afternoon and night, this chemic witchery was accomplished.

Coming home rather late one Saturday night in April from a walk which he had taken about the business heart, in order to escape the regular Saturday night mission services, Clyde found his mother and father worried about the whereabouts of Esta. She had played and sung as usual at this meeting. And all had seemed all right with her. After the meeting she had gone to her room, saying that she was not feeling very well and was going to bed early. But by eleven o'clock, when Clyde returned, her mother had chanced to look into her room and discovered that she was not there nor anywhere about the place. A certain bareness in connection with the room—some trinkets and dresses removed, an old and familiar suitcase gone—had first attracted her mother's attention. Then the house search proving that she was not there, Asa had gone outside to look up and down the street. She sometimes walked out alone, or sat or stood in front of the mission during its idle or closed hours.

This search revealing nothing, Clyde and he had walked to a corner, then along Missouri Avenue. No Esta. At twelve they returned and after that, naturally, the curiosity in regard to her grew momentarily sharper.

At first they assumed that she might have taken an unexplained walk somewhere, but as twelve-thirty, and finally one, and one-thirty, passed and no Esta, they were about to notify the police, when Clyde, going into her room, saw a note pinned to the pillow of her small wooden bed—a missive that had escaped the eye of his mother. At once he went to it, curious and comprehending, for he had often wondered in what way, assuming that he ever wished to depart surreptitiously, he would notify his parents, for he knew they would never countenance his departure unless they were permitted to supervise it in every detail. And now here was Esta missing, and here was undoubtedly some such communication as he might have left. He picked it up, eager to read it, but at that moment his mother came into the room and, seeing it in his hand, exclaimed: "What's that? A note? Is it from her?" He surrendered it and she unfolded it, reading it quickly. He noted that her strong broad face, always tanned a reddish brown, blanched as she turned away toward the outer room. Her biggish mouth was now set in a firm, straight line. Her large, strong hand shook the least bit as it held the small note aloft.

"Asa!" she called, and then tramping into the next room where he was, his frizzled grayish hair curling distractedly above his round head, she said: "Read this."

Clyde, who had followed, saw him take it a little nervously in his pudgy hand, his lips, always weak and beginning to crinkle at the center with age, now working curiously. Any one who had known his life's history would have said it was the expression, slightly emphasized, with which he had received most of the untoward blows of his life in the past.

"Tst! Tst! Tst!" was the only sound he made at first, a sucking sound of the tongue and palate—most weak and inadequate, it seemed to Clyde. Next there was another "Tst! Tst! Tst!", his head beginning to shake from side to side. Then, "Now, what do you suppose could have caused her to do that?" Then he turned and gazed at his wife, who gazed blankly in return. Then, walking to and fro, his hands behind him, his short legs taking unconscious and queerly long steps, his head moving again, he gave vent to another ineffectual "Tst! Tst! Tst!"

Always the more impressive, Mrs. Griffiths now showed herself markedly different and more vital in this trying situation, a kind of irritation or dissatisfaction with life itself, along with an obvious physical distress, seeming to pass through her like a visible shadow. Once her husband had gotten up, she reached out and took the note, then merely glared at it again, her face set in hard yet stricken and disturbing lines. Her manner was that of one who is intensely disquieted and dissatisfied, one who fingers savagely at a material knot and yet cannot undo it, one who seeks restraint and freedom from complaint and yet who would complain bitterly, angrily. For behind her were all those years of religious work and faith, which somehow, in her poorly integrated conscience, seemed dimly to indicate that she should justly have been spared this. Where was her God, her Christ, at this hour when this obvious evil was being done? Why had He not acted for her? How was He to explain this? His Biblical promises! His perpetual guidance! His declared mercies!

In the face of so great a calamity, it was very hard for her, as Clyde could see, to get this straightened out, instantly at least. Although, as Clyde had come to know, it could be done eventually, of course. For in some blind, dualistic way both she and Asa insisted, as do all religionists, in disassociating God from harm and error and misery, while granting Him nevertheless supreme control. They would seek for something else—some malign, treacherous, deceiving power which, in the face of God's omniscience and omnipotence, still beguiles and betrays—and find it eventually in the error and perverseness of the human heart, which God has made, yet which He does not control, because He does not want to control it.

At the moment, however, only hurt and rage were with her, and yet her lips did not twitch as did Asa's, nor did her eyes show that profound distress which filled his. Instead she retreated a step and reëxamined the letter, almost angrily, then said to Asa: "She's run away with some one and she doesn't say——" Then she stopped suddenly, remembering the presence of the children—Clyde, Julia, and Frank, all present and all gazing curiously, intently, unbelievingly. "Come in here," she called to her husband, "I want to talk to you a minute. You children had better go on to bed. We'll be out in a minute."

With Asa then she retired quite precipitately to a small room back of the mission hall. They heard her click the electric bulb. Then their voices were heard in low converse, while Clyde and Julia and Frank looked at each other, although Frank, being so young—only ten—could scarcely be said to have comprehended fully. Even Julia hardly gathered the full import of it. But Clyde, because of his larger contact with life and his mother's statement ("She's run away with some one"), understood well enough. Esta had tired of all this, as had he. Perhaps there was some one, like one of those dandies whom he saw on the streets with the prettiest girls, with whom she had gone. But where? And what was he like? That note told something, and yet his mother had not let him see it. She had taken it away too quickly. If only he had looked first, silently and to himself!

"Do you suppose she's run away for good?" he asked Julia dubiously, the while his parents were out of the room, Julia herself looking so blank and strange.

"How should I know?" she replied a little irritably, troubled by her parents' distress and this secretiveness, as well as Esta's action. "She never said anything to me. I should think she'd be ashamed of herself if she has."

Julia, being colder emotionally than either Esta or Clyde, was more considerate of her parents in a conventional way, and hence sorrier. True, she did not quite gather what it meant, but she suspected something, for she had talked occasionally with girls, but in a very guarded and conservative way. Now, however, it was more the way in which Esta had chosen to leave, deserting her parents and her brothers and herself, that caused her to be angry with her, for why should she go and do anything which would distress her parents in this dreadful fashion. It was dreadful. The air was thick with misery.

And as his parents talked in their little room, Clyde brooded too, for he was intensely curious about life now. What was it Esta had really done? Was it, as he feared and thought, one of those dreadful runaway or sexually disagreeable affairs which the boys on the streets and at school were always slyly talking about? How shameful, if that were true! She might never come back. She had gone with some man. There was something wrong about that, no doubt, for a girl, anyhow, for all he had ever heard was that all decent contacts between boys and girls, men and women, led to but one thing—marriage. And now Esta, in addition to their other troubles, had gone and done this. Certainly this home life of theirs was pretty dark now, and it would be darker instead of brighter because of this.

Presently the parents came out, and then Mrs. Griffiths' face, if still set and constrained, was somehow a little different, less savage perhaps, more hopelessly resigned.

"Esta's seen fit to leave us, for a little while, anyhow," was all she said at first, seeing the children waiting curiously. "Now, you're not to worry about her at all, or think any more about it. She'll come back after a while, I'm sure. She has chosen to go her own way, for a time, for some reason. The Lord's will be done." ("Blessed be the name of the Lord!" interpolated Asa.) "I thought she was happy here with us, but apparently she wasn't. She must see something of the world for herself, I suppose." (Here Asa put in another Tst! Tst! Tst!) "But we mustn't harbor hard thoughts. That won't do any good now— only thoughts of love and kindness." Yet she said this with a kind of sternness that somehow belied it—a click of the voice, as it were. "We can only hope that she will soon see how foolish she has been, and unthinking, and come back. She can't prosper on the course she's going now. It isn't the Lord's way or will. She's too young and she's made a mistake. But we can forgive her. We must. Our hearts must be kept open, soft and tender." She talked as though she were addressing a meeting, but with a hard, sad, frozen face and voice. "Now, all of you go to bed. We can only pray now, and hope, morning, noon and night, that no evil will befall her. I wish she hadn't done that," she added, quite out of keeping with the rest of her statement and really not thinking of the children as present at all—just of Esta.

But Asa!

Such a father, as Clyde often thought, afterwards.

Apart from his own misery, he seemed only to note and be impressed by the more significant misery of his wife. During all this, he had stood foolishly to one side—short, gray, frizzled, inadequate.

"Well, blessed be the name of the Lord," he interpolated from time to time. "We must keep our hearts open. Yes, we mustn't judge. We must only hope for the best. Yes, yes! Praise the Lord—we must praise the Lord! Amen! Oh, yes! Tst! Tst! Tst!"

"If any one asks where she is," continued Mrs. Griffiths after a time, quite ignoring her spouse and addressing the children, who had drawn near her, "we will say that she has gone on a visit to some of my relatives back in Tonawanda. That won't be the truth, exactly, but then we don't know where she is or what the truth is—and she may come back. So we must not say or do anything that will injure her until we know."

"Yes, praise the Lord!" called Asa, feebly.

"So if any one should inquire at any time, until we know, we will say that."

"Sure," put in Clyde, helpfully, and Julia added, "All right."

Mrs. Griffiths paused and looked firmly and yet apologetically at her children. Asa, for his part, emitted another "Tst! Tst! Tst!" and then the children were waved to bed.

At that, Clyde, who really wanted to know what Esta's letter had said, but was convinced from long experience that his mother would not let him know unless she chose, returned to his room again, for he was tired. Why didn't they search more if there was hope of finding her? Where was she now—at this minute? On some train somewhere? Evidently she didn't want to be found. She was probably dissatisfied, just as he was. Here he was, thinking so recently of going away somewhere himself, wondering how the family would take it, and now she had gone before him. How would that affect his point of view and action in the future? Truly, in spite of his father's and mother's misery, he could not see that her going was such a calamity, not from the *going* point of view, at any rate. It was only another something which hinted that things were not right here. Mission work was nothing. All this religious emotion and talk was not so much either. It hadn't saved Esta. Evidently, like himself, she didn't believe so much in it, either.

4

THE EFFECT OF THIS particular conclusion was to cause Clyde to think harder than ever about himself. And the principal result of his thinking was that he must do something for himself and soon. Up to this time the best he had been able to do was to work at such odd jobs as befall all boys between their twelfth and fifteenth years: assisting a man who had a paper route during the summer months of one year, working in the basement of a five-and-ten cent store all one summer long, and on Saturdays, for a period during the winter, opening boxes and unpacking goods, for which he received the munificent sum of five dollars a week, a sum which at the time seemed almost a fortune. He felt himself rich and, in the face of the opposition of his parents, who were opposed to the theater and motion pictures also, as being not only worldly, but sinful, he could occasionally go to one or another of those—in the gallery—a form of diversion which he had to conceal from his parents. Yet that did not deter him. He felt that he had a right to go with his own money; also to take his younger brother Frank, who was glad enough to go with him and say nothing.

Later in the same year, wishing to get out of school because he already felt himself very much belated in the race, he secured a place as an assistant to a soda water clerk in one of the cheaper drug stores of the city, which adjoined a theater and enjoyed not a little patronage of this sort. A sign—"Boy Wanted"—since it was directly on his way to school, first interested him. Later, in conversation with the young man whose assistant he was to be, and from whom he was to learn the trade, assuming that he was sufficiently willing and facile, he gathered that if he mastered this art, he might make as much as fifteen and even eighteen dollars a week. It was rumored that Stroud's at the corner of 14th and Baltimore Streets paid that much to two of their clerks. The particular store to which he was applying paid only twelve, the standard salary of most places.

But to acquire this art, as he was now informed, required time and the friendly help of an expert. If he wished to come here and work for five to begin with—well, six, then, since his face fell—he might soon expect to know a great deal about the art of mixing sweet drinks and decorating a large variety of ice-creams with liquid sweets, thus turning them into sundaes. For the time being apprenticeship meant washing and polishing all the machinery and implements of this particular counter, to say nothing of opening and sweeping out the store at so early an hour as seven-thirty, dusting, and delivering such orders as the owner of this drug store chose to send out by him. At such idle moments as his immediate superior—a Mr. Sieberling—twenty, dashing, self-confident, talkative, was too busy to fill all the orders, he might be called upon to mix such minor drinks—lemonades, coca-colas and the like—as the trade demanded.

Yet this interesting position, after due consultation with his mother, he decided to take. For one thing, it would provide him, as he suspected, with all the ice-cream sodas he desired, free—an advantage not to be disregarded. In the next place, as he saw it at the time, it was an open door to a trade—something which he lacked. Further, and not at all disadvantageously as he saw it, this store required his presence at night as late as twelve o'clock, with certain hours off during the day to compensate for this. And this took him out of his home at night—out of the ten-o'clock-boy class at last. They could not ask him to attend any meetings save on Sunday, and not even then, since he was supposed to work Sunday afternoons and evenings.

Next, the clerk who manipulated this particular soda fountain, quite regularly received passes from the manager of the theater next door, and into the lobby of which one door to the drugstore gave—a most fascinating connection to Clyde. It seemed so interesting to be working for a drug store thus intimately connected with a theater.

And best of all, as Clyde now found to his pleasure, and yet despair at times, the place was visited, just before and after the show on matinée days, by bevies of girls, single and en suite, who sat at the counter and giggled and chattered and gave their hair and their complexions last perfecting touches before the mirror. And Clyde, callow and inexperienced in the ways of the world, and those of the opposite sex, was never weary of observing the beauty, the daring, the self-sufficiency and the sweetness of these, as he saw them. For the first time in his life, while he busied himself with washing glasses, filling the ice-cream and syrup containers, arranging the lemons and oranges in the trays, he had an almost uninterrupted opportunity of studying these girls at close range. The wonder of them! For the most part, they were so well-dressed and smart-looking—the rings, pins, furs, delightful hats, pretty shoes they wore. And so often he overheard them discussing such interesting things—parties, dances, dinners, the shows they had seen, the places in or near Kansas City to which they were soon going, the difference between the styles of this year and last, the fascination of certain actors and actresses—principally actors—who were now playing or soon coming to the city. And to this day, in his own home he had heard nothing of all this.

And very often one or another of these young beauties was accompanied by some male in evening suit, dress shirt, high hat, bow tie, white kid gloves and patent leather shoes, a costume which at that time Clyde felt to be the last word in all true distinction, beauty, gallantry and bliss. To be able to wear such a suit with such ease and air! To be able to talk to a girl after the manner and with the sang-froid of some of these gallants! What a true measure of achievement! No good-looking girl, as it then appeared to him, would have anything to do with him if he did not possess this standard of equipment. It was plainly necessary—the thing. And once he did attain it—was able to wear such clothes as these—well, then was he not well set upon the path that leads to all the blisses? All the joys of life would then most certainly be spread before him. The friendly smiles! The secret handclasps, maybe—an arm about the waist of some one or another—a kiss—a promise of marriage—and then, and then!

And all this as a revealing flash after all the years of walking through the streets with his father and mother to public prayer meeting, the sitting in chapel and listening to queer and nondescript individuals—depressing and disconcerting people—telling how Christ had saved them and what God had done for them. You bet he would get out of that now. He would work and save his money and be somebody. Decidedly this simple and yet idyllic compound of the commonplace had all the luster and wonder of a spiritual transfiguration, the true mirage of the lost and thirsting and seeking victim of the desert.

However, the trouble with this particular position, as time speedily proved, was that much as it might teach him of mixing drinks and how to eventually earn twelve dollars a week, it was no immediate solvent for the yearnings and ambitions that were already gnawing at his vitals. For Albert Sieberling, his immediate superior, was determined to keep as much of his knowledge, as well as the most pleasant parts of the tasks, to himself. And further he was quite at one with the druggist for whom they worked in thinking that Clyde, in addition to assisting him about the fountain, should run such errands as the druggist desired, which kept Clyde industriously employed for nearly all the hours he was on duty.

Consequently there was no immediate result to all this. Clyde could see no way to dressing better than he did. Worse, he was haunted by the fact that he had very little money and very few contacts and connections—so few that, outside his own home, he was lonely and not so very much less than lonely there. The flight of Esta had thrown a chill over the religious work there, and because, as yet, she had not returned—the family, as he now heard, was thinking of breaking up here and moving, for want of a better idea, to Denver, Colorado. But Clyde, by now, was convinced that he did not wish to accompany them. What was the good of it, he asked himself? There would be just another mission there, the same as this one.

He had always lived at home—in the rooms at the rear of the mission in Bickel Street, but he hated it. And since his eleventh year, during all of which time his family had been residing in Kansas City, he had been ashamed to bring boy friends to or near it. For that reason he had always avoided boy friends, and had walked and played very much alone—or with his brothers and sisters.

But now that he was sixteen and old enough to make his own way, he ought to be getting out of this. And yet he was earning almost nothing—not enough to live on, if he were alone—and he had not as yet developed sufficient skill or courage to get anything better.

Nevertheless when his parents began to talk of moving to Denver, and suggested that he might secure work out there, never assuming for a moment that he would not want to go, he began to throw out hints to the effect that it might be better if he did not. He liked Kansas City. What was the use of changing? He had a job now and he might get something better. But his parents, bethinking themselves of Esta and the fate that had overtaken her, were not a little dubious as to the outcome of such early adventuring on his part alone. Once they were away, where would he live? With whom? What sort of influence would enter his life, who would be at hand to aid and council and guide him in the straight and narrow path, as they had done? It was something to think about.

But spurred by this imminence of Denver, which now daily seemed to be drawing nearer, and the fact that not long after this Mr. Sieberling, owing to his too obvious gallantries in connection with the fair sex, lost his place in the drug store, and Clyde came by a new and bony and chill superior who did not seem to want him as an assistant, he decided to quit—not at once, but rather to see, on such errands as took him out of the store, if he could not find something else. Incidentally in so doing, looking here and there, he one day thought he would speak to the manager of the fountain which was connected with the leading drug store in the principal hotel of the city—the latter a great twelve-story affair, which represented, as he saw it, the quintessence of luxury and ease. Its windows were always so heavily curtained; the main entrance (he had never ventured to look beyond that) was a splendiferous combination of a glass and iron awning, coupled with a marble corridor lined with palms. Often he had passed here, wondering with boyish curiosity what the nature of the life of such a place might be. Before its doors, so many taxis and automobiles were always in waiting.

To-day, being driven by the necessity of doing something for himself, he entered the drug store which occupied the principal corner, facing 14th street at Baltimore, and finding a girl cashier in a small glass cage near the door, asked of her who was in charge of the soda fountain. Interested by his tentative and uncertain manner, as well as his deep and rather appealing eyes, and instinctively judging that he was looking for something to do, she observed: "Why, Mr. Secor, there, the manager of the store." She nodded in the direction of a short, meticulously dressed man of about thirty-five, who was arranging an especial display of toilet novelties on the top of a glass case. Clyde approached him, and being still very dubious as to how one went about getting anything in life, and finding him engrossed in what he was doing, stood first on one foot and then on the other, until at last, sensing some one was hovering about for something, the man turned: "Well?" he queried.

"You don't happen to need a soda fountain helper, do you?" Clyde cast at him a glance that said as plain as anything could, "If you have any such place, I wish you would please give it to me. I need it."

"No, no, no," replied this individual, who was blond and vigorous and by nature a little irritable and contentious. He was about to turn away, but seeing a flicker of disappointment and depression pass over Clyde's face, he turned and added, "Ever work in a place like this before?"

"No place as fine as this. No, sir," replied Clyde, rather fancifully moved by all that was about him. "I'm working now down at Mr. Klinkle's store at 7th and Brooklyn, but it isn't anything like this one and I'd like to get something better if I could."

"Uh," went on his interviewer, rather pleased by the innocent tribute to the superiority of his store. "Well, that's reasonable enough. But there isn't anything here right now that I could offer you. We don't make many changes. But if you'd like to be a bell-boy, I can tell you where you might get a place. They're looking for an extra boy in the hotel inside there right now. The captain of the boys was telling me he was in need of one. I should think that would be as good as helping about a soda fountain, any day."

Then seeing Clyde's face suddenly brighten, he added: "But you mustn't say that I sent you, because I don't know you. Just ask for Mr. Squires inside there, under the stairs, and he can tell you all about it."

At the mere mention of work in connection with so imposing an institution as the Green-Davidson, and the possibility of his getting it, Clyde first stared, felt himself tremble the least bit with excitement, then thanking his advisor for his kindness, went direct to a green-marbled doorway which opened from the rear of this drug-store into the lobby of the hotel. Once through it, he beheld a lobby, the like of which, for all his years but because of the timorous poverty that had restrained him from exploring such a world, was more arresting, quite, than anything he had seen before. It was all so lavish. Under his feet was a checkered black-and-white marble floor. Above him a coppered and stained and gilded ceiling. And supporting this, a veritable forest of black marble columns as highly polished as the floor—glassy smooth. And between the columns which ranged away toward three separate entrances, one right, one left and one directly forward toward Dalrymple Avenue—were lamps, statuary, rugs, palms, chairs, divans, tête-à-têtes—a prodigal display. In short it was compact, of all that gauche luxury of appointment which, as some one once sarcastically remarked, was intended to supply "exclusiveness to the masses." Indeed, for an essential hotel in a great and successful American commercial city, it was almost too luxurious. Its rooms and hall and lobbies and restaurants were entirely too richly furnished, without the saving grace of either simplicity or necessity.

As Clyde stood, gazing about the lobby, he saw a large company of people —some women and children, but principally men as he could see—either walking or standing about and talking or idling in the chairs, side by side or alone. And in heavily draped and richly furnished alcoves where were writing-tables, newspaper files, a telegraph office, a haberdasher's shop, and a florist's stand, were other groups. There was a convention of dentists in the city, not a few of whom, with their wives and children, were gathered here; but to Clyde, who was not aware of this nor of the methods and meanings of conventions, this was the ordinary, everyday appearance of this hotel.

He gazed about in awe and amazement, then remembering the name of Squires, he began to look for him in his office "under the stairs." To his right was a grand double-winged black-and-white staircase which swung in two separate flights and with wide, generous curves from the main floor to the one above. And between these great flights was evidently the office of the hotel, for there were many clerks there. But behind the nearest flight, and close to the wall through which he had come, was a tall desk, at which stood a young man of about his own age in a maroon uniform bright with many brass buttons. And on his head was a small, round, pill-box cap, which was cocked jauntily over one ear. He was busy making entries with a lead pencil in a book which lay open before him. Various other boys about his own age, and uniformed as he was, were seated upon a long bench near him, or were to be seen darting here and there, sometimes returning to this one with a slip of paper or a key or note of some kind, and then seating themselves upon the bench to await another call apparently, which seemed to come swiftly enough. A telephone upon the small desk at which stood the uniformed youth was almost constantly buzzing, and after ascertaining what was wanted, this youth struck a small bell before him, or called "front," to which the first boy on the bench, responded. Once called, they went hurrying up one or the other stairs or toward one of the several entrances or elevators, and almost invariably were to be seen escorting individuals whose bags and suitcases and overcoats and golf sticks they carried. There were others who disappeared and returned, carrying drinks on trays or some package or other, which they were taking to one of the rooms above. Plainly this was the work that he should be called upon to do, assuming that he would be so fortunate as to connect himself with such an institution as this.

And it was all so brisk and enlivening that he wished that he might be so fortunate as to secure a position here. But would he be? And where was Mr. Squires? He approached the youth at the small desk: "Do you know where I will find Mr. Squires?" he asked.

"Here he comes now," replied the youth, looking up and examining Clyde with keen, gray eyes.

Clyde gazed in the direction indicated, and saw approaching a brisk and dapper and decidedly sophisticated-looking person of perhaps twenty-nine or thirty years of age. He was so very slender, keen, hatchet-faced and well-dressed that Clyde was not only impressed but overawed at once—a very shrewd and cunning-looking person. His nose was so long and thin, his eyes so sharp, his lips thin, and chin pointed.

"Did you see that tall, gray-haired man with the Scotch plaid shawl who went through here just now?" he paused to say to his assistant at the desk. The assistant nodded. "Well, they tell me that's the Earl of Landreil. He just came in this morning with fourteen trunks and four servants. Can you beat it! He's somebody in Scotland. That isn't the name he travels under, though, I hear. He's registered as Mr. Blunt. Can you beat that English stuff? They can certainly lay on the class, eh?"

"You said it!" replied his assistant deferentially.

He turned for the first time, glimpsing Clyde, but paying no attention to him. His assistant came to Clyde's aid.

"That young fella there is waiting to see you," he explained.

"You want to see me?" queried the captain of the bell-hops, turning to Clyde, and observing his none-too-good clothes, at the same time making a comprehensive study of him.

"The gentleman in the drug store," began Clyde, who did not quite like the looks of the man before him, but was determined to present himself as agreeably as possible, "was saying—that is, he said that I might ask you if there was any chance here for me as a bell-boy. I'm working now at Klinkle's drug-store at 7th and Brooklyn, as a helper, but I'd like to get out of that and he said you might—that is—he thought you had a place open now." Clyde was so flustered and disturbed by the cool, examining eyes of the man before him that he could scarcely get his breath properly, and swallowed hard.

For the first time in his life, it occurred to him that if he wanted to get on he ought to insinuate himself into the good graces of people—do or say something that would make them like him. So now he contrived an eager, ingratiating smile, which he bestowed on Mr. Squires, and added: "If you'd like to give me a chance, I'd try very hard and I'd be very willing."

The man before him merely looked at him coldly, but being the soul of craft and self-acquisitiveness in a petty way, and rather liking anybody who had the skill and the will to be diplomatic, he now put aside an impulse to shake his head negatively, and observed: "But you haven't had any training in this work."

"No sir, but couldn't I pick it up pretty quick if I tried hard?"

"Well, let me see," observed the head of the bell-hops, scratching his head dubiously. "I haven't any time to talk to you now. Come around Monday afternoon. I'll see you then." He turned on his heel and walked away.

Clyde, left alone in this fashion, and not knowing just what it meant, stared, wondering. Was it really true that he had been invited to come back on Monday? Could it be possible that—— He turned and hurried out, thrilling from head to toe. The idea! He had asked this man for a place in the very finest hotel in Kansas City and he had asked him to come back and see him on Monday. Gee! what would that mean? Could it be possible that he would be admitted to such a grand world as this—and that so speedily? Could it really be?

5

THE IMAGINATIVE flights of Clyde in connection with all this—his dreams of what it might mean for him to be connected with so glorious an institution— can only be suggested. For his ideas of luxury were in the main so extreme and mistaken and gauche—mere wanderings of a repressed and unsatisfied fancy, which as yet had had nothing but imaginings to feed it.

He went back to his old duties at the drug-store—to his home after hours in order to eat and sleep—but now for the balance of this Friday and Saturday and Sunday and Monday until late in the day, he walked on air, really. His mind was not on what he was doing, and several times his superior at the drug-store had to remind him to "wake-up." And after hours, instead of going directly home, he walked north to the corner of 14th and Baltimore, where stood this great hotel, and looked at it. There, at midnight even, before each of the three principal entrances—one facing each of three streets—was a doorman in a long maroon coat with many buttons and a high-rimmed and long-visored maroon cap. And inside, behind looped and fluted French silk curtains, were the still blazing lights, the à la carte dining-room and the American grill in the basement near one corner still open. And about them were many taxis and cars. And there was music always—from somewhere.

After surveying it all this Friday night and again on Saturday and Sunday morning, he returned on Monday afternoon at the suggestion of Mr. Squires and was greeted by that individual rather crustily, for by then he had all but forgotten him. But seeing that at the moment he was actually in need of help, and being satisfied that Clyde might be of service, he led him into his small office under the stair, where, with a very superior manner and much actual indifference, he proceeded to question him as to his parentage, where he lived, at what he had worked before and where, what his father did for a living—a poser that for Clyde, for he was proud and so ashamed to admit that his parents conducted a mission and preached on the streets. Instead he replied (which was true at times) that his father canvassed for a washing machine and wringer company—and on Sundays preached—a religious revelation, which was not at all displeasing to this master of boys who were inclined to be anything but home-loving and conservative. Could he bring a reference from where he now was? He could.

Mr. Squires proceeded to explain that this hotel was very strict. Too many boys, on account of the scenes and the show here, the contact with undue luxury to which they were not accustomed—though these were not the words used by Mr. Squires—were inclined to lose their heads and go wrong. He was constantly being forced to discharge boys who, because they made a little extra money, didn't know how to conduct themselves. He must have boys who were willing, civil, prompt, courteous to everybody. They must be clean and neat about their persons and clothes and show up promptly—on the dot—and in good condition for the work every day. And any boy who got to thinking that because he made a little money he could flirt with anybody or talk back, or go off on parties at night, and then not show up on time or too tired to be quick and bright, needn't think that he would be here long. He would be fired, and that promptly. He would not tolerate any nonsense. That must be understood now, once and for all.

Clyde nodded assent often and interpolated a few eager "yes, sirs" and "no, sirs," and assured him at the last that it was the furtherest thing from his thoughts and temperament to dream of any such high crimes and misdemeanors as he had outlined. Mr. Squires then proceeded to explain that this hotel only paid fifteen dollars a month and board—at the servant's table in the basement—to any bell-boy at any time. But, and this information came as a most amazing revelation to Clyde, every guest for whom any of these boys did anything—carried a bag or delivered a pitcher of water or did anything—gave him a tip, and often quite a liberal one—a dime, fifteen cents, a quarter, sometimes more. And these tips, as Mr. Squires explained, taken all together, averaged from four to six dollars a day—not less and sometimes more —most amazing pay, as Clyde now realized. His heart gave an enormous bound and was near to suffocating him at the mere mention of so large a sum. From four to six dollars! Why, that was twenty-eight to forty-two dollars a week! He could scarcely believe it. And that in addition to the fifteen dollars a month and board. And there was no charge, as Mr. Squires now explained, for the handsome uniforms the boys wore. But it might not be worn or taken out of the place. His hours, as Mr. Squires now proceeded to explain, would be as follows: On Mondays, Wednesdays, Fridays and Sundays, he was to work from six in the morning until noon, and then, with six hours off, from six in the evening until midnight. On Tuesdays, Thursdays and Saturdays, he need only work from noon until six, thus giving him each alternate afternoon or evening to himself. But all his meals were to be taken outside his working hours and he was to report promptly in uniform for line-up and inspection by his superior exactly ten minutes before the regular hours of his work began at each watch.

As for some other things which were in his mind at the time, Mr. Squires said nothing. There were others, as he knew, who would speak for him. Instead he went on to add, and then quite climactically for Clyde at that time, who had been sitting as one in a daze: "I suppose you are ready to go to work now, aren't you?"

"Yes, sir, yes, sir," he replied.

"Very good!" Then he got up and opened the door which had shut them in. "Oscar," he called to a boy seated at the head of the bell-boy bench, to which a tallish, rather oversized youth in a tight, neat-looking uniform responded with alacrity. "Take this young man here—Clyde Griffiths is your name, isn't it?—up to the wardrobe on the twelfth and see if Jacobs can find a suit to fit. But if he can't, tell him to alter it by to-morrow. I think the one Silsbee wore ought to be about right for him."

Then he turned to his assistant at the desk who was at the moment looking on. "I'm giving him a trial, anyhow," he commented. "Have one of the boys coach him a little to-night or whenever he starts in. Go ahead, Oscar," he called to the boy in charge of Clyde. "He's green at this stuff, but I think he'll do," he added to his assistant, as Clyde and Oscar disappeared in the direction of one of the elevators. Then he walked off to have Clyde's name entered upon the payroll.

In the meantime, Clyde, in tow of this new mentor, was listening to a line of information such as never previously had come to his ears anywhere.

"You needn't be frightened, if you ain't never worked at anything like dis before," began this youth, whose last name was Hegglund as Clyde later learned, and who hailed from Jersey City, New Jersey, exotic lingo, gestures and all. He was tall, vigorous, sandy-haired, freckled, genial and voluble. They had entered upon an elevator labeled "employees." "It ain't so hard. I got my first job in Buffalo t'ree years ago and I never knowed a t'ing about it up to dat time. All you gotta do is to watch de udders an' see how dey do, see. Yu get dat, do you?"

Clyde, whose education was not a little superior to that of his guide, commented quite sharply in his own mind on the use of such words as "knowed," and "gotta"—also upon "t'ing," "dat," "udders," and so on, but so grateful was he for any courtesy at this time that he was inclined to forgive his obviously kindly mentor anything for his geniality.

"Watch whoever's doin' anyt'ing, at first, see, till you git to know, see. Dat's de way. When de bell rings, if you're at de head of de bench, it's your turn, see, an' you jump up and go quick. Dey like you to be quick around here, see. An' whenever you see any one come in de door or out of an elevator wit a bag, an' you're at de head of de bench, you jump, wedder de captain rings de bell or calls 'front' or not. Sometimes he's busy or ain't lookin' an' he wants you to do dat, see. Look sharp, cause if you don't get no bags, you don't get no tips, see. Everybody dat has a bag or anyt'ing has to have it carried for 'em, unless dey won't let you have it, see.

"But be sure and wait somewhere near de desk for whoever comes in until dey sign up for a room," he rattled on as they ascended in the elevator. "Most every one takes a room. Den de clerk'll give you de key an' after dat all you gotta do is to carry up de bags to de room. Den all you gotta do is to turn on de lights in de batroom and closet, if dere is one, so dey'll know where dey are, see. An' den raise de curtains in de day time or lower 'em at night, an' see if dere's towels in de room, so you can tell de maid if dere ain't, and den if dey don't give you no tip, you gotta go, only most times, unless you draw a stiff, all you gotta do is hang back a little—make a stall, see—fumble wit de door-key or try de transom, see. Den, if dey're any good, dey'll hand you a tip. If dey don't you're out, dat's all, see. You can't even look as dough you was sore, dough—nottin' like dat, see. Den you come down an' unless dey wants ice-water or somepin, you're troo, see. It's back to de bench, quick. Dere ain't much to it. Only you gotta be quick all de time, see, and not let any one get by you comin' or goin'—dat's de main t'ing.

"An' after dey give you your uniform, an' you go to work, don't forgit to give de captain a dollar after every watch before you leave, see—two dollars on de day you has two watches, and a dollar on de day you has one, see? Dat's de way it is here. We work togedder like dat, here, an' you gotta do dat if you wanta hold your job. But dat's all. After dat all de rest is yours."

Clyde saw.

A part of his twenty-four or thirty-two dollars as he figured it was going glimmering, apparently—eleven or twelve all told—but what of it! Would there not be twelve or fifteen or even more left? And there were his meals and his uniform. Kind Heaven! What a realization of paradise! What a consummation of luxury!

Mr. Hegglund of Jersey City escorted him to the twelfth floor and into a room where they found on guard a wizened and grizzled little old man of doubtful age and temperament, who forthwith outfitted Clyde with a suit that was so near a fit that, without further orders, it was not deemed necessary to alter it. And trying on various caps, there was one that fitted him—a thing that sat most rakishly over one ear—only, as Hegglund informed him, "You'll have to get dat hair of yours cut. Better get it clipped behind. It's too long." And with that Clyde himself had been in mental agreement before he spoke. His hair certainly did not look right in the new cap. He hated it now. And going downstairs, and reporting to Mr. Whipple, Mr. Squires' assistant, the latter had said: "Very well. It fits all right, does it? Well, then, you go on here at six. Report at five-thirty and be here in your uniform at five-forty-five for inspection."

Whereupon Clyde, being advised by Hegglund to go then and there to get his uniform and take it to the dressing-room in the basement, and get his locker from the locker-man, he did so, and then hurried most nervously out—first to get a hair-cut and afterwards to report to his family on his great luck.

He was to be a bell-boy in the great Hotel Green-Davidson. He was to wear a uniform and a handsome one. He was to make—but he did not tell his mother at first what he was to make, truly—but more than eleven or twelve at first, anyhow, he guessed—he could not be sure. For now, all at once, he saw economic independence ahead for himself, if not for his family, and he did not care to complicate it with any claims which a confession as to his real salary would most certainly inspire. But he did say that he was to have his meals free —because that meant eating away from home, which was what he wished. And in addition he was to live and move always in the glorious atmosphere of this hotel—not to have to go home ever before twelve, if he did not wish—to have good clothes—interesting company, maybe—a good time, gee!

And as he hurried on about his various errands now, it occurred to him as a final and shrewd and delicious thought that he need not go home on such nights as he wished to go to a theater or anything like that. He could just stay down-town and say he had to work. And that with free meals and good clothes —think of that!

The mere thought of all this was so astonishing and entrancing that he could not bring himself to think of it too much. He must wait and see. He must wait and see just how much he would make here in this perfectly marvelous-marvelous realm.

6

AND AS conditions stood, the extraordinary economic and social inexperience of the Griffiths—Asa and Elvira—dovetailed all too neatly with his dreams. For neither Asa nor Elvira had the least knowledge of the actual character of the work upon which he was about to enter, scarcely any more than he did, or what it might mean to him morally, imaginatively, financially, or in any other way. For neither of them had ever stopped in a hotel above the fourth class in all their days. Neither one had ever eaten in a restaurant of a class that catered to other than individuals of their own low financial level. That there could be any other forms of work or contact than those involved in carrying the bags of guests to and from the door of a hotel to its office, and back again, for a boy of Clyde's years and temperament, never occurred to them. And it was naïvely assumed by both that the pay for such work must of necessity be very small anywhere, say five or six dollars a week, and so actually below Clyde's deserts and his years.

And in view of this, Mrs. Griffiths, who was more practical than her husband at all times, and who was intensely interested in Clyde's economic welfare, as well as that of her other children, was actually wondering why Clyde should of a sudden become so enthusiastic about changing to this new situation, which, according to his own story, involved longer hours and not so very much more pay, if any. To be sure, he had already suggested that it might lead to some superior position in the hotel, some clerkship or other, but he did not know when that would be, and the other had promised rather definite fulfillment somewhat earlier—as to money, anyhow.

But seeing him rush in on Monday afternoon and announce that he had secured the place and that forthwith he must change his tie and collar and get his hair cut and go back and report, she felt better about it. For never before had she seen him so enthusiastic about anything, and it was something to have him more content with himself—not so moody, as he was at times.

Yet, the hours which he began to maintain now—from six in the morning until midnight—with only an occasional early return on such evenings as he chose to come home when he was not working—and when he troubled to explain that he had been let off a little early—together with a certain eager and restless manner—a desire to be out and away from his home at nearly all such moments as he was not in bed or dressing or undressing, puzzled his mother and Asa, also. The hotel! The hotel! He must always hurry off to the hotel, and all that he had to report was that he liked it ever so much, and that he was doing all right, he thought. It was nicer work than working around a soda fountain, and he might be making more money pretty soon—he couldn't tell —but as for more than that he either wouldn't or couldn't say.

And all the time the Griffiths—father and mother—were feeling that because of the affair in connection with Esta, they should really be moving away from Kansas City—should go to Denver. And now more than ever, Clyde was insisting that he did not want to leave Kansas City. They might go, but he had a pretty good job now and wanted to stick to it. And if they left, he could get a room somewhere—and would be all right—a thought which did not appeal to them at all.

But in the meantime what an enormous change in Clyde's life. Beginning with that first evening, when at 5:45, he appeared before Mr. Whipple, his immediate superior, and was approved—not only because of the fit of his new uniform, but for his general appearance—the world for him had changed entirely. Lined up with seven others in the servants' hall, immediately behind the general offices in the lobby, and inspected by Mr. Whipple, the squad of eight marched at the stroke of six through a door that gave into the lobby on the other side of the staircase from where stood Mr. Whipple's desk, then about and in front of the general registration office to the long bench on the other side. A Mr. Barnes, who alternated with Mr. Whipple, then took charge of the assistant captain's desk, and the boys seated themselves—Clyde at the foot—only to be called swiftly and in turn to perform this, that and the other service—while the relieved squad of Mr. Whipple was led away into the rear servants' hall as before, where they disbanded.

"Cling!"

The bell on the room clerk's desk had sounded and the first boy was going.

"Cling!" It sounded again and a second boy leaped to his feet.

"Front!"—"Center door!" called Mr. Barnes, and a third boy was skidding down the long marble floor toward that entrance to seize the bags of an incoming guest, whose white whiskers and youthful, bright tweed suit were visible to Clyde's uninitiated eyes a hundred feet away. A mysterious and yet sacred vision—a tip!

"Front!" It was Mr. Barnes calling again. "See what 913 wants—icewater, I guess." And a fourth boy was gone.

Clyde, steadily moving up along the bench and adjoining Hegglund, who had been detailed to instruct him a little, was all eyes and ears and nerves. He was so tense that he could hardly breathe, and fidgeted and jerked until finally Hegglund exclaimed: "Now, don't git excited. Just hold your horses, will yuh? You'll be all right. You're jist like I was when I begun—all noives. But dat ain't de way. Easy's what you gotta be aroun' here. An' you wants to look as dough you wasn't seein' nobody nowhere—just lookin' to what ya got before ya."

"Front!" Mr. Barnes again. Clyde was scarcely able to keep his mind on what Hegglund was saying. "115 wants some writing paper and pens." A fifth boy had gone.

"Where do you get writing paper and pens if they want em?" He pleaded of his instructor, as one who was about to die might plead.

"Off'n de key desk, I toldja. He's to de left over dere. He'll give 'em to ya. An' you gits ice-water in de hall we lined up in just a minute ago—at dat end over dere, see—you'll see a little door. You gotta give dat guy in dere a dime oncet in a while or he'll get sore."

"Cling!" The room clerk's bell. A sixth boy had gone without a word to supply some order in that direction.

"And now remember," continued Hegglund, seeing that he himself was next, and cautioning him for the last time, "if dey wants drinks of any kind, you get 'em in de grill over dere off'n de dining-room. An' be sure and git de names of de drinks straight or dey'll git sore. An' if it's a room you're showing, pull de shades down to-night and turn on de lights. An' if it's any-t'ing from de dinin'-room you gotta see de head-waiter—he gets de tip, see."

"Front!" He was up and gone.

And Clyde was number one. And number four was already seating himself again by his side—but looking shrewdly around to see if anybody was wanted anywhere.

"Front!" It was Mr. Barnes. Clyde was up and before him, grateful that it was no one coming in with bags, but worried for fear it might be some-thing that he would not understand or could not do quickly.

"See what 882 wants." Clyde was off toward one of the two elevators marked, "employees," the proper one to use, he thought, because he had been taken to the twelfth floor that way, but another boy stepping out from one of the fast passenger elevators cautioned him as to his mistake.

"Goin' to a room?" he called. "Use the guest elevators. Them's for the servants or anybody with bundles."

Clyde hastened to cover his mistake. "Eight," he called. There being no one else on the elevator with them, the negro elevator boy in charge of the car saluted him at once.

"You'se new, ain't you? I ain't seen you around here befo'."

"Yes, I just came on," replied Clyde.

"Well, you won't hate it here," commented this youth in the most friendly way. "No one hates this house, I'll say. Eight did you say?" He stopped the car and Clyde stepped out. He was too nervous to think to ask the direction and now began looking at room numbers, only to decide after a moment that he was in the wrong corridor. The soft brown carpet under his feet; the soft, cream-tinted walls; the snow-white bowl lights set in the ceiling—all seemed to him parts of a perfection and a social superiority which was almost unbelievable—so remote from all that he had ever known.

And finally, finding 882, he knocked timidly and was greeted after a mo-ment by a segment of a very stout and vigorous body in a blue and white striped union suit and a related segment of a round and florid head in which was set one eye and some wrinkles to one side of it.

"Here's a dollar bill, son," said the eye seemingly—and now a hand ap-pared holding a paper dollar. It was fat and red. "You go out to a haber-dasher's and get me a pair of garters—Boston Garters—silk—and hurry back."

"Yes, sir," replied Clyde, and took the dollar. The door closed and he found himself hustling along the hall toward the elevator, wondering what a haberdasher's was. As old as he was—seventeen—the name was new to him.

He had never even heard it before, or noticed it at least. If the man had said a "gents' furnishing store," he would have understood at once, but now here he was told to go to a haberdasher's and he did not know what it was. A cold sweat burst out upon his forehead. His knees trembled. The devil! What would he do now? Could he ask any one, even Hegglund, and not seem——

He pushed the elevator button. The car began to descend. A haberdasher. A haberdasher. Suddenly a sane thought reached him. Supposing he didn't know what a haberdasher was? After all the man wanted a pair of silk Boston garters. Where did one get silk Boston garters—at a store, of course, a place where they sold things for men. Certainly. A gents' furnishing store. He would run out to a store. And on the way down, noting another friendly negro in charge, he asked: "Do you know if there's a gents' furnishing store anywhere around here?"

"One in the building, captain, right outside the south lobby," replied the negro, and Clyde hurried there, greatly relieved. Yet he felt odd and strange in his close-fitting uniform and his peculiar hat. All the time he was troubled by the notion that his small round, tight-fitting hat might fall off. And he kept pressing it furtively and yet firmly down. And bustling into the haberdasher's, which was blazing with lights outside, he exclaimed, "I want to get a pair of Boston silk garters."

"All right, son, here you are," replied a sleek, short man with bright, bald head, pink face and gold-rimmed glasses. "For some one in the hotel, I presume? Well, we'll make that seventy-five cents, and here's a dime for you," he remarked as he wrapped up the package and dropped the dollar in the cash register. "I always like to do the right thing by you boys in there because I know you come to me whenever you can."

Clyde took the dime and the package, not knowing quite what to think. The garters must be seventy-five cents—he said so. Hence only twenty-five cents need to be returned to the man. Then the dime was his. And now, maybe—would the man really give him another tip?

He hurried back into the hotel and up to the elevators. The strains of a string orchestra somewhere were filling the lobby with delightful sounds. People were moving here and there—so well-dressed, so much at ease, so very different from most of the people in the streets or anywhere, as he saw it.

An elevator door flew open. Various guests entered. Then Clyde and another bell-boy who gave him an interested glance. At the sixth floor the boy departed. At the eighth Clyde and an old lady stepped forth. He hurried to the door of his guest and tapped. The man opened it, somewhat more fully dressed than before. He had on a pair of trousers and was shaving.

"Back, eh," he called.

"Yes, sir," replied Clyde, handing him the package and change. "He said it was seventy-five cents."

"He's a damned robber, but you can keep the change, just the same," he replied, handing him the quarter and closing the door. Clyde stood there, quite spellbound for the fraction of a second. "Thirty-five cents"—he thought—"thirty-five cents." And for one little short errand. Could that really be the way things went here? It couldn't be, really. It wasn't possible—not always.

And then, his feet sinking in the soft nap of the carpet, his hand in one pocket clutching the money, he felt as if he could squeal or laugh out loud. Why, thirty-five cents—and for a little service like that. This man had given him a quarter and the other a dime and he hadn't done anything at all.

He hurried from the car at the bottom—the strains of the orchestra once more fascinated him, the wonder of so well-dressed a throng thrilling him—and made his way to the bench from which he had first departed.

And following this he had been called to carry the three bags and two umbrellas of an aged farmer-like couple, who had engaged a parlor, bedroom and bath on the fifth floor. En route they kept looking at him, as he could see, but said nothing. Yet once in their room, and after he had promptly turned on the lights near the door, lowered the blinds and placed the bags upon the bag racks, the middle-aged and rather awkward husband—a decidedly solemn and bewhiskered person—studied him and finally observed: "Young fella, you seem to be a nice, brisk sort of boy—rather better than most we've seen so far, I must say."

"I certainly don't think that hotels are any place for boys," chirped up the wife of his bosom—a large and rotund person, who by this time was busily employed inspecting an adjoining room. "I certainly wouldn't want any of my boys to work in 'em—the way people act."

"But here, young man," went on the elder, laying off his overcoat and fishing in his trousers pocket. "You go down and get me three or four evening papers if there are that many and a pitcher of ice-water, and I'll give you fifteen cents when you get back."

"This hotel's better'n the one in Omaha, Pa," added the wife sententiously. "It's got nicer carpets and curtains."

And as green as Clyde was, he could not help smiling secretly. Openly, however, he preserved a masklike solemnity, seemingly effacing all facial evidence of thought, and took the change and went out. And in a few moments he was back with the ice-water and all the evening papers and departed smilingly with his fifteen cents.

But this, in itself, was but a beginning in so far as this particular evening was concerned, for he was scarcely seated upon the bench again, before he was called to room 529, only to be sent to the bar for drinks—two ginger ales and two syphons of soda—and this by a group of smartly-dressed young men and girls who were laughing and chattering in the room, one of whom opened the door just wide enough to instruct him as to what was wanted. But because of a mirror over the mantel, he could see the party and one pretty girl in a white suit and cap, sitting on the edge of a chair in which reclined a young man who had his arm about her.

Clyde stared, even while pretending not to. And in his state of mind, this sight was like looking through the gates of Paradise. Here were young fellows and girls in this room, not so much older than himself, laughing and talking and drinking even—not ice-cream sodas and the like, but such drinks no doubt as his mother and father were always speaking against as leading to destruction, and apparently nothing was thought of it.

He hustled down to the bar, and having secured the drinks and a charge slip, returned—and was paid—a dollar and a half for the drinks and a quarter for himself. And once more he had a glimpse of the appealing scene. Only now one of the couples was dancing to a tune sung and whistled by the other two.

But what interested him as much as the visits to and glimpses of individuals in the different rooms, was the moving panorama of the main lobby— the character of the clerks behind the main desk—room clerk, key clerk, mail clerk, cashier and assistant cashier. And the various stands about the place— flower stand, news stand, cigar stand, telegraph office, taxicab office, and all manned by individuals who seemed to him curiously filled with the atmosphere of this place. And then around and between all these walking or sitting were such imposing men and women, young men and girls all so fashionably dressed, all so ruddy and contented looking. And the cars or other vehicles in which some of them appeared about dinner time and later. It was possible for him to see them in the flare of the lights outside. The wraps, furs, and other belongings in which they appeared, or which were often carried by these other boys and himself across the great lobby and into the cars or the dining-room or the several elevators. And they were always of such gorgeous textures, as Clyde saw them. Such grandeur. This, then, most certainly was what it meant to be rich, to be a person of consequence in the world—to have money. It meant that you did what you pleased. That other people, like himself, waited upon you. That you possessed all of these luxuries. That you went how, where and when you pleased.

7

AND SO, of all the influences which might have come to Clyde at this time, either as an aid or an injury to his development, perhaps the most dangerous for him, considering his temperament, was this same Green-Davidson, than which no more materially affected or gaudy a realm could have been found anywhere between the two great American mountain ranges. Its darkened and cushioned tea-room, so somber and yet tinted so gayly with colored lights, was an ideal rendezvous, not only for such inexperienced and eager flappers of the period who were to be taken by a show of luxury, but also for those more experienced and perhaps a little faded beauties, who had a thought for their complexions and the advantages of dim and uncertain lights. Also, like most hotels of its kind, it was frequented by a certain type of eager and ambitious male of no certain age or station in life, who counted upon his appearance here at least once, if not twice a day, at certain brisk and interesting hours, to establish for himself the reputation of man-about-town, or rounder, or man of wealth, or taste, or attractiveness, or all.

And it was not long after Clyde had begun to work here that he was informed by these peculiar boys with whom he was associated, one or more of whom was constantly seated with him upon the "hop-bench," as they called it, as to the evidence and presence even here—it was not long before various examples of the phenomena were pointed out to him—of a certain type of social pervert, morally disarranged and socially taboo, who sought to arrest and interest boys of their type, in order to come into some form of illicit relationship with them, which at first Clyde could not grasp. The mere thought of it made him ill. And yet some of these boys, as he was now informed—a certain youth in particular, who was not on the same watch with him at this time—were supposed to be of the mind that "fell for it," as one of the other youths phrased it.

And the talk and the palaver that went on in the lobby and the grill, to say nothing of the restaurants and rooms, were sufficient to convince any inexperienced and none-too-discerning mind that the chief business of life for any one with a little money or social position was to attend a theater, a ball-game in season, or to dance, motor, entertain friends at dinner, or to travel to New York, Europe, Chicago, California. And there had been in the lives of most of these boys such a lack of anything that approached comfort or taste, let alone luxury, that not unlike Clyde, they were inclined to not only exaggerate the import of all that they saw, but to see in this sudden transition an opportunity to partake of it all. Who were these people with money, and what had they done that they should enjoy so much luxury, where others as good seemingly as themselves had nothing? And wherein did these latter differ so greatly from the successful? Clyde could not see. Yet these thoughts flashed through the minds of every one of these boys.

At the same time the admiration, to say nothing of the private overtures of a certain type of woman or girl, who inhibited perhaps by the social milieu in which she found herself, but having means, could invade such a region as this, and by wiles and smiles and the money she possessed, ingratiate herself into the favor of some of the more attractive of these young men here, was much commented upon.

Thus a youth named Ratterer—a hall-boy here—sitting beside him the very next afternoon, seeing a trim, well-formed blonde woman of about thirty enter with a small dog upon her arm, and much bedecked with furs, first nudged him and, with a faint motion of the head indicating her vicinity, whispered, "See her? There's a swift one. I'll tell you about her sometime when I have time. Gee, the things she don't do!"

"What about her?" asked Clyde, keenly curious, for to him she seemed exceedingly beautiful, most fascinating.

"Oh, nothing, except she's been in with about eight different men around here since I've been here. She fell for Doyle"—another hall-boy whom by this time Clyde had already observed as being the quintessence of Chesterfieldian grace and airs and looks, a youth to imitate—"for a while, but now she's got some one else."

"Really?" inquired Clyde, very much astonished and wondering if such luck would ever come to him.

"Surest thing you know," went on Ratterer. "She's a bird that way—never gets enough. Her husbnd, they tell me, has a big lumber business somewhere over in Kansas, but they don't live together no more. She has one of the best suites on the sixth, but she ain't in it half the time. The maid told me."

This same Ratterer, who was short and stocky but good-looking and smiling, was so smooth and bland and generally agreeable that Clyde was instantly drawn to him and wished to know him better. And Ratterer reciprocated that feeling, for he had the notion that Clyde was innocent and inexperienced and that he would like to do some little thing for him if he could.

The conversation was interrupted by a service call, and never resumed about this particular woman, but the effect on Clyde was sharp. The woman was pleasing to look upon and exceedingly well-groomed, her skin clear, her eyes bright. Could what Ratterer had been telling him really be true? She was so pretty. He sat and gazed, a vision of something which he did not care to acknowledge even to himself tingling the roots of his hair.

And then the temperaments and the philosophy of these boys—Kinsella, short and thick and smooth-faced and a little dull, as Clyde saw it, but good-looking and virile, and reported to be a wizard at gambling, who, throughout the first three days at such times as other matters were not taking his attention, had been good enough to continue Hegglund's instructions in part. He was a more suave, better spoken youth than Hegglund, though not so attractive as Ratterer, Clyde thought, without the latter's sympathetic outlook, as Clyde saw it.

And again, there was Doyle—Eddie—whom Clyde found intensely interesting from the first, and of whom he was not a little jealous, because he was so very good-looking, so trim of figure, easy and graceful of gesture, and with so soft and pleasing a voice. He went about with an indescribable air which seemed to ingratiate him instantly with all with whom he came in contact—the clerks behind the counter no less than the strangers who entered and asked this or that question of him. His shoes and collar were so clean and trim, and his hair cut and brushed and oiled after a fashion which would have become a moving-picture actor. From the first Clyde was utterly fascinated by his taste in the matter of dress—the neatest of brown suits, caps, with ties and socks to match. He should wear a brown-belted coat just like that. He should have a brown cap. And a suit as well cut and attractive.

Similarly, a not unrelated and yet different effect was produced by that same youth who had first introduced Clyde to the work here—Hegglund—who was one of the older and more experienced bell-hops, and of considerable influence with the others because of his genial and devil-may-care attitude toward everything, outside the exact line of his hotel duties. Hegglund was neither as schooled nor as attractive as some of the others, yet by reason of a most avid and dynamic disposition—plus a liberality where money and pleasure were concerned, and a courage, strength and daring which neither Doyle nor Ratterer nor Kinsella could match—a strength and daring almost entirely divested of reason at times—he interested and charmed Clyde immensely. As he himself related to Clyde, after a time, he was the son of a Swedish journeyman baker who some years before in Jersey City had deserted his mother and left her to make her way as best she could. In consequence neither Oscar nor his sister Martha had had any too much education or decent social experience of any kind. On the contrary, at the age of fourteen he had left Jersey City in a box car and had been making his way ever since as best he could. And like Clyde, also, he was insanely eager for all the pleasures which he had imagined he saw swirling around him, and was for prosecuting adventures in every direction, lacking, however, the nervous fear of

consequence which characterized Clyde. Also he had a friend, a youth by the
name of Sparser, somewhat older than himself, who was chauffeur to a wealthy
citizen of Kansas City, and who occasionally managed to purloin a car and so
accommodate Hegglund in the matter of brief outings here and there; which
courtesy, unconventional and dishonest though it might be, still caused Hegglund to feel that he was a wonderful fellow and of much more importance
than some of these others, and to lend him in their eyes a luster which had
little of the reality which it suggested to them.

Not being as attractive as Doyle, it was not so easy for him to win the
attention of girls, and those he did succeed in interesting were not of the
same charm or import by any means. Yet he was inordinately proud of such
contacts as he could effect and not a little given to boasting in regard to them,
a thing which Clyde took with more faith than would most, being of less
experience. For this reason Hegglund liked Clyde, almost from the very first,
sensing in him perhaps a pleased and willing auditor.

So, finding Clyde on the bench beside him from time to time, he had
proceeded to continue his instructions. Kansas City was a fine place to be if
you knew how to live. He had worked in other cities—Buffalo, Cleveland,
Detroit, St. Louis—before he came here, but he had not liked any of them any
better, principally—which was a fact which he did not trouble to point out
at the time—because he had not done as well in those places as he had here.
He had been a dish-washer, car-cleaner, plumber's helper and several other
things before finally, in Buffalo, he had been inducted into the hotel business.
And then a youth, working there, but who was now no longer here, had persuaded him to come on to Kansas City. But here:

"Say—de tips in dis hotel is as big as you'll git anywhere, I know dat.
An' what's more, dey's nice people workin' here. You do your bit by dem and
dey'll do right by you. I been here now over a year an' I ain't got no complaint.
Dat guy Squires is all right if you don't cause him no trouble. He's hard, but
he's got to look out for hisself, too—dat's natural. But he don't fire nobody
unless he's got a reason. I know dat, too. And as for de rest dere's no trouble.
An' when your work's troo, your time's your own. Dese fellows here are
good sports, all o' dem. Dey're no four-flushers an' no tightwads, eider. Whenever dere's anyting on—a good time or sumpin' like dat, dere on—nearly all
of 'em. An' dey don't mooch or grouch in case tings don't work out right,
neider. I know dat, cause I been wit 'em now, lots o' times."

He gave Clyde the impression that these youths were all the best of
friends—close—all but Doyle, who was a little stand-offish, but not coldly so.
"He's got too many women chasin' him, dat's all." Also that they went here
and there together on occasion—to a dance hall, a dinner, a certain gambling
joint down near the river, a certain pleasure resort—"Kate Sweeney's"—
where were some peaches of girls—and so on and so forth, a world of such
information as had never previously been poured into Clyde's ear, and that
set him meditating, dreaming, doubting, worrying and questioning as to the
wisdom, charm, delight to be found in all this—also the permissibility of it
in so far as he was concerned. For had he not been otherwise instructed in regard to all this all his life long? There was a great thrill and yet a great question
involved in all to which he was now listening so attentively.

Again there was Thomas Ratterer, who was of a type which at first glance, one would have said, could scarcely prove either inimical or dangerous to any of the others. He was not more than five feet four, plump, with black hair and olive skin, and with an eye that was as limpid as water and as genial as could be. He, too, as Clyde learned after a time, was of a nondescript family, and so had profited by no social or financial advantages of any kind. But he had a way, and was liked by all of these youths—so much so that he was consulted about nearly everything. A native of Wichita, recently moved to Kansas City, he and his sister were the principal support of a widowed mother. During their earlier and formative years, both had seen their very good-natured and sympathetic mother, of whom they were honestly fond, spurned and abused by a faithless husband. There had been times when they were quite without food. On more than one occasion they had been ejected for non-payment of rent. None too continuously Tommy and his sister had been maintained in various public schools. Finally, at the age of fourteen he had decamped to Kansas City, where he had secured different odd jobs, until he succeeded in connecting himself with the Green-Davidson, and was later joined by his mother and sister who had removed from Wichita to Kansas City to be with him.

But even more than by the luxury of the hotel or these youths, whom swiftly and yet surely he was beginning to decipher, Clyde was impressed by the downpour of small change that was tumbling in upon him and making a small lump in his right-hand pants pocket—dimes, nickels, quarters and half-dollars even, which increased and increased even on the first day until by nine o'clock he already had over four dollars in his pocket, and by twelve, at which hour he went off duty, he had over six and a half—as much as previously he had earned in a week.

And of all this, as he then knew, he need only hand Mr. Squires one—no more, Hegglund had said—and the rest, five dollars and a half, for one evening's interesting—yes, delightful and fascinating—work, belonged to himself. He could scarcely believe it. It seemed fantastic, Aladdinish, really. Nevertheless, at twelve, exactly, of that first day a gong had sounded somewhere—a shuffle of feet had been heard and three boys had appeared—one to take Barnes' place at the desk, the other two to answer calls. And at the command of Barnes, the eight who were present were ordered to rise, right dress and march away. And in the hall outside, and just as he was leaving, Clyde approached Mr. Squires and handed him a dollar in silver. "That's right," Mr. Squires remarked. No more. Then, Clyde, along with the others, descended to his locker, changed his clothes and walked out into the darkened streets, a sense of luck and a sense of responsibility as to future luck so thrilling him as to make him rather tremulous—giddy, even.

To think that now, at last, he actually had such a place. To think that he could earn this much every day, maybe. He began to walk toward his home, his first thought being that he must sleep well and so be fit for his duties in the morning. But thinking that he would not need to return to the hotel before 11:30 the next day, he wandered into an all-night beanery to have a cup of coffee and some pie. And now all he was thinking was that he would only need to work from noon until six, when he should be free until the following morning at six. And then he would make more money. A lot of it to spend on himself.

8

THE THING that most interested Clyde at first was how, if at all, he was to keep the major portion of all this money he was making for himself. For ever since he had been working and earning money, it had been assumed that he would contribute a fair portion of all that he received—at least three-fourths of the smaller salaries he had received up to this time—toward the upkeep of the home. But now, if he announced that he was receiving at least twenty-five dollars a week and more—and this entirely apart from the salary of fifteen a month and board—his parents would assuredly expect him to pay ten or twelve.

But so long had he been haunted by the desire to make himself as attractive looking as any other well-dressed boy that, now that he had the opportunity, he could not resist the temptation to equip himself first and as speedily as possible. Accordingly, he decided to say to his mother that all of the tips he received aggregated no more than a dollar a day. And, in order to give himself greater freedom of action in the matter of disposing of his spare time, he announced that frequently, in addition to the long hours demanded of him every other day, he was expected to take the place of other boys who were sick or set to doing other things. And also, he explained that the management demanded of all boys that they look well outside as well as inside the hotel. He could not long be seen coming to the hotel in the clothes that he now wore. Mr. Squires, he said, had hinted as much. But, as if to soften the blow, one of the boys at the hotel had told him of a place where he could procure quite all the things that he needed on time.

And so unsophisticated was his mother in these matters that she believed him.

But that was not all. He was now daily in contact with a type of youth who, because of his larger experience with the world and with the luxuries and vices of such a life as this, had already been inducted into certain forms of libertinism and vice even which up to this time were entirely foreign to Clyde's knowledge and set him agape with wonder and at first with even a timorous distaste. Thus, as Hegglund had pointed out, a certain percentage of this group, of which Clyde was now one, made common cause in connection with quite regular adventures which usually followed their monthly pay night. These adventures, according to their moods and their cash at the time, led them usually either to one of two rather famous and not too respectable all-night restaurants. In groups, as he gathered by degrees from hearing them talk, they were pleased to indulge in occasional late showy suppers with drinks, after which they were wont to go to either some flashy dance hall of the downtown section to pick up a girl, or that failing as a source of group interest, to visit some notorious—or as they would have deemed it reputed —brothel, very frequently camouflaged as a boarding house, where for much less than the amount of cash in their possession they could, as they often boasted, "have any girl in the house." And here, of course, because of their known youth, ignorance, liberality, and uniform geniality and good looks, they were made much of, as a rule, being made most welcome by the various madames and girls of these places who sought, for commercial reasons of course, to interest them to come again.

And so starved had been Clyde's life up to this time and so eager was he for almost any form of pleasure, that from the first he listened with all too eager ears to any account of anything that spelled adventure or pleasure. Not that he approved of these types of adventures. As a matter of fact at first it offended and depressed him, seeing as he did that it ran counter to all he had heard and been told to believe these many years. Nevertheless so sharp a change and relief from the dreary and repressed work in which he had been brought up was it, that he could not help thinking of all this with an itch for the variety and color it seemed to suggest. He listened sympathetically and eagerly, even while at times he was mentally disapproving of what he heard. And seeing him so sympathetic and genial, first one and then another of these youths made overtures to him to go here, there or the other place—to a show, a restaurant, one of their homes, where a card game might be indulged in by two or three of them, or even to one of the shameless houses, contact with which Clyde at first resolutely refused. But by degrees, becoming familiar with Hegglund and Ratterer, both of whom he liked very much, and being invited by them to a joy-night supper—a "blow-out" as they termed it, at Frissell's—he decided to go.

"There's going to be another one of our monthly blow-outs to-morrow night, Clyde, around at Frissell's," Ratterer had said to him. "Don't you want to come along? You haven't been yet."

By this time, Clyde, having acclimated himself to this caloric atmosphere, was by no means as dubious as he was at first. For by now, in imitation of Doyle, whom he had studied most carefully and to great advantage, he had outfitted himself with a new brown suit, cap, overcoat, socks, stickpin and shoes as near like those of his mentor as possible. And the costume became him well—excellently well—so much so that he was far more attractive than he had ever been in his life, and now, not only his parents, but his younger brother and sister, were not a little astonished and even amazed by the change.

How could Clyde have come by all this grandeur so speedily? How much could all this that he wore now have cost? Was he not hypothecating more of his future earnings for this temporary grandeur than was really wise? He might need it in the future. The other children needed things, too. And was the moral and spiritual atmosphere of a place that made him work such long hours and kept him out so late every day, and for so little pay, just the place to work?

To all of which, he had replied, rather artfully for him, that it was all for the best, he was not working too hard. His clothes were not too fine, by any means—his mother should see some of the other boys. He was not spending too much money. And, anyhow, he had a long while in which to pay for all he had bought.

But now, as to this supper. That was a different matter, even to him. How, he asked himself, in case the thing lasted until very late as was expected, could he explain to his mother and father his remaining out so very late. Ratterer had said it might last until three or four, anyhow, although he might go, of course, any time. But how would that look, deserting the crowd? And yet hang it all, most of them did not live at home as he did, or if they did like Ratterer, they had parents who didn't mind what they did. Still, a late supper like that—was it wise? All these boys drank and thought nothing of it—Hegglund, Ratterer, Kinsella, Shiel. It must be silly for him to think that there was so much danger in drinking a little, as they did on these occasions. On the other hand it was true that he need not drink unless he wanted to. He could go, and if anything was said at home, he would say that he had to work late. What difference did it make if he stayed out late once in a while? Wasn't he a man now? Wasn't he making more money than any one else in the family? And couldn't he begin to do as he pleased?

He began to sense the delight of personal freedom—to sniff the air of personal and delicious romance—and he was not to be held back by any suggestion which his mother could now make.

9

AND SO THE interesting dinner, with Clyde attending, came to pass. And it was partaken of at Frissell's, as Ratterer had said. And by now Clyde, having come to be on genial terms with all of these youths, was in the gayest of moods about it all. Think of his new state in life, anyhow. Only a few weeks ago he was all alone, not a boy friend, scarcely a boy acquaintance in the world! And here he was, so soon after, going to this fine dinner with this interesting group.

And true to the illusions of youth, the place appeared far more interesting than it really was. It was little more than an excellent chop-house of the older American order. Its walls were hung thick with signed pictures of actors and actresses, together with playbills of various periods. And because of the general excellence of the food, to say nothing of the geniality of its present manager, it had become the hangout of passing actors, politicians, local business men, and after them, the generality of followers who are always drawn by that which presents something a little different to that with which they are familiar.

And these boys, having heard at one time and another from cab and taxi drivers that this was one of the best places in town, fixed upon it for their monthly dinners. Single plates of anything cost from sixty cents to a dollar. Coffee and tea were served in pots only. You could get anything you wanted to drink. To the left of the main room as you went in was a darker and low-ceilinged room, with a fireplace, to which only men resorted and sat and smoked, and read papers after dinner, and it was for this room that these youths reserved their greatest admiration. Eating here, they somehow felt older, wiser, more important—real men of the world. And both Ratterer and Hegglund, to whom by now Clyde had become very much attached, as well as most of the others, were satisfied that there was not another place in all Kansas City that was really as good.

And so this day, having drawn their pay at noon, and being off at six for the night, they gathered outside the hotel at the corner nearest the drug store at which Clyde had originally applied for work, and were off in a happy, noisy frame of mind—Hegglund, Ratterer, Paul Shiel, Davis Higby, another youth, Arthur Kinsella and Clyde.

"Didja hear de trick de guy from St. Louis pulled on de main office yesterday?" Hegglund inquired of the crowd generally, as they started walking. "Wires last Saturday from St. Louis for a parlor, bedroom and bat for himself and wife, an' orders flowers put in de room. Jimmy, the key clerk, was just tellin' me. Den he comes on here and registers himself an' his girl, see, as man and wife, an', gee, a peach of a lookin' girl, too—I saw 'em. Listen, you fellows, cantcha? Den, on Wednesday, after he's been here tree days and dey're beginnin' to wonder about him a little—meals sent to de room and all dat —he comes down and says dat his wife's gotta go back to St. Louis, and dat he won't need no suite, just one room, and dat dey can transfer his trunk and her bags to de new room until train time for her. But de trunk ain't his at all, see, but hers. And she ain't goin', don't know nuttin about it. But he is. Den he beats it, see, and leaves her and de trunk in de room. And widout a bean, see? Now, dey're holdin' her and her trunk, an' she's cryin' and wirin' friends, and dere's hell to pay all around. Can yau beat dat? An' de flowers, too. Roses. An' six different meals in de room and drinks for him, too."

"Sure, I know the one you mean," exclaimed Paul Shiel. "I took up some drinks myself. I felt there was something phony about that guy. He was too smooth and loud-talking. An' he only come across with a dime at that."

"I remember him, too," exclaimed Ratterer. "He sent me down for all the Chicago papers Monday an' only give me a dime. He looked like a bluff to me."

"Well, dey fell for him up in front, all right." It was Hegglund talking. "An' now dey're tryin' to gouge it outa her. Can you beat it?"

"She didn't look to me to be more than eighteen or twenty, if she's that old," put in Arthur Kinsella, who up to now had said nothing.

"Did you see either of 'em, Clyde?" inquired Ratterer, who was inclined to favor and foster Clyde and include him in everything.

"No," replied Clyde. "I must have missed those two. I don't remember seeing either of 'em."

"Well, you missed seein' a bird when you missed that one. Tall, long black cut-a-way coat, wide, black derby pulled low over his eyes, pearl-gray spats, too. I thought he was an English duke or something at first, the way he walked, and with a cane, too. All they gotta do is pull that English stuff, an' talk loud an' order everybody about an' they git by with it every time."

"That's right," commented Davis Higby. "That's good stuff, that English line. I wouldn't mind pulling some of it myself sometime."

They had now turned two corners, crossed two different streets and, in group formation, were making their way through the main door of Frissell's, which gave in on the reflection of lights upon china and silverware and faces, and the buzz and clatter of a dinner crowd. Clyde was enormously impressed. Never before, apart from the Green-Davidson, had he been in such a place. And with such wise, experienced youths.

They made their way to a group of tables which faced a leather wall-seat. The head-waiter, recognizing Ratterer and Hegglund and Kinsella as old patrons, had two tables put together and butter and bread and glasses brought. About these they arranged themselves, Clyde with Ratterer and Higby occupying the wall-seat; Hegglund, Kinsella and Sheil sitting opposite.

"Now, me for a good old Manhattan, to begin wit'," exclaimed Hegglund avidly, looking about on the crowd in the room and feeling that now indeed he was a person. Of a reddish-tan hue, his eyes keen and blue, his reddish-brown hair brushed straight up from his forehead, he seemed not unlike a large and overzealous rooster.

And similarly, Arthur Kinsella, once he was in here, seemed to perk up and take heart of his present glory. In a sort of ostentatious way, he drew back his coat sleeves, seized a bill of fare, and scanning the drink-list on the back, exclaimed: "Well, a dry Martini is good enough for a start."

"Well, I'm going to begin with a Scotch and soda," observed Paul Sheil, solemnly, examining at the same time the meat orders.

"None of your cocktails for me to-night," insisted Ratterer, genially, but with a note of reserve in his voice. "I said I wasn't going to drink much to-night, and I'm not. I think a glass of Rhine wine and seltzer will be about my speed."

"For de love o' Mike, will you listen to dat, now," exclaimed Hegglund, deprecatingly. "He's goin' to begin on Rhine wine. And him dat likes Manhattans always. What's gettin' into you all of a sudden, Tommy? I tought you said you wanted a good time to-night."

"So I do," replied Ratterer, "but can't I have a good time without lappin' up everything in the place? I want to stay sober to-night. No more call-downs for me in the morning, if I know what I'm about. I came pretty near not showing up last time."

"That's true, too," exclaimed Arthur Kinsella. "I don't want to drink so much I don't know where I'm at, but I'm not going to begin worrying about it now."

"How about you, Higby?" Hegglund now called to the round-eyed youth.

"I'm having a Manhattan, too," he replied, and then, looking up at the waiter who was beside him, added, "How's tricks, Dennis?"

"Oh, I can't complain," replied the waiter. "They're breakin' all right for me these days. How's everything over to the hotel?"

"Fine, fine," replied Higby, cheerfully, studying the bill-of-fare.

"An' you, Griffiths? What are you goin' to have?" called Hegglund, for, as master-of-ceremonies, delegated by the others to look after the orders and pay the bill and tip the waiter, he was now fulfilling the rôle.

"Who, me? Oh, me," exclaimed Clyde, not a little disturbed by this inquiry, for up to now—this very hour, in fact—he had never touched anything stronger than coffee or ice-cream soda. He had been not a little taken back by the brisk and sophisticated way in which these youths ordered cocktails and whisky. Surely he could not go so far as that, and yet, so well had he known long before this, from the conversation of these youths, that on such occasions as this they did drink, that he did not see how he could very well hold back. What would they think of him if he didn't drink something? For ever since he had been among them, he had been trying to appear as much of a man of the world as they were. And yet back of him, as he could plainly feel, lay all of the years in which he had been drilled in the "horrors" of drink and evil companionship. And even though in his heart this long while he had secretly rebelled against nearly all the texts and maxims to which his parents were always alluding, deeply resenting really as worthless and pointless the ragamuffin crew of wasters and failures whom they were always seeking to save, still, now he was inclined to think and hesitate. Should he or should he not drink?

For the fraction of an instant only, while all these things in him now spoke, he hesitated, then added: "Why, I, oh—I think I'll take Rhine wine and seltzer, too." It was the easiest and safest thing to say, as he saw it. Already the rather temperate and even innocuous character of Rhine wine and seltzer had been emphasized by Hegglund and all the others. And yet Ratterer was taking it—a thing which made his choice less conspicuous and, as he felt, less ridiculous.

"Will you listen to dis now?" exclaimed Hegglund, dramatically. "He says he'll have Rhine wine and seltzer, too. I see where dis party breaks up at half-past eight, all right, unless some of de rest of us do someting."

And Davis Higby, who was far more trenchant and roistering than his pleasant exterior gave any indication of, turned to Ratterer and said: "Whatja want to start this Rhine wine and seltzer stuff for, so soon, Tom? Dontcha want us to have any fun at all to-night?"

"Well, I told you why," said Ratterer. "Besides, the last time I went down to that joint I had forty bucks when I went in and not a cent when I came out. I want to know what's goin' on this time."

"That joint," thought Clyde on hearing it. Then, after this supper, when they had all drunk and eaten enough, they were going down to one of those places called a "joint"—a bad-house, really. There was no doubt of it—he knew what the word meant. There would be women there—bad women—evil women. And he would be expected—could he—would he?

For the first time in his life now, he found himself confronted by a choice as to his desire for the more accurate knowledge of the one great fascinating mystery that had for so long confronted and fascinated and baffled and yet frightened him a little. For, despite all his many thoughts in regard to all this and women in general, he had never been in contact with any one of them in this way. And now—now—

All of a sudden he felt faint thrills of hot and cold racing up and down his back and all over him. His hands and face grew hot and then became moist—then his cheeks and forehead flamed. He could feel them. Strange, swift, enticing and yet disturbing thoughts raced in and out of his consciousness. His hair tingled and he saw pictures—bacchanalian scenes—which swiftly, and yet in vain, he sought to put out of his mind. They would keep coming back. And he wanted them to come back. Yet he did not. And through it all he was now a little afraid. Pshaw! Had he no courage at all? These other fellows were not disturbed by the prospects of what was before them. They were very gay. They were already beginning to laugh and kid one another in regard to certain funny things that had happened the last time they were all out together. But what would his mother think if she knew? His mother! He dared not think of his mother or his father either at this time, and put them both resolutely out of his mind.

"Oh, say, Kinsella," called Higby. "Do you remember that little red head in that Pacific Street joint that wanted you to run away to Chicago with her?"

"Do I?" replied the amused Kinsella, taking up the Martini that was just then served him. "She even wanted me to quit the hotel game and let her start me in a business of some kind. 'I wouldn't need to work at all if I stuck by her,' she told me."

"Oh, no, you wouldn't need to work at all, except one way," called Ratterer.

The waiter put down Clyde's glass of Rhine wine and seltzer beside him and, interested and intense and troubled and fascinated by all that he heard, he picked it up, tasted it and, finding it mild and rather pleasing, drank it all down at once. And yet so wrought up were his thoughts that he scarcely realized then that he had drunk it.

"Good for you," observed Kinsella, in a most cordial tone. "You must like that stuff."

"Oh, it's not so bad," said Clyde.

And Hegglund, seeing how swiftly it had gone, and feeling that Clyde, new to this world and green, needed to be cheered and strengthened, called to the waiter: "Here, Jerry! Onc more of these, and make it a big one," he whispered behind his hand.

And so the dinner proceeded. And it was nearly eleven before they had exhausted the various matters of interest to them—stories of past affairs, past jobs, past feats of daring. And by then Clyde had had considerable time to meditate on all of these youths—and he was inclined to think that he was not nearly as green as they thought, or if so, at least shrewder than most of them—of a better mentality, really. For who were they and what were their ambitions? Hegglund, as he could see, was vain and noisy and foolish— a person who could be taken in and conciliated by a little flattery. And Higby and Kinsella, interesting and attractive boys both, were still vain of things he could not be proud of—Higby of knowing a little something about automobiles—he had an uncle in the business—Kinsella of gambling, rolling dice even. And as for Ratterer and Shiel, he could see and had noticed for some time, that they were content with the bell-hop business—just continuing in that and nothing more—a thing which he could not believe, even now, would interest him forever.

At the same time, being confronted by this problem of how soon they would be wanting to go to a place into which he had never ventured before, and to be doing things which he had never let himself think he would do in just this way, he was just a little disturbed. Had he not better excuse himself after they got outside, or perhaps, after starting along with them in whatsoever direction they chose to go, quietly slip away at some corner and return to his own home? For had he not already heard that the most dreadful of diseases were occasionally contracted in just such places—and that men died miserable deaths later because of low vices begun in this fashion? He could hear his mother lecturing concerning all this—yet with scarcely any direct knowledge of any kind. And yet, as an argument per contra, here were all of these boys in nowise disturbed by what was in their minds or moods to do. On the contrary, they were very gay over it all and amused—nothing more.

In fact, Ratterer, who was really very fond of Clyde by now, more because of the way he looked and inquired and listened than because of anything Clyde did or said, kept nudging him with his elbow now and then, asking laughingly, "How about it, Clyde? Going to be initiated to-night?" and then smiling broadly. Or finding Clyde quite still and thinking at times, "They won't do more than bite you, Clyde."

And Hegglund, taking his cue from Ratterer and occasionally desisting from his own self-glorifying diatribes, would add: "You won't ever be de same, Clyde. Dey never are. But we'll all be wid you in case of trouble."

And Clyde, nervous and irritated, would retort: "Ah, cut it out, you two. Quit kidding. What's the use of trying to make out that you know so much more than I do?"

And Ratterer would signal Hegglund with his eyes to let up and would occasionally whisper to Clyde: "That's all right, old man, don't get sore. You know we were just fooling, that's all." And Clyde, very much drawn to Ratterer, would relent and wish they were not so foolish as to show what he actually was thinking about.

At last, however, by eleven o'clock, they had had their fill of conversation and food and drink and were ready to depart, Hegglund leading the way. And instead of the vulgar and secretive mission producing a kind of solemnity and mental or moral self-examination and self-flagellation, they laughed and talked as though there was nothing but a delicious form of amusement before them. Indeed, much to Clyde's disgust and amazement, they now began to reminisce concerning other ventures into this world—of one particular one which seemed to amuse them all greatly, and which seemed to concern some "joint," as they called it, which they had once visited—a place called "Bettina's." They had been led there originally by a certain wild youth by the name of "Pinky" Jones of the staff of another local hotel. And this boy and one other by the name of Birmingham, together with Hegglund, who had become wildly intoxicated, had there indulged in wild pranks which all but led to their arrest—pranks which to Clyde, as he listened to them, seemed scarcely possible to boys of this caliber and cleanly appearance—pranks so crude and disgusting as to sicken him a little.

"Oh, ho, and de pitcher of water de girl on de second floor doused on me as I went out," called Hegglund, laughing heartily.

"And the big fat guy on the second floor that came to the door to see. Remember?" laughed Kinsella. "He thought there was a fire or a riot, I bet."

"And you and that little fat girl, Piggy. 'Member, Ratterer?" squealed Shiel, laughing and choking as he tried to tell it.

"And Ratterer's legs all bent under his load. Yoo-hoo!" yelled Hegglund. "And de way de two of 'em finally slid down de steps."

"That was all your fault, Hegglund," called Higby from Kinsella's side. "If you hadn't tried that switching stuff we never woulda got put out."

"I tell you I was drunk," protested Ratterer. "It was the red-eye they sold in there."

"And that long, thin guy from Texas with the big mustache, will you ever forget him, an' the way he laughed?" added Kinsella. "He wouldn't help nobody 'gainst us. 'Member?"

"It's a wonder we weren't all thrown in the street or locked up. Oh, gee, what a night!" reminisced Ratterer.

By now Clyde was faintly dizzy with the nature of these revelations. "Switchin'." That could mean but one thing.

And they expected him to share in revels such as these, maybe. It could not be. He was not that sort of person. What would his mother and father think if they were to hear of such dreadful things? And yet——

Even as they talked, they had reached a certain house in a dark and rather wide street, the curbs of which for a block or more on either side were sprinkled with cabs and cars. And at the corner, only a little distance away, were some young men standing and talking. And over the way, more men. And not a half a block farther on, they passed two policemen, idling and conversing. And although there was no light visible in any window, nor over any transom, still, curiously, there was a sense of vivid, radiant life. One could feel it in this dark street. Taxis spun and honked and two old-time closed carriages still in use rolled here and there, their curtains drawn. And doors slammed or opened and closed. And now and then a segment of bright inward light pierced the outward gloom and then disappeared again. Overhead on this night were many stars.

Finally, without any comment from any one, Hegglund, accompanied by Higby and Sheil, marched up the steps of this house and rang the bell. Almost instantly the door was opened by a black girl in a red dress. "Good evening. Walk right in, won't you?" was the affable greeting, and the six, having pushed past her and through the curtains of heavy velvet, which separated this small area from the main chambers, Clyde found himself in a bright and rather gaudy general parlor or reception room, the walls of which were ornamented with gilt-framed pictures of nude or semi-nude girls and some very high pier mirrors. And the floor was covered by a bright red thick carpet, over which were strewn many gilt chairs. At the back, before some very bright red hangings, was a gilded upright piano. But of guests or inmates there seemed to be none, other than the black girl.

"Jest be seated, won't you? Make yourselves at home. I'll call the madam." And, running upstairs to the left, she began calling: "Oh, Marie! Sadie! Caroline! They is some young gentlemen in the parlor."

And at that moment, from a door in the rear, there emerged a tall, slim and rather pale-faced woman of about thirty-eight or forty—very erect, very executive, very intelligent and graceful-looking—diaphanously and yet modestly garbed, who said, with a rather wan and yet encouraging smile: "Oh, hello, Oscar, it's you, is it? And you too, Paul. Hello! Hello, Davis! Just make yourselves at home anywhere, all of you. Fannie will be in in a minute. She'll bring you something to drink. I've just hired a new pianist from St. Joe— a negro. Wait'll you hear him. He's awfully clever."

She returned to the rear and called, "Oh, Sam!"

As she did so, nine girls of varying ages and looks, but none apparently over twenty-four or five—came trooping down the stairs at one side in the rear, and garbed as Clyde had never seen any women dressed anywhere. And they were all laughing and talking as they came—evidently very well pleased with themselves and in nowise ashamed of their appearance, which in some instances was quite extraordinary, as Clyde saw it, their costumes ranging from the gayest and flimsiest of boudoir negligées to the somewhat more sober, if no less revealing, dancing and ballroom gowns. And they were of such varied types and sizes and complexions—slim and stout and medium —tall or short—and dark or light or betwixt. And, whatever their ages, all seemed young. And they smiled so warmly and enthusiastically.

"Oh, hello, sweetheart! How are you? Don't you want to dance with me?" or "Wouldn't you like something to drink?"

10

PREPARED AS Clyde was to dislike all this, so steeped had he been in moods and maxims antipathetic to anything of its kind, still so innately sensual and romantic was his own disposition and so starved where sex was concerned, that instead of being sickened, he was quite fascinated. The very fleshly sumptuousness of most of these figures, dull and unromantic as might be the brains that directed them, interested him for the time being. After all, here was beauty of a gross, fleshy character, revealed and purchasable. And there were no difficulties of mood or inhibitions to overcome in connection with any of these girls. One of them, a quite pretty brunette in a black and red costume, with a band of red ribbon across her forehead, seemed to be decidedly at home with Higby, for already she was dancing with him in the back room to a jazz melody most irrationally hammered out upon the piano.

And Ratterer, to Clyde's surprise, was already seated upon one of the gilt chairs and upon his knees was lounging a tall young girl with very light hair and blue eyes. And she was smoking a cigarette and tapping her gold slippers to the melody of the piano. It was really quite an amazing and Aladdin-like scene to him. And here was Hegglund, before whom was standing a German or Scandinavian type, plump and pretty, her arms akimbo and her feet wide apart. And she was asking—with an upward swell of the voice, as Clyde could hear: "You make love to me to-night?" But Hegglund, apparently not very much taken with these overtures, calmly shook his head, after which she went on to Kinsella.

And even as he was looking and thinking, a quite attractive blonde girl of not less than twenty-four, but who seemed younger to Clyde, drew up a chair beside him and seating herself, said: "Don't you dance?" He shook his head nervously. "Want me to show you?"

"Oh, I wouldn't want to try here," he said.

"Oh, it's easy," she continued. "Come on!" But since he would not, though he was rather pleased with her for being agreeable to him, she added: "Well, how about something to drink then?"

"Sure," he agreed, gallantly, and forthwith she signaled the young negress who had returned as waitress, and in a moment a small table was put before them and a bottle of whisky with soda on the side—a sight that so astonished and troubled Clyde that he could scarcely speak. He had forty dollars in his pocket, and the cost of drinks here, as he had heard from the others, would not be less than two dollars each, but even so, think of him buying drinks for such a woman at such a price! And his mother and sisters and brother at home with scarcely the means to make ends meet. And yet he bought and paid for several, feeling all the while that he had let himself in for a terrifying bit of extravagance, if not an orgy, but now that he was here, he must go through with it.

And besides, as he now saw, this girl was really pretty. She had on a Delft blue evening gown of velvet, with slippers and stockings to match. In her ears were blue earrings and her neck and shoulders and arms were plump and smooth. The most disturbing thing about her was that her bodice was cut very low—he dared scarcely look at her there—and her cheeks and lips were painted—most assuredly the marks of the scarlet woman. Yet she did not seem very aggressive, in fact quite human, and she kept looking rather interestedly at his deep and dark and nervous eyes.

"You work over at the Green-Davidson, too, don't you?" she asked.

"Yes," replied Clyde, trying to appear as if all this were not new to him— as if he had been often in just such a place as this, amid such scenes. "How did you know?"

"Oh, I know Oscar Hegglund," she replied. "He comes around here once in a while. Is he a friend of yours?"

"Yes. That is, he works over at the hotel with me."

"But you haven't been here before."

"No," said Clyde, swiftly, and yet with a trace of inquiry in his own mood. Why should she say he hadn't been here before?

"I thought you hadn't. I've seen most of these other boys before, but I never saw you. You haven't been working over at the hotel very long, have you?"

"No," said Clyde, a little irritated by this, his eyebrows and the skin of his forehead rising and falling as he talked—a form of contraction and expansion that went on involuntarily whenever he was nervous or thought deeply. "What of it?"

"Oh, nothing. I just knew you hadn't. You don't look very much like these other boys—you look different." She smiled oddly and rather ingratiatingly, a smile and a mood which Clyde failed to interpret.

"How different?" he inquired, solemnly and contentiously, taking up a glass and drinking from it.

"I'll bet you one thing," she went on, ignoring his inquiry entirely. "You don't care for girls like me very much, do you?"

"Oh, yes, I do, too," he said, evasively.

"Oh, no, you don't either. I can tell. But I like you just the same. I like your eyes. You're not like those other fellows. You're more refined, kinda. I can tell. You don't look like them."

"Oh, I don't know," replied Clyde, very much pleased and flattered, his forehead wrinkling and clearing as before. This girl was certainly not as bad as he thought, maybe. She was more intelligent—a little more refined than the others. Her costume was not so gross. And she hadn't thrown herself upon him as had these others upon Hegglund, Higby, Kinsella and Ratterer. Nearly all of the group by now were seated upon chairs or divans about the room and upon their knees were girls. And in front of every couple was a little table with a bottle of whisky upon it.

"Look who's drinking whisky!" called Kinsella to such of the others as would pay any attention to him, glancing in Clyde's direction.

"Well, you needn't be afraid of me," went on the girl, while Clyde glanced at her arms and neck, at her too much revealed bosom, which quite chilled and yet enticed him. "I haven't been so very long in this business. And I wouldn't be here now if it hadn't been for all the bad luck I've had. I'd rather live at home with my family if I could, only they wouldn't have me, now." She looked rather solemnly at the floor, thinking mainly of the little inexperienced dunce Clyde was—so raw and green. Also of the money she had seen him take out of his pocket—plainly quite a sum. Also how really good-looking he was, not handsome or vigorous, but pleasing. And he was thinking at the instant of Esta, as to where she had gone or was now. What might have befallen her—who could say? What might have been done to her? Had this girl, by any chance, ever had any such unfortunate experience as she had had? He felt a growing, if somewhat grandiose, sympathy, and looked at her as much as to say: "You poor thing." Yet for the moment he would not trust himself to say anything or make any further inquiry.

"You fellows who come into a place like this always think so hard of everybody. I know how you are. But we're not as bad as you think."

Clyde's brows knit and smoothed again. Perhaps she was not as bad as he thought. She was a low woman, no doubt—evil but pretty. In fact, as he looked about the room from time to time, none of the girls appealed to him more. And she thought him better than these other boys—more re-fined—she had detected that. The compliment stuck. Presently she was filling his glass for him and urging him to drink with her. Another group of young men arrived about then—and other girls coming out of the mysterious portals at the rear to greet them—Hegglund and Ratterer and Kinsella and Higby, as he saw, mysteriously disappeared up that back stairs that was heav-ily curtained from the general room. And as these others came in, this girl invited him to come and sit upon a divan in the back room where the lights were dimmer.

And now, seated here, she had drawn very close to him and touched his hands and finally linking an arm in his and pressing close to him, inquired if he didn't want to see how pretty some of the rooms on the second floor were furnished. And seeing that he was quite alone now—not one of all the group with whom he had come around to observe him—and that this girl seemed to lean to him warmly and sympathetically, he allowed himself to be led up that curtained back stair and into a small pink and blue furnished room, while he kept saying to himself that this was an outrageous and dangerous pro-ceeding on his part, and that it might well end in misery for him. He might contract some dreadful disease. She might charge him more than he could

afford. He was afraid of her—himself—everything, really—quite nervous and
almost dumb with his several fears and qualms. And yet he went, and, the
door locked behind him, this interestingly well-rounded and graceful Venus
turned the moment they were within and held him to her, then calmly, and
before a tall mirror which revealed her fully to herself and him, began to
disrobe. . . .

11

THE EFFECT OF this adventure on Clyde was such as might have been expected in connection with one so new and strange to such a world as this. In
spite of all that deep and urgent curiosity and desire that had eventually led
him to that place and caused him to yield, still, because of the moral precepts with which he had so long been familiar, and also because of the nervous
esthetic inhibitions which were characteristic of him, he could not but look
back upon all this as decidedly degrading and sinful. His parents were probably right when they preached that this was all low and shameful. And yet this
whole adventure and the world in which it was laid, once it was all over, was
lit with a kind of gross, pagan beauty or vulgar charm for him. And until other
and more interesting things had partially effaced it, he could not help thinking back upon it with considerable interest and pleasure, even.

In addition he kept telling himself that now, having as much money as he
was making, he could go and do about as he pleased. He need not go there any
more if he did not want to, but he could go to other places that might not be as
low, maybe—more refined. He wouldn't want to go with a crowd like that
again. He would rather have just one girl somewhere if he could find her—a girl
such as those with whom he had seen Sieberling and Doyle associate. And so,
despite all of his troublesome thoughts of the night before, he was thus won
quickly over to this new source of pleasure if not its primary setting. He must
find a free pagan girl of his own somewhere if he could, like Doyle, and spend
his money on her. And he could scarcely wait until opportunity should provide
him with the means of gratifying himself in this way.

But more interesting and more to his purpose at the time was the fact
that both Hegglund and Ratterer, in spite of, or possibly because of, a secret sense of superiority which they detected in Clyde, were inclined to look
upon him with no little interest and to court him and to include him among
all their thoughts of affairs and pleasures. Indeed, shortly after this first
adventure, Ratterer invited him to come to his home, where, as Clyde most
quickly came to see, was a life very different from his own. At the Griffiths all
was so solemn and reserved, the still moods of those who feel the pressure of
dogma and conviction. In Ratterer's home, the reverse of this was nearly true.
The mother and sister with whom he lived, while not without some moral
although no particular religious convictions, were inclined to view life with a
great deal of generosity or, as a moralist would have seen it, laxity. There had
never been any keen moral or characterful direction there at all. And so it
was that Ratterer and his sister Louise, who was two years younger than him-

self, now did about as they pleased, and without thinking very much about it. But his sister chanced to be shrewd or individual enough not to wish to cast herself away on just any one.

The interesting part of all this was that Clyde, in spite of a certain strain of refinement which caused him to look askance at most of this, was still fascinated by the crude picture of life and liberty which it offered. Among such as these, at least, he could go, do, be as he had never gone or done or been before. And particularly was he pleased and enlightened—or rather dubiously liberated—in connection with his nervousness and uncertainty in regard to his charm or fascination for girls of his own years. For up to this very time, and in spite of his recent first visit to the erotic temple to which Hegglund and the others had led him, he was still convinced that he had no skill with or charm where girls were concerned. Their mere proximity or approach was sufficient to cause him to recede mentally, to chill or palpitate nervously, and to lose what little natural skill he had for conversation or poised banter such as other youths possessed. But now, in his visits to the home of Ratterer, as he soon discovered, he was to have ample opportunity to test whether this shyness and uncertainty could be overcome.

For it was a center for the friends of Ratterer and his sister, who were more or less of one mood in regard to life. Dancing, card-playing, love-making rather open and unashamed, went on there. Indeed, up to this time, Clyde would not have imagined that a parent like Mrs. Ratterer could have been as lackadaisical or indifferent as she was, apparently, to conduct and morals generally. He would not have imagined that any mother would have countenanced the easy camaraderie that existed between the sexes in Mrs. Ratterer's home.

And very soon, because of several cordial invitations which were extended to him by Ratterer, he found himself part and parcel of this group—a group which from one point of view—the ideas held by its members, the rather wretched English they spoke—he looked down upon. From another point of view—the freedom they possessed, the zest with which they managed to contrive social activities and exchanges—he was drawn to them. Because, for the first time, these permitted him, if he chose, to have a girl of his own, if only he could summon the courage. And this, owing to the well-meant ministrations of Ratterer and his sister and their friends, he soon sought to accomplish. Indeed the thing began on the occasion of his first visit to the Ratterers.

Louise Ratterer worked in a dry-goods store and often came home a little late for dinner. On this occasion she did not appear until seven, and the eating of the family meal was postponed accordingly. In the meantime, two girl friends of Louise arrived to consult her in connection with something, and finding her delayed, and Ratterer and Clyde there, they made themselves at home, rather impressed and interested by Clyde and his new finery. For he, at once girl-hungry and girl-shy, held himself nervously aloof, a manifestation which they mistook for a conviction of superiority on his part. And in consequence, arrested by this, they determined to show how really interesting they were—vamp him—no less. And he found their crude briskness and effrontery very appealing—so much so that he was soon taken by the charms of one, a certain Hortense Briggs, who, like Louise, was nothing more than a crude shop girl in one of the large stores, but pretty and dark and self-appreciative. And yet from the first, he realized that she was not a little coarse and vulgar —a very long way removed from the type of girl he had been imagining in his dreams that he would like to have.

"Oh, hasn't she come in yet?" announced Hortense, on first being admitted by Ratterer and seeing Clyde near one of the front windows, looking out. "Isn't that too bad? Well, we'll just have to wait a little bit if you don't mind" —this last with a switch and a swagger that plainly said, who would mind having us around? And forthwith she began to primp and admire herself before a mirror which surmounted an ocher-colored mantelpiece that graced a fireless grate in the dining-room. And her friend, Greta Miller, added: "Oh, dear, yes. I hope you won't make us go before she comes. We didn't come to eat. We thought your dinner would be all over by now."

"Where do you get that stuff—'put you out'?" replied Ratterer cynically. "As though anybody could drive you two outa here if you didn't want to go. Sit down and play the victrola or do anything you like. Dinner'll soon be ready and Louise'll be here any minute." He returned to the dining-room to look at a paper which he had been reading, after pausing to introduce Clyde. And the latter, because of the looks and the airs of these two, felt suddenly as though he had been cast adrift upon a chartless sea in an open boat.

"Oh, don't say eat to me!" exclaimed Greta Miller, who was surveying Clyde calmly as though she were debating with herself whether he was worth-while game or not, and deciding that he was: "With all the ice-cream and cake and pie and sandwiches we'll have to eat yet to-night. We was just going to warn Louise not to fill up too much. Kittie Keane's givin' a birthday party, you know, Tom, and she'll have a big cake an' everythin'. You're comin' down, ain't you, afterwards?" she concluded, with a thought of Clyde and his possible companionship in mind.

"I wasn't thinkin' of it," calmly observed Ratterer. "Me and Clyde was thinkin' of goin' to a show after dinner."

"Oh, how foolish," put in Hortense Briggs, more to attract attention to herself and take it away from Greta than anything else. She was still in front of the mirror, but turned now to cast a fetching smile on all, particularly Clyde, for whom she fancied her friend might be angling, "When you could come along and dance. I call that silly."

"Sure, dancing is all you three ever think of—you and Louise," retorted Ratterer. "It's a wonder you don't give yourselves a rest once in a while. I'm on my feet all day an' I like to sit down once in a while." He could be most matter-of-fact at times.

"Oh, don't say sit down to me," commented Greta Miller, with a lofty smile and a gliding, dancing motion of her left foot, "with all the dates we got ahead of us this week. Oh, gee!" Her eyes and eyebrows went up and she clasped her hands dramatically before her. "It's just terrible, all the dancin' we gotta do yet this winter, don't we, Hortense? Thursday night and Friday night and Saturday and Sunday nights." She counted on her fingers most archly. "Oh, gee! It is terrible, really." She gave Clyde an appealing, sympathy-seeking smile. "Guess where we were the other night. Tom. Louise and Ralph Thorpe and Hortense and Bert Gettler, me and Willie Bassick—out to Pegrain's on Webster Avenue. Oh, an' you oughta seen the crowd out there. Sam Shaffer and Tillie Burns was there. And we danced until four in the morning. I thought my knees would break. I ain't been so tired in I don't know when."

"Oh, gee!" broke in Hortense, seizing her turn and lifting her arms dramatically. "I thought I never would get to work the next morning. I could just barely see the customers moving around. And, wasn't my mother fussy! Gee! She hasn't gotten over it yet. She don't mind so much about Saturdays and Sundays, but all these week nights and when I have to get up the next morning at seven—gee—how she can pick!"

"An' I don't blame her, either," commented Mrs. Ratterer, who was just then entering with a plate of potatoes and some bread. "You two'll get sick and Louise, too, if you don't get more rest. I keep tellin' her she won't be able to keep her place or stand it if she don't get more sleep. But she don't pay no more attention to me than Tom does, and that's just none at all."

"Oh, well, you can't expect a fellow in my line to get in early, always, Ma," was all Ratterer said. And Hortense Briggs added: "Gee, I'd die if I had to stay in one night. You gotta have a little fun when you work all day."

What an easy household, thought Clyde. How liberal and indifferent. And the sexy, gay way in which these two girls posed about. And their parents thought nothing of it, evidently. If only he could have a girl as pretty as this Hortense Briggs, with her small, sensuous mouth and her bright hard eyes.

"To bed twice a week early is all I need," announced Greta Miller archly. "My father thinks I'm crazy, but more'n that would do me harm." She laughed jestingly, and Clyde, in spite of the "we was'es" and "I seen's," was most vividly impressed. Here was youth and geniality and freedom and love of life.

And just then the front door opened and in hurried Louise Ratterer, a medium-sized, trim, vigorous little girl in a red-lined cape and a soft blue felt hat pulled over her eyes. Unlike her brother, she was brisk and vigorous and more lithe and as pretty as either of these others.

"Oh, look who's here!" she exclaimed. "You two birds beat me home, didnja? Well, I got stuck to-night on account of some mix-up in my sales-book. And I had to go up to the cashier's office. You bet it wasn't my fault, though. They got my writin' wrong," then noting Clyde for the first time, she announced: "I bet I know who this is—Mr. Griffiths. Tom's talked about you a lot. I wondered why he didn't bring you around here before." And Clyde, very much flattered, mumbled that he wished he had.

But the two visitors, after conferring with Louise in a small front bedroom to which they all retired, reappeared presently and because of strenuous invitations, which were really not needed, decided to remain. And Clyde, because of their presence, was now intensely wrought up and alert—eager to make a pleasing impression and to be received upon terms of friendship here. And these three girls, finding him attractive, were anxious to be agreeable to him, so much so that for the first time in his life they put him at his ease with the opposite sex and caused him to find his tongue.

"We was just going to warn you not to eat so much," laughed Greta Miller, turning to Louise, "and now, see, we are all trying to eat again." She laughed heartily. "And they'll have pies and cakes and everythin' at Kittie's."

"Oh, gee, and we're supposed to dance, too, on top of all this. Well, heaven help me, is all I have to say," put in Hortense.

The peculiar sweetness of her mouth, as he saw it, as well as the way she crinkled it when she smiled, caused Clyde to be quite beside himself with admiration and pleasure. She looked quite delightful—wonderful to him. Indeed her effect on him made him swallow quickly and half choke on the coffee he had just taken. He laughed and felt irrepressibly gay.

At that moment she turned on him and said: "See, what I've done to him now."

"Oh, that ain't all you've done to me," exclaimed Clyde, suddenly being seized with an inspiration and a flow of thought and courage. Of a sudden, because of her effect on him, he felt bold and courageous, albeit a little foolish and added, "Say, I'm gettin' kinda woozy with all the pretty faces I see around here."

"Oh, gee, you don't want to give yourself away that quick around here, Clyde," cautioned Ratterer, genially. "These highbinders'll be after you to make you take 'em wherever they want to go. You better not begin that way." And, sure enough, Louise Ratterer, not to be abashed by what her brother had just said, observed: "You dance, don't you, Mr. Griffiths?"

"No, I don't," replied Clyde, suddenly brought back to reality by this inquiry and regretting most violently the handicap this was likely to prove in this group. "But you bet I wish I did now," he added gallantly and almost appealingly, looking first at Hortense and then at Greta Miller and Louise. But all pretended not to notice his preference, although Hortense titillated with her triumph. She was not convinced that she was so greatly taken with him, but it was something to triumph thus easily and handsomely over these others. And the others felt it. "Ain't that too bad?" she commented, a little indifferently and superiorly now that she realized that she was his preference. "You might come along with us, you and Tom, if you did. There's goin' to be mostly dancing at Kittie's."

Clyde began to feel and look crushed at once. To think that this girl, to whom of all those here he was most drawn, could dismiss him and his dreams and desires thus easily, and all because he couldn't dance. And his accursed home training was responsible for all this. He felt broken and cheated. What a boob he must seem not to be able to dance. And Louise Ratterer looked a little puzzled and indifferent, too. But Greta Miller, whom he liked less than Hortense, came to his rescue with: "Oh, it ain't so hard to learn. I could show you in a few minutes after dinner if you wanted to. It's only a few steps you have to know. And then you could go, anyhow, if you wanted to."

Clyde was grateful and said so—determined to learn here or elsewhere at the first opportunity. Why hadn't he gone to a dancing school before this, he asked himself. But the thing that pained him most was the seeming indifference of Hortense now that he had made it clear that he liked her. Perhaps it was that Bert Gettler, previously mentioned, with whom she had gone to the dance, who was making it impossible for him to interest her. So he was always to be a failure this way. Oh, gee!

But the moment the dinner was over and while the others were still talking, the first to put on a dance record and come over with hands extended was

Hortense, who was determined not to be outdone by her rival in this way. She was not particularly interested or fascinated by Clyde, at least not to the extent of troubling about him as Greta did. But if her friend was going to attempt a conquest in this manner, was it not just as well to forestall her? And so, while Clyde misread her change of attitude to the extent of thinking that she liked him better than he had thought, she took him by the hands, thinking at the same time that he was too bashful. However, placing his right arm about her waist, his other clasped in hers at her shoulder, she directed his attention to her feet and his and began to illustrate the few primary movements of the dance. But so eager and grateful was he—almost intense and ridiculous—she did not like him very much, thought him a little unsophisticated and too young. At the same time, there was a charm about him which caused her to wish to assist him. And soon he was moving about with her quite easily—and afterwards with Greta and then Louise, but wishing always it was Hortense. And finally he was pronounced sufficiently skillful to go, if he would.

And now the thought of being near her, being able to dance with her again, drew him so greatly that, despite the fact that three youths, among them that same Bert Gettler, appeared on the scene to escort them, and although he and Ratterer had previously agreed to go to a theater together, he could not help showing how much he would prefer to follow these others—so much so that Ratterer finally agreed to abandon the theater idea. And soon they were off, Clyde grieving that he could not walk with Hortense, who was with Gettler, and hating his rival because of this; but still attempting to be civil to Louise and Greta, who bestowed sufficient attention on him to make him feel at ease. Ratterer, having noticed his extreme preference and being alone with him for a moment, said: "You better not get too stuck on that Hortense Briggs. I don't think she's on the level with anybody. She's got that fellow Gettler and others. She'll only work you an' you might not get anything, either."

But Clyde, in spite of this honest and well-meant caution, was not to be dissuaded. On sight, and because of the witchery of a smile, the magic and vigor of motion and youth, he was completely infatuated and would have given or done anything for an additional smile or glance or hand pressure. And that despite the fact that he was dealing with a girl who no more knew her own mind than a moth, and who was just reaching the stage where she was finding it convenient and profitable to use boys of her own years or a little older for whatever pleasures or clothes she desired.

The party proved nothing more than one of those ebullitions of the youthful mating period. The house of Kittie Keane was little more than a cottage in a poor street under bare December trees. But to Clyde, because of the passion for a pretty face that was suddenly lit in him, it had the color and the form and gayety of romance itself. And the young girls and boys that he met there—girls and boys of the Ratterer, Hegglund, Hortense stripe—were still of the very substance and texture of that energy, ease and forwardness which he would have given his soul to possess. And curiously enough, in spite of a certain nervousness on his part, he was by reason of his new companions made an integral part of the gayeties.

And on this occasion, he was destined to view a type of girl and youth in action such as previously it had not been his fortune or misfortune, as you will, to see. There was, for instance, a type of sensual dancing which Louise and Hortense and Greta indulged in with the greatest nonchalance and assurance. At the same time, many of these youths carried whisky in a hip flask, from which they not only drank themselves, but gave others to drink—boys and girls indiscriminately.

And the general hilarity for this reason being not a little added to, they fell into more intimate relations—spooning with one and another—Hortense and Louise and Greta included. Also to quarreling at times. And it appeared to be nothing out of the ordinary, as Clyde saw, for one youth or another to embrace a girl behind a door, to hold her on his lap in a chair in some secluded corner, to lie with her on a sofa, whispering intimate and unquestionably welcome things to her. And although at no time did he espy Hortense doing this—still, as he saw, she did not hesitate to sit on the laps of various boys or to whisper with rivals behind doors. And this for a time so discouraged and at the same time incensed him that he felt he could not and would not have anything more to do with her—she was too cheap, vulgar, inconsiderate.

At the same time, having partaken of the various drinks offered him—so as not to seem less worldly wise than the others—until brought to a state of courage and daring not ordinarily characteristic of him, he ventured to half plead with and at the same time half reproach her for her too lax conduct.

"You're a flirt, you are. You don't care who you jolly, do you?" This as they were dancing together after one o'clock to the music of a youth named Wilkens, at the none too toneful piano. She was attempting to show him a new step in a genial and yet coquettish way, and with an amused, sensuous look.

"What do you mean, flirt? I don't get you."

"Oh, don't you?" replied Clyde, a little crossly and still attempting to conceal his real mood by a deceptive smile. "I've heard about you. You jolly 'em all."

"Oh, do I?" she replied quite irritably. "Well, I haven't tried to jolly you very much, have I?"

"Well, now, don't get mad," he half pleaded and half scolded, fearing, perhaps, that he had ventured too far and might lose her entirely now. "I don't mean anything by it. You don't deny that you let a lot of these fellows make love to you. They seem to like you, anyway."

"Oh, well, of course they like me, I guess. I can't help that, can I?"

"Well, I'll tell you one thing," he blurted boastfully and passionately. "I could spend a lot more on you than they could. I got it." He had been thinking only the moment before of fifty-five dollars in bills that snuggled comfortably in his pocket.

"Oh, I don't know," she retorted, not a little intrigued by this cash offer, as it were, and at the same time not a little set up in her mood by the fact that she could thus inflame nearly all youths in this way. She was really a little silly, very lightheaded, who was infatuated by her own charms and looked in every mirror, admiring her eyes, her hair, her neck, her hands, her figure, and practising a peculiarly fetching smile.

At the same time, she was not unaffected by the fact that Clyde was not a little attractive to look upon, although so very green. She liked to tease such beginners. He was a bit of a fool, as she saw him. But he was connected with the Green-Davidson, and he was well-dressed, and no doubt he had all the money he said and would spend it on her. Some of those whom she liked best did not have much money to spend.

"Lots of fellows with money would like to spend it on me." She tossed her head and flicked her eyes and repeated her coyest smile.

At once Clyde's countenance darkened. The witchery of her look was too much for him. The skin of his forehead crinkled and then smoothed out. His eyes burned lustfully and bitterly, his old resentment of life and deprivation showing. No doubt all she said was true. There were others who had more and would spend more. He was boasting and being ridiculous and she was laughing at him.

After a moment, he added, weakly, "I guess that's right, too. But they couldn't want you more than I do."

The uncalculated honesty of it flattered her not a little. He wasn't so bad after all. They were gracefully gliding about as the music continued.

"Oh, well, I don't flirt everywhere like I do here. These fellows and girls all know each other. We're always going around together. You mustn't mind what you see here."

She was lying artfully, but it was soothing to him none the less. "Gee, I'd give anything if you'd only be nice to me," he pleaded, desperately and yet ecstatically. "I never saw a girl I'd rather have than you. You're swell. I'm crazy about you. Why won't you come out to dinner with me and let me take you to a show afterwards? Don't you want to do that, to-morrow night or Sunday? Those are my two nights off. I work other nights."

She hesitated at first, for even now she was not so sure that she wished to continue this contact. There was Gettler, to say nothing of several others, all jealous and attentive. Even though he spent money on her, she might not wish to bother with him. He was already too eager and he might become troublesome. At the same time, the natural coquetry of her nature would not permit her to relinquish him. He might fall into the hands of Greta or Louise. In consequence she finally arranged a meeting for the following Tuesday. But he could not come to the house, or take her home to-night—on account of her escort, Mr. Gettler. But on the following Tuesday, at six-thirty, near the Green-Davidson. And he assured her that they would dine first at Frissell's, and then see "The Corsair," a musical comedy at Libby's, only two blocks away.

12

Now TRIVIAL as this contact may seem to some, it was of the utmost significance to Clyde. Up to this he had never seen a girl with so much charm who would deign to look at him, or so he imagined. And now he had found one, and she was pretty and actually interested sufficiently to accompany him to dinner and to a show. It was true, perhaps, that she was a flirt, and not really sincere with any one, and that maybe at first he could not expect her to center her attentions on him, but who knew—who could tell?

And true to her promise on the following Tuesday she met him at the corner of 14th Street and Wyandotte, near the Green-Davidson. And so excited and flattered and enraptured was he that he could scarcely arrange his jumbled thoughts and emotions in any seemly way. But to show that he was worthy of her, he had made an almost exotic toilet—hair pomaded, a butterfly tie, new silk muffler and silk socks to emphasize his bright brown shoes, purchased especially for the occasion.

But once he had reëncountered Hortense, whether all this was of any import to her he could not tell. For, after all, it was her own appearance, not his, that interested her. And what was more—a trick with her—she chose to keep him waiting until nearly seven o'clock, a delay which brought about in him the deepest dejection of spirit for the time being. For supposing, after all, in the interval, she had decided that she did not care for him and did not wish to see him any more. Well, then he would have to do without her, of course. But that would prove that he was not interesting to a girl as pretty as she was, despite all the nice clothes he was now able to wear and the money he could spend. He was determined that, girl or no girl, he would not have one who was not pretty. Ratterer and Hegglund did not seem to mind whether the girl they knew was attractive or not, but with him it was a passion. The thought of being content with one not so attractive almost nauseated him.

And yet here he was now, on the street corner in the dark—the flare of many signs and lights about, hundreds of pedestrians hurrying hither and thither, the thought of pleasurable intentions and engagements written upon the faces of many—and he, he alone, might have to turn and go somewhere else—eat alone, go to a theater alone, go home alone, and then to work again in the morning. He had just about concluded that he was a failure when out of the crowd, a little distance away, emerged the face and figure of Hortense. She was smartly dressed in a black velvet jacket with a reddish brown collar and cuffs, and a bulgy, round tam of the same material with a red leather buckle on the side. And her cheeks and lips were rouged a little. And her eyes sparkled. And as usual she gave herself all the airs of one very well content with herself.

"Oh, hello, I'm late, ain't I? I couldn't help it. You see, I forgot I had another appointment with a fella, a friend of mine—gee, a peach of a boy, too, and it was only at six I remembered that I had the two dates. Well, I was in a mess then. So I had to do something about one of you. I was just about to call you up and make a date for another night, only I remembered you wouldn't be at your place after six. Tom never is. And Charlie always is in his place till six-thirty, anyhow, sometimes later, and he's a peach of a fella that way—never grouchy or nothing. And he was goin' to take me to the theater and to dinner, too. He has charge of the cigar stand over here at the Orphia. So I called him up. Well, he didn't like it so very much. But I told him I'd make it another night. Now, aintcha glad? Dontcha think I'm pretty nice to you, disappointin' a good-lookin' fella like Charlie for you?"

She had caught a glimpse of the disturbed and jealous and yet fearsome look in Clyde's eyes as she talked of another. And the thought of making him jealous was a delight to her. She realized that he was very much smitten with her. So she tossed her head and smiled, falling into step with him as he moved up the street.

"You bet it was nice of you to come," he forced himself to say, even though the reference to Charlie as a "peach of a fella" seemed to affect his throat and his heart at the same time. What chance had he to hold a girl who was so pretty and self-willed? "Gee, you look swell to-night," he went on, forcing himself to talk and surprising himself a little with his ability to do so. "I like the way that hat looks on you, and your coat too." He looked directly at her, his eyes lit with admiration, an eager yearning filling them. He would have liked to have kissed her—her pretty mouth—only he did not dare here, or anywhere as yet.

"I don't wonder you have to turn down engagements. You're pretty enough. Don't you want some roses to wear?" They were passing a flower store at the moment and the sight of them put the thought of the gift in his mind. He had heard Hegglund say that women liked fellows who did things for them.

"Oh, sure, I would like some roses," she replied, turning into the place. "Or maybe some of those violets. They look pretty. They go better with this jacket, I think."

She was pleased to think that Clyde was sporty enough to think of flowers. Also that he was saying such nice things about her. At the same time she was convinced that he was a boy who had had little, if anything, to do with girls. And she preferred youths and men who were more experienced, not so easily flattered by her—not so easy to hold. Yet she could not help thinking that Clyde was a better type of boy or man than she was accustomed to—more refined. And for that reason, in spite of his gaucheness (in her eyes) she was inclined to tolerate him—to see how he would do.

"Well, these are pretty nifty," she exclaimed, picking up a rather large bouquet of violets and pinning them on. "I think I'll wear these." And while Clyde paid for them, she posed before the mirror, adjusting them to her taste. At last, being satisfied as to their effect, she turned and exclaimed, "Well, I'm ready," and took him by the arm.

Clyde, being not a little overawed by her spirit and mannerisms, was at a loss what else to say for the moment, but he need not have worried—her chief interest in life was herself.

"Gee, I tell you I had a swift week of it last week. Out every night until three. An' Sunday until nearly morning. My, that was some rough party I was to last night, all right. Ever been down to Burkett's at Gifford's Ferry? Oh, a nifty place, all right, right over the Big Blue at 39th. Dancing in summer and you can skate outside when it's frozen in winter or dance on the ice. An' the niftiest little orchestra."

Clyde watched the play of her mouth and the brightness of her eyes and the swiftness of her gestures without thinking so much of what she said—very little.

"Wallace Trone was along with us—gee, he's a scream of a kid—and afterwards when we was sittin' down to eat ice cream, he went out in the kitchen and blacked up an' put on a waiter's apron and coat and then comes back and serves us. That's one funny boy. An' he did all sorts of funny stuff with the dishes and spoons." Clyde sighed because he was by no means as gifted as the gifted Trone.

"An' then, Monday morning, when we all got back it was nearly four, and I had to get up again at seven. I was all in. I coulda chucked my job, and I woulda, only for the nice people down at the store and Mr. Beck. He's the head of my department, you know, and say, how I do plague that poor man. I sure am hard on that store. One day I comes in late after lunch; one of the other girls punched the clock for me with my key, see, and he was out in the hall and he saw her, and he says to me afterwards, about two in the afternoon, 'Say look here, Miss Briggs' (he always calls me Miss Briggs, 'cause I won't let him call me nothing else. He'd try to get fresh if I did), 'that loanin' that key stuff don't go. Cut that stuff out now. This ain't no Follies.' I had to laugh. He does get so sore at times at all of us. But I put him in his place just the same. He's kinda soft on me, you know—he wouldn't fire me for worlds, not him. So I says to him, 'See here, Mr. Beck, you can't talk to me in any such style as that. I'm not in the habit of comin' late often. An' wot's more, this ain't the only place I can work in K.C. If I can't be late once in a while without hearin' about it, you can just send up for my time, that's all, see.' I wasn't goin' to let him get away with that stuff. And just as I thought, he weakened. All he says was, 'Well, just the same, I'm warnin' you. Next time maybe Mr. Tierney'll see you an' then you'll get a chance to try some other store, all right.' He knew he was bluffing and that I did, too. I had to laugh. An' I saw him laughin' with Mr. Scott about two minutes later. But, gee, I certainly do pull some raw stuff around there at times."

By then she and Clyde, with scarcely a word on his part, and much to his ease and relief, had reached Frissell's. And for the first time in his life he had the satisfaction of escorting a girl to a table in such a place. Now he really was beginning to have a few experiences worthy of the name. He was quite on edge with the romance of it. Because of her very high estimate of herself, her very emphatic picture of herself as one who was intimate with so many youths and girls who were having a good time, he felt that up to this hour he had not lived at all. Swiftly he thought of the different things she had told him —Burkett's on the Big Blue, skating and dancing on the ice—Charlie Trone— the young tobacco clerk with whom she had had the engagement for to-night— Mr. Beck at the store who was so struck on her that he couldn't bring himself to fire her. And as he saw her order whatever she liked, without any thought of his purse, he contemplated quickly her face, figure, the shape of her hands, so suggestive always of the delicacy or roundness of the arm, the swell of her bust, already very pronounced, the curve of her eyebrows, the rounded appeal of her smooth cheeks and chin. There was something also about the tone of her voice, unctuous, smooth, which somehow appealed to and disturbed him. To him it was delicious. Gee, if he could only have such a girl all for himself!

And in here, as without, she clattered on about herself, not at all impressed, apparently, by the fact that she was dining here, a place that to him had seemed quite remarkable. When she was not looking at herself in a mirror, she was studying the bill of fare and deciding what she liked—lamb with mint jelly—no omelette, no beef—oh, yes, filet of mignon with mushrooms. She finally compromised on that with celery and cauliflower. And she would like a cocktail. Oh, yes, Clyde had heard Hegglund say that no meal was worth anything without a few drinks, so now he had mildly suggested a cocktail. And having secured that and a second, she seemed warmer and gayer and more gossipy than ever.

But all the while, as Clyde noticed, her attitude in so far as he was concerned was rather distant—impersonal. If for so much as a moment, he ventured to veer the conversation ever so slightly to themselves, his deep personal interest in her, whether she was really very deeply concerned about any other youth, she threw him off by announcing that she liked all the boys, really. They were all so lovely—so nice to her. They had to be. When they weren't, she didn't have anything more to do with them. She "tied a can to them," as she once expressed it. Her quick eyes clicked and she tossed her head defiantly.

And Clyde was captivated by all this. Her gestures, her poses, moues and attitudes were sensuous and suggestive. She seemed to like to tease, promise, lay herself open to certain charges and conclusions and then to withhold and pretend that there was nothing to all of this—that she was very unconscious of anything save the most reserved thoughts in regard to herself. In the main, Clyde was thrilled and nourished by this mere proximity to her. It was torture, and yet a sweet kind of torture. He was full of the most tantalizing thoughts about how wonderful it would be if only he were permitted to hold her close, kiss her mouth, bite her, even. To cover her mouth with his! To smother her with kisses! To crush and pet her pretty figure! She would look at him at moments with deliberate, swimming eyes, and he actually felt a little sick and weak—almost nauseated. His one dream was that by some process, either of charm or money, he could make himself interesting to her.

And yet after going with her to the theater and taking her home again, he could not see that he had made any noticeable progress. For throughout the performance of "The Corsair" at Libby's, Hortense, who, because of her uncertain interest in him was really interested in the play, talked of nothing but similar shows she had seen, as well as of actors and actresses and what she thought of them, and what particular youth had taken her. And Clyde, instead of leading her in wit and defiance and matching her experiences with his own, was compelled to content himself with approving of her.

And all the time she was thinking that she had made another real conquest. And because she was no longer virtuous, and she was convinced that he had some little money to spend, and could be made to spend it on her, she conceived the notion of being sufficiently agreeable—nothing more—to hold him, keep him attentive, if possible, while at the same time she went her own way, enjoying herself as much as possible with others and getting Clyde to buy and do such things for her as might fill gaps—when she was not sufficiently or amusingly enough engaged elsewhere.

13

For a period of four months at least this was exactly the way it worked out. After meeting her in this fashion, he was devoting not an inconsiderable portion of his free time to attempting to interest her to the point where she would take as much interest in him as she appeared to take in others. At the same time he could not tell whether she could be made to entertain a singular affection for any one. Nor could he believe that there was only an innocent camaraderie involved in all this. Yet she was so enticing that he was deliriously moved by the thought that if his worst suspicions were true, she might ultimately favor him. So captivated was he by this savor of sensuality and varietism that was about her, the stigmata of desire manifest in her gestures, moods, voice, the way she dressed, that he could not think of relinquishing her.

Rather, he foolishly ran after her. And seeing this, she put him off, at times evaded him, compelled him to content himself with little more than the crumbs of her company, while at the same time favoring him with descriptions or pictures of other activities and contacts which made him feel as though he could no longer endure to merely trail her in this fashion. It was then he would announce to himself in anger that he was not going to see her any more. She was no good to him, really. But on seeing her again, a cold indifference in everything she said and did, his courage failed him and he could not think of severing the tie.

She was not at all backward at the same time in speaking of things that she needed or would like to have—little things, at first—a new powder puff, a lip stick, a box of powder or a bottle of perfume. Later, and without having yielded anything more to Clyde than a few elusive and evasive endearments— intimate and languorous reclinings in his arms which promised much but always came to nothing—she made so bold as to indicate to him at different times and in different ways, purses, blouses, slippers, stockings, a hat, which she would like to buy if only she had the money. And he, in order to hold her favor and properly ingratiate himself, proceeded to buy them, though at times and because of some other developments in connection with his family, it pressed him hard to do so. And yet, as he was beginning to see toward the end of the fourth month, he was apparently little farther advanced in her favor than he had been in the beginning. In short, he was conducting a feverish and almost painful pursuit without any definite promise of reward.

In the meantime, in so far as his home ties went, the irritations and the depressions which were almost inextricably involved with membership in the Griffiths family were not different from what they had ever been. For, following the disappearance of Esta, there had settled a period of dejection which still endured. Only, in so far as Clyde was concerned, it was complicated with a mystery which was tantalizing and something more—irritating; for when it came to anything which related to sex in the Griffiths family, no parents could possibly have been more squeamish.

And especially did this apply to the mystery which had now surrounded Esta for some time. She had gone. She had not returned. And so far as Clyde and the others knew, no word of any kind had been received from her. However, Clyde had noted that after the first few weeks of her absence, during which time both his mother and father had been most intensely wrought up and troubled, worrying greatly as to her whereabouts and why she did not write, suddenly they had ceased their worries, and had become very much more resigned—at least not so tortured by a situation that previously had seemed to offer no hope whatsoever. He could not explain it. It was quite noticeable, and yet nothing was said. And then one day a little later, Clyde had occasion to note that his mother was in communication with some one by mail—something rare for her. For so few were her social or business connections that she rarely received or wrote a letter.

One day, however, very shortly after he had connected himself with the Green-Davidson, he had come in rather earlier than usual in the afternoon and found his mother bending over a letter which evidently had just arrived and which appeared to interest her greatly. Also it seemed to be connected with something which required concealment. For, on seeing him, she stopped reading at once, and, flustered and apparently nervous, arose and put the letter away without commenting in any way upon what she had been reading. But Clyde for some reason, intuition perhaps, had the thought that it might be from Esta. He was not sure. And he was too far away to detect the character of the handwriting. But whatever it was, his mother said nothing afterwards concerning it. She looked as though she did not want him to inquire, and so reserved were their relations that he would not have thought of inquiring. He merely wondered, and then dismissed it partially, but not entirely, from his mind.

A month or five weeks after this, and just about the time that he was becoming comparatively well-schooled in his work at the Green-Davidson, and was beginning to interest himself in Hortense Briggs, his mother came to him one afternoon with a very peculiar proposition for her. Without explaining what it was for, or indicating directly that now she felt that he might be in a better position to help her, she called him into the mission hall when he came in from work and, looking at him rather fixedly and nervously for her, said: "You wouldn't know, Clyde, would you, how I could raise a hundred dollars right away?"

Clyde was so astonished that he could scarcely believe his ears, for only a few weeks before the mere mention of any sum above four or five dollars in connection with him would have been preposterous. His mother knew that. Yet here she was asking him and apparently assuming that he might be able to assist her in this way. And rightly, for both his clothes and his general air had indicated a period of better days for him.

At the same time his first thought was, of course, that she had observed his clothes and goings-on and was convinced that he was deceiving her about the amount he earned. And in part this was true, only so changed was Clyde's manner of late, that his mother had been compelled to take a very different attitude toward him and was beginning to be not a little dubious as to her further control over him. Recently, or since he had secured this latest place, for some reason he had seemed to her to have grown wiser, more assured, less dubious of himself, inclined to go his own way and keep his own counsel. And while this had troubled her not a little in one sense, it rather pleased her in another. For to see Clyde, who had always seemed because of his sensitiveness and unrest so much of a problem to her, developing in this very interesting way was something; though at times, and in view of his very recent finery, she had been wondering and troubled as to the nature of the company he might be keeping. But since his hours were so long and so absorbing, and whatever money he made appeared to be going into clothes, she felt that she had no real reason to complain. Her one other thought was that perhaps he was beginning to act a little selfish—to think too much of his own comfort—and yet in the face of his long deprivations she could not very well begrudge him any temporary pleasure, either.

Clyde, not being sure of her real attitude, merely looked at her and exclaimed: "Why, where would I get a hundred dollars, Ma?" He had visions of his new-found source of wealth being dissipated by such unheard of and inexplicable demands as this, and distress and distrust at once showed on his countenance.

"I didn't expect that you could get it all for me," Mrs. Griffiths suggested tactfully. "I have a plan to raise the most of it, I think. But I did want you to help me try to think how I would raise the rest. I didn't want to go to your father with this if I could help it, and you're getting old enough now to be of some help." She looked at Clyde approvingly and interestedly enough. "Your father is such a poor hand at business," she went on, "and he gets so worried at times."

She passed a large and weary hand over her face and Clyde was moved by her predicament, whatever it was. At the same time, apart from whether he was willing to part with so much or not, or had it to give, he was decidedly curious about what all this was for. A hundred dollars! Gee whiz!

After a moment or two, his mother added: "I'll tell you what I've been thinking. I must have a hundred dollars, but I can't tell you for what now, you nor any one, and you mustn't ask me. There's an old gold watch of your father's in my desk and a solid gold ring and pin of mine. Those things ought to be worth twenty-five dollars at least, if they were sold or pawned. Then there is that set of solid silver knives and forks and that silver platter and pitcher in there"—Clyde knew the keepsakes well—"that platter alone is worth twenty-five dollars. I believe they ought to bring at least twenty or twenty-five together. I was thinking if I could get you to go to some good pawnshop with them down near where you work, and then if you would let me have five more a week for a while" (Clyde's countenance fell)—"I could get a friend of mine—Mr. Murch who comes here, you know—to advance me enough to make up the hundred, and then I could pay him back out of what you pay me. I have about ten dollars myself."

She looked at Clyde as much as to say: "Now, surely, you won't desert me in my hour of trouble," and Clyde relaxed, in spite of the fact that he had been counting upon using quite all that he earned for himself. In fact, he agreed to take the trinkets to the pawnshop, and to advance her five more for the time being until the difference between whatever the trinkets brought and one hundred dollars was made up. And yet in spite of himself, he could not help resenting this extra strain, for it had only been a very short time that he had been earning so much. And here was his mother demanding more and more, as he saw it—ten dollars a week now. Always something wrong, thought Clyde, always something needed, and with no assurance that there would not be more such demands later.

He took the trinkets, carried them to the most presentable pawnshop he could find, and being offered forty-five dollars for the lot, took it. This, with his mother's ten, would make fifty-five, and with forty-five she could borrow from Mr. Murch, would make a hundred. Only now, as he saw, it would mean that for nine weeks he would have to give her ten dollars instead of five. And that, in view of his present aspirations to dress, live and enjoy himself in a way entirely different from what he previously considered necessary, was by no means a pleasure to contemplate. Nevertheless he decided to do it. After all he owed his mother something. She had made many sacrifices for him and the others in days past and he could not afford to be too selfish. It was not decent.

But the most enduring thought that now came to him was that if his mother and father were going to look to him for financial aid, they should be willing to show him more consideration than had previously been shown him. For one thing he ought to be allowed to come and go with more freedom, in so far as his night hours were concerned. And at the same time he was clothing himself and eating his meals at the hotel, and that was no small item, as he saw it.

However, there was another problem that had soon arisen and it was this. Not so long after the matter of the hundred dollars, he encountered his mother in Montrose Street, one of the poorest streets which ran north from Bickel, and which consisted entirely of two unbroken lines of wooden houses and two-story flats and many unfurnished apartments. Even the Griffiths, poor as they were, would have felt themselves demeaned by the thought of having to dwell in such a street. His mother was coming down the front steps of one of the less tatterdemalion houses of this row, a lower front window of which carried a very conspicuous card which read "Furnished Rooms." And then, without turning or seeing Clyde across the street, she proceeded to another house a few doors away, which also carried a furnished rooms card and, after surveying the exterior interestedly, mounted the steps and rang the bell.

Clyde's first impression was that she was seeking the whereabouts of some individual in whom she was interested and of whose address she was not certain. But crossing over to her at about the moment the proprietress of the house put her head out of the door, he heard his mother say: "You have a room for rent?" "Yes." "Has it a bath?" "No, but there's a bath on the second floor." "How much is it a week?" "Four dollars." "Could I see it?" "Yes, just step in."

Mrs. Griffiths appeared to hesitate while Clyde stood below, not twenty-five feet away, and looked up at her, waiting for her to turn and recognize tim. But she stepped in without turning. And Clyde gazed after her curiously, for while it was by no means inconceivable that his mother might be looking for a room for some one, yet why should she be looking for it in this street when as a rule she usually dealt with the Salvation Army or the Young Women's Christian Association. His first impulse was to wait and inquire of her what she was doing here, but being interested in several errands of his own, he went on.

That night, returning to his own home to dress and seeing his mother in the kitchen, he said to her: "I saw you this morning, Ma, in Montrose Street."

"Yes," his mother replied, after a moment, but not before he had noticed that she had started suddenly as though taken aback by this information. She was paring potatoes and looked at him curiously. "Well, what of it?" she added, calmly, but flushing just the same—a thing decidedly unusual in connection with her where he was concerned. Indeed, that start of surprise interested and arrested Clyde. "You were going into a house there—looking for a furnished room, I guess."

"Yes, I was," replied Mrs. Griffiths, simply enough now. "I need a room for some one who is sick and hasn't much money, but it's not so easy to find either." She turned away as though she were not disposed to discuss this any more, and Clyde, while sensing her mood, apparently, could not resist adding: "Gee, that's not much of a street to have a room in." His new work at the Green-Davidson had already caused him to think differently of how one should live—any one. She did not answer him and he went to his room to change his clothes.

A month or so after this, coming east on Missouri Avenue late one evening, he again saw his mother in the near distance coming west. In the light of one of the small stores which ranged in a row on this street, he saw that she was carrying a rather heavy old-fashioned bag, which had long been about the house but had never been much used by any one. On sight of him approaching (as he afterwards decided) she had stopped suddenly and turned into a hallway of a three-story brick apartment building, and when he came up to it, he found the outside door was shut. He opened it, and saw a flight of steps dimly lit, up which she might have gone. However, he did not trouble to investigate, for he was uncertain, once he reached this place, whether she had gone in to call on some one or not, it had all happened so quickly. But waiting at the next corner, he finally saw her come out again. And then to his increasing curiosity, she appeared to look cautiously about before proceeding as before. It was this that caused him to think that she must have been endeavoring to conceal herself from him. But why?

His first impulse was to turn and follow her, so interested was he by her strange movements. But he decided later that if she did not want him to know what she was doing, perhaps it was best that he should not. At the same time he was made intensely curious by this evasive gesture. Why should his mother not wish him to see her carrying a bag anywhere? Evasion and concealment formed no part of her real disposition (so different from his own). Almost instantly his mind proceeded to join this coincidence with the time he had seen her descending the steps of the rooming house in Montrose Street, together with the business of the letter he had found her reading, and the money she had been compelled to raise—the hundred dollars. Where could she be going? What was she hiding?

He speculated on all this, but he could not decide whether it had any definite connection with him or any member of the family until about a week later, when, passing along Eleventh near Baltimore, he thought he saw Esta, or at least a girl so much like her that she would be taken for her anywhere. She had the same height, and she was moving along as Esta used to walk. Only, now he thought as he saw her, she looked older. Yet, so quickly had she come and gone in the mass of people that he had not been able to make sure. It was only a glance, but on the strength of it, he had turned and sought to catch up with her, but upon reaching the spot she was gone. So convinced was he, however, that he had seen her that he went straight home, and, encountering his mother in the mission, announced that he was positive he had seen Esta. She must be back in Kansas City again. He could have sworn to it. He had seen her near Eleventh and Baltimore, or thought he had. Had his mother heard anything from her?

And then curiously enough he observed that his mother's manner was not exactly what he thought it should have been under the circumstances. His own attitude had been one of commingled astonishment, pleasure, curiosity and sympathy because of the sudden disappearance and now sudden reappearance of Esta. Could it be that his mother had used that hundred dollars to bring her back? The thought had come to him—why or from where, he could not say. He wondered. But if so, why had she not returned to her home, at least to notify the family of her presence here?

He expected his mother would be as astonished and puzzled as he was— quick and curious for details. Instead, she appeared to him to be obviously confused and taken aback by this information, as though she was hearing about something that she already knew and was puzzled as to just what her attitude should be.

"Oh, did you? Where? Just now, you say? At Eleventh and Baltimore? Well, isn't that strange? I must speak to Asa about this. It's strange that she wouldn't come here if she is back." Her eyes, as he saw, instead of looking astonished, looked puzzled, disturbed. Her mouth, always the case when she was a little embarrassed and disconcerted, worked oddly—not only the lips but the jaw itself.

"Well, well," she added, after a pause. "That is strange. Perhaps it was just some one who looked like her."

But Clyde, watching her out of the corner of his eye, could not believe that she was as astonished as she pretended. And, thereafter, Asa coming in, and Clyde not having as yet departed for the hotel, he heard them discussing the matter in some strangely inattentive and unillumined way, as if it was not quite as startling as it had seemed to him. And for some time he was not called in to explain what he had seen.

And then, as if purposely to solve this mystery for him, he encountered his mother one day passing along Spruce Street, this time carrying a small basket on her arm. She had, as he had noticed of late, taken to going out regularly mornings and afternoons or evenings. On this occasion, and long before she had had an opportunity to see him, he had discerned her peculiarly heavy figure draped in the old brown coat which she always wore, and had turned into Myrkel Street and waited for her to pass, a convenient news stand offering him shelter. Once she had passed, he dropped behind her, allowing her to precede him by half a block. And at Dalrymple, she crossed to Beaudry, which was really a continuation of Spruce, but not so ugly. The houses were quite old—quondam residences of an earlier day, but now turned into boarding and rooming houses. Into one of these he saw her enter and disappear, but before doing so she looked inquiringly about her.

After she had entered, Clyde approached the house and studied it with great interest. What was his mother doing in there? Who was it she was going to see? He could scarcely have explained his intense curiosity to himself, and yet, since having thought that he had seen Esta on the street, he had an unconvinced feeling that it might have something to do with her. There were the letters, the one hundred dollars, the furnished room in Montrose Street.

Diagonally across the way from the house in Beaudry Street there was a large-trunked tree, leafless now in the winter wind, and near it a telegraph pole, close enough to make a joint shadow with it. And behind these he was able to stand unseen, and from this vantage point to observe the several windows, side and front and ground and second floor. Through one of the front windows above, he saw his mother moving about as though she were quite at home there. And a moment later, to his astonishment he saw Esta come to one of the two windows and put a package down on the sill. She appeared to have on only a light dressing gown or a wrap drawn about her shoulders. He was not mistaken this time. He actually started as he realized that it was she, also that his mother was in there with her. And yet what had she done that she must come back and hide away in this manner? Had her husband, the man she had run away with, deserted her?

He was so intensely curious that he decided to wait a while outside here to see if his mother might not come out, and then he himself would call on Esta. He wanted so much to see her again—to know what this mystery was all about. He waited, thinking how he had always liked Esta and how strange it was that she should be here, hiding away in this mysterious way.

After an hour, his mother came out, her basket apparently empty, for she held it lightly in her hand. And just as before, she looked cautiously about her, her face wearing that same stolid and yet care-stamped expression which it always wore these days—a cross between an uplifting faith and a troublesome doubt.

Clyde watched her as she proceeded to walk south on Beaudry Street toward the Mission. After she was well out of sight, he turned and entered the house. Inside, as he had surmised, he found a collection of furnished rooms, name plates some of which bore the names of the roomers pasted upon them. Since he knew that the southeast front room upstairs contained Esta, he proceeded there and knocked. And true enough, a light footstep responded within, and presently, after some little delay which seemed to suggest some quick preparation within, the door opened slightly and Esta peeped out —quizzically at first, then with a little cry of astonishment and some confusion. For, as inquiry and caution disappeared, she realized that she was looking at Clyde. At once she opened the door wide.

"Why, Clyde," she called. "How did you come to find me? I was just thinking of you."

Clyde at once put his arms around her and kissed her. At the same time he realized, and with a slight sense of shock and dissatisfaction, that she was considerably changed. She was thinner—paler—her eyes almost sunken, and not any better dressed than when he had seen her last. She appeared nervous and depressed. One of the first thoughts that came to him now was where her husband was. Why wasn't he here? What had become of him? As he looked about and at her, he noticed that Esta's look was one of confusion and uncertainty, not unmixed with a little satisfaction at seeing him. Her mouth was partly open because of a desire to smile and to welcome him, but her eyes showed that she was contending with a problem.

"I didn't expect you here," she added, quickly, the moment he released her. "You didn't see—" Then she paused, catching herself at the brink of some information which evidently she didn't wish to impart.

"Yes, I did, too—I saw Ma," he replied. "That's how I came to know you were here. I saw her coming out just now and I saw you up here through the window." (He did not care to confess that he had been following and watching his mother for an hour.) "But when did you get back?" he went on. "It's a wonder you wouldn't let the rest of us know something about you. Gee, you're a dandy, you are—going away and staying months and never letting any one of us know anything. You might have written me a little something, anyhow. We always got along pretty well, didn't we?"

His glance was quizzical, curious, imperative. She, for her part, felt recessive and thence evasive—uncertain, quite, what to think or say or tell.

She uttered: "I couldn't think who it might be. No one comes here. But, my, how nice you look, Clyde. You've got such nice clothes, now. And you're getting taller. Mamma was telling me you are working at the Green-Davidson."

She looked at him admiringly and he was properly impressed by her notice of him. At the same time he could not get his mind off her condition. He could not cease looking at her face, her eyes, her thin-fat body. And as he looked at her waist and her gaunt face, he came to a very keen realization that all was not well with her. She was going to have a child. And hence the thought recurred to him—where was her husband—or at any rate, the man she had eloped with. Her original note, according to her mother, had said that she was going to get married. Yet now he sensed quite clearly that she was not married. She was deserted, left in this miserable room here alone. He saw it, felt it, understood it.

And he thought at once that this was typical of all that seemed to occur in his family. Here he was just getting a start, trying to be somebody and get along in the world and have a good time. And here was Esta, after her first venture in the direction of doing something for herself, coming to such a finish as this. It made him a little sick and resentful.

"How long have you been back, Esta?" he repeated dubiously, scarcely knowing just what to say now, for now that he was here and she was as she was he began to scent expense, trouble, distress and to wish almost that he had not been so curious. Why need he have been? It could only mean that he must help.

"Oh, not so very long, Clyde. About a month, now, I guess. Not more than that."

"I thought so. I saw you up on Eleventh near Baltimore about a month ago, didn't I? Sure I did," he added a little less joyously—a change that Esta noted. At the same time she nodded her head affirmatively. "I knew I did. I told Ma so at the time, but she didn't seem to think so. She wasn't as surprised as I thought she would be, though. I know why, now. She acted as though she didn't want me to tell her about it either. But I knew I wasn't wrong." He stared at Esta oddly, quite proud of his prescience in this case. He paused though, not knowing quite what else to say and wondering whether what he had just said was of any sense or import. It didn't seem to suggest any real aid for her.

And she, not quite knowing how to pass over the nature of her condition, or to confess it, either, was puzzled what to say. Something had to be done. For Clyde could see for himself that her predicament was dreadful. She could scarcely bear the look of his inquiring eyes. And more to extricate herself than her mother, she finally observed, "Poor Mamma. You mustn't think it strange of her, Clyde. She doesn't know what to do, you see, really. It's all my fault, of course. If I hadn't run away, I wouldn't have caused her all this trouble. She has so little to do with and she's always had such a hard time." She turned her back to him suddenly, and her shoulders began to tremble and her sides to heave. She put her hands to her face and bent her head low— and then he knew that she was silently crying.

"Oh, come now, sis," exclaimed Clyde, drawing near to her instantly and feeling intensely sorry for her at the moment. "What's the matter? What do you want to cry for? Didn't that man that you went away with marry you?"

She shook her head negatively and sobbed the more. And in that instant there came to Clyde the real psychological as well as sociological and biological import of his sister's condition. She was in trouble, pregnant—and with no money and no husband. That was why his mother had been looking for a room. That was why she had tried to borrow a hundred dollars from him. She was ashamed of Esta and her condition. She was ashamed of not only what people outside the family would think, but of what he and Julia and Frank might think—the effect of Esta's condition upon them perhaps—because it was not right, unmoral, as people saw it. And for that reason she had been trying to conceal it, telling stories about it—a most amazing and difficult thing for her, no doubt. And yet, because of poor luck, she hadn't succeeded very well.

And now he was again confused and puzzled, not only by his sister's condition and what it meant to him and the other members of the family here in Kansas City, but also by his mother's disturbed and somewhat unmoral attitude in regard to deception in this instance. She had evaded if not actually deceived him in regard to all this, for she knew Esta was here all the time. At the same time he was not inclined to be too unsympathetic in that respect toward her—far from it. For such deception in such an instance had to be, no doubt, even where people were as religious and truthful as his mother, or so he thought. You couldn't just let people know. He certainly wouldn't want people to know about Esta, if he could help it. What would they think? What would they say about her and him? Wasn't the general state of his family low enough, as it was? And so, now he stood, staring and puzzled the while Esta cried. And she realizing that he was puzzled and ashamed, because of her, cried the more.

"Gee, that is tough," said Clyde, troubled, and yet fairly sympathetic after a time. "You wouldn't have run away with him unless you cared for him though—would you?" (He was thinking of himself and Hortense Briggs.) "I'm sorry for you, Ess. Sure, I am, but it won't do you any good to cry about it now, will it? There's lots of other fellows in the world beside him. You'll come out of it all right."

"Oh, I know," sobbed Esta, "but I've been so foolish. And I've had such a hard time. And now I've brought all this trouble on Mamma and all of you." She choked and hushed a moment. "He went off and left me in a hotel in Pittsburgh without any money," she added. "And if it hadn't been for Mamma, I don't know what I would have done. She sent me a hundred dollars when I wrote her. I worked for a while in a restaurant—as long as I could. I didn't want to write home and say that he had left me. I was ashamed to. But I didn't know what else to do there toward the last, when I began feeling so bad."

She began to cry again; and Clyde, realizing all that his mother had done and sought to do to assist her, felt almost as sorry now for his mother as he did for Esta—more so, for Esta had her mother to look after her and his mother had almost no one to help her.

"I can't work yet, because I won't be able to for a while," she went on. "And Mamma doesn't want me to come home now because she doesn't want Julia or Frank or you to know. And that's right, too, I know. Of course it is. And she hasn't got anything and I haven't. And I get so lonely here, sometimes." Her eyes filled and she began to choke again. "And I've been so foolish."

And Clyde felt for the moment as though he could cry too. For life was so strange, so hard at times. See how it had treated him all these years. He had had nothing until recently and always wanted to run away. But Esta had done so, and see what had befallen her. And somehow he recalled her between the tall walls of the big buildings here in the business district, sitting at his father's little street organ and singing and looking so innocent and good. Gee, life was tough. What a rough world it was anyhow. How queer things went!

He looked at her and the room, and finally, telling her that she wouldn't be left alone, and that he would come again, only she mustn't tell his mother he had been there, and that if she needed anything she could call on him although he wasn't making so very much, either—and then went out. And then, walking toward the hotel to go to work, he kept dwelling on the thought of how miserable it all was—how sorry he was that he had followed his mother, for then he might not have known. But even so, it would have come out. His mother could not have concealed it from hin indefinitely. She would have asked for more money eventually maybe. But what a dog that man was to go off and leave his sister in a big strange city without a dime. He puzzled, thinking now of the girl who had been deserted in the Green-Davidson some months before with a room and board bill unpaid. And how comic it had seemed to him and the other boys at the time—highly colored with a sensual interest in it.

But this, well, this was his own sister. A man had thought so little of his sister as that. And yet, try as he would, he could no longer think that it was as terrible as when he heard her crying in the room. Here was this brisk, bright city about him running with people and effort, and this gay hotel in which he worked. That was not so bad. Besides there was his own love affair, Hortense, and pleasures. There must be some way out for Esta. She would get well again and be all right. But to think of his being part of a family that was always so poor and so little thought of that things like this could happen to it—one thing and another—like street preaching, not being able to pay the rent at times, his father selling rugs and clocks for a living on the streets—Esta running away and coming to an end like this. Gee!

14

THE RESULT of all this on Clyde was to cause him to think more specifically on the problem of the sexes than he ever had before, and by no means in any orthodox way. For while he condemned his sister's lover for thus ruthlessly deserting her, still he was not willing to hold her entirely blameless by any means. She had gone off with him. As he now learned from her, he had been in the city for a week the year before she ran away with him, and it was then that he had introduced himself to her. The following year when he returned for two weeks, it was she who looked him up, or so Clyde suspected, at any rae. And in view of his own interest in and mood regarding Hortense Briggs, it was not for him to say that there was anything wrong with the sex relation in itself.

Rather, as he saw it now, the difficulty lay, not in the deed itself, but in the consequences which followed upon not thinking or not knowing. For had Esta known more of the man in whom she was interested, more of what such a relationship with him meant, she would not be in her present pathetic plight. Certainly such girls as Hortense Briggs, Greta and Louise, would never have allowed themselves to be put in any such position as Esta. Or would they? They were too shrewd. And by contrast with them in his mind, at least at this time, she suffered. She ought, as he saw it, to have been able to manage better. And so, by degrees, his attitude toward her hardened in some measure, though his feeling was not one of indifference either.

But the one influence that was affecting and troubling and changing him now was his infatuation for Hortense Briggs—than which no more agitating influence could have come to a youth of his years and temperament. She seemed, after his few contacts with her, to be really the perfect realization of all that he had previously wished for in a girl. She was so bright, vain, engaging, and so truly pretty. Her eyes, as they seemed to him, had a kind of dancing fire in them. She had a most entrancing way of pursing and parting her lips and at the same time looking straightly and indifferently before her, as though she were not thinking of him, which to him was both flame and fever. It caused him, actually, to feel weak and dizzy, at times, cruelly seared in his veins with minute and wriggling threads of fire, and this could only be described as conscious lust, a torturesome and yet unescapable thing which yet in her case he was unable to prosecute beyond embracing and kissing, a form of reserve and respect in regard to her which she really resented in the very youths in whom she sought to inspire it. The type of boy for whom she really cared and was always seeking was one who could sweep away all such pseudo-ingenuousness and superiorities in her and force her, even against herself, to yield to him.

In fact she was constantly wavering between actual like and dislike of him. And in consequence, he was in constant doubt as to where he stood, a state which was very much relished by her and yet which was never permitted to become so fixed in his mind as to cause him to give her up entirely. After some party or dinner or theater to which she had permitted him to take her, and throughout which he had been particularly tactful—not too assertive —she could be as yielding and enticing in her mood as the most ambitious lover would have liked. And this might last until the evening was nearly over, when suddenly, and at her own door or the room or house of some girl with whom she was spending the night, she would turn, and without rhyme or reason, endeavor to dismiss him with a mere handclasp or a thinly flavored embrace or kiss. At such times, if Clyde was foolish enough to endeavor to force her to yield the favors he craved, she would turn on him with the fury of a spiteful cat, would tear herself away, developing for the moment, seemingly, an intense mood of opposition which she could scarcely have explained to herself. Its chief mental content appeared to be one of opposition to being compelled by him to do anything. And, because of his infatuation and his weak overtures due to his inordinate fear of losing her, he would be forced to depart, usually in a dark and despondent mood.

But so keen was her attraction for him that he could not long remain away, but must be going about to where most likely he would encounter her. Indeed, for the most part these days, and in spite of the peculiar climax which had eventuated in connection with Esta, he lived in a keen, sweet and sensual dream in regard to her. If only she would really come to care for him. At night, in his bed at home, he would lie and think of her—her face —the expressions of her mouth and eyes, the lines of her figure, the motions of her body in walking or dancing—and she would flicker before him as upon a screen. In his dreams, he found her deliciously near him, pressing against him—her delightful body all his—and then in the moment of crisis, when seemingly she was about to yield herself to him completely, he would awake to find her vanished—an illusion only.

Yet there were several things in connection with her which seemed to bode success for him. In the first place, like himself, she was part of a poor family—the daughter of a machinist and his wife, who up to this very time had achieved little more than a bare living. From her childhood she had had nothing, only such gew-gaws and fripperies as she could secure for herself by her wits. And so low had been her social state until very recently that she had not been able to come in contact with anything better than butcher and baker boys—the rather commonplace urchins and small job aspirants of her vicinity. Yet even here she had early realized that she could and should capitalize her looks and charm—and had. Not a few of these had even gone so far as to steal in order to get money to entertain her.

After reaching the age where she was old enough to go to work, and thus coming in contact with the type of boy and man in whom she was now interested, she was beginning to see that without yielding herself too much, but in acting discreetly, she could win a more interesting equipment than she had before. Only, so truly sensual and pleasure-loving was she that she was by no means always willing to divorce her self-advantages from her pleasures. On the contrary, she was often troubled by a desire to like those whom she sought to use, and per contra, not to obligate herself to those whom she could not like.

In Clyde's case, liking him but a little, she still could not resist the desire to use him. She liked his willingness to buy her any little thing in which she appeared interested—a bag, a scarf, a purse, a pair of gloves—anything that she could reasonably ask or take without obligating herself too much. And yet from the first, in her smart, tricky way, she realized that unless she could bring herself to yield to him—at some time or other offer him the definite reward which she knew he craved—she could not hold him indefinitely.

One thought that stirred her more than anything else was that the way Clyde appeared to be willing to spend his money on her she might easily get some quite expensive things from him—a pretty and rather expensive dress, perhaps, or a hat, or even a fur coat such as was then being shown and worn in the city, to say nothing of gold earrings, or a wrist watch, all of which she was constantly and enviously eyeing in the different shop windows.

One day not so long after Clyde's discovery of his sister Esta, Hortense, walking along Baltimore Street near its junction with Fifteenth—the smartest portion of the shopping section of the city—at the noon hour—with Doris Trine, another shop girl in her department store, saw in the window of one of the smaller and less exclusive fur stores of the city, a fur jacket of beaver that to her, viewed from the eye-point of her own particular build, coloring and temperament, was exactly what she needed to strengthen mightily her very limited personal wardrobe. It was not such an expensive coat, worth possibly a hundred dollars—but fashioned in such an individual way as to cause her to imagine that, once invested with it, her own physical charm would register more than it ever had.

Moved by this thought, she paused and exclaimed: "Oh, isn't that just the classiest, darlingest little coat you ever saw! Oh, do look at those sleeves, Doris." She clutched her companion violently by the arm. "Lookit the collar. And the lining! And those pockets! Oh, dear!" She fairly vibrated with the intensity of her approval and delight. "Oh, isn't that just too sweet for words? And the very kind of coat I've been thinking of since I don't know when. Oh, you pitty sing!" she exclaimed, affectedly, thinking all at once as much of her own pose before the window and its effect on the passer-by as of the coat before her. "Oh, if I could only have 'oo."

She clapped her hands admiringly, while Isadore Rubenstein, the elderly son of the proprietor, who was standing somewhat out of the range of her gaze at the moment, noted the gesture and her enthusiasm and decided forthwith that the coat must be worth at least twenty-five or fifty dollars more to her, anyhow, in case she inquired for it. The firm had been offering it at one hundred. "Oh, ha!" he grunted. But being of a sensual and somewhat romantic turn, he also speculated to himself rather definitely as to the probable trading value, affectionally speaking, of such a coat. What, say, would the poverty and vanity of such a pretty girl as this cause her to yield for such a coat?

In the meantime, however, Hortense, having gloated as long as her noontime hour would permit, had gone away, still dreaming and satiating her flaming vanity by thinking of how devastating she would look in such a coat. But she had not stopped to ask the price. Hence, the next day, feeling that she must look at it once more, she returned, only this time alone, and yet with no idea of being able to purchase it herself. On the contrary, she was only vaguely revolving the problem of how, assuming that the coat was sufficiently low in price, she could get it. At the moment she could think of no one. But seeing the coat once more, and also seeing Mr. Rubenstein, Jr., inside eyeing her in a most propitiatory and genial manner, she finally ventured in.

"You like the coat, eh?" was Rubenstein's ingratiating comment as she opened the door. "Well, that shows you have good taste, I'll say. That's one of the nobbiest little coats we've ever had to show in this store yet. A real beauty, that. And how it would look on such a beautiful girl as you!" He took it out of the window and held it up. "I seen you when you was looking at it yesterday." A gleam of greedy admiration was in his eye.

And noting this, and feeling that a remote and yet not wholly unfriendly air would win her more consideration and courtesy than a more intimate one, Hortense merely said, "Yes?"

"Yes, indeed. And I said right away, there's a girl that knows a really swell coat when she sees it."

The flattering unction soothed, in spite of herself.

"Look at that! Look at that!" went on Mr. Rubenstein, turning the coat about and holding it before her. "Where in Kansas City will you find anything to equal that to-day? Look at this silk lining here—genuine Mallinson silk—and these slant pockets. And the buttons. You think those things don't make a different-looking coat? There ain't another one like it in Kansas City to-day—not one. And there won't be. We designed it ourselves and we never repeat our models. We protect our customers. But come back here." (He led the way to a triple mirror at the back.) "It takes the right person to wear a coat like this—to get the best effect out of it. Let me try it on you."

And by the artificial light Hortense was now privileged to see how really fetching she did look in it. She cocked her head and twisted and turned and buried one small ear in the fur, while Mr. Rubenstein stood by, eyeing her with not a little admiration and almost rubbing his hands.

"There now," he continued. "Look at that. What do you say to that, eh? Didn't I tell you it was the very thing for you? A find for you. A pick-up. You'll never get another coat like that in this city. If you do, I'll make you a present of this one." He came very near, extending his plump hands, palms up.

"Well, I must say it does look smart on me," commented Hortense, her vainglorious soul yearning for it. "I can wear anything like this, though." She twisted and turned the more, forgetting him entirely and the effect her interest would have on his cost price. Then she added: "How much is it?"

"Well, it's really a two-hundred-dollar coat," began Mr. Rubenstein artfully. Then noting a shadow of relinquishment pass swiftly over Hortense's face, he added quickly: "That sounds like a lot of money, but of course we don't ask so much for it down here. One hundred and fifty is our price. But if that coat was at Jarek's, that's what you'd pay for it and more. We haven't got the location here and we don't have to pay the high rents. But it's worth every cent of two hundred."

"Why, I think that's a terrible price to ask for it, just awful," exclaimed

Hortense sadly, beginning to remove the coat. She was feeling as though life were depriving her of nearly all that was worth while. "Why, at Biggs and Becks, they have lots of three-quarter mink and beaver coats for that much, and classy styles, too."

"Maybe, maybe. But not that coat," insisted Mr. Rubenstein stubbornly. "Just look at it again. Look at the collar. You mean to say you can find a coat like that up there? If you can, I'll buy the coat for you and sell it to you again for a hundred dollars. Actually, this is a special coat. It's copied from one of the smartest coats that was in New York last summer before the season opened. It has class. You won't find no coat like this coat."

"Oh, well, just the same, a hundred and fifty dollars is more than I can pay," commented Hortense dolefully, at the same time slipping on her old broadcloth jacket with the fur collar and cuffs, and edging toward the door.

"Wait! You like the coat?" wisely observed Mr. Rubenstein, after deciding that even a hundred dollars was too much for her purse, unless it could be supplemented by some man's. "It's really a two-hundred-dollar coat. I'm telling you that straight. Our regular price is one hundred and fifty. But if you could bring me a hundred and twenty-five dollars, since you want it so much, well, I'll let you have it for that. And that's like finding it. A stunning-looking girl like you oughtn't to have no trouble in finding a dozen fellows who would be glad to buy that coat and give it to you. I know I would, if I thought you would be nice to me."

He beamed ingratiatingly up at her, and Hortense, sensing the nature of the overture and resenting it—from him—drew back slightly. At the same time she was not wholly displeased by the compliment involved. But she was not coarse enough, as yet, to feel that just any one should be allowed to give her anything. Indeed not. It must be some one she liked, or at least some one that was enslaved by her.

And yet, even as Mr. Rubenstein spoke, and for some time afterwards, her mind began running upon possible individuals—favorites—who, by the necromancy of her charm for them, might be induced to procure this coat for her. Charlie Wilkens for instance—he of the Orphia cigar store—who was most certainly devoted to her after his fashion, but a fashion, however, which did not suggest that he might do much for her without getting a good deal in return.

And then there was Robert Kain, another youth—very tall, very cheerful and very ambitious in regard to her, who was connected with one of the local electric company's branch offices, but his position was not sufficiently lucrative—a mere entry clerk. Also he was too saving—always talking about his future.

And again, there was Bert Gettler, the youth who had escorted her to the dance the night Clyde first met her, but who was little more than a giddy-headed dancing soul, one not to be relied upon in a crisis like this. He was only a shoe salesman, probably twenty dollars a week, and most careful with his pennies.

But there was Clyde Griffiths, the person who seemed to have real money and to be willing to spend it on her freely. So ran her thoughts swiftly at the time. But could she now, she asked herself, offhand, inveigle him into making such an expensive present as this? She had not favored him so very much—had for the most part treated him indifferently. Hence she was not sure, by any means. Nevertheless as she stood there, debating the cost and the beauty of the coat, the thought of Clyde kept running through her mind. And all the while Mr. Rubenstein stood looking at her, vaguely sensing, after his fashion, the nature of the problem that was confronting her.

"Well, little girl," he finally observed, "I see you'd like to have this coat, all right, and I'd like to have you have it, too. And now I'll tell you what I'll do, and better than that I can't do, and wouldn't for nobody else—not a person in this city. Bring me a hundred and fifteen dollars any time within the next few days—Monday or Wednesday or Friday, if the coat is still here, and you can have it. I'll do even better. I'll save it for you. How's that? Until next Wednesday or Friday. More'n that no one would do for you, now, would they?"

He smiled and shrugged his shoulders and acted as though he were indeed doing her a great favor. And Hortense, going away, felt that if only—only she could take that coat at one hundred and fifteen dollars, she would be capturing a marvelous bargain. Also that she would be the smartest-dressed girl in Kansas City beyond the shadow of a doubt. If only she could in some way get a hundred and fifteen dollars before next Wednesday, or Friday.

15

As HORTENSE well knew Clyde was pressing more and more hungrily toward that ultimate condescension on her part, which, though she would never have admitted it to him, was the privilege of two others. They were never together any more without his insisting upon the real depth of her regard for him. Why was it, if she cared for him the least bit, that she refused to do this, that or the other—would not let him kiss her as much as he wished, would not let him hold her in her arms as much as he would like. She was always keeping dates with other fellows and breaking them or refusing to make them with him. What was her exact relationship toward these others? Did she really care more for them than she did for him? In fact, they were never together anywhere but what this problem of union was uppermost—and but thinly veiled.

And she liked to think that he was suffering from repressed desire for her all of the time; that she tortured him, and that the power to allay his suffering lay wholly in her—a sadistic trait which had for its soil Clyde's own masochistic yearning for her.

However, in the face of her desire for the coat, his stature and interest for her were beginning to increase. In spite of the fact that only the morning before she had informed Clyde, with quite a flourish, that she could not possibly see him until the following Monday—that all her intervening nights were taken—nevertheless, the problem of the coat looming up before her, she now most eagerly planned to contrive an immediate engagement with him without appearing too eager. For by then she had definitely decided to endeavor to persuade him, if possible, to buy the coat for her. Only, of course, she would have to alter her conduct toward him radically. She would have to be much sweeter—more enticing. Although she did not actually say to herself that now she might even be willing to yield herself to him, still basically that was what was in her mind.

For quite a little while she was unable to think how to proceed. How was she to see him this day, or the next at the very latest? How should she go about putting before him the need of this gift, or loan, as she finally worded it to herself? She might hint that he could loan her enough to buy the coat and that later she would pay him back by degrees (yet once in possession of the coat she well knew that that necessity would never confront her). Or, if he did not have so much money on hand at one time, she could suggest that she might arrange with Mr. Rubenstein for a series of time payments which could be met by Clyde. In this connection her mind suddenly turned and began to consider how she could flatter and cajole Mr. Rubenstein into letting her have the coat on easy terms. She recalled that he had said he would be glad to buy the coat for her if he thought she would be nice to him.

Her first scheme in connection with all this was to suggest to Louise Ratterer to invite her brother, Clyde and a third youth by the name of Scull, who was dancing attendance upon Louise, to come to a certain dance hall that very evening to which she was already planning to go with the more favored cigar clerk. Only now she intended to break that engagement and appear alone with Louise and Greta and announce that her proposed partner was ill. That would give her an opportunity to leave early with Clyde and with him walk past the Rubenstein store.

But having the temperament of a spider that spins a web for flies, she foresaw that this might involve the possibility of Louise's explaining to Clyde or Ratterer that it was Hortense who had instigated the party. It might even bring up some accidental mention of the coat on the part of Clyde to Louise later, which, as she felt, would never do. She did not care to let her friends know how she provided for herself. In consequence, she decided that it would not do for her to appeal to Louise nor to Greta in this fashion.

And she was actually beginning to worry as to how to bring about this encounter, when Clyde, who chanced to be in the vicinity on his way home from work, walked into the store where she was working. He was seeking for a date on the following Sunday. And to his intense delight, Hortense greeted him most cordially with a most engaging smile and a wave of the hand. She was busy at the moment with a customer. She soon finished, however, and drawing near, and keeping one eye on her floor-walker who resented callers, exclaimed: "I was just thinking about you. You wasn't thinking about me, was you? Trade last." Then she added, sotto voce, "Don't act like you are talking to me. I see our floor-walker over there."

Arrested by the unusual sweetness in her voice, to say nothing of the warm smile with which she greeted him, Clyde was enlivened and heartened at once. "Was I thinking of you?" he returned gayly. "Do I ever think of any one else? Say! Ratterer says I've got you on the brain."

"Oh, him," replied Hortense, pouting spitefully and scornfully, for Ratterer, strangely enough, was one whom she did not interest very much, and this she knew. "He thinks he's so smart," she added. "I know a lotta girls don't like him."

"Oh, Tom's all right," pleaded Clyde, loyally. "That's just his way of talking. He likes you."

"Oh, no, he don't, either," replied Hortense. "But I don't want to talk about him. Whatcha doin' around six o'clock tonight?"

"Oh, gee!" exclaimed Clyde disappointedly. "You don't mean to say you got to-night free, have you? Well, ain't that tough? I thought you were all dated up. I got to work!" He actually sighed, so depressed was he by the thought that she might be willing to spend the evening with him and he not able to avail himself of the opportunity, while Hortense, noting his intense disappointment, was pleased.

"Well, I gotta date, but I don't want to keep it," she went on with a contemptuous gathering of the lips. "I don't have to break it. I would though if you was free." Clyde's heart began to beat rapidly with delight.

"Gee, I wish I didn't have to work now," he went on, looking at her. "You're sure you couldn't make it to-morrow night? I'm off then. And I was just coming up here to ask you if you didn't want to go for an automobile ride next Sunday afternoon, maybe. A friend of Hegglund's got a car—a Packard —and Sunday we're all off. And he wanted me to get a bunch to run out to Excelsior Springs. He's a nice fellow" (this because Hortense showed signs of not being so very much interested). "You don't know him very well, but he is. But say, I can talk to you about that later. How about to-morrow night? I'm off then."

Hortense, who, because of the hovering floor-walker, was pretending to show Clyde some handkerchiefs, was now thinking how unfortunate that a whole twenty-four hours must intervene before she could bring him to view the coat with her—and so have an opportunity to begin her machinations. At the same time she pretended that the proposed meeting for the next night was a very difficult thing to bring about—more difficult than he could possibly appreciate. She even pretended to be somewhat uncertain as to whether she wanted to do it.

"Just pretend you're examining these handkerchiefs here," she continued, fearing the floor-walker might interrupt. "I gotta nother date for then," she continued thoughtfully, "and I don't know whether I can break it or not. Let me see." She feigned deep thought. "Well, I guess I can," she said finally. "I'll try, anyhow. Just for this once. You be here at Fifteenth and Main at 6.15— no, 6.30's the best you can do, ain't it?—and I'll see if I can't get there. I won't promise, but I'll see and I think I can make it. Is that all right?" She gave him one of her sweetest smiles and Clyde was quite beside himself with satisfaction. To think that she would break a date for him, at last. Her eyes were warm with favor and her mouth wreathed with a smile.

"Surest thing you know," he exclaimed, voicing the slang of the hotel boys. "You bet I'll be there. Will you do me a favor?"

"What is it?" she asked cautiously.

"Wear that little black hat with the red ribbon under your chin, will you? You look so cute in that."

"Oh, you," she laughed. It was so easy to kid Clyde. "Yes, I'll wear it," she added. "But you gotta go now. Here comes that old fish. I know he's going to kick. But I don't care. Six-thirty, eh? So long." She turned to give her attention to a new customer, an old lady who had been patiently waiting to inquire if she could tell her where the muslins were sold. And Clyde, tingling with pleasure because of this unexpected delight vouchsafed him, made his way most elatedly to the nearest exit.

He was not made unduly curious because of this sudden favor, and the next evening, promptly at six-thirty, and in the glow of the overhanging arc-lights showering their glistening radiance like rain, she appeared. As he noted, at once, she had worn the hat he liked. Also she was enticingly ebullient and friendly, more so than at any time he had known her. Before he had time to say that she looked pretty, or how pleased he was because she wore that hat, she began:

"Some favorite you're gettin' to be, *I'll say*, when *I'll* break an engagement and then wear an old hat I don't like just to please you. How do I get that way is what I'd like to know."

He beamed as though he had won a great victory. Could it be that at last he might be becoming a favorite with her?

"If you only knew how cute you look in that hat, Hortense, you wouldn't knock it," he urged admiringly. "You don't know how sweet you do look."

"Oh, ho. In this old thing?" she scoffed. "You certainly are easily pleased, I'll say."

"An' your eyes are just like soft, black velvet," he persisted eagerly. "They're wonderful." He was thinking of an alcove in the Green-Davidson hung with black velvet.

"Gee, you certainly have got 'em to-night," she laughed teasingly. "I'll have to do something about you." Then, before he could make any reply to this, she went off into an entirely fictional account of how, having had a previous engagement with a certain alleged young society man—Tom Keary by name—who was dogging her steps these days in order to get her to dine and dance, she had only this evening decided to "ditch" him, preferring Clyde, of course, for this occasion, anyhow. And she had called Keary up and told him that she could not see him to-night—called it all off, as it were. But just the same, on coming out of the employee's entrance, who should she see there waiting for her but this same Tom Keary, dressed to perfection in a bright gray raglan and spats, and with his closed sedan, too. And he would have taken her to the Green-Davidson, if she had wanted to go. He was a real sport. But she didn't. Not to-night, anyhow. Yet, if she had not contrived to avoid him, he would have delayed her. But she espied him first and ran the other way.

"And you should have just seen my little feet twinkle up Sargent and around the corner into Bailey Place," was the way she narcistically painted her flight. And so infatuated was Clyde by this picture of herself and the wonderful Keary that he accepted all of her petty fabrications as truth.

And then, as they were walking in the direction of Gaspie's, a restaurant in Wyandotte near Tenth which quite lately he had learned was much better than Frissell's, Hortense took occasion to pause and look in a number of windows, saying as she did so that she certainly did wish that she could find a little coat that was becoming to her—that the one she had on was getting worn and that she must have another soon—a predicament which caused Clyde to wonder at the time whether she was suggesting to him that he get her one. Also whether it might not advance his cause with her if he were to buy her a little jacket, since she needed it.

But Rubenstein's coming into view on this same side of the street, its display window properly illuminated and the coat in full view, Hortense paused as she had planned.

"Oh, do look at that darling little coat there," she began, ecstatically, as though freshly arrested by the beauty of it, her whole manner suggesting a first and unspoiled impression. "Oh, isn't that the dearest, sweetest, cutest little thing you ever did see?" she went on, her histrionic powers growing with her desire for it. "Oh, just look at the collar, and those sleeves and those pockets. Aren't they the snappiest things you ever saw? Couldn't I just warm my little hands in those?" She glanced at Clyde out of the tail of her eye to see if he was being properly impressed.

And he, aroused by her intense interest, surveyed the coat with not a little curiosity. Unquestionably it was a pretty coat—very. But, gee, what would a coat like that cost, anyhow? Could it be that she was trying to interest him in the merits of a coat like that in order that he might get it for her? Why, it must be a two-hundred-dollar coat at least. He had no idea as to the value of such things, anyhow. He certainly couldn't afford a coat like that. And especially at this time when his mother was taking a good portion of his extra cash for Esta. And yet something in her manner seemed to bring it to him that that was exactly what she was thinking. It chilled and almost numbed him at first.

And yet, as he now told himself sadly, if Hortense wanted it, she could most certainly find some one who would get it for her—that young Tom Keary, for instance, whom she had just been describing. And, worse luck, she was just that kind of a girl. And if he could not get it for her, some one else could and she would despise him for not being able to do such things for her.

To his intense dismay and dissatisfaction she exclaimed: "Oh, what wouldn't I give for a coat like that!" She had not intended at the moment to put the matter so bluntly, for she wanted to convey the thought that was deepest in her mind to Clyde tactfully.

And Clyde, inexperienced as he was, and not subtle by any means, was nevertheless quite able to gather the meaning of that. It meant—it meant—for the moment he was not quite willing to formulate to himself what it did mean. And now—now—if only he had the price of that coat. He could feel that she was thinking of some one certain way to get the coat. And yet how was he to manage it? How? If he could only arrange to get this coat for her—if he only could promise her that he would get it for her by a certain date, say, if it didn't cost too much, then what? Did he have the courage to suggest to her to-night, or to-morrow, say, after he had learned the price of the coat, that if she would—why then—why then, well, he would get her the coat or anything else she really wanted. Only he must be sure that she was not really fooling him as she was always doing in smaller ways. He wouldn't stand for getting her the coat and then get nothing in return—never!

As he thought of it, he actually thrilled and trembled beside her. And she, standing there and looking at the coat, was thinking that unless he had sense enough now to get her this thing and to get what she meant—how she intended to pay for it—well then, this was the last. He need not think she was going to fool around with any one who couldn't or wouldn't do that much for her. Never.

They resumed their walk toward Gaspie's. And throughout the dinner, she talked of little else—how attractive the coat was, how wonderful it would look on her.

"Believe me," she said at one point, defiantly, feeling that Clyde was perhaps uncertain at the moment about his ability to buy it for her, "I'm going to find some way to get that coat. I think, maybe, that Rubenstein store would let me have it on time if I were to go in there and see him about it, make a big enough payment down. Another girl out of our store got a coat that way once," she lied promptly, hoping thus to induce Clyde to assist her with it. But Clyde, disturbed by the fear of some extraordinary cost in connection with it, hesitated to say just what he would do. He could not even guess the price of such a thing—it might cost two or three hundred, even—and he feared to obligate himself to do something which later he might not be able to do.

"You don't know what they might want for that, do you?" he asked, nervously, at the same time thinking if he made any cash gift to her at this time without some guarantee on her part, what right would he have to expect anything more in return than he had ever received? He knew how she cajoled him into getting things for her and then would not even let him kiss her. He flushed and churned a little internally with resentment at the thought of how she seemed to feel that she could play fast and loose with him. And yet, as he now recalled, she had just said she would do anything for any one who would get that coat for her—or nearly that.

"No-o," she hesitated at first, for the moment troubled as to whether to give the exact price or something higher. For if she asked for time, Mr. Rubenstein might want more. And yet if she said much more, Clyde might not want to help her. "But I know it wouldn't be more than a hundred and twenty-five. I wouldn't pay more than that for it."

Clyde heaved a sigh of relief. After all, it wasn't two or three hundred. He began to think now that if she could arrange to make any reasonable down payment—say, fifty or sixty dollars—he might manage to bring it together within the next two or three weeks anyhow. But if the whole hundred and twenty-five were demanded at once, Hortense would have to wait, and besides he would have to know whether he was to be rewarded or not—definitely.

"That's a good idea, Hortense," he exclaimed without, however, indicating in any way why it appealed to him so much. "Why don't you do that? Why don't you find out first what they want for it, and how much they want down? Maybe I could help you with it."

"Oh, won't that be just too wonderful!" Hortense clapped her hands. "Oh, will you? Oh, won't that be just dandy? Now I just know I can get that coat. I just know they'll let me have it, if I talk to them right."

She was, as Clyde saw and feared, quite forgetting the fact that he was the one who was making the coat possible, and now it would be just as he thought. The fact that he was paying for it would be taken for granted.

But a moment later, observing his glum face, she added: "Oh, aren't you the sweetest, dearest thing, to help me in this way. You just bet I won't forget this either. You just wait and see. You won't be sorry. Now you just wait." Her eyes fairly snapped with gayety and even generosity toward him.

He might be easy and young, but he wasn't mean, and she would reward him, too, she now decided. Just as soon as she got the coat, which must be in a week or two at the latest, she was going to be very nice to him—do something for him. And to emphasize her own thoughts and convey to him what she really meant, she allowed her eyes to grow soft and swimming and to dwell on him promisingly—a bit of romantic acting which caused him to become weak and nervous. The gusto of her favor frightened him even a little, for it suggested, as he fancied, a disturbing vitality which he might not be able to match. He felt a little weak before her now—a little cowardly—in the face of what he assumed her real affection might mean.

Nevertheless, he now announced that if the coat did not cost more than one hundred and twenty-five dollars, that sum to be broken into one payment of twenty-five dollars down and two additional sums of fifty dollars each, he could manage it. And she on her part replied that she was going the very next day to see about it. Mr. Rubenstein might be induced to let her have it at once on the payment of twenty-five dollars down; if not that, then at the end of the second week, when nearly all would be paid.

And then in real gratitude to Clyde she whispered to him, coming out of the restaurant and purring like a cat, that she would never forget this and that he would see—and that she would wear it for him the very first time. If he were not working they might go somewhere to dinner. Or, if not that, then she would have it surely in time for the day of the proposed automobile ride which he, or rather Hegglund, had suggested for the following Sunday, but which might be postponed.

She suggested that they go to a certain dance hall, and there she clung to him in the dances in a suggestive way and afterwards hinted of a mood which made Clyde a little quivery and erratic.

He finally went home, dreaming of the day, satisfied that he would have no trouble in bringing together the first payment, if it were so much as fifty, even. For now, under the spur of this promise, he proposed to borrow as much as twenty-five from either Ratterer or Hegglund, and to repay it after the coat was paid for.

But, ah, the beautiful Hortense. The charm of her, the enormous, compelling, weakening delight. And to think that at last, and soon, she was to be his. It was, plainly, of such stuff as dreams are made of—the unbelievable become real.

16

TRUE TO HER promise, the following day Hortense returned to Mr. Rubenstein, and with all the cunning of her nature placed before him, with many reservations, the nature of the dilemma which confronted her. Could she, by any chance, have the coat for one hundred and fifteen dollars on an easy payment plan? Mr. Rubenstein's head forthwith began to wag a solemn negative. This was not an easy payment store. If he wanted to do business that way he could charge two hundred for the coat and easily get it.

"But I could pay as much as fifty dollars when I took the coat," argued Hortense.

"Very good. But who is to guarantee that I get the other sixty-five, and when?"

"Next week twenty-five, and the week after that twenty-five and the week after that fifteen."

"Of course. But supposin' the next day after you take the coat an automobile runs you down and kills you. Then what? How do I get my money?"

Now that was a poser. And there was really no way that she could prove that any one would pay for the coat. And before that there would have to be all the bother of making out a contract, and getting some really responsible person—a banker, say—to endorse it. No, no, this was not an easy payment house. This was a cash house. That was why the coat was offered to her at one hundred and fifteen, but not a dollar less. Not a dollar.

Mr. Rubenstein sighed and talked on. And finally Hortense asked him if she could give him seventy-five dollars cash in hand, the other forty to be paid in one week's time. Would he let her have the coat then—to take home with her?

"But a week—a week—what is a week then?" argued Mr. Rubenstein. "If you can bring me seventy-five next week or tomorrow, and forty more in another week or ten days, why not wait a week and bring the whole hundred and fifteen? Then the coat is yours and no bother. Leave the coat. Come back to-morrow and pay me twenty-five or thirty dollars on account and I take the coat out of the window and lock it up for you. No one can even see it then. In another week bring me the balance or in two weeks. Then it is yours." Mr. Rubenstein explained the process as though it were a difficult matter to grasp.

But the argument once made was sound enough. It really left Hortense little to argue about. At the same time it reduced her spirit not a little. To think of not being able to take it now. And yet, once out of the place, her vigor revived. For, after all, the time fixed would soon pass and if Clyde performed his part of the agreement promptly, the coat would be hers. The important thing now was to make him give her twenty-five or thirty dollars wherewith to bind this wonderful agreement. Only now, because of the fact that she felt that she needed a new hat to go with the coat, she decided to say that it cost one hundred and twenty-five instead of one hundred and fifteen.

And once this conclusion was put before Clyde, he saw it as a very reasonable arrangement—all things considered—quite a respite from the feeling of strain that had settled upon him after his last conversation with Hortense. For, after all, he had not seen how he was to raise more than thirty-five dollars this first week anyhow. The following week would be somewhat easier, for then, as he told himself, he proposed to borrow twenty or twenty-five from Ratterer if he could, which, joined with the twenty or twenty-five which his tips would bring him, would be quite sufficient to meet the second payment. The week following he proposed to borrow at least ten or fifteen from Hegglund—maybe more—and if that did not make up the required amount to pawn his watch for fifteen dollars, the watch he had bought for himself a few months before. It ought to bring that at least; it cost fifty.

But, he now thought, there was Esta in her wretched room awaiting the most unhappy result of her one romance. How was she to make out, he asked himself, even in the face of the fact that he feared to be included in the financial problem which Esta as well as the family presented. His father was not now, and never had been, of any real financial service to his mother. And yet, if the problem were on this account to be shifted to him, how would he make out? Why need his father always peddle clocks and rugs and preach on the streets? Why couldn't his mother and father give up the mission idea, anyhow?

But, as he knew, the situation was not to be solved without his aid. And the proof of it came toward the end of the second week of his arrangement with Hortense, when, with fifty dollars in his pocket, which he was planning to turn over to her on the following Sunday, his mother, looking into his bedroom where he was dressing, said: "I'd like to see you for a minute, Clyde, before you go out." He noted she was very grave as she said this. As a matter of fact, for several days past, he had been sensing that she was undergoing a strain of some kind. At the same time he had been thinking all this while that with his own resources hypothecated as they were, he could do nothing. Or, if he did it meant the loss of Hortense. He dared not.

And yet what reasonable excuse could he give his mother for not helping her a little, considering especially the clothes he wore, and the manner in which he had been running here and there, always giving the excuse of working, but probably not deceiving her as much as he thought. To be sure, only two months before, he had obligated himself to pay her ten dollars a week more for five weeks, and had. But that only proved to her very likely that he had so much extra to give, even though he had tried to make it clear at the time that he was pinching himself to do it. And yet, however much he chose to waver in her favor, he could not, with his desire for Hortense directly confronting him.

He went out into the living-room after a time, and as usual his mother at once led the way to one of the benches in the mission—a cheerless, cold room these days.

"I didn't think I'd have to speak to you about this, Clyde, but I don't see any other way out of it. I haven't any one but you to depend upon now that you're getting to be a man. But you must promise not to tell any of the others—Frank or Julia or your father. I don't want them to know. But

Esta's back here in Kansas City and in trouble, and I don't know quite what to do about her. I have so very little money to do with, and your father's not very much of a help to me any more."

She passed a weary, reflective hand across her forehead and Clyde knew what was coming. His first thought was to pretend that he did not know that Esta was in the city, since he had been pretending this way for so long. But now, suddenly, in the face of his mother's confession and the need of pretended surprise on his part, if he were to keep up the fiction, he said, "Yes, I know."

"You know?" queried his mother, surprised.

"Yes, I know," Clyde repeated. "I saw you going in that house in Beaudry Street one morning as I was going along there," he announced calmly enough now. "And I saw Esta looking out of the window afterwards, too. So I went in after you left."

"How long ago was that?" she asked, more to gain time than anything else.

"Oh, about five or six weeks ago, I think. I been around to see her a coupla times since then, only Esta didn't want me to say anything about that either."

"Tst! Tst! Tst!" clicked Mrs. Griffiths, with her tongue. "Then you know what the trouble is."

"Yes," replied Clyde.

"Well, what is to be will be," she said resignedly. "You haven't mentioned it to Frank or Julia, have you?"

"No," replied Clyde, thoughtfully, thinking of what a failure his mother had made of attempt to be secretive. She was no one to deceive any one, or his father, either. He thought himself far, far shrewder.

"Well, you mustn't," cautioned his mother solemnly. "It isn't best for them to know, I think. It's bad enough as it is this way," she added with a kind of wry twist to her mouth, the while Clyde thought of himself and Hortense.

"And to think," she added, after a moment, her eyes filling with a sad, all-enveloping gray mist, "she should have brought all this on herself and on us. And when we have so little to do with, as it is. And after all the instruction she has had—the training. 'The way of the transgressor——' "

She shook her head and put her two large hands together and gripped them firmly, while Clyde stared, thinking of the situation and all that it might mean to him.

She sat there, quite reduced and bewildered by her own peculiar part in all this. She had been as deceiving as any one, really. And here was Clyde, now, fully informed as to her falsehoods and strategy, and herself looking foolish and untrue. But had she not been trying to save him from all this—him and the others? And he was old enough to understand that now. Yet she now proceeded to explain why, and to say how dreadful she felt it all to be. At the same time, as she also explained, now she was compelled to come to him for aid in connection with it.

"Esta's about to be very sick," she went on suddenly and stiffly, not being able, or at least willing, apparently, to look at Clyde as she said it, and yet determined to be as frank as possible. "She'll need a doctor very shortly and some one to be with her all the time when I'm not there. I must get money somewhere—at least fifty dollars. You couldn't get me that much in some way, from some of your young men friends, could you, just a loan for a few weeks? You could pay it back, you know, soon, if you would. You wouldn't need to pay me anything for your room until you had."

She looked at Clyde so tensely, so urgently, that he felt quite shaken by the force and the cogency of the request. And before he could add anything to the nervous gloom which shadowed her face, she added: "That other money was for her, you know, to bring her back here after her—her"—she hesitated over the appropriate word but finally added—"husband left her there in Pittsburgh. I suppose she told you that."

"Yes, she did," replied Clyde, heavily and sadly. For after all, Esta's condition was plainly critical, which was something that he had not stopped to meditate on before.

"Gee, Ma," he exclaimed, the thought of the fifty dollars in his pocket and its intended destination troubling him considerably—the very sum his mother was seeking. "I don't know whether I can do that or not. I don't know any of the boys down there well enough for that. And they don't make any more than I do, either. I might borrow a little something, but it won't look very good." He choked and swallowed a little, for lying to his mother in this way was not easy. In fact, he had never had occasion to lie in connection with anything so trying—and so despicably. For here was fifty dollars in his pocket at the moment, with Hortense on the one hand and his mother and sister on the other, and the money would solve his mother's problem as fully as it would Hortense's, and more respectably. How terrible it was not to help her. How could he refuse her, really? Nervously he licked his lips and passed a hand over his brow, for a nervous moisture had broken out upon his face. He felt strained and mean and incompetent under the circumstances.

"And you haven't any money of your own right now that you could let me have, have you?" his mother half pleaded. For there were a number of things in connection with Esta's condition which required immediate cash and she had so little.

"No, I haven't, Ma," he said, looking at his mother shamefacedly, for a moment, then away, and if it had not been that she herself was so distrait, she might have seen the falsehood on his face. As it was, he suffered a pang of commingled self-commiseration and self-contempt, based on the distress he felt for his mother. He could not bring himself to think of losing Hortense. He must have her. And yet his mother looked so lone and so resourceless. It was shameful. He was low, really mean. Might he not, later, be punished for a thing like this?

He tried to think of some other way—some way of getting a little money over and above the fifty that might help. If only he had a little more time —a few weeks longer. If only Hortense had not brought up this coat idea just now.

"I'll tell you what I might do," he went on, quite foolishly and dully the while his mother gave vent to a helpless "Tst! Tst! Tst!" "Will five dollars do you any good?"

"Well, it will be something, anyhow," she replied. "I can use it."

"Well, I can let you have that much," he said, thinking to replace it out of his next week's tips and trust to better luck throughout the week. "And I'll see what I can do next week. I might let you have ten then. I can't say for sure. I had to borrow some of that other money I gave you, and I haven't got through paying for that yet, and if I come around trying to get more, they'll think—well, you know how it is."

His mother sighed, thinking of the misery of having to fall back on her one son thus far. And just when he was trying to get a start, too. What would he think of all this in after years? What would he think of her—of Esta—the family? For, for all his ambition and courage and desire to be out and doing, Clyde always struck her as one who was not any too powerful physically or rock-ribbed morally or mentally. So far as his nerves and emotions were concerned, at times he seemed to take after his father more than he did after her. And for the most part it was so easy to excite him—to cause him to show tenseness and strain—as though he were not so very well fitted for either. And it was she, because of Esta and her husband and their joint and unfortunate lives, that was and had been heaping the greater part of this strain on him.

"Well, if you can't, you can't," she said. "I must try and think of some other way." But she saw no clear way at the moment.

17

IN CONNECTION with the automobile ride suggested and arranged for the following Sunday by Hegglund through his chauffeur friend, a change of plan was announced. The car—an expensive Packard, no less—could not be had for that day, but must be used by this Thursday or Friday, or not at all. For, as had been previously explained to all, but not with the strictest adherence to the truth, the car belonged to a certain Mr. Kimbark, an elderly and very wealthy man who at the time was traveling in Asia. Also, what was not true was that this particular youth was not Mr. Kimbark's chauffeur at all, but rather the rakish, ne'er-do-well son of Sparser, the superintendent of one of Mr. Kimbark's stock farms. This son being anxious to pose as something more than the son of a superintendent of a farm, and as an occasional watchman, having access to the cars, had decided to take the very finest of them and ride in it.

It was Hegglund who proposed that he and his hotel friends be included on some interesting trip. But since the general invitation had been given, word had come that within the next few weeks Mr. Kimbark was likely to return. And because of this, Willard Sparser had decided at once that it might be best not to use the car any more. He might be taken unawares, perhaps, by Mr. Kimbark's unexpected arrival. Laying this difficulty before Hegglund, who was eager for the trip, the latter had scouted the idea. Why not use it once more anyhow? He had stirred up the interest of all of his friends in this and now hated to disappoint them. The following Friday, between noon and six o'clock, was fixed upon as the day. And since Hortense had changed in her plans she now decided to accompany Clyde, who had been invited, of course.

But as Hegglund had explained to Ratterer and Higby since it was being used without the owner's consent, they must meet rather far out—the men in one of the quiet streets near Seventeenth and West Prospect, from which point they could proceed to a meeting place more convenient for the girls, namely, Twentieth and Washington. From thence they would speed via the west Parkway and the Hannibal Bridge north and east to Harlem, North Kansas City, Minaville and so through Liberty and Moseby to Excelsior Springs. Their chief objective there was a little inn—the Wigwam—a mile or two this side of Excelsior which was open the year round. It was really a combination of restaurant and dancing parlor and hotel. A Victrola and Wurlitzer player-piano furnished the necessary music. Such groups as this were not infrequent, and Hegglund as well as Higby, who had been there on several occasions, described it as dandy. The food was good and the road to it excellent. There was a little river just below it where in the summer time at least there was rowing and fishing. In winter some people skated when there was ice. To be sure, at this time—January—the road was heavily packed with snow, but easy to get over, and the scenery fine. There was a little lake not so far from Excelsior, at this time of year also frozen over, and according to Hegglund, who was always unduly imaginative and high-spirited, they might go there and skate.

"Will you listen to who's talkin' about skatin' on a trip like this?" commented Ratterer, rather cynically, for to his way of thinking this was no occasion for any such side athletics, but for love-making exclusively.

"Aw, hell, can't a fellow have a funny idea even without bein' roasted for it?" retorted the author of the idea.

The only one, apart from Sparser, who suffered any qualms in connection with all this was Clyde himself. For to him, from the first, the fact that the car to be used did not belong to Sparser, but to his employer, was disturbing, almost irritatingly so. He did not like the idea of taking anything that belonged to any one else, even for temporary use. Something might happen. They might be found out.

"Don't you think it's dangerous for us to be going out in this car?" he asked of Ratterer a few days before the trip and when he fully understood the nature of the source of the car.

"Oh, I don't know," replied Ratterer, who being accustomed to such ideas and devices as this was not much disturbed by them. "I'm not taking the car and you're not, are you? If he wants to take it, that's his lookout, ain't it? If he wants me to go, I'll go. Why wouldn't I? All I want is to be brought back here on time. That's the only thing that would ever worry me."

And Higby, coming up at the moment, had voiced exactly the same sentiments. Yet Clyde remained troubled. It might not work out right; he might lose his job through a thing like this. But so fascinated was he by the thought of riding in such a fine car with Hortense and with all these other girls and boys that he could not resist the temptation to go.

Immediately after noon on the Friday of this particular week the several participants of the outing were gathered at the points agreed upon. Hegglund, Ratterer, Higby and Clyde at Eighteenth and West Prospect near the railroad yards. Maida Axelrod, Hegglund's girl, Lucille Nickolas, a friend of Ratterer's, and Tina Kogel, a friend of Higby's, also Laura Sipe, another girl who was brought by Tina Kogel to be introduced to Sparser for the occasion, at Twentieth and Washington. Only since Hortense had sent word at the last moment to Clyde that she had to go out to her house for something, and that they were to run out to Forty-ninth and Genesee, where she lived, they did so, but not without grumbling.

The day, a late January one, was inclined to be smoky with lowering clouds, especially within the environs of Kansas City. It even threatened snow at times—a most interesting and picturesque prospect to those within. They liked it.

"Oh, gee, I hope it does," Tina Kogel exclaimed when some one commented on the possibility, and Lucille Nickolas added: "Oh, I just love to see it snow at times." Along the West Bluff Road, Washington and Second Streets, they finally made their way across the Hannibal Bridge to Harlem, and from thence along the winding and hill-sentineled river road to Randolph Heights and Minaville. And beyond that came Moseby and Liberty, to and through which the road bed was better, with interesting glimpses of small homesteads and the bleak snow-covered hills of January.

Clyde, who for all his years in Kansas City had never ventured much beyond Kansas City, Kansas, on the west or the primitive and natural woods of Swope Parks on the east, nor farther along the Kansas or Missouri Rivers than Argentine on the one side and Randolph Heights on the other, was quite fascinated by the idea of travel which appeared to be suggested by all this—distant travel. It was all so different from his ordinary routine. And on this occasion Hortense was inclined to be very genial and friendly. She snuggled down beside him on the seat, and when he, noting that the others had already drawn their girls to them in affectionate embraces, put his arm about her and drew her to him, she made no particular protest. Instead she looked up and said: "I'll have to take my hat off, I guess." The others laughed. There was something about her quick, crisp way which was amusing at times. Besides she had done her hair in a new way which made her look decidedly prettier, and she was anxious to have the others see it.

"Can we dance anywhere out here?" she called to the others, without looking around.

"Surest thing you know," said Higby, who by now had persuaded Tina Kogel to take her hat off and was holding her close. "They got a player-piano and a Victrola out there. If I'd 'a' thought, I'd 'a' brought my cornet. I can play Dixie on that."

The car was speeding at breakneck pace over a snowy white road and between white fields. In fact, Sparser, considering himself a master of car manipulation as well as the real owner of it for the moment, was attempting to see how fast he could go on such a road.

Dark vignettes of woods went by to right and left. Fields away, sentinel hills rose and fell like waves. A wide-armed scarecrow fluttering in the wind, its tall decayed hat awry, stood near at hand in one place. And from near it a flock of crows rose and winged direct toward a distant wood lightly penciled against a foreground of snow.

In the front seat sat Sparser, guiding the car beside Laura Sipe with the air of one to whom such a magnificent car was a commonplace thing. He was really more interested in Hortense, yet felt it incumbent on him, for the time being, anyhow, to show some attention to Laura Sipe. And not to be outdone in gallantry by the others, he now put one arm about Laura Sipe while he guided the car with the other, a feat which troubled Clyde, who was still dubious about the wisdom of taking the car at all. They might all be wrecked by such fast driving. Hortense was only interested by the fact that Sparser had obviously manifested his interest in her; that he had to pay some attention to Laura Sipe whether he wanted to or not. And when she saw him pull her to him and asked her grandly if she had done much automobiling about Kansas City, she merely smiled to herself.

But Ratterer, noting the move, nudged Lucille Nickolas, and she in turn nudged Higby, in order to attract his attention to the affectional development ahead.

"Getting comfortable up front there, Willard?" called Ratterer, genially, in order to make friends with him.

"I'll say I am," replied Sparser, gayly and without turning. "How about you, girlie?"

"Oh, I'm all right," Laura Sipe replied.

But Clyde was thinking that of all the girls present none was really so pretty as Hortense—not nearly. She had come garbed in a red and black dress with a very dark red poke bonnet to match. And on her left cheek, just below her small rouged mouth, she had pasted a minute square of black court plaster in imitation of some picture beauty she had seen. In fact, before the outing began, she had been determined to outshine all the others present, and distinctly she was now feeling that she was succeeding. And Clyde, for himself, was agreeing with her.

"You're the cutest thing here," whispered Clyde, hugging her fondly.

"Gee, but you can pour on the molasses, kid, when you want to," she called out loud, and the others laughed. And Clyde flushed slightly.

Beyond Minaville about six miles the car came to a bend in a hollow where there was a country store and here Hegglund, Higby and Ratterer got out to fetch candy, cigarettes and ice cream cones and ginger ale. And after that came Liberty, and then several miles this side of Excelsior Springs, they sighted the Wigwam which was nothing more than an old two-story farmhouse snuggled against a rise of ground behind it. There was, however, adjoining it on one side a newer and larger one-story addition consisting of the dining-room, the dance floor, and concealed by a partition at one end, a bar. An open fire flickered cheerfully here in a large fireplace. Down in a hollow across the road might be seen the Benton River or creek, now frozen solid.

"There's your river," called Higby cheerfully as he helped Tina Kogel out of the car, for he was already very much warmed by several drinks he had taken en route. They all paused for a moment to admire the stream, winding away among the trees. "I wanted dis bunch to bring dere skates and go down dere," sighed Hegglund, "but dey wouldn't. Well, dat's all right."

By then Lucille Nickolas, seeing a flicker of flame reflected in one of the small windows of the inn, called, "Oh, see, they gotta fire."

The car was parked, and they all trooped into the inn, and at once Higby briskly went over and started the large, noisy, clattery, tinny Nickelodeon with a nickel. And to rival him, and for a prank, Hegglund ran to the Victrola which stood in one corner and put on a record of "The Grizzly Bear," which he found lying there.

At the first sounds of this strain, which they all knew, Tina Kogel called: "Oh, let's all dance to that, will you? Can't you stop that other old thing?" she added.

"Sure, after it runs down," explained Ratterer, laughingly. "The only way to stop that thing is not to feed it any nickels."

But now a waiter coming in, Higby began to inquire what everybody wanted. And in the meantime, to show off her charms, Hortense had taken the center of the floor and was attempting to imitate a grizzly bear walking on its hind legs, which she could do amusingly enough—quite gracefully. And Sparser, seeing her alone in the center of the floor and anxious to interest her now, followed her and tried to imitate her motions from behind. Finding him clever at it, and anxious to dance, she finally abandoned the imitation and giving him her arms went one-stepping about the room most vividly. At once, Clyde, who was by no means as good a dancer, became jealous—painfully so. In his eagerness for her, it seemed unfair to him that he should be deserted by her so early—at the very beginning of things. But she, becoming interested in Sparser, who seemed more worldly-wise, paid no attention at all to Clyde for the time being, but went dancing with her new conquest, his rhythmic skill seeming charmingly to match her own. And then, not to be out of it, the others at once chose partners, Hegglund dancing with Maida, Ratterer with Lucille and Higby with Tina Kogel. This left Laura Sipe for Clyde, who did not like her very much. She was not as perfect as she might be—a plump, pudgy-faced girl with inadequate sensual blue eyes —and Clyde, lacking any exceptional skill, they danced nothing but the conventional one-step while the others were dipping and lurching and spinning.

In a kind of sick fury, Clyde noticed that Sparser, who was still with Hortense, was by now holding her close and looking straight into her eyes. And she was permitting him. It gave him a feeling of lead at the pit of his stomach. Was it possible she was beginning to like this young upstart who had this car? And she had promised to like him for the present. It brought to him a sense of her fickleness—the probability of her real indifference to him. He wanted to do something—stop dancing and get her away from Sparser, but there was no use until this particular record ran out.

And then, just at the end of this, the waiter returned with a tray and put down cocktails, ginger ale and sandwiches upon three small tables which had been joined together. All but Sparser and Hortense quit and came toward it—a fact which Clyde was quick to note. She was a heartless flirt! She really did not care for him after all. And after making him think that she did, so recently—and getting him to help her with that coat. She could go to the devil now. He would show her. And he waiting for her! Wasn't that the limit? Yet, finally, seeing that the others were gathering about the tables, which had been placed near the fire, Hortense and Sparser ceased dancing and approached. Clyde was white and glum. He stood to one side, seemingly indifferent. And Laura Sipe, who had already noted his rage and understood the reason now moved away from him to join Tina Kogel, to whom she explained why he was so angry.

And then noting his glumness, Hortense came over, executing a phase of the "Grizzly" as she did so.

"Gee, wasn't that swell?" she began. "Gee, how I do love to dance to music like that!"

"Sure, it's swell for you," returned Clyde, burning with envy and disappointment.

"Why, what's the trouble?" she asked, in a low and almost injured tone, pretending not to guess, yet knowing quite well why he was angry. "You don't mean to say that you're mad because I danced with him first, do you? Oh, how silly! Why didn't you come over then and dance with me? I couldn't refuse to dance with him when he was right there, could I?"

"Oh, no, of course, you couldn't," replied Clyde sarcastically, and in a low, tense tone, for he, no more than Hortense, wanted the others to hear. "But you didn't have to fall all over him and dream in his eyes, either, did you?" He was fairly blazing. "You needn't say you didn't, because I saw you."

At this she glanced at him oddly, realizing not only the sharpness of his mood, but that this was the first time he had shown so much daring in connection with her. It must be that he was getting to feel too sure of her. She was showing him too much attention. At the same time she realized that this was not the time to show him that she did not care for him as much as she would like to have him believe, since she wanted the coat, already agreed upon.

"Oh, gee, well, ain't that the limit?" she replied angrily, yet more because she was irritated by the fact that what he said was true than anything else. "If you aren't the grouch. Well, I can't help it, if you're going to be as jealous as that. I didn't do anything but dance with him just a little. I didn't think you'd be mad." She moved as if to turn away, but realizing that there was an understanding between them, and that he must be placated if things were to go on, she drew him by his coat lapels out of the range of the hearing of the others, who were already looking and listening, and began.

"Now, see here, you. Don't go acting like this. I didn't mean anything by what I did. Honest, I didn't. Anyhow, everybody dances like that now. And nobody means anything by it. Aren't you goin' to let me be nice to you like I said, or are you?"

And now she looked him coaxingly and winsomely and calculatingly straight in the eye, as though he were the one person among all these present whom she really did like. And deliberately, and of a purpose, she made a pursy, sensuous mouth—the kind she could make—and practised a play of the lips that caused them to seem to want to kiss him—a mouth that tempted him to distraction.

"All right," he said, looking at her weakly and yieldingly. "I suppose I am a fool, but I saw what you did, all right. You know I'm crazy about you, Hortense—just wild! I can't help it. I wish I could sometimes. I wish I wouldn't be such a fool." And he looked at her and was sad. And she, realizing her power over him and how easy it was to bring him around, replied: "Oh, you—you don't, either. I'll kiss you after a while, when the others aren't looking if you'll be good." At the same time she was conscious of the fact that Sparser's eyes were upon her. Also that he was intensely drawn to her and that she liked him more than any one she had recently encountered.

18

THE CLIMAX of the afternoon was reached, however, when after several more dances and drinks, the small river and its possibilities was again brought to the attention of all by Hegglund, who, looking out of one of the windows, suddenly exclaimed: "What's de matter wit de ice down dere? Look at de swell ice. I dare dis crowd to go down dere and slide."

They were off pell-mell—Ratterer and Tina Kogel, running hand in hand, Sparser and Lucille Nickolas, with whom he had just been dancing, Higby and Laura Sipe, whom he was finding interesting enough for a change, and Clyde and Hortense. But once on the ice, which was nothing more than a narrow, winding stream, blown clean in places by the wind, and curving among thickets of leafless trees, the company were more like young satyrs and nymphs of an older day. They ran here and there, slipping and sliding—Higby, Lucille and Maida immediately falling down, but scrambling to their feet with bursts of laughter.

And Hortense, aided by Clyde at first, minced here and there. But soon she began to run and slide, squealing in pretended fear. And now, not only Sparser but Higby, and this in spite of Clyde, began to show Hortense attention. They joined her in sliding, ran after her and pretended to try to trip her up, but caught her as she fell. And Sparser, taking her by the hand, dragged her, seemingly in spite of herself and the others, far upstream and about a curve where they could not be seen. Determined not to show further watchfulness or jealousy Clyde remained behind. But he could not help feeling that Sparser might be taking this occasion to make a date, even to kiss her. She was not incapable of letting him, even though she might pretend to him that she did not want him to. It was agonizing.

In spite of himself, he began to tingle with helpless pain—to begin to wish that he could see them. But Hegglund, having called every one to join hands and crack the whip, he took the hand of Lucille Nickolas, who was holding on to Hegglund's, and gave his other free hand to Maida Axelrod, who in turn gave her free hand to Ratterer. And Higby and Laura Sipe were about to make up the tail when Sparser and Hortense came gliding back—

he holding her by the hand. And they now tacked on at the foot. Then Hegglund and the others began running and doubling back and forth until all beyond Maida had fallen and let go. And, as Clyde noted, Hortense and Sparser,
in falling, skidded and rolled against each other to the edge of the shore
where were snow and leaves and twigs. And Hortense's skirts, becoming
awry in some way, moved up to above her knees. But instead of showing
any embarrassment, as Clyde thought and wished she might, she sat there
for a few moments without shame and even laughing heartily—and Sparser
with her and still holding her hand. And Laura Sipe, having fallen in such a
way as to trip Higby, who had fallen across her, they also lay there laughing
and yet in a most suggestive position, as Clyde thought. He noted, too, that
Laura Sipe's skirts had been worked above her knees. And Sparser, now sitting
up, was pointing to her pretty legs and laughing loudly, showing most of his
teeth. And all the others were emitting peals and squeals of laughter.

"Hang it all!" thought Clyde. "Why the deuce does he always have to be
hanging about her? Why didn't he bring a girl of his own if he wanted to
have a good time? What right have they got to go where they can't be seen?
And she thinks I think she means nothing by all this. She never laughs that
heartily with me, you bet. What does she think I am that she can put that
stuff over on me, anyhow?" He glowered darkly for the moment, but in spite
of his thoughts the line or whip was soon re-formed and this time with Lucille Nickolas still holding his hand. Sparser and Hortense at the tail end
again. But Hegglund, unconscious of the mood of Clyde and thinking only of
the sport, called: "Better let some one else take de end dere, hadn'tcha?"
And feeling the fairness of this, Ratterer and Maida Axelrod and Clyde and
Lucille Nickolas now moved down with Higby and Laura Sipe and Hortense
and Sparser above them. Only, as Clyde noted, Hortense still held Sparser
by the hand, yet she moved just above him and took his hand, he being to
the right, with Sparser next above to her left, holding her other hand
firmly, which infuriated Clyde. Why couldn't he stick to Laura Sipe, the
girl brought out here for him? And Hortense was encouraging him.

He was very sad, and he felt so angry and bitter that he could scarcely play
the game. He wanted to stop and quarrel with Sparser. But so brisk and eager
was Hegglund that they were off before he could even think of doing so.

And then, try as he would, to keep his balance in the face of this, he and
Lucille and Ratterer and Maida Axelrod were thrown down and spun
around on the ice like curling irons. And Hortense, letting go of him at the
right moment, seemed to prefer deliberately to hang on to Sparser. Entangled with these others, Clyde and they spun across forty feet of smooth, green
ice and piled against a snow bank. At the finish, as he found, Lucille Nickolas
was lying across his knees face down in such a spanking position that he was
compelled to laugh. And Maida Axelrod was on her back, next to Ratterer, her
legs straight up in the air; on purpose he thought. She was too coarse and bold
for him. And there followed, of course, squeals and guffaws of delight—so
loud that they could be heard for half a mile. Hegglund, intensely susceptible to humor at all times, doubled to the knees, slapped his thighs and bawled.
And Sparser opened his big mouth and chortled and grimaced until he was
scarlet. So infectious was the result that for the time being Clyde forgot

his jealousy. He too looked and laughed. But Clyde's mood had not changed really. He still felt that she wasn't playing fair.

At the end of all this playing Lucille Nickolas and Tina Kogel being tired, dropped out. And Hortense, also. Clyde at once left the group to join her. Ratterer then followed Lucille. Then the others separating, Hegglund pushed Maida Axelrod before him down stream out of sight around a bend. Higby, seemingly taking his cue from this, pulled Tina Kogel up stream, and Ratterer and Lucille, seeming to see something of interest, struck into a thicket, laughing and talking as they went. Even Sparser and Laura, left to themselves, now wandered off, leaving Clyde and Hortense alone.

And then, as these two wandered toward a fallen log which here paralleled the stream, she sat down. But Clyde, smarting from his fancied wounds, stood silent for the time being, while she, sensing as much, took him by the belt of his coat and began to pull at him.

"Giddap, horsey," she played. "Giddap. My horsey has to skate me now on the ice."

Clyde looked at her glumly, glowering mentally, and not to be diverted so easily from the ills which he felt to be his.

"Whadd'ye wanta let that fellow Sparser always hang around you for?" he demanded. "I saw you going up the creek there with him a while ago. What did he say to you up there?"

"He didn't say anything."

"Oh, no, of course not," he replied cynically and bitterly. "And maybe he didn't kiss you, either."

"I should say not," she replied definitely and spitefully, "I'd like to know what you think I am, anyhow. I don't let people kiss me the first time they see me, smarty, and I want you to know it. I didn't let you, did I?"

"Oh, that's all right, too," answered Clyde; "but you didn't like me as well as you do him, either."

"Oh, didn't I? Well, maybe I didn't, but what right have you to say I like him, anyhow. I'd like to know if I can't have a little fun without you watching me all the time. You make me tired, that's what you do." She was quite angry now because of the proprietary air he appeared to be assuming.

And now Clyde, repulsed and somewhat shaken by this sudden counter on her part, decided on the instant that perhaps it might be best for him to modify his tone. After all, she had never said that she had really cared for him, even in the face of the implied promise she had made him.

"Oh, well," he observed glumly after a moment, and not without a little of sadness in his tone, "I know one thing. If I let on that I cared for any one as much as you say you do for me at times, I wouldn't want to flirt around with others like you are doing out here."

"Oh, wouldn't you?"

"No, I wouldn't."

"Well, who's flirting anyhow, I'd like to know?"

"You are."

"I'm not either, and I wish you'd just go away and let me alone if you can't do anything else but quarrel with me. Just because I danced with him up there in the restaurant, is no reason for you to think I'm flirting. Oh, you make me tired, that's what you do."

"Do I?"

"Yes, you do."

"Well, maybe I better go off and not bother you any more at all then," he returned, a trace of his mother's courage welling up in him.

"Well, maybe you had, if that's the way you're going to feel about me all the time," she answered, and kicked viciously with her toes at the ice. But Clyde was beginning to feel that he could not possibly go through with this—that after all he was too eager about her—too much at her feet. He began to weaken and gaze nervously at her. And she, thinking of her coat again, decided to be civil.

"You didn't look in his eyes, did you?" he asked weakly, his thoughts going back to her dancing with Sparser.

"When?"

"When you were dancing with him?"

"No, I didn't, not that I know of, anyhow. But supposing I did. What of it? I didn't mean anything by it. Gee, criminy, can't a person look in anybody's eyes if they want to?"

"In the way you looked in his? Not if you claim to like anybody else, I say." And the skin of Clyde's forehead lifted and sank, and his eyelids narrowed. Hortense merely clicked impatiently and indignantly with her tongue. "Tst! Tst! Tst! If you ain't the limit!"

"And a while ago back there on the ice," went on Clyde determinedly and yet pathetically. "When you came back from up there, instead of coming up to where I was you went to the foot of the line with him. I saw you. And you held his hand, too, all the way back. And then when you fell down, you had to sit there with him holding your hand. I'd like to know what you call that if it ain't flirting. What else is it? I'll bet he thinks it is, all right."

"Well, I wasn't flirting with him just the same and I don't care what you say. But if you want to have it that way, have it that way. I can't stop you. You're so darn jealous you don't want to let anybody else do anything, that's all the matter with you. How else can you play on the ice if you don't hold hands, I'd like to know? Gee, criminy! What about you and that Lucille Nickolas? I saw her laying across your lap and you laughing. And I didn't think anything of that. What do you want me to do—come out here and sit around like a bump on a log?—follow you around like a tail? Or you follow me? What-a-yuh think I am anyhow? A nut?"

She was being ragged by Clyde, as she thought, and she didn't like it. She was thinking of Sparser who was really more appealing to her at the time than Clyde. He was more materialistic, less romantic, more direct.

He turned and, taking off his cap, rubbed his head gloomily while Hortense, looking at him, thought first of him and then of Sparser. Sparser was more manly, not so much of a cry-baby. He wouldn't stand around and complain this way, you bet. He'd probably leave her for good, have nothing more to do with her. Yet Clyde, after his fashion, was interesting and useful. Who else would do for her what he had? And at any rate, he was not trying to force her to go off with him now as these others had gone and as she had feared he might try to do—ahead of her plan and wish. This quarrel was obviating that.

"Now, see here," she said after a time, having decided that it was best to assuage him and that it was not so hard to manage him after all. "Are we goin' t' fight all the time, Clyde? What's the use, anyhow? Whatja want me to come out here for if you just want to fight with me all the time? I wouldn't have come if I'd 'a' thought you were going to [do] that all day."

She turned and kicked at the ice with the minute toe of her shoes, and Clyde, always taken by her charm again, put his arms about her, and crushed her to him, at the same time fumbling at her breasts and putting his lips to hers and endeavoring to hold and fondle her. But now, because of her suddenly developed liking for Sparser, and partially because of her present mood towards Clyde, she broke away, a dissatisfaction with herself and him troubling her. Why should she let him force her to do anything she did not feel like doing, just now, anyhow, she now asked herself. She hadn't agreed to be as nice to him to-day as he might wish. Not yet. At any rate just now she did not want to be handled in this way by him, and she would not, regardless of what he might do. And Clyde, sensing by now what the true state of her mind in regard to him must be, stepped back and yet continued to gaze gloomily and hungrily at her. And she in turn merely stared at him.

"I thought you said you liked me," he demanded almost savagely now, realizing that his dreams of a happy outing this day were fading into nothing.

"Well, I do when you're nice," she replied, sly and evasively, seeking some way to avoid complication in connection with her original promises to him.

"Yes, you do," he grumbled. "I see how you do. Why, here we are out here now and you won't even let me touch you. I'd like to know what you meant by all that you said, anyhow."

"Well, what did I say?" she countered, merely to gain time.

"As though you didn't know."

"Oh, well. But that wasn't to be right away, either, was it? I thought we said"—she paused dubiously.

"I know what you said," he went on. "But I notice now that you don't like me an' that's all there is to it. What difference would it make if you really cared for me whether you were nice to me now or next week or the week after? Gee whiz, you'd think it was something that depended on what I did for you, not whether you cared for me." In his pain he was quite intense and courageous.

"That's not so!" she snapped, angrily and bitterly, irritated by the truth of what he said. "And I wish you wouldn't say that to me, either. I don't care anything about the old coat now, if you want to know it. And you can just have your old money back, too, I don't want it. And you can just let me alone from now on, too," she added. "I'll get all the coats I want without any help from you." At this, she turned and walked away.

But Clyde, now anxious to mollify her as usual, ran after her. "Don't go, Hortense," he pleaded. "Wait a minute. I didn't mean that either, honest I didn't. I'm crazy about you. Honest I am. Can't you see that? Oh, gee, don't go now. I'm not giving you the money to get something for it. You can have it for nothing if you want it that way. There ain't anybody else in the world like you to me, and there never has been. You can have the money for all I care, all of it. I don't want it back. But, gee, I did think you liked me a little. Don't you care for me at all, Hortense?" He looked cowed and frightened, and she, sensing her mastery over him, relented a little.

"Of course I do," she announced. "But just the same, that don't mean that you can treat me any old way, either. You don't seem to understand that a girl can't do everything you want her to do just when you want her to do it."

"Just what do you mean by that?" asked Clyde, not quite sensing just what she did mean. "I don't get you."

"Oh, yes, you do, too." She could not believe that he did not know.

"Oh, I guess I know what you're talkin' about. I know what you're going to say now," he went on disappointedly. "That's that old stuff they all pull. I know."

He was now reciting almost verbatim the words and intonations even of the other boys at the hotel—Higby, Ratterer, Eddie Doyle—who, having narrated the nature of such situations to him, and how girls occasionally lied out of pressing dilemmas in this way, had made perfectly clear to him what was meant. And Hortense knew now that he did know.

"Gee, but you're mean," she said in an assumed hurt way. "A person can never tell you anything or expect you to believe it. Just the same, it's true, whether you believe it or not."

"Oh, I know how you are," he replied, sadly yet a little loftily, as though this were an old situation to him. "You don't like me, that's all. I see that now, all right."

"Gee, but you're mean," she persisted, affecting an injured air. "It's the God's truth. Believe me or not, I swear it. Honest it is."

Clyde stood there. In the face of this small trick there was really nothing much to say as he saw it. He could not force her to do anything. If she wanted to lie and pretend, he would have to pretend to believe her. And yet a great sadness settled down upon him. He was not to win her after all— that was plain. He turned, and she, being convinced that he felt that she was lying now, felt it incumbent upon herself to do something about it—to win him around to her again.

"Please, Clyde, please," she began now, most artfully, "I mean that. Really, I do. Won't you believe me? But I will next week, sure. Honest, I will. Won't you believe that? I meant everything I said when I said it. Honest, I did. I do like you—a lot. Won't you believe that, too—please?"

And Clyde, thrilled from head to toe by this latest phase of her artistry, agreed that he would. And once more he began to smile and recover his gayety. And by the time they reached the car, to which they were all called a few minutes after by Hegglund, because of the time, and he had held her hand and kissed her often, he was quite convinced that the dream he had been dreaming was as certain of fulfillment as anything could be. Oh, the glory of it when it should come true!

19

FOR THE MAJOR portion of the return trip to Kansas City, there was nothing to mar the very agreeable illusion under which Clyde rested. He sat beside Hortense, who leaned her head against his shoulder. And although Sparser, who had waited for the others to step in before taking the wheel, had squeezed her arm and received an answering and promising look, Clyde had not seen that.

But the hour being late and the admonitions of Hegglund, Ratterer and Higby being all for speed, and the mood of Sparser, because of the looks bestowed upon him by Hortense, being the gayest and most drunken, it was not long before the outlying lamps of the environs began to show. For the car was rushed along the road at break-neck speed. At one point, however, where one of the eastern trunk lines approached the city, there was a long and unexpected and disturbing wait at a grade crossing where two freight trains met and passed. Farther in, at North Kansas City, it began to snow, great soft slushy flakes, feathering down and coating the road surface with a slippery layer of mud which required more caution than had been thus far displayed. It was then half past five. Ordinarily, an additional eight minutes at high speed would have served to bring the car within a block or two of the hotel. But now, with another delay near Hannibal Bridge owing to grade crossing, it was twenty minutes to six before the bridge was crossed and Wyandotte Street reached. And already all four of these youths had lost all sense of the delight of the trip and the pleasure the companionship of these girls had given them. For already they were worrying as to the probability of their reaching the hotel in time. The smug and martinetish figure of Mr. Squires loomed before them all.

"Gee, if we don't do better than this," observed Ratterer to Higby, who was nervously fumbling with his watch, "we're not goin' to make it. We'll hardly have time, as it is, to change."

Clyde, hearing him, exclaimed: "Oh, crickets! I wish we could hurry a little. Gee, I wish now we hadn't come to-day. It'll be tough if we don't get there on time."

And Hortense, noting his sudden tenseness and unrest, added: "Don't you think you'll make it all right?"

"Not this way," he said. But Hegglund, who had been studying the flaked air outside, a world that seemed dotted with falling bits of cotton, called: "Eh, dere Willard. We certainly gotta do better dan dis. It means de razoo for us if we don't get dere on time."

And Higby, for once stirred out of a gambler-like effrontery and calm, added: "We'll walk the plank all right unless we can put up some good yarn. Can't anybody think of anything?" As for Clyde, he merely sighed nervously.

And then, as though to torture them the more, an unexpected crush of vehicles appeared at nearly every intersection. And Sparser, who was irritated by this particular predicament, was contemplating with impatience the warning hand of a traffic policeman, which, at the intersection of Ninth and Wyandotte, had been raised against him. "There goes his mit again," he exclaimed. "What can I do about that! I might turn over to Washington, but I don't know whether we'll save any time by going over there."

A full minute passed before he was signaled to go forward. Then swiftly he swung the car to the right and three blocks over into Washington Street.

But here the conditions were no better. Two heavy lines of traffic moved in opposite directions. And at each succeeding corner several precious moments were lost as the cross-traffic went by. Then the car would tear on to the next corner, weaving its way in and out as best it could.

At Fifteenth and Washington, Clyde exclaimed to Ratterer: "How would it do if we got out at Seventeenth and walked over?"

"You won't save any time if I can turn over there," called Sparser. "I can get over there quicker than you can."

He crowded the other cars for every inch of available space. At Sixteenth and Washington, seeing what he considered a fairly clear block to the left, he turned the car and tore along that thoroughfare to as far as Wyandotte once more. Just as he neared the corner and was about to turn at high speed, swinging in close to the curb to do so, a little girl of about nine, who was running toward the crossing, jumped directly in front of the moving machine. And because there was no opportunity given him to turn and avoid her, she was struck and dragged a number of feet before the machine could be halted. At the same time, there arose piercing screams from at least half a dozen women, and shouts from as many men who had witnessed the accident.

Instantly they all rushed toward the child, who had been thrown under and passed over by the wheels. And Sparser, looking out and seeing them gathering about the fallen figure, was seized with an uninterpretable mental panic which conjured up the police, jail, his father, the owner of the car, severe punishment in many forms. And though by now all the others in the car were up and giving vent to anguished exclamations such as "Oh, God! He hit a little girl"; "Oh, gee, he's killed a kid!" "Oh, mercy!" "Oh, Lord!" "Oh, heavens, what'll we do now?" he turned and exclaimed: "Jesus, the cops! I gotta get outa this with this car."

And, without consulting the others, who were still half standing, but almost speechless with fear, he shot the lever into first, second and then high, and giving the engine all the gas it would endure, sped with it to the next corner beyond.

But there, as at the other corners in this vicinity, a policeman was stationed, and having already seen some commotion at the corner west of him, had already started to leave his post in order to ascertain what it was. As he did so, cries of "Stop that car"—"Stop that car"—reached his ears. And a man, running toward the sedan from the scene of the accident, pointed to it, and called: "Stop that car, stop that car. They've killed a child."

Then gathering what was meant, he turned toward the car, putting his police whistle to his mouth as he did so. But Sparser, having by this time heard the cries and seen the policeman leaving, dashed swiftly past him into Seventeenth Street, along which he sped at almost forty miles an hour, grazing the hub of a truck in one instance, scraping the fender of an automobile in another, and missing by inches and quarter inches vehicles or pedestrians, while those behind him in the car were for the most part sitting bolt upright and tense, their eyes wide, their hands clenched, their faces and lips set—or, as in the case of Hortense and Lucille Nickolas and Tina Kogel, giving voice to repeated, "Oh, Gods!" "Oh, what's going to happen now?"

But the police and those who had started to pursue were not to be outdone so quickly. Unable to make out the license plate number and seeing from the first motions of the car that it had no intention of stopping, the officer blew a loud and long blast on his police whistle. And the policeman at the next corner seeing the car speed by and realizing what it meant, blew on his whistle, then stopped, and springing on the running board of a passing touring car ordered it to give chase. And at this, seeing what was amiss or awind, three other cars, driven by adventurous spirits, joined in the chase, all honking loudly as they came.

But the Packard had far more speed in it than any of its pursuers, and although for the first few blocks of the pursuit there were cries of "Stop that car!" "Stop that car!" still, owing to the much greater speed of the car, these soon died away, giving place to the long wild shrieks of distant horns in full cry.

Sparser by now having won a fair lead and realizing that a straight course was the least baffling to pursue, turned swiftly into McGee, a comparatively quiet thoroughfare along which he tore for a few blocks to the wide and winding Gillham Parkway, whose course was southward. But having followed that at terrific speed for a short distance, he again—at Thirty-first—decided to turn—the houses in the distance confusing him and the suburban country to the north seeming to offer the best opportunity for evading his pursuers. And so now he swung the car to the left into that thoroughfare, his thought here being that amid these comparatively quiet streets it was possible to wind in and out and so shake off pursuit—at least long enough to drop his passengers somewhere and return the car to the garage.

And this he would have been able to do had it not been for the fact that in turning into one of the more outlying streets of this region, where there were scarcely any houses and no pedestrians visible, he decided to turn off his lights, the better to conceal the whereabouts of the car. Then, still speeding east, north, and east and south by turns, he finally dashed into one street where, after a few hundred feet, the pavement suddenly ended. But because another cross street was visible a hundred feet or so further on, and he imagined that by turning into that he might find a paved thoroughfare again, he sped on and then swung sharply to the left, only to crash roughly into a pile of paving stones left by a contractor who was preparing to pave the way. In the absence of the lights he had failed to distinguish this. And diagonally opposite to these, lengthwise of a prospective sidewalk, had been laid a pile of lumber for a house.

Striking the edge of the paving stones at high speed, he caromed, and all but upsetting the car, made directly for the lumber pile opposite, into which he crashed. Only instead of striking it head on, the car struck one end, causing it to give way and spread out, but only sufficiently to permit the right wheels to mount high upon it and so throw the car completely over onto its left side in the grass and snow beyond the walk. Then there, amid a crash of glass and the impacts of their own bodies, the occupants were thrown down in a heap, forward and to the left.

What happened afterwards was more or less of a mystery and a matter of confusion, not only to Clyde, but to all the others. For Sparser and Laura Sipe, being in front, were dashed against the wind-shield and the roof and knocked senseless, Sparser, having his shoulder, hip and left knee wrenched in such a way as to make it necessary to let him lie in the car as he was until an ambulance arrived. He could not possibly be lifted out through the door, which was in the roof as the car now lay. And in the second seat, Clyde, being nearest the door to the left and next to him Hortense, Lucille Nickolas and Ratterer, was pinioned under and yet not crushed by their combined weights. For Hortense in falling had been thrown completely over him on her side against the roof, which was now the left wall. And Lucille, next above her, fell in such a way as to lie across Clyde's shoulders only, while Ratterer, now topmost of the four, had, in falling, been thrown over the seat in front of him. But grasping the steering wheel in front of him as he fell, the same having been wrenched from Sparser's hands, he had broken his fall in part by clinging to it. But even so, his face and hands were cut and bruised and his shoulder, arm and hip slightly wrenched, yet not sufficiently to prevent his being of assistance to the others. For at once, realizing the plight of the others as well as his own, and stirred by their screams, Ratterer was moved to draw himself up and out through the top or side door which he now succeeded in opening, scrambling over the others to reach it.

Once out, he climbed upon the chassis beam of the toppled car, and, reaching down, caught hold of the struggling and moaning Lucille, who like the others was trying to climb up but could not. And exerting all his strength and exclaiming, "Be still, now, honey, I gotcha. You're all right, I'll getcha out," he lifted her to a sitting position on the side of the door, then down in the snow, where he placed her and where she sat crying and feeling her arms and her head. And after her he helped Hortense, her left cheek and forehead and both hands badly bruised and bleeding, but not seriously, although she did not know that at the time. She was whimpering and shivering and shaking—a nervous chill having succeeded the dazed and almost unconscious state which had followed the first crash.

At that moment, Clyde, lifting his bewildered head above the side door of the car, his left cheek, shoulder and arm bruised, but not otherwise injured, was thinking that he too must get out of this as quickly as possible. A child had been killed; a car stolen and wrecked; his job was most certainly lost; the police were in pursuit and might even find them there at any minute. And below him in the car was Sparser, prone where he fell, but already being looked to by Ratterer. And beside him Laura Sipe, also unconscious. He felt called upon to do something—to assist Ratterer, who was reaching down and trying to lay hold of Laura Sipe without injuring her. But so confused were his thoughts that he would have stood there without helping any one had it not been for Ratterer, who called most irritably, "Give us a hand here, Clyde, will you? Let's see if we can get her out. She's fainted." And Clyde, turning now instead of trying to climb out, began to seek to lift her from within, standing on the broken glass window of the side beneath his feet and attempting to draw her body back and up off the body of Sparser. But this was not possible. She was too limp—too heavy. He could only draw her back—off the body of Sparser—and then let her rest there, between the second and first seats on the car's side.

But, meanwhile, at the back, Hegglund, being nearest the top and only slightly stunned, had managed to reach the door nearest him and throw it back. Thus, by reason of his athletic body, he was able to draw himself up and out, saying as he did so: "Oh, Jesus, what a finish! Oh, Christ, dis is de limit! Oh, Jesus, we better beat it outa dis before de cops git here."

At the same time, however, seeing the others below him and hearing their cries, he could not contemplate anything so desperate as desertion. Instead, once out, he turned and making out Maida below him, exclaimed: "Here, for Christ's sake, gimme your hand. We gotta get outa dis, and damn quick, I tell ya." Then turning from Maida, who for the moment was feeling her wounded and aching head, he mounted the top chassis beam again and, reaching down, caught hold of Tina Kogel, who, only stunned, was trying to push herself to a sitting position while resting heavily on top of Higby. But he, relieved of the weight of the others, was already kneeling, and feeling his head and face with his hands.

"Gimme your hand, Dave," called Hegglund. "Hurry! For Christ's sake! We ain't got no time to lose around here. Are ya hurt? Christ, we gotta git outa here, I tell ya. I see a guy comin' acrost dere now an' I doughno wedder he's a cop or not." He started to lay hold of Higby's left hand, but as he did so Higby repulsed him.

"Huh, uh," he exclaimed. "Don't pull. I'm all right. I'll get out by myself. Help the others." And standing up, his head above the level of the door, he began to look about within the car for something on which to place his foot. The back cushion having fallen out and forward, he got his foot on that and raised himself up to the door level on which he sat and drew out his leg. Then looking about, and seeing Hegglund attempting to assist Ratterer and Clyde with Sparser, he went to their aid.

Outside, some odd and confusing incidents had already occurred. For Hortense, who had been lifted out before Clyde, and had suddenly begun to feel her face, had as suddenly realized that her left cheek and forehead were not only scraped but bleeding. And being seized by the notion that her beauty might have been permanently marred by this accident, she was at once thrown into a state of selfish panic which caused her to become completely oblivious, not only to the misery and injury of the others, but to the danger of discovery by the police, the injury to the child, the wreck of this expensive car—in fact everything but herself and the probability or possibility that her beauty had been destroyed. She began to whimper on the instant and wave her hands up and down. "Oh, goodness, goodness, goodness!" she exclaimed desperately. "Oh, how dreadful! Oh, how terrible! Oh, my face is all cut." And feeling an urgent compulsion to do something about it, she suddenly set off (and that without a word to any one and while Clyde was still inside helping Ratterer) south along 35th Street, toward the city where were lights and more populated streets. Her one thought was to reach her own home as speedily as possible in order that she might be able to do something for herself.

Of Clyde, Sparser, Ratterer and the other girls—she really thought nothing. What were they now? It was only intermittently and between thoughts of her marred beauty that she could even bring herself to think of the injured child—the horror of which, as well as the pursuit by the police, maybe, the fact that the car did not belong to Sparser or that it was wrecked, and that they were all liable to arrest in consequence, affecting her but slightly. Her one thought in regard to Clyde was that he was the one who had invited her to this ill-fated journey—hence that he was to blame, really. Those beastly boys—to think they should have gotten her into this and then didn't have brains enough to manage better.

The other girls, apart from Laura Sipe, were not seriously injured—any of them. They were more frightened than anything else, but now that this had happened they were in a panic, lest they be overtaken by the police, arrested, exposed and punished. And accordingly they stood about, exclaiming "Oh, gee, hurry, can't you? Oh, dear, we ought all of us to get away from here. Oh, it's all so terrible." Until at last Hegglund exclaimed: "For Christ's sake, keep quiet, cantcha? We're doin' de best we can, cantcha see? You'll have de cops down on us in a minute as it is."

And then, as if in answer to his comment, a lone suburbanite who lived some four blocks from the scene across the fields and who, hearing the crash and the cries in the night, had ambled across to see what the trouble was, now drew near and stood curiously looking at the stricken group and the car.

"Had an accident, eh?" he exclaimed, genially enough. "Any one badly hurt? Gee, that's too bad. And that's a swell car, too. Can I help any?"

Clyde, hearing him talk and looking out and not seeing Hortense anywhere, and not being able to do more for Sparser than stretch him in the bottom of the car, glanced agonizingly about. For the thought of the police and their certain pursuit was strong upon him. He must get out of this. He must not be caught here. Think of what would happen to him if he were caught —how he would be disgraced and punished probably—all his fine world stripped from him before he could say a word really. His mother would hear —Mr. Squires—everybody. Most certainly he would go to jail. Oh, how terrible that thought was—grinding really like a macerating wheel to his flesh. They could do nothing more for Sparser, and they only laid themselves open to being caught by lingering. So asking, "Where'd Miss Briggs go?" he now began to climb out, then started looking about the dark and snowy fields for her. His thought was that he would first assist her to wherever she might desire to go.

But just then in the distance was heard the horns and the hum of at least two motorcycles speeding swiftly in the direction of this very spot. For already the wife of the suburbanite, on hearing the crash and the cries in the distance, had telephoned the police that an accident had occurred here. And now the suburbanite was explaining: "That's them. I told the wife to telephone for an ambulance." And hearing this, all these others now began to run, for they all realized what that meant. And in addition, looking across the fields one could see the lights of these approaching machines. They reached Thirty-first and Cleveland together. Then one turned south toward this very spot, along Cleveland Avenue. And the other continued east on Thirty-first, reconnoitering for the accident.

"Beat it, for God's sake, all of youse," whispered Hegglund, excitedly. "Scatter!" And forthwith, seizing Maida Axelrod by the hand, he started to run east along Thirty-fifth Street, in which the car then lay—toward the outlying eastern suburbs. But after a moment, deciding that that would not do either, that it would be too easy to pursue him along a street, he cut northeast, directly across the open fields and away from the city.

And now, Clyde, as suddenly sensing what capture would mean—how all his fine thoughts of pleasure would most certainly end in disgrace and probably prison, began running also. Only in his case, instead of following Hegglund or any of the others, he turned south along Cleveland Avenue toward the southern limits of the city. But like Hegglund, realizing that that meant an easy avenue of pursuit for any one who chose to follow, he too took to the open fields. Only instead of running away from the city as before, he now turned southwest and ran toward those streets which lay to the south of Fortieth. Only much open space being before him before he should reach them, and a clump of bushes showing in the near distance, and the light of the motorcycle already sweeping the road behind him, he ran to that and for the moment dropped behind it.

Only Sparser and Laura Sipe were left within the car, she at that moment beginning to recover consciousness. And the visiting stranger, much astounded, was left standing outside.

"Why, the very idea!" he suddenly said to himself. "They must have stolen that car. It couldn't have belonged to them at all."

And just then the first motorcycle reaching the scene, Clyde from his not too distant hiding place was able to overhear. "Well, you didn't get away with it after all, did you? You thought you were pretty slick, but you didn't make it. You're the one we want, and what's become of the rest of the gang, eh? Where are they, eh?"

And hearing the suburbanite declare quite definitely that he had nothing to do with it, that the real occupants of the car had but then run away and might yet be caught if the police wished, Clyde, who was still within earshot of what was being said, began crawling upon his hands and knees at first in the snow south, south and west, always toward some of those distant streets which, lamplit and faintly glowing, he saw to the southwest of him, and among which presently, if he were not captured, he hoped to hide—to lose himself and so escape—if the fates were only kind—the misery and the punishment and the unending dissatisfaction and disappointment which now, most definitely, it all represented to him.

1925

Reading Suggestions

All of Dreiser's novels are available in reprints, many of them in multiple editions: An American Tragedy, The Bulwark, The Financier, The "Genius," Jennie Gerhardt, Sister Carrie, The Stoic, The Titan. Many of his best short stories are included in The Theodore Dreiser Reader and The Best Short Stories *of Theodore Dreiser.* Dreiser's poetry and plays have not been reprinted. He also wrote a number of autobiographical books, including *A Book about Myself* (later reprinted under the title *Newspaper Days*), *A Hoosier Holiday,* and *A Traveller at Forty.* His philosophical views may be found most succinctly expressed in *Living Philosophies: A Series of Intimate Credos.* The best collection of his correspondence has been edited by Robert Elias, *Letters of Theodore Dreiser,* in three volumes. The most extensive bibliography, limited only by the fact that its coverage ends in 1954, is included in the volume of critical essays edited by Kazin and Shapiro, *The Stature of Theodore Dreiser* (1955).

The only reliable biography is *Theodore Dreiser: Apostle of Nature* (1949), by Robert H. Elias. By far the best book-length critical study is F. O. Matthiessen's *Theodore Dreiser* (1951). Charles Shapiro's *Theodore Dreiser: Our Bitter Patriot* (1962) offers a spirited defense of Dreiser's work, taking issue chiefly with early twentieth-century Humanists and later neo-orthodox Christians who have deplored Dreiser's naturalistic philosophy. The volume by Kazin and Shapiro mentioned above is an invaluable resource for the student; it may well be the best work to begin with in reading about Dreiser's fiction. Bringing together most of the classic essays on Dreiser, it also reprints a number of pieces not otherwise easily available, notably "Dreiser's Imagination" by John Berryman and "Dreiser, An Inconsistent Mechanist" by Eliseo Vivas.

One of the most balanced and discriminating brief treatments of Dreiser's work is that of Lionel Trilling in *The Liberal Imagination;* though not unsympathetic to Dreiser, Trilling is impatient with Dreiser's uncritical defenders, such as Burton Roscoe and Dorothy Dudley. Representative of early attacks on Dreiser's naturalism are the essays by Stuart P. Sherman in his *On Contemporary Literature* (1917) and Robert Shafer in Norman Foerster's *Humanism and America* (1930). H. L. Mencken was one of the most vehement and influential spokesmen for the defense in *A Book of Prefaces* (1917). From a later perspective, Philip Rahv in *Image and Idea* (1949) offers a condensed, and perhaps oversimplified, summation of the issues involved in the Dreiser controversy. Malcolm Cowley's "Naturalism in American Literature" in *Evolutionary Thought in America,* edited by Stow Persons, and Harry Levin's "What Is Realism?" in *Comparative Literature* (Summer 1951) are helpful in placing Dreiser's work in a larger context, both philosophic and aesthetic, than is provided by the controversialists. Daniel Aaron's *Writers on the Left: Episodes in American Literary Communism* achieves a comparable enlargement of the political context of which Dreiser's writing is a part. Valuable insights and significant special emphases may also be found in the following: Oscar Cargill, *Intellectual America: Ideas on the March* (1941); Alfred Kazin, *On Native Grounds* (1942); and Charles C. Walcutt, *American Literary Naturalism: A Divided Stream* (1956).

Biography

Few American literary biographies are as closely related to American social history as that of Theodore Dreiser. The seventy-four years of his life were comprehensive of major changes in the American mainstream; and his talent as a writer, strengthened by his experience as a journalist, was constantly reflective of his country's social experience. His work is distinguished by its massive documentation of American society as it has proceeded from agrarianism and regionalism to the complexities of urban life, with its hazards for the individual, its miseries and inequalities, and its brilliant examples of material power and success.

Dreiser was born in Sullivan, Indiana, on August 27, 1871. His father, John Paul Dreiser, a German immigrant to America in 1844, had begun his new life as a peddler. A Roman Catholic with a sternly authoritarian insistence upon divine will, he was later to be remembered by his children as a bigot totally incapable of dealing with the realities of family life. Shortly after his marriage to Sarah Schanab, daughter of a Moravian farmer, he became production manager of a woolen mill at Fort Wayne, Indiana, and then owner of a small weaving industry at Sullivan. His success was abruptly terminated with the loss of his mill, uninsured, through fire. Thereafter he was never able to find regular employment.

With the panic of 1877 the family encountered severe poverty. Sarah Dreiser, who had borne eleven children before Theodore's birth, became the mainstay of her family during various removals to Terre Haute, Vincennes, and Warsaw in Indiana. She took in boarders, and the children worked at odd jobs. Dreiser in maturity was never to forget his mother's fortitude and patience. Her capacity for love became the prototype of womanly generosity of spirit in the heroine of *Jennie Gerhardt* (1911), and in other women of the later fiction.

At the age of fourteen Dreiser left high school after his freshman year and made his first journey alone, to Chicago, in search of work. The significance of the trip by train from Warsaw is memorialized in his first novel, *Sister Carrie* (1900), as the heroine of the book leaves the life of the country for the challenge of the city. In a sense, this journey describes a vast range of American social experience, as Dreiser saw it. For a time he worked as a shipping clerk and truck driver. A teacher he had known in Warsaw intervened to support him for a year as a special student at Indiana University. The youth felt that the year had been a failure. Actually, it was significant because it introduced him to the theory of Herbert Spencer, and that of Huxley and other philosophers. Though Dreiser never became a systematic proponent of naturalism, his view of society and the individual was consistently shaped by Spencer's famous doctrine of "the survival of the fittest."

An older brother Paul, who spelled the family name Dresser, had become a successful song writer (for example, "My Gal Sal," "On the Banks of the Wabash"). The extent of Paul's material aid to the family is not certain, but it is clear that his identification with city life acted as a spur to the aspirations of his brother. Encouraged by his teachers to think of writing as a career, Theodore Dreiser began work as a newspaper reporter with the Chicago *Globe*, and at the age of twenty-one proceeded to St. Louis, where he served as a feature writer for the *Globe-Democrat* and the *Republic*. At the urging of his brother Paul, he left St. Louis in 1894, and began a slow professional journey toward New York. His interim positions included assignments on the Toledo *Blade* and the Pittsburgh *Dispatch*. In Toledo he made one of the firm friendships of his mature years with the city editor of the *Blade*, Arthur Henry. The counsel which he received from Henry was perhaps secondary only to the encouragement which he was later to receive from H. L. Mencken.

Within a few months after his departure from St. Louis Dreiser was at work as a police reporter for the New York *World*. His brother Paul introduced him to the city which was to be his home for forty years; and it was with Paul's assistance through a position obtained for him as editor of a music publishers' magazine that he was allowed time for free-lance writing. Following his marriage in 1898 to Sara White of St. Louis, he established himself in New York as a writer of short stories, some of which, including "Old Rogaum and His Theresa" and "Nigger Jeff," remain among his best-known shorter pieces.

Dreiser's first novel, *Sister Carrie*, was rejected by Harper's in 1900, on grounds of immoral subject matter, and then accepted by Doubleday's. It was published in November of that year, in an issue of 1000 copies. The head of the firm was in Europe at the time of the appearance of the book. On his return, the novel was immediately suppressed as unfit for distribution under the Doubleday name. Dreiser's disappointment very nearly led to his suicide. He left New York for several months, wandered in Virginia and to Philadelphia, and then moved to Brooklyn where, for a time, he re-enacted the final disillusionment and defeat of his character Hurstwood of *Sister Carrie*. With the assistance of his brother Paul he was sent to a sanatorium for recuperation.

It appears that in this year of crisis Dreiser resolved first to conquer the world of the city before he returned to fiction. From 1902 to 1908 he devoted his entire time to a career in editing, first for the Street and Smith publications and eventually, at $10,000 a year, for the Butterick magazines. *Sister Carrie* was successfully reissued by B. W. Dodge in 1907. The conquest of the city was for the moment complete. Dreiser resigned his position at Butterick's in 1909, to work on *Jennie Gerhardt*. In *Sister Carrie* he had relived aspects of his own life, and the life of a sister who had been supported by an illicit lover in Chicago. In *Jennie Gerhardt*, published in 1911, he exploited again the suffering of his family. Jennie's character is founded upon his memories of his mother's courage and generosity. Old Gerhardt is a reincarnation of his authoritarian father.

These first novels are reckonings with the past, Dreiser's past and in the larger sense the immediate American past, of country life and country ways giving place to the machinery of urban society. With the publication of *The Financier* in 1912 and *The Titan* in 1914 Dreiser turned to a more spacious architecture of the novel. In his character Cowperwood, based on the life of the financier Charles T. Yerkes, he concerned himself with the American success story and with the character of American financial power. (The two form parts of a massive trilogy, which was not to be completed until the posthumous appearance of *The Stoic* in 1947.) The city is authoritative again in *The "Genius,"* published in 1915. Here Dreiser turned to the problem of the artist in society; and here he identified his image of the city with that of the so-called Ash-Can school of American painters—Luks, Glackens, Sloan and Shinn—in his insistence upon raw realism. Throughout this initial period of full devotion to the novel, Dreiser made wide use of his reportorial experience. Society is taken to be the author of both the individual and the course of his experience. Dreiser's method in the documentary style was clearly formulated during this period. It was to reach its highest achievement with the publication of *An American Tragedy* in 1925.

The fate of *The "Genius"* was similar to that of *Sister Carrie*. For five years after its publication (1915) it was withheld in the warehouse of the publisher (John Lane) while court injunctions against it, originally provoked by the Western Society for the Prevention of Vice, were answered. Its sale began in 1923 after defenses of Dreiser had been made by some of his eminent literary contemporaries, including Robert Frost and Ezra Pound. In the years intervening Dreiser continued writing plays, most notably *The Hand of the Potter* (produced amid controversy in 1916), stories (*Free and Other Stories*, 1918; *Twelve Men*, 1919), and philosophical essays (*Hey-rub-a-dub-dub*, 1920). Retrospective accounts of his early life as a reporter appeared in 1922, in *A Book about Myself* (reprinted in 1931 as *Newspaper Days*) and in 1923 in *The Color of a Great City*.

The release of *The "Genius"* in 1923 prompted Dreiser's renewed attention to the novel. He began sketches for *An American Tragedy* at about this time, in California where he was living with the actress Helen Richardson. (Mrs. Dreiser refused a divorce, and the two were not married until after her death in 1942). The appearance of the novel in 1925 was a literary sensation. It immediately took its place as the apotheosis of Dreiser's social determinism. He intended in Clyde Griffiths, he said, "a victim of the contemporary American dream." The book was soon made into a play for the New York stage, and it was later accorded two movie versions. It marked the arrival of Dreiser's real affluence as a successful novelist of the city. It marked, as well, his full reputation as a spokesman on the larger problems of social justice. The remainder of his life was strongly colored by his role as a theorist.

Dreiser traveled in Russia on invitation from the Soviet government in 1927. His impressions of this journey are recorded in *Dreiser Looks at Russia*. From 1930 onward he participated in political and social issues of major range on the American scene. In 1931 he took the chairmanship of the National Committee for the Defense of Political Prisoners; he went to the coal fields of Harlan, Kentucky, to investigate the terrorizing of union organizers among the miners; he was involved in movements against anti-Semitism. In *America Is Worth Saving* (1940) he expressed strong views against the involvement of the United States in World War II, and prejudices against Franklin D. Roosevelt, whose foreign policy he could not condone.

Dreiser's last work as a novelist was accomplished during the final four years of his life. He completed work on *The Stoic* (published posthumously in 1947); and he expressed the religious fervor of his last reflections in *The Bulwark* (1946). How much of Dreiser's life is typical of the American experience recorded in literature may be seen finally in his turning in *The Bulwark* to Oriental philosophy, that of China and India, for ultimate spiritual realities. He was not a professional Orientalist, in any sense. But, like Melville and Whitman before him, and like his contemporary Ezra Pound, he concluded that the Judaeo-Christian heritage alone was insufficient for Western civilization. He believed that this civilization had yet to learn how man, solitary in the midst of hostile nature, can learn compassion as his first duty.

Dreiser died in New York City on December 27, 1945.

The Reading Suggestions for Dreiser were prepared by Hyatt H. Waggoner, and the Biography by James Baird.

Anderson continually emphasized
mood and nuance rather than
full dramatic exposition.
Produced handful of s.s.

SHERWOOD ANDERSON ❖
1876-1941

Lacks ability to write
sustained narrative and to
construct a fully articulated plot

all his novels have a basic
structural weakness

Best when writing about subjects
   and people of his Middle Western youth
      cabbage farming
      bicycle factories
      county fairs
      race tracks
      horse racing
      frustrated inhabitants of villages +
                                        hamlets

In depicting small-town life, Anderson generally adopted neither a satirical nor a tragic point of view. He was primarily concerned with the inhibitions which prevent people from leading simple, honest lives, and he strove to present these frustrations with sympathy and insight.

Winesburg, Ohio my be read as a fable of American estrangement, its theme the loss of love.

Characters are alienated from nature
from the community in which they live
from human society (saddest of all)

Introduction

Sherwood Anderson is too often underestimated nowadays. It has been his misfortune to be eclipsed by the writers of the next generation. True, he lacks the elegance and deftness of touch of Scott Fitzgerald, and he never attained the vigor and conciseness of Hemingway or the depth and tortured violence of Faulkner. Yet he was an admirable pioneer to whom his successors were greatly indebted. Faulkner acknowledged it publicly:

He was the father of my generation of American writers and the tradition of American writing which our successors will carry on. He has never received his proper evaluation. Dreiser is his older brother and Mark Twain the father of them both.

Hemingway, too, though he later cruelly parodied his master in *The Torrents of Spring*, was nevertheless obliged to admit that Sherwood Anderson had helped him to find himself.

I

Though a bold innovator in some respects and a self-taught writer who started late in life, Sherwood Anderson, as Faulkner pointed out, was himself indebted to a number of his predecessors. As a boy and a young man, he read voraciously from James Fenimore Cooper's and Mark Twain's works to H. G. Wells's and George Moore's early novels, from the Bible to Dickens. When he settled in Chicago in 1913 with the intention of becoming a writer, he found himself in the middle of a literary renaissance. It was only a "Robin's Egg Renaissance," as he later called it, but still it put him in touch with Edgar Lee Masters, who had just published his *Spoon River Anthology*, with Floyd Dell, Carl Sandburg, and lesser figures. All of these writers were in revolt against social conventions, bourgeois morality, Midwestern philistinism, and materialism. This atmosphere stimulated him. Until then he had written two unoriginal novels, *Windy McPherson's Son,* which was indeed rather loose and windy, and *Marching Men,* in which the men of the title did not know exactly where to march. His contact with other writers made him conscious of his own peculiarities and helped him to find his way to *Winesburg, Ohio.* It was a crucial experience, for not only was he encouraged by the example of his friends to write about his native Middle West, but he became acquainted through them with authors who were to have a determining influence on his art: Tolstoi, Dostoyevski, Turgenev, Chekhov, in whose works, he said, "one feels life everywhere, in every page," and Gertrude Stein, from whom he learned the necessity of self-control and craftsmanship as a preliminary condition for telling the truth.

However, naturalism was by far the dominating factor in Anderson's development as an artist. Dreiser, who had doubly triumphed in 1911 with the publication of *Jenny Gerhardt* and the reissue of *Sister Carrie,* suppressed since 1900, was the most famous product of the Chicago school and a tempting model for a beginner from the Middle West. Sherwood Anderson absorbed his writings and assimilated his spirit. No wonder that, when *Winesburg, Ohio* appeared, Francis Hackett, the Chicago critic, described its author as "a naturalist with a skirl of music." He was right. Outwardly the book consists of a series of slices of life in the naturalistic manner. It offers a cross section of village life and carefully relates the various characters to their environment. Also, these narratives are based on a solid realistic substratum. Winesburg is the Clyde, Ohio, of Sherwood Anderson's boyhood, with hardly any change at all. (Even the name is not entirely imaginary, contrary to what Anderson thought. There is such a town, to which he may have sent "Roof–Fix" when he dealt in paint in Elyria.) Thanks to this careful use of an actual place, the village is so real that one could draw a map of it.

Not only is the background of the book a faithful and only slightly modified reproduction of reality, but the stories themselves are often told with absolute detachment and perfect objectivity, as though the author were a scientist observing physical or chemical phenomena with total unconcern. When, for instance, he describes Wing Biddlebaum being beaten by the father of one of his pupils, he shows no emotion whatever but remains, on the contrary, as impassive as the lens of a camera and as neutral as a tape recorder. As a rule, like a true realist or naturalist, he abstains from taking sides and steadfastly refuses to gloss over facts. Wash Williams, the hero of "Respectability," is depicted as a repulsive, bleary-eyed, dirty old man. "Everything about him was unclean. Even the whites of his eyes looked soiled." Louise Trunnion, one of George Willard's sweethearts, had "a black smudge on the side of her nose" and George "thought she must have rubbed her nose with her finger after she had been handling some of the kitchen-pots." It is not a world of glossy red apples, as on colored advertisements, but of "gnarled, twisted apples." And the section of town inhabited by day laborers is not left out of the picture. In "An Awakening" George Willard is described walking among its cheap wooden houses and stinking pigsties. There is indeed no idealization, no smoothing over of unpleasant details in *Winesburg, Ohio*.

Yet, in spite of appearances, the book is more than merely realistic in the usual sense. For one thing, it is too laconic. True realists are prolix and indulge in long and minute descriptions of external reality based on careful observations methodically recorded in notebooks. Arnold Bennett would thus note after a walk: "I passed 68 gulls sitting on the railings." The idea of counting gulls would never have occurred to Sherwood Anderson. "The writer with a notebook in his hand," he once wrote, "is always a bad workman, a man who distrusts his imagination." And, though he gives us a candid picture of the sexual life of his characters, Anderson refrains from entering into unnecessary detail. For all his boldness and candor, he always remains discreet and tactful on such topics.

Moreover, though he describes the surface of reality with as much objectivity and frankness as he can, his real purpose was to go below the mere surface. He dedicated *Winesburg, Ohio* to the memory of his mother, because, he said, she awoke in him "the hunger to see beneath the surface of lives." And indeed we see this hunger at work in the book. George Willard feels it. It makes him want to know in particular what lurks behind "the hideous leering face" of Wash Williams. And, as a result, whereas a realist would have seen nothing in Wash Williams but a filthy old man, Sherwood Anderson makes his hero imagine, or rather he himself imagines, that Wash Williams is changed into "a comely young man with black hair and black shining eyes." "The telegraph operator of Winesburg, sitting in the darkness on the railroad ties had become a poet." The railroad ties remain, but the hideous old man has been metamorphosed, transfigured into a comely young poet—a surprising transmutation of lead into gold, of reality into dreams. It is clear here that realism, the mere reproduction of facts, is not an end in itself for Sherwood Anderson, but only a means to an end.

This end is not the description of everyday life, in which on the contrary naturalists are engrossed. "Down with realism! A bas naturalism! Up with fantasy!" Sherwood Anderson wrote to a friend in 1922. He is not interested in the standard reactions of commonplace people under ordinary circumstances, but in the secret thoughts of men and women who live in their dreams or who dream aloud at night, when darkness frees them from the tyranny of society—and that is why, incidentally, such a large part of the book is set in twilight or complete darkness. In his *Memoirs* Anderson announced, "I would like to write a book of the life of the mind and of the imagination. Facts elude me. I cannot remember dates. When I deal in facts, at once I begin to lie. I can't help it." To some extent he did write this ideal book. It is *Winesburg, Ohio;* for the stories which compose it are not meant to describe external reality, but to explore the innermost recesses of a number of souls. As he jotted down in a notebook, "I do not intend to lift you *out of* yourself. What I intend is to lift you *into* yourself." In other words, he wanted above all to reveal what his characters keep hidden or unexpressed in their souls for fear of being laughed at or despised or even punished by the community in which they live.

Each of the characters of *Winesburg, Ohio*, except George Willard (as he points out in the "Book of the Grotesque," which serves as a kind of prologue to the other stories), "took one of the truths to himself." Each one took "the truth of virginity and the truth of passion, the truth of wealth and of poverty, of thrift and of profligacy, of carelessness and abandon"; he "tried to live his life by it, he became a grotesque." That is to say, each of these characters has become a monomaniac secretly obsessed with one preoccupation which he does not dare to confess or express either in word or action. As a result of this suppression, their personalities have been warped, twisted, and they are tortured, "crucified," as Dr. Parcival puts it in "The Philosopher." As a girl, Mrs. Willard was tormented by "the truth of passion" and desperately tried to find herself, to find something which she could not define, and she failed. Louise Bentley behaves hysterically, has become a "neurotic," because she grew up an orphan in a home where she was not wanted and because later her husband never gave her the love she craved. They could all say, like Tom Hard, the dipsomaniac in "Tandy," "I am a lover and have not found my thing to love." And so they all live shut up in their own thoughts, cut off from the others, unable to communicate even with those they love.

Sherwood Anderson sympathetically explores all these tortured souls, and his diagnosis is consonant with the findings of psychoanalysis: all these grotesques suffer because they have failed to satisfy their craving for love. However, though like Freud he was aware of "the terrible importance of the flesh in human relations" and illustrated it with the examples of Kate Swift, the Reverend Hartman, and Alice Hindman (who are all driven frantic by their unsatisfied sexual instincts), the love his characters are hungry for is not mere sexual love. It is something more, a passionate tenderness similar to the one which a mother experiences for her son, or which Tom Hard experiences for the little girl whose name, Tandy, curiously and mysteriously recalls both candy and tenderness. In a way, Tom Hard formulates the moral of the book when he pleads, "Dare to be strong and courageous. . . . Be brave enough to dare to be loved. Be something more than man or woman. Be Tandy."

Love, whether suppressed or expressed, is thus the major theme of *Winesburg, Ohio*. What matters is not George Willard or the grotesques whom he meets, but the love which they all hide in their hearts. And the book is indirectly a declaration of love to mankind paralleling what Sherwood Anderson more explicitly, but rather awkwardly, proclaimed in some of his poems, in "Song of Theodore," for instance: "O my beloved—men and women—I come into your presence. It is night and I am alone and I come to you. . . . I am a lover and I would touch you with the fingers of my hands." *Winesburg, Ohio* is thus essentially poetry in the form of fiction. For Anderson, stories were substitutes for poems, and literature a substitute for religion. When describing Dr. Reefy in "Death," he was probably thinking of himself:

He was almost a poet in his old age and his notion of what happened took a poetic turn. "I had come to a time in my life, when prayer became necessary and so I invented gods and prayed to them," he said. "I did not say my prayers in words nor did kneel down but sat perfectly still in my chair."

II

So what counts most in *Winesburg, Ohio* is not what is said in words but what is left unsaid, what is only suggested. The grotesques are not merely the queer creatures they seem to be; they are symbols of thwarted or unfulfilled love. Similarly, many other things in Winesburg are not merely what they seem to be. The hands of Wing Biddlebaum, for instance, are not mere hands; they soon become "the piston-rods of his machinery of expression," and later "the wings of an imprisoned bird" trying to escape. A little further, they are metamorphosed into "fluttering pennants of promise," recalling the "fluttering pennants of joy" in Whitman's "Song of the Open Road." Their external appearance does not matter. They are interesting only insofar as they express something hidden, the love which their owner is obliged to repress. These comparisons are not based on physical resemblances. They have hardly any plastic value at all and are not intended to describe the outside, but to suggest the inside of things. They are symbols, symbols of the possibility of communication between men, as we find out in "Sophistication," where, speaking of George Willard, Sherwood Anderson writes, "With all his heart, he wants to come close to some other human, touch with his hands, be touched by the hands of another."

Throughout the book there are thus constant correspondences between the so-called real world and the spiritual world of love which it hides. Rooms, walls, curtains, for instance, are meant to suggest, as opposed to hands, the isolation of the individual. "Loneliness, we are told, is in fact the story of a room" where Enoch Robinson "began to feel choked and walled-in." Mary Hardy similarly felt that "for her there was no way to break through the wall that had shut her off from the joy of life." All the characters crave love, and their craving is compared to hunger. The words "to hunger" and its corollary "to feed" recur again and again, as well as the words "scar" and "wound," suggesting the wounds inflicted by life.

But sometimes the symbols used by Anderson are not so transparent and banal. This is true, for instance, of the stained-glass window in the study of the Reverend Curtis Hartman. "On the window, made of little leaded panes, was a design showing the Christ laying his hand upon the head of a child." We soon hear that the tortured clergyman, in order to watch a young lady in her bedroom across the street, has broken a corner of the window with a stone. By a curious coincidence the broken pane happens to be the bare heel of the boy "standing motionless and looking with rapt eyes into the face of the Christ." What did Sherwood Anderson want to suggest by this? He probably had in mind Genesis 3: 14-15: "And the Lord God said unto the serpent . . . I will put enmity between thee and the woman, and between thy seed and her seed; it shall bruise thy head; and thou shalt bruise his heel." The heel therefore represents man's vulnerability to evil. It is through the heel that the serpent's poison enters us. So it is only natural that evil thoughts should enter the clergyman's mind through the heel of the boy on the stained-glass window. Later, however, the Reverend Hartman overcomes temptation and smashes the glass of the window with his fist because he catches sight of the woman kneeling on her bed and praying and "in the lamplight, her figure, slim and strong, looked like the figure of the boy in the presence of the Christ on the leaded window." This image of purity and innocence saves him.

Other episodes cannot be deciphered so easily. In "Mother," for example, Mrs. Willard observes from her window the feud between the baker and the druggist's grey cat. The cat keeps invading the bakery, and the baker invariably chases her, swearing and throwing things at her. It is a trivial occurrence, but it makes Mrs. Willard cry because "it seemed like a rehearsal of her own life, terrible in its vividness." It is probably meant to symbolize the cruelty and meaninglessness of life. But we are not told the meaning of the strange metamorphoses undergone by Mrs. Willard's lovers in her youth. After sexual intercourse she always thought—even when they were large and bearded—that they had suddenly become little boys, and she sobbed and sobbed and wondered why they did not sob too. This may be intended to suggest the fundamental innocence of love—before the fall. But we do not know for certain. Sherwood Anderson does not tell us.

In a way his stories are like the pictures painted by Enoch Robinson. His friends did not understand what they were supposed to represent, and it drove him frantic. "You don't get the point," he wanted to explain, "the picture you see doesn't consist of the things you see and say words about. There is something else, something you don't see at all, something you are not intended to see. Look at this one over here. . . . The dark spot by the road that you might not notice at all is, you see, the beginning of everything. There is a clump of elders there such as used to grow beside the road before our house back in Winesburg, Ohio, and in among the elders there is something hidden. It is a woman, that's what it is. She has been thrown from a horse and the horse has run away out of sight. . . . It's a woman and, oh, she is lovely! She is hurt and suffering, but she makes no sound. Don't you see how it is? She lies quite still, white and still, and the beauty comes out of her and spreads over everything. . . . I didn't try to paint the woman, of course. She is too beautiful to be painted. . . ."

Thus, when we read *Winesburg, Ohio*, we have to look for the beautiful woman hidden in the cluster of elders, for the secret meaning concealed under the fiction and the images. Outwardly they are tales of failure illustrating the absurdity of life, but a closer examination reveals their real contents. They are intended to express the love of the author for all that exists, but it is impossible for him to express such a feeling directly; he can only suggest it. In short, all these stories are so many meditations on life in the form of fables. They reflect Sherwood Anderson's twofold attitude, made of hope and despair, of disgust and love. He defines it explicitly in "Sophistication": "One shudders at the thought of the meaninglessness of life while at the same instant . . . one loves life so intensely that tears come into the eyes." This intense feeling of love and wonder spreads over the whole book and gives it its melancholy beauty.

III

Sherwood Anderson's main purpose being to make the reader realize the beauty and wonder of life, he was interested only in the privileged moments when he felt it himself with exceptional intensity and he wanted above all to record such rare intuitions. For this reason he wrote in *A Story Teller's Story*, "I have come to think that the true history of life is but a history of moments. It is only at rare moments that we live." Consequently, there was no point in writing a novel. Only short stories answered his purpose. "The novel form," he explained in his *Memoirs*, "does not fit an American writer. . . . What is wanted is a new looseness; and in *Winesburg* I . . . made my own form." So, just as Whitman had rejected the conventions of poetry, Anderson rejected the conventions of storytelling which Poe and O. Henry in particular had helped to establish. Not only did he decide to do without the novel form, but he also made up his mind to write short stories without any plot at all, since, as he said, "there are no plot-stories in life."

As a result of this attitude, his stories are the very opposite of "the story with a kick in it." They are apparently pointless. Nothing happens in them. They take place either long after the crisis, as in "Hands" and "Respectability"; or they announce a crisis to come, as in "Adventure," which is really no adventure at all since no one sees Alice Hindman as she goes out stark naked in the rain, and we shall never know whether she will eventually do "something dreadful," to take up her own phrase. Most of these tales thus fizzle out. The characters never kill or get killed. They always stop half way, because it was not Sherwood Anderson's intention to write tragic or dramatic stories but to describe states of feeling. Yet, however inconclusive these stories may seem, they are not formless. Each of them follows a parabola, describes the rise and fall of some lyrical excitement in the soul of one of the grotesques, generally in the presence of George Willard. Each of them, too, has a unity of its own, since it is devoted to one particular character and one particular "truth," as Sherwood Anderson explains in "The Book of the Grotesque." This impression of unity is further reinforced by the imagery, for each tale is built round one symbolical image: hands in the story by that name; "twisted apples" in "Paper Pills"; "a harnessed draught horse" in "The Untold Lie," and so forth.

Moreover, the book itself is not a loose collection of short stories. It also has form and a unity of its own. All the stories, despite their centrifugal tendency, are devoted to a central theme: the isolation of the individual who craves love and cannot for all his efforts satisfy his craving and communicate with others. Besides, all the stories take place in Winesburg, and nearly all of them directly or indirectly involve a central character, George Willard, who is now a mere witness and now an actor. In a way, the book could be entitled *The Education of George Willard*, for it shows his passage from the relative innocence of puberty to the "Sophistication" of young manhood through his experience of love with various girls (Louise Trunnion, Kate Swift, Helen White) and of death with the death of his mother, which liberates him and brings his childhood and the book to an end. In this respect, *Winesburg, Ohio* may even be considered a novel rather than a collection of short stories, for it has the temporal density of a novel, which is to say that, though made up of desultory episodes, the work gives an impression of progression and living duration.

Winesburg, Ohio is thus a much more complex book than it appears to be on a first reading, and Sherwood Anderson a far more subtle artist than he seems to the surface reader. The complexities also hold true on the level of language. Like Whitman, Anderson loved words for their own sake. "If you put words together in just a certain way," he wrote in *Tar*, "they sound nice even though you don't know what they mean." And Tar, who was one of his projections, "loved to say horses' names, racing words, horse words. . . ." In *Winesburg, Ohio*, however, Sherwood Anderson did not give full play to his love of words, first, because he realized that a writer must not be a "mere peddler of words," as Kate Swift points out in "The Teacher," and, second, because he was less interested in outer than in inner reality. He preferred to lay emphasis on emotions, feelings, and subjective impressions rather than on sensations. His vocabulary is less emotional than sensuous. On the other hand, though some passages, especially in the four episodes of "Godliness" and in "The Strength of God," have a Biblical flavor, and one occasionally encounters such technical words as "piston-rods" or "galvanized," the language used by Anderson in *Winesburg* is remarkably unaffected and nonliterary. It is even frequently colloquial. He never hesitates to resort to such phrases as "she got nowhere" or to rustic archaisms like "afoot," "abloom," "afire." And such a vague and trite word as "thing" frequently recurs several times on the same page.

His style is equally unpretentious. Its most obvious characteristic is its extreme syntactic simplicity. It is the very reverse of a periodic style. It proceeds by juxtaposition and accumulation, never, or hardly ever, by subordination. Sherwood Anderson's stories are strings of simple statements held together with *and's*. The reader thus has the impression of listening to a spoken narrative told by some farmer in the general store of a midwestern village. And yet, in spite of its simple structure and distinctly oral character, in spite even of its colloquialisms, Anderson's style is not really colloquial. It always has a certain stiffness and formality. The author, one feels, does not let himself go. His prose is not real spoken prose, but rather stylized spoken prose, as can be seen in particular in his avoidance of pronouns, whether personal or relative. He systematically prefers to repeat the nouns, which give both independence and dignity to each of his sentences. He also uses the same tone and manner in the straight narrative parts as in the dialogues, and on the whole makes all his characters speak in the same way, that is to say, like himself. This result was consonant with his aim, which was to project his dreams rather than give a photographic reproduction of reality or an authentic recording of real conversations. "People do not converse in the book world as they do in life," he noted in "A Writer's Conception of Realism"; "scenes of the imaginative world are not real scenes."

So this style was perfectly adapted to the author's purpose, but it is far from perfect all the same. Besides being somewhat monotonous, it is often diffuse and encumbered with unnecessary repetitions. In the last six lines of "Adventure," for instance, the word "face" recurs three times. Though he admired Gertrude Stein, whom he called "an artist in phrase making," Sherwood Anderson, unlike her, never tried to write "perfect" sentences. And this attitude partly explains Hemingway's revulsion from him. But Anderson's purpose was different. His ambition was not to carve enduring stories in dense prose, but to make his readers share certain experiences. Like Whitman, he wanted above all to sing himself, but he did so in stories told in the third person rather than in poems about his "Self." In spite of appearances, he was fundamentally a lyric poet in prose rather than a storyteller.

IV

Such was the art of this passionately sincere improviser who confessed in his *Memoirs* that he could not correct, fill in, rework his stories but preferred to throw them away when he had failed and rewrite them completely as much as ten or twelve times. He despised finish and equated art with artifice. He believed in inspiration rather than in rules, but he knew that his inspiration obeyed secret laws which gave form and meaning to what he wrote. "There are laws . . . that ride over the laws," he claimed; "this thing called form in art, it exists, of course. It is the force that holds the things of loveliness together." He was right. The stories which make up *Winesburg, Ohio*, are held together by such a force, which fuses his inner contradictions into one and enables him to express both "the truth of virginity and the truth of passion," to reconcile the innocence of the adolescent he never ceased to be with the experience of the "slick fellow" he later became, and so, in short, to make us feel both the meaninglessness and the wonder of life.

ROGER ASSELINEAU

A Note on the Text.   The text of *Winesburg, Ohio* here followed is that of the first edition (New York: B. W. Huebsch, 1919) as revised by Malcolm Cowley (New York: The Viking Press, Inc., 1960).

"Hands" which was originally published in *The Masses*, 1916, became the initial story of *Winesburg, Ohio*. The pathetic Wing Biddlebaum yearns for companionship and understanding. Tries to express his dreams & his visions through his graceful sensitive hands.

WINESBURG, OHIO

Hands

UPON THE HALF decayed veranda[1] of a small frame house that stood near the edge of a ravine near the town of Winesburg, Ohio, a fat little old man walked nervously up and down. Across a long field that had been seeded for clover but that had produced only a dense crop of yellow mustard weeds, he could see the public highway along which went a wagon filled with berry pickers returning from the fields. The berry pickers, youths and maidens, laughed and shouted boisterously. A boy clad in a blue shirt leaped from the wagon and attempted to drag after him one of the maidens, who screamed and protested shrilly. The feet of the boy in the road kicked up a cloud of dust that floated across the face of the departing sun. Over the long field came a thin girlish voice. "Oh, you Wing Biddlebaum, comb your hair, it's falling into

The nine stories here reprinted are from *Winesburg, Ohio*, by Sherwood Anderson. Copyright 1919 by B. W. Huebsch, 1947 by Eleanor Copenhaver Anderson. Reprinted by permission of the Viking Press, Inc.

[1] In the manuscript the story originally began with "Upon the veranda . . . ."

In the end wing's hands, providing the body with physical nourishment, suggest the head wanting of the devotee seeking spiritual solace.

your eyes," commanded the voice to the man, who was bald and whose nervous little hands fiddled about the bare white forehead as though arranging a mass of tangled locks.

Wing Biddlebaum, forever frightened and beset by a ghostly band of doubts, did not think of himself as in any way a part of the life of the town where he had lived for twenty years. Among all the people of Winesburg but one had come close to him. With George Willard, son of Tom Willard, the proprietor of the New Willard House, he had formed something like[2] a friendship. George Willard was the reporter on the *Winesburg Eagle* and sometimes in the evenings he walked out along the highway to Wing Biddlebaum's house. Now as the old man walked up and down on the veranda, his hands moving nervously about, he was hoping that George Willard would come and spend the evening with him. After the wagon containing the berry pickers had passed, he went across the field through the tall mustard weeds and climbing a rail fence peered anxiously along the road to the town. For a moment he stood thus, rubbing his hands together and looking up and down the road, and then, fear overcoming him, ran back to walk again upon the porch on his own house.

In the presence of George Willard, Wing Biddlebaum, who for twenty years had been the town mystery, lost something of his timidity, and his shadowy personality, submerged in a sea of doubts, came forth to look at the world. With the young reporter at his side, he ventured in the light of day into Main Street or strode up and down on the rickety front porch of his own house, talking excitedly. The voice that had been low and trembling became shrill and loud. The bent figure straightened. With a kind of wriggle, like a fish returned to the brook by the fisherman, Biddlebaum the silent began to talk, striving to put into words the ideas that had been accumulated by his mind during long years of silence.

Wing Biddlebaum talked much with his hands. The slender expressive fingers, forever active, forever striving to conceal themselves in his pockets or behind his back, came forth and became the piston rods of his machinery of expression.

The story of Wing Biddlebaum is a story of hands.[3] Their restless activity, like unto the beating of the wings of an imprisoned bird,[4] had given him his name. Some obscure poet of the town had thought of it. The hands alarmed their owner. He wanted to keep them hidden away and looked with amazement at the quiet inexpressive hands of other men who worked beside him in the fields, or passed, driving sleepy teams on country roads.

When he talked to George Willard, Wing Biddlebaum closed his fists and beat with them upon a table or on the walls of his house. The action made him more comfortable. If the desire to talk came to him when the two were walking in the fields, he sought out a stump or the top board of a fence and with his hands pounding busily talked with renewed ease.

[2] The manuscript shows that "something like" was added by Anderson as a corrective.

[3] In the manuscript this sentence originally concluded: "a story of his hands." The deletion of "his" makes the hands seem more impersonal.

[4] The word "imprisoned" was added later in the manuscript.

The story of Wing Biddlebaum's hands is worth a book in itself. Sympathetically set forth it would tap many strange, beautiful qualities in obscure men. It is a job for a poet. In Winesburg the hands had attracted attention merely because of their activity. With them Wing Biddlebaum had picked as high as a hundred and forty quarts of strawberries in a day. They became his distinguishing feature, the source of his fame. Also they made more grotesque an already grotesque and elusive individuality. Winesburg was proud of the hands of Wing Biddlebaum in the same spirit in which it was proud of Banker White's new stone house and Wesley Moyer's bay stallion, Tony Tip, that had won the two-fifteen trot at the fall races in Cleveland.

As for George Willard, he had many times wanted to ask about the hands. At times an almost overwhelming curiosity had taken hold [5] of him. He felt that there must be a reason for their strange activity and their inclination to keep hidden away and only a growing respect for Wing Biddlebaum kept him from blurting out the questions that were often in his mind.

Once he had been on the point of asking. The two were walking in the fields on a summer afternoon and had stopped to sit upon a grassy bank. All afternoon Wing Biddlebaum had talked as one inspired. By a fence he had stopped and beating like a giant woodpecker upon the top board had shouted at George Willard, condemning his tendency to be too much influenced by the people about him. "You are destoying yourself," he cried. "You have the inclination to be alone and to dream and you are afraid of dreams. You want to be like others in town here. You hear them talk and you try to imitate them."

On the grassy bank Wing Biddlebaum had tried again to drive his point home. His voice became soft and reminiscent, and with a sigh of contentment he launched into a long rambling talk, speaking as one lost in a dream.

Out of the dream Wing Biddlebaum made a picture for George Willard. In the picture men lived again in a kind of pastoral golden age. Across a green open country came clean-limbed young men, some afoot, some mounted upon horses. In crowds the young men came to gather about the feet of an old man who sat beneath a tree in a tiny garden and who talked to them.

Wing Biddlebaum became wholly inspired. For once he forgot the hands. Slowly they stole forth and lay upon George Willard's shoulders.[6] Something new and bold came into the voice that talked. "You must try to forget all you have learned," said the old man. "You must begin to dream. From this time on you must shut your ears to the roaring of the voices."

Pausing in his speech, Wing Biddlebaum looked long and earnestly at George Willard. His eyes glowed. Again he raised the hands[7] to caress the boy and then a look of horror swept over his face.

With a convulsive movement of his body, Wing Biddlebaum sprang to his feet and thrust his hands deep into his trousers pockets. Tears came to his eyes. "I must be getting along home. I can talk no more with you," he said nervously.

Without looking back, the old man had hurried down the hillside and

---

[5] Sherwood Anderson had originally written "possession" instead of "hold."

[6] The sentence originally read, ". . . stole to George Willard's shoulders."

[7] Sherwood Anderson first wrote, "Again he raised his hands. . . ."

across a meadow, leaving George Willard perplexed and frightened upon the grassy slope. With a shiver of dread the boy arose and went along the road toward town. "I'll not ask him about his hands," he thought, touched by the memory of the terror he had seen in the man's eyes. "There's something wrong, but I don't want to know what it is. His hands have something to do with his fear of me and of everyone."

And George Willard was right. Let us look briefly into the story of the hands. Perhaps our talking of them will arouse the poet who will tell the hidden wonder story of the influence for which the hands were but fluttering pennants of promise.

In his youth Wing Biddlebaum had been a school teacher in a town in Pennsylvania. He was not then known as Wing Biddlebaum, but went by the less euphonic name of Adolph Myers. As Adolph Myers he was much loved by the boys of his school.

Adolph Myers was meant by nature to be a teacher of youth. He was one of those rare, little-understood men who rule by a power so gentle that it passes as a lovable weakness. In their feeling for the boys under their charge such men are not unlike the finer sort of women in their love of men.

And yet that is but crudely stated. It needs the poet there. With the boys of his school, Adolph Myers had walked in the evening or had sat talking until dusk upon the schoolhouse steps lost in a kind of dream. Here and there went his hands, caressing the shoulders of the boys, playing about the tousled heads. As he talked his voice became soft and musical. There was a caresss in that also. In a way the voice and the hands, the stroking of the shoulders and the touching of the hair were a part of the schoolmaster's effort to carry a dream into the young minds. By the caress that was in his fingers he expressed himself. He was one of those men in whom the force that creates life is diffused, not centralized. Under the caress of his hands doubt and disbelief went out of the minds of the boys and they began also to dream.

And then the tragedy. A half-witted boy of the school became enamored of the young master. In his bed at night he imagined unspeakable things and in the morning went forth to tell his dreams as facts. Strange, hideous accusations fell from his loose-hung lips. Through the Pennsylvania town went a shiver. Hidden, shadowy doubts that had been in men's minds concerning Adolph Myers were galvanized into beliefs.

The tragedy did not linger. Trembling lads were jerked out of bed and questioned. "He put his arms about me," said one. "His fingers were always playing in my hair," said another.

One afternoon a man of the town, Henry Bradford, who kept a saloon, came to the schoolhouse door. Calling Adolph Myers into the school yard he began to beat him with his fists. As his hard knuckles beat down into the frightened face of the schoolmaster, his wrath became more and more terrible. Screaming with dismay, the children ran here and there like disturbed insects. "I'll teach you to put your hands on my boy, you beast," roared the saloon keeper, who, tired of beating the master, had begun to kick him about the yard.

Adolph Myers was driven from the Pennsylvania town in the night. With lanterns in their hands a dozen men came to the door of the house where he lived alone and commanded that he dress and come forth. It was raining and one of the men had a rope in his hands. They had intended to hang the schoolmaster, but something in his figure, so small, white, and pitiful, touched their hearts and they let him escape. As he ran away into the darkness they repented of their weakness and ran after him, swearing and throwing sticks and great balls of soft mud at the[8] figure that screamed and ran faster and faster into the darkness.

For twenty years Adolph Myers had lived alone in Winesburg. He was but forty but looked sixty-five. The name of Biddlebaum he got from a box of goods seen at a freight station as he hurried through an eastern Ohio town. He had an aunt in Winesburg, a black-toothed old woman who raised chickens, and with her he lived until she died. He had been ill for a year after the experience in Pennsylvania, and after his recovery worked as a day laborer in the fields, going timidly about and striving to conceal his hands. Although he did not understand what had happened he felt that the hands must be to blame. Again and again the fathers of the boys had talked of the hands. "Keep your hands to yourself," the saloon keeper had roared, dancing with fury in the schoolhouse yard.

Upon the veranda of his house by the ravine, Wing Biddlebaum continued to walk up and down until the sun had disappeared and the road beyond the field was lost in the grey shadows. Going into his house he cut slices of bread and spread honey upon them. When the rumble of the evening train that took away the express cars loaded with the day's harvest of berries had passed and restored the silence of the summer night, he went again to walk upon the veranda. In the darkness he could not see the hands and they became quiet. Although he still hungered for the presence of the boy,[9] who was the medium through which he expressed his love of man, the hunger became again a part of his loneliness and his waiting. Lighting a lamp, Wing Biddlebaum washed the few dishes soiled by his simple meal and, setting up a folding cot by the screen door that led to the porch, prepared to undress for the night. A few stray white bread crumbs lay on the cleanly washed floor by the table; putting the lamp upon a low stool he began to pick up the crumbs, carrying them to his mouth one by one with unbelievable rapidity. In the dense blotch of light beneath the table, the kneeling figure looked like a priest engaged in some service of his church. The nervous expressive fingers, flashing in and out of the light, might well have been mistaken for the fingers of the devotee going swiftly through decade after decade of his rosary.

Paper Pills

HE WAS AN old man with a white beard and huge nose and hands. Long before the time during which we will know him, he was a doctor and drove

[8] Originally "his" in the manuscript.

[9] This sentence originally read, "Although he still hungered for the boy. . . ."

a jaded white horse from house to house through the streets of Winesburg. Later he married a girl who had money. She had been left a large fertile farm when her father died. The girl was quiet, tall, and dark, and to many people she seemed very beautiful. Everyone in Winesburg wondered why she married the doctor. Within a year after the marriage she died.

The knuckles of the doctor's hands were extraordinarily large. When the hands were closed they looked like clusters of unpainted wooden balls as large as walnuts fastened together by steel rods. He smoked a cob pipe and after his wife's death sat all day in his empty office close by a window that was covered with cobwebs. He never opened the window. Once on a hot day in August he tried but found it stuck fast and after that he forgot all about it.

Winesburg had forgotten the old man, but in Doctor Reefy there were the seeds of something very fine. Alone in his musty office in the Heffner Block[1] above the Paris Dry Goods Company's store, he worked ceaselessly, building up something that he himself destroyed. Little pyramids of truth he erected and after erecting knocked them down again that he might have the truths to erect other pyramids.

Doctor Reefy was a tall man who had worn one suit of clothes for ten years. It was frayed at the sleeves and little holes had appeared at the knees and elbows. In the office he wore also a linen duster with huge pockets into which he continually stuffed scraps of paper. After some weeks the scraps of paper became little hard round balls, and when the pockets were filled he dumped them out upon the floor. For ten years he had but one friend, another old man named John Spaniard who owned a tree nursery.[2] Sometimes, in a playful mood, old Doctor Reefy took from his pockets a handful of the paper balls and threw them at the nursery man. "That is to confound you, you blithering old sentimentalist," he cried, shaking with laughter.

The story of Doctor Reefy and his courtship of the tall dark girl who became his wife and left her money to him is a very curious story. It is delicious, like the twisted little apples that grow in the orchards of Winesburg. In the fall one walks in the orchards and the ground is hard with frost underfoot. The apples have been taken from the trees by the pickers. They have been put in barrels and shipped to the cities where they will be eaten in apartments that are filled with books, magazines, furniture, and people. On the trees are only a few gnarled apples that the pickers have rejected. They look like the knuckles of Doctor Reefy's hands. One nibbles at them and they are delicious. Into a little round place at the side of the apple has been gathered all of its sweetness. One runs from tree to tree over the frosted ground picking the gnarled, twisted apples and filling his pockets with them. Only the few know the sweetness of the twisted apples.

The girl and Doctor Reefy began their courtship on a summer afternoon. He was forty-five then and already he had begun the practice of filling his pockets with the scraps of paper that became hard balls and were thrown away. The habit had been formed as he sat in his buggy behind the jaded grey

---

[1] This was the name of an actual block of buildings in Clyde, Ohio, Anderson's boyhood home.

[2] There was a nurseryman named French in Clyde, Ohio.

horse and went slowly along country roads. On the papers were written thoughts, ends of thoughts, beginnings of thoughts.

One by one the mind of Doctor Reefy had made the thoughts. Out of many of them he formed a truth that arose gigantic in his mind. The truth clouded the world. It became terrible and then faded away and the little thoughts began again.

The tall dark girl came to see Doctor Reefy because she was in the family way and had become frightened. She was in that condition because of a series of circumstances also curious.

The death of her father and mother and the rich acres of land that had come down to her had set a train of suitors on her heels. For two years she saw suitors almost every evening. Except two they were all alike. They talked to her of passion and there was a strained eager quality in their voices and in their eyes when they looked at her. The two who were different were much unlike each other. One of them, a slender young man with white hands, the son of a jeweler in Winesburg, talked continually of virginity. When he was with her he was never off the subject. The other, a black-haired boy with large ears, said nothing at all but always managed to get her into the darkness, where he began to kiss her.

For a time the tall dark girl thought she would marry the jeweler's son. For hours she sat in silence listening as he talked to her and then she began to be afraid of something. Beneath his talk of virginity she began to think there was a lust greater than in all the others. At times it seemed to her that as he talked he was holding her body in his hands. She imagined him turning it slowly about in the white hands and staring at it. At night she dreamed that he had bitten into her body and that his jaws were dripping. She had the dream three times, then she became in the family way to the one who said nothing at all but who in the moment of his passion actually did bite her shoulder so that for days the marks of his teeth showed.

After the tall dark girl came to know Doctor Reefy it seemed to her that she never wanted to leave him again. She went into his office one morning and without her saying anything he seemed to know what had happened to her.

In the office of the doctor there was a woman, the wife of the man who kept the bookstore in Winesburg. Like all old-fashioned country practitioners, Doctor Reefy pulled teeth, and the woman who waited held a handkerchief to her teeth and groaned. Her husband was with her and when the tooth was taken out they both screamed and blood ran down on the woman's white dress. The tall dark girl did not pay any attention. When the woman and the man had gone the doctor smiled. "I will take you driving into the country with me," he said.

For several weeks the tall dark girl and the doctor were together almost every day. The condition that had brought her to him passed in an illness, but she was like one who has discovered the sweetness of the twisted apples, she could not get her mind fixed again upon the round perfect fruit that is eaten in the city apartments. In the fall after the beginning of her acquaintanceship with him she married Doctor Reefy and in the following spring she died. During the winter he read to her all of the odds and ends of thoughts he had scribbled on the bits of paper. After he had read them he laughed and stuffed them away in his pockets to become round hard balls.

Mother

ELIZABETH WILLARD, the mother of George Willard, was tall and gaunt and her face was marked with smallpox scars. Although she was but forty-five, some obscure disease had taken the fire out of her figure. Listlessly she went about the disorderly old hotel looking at the faded wall-paper and the ragged carpets and, when she was able to be about, doing the work of a chambermaid among beds soiled by the slumbers of fat traveling men. Her husband, Tom Willard, a slender, graceful man with square shoulders, a quick military step, and a black mustache trained to turn sharply up at the ends, tried to put the wife out of his mind. The presence of the tall ghostly figure, moving slowly through the halls, he took as a reproach to himself. When he thought of her he grew angry and swore. The hotel was unprofitable and forever on the edge of failure and he wished himself out of it. He thought of the old house and the woman who lived there with him as things defeated and done for. The hotel in which he had begun life so hopefully as now a mere ghost of what a hotel should be. As he went spruce and business-like through the streets of Winesburg, he sometimes stopped and turned quickly about as though fearing that the spirit of the hotel and of the woman would follow him even into the streets. "Damn such a life, damn it!" he sputtered aimlessly.

Tom Willard had a passion for village politics and for years had been the leading Democrat in a strongly Republican community. Some day, he told himself, the tide of things political will turn in my favor and the years of ineffectual service count big in the bestowal of rewards. He dreamed of going to Congress and even of becoming governor. Once when a younger member of the party arose at a political conference and began to boast of his faithful service, Tom Willard grew white with fury. "Shut up, you," he roared, glaring about. "What do you know of service? What are you but a boy? Look at what I've done here! I was a Democrat here in Winesburg when it was a crime to be a Democrat. In the old days they fairly hunted us with guns."

Between Elizabeth and her one son George there was a deep unexpressed bond of sympathy, based on a girlhood dream that had long ago died. In the son's presence she was timid and reserved, but sometimes while he hurried about town intent upon his duties as a reporter, she went into his room and closing the door knelt by a little desk, made of a kitchen table, that sat near a window. In the room by the desk she went through a ceremony that was half a prayer, half a demand, addressed to the skies. In the boyish figure she yearned to see something half forgotten that had once been a part of herself re-created. The prayer concerned that. "Even though I die, I will in some way keep defeat from you," she cried, and so deep was her determination that her whole body shook. Her eyes glowed and she clenched her fists. "If I am dead and see him becoming a meaningless drab figure like myself, I will come back," she declared. "I ask God now to give me that privilege. I demand it. I will pay for it. God may beat me with his fists. I will take any blow that may befall if but this my boy be allowed to express something for us both." Pausing uncertainly, the woman stared about the boy's room. "And do not let him become smart and successful either," she added vaguely.

The communion between George Willard and his mother was outwardly a formal thing without meaning. When she was ill and sat by the window in her room he sometimes went in the evening to make her a visit. They sat by a window that looked over the roof of a small frame building into Main Street. By turning their heads they could see through another window, along an alleyway that ran behind the Main Street stores and into the back door of Abner Groff's bakery. Sometimes as they sat thus a picture of village life presented itself to them. At the back door of his shop appeared Abner Groff with a stick or an empty milk bottle in his hand. For a long time there was a feud between the baker and a grey cat that belonged to Sylvester West, the druggist. The boy and his mother saw the cat creep into the door of the bakery and presently emerge followed by the baker, who swore and waved his arms about. The baker's eyes were small and red and his black hair and beard were filled with flour dust. Sometimes he was so angry that, although the cat had disappeared, he hurled sticks, bits of broken glass, and even some of the tools of his trade about. Once he broke a window at the back of Sinning's Hardware Store. In the alley the grey cat crouched behind barrels filled with torn paper and broken bottles above which flew a black swarm of flies. Once when she was alone, and after watching a prolonged and ineffectual outburst on the part of the baker, Elizabeth Willard put her head down on her long white hands and wept. After that she did not look along the alleyway any more, but tried to forget the contest between the bearded man and the cat. It seemed like a rehearsal of her own life, terrible in its vividness.

In the evening when the son sat in the room with his mother, the silence made them both feel awkward. Darkness came on and the evening train came in at the station. In the street below feet tramped up and down upon a board sidewalk. In the station yard, after the evening train had gone, there was a heavy silence. Perhaps Skinner Leason,[1] the express agent, moved a truck the length of the station platform. Over on Main Street sounded a man's voice, laughing. The door of the express office banged. George Willard arose and crossing the room fumbled for the doorknob. Sometimes he knocked against a chair, making it scrape along the floor. By the window sat the sick woman, perfectly still, listless. Her long hands, white and bloodless, could be seen drooping over the ends of the arms of the chair. "I think you had better be out among the boys. You are too much indoors," she said, striving to relieve the embarrassment of the departure. "I thought I would take a walk," replied George Willard, who felt awkward and confused.

One evening in July, when the transient guests who made the New Willard House their temporary home had become scarce, and the hallways, lighted only by kerosene lamps turned low, were plunged in gloom, Elizabeth Willard had an adventure. She had been ill in bed for several days and her son

---

[1] There was a Skinner Letson in Clyde, Ohio, and Sherwood Anderson first wrote his actual name on the manuscript, but changed it to "Leason" afterward.

had not come to visit her. She was alarmed. The feeble blaze of life that remained in her body was blown into a flame by her anxiety and she crept out of bed, dressed and hurried along the hallway toward her son's room, shaking with exaggerated fears. As she went along she steadied herself with her hand, slipped along the papered walls of the hall and breathed with difficulty. The air whistled through her teeth. As she hurried forward she thought how foolish she was. "He is concerned with boyish affairs," she told herself. "Perhaps he has now begun to walk about in the evening with girls."

Elizabeth Willard had a dread of being seen by guests in the hotel that had once belonged to her father and the ownership of which still stood recorded in her name in the county courthouse. The hotel was continually losing patronage because of its shabbiness and she thought of herself as also shabby. Her own room was in an obscure corner and when she felt able to work she voluntarily worked among the beds, preferring the labor that could be done when the guests were abroad seeking trade among the merchants of Winesburg.

By the door of her son's room the mother knelt upon the floor and listened for some sound from within. When she heard the boy moving about and talking in low tones a smile came to her lips. George Willard had a habit of talking aloud to himself and to hear him doing so had always given his mother a peculiar pleasure. The habit in him, she felt, strengthened the secret bond that existed between them. A thousand times she had whispered to herself of the matter. "He is groping about, trying to find himself," she thought. "He is not a dull clod, all words and smartness. Within him there is a secret something that is striving to grow. It is the thing I let be killed in myself."

In the darkness in the hallway by the door the sick woman arose and started again toward her own room. She was afraid that the door would open and the boy come upon her. When she had reached a safe distance and was about to turn a corner into a second hallway she stopped and bracing herself with her hands waited, thinking to shake off a trembling fit of weakness that had come upon her. The presence of the boy in the room had made her happy. In her bed, during the long hours alone, the little fears that had visited her had become giants. Now they were all gone. "When I get back to my room I shall sleep," she murmured gratefully.

But Elizabeth Willard was not to return to her bed and to sleep. As she stood trembling in the darkness the door of her son's room opened and the boy's father, Tom Willard, stepped out. In the light that streamed out at the door he stood with the knob in his hand and talked. What he said infuriated the woman.

Tom Willard was ambitious for his son. He had always thought of himself as a successful man, although nothing he had ever done had turned out successfully. However, when he was out of sight of the New Willard House and had no fear of coming upon his wife, he swaggered and began to dramatize himself as one of the chief men of the town. He wanted his son to succeed. He it was who had secured for the boy the position on the *Winesburg Eagle*. Now, with a ring of earnestness in his voice, he was advising concerning some course of conduct. "I tell you what, George, you've got to wake up," he said sharply. "Will Henderson has spoken to me three times concerning the matter. He says you go along for hours not hearing when you are spoken to and acting like a gawky girl. What ails you?" Tom Willard laughed good-naturedly. "Well, I guess you'll get over it," he said. "I told Will that. You're not a fool and you're not a woman. You're Tom Willard's son and you'll wake up. I'm not afraid. What you say clears things up. If being a newspaper man had put the notion of becoming a writer into your mind that's all right. Only I guess you'll have to wake up to do that too, eh?"

Tom Willard went briskly along the hallway and down a flight of stairs to the office. The woman in the darkness could hear him laughing and talking with a guest who was striving to wear away a dull evening by dozing in a chair by the office door. She returned to the door of her son's room. The weakness had passed from her body as by a miracle and she stepped boldly along. A thousand ideas raced through her head. When she heard the scraping of a chair and the sound of a pen scratching upon paper, she again turned and went back along the hallway to her own room.

A definite determination had come into the mind of the defeated wife of the Winesburg hotel keeper. The determination was the result of long years of quiet and rather ineffectual thinking. "Now," she told herself, "I will act. There is something threatening my boy and I will ward it off." The fact that the conversation between Tom Willard and his son had been rather quiet and natural, as though an understanding existed between them, maddened her. Although for years she had hated her husband, her hatred had always before been a quite impersonal thing. He had been merely a part of something else that she hated. Now, and by the few words at the door, he had become the thing personified. In the darkness of her own room she clenched her fists and glared about. Going to a cloth bag that hung on a nail by the wall she took out a long pair of sewing scissors and held them in her hand like a dagger. "I will stab him," she said aloud. "He has chosen to be the voice of evil and I will kill him. When I have killed him something will snap within myself and I will die also. It will be a release for all of us."

In her girlhood and before her marriage with Tom Willard, Elizabeth had borne a somewhat shaky reputation in Winesburg. For years she had been what is called "stage-struck" and had paraded through the streets with traveling men guests at her father's hotel, wearing loud clothes and urging them to tell her of life in the cities out of which they had come. Once she startled the town by putting on men's clothes and riding a bicycle down Main Street.

In her own mind the tall dark girl had been in those days much confused. A great restlessness was in her and it expressed itself in two ways. First there was an uneasy desire for change, for some big definite movement to her life. It was this feeling that had turned her mind to the stage. She dreamed of joining some company and wandering over the world, seeing always new faces and giving something out of herself to all people. Sometimes at night she was quite beside herself with the thought, but when she tried to talk of the matter to the members of the theatrical companies that came to Winesburg and stopped at her father's hotel, she got nowhere. They did not seem to know what she meant, or if she did get something of her passion expressed, they only laughed. "It's not like that," they said. "It's as dull and uninteresting as this here. Nothing comes of it."

With the traveling men when she walked about with them, and later with Tom Willard, it was quite different. Always they seemed to understand and sympathize with her. On the side streets of the village, in the darkness under the trees, they took hold of her hand and she thought that something unexpressed in herself came forth and became a part of an unexpressed something in them.

And then there was the second expression of her restlessness. When that came she felt for a time released and happy. She did not blame the men who walked with her and later she did not blame Tom Willard. It was always the same, beginning with kisses and ending, after strange wild emotions, with peace and then sobbing repentance. When she sobbed she put her hand upon the face of the man and had always the same thought. Even though he were large and bearded she thought he had become suddenly a little boy. She wondered why he did not sob also.

In her room, tucked away in a corner of the old Willard House, Elizabeth Willard lighted a lamp and put it on a dressing table that stood by the door. A thought had come into her mind and she went to a closet and brought out a small square box and set it on the table. The box contained material for make-up and had been left with other things by a theatrical company that had once been stranded in Winesburg. Elizabeth Willard had decided that she would be beautiful. Her hair was still black and there was a great mass of it braided and coiled about her head. The scene that was to take place in the office below began to grow in her mind. No ghostly worn-out figure should confront Tom Willard, but something quite unexpected and startling. Tall and with dusky cheeks and hair that fell in a mass from her shoulders, a figure should come striding down the stairway before the startled loungers in the hotel office. The figure would be silent—it would be swift and terrible. As a tigress whose cub had been threatened would she appear, coming out of the shadows, stealing noiselessly along and holding the long wicked scissors in her hand.

With a little broken sob in her throat, Elizabeth Willard blew out the light that stood upon the table and stood weak and trembling in the darkness. The strength that had been as a miracle in her body left and she half reeled across the floor, clutching at the back of the chair in which she had spent so many long days staring out over the tin roofs into the main street of Winesburg. In the hallway there was the sound of footsteps and George Willard came in at the door. Sitting in a chair beside his mother he began to talk. "I'm going to get out of here," he said. "I don't know where I shall go or what I shall do but I am going away."

The woman in the chair waited and trembled. An impulse came to her. "I suppose you had better wake up," she said. "You think that? You will go to the city and make money, eh? It will be better for you, you think, to be a business man, to be brisk and smart and alive?" She waited and trembled.

The son shook his head. "I suppose I can't make you understand, but oh, I wish I could," he said earnestly. "I can't even talk to father about it. I don't try. There isn't any use. I don't know what I shall do. I just want to go away and look at people and think."

Silence fell upon the room where the boy and woman sat together. Again, as on the other evenings, they were embarrassed. After a time the boy tried again to talk. "I suppose it won't be for a year or two but I've been thinking about it," he said, rising and going toward the door. "Something father said makes it sure that I shall have to go away." He fumbled with the door knob. In the room the silence became unbearable to the woman. She wanted to cry out with joy because of the words that had come from the lips of her son, but the expression of joy had become impossible to her. "I think you had better go out among the boys. You are too much indoors," she said. "I thought I would go for a little walk," replied the son stepping awkwardly out of the room and closing the door.

*   *   *

The Strength of God

THE REVEREND CURTIS HARTMAN was pastor of the Presbyterian Church of Winesburg, and had been in that position ten years. He was forty years old, and by his nature very silent and reticent. To preach, standing in the pulpit before the people, was always a hardship for him and from Wednesday morning until Saturday evening he thought of nothing but the two sermons that must be preached on Sunday. Early on Sunday morning he went into a little room called a study in the bell tower of the church and prayed. In his prayers there was one note that always predominated. "Give me strength and courage for Thy work, O Lord!" he pleaded, kneeling on the bare floor and bowing his head in the presence of the task that lay before him.

The Reverend Hartman was a tall man with a brown beard. His wife, a stout, nervous woman, was the daughter of a manufacturer of underwear at Cleveland, Ohio. The minister himself was rather a favorite in the town. The elders of the church liked him because he was quiet and unpretentious and Mrs. White, the banker's wife, thought him scholarly and refined.

The Presbyterian Church held itself somewhat aloof from the other churches of Winesburg. It was larger and more imposing and its minister was better paid. He even had a carriage of his own and on summer evenings sometimes drove about town with his wife. Through Main Street and up and down Buckeye Street he went, bowing gravely to the people, while his wife, afire with secret pride, looked at him out of the corners of her eyes and worried lest the horse become frightened and run away.

For a good many years after he came to Winesburg things went well with Curtis Hartman. He was not one to arouse keen enthusiasm among the worshippers in his church but on the other hand he made no enemies. In reality he was much in earnest and sometimes suffered prolonged periods of remorse because he could not go crying the word of God in the highways and byways of the town. He wondered if the flame of the spirit really burned in him and dreamed of a day when a strong sweet new current of power would come like a great wind into his voice and his soul and the people would tremble before the spirit of God made manifest in him. "I am a poor stick and that will never really happen to me," he mused dejectedly, and then a patient smile lit up his features. "Oh well, I suppose I'm doing well enough," he added philosophically.

The room in the bell tower of the church, where on Sunday mornings the minister prayed for an increase in him of the power of God, had but one window. It was long and narrow and swung outward on a hinge like a door. On the window, made of little leaded panes, was a design showing the Christ laying his hand upon the head of a child. One Sunday morning in the summer as he sat by his desk in the room with a large Bible opened before him, and the sheets of his sermon scattered about, the minister was shocked to see, in the upper room of the house next door, a woman lying in her bed and smoking a cigarette while she read a book. Curtis Hartman went on tiptoe to the window and closed it softly. He was horror stricken at the thought of a woman smoking and trembled also to think that his eyes, just raised from the pages of the book of God, had looked upon the bare shoulders and white throat of a woman. With his brain in a whirl he went down into the pulpit and preached a long sermon without once thinking of his gestures or his voice. The sermon attracted unusual attention because of its power and clearness. "I wonder if she is listening, if my voice is carrying a message into her soul," he thought and began to hope that on future Sunday mornings he might be able to say words that would touch and awaken the woman apparently far gone in secret sin.

The house next door to the Presbyterian Church, through the windows of which the minister had seen the sight that had so upset him, was occupied by two women. Aunt Elizabeth Swift, a grey competent-looking widow with money in the Winesburg National Bank, lived there with her daughter Kate Swift, a school teacher. The school teacher was thirty years old and had a neat trim-looking figure. She had few friends and bore a reputation of having a sharp tongue. When he began to think about her, Curtis Hartman remembered that she had been to Europe and had lived for two years in New York City. "Perhaps after all her smoking means nothing," he thought. He began to remember that when he was a student in college and occasionally read novels, good although somewhat worldly women, had smoked through the pages of a book that had once fallen into his hands. With a rush of new determination he worked on his sermons all through the week and forgot, in his zeal to reach the ears and the soul of this new listener, both his embarrassment in the pulpit and the necessity of prayer in the study on Sunday mornings.

Reverend Hartman's experience with women had been somewhat limited. He was the son of a wagon maker from Muncie, Indiana, and had worked his way through college. The daughter of the underwear manufacturer had boarded in a house where he lived during his school days and he had married her after a formal and prolonged courtship, carried on for the most part by the girl herself. On his marriage day the underwear manufacturer had given his daughter five thousand dollars and he promised to leave her at least twice that amount in his will. The minister had thought himself fortunate in marriage and had never permitted himself to think of other women. He did not want to think of other women. What he wanted was to do the work of God quietly and earnestly.

In the soul of the minister a struggle awoke. From wanting to reach the ears of Kate Swift, and through his sermons to delve into her soul, he began to want also to look again at the figure lying white and quiet in the bed. On a Sunday morning when he could not sleep because of his thoughts he arose and went to walk in the streets. When he had gone along Main Street almost to the old Richmond place he stopped and picking up a stone rushed off to the room in the bell tower. With the stone he broke out a corner of the window and then locked the door and sat down at the desk before the open Bible to wait. When the shade of the window to Kate Swift's room was raised he could see, through the hole, directly into her bed, but she was not there. She also had arisen and had gone for a walk and the hand that raised the shade was the hand of Aunt Elizabeth Swift.

The minister almost wept with joy at this deliverance from the carnal desire to "peep" and went back to his own house praising God. In an ill moment he forgot, however, to stop the hole in the window. The piece of glass broken out at the corner of the window just nipped off the bare heel of the boy standing motionless and looking with rapt eyes into the face of the Christ.

Curtis Hartman forgot his sermon on that Sunday morning. He talked to his congregation and in his talk said that it was a mistake for people to think of their minister as a man set aside and intended by nature to lead a blameless life. "Out of my own experience I know that we, who are the ministers of God's word, are beset by the same temptations that assail you," he declared. "I have been tempted and have surrendered to temptation. It is only the hand of God, placed beneath my head, that has raised me up. As he has raised me so also will he raise you. Do not despair. In your hour of sin raise your eyes to the skies and you will be again and again saved."

Resolutely the minister put the thoughts of the woman in the bed out of his mind and began to be something like a lover in the presence of his wife. One evening when they drove out together he turned the horse out of Buckeye Street and in the darkness on Gospel Hill, above Waterworks Pond, put his arm about Sarah Hartman's waist. When he had eaten breakfast in the morning and was ready to retire to his study at the back of his house he went around the table and kissed his wife on the cheek. When thoughts of Kate Swift came into his head, he smiled and raised his eyes to the skies. "Intercede for me, Master," he muttered, "keep me in the narrow path intent on Thy work."

And now began the real struggle in the soul of the brown-bearded minister. By chance he discovered that Kate Swift was in the habit of lying in her bed in the evenings and reading a book. A lamp stood on a table by the side of the bed and the light streamed down upon her white shoulders and bare throat. On the evening when he made the discovery the minister sat at the desk in the study from nine until after eleven and when her light was put out stumbled out of the church to spend two more hours walking and praying in the streets. He did not want to kiss the shoulders and the throat of Kate Swift and had not allowed his mind to dwell on such thoughts. He did not know what he wanted. "I am God's child and he must save me from myself," he cried, in the darkness under the trees as he wandered in the streets. By a tree he stood and looked at the sky that was covered with hurrying clouds. He began to talk to God intimately and closely. "Please, Father, do not forget me. Give me power to go tomorrow and repair the hole in the window. Lift my eyes again to the skies. Stay with me, Thy servant, in his hour of need."

Up and down through the silent streets walked the minister and for days and weeks his soul was troubled. He could not understand the temptation that had come to him nor could he fathom the reason for its coming. In a way he began to blame God, saying to himself that he had tried to keep his feet in the true path and had not run about seeking sin. "Through my days as a young man and all through my life here I have gone quietly about my work," he declared. "Why now should I be tempted? What have I done that this burden should be laid on me?"

Three times during the early fall and winter of that year Curtis Hartman crept out of his house to the room in the bell tower to sit in the darkness looking at the figure of Kate Swift lying in her bed and later went to walk and pray in the streets. He could not understand himself. For weeks he would go along scarcely thinking of the school teacher and telling himself that he had conquered the carnal desire to look at her body. And then something would happen. As he sat in the study of his own house, hard at work on a sermon, he would become nervous and begin to walk up and down the room. "I will go out into the streets," he told himself and even as he let himself in at the church door he persistently denied to himself the cause of his being there. "I will not repair the hole in the window and I will train myself to come here at night and sit in the presence of this woman without raising my eyes. I will not be defeated in this thing. The Lord has devised this temptation as a test of my soul and I will grope my way out of darkness into the light of righteousness."

One night in January when it was bitter cold and snow lay deep on the streets of Winesburg Curtis Hartman paid his last visit to the room in the bell tower of the church. It was past nine o'clock when he left his own house and he set out so hurriedly that he forgot to put on his overshoes. In Main Street no one was abroad but Hop Higgins the night watchman and in the whole town no one was awake but the watchman and young George Willard, who sat in the office of the *Winesburg Eagle* trying to write a story. Along the street to the church went the minister, plowing through the drifts and thinking that this time he would utterly give way to sin. "I want to look at the woman and to think of kissing her shoulders and I am going to let myself think what I choose," he declared bitterly and tears came into his eyes. He began to think that he would get out of the ministry and try some other way of life. "I shall go to some city and get into business," he declared. "If my nature is such that I cannot resist sin, I shall give myself over to sin. At least I shall not be a hypocrite, preaching the word of God with my mind thinking of the shoulders and neck of a woman who does not belong to me."

It was cold in the room of the bell tower of the church on that January night and almost as soon as he came into the room Curtis Hartman knew that if he stayed he would be ill. His feet were wet from tramping in the snow and there was no fire. In the room in the house next door Kate Swift had not yet appeared. With grim determination the man sat down to wait. Sitting in the chair and gripping the edge of the desk on which lay the Bible he stared into the darkness thinking the blackest thoughts of his life. He thought of his wife and for the moment almost hated her. "She has always been ashamed of passion and has cheated me," he thought. "Man has a right to expect living passion and beauty in a woman. He has no right to forget that he is an animal and in me there is something that is Greek. I will throw off the woman of my bosom and seek other women. I will besiege this school teacher. I will fly in the face of all men and if I am a creature of carnal lusts I will live then for my lusts."

The distracted man trembled from head to foot, partly from cold, partly from the struggle in which he was engaged. Hours passed and a fever assailed his body. His throat began to hurt and his teeth chattered. His feet on the study floor felt like two cakes of ice. Still he would not give up. "I will see this woman and will think the thoughts I have never dared to think," he told himself, gripping the edge of the desk and waiting.

Curtis Hartman came near dying from the effects of that night of waiting in the church, and also he found in the thing that happened what he took to be the way of life for him. On other evenings when he had waited he had not been able to see, through the little hole in the glass, any part of the school teacher's room except that occupied by her bed. In the darkness he had waited until the woman suddenly appeared sitting in the bed in her white night-robe. When the light was turned up she propped herself up among the pillows and read a book. Sometimes she smoked one of the cigarettes. Only her bare shoulders and throat were visible.

On the January night, after he had come near dying with cold and after his mind had two or three times actually slipped away into an odd land of fantasy so that he had by an exercise of will power to force himself back into consciousness, Kate Swift appeared. In the room next door a lamp was lighted and the waiting man stared into an empty bed. Then upon the bed before his eyes a naked woman threw herself. Lying face downward she wept and beat with her fists upon the pillow. With a final outburst of weeping she half arose, and in the presence of the man who had waited to look and to think thoughts the woman of sin began to pray. In the lamplight her figure, slim and strong, looked like the figure of the boy in the presence of the Christ on the leaded window.

Curtis Hartman never remembered how he got out of the church. With a cry he arose, dragging the heavy desk along the floor. The Bible fell, making a great clatter in the silence. When the light in the house next door went out he stumbled down the stairway and into the street. Along the street he went and ran in at the door of the *Winesburg Eagle*. To George Willard, who was tramping up and down in the office undergoing a struggle of his own, he began to talk half incoherently. "The ways of God are beyond human understanding," he cried, running in quickly and closing the door. He began to advance upon the young man, his eyes glowing and his voice ringing with fervor. "I have found the light," he cried. "After ten years in this town, God has manifested himself to me in the body of a woman." His voice dropped and he began to whisper. "I did not understand," he said. "What I took to be a trial of my soul was only a preparation for a new and more beautiful fervor of the spirit. God has appeared to me in the person of Kate Swift, the school teacher, kneeling naked on a bed. Do you know Kate Swift? Although she may not be aware of it, she is an instrument of God, bearing the message of truth."

Reverend Curtis Hartman turned and ran out of the office. At the door he stopped, and after looking up and down the deserted street, turned again to George Willard. "I am delivered. Have no fear." He held up a bleeding fist for the young man to see. "I smashed the glass of the window," he cried. "Now it will have to be wholly replaced. The strength of God was in me and I broke it with my fist."

The Teacher

SNOW LAY DEEP in the streets of Winesburg. It had begun to snow about ten o'clock in the morning and a wind sprang up and blew the snow in clouds along Main Street. The frozen mud roads that led into town were fairly smooth and in places ice covered the mud. "There will be good sleighing," said Will Henderson, standing by the bar in Ed Griffith's saloon. Out of the saloon he went and met Sylvester West the druggist stumbling along in the kind of heavy overshoes called arctics. "Snow will bring the people into town on Saturday," said the druggist. The two men stopped and discussed their affairs. Will Henderson, who had on a light overcoat and no overshoes, kicked the heel of his left foot with the toe of the right. "Snow will be good for the wheat," observed the druggist sagely.

Young George Willard, who had nothing to do, was glad because he did not feel like working that day. The weekly paper had been printed and taken to the post office Wednesday evening and the snow began to fall on Thursday. At eight o'clock, after the morning train had passed, he put a pair of skates in his pocket and went up to Waterworks Pond but did not go skating. Past the pond and along a path that followed Wine Creek he went until he came to a grove of beech trees. There he built a fire against the side of a log and sat down at the end of the log to think. When the snow began to fall and the wind to blow he hurried about getting fuel for the fire.

The young reporter was thinking of Kate Swift, who had once been his school teacher. On the evening before he had gone to her house to get a book she wanted him to read and had been alone with her for an hour. For the fourth or fifth time the woman had talked to him with great earnestness and he could not make out what she meant by her talk. He began to believe she might be in love with him and the thought was both pleasing and annoying.

Up from the log he sprang and began to pile sticks on the fire. Looking about to be sure he was alone he talked aloud pretending he was in the presence of the woman. "Oh, you're just letting on, you know you are," he declared. "I am going to find out about you. You wait and see."

The young man got up and went back along the path toward town leaving the fire blazing in the wood. As he went through the streets the skates clanked in his pocket. In his own room in the New Willard House he built a fire in the stove and lay down on top of the bed. He began to have lustful thoughts and pulling down the shade of the window closed his eyes and turned his face to the wall. He took a pillow into his arms and embraced it thinking first of the school teacher, who by her words had stirred something within him, and later of Helen White, the slim daughter of the town banker, with whom he had been for a long time half in love.

By nine o'clock of that evening snow lay deep in the streets and the weather had become bitter cold. It was difficult to walk about. The stores were dark and the people had crawled away to their houses. The evening train from Cleveland was very late but nobody was interested in its arrival. By ten o'clock all but four of the eighteen hundred citizens of the town were in bed.

Hop Higgins, the night watchman, was partially awake. He was lame and carried a heavy stick. On dark nights he carried a lantern. Between nine and ten o'clock he went his rounds. Up and down Main Street he stumbled through the drifts trying the doors of the stores. Then he went into alleyways and tried the back doors. Finding all tight he hurried around the corner to the New Willard House and beat on the door. Through the rest of the night he intended to stay by the stove. "You go to bed. I'll keep the stove going," he said to the boy who slept on a cot in the hotel office.

Hop Higgins sat down by the stove and took off his shoes. When the boy had gone to sleep he began to think of his own affairs. He intended to paint his house in the spring and sat by the stove calculating the cost of paint and labor. That led him into other calculations. The night watchman was sixty years old and wanted to retire. He had been a soldier in the Civil War and drew a small pension. He hoped to find some new method of making a living and aspired to become a professional breeder of ferrets. Already he had four of the strangely shaped savage little creatures, that are used by sportsmen in the pursuit of rabbits, in the cellar of his house. "Now I have one male and three females," he mused. "If I am lucky by spring I shall have twelve or fifteen. In another year I shall be able to begin advertising ferrets for sale in the sporting papers."

The night watchman settled into his chair and his mind became a blank. He did not sleep. By years of practice he had trained himself to sit for hours through the long nights neither asleep nor awake. In the morning he was almost as refreshed as though he had slept.

With Hop Higgins safely stowed away in the chair behind the stove only three people were awake in Winesburg. George Willard was in the office of the *Eagle* pretending to be at work on the writing of a story but in reality continuing the mood of the morning by the fire in the wood. In the bell tower of the Presbyterian Church the Reverend Curtis Hartman was sitting in the darkness preparing himself for a revelation from God, and Kate Swift, the school teacher, was leaving her house for a walk in the storm.

It was past ten o'clock when Kate Swift set out and the walk was unpremeditated. It was as though the man and the boy, by thinking of her, had driven her forth into the wintry streets. Aunt Elizabeth Swift had gone to the county seat concerning some business in connection with mortgages in which she had money invested and would not be back until the next day. By a huge stove, called a base burner, in the living room of the house sat the daughter reading a book. Suddenly she sprang to her feet and, snatching a cloak from a rack by the front door, ran out of the house.

At the age of thirty Kate Swift was not known in Winesburg as a pretty woman. Her complexion was not good and her face was covered with blotches that indicated ill health. Alone in the night in the winter streets she was lovely. Her back was straight, her shoulders square, and her features were as the features of a tiny goddess on a pedestal in a garden in the dim light of a summer evening.

During the afternoon the school teacher had been to see Doctor Welling concerning her health. The doctor had scolded her and had declared she was in danger of losing her hearing. It was foolish for Kate Swift to be abroad in the storm, foolish and perhaps dangerous.

The woman in the streets did not remember the words of the doctor and would not have turned back had she remembered. She was very cold but after walking for five minutes no longer minded the cold. First she went to the end of her own street and then across a pair of hay scales set in the ground before a feed barn and into Trunion Pike. Along Trunion Pike she went to Ned Winters' barn and turning east followed a street of low frame houses that led over Gospel Hill and into Sucker Road that ran down a shallow valley past Ike Smead's chicken farm to Waterworks Pond. As she went along, the bold, excited mood that had driven her out of doors passed and then returned again.

There was something biting and forbidding in the character of Kate Swift. Everyone felt it. In the schoolroom she was silent, cold, and stern, and yet in an odd way very close to her pupils. Once in a long while something seemed to have come over her and she was happy. All of the children in the school-room felt the effect of her happiness. For a time they did not work but sat back in their chairs and looked at her.

With hands clasped behind her back the school teacher walked up and down in the schoolroom and talked very rapidly. It did not seem to matter what subject came into her mind. Once she talked to the children of Charles Lamb and made up strange, intimate little stories concerning the life of the dead writer. The stories were told with the air of one who had lived in a house with Charles Lamb and knew all the secrets of his private life. The children were somewhat confused, thinking Charles Lamb must be someone who had once lived in Winesburg.

On another occasion the teacher talked to the children of Benvenuto Cellini. That time they laughed. What a bragging, blustering, brave, lovable fellow she made of the old artist! Concerning him also she invented anecdotes. There was one of a German music teacher who had a room above Cellini's lodgings in the city of Milan that made the boys guffaw. Sugars McNutts, a fat boy with red cheeks, laughed so hard that he became dizzy and fell off his seat and Kate Swift laughed with him. Then suddenly she became again cold and stern.

On the winter night when she walked through the deserted snow-covered streets, a crisis had come into the life of the school teacher. Although no one in Winesburg would have suspected it, her life had been very adventurous. It was still adventurous. Day by day as she worked in the schoolroom or walked in the streets, grief, hope, and desire fought within her. Behind a cold exterior the most extraordinary events transpired in her mind. The people of the town thought of her as a confirmed old maid and because she spoke sharply and went her own way thought her lacking in all the human feeling that did so much to make and mar their own lives. In reality she was the most eagerly passionate soul among them, and more than once, in the five years since she had come back from her travels to settle in Winesburg and become a school teacher, had been compelled to go out of the house and walk half through the night fighting out some battle raging within. Once on a night when it rained she had stayed out six hours and when she came home had a quarrel with Aunt Elizabeth Swift. "I am glad you're not a man," said the mother sharply. "More than once I've waited for your father to come home, not knowing what new mess he had got into. I've had my share of uncertainty and you cannot blame me if I do not want to see the worst side of him reproduced in you."

* * *

Kate Swift's mind was ablaze with thoughts of George Willard. In something he had written as a school boy she thought she had recognized the spark of genius and wanted to blow on the spark. One day in the summer she had gone to the *Eagle* office and finding the boy unoccupied had taken him out Main Street to the Fair Ground, where the two sat on a grassy bank and talked. The school teacher tried to bring home to the mind of the boy some conception of the difficulties he would have to face as a writer. "You will have to know life," she declared, and her voice trembled with earnestness. She took hold of George Willard's shoulders and turned him about so that she could look into his eyes. A passer-by might have thought them about to embrace. "If you are to become a writer you'll have to stop fooling with words," she explained. "It would be better to give up the notion of writing until you are better prepared. Now it's time to be living. I don't want to frighten you, but I would like to make you understand the import of what you think of attempting. You must not become a mere peddler of words. The thing to learn is to know what people are thinking about, not what they say."

On the evening before that stormy Thursday night when the Reverend Curtis Hartman sat in the bell tower of the church waiting to look at her body, young Willard had gone to visit the teacher and to borrow a book. It was then the thing happened that confused and puzzled the boy. He had the book under his arm and was preparing to depart. Again Kate Swift talked with great earnestness. Night was coming on and the light in the room grew dim. As he turned to go she spoke his name softly and with an impulsive movement took hold of his hand. Because the reporter was rapidly becoming a man something of his man's appeal, combined with the winsomeness of the boy, stirred the heart of the lonely woman. A passionate desire to have him understand the import of life, to learn to interpret it truly and honestly, swept over her. Leaning forward, her lips brushed his cheek. At the same moment he for the first time became aware of the marked beauty of her features. They were both embarrassed, and to relieve her feeling she became harsh and domineering. "What's the use? It will be ten years before you begin to understand what I mean when I talk to you," she cried passionately.

* * *

On the night of the storm and while the minister sat in the church waiting for her, Kate Swift went to the office of the *Winesburg Eagle,* intending to have another talk with the boy. After the long walk in the snow she was cold, lonely, and tired. As she came through Main Street she saw the light from the printshop window shining on the snow and on an impulse opened the door and went in. For an hour she sat by the stove in the office talking of life. She talked with passionate earnestness. The impulse that had driven her out into the snow poured itself out into talk. She became inspired as she sometimes did in the presence of the children in school. A great eagerness to open the door of life to the boy, who had been her pupil and who she thought might possess a talent for the understanding of life, had possession of her. So strong was her passion that it became something physical. Again her hands took hold of his shoulders and she turned him about. In the dim light her eyes blazed. She arose and laughed, not sharply as was customary with her, but in a queer, hesitating way. "I must be going," she said. "In a moment, if I stay, I'll be wanting to kiss you."

In the newspaper office a confusion arose. Kate Swift turned and walked to the door. She was a teacher but she was also a woman. As she looked at George Willard, the passionate desire to be loved by a man, that had a thousand times before swept like a storm over her body, took possession of her. In the lamplight George Willard looked no longer a boy, but a man ready to play the part of a man.

The school teacher let George Willard take her into his arms. In the warm little office the air became suddenly heavy and the strength went out of her body. Leaning against a low counter by the door she waited. When he came and put a hand on her shoulder she turned and let her body fall heavily against him. For George Willard the confusion was immediately increased. For a moment he held the body of the woman tightly against his body and then it stiffened. Two sharp little fists began to beat on his face. When the school teacher had run away and left him alone, he walked up and down in the office swearing furiously.

It was into this confusion that the Reverend Curtis Hartman protruded himself. When he came in George Willard thought the town had gone mad. Shaking a bleeding fist in the air, the minister proclaimed the woman George had only a moment before held in his arms an instrument of God bearing a message of truth.[1]

* * *

George blew out the lamp by the window and locking the door of the printshop went home. Through the hotel office, past Hop Higgins lost in his

[1] Compare the closing lines of "The Strength of God."

dream of the raising of ferrets, he went and up into his own room. The fire in the stove had gone out and he undressed in the cold. When he got into bed the sheets were like blankets of dry snow.

George Willard rolled about in the bed on which he had lain in the afternoon hugging the pillow and thinking thoughts of Kate Swift. The words of the minister, who he thought had gone suddenly insane, rang in his ears. His eyes stared about the room. The resentment, natural to the baffled male, passed and he tried to understand what had happened. He could not make it out. Over and over he turned the matter in his mind. Hours passed and he began to think it must be time for another day to come. At four o'clock he pulled the covers up about his neck and tried to sleep. When he became drowsy and closed his eyes, he raised a hand and with it groped about in the darkness. "I have missed something. I have missed something Kate Swift was trying to tell me," he muttered sleepily. Then he slept and in all Winesburg he was the last soul on that winter night to go to sleep.

Loneliness

HE WAS THE SON of Mrs. Al Robinson who once owned a farm on a side road leading off Trunion Pike, east of Winesburg and two miles beyond the town limits. The farmhouse was painted brown and the blinds to all of the windows facing the road were kept closed. In the road before the house a flock of chickens, accompanied by two guinea hens, lay in the deep dust. Enoch lived in the house with his mother in those days and when he was a young boy went to school at the Winesburg High School. Old citizens remembered him as a quiet, smiling youth inclined to silence. He walked in the middle of the road when he came into town and sometimes read a book. Drivers of teams had to shout and swear to make him realize where he was so that he would turn out of the beaten track and let them pass.

When he was twenty-one years old Enoch went to New York City and was a city man for fifteen years. He studied French and went to an art school, hoping to develop a faculty he had for drawing. In his own mind he planned to go to Paris and to finish his art education among the masters there, but that never turned out.

Nothing ever turned out for Enoch Robinson. He could draw well enough and he had many odd delicate thoughts hidden away in his brain that might have expressed themselves through the brush of a painter, but he was always a child and that was a handicap to his worldly development. He never grew up and of course he couldn't understand people and he couldn't make people understand him. The child in him kept bumping against things, against actualities like money and sex and opinions. Once he was hit by a street car and thrown against an iron post. That made him lame. It was one of the many things that kept things from turning out for Enoch Robinson.

In New York City, when he first went there to live and before he became confused and disconcerted by the facts of life, Enoch went about a good deal with young men. He got into a group of other young artists, both men and women, and in the evenings they sometimes came to visit him in his room. Once he got drunk and was taken to a police station where a police magistrate frightened him horribly, and once he tried to have an affair with a woman of the town met on the sidewalk before his lodging house. The woman and Enoch walked together three blocks and then the young man grew afraid and ran away. The woman had been drinking and the incident amused her. She leaned against the wall of a building and laughed so heartily that another man stopped and laughed with her. The two went away together, still laughing, and Enoch crept off to his room trembling and vexed.

The room in which young Robinson lived in New York faced Washington Square and was long and narrow like a hallway. It is important to get that fixed in your mind. The story of Enoch is in fact the story of a room almost more than it is the story of a man.

And so into the room in the evening came young Enoch's friends. There was nothing particularly striking about them except that they were artists of the kind that talk. Everyone knows of the talking artists. Throughout all of the known history of the world they have gathered in rooms and talked. They talk of art and are passionately, almost feverishly, in earnest about it. They think it matters much more than it does.

And so these people gathered and smoked cigarettes and talked and Enoch Robinson, the boy from the farm near Winesburg, was there. He stayed in a corner and for the most part said nothing. How his big blue childlike eyes stared about! On the walls were pictures he had made, crude things, half finished. His friends talked of these. Leaning back in their chairs, they talked and talked with their heads rocking from side to side. Words were said about line and values and composition, lots of words, such as are always being said.

Enoch wanted to talk too but he didn't know how. He was too excited to talk coherently. When he tried he sputtered and stammered and his voice sounded strange and squeaky to him. That made him stop talking. He knew what he wanted to say, but he knew also that he could never by any possibility say it. When a picture he had painted was under discussion, he wanted to burst out with something like this: "You don't get the point," he wanted to explain; "the picture you see doesn't consist of the things you see and say words about. There is something else, something you don't see at all, something you aren't intended to see. Look at this one over here, by the door here, where the light from the window falls on it. The dark spot by the road that you might not notice at all is, you see, the beginning of everything. There is a clump of elders there such as used to grow beside the road before our house back in Winesburg, Ohio, and in among the elders there is something hidden. It is a woman, that's what it is. She has been thrown from a horse and the horse has run away out of sight. Do you not see how the old man who drives a cart looks anxiously about? That is Thad Grayback who has a farm up the road. He is taking corn to Winesburg to be ground into meal at Comstock's mill. He knows there is something in the elders, something hidden away, and yet he doesn't quite know.

"It's a woman you see, that's what it is! It's a woman and, oh, she is lovely! She is hurt and is suffering but she makes no sound. Don't you see

how it is? She lies quite still, white and still, and the beauty comes out from
her and spreads over everything. It is in the sky back there and all around
everywhere. I didn't try to paint the woman, of course. She is too beautiful to
be painted. How dull to talk of composition and such things! Why do you not
look at the sky and then run away as I used to do when I was a boy back there in
Winesburg, Ohio?"

That is the kind of thing young Enoch Robinson trembled to say to the
guests who came into his room when he was a young fellow in New York City,
but he always ended by saying nothing. Then he began to doubt his own
mind. He was afraid the things he felt were not getting expressed in the pictures he painted. In a half indignant mood he stopped inviting people into
his room and presently got into the habit of locking the door. He began to
think that enough people had visited him, that he did not need people any
more. With quick imagination he began to invent his own people to whom he
could really talk and to whom he explained the things he had been unable to
explain to living people. His room began to be inhabited by the spirits of men
and women among whom he went, in his turn saying words. It was as though
everyone Enoch Robinson had ever seen had left with him some essence of
himself, something he could mould and change to suit his own fancy, something that understood all about such things as the wounded woman behind
the elders in the pictures.

The mild, blue-eyed young Ohio boy was a complete egotist, as all children are egotists. He did not want friends for the quite simple reason that no
child wants friends. He wanted most of all the people of his own mind, people with whom he could really talk, people he could harangue and scold by
the hour, servants, you see, to his fancy. Among these people he was always
self-confident and bold. They might talk, to be sure, and even have opinions
of their own, but always he talked last and best. He was like a writer busy
among the figures of his brain, a kind of tiny blue-eyed king he was, in a six-
dollar room facing Washington Square in the city of New York.

Then Enoch Robinson got married. He began to get lonely and to want to
touch actual flesh-and-bone people with his hands. Days passed when his
room seemed empty. Lust visited his body and desire grew in his mind. At
night strange fevers, burning within, kept him awake. He married a girl who
sat in a chair next to his own in the art school and went to live in an apartment
house in Brooklyn. Two children were born to the woman he married, and
Enoch got a job in a place where illustrations are made for advertisements.

That began another phase of Enoch's life. He began to play at a new
game. For a while he was very proud of himself in the role of producing
citizen of the world. He dismissed the essence of things and played with realities. In the fall he voted at an election and he had a newspaper thrown on
his porch each morning. When in the evening he came home from work he
got off a streetcar and walked sedately along behind some business man,
striving to look very substantial and important. As a payer of taxes he
thought he should post himself on how things are run. "I'm getting to be of
some moment, a real part of things, of the state and the city and all that," he
told himself with an amusing miniature air of dignity. Once, coming home

from Philadelphia, he had a discussion with a man met on a train. Enoch talked about the advisability of the government's owning and operating the railroads and the man gave him a cigar. It was Enoch's notion that such a move on the part of the government would be a good thing, and he grew quite excited as he talked. Later he remembered his own words with pleasure. "I gave him something to think about, that fellow," he muttered to himself as he climbed the stairs to his Brooklyn apartment.

To be sure, Enoch's marriage did not turn out. He himself brought it to an end. He began to feel choked and walled in by the life in the apartment, and to feel toward his wife and even toward his children as he had felt concerning the friends who once came to visit him. He began to tell little lies about business engagements that would give him freedom to walk alone in the street at night and, the chance offering, he secretly re-rented the room facing Washington Square. Then Mrs. Al Robinson died on the farm near Winesburg, and he got eight thousand dollars from the bank that acted as trustee of her estate. That took Enoch out of the world of men altogether. He gave the money to his wife and told her he could not live in the apartment any more. She cried and was angry and threatened, but he only stared at her and went his own way. In reality the wife did not care much. She thought Enoch slightly insane and was a little afraid of him. When it was quite sure that he would never come back, she took the two children and went to a village in Connecticut where she had lived as a girl. In the end she married a man who bought and sold real estate and was contented enough.

And so Enoch Robinson stayed in the New York room among the people of his fancy, playing with them, talking to them, happy as a child is happy. They were an odd lot, Enoch's people. They were made, I suppose, out of real people he had seen and who had for some obscure reason made an appeal to him. There was a woman with a sword in her hand, an old man with a long white beard who went about followed by a dog, a young girl whose stockings were always coming down and hanging over her shoe tops. There must have been two dozen of the shadow people, invented by the child-mind of Enoch Robinson, who lived in the room with him.

And Enoch was happy. Into the room he went and locked the door. With an absurd air of importance he talked aloud, giving instructions, making comments on life. He was happy and satisfied to go on making his living in the advertising place until something happened. Of course something did happen. That is why he went back to live in Winesburg and why we know about him. The thing that happened was a woman. It would be that way. He was too happy. Something had to come into his world. Something had to drive him out of the New York room to live out his life an obscure, jerky little figure, bobbing up and down on the streets of an Ohio town at evening when the sun was going down behind the roof of Wesley Moyer's livery barn.

About the thing that happened. Enoch told George Willard about it one night. He wanted to talk to someone, and he chose the young newspaper reporter because the two happened to be thrown together at a time when the younger man was in a mood to understand.

Youthful sadness, young man's sadness, the sadness of a growing boy in a village at the year's end, opened the lips of the old man. The sadness was in the heart of George Willard and was without meaning, but it appealed to Enoch Robinson.

It rained on the evening when the two met and talked, a drizzly wet October rain. The fruition of the year had come and the night should have been fine with a moon in the sky and the crisp sharp promise of frost in the air, but it wasn't that way. It rained and little puddles of water shone under the street lamps on Main Street. In the woods in the darkness beyond the Fair Ground water dripped from the black trees. Beneath the trees wet leaves were pasted against tree roots that protruded from the ground. In gardens back of houses in Winesburg dry shriveled potato vines lay sprawling on the ground. Men who had finished the evening meal and who had planned to go uptown to talk the evening away with other men at the back of some store changed their minds. George Willard tramped about in the rain and was glad that it rained. He felt that way. He was like Enoch Robinson on the evenings when the old man came down out of his room and wandered alone in the streets. He was like that only that George Willard had become a tall young man and did not think it manly to weep and carry on. For a month his mother had been very ill and that had something to do with his sadness, but not much. He thought about himself and to the young that always brings sadness.

Enoch Robinson and George Willard met beneath a wooden awning that extended out over the sidewalk before Voight's wagon shop on Maumee Street just off the main street of Winesburg. They went together from there through the rain-washed streets to the older man's room on the third floor of the Heffner Block. The young reporter went willingly enough. Enoch Robinson asked him to go after the two had talked for ten minutes. The boy was a little afraid but had never been more curious in his life. A hundred times he had heard the old man spoken of as a little off his head and he thought himself rather brave and manly to go at all. From the very beginning, in the street in the rain, the old man talked in a queer way, trying to tell the story of the room in Washington Square and of his life in the room. "You'll understand if you try hard enough," he said conclusively. "I have looked at you when you went past me on the street and I think you can understand. It isn't hard. All you have to do is to believe what I say, just listen and believe, that's all there is to it."

It was past eleven o'clock that evening when old Enoch, talking to George Willard in the room in the Heffner Block, came to the vital thing, the story of the woman and of what drove him out of the city to live out his life alone and defeated in Winesburg. He sat on a cot by the window with his head in his hand and George Willard was in a chair by a table. A kerosene lamp sat on the table and the room, although almost bare of furniture, was scrupulously clean. As the man talked George Willard began to feel that he would like to get out of the chair and sit on the cot also. He wanted to put his arms about the little old man. In the half darkness the man talked and the boy listened, filled with sadness.

"She got to coming in there after there hadn't been anyone in the room for years," said Enoch Robinson. "She saw me in the hallway of the house and we got acquainted. I don't know just what she did in her own room. I never went there. I think she was a musician and played a violin. Every now and then she came and knocked at the door and I opened it. In she came and sat down beside me, just sat and looked about and said nothing. Anyway, she said nothing that mattered."

The old man arose from the cot and moved about the room. The overcoat he wore was wet from the rain and drops of water kept falling with a soft thump on the floor. When he again sat upon the cot George Willard got out of the chair and sat beside him.

"I had a feeling about her. She sat there in the room with me and she was too big for the room. I felt that she was driving everything else away. We just talked of little things, but I couldn't sit still. I wanted to touch her with my fingers and to kiss her. Her hands were so strong and her face was so good and she looked at me all the time."

The trembling voice of the old man became silent and his body shook as from a chill. "I was afraid," he whispered. "I was terribly afraid. I didn't want to let her come in when she knocked at the door but I couldn't sit still. 'No, no,' I said to myself, but I got up and opened the door just the same. She was so grown up, you see. She was a woman. I thought she would be bigger than I was there in that room."

Enoch Robinson stared at George Willard, his childlike blue eyes shining in the lamplight. Again he shivered. "I wanted her and all the time I didn't want her," he explained. "Then I began to tell her about my people, about everything that meant anything to me. I tried to keep quiet, to keep myself to myself, but I couldn't. I felt just as I did about opening the door. Sometimes I ached to have her go away and never come back any more."

The old man sprang to his feet and his voice shook with excitement. "One night something happened. I became mad to make her understand me and to know what a big thing I was in that room. I wanted her to see how important I was. I told her over and over. When she tried to go away, I ran and locked the door. I followed her about. I talked and talked and then all of a sudden things went to smash. A look came into her eyes and I knew she did understand. Maybe she had understood all the time. I was furious. I couldn't stand it. I wanted her to understand but, don't you see, I couldn't let her understand. I felt that then she would know everything, that I would be submerged, drowned out, you see. That's how it is. I don't know why."

The old man dropped into a chair by the lamp and the boy listened, filled with awe. "Go away, boy," said the man. "Don't stay here with me any more. I thought it might be a good thing to tell you but it isn't. I don't want to talk any more. Go away."

George Willard shook his head and a note of command came into his voice. "Don't stop now. Tell me the rest of it," he commanded sharply. "What happened? Tell me the rest of the story."

Enoch Robinson sprang to his feet and ran to the window that looked down into the deserted main street of Winesburg. George Willard followed. By the window the two stood, the tall awkward boy-man and the little wrinkled man-boy. The childish, eager voice carried forward the tale. "I swore at her," he explained. "I said vile words. I ordered her to go away and not to come back. Oh, I said terrible things. At first she pretended not to understand but I kept at it. I screamed and stamped on the floor. I made the house ring with my curses. I didn't want ever to see her again and I knew, after some of the things I said, that I never would see her again."

The old man's voice broke and he shook his head. "Things went to smash," he said quietly and sadly. "Out she went through the door and all the life there had been in the room followed her out. She took all of my people away. They all went out through the door after her. That's the way it was."

George Willard turned and went out of Enoch Robinson's room. In the darkness by the window, as he went through the door, he could hear the thin old voice whimpering and complaining. "I'm alone, all alone here," said the voice. "It was warm and friendly in my room but now I'm all alone."

*   *   *

Death

THE STAIRWAY leading up to Doctor Reefy's office, in the Heffner Block above the Paris Dry Goods store, was but dimly lighted. At the head of the stairway hung a lamp with a dirty chimney that was fastened by a bracket to the wall. The lamp had a tin reflector, brown with rust and covered with dust. The people who went up the stairway followed with their feet the feet of many who had gone before. The soft boards of the stairs had yielded under the pressure of feet and deep hollows marked the way.

At the top of the stairway a turn to the right brought you to the doctor's door. To the left was a dark hallway filled with rubbish. Old chairs, carpenter's horses, step ladders and empty boxes lay in the darkness waiting for shins to be barked. The pile of rubbish belonged to the Paris Dry Goods Company. When a counter or a row of shelves in the store became useless, clerks carried it up the stairway and threw it on the pile.

Doctor Reefy's office was as large as a barn. A stove with a round paunch sat in the middle of the room. Around its base was piled sawdust, held in place by heavy planks nailed to the floor. By the door stood a huge table that had once been a part of the furniture of Herrick's Clothing Store and that had been used for displaying custom-made clothes. It was covered with books, bottles, and surgical instruments. Near the edge of the table lay three or four apples left by John Spaniard, a tree nurseryman who was Doctor Reefy's friend, and who had slipped the apples out of his pocket as he came in at the door.[1]

At middle age Doctor Reefy was tall and awkward. The grey beard he later wore had not yet appeared, but on the upper lip grew a brown mustache. He was not a graceful man, as when he grew older, and was much occupied with the problem of disposing of his hands and feet.

On summer afternoons, when she had been married many years and when her son George was a boy of twelve or fourteen, Elizabeth Willard some-

---

[1] Compare "Paper Pills."

times went up the worn steps to Doctor Reefy's office. Already the woman's
naturally tall figure had begun to droop and to drag itself listlessly about. Ostensibly she went to see the doctor because of her health, but on the half
dozen occasions when she had been to see him the outcome of the visits did
not primarily concern her health. She and the doctor talked of that but they
talked most of her life, of their two lives and of the ideas that had come to
them as they lived their lives in Winesburg.

In the big empty office the man and the woman sat looking at each other
and they were a good deal alike. Their bodies were different, as were also the
color of their eyes, the length of their noses, and the circumstances of their
existence, but something inside them meant the same thing, wanted the same
release, would have left the same impression on the memory of an onlooker.
Later, and when he grew older and married a young wife, the doctor often
talked to her of the hours spent with the sick woman and expressed a good
many things he had been unable to express to Elizabeth. He was almost a poet
in his old age and his notion of what happened took a poetic turn. "I had
come to the time in my life when prayer became necessary and so I invented
gods and prayed to them," he said. "I did not say my prayers in words nor did
I kneel down but sat perfectly still in my chair. In the late afternoon when it
was hot and quiet on Main Street or in the winter when the days were
gloomy, the gods came into the office and I thought no one knew about them.
Then I found that this woman Elizabeth knew, that she worshipped also the
same gods. I have a notion that she came to the office because she thought
the gods would be there but she was happy to find herself not alone just the
same. It was an experience that cannot be explained, although I suppose it is
always happening to men and women in all sorts of places."

*   *   *

On the summer afternoons when Elizabeth and the doctor sat in the office
and talked of their two lives they talked of other lives also. Sometimes the
doctor made philosophic epigrams. Then he chuckled with amusement. Now
and then after a period of silence, a word was said or a hint given that strangely
illuminated the life of the speaker, a wish became a desire, or a dream, half
dead, flared suddenly into life. For the most part the words came from the
woman and she said them without looking at the man.

Each time she came to see the doctor the hotel keeper's wife talked a little
more freely and after an hour or two in his presence went down the stairway
into Main Street feeling renewed and strengthened against the dullness of her
days. With something approaching a girlhood swing to her body she walked
along, but when she had got back to her chair by the window of her room and
when darkness had come on and a girl from the hotel dining room brought
her dinner on a tray, she let it grow cold. Her thoughts ran away to her girlhood
with its passionate longing for adventure and she remembered the arms of
men that had held her when adventure was a possible thing for her. Particularly she remembered one who had for a time been her lover and who in the
moment of his passion had cried out to her more than a hundred times, saying

the same words madly over and over: "You dear! You dear! You lovely dear!" The words, she thought, expressed something she would have liked to have achieved in life.

In her room in the shabby old hotel the sick wife of the hotel keeper began to weep and, putting her hands to her face, rocked back and forth. The words of her one friend, Doctor Reefy, rang in her ears. "Love is like a wind stirring the grass beneath trees on a black night," he had said. "You must not try to make love definite. It is the divine accident of life. If you try to be definite and sure about it and to live beneath the trees, where soft night winds blow, the long hot day of disappointment comes swiftly and the gritty dust from passing wagons gathers upon lips inflamed and made tender by kisses."

Elizabeth Willard could not remember her mother who had died when she was but five years old. Her girlhood had been lived in the most haphazard manner imaginable. Her father was a man who had wanted to be let alone and the affairs of the hotel would not let him alone. He also had lived and died a sick man. Every day he arose with a cheerful face, but by ten o'clock in the morning all the joy had gone out of his heart. When a guest complained of the fare in the hotel dining room or one of the girls who made up the beds got married and went away, he stamped on the floor and swore. At night when he went to bed he thought of his daughter growing up among the stream of people that drifted in and out of the hotel and was overcome with sadness. As the girl grew older and began to walk out in the evening with men he wanted to talk to her, but when he tried was not successful. He always forgot what he wanted to say and spent the time complaining of his own affairs.

In her girlhood and young womanhood Elizabeth had tried to be a real adventurer in life. At eighteen life had so gripped her that she was no longer a virgin but, although she had a half dozen lovers before she married Tom Willard, she had never entered upon an adventure prompted by desire alone. Like all the women in the world, she wanted a real lover. Always there was something she sought blindly, passionately, some hidden wonder in life. The tall beautiful girl with the swinging stride who had walked under the trees with men was forever putting out her hand into the darkness and trying to get hold of some other hand. In all the babble of words that fell from the lips of the men with whom she adventured she was trying to find what would be for her the true word.

Elizabeth had married Tom Willard, a clerk in her father's hotel, because he was at hand and wanted to marry at the time when the determination to marry came to her. For a while, like most young girls, she thought marriage would change the face of life. If there was in her mind a doubt of the outcome of the marriage with Tom she brushed it aside. Her father was ill and near death at the time and she was perplexed because of the meaningless outcome of an affair in which she had just been involved. Other girls of her age in Winesburg were marrying men she had always known, grocery clerks or young farmers. In the evening they walked in Main Street with their husbands and when she passed they smiled happily. She began to think that the fact of marriage might be full of some hidden significance. Young wives with whom she talked spoke softly and shyly. "It changes things to have a man of your own," they said.

On the evening before her marriage the perplexed girl had a talk with her father. Later she wondered if the hours alone with the sick man had not led to her decision to marry. The father talked of his life and advised the daughter to avoid being led into another such muddle. He abused Tom Willard, and that led Elizabeth to come to the clerk's defense. The sick man became excited and tried to get out of bed. When she would not let him walk about he began to complain. "I've never been let alone," he said. "Although I've worked hard I've not made the hotel pay. Even now I owe money at the bank. You'll find that out when I'm gone."

The voice of the sick man became tense with earnestness. Being unable to arise, he put out his hand and pulled the girl's head down beside his own. "There's a way out," he whispered. "Don't marry Tom Willard or anyone else here in Winesburg. There is eight hundred dollars in a tin box in my trunk. Take it and go away."

Again the sick man's voice became querulous. "You've got to promise," he declared. "If you won't promise not to marry, give me your word that you'll never tell Tom about the money. It is mine and if I give it to you I've the right to make that demand. Hide it away. It is to make up to you for my failure as a father. Some time it may prove to be a door, a great open door to you. Come now, I tell you I'm about to die, give me your promise."

* * *

In Doctor Reefy's office, Elizabeth, a tired gaunt old woman at forty-one, sat in a chair near the stove and looked at the floor. By a small desk near the window sat the doctor. His hands played with a lead pencil that lay on the desk. Elizabeth talked of her life as a married woman. She became impersonal and forgot her husband, only using him as a lay figure to give point to her tale. "And then I was married and it did not turn out at all," she said bitterly. "As soon as I had gone into it I began to be afraid. Perhaps I knew too much before and then perhaps I found out too much during my first night with him. I don't remember.

"What a fool I was. When father gave me the money and tried to talk me out of the thought of marriage, I would not listen. I thought of what the girls who were married had said of it and I wanted marriage also. It wasn't Tom I wanted, it was marriage. When father went to sleep I leaned out of the window and thought of the life I had led. I didn't want to be a bad woman. The town was full of stories about me. I even began to be afraid Tom would change his mind."

The woman's voice began to quiver with excitement. To Doctor Reefy, who without realizing what was happening had begun to love her, there came an odd illusion. He thought that as she talked the woman's body was changing, that she was becoming younger, straighter, stronger. When he could not shake off the illusion his mind gave it a professional twist. "It is good for both her body and her mind, this talking," he muttered.

The woman began telling of an incident that had happened one afternoon a few months after her marriage. Her voice became steadier. "In the late afternoon I went for a drive alone," she said. "I had a buggy and a little grey pony

I kept in Moyer's Livery. Tom was painting and repapering rooms in the hotel. He wanted money and I was trying to make up my mind to tell him
about the eight hundred dollars father had given to me. I couldn't decide to
do it. I didn't like him well enough. There was always paint on his hands and
face during those days and he smelled of paint. He was trying to fix up the old
hotel, make it new and smart."

The excited woman sat up very straight in her chair and made a quick
girlish movement with her hand as she told of the drive alone on the spring
afternoon. "It was cloudy and a storm threatened," she said. "Black clouds
made the green of the trees and the grass stand out so that the colors hurt my
eyes. I went out Trunion Pike a mile or more and then turned into a side road.
The little horse went quickly along up hill and down. I was impatient.
Thoughts came and I wanted to get away from my thoughts. I began to beat
the horse. The black clouds settled down and it began to rain. I wanted to
go at a terrible speed, to drive on and on forever. I wanted to get out of town,
out of my clothes, out of my marriage, out of my body, out of everything. I
almost killed the horse, making him run, and when he could not run any more
I got out of the buggy and ran afoot into the darkness until I fell and hurt my
side. I wanted to run away from everything but I wanted to run towards something too. Don't you see, dear, how it was?"

Elizabeth sprang out of the chair and began to walk about in the office.
She walked as Doctor Reefy thought he had never seen anyone walk before.
To her whole body there was a swing, a rhythm that intoxicated him. When
she came and knelt on the floor beside his chair he took her into his arms and
began to kiss her passionately. "I cried all the way home," she said, as she
tried to continue the story of her wild ride, but he did not listen. "You dear!
You lovely dear! Oh you lovely dear!" he muttered and thought he held in his
arms not the tired-out woman of forty-one but a lovely and innocent girl who
had been able by some miracle to project herself out of the husk of the body
of the tired-out woman.

Doctor Reefy did not see the woman he had held in his arms again until
after her death. On the summer afternoon in the office when he was on the
point of becoming her lover a half grotesque little incident brought his love-
making quickly to an end. As the man and woman held each other tightly
heavy feet came tramping up the office stairs. The two sprang to their feet
and stood listening and trembling. The noise on the stairs was made by a
clerk from the Paris Dry Goods Company. With a loud bang he threw an
empty box on the pile of rubbish in the hallway and then went heavily down
the stairs. Elizabeth followed him almost immediately. The thing that had
come to life in her as she talked to her one friend died suddenly. She was
hysterical, as was also Doctor Reefy, and did not want to continue the talk.
Along the street she went with the blood still singing in her body, but when she
turned out of Main Street and saw ahead the lights of the New Willard House,
she began to tremble and her knees shook so that for a moment she thought she
would fall in the street.

The sick woman spent the last few months of her life hungering for death.
Along the road of death she went, seeking, hungering. She personified the fig-

ure of death and made him now a strong black-haired youth running over hills, now a stern quiet man marked and scarred by the business of living. In the darkness of her room she put out her hand, thrusting it from under the covers of her bed, and she thought that death like a living thing put out his hand to her. "Be patient, lover," she whispered. "Keep yourself young and beautiful and be patient."

On the evening when disease laid its heavy hand upon her and defeated her plans for telling her son George of the eight hundred dollars hidden away, she got out of bed and crept half across the room pleading with death for another hour of life. "Wait, dear! The boy! The boy! The boy!" she pleaded as she tried with all of her strength to fight off the arms of the lover she had wanted so earnestly.

*   *   *

Elizabeth died one day in March in the year when her son George became eighteen, and the young man had but little sense of the meaning of her death. Only time could give him that. For a month he had seen her lying white and still and speechless in her bed, and then one afternoon the doctor stopped him in the hallway and said a few words.

The young man went into his own room and closed the door. He had a queer empty feeling in the region of his stomach. For a moment he sat staring at the floor and then jumping up went for a walk. Along the station platform he went, and around through residence streets past the high-school building, thinking almost entirely of his own affairs. The notion of death could not get hold of him and he was in fact a little annoyed that his mother had died on that day. He had just received a note from Helen White, the daughter of the town banker, in answer to one from him. "Tonight I could have gone to see her and now it will have to be put off," he thought half angrily.

Elizabeth died on a Friday afternoon at three o'clock. It had been cold and rainy in the morning but in the afternoon the sun came out. Before she died she lay paralyzed for six days unable to speak or move and with only her mind and her eyes alive. For three of the six days she struggled, thinking of her boy, trying to say some few words in regard to his future, and in her eyes there was an appeal so touching that all who saw it kept the memory of the dying woman in their minds for years. Even Tom Willard, who had always half resented his wife, forgot his resentment and the tears ran out of his eyes and lodged in his mustache. The mustache had begun to turn grey and Tom colored it with dye. There was oil in the preparation he used for the purpose and the tears, catching in the mustache and being brushed away by his hand, formed a fine mist-like vapor. In his grief Tom Willard's face looked like the face of a little dog that has been out a long time in bitter weather.

George came home along Main Street at dark on the day of his mother's death and, after going to his own room to brush his hair and clothes, went along the hallway and into the room where the body lay. There was a candle on the dressing table by the door and Doctor Reefy sat in a chair by the bed. The doctor arose and started to go out. He put out his hand as though to greet the younger man and then awkwardly drew it back again. The air of the room was heavy with the presence of the two self-conscious human beings, and the man hurried away.

The dead woman's son sat down in a chair and looked at the floor. He again thought of his own affairs and definitely decided he would make a change in his life, that he would leave Winesburg. "I will go to some city. Perhaps I can get a job on some newspaper," he thought, and then his mind turned to the girl with whom he was to have spent this evening and again he was half angry at the turn of events that had prevented his going to her.

In the dimly lighted room with the dead woman the young man began to have thoughts. His mind played with thoughts of life as his mother's mind had played with the thought of death. He closed his eyes and imagined that the red young lips of Helen White touched his own lips. His body trembled and his hands shook. And then something happened. The boy sprang to his feet and stood stiffly. He looked at the figure of the dead woman under the sheets and shame for his thoughts swept over him so that he began to weep. A new notion came into his mind and he turned and looked guiltily about as though afraid he would be observed.

George Willard became possessed of a madness to lift the sheet from the body of his mother and look at her face. The thought that had come into his mind gripped him terribly. He became convinced that not his mother but someone else lay in the bed before him. The conviction was so real that it was almost unbearable. The body under the sheets was long and in death looked young and graceful. To the boy, held by some strange fancy, it was unspeakably lovely. The feeling that the body before him was alive, that in another moment a lovely woman would spring out of the bed and confront him, became so overpowering that he could not bear the suspense. Again and again he put out his hand. Once he touched and half lifted the white sheet that covered her, but his courage failed and he, like Doctor Reefy, turned and went out of the room. In the hallway outside the door he stopped and trembled so that he had to put a hand against the wall to support himself. "That's not my mother. That's not my mother in there," he whispered to himself and again his body shook with fright and uncertainty. When Aunt Elizabeth Swift, who had come to watch over the body, came out of an adjoining room he put his hand into hers and began to sob, shaking his head from side to side, half blind with grief. "My mother is dead," he said, and then forgetting the woman he turned and stared at the door through which he had just come. "The dear, the dear, oh the lovely dear," the boy, urged by some impulse outside himself, muttered aloud.

*   *   *

As for the eight hundred dollars the dead woman had kept hidden so long and that was to give George Willard his start in the city, it lay in the tin box behind the plaster by the foot of his mother's bed. Elizabeth had put it there a week after her marriage, breaking the plaster away with a stick. Then she got one of the workmen her husband was at that time employing about the hotel to mend the wall. "I jammed the corner of the bed against it," she had explained to her husband, unable at the moment to give up her dream of release, the release that after all came to her but twice in her life, in the moments when her lovers Death and Doctor Reefy held her in their arms.

Sophistication

IT WAS EARLY evening of a day in the late fall and the Winesburg County Fair had brought crowds of country people into town. The day had been clear and the night came on warm and pleasant. On the Trunion Pike, where the road after it left town stretched away between berry fields now covered with dry brown leaves, the dust from passing wagons arose in clouds. Children, curled into little balls, slept on the straw scattered on wagon beds. Their hair was full of dust and their fingers black and sticky. The dust rolled away over the fields and the departing sun set it ablaze with colors.

In the main street of Winesburg crowds filled the stores and the sidewalks. Night came on, horses whinnied, the clerks in the stores ran madly about, children became lost and cried lustily, an American town worked terribly at the task of amusing itself.

Pushing his way through the crowds in Main Street, young George Willard concealed himself in the stairway leading to Doctor Reefy's office and looked at the people. With feverish eyes he watched the faces drifting past under the store lights. Thoughts kept coming into his head and he did not want to think. He stamped impatiently on the wooden steps and looked sharply about. "Well, is she going to stay with him all day? Have I done all this waiting for nothing?" he muttered.

George Willard, the Ohio village boy, was fast growing into manhood and new thoughts had been coming into his mind. All that day, amid the jam of people at the Fair, he had gone about feeling lonely. He was about to leave Winesburg to go away to some city where he hoped to get work on a city newspaper and he felt grown up. The mood that had taken possession of him was a thing known to men and unknown to boys. He felt old and a little tired. Memories awoke in him. To his mind his new sense of maturity set him apart, made of him a half-tragic figure. He wanted someone to understand the feeling that had taken possession of him after his mother's death.

There is a time in the life of every boy when he for the first time takes the backward view of life. Perhaps that is the moment when he crosses the line into manhood. The boy is walking through the street of his town. He is thinking of the future and of the figure he will cut in the world. Ambitions and regrets awake within him. Suddenly something happens; he stops under a tree and waits as for a voice calling his name. Ghosts of old things creep into his consciousness; the voices outside of himself whisper a message concerning the limitations of life. From being quite sure of himself and his future he becomes not at all sure. If he be an imaginative boy a door is torn open and for the first time he looks out upon the world, seeing, as though they marched in procession before him, the countless figures of men who before his time have come out of nothingness into the world, lived their lives and again disappeared into nothingness. The sadness of sophistication has come to the boy. With a little gasp he sees himself as merely a leaf blown by the wind through the streets of his village. He knows that in spite of all the stout talk of his fellows he must live and die in uncertainty, a thing blown by the winds, a thing destined like corn to wilt in the sun. He shivers and looks eagerly about. The eighteen years he has lived seem but a moment, a breathing space in the long march of humanity. Already he hears death calling. With all his heart he wants to come close to some other human, touch someone with his hands, be touched by the hand of another. If he prefers that the other be a woman, that is because he believes that a woman will be gentle, that she will understand. He wants, most of all, understanding.

When the moment of sophistication came to George Willard his mind turned to Helen White, the Winesburg banker's daughter. Always he had been conscious of the girl growing into womanhood as he grew into manhood. Once on a summer night when he was eighteen, he had walked with her on a country road and in her presence had given way to an impulse to boast, to make himself appear big and significant in her eyes. Now he wanted to see her for another purpose. He wanted to tell her of the new impulses that had come to him. He had tried to make her think of him as a man when he knew nothing of manhood and now he wanted to be with her and to try to make her feel the change he believed had taken place in his nature.

As for Helen White, she also had come to a period of change. What George felt, she in her young woman's way felt also. She was no longer a girl and hungered to reach into the grace and beauty of womanhood. She had come home from Cleveland, where she was attending college, to spend a day at the Fair. She also had begun to have memories. During the day she sat in the grand-stand with a young man, one of the instructors from the college, who was a guest of her mother's. The young man was of a pedantic turn of mind and she felt at once he would not do for her purpose. At the Fair she was glad to be seen in his company as he was well dressed and a stranger. She knew that the fact of his presence would create an impression. During the day she was happy, but when night came on she began to grow restless. She wanted to drive the instructor away, to get out of his presence. While they sat together in the grand-stand and while the eyes of former schoolmates were upon them, she paid so much attention to her escort that he grew interested. "A scholar needs money. I should marry a woman with money," he mused.

Helen White was thinking of George Willard even as he wandered gloomily through the crowds thinking of her. She remembered the summer evening when they had walked together and wanted to walk with him again. She thought that the months she had spent in the city, the going to theaters and the seeing of great crowds wandering in lighted thoroughfares, had changed her profoundly. She wanted him to feel and be conscious of the change in her nature.

The summer evening together that had left its mark on the memory of both the young man and woman had, when looked at quite sensibly, been rather stupidly spent. They had walked out of town along a country road. Then they had stopped by a fence near a field of young corn and George had taken off his coat and let it hang on his arm. "Well, I've stayed here in Winesburg—yes—I've not yet gone away but I'm growing up," he had said. "I've been reading books and I've been thinking. I'm going to try to amount to something in life.

"Well," he explained, "that isn't the point. Perhaps I'd better quit talking."

The confused boy put his hand on the girl's arm. His voice trembled. The two started to walk back along the road toward town. In his desperation George boasted, "I'm going to be a big man, the biggest that ever lived here in Winesburg," he declared. "I want you to do something, I don't know what. Perhaps it is none of my business. I want you to try to be different from other women. You see the point. It's none of my business I tell you. I want you to be a beautiful woman. You see what I want."

The boy's voice failed and in silence the two came back into town and went along the street to Helen White's house. At the gate he tried to say something impressive. Speeches he had thought out came into his head, but they seemed utterly pointless. "I thought—I used to think—I had it in my mind you would marry Seth Richmond. Now I know you won't," was all he could find to say as she went through the gate and toward the door of her house.

On the warm fall evening as he stood in the stairway and looked at the crowd drifting through Main Street, George thought of the talk beside the field of young corn and was ashamed of the figure he had made of himself. In the street the people surged up and down like cattle confined in a pen. Buggies and wagons almost filled the narrow thoroughfare. A band played and small boys raced along the sidewalk, diving between the legs of men. Young men with shining red faces walked awkwardly about with girls on their arms. In a room above one of the stores, where a dance was to be held, the fiddlers tuned their instruments. The broken sounds floated down through an open window and out across the murmur of voices and the loud blare of the horns of the band. The medley of sounds got on young Willard's nerves. Everywhere, on all sides, the sense of crowding, moving life closed in about him. He wanted to run away by himself and think. "If she wants to stay with that fellow she may. Why should I care? What difference does it make to me?" he growled and went along Main Street and through Hern's Grocery into a side street.

George felt so utterly lonely and dejected that he wanted to weep but pride made him walk rapidly along, swinging his arms. He came to Wesley Moyer's livery barn and stopped in the shadows to listen to a group of men who talked of a race Wesley's stallion, Tony Tip, had won at the Fair during the afternoon. A crowd had gathered in front of the barn and before the crowd walked Wesley, prancing up and down and boasting. He held a whip in his hand and kept tapping the ground. Little puffs of dust arose in the lamplight. "Hell, quit your talking," Wesley exclaimed. "I wasn't afraid, I knew I had 'em beat all the time. I wasn't afraid."

Ordinarily George Willard would have been intensely interested in the boasting of Moyer, the horseman. Now it made him angry. He turned and hurried away along the street. "Old windbag," he sputtered. "Why does he want to be bragging? Why don't he shut up?"

George went into a vacant lot and, as he hurried along, fell over a pile of rubbish. A nail protruding from an empty barrel tore his trousers. He sat down on the ground and swore. With a pin he mended the torn place and then arose and went on. "I'll go to Helen White's house, that's what I'll do. I'll walk right in. I'll say that I want to see her. I'll walk right in and sit down, that's what I'll do," he declared, climbing over a fence and beginning to run.

On the veranda of Banker White's house Helen was restless and distraught. The instructor sat between the mother and daughter. His talk wearied the girl. Although he had also been raised in an Ohio town, the instructor began to put on the airs of the city. He wanted to appear cosmopolitan. "I like the chance you have given me to study the background out of which most of our girls come," he declared. "It was good of you, Mrs. White, to have me down for the day." He turned to Helen and laughed. "Your life is still bound up with the life of this town?" he asked. "There are people here in whom you are interested?" To the girl his voice sounded pompous and heavy.

Helen arose and went into the house. At the door leading to a garden at the back she stopped and stood listening. Her mother began to talk. "There is no one here fit to associate with a girl of Helen's breeding," she said.

Helen ran down a flight of stairs at the back of the house and into the garden. In the darkness she stopped and stood trembling. It seemed to her that the world was full of meaningless people saying words. Afire with eagerness she ran through a garden gate and, turning a corner by the banker's barn, went into a little side street. "George! Where are you, George?" she cried, filled with nervous excitement. She stopped running, and leaned against a tree to laugh hysterically. Along the dark little street came George Willard, still saying words. "I'm going to walk right into her house. I'll go right in and sit down," he declared as he came up to her. He stopped and stared stupidly. "Come on," he said and took hold of her hand. With hanging heads they walked away along the street under the trees. Dry leaves rustled under foot. Now that he had found her George wondered what he had better do and say.

* * *

At the upper end of the Fair Ground, in Winesburg, there is a half decayed old grand-stand. It has never been painted and the boards are all warped out of shape. The Fair Ground stands on top of a low hill rising out of the valley of Wine Creek and from the grand-stand one can see at night, over a cornfield, the lights of the town reflected against the sky.

George and Helen climbed the hill to the Fair Ground, coming by the path past Waterworks Pond. The feeling of loneliness and isolation that had come to the young man in the crowded streets of his town was both broken and intensified by the presence of Helen. What he felt was reflected in her.

In youth there are always two forces fighting in people. The warm unthinking little animal struggles against the thing that reflects and remembers, and the older, the more sophisticated thing had possession of George Willard. Sensing his mood, Helen walked beside him filled with respect. When they got to the grand-stand they climbed up under the roof and sat down on one of the long bench-like seats.

There is something memorable in the experience to be had by going into a fair ground that stands at the edge of a Middle Western town on a night after the annual fair has been held. The sensation is one never to be forgotten. On all sides are ghosts, not of the dead, but of living people. Here, during the day just passed, have come the people pouring in from the town and the country around. Farmers with their wives and children and all the people from the hundreds of little frame houses have gathered within these board walls. Young girls have laughed and men with beards have talked of the affairs of their lives. The place has been filled to overflowing with life. It has itched and squirmed with life and now it is night and the life has all gone away. The silence is almost terrifying. One conceals oneself standing silently beside the trunk of a tree and what there is of a reflective tendency in his nature is intensified. One shudders at the thought of the meaninglessness of life while at the same instant, and if the people of the town are his people, one loves life so intensely that tears come into the eyes.

In the darkness under the roof of the grand-stand, George Willard sat beside Helen White and felt very keenly his own insignificance in the scheme of existence. Now that he had come out of town where the presence of the people stirring about, busy with a multitude of affairs, had been so irritating, the irritation was all gone. The presence of Helen renewed and refreshed him. It was as though her woman's hand was assisting him to make some minute readjustment of the machinery of his life. He began to think of the people in the town where he had always lived with something like reverence. He had reverence for Helen. He wanted to love and to be loved by her, but he did not want at the moment to be confused by her womanhood. In the darkness he took hold of her hand and when she crept close put a hand on her shoulder. A wind began to blow and he shivered. With all his strength he tried to hold and to understand the mood that had come upon him. In that high place in the darkness the two oddly sensitive human atoms held each other tightly and waited. In the mind of each was the same thought. "I have come to this lonely place and here is this other," was the substance of the thing felt.

In Winesburg the crowded day had run itself out into the long night of the late fall. Farm horses jogged away along lonely country roads pulling their portion of weary people. Clerks began to bring samples of goods in off the sidewalks and lock the doors of stores. In the Opera House a crowd had gathered to see a show and further down Main Street the fiddlers, their instruments tuned, sweated and worked to keep the feet of youth flying over a dance floor.

In the darkness in the grand-stand Helen White and George Willard remained silent. Now and then the spell that held them was broken and they turned and tried in the dim light to see into each other's eyes. They kissed but that impulse did not last. At the upper end of the Fair Ground a half dozen men worked over horses that had raced during the afternoon. The men had built a fire and were heating kettles of water. Only their legs could be seen as they passed back and forth in the light. When the wind blew the little flames of the fire danced crazily about.

George and Helen arose and walked away into the darkness. They went along a path past a field of corn that had not yet been cut. The wind whispered among the dry corn blades. For a moment during the walk back into town the spell that held them was broken. When they had come to the crest of Water-works Hill they stopped by a tree and George again put his hands on the girl's shoulders. She embraced him eagerly and then again they drew quickly back from that impulse. They stopped kissing and stood a little apart. Mutual respect grew big in them. They were both embarrassed and to relieve their embarrassment dropped into the animalism of youth. They laughed and began to pull and haul at each other. In some way chastened and purified by the mood they had been in, they became, not man and woman, not boy and girl, but excited little animals.

It was so they went down the hill. In the darkness they played like two splendid young things in a young world. Once, running swiftly forward, Helen tripped George and he fell. He squirmed and shouted. Shaking with laughter, he rolled down the hill. Helen ran after him. For just a moment she stopped in the darkness. There is no way of knowing what woman's thoughts went through her mind but, when the bottom of the hill was reached and she came up to the boy, she took his arm and walked beside him in dignified silence. For some reason they could not have explained they had both got from their silent evening together the thing needed. Man or boy, woman or girl, they had for a moment taken hold of the thing that makes the mature life of men and women in the modern world possible.

Departure

YOUNG GEORGE WILLARD got out of bed at four in the morning. It was April and the young tree leaves were just coming out of their buds. The trees along the residence streets in Winesburg are maple and the seeds are winged. When the wind blows they whirl crazily about, filling the air and making a carpet underfoot.

George came downstairs into the hotel office carrying a brown leather bag. His trunk was packed for departure. Since two o'clock he had been awake thinking of the journey he was about to take and wondering what he would find at the end of his journey. The boy who slept in the hotel office lay on a cot by the door. His mouth was open and he snored lustily. George crept past the cot and went out into the silent deserted main street. The east was pink with the dawn and long streaks of light climbed into the sky where a few stars still shone.

Beyond the last house on Trunion Pike in Winesburg there is a great stretch of open fields. The fields are owned by farmers who live in town and drive homeward at evening along Trunion Pike in light creaking wagons. In the fields are planted berries and small fruits. In the late afternoon in the hot summers when the road and the fields are covered with dust, a smoky haze lies over the great flat basin of land. To look across it is like looking out across the sea. In the spring when the land is green the effect is somewhat different. The land becomes a wide green billiard table on which tiny human insects toil up and down.

All through his boyhood and young manhood George Willard had been

in the habit of walking on Trunion Pike. He had been in the midst of the
great open place on winter nights when it was covered with snow and only
the moon looked down at him; he had been there in the fall when bleak
winds blew and on summer evenings when the air vibrated with the song of
insects. On the April morning he wanted to go there again, to walk again
in the silence. He did walk to where the road dipped down by a little stream
two miles from town and then turned and walked silently back again. When
he got to Main Street clerks were sweeping the sidewalks before the stores.
"Hey, you George. How does it feel to be going away?" they asked.

The westbound train leaves Winesburg at seven forty-five in the morning.
Tom Little is conductor. His train runs from Cleveland to where it connects
with a great trunk line railroad with terminals in Chicago and New York.
Tom has what in railroad circles is called an "easy run." Every evening he
returns to his family. In the fall and spring he spends his Sundays fishing in
Lake Erie. He has a round red face and small blue eyes. He knows the people in the towns along his railroad better than a city man knows the people
who live in his apartment building.

George came down the little incline from the New Willard House at
seven o'clock. Tom Willard carried his bag. The son had become taller than
the father.

On the station platform everyone shook the young man's hand. More
than a dozen people waited about. Then they talked of their own affairs.
Even Will Henderson, who was lazy and often slept until nine, had got out
of bed. George was embarrassed. Gertrude Wilmot, a tall thin woman of
fifty who worked in the Winesburg post office, came along the station platform. She had never before paid any attention to George. Now she stopped
and put out her hand. In two words she voiced what everyone felt. "Good
luck," she said sharply and then turning went on her way.

When the train came into the station George felt relieved. He scampered
hurriedly aboard. Helen White came running along Main Street hoping to have
a parting word with him, but he had found a seat and did not see her. When
the train started Tom Little punched his ticket, grinned and, although he
knew George well and knew on what adventure he was just setting out, made
no comment. Tom had seen a thousand George Willards go out of their
towns to the city. It was a commonplace enough incident with him. In the
smoking car there was a man who had just invited Tom to go on a fishing trip
to Sandusky Bay. He wanted to accept the invitation and talk over details.

George glanced up and down the car to be sure no one was looking, then
took out his pocketbook and counted his money. His mind was occupied with
a desire not to appear green. Almost the last words his father had said to him
concerned the matter of his behavior when he got to the city. "Be a sharp
one," Tom Willard had said. "Keep your eyes on your money. Be awake.
That's the ticket. Don't let anyone think you're a greenhorn."

After George counted his money he looked out of the window and was
surprised to see that the train was still in Winesburg.

The young man, going out of his town to meet the adventure of life,
began to think but he did not think of anything very big or dramatic. Things
like his mother's death, his departure from Winesburg, the uncertainty of

his future life in the city, the serious and larger aspects of his life did not come into his mind.

He thought of little things—Turk Smollet wheeling boards through the main street of his town in the morning, a tall woman, beautifully gowned, who had once stayed overnight at his father's hotel, Butch Wheeler the lamp lighter of Winesburg hurrying through the streets on a summer evening and holding a torch in his hand, Helen White standing by a window in the Winesburg post office and putting a stamp on an envelope.

The young man's mind was carried away by his growing passion for dreams. One looking at him would not have thought him particularly sharp. With the recollection of little things occupying his mind he closed his eyes and leaned back in the car seat. He stayed that way for a long time and when he aroused himself and again looked out of the car window the town of Winesburg had disappeared and his life there had become but a background on which to paint the dreams of his manhood.

1919

Reading Suggestions

Though *Winesburg, Ohio* is generally considered Anderson's masterpiece because it is a well-knit and homogeneous collection of short stories, some of his very best stories are actually to be found in *The Triumph of the Egg* and *Horses and Men*. Unfortunately these, like nearly all of Sherwood Anderson's books, have never been reprinted. So students who want to broaden their knowledge of his works should use two excellent selections: *The Sherwood Anderson Reader*, edited with an introduction by Paul Rosenfeld (1947), and *The Portable Sherwood Anderson*, edited with an introduction by Horace Gregory (1949); reprinted as a paperbound portable (Viking). The former is the richer and contains in particular specimens of Anderson's poetry and his essay entitled "A Writer's Conception of Realism."

The Letters of Sherwood Anderson, selected and edited, with an introduction and notes, by Howard M. Jones in association with Walter B. Rideout (1953), is quite worth reading too for the light it throws on his personality and on his aesthetics.

There are two good critical biographies of Anderson: James E. Schevill's *Sherwood Anderson, His Life and Work* (1951) and Irving Howe's *Sherwood Anderson* (1951).

But the best critical estimates have appeared in the form of articles or as parts of books: Lionel Trilling, "Sherwood Anderson," *Kenyon Review* (Summer 1941), reprinted in *The Liberal Imagination* (1950); Alfred Kazin, "The New Realism: Sherwood Anderson and Sinclair Lewis," *On Native Grounds* (1942); Robert M. Lovett, "Sherwood Anderson, American," *Virginia Quarterly Review* (Summer 1941), reprinted in *Literary Opinion in America*, edited by Morton D. Zabel (1951). The realistic substratum of *Winesburg, Ohio* has been very searchingly studied by William L. Phillips in "How Sherwood Anderson Wrote *Winesburg, Ohio*," *American Literature* (March 1951).

The most complete and up-to-date bibliography is that of Eugene Sheehy and Kenneth Lohf: *Sherwood Anderson: A Bibliography* (1960).

Biography

Sherwood Anderson made a late start as a writer. At thirty-six years of age, he had not yet published a single book and hardly written anything except advertisements. But this is not surprising, considering his background. He was born in Camden, Ohio, and spent all his boyhood in small midwestern towns. His father, who was rather ineffective as a breadwinner, made a living as a harness maker, later as a house and sign painter, and the family drifted with him from town to town, living mostly in poverty. Young Sherwood Anderson picked up nearly all the formal education he ever had from various public schools, but, as soon as he entered his teens, he was always on the lookout for part-time jobs to supplement the family income and relieve his mother, whom he loved. He even became known as "Jobby" Anderson among his friends. At fourteen he stopped school altogether and worked as an errand boy, a cow driver, and a stable groom. When his mother died of tuberculosis and exhaustion at the age of forty-three, like the hero of *Winesburg, Ohio*, he left home for the big city and at the age of nineteen became a laborer in Chicago.

In 1898, when the war with Spain broke out, he enlisted to escape this drudgery, spent four months in Cuba, saw no fighting, returned to Ohio and then, thanks to his elder brother's generosity, studied for a year at Wittenberg Academy (Springfield, Ohio). This helped him to get a job as a copy writer in an advertising agency in Chicago. His lively imagination and his energy made him a success. After his marriage, in order further to improve his status, he launched out into business and became manager of a mail-order firm specializing in a roof paint called "Roof-Fix," at Elyria, Ohio. But he wanted more and more urgently to write, and on November 27, 1912, he broke down under the strain of the double career he was trying to follow and suddenly left his factory and his family. This was the crisis of his life.

After this dramatic gesture he gradually disentangled himself from his business and family obligations and settled in Chicago, where he mixed with the writers who were taking part in the "Chicago Renaissance": Floyd Dell, Harriett Monroe, Margaret Anderson, Carl Sandburg. But he had once more to work as a copy writer in an advertising agency to support himself. His first two books, *Windy McPherson's Son* and *Marching Men*, were not successful. His third one, *Mid-American Chants* (poems in free verse), was even a failure. It was only with *Winesburg, Ohio* (1919) that he won recognition. From then on he was able to make a living by his pen. He spent a summer in Paris, where he made friends with Gertrude Stein and James Joyce, lived for several months in New Orleans, where he encouraged Faulkner to write, and traveled restlessly about. Yet it was the most productive period of his career. He wrote book after book: novels like *Poor White*, a description of the coming of the machine age to the Middle West, and *Many Marriages*; collections of short stories like *The Triumph of the Egg* and *Horses and Men*; and disguised autobiographies like *A Story Teller's Story* and *Tar: A Midwest Childhood*. After the success of *Dark Laughter*, which was the only one of his books to become a best-seller, he settled for a time at Marion, Virginia. There he owned and edited two local weekly newspapers and built himself a beautiful stone house.

He did not take root, however, and in 1929 he married for the fourth time and resumed his wandering life. Under the impact of the Depression and the influence of his new wife he became interested in social questions and in the denunciation of what he considered the evils of industrialism. He tried to write books about them: *Perhaps Women, Beyond Desire, Kit Brandon.* But, as he had no direct experience of the life of the urban proletariat, his works of this period are not quite convincing. He died of peritonitis at Colon, Panama, on his way to South America in February 1941. He had become a classic in his lifetime with the inclusion of *Winesburg, Ohio* in the Modern Library in the very year of its first publication, but he was never able to repeat this perform- ance, and after 1930, for all his efforts, his career was a steady decline.

impt.

At the very heart of Am. Lit.

Must keep in mind that Puritan Theocracy is the all-influential fact in the history of the Am. mind — the Puritan conception of the Diety is not alone all-determining but precisely responsible for the practical affairs of the race.

On one hand: The current of Transcendentalism originating in the piety of the Puritans becoming a philosophy in Jonathan Edwards, passing through Emerson, producing the fastidious refinement and aloofness of the chief Am. Writers

On other hand: Current catch penny opportunism becoming a philosophy in Franklin, passing through Am. humorists and resulting in atmosphere of contemporary business life.

His attitude toward poetry: "that
it may be enjoyed, valued, and
sensed long before it is fully
comprehensible."

Deceased Jan. 4, 1964 London

THOMAS STEARNS ELIOT ✢
1888- 1965

A writer of dramatic
prose.

Shares with Eugene O'Neill the same
sense of Waste land, quality in modern
life and culture, a curse of sterility
that demanded some new birth of
spiritual and creative power if life
and culture were to go on.

Two books to read in conjunction
with T. S. Eliot:
Sir James Frazer, The Golden Bough
Jessie L. Weston, From Ritual to Romance

Eliot's dominant characteristics or tendencies:

1. Strong feeling for the _Past_
(especially literary and religious traditions)
To Eliot the past is not something dead, but a memory vigoriously manifested in present events.
To him mythology transcends time.

2. fascinated with Symbols
especially mental symbols called the archtypes (images which relate to problems of man's nature or social environment.)
Frequently concerned with fertility fetishes or with man's erotic nature.

3. a political conservative
(anti-democratic on intellectual grounds)
he feels little kinship with the unlettered masses — believes the impt. forces of society to lie in the educated, the talented, and the aristocratic.

4. often portrays inadequate characters who feel a sense of their own impotence and the banality of their lives, who seek to rebel in an heroic fashion against their situations (sometimes called the Prufrock motif)

5. in poetic techniques takes his departure from the Imagists and evolves toward a more personal and more original style. Uses free verse, copious allusions, juxtaposition of ancient and modern, and writes for a small audience.

Poetry "aims . . . at the reformation of the poet, as prayer does. In the grand cases—as, in our century, Yeats and Eliot—it enables the poet gradually, again and again, to become almost another man; but something of the sort happens, on a small scale, a freeing, with the creation of every real poem."

JOHN BERRYMAN

Eliot is the dominant figure of the reactionary movement of his literary era.

Introduction

Eliot's career can best be understood as a long process of self-discovery with integration and fulfillment as the goals. But since the self is not independent of reality, of the world, the searching of and for the self has been accompanied, inevitably, by a search for a viable conception of the Other, Nature, the total reality outside the self. The psychological and the theological meanings of the poetry are two reflections of the same development.

Roots of his thought and art lay deep in the British-American tradition.

The image of a pilgrimage may help us to discern the shape of the career as a whole. The pilgrim journeys to an external shrine, but not for external reasons. He seeks redemption of the self, he wants to be a new man. Or again, to shift the figure, the image of the quest may help. The object of the knight's quest, the Holy Grail or cup used at the Last Supper, is at once a religious relic with "magical" properties and a female phallic image. Though there is a sense in which the life of any poet, or indeed of any person, may be thought of as a quest, this archetypal image of the human search for renewal is more clearly relevant to Eliot's career than to that of most poets.

The poet's quest has taken him back to the origins, down to the roots, eastward to the sources. Born on the banks of the Mississippi, he was the grandson of a Unitarian minister who brought with him into the West both New England's lasting faith in education—he founded Washington University—and Boston's nineteenth-century preference for "liberal Christianity." But Eliot reversed the direction of the family migration, both geographical and religious, to go east, not just to college in Cambridge, or even just to visit the ancestral village of East Coker, but to find a spiritual home at Little Gidding, the seventeenth-century English church in which the Anglican mystic Nicholas Ferrar prayed and meditated.

Rejecting modern scientific rationalism and naturalism as well as the rationalistic religious optimism of his Unitarian grandfather, Eliot sought the conditions of a viable affirmation in the seventeenth century and ear-

811

lier, going back to the time before "the wrong turning" was made. No reaction against the modern world, and particularly against the direction of the liberal currents of thought of the age of Emerson and Whitman, could, seemingly, have been more complete and extreme than his. Yet, paradoxically, that reaction turned out to be a way of finally reaffirming, in different terms, the fundamental ideals and convictions of Emerson and Whitman and the liberal grandfather.

For they had lived and died in the faith that human life is intrinsically meaningful, not with some meaning we temporarily create, but fundamentally, essentially, eternally; meaningful because embedded in a structure of ultimate meaning in a purposive universe. Moving beyond religious orthodoxy, they had found the General Revelation offered by Nature to intuition and reason an adequate substitute for a Scriptural Revelation they no longer trusted. Properly interpreted, both revelations, they thought, had the same thing to say. Christ might not be divine for them—or at least no more so than all of us—but nature itself was best understood as supernatural, and all reality was ultimately spiritual, even miraculous, in its tendency and meaning.

But Eliot had grown up in the world reflected in "Preludes" and known by Prufrock, where this vision of a diffused divinity, this "natural supernaturalism," was quite lost. What he seemed to know from his own experience was the reality of hollow men in a meaningless universe. One could imagine but not experience the glow of romantic idealism, could dream, with Prufrock, of mermaids but could see only bits of paper blowing in the streets. Nature had been "neutralized": it consisted of "facts." Faced with full honesty, without any subjective illusions, experience seemed to offer no reason at all for supposing grandfather's rational, coherent, and hopeful world to be the real one. Experience seemed rather to suggest that reality objectively perceived was irrational, inhuman, nightmarish.

But by the time of *The Four Quartets*, the really fundamental elements in the faith of the grandfather had been reaffirmed. Nature, in the later poetry, *does* grant us epiphanies, if we have eyes that see and ears that hear, and human life *is* finally meaningful, despite the terrible reality of the natural and moral evil that the age of Emerson had chosen to minimize. By the time of *The Elder Statesman* Eliot was saying that human love is an analogue of and preparation for divine love, indeed the chief means of our salvation—a position the liberal grandfather would have embraced wholeheartedly. Eliot's "reactionary" pilgrimage was more of a quest than a rejection from the very beginning, and it finally brought him full circle.

I

Eliot began where Henry Adams did, with a whole world of meaning in ruins, as the use the poet made of *The Education* in "Gerontion" might remind us. Melville had stared in horrified fascination at the Nothingness revealed, apparently, by objective knowledge. At the end of the chapter on the whiteness of the whale, the world looked to Ishmael dead white, a charnel house in which all meaning and value are purely subjective and evanescent. The only *really* real things in such a world are the "primary" qualities of classical or Newtonian physics—mass, motion, the properties of "things." These are real, but purpose, meaning, growth, indeed all the values man lives by, are "epiphenomenal," derivative, subjective. Man is a curious temporary accident in an essentially meaningless world. In 1903 Bertrand Russell urged us to accustom ourselves to this world revealed by science, to summon all our courage and accept ultimate nothingness. This, he thought, was the only honest form "a free man's worship" could take. God, as Nietzsche had proclaimed some years before, was dead. One must discipline himself to see in Nature "Nothing that is not there and the nothing that is."

But if Eliot began in disillusion produced by new science, he matured under the guidance of new philosophy and new theology. Many of the best philosophers of our century have responded by saying that this world supposedly revealed by science is not the world of reality at all but a world of specialized abstractions. Bergson, whose influence on Eliot was considerable, transferred the center of reality from physics to biology, making life and consciousness the key to the ultimately real. Whitehead accused scientific philosophers of committing "the fallacy of misplaced concreteness," of attributing to the abstractions of science a kind of reality they did not in fact have and using them to discredit the validity of concrete, existential experience. "I hold," he wrote, "that the ultimate appeal [in discussions of the nature of reality] is to naive experience, and that is why I lay such stress on the evidence of poetry." Heidegger and other Existentialist philosophers developed a more radically subjective and antirationalist answer to naturalistic materialism. Existentialists begin in doubt—by doubting the truth-claims not only of a philosophy built on classical physics, as Whitehead did, but equally of all rationalist metaphysics. They doubt that we can know anything certain about the ultimate "essences" of things: all we can really know is "existence," the "naive experience" of Whitehead before it is rationalized. The toothache experienced is really real, even if orthodontic theory suggests that the origin is psychosomatic rather than structural. If so, the poet can tell us something about toothaches that no dentist, unless he be also a poet, can; and what the poet can tell us must not be discredited as "merely subjective."

Man lives, the Existentialists think, more in the world of experienced ("existential") toothaches than of orthodontic theory. Thrown into a world he never made and that does not, of itself, make sense, unless he somehow makes sense of it, he has to live, and to live as a human being, not as a thing, even if he no longer hopes wholly to understand. His situation is absurd, and his anxiety is the mark, not of an abnormal neurosis, but of his very humanity. If God exists, his existence cannot be proved, but if he does not exist the only final reality for man is nothingness. Despair is the badge of honesty and the beginning of authentic experience and reflection. Religious Existentialists, like Kierkegaard in the nineteenth century and Marcel in ours, would add that it is also the first step toward authentic religious faith. At any rate, with or without the hope of ultimate meaning, man must commit himself and act if he is to achieve any meaning at all. It is implicit in the very nature of man's situation that life should be tragic, but whether or not it should be totally meaningless for the individual depends on the decisions he makes in his freedom.

Eliot's early poetry is significantly illuminated by Existentialist philosophy. Life in the poems is seen as pointless, ironic, absurd. People are seen as things—as bits of paper in "Gerontion," as falling apart, losing their humanity in "Sweeney among the Nightingales." (The Existentialists believe that man is indeed just a "thing," except as in free decisions he commits himself to action.) Man in the poems is as divided, as lacking in wholeness, as the world he perceives, divided within himself ("Prufrock") and from others and from nature ("The Waste Land"). If he fails to recognize the reality of his situation he cannot rise to the authentically human (Sweeney), but if he does he may still be paralyzed by his recognition of the Absurd and so be unable to commit himself and act (Prufrock). The speaker in "The Waste Land" has understood the voice of the thunder, but whether he will set his lands in order, and just how meaningful an act that would be if he did, are not clear at the end of the poem. Alienation, fragmentation, meaninglessness confront us with an immediacy not to be denied by any except the dishonest or the insensitive. Anything else can only be hoped for, at best.

The atheist Existentialists like Sartre and Camus see any religious faith as incompatible with Existentialism, but many Existentialists have in fact moved on or through to religious commitments, among them Jaspers, Marcel, Buber, Bultmann, and Tillich. The thought of the religious Existentialists is particularly helpful for an understanding of Eliot's later poetry, in which we witness the difficulties of a thoroughly modern mind groping toward faith. Here, as in the humanistic theism of Buber and the radical Protestantism of Tillich, religious meaning cannot be inherited or assumed but must be discovered and experienced. God does not overpower us or come when we are not ready. Religious meaning is not like scientific meaning, which—by comparison, at least—may be grasped without decision and commitment. Not that God is a merely subjective experience but that between religion and science, as between religion and magic, there is a sharp distinction. A valid religious faith cannot be simply "learned," and there is no religious technique that when mastered will produce results. Religion and the arts are much closer together than religion and science or religion and magic. There was a real (not merely subjective) epiphany in the garden experience remembered in "Burnt Norton," but it was not until long after the "experience" that the speaker was ready to perceive it, and even then, what he perceived was the sort of thing that could be conveyed only by poetry, so far as it could be conveyed at all.

Eliot's High Church position might have been expected to lead him to objectivize and externalize religious experience in his poetry, but that has not in fact happened. The religious meanings of the later poetry are Existential, though the doctrinal background, usually implied rather than expressed, is orthodox enough and sometimes recognizably Catholic. The "essentialist" aspects of the poet's thought have been expressed chiefly in his prose, not in his poetry.

II

Jamesian in subject, in the manner of its dramatic development, and in tone, "Portrait of a Lady" may be described as a series of gradual revelations. We see first the romantic, sentimental, pathetic "lady," arranging her flowers and her scenes; then the sensitive, embarrassed, egocentric young man. We share his embarrassment at her overtures and self-revelations; we see how he has been put "in the wrong" not by anything he has said or done but by what she has said and he has not said. We see finally that a judgment must be made not simply of her but—and even more significantly—of him. She is not facing reality, but he is not facing her—as a human being. True, he sees her with great clarity and his implicit judgments are correct (her taste in music, for instance, tells us this); but it should have been possible for him to respond to her as a human being if not as a lover. Instead, the clarity and perceptiveness of his vision and the paralysis of his emotions combine to "objectivize" her: there is no meeting of persons here, no "I-thou" relationship, to use Buber's term, but only an observer and an observed.

The most interesting thing about the poem, brilliant as it is in other respects, is the way the implicit self-judgment is expressed. Should the speaker, who has been so correct in all his actions and so right in his judgments of the lady, have the right to smile if she were to die? That he is indeed "in the wrong," and not just in the initial sense that produced his embarrassment, is suggested by a comparison with Matthew Arnold's "The Buried Life," which is echoed in "Portrait." Arnold's poem laments the fact of human isolation: "Are even lovers powerless to reveal/ To one another what indeed they feel?" Arnold had asked. But the speaker here has made no effort to reveal anything at all of himself to the lady: he has pinned her like an insect for study, as Prufrock was later to imagine people pinning and studying him. He knows this and so asks his crucial question at the end, but he is unable to do anything about it. The artist triumphs but the man is defective.

Like the young man in the "Portrait," Prufrock "knows too much," with a special kind of "objective" knowledge, ever to sing his love song. Like the speaker in the earlier poem, Prufrock is quite right in his judgments, objectively speaking. He would not be amused or interested by the talk of Michelangelo, by the persiflage over the teacups: he really *has* heard it all already. He is a very sophisticated, very intelligent, no longer very young, man: he can see through romantic illusion all too easily. The "facts" he "knows" destroy the "values" he longs for. Feminine arms have hair on them, and the magic lantern (fluoroscope, we should say today) of knowledge reveals the mechanisms of human response as it does the structure of the nervous system. As devastating in his judgment of himself as he is in his judgment of others, he sees himself correctly as thin and bald, but he knows an even sadder truth than that, too: that even if he were not, what he does or does not do would not in the end make any difference. Nature has been neutralized, and it is not only the thin and bald who "drown."

Prufrock already knows all that Joseph Wood Krutch was to expound a decade later in *The Modern Temper* as having been established by science. He knows that man is only a complicated mechanism, that the soul has not been found in the laboratory and that freedom does not exist, that love as a romantic value has been shown to be an illusion and that nature is lifeless and purposeless. The deeper irony behind his wondering if he dares disturb the universe is that he knows too well that nothing at all that he can do will "disturb" it. Knowing this, he cannot imagine any possible solution to the problem of what the psychologist Jung has called, in the title of one of his books, "the place of value in a world of fact." When he dreams of a more meaningful world, he can dream only of *mermaids:* his myth is sheer fantasy. If mermaids existed, man and nature would be joined and harmonious, but they are obviously not. Nature has been stripped of purpose and meaning and man left with his romantic and purely subjective daydreams. The voices of human knowledge have waked us from our dreams of a humanly meaningful world. We drown in water that once both cleansed us and brought renewal. Prufrock may be neurotic, but his neurosis is the neurosis of modern man.

Prufrock knows but cannot act. Sweeney acts but does not know. Types of the modern intellectual and the mass man, living without communication in separate worlds, they may also be thought of as soul and body, mind and matter, value and fact, separated and so rendered equally impotent. The voice that speaks to us in "Sweeney Erect" is again that of Prufrock, though he is not named, a Prufrock still longing for a more significant, a less naturalistic, world. He perceives the scene with perfectly objective clarity and thinks of analogues from literature and myth. Emerson's naive idealism, he thinks, could survive only because Emerson had not seen either brute fact or brute man in all their naked sordidness.

The reason Sweeney is able to act—in this case to go on shaving—is precisely that he does not *know*, is not aware of his real situation. Without awareness, he is not, like Prufrock, troubled by any sense of a loss of purpose. A man who cannot distinguish between an epileptic fit and seductive posturing is not likely to be disturbed by any threat of ultimate meaninglessness. Sweeney is Prufrock's answer to those who smile at him and call him neurotic, dismissing his problem as merely private. They may be more intelligent than Sweeney, but like him they are content with a naturalistic world only because they do not know what it implies, as Sweeney is unaware here and in "Sweeney among the Nightingales."

This second poem is much more complex than the first, but Sweeney himself remains the same "man without a soul" of the naturalistic vision. A sordid Agamemnon in a sordid setting, where everything is falling to pieces and even people are disintegrating to bundles of reflexes, he is unaware not only of the nightingales singing nearby but of his own personal danger. But if Sweeney does not hear the singing, the speaker in the poem, and the reader, do. The poignant beauty of the song recalls a world that Sweeney knows nothing of and that seems lost as we concentrate, in the "close-ups," on the scene immediately before us. The lost world is at once the same as, and different from, this one: the same because in it too there were violence and lust and betrayal, different because these and all other facts were once seen and implicitly judged within a framework of values believed in even by those whose actions ran counter to them; different, in short, because where once there were sin and tragedy—moral meaning— now there is only sordid meaninglessness.

Different too because where once there was hope of renewal, of resurrection, there is now no such hope. To the reader aware of classic myth, the nightingales recall the story of Philomel, who was raped and murdered by Tereus, her brother-in-law, but was then changed by the gods into a nightingale, to remind us forever by its song of the persistence of beauty and love. The poem is filled with allusions to slain and risen gods, from Dionysus to Jesus, and it may be fun to track some of them down as one critic has.[1] But that it is not necessary to have them all in mind to appreciate the poem is suggested by their very profusion, and by the fact that they all point in the same direction. They suggest that the natural world continually betrays the world of spirit, and that if we hold to a merely naturalistic philosophy, that is the end of the matter. They keep before us a world of religious myth in which transcendent values were firmly attached to natural facts, not obliterating them but giving them meaning in another dimension. The sense of foreboding that Eliot has said is all he was trying to express in the poem is the deepest foreboding man can know:

that man is only a nasty animal; that the dead may not rise; that God's death may be, as Yeats said, "but a play"; that art is merely the child's fouling of his crib.[2]

[1] Stanley Edgar Hyman, *Poetry and Criticism*, New York, 1961, chap. 4.
[2] *Ibid.*, p. 168.

(The "liquid siftings" of the singer, the poet, the artist, are perhaps merely excrement after all.)

The situation of the artist, implicit here as a minor theme in the analogue between the nightingale and the poet, who keep alive for us memories of a different world, is more clearly a central theme in "La Figlia che Piange," the girl who weeps. If John Berryman is right, the poet as artist and the poet as man cannot finally be separated, yet for some purposes and at some times they must be. Here the speaker is divided within himself. As artist, he appreciates the romantic beauty of the parting scene, would indeed if he could rearrange it to make it even more strikingly dramatic, but he feels no involvement in it. He is not interested in human values as such: the girl is an aesthetic object for him. But the speaker is aware of something missing in this approach. As moral man he is not content to "appreciate" the scene. Is he not betraying the very values he holds dearest, as he yearns for a world of greater beauty, heroism, and romance than any actual scene provides?

The "cogitations" that trouble his nights are very like those that troubled the younger Prufrock figure in "Portrait of a Lady." How are objectivity and commitment related in artist and man? What is the connection between art and belief? We shall understand not only this poem but Eliot's career as a whole better if we think of it in connection with the self-directed humor and objectivity of one of the minor poems, "Mélange Adultère de Tout." Which is not at all to suggest that the religious belief was adopted for merely artistic reasons. Artist and moral man *are* finally one.

The voice that speaks to us in "The Waste Land" is the same weary, disillusioned, dispassionate voice we have heard before. The world he knows and pictures is an arid waste land because in it there is no love, no communication even, much less communion, and there is no integration, no wholeness. (The first, it is implied, cannot exist without the second.) Everywhere there is fragmentation, division, alienation, a multitude of individuals, each in his prison. The speaker sees all this clearly, as the speaker saw Sweeney, but now he in no way separates himself from what he sees. He too is incapable of wholeness and love. He never again meets the girl with whom he talked in the Hofgarten, and he rejects the proffered love of the hyacinth girl, looking not into her eyes but beyond her into the empty and blank heart of light which is at the same time a heart of darkness, into the nothingness of existence. He knows that his awareness of the nothingness that frames all human activity is connected with his inability to love. Faith and hope in St. Paul's list are prior to and necessary for "the greatest of these," love.

For men of the waste land the Incarnation did not occur, and so there is no incarnation in their lives: logos and history, meaning and fact, spirit and flesh are forever separated. Sexual activity is without transcendent or personal value and *love* occurs merely in dream and myth. Deprived of its connections, isolated in a world where all is isolated, sexuality fails to give even excitement: the typist has failed to find not only "love" but even passion, and the girls in the canoes are merely bored and tired. In the waste land there is impotence and there is sexual activity, but there is no love.

Behind this "immense panorama of futility and anarchy," as Eliot described the modern world in his review of Joyce's *Ulysses*, we glimpse a different sort of world—whether lost for good or not is the question. The many allusions to *The Tempest*, for instance—"Those are pearls that were his eyes"—recall Shakespeare's celebration of forgiveness and triumphant love. In the world of the play, isolation is followed by reunion, death by resurrection. The two sets of religious myths Eliot refers to in the notes to the poem—notes he prepared on request of the publisher—have the same effect. The vegetation myths he found in *The Golden Bough* point to a seasonal rhythm of death and resurrection and to sacrifice as a means to renewal: the dying god's rebirth brought with it the new growth of the crops as the waters of the Nile rose in flood. Ancient man saw death as a part of and necessity for life, not as the men of the waste land see it. In the Grail legends that make up the other chief strand of mythic material in the poem, the knight must risk his life in his quest of the Grail, which, when found, will renew his life. He must journey far into an unknown land, endure ordeals, ask the right questions, and finally face death in the Chapel Perilous.

The Sanskrit words meaning "give," "sympathize," and "control" spoken by the voice of the thunder at the end of the poem contain sufficient clues to guide the protagonist out of the waste land, but it is significant that they are uttered in a little-known language and that they are followed by a rush of fragments of the memories he has been living through, bits and pieces more fragmentary and disordered than ever. Though there have been thunder and a "damp gust," the life-giving rain has not yet fallen and the speaker is still fishing in the dull canal. The contemporary tendency to read back into *The Waste Land* all the meanings associated with Eliot's later religious development may encourage a misreading at this point. The irony of the ending cannot be wholly dissolved without ignoring the tone. We cannot get out of the waste land merely by wishing to, or simply by understanding, intellectually, what sorts of beliefs would, if held, give life more meaning for us. Myth known as a result of scholarly inquiry and myth held as truth are two quite different things. The vegetation myths once gave man a sense of direction and purpose, reconciled him to life, but they are simply not available to us. Knowing about them is no help. The "Shantih," peace, with which the poem closes may remain a hollow mockery for us. If it should really come to us, it will pass, exceed and upset, all our understanding.

"The Journey of the Magi," written after Eliot's conversion, may be read as a dramatic presentation of one aspect of the same speaker's quest for a valid faith. "Lord, I believe; help Thou mine unbelief." It presents the difficulty, the loneliness, the recurrent doubts. "A cold coming" the speaker had, in "the very dead of winter," with no miraculous transformation at the end of the journey. The deed has been done, the step taken, but where is the hoped-for newness of life? Courage and endurance are still needed. "I had seen birth and death,/ But had thought they were different."

In "Marina" they are different, both from each other and from what was expected. A poem of joyous fulfillment, "Marina" rests its affirmation on a base of dream and intuition. Here there is none of the speculative rumination of the wise men. The speaker awakens, or perhaps seems in a dream to awaken, to the sound of water and the song of the woodthrush. Nature, once etherized for Prufrock, is no longer alien but vital and instinct with value. The grossness and sinfulness of the world, once overwhelmingly present in the center of the speaker's attention, have been "dissolved" by the grace, or gift, of the vision. The speaker has been transformed by the experience summed up for him by "this form, this face, this life."

The difference between the voice once named Prufrock and the voice that speaks here is apparent in many ways but in none more significantly than in the fact that the Philomel of the earlier poems has become the woodthrush. An allusion to a myth preserved only in literature has given way to a significant memory. (Eliot summered, when young, on the coast of New England and must have heard the woodthrush.) By comparison, Philomel was a device, the woodthrush an experience—an experience carrying with it a meaning no longer lost, no longer merely putative. In our own world, in our own experience, there are possibilities of discovering the values once associated with the Philomel myth.

The description of the boat in which the speaker is journeying points in the same direction. Symbolizing religiously the newly won faith, psychologically the new self, the vessel is very far from being all that one could desire. But though in need of a good deal of repair, it has brought the speaker to the place where he can hear the thrush and see the face, and rather than concentrate on its defects, as Prufrock concentrated on his defects and those of his world, the speaker now is thankful for his arrival at a spot not on any map, a shore at once strange and familiar. If there is no certainty about its location—in dream? in history?—certainty is not demanded. The experience may result in or be connected with a theology, but the experience is its own justification, and what the poem presents is the experience and not a theory: "My daughter," a new life.

"Marina" draws upon dream and the subconscious to present a vision and the joy of living in the light of that vision. But visions fade and periods of active faith are followed by dry periods. One must understand the faith as well as welcome it when it comes, like a gift. *The Four Quartets* is a theological and philosophical poem as well as a kind of spiritual autobiography. Though the main Christian doctrines are reflected in it, its emphasis is not doctrinal but speculative, experiential, and personal. Its four meditations on the theme of time and eternity begin with a vision of time as unredeemable and end beyond time as we know it in the ordinary sense, where the fire and the rose, redemptive suffering and love, are one.

But to skip to the end this way is not only to caricature the poem, transforming it into an argument leading to a conclusion, but to miss most of the meaning of the conclusion itself. How can suffering be redemptive when it is so clearly, most of the time, destructive? What is meant by love? The garden experience related in "Burnt Norton" was missed when it was had and is already long in the past when memory turns to it again. The speaker cannot literally go back and relive the experience, to appropriate the values he once missed. The pool is empty and dry and will not be filled again. Indeed, he wonders at first whether it is not merely sentimental to indulge the memory at all. But he cannot free himself from the thought that all he needed, all he has since in some degree (but not wholly satisfactorily) achieved or been given, was there for the recognizing. Psychologically, the experience demanded the power of emotional response; religiously, the epiphany demanded the spiritual sensitivity to receive it. But the power and the insight were lacking, and simply to dwell now on the lost opportunity is merely to sharpen the pain of reality.

What follows is what we may call the creative use of memory, history recreated and transformed, not wishfully—that would be delusion, insanity —but personally, vitally. What is involved is more than mere recalling, and more than mere speculation on the meaning of what is recalled, though both recall and analysis are involved. The will comes into play, for it is necessary to give up what cannot be recovered and to accept what cannot be undone. The speaker must accept his own unsatisfactory self and move willingly into an unknown future, if the meaning of the past is to be realized and its values made available.

> We shall not cease from exploration
> And the end of all our exploring
> Will be to arrive where we started
> And know the place for the first time.

These lines from "Little Gidding," the last section of *The Four Quartets*, may serve to give us entry into the earlier section. "Burnt Norton" begins in speculative recounting of several theories of the nature of time, moves to personal memory and then back to speculation again, and ends in personal experience. Like the lines just quoted from "Little Gidding," the affirmation of the ending rests on paradox: we must journey forward to go back, and going back takes us forward. Eternity was revealed (in a revelation that was missed) in the past, but can be discovered only in the present, since the present is all that is available to us. Though the past determines the present and the present the future, we must still choose, and by our choices in the present we alter not only the future but the past. A purely rational view of time leads to deterministic conclusions, but only in time is time transcended. For us personally, the logos must enter history, spirit be enfleshed, again and again, continually, in a never-ending present. The Incarnation, or perfect union of value and fact, both occurred once for all and is forever recurring. The present contains all the revelation we need: the laughter of the children hidden in the bushes among those "accepting and accepted" is not lost but

> Quick now, here, now, always—
> Ridiculous the waste sad time
> Stretching before and after.

As readers we have been brought to an acceptance of this interpretation of the meaning of the garden epiphany—we have been brought to it, that is, so far as the poem has worked with us—by a complex structure highly resistant to paraphrase. Though there is a sense in which the verse in *The Four Quartets* is more open, less dense and allusive, than Eliot's earlier work, there is another sense in which it is more difficult: less is revealed here by tracking down the sources of the images. Once we know the Philomel myth, for instance, its implication in *The Waste Land* is quite clear, but the image of the wheel here is of a different sort, and no brief comment on it is likely to be very satisfactory. It suggests both the classical conception of history's endless and seemingly pointless cycles of repetition and the Oriental mandala image of the relation of time and eternity. When we are on the rim of the wheel, wholly caught up in life's temporal activities, we move farther in its revolutions, without ever approaching reality, than when we are nearer the center, the still point, where ultimate meaning is.

Or another image, the dance. A dance is a pattern of motion in relation to rest. Its motions must be organized, meaningful, not chaotic, and must involve both repetition and variation or newness, the unexpected. It is, the poem seems to imply, a paradox very like that of the Incarnation: its exploitation of motion rests upon the possibility of stillness, its achievement of novelty upon the fact of repetition. The necessary Revelation is both given once for all and endlessly repeated, and history and the eternal are both inconceivable without the other. Without the stillness there could be no dance, and without the dance there could be no meaning, no redemption.

But paraphrase does not work. The speaker of the poem confesses his words inadequate: "Only by the form, the pattern,/ Can words or music reach/ The stillness." A single example: it is only in and through the simultaneity of meanings that the lyric of section four really works its spell on us. On one level, it takes us from the light of day down into the chill darkness of the grave, from life into death and time into eternity, and then back up and out again into the light—but into a transformed light, or a light freshly seen. This over-all life-death-resurrection pattern has both a specifically

"religious" (more precisely, a liturgical) meaning and a "natural" one: images of nature and of the Mass or Holy Communion reinforce one another,
as the General Revelation and the Biblical Revelation do. On the one hand,
we experience a momentary overcast on a sunny day. After the cloud
passes, the light flashes once more on the kingfisher's wing. Nature, truly
understood in its implications of transcendence, points to, will lead us to,
God. The light on the wing has "answered," reflected, another, in itself
invisible, light.

While these patterns of nature imagery have been developing, we have
also been at Mass. The bell is the Sanctus bell, rung to announce the words
in the service that tell of Christ's death. The clematis, also called "Virgin's bower," is blue—"Mary's color." The yew is an evergreen tree, symbolic of the unchanging eternal and of personal immortality because it
does not participate in the seasonal "death" of the trees that shed their
leaves. The descent into the grave is re-enacted at every Mass: the believer,
as St. Paul said and as the service reminds the participant, must die with
Christ in order to live with Him, must accept death in order to know life.
The life-death-resurrection pattern of the lyric has meanings at once specifically Anglo-Catholic, more broadly Christian, and, more still broadly,
archetypal and universal.

We are a long way here from Prufrock and his problems. "The modern
temper" has been left behind in Eliot's paradoxical journey backward in
time, a journey undertaken that he might go forward. "The neutralization
of nature" has been undone: nature is no longer dead and meaningless,
April no longer cruel in its reminder that we do not participate in the seasonal rebirth. What Prufrock and Gerontion could not believe is now affirmed, that experience contains potentially the meanings needed to give
our lives meaning, to save us from futility, if we will only see and respond to
the meanings. And another fact that Prufrock understood but could do
nothing about is implied, that knowledge alone is not sufficient to accomplish our redemption from meaninglessness. The speaker in "The Waste
Land" "knew," theoretically, all he needed to know, but his knowledge did
not help him. The new self, it is implied in *The Four Quartets*, begins, not
with an act of pure objective knowledge, but with an act of risk in commitment, with, as Buber would say, a response in dialogue. Once again, Existentialist philosophy illuminates the poetry. The poem implies the need to
change Descartes' formula as Heinemann has suggested, from "Cogito,
ergo sum" to "Respondeo, ergo sum"—from "I think, therefore I exist," to
"I respond, therefore I exist."

III

Eliot's work, in each of the several fields in which he has created, has
been both deeply expressive of and profoundly influential on the age. The
Imagist base of the earlier poetry is expressive of the attitudes of an age

characterized by its "realism," its concern with fact and desire to avoid specious idealization. The stream of consciousness method of poems like "Prufrock" reflects an age fundamentally altered by both the discoveries and the methods of psychology. The impersonal concept of the arts, resulting in the early poetry in a predominantly dramatic technique, expresses the reaction of our century against the nineteenth century's excesses of individualism. The mythological method is a response to an age both characterized and altered by the rise of anthropology among the older sciences. Its effect—letting the artist deal with significant values while remaining, himself, in the background, invisible—is connected with the great twentieth-century critical debate on the relations of science and poetry. The New Criticism which Eliot and Richards fathered has, similarly, been an attempt to be objective in an age of science and yet to deal fruitfully with those values in literature that a narrowly "scientific" approach to literature could not reach.

In what is perhaps its broadest significance, Eliot's work as a whole represents a reaction against nineteenth-century atomistic individualism and a rediscovery of community, in time as well as in space. History is now, here; all time and all meanings are present. All experience points to one end and all movements are defined by their relation to one center: the still point at the center of the wheel of history is both the object of mystic contemplation and the center of the human community. Buddha and Christ, Heraclitus and Vergil agree on the essentials. There is one human truth to which, properly understood, they all testify.

In an age of multiplicity and relativism, this is either reactionary or radical doctrine, depending on how we choose to name it. The impulse behind it, and the usefulness of it, are essentially redemptive, not descriptive, pointed toward saving action, not objective perception. (But, once again, in an age that has discovered that you cannot leave the experimenter out of the experiment if you are going to understand the results, the poet's stance is expressive and appropriate.) If history is really altered by what we do now, then an individual and a culture can escape from imprisonment in the mistakes and failures of the past. Freedom and creativity are real, and redemption from meaninglessness is possible. The individual talent can truly express itself not because it has no past, no controlling conditions, but because it can work within and modify a tradition which, paradoxically, at once controls and is chosen. The individual can move forward toward fulfillment not because he has no ties with others but because he recognizes himself as bound to those both past and present who make up the one human community that exists *sub specie aeternitatis*.

The twentieth century might be said to have begun in American literature with Henry Adams's discovery of fragmentation, diversity, incoherence, and futility—with the disappearance of a *universe* of meaning. In Eliot's work as poet, critic, and dramatist we discover a powerfully thought

Frame of his thought — conservative.
But picture in frame comes close to modern art as Picasso.

and felt answer to Adam's "discoveries." In any age concerned with ultimate human values, this body of work is not likely to lose its relevance.

His principal symbols:
time that merges with the past and present
in a world that is a waste land.

HYATT H. WAGGONER

A Note on the Text. The texts of Eliot's work used in this anthology are,
for the poetry, *The Complete Poems and Plays* (New York: Harcourt,
Brace & World, Inc., 1952); for the essays, *Selected Essays: New Edition*
(New York: Harcourt, Brace & World, Inc., 1950) and *On Poetry and
Poets* (New York: Farrar, Straus & Giroux, 1957).

*Speaker a young man; his companion
is a lady, somewhat older. She realizes
she cannot hold him permanently.
Young man torn between sympathy
and a longing for freedom.*

PORTRAIT OF A LADY 1917

*Lady lives a highly artificial life among
her flowers, her Chopin recitals and her "few
friends."*

[This is one of Eliot's earliest poems, written in 1909–1910. It stands in ironic
relation with James's novel of the same name. A comparison with Pound's "Portrait d'une Femme," a scathing satire, is also interesting. Eliot's poem has not only
more depth and complexity but greater compassion.

The epigraph struck a responsive chord among modern writers, the most famous
of whom is Hemingway, who called one of his finest short stories "In Another Country" and entitled the German edition of *A Farewell to Arms, In Andern Land*. Many
of those who have used or alluded to the quotation found it in Eliot's poem rather
than in Marlowe's play, as their following of Eliot's punctuation rather than Marlowe's
shows.]

> Thou hast committed—
> Fornication: but that was in another country,
> And besides, the wench is dead.
> —*The Jew of Malta*

I

Among the smoke and fog of a December afternoon
You have the scene arrange itself—as it will seem to do—
With "I have saved this afternoon for you";
And four wax candles in the darkened room,
Four rings of light upon the ceiling overhead,   5

*Eliot believed that he revived the
metaphysical poetry of the 17th century —
argued for unity of feeling and intellect.*

An atmosphere of Juliet's tomb
Prepared for all the things to be said, or left unsaid.
We have been, let us say, to hear the latest Pole[1]
Transmit the Preludes, through his hair and fingertips.
"So intimate, this Chopin, that I think his soul   10
Should be resurrected [2] only among friends
Some two or three, who will not touch the bloom
That is rubbed and questioned in the concert room."
—And so the conversation slips
Among velleities and carefully caught regrets   15
Through attenuated tones of violins
Mingled with remote cornets
And begins.
"You do not know how much they mean to me, my friends,
And how, how rare and strange it is, to find   20
In a life composed so much, so much of odds and ends,
[For indeed I do not love it . . . you knew? you are not blind!
How keen you are!]
To find a friend who has these qualities,
Who has, and gives   25
Those qualities upon which friendship lives.
How much it means that I say this to you—
Without these friendships—life, what *cauchemar!*"

    Among the windings of the violins
And the ariettes   30
Of cracked cornets
Inside my brain a dull tom-tom begins
Absurdly hammering a prelude of its own,
Capricious monotone
That is at least one definite "false note."   35
—Let us take the air, in a tobacco trance,
Admire the monuments,
Discuss the late events,
Correct our watches by the public clocks.
Then sit for half an hour and drink our bocks.   40

II

Now that lilacs are in bloom
She has a bowl of lilacs in her room
And twists one in her fingers while she talks.

[1] Chopin would have been considered excessively romantic by the speaker's more sophisticated friends. The speaker's reservations and the lady's admiration—and the terms in which it is expressed—not only characterize the two people but, in context, justify his feeling of superiority: his *taste* is so much better, he *knows* so much more. Compare the talk about Michelangelo in "Prufrock."

[2] One of the first indications that the poem will concern, at its deepest level, a sort of death of the spirit. Compare the closing verse paragraph.

[handwritten: "Wisdom is Knows when you can't be wise"
Paul Engle, Natl. Council for the Humanities] 827

PORTRAIT OF A LADY

"Ah, my friend, you do not know, you do not know
What life is, you who hold it in your hands";   45
(Slowly twisting the lilac stalks)
"You let it flow from you, you let it flow,
And youth is cruel, and has no remorse
And smiles at situations which it cannot see."
I smile, of course,   50
And go on drinking tea.
"Yet with these April sunsets, that somehow recall
My buried life,[3] and Paris in the Spring,
I feel immeasurably at peace, and find the world
To be wonderful and youthful, after all."   55

     The voice returns like the insistent out-of-tune
Of a broken violin on an August afternoon:
"I am always sure that you understand
My feelings, always sure that you feel,
Sure that across the gulf you reach your hand.   60
     You are invulnerable, you have no Achilles' heel.
You will go on, and when you have prevailed
You can say: at this point many a one has failed.
But what have I, but what have I, my friend,
To give you, what can you receive from me?   65
Only the friendship and the sympathy
Of one about to reach her journey's end.

     I shall sit here, serving tea to friends. . . ."

     I take my hat: how can I make a cowardly amends
For what she has said to me?   70
You will see me any morning in the park
Reading the comics and the sporting page.
Particularly I remark
An English countess goes upon the stage.
A Greek was murdered at a Polish dance,   75
Another bank defaulter has confessed.
I keep my countenance,
I remain self-possessed
Except when a street piano, mechanical and tired
Reiterates some worn-out common song   80
With the smell of hyacinths[4] across the garden
Recalling things that other people have desired.
Are these ideas right or wrong?

[3] An allusion to Arnold's "The Buried Life."

[4] The blue spike of the hyacinth flower has often been seen as a male phallic image. Is the speaker capable of love? Or indeed of any significant action—such as those of the people he reads about in the newspapers? Compare Prufrock's decision to eat a peach (another sex symbol) and to roll his trousers and walk on the beach.

III

The October night comes down; returning as before
Except for a slight sensation of being ill at ease   85
I mount the stairs and turn the handle of the door
And feel as if I had mounted on my hands and knees.
"And so you are going abroad; and when do you return?
But that's a useless question.
You hardly know when you are coming back,
You will find so much to learn."   90
My smile falls heavily among the bric-à-brac.

   "Perhaps you can write to me."
My self-possession flares up for a second;
This is as I had reckoned.   95
"I have been wondering frequently of late
(But our beginnings never know our ends!)
Why we have not developed into friends."
I feel like one who smiles, and turning shall remark
Suddenly, his expression in a glass.   100
My self-possession gutters; we are really in the dark.

the penultimate stanza
   "For everybody said so, all our friends,
They all were sure our feelings would relate
So closely! I myself can hardly understand.
We must leave it now to fate.   105
You will write, at any rate.
Perhaps it is not too late.
I shall sit here, serving tea to friends."

   And I must borrow every changing shape
To find expression . . . dance, dance   110
Like a dancing bear,
Cry like a parrot, chatter like an ape.
Let us take the air, in a tobacco trance—

   Well! and what if she should die some afternoon,
Afternoon grey and smoky, evening yellow and rose;   115
Should die and leave me sitting pen in hand
With the smoke coming down above the housetops;
Doubtful, for a while
Not knowing what to feel or if I understand
Or whether wise or foolish, tardy or too soon . . .   120
Would she not have the advantage, after all?
This music is successful with a "dying fall"
Now that we talk of dying—
And should I have the right to smile?

1917

Lady scarcely conceals her anguish at parting yet the young man realizes it is to her permanent

[handwritten: Eliot's conception of 20th century intellectual — timid, blasé, mediocre, defective.]

[handwritten: His most successful poem.]

THE LOVE SONG OF J. ALFRED PRUFROCK

[handwritten: Middle aged man]

[The title presents the first of the ironies of which the poem is compounded. One would hardly expect to hear a man with such a name singing a love song. The epigraph, from Dante's *Inferno*, Canto 27, presents one of the dead speaking to Dante and explaining why he thinks he can afford to speak frankly: "If I believed that my reply would be heard by one who would return to the world [of the living], this flame would shake no more. But if I hear truly, my words will never reach anyone who will return alive from this pit to make me infamous." Only "intellectuals" will read and understand Prufrock's "song," and they are as dead emotionally and spiritually as he. This is one of the many indications in the poem that it was not Eliot's intention to portray in Prufrock a merely private neurosis.]

[handwritten: A dramatic monolog.]

[handwritten: A lesson in abjectivity.] *[handwritten: Horror of being sentimental. Revolt & Victorian Age — wants to be direct. Not high seriousness — this age had no answer. Note the love he has known.]*

S'io credesse che mia risposta fosse
A persona che mai tornasse al mondo,
Questa fiamma staria senza più scosse.
Ma per ciò che giammai di questo fondo
Non tornò vivo alcun, s'i' odo il vero,
Senza tema d'infamia ti rispondo.

[handwritten: Famous metaphor — actually similes]

Let us go then, you and I,
When the evening is spread out against the sky
Like a patient etherised upon a table;
Let us go, through certain half-deserted streets,
The muttering retreats   5
Of restless nights in one-night cheap hotels
And sawdust restaurants with oyster-shells:
Streets that follow like a tedious argument
Of insidious intent
To lead you to an overwhelming question. . . .   10
Oh, do not ask, "What is it?"
Let us go and make our visit.

[handwritten: Passion is played against reasoning to the point of stalemate.]

In the room the other women come and go
Talking of Michelangelo.[1]
The yellow fog that rubs its back upon the window-panes,   15

[handwritten: organized around these lines]

[1] A painter noted for the "fleshly" quality of his portrayals, even when they were in religious scenes. Prufrock would probably prefer painters of a more ascetic school. Also, a reaction against Michelangelo's style of painting and in favor of earlier, less "humanistic," painters had already set in at the time the poem was written. To Prufrock, Michelangelo is simply not interesting: the subject is banal. Prufrock's sense of superiority in aesthetic matters is no mere conceit. His problem would be more easily solved if it were.

[handwritten: Prufrock is a rather pathetic aging man-about-town. We see & sympathize with him — but in a larger sense he is a damned soul]

The sea imagery becomes a symbol
of the release of the spirit.

THOMAS STEARNS ELIOT

The yellow smoke that rubs its muzzle on the window-panes   *torn with*
Licked its tongue into the corners of the evening,
Lingered upon the pools that stand in drains,
Let fall upon its back the soot that falls from chimneys,
Slipped by the terrace, made a sudden leap,   20
And seeing that it was a soft October night,
Curled once about the house, and fell asleep.

And indeed there will be time
For the yellow smoke that slides along the street
Rubbing its back upon the window-panes;   25
Psychological There will be time, there will be time
insight To prepare a face to meet the faces that you meet;
There will be time to murder and create,
And time for all the works and days of hands
That lift and drop a question on your plate;   *is not a tangible*   30
Time for you and time for me,   *thing but when*
And time yet for a hundred indecisions,   *you put it on*
And for a hundred visions and revisions,   *the plate now do*
Before the taking of a toast and tea.

In the room the women come and go   35
Talking of Michelangelo.

And indeed there will be time
To wonder, "Do I dare?" and, "Do I dare?"
Time to turn back and descend the stair,
With a bald spot in the middle of my hair—   40
[They will say: "How his hair is growing thin!"]
My morning coat, my collar mounting firmly to the chin,
My necktie rich and modest, but asserted by a simple pin—
[They will say: "But how his arms and legs are thin!"]
Do I dare   45
Disturb the universe?
In a minute there is time
For decisions and revisions which a minute will reverse.

For I have known them all already, known them all—
Have known the evenings, mornings, afternoons,   50
a much loved I have measured out my life with coffee spoons;   *the trough*
I know the voices dying with a dying fall   *of it all —*
Beneath the music from a farther room.   *Knowing this*
    So how should I presume?

And I have known the eyes already, known them all—   55
The eyes that fix you in a formulated phrase,
And when I am formulated, sprawling on a pin,
When I am pinned and wriggling on the wall,
Then how should I begin
To spit out all the butt-ends of my days and ways?   60
    And how should I presume?

The irony is from the half seriousness. (handwritten)

A psychological portrait. (handwritten)

And I have known the arms already, known them all—
Arms that are braceleted and white and bare
[But in the lamplight, downed with light brown hair!]
Is it perfume from a dress   *Seems never to go* (handwritten)
That makes me so digress?   *beyond this —* (handwritten)   65
Arms that lie along a table, or wrap about a shawl.   *Uses the stream of* (handwritten)
    And should I then presume?   *consciousness — a* (handwritten)
    And how should I begin?   *climax* (handwritten)   *psychological trend* (handwritten)

                    *   *   *   70

Shall I say, I have gone at dusk through narrow streets
And watched the smoke that rises from the pipes
Of lonely men in shirt-sleeves, leaning out of windows? . . .

I should have been a pair of ragged claws
Scuttling across the floors of silent seas.

                    *   *   *

And the afternoon, the evening, sleeps so peacefully!   75
Smoothed by long fingers,
Asleep . . . tired . . . or it malingers,
Stretched on the floor, here beside you and me.
Should I, after tea and cakes and ices,
Have the strength to force the moment to its crisis?   80
But though I have wept and fasted, wept and prayed,
Though I have seen my head [grown slightly bald]
    brought in upon a platter,
I am no prophet[2]—and here's no great matter;   *Evil in this time — one tells* (handwritten)
I have seen the moment of my greatness flicker,   *Herod's wife does not warn* (handwritten)
And I have seen the eternal Footman hold my coat, and snicker,   *about*   *death* (handwritten)   85
And in short, I was afraid.   *Prufrock knows* (handwritten)
And would it have been worth it, after all,   *evil & can wd* (handwritten)
After the cups, the marmalade, the tea,   *wont tell* (handwritten)   90
Among the porcelain, among some talk of you and me,
Would it have been worth while,
To have bitten off the matter with a smile,
To have squeezed the universe into a ball
To roll it toward some overwhelming question,

    [2] The prophet John the Baptist was beheaded and his head exhibited "on a charger," as the King James Version puts it. Prufrock's comparisons of himself with John the Baptist, Hamlet, and Lazarus all contain an ironic similarity in difference. Insofar as Prufrock's difficulties are typical of those of intellectuals, in exposing his own dilemma he becomes a kind of prophet, but without any heroic stature or claim to divine backing. Insofar as he is indecisive, he is like Hamlet, or at least like Hamlet as the play is sometimes interpreted; but he is not a prince and will not, like Hamlet, finally act. Insofar as he is already spiritually dead, he is like Lazarus, but he has no hope of coming back to life.

To say: "I am Lazarus, come from the dead,
Come back to tell you all, I shall tell you all"—
If one, settling a pillow by her head,
  Should say: "That is not what I meant at all.
   That is not it, at all."   95

And would it have been worth it, after all,
Would it have been worth while,   100
After the sunsets and the dooryards and the sprinkled streets,
After the novels, after the teacups, after the skirts that
     trail along the floor—
And this, and so much more?—
It is impossible to say just what I mean!
But as if a magic lantern threw the nerves in patterns on a screen: 105
Would it have been worth while
If one, settling a pillow or throwing off a shawl,
And turning toward the window, should say:
  "That is not it at all,
  That is not what I meant, at all."   110

        *   *   *

No! I am not Prince Hamlet, nor was meant to be;
Am an attendant lord, one that will do
To swell a progress, start a scene or two,
Advise the prince; no doubt, an easy tool,
Deferential, glad to be of use,   115
Politic, cautious, and meticulous;
Full of high sentence, but a bit obtuse;
At times, indeed, almost ridiculous—
Almost, at times, the Fool.

I grow old . . . I grow old . . .   120
I shall wear the bottoms of my trousers rolled.[3]

Shall I part my hair behind? Do I dare to eat a peach?
I shall wear white flannel trousers, and walk upon the beach.
I have heard the mermaids singing, each to each.

I do not think that they will sing to me.   125

I have seen them riding seaward on the waves
Combing the white hair of the waves blown back
When the wind blows the water white and black.

[3] Note the tightening of the meter and the increase in the regularity of the rhyme from this point on. At the end of Prufrock's meditations, as he faces the full implications of his situation, there is an increase in tension, a sharpening of emotional urgency. After the sexual implications of the peach, he dreams of mermaids—half "animal," half human, the objects of desire in many a romantic tale—and of love; and does so in lines marked by traditional poetic figures and cadences, lines sharply in contrast with the dry tones and conversational rhythms that predominate earlier.

Eliot: You prepare faces for the face one meets.

We have lingered in the chambers of the sea
By sea-girls wreathed with seaweed red and brown   130
Till human voices wake us, and we drown.

1917

SWEENEY AMONG THE NIGHTINGALES

✤ [The poem has been memorably characterized by Donald Stauffer as "a narrative of betrayal by the brute lust of the world." The song of the nightingales does not penetrate the consciousness of Sweeney and his companions. Without being aware of what they are doing, they are repeating the rape of Philomel. (For the story of Philomel, see the general introduction to Eliot.) Sweeney's sordid companions intend to betray Sweeney; unintentionally, they are betraying mankind by their obliviousness of man's heritage.

In the suggestion that Sweeney is the modern Agamemnon—a poor substitute perhaps, but still a fighter and still betrayed—and in the other reminders that the same acts of violence and betrayal have gone on always, as the nightingales have sung then and sing now, we see another aspect of the meaning of the poem. The essential difference between the several worlds contrasted with the immediate scene and Sweeney's world is not in what *happens* but how it is interpreted; not in brute fact but in frames of reference, perspectives, modes of interpretation. Agamemnon was betrayed more savagely than Sweeney is likely to be, but the betrayal was recognized for what it was. There was tragedy in the world of Greek and Christian myth, but life was not without meaning. What is going on in this South Boston joint, by contrast, is simply sordid and meaningless. Everything here is falling down, disintegrating to a subhuman level where distinctively *human* meanings are inapplicable. But this situation is not caused by changes in human nature or in the pattern of events but by changes in *belief* about nature and human nature.

The epigraph, from Aeschylus' *Agamemnon,* may be translated, "It dealt me a blow to the heart." The implication is that the picture drawn in the poem should deal *us* a blow to the heart. If the naturalistic picture here is a true portrayal of "nature"— that is, of the ultimately real—then man's heart has been betrayed indeed.

"The hornèd gate": in the *Odyssey* we read of two doors or gates to the underworld, the world of the dead—one of horn and one of ivory. "True dreams," dreams that could be trusted, came through the gate of horn, false dreams through the gate of ivory. A possible interpretation here is that, ironically, only the Sweeneys of this world "guard"—that is, defend and maintain—man's "true dreams"—the values associated with the convent and Philomel. Sweeney is Boston Irish, and Roman Catholic; he does not know, understand, appreciate the values he nominally maintains. Though he nominally "guards" them, they are lost to and on him.

If it is possible for a poem to be over-explicated, explained too much, this poem has been. To get the effect of the references to geography, geology, astrology, and classic literature (Homer and Dante) in the second and third stanzas it is not necessary to assign precise values to each reference. Combined, the allusions establish a *perspective*: against this cosmic background Sweeney's little drama is acted out. The effect is somewhat like that achieved in the movies by a juxtaposition of close-ups of interior scenes and distant views of nature. We have just looked closely at Sweeney laughing. Now we look off and see clouds, the constellations, "the heavens," the sea; in a sense we ourselves move off in time and space and look at Sweeney from afar, from

the perspective of life and death and nature, as well as that of Dante and Homer.
Nature and myth combine to create a frame for the picture immediately before us.]

ὤμοι, πέπληγμαι καιρίαν πληγὴν ἔσω

Apeneck Sweeney spreads his knees
Letting his arms hang down to laugh,
The zebra stripes along his jaw
Swelling to maculate giraffe.

The circles of the stormy moon   5
Slide westward toward the River Plate,
Death and the Raven drift above
And Sweeney guards the hornèd gate.

Gloomy Orion and the Dog
Are veiled; and hushed the shrunken seas;   10
The person in the Spanish cape
Tries to sit on Sweeney's knees

Slips and pulls the table cloth
Overturns a coffee-cup,
Reorganized upon the floor   15
She yawns and draws a stocking up;

The silent man in mocha brown
Sprawls at the window-sill and gapes;
The waiter brings in oranges
Bananas figs and hothouse grapes;   20

The silent vertebrate in brown[1]
Contracts and concentrates, withdraws;
Rachel *née* Rabinovitch[2]
Tears at the grapes with murderous paws;

[1] Biology classifies living things as vertebrate and invertebrate; men and mice are
vertebrates. But is man *only* one of the "higher" (vertebrate) animals? Is such a
classification in terms of his place in nature the most significant thing about him? Or
should we define him, as the Existentialists do, in terms of his freedom, his capacity for
transcendence? The picture presented by the poem is drawn in naturalistic terms, with
the implication that it is the view held by the modern world. This, the poem seems
to say, is the way it is, if this is the way you look at it. Agamemnon's story too could
be so interpreted.

[2] Rachel has changed her name but not her nature. She has cut the ties that bound
her to a defining tradition, become "assimilated" to modernism, but she continues
blindly to fulfill her role as a modern Maenad. The Maenads of classic myth accom-

She and the lady in the cape   25
Are suspect, thought to be in league;
Therefore the man with heavy eyes
Declines the gambit, shows fatigue,

Leaves the room and reappears
Outside the window, leaning in,   30
Branches of wistaria
Circumscribe a golden grin;

The host with someone indistinct[3]
Converses at the door apart,
The nightingales are singing near   35
The Convent of the Sacred Heart,[4]

And sang within the bloody wood
When Agamemnon cried aloud,
And let their liquid siftings fall [5]
To stain the stiff dishonoured shroud.   40

1919

---

panied and periodically tore to pieces Dionysus or Bacchus, god of the grape and inspiration. As Rachel tears at the grapes she is killing the god. But in the myth, Dionysus was always reborn after being slain; here we may anticipate no resurrection.

[3] Probably a reference to Christ (another "slain god"), who was unrecognized by his disciples as he walked with them on the road to Emmaus after the Crucifixion and the Resurrection. If the word is interpreted this way, the image reinforces the nightingale image: the nightingale sings now as it always has, and the saving presence is always beside us, but if our vision is wholly contained by the foreground scene, we do not hear the one or see the other. This interpretation also reinforces the earlier reference to Dionysus: both Christ and Dionysus are resurrected after being slain, although in the modern world of the naturalistic view the cycle is incomplete. That this may be the real world, as contrasted with the world of "dream," is the essence of the speaker's foreboding.

[4] Within the areas of relevance established by the poem, the meanings of the Philomel myth and of the Christian faith (the Convent) are the same. Both are resurrection stories; both ground man's hope of rebirth and renewal in the very nature of things, of the gods or of God, who will not permit the betrayal to be final, will not allow the permanent destruction of the highest values.

[5] At the end of the poem the irony that begins in its title is not resolved but deepens. Is this the "liquid" sound of the song, or the birds' liquid excrement? Which is the "real" world, the world of Sweeney or the world of the nightingales? The artist, the poet, is also a "singer," and like the nightingales he has been reminding us of the values embodied in classic myth. Is his song also perhaps mere "excrement," a product of neurosis, having nothing to do with truth? If this "Freudian" interpretation of art is the correct one, the speaker's response to the song of the nightingale is a sign, not that his values are superior to Sweeney's, but that he is sick.

SWEENEY ERECT

✣ [In addition to the sexual meaning of the pun in the title, there is an ironic play on the definition of man as the ape who walks erect. Sweeney stands erect in the poem, shaving, unaware of what is really going on around him. He is not "homo sapiens" but "homo erectus." He does not lack what was for Emerson the most necessary virtue, self-reliance, and we may conceive him joining with others of his kind in a revolt of the masses that would make history.

The epigraph is from Beaumont and Fletcher's *The Maid's Tragedy*. The lines are spoken by a lovelorn maiden, Aspatia, as she looks at a tapestry depicting Ariadne, another lovelorn maiden. Since there is also a "love-lorn maiden" on the bed in the poem, the epigraph has the effect of making this a picture of a picture of a picture, each picture treating love—and loyalty in love—a little differently, each throwing a different light on it. The foreground picture might be called "naturalistic," but there is no suggestion that this perspective is absolute.

The effect of Aspatia's words is to say, let nature grieve too when love is betrayed. But has there been any "love" between the girl on the bed and Sweeney? (What do we mean by "love"?) Can Sweeney be said to have "betrayed" her? In one sense no, since he has no doubt paid, or will pay, for her services; but in another sense yes, since both she and all humanity are betrayed by his blind and brutal sensuality. In the opening lines Aspatia asks her handmaidens to paint this scene of desolation and grief for her; the poet will paint such a scene, done in the contemporary manner, for us.]

And the trees about me,
Let them be dry and leafless; let the rocks
Groan with continual surges; and behind me
Make all a desolation. Look, look, wenches!

Paint me a cavernous waste shore
Cast in the unstilled Cyclades,
Paint me the bold anfractuous rocks
Faced by the snarled and yelping seas.

Display me Aeolus above
Reviewing the insurgent gales
Which tangle Ariadne's hair
And swell with haste the perjured sails.

Morning stirs the feet and hands
(Nausicaa and Polypheme).[1]   10

[1] Nausicaa is another "love-lorn maiden," this time from the *Odyssey*. Ulysses loved her and left her. (Sweeney is no Ulysses.) Polyphemus is a repulsive and bestial one-eyed giant in the *Odyssey*. Ulysses escaped from him by putting out his one eye, thus leaving him totally blind. Sweeney too is blind. Sight, insight, vision—Sweeney lacks

Gesture of orang-outang
    Rises from the sheets in steam.

This withered root of knots of hair
    Slitted below and gashed with eyes,
The oval O cropped out with teeth:
    The sickle motion from the thighs

Jackknifes upward at the knees
    Then straightens out from heel to hip
Pushing the framework of the bed
    And clawing at the pillow slip.

Sweeney addressed full length to shave
    Broadbottomed, pink from nape to base,
Knows the female temperament
    And wipes the suds around his face.

(The lengthened shadow of a man
    Is history, said Emerson
Who had not seen the silhouette
    Of Sweeney straddled in the sun.)

Tests the razor on his leg
    Waiting until the shriek subsides.
The epileptic on the bed
    Curves backward, clutching at her sides.

The ladies of the corridor
    Find themselves involved, disgraced,
Call witness to their principles
    And deprecate the lack of taste

Observing that hysteria
    Might easily be misunderstood;
Mrs. Turner intimates
    It does the house no sort of good.[2]

But Doris, towelled from the bath,
    Enters padding on broad feet,
Bringing sal volatile
    And a glass of brandy neat.

1920

---

them all except, in the strictly literal sense, sight. In the biblical figure, though he has eyes, he sees not. His actions therefore, unguided by vision, are random, humanly meaningless.

[2] Faulkner has drawn upon these stanzas in the scene between the two madams in *Sanctuary*. A comparison of the poem and the novel suggests something of the nature of Eliot's influence on modern literature. Even prostitutes have their standards of propriety, their codes; but how adequate a code is it, what estimate of human nature and what final values does it imply?

[handwritten top left: There is the significance in terms of Fertility Ritual.]

THOMAS STEARNS ELIOT

[handwritten: How there is no antagonism]

[handwritten above title: Much disorganization, however, this reflect the present state of civilization]

THE WASTE LAND 1922

[handwritten left margin: culture and traditions are intermingled.]

[For a generation the title supplied an epithet for what seemed a sterile society, without faith of any sort and without hope of renewal. The epigraph suggests the reason, implied in the poem, for the age's sterility. Taken from *The Satyricon* of Petronius, it may be freely rendered: "I have seen with my own eyes the well-known Cumaean Sibyl hanging in a jar, and when the young men asked her what she wanted, she said she wanted to die." The famous prophetess of classic myth was granted endless life but not lasting youth. She withered and shrank with age and was finally exhibited in a jar as a curiosity. Here drunken and scornful youths mock her. The voices of prophesy are no longer listened to, the prophets themselves no longer respected. Compare Madame Sosostris with her bad cold, which muffles her voice.

The title of the first section is taken from the Book of Common Prayer. The relation between the poem and the burial service is of course ironic. St. Paul's analogy between man and the grain of wheat which, when put in the ground, must die as itself in order to be reborn as a new plant, is at the heart of the service. Here in the poem it is not wheat but a corpse that is "planted," and though it may be dug up, it will not sprout. The implication is that St. Paul's analogy is false; the promise of resurrection does not apply to man. April, the time of Easter and of the seasonal rebirth in the natural world, is therefore the cruelest month because man is excluded from its promise.

[handwritten left margin: much rendering conscious]

The title of the second section suggests that the naturalistic ethic of the modern world conceives life as a game played for personal advantage. A best-selling book of a few years ago was entitled *How to Win Friends and Influence People*; in it traditional moral "absolutes" were recommended as profitable. Between a religious ethic and any such prudential morality there is a great chasm, but of course neonaturalistic ethics need not be narrowly prudential. At any rate, the people in this section of the poem are incapable of love or sacrifice. Each is alone, maneuvering in a game he hopes to win. What may not be clear to them but is clear to the reader is that in such a game no one wins.

[handwritten left margin: The mind latches on to seemingly unrelated observations, an object, a sensation, a series of experiences & pulls them together; as a whole.]

The third section, taking its title from Buddha and its closing lines from St. Augustine, pictures the various perversions and degradations of man's sexuality. The central core of meaning is similar in all the great religions, in Eliot's view. In the passages alluded to, both Buddha and St. Augustine recommended asceticism. But that asceticism is not the only alternative to sordidness is suggested by the opening lines, which echo Spenser's "Prothalamion," or marriage song. Spenser's position may be described as that of a Christian humanist: he saw married love as analogous to and preparatory for divine love. The use Eliot has made of Spenser here thus foreshadows *The Elder Statesman*, in which human love is pictured as redemptive. Eliot has recognized—and deplored—in himself what he calls a "Puritan" tendency, which, as his critics have often noted, finds frequent expression in his early work. But it seems never to have been his intention to recommend a "Puritan" view of life—that is, a sharply dualistic view in which it is thought that man's "lower" nature ought to be suppressed, because "flesh," matter, the natural world, is corrupt and corrupting.

Eliot's note on Tiresias (what he sees "is the substance of the poem") makes the author's *intention* clear. But the achieved meaning of a poem may not perfectly coincide with the intended meaning. It is possible reasonably to read *The Waste Land* in such a way that the drowned Phoenician sailor of the next section, rather than the blind seer of Greek myth, becomes the "most important personage" of the poem. If we read the work primarily in moral terms, as a diagnosis and indictment of the moral failures of a society, then Eliot's note seems justified. But if we read it in philosophic, as contrasted with moral, terms, then it may seem that Phlebas should be considered central and his section, "Death by Water," the turning point of the poem. For his death raises the whole question of the existence of God or of a purposive, meaningful universe. "Consider Phlebas, who was once handsome and tall as you."

The Shakespearean sonnet which begins with line 235 is followed by another beginning with line 249, which disintegrates before it ends. That this sordid and meaningless "love" scene should be conveyed by a poetic form associated traditionally with the expression of idealized love is, ironically, very appropriate. That the second sonnet should be lost before coming to the climax in the couplet is also appropriate: it parallels formally the typist's sexual experience.

The title of the last section alludes to Roman religious myth, the opening lines remind us of Christ's agony in the Garden of Gethsemane, and the closing lines are taken from the Hindu Scriptures. Thus once again we are reminded of Eliot's view that the higher religions agree in large part: there is a central core of meaning of all religious myth. But can we respond to that meaning? Can we even understand it? The Roman god Jupiter was known as the Thunderer, but everybody today knows that the Roman gods were only "mythical." What shall we make of this voice that speaks to us here stammering in unfamiliar languages?

This question may provide a clue to the meaning of a line that has struck many readers as obscure—"Why then Ile. . . ." The line is taken from Kyd's *The Spanish Tragedy*, the subtitle of which is "Hieronymo's mad againe." Like Hamlet, Hieronymo in Kyd's play pretends to be mad to discover truth. A possible reading of the line in the poem might then be, "What I have written may seem to you, reader, nonsensical, or even mad; but if so, think again." If we read it this way and then recall that the first American review of the poem declared it to be a hoax, the line seems prophetic.]

> "Nam Sibyllam quidem Cumis ego ipse oculis meis
> vidi in ampulla pendere, et cum illi pueri dicerent:
> Σίβυλλα τί θέλεις; respondebat illa: ἀποθανεῖν θέλω."

> For Ezra Pound
> il miglior fabbro.

[handwritten margin: these words... Eliot moving to psychology, toward chaos and away from conventional meaning]

I. THE BURIAL OF THE DEAD

April is the cruellest month, breeding
Lilacs out of the dead land, mixing
Memory and desire, stirring
Dull roots with spring rain.
Winter kept us warm, covering
Earth in forgetful snow, feeding
A little life with dried tubers.
Summer surprised us, coming over the Starnbergersee
With a shower of rain; we stopped in the colonnade,
And went on in sunlight, into the Hofgarten,   10
And drank coffee, and talked for an hour.

[handwritten margin: Not a great poem, but impt. Much like "Emperor's New Clothes"]

[handwritten footer: Vegetation cults, fertility rituals, with their sympathetic magic, represent a harmony of human culture with the natural environment, and express an extreme sense of the unity of life.]

Bin gar keine Russin, stamm' aus Litauen, echt deutsch.
And when we were children, staying at the arch-duke's,
My cousin's, he took me out on a sled,
And I was frightened. He said, Marie,   15
Marie, hold on tight. And down we went.
In the mountains, there you feel free.
I read, much of the night, and go south in the winter.

What are the roots that clutch, what branches grow
Out of this stony rubbish? Son of man,   20
You cannot say, or guess, for you know only
A heap of broken images, where the sun beats,
And the dead tree gives no shelter, the cricket no relief,
And the dry stone no sound of water. Only
There is shadow under this red rock   25
(Come in under the shadow of this red rock),
And I will show you something different from either
Your shadow at morning striding behind you
Or your shadow at evening rising to meet you;
I will show you fear in a handful of dust.   30

      Frisch weht der Wind
      Der Heimat zu
      Mein Irisch Kind,
      Wo weilest du?

"You gave me hyacinths first a year ago;   35
"They called me the hyacinth girl."
—Yet when we came back, late, from the Hyacinth garden,
Your arms full, and your hair wet, I could not
Speak, and my eyes failed, I was neither
Living or dead, and I knew nothing,   40
Looking into the heart of light, the silence.
Oed' und leer das Meer.

Madame Sosostris, famous clairvoyante,
Had a bad cold, nevertheless
Is known to be the wisest woman in Europe,   45
With a wicked pack of cards. Here, said she,
Is your card, the drowned Phoenician Sailor,
(Those are pearls that were his eyes. Look!)
Here is Belladonna, the Lady of the Rocks,
The lady of situations.   50
Here is the man with three staves, and here the Wheel
And here is the one-eyed merchant, and this card,
Which is blank, is something he carries on his back,
Which I am forbidden to see. I do not find
The Hanged Man. Fear death by water.   55
I see crowds of people, walking round in a ring.
Thank you. If you see dear Mrs. Equitone,

[Handwritten marginalia:]

Not only the agony in the garden but also agony of the Waste Land

Modern sordid affairs — material that shows passion of person.

one of Wasteland figures

represents something & cosmopolitan "high life"

Deep under fire & fake

Eliot says, "he is associated with the Hanged God of Frazer and the hooded figure in passage of the disciples to Emmaus in Part V"

[handwritten top margin: The Wounded man has become Christ, the Vegetation God, and the Journey through the Waste Land along "the Sorry road" becomes the Journey to Emmaus.]

Tell her I bring the horoscope myself:
One must be so careful these days.

Unreal City, *[handwritten: urban background]*
Under the brown fog of a winter dawn,
A crowd flowed over London Bridge, so many,
I had not thought death had undone so many. *[handwritten left margin: Relove to Dante]*
Sighs, short and infrequent, were exhaled,
And each man fixed his eyes before his feet.
Flowed up the hill and down King William Street,
To where Saint Mary Woolnoth kept the hours
With a dead sound on the final stroke of nine.
There I saw one I knew, and stopped him, crying: "Stetson!
"You who were with me in the ships at Mylae!
"That corpse you planted last year in your garden,
"Has it begun to sprout? Will it bloom this year?
"Or has the sudden frost disturbed its bed?
"Oh keep the Dog far hence, that's friend to men,
"Or with his nails he'll dig it up again!
"You! hypocrite lecteur!—mon semblable,—mon frère!"

[handwritten right margin: The city turns into the intense but meaningless horror, the absurd inconsequence, of night mares.]

60

65

70

75

[handwritten: Pick up theme again — Corpse acquire association with slain god & The Guild]

II. A GAME OF CHESS

The Chair she sat in, like a burnished throne,
Glowed on the marble, where the glass
Held up by standards wrought with fruited vines
From which a golden Cupidon peeped out
(Another hid his eyes behind his wing)
Doubled the flames of sevenbranched candelabra
Reflecting light upon the table as
The glitter of her jewels rose to meet it,
From satin cases poured in rich profusion;
In vials of ivory and coloured glass
Unstoppered, lurked her strange synthetic perfumes,
Unguent, powdered, or liquid—troubled, confused
And drowned the sense in odours; stirred by the air
That freshened from the window, these ascended
In fattening the prolonged candle-flames,
Flung their smoke into the laquearia,
Stirring the pattern on the coffered ceiling.
Huge sea-wood fed with copper
Burned green and orange, framed by the coloured stone,
In which sad light a carvèd dolphin swam.
Above the antique mantel was displayed
As though a window gave upon the sylvan scene
The change of Philomel, by the barbarous king
So rudely forced; yet there the nightingale
Filled all the desert with inviolable voice
And still she cried, and still the world pursues,

[handwritten right margin: A Knowledge & Bough Anthony and Cleopatra is assumed.]

80

85

90

95

100

[handwritten bottom: → Focus of attention shifts to the outer disintegration in its large, obvious aspects, and the reference to Russia and to post war Europe in general are plain.]

"Jug Jug" to dirty ears.
And other withered stumps of time
Were told upon the walls; staring forms   105
Leaned out, leaning, hushing the room enclosed.
Footsteps shuffled on the stair.
Under the firelight, under the brush, her hair
Spread out in fiery points
Glowed into words, then would be savagely still.   110

"My nerves are bad to-night. Yes, bad. Stay with me.
"Speak to me. Why do you never speak. Speak.
    "What are you thinking of? What thinking? What?
"I never know what you are thinking. Think."

I think we are in rats' alley   115
Where the dead men lost their bones.

Hallucinatory "What is that noise?"
quality
which adds   The wind under the door.
to the   "What is that noise now? What is the wind doing?"
neurasthenic   Nothing again nothing.   120
episode.   "Do
              "You know nothing? Do you see nothing? Do you remember
              "Nothing?"
                  I remember
              Those are pearls that were his eyes.   125
              "Are you alive, or not? Is there nothing in your head?"
                                                              But

O O O O that Shakespeherian Rag—
It's so elegant
So intelligent   130
Several   "What shall I do now? What shall I do?"
talking   "I shall rush out as I am, and walk the street
at same   "With my hair down, so. What shall we do tomorrow?
time.   "What shall we ever do?"
                              The hot water at ten.   135
              And if it rains, a closed car at four.   *Hurry up*
              And we shall play a game of chess,
              Pressing lidless eyes and waiting for a knock upon the door.

When Lil's husband got demobbed, I said—
I didn't mince my words, I said to her myself,   140
HURRY UP PLEASE ITS TIME
Now Albert's coming back, make yourself a bit smart.
He'll want to know what you done with that money he gave you
To get yourself some teeth. He did, I was there.
You have them all out, Lil, and get a nice set,   145
He said, I swear, I can't bear to look at you.
And no more can't I, I said, and think of poor Albert,

Note compressed description — so tight. one has to have time for it to unfold 843 in his mind.

He's been in the army four years, he wants a good time,
And if you don't give it him, there's others will, I said.
Oh is there, she said. Something o' that, I said.   150
Then I'll know who to thank, she said, and give me a straight look.
HURRY UP PLEASE ITS TIME
If you don't like it you can get on with it, I said.   *If you don't show him a good time, then I will.*
Others can pick and choose if you can't.
But if Albert makes off, it won't be for lack of telling.   155
You ought to be ashamed, I said, to look so antique.
(And her only thirty-one.)
I can't help it, she said, pulling a long face,
It's them pills I took, to bring it off, she said.
(She's had five already, and nearly died of young George.)   160
The chemist said it would be all right, but I've never been the same.
You *are* a proper fool, I said.
Well, if Albert won't leave you alone, there it is, I said,
What you get married for if you don't want children?
HURRY UP PLEASE ITS TIME   165
Well, that Sunday Albert was home, they had a hot gammon,
And they asked me in to dinner, to get the beauty of it hot—
HURRY UP PLEASE ITS TIME
HURRY UP PLEASE ITS TIME
Goonight Bill. Goonight Lou. Goonight May. Goonight.   170
Ta ta. Goonight. Goonight.
Good night, ladies, good night, sweet ladies, good night, good night.

Ophelia these also

Thames — described in ugly detail.

III. THE FIRE SERMON

The river's tent is broken: the last fingers of leaf
Clutch and sink into the wet bank. The wind   *Structural analogy*
Crosses the brown land, unheard. The nymphs are departed.   *in letting*   175
Sweet Thames, run softly, till I end my song.   *stony*
The river bears no empty bottles, sandwich papers,
Silk handkerchiefs, cardboard boxes, cigarette ends
Or other testimony of summer nights. The nymphs are departed.
And their friends, the loitering heirs of city directors—   180
Departed, have left no addresses.
By the waters of Leman I sat down and wept . . .
Sweet Thames, run softly till I end my song,   *Spenser's*
Sweet Thames, run softly, for I speak not loud or long.
But at my back in a cold blast I hear   185   *Pope*
The rattle of the bones, and chuckle spread from ear to ear.
A rat crept softly through the vegetation
Dragging its slimy belly on the bank
While I was fishing in the dull canal
On a winter evening round behind the gashouse   *Last Judgment* 190
Musing upon the king my brother's wreck   *must be qualified*
And on the king my father's death before him.
                                                                   Last 2 lines too much quality of caricature.

Read many times before one sees the complete picture of the desolation.

White bodies naked on the low damp ground
And bones cast in a little low dry garret,
Rattled by the rat's foot only, year to year.   195
But at my back from time to time I hear
The sound of horns and motors, which shall bring
Sweeney to Mrs. Porter in the spring.
O the moon shone bright on Mrs. Porter
And on her daughter   200
They wash their feet in soda water
Et O ces voix d'enfants, chantant dans la coupole!
Twit twit twit
Jug jug jug jug jug jug
So rudely forc'd.   205

Tereu

Unreal City
Under the brown fog of a winter noon
Mr. Eugenides, the Smyrna merchant
Unshaven, with a pocket full of currants   210
C.i.f. London: documents at sight,
Asked me in demotic French
To luncheon at the Cannon Street Hotel
Followed by a weekend at the Metropole.

At the violet hour, when the eyes and back   215
Turn upward from the desk, when the human engine waits
Like a taxi throbbing waiting,
I Tiresias, though blind, throbbing between two lives,
Old man with wrinkled female breasts, can see
At the violet hour, the evening hour that strives   220
Homeward, and brings the sailor home from sea,
The typist home at teatime, clears her breakfast, lights
Her stove, and lays out food in tins.
Out of the window perilously spread
Her drying combinations touched by the sun's last rays,   225
On the divan are piled (at night her bed)
Stockings, slippers, camisoles, and stays.
I Tiresias, old man with wrinkled dugs
Perceived the scene, and foretold the rest—
I too awaited the expected guest.   230
He, the young man carbuncular, arrives,
A small house agent's clerk, with one bold stare,
One of the low on whom assurance sits
As a silk hat on a Bradford millionaire.
The time is now propitious, as he guesses,   235
The meal is ended, she is bored and tired,
Endeavours to engage her in caresses
Which still are unreproved, if undesired.

Flushed and decided, he assaults at once;   240
Exploring hands encounter no defence;
His vanity requires no response,
And makes a welcome of indifference.
(And I Tiresias have foresuffered all
Enacted on this same divan or bed;   245
I who have sat by Thebes below the wall
And walked among the lowest of the dead.)
Bestows one final patronising kiss,
And gropes his way, finding the stairs unlit . . .

She turns and looks a moment in the glass,   250
Hardly aware of her departed lover;
Her brain allows one half-formed thought to pass:
"Well now that's done: and I'm glad it's over."
When lovely woman stoops to folly and
Paces about her room again, alone,   255
She smoothes her hair with automatic hand,
And puts a record on the gramophone.

"This music crept by me upon the waters"
And along the Strand, up Queen Victoria Street.
O City city, I can sometimes hear   260
Beside a public bar in Lower Thames Street,
The pleasant whining of a mandoline
And a clatter and a chatter from within
Where fishmen lounge at noon: where the walls
Of Magnus Martyr hold   265
Inexplicable splendour of Ionian white and gold.

        The river sweats
        Oil and tar
        The bargest drift
        With the turning tide
        Red sails   270
        Wide
        To leeward, swing on the heavy spar.
        The barges wash
        Drifting logs
        Down Greenwich reach   275
        Past the Isle of Dogs.
                Weialala leia
                Wallala leialala
        Elizabeth and Leicester
        Beating oars   280
        The stern was formed
        A gilded shell
        Red and gold
        The brisk swell

Both oriental and occidental – both
say restraint Poor last. Not

Rippled both shores   hinting to Christian   285
Southwest wind   religion. When
Carried down stream   thunder comes, we
The peal of bells   get answer.
White towers
    Weialala leia   290
    Wallala leialala

"Trams and dusty trees.
Highbury bore me. Richmond and Kew
Undid me. By Richmond I raised my knees
Supine on the floor of a narrow canoe."   295
"My feet are at Moorgate, and my heart
Under my feet. After the event
He wept. He promised 'a new start.'
I made no comment. What should I resent?"

"On Margate Sands.   300
I can connect
Nothing with nothing.
The broken fingernails of dirty hands.
My people humble people who expect
Nothing."   305
    la la
Fire Sermon   To Carthage then I came   Lifter 2 lines
soul &   Buddha   from St. Augustine
poetic   Burning burning burning burning and 2 from
economy   Oh Lord Thou pluckest me out   fire scene &
the eastern & western O Lord Thou pluckest   310
asceticism   burning   the Buddha.

IV. DEATH BY WATER

He intends
for St.   Phlebas the Phoenician, a fortnight dead,
Augustine   Forgot the cry of gulls, and the deep sea swell
and the   And the profit and loss.
Buddha   A current under sea   315
to be   Picked his bones in whispers. As he rose and fell
actively   He passed the stages of his age and youth
present here. Entering the whirlpool.
                          Gentile or Jew
              O you who turn the wheel and look to windward,   320
              Consider Phlebas, who was once handsome and tall as you.

V. WHAT THE THUNDER SAID

The drouth
becomes   After the torchlight red on sweaty faces
as thirst   After the frosty silence in the gardens
for the   After the agony in stony places
              The shouting and the crying   325
waters of faith and healing, and the
specifically religious enters into the
orchestration of the poem.

Stated negatively — this is what we have not done by sympathy.

Prison and palace and reverberation
Of thunder of spring over distant mountains
He who was living is now dead
We who were living are now dying
With a little patience

"The thunder is the "dry, sterile thunder without rain" 330

Here is no water but only rock
Rock and no water and the sandy road
The road winding above among the mountains
Which are mountains of rock without water
If there were water we should stop and drink
Amongst the rock one cannot stop or think
Sweat is dry and feet are in the sand
If there were only water amongst the rock
Dead mountain mouth of carious teeth that cannot spit
Here one can neither stand nor lie nor sit
There is not even silence in the mountains
But dry sterile thunder without rain
There is not even solitude in the mountains
But red sullen faces sneer and snarl
From doors of mudcracked houses

There is no resurrection or renewal 335

here there is no buoyancy but a dragging, persistent movement of hopeless exhaustion. 340 345

The imagined sound & If there were water
And no rock *water*
If there were rock *suggest fever.*
And also water
And water
A spring
A pool among the rock
If there were the sound of water only
Not the cicada
And dry grass singing
But sound of water over a rock
Where the hermit-thrush sings in the pine trees
Drip drop drip drop drop drop drop
But there is no water

350

355

Who is the third who walks always beside you? 360
When I count, there are only you and I together
But when I look ahead up the white road
There is always another one walking beside you
Gliding wrapt in a brown mantle, hooded
I do not know whether a man or a woman
—But who is that on the other side of you?

Christ, the hooded one 365

What is that sound high in the air
Murmur of maternal lamentation
Who are those hooded hordes swarming
Over endless plains, stumbling in cracked earth
Ringed by the flat horizon only

here one passes into hallucinated vision and then into nightmare 370

Here also a peculiar menacing undertone.

What is the city over the mountains
Cracks and reforms and bursts in the violet air
Falling towers
Jerusalem Athens Alexandria   375
Vienna London
Unreal

A woman drew her long black hair out tight
And fiddled whisper music on those strings
And bats with baby faces in the violet light   380
Whistled, and beat their wings
And crawled head downward down a blackened wall
And upside down in air were towers
Tolling reminiscent bells, that kept the hours
And voices singing out of empty cisterns and exhausted wells.   385

In this decayed hole among the mountains
In the faint moonlight, the grass is singing
Over the tumbled graves, about the chapel
There is the empty chapel, only the wind's home.
It has no windows, and the door swings,   390
Dry bones can harm no one.
Only a cock stood on the rooftree
Co co rico co co rico
In a flash of lightning. Then a damp gust
Bringing rain   395
Ganga was sunken, and the limp leaves
Waited for rain, while the black clouds
Gathered far distant, over Himavant.
The jungle crouched, humped in silence.
Then spoke the thunder   400
Da
Datta: what have we given?
My friend, blood shaking my heart
The awful daring of a moment's surrender
Which an age of prudence can never retract   405
By this, and this only, we have existed
Which is not to be found in our obituaries
Or in memories draped by the beneficent spider
Or under seals broken by the lean solicitor
In our empty rooms   410
Da
Dayadhvam: I have heard the key
Turn in the door once and turn once only
We think of the key, each in his prison
Thinking of the key, each confirms a prison   415
Only at nightfall, aethereal rumours
Revive for a moment a broken Coriolanus
Da

[Handwritten at top:] The whole poem is a self-subsistent Poem. It is a new start for Eng. poetry. Despite the fact that much depends upon Eliot's notes. ¶ From Ritual to Romance. Jessie L. Weston ¶ we return to the individual giving + self without getting involved → when we give up, Don't give up ¶ 1922 refrain and become involved in look.

> *Damyata:* The boat responded *[handwritten:]* Control
> Gaily, to the hand expert with sail and oar
> The sea was calm, your heart would have responded   *[hw:]* 42?
> Gaily, when invited, beating obedient
> To controlling hands
>   I sat upon the shore
> Fishing, with the arid plain behind me
> Shall I at least set my lands in order?
> London Bridge is falling down falling down falling down
> *Poi s'ascose nel foco che gli affina*
> *Quando fiam uti chelidon*—O swallow swallow
> *Le Prince d'Aquitaine à la tour abolie*   *[hw:]* 430
> These fragments I have shored against my ruins
> Why then Ile fit you. Hieronymo's mad againe.
> Datta. Dayadhvam. Damyata.
>   Shantih   shantih   shantih

[Handwritten left:] 425 ... The answer and sums it up,   →   1922

NOTES ON "THE WASTE LAND"

[T. S. Eliot]

Not only the title, but the plan and a good deal of the incidental symbolism of the poem were suggested by Miss Jessie L. Weston's book on the Grail legend: *From Ritual to Romance* (Cambridge). Indeed, so deeply am I indebted, Miss Weston's book will elucidate the difficulties of the poem much better than my notes can do; and I recommend it (apart from the great interest of the book itself) to any who think such elucidation of the poem worth the trouble. To another work of anthropology I am indebted in general, one which has influenced our generation profoundly; I mean *The Golden Bough*; I have used especially the two volumes *Adonis, Attis, Osiris*. Anyone who is acquainted with these works will immediately recognise in the poem certain references to vegetation ceremonies.

I. THE BURIAL OF THE DEAD

Line 20   Cf. Ezekiel II, i.

23.   Cf. Ecclesiastes XII, v.

31.   V. Tristan und Isolde, I, verses 5–8.

42.   Id. III, verse 24.

46.   I am not familiar with the exact constitution of the Tarot pack of cards, from which I have obviously departed to suit my own convenience. The Hanged Man, a member of the traditional pack, fits my purpose in two ways: because he is associated in my mind with the Hanged God of Frazer, and because I associate him with the hooded figure in the passage of the disciples to Emmaus in Part V. The Phoenician Sailor and the Merchant appear later; also the "crowd of people," and Death by Water is executed in Part IV. The Man with Three Staves (an authentic member of the Tarot pack) I associate, quite arbitrarily, with the Fisher King himself.

60.   Cf. Baudelaire:

> "Fourmillante cité, cité pleine de rêves,
> "Où le spectre en plein jour raccroche le passant."

63.   Cf. Inferno III, 55–57:

> "si lunga tratta
> di gente, ch'io non avrei mai creduto
> che morte tanta n'avesse disfatta."

64.   Cf. Inferno IV, 25–27:

> "Quivi, secondo che per ascolatare,
> "non avea pianto, ma' che di sospiri,
> "che l'aura eterna facevan tremare."

68.   A phenomenon which I have often noticed.

74.   Cf. the Dirge in Webster's *White Devil*.

76.   V. Baudelaire, Preface to *Fleurs du Mal*.

II. A GAME OF CHESS

77.   Cf. *Antony and Cleopatra*, II, ii, 1. 190.

92.   Laquearia. V. *Aeneid*, I, 726:

> dependent lychni laquearibus aureis incensi, et noctem
> flammis funalia vincunt.

98.   Sylvan scene. V. Milton, *Paradise Lost*, IV, 140.

99.   V. Ovid, *Metamorphoses*, VI, Philomela.

100.   Cf. Part III, 1. 204.

115.   Cf. Part III, 1. 195.

118.   Cf. Webster: "Is the wind in that door still?"

126.   Cf. Part I, 1. 37, 48.

138.   Cf. the game of chess in Middleton's *Women beware Women*.

III. THE FIRE SERMON

176.   V. Spenser, *Prothalamion*.

192.   Cf. *The Tempest*, I, ii.

196.   Cf. Marvell, *To His Coy Mistress*.

197.   Cf. Day, *Parliament of Bees*:

> "When of the sudden, listening, you shall hear,
> "A noise of horns and hunting, which shall bring
> "Actaeon to Diana in the spring,
> "Where all shall see her naked skin . . ."

199.   I do not know the origin of the ballad from which these lines are taken: it was reported to me from Sydney, Australia.

202.   V. Verlaine, *Parsifal*.

210.   The currants were quoted at a price "carriage and insurance free to London"; and the Bill of Lading etc. were to be handed to the buyer upon payment of the sight draft.

218.   Tiresias, although a mere spectator and not indeed a "character," is yet the most important personage in the poem, uniting all the rest. Just as the one-eyed merchant,

seller of currants, melts into the Phoenician Sailor, and the latter is not wholly distinct from Ferdinand Prince of Naples, so all the women are one woman, and the two sexes meet in Tiresias. What Tiresias *sees*, in fact, is the substance of the poem. The whole passage from Ovid is of great anthropological interest:

> ". . . Cum Iunone iocos et maior vestra profecto est
> Quam, quae contingit maribus," dixisse, "voluptas."
> Illa negat; placuit quae sit sententia docti
> Quaerere Tiresiae: venus huic erat utraque nota.
> Nam duo magnorum viridi coeuntia silva
> Corpora serpentum baculi violaverat ictu
> Deque viro factus, mirabile, femina septem
> Egerat autumnos; octavo rursus eosdem
> Vidit et "est vestrae si tanta potentia plagae,"
> Dixit "ut auctoris sortem in contraria mutet,
> Nunc quoque vos feriam!" percussis anguibus isdem
> Forma prior rediit genetivaque venit imago.
> Arbiter hic igitur sumptus de lite iocosa
> Dicta Iovis firmat; gravius Saturnia iusto
> Nec pro materia fertur doluisse suique
> Iudicis aeterna demnavit lumina nocte,
> At pater omnipotens (neque enim licet inrita cuiquam
> Facta dei fecisse deo) pro lumine adempto
> Scire futura dedit poenamque levavit honore.

221. This may not appear as exact as Sappho's lines, but I had in mind the "long-shore" or "dory" fisherman, who returns at nightfall.

253. V. Goldsmith, the song in *The Vicar of Wakefield*.

257. V. *The Tempest*, as above.

264. The interior of St. Magnus Martyr is to my mind one of the finest among Wren's interiors. See *The Proposed Demolition of Nineteen City Churches*: (P. S. King & Son, Ltd.).

266. The Song of the (three) Thames-daughters begins here. From line 292 to 306 inclusive they speak in turn. V. *Gotterdammerung*, III, i: the Rhine-daughters.

279. V. Froude, *Elizabeth*, Vol. I, ch. iv, letter of De Quadra to Philip of Spain:
"In the afternoon we were in a barge, watching the games on the river. (The queen) was alone with Lord Robert and myself on the poop, when they began to talk non-sense, and went so far that Lord Robert at last said, as I was on the spot there was no reason why they should not be married if the queen pleased."

293. Cf. *Purgatorio*, V, 133:

> "Ricorditi di me, che son la Pia;
> "Siena mi fe', disfecemi Maremma."

307. V. St. Augustine's *Confessions*: "to Carthage then I came, where a cauldron of unholy loves sang all about mine ears."

308. The complete text of the Buddha's Fire Sermon (which corresponds in importance to the Sermon on the Mount) from which these words are taken, will be found translated in the late Henry Clarke Warren's *Buddhism in Translation* (Harvard Oriental Series). Mr. Warren was one of the great pioneers of Buddhist studies in the Occident.

309. From St. Augustine's *Confessions* again. The collocation of these two representatives of eastern and western asceticism, as the culmination of this part of the poem, is not an accident.

V. WHAT THE THUNDER SAID

In the first part of Part V three themes are employed: the journey to Emmaus, the approach to the Chapel Perilous (see Miss Weston's book) and the present decay of eastern Europe.

357. This is *Turdus aonalaschkae pallasii*, the hermit-thrush which I have heard in Quebec Province. Chapman says (*Handbook of Birds of Eastern North America*) "it is most at home in secluded woodland and thickety retreats. . . . Its notes are not remarkable for variety or volume, but in purity and sweetness of tone and exquisite modulation they are unequalled." Its "water-dripping song" is justly celebrated.

360. The following lines were stimulated by the account of one of the Antarctic expeditions (I forget which, but I think one of Shackleton's); it was related that the party of explorers, at the extremity of their strength, had the constant delusion that there was *one more member* than could actually be counted.

366-76. Cf. Hermann Hesse, *Blick ins Chaos:* "Schon ist halb Europa, schon ist zumindest der halbe Osten Europas auf dem Wege zum Chaos, fährt betrunken im heiligem Wahn am Abgrund entlang und singt dazu, singt betrunken und hymnisch wie Dmitri Karamasoff sang. Ueber diese Lieder lacht der Bürger beleidigt, der Heilige und Seher hört sie mit Tränen."

401. "Data, dayadhvam, damyata" (Give, sympathise, control). The fable of the meaning of the Thunder is found in the *Brihadaranyaka—Upanishad*, 5, 1. A translation is found in Deussen's *Sechzig Upanishads des Veda*, p. 489.

407. Cf. Webster, *The White Devil*, V, vi:

> ". . . they'll remarry
> Ere the worm pierce your winding-sheet, ere the spider
> Make a thin curtain for your epitaphs."

411. Cf. *Inferno*, XXXIII, 46:

> "ed io sentii chiavar l'uscio di sotto
> all'orribile torre."

Also F. H. Bradley, *Appearance and Reality*, p. 346.

"My external sensations are no less private to myself than are my thoughts or my feelings. In either case my experience falls within my own circle, a circle closed on the outside; and, with all its elements alike, every sphere is opaque to the others which surround it. . . . In brief, regarded as an existence which appears in a soul, the whole world for each is peculiar and private to that soul."

424. V. Weston: *From Ritual to Romance*; chapter on the Fisher King.

427. V. *Purgatorio*, XXVI, 148.

> " 'Ara vos prec per aquella valor
> 'que vos guida al som de l'escalina,
> 'sovegna vos a temps dê ma dolor.'
> Poi s'ascose nel foco che gli affina."

428. V. *Pervigilium Veneris*. Cf. Philomela in Parts II and III.

429. V. Gerard de Nerval, Sonnet *El Desdichado*.

431. V. Kyd's *Spanish Tragedy*.

433. Shantih. Repeated as here, a formal ending to an Upanishad. "The Peace which passeth understanding" is our equivalent to this word.

MARINA

❀ [The title and the epigraph stand in ironic relation. In Shakespeare's *Pericles*,
Pericles awakes to discover his daughter Marina alive, not dead as he had
thought. The epigraph may be translated, "What place is this, what region, what part
of the world?" In Seneca's *Hercules Furens*, from which the epigraph is quoted, Hercules awakes to discover that he has slain his wife and children. If the meaning of the
poem were entirely dependent on the title and the epigraph, with the implications these
carry with them from their original contexts, the two recognition scenes would cancel
each other.

But the poem itself is not structured in ironic terms. It presents an experience filled
with joy; it does not present, or even imply, either the logic of, or an argument for,
religious belief. The implication of the suggestions carried by the title and epigraph,
taken together with the poem that follows, would seem to be that we cannot *know*, in
any purely rational or objective sense, that experiences such as this are true revelations
of reality. They may be merely "psychological." Elizabeth Drew has called this "the
only purely joyous poem Eliot has ever written," but it does not minimize the ambiguity of the religious experience. The speaker *accepts* the ambiguity, the "not knowing."]

Quis hic locus, quae regio, quae mundi plaga?

What seas what shores what grey rocks and what islands
What water lapping the bow
And scent of pine and the woodthrush singing through the fog
What images return
O my daughter.   5

Those who sharpen the tooth of the dog, meaning
Death[1]
Those who glitter with the glory of the hummingbird, meaning
Death
Those who sit in the stye of contentment, meaning   10
Death
Those who suffer the ecstasy of the animals, meaning
Death

[1] A deliberately vague and generalized catalogue of some of the more worldly sins.
Their lack of sharpness and clarity is a part of the meaning of the passage: they have
become, for the speaker, "unsubstantial." Compare the precise clarity of Prufrock's
thoughts of *his* world, or the vivid details registered in the mind of the speaker in
"Sweeney Erect."

Are become unsubstantial, reduced by a wind,
A breath of pine, and the woodsong fog   15
By this grace dissolved in place

What is this face, less clear and clearer
The pulse in the arm, less strong and stronger—
Given or lent? more distant than stars and nearer than the eye

Whispers and small laughter between leaves and hurrying feet   20
Under sleep, where all the waters meet.

Bowsprit cracked with ice and paint cracked with heat.
I made this, I have forgotten
And remember.
The rigging weak and the canvas rotten   25
Between one June and another September.
Made this unknowing, half conscious, unknown, my own.
The garboard strake leaks, the seams need caulking.
This form, this face, this life
Living to live in a world of time beyond me; let me   30
Resign my life for this life, my speech for that unspoken,
The awakened, lips parted, the hope, the new ships.

What seas what shores what granite islands towards my timbers
And woodthrush calling through the fog
My daughter.   35

                                                                    1930

BURNT NORTON

[The title of the poem is the name of an estate Eliot is said to have visited as
a young man. *The Four Quartets* has been called Wordsworthian, and this personal reference, like the reference to the Mississippi in "The Dry Salvages," may serve
to remind us of the extent to which Eliot's later poetry departs from the impersonal
manner of the early poetry, to anticipate the neoromanticism of the poetry of the
fifties and sixties.

The epigraphs may be translated, "There is a Universal Reason, but most men live
as though they were a law unto themselves," and "The way up and the way down are
one and the same." There are a number of suggestions here: that the testimony of
non-Christian philosophers corroborates Christian belief—the "Universal Reason" of
Heraclitus, a pre-Socratic philosopher, may be associated with the conception of Christ
as the Logos, or Word, or Meaning, put forth in John's Gospel; that the testimony of
the philosophers and that of the mystics support each other; and that the affirmative
way of the mystics, the way up, arrives at the same end as the negative way, the way
down.

Unlike Hart Crane's "The Bridge," "Burnt Norton" should probably not be called
a "mystical" poem—that is, it does not attempt to describe the speaker's experience of
the mystical state. Rather, it is a poetic meditation on time and eternity as they are
illuminated by the experiences of the mystics, the doctrines of philosophy, and the

historical facts and doctrines of the Christian religion, all in relation to the speaker's own experience.]

τοῦ λόγου δ'ἐόντος ξυνοῦ ζώουσιν οἱ πολλοί
ὡς ἰδίαν ἔχοντες φρόνησιν.
                                          I. p. 77. Fr. 2.

ὁδὸς ἄνω κάτω μία καὶ ωὐτή.
                                          I. p. 89. Fr. 60.

Diels: *Die Fragmente der Vorsokratiker* (Herakleitos)

I

Time present and time past
Are both perhaps present in time future,
And time future contained in time past.
If all time is eternally present
All time is unredeemable.[1]   5
What might have been is an abstraction
Remaining a perpetual possibility
Only in a world of speculation.
What might have been and what has been
Point to one end, which is always present.   10
Footfalls echo in the memory
Down the passage which we did not take[2]
Towards the door we never opened
Into the rose-garden. My words echo
Thus, in your mind.
                    But to what purpose   15
Disturbing the dust on a bowl of rose-leaves
I do not know.
                Other echoes
Inhabit the garden. Shall we follow?
Quick, said the bird, find them, find them,
Round the corner. Through the first gate,   20
Into our first world, shall we follow

[1] Determinism and its consequences are here presented and explored. If every effect has its cause and every cause its effect, how can there be any freedom of choice? And if there is none, are we not simply products of the past, and is not the future already determined? If all time is present in this sense, then time is unredeemable.

[2] The lost opportunity, the rejected relation, the spurned love: compare the hyacinth girl scene in "The Waste Land." "The door": compare Christ's "I stand at the door and knock." "The rose-garden": the rose is the immemorial symbol of love; the garden is both the garden of personal experience ("Burnt Norton") and a reminder of the Garden of Eden, where innocence was lost and God's love rejected.

The deception of the thrush? [3] Into our first world.
There they were, dignified, invisible,
Moving without pressure, over the dead leaves,
In the autumn heat, through the vibrant air,   25
And the bird called, in response to
The unheard music[4] hidden in the shrubbery,
And the unseen eyebeam crossed, for the roses
Had the look of flowers that are looked at.
There they were as our guests, accepted and accepting.   30
So we moved, and they, in a formal pattern,
Along the empty alley, into the box circle,
To look down into the drained pool.
Dry the pool, dry concrete, brown edged,
And the pool was filled with water out of sunlight   35
And the lotos rose, quietly, quietly,
The surface glittered out of heart of light,
And they were behind us,[5] reflected in the pool.
Then a cloud passed, and the pool was empty.
Go, said the bird, for the leaves were full of children,   40
Hidden excitedly, containing laughter.
Go, go, go, said the bird: human kind
Cannot bear very much reality.
Time past and time future
What might have been and what has been   45
Point to one end, which is always present.

II

Garlic and sapphires in the mud
Clot the bedded axle-tree.[6]
The trilling wire in the blood
Sings below inveterate scars   50

[3] Compare Philomel of the earlier poems and the wood thrush of "Marina." To the unregenerate mind, the meaning of the bird's song seems a "deception" (Philomel's story is a "mere myth"). Compare Whitman's use of the song of the thrush in "When Lilacs Last in the Dooryard Bloom'd."

[4] The one who remembers never simply "relives"; he is aware of himself as remembering, aware therefore of the present in which the remembering is being done (and in which the pool is empty, the people gone or dead) as well as of the past which is being recalled. Memory therefore mixes past and present, as this passage does.

[5] There would seem to be two suggestions here, one temporal, one spatial; one historical, one personal. So far as the garden is Eden, they preceded us in time, were "behind" in the sense of at our backs as we face the future. So far as the garden is the site of a personal experience, the speaker didn't respond, turned away. The question for the speaker is whether the effects of this rejection can ever be undone.

[6] God, "the still point," is not remote and uninvolved, the "First Cause" of the Deists, but "embedded" in the mud of the world. All created nature, of which man is a part, reveals Him. For another statement of man's involvement with natural processes—even while he must in some sense, if he is to reach his full potential, transcend them—see the second verse paragraph of "The Dry Salvages," "the river is within us."

And reconciles forgotten wars.
The dance along the artery
The circulation of the lymph
Are figured in the drift of stars
Ascend to summer in the tree   55
We move above the moving tree
In light upon the figured leaf
And hear upon the sodden floor
Below, the boarhound and the boar
Pursue their pattern as before   60
But reconciled among the stars.

    At the still point of the turning world. Neither flesh nor fleshless;[7]
Neither from nor towards; at the still point, there the dance is,
But neither arrest nor movement. And do not call it fixity,
Where past and future are gathered. Neither movement from
       nor towards,   65
Neither ascent nor decline. Except for the point, the still point,
There would be no dance, and there is only the dance.
I can only say, *there* we have been: but I cannot say where.
And I cannot say, how long, for that is to place it in time.

    The inner freedom from the practical desire,   70
The release from action and suffering, release from the inner
And the outer compulsion, yet surrounded
By a grace of sense, a white light still and moving,
Erhebung without motion, concentration
Without elimination, both a new world   75
And the old made explicit, understood
In the completion of its partial ecstasy,
The resolution of its partial horror.
Yet the enchainment of past and future
Woven in the weakness of the changing body,   80
Protects mankind from heaven and damnation
Which flesh cannot endure.
                Time past and time future
Allow but a little consciousness.
To be conscious is not to be in time[8]

---

[7] "Neither flesh nor fleshless": neither "mere" flesh nor disembodied spirit. In and through God's action in the Incarnation—and in the many incarnations revealed to intuition and reason by nature—the dualisms of mind-body, spirit-matter, meaning-fact are broken down. Prufrock's problem—the divorce between value and fact, between Logos and History—has been resolved. In a paradoxical sense which must remain a mystery, the eternal and the temporal are one "at the still point." Redeemed life, like a dance, imitates or repeats this mystery, being composed of movements which, as a *pattern* of movement, are "unmoving," unlike the random, disintegrative, meaningless movements of "Sweeney among the Nightingales."

[8] One of a number of indications in Eliot's work of his indebtedness to Bergson, who argued that the scientific or mathematical ("rational") conception of time on the

But only in time can the moment in the rose-garden,   85
The moment in the arbour where the rain beat,
The moment in the draughty church at smokefall
Be remembered; involved with past and future.
Only through time time is conquered.[9]

III

Here is a place of disaffection   90
Time before and time after
In a dim light: neither daylight
Investing form with lucid stillness
Turning shadow into transient beauty
With slow rotation suggesting permanence   95
Nor darkness to purify the soul
Emptying the sensual with deprivation
Cleansing affection from the temporal.
Neither plenitude nor vacancy. Only a flicker
Over the strained time-ridden faces   100
Distracted from distraction by distraction
Filled with fancies and empty of meaning
Tumid apathy with no concentration
Men and bits of paper, whirled by the cold wind
That blows before and after time,   105
Wind in and out of unwholesome lungs
Time before and time after.
Eructation of unhealthy souls
Into the faded air, the torpid
Driven on the wind that sweeps the gloomy hills of London,   110
Hampstead and Clerkenwell, Campden and Putney,
Highgate, Primrose and Ludgate. Not here
Not here the darkness, in this twittering world.

  Descend lower, descend only
Into the world of perpetual solitude,   115

---

analogy of a line drawn in space, and thus infinitely divisible, is a distortion not only of time as we experience it but of "real" time. To be conscious is not to be in *this* time. Consciousness is fluid rather than static, more like a flowing stream than a mathematical line, and not really divisible into separate units called past, present, and future.

  [9] "Only through time": yet there is a sense in which we are involved in time as thus apprehended by the mind. The problem is not to try to *escape* from ordinary time—to leap out of history, as it were—but to redeem it. Theologically, this means that there had to be an Incarnation; philosophically, that man both is and is not contained by "clock-measured" time. The section that follows shows us involvement in the world's time without transcendence—living in terms of the "abstractions" of past and future, the one gone, the other not yet come, both therefore "unreal." The past brings its burden of guilt, the future its burden of anxiety. For an interesting parallel with the image of the "cold wind" that whirls men and bits of paper, see Saint-John Perse's *Winds.*

World not world, but that which is not world.
Internal darkness, deprivation
And destitution of all property,
Desiccation of the world of sense,
Evacuation of the world of fancy,   120
Inoperancy of the world of spirit;
This is the one way,[10] and the other
Is the same, not in movement
But abstention from movement; while the world moves
In appetency, on its metalled ways   125
Of time past and time future.

                               I V

Time and the bell have buried the day,[11]
The black cloud carries the sun away.
Will the sunflower turn to us, will the clematis
Stray down, bend to us; tendril and spray   130
Clutch and cling?
Chill
Fingers of yew be curled
Down on us? After the kingfisher's wing
Has answered light to light, and is silent, the light is still   135
At the still point of the turning world.

                                V

Words move, music moves
Only in time; but that which is only living
Can only die. Words, after speech, reach
Into the silence. Only by the form, the pattern,   140
Can words or music reach

---

[10] The "way down" of the epigraph, the *via negativa* or "negation of images" of the mystics. Connected with the Augustinian tradition in theology (compare Karl Barth today), the *via negativa* implies that nothing in our experience can give us an adequate idea of God. God is therefore not only beyond the world but beyond reason. The Thomistic tradition, on the other hand, encouraged "the way up" or "the affirmation of images." It implies that reasoning by analogy gives valid results, that we may infer the nature of God from the evidences of his creation. This tradition may lead finally either to pure rationalism, as it tended to in the Age of Reason, or to mysticism of the type exemplified by Emerson, Whitman, and Hart Crane—or Vaughan and Wordsworth. Eliot's natural tendency seems to be to present the negative way more forcefully, though theoretically, as in the epigraph and in this passage, he admits the two ways as equally valid. It should be noted that the "argument" of *The Four Quartets* as a whole rests on the way of the affirmation of images—on finding in nature as experienced the meanings necessary if we are to "conquer" time, redeem it from meaninglessness.

[11] In the movement of this lyric, the "way down" and the "way up" prove to be "one and the same."

The stillness, as a Chinese jar still
Moves perpetually in its stillness.[12]
Not the stillness of the violin, while the note lasts,
Not that only, but the co-existence,   145
Or say that the end precedes the beginning,
And the end and the beginning were always there
Before the beginning and after the end.
And all is always now. Words strain,
Crack and sometimes break, under the burden,   150
Under the tension, slip, slide, perish,
Decay with imprecision, will not stay in place,
Will not stay still. Shrieking voices
Scolding, mocking, or merely chattering,
Always assail them. The Word in the desert   155
Is most attacked by voices of temptation,
The crying shadow in the funeral dance,
The loud lament of the disconsolate chimera.

    The detail of the pattern is movement,
As in the figure of the ten stairs.   160
Desire itself is movement
Not in itself desirable;
Love is itself unmoving,
Only the cause and end of movement,
Timeless, and undesiring   165
Except in the aspect of time
Caught in the form of limitation
Between un-being and being.
Sudden in a shaft of sunlight
Even while the dust moves   170
There rises the hidden laughter
Of children in the foliage
Quick now, here, now, always—
Ridiculous the waste sad time
Stretching before and after.   175

1936

[12] The analogy of art, in which a "timeless" aspect, the *form*, gives meaning and, in the aesthetic sense, reality, to the work. A poem is made up of words, as a musical composition is made up of notes, but the poem is not the *sum* of its words or the composition the *sum* of its notes. Art is *essentially* form, pattern, and form is not "temporal" in the same sense that the parts making it up are. This passage makes clear what is meant by the way of analogy and transcendence, the "affirmative way" of mystic experience: the analogy between art and religion gives us, it is implied here, valid knowledge of religious realities that cannot be more directly apprehended or expressed. In its admission of the validity of both ways but its final emphasis on the way up—its affirmation that the values found in the personal experience in the garden reveal ultimate reality—"Burnt Norton" is solidly within the Anglican tradition of Christianity.

TRADITION AND THE INDIVIDUAL TALENT

1

IN ENGLISH writing we seldom speak of tradition, though we occasionally apply its name in deploring its absence. We cannot refer to "the tradition" or to "a tradition"; at most, we employ the adjective in saying that the poetry of So-and-so is "traditional" or even "too traditional." Seldom, perhaps, does the word appear except in a phrase of censure. If otherwise, it is vaguely approbative, with the implication, as to the work approved, of some pleasing archæological reconstruction. You can hardly make the word agreeable to English ears without this comfortable reference to the reassuring science of archæology.

Certainly the word is not likely to appear in our appreciations of living or dead writers. Every nation, every race, has not only its own creative, but its own critical turn of mind; and is even more oblivious of the shortcomings and limitations of its critical habits than of those of its creative genius. We know, or think we know, from the enormous mass of critical writing that has appeared in the French language the critical method or habit of the French; we only conclude (we are such unconscious people) that the French are "more critical" than we, and sometimes even plume ourselves a little with the fact, as if the French were the less spontaneous. Perhaps they are; but we might remind ourselves that criticism is as inevitable as breathing, and that we should be none the worse for articulating what passes in our minds when we read a book and feel an emotion about it, for criticizing our own minds in their work of criticism. One of the facts that might come to light in this process is our tendency to insist, when we praise a poet, upon those aspects of his work in which he least resembles anyone else. In these aspects or parts of his work we pretend to find what is individual, what is the peculiar essence of the man. We dwell with satisfaction upon the poet's difference from his predecessors, especially his immediate predecessors; we endeavour to find something that can be isolated in order to be enjoyed. Whereas if we approach a poet without this prejudice we shall often find that not only the best, but the most individual parts of his work may be those in which the dead poets, his ancestors, assert their immortality most vigorously. And I do not mean the impressionable period of adolescence, but the period of full maturity.

Yet if the only form of tradition, of handing down, consisted in following the ways of the immediate generation before us in a blind or timid adherence to its successes, "tradition" should positively be discouraged. We have seen many such simple currents soon lost in the sand; and novelty is better than repetition. Tradition is a matter of much wider significance. It cannot be inherited, and if you want it you must obtain it by great labour. It involves, in the first place, the historical sense, which we may call nearly indispensable to anyone who would continue to be a poet beyond his twenty-fifth year; and the historical sense involves a perception, not only of the pastness of the past, but of its presence; the historical sense compels a man to write not merely with his own generation in his bones, but with a feeling that the whole of the literature of Europe from Homer and within it the whole of the literature of his own country has a simultaneous existence and composes a simultaneous order. This historical sense, which is a sense of the timeless as well as of the temporal and of the timeless and of the temporal together, is what makes a writer traditional. And it is at the same time what makes a writer most acutely conscious of his place in time, of his own contemporaneity.

No poet, no artist of any art, has his complete meaning alone. His significance, his appreciation is the appreciation of his relation to the dead poets and artists. You cannot value him alone; you must set him, for contrast and comparison, among the dead. I mean this as a principle of aesthetic, not merely historical, criticism. The necessity that he shall conform, that he shall cohere, is not one-sided; what happens when a new work of art is created is something that happens simultaneously to all the works of art which preceded it. The existing monuments form an ideal order among themselves, which is modified by the introduction of the new (the really new) work of art among them. The existing order is complete before the new work arrives; for order to persist after the supervention of novelty, the *whole* existing order must be, if ever so slightly, altered; and so the relations, proportions, values of each work of art toward the whole are readjusted; and this is conformity between the old and the new. Whoever has approved this idea of order, of the form of European, of English literature, will not find it preposterous that the past should be altered by the present as much as the present is directed by the past. And the poet who is aware of this will be aware of great difficulties and responsibilities.

In a peculiar sense he will be aware also that he must inevitably be judged by the standards of the past. I say judged, not amputated, by them; not judged to be as good as, or worse or better than, the dead; and certainly not judged by the canons of dead critics. It is a judgment, a comparison, in which two things are measured by each other. To conform merely would be for the new work not really to conform at all; it would not be new, and would therefore not be a work of art. And we do not quite say that the new is more valuable because it fits in; but its fitting in is a test of its value—a test, it is true, which can only be slowly and cautiously applied, for we are none of us infallible judges of conformity. We say: it appears to conform, and is perhaps individual, or it appears individual, and may conform; but we are hardly likely to find that it is one and not the other.

To proceed to a more intelligible exposition of the relation of the poet to the past: he can neither take the past as a lump, an indiscriminate bolus, nor can he form himself wholly on one or two private admirations, nor can he form himself wholly upon one preferred period. The first course is inadmissible, the second is an important experience of youth, and the third is a pleasant and highly desirable supplement. The poet must be very conscious of the main current, which does not at all flow invariably through the most distinguished reputations. He must be quite aware of the obvious fact that art never improves, but that the material of art is never quite the same. He must be aware that the mind of Europe—the mind of his own country—a mind which he learns in time to be much more important than his own private mind—is a mind which changes, and that this change is a development which abandons nothing *en route*, which does not superannuate either Shakespeare, or Homer, or the rock drawing of the Magdalenian draughtsmen. That this development, refinement perhaps, complication certainly, is not, from the point of view of the artist, any improvement. Perhaps not even an improvement from the point of view of the psychologist or not to the extent which we imagine; perhaps only in the end based upon a complication in economics and machinery. But the difference between the present and the past is that the conscious present is an awareness of the past in a way and to an extent which the past's awareness of itself cannot show.

Someone said: "The dead writers are remote from us because we *know* so much more than they did." Precisely, and they are that which we know.

I am alive to a usual objection to what is clearly part of my programme for the *métier* of poetry. The objection is that the doctrine requires a ridiculous amount of erudition (pedantry), a claim which can be rejected by appeal to the lives of poets in any pantheon. It will even be affirmed that much learning deadens or perverts poetic sensibility. While, however, we persist in believing that a poet ought to know as much as will not encroach upon his necessary receptivity and necessary laziness, it is not desirable to confine knowledge to whatever can be put into a useful shape for examinations, drawing-rooms, or the still more pretentious modes of publicity. Some can absorb knowledge, the more tardy must sweat for it. Shakespeare acquired more essential history from Plutarch than most men could from the whole British Museum. What is to be insisted upon is that the poet must develop or procure the consciousness of the past and that he should continue to develop this consciousness throughout his career.

What happens is a continual surrender of himself as he is at the moment to something which is more valuable. The progress of an artist is a continual self-sacrifice, a continual extinction of personality.

There remains to define this process of depersonalization and its relation to the sense of tradition. It is in this depersonalization that art may be said to approach the condition of science. I therefore invite you to consider, as a suggestive analogy, the action which takes place when a bit of finely filiated platinum is introduced into a chamber containing oxygen and sulphur dioxide.

2

Honest criticism and sensitive appreciation are directed not upon the poet but upon the poetry. If we attend to the confused cries of the newspaper critics and the susurrus of popular repetition that follows, we shall hear the names of poets in great numbers; if we seek not Blue-book knowledge but the enjoyment of poetry, and ask for a poem, we shall seldom find it. I have tried to point out the importance of the relation of the poem to other poems by other authors, and suggested the conception of poetry as a living whole of all the poetry that has ever been written. The other aspect of this Impersonal theory of poetry is the relation of the poem to its author. And I hinted, by an analogy, that the mind of the mature poet differs from that of the immature one not precisely in any valuation of "personality," not being necessarily more interesting, or having "more to say," but rather by being a more finely perfected medium in which special, or very varied, feelings are at liberty to enter into new combinations.

The analogy was that of the catalyst. When the two gases previously mentioned are mixed in the presence of a filament of platinum, they form sulphurous acid. This combination takes place only if the platinum is present; nevertheless the newly formed acid contains no trace of platinum, and the platinum itself is apparently unaffected; has remained inert, neutral, and unchanged. The mind of the poet is the shred of platinum. It may partly or exclusively operate upon the experience of the man himself; but, the more perfect the artist, the more completely separate in him will be the man who suffers and the mind which creates; the more perfectly will the mind digest and transmute the passions which are its material.

The experience, you will notice, the elements which enter the presence of the transforming catalyst, are of two kinds: emotions and feelings. The effect of a work of art upon the person who enjoys it is an experience different in kind from any experience not of art. It may be formed out of one emotion, or may be a combination of several; and various feelings, inhering for the writer in particular words or phrases or images, may be added to compose the final result. Or great poetry may be made without the direct use of any emotion whatever: composed out of feelings solely. Canto XV of the *Inferno* (Brunetto Latini) is a working up of the emotion evident in the situation; but the effect, though single as that of any work of art, is obtained by considerable complexity of detail. The last quatrain gives an image, a feeling attaching to an image, which "came," which did not develop simply out of what precedes, but which was probably in suspension in the poet's mind until the proper combination arrived for it to add itself to. The poet's mind is in fact a receptacle for seizing and storing up numberless feelings, phrases, images, which remain there until all the particles which can unite to form a new compound are present together.

If you compare several representative passages of the greatest poetry you see how great is the variety of types of combination, and also how completely any semi-ethical criterion of "sublimity" misses the mark. For it is not the "greatness," the intensity, of the emotions, the components, but the intensity of the artistic process, the pressure, so to speak, under which the fusion takes place, that counts. The episode of Paolo and Francesca employs a definite emotion, but the intensity of the poetry is something quite different from whatever intensity in the supposed experience it may give the impression of. It is no more intense, furthermore, than Canto XXVI, the voyage of

Ulysses, which has not the direct dependence upon an emotion. Great variety is possible in the process of transmutation of emotion: the murder of Agamemnon, or the agony of Othello, gives an artistic effect apparently closer to a possible original than the scenes from Dante. In the *Agamemnon*, the artistic emotion approximates to the emotion of an actual spectator; in *Othello* to the emotion of the protagonist himself. But the difference between art and the event is always absolute; the combination which is the murder of Agamemnon is probably as complex as that which is the voyage of Ulysses. In either case there has been a fusion of elements. The ode of Keats contains a number of feelings which have nothing particular to do with the nightingale, but which the nightingale, partly, perhaps, because of its attractive name, and partly because of its reputation, served to bring together.

The point of view which I am struggling to attack is perhaps related to the metaphysical theory of the substantial unity of the soul: for my meaning is, that the poet has, not a "personality" to express, but a particular medium, which is only a medium and not a personality, in which impressions and experiences combine in peculiar and unexpected ways. Impressions and experiences which are important for the man may take no place in the poetry, and those which become important in the poetry may play quite a negligible part in the man, the personality.

I will quote a passage which is unfamiliar enough to be regarded with fresh attention in the light—or darkness—of these observations:

> And now methinks could e'en chide myself
> For doating on her beauty, though her death
> Shall be revenged after no common action.
> Does the silkworm expend her yellow labours
> For thee? For thee does she undo herself?
> Are lordships sold to maintain ladyships
> For the poor benefit of a bewildering minute?
> Why does yon fellow falsify highways,
> And put his life between the judge's lips,
> To refine such a thing—keeps horse and men
> To beat their valours for her? . . .

In this passage (as is evident if it is taken in its context) there is a combination of positive and negative emotions: an intensely strong attraction toward beauty and an equally intense fascination by the ugliness which is contrasted with it and which destroys it. This balance of contrasted emotion is in the dramatic situation to which the speech is pertinent, but that situation alone is inadequate to it. This is, so to speak, the structural emotion, provided by the drama. But the whole effect, the dominant tone, is due to the fact that a number of floating feelings, having an affinity to this emotion by no means superficially evident, have combined with it to give us a new art emotion.

It is not in his personal emotions, the emotions provoked by particular events in his life, that the poet is in any way remarkable or interesting. His particular emotions may be simple, or crude, or flat. The emotion in his poetry will be a very complex thing, but not with the complexity of the emotions of people who have very complex or unusual emotions in life. One error, in fact, of eccentricity in poetry is to seek for new human emotions to express; and in this search for novelty in the wrong place it discovers the perverse. The business of the poet is not to find new emotions, but to use the ordinary ones and, in working them up into poetry, to express feelings which are not in actual emotions at all. And emotions which he has never experienced will serve his turn as well as those familiar to him. Consequently, we must believe that "emotion recollected in tranquillity" is an inexact formula. For it is neither emotion, nor recollection, nor, without distortion of meaning, tranquillity. It is a concentration, and a new thing resulting from the concentration, of a very great number of experiences which to the practical and active person would not seem to be experiences at all; it is a concentration which does not happen consciously or of deliberation. These experiences are not "recollected," and they finally unite in an atmosphere which is "tranquil" only in that it is a passive attending upon the event. Of course this is not quite the whole story. There is a great deal, in the writing of poetry, which must be conscious and deliberate. In fact, the bad poet is usually unconscious where he ought to be conscious, and conscious where he ought to be unconscious. Both errors tend to make him "personal." Poetry is not a turning loose of emotion, but an escape from emotion; it is not the expression of personality, but an escape from personality. But, of course, only those who have personality and emotions know what it means to want to escape from these things.

3

ὁ δὲ νοῦς ἴσως θειότερόν τι καὶ ἀπαθές ἐστιν [1]

This essay proposes to halt at the frontier of metaphysics or mysticism, and confine itself to such practical conclusions as can be applied by the responsible person interested in poetry. To divert interest from the poet to the poetry is a laudable aim: for it would conduce to a juster estimation of actual poetry, good and bad. There are many people who appreciate the expression of sincere emotion in verse, and there is a smaller number of people who can appreciate technical excellence. But very few know when there is expression of *significant* emotion, emotion which has its life in the poem and not in the history of the poet. The emotion of art is impersonal. And the poet cannot reach this impersonality without surrendering himself wholly to the work to be done. And he is not likely to know what is to be done unless he lives in what is not merely the present, but the present moment of the past, unless he is conscious, not of what is dead, but of what is already living.

1920

---

[1] Aristotle, *De Anima*, I.4: "And reason is perhaps something more divine and not subject to change."

THE MUSIC OF POETRY

THE POET, WHEN he talks or writes about poetry, has peculiar qualifications and peculiar limitations: if we allow for the latter we can better appreciate the former—a caution which I recommend to poets themselves as well as to the readers of what they say about poetry. I can never re-read any of my own prose writings without acute embarrassment: I shirk the task, and consequently may not take account of all the assertions to which I have at one time or another committed myself; I may often repeat what I have said before, and I may often contradict myself. But I believe that the critical writings of poets, of which in the past there have been some very distinguished examples, owe a great deal of their interest to the fact that the poet, at the back of his mind, if not as his ostensible purpose, is always trying to defend the kind of poetry he is writing, or to formulate the kind that he wants to write. Especially when he is young, and actively engaged in battling for the kind of poetry which he practises, he sees the poetry of the past in relation to his own: and his gratitude to those dead poets from whom he has learned, as well as his indifference to those whose aims have been alien to his own, may be exaggerated. He is not so much a judge as an advocate. His knowledge even is likely to be partial: for his studies will have led him to concentrate on certain authors to the neglect of others. When he theorizes about poetic creation, he is likely to be generalizing one type of experience; when he ventures into aesthetics, he is likely to be less, rather than more competent than the philosopher; and he may do best merely to report, for the information of the philosopher, the data of his own introspection. What he writes about poetry, in short, must be assessed in relation to the poetry he writes. We must return to the scholar for ascertainment of facts, and to the more detached critic for impartial judgment. The critic, certainly, should be something of a scholar, and the scholar something of a critic. Ker, whose attention was devoted mainly to the literature of the past, and to problems of historical relationship, must be put in the category of scholars; but he had in a high degree the sense of value, the good taste, the understanding of critical canons and the ability to apply them, without which the scholar's contribution can be only indirect.

There is another, more particular respect in which the scholar's and the practitioner's acquaintance with versification differ. Here, perhaps, I should be prudent to speak only of myself. I have never been able to retain the names of feet and metres, or to pay the proper respect to the accepted rules of scansion. At school, I enjoyed very much reciting Homer or Virgil—in my own fashion. Perhaps I had some instinctive suspicion that nobody really knew how Greek ought to be pronounced, or what interweaving of Greek and native rhythms the Roman ear might appreciate in Virgil; perhaps I had only an instinct of protective laziness. But certainly, when it came to applying rules of scansion to English verse, with its very different stresses and variable syllabic values, I wanted to know why one line was good and another bad; and this, scansion could not tell me. The only way to learn to manipulate any kind of English verse seemed to be by assimilation and imitation, by becoming so engrossed in the work of a particular poet that one could produce a recognizable derivative. This is not to say that I consider the analytical study of metric, of the abstract forms which sound so extraordinarily different when handled by different poets, to be an utter waste of time. It is only that a study of anatomy will not teach you how to make a hen lay eggs. I do not recommend any other way of beginning the study of Greek and Latin verse than with the aid of those rules of scansion which were established by grammarians after most of the poetry had been written; but if we could revive those languages sufficiently to be able to speak and hear them as the authors did, we could regard the rules with indifference. We have to learn a dead language by an artificial method, and we have to approach its versification by an artificial method, and our methods of teaching have to be applied to pupils most of whom have only a moderate gift for language. Even in approaching the poetry of our own language, we may find the classification of metres, of lines with different numbers of syllables and stresses in different places, useful at a preliminary stage, as a simplified map of a complicated territory: but it is only the study, not of poetry but of poems, that can train our ear. It is not from rules, or by cold-blooded imitation of style, that we learn to write: we learn by imitation indeed, but by a deeper imitation than is achieved by analysis of style. When we imitated Shelley, it was not so much from a desire to write as he did, as from an invasion of the adolescent self by Shelley, which made Shelley's way, for the time, the only way in which to write.

The practice of English versification has, no doubt, been affected by awareness of the rules of prosody: it is a matter for the historical scholar to determine the influence of Latin upon the innovators Wyatt and Surrey. The great grammarian Otto Jespersen has maintained that the structure of English grammar has been misunderstood in our attempts to make it conform to the categories of Latin—as in the supposed "subjunctive." In the history of versification, the question whether poets have misunderstood the rhythms of the language in imitating foreign models does not arise: we must accept the practices of great poets of the past, because they are practices upon which our ear has been trained and must be trained. I believe that a number of foreign influences have gone to enrich the range and variety of English verse. Some classical scholars hold the view—this is a matter beyond my competence—that the native measure of Latin poetry was accentual rather than syllabic, that it was overlaid by the influence of a very different language—Greek—and that it reverted to something approximating to its early form, in poems such as the *Pervigilium Veneris* and the early Christian hymns. If so, I cannot help suspecting that to the cultivated audience of the age of Virgil, part of the pleasure in the poetry arose from the presence in it of two metrical schemes in a kind of counterpoint: even though the audience may not necessarily have been able to analyse the experience. Similarly, it may be possible that the beauty of some English poetry is due to the presence of more than one metrical structure in it. Deliberate attempts to devise English metres on Latin models are usually very frigid. Among the most successful are a few exercises by Campion, in his brief but too little read treatise on metrics; among the most eminent failures, in my opinion, are the experiments of Robert Bridges—I would give all his ingenious inventions for his earlier and more traditional lyrics. But when a poet has so thoroughly absorbed Latin poetry that its movement informs his verse without deliberate artifice—as with Milton and in some of Tennyson's poems—the result can be among the great triumphs of English versification.

What I think we have, in English poetry, is a kind of amalgam of systems of divers sources (though I do not like to use the word "system," for it has a suggestion of conscious invention rather than growth): an amalgam like the amalgam of races, and indeed partly due to racial origins. The rhythms of Anglo-Saxon, Celtic, Norman French, of Middle English and Scots, have all made their mark upon English poetry, together with the rhythms of Latin, and, at various periods, of French, Italian and Spanish. As with human beings in a composite race, different strains may be dominant in different individuals, even in members of the same family, so one or another element in the poetic compound may be more congenial to one or another poet or to one or another period. The kind of poetry we get is determined, from time to time, by the influence of one or another contemporary literature in a foreign language; or by circumstances which make one period of our own past more sympathetic than another; or by the prevailing emphasis in education. But there is one law of nature more powerful than any of these varying currents, or influences from abroad or from the past: the law that poetry must not stray too far from the ordinary everyday language which we use and hear. Whether poetry is accentual or syllabic, rhymed or rhymeless, formal or free, it cannot afford to lose its contact with the changing language of common intercourse.

It may appear strange, that when I profess to be talking about the "music" of poetry, I put such emphasis upon conversation. But I would remind you, first, that the music of poetry is not something which exists apart from the meaning. Otherwise, we could have poetry of great musical beauty which made no sense, and I have never come across such poetry. The apparent exceptions only show a difference of degree: there are poems in which we are moved by the music and take the sense for granted, just as there are poems in which we attend to the sense and are moved by the music without noticing it. Take an apparently extreme example—the nonsense verse of Edward Lear. His non-sense is not vacuity of sense: it is a parody of sense, and that is the sense of it. *The Jumblies* is a poem of adventure, and of nostalgia for the romance of foreign voyage and exploration; *The Yongy-Bongy Bo* and *The Dong with a Luminous Nose* are poems of unrequited passion—"blues" in fact. We enjoy the music, which is of a high order, and we enjoy the feeling of irresponsibility towards the sense. Or take a poem of another type, the *Blue Closet* of William Morris. It is a delightful poem, though I cannot explain what it means and I doubt whether the author could have explained it. It has an effect somewhat like that of a rune or charm, but runes and charms are very practical formulae designed to produce definite results, such as getting a cow out of a bog. But its obvious intention (and I think the author succeeds) is to produce the effect of a dream. It is not necessary, in order to enjoy the poem, to know what the dream means; but human beings have an unshakeable belief that dreams mean something: they used to believe—and many still believe—that dreams disclose the secrets of the future; the orthodox modern faith is that they reveal the secrets—or at least the more horrid secrets—of the past. It is a commonplace to observe that the meaning of a poem may wholly escape paraphrase. It is not quite so commonplace to observe that the meaning of a poem may be something larger than its author's conscious purpose, and something remote from its origins. One of the more obscure of modern poets was the French writer Stéphane Mallarmé, of whom the French sometimes say that his language is so peculiar that it can be understood only by foreigners. The late Roger Fry, and his friend Charles Mauron, published an English translation with notes to unriddle the meanings: when I learn that a difficult sonnet was inspired by seeing a painting on the ceiling reflected on the polished top of a table, or by seeing the light reflected from the foam on a glass of beer, I can only say that this may be a correct embryology, but it is not the meaning. If we are moved by a poem, it has meant something, perhaps something important, to us; if we are not moved, then it is, as poetry, meaningless. We can be deeply stirred by hearing the recitation of a poem in a language of which we understand no word; but if we are then told that the poem is gibberish and has no meaning, we shall consider that we have been deluded—this was no poem, it was merely an imitation of instrumental music. If, as we are aware, only a part of the meaning can be conveyed by paraphrase, that is because the poet is occupied with frontiers of consciousness beyond which words fail, though meanings still exist. A poem may appear to mean very different things to different readers, and all of these meanings may be different from what the author thought he meant. For instance, the author may have been writing some peculiar personal experience, which he saw quite unrelated to anything outside; yet for the reader the poem may become the expression of a general situation, as well as of some private experience of his own. The reader's interpretation may differ from the author's and be equally valid—it may even be better. There may be much more in a poem than the author was aware of. The different interpretations may all be partial formulations of one thing; the ambiguities may be due to the fact that the poem means more, not less, than ordinary speech can communicate.

So, while poetry attempts to convey something beyond what can be conveyed in prose rhythms, it remains, all the same, one person talking to another; and this is just as true if you sing it, for singing is another way of talking. The immediacy of poetry to conversation is not a matter on which we can lay down exact laws. Every revolution in poetry is apt to be, and sometimes to announce itself to be, a return to common speech. That is the revolution which Wordsworth announced in his prefaces, and he was right: but the same revolution had been carried out a century before by Oldham, Waller, Denham and Dryden; and the same revolution was due again something over a century later. The followers of a revolution develop the new poetic idiom in one direction or another; they polish or perfect it; meanwhile the spoken language goes on changing, and the poetic idiom goes out of date. Perhaps we do not realize how natural the speech of Dryden must have sounded to the most sensitive of his contemporaries. No poetry, of course, is ever exactly the same speech that the poet talks and hears: but it has to be in such a relation to the speech of his time that the listener or reader can say "that is how I should talk if I could talk poetry." This is the reason why the best contemporary poetry can give us a feeling of excitement and a sense of fulfilment different from any sentiment aroused by even very much greater poetry of a past age.

The music of poetry, then, must be a music latent in the common speech of its time. And that means also that it must be latent in the common speech of the poet's *place*. It would not be to my present purpose to inveigh against the ubiquity of standardized, or "B.B.C." English. If we all came to talk alike there would no longer be any point in our not writing alike: but until that time comes—and I hope it may be long postponed—it is the poet's business to use the speech which he finds about him, that with which he is most familiar. I shall always remember the impression of W. B. Yeats reading poetry aloud. To hear him read his own works was to be made to recognize how much the Irish way of speech is needed to bring out the beauties of Irish poetry: to hear Yeats reading William Blake was an experience of a different kind, more astonishing than satisfying. Of course, we do not want the poet merely to reproduce exactly the conversational idiom of himself, his family, his friends and his particular district: but what he finds there is the material out of which he must make his poetry. He must, like the sculptor, be faithful to the material in which he works; it is out of sounds that he has heard that he must make his melody and harmony.

It would be a mistake, however, to assume that all poetry ought to be melodious, or that melody is more than one of the components of the music of words. Some poetry is meant to be sung; most poetry, in modern times, is meant to be spoken—and there are many other things to be spoken of besides the murmur of innumerable bees or the moan of doves in immemorial elms. Dissonance, even cacophony, has its place: just as, in a poem of any length, there must be transitions between passages of greater and less intensity, to give a rhythm of fluctuating emotion essential to the musical structure of the whole; and the passages of less intensity will be, in relation to the level on which the total poem operates, prosaic—so that, in the sense implied by that context, it may be said that no poet can write a poem of amplitude unless he is a master of the prosaic.[1]

What matters, in short, is the whole poem: and if the whole poem need not be, and often should not be, wholly melodious, it follows that a poem is not made only out of "beautiful words." I doubt whether, from the point of view of *sound* alone, any word is more or less beautiful than another— within its own language, for the question whether some languages are not more beautiful than others is quite another question. The ugly words are the

[1] This is the complementary doctrine to that of the "touchstone" line or passage of Matthew Arnold: this test of the greatness of a poet is the way he writes his less intense, but structurally vital, matter. [T.S.E.]

words not fitted for the company in which they find themselves; there are words which are ugly because of rawness or because of antiquation; there are words which are ugly because of foreignness or ill-breeding (e.g., *television*): but I do not believe that any word well-established in its own language is either beautiful or ugly. The music of a word is, so to speak, at a point of intersection: it arises from its relation first to the words immediately preceding and following it, and indefinitely to the rest of its context; and from another relation, that of its immediate meaning in that context to all the other meanings which it has had in other contexts, to its greater or less wealth of association. Not all words, obviously, are equally rich and well-connected: it is part of the business of the poet to dispose the richer among the poorer, at the right points, and we cannot afford to load a poem too heavily with the former—for it is only at certain moments that a word can be made to insinuate the whole history of a language and a civilization. This is an "allusiveness" which is not the fashion or eccentricity of a peculiar type of poetry; but an allusiveness which is in the nature of words, and which is equally the concern of every kind of poet. My purpose here is to insist that a "musical poem" is a poem which has a musical pattern of sound and a musical pattern of the secondary meanings of the words which compose it, and that these two patterns are indissoluble and one. And if you object that it is only the pure sound, apart from the sense, to which the adjective "musical" can be rightly applied, I can only reaffirm my previous assertion that the sound of a poem is as much an abstraction from the poem as is the sense.

The history of blank verse illustrates two interesting and related points: the dependence upon speech and the striking difference, in what is prosodically the same form, between dramatic blank verse and blank verse employed for epical, philosophical, meditative and idyllic purposes. The dependence of verse upon speech is much more direct in dramatic poetry than in any other. In most kinds of poetry, the necessity for its reminding us of contemporary speech is reduced by the latitude allowed for personal idiosyncrasy: a poem by Gerard Hopkins, for instance, may sound pretty remote from the way in which you and I express ourselves—or rather, from the way in which our fathers and grandfathers expressed themselves: but Hopkins does give the impression that his poetry has the necessary fidelity to his way of thinking and talking to himself. But in dramatic verse the poet is speaking in one character after another, through the medium of a company of actors trained by a producer, and of different actors and different producers at different times: his idiom must be comprehensive of all the voices, but present at a deeper level than is necessary when the poet speaks only for himself. Some of Shakespeare's later verse is very elaborate and peculiar: but it remains the language, not of one person, but of a world of persons. It is based upon the speech of three hundred years ago, yet when we hear it well rendered we can forget the distance of time—as is brought home to us most patently in one of those plays, of which *Hamlet* is the chief, which can be fittingly produced in modern dress. By the time of Otway dramatic blank verse has become artificial and at best reminiscent; and when we get to the verse plays by nineteenth-century poets, of which the greatest is probably *The Cenci*, it is difficult to preserve any illusion of reality. Nearly all the greater poets of

the last century tried their hands at verse plays. These plays, which few people read more than once, are treated with respect as fine poetry; and their in-
sipidity is usually attributed to the fact that the authors, though great poets,
were amateurs in the theatre. But even if the poets had had greater natural
gifts for the theatre, or had toiled to acquire the craft, their plays would have
been just as ineffective, unless their theatrical talent and experience had
shown them the necessity for a different kind of versification. It is not primarily lack of plot, or lack of action and suspense, or imperfect realization
of character, or lack of anything of what is called "theatre," that makes
these plays so lifeless: it is primarily that their rhythm of speech is something
that we cannot associate with any human being except a poetry reciter.

Even under the powerful manipulation of Dryden dramatic blank verse
shows a grave deterioration. There are splendid passages in *All for Love*: yet
Dryden's characters talk more naturally at times in the heroic plays which he
wrote in rhymed couplets, than they do in what would seem the more natural form of blank verse—though less naturally than do the characters of
Corneille and Racine in French. The causes for the rise and decline of any
form of art are always complex, and we can trace a number of contributory
causes, while there seems to remain some deeper cause incapable of formulation: I should not care to advance any one reason why prose came to super-
sede verse in the theatre. But I feel sure that one reason why blank verse
cannot be employed now in the drama is that so much non-dramatic poetry,
and great non-dramatic poetry, has been written in it in the last three hundred years. Our minds are saturated in these non-dramatic works in what is
formally the same kind of verse. If we can imagine, as a flight of fancy, Milton
coming before Shakespeare, Shakespeare would have had to discover quite
a different medium from that which he used and perfected. Milton handled
blank verse in a way which no one has ever approached or ever will approach:
and in so doing did more than anyone or anything else to make it impossible
for the drama: though we may also believe that dramatic blank verse had
exhausted its resources, and had no future in any event. Indeed, Milton almost made blank verse impossible for any purpose for a couple of generations.
It was the precursors of Wordsworth—Thompson, Young, Cowper—who
made the first efforts to rescue it from the degradation to which the eighteenth-century imitators of Milton had reduced it. There is much, and varied,
fine blank verse in the nineteenth century: the nearest to colloquial speech is
that of Browning—but, significantly, in his monologues rather than in his
plays.

To make a generalization like this is not to imply any judgment of the
relative stature of poets. It merely calls attention to the profound difference
between dramatic and all other kinds of verse: a difference in the music,
which is a difference in the relation to the current spoken language. It leads
to my next point: which is that the task of the poet will differ, not only according to his personal constitution, but according to the period in which
he finds himself. At some periods, the task is to explore the musical possibilities of an established convention of the relation of the idiom of verse to that
of speech; at other periods, the task is to catch up with the changes in colloquial speech, which are fundamentally changes in thought and sensibility. This

cyclical movement also has a very great influence upon our critical judgment. At a time like ours, when a refreshment of poetic diction similar to that brought about by Wordsworth had been called for (whether it has been satisfactorily accomplished or not) we are inclined, in our judgments upon the past, to exaggerate the importance of the innovators at the expense of the reputation of the developers.

I have said enough, I think, to make clear that I do not believe that the task of the poet is primarily and always to effect a revolution in language. It would not be desirable, even if it were possible, to live in a state of perpetual revolution: the craving for continual novelty of diction and metric is as unwholesome as an obstinate adherence to the idiom of our grandfathers. There are times for exploration and times for the development of the territory acquired. The poet who did most for the English language is Shakespeare: and he carried out, in one short lifetime, the task of two poets. I can only say here, briefly, that the development of Shakespeare's verse can be roughly divided into two periods. During the first, he was slowly adapting his form to colloquial speech: so that by the time he wrote *Antony and Cleopatra* he had devised a medium in which everything that any dramatic character might have to say, whether high or low, "poetical" or "prosaic," could be said with naturalness and beauty. Having got to this point, he began to elaborate. The first period—of the poet who began with *Venus and Adonis*, but who had already, in *Love's Labours Lost*, begun to see what he had to do—is from artificiality to simplicity, from stiffness to suppleness. The later plays move from simplicity towards elaboration. The late Shakespeare is occupied with the other task of the poet—that of experimenting to see how elaborate, how complicated, the music could be made without losing touch with colloquial speech altogether, and without his characters ceasing to be human beings. This is the poet of *Cymbeline, The Winter's Tale, Pericles,* and *The Tempest.* Of those whose exploration took them in this one direction only, Milton is the greatest master. We may think that Milton, in exploring the orchestral music of language, sometimes ceases to talk a social idiom at all; we may think that Wordsworth, in attempting to recover the social idiom, sometimes oversteps the mark and becomes pedestrian: but it is often true that only by going too far can we find out how far we can go; though one has to be a very great poet to justify such perilous adventures.

So far, I have spoken only of versification and not of poetic structure; and it is time for a reminder that the music of verse is not a line by line matter, but a question of the whole poem. Only with this in mind can we approach the vexed question of formal pattern and free verse. In the plays of Shakespeare a musical design can be discovered in particular scenes, and in his more perfect plays as wholes. It is a music of imagery as well as sound: Mr. Wilson Knight has shown in his examination of several of the plays, how much the use of recurrent imagery and dominant imagery, throughout one play, has to do with the total effect. A play of Shakespeare is a very complex musical structure; the more easily grasped structure is that of forms such as the sonnet, the formal ode, the ballade, the villanelle, rondeau or sestina. It is sometimes assumed that modern poetry has done away with forms like these. I have seen signs of a return to them; and indeed I believe that the tendency to return to set, and even elaborate patterns is permanent, as permanent as the need for a refrain or a chorus to a popular song. Some forms are more appropriate to some languages than to others, and any form may be more appropriate to some periods than to others. At one stage the stanza is a right and natural formalization of speech into pattern. But the stanza—and the more elaborate it is, the more rules to be observed in its proper execution, the more surely this happens—tends to become fixed to the idiom of the moment of its perfection. It quickly loses contact with the changing collo-quial speech, being possessed by the mental outlook of a past generation; it becomes discredited when employed solely by those writers who, having no impulse to form within them, have recourse to pouring their liquid senti-ment into a ready-made mould in which they vainly hope that it will set. In a perfect sonnet, what you admire is not so much the author's skill in adapt-ing himself to the pattern as the skill and power with which he makes the pattern comply with what he has to say. Without this fitness, which is contingent upon period as well as individual genius, the rest is at best virtu-osity: and where the musical element is the only element, that also vanishes. Elaborate forms return: but there have to be periods during which they are laid aside.

As for "free verse," I expressed my view twenty-five years ago by saying that no verse is free for the man who wants to do a good job. No one has better cause to know than I, that a great deal of bad prose has been writ-ten under the name of free verse; though whether its authors wrote bad prose or bad verse, or bad verse in one style or in another, seems to me a matter of indifference. But only a bad poet could welcome free verse as a liberation from form. It was a revolt against dead form, and a preparation for new form or for the renewal of the old; it was an insistence upon the inner unity which is unique to every poem, against the outer unity which is typical. The poem comes before the form, in the sense that a form grows out of the attempt of somebody to say something; just as a system of prosody is only a formulation of the identities in the rhythms of a succession of poets influenced by each other.

Forms have to be broken and remade: but I believe that any language, so long as it remains the same language, imposes its laws and restrictions and permits its own licence, dictates its own speech rhythms and sound patterns. And a language is always changing; its developments in vocabulary, in syntax, pronunciation and intonation—even, in the long run, its deterioration—must be accepted by the poet and made the best of. He in turn has the privilege of contributing to the development and maintaining the quality, the ca-pacity of the language to express a wide range, and subtle gradation, of feeling and emotion; his task is both to respond to change and make it conscious, and to battle against degradation below the standards which he has learnt from the past. The liberties that he may take are for the sake of order.

At what stage contemporary verse now finds itself, I must leave you to judge for yourselves. I suppose that it will be agreed that if the work of the last twenty years is worthy of being classified at all, it is as belonging to a period of search for a proper modern colloquial idiom. We have still a good way to go in the invention of a verse medium for the theatre, a medium in which we shall be able to hear the speech of contemporary human beings, in which dramatic characters can express the purest poetry without high-falutin and in which they can convey the most commonplace message without absurdity. But when we reach a point at which the poetic idiom can be stabilized, then a period of musical elaboration can follow. I think that a poet may gain much from the study of music: how much technical knowledge of musical form is desirable I do not know, for I have not that technical knowledge myself. But I believe that the properties in which music concerns the poet most nearly, are the sense of rhythm and the sense of structure. I think that it might be possible for a poet to work too closely to musical analogies: the result might be an effect of artificiality; but I know that a poem, or a passage of a poem, may tend to realize itself first as a particular rhythm before it reaches expression in words, and that this rhythm may bring to birth the idea and the image; and I do not believe that this is an experience peculiar to myself. The use of recurrent themes is as natural to poetry as to music. There are possibilities for verse which bear some analogy to the development of a theme by different groups of instruments; there are possibilities of transitions in a poem comparable to the different movements of a symphony or a quartet; there are possibilities of contrapuntal arrangement of subject-matter. It is in the concert room, rather than in the opera house, that the germ of a poem may be quickened. More than this I cannot say, but must leave the matter here to those who have had a musical education. But I would remind you again of the two tasks of poetry, the two directions in which language must at different times be worked: so that however far it may go in musical elaboration, we must expect a time to come when poetry will have again to be recalled to speech. The same problems arise, and always in new forms; and poetry has always before it, as F. S. Oliver said of politics, an "endless adventure."

1942

THE SOCIAL FUNCTION OF POETRY

The title of this essay is so likely to suggest different things to different people, that I may be excused for explaining first what I do not mean by it before going on to try to explain what I do mean. When we speak of the "function" of anything we are likely to be thinking of what that thing *ought* to do rather than of what it does do or has done. That is an important distinction, because I do not intend to talk about what I think poetry *ought* to do. People who tell us what poetry ought to do, especially if they are poets themselves, usually have in mind the particular kind of poetry that they would like to write. It is always possible, of course, that poetry may have a different task in the future from what it has had in the past; but even if that is so, it is worth while to decide first what function it has had in the past, both at one time or another in one language or another, and universally. I could easily write about what I do with poetry myself, or what I should like to do, and then try to persuade you that this is exactly what all good poets have tried to do, or ought to have done, in the past—only they have not succeeded completely, but perhaps that is not their fault. But it seems to me probable that if poetry—and I mean *all* great poetry—has had no social function in the past, it is not likely to have any in the future.

When I say *all* great poetry I mean to avoid another way in which I might treat the subject. One might take up the various kinds of poetry, one after another, and discuss the social function of each kind in turn without reaching the general question of what is the function of poetry as poetry. I want to distinguish between the general and particular functions, so that we shall know what we are not talking about. Poetry may have a deliberate, conscious social purpose. In its more primitive forms this purpose is often quite clear. There are, for example, early runes and chants, some of which had very practical magical purposes—to avert the evil eye, to cure some disease, or to propitiate some demon. Poetry is early used in religious ritual, and when we sing a hymn we are still using poetry for a particular social purpose. The early forms of epic and saga may have transmitted what was held to be history before surviving for communal entertainment only; and before the use of written language a regular verse form must have been extremely helpful to the memory—and the memory of primitive bards, storytellers and scholars must have been prodigious. In more advanced societies, such as that of ancient Greece, the recognized social functions of poetry are also very conspicuous. The Greek drama develops out of religious rites, and remains a formal public ceremony associated with traditional religious celebrations; the pindaric ode develops in relation to a particular social occasion. Certainly, these definite uses of poetry gave poetry a framework which made possible the attainment of perfection in particular kinds.

In more modern poetry some of these forms remain, such as that of the religious hymn which I have mentioned. The meaning of the term *didactic* poetry has undergone some change. *Didactic* may mean "conveying information," or it may mean "giving moral instruction," or it may mean something which comprehends both. Virgil's *Georgics*, for instance, are very beautiful poetry, and contain some very sound information about good farming. But it would seem impossible, at the present day, to write an up-to-date book about farming which should also be fine poetry: for one thing the subject itself has become much more complicated and scientific; and for another, it can be handled more readily in prose. Nor should we, as the Romans did, write astronomical and cosmological treatises in verse. The poem, the ostensible aim of which is to convey information, has been superseded by prose. Didactic poetry has gradually become limited to poetry of moral exhortation, or poetry which aims to *persuade* the reader to the author's point of view about something. It therefore includes a great deal of what can be called *satire*, though satire overlaps with burlesque and parody, the purpose of which is primarily to cause mirth. Some of Dryden's poems, in the seventeenth century, are satires in the sense that they aim to ridicule the objects against which they are directed, and also didactic in the aim to persuade the reader to a particular political or religious point of view; and in doing this they also make use of the allegorical method of disguising reality as fiction: *The Hind and the Panther*, which aims to persuade the reader that right was on the side of the Church of Rome against the Church of England, is his most remarkable poem in this kind. In the nineteenth century a good deal of the poetry of Shelley is inspired by a zeal for social and political reforms.

As for *dramatic* poetry, that has a social function of a kind now peculiar to itself. For whereas most poetry to-day is written to be read in solitude, or to be read aloud in a small company, dramatic verse alone has as its function the making an immediate, collective impression upon a large number of people gathered together to look at an imaginary episode acted upon a stage. Dramatic poetry is different from any other, but as its special laws are those of the drama its function is merged into that of the drama in general, and I am not here concerned with the special social function of the drama.

As for the special function of philosophical poetry, that would involve an analysis and an historical account of some length. I have, I think, already mentioned enough kinds of poetry to make clear that the special function of each is related to some other function: of dramatic poetry to drama, of didactic poetry of information to the function of its subject-matter, of didactic poetry of philosophy or religion or politics or morals to the function of these subjects. We might consider the function of any of these kinds of poetry and still leave untouched the question of the function of *poetry*. For all these things can be dealt with in prose.

But before proceeding I want to dismiss one objection that may be raised. People sometimes are suspicious of any poetry that has a particular purpose: poetry in which the poet is advocating social, moral, political or religious views. And they are much more inclined to say that it isn't poetry when they dislike the particular views; just as other people often think that something is real poetry because it happens to express a point of view which they like. I should say that the question of whether the poet is using his poetry to advocate or attack a social attitude does not matter. Bad verse may have a transient vogue when the poet is reflecting a popular attitude of the moment; but real poetry survives not only a change of popular opinion but the complete extinction of interest in the issues with which the poet was passionately concerned. Lucretius' poem remains a great poem, though his notions of physics and astronomy are discredited; Dryden's, though the political quarrels of the seventeenth century no longer concern us; just as a great poem of the past may still give great pleasure, though its subject-matter is one which we should now treat in prose.

Now if we are to find the essential social function of poetry we must look first at its more obvious functions, those which it must perform if it is to perform any. The first, I think, that we can be sure about is that poetry has to give pleasure. If you ask what kind of pleasure then I can only answer, the kind of pleasure that poetry gives: simply because any other answer would take us far afield into aesthetics, and the general question of the nature of art.

I suppose it will be agreed that every good poet, whether he be a great poet or not, has something to give us besides pleasure: for if it were only pleasure, the pleasure itself could not be of the highest kind. Beyond any specific intention which poetry may have, such as I have already instanced in the various kinds of poetry, there is always the communication of some new experience, or some fresh understanding of the familiar, or the expression of something we have experienced but have no words for, which enlarges our consciousness or refines our sensibility. But it is not with such individual benefit from poetry, any more than it is with the quality of individual pleasure, that this paper is concerned. We all understand, I think, both the kind of pleasure which poetry can give, and the kind of difference, beyond the pleasure, which it makes to our lives. Without producing these two effects it simply is not poetry. We may acknowledge this, but at the same time overlook something which it does for us collectively, as a society. And I mean that in the widest sense. For I think it is important that every people should have its own poetry, not simply for those who enjoy poetry—such people could always learn other languages and enjoy their poetry—but because it actually makes a difference to the society as a whole, and that means to people who do not enjoy poetry. I include even those who do not know the names of their own national poets. That is the real subject of this paper.

We observe that poetry differs from every other art in having a value for the people of the poet's race and language, which it can have for no other. It is true that even music and painting have a local and racial character: but certainly the difficulties of appreciation in these arts, for a foreigner, are much less. It is true on the other hand that prose writings have significance in their own language which is lost in translation; but we all feel that we lose much less in reading a novel in translation than in reading a poem; and in a translation of some kinds of scientific work the loss may be virtually nil. That poetry is much more local than prose can be seen in the history of European languages. Through the Middle Ages to within a few hundred years ago Latin remained the language for philosophy, theology, and science. The impulse towards the literary use of the languages of the peoples began with poetry. And this appears perfectly natural when we realize that poetry has primarily to do with the expression of feeling and emotion; and that feeling and emotion are particular, whereas thought is general. It is easier to think in a foreign language than it is to feel in it. Therefore no art is more stubbornly national than poetry. A people may have its language taken away from it, suppressed, and another language compelled upon the schools; but unless you teach that people to *feel* in a new language, you have not eradicated the old one, and it will reappear in poetry, which is the vehicle of feeling. I have just said "feel in a new language," and I mean something more than merely "express their feelings in a new language." A thought expressed in a different language may be practically the same thought, but a feeling or emotion expressed in a different language is not the same feeling or emotion. One of the reasons for learning at least one foreign language well is that we acquire a kind of supplementary personality; one of the reasons for not acquiring a new language *instead* of our own is that most of us do not want to become a different person. A superior language can seldom be exterminated except by the extermination of the people who speak it. When one language supersedes another it is usually because that language has advantages which commend it, and which offer not merely a difference but a wider and more refined range, not only for thinking but for feeling, than the more primitive language.

Emotion and feeling, then, are best expressed in the common language of the people—that is, in the language common to all classes: the structure, the rhythm, the sound, the idiom of a language, express the personality of the people which speaks it. When I say that it is poetry rather than prose that is concerned with the expression of emotion and feeling, I do not mean that poetry need have no intellectual content or meaning, or that great poetry does not contain more of such meaning than lesser poetry. But to develop this investigation would take me away from my immediate purpose. I will take it as agreed that people find the most conscious expression of their deepest feelings in the poetry of their own language rather than in any other art or in the poetry of other languages. This does not mean, of course, that true poetry is limited to feelings which everyone can recognize and understand; we must not limit poetry to *popular* poetry. It is enough that in a homogeneous people the feelings of the most refined and complex have something in common with those of the most crude and simple, which they have not in common with those of people of their own level speaking another language. And, when a civilization is healthy, the great poet will have something to say to his fellow countrymen at every level of education.

We may say that the duty of the poet, as poet, is only indirectly to his people: his direct duty is to his *language*, first to preserve, and second to extend and improve. In expressing what other people feel he is also changing the feeling by making it more conscious; he is making people more aware of what they feel already, and therefore teaching them something about themselves. But he is not merely a more conscious person than the others; he is also individually different from other people, and from other poets too, and can make his readers share consciously in new feelings which they had not experienced before. That is the difference between the writer who is merely eccentric or mad and the genuine poet. The former may have feelings which are unique but which cannot be shared, and are therefore useless; the latter discovers new variations of sensibility which can be appropriated by others. And in expressing them he is developing and enriching the language which he speaks.

I have said quite enough about the impalpable differences of feeling between one people and another, differences which are affirmed in, and developed by, their different languages. But people do not only experience the world differently in different places, they experience it differently at different times. In fact, our sensibility is constantly changing, as the world about us changes: ours is not the same as that of the Chinese or the Hindu, but also it is not the same as that of our ancestors several hundred years ago. It is not the same as that of our fathers; and finally, we ourselves are not quite the same persons that we were a year ago. This is obvious; but what is not so obvious is that this is the reason why we cannot afford to *stop* writing poetry. Most educated people take a certain pride in the great authors of their language, though they may never read them, just as they are proud of any other distinction of their country: a few authors even become celebrated enough to be mentioned occasionally in political speeches. But most people do not realize that this is not enough; that unless they go on producing great authors, and especially great poets, their langue will deteriorate, their culture will deteriorate and perhaps become absorbed in a stronger one.

One point is, of course, that if we have no living literature we shall become more and more alienated from the literature of the past; unless we keep up continuity, our literature of the past will become more and more remote from us until it is as strange to us as the literature of a foreign people. For our language goes on changing; our way of life changes, under the pressure of material changes in our environment in all sorts of ways; and unless we have those few men who combine an exceptional sensibility with an exceptional power over words, our own ability, not merely to express, but even to feel any but the crudest emotions, will degenerate.

It matters little whether a poet had a large audience in his own time. What matters is that there should always be at least a small audience for him in every generation. Yet what I have just said suggests that his importance is for his own time, or that dead poets cease to be of any use to us unless we have living poets as well. I would even press my first point and say that if a poet gets a large audience very quickly, that is a rather suspicious circumstance: for it leads us to fear that he is not really doing anything new, that he is only giving people what they are already used to, and therefore what they have already had from the poets of the previous generation. But that a poet should have the right, small audience in his own time *is* important. There should always be a small vanguard of people, appreciative of poetry, who are independent and somewhat in advance of their time or ready to assimilate novelty more quickly. The development of culture does not mean bringing everybody up to the front, which amounts to no more than making everyone keep step: it means the maintenance of such an *élite*, with the main, and more passive body of readers not lagging more than a generation or so behind. The changes and developments of sensibility which appear first in a few will work themselves into the language gradually, through their influence on other, and more readily popular authors; and by the time they have become well established, a new advance will be called for. It is, moreover, through the living authors that the dead remain alive. A poet like Shakespeare has influenced the English language very deeply, not only by his influence on his immediate successors. For the greatest poets have aspects which do not come to light at once; and by exercising a direct influence on other poets centuries later, they continue to affect the living language. Indeed, if an English poet is to learn how to use words in our time, he must devote close study to those who have used them best in *their* time; to those who, in their own day, have made the language new.

So far I have only suggested the final point to which I think the influence of poetry may be said to extend; and that can be put best by the assertion that, in the long run, it makes a difference to the speech, to the sensibility, to the lives of all the members of a society, to all the members of the community, to the whole people, whether they read and enjoy poetry or not: even, in fact, whether they know the names of their greatest poets or not. The influence of poetry, at the furthest periphery, is of course very diffused, very indirect, and very difficult to prove. It is like following the course of a bird or an aeroplane in a clear sky: if you have seen it when it was quite near, and kept your eye on it as it flew farther and farther away, you can still see it at a great distance, a distance at which the eye of another person, to whom you try to point it out, will be unable to find it. So, if you follow the influence of poetry, through those readers who are most affected by it, to those people who never read at all, you will find it present everywhere. At least you will find it if the national culture is living and healthy, for in a healthy society there is a continuous reciprocal influence and interaction of each part upon the others. And this is what I mean by the social function of poetry in its largest sense: that it does, in proportion to its excellence and vigour, affect the speech and the sensibility of the whole nation.

You must not imagine me to be saying that the language which we speak is determined exclusively by our poets. The structure of culture is much more complex than that. Indeed it will equally be true that the quality of our poetry is dependent upon the way in which the people use their language: for a poet must take as his material his own language as it is actually spoken around him. If it is improving, he will profit; if it is deteriorating, he must make the best of it. Poetry can to some extent preserve, and even restore, the beauty of a language; it can and should also help it to develop, to be just as subtle and precise in the more complicated conditions and for the changing purposes of modern life, as it was in and for a simpler age. But poetry, like every other single element in that mysterious social personality which we call our "culture," must be dependent upon a great many circumstances which are beyond its control.

This leads me to a few after-thoughts of a more general nature. My emphasis to this point has been upon the national and local function of poetry; and this must be qualified. I do not wish to leave the impression that the function of poetry is to divide people from people, for I do not believe that the cultures of the several nations of Europe can flourish in isolation from each other. There have been, no doubt, in the past, high civilizations producing great art, thought and literature, which have developed in isolation. Of that I cannot speak with assurance, for some of them may not have been so isolated as at first appears. But in the history of Europe this has not been so. Even Ancient Greece owed much to Egypt, and something to the Asiatic frontiers; and in the relations of the Greek states to each other, with their different dialects and different manners, we may find a reciprocal influence and stimulus analogous to that of the countries of Europe upon each other. But the history of European literature will not show that any has been independent of the others; rather that there has been a constant give and take, and that each has in turn, from time to time, been revitalized by stimulation from outside. A general *autarky* in culture simply will not work: the hope of perpetuating the culture of any country lies in communication with others. But if separation of cultures within the unity of Europe is a danger, so also would be a unification which led to uniformity. The variety is as essential as the unity. For instance, there is much to be said, for certain limited purposes, for a universal *lingua franca* such as Esperanto or Basic English. But supposing that all communication between nations was carried on in such an artificial language, how imperfect it would be! Or rather, it would be wholly adequate in some respects, and there would be a complete lack of communication in others. Poetry is a constant reminder of all the things that can only be said in one language, and are untranslatable. The *spiritual* communication between people and people cannot be carried on without the individuals who take the trouble to learn at least one foreign language as well as one can learn any language but one's own, and who consequently are able, to a greater or less degree, to *feel* in another language as well as in their own. And one's understanding of another people, in this way, needs to be supplemented by the understanding of those individuals among that people who have gone to the pains to learn one's own language.

Incidentally, the study of another people's poetry is peculiarly instructive. I have said that there are qualities of the poetry of every language, which only those to whom the language is native can understand. But there is another side to this too. I have sometimes found, in trying to read a language which I did not know very well, that I did not understand a piece of prose until I understood it according to the standards of the school teacher: that is, I had to be sure of the meaning of every word, grasp the grammar and syntax, and then I could think the passage out in English. But I have also found sometimes that a piece of poetry, which I could not translate, containing many words unfamiliar to me, and sentences which I could not construe, conveyed something immediate and vivid, which was unique, different from anything in English— something which I could not put into words and yet felt that I understood. And on learning that language better I found that this impression was not an illusion, not something which I had imagined to be in the poetry, but something that was really there. So in poetry you can, now and then, penetrate into another country, so to speak, before your passport has been issued or your ticket taken.

The whole question of the relation of countries of different language but related culture, within the ambit of Europe, is therefore one into which we are led, perhaps unexpectedly, by inquiring into the social function of poetry. I certainly do not intend to pass from this point into purely political questions; but I could wish that those who are concerned with political questions would more often cross the frontier into these which I have been considering. For these give the spiritual aspect of problems the material aspect of which is the concern of politics. On my side of the line one is concerned with living things which have their own laws of growth, which are not always reasonable, but must just be accepted by the reason: things which cannot be neatly planned and put into order any more than the winds and the rains and the seasons can be disciplined.

If, finally, I am right in believing that poetry has a "social function" for the whole of the people of the poet's language, whether they are aware of his existence or not, it follows that it matters to each people of Europe that the others should continue to have poetry. I cannot read Norwegian poetry, but if I were told that no more poetry was being written in the Norwegian language I should feel an alarm which would be much more than generous sympathy. I should regard it as a spot of malady which was likely to spread over the whole Continent; the beginning of a decline which would mean that people everywhere would cease to be able to express, and consequently be able to feel, the emotions of civilized beings. This of course might happen. Much has been said everywhere about the decline of religious belief; not so much notice has been taken of the decline of religious sensibility. The trouble of the modern age is not merely the inability to believe certain things about God and man which our forefathers believed, but the inability to *feel* towards God and man as they did. A belief in which you no longer believe is something which to some extent you can still understand; but when religious feeling disappears, the words in which men have struggled to express it become meaningless. It is true that religious feeling varies naturally from country to country, and from age to age, just as poetic feeling does; the feeling varies, even when the belief, the doctrine, remains the same. But this is a condition of human life, and what I am apprehensive of is death. It is equally possible that the feeling for poetry, and the feelings which are the material of poetry, may disappear everywhere: which might perhaps help to facilitate that unification of the world which some people consider desirable for its own sake.

1945

Reading Suggestions

For many students, probably the most rewarding sort of further reading will consist of reading more works by Eliot himself. Among the poems, "Preludes" helps to supply a background for Prufrock's desiccated thoughts and feelings, and *The Hollow Men* shows us, from within, what it feels like to live in the waste land. "Burnt Norton" is much more meaningful when read in the context of the other three of *The Four Quartets*. Among the plays, *Murder in the Cathedral* is probably the best, and *The Cocktail Party* one of the most interesting, but *The Elder Statesman* might be read for its clarification of one of the major themes of *The Four Quartets*, the relation of love of man and love of God. Among the essays, "Music and Poetry," "The Function of Criticism" (1923) and "The Frontiers of Criticism" (1956) are good ones to begin with.

In a very large body of useful criticism of Eliot's poetry, the following titles stand out as most likely to be helpful to a beginning student of the subject: Elizabeth Drew, *T. S. Eliot: The Design of His Poetry* (1949), an approach through Jungian psychology; Helen Gardner, *The Art of T. S. Eliot* (1950), especially good on "the auditory imagination" and on *The Four Quartets*; F. O. Matthiessen, *The Achievement of T. S. Eliot*, Galaxy paperback (one of the first books on the subject but still helpful, especially after one has read the poetry and, if possible, the Drew and Gardner books; its method is generalized and comparative, and it assumes a considerable knowledge of modern literature and culture); Grover Smith, Jr., *T. S. Eliot's Poetry and Plays: A Study in Sources and Meaning* (1956).

Eliot's significance in "the revolution of modernism" and the relation between his critical theory and his poetic practice, with "Tradition and the Individual Talent" and "Sweeney among the Nightingales" used as examples, have recently been well set forth by Stanley Edgar Hyman in *Poetry and Criticism: Four Revolutions in Literary Taste* (1961), chapter 4. Raymond Preston, *Four Quartets Rehearsed* (1946), presents a usually helpful close reading of the poem. Two collections of critical essays are noteworthy: edited by Leonard Unger, *T. S. Eliot: A Selected Critique* (1948); and, edited by B. Rajan, *T. S. Eliot: A Study of His Writings by Several Hands* (1947).

There is much less good criticism on the plays than on the poetry, but the following items are recommended, in addition to the appropriate chapters in the books by Gardner, Matthiessen, and Smith, above: William Arrowsmith, "English Verse Drama: *The Cocktail Party*," *Hudson Review* (Autumn 1950), and John Edward Hardy, "An Antic Disposition," *Sewanee Review* (Winter 1957). These two articles should be read together; the second answers the first. Also recommended are Maud Bodkin, *The Quest for Salvation in Two Plays* (1941), on the *Eumenides* of Aeschylus and Eliot's *The Family Reunion*; and Robert A. Colby, "Orpheus in the Counting House: The Confidential Clerk," *Publications of the Modern Language Association* (September 1957).

By far the soundest and most helpful treatment of Eliot's literary criticism is that by Rene Wellek in "The Criticism of T. S. Eliot," *Sewanee Review* (Summer 1956). An intelligent hostile analysis of Eliot's critical ideas and practice may be found in Yvor Winters, *In Defense of Reason* (1947), also to be found reprinted in the Unger collection cited above. On the significance of Eliot's concept of the "objective correlative," Eliseo Vivas is helpful in his *Creation and Discovery* (1955).

Reactions to Eliot as a person and as a literary personality have been sharply divided, often, one suspects, on religious and philosophical, or on political and social, grounds. An entry into the subject may be made by starting with the following: Arthur Mizener, "To Meet Mr. Eliot," *Sewanee Review* (Winter 1957); Malcolm Cowley, editor, *Writers at Work* (1958), an interview with Eliot; the Unger collection, above; and Neville Braybrooke, editor, *T. S. Eliot: A Symposium for His Seventieth Birthday* (1958).

Biography

Thomas Stearns Eliot was born in 1888 in St. Louis, of a family prominent both there and in New England, where it settled in the seventeenth century. After graduating from Harvard in 1910, he studied philosophy at the Sorbonne and at Oxford and for a time was instructor in philosophy at Harvard. Though he did not take his doctorate, he wrote a thesis on F. H. Bradley. The anthropological, philosophical, and theological learning in his poetry is not something he had to "work up" for the occasion.

Since 1914 Eliot has lived in England. In the early European years he taught for a while, then clerked in a bank, and finally became an editor for the publishing firm of Faber & Faber. Meanwhile he wrote his poetry in the evening and edited *The Criterion*, one of the most influential little magazines of the time. In 1927 he became a British subject, a gesture not unlike that of Henry James, with whom he has much in common. When he renounced his American citizenship, he declared his position to be that of Anglo-Catholic in religion, Royalist in politics, and Classicist in literature—a "reactionary" set of attitudes that defiantly and somewhat quixotically defined his differences with what he took to be the ruling cultural orthodoxy.

As a man of letters Eliot has been a profoundly formative influence in the shaping of the literature of the period between 1920 and 1950, the literature of "modernism." He is the most important, and probably the most influential, literary critic of the century so far. Though most of his critical writing has been of an occasional nature and he has not pursued systematically the implications of his own critical pronouncements, his early reviews and essays initiated a revolution in taste. He and I. A. Richards fathered the most significant critical movement of the century, the "New Criticism," though his own critical writings are generally more "scholarly" (in the British manner of literary scholarship) and "appreciative" than closely analytical in the manner of the New Critics. When he turned from lyric poetry to poetic drama in the later part of his career, he stimulated the mid-century revival of interest in drama that is "poetic," whether written in verse or in prose.

But it is probably as a lyric poet and a critic that the future will chiefly remember him. His early poems, especially "The Love Song of J. Alfred Prufrock" and "The Waste Land," were largely responsible for creating a literary epoch. Their irony, their picture of a world in fragments, their expression of a sense of alienation and futility, all became standard ingredients of modern writing—in part at least because they reflected deep social realities. The later work, after the conversion, especially *The Four Quartets*, anticipated and played a part in shaping the changes in the cultural climate of the forties and fifties that produced, among other things, the religious revolution associated with neo-orthodoxy. The poet who was first read as a spokesman for the "lost generation" moved on to become a formative influence on the age for which Reinhold Niebuhr and Paul Tillich are more representative spokesmen than John Dewey. Young poets today are still struggling to free themselves from his influence. The frequent violence of their reaction suggests the difficulty of their attempt.

R. P. Blackmur, in an essay on
Wallace Stevens, shows how the difficulty in
reading him would be greatly reduced
if one did the usual thing and
looked up the unusual or puzzling
words — thus he would be more
easily understood.

WALLACE STEVENS ✦

1879-1955

Stevens believed that a poem
is like an invitation or proposal.
(might use "The Plot against the Giant"
pp. 68-69
Chas. B. Wheeler, The Design of Poetry
(New York: W. W. Norton + Co., Inc., 1966),
pp. 68-69.

Not even blank verse is endlessly
variable — after Stevens and Frost
where do we go?

Peter Quince at the Clavier

The tension felt between art
and nature.

Art is music in poem — plays a
double role.

1. Furnishes the material to carry
   the conceptual meaning — music
   and things associated with it
   one the chief sources of imagery
2. attention of reader is brought
   to the meter and rhyme by
   constant and subtle variations,
   always motivated by some
   change in the character or twist
   in the plot of the story.

Handwritten note at top of page:
Wallace Stevens is both a successful business man and a poet.

Introduction

The nature of poetry, contended Wallace Stevens, is "an interdependence of the imagination and reality as equals." [1] Any comprehension of his intent and his experience as an artist must begin with his definition. He had in mind two forms of consciousness at the sources of modern poetry. One may be called the consciousness of public knowledge, that knowledge of the world expressed in the commonly shared facts of public existence. Every age knows a public reality, compounded of its total experience: the limits and the content of its scientific knowledge, the urgencies of its faith and its skepticism, the toil of its living and earning, its pride of place in its natural and constructed settings, its fear of cataclysm and pain. The totality of the world, insofar as this may be comprehended by its citizens, is reality in the view of Stevens.

The other consciousness is that of private vision. It is awareness brought to life through the individual imagination. Stevens' definition of the nature of poetry was published in the first year of World War II. He was thinking, he said, of the pressure of reality, "of life in a state of violence, not physically violent, as yet, for us in America, but physically violent for millions of our friends and for still more millions of our enemies and spiritually violent . . . for everyone alive." [2] The reality of physical violence is the mounting capacity of the human being, wherever he lives on the planet, to destroy himself and his world; the reality of spiritual violence is the chaos at the center of our private lives, a center frequently destitute of faith in anything save power and material possessions. It should be carefully noted that Stevens chose to speak of modern poetry as an interdependence of the imagination and reality as *equals*. The individual must meet his violent world with imagination. He must somehow, through the transforming imagina-

[1] See his address, "The Noble Rider and the Sound of Words," reprinted here. It was delivered at Princeton in 1942, and then published by the University.
[2] *Ibid.*

889

tion, make the violence, and hence life, tolerable. But poetry must encompass both equally. It must, then, spring to being out of the tension between the individual and his world.

The difficulties of reading Stevens' poetry have been widely proclaimed. Yet they are no more formidable than those peculiar to the work of his major American contemporaries in the poetic art: Eliot, Pound, and Frost. For each of these, poetry has been an art descriptive of degrees and kinds of reality in a world which knows a time of fragmented traditions; and each has made his art upon his independent vision of that world. Eliot and Pound have chosen to interpret the present through history, and to establish a poetic imagery of interpretation upon the scholar's view. A full understanding of the expression of each must always presuppose for the student a considerable knowledge of past realities as well as those of the present. Both Eliot and Pound have given us poetic descriptions of their convictions: a return to the continuity of tradition in the Western world is the only means we have of combating modern spiritual violence. The learning of Frost, although it is no less impressive in fact, has been directed toward a different end in poetic expression. This end is a reality which never changes for humanity, no matter what history is spoken of: perfection and completeness, fulfillment and satisfaction in individual existence are illusions of the human mind. In the human need to admit to these illusions and yet, paradoxically, to confess the truth of life's incompleteness the poet discovers the poignancy and beauty of our common humanity. This is the universality of Frost, which transcends New England; within it is the sense of the insufficient in existence which often makes the poetry of Frost most difficult when it seems most simple. Eliot and Pound, even at their most erudite, have not objected to the search for absolute meaning in their poetry. Frost has frequently disclaimed any values in a precision of meaning. He was an artist intent upon what it is to sense fully the limitations of human experience and the solitariness of the individual. Poetry, in Frost's conviction, is the only means we have of describing these limitations.

But the art of Stevens has, of course, its own special difficulties. He shares very little, if at all, with Eliot and Pound in respect for learning per se or for the perseverance of ideas in the flow of human history. He insists upon modern man as different from his predecessors, and unique, save for his possession of the power to imagine, which he shares with all men of the past. In other words, this century is a special case in history: its reality is more violent than any other heretofore known; its spiritual loss is the total loss of the substructures of myth and faith which formerly compelled the unity of cultures; and to dream that a return to any tradition might be salvation is idle. Each modern man stands alone, as Stevens saw him, alone until heroic acts of the imagination create a new myth and a new faith in an age yet to come. Each man must find his salvation as he can, and discover his humanity in his own terms. At this point Stevens differs from

Frost, as well. In Stevens' conviction there is a completeness of being which lies within the grasp of the solitary individual. It is his salvation from confusion and violence, from insufficiency in the widest sense, through the development and the exercise of his unique imagination, an imagination entirely his own, unlike that of any other man. If he is an artist, it is this imagination which plots and achieves the architecture of his life. He is the master builder in defiance of a violent world.

It is idle to speak of Stevens as a poet who refused to acknowledge his involvement in the human condition of his century. He cannot assume with Frost that a necessity of humanity, our knowing and accepting the insufficiencies of our world, must be the great subject of modern poetry. But no more does he assume that the saving power of the imagination is denied any modern man who would exercise it, whether or not he is an artist. The distinguishing attitude of Stevens is that the individual who confronts the violence of modern reality brings with him the equal power of an imagination not exactly like that of any other man. Each perceiver must make his world. "What is his [the poet's] function?" Stevens asked. "Certainly it is not to lead people out of the confusion in which they find themselves . . . . His role, in short, is to help people to live their lives." [3] In this sense the poet is not the maker of a book of wisdom; he is not a moralist. He is the maker of an example of imagination in its acts of playing upon common reality, of heightening the color and the interest of the world. "To help people to live their lives" was for Stevens to help one's contemporaries to exert imagination vigorously and individually, and to rejoice in the physical beauty of a physical world, illuminated by the light of the unfailing sun.

I

These remarks have been concerned with what may be called the poet's conceptual understanding of his art, including both his power as a poet and the objectives to which he addresses himself. They are intended to suggest ways toward understanding certain differences among four major poets of our century (and it may perhaps be assumed that future comparative studies will find the differences between Frost and Stevens of first importance). The naming of Wallace Stevens among these artists requires our notice of his chief distinction: he was a romantic poet, perhaps the last of the great American romantics. The American settings occurring in the art of this poet are deeply native, as deeply so as those of Whitman, for example. American seacoasts and cities, American rivers, mountains and plains take their majestic situations in his work. No American poet has revealed a greater pride of place on American soil. But it is not American history which is of first importance to Stevens; it is the beauty of the land. He accepts and magnifies his American origin. His distinction as an American

[3] *Ibid.*

poet lies in what he chose to do with the American scene. The choice is
clearly romantic. So he admits of himself in his notebook: "The whole effort of the imagination is toward the production of the romantic." [4]

Lest there be confusion here in an understanding of this admission, the
kind of romanticism in question must be defined. Stevens' reach is a long
one: he grasps the heart of English romanticism in his faith that the poet's
imagination is a power sufficient to make the world his own, and the heart
of American transcendentalism, as well, in his conviction that the imagining individual is an architect of life. He takes the shaping power of the imagination to be quite literally godlike. In this sense, he is one of the romantic gods of literature in English; and the student of poetry who feels the
passion of John Keats's commitment to the imagination will read Stevens with the excitement of recognition.

Very probably Keats is our best English spokesman for the doctrine of
imagination as salvation. In "Sleep and Poetry" (1817) he asks, "Is there
so small a range/In the present strength of manhood, that the high/Imag-
ination cannot freely fly/As she was wont of old? prepare her steeds,/Paw
up against the light, and do strange deeds/Upon the clouds?" (11.163 ff.)
The light and the clouds are images of setting for the poet's imagination
in reaching *upward*, from the world. The reality of the poetry sought is to
be the achievement of the imagination. The life of the imagination is the
only life. The testament of Keats's brief career in poetry certainly does
not suggest Stevens' required meeting of the world and the imagination as
equals. But Stevens is wholly devoted to the major romantic conviction
here: the imagination alone makes the world endurable. There is clear
evidence in Stevens' poetry that he was thoroughly familiar with Wordsworth, Coleridge, and Shelley as theorists of the imagination. Yet he must
be taken to agree with Keats rather than with this great English triumvi-
rate. The commonly shared position of these three is basically Platonic:
the exercise of the imagination leads through poetic vision to universal
truth, a truth of a spiritual reality beyond the phenomena of the physical
world. Stevens' commitment in the manner of Keats excludes the reach of
poetry to universal truth, and insists only upon a universal human need for
beauty. Through the exertion of the imagination each man's truth is perforce his own.

English romanticism in its doctrines of the imagination became a
major source of the American transcendental view of the individual. In the
historical context, this great source derives its energies from the central
tenets concerning human liberties and the rights of man in the revolutionary thought of the eighteenth century. From the time of the appearance of Emerson's *Nature* in 1836, no single attribute of American
transcendentalism is more strongly distinguished than its unyielding
insistence upon every man as an imagining man, the maker of his world.

---

[4] See *Opus Posthumous*, ed. Samuel F. Morse (1957), p. 215.

If the individual is an artist, so much the greater his uniqueness as a master of imagination. In the transcendental view, he becomes the architect of the supreme structure: his own life. And if that life is like no other life, assuming that it was made in morality and decency, his making it as he wills is his right in a free society. There is, for example, a beautiful correspondence between Thoreau's two acts of building in *Walden*. The artist, the maker of a life, goes to a stand of pines beside a pond. He builds a modest shelter, a house to protect him from severe weather. Thereafter, chapter by chapter, Thoreau builds a life structure, as his imagination invades the realm of natural forms surrounding the house. The imagination, working with architectural skill, chooses among the forms; it magnifies them; it establishes relations; it joins together and elevates the elements of spiritual existence which it selects as materials. The book of Thoreau becomes an edifice itself, and its maker is the master of his house. The labor of a man wielding axe and hammer made the shelter standing in a physical domain; the exertion of his imagination made his house of the spirit.

The art of Wallace Stevens stands today as perhaps a final American exertion of the great transcendental prerogative to be studied in such acts of design and structure as Thoreau's. It is principally related to the commitments of Stevens' predecessors in the sense of an American freedom to shape the very quality of existence. One may advance here as examples among his forebears Emerson, Thoreau, Emily Dickinson, and Henry James.

Stevens' view of nature does not differ appreciably from Emerson's, who found it to be "the all that is the NOT ME" (Introduction to *Nature*). He simply names "nature" for us as the whole of reality which the imagination must advance to meet. His conviction of the power of the imagination to dominate and to order the particulars of the actual in life will be found to accord with Thoreau's faith in that "most glorious" of acts: ". . . to carve and paint the very atmosphere through which we look . . . . To affect the quality of the day, that is the highest of arts" (*Walden*, "What I Lived For"). In his contention, entered in his notebook, "God and the imagination are one," [5] Stevens seems to meet Emily Dickinson's belief, apparent throughout all her religious lyrics, that the making of poetry is man's imaginative reach toward a definition of God. The sense of both poets is clear: human freedom to create through the imagination is the equivalent of the idea of God. It is again the *quality* of existence achieved by the imagination, whether this be the artist's own or that envisioned for one of his characters, which Henry James celebrates as he writes in *The Art of Fiction*: ". . . when the mind is imaginative—much more when it happens to be that of a man of genius—it takes to itself the faintest hints of life, it converts the very pulses of the air into revelations." This revelatory power of mind in its role as imagination is rooted in the major presuppositions of American aesthetic tradition. As an inheritor of the concept, Wallace Ste-

[5] *Ibid.*, p. 178.

vens came to regard poetry as modern revelation. What is revealed? The answer is heard from his poetry: it is the heroism of modern man who wills to redeem his existence as an individual from the pressure of modern reality, from its violence, or, in its less severe moments, from its grayness and its monotony. It is the revelation which preserves him from the commonplaceness and the crassness of the ordinary. It saves him from anonymity. As an art of revelation it is also a particular record of *how* an individual met his world.

Finally, it must be understood that an approach to Stevens can have no sympathy with that kind of romanticism which proposes fantastic invention alone as the work of imagination. Fantasy as art was intolerable to him. It is sometimes claimed that his aesthetic is related to that of Poe. To assert as much is to urge that he would have been sympathetic to Poe's creative act in writing "The City in the Sea," or "Ulalume," or "Ligeia." He could scarcely have been so. His insistence upon the meeting of reality and imagination as equals, upon what has been called here the interplay of public knowledge and private vision, would have been compromised in an acceptance of Poe's wholly exclusive world of fantasy. Toward a realm of fantasy in the art of his own time Stevens was entirely unsympathetic. Surrealism was to him invention without discovery; that is, it is committed totally to the work of imagination exerted in utter indifference to public reality. In his notebook he wrote, "To make a clam play an accordion is to invent, not to discover." [6]

Students of Stevens who would make much of the proposed influence of the French Symbolist school of poetry upon him (for he read widely in this poetry) should be careful to distinguish between its manifestations as a literature of imagination, in the sense of Stevens, and as one of pure fantasy. For Wallace Stevens there could be no true poetry without the world. For him, as well, it was possible to be the master builder, even in prospect of violence. There is a gray obdurateness in the factualness of the world. It is a stern reality for us today, but a reality, as Stevens saw it, like a gray rock, where we must live amid the grim human events marking it. Stevens intended for himself a life in poetry which would achieve an architecture of the spirit, a total structure. By imagination the rock and the life lived upon it can be colored and made endurable, even beautiful. The most revealing of all his purposes is simply stated in a line from his notebook: "The gold dome of things is the perfected spirit." [7] If the world must be found and known as imperfect, insufficient, violent, chaotic, there is yet a redemption in the gold dome, the bright canopy flung across it by imagination. Terror will still be there, and the threat of nothingness; but the human need for beauty is answered.

[6] *Ibid.*, p. 177.
[7] *Ibid.*, p. 168.

II

Thus Stevens lived in scrupulous regard for the two elements of poetry as he understood it: he was a man of the world of human affairs, and a man of the imagination. Deliberately and unswervingly, he was a businessman by day, perceiving with keen intelligence the facts of that reality we call "the world," and a poet by night. Or, to propose another image of this "double" life, he was another American traveler standing in prospect of the facts of shore and sea in Florida or in Maine, and in poetic retreat from this holiday leisure, a man transforming the huge facts of physical nature into art springing from the interplay of imagination and reality as equals. Stevens came late to the eminence of reputation. His first volume of poetry did not appear until his forty-fourth year. Yet from his earliest practice at the New York bar (beginning in 1904) and through his long career as a specialist-administrator in investment banking for the Hartford Accident and Indemnity Company (from 1916 until his death in 1955) his need as a poet was clear to him. He had, as a man, to live the *real* world in order to perceive the rock upon which imagination might exert itself. The life of his art could not be an Olympian withdrawal. As much as Emily Dickinson, deliberately choosing the life of a poet's solitude, he was entirely purposive. He knew with brilliant self-knowledge what he required as an artist. (One may suppose that Emerson's sharp command, "Know thyself," was never more fully answered in the history of American literature in its maturity.)

In a late poem, "The Bouquet," Stevens distinguishes between the two lives which he exacted of himself. The poet's eye perceives in two ways. There is the physical fact of the bouquet. It is of the real world. Yet it stands as an object potential of change. It will be changed by the second way, through imagination, and thus appropriated to the poet's sovereignty. There is a "growth of the reality of the eye," there is an "artifice." As in the method of Braque, a painter of the modern idiom whom Stevens studied, the bouquet is transformed from physical fact to personal experience. Its form and its color are altered as the artist wills; it is fully claimed by his purpose.

Once one has grasped Stevens' objective of "double" reference in his poetry—reference to the initial world of reality and to the appropriating act of imagination—the difficulties in perceiving the singular beauty of his art begin to disappear. Stevens has been accused by those who have not comprehended his poetic stature, and his manner of expression, of indifference to the realities of human suffering. The charge proceeds from ignorance. The whole range of Stevens' poetry is again and again marked with images from a majestic yet somber vision: it is the certainty of pain and of death which emphasizes and makes urgent the human need for beauty. War comes upon us, a reality more huge and hideous in each mounting instance; and the war that threatens us now, after the last great holocaust of the 1940's, would be the one, as he writes in "Page from a Tale," of the last and supreme violence, the one to "spill night out in brilliant vanishings,/Whirlpools of darkness in whirlwinds of light . . . ." It was of World War II that he wrote in his long poem, "Esthétique du Mal" (The Aesthetic of Evil), the first word of the title used in its radical meaning, from the Greek verb *aisthanomai*, to *perceive*). What is it to perceive evil in our time? The lines of section xi of the poem disclose the range of Stevens' feeling as a human being. "Life is a bitter aspic. We are not/At the centre of a diamond. At dawn,/The paratroopers fall . . . . A vessel sinks in waves/Of people, as big bell-billows from its bell/Bell-bellow in the village steeple . . . ." Life with its certainties of evil and destruction is not an elixir; it is a bitter savory. We do not live it in the flawless splendor of the rarest jewel. War thrusts men from the skies; it sinks a ship in waves of men, undulating on the sea-surface; and lamenting bells ring on the shore. Yet it was a part of the violence of the poet's world. Being of his span of existence, it had to be known. What possible human counteraction can there be, to make life endurable at all? The answer comes immediately in the lines following this passage of terror: "Natives of poverty, children of malheur,/The gaiety of language is our seigneur." We are children of unhappiness. But in our poverty and our sorrow there is left to us the power to discover words fit to make the poem of our pain. The *gaiety* of the poet's language (Stevens uses the word in the sense of *liveliness*, not *merriment*) is our lord, whoever the poet may be, honored in the world, or unknown. The contention can in no sense be strange. For certainly it is the vividness of language which endows both pain and evil with a terrible beauty in John Milton's descriptions of the fallen Lucifer in *Paradise Lost*.

Or there is Stevens the poet-traveler, standing before the facts of wind and sea at Key West: "The meaningless plungings of water and the wind." It is he, an imagining man, who wrests his own order from this awesome interplay of force. He assumes the role of a singer by the sea; he becomes "the single artificer of the world" ("The Idea of Order at Key West"). A dark sea beating on an American coast is made his through his poet's music, his private vision. The awesomeness of the world becomes significance through an act of art. Or again he stands in prospect of American seas in Maine, water of Monhegan and of Pemaquid: "It is cold to be forever young,/To come to tragic shores and flow,/In sapphire, round the sun-bleached stones,/Being, for old men, time of their time" ("Variations on a Summer Day," section vi). The water is a fact of reality. It is forever young in the sense that it is physically unchanging. It is the imagination which orders the cold sea to flow in sapphire, around the stones of the rocky coast. The sea becomes a metaphor of eternal youth in the poet's imagination; the stones become metaphors of aging men. Who can say how closely Stevens may have known his proximity here to Emerson? Nature becomes for him a metaphor of being; he seems to recall Emerson's dictum for the poet, that he is the namer of spiritual fact. Yet Stevens totally rejects the Emersonian claim that a spiritual absolute lies beyond the metaphor. Almost immediately, in the same poem, he contends: ". . . one looks at the sea / As one improvises, on the piano." One of Stevens' most frequently recurring images of the poet is that of the musician (player of the piano, the clavier, the guitar, or singer). To know the ranges of the imagination playing upon reality and to make poetry of these ranges is to improvise upon a theme chosen in the poet's act of will. Hence the title here, *Variations* on a Summer Day.

III

The poetry of Wallace Stevens is the biography of an imagination in its encounter with modern reality. There is perhaps no prototype for it in the range of poetry in English save *The Prelude* of Wordsworth. The subtitle of Wordsworth's massive work, it will be remembered, is "Growth of a Poet's Mind." Its final attainment in Book XIV is Wordsworth's description of the universal truth of man's soul as immortal. The biography of an imagination of the twentieth century left us by Stevens might be titled "A Poet's Sense of the Modern World." Its final attainment is a description of the poet's full realization, full as he believed it to be, of his humanity. Wordsworth's method was formed in Platonic idealism wedded to Christian faith: dependence upon sensuous experience is transcended, and pure intellect is the poet's achievement. Stevens' method is revealed constantly in his insistence upon a lifetime of dependence upon sense perception. The world is good, when it is good at all, because we perceive its beauty through the senses. From the data provided by the senses, art may be made through the full play of a finely developed imagination upon them. There is no absolute and universal truth lying beyond them; and hence there is no transcendence. The imagination, like the human body, knows its life of rising vigor, its mature energy, and its decline into weakness and pale reflection with old age. Like the gold dome flung over the rock of existence, the imagination describes an arc through its life. It springs from the rock toward the sun; it declines to earth.

An intent reading of Stevens will disclose the signs of the imagination at work. Three of these require notice here. The first is the sign of the imagination's power to color reality through the exercise of its own freedom. One can best understand the acts of Wallace Stevens as a colorist by following the analogy of his poetry to the idiom of modern painting. In his notebook the following observation appears, a conviction fully developed in an address which he delivered at the Museum of Modern Art in New York in 1951: "To a large extent, the problems of poets are the problems of painters, and poets must often turn to the literature of painting for a discussion of their own problems." [8]

Students of French aesthetics of the nineteenth century will be tempted to relate Stevens to the famous doctrine of *correspondance*, conspicuous in the work of Théophile Gautier and Baudelaire, as examples, a doctrine holding that all the fine arts are susceptible of being brought into a single unity. This error should be avoided. Stevens' direction is a new one. Since he believed that the reality of the world provides the material for imaginative acts (*materia poetica*, as he called it), he saw that the arts of music, sculpture, and architecture are provinces of imagination working upon the basic rhythms of existence which nature provides. Yet each of these arts is sovereign. Unity is neither possible nor desirable.

Painting and poetry stand in an artistic proximity, as Stevens regarded them, solely because each, in its modern idiom, is intent upon conferring original design and original color upon the material of the real world. And each is so exerted as an art because each must recognize that the power of perception which we have is made possible by light—for men of earth, the light of the sun. This light of modern perceivers is quite different from John Milton's symbol of light (as in the "Ode on the Morning of Christ's Nativity" and *Paradise Lost*), of the beneficent majesty of God streaming from His throne. It is a physical light in a physical world in a physical universe. Because we have this light, we have the power to perceive and to confer color.

Stevens believed that the major painters of our century have worked in full acknowledgment of this great physical principle. He purposed to work in the same truth. Thus he begins his longest poem, *Notes toward a Supreme Fiction*, perhaps the greatest poem in praise of man's physical existence in American literature, with these lines: "Begin, ephebe, by perceiving the idea/Of this invention, this invented world,/The inconceivable idea of the sun." The youth addressed is called *ephebe*, from the Greek, a youth about to take his majority as a citizen. The *supreme fiction* is the individual's life itself, the life to be made noble and complete by the work of the imagination. Where does one begin in youth as an imagining man? He begins in full rejoicing in the idea of light. The sun is the source of our physical being, and from its light we enjoy the power to discern the physicality of the world about us, and to imagine color. Students of modern painting need not be reminded that one of the distinguishing aspects of this modern art is the liberty reserved by the individual creator to color his view of the world as he wills.

Insofar as Stevens is indebted to any American predecessor in this splendid doctrine of light in the supreme fiction, scholars interpreting his work will find him turning to the philosopher, George Santayana. It was the theory of Santayana, who was teaching at Harvard when Stevens studied there

[8] *Ibid.*, p. 160.

as an undergraduate, and whom Stevens celebrates in the poem "To an Old Philosopher in Rome," that sight is our primary perception. We are indebted to light first for all our imagining, because the fittest material for imaginative acts comes to us through the eye. (See Santayana's *The Sense of Beauty*, first published in 1894.) One can scarcely suppose that this admission suggests other than a world of *imagined* color. Such a world, more frequently than not, is the world of modern painting, which declines to obligate itself to exact representations of reality.

Wallace Stevens was not a symbolist by profession. He was not a poet of what we are often pleased to call moral values. But he adhered faithfully to a symbolism of color throughout the whole body of his poetry. We may be reasonably sure at all times of the following symbols of Stevens, the colorist, as we encounter them in his work: blue, for the imagination; green, for the primitive vitality of nature, the potential of raw reality subject to the transforming poet's hand; red, for the bloodedness, the vitality of imagining man; white, the non-hue, for the absence of imaginative vigor; black, for the certainty of death; yellow or gold, for the light of the sun, and for the achievement of art; bronze, for the antiquity of man; purple, for ceremony, myth, and rite.

A second sign of the imagination at work in the poetry of Stevens is discovered in a second range of symbols. They all refer to music, specifically to the dynamic power of music in modulation. Because the imagination builds at will, it has the analogous power of ordering metamorphosis, change. Stevens' images of the poet as singer or musician, most frequently the player of the guitar (an image which he deliberately borrows from the canvases of many of the Cubist painters and from the famous "Blue" period of Pablo Picasso), are consistently employed as signs of modulation in theme and in imaginative vision. In the poem "Peter Quince at the Clavier," for instance, he intends a record of imagination at work under the symbolic sign of Shakespeare's character of A *Midsummer-Night's Dream*, Peter Quince, the master of the revels. But Stevens, of course, alters Peter's dramatic function by seating him at a keyboard instrument; and we understand that Peter represents the poet himself. Peter is the sign of the imagination acting upon the facts of reality, transforming, changing, amplifying, coloring, precisely as though the poet were the director of the changes in a masquerade. The poet presents himself to us as a man seated at the clavier. A beautiful woman is at the center of the scene. She appears in *blue-*shadowed silk. She is desirable. And on this theme of desire the poet-musician imposes the old legend from biblical literature of Susanna and the elders.

But it is not simply legend recounted, used analogously. It is changed and colored anew by the imagination. The music is the sign of the poet's intention. In *Notes toward a Supreme Fiction* the poet thinks of human beings who live in an intolerable lack of imagination. They know only "A single text, granite monotony . . . ." "These are of minstrels lack-ing minstrelsy,/ Of an earth in which the first leaf is the tale/Of leaves, in which the sparrow is a bird/Of stone, that never changes" (Part II, section vi). The minstrelsy named here is the sign of the musician-poet who modulates and changes the aspect of leaves, of sparrows, at will. The play of the imagination upon such natural facts as these makes a variety of life, a fiction both bearable and beautiful.

A third sign of the imagination at work is directly related to Stevens' delight in language, his poet's joy in play with words. He is an innovator. Readers of Whitman and Emily Dickinson know how the same joy radiates from the poetic language of these eminent Americans. In "Variations on a Summer Day" (section xiv) Stevens defined the function of words in a poet's perception. To love words is to enlarge perception: "Words add to the senses. The words for the dazzle/Of mica, the dithering of grass,/The Arachne integument of dead trees,/Are the eye grown larger, more intense." It is Wallace Stevens enamored of the sound of words of his own devis-ing whom we hear in the *dithering* of grass, or in the first lines of his "Au-tumn Refrain": "The skreak and skritter of evening gone/And grackles gone and sorrows of the sun . . . ."

What necessity evokes this *skreak* and *skritter*? It is a modern poet's necessity in an age which has produced painters who invent their own colors to express private perception, and musicians whose dissonances are of our time, descriptive of individual imagining, and owing no allegiance to the laws of harmony which earlier generations honored. The necessity lies in the poet's feeling. He improvises upon an ancient theme in the his-tory of all the poetry ever written, of whatever age or country: the melan-choly of autumn. He makes a *skreak* and *skritter*, related to the image of the grackles. It is an image of the grackle's cry, heard in the evenings of a late summer, now gone. The desolate season comes, a time (for some poets) of writing of the nightingale one has never heard, of imagining a bird of sum-mer to fend off the reality of autumn death and decay. But not for him, this nightingale. He must take the stillness. He must confront the reality of autumn; and he must write of an American bird he knows. He must make words only for what he experienced. On this same theme of autumn melan-choly he is the innovator of language in another poem bearing the title "Metamorphosis." The year advances to its end. In the first stanza "the wind spells out/Sep-tem-ber . . ." The time of melancholy advances to the next month in the second stanza: "Oto-otu-bre." Next "The sky/Falls and lies with the worms." In the fourth and final stanza only the November street lamps are left, in a cold twilight, in "Niz-nil-imbo." The last word of Stevens' own making is a marvel of his innovation: November leaves us in *limbo*. We dangle there, until another spring. To live is to experience end-less change. Language makes the beauty of this metamorphosis we know, and endure.

IV

The poems appearing in the following selection which have not earlier been referred to invite brief introductory comment. Each reader must assume the freedom which Stevens insisted upon for poetry. To perceive poetry is to find what one's imagination directs as one reads. Certain suggestions pertaining to the theme of each poem may, however, be useful. "The Paltry Nude Starts on a Spring Voyage" presents a picture of an impoverished Venus. The old goddess, having lost the sanction of imagining human beings, who imagined her into being, is now paltry. Let us then use her as an image for oncoming spring, to be succeeded by summer. She is good for nothing else. Her myth is dead. "Sunday Morning" is a lyrical tribute to the temporality of the self. Stevens did not accept the doctrine of immortality. "A Postcard from the Volcano" projects an image of our age as it will be regarded in a time of the future: what we were was only what we imagined of the world. In the piece entitled "Of Modern Poetry" Stevens is intent upon the problem of poetry in our time. Tradition and myth have been lost. The poet must find his own independent vision and create his own order. In "Less and Less Human, O Savage Spirit" he thinks of man as the only master of man; the gods are imagined. "This Solitude of Cataracts" creates a scene of antiquity: man at the center when the world (reality) was new and he was free to make original images of his condition as man. The painterly poem, "Bouquet of Roses in Sunlight," is developed upon the most frequently displayed theme in Stevens' work: things are to each beholder what they are made to be by each imagination. The stanzas for "The Man with the Blue Guitar" reflect the poet's roles as colorist and musician, altering reality as he wills. "The Green Plant" celebrates the green of primitive vitality, encompassed in Stevens' symbolism of color. It is this "barbaric green" which must be relinquished as the imagination loses vitality with old age.

Wallace Stevens' total career in poetry is closely related to a metaphor which he takes from nature. The year knows its seasons. In spring the poet perceives the vibrancy of existence, and he colors brilliantly the reality which he knows. In summer he is at the zenith of imaginative power and of his craft as an artist. In autumn he feels his energy begin to wane. He becomes reflective. He prepares for his final acceptance of reality, his own end. So there must be a "Final Soliloquy of the Interior Paramour" (the imagination). So must the poet go earthward, to the reality of the obdurate rock. In the brilliant meditation which he named "Things of August" he thinks of men of our time and their records of this modern reality. "A text of intelligent men/At the centre of the unintelligible,/As in a hermitage, for us to think/Writing and reading the rigid inscription" (section ix). The text of Stevens at the center of the unintelligible is his poetry. In his later poem, almost his valedictory, "The Rock," he again advances this "text," the poetry of a modern man's making, but this time as salvation. The leaves (individual poems) spread upon the rock of being are a salvation in the midst of existence. They may be "a cure of the ground" itself. Human beings, having only themselves to acknowledge as masters of this world, may learn through imagination to alter reality, that man-made violence of reality which we know.

JAMES BAIRD

A Note on the Text.   The texts here used are as follows: "The Noble Rider and the Sound of Words" is taken from the collection of Stevens' essays, *The Necessary Angel* (New York: Alfred A. Knopf, Inc., 1951); the poems, with the exception noted below, are from *The Collected Poems of Wallace Stevens* (New York: Alfred A. Knopf, Inc., 1954); "Stanzas for 'The Man with the Blue Guitar'" and the selections from "Adagia" are from *Opus Posthumous*, edited by Samuel French Morse (New York: Alfred A. Knopf, Inc., 1957).

THE NOBLE RIDER AND THE
SOUND OF WORDS

IN THE *Phaedrus*, Plato speaks of the soul in a figure. He says:

> Let our figure be of a composite nature—a pair of winged horses and a charioteer. Now the winged horses and the charioteer of the gods are all of them noble, and of noble breed, while ours are mixed; and we have a charioteer who drives them in a pair, and one of them is noble and of noble origin, and the other is ignoble and of ignoble origin; and, as might be expected, there is a great deal of trouble in managing them. I will endeavor to explain to you in what way the mortal differs from the immortal creature. The soul or animate being has the care of the inanimate, and traverses the whole heaven in divers forms appearing;—when perfect and fully winged she soars upward, and is the ruler of the universe; while the imperfect soul loses her feathers, and drooping in her flight at last settles on the solid ground.

We recognize at once, in this figure, Plato's pure poetry; and at the same time we recognize what Coleridge called Plato's dear, gorgeous nonsense. The truth is that we have scarcely read the passage before we have identified ourselves with the charioteer, have, in fact, taken his place and, driving his winged horses, are traversing the whole heaven. Then suddenly we remember, it may be, that the soul no longer exists and we droop in our flight and at last settle on the solid ground. The figure becomes antiquated and rustic.

1

What really happens in this brief experience? Why does this figure, potent for so long, become merely the emblem of a mythology, the rustic memorial of a belief in the soul and in a distinction between good and evil? The answer to these questions is, I think, a simple one.

I said that suddenly we remember that the soul no longer exists and we droop in our flight. For that matter, neither charioteers nor chariots any longer exist. Consequently, the figure does not become unreal because we are troubled about the soul. Besides, unreal things have a reality of their own, in poetry as elsewhere. We do not hesitate, in poetry, to yield ourselves to the unreal, when it is possible to yield ourselves. The existence of the soul, of charioteers and chariots and of winged horses is immaterial. They did not exist for Plato, not even the charioteer and chariot; for certainly a charioteer driving his chariot across the whole heaven was for Plato precisely what he is for us. He was unreal for Plato as he is for us. Plato, however, could yield himself, was free to yield himself, to this gorgeous nonsense. We cannot yield ourselves. We are not free to yield ourselves.

Just as the difficulty is not a difficulty about unreal things, since the imagination accepts them, and since the poetry of the passage is, for us, wholly the poetry of the unreal, so it is not an emotional difficulty. Something else than the imagination is moved by the statement that the horses of the gods are all of them noble, and of noble breed or origin. The statement is a moving statement and is intended to be so. It is insistent and its insistence moves us. Its insistence is the insistence of a speaker, in this case Socrates, who, for the moment, feels delight, even if a casual delight, in the nobility and noble breed. Those images of nobility instantly become nobility itself and determine the emotional level at which the next page or two are to be read. The figure does not lose its vitality because of any failure of feeling on Plato's part. He does not communicate nobility coldly. His horses are not marble horses, the reference to their breed saves them from being that. The fact that the horses are not marble horses helps, moreover, to save the charioteer from being, say, a creature of cloud. The result is that we recognize, even if we cannot realize, the feelings of the robust poet clearly and fluently noting the images in his mind and by means of his robustness, clearness and fluency communicating much more than the images themselves. Yet we do not quite yield. We cannot. We do not feel free.

In trying to find out what it is that stands between Plato's figure and ourselves, we have to accept the idea that, however legendary it appears to be, it has had its vicissitudes. The history of a figure of speech or the history of an idea, such as the idea of nobility, cannot be very different from the history of anything else. It is the episodes that are of interest, and here the epi-

sode is that of our diffidence. By us and ourselves, I mean you and me; and
yet not you and me as individuals but as representatives of a state of mind.
Adams in his work on Vico[1] makes the remark that the true history of the
human race is a history of its progressive mental states. It is a remark of interest in this relation. We may assume that in the history of Plato's figure
there have been incessant changes of response; that these changes have been
psychological changes, and that our own diffidence is simply one more state
of mind due to such a change.

The specific question is partly as to the nature of the change and partly as
to the cause of it. In nature, the change is as follows: The imagination loses
vitality as it ceases to adhere to what is real. When it adheres to the unreal and
intensifies what is unreal, while its first effect may be extraordinary, that
effect is the maximum effect that it will ever have. In Plato's figure, his imagination does not adhere to what is real. On the contrary, having created something unreal, it adheres to it and intensifies its unreality. Its first effect, its
effect at first reading, is its maximum effect, when the imagination, being
moved, puts us in the place of the charioteer, before the reason checks us. The
case is, then, that we concede that the figure is all imagination. At the same
time, we say that it has not the slightest meaning for us, except for its nobility.
As to that, while we are moved by it, we are moved as observers. We recognize
it perfectly. We do not realize it. We understand the feeling of it, the robust
feeling, clearly and fluently communicated. Yet we understand it rather than
participate in it.

As to the cause of the change, it is the loss of the figure's vitality. The
reason why this particular figure has lost its vitality is that, in it, the imagination adheres to what is unreal. What happened, as we were traversing the
whole heaven, is that the imagination lost its power to sustain us. It has the
strength of reality or none at all.

2

What has just been said demonstrates that there are degrees of the imagination, as, for example, degrees of vitality and, therefore, of intensity. It is an
implication that there are degrees of reality. The discourse about the two
elements seems endless. For my own part, I intend merely to follow, in a very
hasty way, the fortunes of the idea of nobility as a characteristic of the imagination, and even as its symbol or alter ego, through several of the episodes in its history, in order to determine, if possible, what its fate has been
and what has determined its fate. This can be done only on the basis of the
relation between the imagination and reality. What has been said in respect
to the figure of the charioteer illustrates this.

I should like now to go on to other illustrations of the relation between
the imagination and reality and particularly to illustrations that constitute
episodes in the history of the idea of nobility. It would be agreeable to pass
directly from the charioteer and his winged horses to Don Quixote. It would

[1] Giovanni Battista Vico, 1668-1744, Italian philosopher and jurist of Naples. The
reference is to The Life and Writings of Giambattista Vico, by Henry Packwood
Adams (1935).

be like a return from what Plato calls "the back of heaven" to one's own spot. Nevertheless, there is Verrocchio[2] (as one among others) with his statue of Bartolommeo Colleoni,[3] in Venice, standing in the way. I have not selected him as a Neo-Platonist[4] to relate us back from a modern time to Plato's time, although he does in fact so relate us, just as through Leonardo,[5] his pupil, he strengthens the relationship. I have selected him because there, on the edge of the world in which we live today, he established a form of such nobility that it has never ceased to magnify us in our own eyes. It is like the form of an invincible man, who has come, slowly and boldly, through every warlike opposition of the past and who moves in our midst without dropping the bridle of the powerful horse from his hand, without taking off his helmet and without relaxing the attitude of a warrior of noble origin. What man on whose side the horseman fought could ever be anything but fearless, anything but indomitable? One feels the passion of rhetoric begin to stir and even to grow furious; and one thinks that, after all, the noble style, in whatever it creates, merely perpetuates the noble style. In this statue, the apposition between the imagination and reality is too favorable to the imagination. Our difficulty is not primarily with any detail. It is primarily with the whole. The point is not so much to analyze the difficulty as to determine whether we share it, to find out whether it exists, whether we regard this specimen of the genius of Verrocchio and of the Renaissance as a bit of uncommon panache, no longer quite the appropriate thing outdoors, or whether we regard it, in the language of Dr. Richards,[6] as something inexhaustible to meditation or, to speak for myself, as a thing of a nobility responsive to the most minute demand. It seems, nowadays, what it may very well not have seemed a few years ago, a little overpowering, a little magnificent.

Undoubtedly, Don Quixote could be Bartolommeo Colleoni in Spain. The tradition of Italy is the tradition of the imagination. The tradition of Spain is the tradition of reality. There is no apparent reason why the reverse should not be true. If this is a just observation, it indicates that the relation between the imagination and reality is a question, more or less, of precise equilibrium. Thus it is not a question of the difference between grotesque extremes. My purpose is not to contrast Colleoni with Don Quixote. It is to say that one passed into the other, that one became and was the other. The difference between them is that Verrocchio believed in one kind of nobility and Cervantes,[7] if he believed in any, believed in another kind. With Verrocchio it was an affair of the noble style, whatever his prepossession respecting the nobility of man as a real animal may have been. With Cervantes, nobility was not a thing of the imagination. It was a part of reality, it was something

[2] Andrea del Verrocchio, 1435-1488, Renaissance sculptor of Florence.

[3] Italian soldier of fortune, 1400-1475, eventually generalissimo of Venice.

[4] An exponent of a school of thought founded by Plotinus in the third century A.D. and designed to harmonize the philosophy of Plato with Hebrew religious thought.

[5] Leonardo da Vinci, 1452-1519, Italian painter, sculptor, architect, musician, engineer, and scientist.

[6] I. A. Richards (b. 1893), British-born literary critic, philologist, and philosopher.

[7] Miguel de Cervantes Saavedra, 1547-1616, Spanish novelist, dramatist, and poet, author in 1605 of the famous Don Quixote de la Mancha.

that exists in life, something so true to us that it is in danger of ceasing to exist, if we isolate it, something in the mind of a precarious tenure. These may be words. Certainly, however, Cervantes sought to set right the balance between the imagination and reality. As we come closer to our own times in Don Quixote and as we are drawn together by the intelligence common to the two periods, we may derive so much satisfaction from the restoration of reality as to become wholly prejudiced against the imagination. This is to reach a conclusion prematurely, let alone that it may be to reach a conclusion in respect to something as to which no conclusion is possible or desirable.

There is in Washington, in Lafayette Square, which is the square on which the White House faces, a statue of Andrew Jackson, riding a horse with one of the most beautiful tails in the world. General Jackson is raising his hat in a gay gesture, saluting the ladies of his generation. One looks at this work of Clark Mills[8] and thinks of the remark of Bertrand Russell [9] that to acquire immunity to eloquence is of the utmost importance to the citizens of a democracy. We are bound to think that Colleoni, as a mercenary, was a much less formidable man than General Jackson, that he meant less to fewer people and that, if Verrocchio could have applied his prodigious poetry to Jackson, the whole American outlook today might be imperial. This work is a work of fancy. Dr. Richards cites Coleridge's theory of fancy as opposed to imagination. Fancy is an activity of the mind which puts things together of choice, *not* the will, as a principle of the mind's being, striving to realize itself in knowing itself. Fancy, then, is an exercise of selection from among objects already supplied by association, a selection made for purposes which are not then and therein being shaped but have been already fixed. We are concerned then with an object occupying a position as remarkable as any that can be found in the United States in which there is not the slightest trace of the imagination. Treating this work as typical, it is obvious that the American will as a principle of the mind's being is easily satisfied in its efforts to realize itself in knowing itself. The statue may be dismissed, not without speaking of it again as a thing that at least makes us conscious of ourselves as we were, if not as we are. To that extent, it helps us to know ourselves. It helps us to know ourselves as we were and that helps us to know ourselves as we are. The statue is neither of the imagination nor of reality. That it is a work of fancy precludes it from being a work of the imagination. A glance at it shows it to be unreal. The bearing of this is that there can be works, and this includes poems, in which neither the imagination nor reality is present.

The other day I was reading a note about an American artist who was said to have "turned his back on the aesthetic whims and theories of the day, and established headquarters in lower Manhattan." Accompanying this note was a reproduction of a painting called *Wooden Horses*. It is a painting of a merry-go-round, possibly of several of them. One of the horses seems to be prancing. The others are going lickety-split, each one struggling to get the bit in his teeth. The horse in the center of the picture, painted yellow, has two riders, one a man, dressed in a carnival costume, who is seated in the saddle, the other a blonde, who is seated well up the horse's neck. The man

---

[8] American sculptor, 1810-1883, chiefly renowned for this equestrian statue.

[9] English philosopher and mathematician (*b.* 1872).

has his arms under the girl's arms. He holds himself stiffly in order to keep his cigar out of the girl's hair. Her feet are in a second and shorter set of stirrups. She has the legs of a hammer-thrower. It is clear that the couple are accustomed to wooden horses and like them. A little behind them is a younger girl riding alone. She has a strong body and streaming hair. She wears a short-sleeved, red waist, a white skirt and an emphatic bracelet of pink coral. She has her eyes on the man's arms. Still farther behind, there is another girl. One does not see much more of her than her head. Her lips are painted bright red. It seems that it would be better if someone were to hold her on her horse. We, here, are not interested in any aspect of this picture except that it is a picture of ribald and hilarious reality. It is a picture wholly favorable to what is real. It is not without imagination and it is far from being without aesthetic theory.

3

These illustrations of the relation between the imagination and reality are an outline on the basis of which to indicate a tendency. Their usefulness is this: that they help to make clear, what no one may ever have doubted, that just as in this or that work the degrees of the imagination and of reality may vary, so this variation may exist as between the works of one age and the works of another. What I have said up to this point amounts to this: that the idea of nobility exists in art today only in degenerate forms or in a much diminished state, if, in fact, it exists at all or otherwise than on sufferance; that this is due to failure in the relation between the imagination and reality. I should now like to add that this failure is due, in turn, to the pressure of reality.

A variation between the sound of words in one age and the sound of words in another age is an instance of the pressure of reality. Take the statement by Bateson[10] that a language, considered semantically, evolves through a series of conflicts between the denotative and the connotative forces in words; between an asceticism tending to kill language by stripping words of all association and a hedonism tending to kill language by dissipating their sense in a multiplicity of associations. These conflicts are nothing more than changes in the relation between the imagination and reality. Bateson describes the seventeenth century in England as predominantly a connotative period. The use of words in connotative senses was denounced by Locke[11] and Hobbes,[12] who desired a mathematical plainness; in short, perspicuous words. There followed in the eighteenth century an era of poetic diction. This was not the language of the age but a language of poetry peculiar to itself. In time, Wordsworth came to write the preface to the second edition of the *Lyrical Ballads* (1800), in which he said that the first volume had been published, "as an experiment, which, I hoped, might be of some use to ascertain how

[10] Frederick W. Bateson (b. 1901), critic and literary historian, author of *English Poetry and the English Language* (1934).

[11] John Locke, 1632-1704, English philosopher and founder of British empiricism.

[12] Thomas Hobbes, 1588-1679, English mathematician, physicist, and exponent of rationalism.

far, by fitting to metrical arrangement a selection of the real language of man in a state of vivid sensation, that sort of pleasure and that quantity of pleasure may be imparted, which a Poet may rationally endeavour to impart."

As the nineteenth century progressed, language once more became connotative. While there have been intermediate reactions, this tendency toward the connotative is the tendency today. The interest in semantics is evidence of this. In the case of some of our prose writers, as, for example, Joyce,[13] the language, in quite different ways, is wholly connotative. When we say that Locke and Hobbes denounced the connotative use of words as an abuse, and when we speak of reactions and reforms, we are speaking, on the one hand, of a failure of the imagination to adhere to reality, and, on the other, of a use of language favorable to reality. The statement that the tendency toward the connotative is the tendency today is disputable. The general movement in the arts, that is to say, in painting and in music, has been the other way. It is hard to say that the tendency is toward the connotative in the use of words without also saying that the tendency is toward the imagination in other directions. The interest in the subconscious and in surrealism shows the tendency toward the imaginative. Boileau's[14] remark that Descartes[15] had cut poetry's throat is a remark that could have been made respecting a great many people during the last hundred years, and of no one more aptly than of Freud,[16] who, as it happens, was familiar with it and repeats it in his *Future of an Illusion*. The object of that essay was to suggest a surrender to reality. His premise was that it is the unmistakable character of the present situation not that the promises of religion have become smaller but that they appear less credible to people. He notes the decline of religious belief and disagrees with the argument that man cannot in general do without the consolation of what he calls the religious illusion and that without it he would not endure the cruelty of reality. His conclusion is that man must venture at last into the hostile world and that this may be called education to reality. There is much more in that essay inimical to poetry and not least the observation in one of the final pages that "The voice of the intellect is a soft one, but it does not rest until it has gained a hearing." This, I fear, is intended to be the voice of the realist.

A tendency in language toward the connotative might very well parallel a tendency in other arts toward the denotative. We have just seen that that is in fact the situation. I suppose that the present always appears to be an illogical complication. The language of Joyce goes along with the dilapidations of Braque and Picasso[17] and the music of the Austrians.[18] To the extent that this painting and this music are the work of men who regard it as part of

[13] James Joyce, 1882-1941, the famous Irish novelist.

[14] Nicolas Boileau-Despréaux, 1636-1711, French literary critic and poet.

[15] René Descartes, 1596-1650, French philosopher and scientist.

[16] Sigmund Freud, 1856-1939, Austrian psychiatrist, and founder of psychoanalysis.

[17] Georges Braque, French painter (1882-1963), and Pablo Picasso, Spanish painter (*b.* 1881), founders in 1908 of cubism.

[18] Stevens here refers to the Austrian modernist school of composers, represented by Arnold Schönberg, 1874-1951, and his pupil Alban Berg, 1885-1935.

the science of painting and the science of music it is the work of realists. Actually its effect is that of the imagination, just as the effect of abstract painting is so often that of the imagination, although that may be different. Busoni said, in a letter to his wife, "I have made the painful discovery that nobody loves and feels music." Very likely, the reason there is a tendency in language toward the connotative today is that there are many who love it and feel it. It may be that Braque and Picasso love and feel painting and that Schönberg loves and feels music, although it seems that what they love and feel is something else.

A tendency toward the connotative, whether in language or elsewhere, cannot continue against the pressure of reality. If it is the pressure of reality that controls poetry, then the immediacy of various theories of poetry is not what it was. For instance, when Rostrevor Hamilton[19] says, "The object of contemplation is the highly complex and unified content of consciousness, which comes into being through the developing subjective attitude of the percipient," he has in mind no such "content of consciousness" as every newspaper reader experiences today.

By way of further illustration, let me quote from Croce's[20] Oxford lecture of 1933. He said: "If . . . poetry is intuition and expression, the fusion of sound and imagery, what is the material which takes on the form of sound and imagery? It is the whole man: the man who thinks and wills, and loves, and hates; who is strong and weak, sublime and pathetic, good and wicked; man in the exultation and agony of living; and together with the man, integral with him, it is all nature in its perpetual labour of evolution. . . . Poetry . . . is the triumph of contemplation. . . . Poetic genius chooses a strait path in which passion is calmed and calm is passionate."

Croce cannot have been thinking of a world in which all normal life is at least in suspense, or, if you like, under blockage. He was thinking of normal human experience.

Quite apart from the abnormal aspect of everyday life today, there is the normal aspect of it. The spirit of negation has been so active, so confident and so intolerant that the commonplaces about the romantic provoke us to wonder if our salvation, if the way out, is not the romantic. All the great things have been denied and we live in an intricacy of new and local mythologies, political, economic, poetic, which are asserted with an ever-enlarging incoherence. This is accompanied by an absence of any authority except force, operative or imminent. What has been called the disparagement of reason is an instance of the absence of authority. We pick up the radio and find that comedians regard the public use of words of more than two syllables as funny. We read of the opening of the National Gallery at Washington and we are convinced, in the end, that the pictures are counterfeit, that museums are impositions and that Mr. Mellon[21] was a monster. We turn to a recent transla-

[19] Author of *The World to Come* (1939), a book admired by Stevens.

[20] Benedetto Croce, 1866-1952, Italian philosopher and critic, noted particularly for his work in aesthetics.

[21] Andrew W. Mellon, 1855-1937, American financier and industrialist of Pittsburgh. In 1937 he gave his art collection to the American people, together with funds for the erection of a building to house it.

tion of Kierkegaard [22] and we find him saying: "A great deal has been said about poetry reconciling one with existence; rather it might be said that it arouses one against existence; for poetry is unjust to men . . . it has use only for the elect, but that is a poor sort of reconciliation. I will take the case of sickness. Aesthetics replies proudly and quite consistently, 'That cannot be employed, poetry must not become a hospital.' Aesthetics culminates . . . by regarding sickness in accordance with the principle enunciated by Friedrich Schlegel: [23] 'Nur Gesundheit ist liebenswürdig.' (Health alone is lovable.)"

The enormous influence of education in giving everyone a little learning, and in giving large groups considerably more: something of history, something of philosophy, something of literature; the expansion of the middle class with its common preference for realistic satisfactions; the penetration of the masses of people by the ideas of liberal thinkers, even when that penetration is indirect, as by the reporting of the reasons why people oppose the ideas that they oppose,—these are normal aspects of everyday life. The way we live and the way we work alike cast us out on reality. If fifty private houses were to be built in New York this year, it would be a phenomenon. We no longer live in homes but in housing projects and this is so whether the project is literally a project or a club, a dormitory, a camp or an apartment in River House. [24] It is not only that there are more of us and that we are actually close together. We are close together in every way. We lie in bed and listen to a broadcast from Cairo, and so on. There is no distance. We are intimate with people we have never seen and, unhappily, they are intimate with us. Democritus [25] plucked his eye out because he could not look at a woman without thinking of her as a woman. If he had read a few of our novels, he would have torn himself to pieces. Dr. Richards has noted "the widespread increase in the aptitude of the average mind for self-dissolving introspection, the generally heightened awareness of the goings-on of our own minds, *merely as goings-on*." This is nothing to the generally heightened awareness of the goings-on of other people's minds, *merely as goings-on*. The way we work is a good deal more difficult for the imagination than the highly civilized revolution that is occurring in respect to work indicates. It is, in the main, a revolution for more pay. We have been assured, by every visitor, that the American businessman is absorbed in his business and there is nothing to be gained by disputing it. As for the workers, it is enough to say that the word has grown to be literary. They have become, at their work, in the face of the machines, something approximating an abstraction, an energy. The time must be coming when, as they leave the factories, they will be passed through an air-chamber or a bar to revive them for riot and reading. I am sorry to have to add that to one that

[22] Søren Kierkegaard, 1813-1855, Danish theologian and early exponent of existentialism.

[23] German critic and philosopher, 1772-1829, most prominent of the founders of the romantic school.

[24] An expensive residential apartment building of the fashionable East Side of Manhattan, New York City.

[25] Greek philosopher and scientist, c. 460-c. 370 B.C., founder of early atomic theory, and advocate of thought alone as capable of apprehending the nature of things.

thinks, as Dr. Richards thinks, that poetry is the supreme use of language, some of the foreign universities in relation to our own appear to be, so far as the things of the imagination are concerned, as Verrocchio is to the sculptor of the statue of General Jackson.

These, nevertheless, are not the things that I had in mind when I spoke of the pressure of reality. These constitute the drift of incidents, to which we accustom ourselves as to the weather. Materialism is an old story and an indifferent one. Robert Wolseley[26] said: "True genius . . . will enter into the hardest and dryest thing, enrich the most barren Soyl, and inform the meanest and most uncomely matter . . . the baser, the emptier, the obscurer, the fouler, and the less susceptible of Ornament the subject appears to be, the more is the Poet's Praise . . . who, as Horace says of Homer, can fetch Light out of Smoak, Roses out of Dunghills, and give a kind of Life to the inanimate . . . " (Preface to Rochester's *Valentinian*, 1685, *English Association Essays and Studies*, 1939). By the pressure of reality, I mean the pressure of an external event or events on the consciousness to the exclusion of any power of contemplation. The definition ought to be exact and, as it is, may be merely pretentious. But when one is trying to think of a whole generation and of a world at war, and trying at the same time to see what is happening to the imagination, particularly if one believes that that is what matters most, the plainest statement of what is happening can easily appear to be an affectation.

For more than ten years now, there has been an extraordinary pressure of news—let us say, news incomparably more pretentious than any description of it, news, at first, of the collapse of our system, or, call it, of life; then of news of a new world, but of a new world so uncertain that one did not know anything whatever of its nature, and does not know now, and could not tell whether it was to be all-English, all-German, all-Russian, all-Japanese, or all-American, and cannot tell now; and finally news of a war, which was a renewal of what, if it was not the greatest war, became such by this continuation. And for more than ten years, the consciousness of the world has concentrated on events which have made the ordinary movement of life seem to be the movement of people in the intervals of a storm. The disclosures of the impermanence of the past suggested, and suggest, an impermanence of the future. Little of what we have believed has been true. Only the prophecies are true. The present is an opportunity to repent. This is familiar enough. The war is only a part of a war-like whole. It is not possible to look backward and to see that the same thing was true in the past. It is a question of pressure, and pressure is incalculable and eludes the historian. The Napoleonic era is regarded as having had little or no effect on the poets and the novelists who lived in it. But Coleridge and Wordsworth and Sir Walter Scott and Jane Austen did not have to put up with Napoleon and Marx and Europe, Asia and Africa all at one time. It seems possible to say that they knew of the events of their day much as we know of the bombings in the interior of China and not at all as we know of the bombings of London, or, rather, as we should

26 1649-1697, English barrister, and a champion of poetry in his age. He was the eldest son of Sir Charles Wolseley, an eminent politician during the civil war, and a counselor to Cromwell.

know of the bombings of Toronto or Montreal. Another part of the war-like whole to which we do not respond quite as we do to the news of war is the income tax. The blanks are specimens of mathematical prose. They titillate the instinct of self-preservation in a class in which that instinct has been forgotten. Virginia Woolf [27] thought that the income tax, if it continued, would benefit poets by enlarging their vocabularies and I dare say that she was right.

If it is not possible to assert that the Napoleonic era was the end of one era in the history of the imagination and the beginning of another, one comes closer to the truth by making that assertion in respect to the French Revolution. The defeat or triumph of Hitler are parts of a war-like whole but the fate of an individual is different from the fate of a society. Rightly or wrongly, we feel that the fate of a society is involved in the orderly disorders of the present time. We are confronting, therefore, a set of events, not only beyond our power to tranquillize them in the mind, beyond our power to reduce them and metamorphose them, but events that stir the emotions to violence, that engage us in what is direct and immediate and real, and events that involve the concepts and sanctions that are the order of our lives and may involve our very lives; and these events are occurring persistently with increasing omen, in what may be called our presence. These are the things that I had in mind when I spoke of the pressure of reality, a pressure great enough and prolonged enough to bring about the end of one era in the history of the imagination and, if so, then great enough to bring about the beginning of another. It is one of the peculiarities of the imagination that it is always at the end of an era. What happens is that it is always attaching itself to a new reality, and adhering to it. It is not that there is a new imagination but that there is a new reality. The pressure of reality may, of course, be less than the general pressure that I have described. It exists for individuals according to the circumstances of their lives or according to the characteristics of their minds. To sum it up, the pressure of reality is, I think, the determining factor in the artistic character of an era and, as well, the determining factor in the artistic character of an individual. The resistance to this pressure or its evasion in the case of individuals of extraordinary imagination cancels the pressure so far as those individuals are concerned.

4

Suppose we try, now, to construct the figure of a poet, a possible poet. He cannot be a charioteer traversing vacant space, however ethereal. He must have lived all of the last two thousand years, and longer, and he must have instructed himself, as best he could, as he went along. He will have thought that Virgil, Dante, Shakespeare, Milton placed themselves in remote lands and in remote ages; that their men and women were the dead—and not the dead lying in the earth, but the dead still living in their remote lands and in their remote ages, and living in the earth or under it, or in the heavens— and he will wonder at those huge imaginations, in which what is remote becomes near, and what is dead lives with an intensity beyond any experience

[27] English novelist and literary critic, 1882-1941.

of life. He will consider that although he has himself witnessed, during the long period of his life, a general transition to reality, his own measure as a poet, in spite of all the passions of all the lovers of the truth, is the measure of his power to abstract himself, and to withdraw with him into his abstraction the reality on which the lovers of truth insist. He must be able to abstract himself and also to abstract reality, which he does by placing it in his imagination. He knows perfectly that he cannot be too noble a rider, that he cannot rise up loftily in helmet and armor on a horse of imposing bronze. He will think again of Milton and of what was said about him: that "the necessity of writing for one's living blunts the appreciation of writing when it bears the mark of perfection. Its quality disconcerts our hasty writers; they are ready to condemn it as preciosity and affectation. And if to them the musical and creative powers of words convey little pleasure, how out of date and irrelevant they must find the . . . music of Milton's verse." Don Quixote will make it imperative for him to make a choice, to come to a decision regarding the imagination and reality; and he will find that it is not a choice of one over the other and not a decision that divides them, but something subtler, a recognition that here, too, as between these poles, the universal interdependence exists, and hence his choice and his decision must be that they are equal and inseparable. To take a single instance: When Horatio says,

> Now cracks a noble heart. Good night, sweet prince,
> And flights of angels sing thee to thy rest! [28]

are not the imagination and reality equal and inseparable? Above all, he will not forget General Jackson or the picture of the *Wooden Horses.*

I said of the picture that it was a work in which everything was favorable to reality. I hope that the use of that bare word has been enough. But without regard to its range of meaning in thought, it includes all its natural images, and its connotations are without limit. Bergson[29] describes the visual perception of a motionless object as the most stable of internal states. He says: "The object may remain the same, I may look at it from the same side, at the same angle, in the same light; nevertheless, the vision I now have of it differs from that which I have just had, even if only because the one is an instant later than the other. My memory is there, which conveys something of the past into the present."

Dr. Joad's[30] comment on this is: "Similarly with external things. Every body, every quality of a body resolves itself into an enormous number of vibrations, movements, changes. What is it that vibrates, moves, is changed? There is no answer. Philosophy has long dismissed the notion of substance and modern physics has endorsed the dismissal. . . . How, then, does the world come to appear to us as a collection of solid, static objects extended in space? Because of the intellect, which presents us with a false view of it."

The poet has his own meaning for reality, and the painter has, and the musician has; and besides what it means to the intelligence and to the senses,

---

[28] Shakespeare, *Hamlet,* Act V, sc. ii.
[29] Henri Bergson, French philosopher, 1859-1941.
[30] Cyril Edwin Mitchinson Joad (*b.* 1891), English philosopher.

it means something to everyone, so to speak. Notwithstanding this, the word
in its general sense, which is the sense in which I have used it, adapts itself
instantly. The subject-matter of poetry is not that "collection of solid, static
objects extended in space" but the life that is lived in the scene that it composes; and so reality is not that external scene but the life that is lived in it.
Reality is things as they are. The general sense of the word proliferates its
special senses. It is a jungle in itself. As in the case of a jungle, everything
that makes it up is pretty much of one color. First, then, there is the reality that
is taken for granted, that is latent and, on the whole, ignored. It is the comfortable American state of life of the eighties, the nineties and the first ten
years of the present century. Next, there is the reality that has ceased to be
indifferent, the years when the Victorians had been disposed of and intellectual minorities and social minorities began to take their place and to convert
our state of life to something that might not be final. This much more vital
reality made the life that had preceded it look like a volume of Ackermann's[31] colored plates or one of Töpfer's[32] books of sketches in Switzerland.
I am trying to give the feel of it. It was the reality of twenty or thirty years
ago. I say that it was a vital reality. The phrase gives a false impression. It was
vital in the sense of being tense, of being instinct with the fatal or with what
might be the fatal. The minorities began to convince us that the Victorians had left nothing behind. The Russians followed the Victorians, and the
Germans, in their way, followed the Russians. The British Empire, directly
or indirectly, was what was left and as to that one could not be sure whether it
was a shield or a target. Reality then became violent and so remains. This
much ought to be said to make it a little clearer that in speaking of the pressure of reality, I am thinking of life in a state of violence, not physically
violent, as yet, for us in America, but physically violent for millions of our
friends and for still more millions of our enemies and spiritually violent, it
may be said, for everyone alive.

A possible poet must be a poet capable of resisting or evading the pressure of the reality of this last degree, with the knowledge that the degree of
today may become a deadlier degree tomorrow. There is, however, no point
to dramatizing the future in advance of the fact. I confine myself to the outline of a possible poet, with only the slightest sketch of his background.

5

Here I am, well-advanced in my paper, with everything of interest that
I started out to say remaining to be said. I am interested in the nature of
poetry and I have stated its nature, from one of the many points of view
from which it is possible to state it. It is an interdependence of the imagination and reality as equals. This is not a definition, since it is incomplete. But
it states the nature of poetry. Then I am interested in the role of the poet and
this is paramount. In this area of my subject I might be expected to speak
of the social, that is to say sociological or political, obligation of the poet. He

[31] Rudolph Ackermann, 1764-1834, acquatint engraver, noted for his *Picturesque
Tour of the English Lakes* (1821).

[32] Rodolphe Töpfer, 1799-1846, Swiss artist and writer of travel sketches.

has none. That he must be contemporaneous is as old as Longinus[33] and I dare say older. But that he *is* contemporaneous is almost inevitable. How contemporaneous in the direct sense in which being contemporaneous is intended were the four great poets of whom I spoke a moment ago? I do not think that a poet owes any more as a social obligation than he owes as a moral obligation, and if there is anything concerning poetry about which people agree it is that the role of the poet is not to be found in morals. I cannot say what that wide agreement amounts to because the agreement (in which I do not join) that the poet is under a social obligation is equally wide. Reality is life and life is society and the imagination and reality; that is to say, the imagination and society are inseparable. That is pre-eminently true in the case of the poetic drama. The poetic drama needs a terrible genius before it is anything more than a literary relic. Besides the theater has forgotten that it could ever be terrible. It is not one of the instruments of fate, decidedly. Yes: the all-commanding subject-matter of poetry is life, the never-ceasing source. But it is not a social obligation. One does not love and go back to one's ancient mother as a social obligation. One goes back out of a suasion not to be denied. Unquestionably if a social movement moved one deeply enough, its moving poems would follow. No politician can command the imagination, directing it to do this or that. Stalin might grind his teeth the whole of a Russian winter and yet all the poets in the Soviets might remain silent the following spring. He might excite their imaginations by something he said or did. He would not command them. He is singularly free from that "cult of pomp," which is the comic side of the European disaster; and that means as much as anything to us. The truth is that the social obligation so closely urged is a phase of the pressure of reality which a poet (in the absence of dramatic poets) is bound to resist or evade today. Dante in Purgatory and Paradise was still the voice of the Middle Ages but not through fulfilling any social obligation. Since that is the role most frequently urged, if that role is eliminated, and if a possible poet is left facing life without any categorical exactions upon him, what then? What is his function? Certainly it is not to lead people out of the confusion in which they find themselves. Nor is it, I think, to comfort them while they follow their readers to and fro. I think that his function is to make his imagination theirs and that he fulfills himself only as he sees his imagination become the light in the minds of others. His role, in short, is to help people to live their lives. Time and time again it has been said that he may not address himself to an élite. I think he may. There is not a poet whom we prize living today that does not address himself to an élite. The poet will continue to do this: to address himself to an élite even in a classless society, unless, perhaps, this exposes him to imprisonment or exile. In that event he is likely not to address himself to anyone at all. He may, like Shostakovich,[34] content himself with pretence. He will,

[33] Dionysius Cassius Longinus, c. A.D. 213-273, eminent Greek rhetorician and philosopher of the Platonic school.

[34] Dmitri Shostakovich (*b.* 1906), Russian composer. It is worth noting that Stevens detested every representative of Soviet totalitarianism, particularly with respect to the Soviet requirement of conformity of all imaginative achievment in the arts to the ends of the state.

nevertheless, still be addressing himself to an élite, for all poets address themselves to someone and it is of the essence of that instinct, and it seems to amount to an instinct, that it should be to an élite, not to a drab but to a woman with the hair of a pythoness, not to a chamber of commerce but to a gallery of one's own, if there are enough of one's own to fill a gallery. And that élite, if it responds, not out of complaisance, but because the poet has quickened it, because he has educed from it that for which it was searching in itself and in the life around it and which it had not yet quite found, will thereafter do for the poet what he cannot do for himself, that is to say, receive his poetry.

I repeat that his role is to help people to live their lives. He has had immensely to do with giving life whatever savor it possesses. He has had to do with whatever the imagination and the senses have made of the world. He has, in fact, had to do with life except as the intellect has had to do with it and, as to that, no one is needed to tell us that poetry and philosophy are akin. I want to repeat for two reasons a number of observations made by Charles Mauron.[35] The first reason is that these observations tell us what it is that a poet does to help people to live their lives and the second is that they prepare the way for a word concerning escapism. They are: that the artist transforms us into epicures; that he has to discover the possible work of art in the real world, then to extract it, when he does not himself compose it entirely; that he is *un amoureux perpétuel* of the world that he contemplates and thereby enriches; that art sets out to express the human soul; and finally that everything like a firm grasp of reality is eliminated from the aesthetic field. With these aphorisms in mind, how is it possible to condemn escapism? The poetic process is psychologically an escapist process. The chatter about escapism is, to my way of thinking, merely common cant. My own remarks about resisting or evading the pressure of reality mean escapism, if analyzed. Escapism has a pejorative sense, which it cannot be supposed that I include in the sense in which I use the word. The pejorative sense applies where the poet is not attached to reality, where the imagination does not adhere to reality, which, for my part, I regard as fundamental. If we go back to the collection of solid, static objects extended in space, which Dr. Joad posited, and if we say that the space is blank space, nowhere, without color, and that the objects, though solid, have no shadows and, though static, exert a mournful power, and, without elaborating this complete poverty, if suddenly we hear a different and familiar description of the place:

> This City now doth, like a garment, wear
> The beauty of the morning, silent, bare,
> Ships, towers, domes, theatres, and temples lie
> Open unto the fields, and to the sky;
> All bright and glittering in the smokeless air;[36]

if we have this experience, we know how poets help people to live their lives. This illustration must serve for all the rest. There is, in fact, a world of

---

[35] A contemporary French psychologist and literary critic, noted for his psychoanalytic studies of French art and poetry of recent years.

[36] Lines 4-8 of the celebrated sonnet of William Wordsworth, "Composed upon Westminster Bridge," September 3, 1802.

poetry indistinguishable from the world in which we live, or, I ought to say, no doubt, from the world in which we shall come to live, since what makes the poet the potent figure that he is, or was, or ought to be, is that he creates the world to which we turn incessantly and without knowing it and that he gives to life the supreme fictions without which we are unable to conceive of it.

And what about the sound of words? What about nobility, of which the fortunes were to be a kind of test of the value of the poet? I do not know of anything that will appear to have suffered more from the passage of time than the music of poetry and that has suffered less. The deepening need for words to express our thoughts and feelings which, we are sure, are all the truth that we shall ever experience, having no illusions, makes us listen to words when we hear them, loving them and feeling them, makes us search the sound of them, for a finality, a perfection, an unalterable vibration, which it is only within the power of the acutest poet to give them. Those of us who may have been thinking of the path of poetry, those who understand that words are thoughts and not only our own thoughts but the thoughts of men and women ignorant of what it is that they are thinking, must be conscious of this: that, above everything else, poetry is words; and that words, above everything else, are, in poetry, sounds. This being so, my time and yours might have been better spent if I had been less interested in trying to give our possible poet an identity and less interested in trying to appoint him to his place. But unless I had done these things, it might have been thought that I was rhetorical, when I was speaking in the simplest way about things of such importance that nothing is more so. A poet's words are of things that do not exist without the words. Thus, the image of the charioteer and of the winged horses, which has been held to be precious for all of time that matters, was created by words of things that never existed without the words. A description of Verrocchio's statue could be the integration of an illusion equal to the statute itself. Poetry is a revelation in words by means of the words. Croce was not speaking of poetry in particular when he said that language is perpetual creation. About nobility I cannot be sure that the decline, not to say the disappearance of nobility is anything more than a maladjustment between the imagination and reality. We have been a little insane about the truth. We have had an obsession. In its ultimate extension, the truth about which we have been insane will lead us to look beyond the truth to something in which the imagination will be the dominant complement. It is not only that the imagination adheres to reality, but, also, that reality adheres to the imagination and that the interdependence is essential. We may emerge from our *bassesse*[37] and, if we do, how would it happen if not by the intervention of some fortune of the mind? And what would that fortune of the mind happen to be? It might be only commonsense but even that, a commonsense beyond the truth, would be a nobility of long descent.

The poet refuses to allow his task to be set for him. He denies that he has a task and considers that the organization of materia poetica is a contradiction in terms. Yet the imagination gives to everything that it touches a peculiarity, and it seems to me that the peculiarity of the imagination is

[37] A French term, to be rendered literally into English as *baseness* or *servility*, used here by Stevens in the sense of our modern *limitation* or *impoverishment*.

nobility, of which there are many degrees. This inherent nobility is the natural source of another, which our extremely headstrong generation regards as false and decadent. I mean that nobility which is our spiritual height and depth; and while I know how difficult it is to express it, nevertheless I am bound to give a sense of it. Nothing could be more evasive and inaccessible. Nothing distorts itself and seeks disguise more quickly. There is a shame of disclosing it and in its definite presentations a horror of it. But there it is. The fact that it is there is what makes it possible to invite to the reading and writing of poetry men of intelligence and desire for life. I am not thinking of the ethical or the sonorous or at all of the manner of it. The manner of it is, in fact, its difficulty, which each man must feel each day differently, for himself. I am not thinking of the solemn, the portentous or demoded. On the other hand, I am evading a definition. If it is defined, it will be fixed and it must not be fixed. As in the case of an external thing, nobility resolves itself into an enormous number of vibrations, movements, changes. To fix it is to put an end to it. Let me show it to you unfixed.

Late last year Epstein[38] exhibited some of his flower paintings at the Leicester Galleries in London. A commentator in *Apollo* said: "*How with this rage can beauty hold a plea* . . . The quotation from Shakespeare's 65th sonnet prefaces the catalogue. . . . It would be apropos to any other flower paintings than Mr. Epstein's. His make no pretence to fragility. They shout, explode all over the picture space and generally oppose the rage of the world with such a rage of form and colour as no flower in nature or pigment has done since Van Gogh." [39]

What ferocious beauty the line from Shakespeare puts on when used under such circumstances! While it has its modulation of despair, it holds its plea and its plea is noble. There is no element more conspicuously absent from contemporary poetry than nobility. There is no element that poets have sought after, more curiously and more piously, certain of its obscure existence. Its voice is one of the inarticulate voices which it is their business to overhear and to record. The nobility of rhetoric is, of course, a lifeless nobility. Pareto's[40] epigram that history is a cemetery of aristocracies easily becomes another: that poetry is a cemetery of nobilities. For the sensitive poet, conscious of negations, nothing is more difficult than the affirmations of nobility and yet there is nothing that he requires of himself more persistently, since in them and in their kind, alone, are to be found those sanctions that are the reasons for his being and for that occasional ecstasy, or ecstatic freedom of the mind, which is his special privilege.

It is hard to think of a thing more out of time than nobility. Looked at plainly it seems false and dead and ugly. To look at it at all makes us realize sharply that in our present, in the presence of our reality, the past looks false and is, therefore, dead and is, therefore, ugly; and we turn away from it as from something repulsive and particularly from the characteristic that it has a way of assuming: something that was noble in its day, grandeur that was, the rhetorical once. But as a wave is a force and not the water of which it is

[38] Presumably Jacob Epstein (*b.* 1880), the Russian-Polish artist and sculptor, who has worked chiefly in England.

[39] Vincent van Gogh, 1853-1890, eminent postimpressionist Dutch painter.

[40] Vilfredo Pareto, 1848-1923, Italian economist and sociologist.

a lyric poem but also a dramatic monologue.

PETER QUINCE AT THE CLAVIER   919

Personae: Stevens – poet and man Quince – narrator and man Reader – receiver and man

composed, which is never the same, so nobility is a force and not the manifestations of which it is composed, which are never the same. Possibly this
description of it as a force will do more than anything else I can have said
about it to reconcile you to it. It is not an artifice that the mind has added to
human nature. The mind has added nothing to human nature. It is a violence from within that protects us from a violence without. It is the imagination pressing back against the pressure of reality. It seems, in the last analysis, to have something to do with our self-preservation; and that, no doubt, is
why the expression of it, the sound of its words, helps us to live our lives.

1941-1942

Keyboard of a piano or organ.

Musical phrasings here.

Peter Quince is a rustic carpenter who manages the play, employing such paradoxical language as "laughable tragedy, lamentable comedy, and tragic mirth," to describe it.

PETER QUINCE[1] AT THE CLAVIER

I

Just as my fingers on these keys
Make music, so the selfsame sounds
On my spirit make a music, too.
Statement & realisation.
Music is feeling, then, not sound;
And thus it is that what I feel,
Here in this room, desiring you,   *maybe present (see lines 4-8)*

Thinking of your blue-shadowed silk,   5
Is music. It is like the strain   *Suggest she is absent*
Waked in the elders by Susanna.[2]

Of a green evening, clear and warm,   *Didactic*   10
She bathed in her still garden, while
The red-eyed elders watching, felt

The basses of their beings throb   *Part I describes*
In witching chords, and their thin blood *feelings that are*
Pulse pizzicati[3] of Hosanna.   *the same.*

"Peter Quince at the Clavier" and the following two poems, "The Paltry Nude Starts on a Spring Voyage" and "Sunday Morning," are from *The Collected Poems of Wallace Stevens*, by permission of Alfred A. Knopf, Inc. Copyright 1923, 1951 by Wallace Stevens.

[1] Peter Quince, the carpenter and the master of the revels in Shakespeare's *A Midsummer-Night's Dream.*

[2] Of the Apocryphal Story of Susanna, attached to the Book of Daniel. For a copy of the text with emendations, see R. H. Charles, *The Apocrypha and Pseudepigrapha of the Old Testament* (1913).

[3] Pluckings of strings of musical instruments.

Section 1 begins in conscious thought as simile and metaphor introduce the extended metaphor of the poem.

As thought leads on to thought,
Quince considers his immediate occupation,
the loved one,
the nature of passion

Theme but stated in terms of Quince's experience

iambic dimeter comes after alternating trimeter —

to be read as one breath.

II

In the green water, clear and warm, — *both*
Susanna lay.
She searched
The touch of springs,
And found
Concealed imaginings.
She sighed,
For so much melody.

imagery and rhythm — essentially sensual   20

Upon the bank, she stood
In the cool
Of spent emotions.
She felt, among the leaves,
The dew
Of old devotions.

Pt. II
Description of Susanna   25

She walked upon the grass,   30
Still quavering.
The winds were like her maids,
On timid feet,
Fetching her woven scarves,
Yet wavering.   35

A breath upon her hand
Muted the night.
She turned—
A cymbal crashed,
And roaring horns.   40

III

A ballet with exotic oriental dancers.

Soon, with a noise like tambourines,
Came her attendant Byzantines.

They wondered why Susanna cried
Against the elders by her side;

And as they whispered, the refrain   45
Was like a willow swept by rain.

Anon, their lamps' uplifted flame
Revealed Susanna and her shame.

And then, the simpering Byzantines
Fled, with a noise like tambourines.   50

IV

begins with a line of prose,

Beauty is momentary in the mind—
The fitful tracing of a portal;
But in the flesh it is immortal.

The body dies; the body's beauty lives.   *a series of*
So evenings die, in their green going,   *observations follow.*
A wave, interminably flowing.
So gardens die, their meek breath scenting
The cowl of winter, done repenting.
So maidens die, to the auroral   *Note use of*
Celebration of a maiden's choral.
Susanna's music touched the bawdy strings   *feminine rhyme*
Of those white elders; but, escaping,
Left only Death's ironic scraping.
Now, in its immortality, it plays
On the clear viol [4] of her memory,   65
And makes a constant sacrament of praise.

1915

THE PALTRY NUDE
STARTS ON A SPRING VOYAGE

But not on a shell,[5] she starts,
Archaic, for the sea.
But on the first-found weed
She scuds the glitters,
Noiselessly, like one more wave.   5

She too is discontent
And would have purple stuff upon her arms,
Tired of the salty harbors,
Eager for the brine and bellowing
Of the high interiors of the sea.   10

The wind speeds her,
Blowing upon her hands
And watery back.
She touches the clouds, where she goes
In the circle of her traverse of the sea.   15

Yet this is meagre play
In the scurry and water-shine,
As her heels foam—

[4] The constant use of musical terms and images throughout the poem should be carefully noted as descriptive of the imagination in the act of playing upon the theme of beauty.

[5] The poem recalls the myth of Venus as represented by the Italian painter Sandro Botticelli (1447?-1510) in his "The Birth of Venus." The goddess is shown in the nude, standing in the cup of a water-borne shell as the four winds blow her gently to the shore. Venus, beyond her function as goddess of love, was also goddess of gardens and bloom in Roman mythology. Stevens associates her here with the coming of spring.

Not as when the goldener nude
Of a later day   20

Will go, like the centre of sea-green pomp,
In an intenser calm,
Scullion of fate,
Across the spick torrent, ceaselessly,
Upon her irretrievable way.   25

1919

SUNDAY MORNING

I

Complacencies of the peignoir, and late
Coffee and oranges in a sunny chair,
And the green freedom of a cockatoo
Upon a rug mingle to dissipate
The holy hush of ancient sacrifice.   5
She dreams a little, and she feels the dark
Encroachment of that old catastrophe,
As a calm darkens among water-lights.
The pungent oranges and bright, green wings
Seem things in some procession of the dead,   10
Winding across wide water, without sound.
The day is like wide water, without sound,
Stilled for the passing of her dreaming feet
Over the seas, to silent Palestine,
Dominion of the blood and sepulchre.   15

II

Why should she give her bounty to the dead?
What is divinity if it can come
Only in silent shadows and in dreams?
Shall she not find in comforts of the sun,
In pungent fruit and bright, green wings, or else   20
In any balm or beauty of the earth,
Things to be cherished like the thought of heaven?
Divinity must live within herself:
Passions of rain, or moods in falling snow;
Grievings in loneliness, or unsubdued   25
Elations when the forest blooms; gusty
Emotions on wet roads on autumn nights;
All pleasures and all pains, remembering
The bough of summer and the winter branch.
These are the measures destined for her soul.   30

III

Jove in the clouds had his inhuman birth.
No mother suckled him, no sweet land gave
Large-mannered motions to his mythy mind.
He moved among us, as a muttering king,   35
Magnificent, would move among his hinds,
Until our blood, commingling, virginal,
With heaven, brought such requital to desire
The very hinds discerned it, in a star.
Shall our blood fail? Or shall it come to be   40
The blood of paradise? And shall the earth
Seem all of paradise that we shall know?
The sky will be much friendlier then than now,
A part of labor and a part of pain,
And next in glory to enduring love,   45
Not this dividing and indifferent blue.

IV

She says, "I am content when wakened birds,
Before they fly, test the reality
Of misty fields, by their sweet questionings;
But when the birds are gone, and their warm fields   50
Return no more, where, then, is paradise?"
There is not any haunt of prophecy,
Nor any old chimera[1] of the grave,
Neither the golden underground, nor isle
Melodious, where spirits gat them home,   55
Nor visionary south, nor cloudy palm
Remote on heaven's hill, that has endured
As April's green endures; or will endure
Like her remembrance of awakened birds,
Or her desire for June and evening, tipped   60
By the consummation of the swallow's wings.

V

She says, "But in contentment I still feel
The need of some imperishable bliss."
Death is the mother of beauty; hence from her,
Alone, shall come fulfilment to our dreams
And our desires. Although she strews the leaves   65
Of sure obliteration on our paths,
The path sick sorrow took, the many paths
Where triumph rang its brassy phrase, or love
Whispered a little out of tenderness,
She makes the willow shiver in the sun   70
For maidens who were wont to sit and gaze

[1] A devouring she-monster of Greek mythology.

Upon the grass, relinquished to their feet.
She causes boys to pile new plums and pears
On disregarded plate. The maidens taste
And stray impassioned in the littering leaves.   75

VI

Is there no change of death in paradise?
Does ripe fruit never fall? Or do the boughs
Hang always heavy in that perfect sky,
Unchanging, yet so like our perishing earth,
With rivers like our own that seek for seas   80
They never find, the same receding shores
That never touch with inarticulate pang?
Why set the pear upon those river-banks
Or spice the shores with odors of the plum?
Alas, that they should wear our colors there,   85
The silken weavings of our afternoons,
And pick the strings of our insipid lutes!
Death is the mother of beauty, mystical,
Within whose burning bosom we devise
Our earthly mothers waiting, sleeplessly.   90

VII

barbaric
Splendor

Supple and turbulent, a ring of men
Shall chant in orgy on a summer morn
Their boisterous devotion to the sun,
Not as a god, but as a god might be,
Naked among them, like a savage source.   95
Their chant shall be a chant of paradise,
Out of their blood, returning to the sky;
And in their chant shall enter, voice by voice,
The windy lake wherein their lord delights,
The trees, like serafin, and echoing hills,   100
That choir among themselves long afterward.
They shall know well the heavenly fellowship
Of men that perish and of summer morn.
And whence they came and whither they shall go
The dew upon their feet shall manifest.   105

VIII

She hears, upon that water without sound,
A voice that cries, "The tomb in Palestine
Is not the porch of spirits lingering.
It is the grave of Jesus, where he lay."
We live in an old chaos of the sun,   110
Or old dependency of day and night,
Or island solitude, unsponsored, free,
Of that wide water, inescapable.

> Deer walk upon our mountains, and the quail
> Whistle about us their spontaneous cries;   115
> Sweet berries ripen in the wilderness;
> And, in the isolation of the sky,
> At evening, casual flocks of pigeons make
> Ambiguous undulations as they sink,
> Downward to darkness, on extended wings.   120

1915, 1923

THE IDEA OF ORDER AT KEY WEST

> She sang beyond the genius of the sea.
> The water never formed to mind or voice,
> Like a body wholly body, fluttering
> Its empty sleeves; and yet its mimic motion
> Made constant cry, caused constantly a cry,   5
> That was not ours although we understood,
> Inhuman, of the veritable ocean.
>
> The sea was not a mask. No more was she.
> The song and water were not medleyed sound
> Even if what she sang was what she heard,   10
> Since what she sang was uttered word by word.
> It may be that in all her phrases stirred
> The grinding water and the gasping wind;
> But it was she and not the sea we heard.
>
> For she was the maker of the song she sang.   15
> The ever-hooded, tragic-gestured sea
> Was merely a place by which she walked to sing.
> Whose spirit is this? we said, because we knew
> It was the spirit that we sought and knew
> That we should ask this often as she sang.   20
>
> If it was only the dark voice of the sea
> That rose, or even colored by many waves;
> If it was only the outer voice of sky
> And cloud, of the sunken coral water-walled,
> However clear, it would have been deep air,   25
> The heaving speech of air, a summer sound
> Repeated in a summer without end
> And sound alone. But it was more than that,
> More even than her voice, and ours, among

The meaningless plungings of water and the wind,   30
Theatrical distances, bronze shadows heaped
On high horizons, mountainous atmospheres
Of sky and sea.
                    It was her voice that made
The sky acutest at its vanishing.
She measured to the hour its solitude.   35
She was the single artificer of the world
In which she sang. And when she sang, the sea,
Whatever self it had, became the self
That was her song, for she was the maker. Then we,
As we beheld her striding there alone,   40
Knew that there never was a world for her
Except the one she sang and, singing, made.

Ramon Fernandez,[1] tell me, if you know,
Why, when the singing ended and we turned
Toward the town, tell why the glassy lights,   45
The lights in the fishing boats at anchor there,
As the night descended, tilting in the air,
Mastered the night and portioned out the sea,
Fixing emblazoned zones and fiery poles,
Arranging, deepening, enchanting night.   50

Oh! Blessed rage for order, pale Ramon,
The maker's rage to order words of the sea,
Words of the fragrant portals, dimly-starred,
And of ourselves and of our origins,
In ghostlier demarcations, keener sounds.   55

                                                    1934

STANZAS FOR
"THE MAN WITH THE BLUE GUITAR"

I

The day is green and the wind is young.
The world is young and I play my guitar.

The skeletons[2] sit on the wall. They drop
Red mango peels and I play my guitar.

From *Opus Posthumous* by Wallace Stevens, by permission of Alfred A. Knopf, Inc.
Copyright 1935 by Wallace Stevens.

  [1] A fictitious name. He should be regarded as a dramatic character in the scene, a
companion of the speaker. The poet assumes two roles here, that of the singer and
that of the narrator.
  [2] See footnote 2 in the selections from the "Adagia" following.

The gate is not jasper. It is not bone.
It is mud and mud long baked in the sun,

An eighteenth century fern or two
And the dewiest beads of insipid fruit

And honey from thorns and I play my guitar.
The negro with laundry passes me by.   10

The boatman goes humming. He smokes a cigar
And I play my guitar. The vines have grown wild.

The oranges glitter as part of the sky,
A tiara from Cohen's,[3] this summer sea.

II

I play them on a blue guitar   15
And then things are not as they are.

The shapings of the instrument
Distort the shape of what I meant,

Which takes a shape by accident.   20
Yet what I mean I always say.

The accident is how I play.
I still intend things as they are.

The greenish quaverings of day
Quiver upon the blue guitar.

III

To ride an old mule round the keys—   25
Mature emotional gesture, that—

Blond weather. One is born a saint,
Complete in wind-sucked poverty.

In such an air, poor as one's mule.   30
Here, if there was a peak to climb,

One could watch the blue sea's blueness flow
And blacken into indigo.

But squint and squeak, where no people are:
On such a peak, the blue guitar—

Blond weather. Give the mule his hay.   35.
True, things are people as they are.

1935-1936

---

[3] A fictitious shop, very probably intended by the poet as the equivalent of a typical
American dime store. The sea glitters with the raw colors of glass jewelry.

A POSTCARD FROM THE VOLCANO

Children picking up our bones
Will never know that these were once
As quick as foxes on the hill;

And that in autumn, when the grapes
Made sharp air sharper by their smell   5
These had a being, breathing frost;

And least will guess that with our bones
We left much more, left what still is
The look of things, left what we felt

At what we saw. The spring clouds blow   10
Above the shuttered mansion-house,
Beyond our gate and the windy sky

Cries out a literate despair.
We knew for long the mansion's look
And what we said of it became   15

A part of what it is . . . Children,
Still weaving budded aureoles,
Will speak our speech and never know,

Will say of the mansion that it seems
As if he that lived there left behind   20
A spirit storming in blank walls,

A dirty house in a gutted world,
A tatter of shadows peaked to white,
Smeared with the gold of the opulent sun.

1936

OF MODERN POETRY

The poem of the mind in the act of finding
What will suffice. It has not always had
To find: the scene was set; it repeated what
Was in the script.
                    Then the theatre was changed

To something else. Its past was a souvenir.
It has to be living, to learn the speech of the place.
It has to face the men of the time and to meet
The women of the time. It has to think about war
And it has to find what will suffice. It has
To construct a new stage. It has to be on that stage   10
And, like an insatiable actor, slowly and
With meditation, speak words that in the ear,
In the delicatest ear of the mind, repeat,
Exactly, that which it wants to hear, at the sound
Of which, an invisible audience listens,   15
Not to the play, but to itself, expressed
In an emotion as of two people, as of two
Emotions becoming one. The actor is
A metaphysician in the dark, twanging
An instrument, twanging a wiry string that gives   20
Sounds passing through sudden rightnesses, wholly
Containing the mind, below which it cannot descend,
Beyond which it has no will to rise.
                                        It must
Be the finding of a satisfaction, and may
Be of a man skating, a woman dancing, a woman   25
Combing. The poem of the act of the mind.

                                   1940

VARIATIONS ON A SUMMER DAY

I

Say of the gulls that they are flying
In light blue air over dark blue sea.

II

A music more than a breath, but less
Than the wind, sub-music like sub-speech,
A repetition of unconscious things,   5
Letters of rock[1] and water, words
Of the visible elements and of ours.

III

The rocks of the cliffs are the heads of dogs
That turn into fishes and leap
Into the sea.   10

---

[1] Compare this and succeeding images of rock with the poet's "rock of reality" discussed in the Introduction.

IV

Star over Monhegan,[2] Atlantic star,
Lantern without a bearer, you drift,
You, too, are drifting, in spite of your course;
Unless in the darkness, brightly-crowned,
You are the will, if there is a will,   15
Or the portent of a will that was,
One of the portents of the will that was.

V

The leaves of the sea are shaken and shaken.
There was a tree that was a father,
We sat beneath it and sang our songs.   20

VI

It is cold to be forever young,
To come to tragic shores and flow,
In sapphire, round the sun-bleached stones,
Being, for old men, time of their time.

VII

One sparrow is worth a thousand gulls,   25
When it sings. The gull sits on chimney-tops.
He mocks the guinea, challenges
The crow, inciting various modes.
The sparrow requites one, without intent.

VIII

An exercise in viewing the world.   30
On the motive! But one looks at the sea
As one improvises, on the piano.[3]

IX

This cloudy world, by aid of land and sea,
Night and day, wind and quiet, produces
More nights, more days, more clouds, more worlds.   35

X

To change nature, not merely to change ideas,
To escape from the body, so to feel
Those feelings that the body balks,
The feelings of the natures round us here:
As a boat feels when it cuts blue water.   40

[2] An island off the coast of Maine.
[3] For comment on this improvisation, see the Introduction.

XI

Now, the timothy at Pemaquid [4]
That rolled in heat is silver-tipped
And cold. The moon follows the sun like a French
Translation of a Russian poet.

XII

Everywhere the spruce trees bury soldiers: 45
Hugh March,[5] a sergeant, a redcoat, killed,
With his men, beyond the barbican.[6]
Everywhere spruce trees bury spruce trees.

XIII

Cover the sea with the sand rose. Fill
The sky with the radiantiana[7]   50
Of spray. Let all the salt be gone.

XIV

Words add to the senses. The words for the dazzle
Of mica,[8] the dithering of grass,
The Arachne[9] integument of dead trees,
Are the eye grown larger, more intense.   55

XV

The last island and its inhabitant,
The two alike, distinguish blues,
Until the difference between air
And sea exists by grace alone,
In objects, as white this, white that.   60

XVI

Round and round goes the bell of the water
And round and round goes the water itself
And that which is the pitch of its motion,
The bell of its dome, the patron of sound.

[4] A small peninsula of the Maine coast, south of Damariscotta.
[5] Presumably an English soldier killed in a skirmish of the Revolutionary War. The coast of the Pemaquid Peninsula is distinguished by spruce trees.
[6] A tower at a gate or bridge of a fortification.
[7] A striking example of Stevens's power of innovation in poetic language.
[8] A mineral silicate easily separated into thin leaves, often transparent, as in isinglass.
[9] A Lydian girl who defeated Minerva, in Roman mythology, in a contest in weaving, and was changed into a spider.

XVII

Pass through the door and through the walls,   65
Those bearing balsam, its field fragrance,
Pine-figures bringing sleep to sleep.

XVIII

Low tide, flat water, sultry sun.
One observes profoundest shadows rolling.
Damariscotta[10] da da doo.   70

XIX

One boy swims under a tub, one sits
On top. Hurroo, the man-boat comes,
In a man-makenesse, neater than Naples.

XX

You could almost see the brass on her gleaming,
Not quite. The mist was to light what red   75
Is to fire. And her mainmast tapered to nothing,
Without teetering a millimeter's measure.
The beads on her rails seemed to grasp at transparence.
It was not yet the hour to be dauntlessly leaping.

                                                        1940

LES PLUS BELLES PAGES[11]

The milkman came in the moonlight and the moonlight
Was less than moonlight. Nothing exists by itself.
The moonlight seemed to.

[10] Damariscotta, a town lying near the coast of central Maine, is the point of intersection for the route to the Pemaquid Peninsula. The poet suggests here his fascination
with the sound of the name.

[11] For this poem Stevens wrote one of the few notes of his career with respect to the
meaning which he had in mind in composition. The note, printed by Samuel F. Morse
in *Opus Posthumous* (1957) follows. (Copyright 1957 by Elsie Stevens and Holly
Stevens.)

Apparently the poem means that the conjunction of milkman and moonlight
is the equivalent of the conjunction of logician and saint. What it really means
is that the inter-relation between things is what makes them fecund. Interaction is
the source of poetry. Sex is an illustration. But the principle is not confined to
the illustration. The milkman and the moonlight are an illustration. The two people, the three horses, etc., are illustrations. The principle finds its best illustration
in the interaction of our faculties or of our thoughts and emotions. Aquinas is a
classic example: a figure of great modern interest, whose special force seems to
come from the interaction of his prodigious love of God. The idea that his theology, as such, is involved is dismissed in the last line. That the example is not of

Two people, three horses, an ox
And the sun, the waves together in the sea.

The moonlight and Aquinas seemed to. He spoke,
Kept speaking, of God. I changed the word to man.   5
The automaton, in logic self-contained,
Existed by itself. Or did the saint survive?
Did several spirits assume a single shape?

Theology after breakfast sticks to the eye.

1941

LESS AND LESS HUMAN, O SAVAGE SPIRIT

If there must be a god in the house, must be,
Saying things in the rooms and on the stair,

Let him move as the sunlight moves on the floor,
Or moonlight, silently, as Plato's ghost

Or Aristotle's skeleton. Let him hang out   5
His stars on the wall. He must dwell quietly.

He must be incapable of speaking, closed,
As those are: as light, for all its motion, is;

As color, even the closest to us, is;
As shapes, though they portend us, are.   10

It is the human that is the alien,
The human that has no cousin in the moon.

It is the human that demands his speech
From beasts or from the incommunicable mass.

If there must be a god in the house, let him be one   15
That will not hear us when we speak: a coolness,

A vermilioned nothingness, any stick of the mass
Of which we are too distantly a part.

1944

---

scholarly choice is indicated by the title. But the title also means that les plus belles pages are those in which things do not stand alone, but are operative as the result of interaction, inter-relation. This is an idea of some consequence, not a casual improvisation. The inter-relation between reality and the imagination is the basis of the character of literature. The inter-relation between reality and the emotions is the basis of the vitality of literature, between reality and thought, the basis of its power.

BOUQUET OF ROSES IN SUNLIGHT

Say that it is a crude effect, black reds,
Pink yellows, orange whites, too much as they are
To be anything else in the sunlight of the room,

Too much as they are to be changed by metaphor,
Too actual, things that in being real   5
Make any imaginings of them lesser things.

And yet this effect is a consequence of the way
We feel and, therefore, is not real, except
In our sense of it, our sense of the fertilest red,

Of yellow as first color and of white,   10
In which the sense lies still, as a man lies,
Enormous, in a completing of his truth.

Our sense of these things changes and they change,
Not as in metaphor, but in our sense
Of them. So sense exceeds all metaphor.   15

It exceeds the heavy changes of the light.
It is like a flow of meanings with no speech
And of as many meanings as of men.

We are two that use these roses as we are,
In seeing them. This is what makes them seem   20
So far beyond the rhetorician's touch.

1947

THIS SOLITUDE OF CATARACTS

He never felt twice the same about the flecked river,
Which kept flowing and never the same way twice, flowing

Through many places, as if it stood still in one,
Fixed like a lake on which the wild ducks fluttered,

Ruffling its common reflections, thought-like Monadnocks.[1]   5
There seemed to be an apostrophe that was not spoken.

There was so much that was real that was not real at all.
He wanted to feel the same way over and over.

[1] From Mount Monadnock, in southwestern New Hampshire.

He wanted the river to go on flowing the same way,
To keep on flowing. He wanted to walk beside it, 10

Under the buttonwoods, beneath a moon nailed fast.
He wanted his heart to stop beating and his mind to rest

In a permanent realization, without any wild ducks
Or mountains that were not mountains, just to know how it would be,

Just to know how it would feel, released from destruction, 15
To be a bronze man breathing under archaic lapis,

Without the oscillations of planetary pass-pass,
Breathing his bronzen breath at the azury centre of time.

1948

THINGS OF AUGUST

I

These locusts by day, these crickets by night
Are the instruments on which to play
Of an old and disused ambit of the soul
Or of a new aspect, bright in discovery—

A disused ambit of the spirit's way, 5
The sort of thing that August crooners sing,
By a pure fountain, that was a ghost, and is,
Under the sun-slides of a sloping mountain;

Or else a new aspect, say the spirit's sex,
Its attitudes, its answers to attitudes 10
And the sex of its voices, as the voice of one
Meets nakedly another's naked voice.

Nothing is lost, loud locusts. No note fails.
These sounds are long in the living of the ear.
The honky-tonk out of the somnolent grasses 15
Is a memorizing, a trying out, to keep.

II

We make, although inside an egg,
Variations on the words spread sail.

The morning-glories grow in the egg.
It is full of the myrrh and camphor of summer 20

And Adirondack glittering. The cat hawks it
And the hawk cats it and we say spread sail,

Spread sail, we say spread white, spread way.
The shell is a shore. The egg of the sea

And the egg of the sky are in shells, in walls, in skins   25
And the egg of the earth lies deep within an egg.

Spread outward. Crack the round dome. Break through.
Have liberty not as the air within a grave

Or down a well. Breathe freedom, oh, my native,
In the space of horizons that neither love nor hate.   30

III

High poetry and low:
Experience in perihelion[1]
Or in the penumbra[2] of summer night—

The solemn sentences,
Like interior intonations,   35
The speech of truth in its true solitude,
A nature that is created in what it says,
The peace of the last intelligence;
Or the same thing without desire,
He that in this intelligence   40
Mistakes it for a world of objects,
Which, being green and blue, appease him,
By chance, or happy chance, or happiness,
According to his thought, in the Mediterranean
Of the quiet of the middle of the night,   45
With the broken statues standing on the shore.

IV

The sad smell of the lilacs—one remembered it,
Not as the fragrance of Persephone,[3]
Nor of a widow Dooley,[4]
But as of an exhumation returned to earth,   50

---

[1] The point of the path of a celestial body which is nearest the sun.

[2] The space of partial illumination, as in an eclipse, between the umbra, or perfect shadow, on all sides, and the full light.

[3] In Greek mythology the daughter of Zeus and Demeter, wife of Hades and queen of the infernal regions. The fragrance of the lilac in our time has no relation to myth of any sort, but merely to the rich earth from which it comes. This is the sense of *not* and *nor*.

[4] Presumably of no importance as a name, but suggestive merely of an idle, superficial, and perhaps predatory woman of our contemporary culture. The theme of the lilac here suggests another poem of the century in which it receives a quite different use: T. S. Eliot's "Portrait of a Lady." No assertion may be made, however, that Stevens has Eliot's poem in mind here.

The rich earth, of its own self made rich,
Fertile of its own leaves and days and wars,
Of its brown wheat rapturous in the wind,
The nature of its women in the air,

The stern voices of its necessitous men,   55
This chorus as of those that wanted to live.
The sentiment of the fatal is a part
Of filial love. Or is it the element,

An approximation of an element,
A little thing to think of on Sunday walks,   60
Something not to be mentioned to Mrs. Dooley,
An arrogant dagger darting its arrogance,

In the parent's hand, perhaps parental love?
One wished that there had been a season,
Longer and later, in which the lilacs opened   65
And spread about them a warmer, rosier odor.

V

We'll give the week-end to wisdom, to Weisheit,[5] the rabbi,
Lucidity of his city, joy of his nation,
The state of circumstance.

The thinker as reader reads what has been written.   70
He wears the words he reads to look upon
Within his being,

A crown within him of crispest diamonds,
A reddened garment falling to his feet,
A hand of light to turn the page,   75

A finger with a ring to guide his eye
From line to line, as we lie on the grass and listen
To that which has no speech,

The voluble intentions of the symbols,
The ghostly celebrations of the picnic,   80
The secretions of insight.

VI

The world images for the beholder.
He is born the blank mechanic of the mountains,

The blank frere of fields, their matin laborer.
He is the possessed of sense not the possessor.   85

[5] A German term meaning *wisdom* which Stevens often uses in a symbolic sense as *professional wisdom* or *doctrine*, as though to satirize the notion that doctrine alone may save the human being from meaninglessness. The accompanying symbol in *rabbi* here recalls his like usage elsewhere: *rabbi* as the *professional* theologian and the maker of doctrine, and dogma.

He does not change the sea from crumpled tinfoil
To chromatic crawler. But it is changed.

He does not raise the rousing of fresh light
On the still, black-slatted eastward shutters.

The woman is chosen but not by him,   90
Among the endlessly emerging accords.

The world? The inhuman as human? That which thinks not,
Feels not, resembling thought, resembling feeling?

It habituates him to the invisible,
By its faculty of the exceptional,   95

The faculty of ellipses and deviations,
In which he exists but never as himself.

VII

He turned from the tower to the house,
From the spun sky and the high and deadly view,
To the novels on the table,   100
The geraniums on the sill.

He could understand the things at home.
And being up high had helped him when up high,
As if on a taller tower
He would be certain to see   105

That, in the shadowless atmosphere,
The knowledge of things lay round but unperceived:
The height was not quite proper;
The position was wrong.

It was curious to have to descend   110
And, seated in the nature of his chair,
To feel the satisfactions
Of that transparent air.

VIII

When was it that the particles became
The whole man, that tempers and beliefs became   115
Temper and belief and that differences lost
Difference and were one? It had to be
In the presence of a solitude of the self,
An expanse and the abstraction of an expanse,
A zone of time without the ticking of clocks,   120
A color that moved us with forgetfulness.
When was it that we heard the voice of union?

Was it as we sat in the park and the archaic form
Of a woman with a cloud on her shoulder rose

Against the trees and then against the sky   125
And the sense of the archaic touched us at once
In a movement of the outlines of similarity?
We resembled one another at the sight.
The forgetful color of the autumn day
Was full of these archaic forms, giants   130
Of sense, evoking one thing in many men,
Evoking an archaic space, vanishing
In the space, leaving an outline of the size
Of the impersonal person, the wanderer,
The father, the ancestor, the bearded peer,   135
The total of human shadows bright as glass.

IX

A new text of the world,
A scribble of fret and fear and fate,
From a bravura of the mind,
A courage of the eye,   140
In which, for all the breathings
From the edge of night,
And for all the white voices
That were rosen once,

The meanings are our own—   145
It is a text that we shall be needing,
To be the footing of noon,
The pillar of midnight,

That comes from ourselves, neither from knowing
Nor not knowing, yet free from question,   150
Because we wanted it so
And it had to be,

A text of intelligent men
At the centre of the unintelligible,
As in a hermitage, for us to think,   155
Writing and reading the rigid inscription.

X

The mornings grow silent, the never-tiring wonder.
The trees are reappearing in poverty.

Without rain, there is the sadness of rain
And an air of lateness. The moon is a tricorn   160

Waved in pale adieu. The rex Impolitor[6]
Will come stamping here, the ruler of less than men,

[6] In Latin, literally "the uncouth king." Stevens clearly intends a personification: Death.

In less than nature. He is not here yet.
Here the adult one is still banded with fulgor,

Is still warm with the love with which she came,   165
Still touches solemnly with what she was

And willed. She has given too much, but not enough.
She is exhausted and a little old.

1949

THE ROCK

SEVENTY YEARS LATER

It is an illusion that we were ever alive,
Lived in the houses of mothers, arranged ourselves
By our own motions in a freedom of air.

Regard the freedom of seventy years ago.
It is no longer air. The houses still stand,   5
Though they are rigid in rigid emptiness.

Even our shadows, their shadows, no longer remain.
The lives these lived in the mind are at an end.
They never were . . . The sounds of the guitar

Were not and are not. Absurd. The words spoken   10
Were not and are not. It is not to be believed.
The meeting at noon at the edge of the field seems like

An invention, an embrace between one desperate clod
And another in a fantastic consciousness,
In a queer assertion of humanity: 15

A theorem proposed between the two—
Two figures in a nature of the sun,
In the sun's design of its own happiness,

As if nothingness contained a métier,
A vital assumption, an impermanence   20
In its permanent cold, an illusion so desired

That the green leaves came and covered the high rock,
That the lilacs came and bloomed, like a blindness cleaned,
Exclaiming bright sight, as it was satisfied,

In a birth of sight. The blooming and the musk   25
Were being alive, an incessant being alive,
A particular of being, that gross universe.

II. THE POEM AS ICON[1]

It is not enough to cover the rock with leaves.
We must be cured of it by a cure of the ground
Or a cure of ourselves, that is equal to a cure   30

Of the ground, a cure beyond forgetfulness.
And yet the leaves, if they broke into bud,
If they broke into bloom, if they bore fruit,

And if we ate the incipient colorings
Of their fresh culls might be a cure of the ground.   35
The fiction of the leaves is the icon

Of the poem, the figuration of blessedness,
And the icon is the man. The pearled chaplet of spring,
The magnum wreath of summer, time's autumn snood,

Its copy of the sun, these cover the rock.   40
These leaves are the poem, the icon and the man.
These are a cure of the ground and of ourselves,

In the predicate that there is nothing else.
They bud and bloom and bear their fruit without change.
They are more than leaves that cover the barren rock   45

They bud the whitest eye, the pallidest sprout,
New senses in the engenderings of sense,
The desire to be at the end of distances,

The body quickened and the mind in root.
They bloom as a man loves, as he lives in love.   50
They bear their fruit so that the year is known,

As if its understanding was brown skin,
The honey in its pulp, the final found,
The plenty of the year and of the world.

In this plenty, the poem makes meanings of the rock,   55
Of such mixed motion and such imagery
That its barrenness becomes a thousand things

And so exists no more. This is the cure
Of leaves and of the ground and of ourselves.
His words are both the icon and the man.   60

---

1 From the Greek *eikōn*, an image or representation. In the Eastern Orthodox Church, the term designates an image of Christ, the Virgin Mary, or a saint, usually in the form of a picture. Stevens' regard for the making of poetry as the making of an icon accords with his view of poetry as salvation. (See the Introduction preceding this selection of Stevens' poems.)

III. FORMS OF THE ROCK IN A NIGHT-HYMN

The rock is the gray particular of man's life,
The stone from which he rises, up—and—ho,
The step to the bleaker depths of his descents . . .

The rock is the stern particular of the air,
The mirror of the planets, one by one,   65
But through man's eye, their silent rhapsodist,

Turquoise the rock, at odious evening bright
With redness that sticks fast to evil dreams;
The difficult rightness of half-risen day.

The rock is the habitation of the whole,   70
Its strength and measure, that which is near, point A
In a perspective that begins again

At B: the origin of the mango's rind.
It is the rock where tranquil must adduce
Its tranquil self, the main of things, the mind,   75

The starting point of the human and the end,
That in which space itself is contained, the gate
To the enclosure, day, the things illumined

By day, night and that which night illumines,
Night and its midnight-minting fragrances,   80
Night's hymn of the rock, as in a vivid sleep.

                                   1950

FINAL SOLILOQUY OF THE INTERIOR PARAMOUR

Light the first light of evening, as in a room
In which we rest and, for small reason, think
The world imagined is the ultimate good.

This is, therefore, the intensest rendezvous.
It is in that thought that we collect ourselves,   5
Out of all the indifferences, into one thing:

Within a single thing, a single shawl
Wrapped tightly round us, since we are poor, a warmth,
A light, a power, the miraculous influence.

Here, now, we forget each other and ourselves.   10
We feel the obscurity of an order, a whole,
A knowledge, that which arranged the rendezvous.

Within its vital boundary, in the mind.
We say God and the imagination are one . . .
How high that highest candle lights the dark.   15

Out of this same light, out of the central mind,
We make a dwelling in the evening air,
In which being there together is enough.

1951

THE GREEN PLANT

Silence is a shape that has passed.
Otu-bre's lion-roses have turned to paper
And the shadows of the trees
Are like wrecked umbrellas.

The effete vocabulary of summer   5
No longer says anything.
The brown at the bottom of red
The orange far down in yellow,

Are falsifications from a sun
In a mirror, without heat,   10
In a constant secondariness,
A turning down toward finality—

Except that a green plant glares, as you look
At the legend of the maroon and olive forest,
Glares, outside of the legend, with the barbarous green   15
Of the harsh reality of which it is part.

1952

TO AN OLD PHILOSOPHER[1] IN ROME

On the threshold of heaven, the figures in the street
Become the figures of heaven, the majestic movement
Of men growing small in the distances of space,

"The Green Plant" and the following poem, "To an Old Philosopher in Rome," are from *The Collected Poems of Wallace Stevens*, by permission of Alfred A. Knopf, Inc. Copyright 1952 by Wallace Stevens.

[1] In tribute to George Santayana (1863-1952), Spanish-American philosopher, poet, and novelist, one-time professor at Harvard. As an undergraduate at Harvard, Stevens came under his influence. (See the Introduction.) In his final illness Santayana was cared for by nuns in a convent in Rome, where he died in September 1952. Stevens intends chiefly to praise here the power of Santayana as the fashioner of a structure, "a total edifice" of his life.

Singing, with smaller and still smaller sound,
Unintelligible absolution and an end—   5

The threshold, Rome, and that more merciful Rome
Beyond, the two alike in the make of the mind.
It is as if in a human dignity
Two parallels become one, a perspective, of which
Men are part both in the inch and in the mile.   10

How easily the blown banners change to wings . . .
Things dark on the horizons of perception,
Become accompaniments of fortune, but
Of the fortune of the spirit, beyond the eye,
Not of its sphere, and yet not far beyond,   15

The human end in the spirit's greatest reach,
The extreme of the known in the presence of the extreme
Of the unknown. The newsboys' muttering
Becomes another murmuring; the smell
Of medicine, a fragrantness not to be spoiled . . .   20

The bed, the books, the chair, the moving nuns,
The candle as it evades the sight, these are
The sources of happiness in the shape of Rome,
A shape within the ancient circles of shapes,
And these beneath the shadow of a shape   25

In a confusion on bed and books, a portent
On the chair, a moving transparence on the nuns,
A light on the candle tearing against the wick
To join a hovering excellence, to escape
From fire and be part only of that of which   30

Fire is the symbol: the celestial possible.
Speak to your pillow as if it was yourself.
Be orator but with an accurate tongue
And without eloquence, O, half-asleep,
Of the pity that is the memorial of this room,   35

So that we feel, in this illumined large,
The veritable small, so that each of us
Beholds himself in you, and hears his voice
In yours, master and commiserable man,
Intent on your particles of nether-do,   40

Your dozing in the depths of wakefulness,
In the warmth of your bed, at the edge of your chair, alive
Yet living in two worlds, impenitent
As to one, and, as to one, most penitent,
Impatient for the grandeur that you need   45

In so much misery; and yet finding it
Only in misery, the afflatus of ruin,

Profound poetry of the poor and of the dead,
As in the last drop of the deepest blood,
As it falls from the heart and lies there to be seen,   50

Even as the blood of an empire, it might be,
For a citizen of heaven though still of Rome.
It is poverty's speech that seeks us out the most.
It is older than the oldest speech of Rome.
This is the tragic accent of the scene.   55

And you—it is you that speak it, without speech,
The loftiest syllables among loftiest things,
The one invulnerable man among
Crude captains, the naked majesty, if you like,
Of bird-nest arches and of rain-stained-vaults.   60

The sounds drift in. The buildings are remembered.
The life of the city never lets go, nor do you
Ever want it to. It is part of the life in your room.
Its domes are the architecture of your bed.
The bells keep on repeating solemn names   65

In choruses and choirs of choruses,
Unwilling that mercy should be a mystery
Of silence, that any solitude of sense
Should give you more than their peculiar chords
And reverberations clinging to whisper still.   70

It is a kind of total grandeur at the end,
With every visible thing enlarged and yet
No more than a bed, a chair and moving nuns,
The immensest theatre, the pillared porch
The book and candle in your ambered room,   75

Total grandeur of a total edifice,
Chosen by an inquisitor of structures
For himself. He stops upon this threshold,
As if the design of all his words takes form
And frame from thinking and is realized.   80

1952

FROM THE "ADAGIA"[1]

To GIVE a sense of the freshness or vividness of life is a valid purpose for poetry. A didactic purpose justifies itself in the mind of the teacher; a philosophical purpose justifies itself in the mind of the philosopher. It is not that one purpose is as justifiable as another but that some purposes are pure, others impure. Seek those purposes that are purely the purposes of the pure poet.

Merit in poets is as boring as merit in people.

To a large extent, the problems of poets are the problems of painters, and poets must often turn to the literature of painting for a discussion of their own problems.

Weather is a sense of nature. Poetry is a sense.

Politics is the struggle for existence.

In poetry, you must love the words, the ideas and the images and rhythms with all your capacity to love anything at all.

Sentimentality is a failure of feeling.

Wine and music are not good until afternoon. But poetry is like prayer in that it is most effective in solitude and in the times of solitude as, for example, in the earliest morning.

Intolerance respecting other people's religion is toleration itself in comparison with intolerance respecting other people's art.

It is the explanations of things what we make to ourselves that disclose our character: The subjects of one's poems are the symbols of one's self or of one of one's selves.

War is the periodical failure of politics.

Poetry is an effort of a dissatisfied man to find satisfaction through words, occasionally of the dissatisfied thinker to find satisfaction through his emotions.

Poetry is the scholar's art.

When one is young everything is physical; when one is old everything is psychic.

The gold dome of things is the perfected spirit.

Aristotle is a skeleton.[2]

[1] A name given by Stevens to a collection of aphorisms of his own devising contained in a manuscript notebook found among his papers at the time of his death, and published by Samuel F. Morse in *Opus Posthumous* (1957).

[2] Compare the use of "skeletons" in "Stanzas for 'The Man with the Blue Guitar.'" Stevens' usage refers to both the makers and the embodiments of ideas of a dead past.

The body is the great poem.[3]

The world is myself. Life is myself.[4]

The poet is a god, or, the young poet is a god. The old poet is a tramp.

Every poem is a poem within a poem: the poem of the idea within the poem of the words.

Nothing could be more inappropriate to American literature than its English source since the Americans are not British in sensibility.

The essential fault of surrealism is that it invents without discovering. To make a clam play an accordion is to invent not to discover. The observation of the unconscious, so far as it can be observed, should reveal things of which we have previously been unconscious, not the familiar things of which we have been conscious plus imagination.

Poetry is (and should be) for the poet a source of pleasure and satisfaction, not a source of honors.

Gaiety in poetry is a precious characteristic but it should be a characteristic of diction.[5]

[3] Readers of Whitman will recognize here a strong affinity with the major theme of "Song of Myself," even though Stevens does not regard the body as a symbol of spirit.

[4] Compare the transcendental theory of the self set forth by Emerson in *Nature* and "Self Reliance."

[5] Here and throughout the "Adagia" readers of Stevens who know the Pennsylvania Dutch country of his origin will sense a particular appropriateness in the form which he gives to these reflections. A strong German-Dutch fondness for proverbs marks all of them. See Michael Lafferty, "Wallace Stevens: A Man of Two Worlds," *Historical Review of Berks County* (Reading, Pennsylvania), XXIV, No. 4 (1959), p. 112. Mr. Lafferty's article is indispensable to students of Stevens for biographical data. The biographical summary at the conclusion of this volume is indebted to Mr. Lafferty's collection of facts pertaining to the life of Stevens prior to his residence in Hartford.

Reading Suggestions

The published work of Wallace Stevens is contained in the following authorized editions: *The Necessary Angel* (1951); *The Collected Poems of Wallace Stevens* (1955); *Opus Posthumous*, edited by Samuel French Morse (1957). An inexpensive paperback selection from the poems, edited with an introduction by Samuel French Morse, has been issued (Vintage Books).

Six studies of book length presenting a critical appraisal of various aspects of the poetry have appeared: John J. Enck, *Wallace Stevens: Images and Judgments* (1964); Daniel Fuchs, *The Comic Spirit of Wallace Stevens* (1963); Frank Kermode, *Wallace Stevens* (1960); William V. O'Connor, *The Shaping Spirit: A Study of Wallace Stevens* (1950); Robert Pack, *Wallace Stevens: An Approach to His Poetry and Thought* (1958); Henry W. Wells, *Introduction to Wallace Stevens* (1964). Roy Harvey Pearce's *The Continuity of American Poetry* (1961) contains a particularly skillful and perceptive judgment of the place of Stevens in American literature of the twentieth century. A brief essay by William Y. Tindall, *Wallace Stevens*, No. 11, University of Minnesota Pamphlets on American Writers (1961), is useful.

Studies in the form of articles are most numerous. The following have been selected with attention to the scope of the critical view presented: Marius Bewley, "The Poetry of Wallace Stevens," *Partisan Review* (September 1949); Randall Jarrell, "Reflections on Wallace Stevens," *Partisan Review* (May–June 1951); Louis L. Martz, "Wallace Stevens: 'The World as Meditation,'" *Literature and Belief*, English Institute Essays, 1957 (1958); Ralph J. Mills, Jr., "Wallace Stevens: The Image of the Rock," *Accent* (Spring 1958); Roy H. Pearce, "Wallace Stevens: The Life of Imagination," *Publications of the Modern Language Association* (September 1951); Joseph N. Riddel, "Wallace Stevens' 'Visibility of Thought,'" *Publications of the Modern Language Association* (September 1962). A critical biography is being prepared by Samuel French Morse; and the publication of the private correspondence is anticipated.

Biography

Wallace Stevens was born in the so-called "Dutch" country of Pennsylvania in the city of Reading on October 2, 1879. His father, Garrett B. Stevens, was of Holland Dutch ancestry, a rugged man who left the family farm in Bucks County to become a successful attorney in Reading, where he practiced at the bar until his death in 1911. His mother, Mary Catherine Zeller Stevens, was of equally hardy origins, her forebears having been vigorous German settlers of the area. There were five children, all of whom apparently inherited and enjoyed the strong individuality of the parents, abundant health, and a certain sturdiness of manner which distinguished the family in Reading and throughout the surrounding countryside. Throughout his life Stevens, the poet, thought of his native region of Pennsylvania as home. Its people remained in his memory as characteristically and vigorously American.

In 1897 Stevens graduated from the Reading Boys' High School, already committed to his father's profession in his resolve to prepare for a career in law. He proceeded to Harvard in the same year, entering as a special student in prospect of entering law school after a three-year course of study in the liberal arts. An early interest from his high school years in Reading led him to try his hand again at writing. Using various pseudonyms, he became a contributor to the undergraduate literary journal *The Harvard Advocate*. He became president of the publication in 1900, shortly before his departure for New York.

For a time Stevens was employed as a reporter by the *New York Herald Tribune* and later by the magazine *The World's Work*. But his first intention to enter legal training soon claimed his purpose. He entered the New York Law School in the fall of 1901, and graduated with the degree of Bachelor of Laws in June 1903. He was admitted to the New York bar in 1904, and immediately entered the bond claim field with the American Bonding Company, a special area of finance in which he was to become an expert. He married Elsie Viola Kachel of Reading in 1909, and the two returned to New York for a residence of seven years.

During this period of early marriage Stevens and his wife were living near Greenwich Village, where college friends of Stevens were writing and painting. Among these artists of the avant garde were Walter Arensberg, Pitts Sandborn, and Witter Bynner, all of whom were in their separate ways to reach distinction in the American twentieth-century renaissance of the arts. Stevens had been writing verse in New York sporadically since the beginning of his legal practice. But by 1914 he was working in earnest. In that year, at the age of thirty-five, he won a prize of $100 offered by *Poetry* magazine for poems published in a special war number. He had won the admiration of the famous editor of *Poetry*, Harriet Monroe; and it was Miss Monroe's interest and that of the anthologist and critic Alfred Kreymborg which no doubt assured the publication of many of his early poems (later to appear in his first collected work, *Harmonium,* in 1923) and his ventures in the writing of verse drama. His plays, *Three Travelers Watch a Sunrise* (published in *Poetry* in 1916) and *Carlos among the Candles* (produced by the Wisconsin Players in the season of 1917-1918) he did not regard as successful; and he abandoned writing in dramatic form.

In 1916 Stevens became a member of the legal staff of the Hartford Accident and Indemnity Company. He removed to Hartford, and founded the company's claim department, which he headed until his death almost forty years later. A daughter Holly was born in Hartford in August 1924.

There is little yet known of an artist's distinctive life on the part of this quiet and efficient business executive in Hartford. After the publication of *Harmonium* in 1923 he entered a long period of literary silence. But within his solitude he continued to answer the claims of poetry, and very probably he read much during the twelve years that followed this first volume. Stevens re-emerged as a poet of full and mature power in 1936 with *Ideas of Order.* Only a year before this volume, he had been elected a vice-president of the Hartford Accident and Indemnity Company. No doubt his return to poetry was assured by the consolidation of his position in the world of business. In the twenty succeeding years left to him, his publication was copious: *Owl's Clover* in 1936; *The Man with the Blue Guitar* in the year following; *Parts of a World* and *Notes toward a Supreme Fiction* in 1942; *Transport to Summer* in 1947; and *The Auroras of Autumn* in 1950. During the 1940's he added to his literary activities by lecturing on poetic theory. Throughout the long span of the Hartford years he traveled occasionally. He knew Florida from vacation trips, and he had been to Havana; at times he traveled in summer holidays in New York state and in New England. He never went to Europe. He enjoyed his friends; but these were often people of interests other than the arts. His life was a quiet and thoroughly disciplined one; his claims for attention as a poet were modest in the extreme.

By the mid-1940's Stevens' reputation as one of the master poets in the language was fully assured. He was elected to the National Institute of Arts and Letters in 1946; he received the National Book Award and the Bollingen Award in 1950; in 1955 he was awarded the Pulitzer Prize for poetry. He was honored by degrees from Bard, Columbia, Harvard, Mount Holyoke, Wesleyan, and Yale, the last of these from Yale having been conferred upon him less than two months before his death in Hartford on August 2, 1955.

SCOTT FITZGERALD ✤
1896-1940

Introduction

"I didn't have the two top things: great animal magnetism or money," Fitzgerald wrote in his *Note-Books*. "I had the two second things, though: good looks and intelligence." This is scarcely an order of virtues to impress the early Church Fathers, or the old Romans for that matter. One of a hundred-odd entries under the loose heading of "Observations," this is presumably of more concern to the biographer than to the critic. But Fitzgerald's life is so intricately bound up in his writings one cannot help speculating on the significance of such a summing up of desiderata by a creative artist. The only item that seems immediately relevant to the needs of an author, "intelligence," is placed last on his list. And it is a serious question of just how much and what kind of intelligence Fitzgerald had. He certainly did not have the balanced mind of James, the erudition of Eliot, or the intellectuality of Stevens. What he had was a clever alertness for picking up the revealing details on the surface of life, and a marked sensitivity to people and the human situation in general that enabled him to perceive and render meanings even when he did not understand them rationally.

Two of the top things on his list, "good looks" and "animal magnetism," were definite hindrances to his literary work. The latter quality he disclaimed, but if he meant by it personal charm he had it in abundance. His attractive appearance and personality led him into a web of superficial social relations that dissipated his energies and turned his talents away from serious authorship. The final item, "money," is the ambivalent center of his whole life and artistic career. Financial security that frees the author from the market place is one thing. But Fitzgerald's obsession with lack of money was another. It led him to envy the rich, then to consume himself writing for high pay, so he could make and spend money as lavishly as they. He kept persuading himself that he could ride two horses at once, one a hack and the other Pegasus, until he had a fatal crack-up in the end. Yet his fascination with wealth became the most fruitful subject of his fictions. When he gained the needed perspective and could see simultaneously what it did *to* people as well as *for* them, he discovered his one great theme.

I

In his best fictions Fitzgerald renders deeply felt experiences with such immediacy as to make them seem personal, yet at the same time with a quality of the universal about them achieved by objectifying his materials. But writing so close to autobiography had its dangers. When not transmuted by the imagination, his writings are mere transcripts from his own life. These are at best "period pieces," of considerable interest in the twenties because they seemed to mirror the age, especially in its jazziest aspects, but of faded interest today for the very reason of their former timeliness. The curve of his contemporary popularity proves how superficial his success was. The two novels that shot him to fame, *This Side of Paradise* (1920) and *The Beautiful and Damned* (1922), were based all too literally on his prep school and college days and on the flashy years of his early married life in New York. The two volumes of short stories published in the same years, *Flappers and Philosophers* and *Tales of the Jazz Age*, drew directly on episodes from his own life and that of his friends. This astonishing performance between the ages of twenty-four and twenty-six made Fitzgerald the darling of the hour, the spokesman of a postwar generation disillusioned and hell-bent for pleasure. Though the value of these early fictions as serious literary art is open to question, they are not without merit compared to the admitted hackwork that poured from his pen during the same period and later. But his permanent achievement is small: *The Great Gatsby* (1925) and a few superb stories, products of those rare occasions when the artist brought the personality under control.

The relation of autobiography to fiction in Fitzgerald's writings at once calls to mind the similar problem in the works of a slightly younger contemporary who was soon to eclipse him, if not in popularity at least in winning high critical acclaim at the same time that he reached a fairly wide audience. The fictions of Hemingway parallel even more closely the external experiences of their author, but in the best ones he managed to keep free of emotional involvement with his characters. He achieved this artistic distance by being in command of his creative techniques from the start. So the internal lives of his heroes are projections of how he *might* have been affected by all that happened to him in the cataclysmic decade of 1914-1924 if he had really been a Nick Adams, Jake Barnes, or Lieutenant Henry. That their outer lives follow segments of his own enabled him to endow time and place, situation and event, with authentic immediacy. That they were not transcriptions of the actual Hemingway but transmutations, emotionally and spiritually, is proved by the objectivity with which he could record their long night journeys in dramatically controlled stories. They were successive masks that the artist could put on at will to evaluate the potentialities of his experiences, and so they differ internally from one another as well as from their author. Hemingway's disciplined techniques in language, structure, and point of view for rendering all this are the precise measure of his success as a creator.

With Fitzgerald the situation was almost exactly opposite, nearer to Thomas Wolfe in the relation of his life to his work. Change as he would the outer careers of his heroes, they were all Fitzgerald inside. Hopelessly entangled in their confusions, he could not understand their emotional states, could not give meaning to either their revolt from an old order or their deterioration under the disorder of modern times. So the reader rarely discovers what their stories are all about, even though the surface of their lives and their world shines with marvelous verisimilitude. When he did achieve perspective by divorcing himself from his materials, we have the fulfillment of a talent that usually floundered through failure to master the techniques of his craft.

Considering the ignorance of method as well as theory with which Fitzgerald began his career as a novelist, the progress he made in the first five years was nothing short of remarkable. A convincing explanation of how this development in technique came about has been formulated by his most able interpreter.[1] When he wrote *This Side of Paradise* in 1920 he was blindly following the novels of H. G. Wells and Compton Mackenzie, his literary idols at that time. By 1925, in *The Great Gatsby*, he had swung to an opposite tradition, represented by Conrad and James. This opposition was dramatized by a controversy that began in London in 1915 and was continued in New York during the early twenties, the crucial years for the "new novel" in America. Both Wells and James had previously stated their theories of novel writing in essays, and their differences were so fundamental they soon broke out in an open debate that ran through several exchanges, detailed and in the end bitter. Wells wanted the novel to be a literal transcription, a slice of life, in order to imitate its diversity; James a method for framing that would give the illusion of life's complexity without undue documentation. Wells advocated the loosely constructed novel, James the tight—shaped by a "center of interest" and a "controlling idea." The emphasis of both on manner and method raised the prime question of how the story is to be told. What they were arguing about turned out to be the basic split in twentieth-century fiction.

Though Wells set himself up as defender of the discursive novel, his points also were concerned with technique. His four main principles were an emphasis on character rather than plot; unity to be achieved through mood, with only the loosest relevancy of events; the use of author-

[1] See the entry under James Miller in Reading Suggestions, a study that has been useful in the following pages.

intrusion so the book would be a reflection of his personality; and a clearly
stated purpose, since the novel should be a vehicle for social, economic,
and political ideas. It was this kind of fiction, dominant in 1915, that
James attacked as "the novel of saturation." His term for the kind of fiction
he championed was "the novel of selection." As examples of the former
school he chose for analysis the novels of Mackenzie and those of his antagonist Wells; for the latter his exemplar was Conrad (and by implication
himself).

It is no accident that these are exactly the models followed by Fitzgerald at the beginning and end of his one great period of development.
Just as his letters record his enthusiastic reading of the fiction of these authors, so his own first three novels show clearly enough by their method his
shift of allegiance. There is also evidence that he was acquainted with the
debate on theory in London and its echo in New York. Especially pertinent
to his purposes was a symposium, "The Novel of Tomorrow," published in
a special issue of the *New Republic* in April 1922. Though these essays
leaned heavily on the side of the saturation school, typified in America by
the work of novelists like Sinclair Lewis and Dreiser, there was a growing
concern on the part of younger writers for form and method. The Jamesian side was ably represented by Willa Cather's essay calling for selection
rather than amplitude and by a review of Percy Lubbock's *The Craft of Fiction,* which emphasized the technique of point of view as all important. In
the three years between the appearance of this symposium and the publication of *The Great Gatsby* Fitzgerald made a clean break with the older
method of novel writing in favor of the new.

When *This Side of Paradise* appeared in 1920, in spite of its immediate
popular success a few critics pointed out not only that it was imitative but
that it imitated an inferior model, Mackenzie's *Sinister Street.* This was the
very novel James had singled out as the epitome of the "saturation" school
he disapproved of, characterizing it as "a boy's experience . . . given us for
its face value simply, . . . from beginning to end the remembered and reported thing, that thing alone"; its fatal weakness, he found, was that it
failed "to converge to an idea." This description makes an exact critique
of Fitzgerald's first novel, published five years later. He denied the charge
of imitation, even though the novel in question was named as his hero's
favorite, saying that his book was modeled instead on his own life and that
of friends. But this misses the point altogether, since what he had borrowed
from discursive novels, in general and in particular, was their manner
rather than their matter. The technique of the slice-of-life school encouraged just such autobiographical unloading, a sequence of loosely related
events with no unifying plan other than a chronicle of the hero's life and
no apparent purpose other than to set down his experiences for their own
sake.

This Side of Paradise is a transcript of episodes from the life of Fitzgerald during school, college, and army years. They are slightly fictionalized under the character of Amory Blaine, so as to suggest a representative "story of the youth of our generation," according to the author's claim. Actually, it is such a ragbag of autobiographical fragments that it includes even poems and sketches written at Princeton before the novel was ever conceived, so that one reviewer called the book "the collected works of F. Scott Fitzgerald." The Wellsian formula for novel writing is followed not only in the looseness of structure but also in the tacking on at the end a discussion of social problems in a desperate effort to find a theme. But the hero's turn to reform, in a sudden impulse to use his talents for other than selfish purposes, is totally unconvincing. The questioning of American economic and political institutions is sophomoric. And the revolt against the sexual code, the most timely topic, is negatived by the hero's ambivalence: as soon as it threatens to go beyond the promiscuous kiss, he retreats in fastidious horror. A novel cannot be made a vehicle of ideas if all its ideas are banal or blurred. The very vagueness of this rebellion is what captured the public fancy in the twenties. But Edmund Wilson, Fitzgerald's close friend, called this its chief weakness: "it is not really *about* anything; intellectually it amounts to little more than a gesture—a gesture of indefinite revolt." In conclusion he found the one note of praise possible, that though it has almost every fault a novel can have it does not commit the unpardonable sin, "it does not fail to live."

Fitzgerald's second novel, *The Beautiful and Damned* (1922), is likewise flawed by immature, even bogus ideas. He had by then come under a new influence, that of H. L. Mencken, who held that the superior novel is not made by artistry but by the character of its hero. He is defined as a sensitive and intelligent man "in revolt against the inexplicable tragedy of existence"—always defeated, usually destroyed. This is the formula for Anthony Patch, who is convinced of "the meaninglessness of life." With this as his philosophy, he and his beautiful wife indulge in a purposeless round of dissipation while waiting to inherit a fortune from his grandfather. The old man cuts them off because of their debaucheries, and by the time they break his will and win their millions Gloria's beauty has faded and Anthony is broken physically and mentally. As far as the novel has a theme it is again the revolt of youth. What they are "against," by way of improvement over Blaine, is concretely embodied in the Victorianism of the grandfather. But their shallow philosophy of meaninglessness deprives their rebellion of significance. When they try to put into words what they are "for," all we get is a superficial and at times even sinister sophistication.

It is disconcerting to discover that Fitzgerald, in a letter, claimed these ideas as his own. Certainly one of his handicaps as a writer was his immaturity of mind. Near the end of his life he wrote to the same friend, Wilson, "I am still the ignoramus that you . . . wrote about at Princeton." Again, in "The Crack-Up," his astonishingly frank self-diagnosis at the age of forty, he confessed, "I wondered whether I had ever thought," then concluded, "I had done very little thinking, save within the problems of my craft." But failure to be an intellectual is chiefly a handicap to the novelist of ideas, and the important thing for Fitzgerald to learn was that this kind of fiction was simply not his metier.

Meantime, even *The Beautiful and Damned* showed some advance in the very matter of craft. Though it was still too much of a documentary novel, there was some real design in the central action, which is concerned with the relations between two characters (rather than the chronicle of an isolated hero, as in his first novel). This served as a basis for judging relevancy and so was a step toward the novel of selection. Besides, the minor technical devices he had been experimenting with—impressionistic episodes in the stream-of-consciousness manner, scenes cast in play form, strategies like the use of diaries and letters to reduce narrative amplitude— these were now being made functional to the story instead of tricks to show the author's virtuosity. What remained to be learned was the crucial relation of technique to the whole problem of plot and theme. The basic flaw in his first two novels was lack of a point of view. Without it Fitzgerald could not gain the proper distance from his autobiographical experiences so he could objectify them and understand their meaning for him. It was a failure of form—a failure to discover how the story should be told.

II

The mastery of form is a simpler matter in the short story than in the novel, and some of Fitzgerald's experiments in this genre during the years prior to *The Great Gatsby* show transitional stages in his technical development. Most of the stories were written deliberately to sell to the high-paying slick magazines, but a few were serious. They had a negative advantage to begin with, that the saturation method was forbidden by the rule of thumb that had prevailed since Poe's definition: the short story must aim at a single unified effect. Three of them can be singled out as positive steps toward his new method. "May Day" employs an unusual technique, well adapted to the difficult task of giving coherence to large blocks of material. It consists of the independent but simultaneous development of three originally unrelated lines of action, occasionally merged in apparently accidental ways. Faulkner was to use this structure with brilliant success in a full-length novel, *Light in August*. Dos Passos was to use it on an even larger scale in his trilogy, *U.S.A.*, employing numerous ingenious devices to hold his unwieldy materials together. But it takes great artistic skill to maintain suspense in a long fiction without a single continuous action. Perhaps Fitzgerald lacked the talent to translate this three-part structure into novel form, though there is a certain embryonic relation between "May Day" and *The Great Gatsby*. In that novel there are also three sto-

ries, those of Gatsby aind Nick and Daisy, but though their coming together on Long Island has the appearance of an accident, at least two of
the three pairs have relations that extend far back into the past, so that the
interweaving of their lives during one fated summer presented fewer technical problems.

"May Day," called a novelette on its publication in the *Smart Set* (July
1920), was an ideal length for him because it allowed space for full development of his several "stories" without losing reader interest through lack
of a central plot. Fitzgerald's account of its source in real life indicates the
nature of his problem: "Each of these events made a great impression upon
me. In life they were unrelated, except by the general hysteria of that spring
[1919] which inaugurated the Age of Jazz, but in my story I have tried, un-
successfully I fear, to weave them into a pattern. [It was my purpose to
render] the effect of those months in New York as they appeared to . . .
the younger generation." [2] This implies an attempt to unify these separate
lines of action merely by relating them to an atmosphere, the general disillusionment following World War I. The introductory paragraphs do just
this. They provide a setting without specifying time or place, just "a great
city" after "a war," that lends universality to the mood of purposeless excitement covering an utter confusion of values.

"May Day" is also unified thematically as well as atmospherically. It
presents an image of the ways of wealth gone astray: in the shallow gaiety
of the leisure class, the violence and stupidity of the down-and-outers, the
ineffectualness of sporadic efforts at economic reform. And the disparate
groups illustrating these several aspects are brought together with convincing casualness by the very nature of the occasion, a wild celebration in a big
city. Such a time and place make accidental meetings seem natural, as in
the drunken party at Delmonico's, the aimless processions, and the rioting.
In two instances the machinery creaks a bit under the need to make these
widely separated lines of action converge: the all too conveniently located
newspaper office where the socialite brother of one of the debutantes has
turned socialist, and the coincidence of Sterrett's tawdry affair with his mistress reaching its crisis on the same night as the other climaxes. But on the
whole the cinematic flicker of scenes and the surface motion sweep the
stories along and make them coalesce.

The nearest that "May Day" comes to having a plot is in the story of
Gordon Sterrett, but his deterioration is too rapid and his exit too melodramatic to be convincing. For all that, it is astonishingly prophetic of Fitzgerald's own "crack-up," though in real life (or at least as the artist in that
late creation) he refused to go out with either a bang or a whimper. More
important for his art than any structural originality in this story is his initiation of a major theme, the outside versus the inside of wealth. The hard
bright shallowness of the social set at the Yale dance has the excuse of

[2] Preface, *Tales of the Jazz Age*, 1922.

youth here, but it is a signpost to those who will become the beautiful and damned at maturity, and to the cushioned but empty lives of the conventional Buchanans in *The Great Gatsby*. Fitzgerald was to explore all the possibilities of this theme, though he wisely bypassed the have-nots and economic protest as outside his ken. Far too drawn personally to the glamour and luxury of the wealthy, he yet saw clearly the cruel side, the dullness, and the degraded sensibilities. Even in "May Day" he recorded not only the superficial aspects of gilded youths but the very pitch and beat of their meaningless lives. With its almost glacial impartiality toward both glitter and falsity, as one critic has said, it brings "the bitter brackish dry taste of decay fully to the mouth."

The most important advance in fictional technique made by the story is in its use of symbolism. This begins in the title itself, "May Day," which is traditionally a day of celebration for the full advent of spring, with fertility rites as well as those of rebirth. Since the outer picture is of young love, the sexual implications are restrained, with only overtones of the Bacchanal. But this is echoed in a lower key by Sterrett's involvement with Jewel Hudson, the gem of Manhattan. The Bacchanalian theme is repeated in the drunken celebration the two returned soldiers take part in. This makes a link with the second significance of the title. Since 1917, May Day has taken on a new meaning, celebration of the triumph of Communism in Russia. Now in New York, two years later, this turned into an anti-Communist riot. But the veterans back from a war to make the world safe for Democracy simply indulge in a senseless attack on a Socialist newspaper, unaware they are attacking the freedom of the press. Jobless themselves, they also make a farce out of the serious new challenge to the privilege and waste of the capitalist system. Even the revolt for sexual freedom is superficial, as the jazz bands play on.

There is no brave renewal of the world on this May Day—instead, a modern travesty on the revels of a famous midsummer night's dream. All is as meaningless as the drunken antics of "Mr. In and Mr. Out" (the one specifically autobiographical episode), satirizing the meaninglessness of modern society. As they go up on the elevator, telling the operator that heaven is their destination, they symbolize all those characters in Fitzgerald's fictions who are headed for a very secular place well this side of paradise. As they weave through the streets of New York, the signs from Delmonico's coatrooms fixed to their chests, they are the comic representatives of those who are "in" society, just as the drunken mob are "out." Of those who were once in, Sterrett is now fading out through weakness, and the debutante's Socialist brother has bailed himself out in a futile gesture. The curtain comes down on a scene outside Childs Restaurant where the revelers are sobering up. The rising sun shines on the statue in Columbus Circle as an ironic reference to the lost dream of America, on its first discovery, the dawn of a new Eden in the West. Much of this symbolism, perhaps too obvious here, reappears with striking effect in *The Great Gatsby*.

In order to achieve perspective on the problem of wealth, Fitzgerald blew it up to the proportions of extravaganza in "The Diamond as Big as the Ritz" (1922). This story shows two technical advances that point toward the triumph of his second manner. The theme is again the attraction-repulsion of great wealth, both its luxurious outside and the corruption behind it, but this time viewed simultaneously and through a single consciousness. Since the reaction is that of a character who is observer rather than principal actor, he gains distance from his material. And since the story is told in retrospect, this allows for selection of just those details that created the impact, first of awe and then of horror.

A schoolboy named Unger goes to visit his classmate on the estate his father, Braddock Washington, has built on a diamond mountain in Montana. It is literally that, so that the stones can be cut in size from a carat up to a ton or more. The trouble with such fabulous wealth is that it can be founded only on cruel exploitation, maintained only by separating oneself from humanity in order to guard against the greed of others. In this way the egotistical father has transformed himself into a moral monster, and the whole family is tainted by the same guilt. The reader is left to imply whether this differs except in degree from all craving for wealth. The action consists in the visitor's progress from being overwhelmed at what fantastic riches can buy in the way of beauty and "civilization" to his stupefaction at the evil on which it all rests. The second device that leads toward selectivity is the use of symbolism that is functional to the story line rather than merely ornamental. This allows for narrative economy and extension of meaning, as in the closing scene. There, his estate under bombing attack, Washington tries to bribe God with the "greatest diamond in the world," offered for sacrifice at a jeweled altar in blasphemous parody of a religious rite. Such is the corruption of fabulous wealth created by disregarding all human and divine law.

Spun out to a novel, this mode would crack under its own artificiality. Allegory is one thing, modern fiction another, especially in its longer forms. Besides, Fitzgerald still had not learned any way to order his stories other than by the straight chronicle. The way to gain compactness and force, he was learning from Conrad and possibly James, could be found only in dramatic framing. A final experiment in the short story, "Absolution," brought him a long step toward that form. Originally conceived as a prologue to *The Great Gatsby*, it was detached from that novel and published separately in 1924. The first and last sections, in the present tense, render a scene where the young hero tries to confess his "terrible sin" in a priest's study, is baffled in his attempt by an extraordinary occurrence, then feels he has received an acceptable substitute for absolution. In the three intervening sections several incidents from his recent past are given as flash backs— at church, in the confessional booth, and at home—that form the background of his present troubled conscience. By the selective processes of memory the narrative is thus foreshortened and focused on the moment of crisis. But the opening and closing sections serve as a frame in another and more literal sense. The window of the priest's study looks out on the Dakota wheat fields where in the hot summer afternoon young Swedish girls with yellow hair "walked sensuously along roads that bounded the fields, calling innocent, exciting things to the young men" who were working there. This impressionistic tableau, given twice, symbolizes the frustration of the old celibate and at the same time the confused adolescent stirrings of the eleven-year-old boy. Realizing that the priest also is subject to temptations of the flesh, he feels no further need of being absolved from his sins. So a story of confession is changed into one of awakening and growing up. And this shift of meaning is achieved by the art of "magic suggestiveness," another technique he had learned from Conrad.

III

Fitzgerald was now ready to write *The Great Gatsby*. For during this same period, in addition to his own experiments in the short story and possibly motivating them, came his eager reading in the theory and practice of several masters of the novel of selection. In an interview, some months before the publication of his masterpiece, he said, "My third novel . . . is just finished and quite different from the other two in that it is an attempt at form. . . . The writer, if he has any aspiration toward art, should try to convey the feel of his scenes, places and people directly—as Conrad does." Just before beginning the *Gatsby* he had reread the preface to *The Nigger of the Narcissus*. In this artist's manifesto Conrad defined his purpose: "I am trying . . . by the power of the written word to make you hear, to make you feel— . . . before all, to make you *see*. That—and no more, and it is everything." In his novels he accomplished this by the suggestiveness of symbolism, by reordering chronology so as to dramatize climactic scenes, by using a narrator-observer as the point of view for telling the story. The last was Fitzgerald's chief instrument for mastering form in his one great novel. It gave him the much-needed distance from his materials. At the same time it removed the author as an obstruction between readers and the story itself. Further, the partial knowledge and spotty contacts of this observer, sympathetically involved in the action though he is, made him a natural device for selectivity.

A further influence in these matters is suggested by the letter with which T. S. Eliot greeted *The Great Gatsby*: "It has interested and excited me more than any new novel I have seen, either English or American, for a number of years. . . . In fact it seems to me to be the first step that American fiction has taken since Henry James." It is not clear just when Fitzgerald did read James, but he could have learned much of the Jamesian mode through reading the novels of his two chief American disciples, Willa Cather and Edith Wharton, as he was doing between 1922 and 1924. Fictional technique is what he was borrowing from his new masters, just as it is what he was discarding from his old ones, Wells and Mackenzie. Comparison of a story written at the beginning of this period ("Winter Dreams") with the novel that brought it to an end shows how great the difference in achievement can be by using different techniques for an identical theme, by using the art of selection rather than saturation.

The distinction of *The Great Gatsby* does not lie in its discovery of a new theme, though Fitzgerald does play a new variation on the old one of wealth, its glamorous outside and its empty inside. This time there is no didactic contrast between beauty and evil, even if Gatsby's fortune is made in the underworld and the inherited riches of the Buchanans presumably rest on exploitation. The theme is now more subtle. Wealth has robbed the leisure class in America of the faculty of imagination, of "a heightened sensitivity to the promises of life," to use the phrase from James that Fitzgerald applies to his hero in the prologue. Thus Gatsby, the most ostentatiously rich and the most blatant offender against the ethics of money making, is by all odds "the best of the whole sorry lot," as the narrator says. He at least has lived by his dream, fantastic and absurd as it is. It is not a vision of money and power but of beauty and love. His only purpose in building up an empire of wealth is to win back Daisy, the dream-girl beyond his reach whom he had won for a moment as a young man, his hick background disguised in the anonymity of an army uniform. The war soon separates them, and Daisy, though she still loves him, marries Tom Buchanan of her own wealthy set. In desperation Gatsby becomes a bootlegger and racketeer; yet, heel of the underworld as he is, his heart remains uncorrupted. His drive toward fulfillment of his dream has never deviated for a moment. But none of this past narrative is revealed except by flash backs buried at the center of the novel. *The Great Gatsby* is not a story of rags to riches, and what became of the poor-rich boy. It is a tragedy of the conflict between undisciplined imagination and the spiritual bankruptcy of great wealth.

Gatsby first looms before the reader as a mystery man living in lone splendor in a pretentious "palace" at West Egg, Long Island. Everything is seen through the eyes of Nick Carraway, who becomes acquainted with him by the accident of proximity. Having come to New York to make a career in the investment business, Nick has rented a cottage near by because his cousin Daisy Buchanan lives not far away in more fashionable East Egg. Fascinated by the fabulous parties next door, to which everybody yet "nobody" comes, his curiosity about the mansion's owner is mildly whetted. On his part Gatsby, learning of Nick's relation to Daisy, becomes more than interested in his neighbor. Not only are all the events of this summer related by Nick—rising from the idle entertainments of the rich through climax after climax—but also the threads of an almost incredible past are picked up by him and woven into the legend that is the true story of Gatsby's life. More important, the significance of it all is filtered through Nick's consciousness, and his final understanding of its meaning is the story of his own development.

The Buchanans represent the "ins" of this story, yet so dulled in sensibility they understand neither their own world of inherited wealth nor any other outside it. Jay Gatsby is the epitome of the man who was born an "out," trying to crash this exclusive world which he sees through a romantic haze only because it contains Daisy, at the same time that his own reality as a nobody named James Gatz has faded from his memory because it got in the way of his dream. Nick Carraway is the only one who lives simultaneously in the two worlds of wealth and of imagination, and this is what makes him such a fine center of consciousness. He is both "Mr. In" and "Mr. Out." Born to the same background as Daisy and Tom, he has been able to detach himself from it because he no longer believes in it wholeheartedly, even at the opening of the story. As the tragedy of Gatsby unfolds before his eyes he sees the society in which he has moved for the dead and empty thing it is. With the final revelation at the end, he leaves the East and Wall Street to become an author, at least the author of this novel, deserting the world of wealth for the world of imagination. His own story, though muted to the surface tragedy, is equally significant.

These are the techniques that give *The Great Gatsby* its dramatic impact. By framing the whole of a fabulous career in the tightly packed events of one summer, Fitzgerald achieves the utmost in narrative economy. By seeing all through a narrator-observer, he achieves distance from his materials. And letting Nick tell the story in retrospect provides a natural device for selection of details and organization of the plot. The novel assumes a pyramidal shape, reaching its apex in the reunion of Daisy and Gatsby at Nick's house. Ascending and descending on either side are a series of small encompassing climaxes. These episodes are balanced in pairs: Nick's first ride into town when he meets Tom's mistress, and his fatal last ride when, with Daisy driving Gatsby's car, Myrtle is accidentally run down and killed; the first party at the mistress's sordid flat, and the inner climax in the hotel room where the falsity of the Buchanans' hearts and the desperate truth of Gatsby's are revealed. There are similarly balanced pairs of scenes: Gatsby standing beside his marble swimming pool early in the story alone but filled with his romantic vision, and at the end his body floating in the same pool after he has been murdered by Myrtle's husband through a mistake connived at by Tom; the former's vulgar new mansion at West Egg, the quiet luxury of the latter's home at East Egg.

All of these achieve the suggestiveness of symbols, two pairs of them especially. The lyrical description of Long Island, in all the lush greenness of early June, seems like the prologue to a summer idyl; contrasted with this is the Valley of Ashes through which the motor trips are made to town in hot dry August, a concrete embodiment of the modern waste land. Then the framing pair, most effective of all: Gatsby on his dock looking across the bay with yearning to the green light shining on Daisy's; Nick on the same dock at the end looking across to Manhattan, "aware of the old island that flowered here once for Dutch sailors' eyes—a fresh green breast of the new world." But that world has vanished, and the book is over. On the last page Nick muses on the meaning of the story he has told: "Gatsby believed in the green light, the orgiastic future that year by year recedes before us. . . . So we beat on, boats against the current, borne back ceaselessly into the past." This is magic suggestiveness such as Conrad would have approved of, dramatized in a compact form that would do justice to James.

After such a triumph, based on five years of hard work at his craft, Fitzgerald was prepared to go on to others. He had had, from the first, an almost inexhaustible subject and a theme capable of endless variations. Now he had found the techniques admirably suited for rendering them. But the remaining fifteen years of his career are marked instead by wasted energies and talents. He kept writing at a furious pace, but more and more of his work was aimed at the money market to pay the ever-mounting bills of spendthrift living. And the way of life thus supported drained away his strength and dulled his imagination. The record of the decade following the *Gatsby* is crucial for the biographer, but it offers little to the critic. There were a few short stories of real merit, two of which may be noted. "The Rich Boy" (1926) is a kind of coda to the novel, a biography of the Complete Egotist so encased in his sense of superiority, because of inherited wealth and position, that he gradually insulates himself from every human relation. He has good looks, charm, money, even intelligence—everything but imagination, and a heart. "Babylon Revisited" (1931) is a kind of preview of the author's own impending disintegration. It is the moving story of a man who returns to Paris during the Depression in an attempt to pick up the broken fragments of his life, only to discover, paradoxically, that it was during the Boom of the twenties he had "lost everything he wanted." Fitzgerald was making the same discovery about himself in the thirties.

The one sustained effort of these years, *Tender Is the Night* (1934), was his most complex novel and his most magnificent failure, if one judges it by the standard of his masterpiece. The author's growing uncertainty of direction is reflected in the many versions through which it passed before he released it for publication, not to mention a "final version" he left at his death six years later in a last effort to bring it to form. The contents also reflect his autobiographical situation at the time. Dick Diver is a once-brilliant psychiatrist who, in his loneliness in Europe and his feeling of isolation from the world he had formerly known, marries one of his rich neurotic patients. Gradually all his promise and resources are sapped from

him by the leeches in her aimless dissipated circle of expatriates. Intended
as a tragedy, it achieves only pathos. But it holds genuine interest for the
student of literature because of its ambitious scope and the partial success
of its execution.

IV

Near the end of his battered career, strewn with the bits and pieces of a
fine talent and a life begun in high hopes, Fitzgerald subjected himself to a
grim stocktaking. The result was a three-part essay entitled "The Crack-
Up," diagnosing the physical, moral, and spiritual dead end he had
reached. It is an astonishing piece of writing on any score. Though widely
praised by critics and biographers, it has been valued chiefly as a kind of redemptive testament for the man Fitzgerald. The personality that had
gone to pieces under success seemed at last to have drawn itself together in
defeat. A life wasted in folly was now being husbanded with dignity as
death stared him down. Even his best literary critic seems impressed by the
personal aspect of this painful revelation, that he "does not envision himself in heroic terms but rather in domestic metaphor, as simply a cracked
plate." It is indeed modest of the author who had been the sensation of his
age a decade before to figure himself now as a piece of broken crockery
that will never again "be brought out for company" but merely kept in
the pantry "as a household necessity, . . . to go into the ice box under left-
overs." But the really important thing about this elaborated metaphor,
since its purpose is to present the crack-up of a man who was a literary
artist, is the fact that it is a metaphor.

Though published under the guise of an essay, this self-analysis has
many touches that suggest the hand of a creator. The metaphorical mode
set by the main title is sustained by the subtitles: "Handle with Care" and
"Pasting It Together." The style, by an author who formerly tended to be
gushing and slovenly, has tightened into an instrument as keen and flexible
as a sword. In economy and force it is the most effective thing he ever wrote
except the *Gatsby*. Is it possible then that "The Crack-Up," closely as it followed a skeleton of facts, was shaped by the artist into a kind of fictional
autobiography, just as most of the stories and novels are autobiographical
fictions? Two emotional experiences, given as crucial turning points in his
career, can be used as a check. The first tells of his being forced to drop out
of Princeton during his junior year because of illness—"diagnosed as malaria," though it later turned out to be tuberculosis—and thus losing "every
single thing I wanted." The effect of this on him he described as "a harsh
and bitter business," knowing "that my career as a leader of men was over"
—melodramatic enough on its face, when one remembers that all he had
lost were simply college honors and offices and medals. These histrionics

are deflated by the sober words of his latest biographer,[3] recording a conversation with a classmate at the time which was conveniently forgotten by the author in his remembrance of things past:

Fitzgerald told Arrott that the Dean's office was hounding him about his grades. When Arrott said it took only a little time each day to do passing work, Fitzgerald agreed but said he couldn't find the time. It seemed likely he would flunk out at midyears, and using his sickness as a pretext he withdrew from college in December.

The second experience, having a pervasive relation to his fictions, is even more central:

It was one of those tragic loves doomed for lack of money, and one day the girl closed it out on the basis of common sense. During a long summer of despair I wrote a novel instead of letters, so it came out all right, but it came out all right for a different person [that is, for a changed Fitzgerald]. The man with the jingle of money in his pocket who married the girl a year later would always cherish an abiding distrust, an animosity, toward the leisure class—not the conviction of a revolutionist but the smouldering hatred of a peasant. In the years since then I have never been able to stop wondering where my friends' money came from, nor to stop thinking that at one time a sort of *droit de seigneur* might have been exercised to give one of them my girl.

There is a very real source for this in Fitzgerald's life. In fact, the interesting point is that there are two sources. This emotional crisis in "The Crack-Up" is clearly a composite of his love affair with Ginevra King from 1915 to 1917, and the ups and downs of his courtship of Zelda Sayre from 1918 until their marriage in 1920. The first girl "closed it out" because, as a daughter of the moneyed aristocracy of Chicago, she preferred a life of greater luxury than he seemed likely to provide; in wanting a millionairess he was simply reaching beyond his grasp. The second, an Alabama girl of good family but not of wealth, broke her engagement because as a beginning author he had no adequate income at the moment; she renewed it when fame and money came with the publication of *This Side of Paradise*.

Not only is the passage about "tragic" young love in "The Crack-Up" thus composed; it is deliberately heightened in several ways. One of the most obvious is sounding the overtones of hierarchical feudalism: his feeling toward potential rivals among the wealthy becomes "the smouldering hatred of a peasant," because one of them might have exercised the lord's right of seducing his girl away from him. The metaphorical language here is what lifts it quite above the matter-of-fact tone of a letter written near the end of his life:

[3] See the entry under Andrew Turnbull in Reading Suggestions for the biographical facts on this and succeeding pages.

That was always my experience—a poor boy in a rich town; a poor boy in a rich boy's school; a poor boy in a rich man's club at Princeton. . . . I have never been able to forgive the rich for being rich, and it has colored my entire life and works. . . . The whole idea of Gatsby is the unfairness of a poor young man not being able to marry a girl with money. This theme comes up again and again because I lived it.

Actually, Fitzgerald was not in any sense a "poor young man" except by contrast with the rich. His family was well enough off financially to give him a far better than average launching, and by the age of twenty-five he was making big money as a best-selling author. Yet he was always in debt and always envying the rich. Besides, there is nothing really "unfair" in a rich girl refusing to marry a poor boy, if such had been the case. The literal facts in the life of a creative author are less important than what he makes of them in his fictions. After quoting the above letter, his biographer comments: "Thus Gatsby's love for Daisy was Fitzgerald's love for Zelda—and before her, Ginevra—decked out in a Keatsian prose." This last phrase describes the manner of presentation in "The Crack-Up" quite as accurately as that in the novel, and in the several short stories on the same theme.

Perhaps one can think of "The Crack-Up," therefore, as another mask Fitzgerald tried on in his last years, the mask of the hard-boiled egotist. If he had known simply as a man that this was his last resort, he would have tried to become one without talking about it. But his letters to friends and daughter in the remaining brief span of his life, 1936 to 1940, do not bear this out. Since he was also an artist who had frittered his talents away in all directions, he had to create this role as a protective covering and express it in words so he could explore its usefulness for the rest of his career. It was probably the chief prop that held him up while trying to finish his last novel, *The Great Tycoon*, in which the egotist masquerades as a movie director controlling the lives of his puppets. The egotist in various disguises is the type of all his fictional projections of himself. The first version of *This Side of Paradise* was actually entitled "The Romantic Egotist," and it is as such that Amory Blaine launches the Fitzgerald hero. In *The Beautiful and Damned* he could be labeled the egotist-as-cynic, in *The Great Gatsby* the egotist-as-dreamer. It is interesting that in the one novel he produced in the next decade, *Tender Is the Night*, the egotist is cast in the role of a psychoanalyst, probing the crack-ups of other people. Two years later he turned the analysis on himself, in what is both his most remarkable essay and one of his finest pieces of literary composition.

There is no question about the courage with which Fitzgerald faced his breakdown in 1936, and the honesty with which he confessed the worst aspects of himself—or at least some of them. But one remembers how in his early story "Absolution," based on an autobiographical experience, the young hero in unburdening to a priest maneuvers the truth "to make things finer in the confessional, brightening up the dinginess of his admissions by saying a thing radiant and proud." There is evidence of similar strategies at work in the public confession of the forty-year-old author. By deletions from the record, and additions to it, Fitzgerald certainly adds to the dramatic impact of the emotional experiences that contributed to "The Crack-Up." What is remarkable is the way he makes the normal setbacks everybody is subject to—loss of honors one has not earned and of dream-girls over the horizon—seem like blows of fate. With these as auguries, he reconstructs a career of high promise that goes down in shipwreck, then diagnoses the nature of his plight and creates the new stance by which he will cope with it and salvage what he can. All this is achieved by the careful selection and manipulation of autobiographical fact to suit his purposes and by controlling his effects through skillful use of language, imagery, and structure. A full explication of these techniques as applied in the "essay" would make an interesting piece of literary criticism. Such a reading of his last testament is not intended as blame for the man but praise for the artist. In "The Crack-Up" Fitzgerald made a final dramatization of himself that is a splendid creation, though the scale is miniature.

That all his best writings were autobiographical he himself was well aware. As early as 1933 he published an essay, "One Hundred False Starts," containing a sort of apologia for this limitation. His talents were already getting submerged in riotous living and in his desperate efforts to write more and more best-selling stuff to foot the bills for this extravagance. Though he knew his vogue was slipping, because the Depression had turned public interest to social themes, he still saw with clear eyes that his true forte remained the self-portrait:

Mostly, we authors must repeat ourselves—that's the truth. We have two or three great and moving experiences in our lives—experiences so great and moving that it doesn't seem at the time that anyone else has been so caught up and pounded and dazzled and astonished and beaten and broken and rescued and illuminated and rewarded and humbled in just that way ever before.

Then we learn our trade, well or less well, and we tell our two or three stories—each time in a new disguise—maybe ten times, maybe a hundred, as long as people will listen.

In his *Note-Books* he specified his kinship to the heroes in the principal versions of his central story:

Books are like brothers. I am an only child. Gatsby my imaginary eldest brother, Amory my younger, Anthony my worry, Dick my comparatively good brother, but all of them far from home. When I have the courage to put the old white light on the home of my heart, then . . . .

Written about the time of his "Crack-Up," this broken-off last sentence has a ring of poignance about it. The final touch comes in a letter to his daughter, just six months before his death, showing his awareness of both his one great victory and the waste of his last fifteen years:

What little I've accomplished has been by the most laborious and up-hill work, and I wish now I'd *never* relaxed or looked back—but said at the end of *The Great Gastby:* "I've found my line—from now on this comes first. This is my immediate duty—without this I am nothing."

CHARLES R. ANDERSON

A Note on the Text. The text followed here for "May Day" is that of its first publication in book form in *Tales of the Jazz Age* (New York: Charles Scribner's Sons, 1922)—"prestiged" has been changed to "presaged" (p. 984), as in later editions; for "The Crack-Up," the text in the volume by that name edited by Edmund Wilson (New York: New Directions, 1945).

MAY DAY

THERE HAD BEEN a war fought and won and the great city of the conquering people was crossed with triumphal arches and vivid with thrown flowers of white, red, and rose. All through the long spring days the returning soldiers marched up the chief highway behind the strump of drums and the joyous, resonant wind of the brasses, while merchants and clerks left their bickerings and figurings and, crowding to the windows, turned their white-bunched faces gravely upon the passing battalions.

Never had there been such splendor in the great city, for the victorious war had brought plenty in its train, and the merchants had flocked thither from the South and West with their households to taste of all the luscious feasts and witness the lavish entertainments prepared—and to buy for their women furs against the next winter and bags of golden mesh and varicolored slippers of silk and silver and rose satin and cloth of gold.

So gaily and noisily were the peace and prosperity impending hymned by the scribes and poets of the conquering people that more and more spenders had gathered from the provinces to drink the wine of excitement, and faster and faster did the merchants dispose of their trinkets and slippers until they sent up a mighty cry for more trinkets and more slippers in order that they might give in barter what was demanded of them. Some even of them flung up their hands helplessly, shouting:

"Alas! I have no more slippers! and alas! I have no more trinkets! May Heaven help me, for I know not what I shall do!"

But no one listened to their great outcry, for the throngs were far too busy—day by day, the foot-soldiers trod jauntily the highway and all exulted because the young men returning were pure and brave, sound of tooth and pink of cheek, and the young women of the land were virgins and comely both of face and of figure.

So during all this time there were many adventures that happened in the great city, and, of these, several—or perhaps one—are here set down.

1

At nine o'clock on the morning of the first of May, 1919, a young man spoke to the room clerk at the Biltmore Hotel, asking if Mr. Philip Dean were registered there, and if so, could he be connected with Mr. Dean's rooms. The inquirer was dressed in a well-cut, shabby suit. He was small, slender, and darkly handsome; his eyes were framed above with unusually long eyelashes and below with the blue semicircle of ill health, this latter effect heightened by an unnatural glow which colored his face like a low, incessant fever.

Mr. Dean was staying there. The young man was directed to a telephone at the side.

After a second his connection was made; a sleepy voice hello'd from somewhere above.

"Mr. Dean?"—this very eagerly—"it's Gordon, Phil. It's Gordon Sterrett. I'm down-stairs. I heard you were in New York and I had a hunch you'd be here."

The sleepy voice became gradually enthusiastic. Well, how was Gordy, old boy! Well, he certainly was surprised and tickled! Would Gordy come right up, for Pete's sake!

A few minutes later Philip Dean, dressed in blue silk pajamas, opened his door and the two young men greeted each other with a half-embarrassed exuberance. They were both about twenty-four, Yale graduates of the year before the war; but there the resemblance stopped abruptly. Dean was blond, ruddy, and rugged under his thin pajamas. Everything about him radiated fitness and bodily comfort. He smiled frequently, showing large and prominent teeth.

"I was going to look you up," he cried enthusiastically. "I'm taking a couple of weeks off. If you'll sit down a sec I'll be right with you. Going to take a shower."

As he vanished into the bathroom his visitor's dark eyes roved nervously around the room, resting for a moment on a great English travelling bag in the corner and on a family of thick silk shirts littered on the chairs amid impressive neckties and soft woollen socks.

Gordon rose and, picking up one of the shirts, gave it a minute examination. It was of very heavy silk, yellow with a pale blue stripe—and there were nearly a dozen of them. He stared involuntarily at his own shirt-cuffs—they were ragged and linty at the edges and soiled to a faint gray. Dropping the silk shirt, he held his coat-sleeves down and worked the frayed shirt-cuffs up till they were out of sight. Then he went to the mirror and looked at himself with listless, unhappy interest. His tie, of former glory, was faded and thumb-creased—it served no longer to hide the jagged buttonholes of his collar. He thought, quite without amusement, that only three years before he had received a scattering vote in the senior elections at college for being the best-dressed man in his class.

Dean emerged from the bathroom polishing his body.

"Saw an old friend of yours last night," he remarked. "Passed her in the lobby and couldn't think of her name to save my neck. That girl you brought up to New Haven senior year."

Gordon started.

"Edith Bradin? That who you mean?"

" 'At's the one. Damn good looking. She's still sort of a pretty doll—you know what I mean: as if you touched her she'd smear."

He surveyed his shining self complacently in the mirror, smiled faintly, exposing a section of teeth.

"She must be twenty-three anyway," he continued.

"Twenty-two last month," said Gordon absently.

"What? Oh, last month. Well, I imagine she's down for the Gamma Psi dance. Did you know we're having a Yale Gamma Psi dance tonight at Delmonico's? You better come up, Gordy. Half of New Haven'll probably be there. I can get you an invitation."

Draping himself reluctantly in fresh underwear, Dean lit a cigarette and sat down by the open window, inspecting his calves and knees under the morning sunshine which poured into the room.

"Sit down, Gordy," he suggested, "and tell me all about what you've been doing and what you're doing now and everything."

Gordon collapsed unexpectedly upon the bed; lay there inert and spiritless. His mouth, which habitually dropped a little open when his face was in repose, became suddenly helpless and pathetic.

"What's the matter?" asked Dean quickly.

"Oh, God!"

"What's the matter?"

"Every God damn thing in the world," he said miserably. "I've absolutely gone to pieces, Phil. I'm all in."

"Huh?"

"I'm all in." His voice was shaking.

Dean scrutinized him more closely with appraising blue eyes.

"You certainly look all shot."

"I am. I've made a hell of a mess of everything." He paused. "I'd better start at the beginning—or will it bore you?"

"Not at all; go on." There was, however, a hesitant note in Dean's voice. This trip East had been planned for a holiday—to find Gordon Sterrett in trouble exasperated him a little.

"Go on," he repeated, and then added half under his breath, "Get it over with."

"Well," began Gordon unsteadily, "I got back from France in February, went home to Harrisburg for a month, and then came down to New York to get a job. I got one—with an export company. They fired me yesterday."

"Fired you?"

"I'm coming to that, Phil. I want to tell you frankly. You're about the only man I can turn to in a matter like this. You won't mind if I just tell you frankly, will you, Phil?"

Dean stiffened a bit more. The pats he was bestowing on his knees grew perfunctory. He felt vaguely that he was being unfairly saddled with responsibility; he was not even sure he wanted to be told. Though never surprised at finding Gordon Sterrett in mild difficulty, there was something in this present misery that repelled him and hardened him, even though it excited his curiosity.

"Go on."

"It's a girl."

"Hm." Dean resolved that nothing was going to spoil his trip. If Gordon was going to be depressing, then he'd have to see less of Gordon.

"Her name is Jewel Hudson," went on the distressed voice from the bed. "She used to be 'pure,' I guess, up to about a year ago. Lived here in New York—poor family. Her people are dead now and she lives with an old aunt. You see it was just about the time I met her that everybody began to come back from France in droves—and all I did was to welcome the newly arrived and go on parties with 'em. That's the way it started, Phil, just from being glad to see everybody and having them glad to see me."

"You ought to've had more sense."

"I know," Gordon paused, and then continued listlessly. "I'm on my own now, you know, and Phil, I can't stand being poor. Then came this darn girl. She sort of fell in love with me for a while and, though I never intended to get so involved, I'd always seem to run into her somewhere. You can imagine the sort of work I was doing for those exporting people—of course, I always intended to draw; do illustrating for magazines; there's a pile of money in it."

"Why didn't you? You've got to buckle down if you want to make good," suggested Dean with cold formalism.

"I tried, a little, but my stuff's crude. I've got talent, Phil; I can draw—but I just don't know how. I ought to go to art school and I can't afford it. Well, things came to a crisis about a week ago. Just as I was down to about my last dollar this girl began bothering me. She wants some money; claims she can make trouble for me if she doesn't get it."

"Can she?"

"I'm afraid she can. That's one reason I lost my job—she kept calling up the office all the time, and that was sort of the last straw down there. She's got a letter all written to send to my family. Oh, she's got me, all right. I've got to have some money for her."

There was an awkward pause. Gordon lay very still, his hands clenched by his side.

"I'm all in," he continued, his voice trembling. "I'm half crazy, Phil. If I hadn't known you were coming East, I think I'd have killed myself. I want you to lend me three hundred dollars."

Dean's hands, which had been patting his bare ankles, were suddenly quiet —and the curious uncertainty playing between the two became taut and strained.

After a second Gordon continued:

"I've bled the family until I'm ashamed to ask for another nickel."
Still Dean made no answer.

"Jewel says she's got to have two hundred dollars."

"Tell her where she can go."

"Yes, that sounds easy, but she's got a couple of drunken letters I wrote her. Unfortunately she's not at all the flabby sort of person you'd expect."

Dean made an expression of distaste.

"I can't stand that sort of woman. You ought to have kept away."

"I know," admitted Gordon wearily.

"You've got to look at things as they are. If you haven't got money you've got to work and stay away from women."

"That's easy for you to say," began Gordon, his eyes narrowing. "You've got all the money in the world."

"I most certainly have not. My family keep darn close tab on what I spend. Just because I have a little leeway I have to be extra careful not to abuse it."

He raised the blind and let in a further flood of sunshine.

"I'm no prig, Lord knows," he went on deliberately. "I like pleasure—and I like a lot of it on a vacation like this, but you're—you're in awful shape. I never heard you talk just this way before. You seem to be sort of bankrupt—morally as well as financially."

"Don't they usually go together?"

Dean shook his head impatiently.

"There's a regular aura about you that I don't understand. It's a sort of evil."

"It's an air of worry and poverty and sleepless nights," said Gordon, rather defiantly.

"I don't know."

"Oh, I admit I'm depressing. I depress myself. But, my God, Phil, a week's rest and a new suit and some ready money and I'd be like—like I was. Phil, I can draw like a streak, and you know it. But half the time I haven't had the money to buy decent drawing materials—and I can't draw when I'm tired and discouraged and all in. With a little ready money I can take a few weeks off and get started."

"How do I know you wouldn't use it on some other woman?"

"Why rub it in?" said Gordon quietly.

"I'm not rubbing it in. I hate to see you this way."

"Will you lend me the money, Phil?"

"I can't decide right off. That's a lot of money and it'll be darn inconvenient for me."

"It'll be hell for me if you can't—I know I'm whining, and it's all my own fault but—that doesn't change it."

"When could you pay it back?"

This was encouraging. Gordon considered. It was probably wisest to be frank.

"Of course, I could promise to send it back next month, but—I'd better say three months. Just as soon as I start to sell drawings."

"How do I know you'll sell any drawings?"

A new hardness in Dean's voice sent a faint chill of doubt over Gordon. Was it possible that he wouldn't get the money?

"I supposed you had a little confidence in me."

"I did have—but when I see you like this I begin to wonder."

"Do you suppose if I wasn't at the end of my rope I'd come to you like this? Do you think I'm enjoying it?" He broke off and bit his lip, feeling that he had better subdue the rising anger in his voice. After all, he was the suppliant.

"You seem to manage it pretty easily," said Dean angrily. "You put me in the position where, if I don't lend it to you, I'm a sucker—oh, yes, you do. And let me tell you it's no easy thing for me to get hold of three hundred dollars. My income isn't so big but that a slice like that won't play the deuce with it."

He left his chair and began to dress, choosing his clothes carefully. Gordon stretched out his arms and clenched the edges of the bed, fighting back a desire to cry out. His head was splitting and whirring, his mouth was dry and bitter and he could feel the fever in his blood resolving itself into innumerable regular counts like a slow dripping from a roof.

Dean tied his tie precisely, brushed his eyebrows, and removed a piece of tobacco from his teeth with solemnity. Next he filled his cigarette case, tossed the empty box thoughtfully into the waste basket, and settled the case in his vest pocket.

"Had breakfast?" he demanded.

"No; I don't eat it any more."

"Well, we'll go out and have some. We'll decide about that money later. I'm sick of the subject. I came East to have a good time.

"Let's go over to the Yale Club," he continued moodily, and then added with an implied reproof: "You've given up your job. You've got nothing else to do."

"I'd have a lot to do if I had a little money," said Gordon pointedly.

"Oh, for Heaven's sake drop the subject for a while! No point in glooming on my whole trip. Here, here's some money."

He took a five-dollar bill from his wallet and tossed it over to Gordon, who folded it carefully and put it in his pocket. There was an added spot of color in his cheeks, an added glow that was not fever. For an instant before they turned to go out their eyes met and in that instant each found something that made him lower his own glance quickly. For in that instant they quite suddenly and definitely hated each other.

2

Fifth Avenue and Forty-fourth Street swarmed with the noon crowd. The wealthy, happy sun glittered in transient gold through the thick windows of the smart shops, lighting upon mesh bags and purses and strings of pearls in gray velvet cases; upon gaudy feather fans of many colors; upon the laces and silks of expensive dresses; upon the bad paintings and the fine period furniture in the elaborate show rooms of interior decorators.

Working-girls, in pairs and groups and swarms, loitered by the windows, choosing their future boudoirs from some resplendent display which included even a man's silk pajamas laid domestically across the bed. They stood in front of the jewelry stores and picked out their engagement rings, and their wedding rings and their platinum wrist watches, and then drifted on to inspect the feather fans and opera cloaks; meanwhile digesting the sandwiches and sundaes they had eaten for lunch.

All through the crowd were men in uniform, sailors from the great fleet anchored in the Hudson, soldiers with divisional insignia from Massachusetts to California wanting fearfully to be noticed, and finding the great city thoroughly fed up with soldiers unless they were nicely massed into pretty formations and uncomfortable under the weight of a pack and rifle.

Through this medley Dean and Gordon wandered; the former interested, made alert by the display of humanity at its frothiest and gaudiest; the latter reminded of how often he had been one of the crowd, tired, casually fed, overworked, and dissipated. To Dean the struggle was significant, young, cheerful; to Gordon it was dismal, meaningless, endless.

In the Yale Club they met a group of their former classmates who greeted the visiting Dean vociferously. Sitting in a semicircle of lounges and great chairs, they had a highball all around.

Gordon found the conversation tiresome and interminable. They lunched together *en masse*, warmed with liquor as the afternoon began. They were all going to the Gamma Psi dance that night—it promised to be the best party since the war.

"Edith Bradin's coming," said some one to Gordon. "Didn't she used to be an old flame of yours? Aren't you both from Harrisburg?"

"Yes." He tried to change the subject. "I see her brother occasionally. He's sort of a socialistic nut. Runs a paper or something here in New York."

"Not like his gay sister, eh?" continued his eager informant. "Well, she's coming to-night with a junior named Peter Himmell."

Gordon was to meet Jewel Hudson at eight o'clock—he had promised to have some money for her. Several times he glanced nervously at his wrist watch. At four, to his relief, Dean rose and announced that he was going over to Rivers Brothers to buy some collars and ties. But as they left the Club another of the party joined them, to Gordon's great dismay. Dean was in a jovial mood now, happy, expectant of the evening's party, faintly hilarious. Over in Rivers' he chose a dozen neckties, selecting each one after long consultations with the other man. Did he think narrow ties were coming back? And wasn't it a shame that Rivers couldn't get any more Welsh Margotson collars? There never was a collar like the "Covington."

Gordon was in something of a panic. He wanted the money immediately. And he was now inspired also with a vague idea of attending the Gamma Psi dance. He wanted to see Edith—Edith whom he hadn't met since one romantic night at the Harrisburg Country Club just before he went to France. The affair had died, drowned in the turmoil of the war and quite forgotten in the arabesque of these three months, but a picture of her, poignant, debonnaire, immersed in her own inconsequential chatter, recurred to him unexpectedly and brought a hundred memories with it. It was Edith's face that he had cherished through college with a sort of detached yet affectionate admiration. He had loved to draw her—around his room had been a dozen sketches of her—playing golf, swimming—he could draw her pert, arresting profile with his eyes shut.

They left Rivers' at five-thirty and paused for a moment on the sidewalk.

"Well," said Dean genially, "I'm all set now. Think I'll go back to the hotel and get a shave, haircut, and massage."

"Good enough," said the other man, "I think I'll join you."

Gordon wondered if he was to be beaten after all. With difficulty he restrained himself from turning to the man and snarling out, "Go on away, damn you!" In despair he suspected that perhaps Dean had spoken to him, was keeping him along in order to avoid a dispute about the money.

They went into the Biltmore—a Biltmore alive with girls—mostly from the West and South, the stellar débutantes of many cities gathered for the dance of a famous fraternity of a famous university. But to Gordon they were faces in a dream. He gathered together his forces for a last appeal, was about to come out with he knew not what, when Dean suddenly excused himself to the other man and taking Gordon's arm led him aside.

"Gordy," he said quickly, "I've thought the whole thing over carefully and I've decided that I can't lend you that money. I'd like to oblige you, but I don't feel I ought to—it'd put a crimp in me for a month."

Gordon, watching him dully, wondered why he had never before noticed how much those upper teeth projected.

"—I'm mighty sorry, Gordon," continued Dean, "but that's the way it is."

He took out his wallet and deliberately counted out seventy-five dollars in bills.

"Here," he said, holding them out, "here's seventy-five; that makes eighty all together. That's all the actual cash I have with me, besides what I'll actually spend on the trip."

Gordon raised his clenched hand automatically, opened it as though it were a tongs he was holding, and clenched it again on the money.

"I'll see you at the dance," continued Dean. "I've got to get along to the barber shop."

"So-long," said Gordon in a strained and husky voice.

"So-long."

Dean began to smile, but seemed to change his mind. He nodded briskly and disappeared.

But Gordon stood there, his handsome face awry with distress, the roll of bills clenched tightly in his hand. Then, blinded by sudden tears, he stumbled clumsily down the Biltmore steps.

3

About nine o'clock of the same night two human beings came out of a cheap restaurant in Sixth Avenue. They were ugly, ill-nourished, devoid of all except the very lowest form of intelligence, and without even that animal exuberance that in itself brings color into life; they were lately vermin-ridden, cold, and hungry in a dirty town of a strange land; they were poor, friendless; tossed as driftwood from their births, they would be tossed as driftwood to their deaths. They were dressed in the uniform of the United States Army, and on the shoulder of each was the insignia of a drafted division from New Jersey, landed three days before.

The taller of the two was named Carrol Key, a name hinting that in his veins, however thinly diluted by generations of degeneration, ran blood of some potentiality. But one could stare endlessly at the long, chinless face, the dull, watery eyes, and high cheek-bones, without finding a suggestion of either ancestral worth or native resourcefulness.

His companion was swart and bandy-legged, with rat-eyes and a much-broken hooked nose. His defiant air was obviously a pretense, a weapon of protection borrowed from that world of snarl and snap, of physical bluff and physical menace, in which he had always lived. His name was Gus Rose.

Leaving the café they sauntered down Sixth Avenue, wielding toothpicks with great gusto and complete detachment.

"Where to?" asked Rose, in a tone which implied that he would not be surprised if Key suggested the South Sea Islands.

"What you say we see if we can getta holda some liquor?" Prohibition was not yet. The ginger in the suggestion was caused by the law forbidding the selling of liquor to soldiers.

Rose agreed enthusiastically.

"I got an idea," continued Key, after a moment's thought, "I got a brother somewhere."

"In New York?"

"Yeah. He's an old fella." He meant that he was an elder brother. "He's a waiter in a hash joint."

"Maybe he can get us some."

"I'll say he can!"

"B'lieve me, I'm goin' to get this darn uniform off me to-morra. Never get me in it again, neither. I'm goin' to get me some regular clothes."

"Say, maybe I'm not."

As their combined finances were something less than five dollars, this intention can be taken largely as a pleasant game of words, harmless and consoling. It seemed to please both of them, however, for they reinforced it with chuckling and mention of personages high in biblical circles, adding such further emphasis as "Oh, boy!" "You know!" and "I'll say so!" repeated many times over.

The entire mental pabulum of these two men consisted of an offended nasal comment extended through the years upon the institution—army, business, or poorhouse—which kept them alive, and toward their immediate superior in that institution. Until that very morning the institution had been the "government" and the immediate superior had been the "Cap'n"—from these two they had glided out and were now in the vaguely uncomfortable state before they should adopt their next bondage. They were uncertain, resentful, and somewhat ill at ease. This they hid by pretending an elaborate relief at being out of the army, and by assuring each other that military discipline should never again rule their stubborn, liberty-loving wills. Yet, as a matter of fact, they would have felt more at home in a prison than in this new-found and unquestionable freedom.

Suddenly Key increased his gait. Rose, looking up and following his glance, discovered a crowd that was collecting fifty yards down the street. Key chuckled and began to run in the direction of the crowd; Rose thereupon also chuckled and his short bandy legs twinkled beside the long, awkward strides of his companion.

Reaching the outskirts of the crowd they immediately became an indistinguishable part of it. It was composed of ragged civilians somewhat the worse for liquor, and of soldiers representing many divisions and many stages of sobriety, all clustered around a gesticulating little Jew with long black whiskers, who was waving his arms and delivering an excited but succinct harangue. Key and Rose, having wedged themselves into the approximate parquet, scrutinized him with acute suspicion, as his words penetrated their common consciousness.

"—What have you got outa the war?" he was crying fiercely. "Look arounja, look arounja! Are you rich? Have you got a lot of money offered you? —no; you're lucky if you're alive and got both your legs; you're lucky if you came back an' find your wife ain't gone off with some other fella that had the money to buy himself out of the war! That's when you're lucky! Who got anything out of it except J. P. Morgan an' John D. Rockerfeller?"

At this point the little Jew's oration was interrupted by the hostile impact of a fist upon the point of his bearded chin and he toppled backward to a sprawl on the pavement.

"God damn Bolsheviki!" cried the big soldier-blacksmith who had delivered the blow. There was a rumble of approval, the crowd closed in nearer.

The Jew staggered to his feet, and immediately went down again before a half-dozen reaching-in fists. This time he stayed down, breathing heavily, blood oozing from his lip where it was cut within and without.

There was a riot of voices, and in a minute Rose and Key found themselves flowing with the jumbled crowd down Sixth Avenue under the leadership of a thin civilian in a slouch hat and the brawny soldier who had summarily ended the oration. The crowd had marvelously swollen to formidable proportions and a stream of more noncommittal citizens followed it along the sidewalks lending their moral support by intermittent huzzas.

"Where we goin'?" yelled Key to the man nearest him.

His neighbor pointed up to the leader in the slouch hat.

"That guy knows where there's a lot of 'em! We're goin' to show 'em!"

"We're goin' to show 'em!" whispered Key delightedly to Rose, who repeated the phrase rapturously to a man on the other side.

Down Sixth Avenue swept the procession, joined here and there by soldiers and marines, and now and then by civilians, who came up with the inevitable cry that they were just out of the army themselves, as if presenting it as a card of admission to a newly formed Sporting and Amusement Club.

Then the procession swerved down a cross street and headed for Fifth Avenue and the word filtered here and there that they were bound for a Red meeting at Tolliver Hall.

"Where is it?"

The question went up the line and a moment later the answer floated back. Tolliver Hall was down on Tenth Street. There was a bunch of other sojers who was goin' to break it up and was down there now!

But Tenth Street had a faraway sound and at the word a general groan went up and a score of the procession dropped out. Among these were Rose and Key, who slowed down to a saunter and let the more enthusiastic sweep on by.

"I'd rather get some liquor," said Key as they halted and made their way to the sidewalk amid cries of "Shell hole!" and "Quitters!"

"Does your brother work around here?" asked Rose, assuming the air of one passing from the superficial to the eternal.

"He oughta," replied Key. "I ain't seen him for a coupla years. I been out to Pennsylvania since. Maybe he don't work at night anyhow. It's right along here. He can get us some o'right if he ain't gone."

They found the place after a few minutes' patrol of the street—a shoddy tablecloth restaurant between Fifth Avenue and Broadway. Here Key went inside to inquire for his brother George, while Rose waited on the sidewalk.

"He ain't here no more," said Key emerging. "He's a waiter up to Delmonico's."

Rose nodded wisely, as if he'd expected as much. One should not be surprised at a capable man changing jobs occasionally. He knew a waiter once— there ensued a long conversation as they walked as to whether waiters made more in actual wages than in tips—it was decided that it depended on the social tone of the joint wherein the waiter labored. After having given each other vivid pictures of millionaires dining at Delmonico's and throwing away fifty-dollar bills after their first quart of champagne, both men thought privately of becoming waiters. In fact, Key's narrow brow was secreting a resolution to ask his brother to get him a job.

"A waiter can drink up all the champagne those fellas leave in bottles," suggested Rose with some relish, and then added as an afterthought, "Oh, boy!"

By the time they reached Delmonico's it was half past ten, and they were surprised to see a stream of taxis driving up to the door one after the other and emitting marvelous, hatless young ladies, each one attended by a stiff young gentleman in evening clothes.

"It's a party," said Rose with some awe. "Maybe we better not go in. He'll be busy."

"No, he won't. He'll be o'right."

After some hesitation they entered what appeared to them to be the least elaborate door and, indecision falling upon them immediately, stationed themselves nervously in an inconspicuous corner of the small dining-room in which they found themselves. They took off their caps and held them in their hands. A cloud of gloom fell upon them and both started when a door at one end of the room crashed open, emitting a comet-like waiter who streaked across the floor and vanished through another door on the other side.

There had been three of these lightning passages before the seekers mustered the acumen to hail a waiter. He turned, looked at them suspiciously, and then approached with soft, catlike steps, as if prepared at any moment to turn and flee.

"Say," began Key, "say, do you know my brother? He's a waiter here."

"His name is Key," annotated Rose.

Yes, the waiter knew Key. He was up-stairs, he thought. There was a big dance going on in the main ballroom. He'd tell him.

Ten minutes later George Key appeared and greeted his brother with the utmost suspicion; his first and most natural thought being that he was going to be asked for money.

George was tall and weak chinned, but there his resemblance to his brother ceased. The waiter's eyes were not dull, they were alert and twinkling, and his manner was suave, in-door, and faintly superior. They exchanged formalities. George was married and had three children. He seemed fairly interested, but not impressed by the news that Carrol had been abroad in the army. This disappointed Carrol.

"George," said the younger brother, these amenities having been disposed of, "we want to get some booze, and they won't sell us none. Can you get us some?"

George considered.

"Sure. Maybe I can. It may be half an hour, though."

"All right," agreed Carrol, "we'll wait."

At this Rose started to sit down in a convenient chair, but was hailed to his feet by the indignant George.

"Hey! Watch out, you! Can't sit down here! This room's all set for a twelve o'clock banquet."

"I ain't goin' to hurt it," said Rose resentfully. "I been through the delouser."

"Never mind," said George sternly, "if the head waiter seen me here talkin' he'd romp all over me."

"Oh."

The mention of the head waiter was full explanation to the other two; they fingered their overseas caps nervously and waited for a suggestion.

"I tell you," said George, after a pause, "I got a place you can wait; you just come here with me."

They followed him out the far door, through a deserted pantry and up a pair of dark winding stairs, emerging finally into a small room chiefly furnished by piles of pails and stacks of scrubbing brushes, and illuminated by a single dim electric light. There he left them, after soliciting two dollars and agreeing to return in half an hour with a quart of whiskey.

"George is makin' money, I bet," said Key gloomily as he seated himself on an inverted pail. "I bet he's making fifty dollars a week."

Rose nodded his head and spat.

"I bet he is, too."

"What'd he say the dance was of?"

"A lot of college fellas. Yale College."

They both nodded solemnly at each other.

"Wonder where that crowda sojers is now?"

"I don't know. I know that's too damn long to walk for me."

"Me too. You don't catch me walkin' that far."

Ten minutes later restlessness seized them.

"I'm goin' to see what's out here," said Rose, stepping cautiously toward the other door.

It was a swinging door of green baize and he pushed it open a cautious inch.

"See anything?"

For answer Rose drew in his breath sharply.

"Doggone! Here's some liquor I'll say!"

"Liquor?"

Key joined Rose at the door, and looked eagerly.

"I'll tell the world that's liquor," he said, after a moment of concentrated gazing.

It was a room about twice as large as the one they were in—and in it was prepared a radiant feast of spirits. There were long walls of alternating bottles set along two white covered tables; whiskey, gin, brandy, French and Italian vermouths, and orange juice, not to mention an array of syphons and two great empty punch bowls. The room was as yet uninhabited.

"It's for this dance they're just starting," whispered Key; "hear the violins playin'? Say, boy, I wouldn't mind havin' a dance."

They closed the door softly and exchanged a glance of mutual comprehension. There was no need of feeling each other out.

"I'd like to get my hands on a coupla those bottles," said Rose emphatically,

"Me too."

"Do you suppose we'd get seen?"

Key considered.

"Maybe we better wait till they start drinkin' 'em. They got 'em all laid out now, and they know how many of them there are."

They debated this point for several minutes. Rose was all for getting his hands on a bottle now and tucking it under his coat before any one came into the room. Key, however, advocated caution. He was afraid he might get his brother in trouble. If they waited till some of the bottles were opened it'd be all right to take one, and everybody'd think it was one of the college fellas.

While they were still engaged in argument George Key hurried through the room and, barely grunting at them, disappeared by way of the green baize door. A minute later they heard several corks pop, and then the sound of crackling ice and splashing liquid. George was mixing the punch.

The soldiers exchanged delighted grins.

"Oh, boy!" whispered Rose.

George reappeared.

"Just keep low, boys," he said quickly. "I'll have your stuff for you in five minutes."

He disappeared through the door by which he had come.

As soon as his footsteps receded down the stairs, Rose, after a cautious look, darted into the room of delights and reappeared with a bottle in his hand.

"Here's what I say," he said, as they sat radiantly digesting their first drink. "We'll wait till he comes up, and we'll ask him if we can't just stay here and drink what he brings us—see. We'll tell him we haven't got any place to drink it—see. Then we can sneak in there whenever there ain't nobody in that there room and tuck a bottle under our coats. We'll have enough to last us a coupla days—see?"

"Sure," agreed Rose enthusiastically. "Oh, boy! And if we want to we can sell it to sojers any time we want to."

They were silent for a moment thinking rosily of this idea. Then Key reached up and unhooked the collar of his O.D. coat.

"It's hot in here, ain't it?"

Rose agreed earnestly.

"Hot as hell."

4

She was still quite angry when she came out of the dressing-room and crossed the intervening parlor of politeness that opened onto the hall—angry not so much at the actual happening which was, after all, the merest commonplace of her social existence, but because it had occurred on this particular night. She had no quarrel with herself. She had acted with that correct mixture of dignity and reticent pity which she always employed. She had succinctly and deftly snubbed him.

It had happened when their taxi was leaving the Biltmore—hadn't gone half a block. He had lifted his right arm awkwardly—she was on his right side—and attempted to settle it snugly around the crimson fur-trimmed opera cloak she wore. This in itself had been a mistake. It was inevitably more graceful for a young man attempting to embrace a young lady of whose acquiescence he was not certain, to first put his far arm around her. It avoided that awkward movement of raising the near arm.

His second *faux pas* was unconscious. She had spent the afternoon at the hairdresser's; the idea of any calamity overtaking her hair was extremely repugnant—yet as Peter made his unfortunate attempt the point of his elbow had just faintly brushed it. That was his second *faux pas*. Two were quite enough.

He had begun to murmur. At the first murmur she had decided that he was nothing but a college boy—Edith was twenty-two, and anyhow, this dance, first of its kind since the war, was reminding her, with the accelerating rhythm of its associations, of something else—of another dance and another man, a man for whom her feelings had been little more than a sad-eyed, adolescent mooniness. Edith Bradin was falling in love with her recollection of Gordon Sterrett.

So she came out of the dressing-room at Delmonico's and stood for a second in the doorway looking over the shoulders of a black dress in front of her at the groups of Yale men who flitted like dignified black moths around the head of the stairs. From the room she had left drifted out the heavy fragrance left by the passage to and fro of many scented young beauties—rich perfumes and the fragile memory-laden dust of fragrant powders. This odor drifting out acquired the tang of cigarette smoke in the hall, and then settled sensuously down the stairs and permeated the ballroom where the Gamma Psi dance was to be held. It was an odor she knew well, exciting, stimulating, restlessly sweet—the odor of a fashionable dance.

She thought of her own appearance. Her bare arms and shoulders were powdered to a creamy white. She knew they looked very soft and would gleam like milk against the black backs that were to silhouette them tonight. The hairdressing had been a success; her reddish mass of hair was piled and crushed and creased to an arrogant marvel of mobile curves. Her lips were finely made of deep carmine; the irises of her eyes were delicate, breakable blue, like china eyes. She was a complete, infinitely delicate, quite perfect thing of beauty, flowing in an even line from a complex coiffure to two small slim feet.

She thought of what she would say to-night at this revel, faintly presaged already by the sounds of high and low laughter and slippered footsteps, and movements of couples up and down the stairs. She would talk the language she had talked for many years—her line—made up of the current expressions, bit of journalese and college slang strung together into an intrinsic whole, careless, faintly provocative, delicately sentimental. She smiled faintly as she heard a girl sitting on the stairs near her say: "You don't know the half of it, dearie!"

And as she smiled her anger melted for a moment, and closing her eyes she drew in a deep breath of pleasure. She dropped her arms to her side until they were faintly touching the sleek sheath that covered and suggested her figure. She had never felt her own softness so much nor so enjoyed the whiteness of her own arms.

"I smell sweet," she said to herself simply, and then came another thought —"I'm made for love."

She liked the sound of this and thought it again; then in inevitable succession came her new-born riot of dreams about Gordon. The twist of her imagination which, two months before, had disclosed to her her unguessed desire to see him again, seemed now to have been leading up to this dance, this hour.

For all her sleek beauty, Edith was a grave, slow-thinking girl. There was a streak in her of that same desire to ponder, of that adolescent idealism that had turned her brother socialist and pacifist. Henry Bradin had left Cornell, where he had been an instructor in economics, and had come to New York to pour the latest cures for incurable evils into the columns of a radical weekly newspaper.

Edith, less fatuously, would have been content to cure Gordon Sterrett. There was a quality of weakness in Gordon that she wanted to take care of; there was a helplessness in him that she wanted to protect. And she wanted someone she had known a long while, someone who had loved her a long while. She was a little tired; she wanted to get married. Out of a pile of letters, half a dozen pictures and as many memories, and this weariness, she had decided that next time she saw Gordon their relations were going to be changed. She would say something that would change them. There was this evening. This was her evening. All evenings were her evenings.

Then her thoughts were interrupted by a solemn undergraduate with a hurt look and an air of strained formality who presented himself before her and bowed unusually low. It was the man she had come with, Peter Himmel. He was tall and humorous, with horned-rimmed glasses and an air of attractive whimsicality. She suddenly rather disliked him—probably because he had not succeeded in kissing her.

"Well," she began, "are you still furious at me?"

"Not at all."

She stepped forward and took his arm.

"I'm sorry," she said softly. "I don't know why I snapped out that way. I'm in a bum humor to-night for some strange reason. I'm sorry."

"S'all right," he mumbled, "don't mention it."

He felt disagreeably embarrassed. Was she rubbing in the fact of his late failure?

"It was a mistake," she continued, on the same consciously gentle key. "We'll both forget it." For this he hated her.

A few minutes later they drifted out on the floor while the dozen swaying, sighing members of the specially hired jazz orchestra informed the crowded ballroom that "if a saxophone and me are left alone why then two is compan-ee!"

A man with a mustache cut in.

"Hello," he began reprovingly. "You don't remember me."

"I can't just think of your name," she said lightly—"and I know you so well."

"I met you up at—" His voice trailed disconsolately off as a man with very fair hair cut in. Edith murmured a conventional "Thanks, loads—cut in later," to the *inconnu*.

The very fair man insisted on shaking hands enthusiastically. She placed him as one of the numerous Jims of her acquaintance—last name a mystery. She remembered even that he had a peculiar rhythm in dancing and found as they started that she was right.

"Going to be here long?" he breathed confidentially.

She leaned back and looked up at him.

"Couple of weeks."

"Where are you?"

"Biltmore. Call me up some day."

"I mean it," he assured her. "I will. We'll go to tea."

"So do I—Do."

A dark man cut in with intense formality.

"You don't remember me, do you?" he said gravely.

"I should say I do. Your name's Harlan."

"No-ope. Barlow."

"Well, I knew there were two syllables anyway. You're the boy that played the ukulele so well up at Howard Marshall's house party."

"I played—but not——"

A man with prominent teeth cut in. Edith inhaled a slight cloud of whiskey. She liked men to have had something to drink; they were so much more cheerful, and appreciative and complimentary—much easier to talk to.

"My name's Dean, Philip Dean," he said cheerfully. "You don't remember me, I know, but you used to come up to New Haven with a fellow I roomed with senior year, Gordon Sterrett."

Edith looked up quickly.

"Yes, I went up with him twice—to the Pump and Slipper and the Junior prom."

"You've seen him, of course," said Dean carelessly. "He's here tonight. I saw him just a minute ago."

Edith started. Yet she had felt quite sure he would be here.

"Why, no, I haven't——"

A fat man with red hair cut in.

"Hello, Edith," he began.

"Why—hello there——"

She slipped, stumbled lightly.

"I'm sorry, dear," she murmured mechanically.

She had seen Gordon—Gordon very white and listless, leaning against the side of a doorway, smoking and looking into the ballroom. Edith could see that his face was thin and wan—that the hand he raised to his lips with a cigarette was trembling. They were dancing quite close to him now.

"—They invite so darn many extra fellas that you—" the short man was saying.

"Hello, Gordon," called Edith over he partner's shoulder. Her heart was pounding wildly.

His large dark eyes were fixed on her. He took a step in her direction. Her partner turned her away—she heard his voice bleating——

"—but half the stags get lit and leave before long, so——"

Then a low tone at her side.

"May I, please?"

She was dancing suddenly with Gordon; one of his arms was around her; she felt it tighten spasmodically; felt his hand on her back with the fingers spread. Her hand holding the little lace handkerchief was crushed in his.

"Why Gordon," she began breathlessly.

"Hello, Edith."

She slipped again—was tossed forward by her recovery until her face touched the black cloth of his dinner coat. She loved him—she knew she loved him—then for a minute there was silence while a strange feeling of uneasiness crept over her. Something was wrong.

Of a sudden her heart wrenched, and turned over as she realized what it was. He was pitiful and wretched, a little drunk, and miserably tired.

"Oh—" she cried involuntarily.

His eyes looked down at her. She saw suddenly that they were blood-streaked and rolling uncontrollably.

"Gordon," she murmured, "we'll sit down, I want to sit down."

They were nearly in mid-floor, but she had seen two men start toward her from opposite sides of the room, so she halted, seized Gordon's limp hand and led him bumping through the crowd, her mouth tight shut, her face a little pale under her rouge, her eyes trembling with tears.

She found a place high up on the soft-carpeted stairs, and he sat down heavily beside her.

"Well," he began, staring at her unsteadily, "I certainly am glad to see you, Edith."

She looked at him without answering. The effect of this on her was immeasurable. For years she had seen men in various stages of intoxication, from uncles all the way down to chauffeurs, and her feelings had varied from amusement to disgust, but here for the first time she was seized with a new feeling—an unutterable horror.

"Gordon," she said accusingly and almost crying, "you look like the devil."

He nodded. "I've had trouble, Edith."

"Trouble?"

"All sorts of trouble. Don't you say anything to the family, but I'm all gone to pieces. I'm a mess, Edith."

His lower lip was sagging. He seemed scarcely to see her.

"Can't you—can't you," she hesitated, "can't you tell me about it, Gordon? You know I'm always interested in you."

She bit her lip—she had intended to say something stronger, but found at the end that she couldn't bring it out.

Gordon shook his head dully. "I can't tell you. You're a good woman. I can't tell a good woman the story."

"Rot," she said, defiantly. "I think it's a perfect insult to call any one a good woman in that way. It's a slam. You've been drinking, Gordon."

"Thanks." He inclined his head gravely. "Thanks for the information."

"Why do you drink?"

"Because I'm so damn miserable."

"Do you think drinking's going to make it any better?"

"What you doing—trying to reform me?"

"No; I'm trying to help you, Gordon. Can't you tell me about it?"

"I'm in an awful mess. Best thing you can do is to pretend not to know me."

"Why, Gordon?"

"I'm sorry I cut in on you—it's unfair to you. You're pure woman—and all that sort of thing. Here, I'll get some one else to dance with you."

He rose clumsily to his feet, but she reached up and pulled him down beside her on the stairs.

"Here, Gordon. You're ridiculous. You're hurting me. You're acting like a —like a crazy man——"

"I admit it. I'm a little crazy. Something's wrong with me, Edith. There's something left me. It doesn't matter."

"It does, tell me."

"Just that. I was always queer—little bit different from other boys. All right in college, but now it's all wrong. Things have been snapping inside me for four months like little hooks on a dress, and it's about to come off when a few more hooks go. I'm very gradually going loony."

He turned his eyes full on her and began to laugh, and she shrank away from him.

"What *is* the matter?"

"Just me," he repeated. "I'm going loony. This whole place is like a dream to me—this Delmonico's——"

As he talked she saw he had changed utterly. He wasn't at all light and gay and careless—a great lethargy and discouragement had come over him. Revulsion seized her, followed by a faint, surprising boredom. His voice seemed to come out of a great void.

"Edith," he said, "I used to think I was clever, talented, an artist. Now I know I'm nothing. Can't draw, Edith. Don't know why I'm telling you this."

She nodded absently.

"I can't draw, I can't do anything. I'm poor as a church mouse." He laughed, bitterly and rather too loud. "I've become a damn beggar, a leech on my friends. I'm a failure. I'm poor as hell."

Her distaste was growing. She barely nodded this time, waiting for her first possible cue to rise.

Suddenly Gordon's eyes filled with tears.

"Edith," he said, turning to her with what was evidently a strong effort at self-control, "I can't tell you what it means to me to know there's one person left who's interested in me."

He reached out and patted her hand, and involuntarily she drew it away.

"It's mighty fine of you," he repeated.

"Well," she said slowly, looking him in the eye, "any one's always glad to see an old friend—but I'm sorry to see you like this, Gordon."

There was a pause while they looked at each other, and the momentary eagerness in his eyes wavered. She rose and stood looking at him, her face quite expressionless.

"Shall we dance?" she suggested, coolly.

—Love is fragile—she was thinking—but perhaps the pieces are saved, the things that hovered on lips, that might have been said. The new love words, the tendernesses learned, are treasured up for the next lover.

5

Peter Himmel, escort to the lovely Edith, was unaccustomed to being snubbed; having been snubbed, he was hurt and embarrassed, and ashamed of himself. For a matter of two months he had been on special delivery terms with Edith Bradin and knowing that the one excuse and explanation of the special delivery letter is its value in sentimental correspondence, he had believed himself quite sure of his ground. He searched in vain for any reason why she should have taken this attitude in the matter of a simple kiss.

Therefore when he was cut in on by the man with the mustache he went out into the hall and, making up a sentence, said it over to himself several times. Considerably deleted, this was it:

"Well, if any girl ever led a man on and then jolted him, she did—and she has no kick coming if I go out and get beautifully boiled."

So he walked through the supper room into a small room adjoining it, which he had located earlier in the evening. It was a room in which there were several large bowls of punch flanked by many bottles. He took a seat beside the table which held the bottles.

At the second highball, boredom, disgust, the monotony of time, the turbidity of events, sank into a vague background before which glittering cobwebs formed. Things became reconciled to themselves, things lay quietly on their shelves; the troubles of the day arranged themselves in trim formation and at his curt wish of dismissal, marched off and disappeared. And with the departure of worry came brilliant, permeating symbolism. Edith became a flighty, negligible girl, not to be worried over; rather to be laughed at. She fitted like a figure of his own dream into the surface world forming about him. He himself became in a measure symbolic, a type of the continent bacchanal, the brilliant dreamer at play.

Then the symbolic mood faded and as he sipped his third highball his imagination yielded to the warm glow and he lapsed into a state similar to floating on his back in pleasant water. It was at this point that he noticed that a green baize door near him was open about two inches, and that through the aperture a pair of eyes were watching him intently.

"Hm," murmured Peter calmly.

The green door closed—and then opened again—a bare half inch this time.

"Peek-a-boo," murmured Peter.

The door remained stationary and then he became aware of a series of tense intermittent whispers.

"One guy."

"What's he doin'?"

"He's sittin' lookin'."

"He better beat it off. We gotta get another li'l' bottle."

Peter listened while the words filtered into his consciousness.

"Now this," he thought, "is most remarkable."

He was excited. He was jubilant. He felt that he had stumbled upon a mystery. Affecting an elaborate carelessness he arose and walked around the table—then, turning quickly, pulled open the green door, precipitating Private Rose into the room.

Peter bowed.

"How do you do?" he said.

Private Rose set one foot slightly in front of the other, poised for fight, flight, or compromise.

"How do you do?" repeated Peter politely.

"I'm o'right."

"Can I offer you a drink?"

Private Rose looked at him searchingly, suspecting possible sarcasm.

"O'right," he said finally.

Peter indicated a chair.

"Sit down."

"I got a friend," said Rose, "I got a friend in there." He pointed to the green door.

"By all means let's have him in."

Peter crossed over, opened the door and welcomed in Private Key, very suspicious and uncertain and guilty. Chairs were found and the three took their seats around the punch bowl. Peter gave them each a highball and offered them a cigarette from his case. They accepted both with some diffidence.

"Now," continued Peter easily, "may I ask why you gentlemen prefer to lounge away your leisure hours in a room which is chiefly furnished, as far as I can see, with scrubbing brushes. And when the human race has progressed to the stage where seventeen thousand chairs are manufactured on every day except Sunday—" he paused. Rose and Key regarded him vacantly. "Will you tell me," went on Peter, "why you choose to rest yourselves on articles intended for the transportation of water from one place to another?"

At this point Rose contributed a grunt to the conversation.

"And lastly," finished Peter, "will you tell me why, when you are in a building beautifully hung with enormous candelabra, you prefer to spend these evening hours under one anemic electric light?"

Rose looked at Key; Key looked at Rose. They laughed; they laughed uproariously; they found it was impossible to look at each other without laughing. But they were not laughing with this man—they were laughing at him. To them a man who talked after this fashion was either raving drunk or raving crazy.

"You are Yale men, I presume," said Peter, finishing his highball and preparing another.

They laughed again.

"Na-ah."

"So? I thought perhaps you might be members of that lowly section of the university known as the Sheffield Scientific School."

"Na-ah."

"Hm. Well, that's too bad. No doubt you are Harvard men, anxious to preserve your incognito in this—this paradise of violet blue, as the newspapers say."

"Na-ah," said Key scornfully, "we was just waitin' for somebody."

"Ah," exclaimed Peter, rising and filling their glasses, "very interestin'. Had a date with a scrublady, eh?"

They both denied this indignantly.

"It's all right," Peter reassured them, "don't apologize. A scrublady's as good as any lady in the world. Kipling says 'Any lady and Judy O'Grady under the skin.' "

"Sure," said Key, winking broadly at Rose.

"My case, for instance," continued Peter, finishing his glass. "I got a girl up there that's spoiled. Spoildest darn girl I ever saw. Refused to kiss me; no reason whatsoever. Led me on deliberately to think sure I want to kiss you and then plunk! Threw me over! What's the younger generation comin' to?"

"Say tha's hard luck," said Key—"that's awful hard luck."

"Oh boy!" said Rose.

"Have another?" said Peter.

"We got in a sort of fight for a while," said Key after a pause, "but it was too far away."

"A fight?—tha's stuff!" said Peter, seating himself unsteadily. "Fight 'em all! I was in the army."

"This was with a Bolshevik fella."

"Tha's stuff!" exclaimed Peter, enthusiastic. "That's what I say! Kill the Bolshevik! Exterminate 'em!"

"We're Americuns," said Rose, implying a sturdy, defiant patriotism.

"Sure," said Peter. "Greatest race in the world! We're all Americuns! Have another."

They had another.

6

At one o'clock a special orchestra, special even in a day of special orchestras, arrived at Delmonico's, and its members, seating themselves arrogantly around the piano, took up the burden of providing music for the Gamma Psi Fraternity. They were headed by a famous flute-player, distinguished throughout New York for his feat of standing on his head and shimmying with his shoulders while he played the latest jazz on his flute. During his performance the lights were extinguished except for the spotlight on the flute-player and another roving beam that threw flickering shadows and changing kaleidoscopic colors over the massed dancers.

Edith had danced herself into that tired, dreamy state habitual only with débutantes, a state equivalent to the glow of a noble soul after several long highballs. Her mind floated vaguely on the bosom of her music; her partners changed with the unreality of phantoms under the colorful shifting dusk, and to her present coma it seemed as if days had passed since the dance began. She had talked on many fragmentary subjects with many men. She had been kissed once and made love to six times. Earlier in the evening different undergraduates had danced with her, but now, like all the more popular girls there, she had her own entourage—that is, half a dozen gallants had singled her out or were alternating her charms with those of some other chosen beauty; they cut in on her in regular, inevitable succession.

Several times she had seen Gordon—he had been sitting a long time on the stairway with his palm to his head, his dull eyes fixed at an infinite speck on the floor before him, very depressed, he looked, and quite drunk—but Edith each time had averted her glance hurriedly. All that seemed long ago; her mind was passive now, her senses were lulled to trance-like sleep; only her feet danced and her voice talked on in hazy sentimental banter.

But Edith was not nearly so tired as to be incapable of moral indignation when Peter Himmel cut in on her, sublimely and happily drunk. She gasped and looked up at him.

"Why, *Peter!*"

"I'm a li'l' stewed, Edith."

"Why, Peter, you're a *peach*, you are! Don't you think it's a bum way of doing—when you're with me?"

Then she smiled unwillingly, for he was looking at her with owlish sentimentality varied with a silly spasmodic smile.

"Darlin' Edith," he began earnestly, "you know I love you, don't you?"

"You tell it well."

"I love you—and I merely wanted you to kiss me," he added sadly.

His embarrassment, his shame, we're both gone. She was a mos' beautiful girl in whole worl'. Mos' beautiful eyes, like stars above. He wanted to 'pologize—firs', for presuming try to kiss her; second, for drinking—but he'd been so discouraged 'cause he had thought she was mad at him——

The red-fat man cut in, and looking up at Edith smiled radiantly.

"Did you bring any one?" she asked.

No. The red-fat man was a stag.

"Well, would you mind—would it be an awful bother for you to—to take me home to-night?" (this extreme diffidence was a charming affectation on Edith's part—she knew that the red-fat man would immediately dissolve into a paroxysm of delight).

"Bother? Why, good Lord, I'd be darn glad to! You know I'd be darn glad to."

"Thanks *loads!* You're awfully sweet."

She glanced at her wrist-watch. It was half-past one. And, as she said "half-past one" to herself, it floated vaguely into her mind that her brother had told her at luncheon that he worked in the office of his newspaper until after one-thirty every evening.

Edith turned suddenly to her current partner.

"What street is Delmonico's on, anyway?"

"Street? Oh, why Fifth Avenue, of course."

"I mean, what cross street?"

"Why—let's see—it's on Forty-fourth Street."

This verified what she had thought. Henry's office must be across the street and just around the corner, and it occurred to her immediately that she might slip over for a moment and surprise him, float in on him, a shimmering marvel in her new crimson opera cloak and "cheer him up." It was exactly the sort of thing Edith revelled in doing—an unconventional, jaunty thing. The idea reached out and gripped at her imagination—after an instant's hesitation she had decided.

"My hair is just about to tumble entirely down," she said pleasantly to her partner; "would you mind if I go and fix it?"

"Not at all."

"You're a peach."

A few minutes later, wrapped in her crimson opera cloak, she flitted down a side-stairs, her cheeks glowing with excitement at her little adventure. She ran by a couple who stood at the door—a weak-chinned waiter and an over-rouged young lady, in hot dispute—and opening the outer door stepped into the warm May night.

7

The over-rouged young lady followed her with a brief, bitter glance—then turned again to the weak-chinned waiter and took up her argument.

"You better go up and tell him I'm here," she said defiantly, "or I'll go up myself."

"No, you don't!" said George sternly.

The girl smiled sardonically.

"Oh, I don't, don't I? Well, let me tell you I know more college fellas and more of 'em know me, and are glad to take me out on a party, than you ever saw in your whole life."

"Maybe so——"

"Maybe so," she interrupted. "Oh, it's all right for any of 'em like that one that just ran out—God knows where *she* went—it's all right for them that are asked here to come or go as they like—but when I want to see a friend they have some cheap, ham-slinging, bring-me-a-doughnut waiter to stand here and keep me out."

"See here," said the elder Key indignantly, "I can't lose my job. Maybe this fella you're talkin' about doesn't want to see you."

"Oh, he wants to see me all right."

"Anyway, how could I find him in all that crowd?"

"Oh, he'll be there," she asserted confidently. "You just ask anybody for Gordon Sterrett and they'll point him out to you. They all know each other, those fellas."

She produced a mesh bag, and taking out a dollar bill handed it to George.

"Here," she said, "here's a bribe. You find him and give him my message. You tell him if he isn't here in five minutes I'm coming up."

George shook his head pessimistically, considered the question for a moment, wavered violently, and then withdrew.

In less than the allotted time Gordon came down-stairs. He was drunker than he had been earlier in the evening and in a different way. The liquor seemed to have hardened on him like a crust. He was heavy and lurching —almost incoherent when he talked.

"'Lo, Jewel," he said thickly. "Came right away. Jewel, I couldn't get that money. Tried my best."

"Money nothing!" she snapped. "You haven't been near me for ten days. What's the matter?"

He shook his head slowly.

"Been very low, Jewel. Been sick."

"Why didn't you tell me if you were sick. I don't care about the money that bad. I didn't start bothering you about it at all until you began neglecting me."

Again he shook his head.

"Haven't been neglecting you. Not at all."

"Haven't! You haven't been near me for three weeks, unless you been so drunk you didn't know what you were doing."

"Been sick, Jewel," he repeated, turning his eyes upon her wearily.

"You're well enough to come and play with your society friends here all right. You told me you'd meet me for dinner, and you said you'd have some money for me. You didn't even bother to ring me up."

"I couldn't get any money."

"Haven't I just been saying that doesn't matter? I wanted to see *you*, Gordon, but you seem to prefer your somebody else."

He denied this bitterly.

"Then get your hat and come along," she suggested.

Gordon hesitated—and she came suddenly close to him and slipped her arms around his neck.

"Come on with me, Gordon," she said in a half whisper. "We'll go over to Devineries' and have a drink, and then we can go up to my apartment."

"I can't, Jewel,——"

"You can," she said intensely.

"I'm sick as a dog!"

"Well, then, you oughtn't to stay here and dance."

With a glance around him in which relief and despair were mingled,

Gordon hesitated; then she suddenly pulled him to her and kissed him with soft, pulpy lips.

"All right," he said heavily. "I'll get my hat."

8

When Edith came out into the clear blue of the May night she found the Avenue deserted. The windows of the big shops were dark; over their doors were drawn great iron masks until they were only shadowy tombs of the late day's splendor. Glancing down toward Forty-second Street she saw a commingled blur of lights from the all-night restaurants. Over on Sixth Avenue the elevated, a flare of fire, roared across the street between the glimmering parallels of light at the station and streaked along into the crisp dark. But at Forty-fourth Street it was very quiet.

Pulling her cloak close about her Edith darted across the Avenue. She started nervously as a solitary man passed her and said in a hoarse whisper —"Where bound, kiddo?" She was reminded of a night in her childhood when she had walked around the block in her pajamas and a dog had howled at her from a mystery-big back yard.

In a minute she had reached her destination, a two-story, comparatively old building on Forty-fourth, in the upper windows of which she thankfully detected a wisp of light. It was bright enough outside for her to make out the sign beside the window—the *New York Trumpet*. She stepped inside a dark hall and after a second saw the stairs in the corner.

Then she was in a long, low room furnished with many desks and hung on all sides with file copies of newspapers. There were only two occupants. They were sitting at different ends of the room, each wearing a green eye-shade and writing by a solitary desk light.

For a moment she stood uncertainly in the doorway, and then both men turned around simultaneously and she recognized her brother.

"Why, Edith!" He rose quickly and approached her in surprise, removing his eye-shade. He was tall, lean, and dark, with black, piercing eyes under very thick glasses. They were far-away eyes that seemed always fixed just over the head of the person to whom he was talking.

He put his hands on her arms and kissed her cheek.

"What is it?" he repeated in some alarm.

"I was at a dance across at Delmonico's, Henry," she said excitedly, "and I couldn't resist tearing over to see you."

"I'm glad you did." His alertness gave way quickly to a habitual vagueness. "You oughtn't to be out alone at night though, ought you?"

The man at the other end of the room had been looking at them curiously, but at Henry's beckoning gesture he approached. He was loosely fat with little twinkling eyes, and, having removed his collar and tie, he gave the impression of a Middle-Western farmer on a Sunday afternoon.

"This is my sister," said Henry. "She dropped in to see me."

"How do you do?" said the fat man, smiling. "My name's Bartholomew, Miss Bradin. I know your brother has forgotten it long ago."

Edith laughed politely.

"Well," he continued, "not exactly gorgeous quarters we have here, are they?"

Edith looked around the room.

"They seem very nice," she replied. "Where do you keep the bombs?"

"The bombs?" repeated Batholomew, laughing. "That's pretty good—the bombs. Did you hear her, Henry? She wants to know where we keep the bombs. Say, that's pretty good."

Edith swung herself around onto a vacant desk and sat dangling her feet over the edge. Her brother took a seat beside her.

"Well," he asked, absent-mindedly, "how do you like New York this trip?"

"Not bad. I'll be over at the Biltmore with the Hoyts until Sunday. Can't you come to luncheon to-morrow?"

He thought a moment.

"I'm especially busy," he objected, "and I hate women in groups."

"All right," she agreed, unruffled. "Let's you and me have luncheon together."

"Very well."

"I'll call for you at twelve."

Bartholomew was obviously anxious to return to his desk, but apparently considered that it would be rude to leave without some parting pleasantry.

"Well"—he began awkwardly.

They both turned to him.

"Well, we—we had an exciting time earlier in the evening."

The two men exchanged glances.

"You should have come earlier," continued Bartholomew, somewhat encouraged. "We had a regular vaudeville."

"Did you really?"

"A serenade," said Henry. "A lot of soldiers gathered down there in the street and began to yell at the sign."

"Why?" she demanded.

"Just a crowd," said Henry, abstractedly. "All crowds have to howl. They didn't have anybody with much initiative in the lead, or they'd probably have forced their way in here and smashed things up."

"Yes," said Bartholomew, turning again to Edith, "you should have been here."

He seemed to consider this a sufficient cue for withdrawal, for he turned abruptly and went back to his desk.

"Are the soldiers all set against the Socialists?" demanded Edith of her brother. "I mean do they attack you violently and all that?"

Henry replaced his eye-shade and yawned.

"The human race has come a long way," he said casually, "but most of us are throw-backs; the soldiers don't know what they want, or what they hate, or what they like. They're used to acting in large bodies, and they seem to have to make demonstrations. So it happens to be against us. There've been riots all over the city to-night. It's May Day, you see."

"Was the disturbance here pretty serious?"

"Not a bit," he said scornfully. "About twenty-five of them stopped in the street about nine o'clock, and began to bellow at the moon."

"Oh"— She changed the subject. "You're glad to see me, Henry?"

"Why, sure."

"You don't seem to be."

"I am."

"I suppose you think I'm a—a waster. Sort of the World's Worst Butterfly."

Henry laughed.

"Not at all. Have a good time while you're young. Why? Do I seem like the priggish and earnest youth?"

"No—" She paused, "—but somehow I began thinking how absolutely different the party I'm on is from—from all your purposes. It seems sort of —of incongruous, doesn't it?—me being at a party like that, and you over here working for a thing that'll make that sort of party impossible ever any more, if your ideas work."

"I don't think of it that way. You're young, and you're acting just as you were brought up to act. Go ahead—have a good time."

Her feet, which had been idly swinging, stopped and her voice dropped a note.

"I wish you'd—you'd come back to Harrisburg and have a good time. Do you feel sure that you're on the right track——"

"You're wearing beautiful stockings," he interrupted. "What on earth are they?"

"They're embroidered," she replied, glancing down. "Aren't they cunning?" She raised her skirts and uncovered slim, silk-sheathed calves. "Or do you disapprove of silk stockings?"

He seemed slightly exasperated, bent his dark eyes on her piercingly.

"Are you trying to make me out as criticizing you in any way, Edith?"

"Not at all——"

She paused. Bartholomew had uttered a grunt. She turned and saw that he had left his desk and was standing at the window.

"What is it?" demanded Henry.

"People," said Bartholomew, and then after an instant: "Whole jam of them. They're coming from Sixth Avenue."

"People."

The fat man pressed his nose to the pane.

"Soldiers, by God!" he said emphatically. "I had an idea they'd come back."

Edith jumped to her feet, and running over joined Bartholomew at the window.

"There's a lot of them!" she cried excitedly. "Come here, Henry!"

Henry readjusted his shade, but kept his seat.

"Hadn't we better turn out the lights?" suggested Bartholomew.

"No. They'll go away in a minute."

"They're not," said Edith, peering from the window. "They're not even thinking of going away. There's more of them coming. Look—there's a whole crowd turning the corner of Sixth Avenue."

By the yellow glow and blue shadows of the street lamp she could see that the sidewalk was crowded with men. They were mostly in uniform, some sober, some enthusiastically drunk, and over the whole swept an incoherent clamor and shouting.

Henry rose, and going to the window exposed himself as a long silhouette against the office lights. Immediately the shouting became a steady yell, and a rattling fusillade of small missiles, corners of tobacco plugs, cigarette-boxes, and even pennies beat against the window. The sounds of the racket now began floating up the stairs as the folding doors revolved.

"They're coming up!" cried Bartholomew.

Edith turned anxiously to Henry.

"They're coming up, Henry."

From down-stairs in the lower hall their cries were now quite audible.

"—God damn Socialists!"

"Pro-Germans! Boche-lovers!"

"Second floor, front! Come on!"

"We'll get the sons——"

The next five minutes passed in a dream. Edith was conscious that the clamor burst suddenly upon the three of them like a cloud of rain, that there was a thunder of many feet on the stairs, that Henry had seized her arm and drawn her back toward the rear of the office. Then the door opened and an overflow of men were forced into the room—not the leaders, but simply those who happened to be in front.

"Hello, Bo!"

"Up late, ain't you?"

"You an' your girl. Damn *you!*"

She noticed that two very drunken soldiers had been forced to the front, where they wobbled fatuously—one of them was short and dark, the other was tall and weak of chin.

Henry stepped forward and raised his hand.

"Friends!" he said.

The clamor faded into a momentary stillness, punctuated with mutterings.

"Friends!" he repeated, his far-away eyes fixed over the heads of the crowd, "you're injuring no one but yourselves by breaking in here to-night. Do we look like rich men? Do we look like Germans? I ask you in all fairness——"

"Pipe down!"

"I'll say you do!"

"Say, who's your lady friend, buddy?"

A man in civilian clothes, who had been pawing over a table, suddenly held up a newspaper.

"Here it is!" he shouted. "They wanted the Germans to win the war!"

A new overflow from the stairs was shouldered in and of a sudden the room was full of men all closing around the pale little group at the back. Edith saw that the tall soldier with the weak chin was still in front. The short dark one had disappeared.

She edged slightly backward, stood close to the open window, through which came a clear breath of cool night air.

Then the room was a riot. She realized that the soldiers were surging forward, glimpsed the fat man swinging a chair over his head—instantly the lights went out, and she felt the push of warm bodies under rough cloth, and her ears were full of shouting and trampling and hard breathing.

A figure flashed by her out of nowhere, tottered, was edged sideways, and of a sudden disappeared helplessly out through the open window with a frightened, fragmentary cry that died staccato on the bosom of the clamor. By the faint light streaming from the building backing on the area Edith had a quick impression that it had been the tall soldier with the weak chin.

Anger rose astonishingly in her. She swung her arms wildly, edged blindly toward the thickest of the scuffling. She heard grunts, curses, the muffled impact of fists.

"Henry!" she called frantically, "Henry!"

Then, it was minutes later, she felt suddenly that there were other figures in the room. She heard a voice, deep, bullying, authoritative; she saw yellow rays of light sweeping here and there in the fracas. The cries became more scattered. The scuffling increased and then stopped.

Suddenly the lights were on and the room was full of policemen, clubbing left and right. The deep voice boomed out:

"Here now! Here now! Here now!"

And then:

"Quiet down and get out! Here now!"

The room seemed to empty like a wash-bowl. A policeman fast-grappled in the corner released his hold on his soldier antagonist and started him with a shove toward the door. The deep voice continued. Edith perceived now that it came from a bull-necked police captain standing near the door.

"Here now! This is no way! One of your own sojers got shoved out of the back window an' killed hisself!"

"Henry!" called Edith, "Henry!"

She beat wildly with her fists on the back of the man in front of her; she brushed between two others; fought, shrieked, and beat her way to a very pale figure sitting on the floor close to a desk.

"Henry," she cried passionately, "what's the matter? What's the matter? Did they hurt you?"

His eyes were shut. He groaned and then looking up said disgustedly——

"They broke my leg. My God, the fools!"

"Here now!" called the police captain. "Here now! Here now!"

9

"Childs', Fifty-ninth Street," at eight o'clock of any morning differs from its sisters by less than the width of their marble tables or the degree of polish on the frying-pans. You will see there a crowd of poor people with sleep in the corners of their eyes, trying to look straight before them at their food so as not to see the other poor people. But Childs', Fifty-ninth, four hours earlier is quite unlike any Childs' restaurant from Portland, Oregon, to Portland, Maine. Within its pale but sanitary walls one finds a noisy medley of chorus girls, college boys, débutantes, rakes, *filles de joie*—a not unrepresentative mixture of the gayest of Broadway, and even of Fifth Avenue.

In the early morning of May the second it was unusually full. Over the marble-topped tables were bent the excited faces of flappers whose fathers owned individual villages. They were eating buckwheat cakes and scrambled eggs with relish and gusto, an accomplishment that it would have been utterly impossible for them to repeat in the same place four hours later.

Almost the entire crowd were from the Gamma Psi dance at Delmonico's except for several chorus girls from a midnight revue who sat at a side table and wished they'd taken off a little more make-up after the show. Here and there a drab, mouse-like figure, desperately out of place, watched the butterflies with a weary, puzzled curiosity. But the drab figure was the exception. This was the morning after May Day, and celebration was still in the air.

Gus Rose, sober but a little dazed, must be classed as one of the drab figures. How he had got himself from Forty-fourth Street to Fifty-ninth Street after the riot was only a hazy half-memory. He had seen the body of Carrol Key put in an ambulance and driven off, and then he had started up town with two or three soldiers. Somewhere between Forty-fourth Street and Fifty-ninth Street the other soldiers had met some women and disappeared. Rose had wandered to Columbus Circle and chosen the gleaming lights of Childs' to minister to his craving for coffee and doughnuts. He walked in and sat down.

All around him floated airy, inconsequential chatter and high-pitched laughter. At first he failed to understand, but after a puzzled five minutes he realized that this was the aftermath of some gay party. Here and there a restless, hilarious young man wandered fraternally and familiarly between the tables, shaking hands indiscriminately and pausing occasionally for a facetious chat, while excited waiters, bearing cakes and eggs aloft, swore at him silently, and bumped him out of the way. To Rose, seated at the most inconspicuous and least crowded table, the whole scene was a colorful circus of beauty and riotous pleasure.

He became gradually aware, after a few moments, that the couple seated diagonally across from him, with their backs to the crowd, were not the least interesting pair in the room. The man was drunk. He wore a dinner coat with a dishevelled tie and shirt swollen by spillings of water and wine. His eyes, dim and bloodshot, roved unnaturally from side to side. His breath came short between his lips.

"He's been on a spree!" thought Rose.

The woman was almost if not quite sober. She was pretty, with dark eyes and feverish high color, and she kept her active eyes fixed on her companion with the alertness of a hawk. From time to time she would lean and whisper intently to him, and he would answer by inclining his head heavily or by a particularly ghoulish and repellent wink.

Rose scrutinized them dumbly for some minutes, until the woman gave him a quick, resentful look; then he shifted his gaze to two of the most conspicuously hilarious of the promenaders who were on a protracted circuit of the tables. To his surprise he recognized in one of them the young man by whom he had been so ludicrously entertained at Delmonico's. This started him thinking of Key with a vague sentimentality, not unmixed with awe.

Key was dead. He had fallen thirty-five feet and split his skull like a cracked cocoanut.

"He was a darn good guy," thought Rose mournfully. "He was a darn good guy, o'right. That was awful hard luck about him."

The two promenaders approached and started down between Rose's table and the next, addressing friends and strangers alike with jovial familiarity. Suddenly Rose saw the fair-haired one with the prominent teeth stop, look unsteadily at the man and girl opposite, and then begin to move his head disapprovingly from side to side.

The man with the blood-shot eyes looked up.

"Gordy," said the promenader with the prominent teeth, "Gordy."

"Hello," said the man with the stained shirt thickly.

Prominent Teeth shook his finger pessimistically at the pair, giving the woman a glance of aloof condemnation.

"What'd I tell you Gordy?"

Gordon stirred in his seat.

"Go to hell!" he said.

Dean continued to stand there shaking his finger. The woman began to get angry.

"You go away!" she cried fiercely. "You're drunk, that's what you are!"

"So's he," suggested Dean, staying the motion of his finger and pointing it at Gordon.

Peter Himmel ambled up, owlish now and oratorically inclined.

"Here now," he began as if called upon to deal with some petty dispute between children. "Wha's all trouble?"

"You take your friend away," said Jewel tartly. "He's bothering us."

"What's 'at?"

"You heard me!" she said shrilly. "I said to take your drunken friend away."

Her rising voice rang out above the clatter of the restaurant and a waiter came hurrying up.

"You gotta be more quiet!"

"That fella's drunk," she cried. "He's insulting us."

"Ah-ha, Gordy," persisted the accused. "What'd I tell you." He turned to the waiter. "Gordy an' I friends. Been tryin' help him, haven't I, Gordy?"

Gordy looked up.

"Help me? Hell, no!"

Jewel rose suddenly, and seizing Gordon's arm assisted him to his feet.

"Come on, Gordy!" she said, leaning toward him and speaking in a half whisper. "Let's us get out of here. This fella's got a mean drunk on."

Gordon allowed himself to be urged to his feet and started toward the door. Jewel turned for a second and addressed the provoker of their flight.

"I know all about you!" she said fiercely. "Nice friend, you are, I'll say. He told me about you."

Then she seized Gordon's arm, and together they made their way through the curious crowd, paid their check, and went out.

"You'll have to sit down," said the waiter to Peter after they had gone.

"What's 'at? Sit down?"

"Yes—or get out."

Peter turned to Dean.

"Come on," he suggested. "Let's beat up this waiter."

"All right."

They advanced toward him, their faces grown stern. The waiter retreated.

Peter suddenly reached over to a plate on the table beside him and picking up a handful of hash tossed it into the air. It descended as a languid parabola in snowflake effect on the heads of those near by.

"Hey! Ease up!"

"Put him out!"

"Sit down, Peter!"

"Cut out that stuff!"

Peter laughed and bowed.

"Thank you for your kind applause, ladies and gents. If some one will lend me some more hash and a tall hat we will go on with the act."

The bouncer hustled up.

"You've gotta get out!" he said to Peter.

"Hell, no!"

"He's my friend!" put in Dean indignantly.

A crowd of waiters were gathering. "Put him out!"

"Better go, Peter."

There was a short struggle and the two were edged and pushed toward the door.

"I got a hat and a coat here!" cried Peter.

"Well, go get 'em and be spry about it!"

The bouncer released his hold on Peter, who, adopting a ludicrous air of extreme cunning, rushed immediately around to the other table, where he burst into derisive laughter and thumbed his nose at the exasperated waiters.

"Think I just better wait a l'il' longer," he announced.

The chase began. Four waiters were sent around one way and four another. Dean caught hold of two of them by the coat, and another struggle took place before the pursuit of Peter could be resumed; he was finally pinioned after overturning a sugar-bowl and several cups of coffee. A fresh argument ensued at the cashier's desk, where Peter attempted to buy another dish of hash to take with him and throw at policemen.

But the commotion upon his exit proper was dwarfed by another phenomenon which drew admiring glances and a prolonged involuntary "Ohh-h!" from every person in the restaurant.

The great plate-glass front had turned to a deep creamy blue, the color of a Maxfield Parrish moonlight—a blue that seemed to press close upon the pane as if to crowd its way into the restaurant. Dawn had come up in Columbus Circle, magical, breathless dawn, silhouetting the great statue of the immortal Christopher, and mingling in a curious and uncanny manner with the fading yellow electric light inside.

10

Mr. In and Mr. Out are not listed by the census-taker. You will search for them in vain through the social register or the births, marriages, and deaths, or the grocer's credit list. Oblivion has swallowed them and the testimony that they ever existed at all is vague and shadowy, and inadmissible in a court of law. Yet I have it upon the best authority that for a brief space Mr. In and Mr. Out lived, breathed, answered to their names and radiated vivid personalities of their own.

During the brief span of their lives they walked in their native garments down the great highway of a great nation; were laughed at, sworn at, chased, and fled from. Then they passed and were heard of no more.

They were already taking form dimly, when a taxicab with the top open breezed down Broadway in the faintest glimmer of May dawn. In this car sat the souls of Mr. In and Mr. Out discussing with amazement the blue light that had so precipitately colored the sky behind the statue of Christopher Columbus, discussing with bewilderment the old, gray faces of the early risers which skimmed palely along the street like blown bits of paper on a gray lake. They were agreed on all things, from the absurdity of the bouncer in Childs' to the absurdity of the business of life. They were dizzy with the extreme maudlin happiness that the morning had awakened in their glowing souls. Indeed, so fresh and vigorous was their pleasure in living that they felt it should be expressed by loud cries.

"Ye-ow-ow!" hooted Peter, making a megaphone with his hands—and Dean joined in with a call that, though equally significant and symbolic, derived its resonance from its very inarticulateness.

"Yo-ho! Yea! Yoho! Yo-buba!"

Fifty-third Street was a bus with a dark, bobbed-hair beauty atop; Fifty-second was a street cleaner who dodged, escaped, and sent up a yell of "Look where you're aimin'!" in a pained and grieved voice. At Fiftieth Street a group of men on a very white sidewalk in front of a very white building turned to stare after them, and shouted:

"Some party, boys!"

At Forty-ninth Street Peter turned to Dean. "Beautiful morning," he said gravely, squinting up his owlish eyes.

"Probably is."

"Go get some breakfast, hey?"

Dean agreed—with additions.

"Breakfast and liquor."

"Breakfast and liquor," repeated Peter, and they looked at each other, nodding. "That's logical."

Then they both burst into loud laughter.

"Breakfast and liquor! Oh, gosh!"

"No such thing," announced Peter.

"Don't serve it? Ne'mind. We force 'em serve it. Bring pressure bear."

"Bring logic bear."

The taxi cut suddenly off Broadway, sailed along a cross street, and stopped in front of a heavy tomb-like building in Fifth Avenue.

"What's idea?"

The taxi-driver informed them that this was Delmonico's.

This was somewhat puzzling. They were forced to devote several minutes to intense concentration, for if such an order had been given there must have been a reason for it.

"Somep'm 'bouta coat," suggested the taxi-man.

That was it. Peter's overcoat and hat. He had left them at Delmonico's. Having decided this, they disembarked from the taxi and strolled toward the entrance arm in arm.

"Hey!" said the taxi-driver.

"Huh?"

"You better pay me."

They shook their heads in shocked negation.

"Later, not now—we give orders, you wait."

The taxi-driver objected; he wanted his money now. With the scornful condescension of men exercising tremendous self-control they paid him.

Inside Peter groped in vain through a dim, deserted check-room in search of his coat and derby.

"Gone, I guess. Somebody stole it."

"Some Sheff student."

"All probability."

"Never mind," said Dean, nobly. "I'll leave mine here too—then we'll both be dressed the same."

He removed his overcoat and hat and was hanging them up when his roving glance was caught and held magnetically by two large squares of cardboard tacked to the two coat-room doors. The one on the left-hand door bore the word "In" in big black letters, and the one on the right-hand door flaunted the equally emphatic word "Out."

"Look!" he exclaimed happily——

Peter's eyes followed his pointing finger.

"What?"

"Look at the signs. Let's take 'em."

"Good idea."

"Probably pair very rare an' valuable signs. Probably come in handy."

Peter removed the left-hand sign from the door and endeavored to conceal it about his person. The sign being of considerable proportions, this was a matter of some difficulty. An idea flung itself at him, and with an air of dignified mystery he turned his back. After an instant he wheeled dramatically around, and stretching out his arms displayed himself to the admiring Dean. He had inserted the sign in his vest, completely covering his shirt front. In effect, the word "In" had been painted upon his shirt in large black letters.

"Yoho!" cheered Dean. "Mister In."

He inserted his own sign in like manner.

"Mister Out!" he announced triumphantly. "Mr. In meet Mr. Out."

They advanced and shook hands. Again laughter overcame them and they rocked in a shaken spasm of mirth.

"Yoho!"

"We probably get a flock of breakfast."

"We'll go—go to the Commodore."

Arm in arm they sallied out the door, and turning east in Forty-fourth Street set out for the Commodore.

As they came out a short dark soldier, very pale and tired, who had been wandering listlessly along the sidewalk, turned to look at them.

He started over as though to address them, but as they immediately bent on him glances of withering unrecognition, he waited until they had started unsteadily down the street, and then followed at about forty paces, chuckling to himself and saying, "Oh, boy!" over and over under his breath, in delighted, anticipatory tones.

Mr. In and Mr. Out were meanwhile exchanging pleasantries concerning their future plans.

"We want liquor; we want breakfast. Neither without the other. One and indivisible."

"We want both 'em!"

"Both 'em!"

It was quite light now, and passers-by began to bend curious eyes on the pair. Obviously they were engaged in a discussion, which afforded each of them intense amusement, for occasionally a fit of laughter would seize upon them so violently that, still with their arms interlocked, they would bend nearly double.

Reaching the Commodore, they exchanged a few spicy epigrams with the sleepy-eyed doorman, navigated the revolving door with some difficulty, and then made their way through a thinly populated but startled lobby to the dining-room, where a puzzled waiter showed them an obscure table in a corner. They studied the bill of fare helplessly, telling over the items to each other in puzzled mumbles.

"Don't see any liquor here," said Peter reproachfully.

The waiter became audible but unintelligible.

"Repeat," continued Peter, with patient tolerance, "that there seems to be unexplained and quite distasteful lack of liquor upon bill of fare."

"Here!" said Dean confidently, "let me handle him." He turned to the waiter—"Bring us—bring us—" he scanned the bill of fare anxiously, "Bring us a quart of champagne and a—a—probably ham sandwich."

The waiter looked doubtful.

"Bring it!" roared Mr. In and Mr. Out in chorus.

The waiter coughed and disappeared. There was a short wait during which they were subjected without their knowledge to a careful scrutiny by the head-waiter. Then the champagne arrived, and at the sight of it Mr. In and Mr. Out became jubilant.

"Imagine their objecting to us having champagne for breakfast—jus' imagine."

They both concentrated upon the vision of such an awesome possibility, but the feat was too much for them. It was impossible for their joint imaginations to conjure up a world where any one might object to any one else having champagne for breakfast. The waiter drew the cork with an enormous *pop*—and their glasses immediately foamed with pale yellow froth.

"Here's health, Mr. In."

"Here's the same to you, Mr. Out."

The waiter withdrew; the minutes passed; the champagne became low in the bottle.

"It's—it's mortifying," said Dean suddenly.

"Wha's mortifying?"

"The idea their objecting us having champagne breakfast."

"Mortifying?" Peter considered. "Yes, tha's word—mortifying."

Again they collapsed into laughter, howled, swayed, rocked back and forth in their chairs, repeating the word "mortifying" over and over to each other— each repetition seeming to make it only more brilliantly absurd.

After a few more gorgeous minutes they decided on another quart. Their anxious waiter consulted his immediate superior, and this discreet person gave implicit instructions that no more champagne should be served. Their check was brought.

Five minutes later, arm in arm, they left the Commodore and made their way through a curious, staring crowd along Forty-second Street, and up Vanderbilt Avenue to the Biltmore. There, with sudden cunning, they rose to the occasion and traversed the lobby, walking fast and standing unnaturally erect.

Once in the dining-room they repeated their performance. They were torn between intermittent convulsive laughter and sudden spasmodic discussions of politics, college, and the sunny state of their dispositions. Their watches told them that it was now nine o'clock, and a dim idea was born in them that they were on a memorable party, something that they would remember always. They lingered over the second bottle. Either of them had only to mention the word "mortifying" to send them both into riotous gasps. The dining-room was whirring and shifting now; a curious lightness permeated and rarefied the heavy air.

They paid their check and walked out into the lobby.

It was at this moment that the exterior doors revolved for the thousandth time that morning, and admitted into the lobby a very pale young beauty with dark circles under her eyes, attired in a much-rumpled evening dress. She was accompanied by a plain stout man, obviously not an appropriate escort.

At the top of the stairs this couple encountered Mr. In and Mr. Out.

"Edith," began Mr. In, stepping toward her hilariously and making a sweeping bow, "darling, good morning."

The stout man glanced questioningly at Edith, as if merely asking her permission to throw this man summarily out of the way.

" 'Scuse familiarity," added Peter, as an afterthought. "Edith, good-morning."

He seized Dean's elbow and impelled him into the foreground.

"Meet Mr. In, Edith, my bes' frien'. Inseparable. Mr. In and Mr. Out."

Mr. Out advanced and bowed; in fact, he advanced so far and bowed so low that he tipped slightly forward and only kept his balance by placing a hand lightly on Edith's shoulder.

"I'm Mr. Out, Edith," he mumbled pleasantly, "S'misterin Misterout."

" 'Smisterinanout," said Peter proudly.

But Edith stared straight by them, her eyes fixed on some infinite speck in the gallery above her. She nodded slightly to the stout man, who advanced bull-like and with a sturdy brisk gesture pushed Mr. In and Mr. Out to either side. Through this alley he and Edith walked.

But ten paces farther on Edith stopped again—stopped and pointed to a short, dark soldier who was eyeing the crowd in general, and the tableau of Mr. In and Mr. Out in particular, with a sort of puzzled, spell-bound awe.

"There," cried Edith. "See there!"

Her voice rose, became somewhat shrill. Her pointing finger shook slightly.

"There's the soldier who broke my brother's leg."

There were a dozen exclamations; a man in a cutaway coat left his place near the desk and advanced alertly; the stout person made a sort of lightning-like spring toward the short, dark soldier, and then the lobby closed around the little group and blotted them from the sight of Mr. In and Mr. Out.

But to Mr. In and Mr. Out this event was merely a particolored iridescent segment of a whirring, spinning world.

They heard loud voices; they saw the stout man spring; the picture suddenly blurred.

Then they were in an elevator bound skyward.

"What floor, please?" said the elevator man.

"Any floor," said Mr. In.

"Top floor," said Mr. Out.

"This is the top floor," said the elevator man.

"Have another floor put on," said Mr. Out.

"Higher," said Mr. In.

"Heaven," said Mr. Out.

11

In a bedroom of a small hotel just off Sixth Avenue Gordon Sterrett awoke with a pain in the back of his head and a sick throbbing in all his veins. He looked at the dusky gray shadows in the corners of the room and at a raw place on a large leather chair in the corner where it had long been in use. He saw clothes, dishevelled, rumpled clothes on the floor and he smelt stale cigarette smoke and stale liquor. The windows were tight shut. Outside the bright sunlight had thrown a dust-filled beam across the sill—a beam broken by the head of the wide wooden bed in which he had slept. He lay very quiet —comatose, drugged, his eyes wide, his mind clicking wildly like an unoiled machine.

It must have been thirty seconds after he perceived the sunbeam with the dust on it and the rip on the large leather chair that he had the sense of life close beside him, and it was another thirty seconds after that before he realized he was irrevocably married to Jewel Hudson.

He went out half an hour later and bought a revolver at a sporting goods store. Then he took a taxi to the room where he had been living on East Twenty-seventh Street, and, leaning across the table that held his drawing materials, fired a cartridge into his head just behind the temple.

1920

THE CRACK-UP

February, 1936

OF COURSE ALL LIFE is a process of breaking down, but the blows that do the dramatic side of the work—the big sudden blows that come, or seem to come, from outside—the ones you remember and blame things on and, in moments of weakness, tell your friends about, don't show their effect all at once. There is another sort of blow that comes from within—that you don't feel until it's too late to do anything about it, until you realize with finality that in some regard you will never be as good a man again. The first sort of breakage seems to happen quick—the second kind happens almost without your knowing it but is realized suddenly indeed.

Before I go on with this short history let me make a general observation—the test of a first-rate intelligence is the ability to hold two opposed ideas in the mind at the same time, and still retain the ability to function. One should, for example, be able to see that things are hopeless and yet be determined to make them otherwise. This philosophy fitted on to my early adult life, when I saw the improbable, the implausible, often the "impossible" come true. Life was something you dominated if you were any good. Life yielded easily to intelligence and effort, or to what porportion could be mustered of both. It seemed a romantic business to be a successful literary man—you were not ever going to be as famous as a movie star but what note you had was probably longer-lived—you were never going to have the power of a man of strong political or religious convictions but you were certainly more independent. Of course within the practice of your trade you were forever unsatisfied—but I, for one, would not have chosen any other.

As the twenties passed, with my own twenties marching a little ahead of them, my two juvenile regrets—at not being big enough (or good enough) to play football in college, and at not getting overseas during the war—resolved themselves into childish waking dreams of imaginary heroism that were good enough to go to sleep on in restless nights. The big problems of life seemed to solve themselves, and if the business of fixing them was difficult, it made one too tired to think of more general problems.

Life, ten years ago, was largely a personal matter. I must hold in balance the sense of the futility of effort and the sense of the necessity to struggle; the conviction of the inevitability of failure and still the determination to "succeed"—and, more than these, the contradiction between the dead hand of the past and the high intentions of the future. If I could do this through the common ills—domestic, professional and personal—then the ego would continue as an arrow shot from nothingness to nothingness with such force that only gravity would bring it to earth at last.

For seventeen years, with a year of deliberate loafing and resting out in the center—things went on like that, with a new chore only a nice prospect for the next day. I was living hard too, but: "Up to forty-nine it'll be all right," I said. "I can count on that. For a man who's lived as I have, that's all you could ask."

—And then, ten years this side of forty-nine, I suddenly realized that I had prematurely cracked.

Now a man can crack in many ways—can crack in the head—in which case the power of decision is taken from you by others! or in the body when one can but submit to the white hospital world—or in the nerves. William Seabrook in an unsympathetic book tells, with some pride and a movie ending, of how he became a public charge. What led to his alcoholism or was bound up with it, was a collapse of his nervous system. Though the present writer was not so entangled—having at the time not tasted so much as a glass of beer for six months—it was his nervous reflexes that were giving way—too much anger and too many tears.

Moreover, to go back to my thesis that life has a varying offensive, the realization of having cracked was not simultaneous with a blow, but with a reprieve.

Not long before, I had sat in the office of a great doctor and listened to a grave sentence. With what, in retrospect, seems some equanimity, I had gone on about my affairs in the city where I was then living, not caring much, not thinking how much had been left undone, or what would become of this and that responsibility, like people do in books; I was well insured and anyhow I had been only a mediocre caretaker of most of the things left in my hands, even of my talent.

But I had a strong sudden instinct that I must be alone. I didn't want to see any people at all. I had seen so many people all my life—I was an average mixer, but more than average in a tendency to identify myself, my ideas, my destiny with those of all classes that I came in contact with. I was always saving or being saved—in a single morning I would go through the emotions ascribable to Wellington at Waterloo. I lived in a world of inscrutable hostiles and unalienable friends and supporters.

But now I wanted to be absolutely alone and so arranged a certain insulation from ordinary cares.

It was not an unhappy time. I went away and there were fewer people. I found I was good-and-tired. I could lie around and was glad to, sleeping or dozing sometimes twenty hours a day and in the intervals trying resolutely not to think—instead I made lists—made lists and tore them up, hundreds of lists: of cavalry leaders and football players and cities, and popular tunes and pitchers, and happy times, and hobbies and houses lived in and how many suits since I left the army and how many pairs of shoes (I didn't count the suit I bought in Sorrento that shrunk, nor the pumps and dress shirt and collar that I carried around for years and never wore because the pumps got damp and grainy and the shirt and collar got yellow and starch-rotted). And lists of women I'd liked, and of the times I had let myself be snubbed by people who had not been my betters in character or ability.

—And then suddenly, surprisingly I got better.

—And cracked like an old plate as soon as I heard the news.

That is the real end of this story. What was to be done about it will have to rest in what used to be called the "womb of time." Suffice it to say that after about an hour of solitary pillow-hugging, I began to realize that for two years my life had been a drawing on resources that I did not possess, that I had been mortgaging myself physically and spiritually up to the hilt. What was the small gift of life given back in comparison to that?—when there had once been a pride of direction and a confidence in enduring independence.

I realized that in those two years in order to preserve something—an inner hush maybe, maybe not—I had weaned myself from all the things I used to love—that every act of life from the morning toothbrush to the friend at dinner had become an effort. I saw that for a long time I had not liked people and things, but only followed the rickety old pretense of liking. I saw that even my love for those closest to me was become only an attempt to love, that my casual relations—with an editor, a tobacco seller, the child of a friend, were only what I remembered I *should* do, from other days. All in the same month I became bitter about such things as the sound of the radio, the advertisements in the magazines, the screech of tracks, the dead silence of the country—contemptuous at human softness, immediately (if secretively) quarrelsome toward hardness—hating the night when I couldn't sleep and hating the day because it went toward night. I slept on the heart side now because I knew that the sooner I could tire that out, even a little, the sooner would come that blessed hour of nightmare which, like a catharsis, would enable me to better meet the new day.

There were certain spots, certain faces I could look at. Like most Middle-Westerners I have never had any but the vaguest race prejudices—I always had a secret yen for the lovely Scandinavian blondes who sat on porches in St. Paul but hadn't emerged enough economically to be part of what was then society. They were too nice to be "chickens" and too quickly off the farmlands to seize a place in the sun, but I remember going round blocks to catch a single glimpse of shining hair—the bright shock of a girl I'd never known. This is urban, unpopular talk. It strays afield from the fact that in these latter days I couldn't stand the sight of Celts, English, Politicians, Strangers, Virginians, Negroes (light or dark), Hunting People, all retail clerks, and middlemen in general, all writers (I avoided writers very carefully because they can perpetuate trouble as no one else can)—and all the classes as classes and most of them as members of their class . . .

Trying to cling to something, I liked doctors and girl children up to the age of about thirteen and well-brought-up boy children from about eight years old on. I could have peace and happiness with these few categories of people. I forgot to add that I liked old men—men over seventy, sometimes over sixty if their faces looked seasoned. I liked Katherine Hepburn's face on the screen, no matter what was said about her pretentiousness, and Miriam Hopkins' face, and old friends if I only saw them once a year and could remember their ghosts.

All rather inhuman and undernourished, isn't it? Well, that, children, is the true sign of cracking up.

It is not a pretty picture. Inevitably it was carted here and there within its frame and exposed to various critics. One of them can only be described as a person whose life makes other people's lives seem like death—even this time when she was cast in the usually unappealing role of Job's comforter. In spite of the fact that this story is over, let me append our conversation as a sort of post-script:

"Instead of being so sorry for yourself, listen—" she said. (She always says "Listen," because she thinks while she talks—*really* thinks.) So she said: "Listen. Suppose this wasn't a crack in you—suppose it was a crack in the Grand Canyon."

"The crack's in me," I said heroically.

"Listen! The world only exists in your eyes—your conception of it. You can make it as big or as small as you want to. And you're trying to be a little puny individual. By God, if I ever cracked I'd try to make the world crack with me. Listen! The world only exists through your apprehension of it, and so it's much better to say that it's not you that's cracked—it's the Grand Canyon."

"Baby et up all her Spinoza?"

"I don't know anything about Spinoza. I know—" She spoke, then, of old woes of her own, that seemed, in the telling, to have been more dolorous than mine, and how she had met them, overridden them, beaten them.

I felt a certain reaction to what she said, but I am a slow-thinking man, and it occurred to me simultaneously that of all natural forces, vitality is the incommunicable one. In days when juice came into one as an article without duty, one tried to distribute it—but always without success; to further mix metaphors, vitality never "takes." You have it or you haven't it, like health or brown eyes or honor or a baritone voice. I might have asked some of it from her, neatly wrapped and ready for home cooking and digestion, but I could never have got it—not if I'd waited around for a thousand hours with the tin cup of self-pity. I could only walk from her door, holding myself very carefully like cracked crockery, and go away into the world of bitterness, where I was making a home with such materials as are found there—and quote to myself after I left her door:

"*Ye are the salt of the earth. But if the salt hath lost its savour, wherewith shall it be salted?*"
Matthew 5-13.

Handle with Care

March 1936

In a previous article this writer told about his realization that what he had before him was not the dish that he had ordered for his forties. In fact—since he and the dish were one, he described himself as a cracked plate, the kind that one wonders whether it is worth preserving. Your editor thought that the article suggested too many aspects without regarding them closely, and probably many readers felt the same way—and there are always those to whom all self-revelation is contemptible, unless it ends with a noble thanks to the gods for the Unconquerable Soul.

But I had been thanking the gods too long, and thanking them for nothing. I wanted to put a lament into my record, without even the background of the Euganean Hills to give it color. There weren't any Euganean Hills that I could see.

Sometimes, though, the cracked plate has to be retained in the pantry, has to be kept in service as a household necessity. It can never again be warmed on the stove nor shuffled with the other plates in the dishpan; it will not be brought out for company, but it will do to hold crackers late at night or to go into the ice box under left-overs . . .

Hence this sequel—a cracked plate's further history.

Now the standard cure for one who is sunk is to consider those in actual destitution or physical suffering—this is an all-weather beatitude for gloom in general and fairly salutory day-time advice for everyone. But at three o'clock in the morning, a forgotten package has the same tragic importance as a death sentence, and the cure doesn't work—and in a real dark night of the soul it is always three o'clock in the morning, day after day. At that hour the tendency is to refuse to face things as long as possible by retiring into an infantile dream—but one is continually startled out of this by various contacts with the world. One meets these occasions as quickly and carelessly as possible and retires once more back into the dream, hoping that things will adjust themselves by some great material or spiritual bonanza. But as the withdrawal persists there is less and less chance of the bonanza—one is not waiting for the fade-out of a single sorrow, but rather being an unwilling witness of an execution, the disintegration of one's own personality . . .

Unless madness or drugs or drink come into it, this phase comes to a dead-end, eventually, and is succeeded by a vacuous quiet. In this you can try to estimate what has been sheared away and what is left. Only when this quiet came to me, did I realize that I had gone through two parallel experiences.

The first time was twenty years ago, when I left Princeton in junior year with a complaint diagnosed as malaria (it transpired, through an X-ray taken a dozen years later, that it had been tuberculosis—a mild case), and after a few months of rest I went back to college. But I had lost certain offices, the chief one was the presidency of the Triangle Club, a musical comedy idea, and also I dropped back a class. To me college would never be the same. There were to be no badges of pride, no medals after all. It seemed on one March afternoon that I had lost every single thing I wanted—and that night was the first time that I hunted down the specter of womanhood that, for a little while, makes everything else seem unimportant.

Years later I realized that my failure as a big shot in college was all right—instead of serving on committees, I took a beating on English poetry; when I got the idea of what it was all about, I set about learning how to write. On Shaw's principle that "If you don't get what you like, you better like what you get," it was a lucky break—at the moment it was a harsh and bitter business to know that my career as a leader of men was over.

Since that day I have not been able to fire a bad servant, and I am astonished and impressed by people who can. Some old desire for personal dominance was broken and gone. Life around me was a solemn dream, and I lived on the letters I wrote to a girl in another city. A man does not recover from such jolts—he becomes a different person and, eventually, the new person finds new things to care about.

The other episode parallel to my current situation took place after the war, when I had again over-extended my flank. It was one of those tragic loves doomed for lack of money, and one day the girl closed it out on the basis of common sense. During a long summer of despair I wrote a novel instead of letters, so it came out all right, but it came out all right for a different person. The man with the jingle of money in his pocket who married the girl a year later would always cherish an abiding distrust, an animosity, toward the leisure class—not the conviction of a revolutionist but the smouldering hatred of a peasant. In the years since then I have never been able to stop wondering where my friends' money came from, nor to stop thinking that at one time a sort of *droit de seigneur* might have been exercised to give one of them my girl.

For sixteen years I lived pretty much as this latter person, distrusting the rich, yet working for money with which to share their mobility and the grace that some of them brought into their lives. During this time I had plenty of the usual horses shot from under me—I remember some of their names—*Punctured Pride, Thwarted Expectation, Faithless, Show-off, Hard Hit, Never Again.* And after awhile I wasn't twenty-five, then not even thirty-five, and nothing was quite as good. But in all these years I don't remember a moment of discouragement. I saw honest men through moods of suicidal gloom —some of them gave up and died; others adjusted themselves and went on to a larger success than mine; but my morale never sank below the level of self-disgust when I had put on some unsightly personal show. Trouble has no necessary connection with discouragement—discouragement has a germ of its own, as different from trouble as arthritis is different from a stiff joint.

When a new sky cut off the sun last spring, I didn't at first relate it to what had happened fifteen or twenty years ago. Only gradually did a certain family resemblance come through—an over-extension of the flank, a burning of the candle at both ends; a call upon physical resources that I did not command, like a man over-drawing at his bank. In its impact this blow was more violent than the other two but it was the same in kind—a feeling that I was standing at twilight on a deserted range, with an empty rifle in my hands and the targets down. No problem set—simply a silence with only the sound of my own breathing.

In this silence there was a vast irresponsibility toward every obligation, a deflation of all my values. A passionate belief in order, a disregard of motives or consequences in favor of guess work and prophecy, a feeling that craft and industry would have a place in any world—one by one, these and other convictions were swept away. I saw that the novel, which at my maturity was the strongest and supplest medium for conveying thought and emotion from one human being to another, was becoming subordinated to a mechanical and communal art that, whether in the hands of Hollywood merchants or Russian idealists, was capable of reflecting only the tritest thought, the most obvious emotion. It was an art in which words were subordinate to images, where personality was worn down to the inevitable low gear of collaboration. As long past as 1930, I had a hunch that the talkies would make even the best selling novelist as archaic as silent pictures. People still read, if only Professor Canby's book of the month—curious children nosed at the slime of Mr. Tiffany Thayer in the drug-store libraries—but there was a rankling indignity, that to me has become almost an obsession, in seeing the power of the written word subordinated to another power, a more glittering, a grosser power . . .

I set that down as an example of what haunted me during the long night— this was something I could neither accept nor struggle against, something which tended to make my efforts obsolescent, as the chain stores have crippled the small merchant, an exterior force, unbeatable—

(I have the sense of lecturing now, looking at a watch on the desk before me and seeing how many more minutes—)

Well, when I had reached this period of silence, I was forced into a measure that no one ever adopts voluntarily: I was impelled to think. God, was it difficult! The moving about of great secret trunks. In the first exhausted halt, I wondered whether I had ever thought. After a long time I came to these conclusions, just as I write them here:

(1) That I had done very little thinking, save within the problems of my craft. For twenty years a certain man had been my intellectual conscience. That was Edmund Wilson.

(2) That another man resented my sense of the "good life," though I saw him once in a decade, and since then he might have been hung. He is in the fur business in the Northwest and wouldn't like his name set down here. But in difficult situations I had tried to think what *he* would have thought, how *he* would have acted.

(3) That a third contemporary had been an artistic conscience to me— I had not imitated his infectious style, because my own style, such as it is, was formed before he published anything, but there was an awful pull toward him when I was on a spot.

(4) That a fourth man had come to dictate my relations with other people when these relations were successful: how to do, what to say. How to make people at least momentarily happy (in opposition to Mrs. Post's theories of how to make everyone thoroughly uncomfortable with a sort of systematized vulgarity). This always confused me and made me want to go out and get drunk, but this man had seen the game, analyzed it and beaten it, and his word was good enough for me.

(5) That my political conscience had scarcely existed for ten years save as an element of irony in my stuff. When I became again concerned with the system I should function under, it was a man much younger than myself who brought it to me, with a mixture of passion and fresh air.

So there was not an "I" any more—not a basis on which I could organize my self-respect—save my limitless capacity for toil that it seemed I possessed no more. It was strange to have no self—to be like a little boy left alone in a big house, who knew that now he could do anything he wanted to do, but found that there was nothing that he wanted to do—

(The watch is past the hour and I have barely reached my thesis. I have some doubts as to whether this is of general interest but if anyone wants more, there is plenty left, and your editor will tell me. If you've had enough, say so—but not too loud, because I have the feeling that someone, I'm not sure who, is sound asleep—someone who could have helped me to keep my shop open. It wasn't Lenin, and it wasn't God.)

Pasting It Together

April 1936

I have spoken in these pages of how an exceptionally optimistic young man experienced a crack-up of all values, a crack-up that he scarcely knew of until long after it occurred. I told of the succeeding period of desolation and of the necessity of going on, but without benefit of Henley's familiar hero-ics, "my head is bloody but unbowed." For a check-up of my spiritual liabili-ties indicated that I had no particular head to be bowed or unbowed. Once I had had a heart but that was about all I was sure of.

This was at least a starting place out of the morass in which I floundered: "I felt—therefore I was." At one time or another there had been many people who had leaned on me, come to me in difficulties or written me from afar, believed implicity in my advice and my attitude toward life. The dullest platitude monger or the most unscrupulous Rasputin who can influence the destinies of many people must have some individuality, so the question be-came one of finding why and where I had changed, where was the leak through which, unknown to myself, my enthusiasm and my vitality had been steadily and prematurely trickling away.

One harassed and despairing night I packed a brief case and went off a thousand miles to think it over. I took a dollar room in a drab little town where I knew no one and sunk all the money I had with me in a stock of potted meat, crackers and apples. But don't let me suggest that the change from a rather overstuffed world to a comparative asceticism was any Research Mag-nificent—I only wanted absolute quiet to think out why I had developed a sad attitude toward sadness, a melancholy attitude toward melancholy and a tragic attitude toward tragedy—*why I had become identified with the objects of my horror or compassion.*

Does this seem a fine distinction? It isn't: identification such as this spells the death of accomplishment. It is something like this that keeps insane people from working. Lenin did not willingly endure the sufferings of his proletariat, nor Washington of his troops, nor Dickens of his London poor. And when Tolstoi tried some such merging of himself with the objects of his attention it was a fake and a failure. I mention these because they are the men best known to us all.

It was dangerous mist. When Wordsworth decided that "there had passed away a glory from the earth" he felt no compulsion to pass away with it, and the Fiery Particle Keats never ceased his struggle against t. b. nor in his last moments relinquished his hope of being among the English poets.

My self-immolation was something sodden-dark. It was very distinctly not modern—yet I saw it in others, saw it in a dozen men of honor and industry since the war. (I heard you, but that's too easy—there were Marxians among these men.) I had stood by while one famous contemporary of mine played with the idea of the Big Out for half a year; I had watched when another, equally eminent, spent months in an asylum unable to endure any contact with his fellow men. And of those who had given up and passed on I could list a score.

This led me to the idea that the ones who had survived had made some sort of clean break. This is a big word and is no parallel to a jail-break when one is probably headed for a new jail or will be forced back to the old one. The famous "Escape" or "run away from it all" is an excursion in a trap even if the trap includes the south seas, which are only for those who want to paint them or sail them. A clean break is something you cannot come back from; that is irretrievable because it makes the past cease to exist. So, since I could no longer fulfill the obligations that life had set for me or that I had set for myself, why not slay the empty shell who had been posturing at it for four years? I must continue to be a writer because that was my only way of life, but I would cease any attempts to be a person—to be kind, just or generous. There were plenty of counterfeit coins around that would pass instead of these and I knew where I could get them at a nickel on the dollar. In thirty-nine years an observant eye has learned to detect where the milk is watered and sugar is sanded, the rhinestone passed for diamond and the stucco for stone. There was to be no more giving of myself—all giving was to be outlawed henceforth under a new name, and that name was Waste.

The decision made me rather exuberant, like anything that is both real and new. As a sort of beignning there was a whole shaft of letters to be tipped into the waste basket when I went home, letters that wanted something for nothing—to read this man's manuscript, market this man's poem, speak free on the radio, indite notes of introduction, give this interview, help with the plot of this play, with this domestic situation, perform this act of thoughtfulness or charity.

The conjuror's hat was empty. To draw things out of it had long been a sort of sleight of hand, and now, to change the metaphor, I was off the dispensing end of the relief roll forever.

The heady villainous feeling continued.

I felt like the beady-eyed men I used to see on the commuting train from Great Neck fifteen years back—men who didn't care whether the world tumbled into chaos tomorrow if it spared their houses. I was one with them now, one with the smooth articles who said:

"I'm sorry but business is business."

Or:

"You ought to have thought of that before you got into this trouble."

Or:

"I'm not the person to see about that."

And a smile—ah, I would get me a smile. I'm still working on that smile. It is to combine the best qualities of a hotel manager, an experienced old social weasel, a headmaster on visitors' day, a colored elevator man, a pansy pulling a profile, a producer getting stuff at half its market value, a trained nurse coming on a new job, a body-vendor in her first rotogravure, a hopeful extra swept near the camera, a ballet dancer with an infected toe, and of course the great beam of loving kindness common to all those from Washington to Beverly Hills who must exist by virtue of the contorted pan.

The voice too—I am working with a teacher on the voice. When I have perfected it the larynx will show no ring of conviction except the conviction of the person I am talking to. Since it will be largely called upon for the elicitation of the word "Yes," my teacher (a lawyer) and I are concentrating on that, but in extra hours. I am learning to bring into it that polite acerbity that makes people feel that far from being welcome they are not even tolerated and are under continual and scathing analysis at every moment. These times will of course not coincide with the smile. This will be reserved exclusively for those from whom I have nothing to gain, old worn-out people or young struggling people. They won't mind—what the hell, they get it most of the time anyhow.

But enough. It is not a matter of levity. If you are young and you should write asking to see me and learn how to be a somber literary man writing pieces upon the state of emotional exhaustion that often overtakes writers in their prime—if you should be so young and so fatuous as to do this, I would not do so much as acknowledge your letter, unless you were related to someone very rich and important indeed. And if you were dying of starvation outside my window I would go out quickly and give you the smile and the voice (if no longer the hand) and stick around till somebody raised a nickel to phone for the ambulance, that is if I thought there would be any copy in it for me.

I have now at last become a writer only. The man I had persistently tried to be became such a burden that I have "cut him loose" with as little compunction as a Negro lady cuts loose a rival on Saturday night. Let the good people function as such—let the over-worked doctors die in harness, with one week's "vacation" a year that they can devote to straightening out their family affairs and let the under-worked doctors scramble for cases at one dollar a throw; let the soldiers be killed and enter immediately into the Valhalla of their profession. That is their contract with the gods. A writer need have no such ideals unless he makes them for himself, and this one has quit. The old dream of being an entire man in the Goethe-Byron-Shaw tradition, with an opulent American touch, a sort of combination of J. P. Morgan, Topham Beauclerk and St. Francis of Assisi has been relegated to the junk heap of the shoulder pads worn for one day on the Princeton freshman football field and the overseas cap never worn overseas.

So what? This is what I think now: that the natural state of the sentient adult is a qualified unhappiness. I think also that in an adult the desire to be finer in grain than you are, "a constant striving" (as those people say who gain their bread by saying it) only adds to this unhappiness in the end—that end that comes to our youth and hope. My own happiness in the past often approached such an ecstasy that I could not share it even with the person dearest to me but had to walk it away in quiet streets and lanes with only fragments of it to distill into little lines in books—and I think that my happiness, or talent for self-delusion or what you will, was an exception. It was not the natural thing but the unnatural—unnatural as the Boom; and my recent experience parallels the wave of despair that swept the nation when the Boom was over.

I shall manage to live with the new dispensation, though it has taken some months to be certain of the fact. And just as the laughing stoicism which has enabled the American negro to endure the intolerable conditions of his existence has cost him his sense of the truth—so in my case there is a price to pay. I do not any longer like the postman, nor the grocer, nor the editor, nor the cousin's husband, and he in turn will come to dislike me, so that life will never be very pleasant again, and the sign *Cave Canem* is hung permanently just above my door. I will try to be a correct animal though, and if you throw me a bone with enough meat on it I may even lick your hand.

Reading Suggestions

In addition to "May Day" the best short stories of Fitzgerald can be found in a Scribner paperback, *Babylon Revisited and Other Stories* (1960), including in addition to the title story: "The Diamond as Big as the Ritz," "Absolution," and "The Rich Boy." Though there is no collected edition of his works, all his novels can be found in trade editions, *The Great Gatsby* being also available in a paperback. *The Crack-Up*, edited by Edmund Wilson (New Directions, 1946—reprinted as a paperback) contains some interesting miscellaneous writings in addition to the title essay: Fitzgerald's *Note-Books*, running to 150 pages; about fifty of his letters, mostly to Edmund Wilson, John Peale Bishop, and the author's daughter; half-a-dozen uncollected essays by Fitzgerald and several about him. A check list of his writings, giving place and date for the separate publication of all his fictions and essays, is included at the end of Arthur Mizener's *The Far Side of Paradise: A Biography of F. Scott Fitzgerald* (1951).

Mizener's book was the pioneer study of Fitzgerald. It attempts a combination of biography and criticism, though the latter is largely confined to running commentary on the novels and stories. A more detailed biography, though not superseding Mizener's, is Andrew Turnbull's *Scott Fitzgerald* (1962). This is supplemented by *The Letters of F. Scott Fitzgerald* (1963), edited by Turnbull. By all odds the best critical interpretation of the novels is James Miller's *The Fictional Techniques of Scott Fitzgerald* (1957), an illuminating analysis of his artistic development. Critics have been slower in turning their attention to Fitzgerald than to Hemingway and Faulkner, for example. At the time the first collection of essays about him appeared, edited by Alfred Kazin, *F. Scott Fitzgerald; The Man and His Work* (1951), there was not too much to choose from. Among the most useful in this volume are the essays by two older contemporaries, Edmund Wilson and Glenway Westcott, to which should be added those by the editor himself, by William Troy, and by Lionel Trilling. Ten years later there were enough critical articles to fill a long check list in *Modern Fiction Studies* (Spring 1961). As a result, the next two volumes of selections offer richer fare. *F. Scott Fitzgerald: A Collection of Critical Essays* (1963), edited by Arthur Mizener contains twenty articles (including those named above), many of high caliber, covering the career of the author and most of his important works. *The Great Gatsby: A Study* (a Scribner paperback), edited by Frederick Hoffman, concentrates on Fitzgerald's masterpiece but uses a valuable method of approach. In addition to ten essays focused on the *Gatsby* and several others on earlier fictions leading up to it, there are some unique features: liberal quotations from the novel itself, the author's introduction to the 1934 edition, letters by and to him concerning it, several of his related stories and essays, and two items that throw light on the all-important influence of Conrad on Fitzgerald.

Biography

Biography and fiction are so entangled in the career of Fitzgerald it is hard to write about one without writing about the other. The scenes that figure most prominently in his works were also the centers of importance in his life: St. Paul (Minnesota), Princeton, New York, Europe (especially Paris), and finally Hollywood. At least one of his novels, as well as numerous stories, has its setting in each of these places that meant so much to him—all except the Minnesota city where he was born on September 24, 1896. Drawn irresistibly to the East, he never really exploited his boyhood in the West, though it is the scene of several short fictions and his first full-scale hero takes off from there, like him, never to return. But St. Paul had a strong influence on his character and personality, out of proportion to the short time he lived there. When he was only two the family moved to Buffalo, not returning to St. Paul until he was twelve. Then from the age of fifteen on he was only at home during vacations from school and college. After that he was gone for good. Yet this particular community and his family's place in it conditioned him in many ways.

Fitzgerald's maternal grandfather was an Irish immigrant who made a small fortune as a wholesale grocer in St. Paul during the period just before and after the Civil War. So his mother came from a respectable Catholic family, reasonably prosperous but not fashionable. His father was the son of an old Maryland family, handsome and gentlemanly, but not successful. His business failed in 1898, and after ten years as a salesman in upstate New York he lost his job and returned to St. Paul. By that time his wife's inheritance was adequate to live on, yielding an income of $5,000 a year—equivalent to about $20,000 in spending value today. They could afford a comfortable house with servants and private schools for the children, all of which threw them in contact with a circle beyond their means. For the city of St. Paul was full of new money in those days, typified by the fortune of the railroad tycoon James J. Hill, with a tendency to lavish display in mansions and social activities.

This particular aspect of the local environment was enhanced when young Scott was sent back East in 1911 to Newman, a preparatory school in New Jersey for the sons of rich Catholic families; and further extended when he went on from there to Princeton, where he joined one of the clubs dedicated to the wealthy. The attraction-repulsion of wealth had now become a fixed trait in Fitzgerald's make-up. Part of his energies in college were drawn off by high-flying social life, part by his sporadic attachment to classmates like Edmund Wilson and John Peale Bishop, both of whom were to make enviable names in the intellectual world. Fitzgerald alternated between being a playboy and a half-serious writer, contributing stories to the literary periodicals and musical comedy scripts for the Triangle Club. But he was an indifferent student. He lost a year when both failing grades and sickness caused him to drop out, and in 1917 he left before graduating to join the army.

Since Fitzgerald never got overseas, he took advantage of his spare time during the war to write the first draft of a novel based on his life in St. Paul, at school, and at college. The other important experience of these years was the beginning of his love affair with Zelda Sayre, a judge's daughter whom he met during an encampment in Alabama. (A previous affair with Ginevra King, a Chicago millionairess beyond his reach, had come to an end just before he entered the army.) Discharged in the winter of 1919, he went to New York, armed with his manuscript and his pride in being engaged to a society belle. Fitzgerald had great confidence in his powers as a ladies' man and as an author, but both received a brief setback. Unable to get work as a journalist while he completed his novel, he had to take a grubbing job in an advertising agency. By June his fiancée had broken off, unconvinced of his future. Stung by the double defeat, he returned to his home town, finished the novel, and by the end of the summer could announce that Scribner's had accepted it. The engagement was on again, and the following spring saw publication and marriage in rapid sequence.

Both were sensational successes. The novel and the young couple became the talk of the town. *This Side of Paradise* (1920) made such a hit the publishers followed it in a few months with a collection of his short stories, *Flappers and Philosophers*. The Fitzgeralds took up residence first at Westport and then in an apartment near the Plaza, were swept into a mad round of parties and drunken pranks, and became in the public eye a living embodiment of the Jazz Age depicted in his fictions. Their life for the next ten years was full of excitement for them, but it makes dull reading for the literary biographer. Nothing could be more repetitious than dissipation, nothing more superficial than the transient contacts of such social high jinks. The amazing thing is how in the midst of this endless carousing he got so much writing done, trashy as most of it was. Yet in the spring of 1922 his second novel, *The Beautiful and Damned*, was published, closely based on their married life in New York, and six months later the best of his new stories were collected as *Tales of the Jazz Age*. Both his novels reached sales over 40,000, which in the years before mammoth promotional schemes put them at the top of best-seller lists. His stories in the *Saturday Evening Post* were bringing fees up to $3,500, a new high in that day. His annual income during the whole decade was in excess of $25,000 —a figure that must be multiplied by two or three for its equivalent today. But he threw away money faster than he could make it, and extravagant living kept him continually in debt.

The pace was stepped up when they rented a house at Great Neck, Long Island, among the estates of celebrities and the really rich, nouveau and otherwise. The next two years were riotous ones. The scale of living and the fabulous parties were providing material for his next novel, but Fitzgerald, still the darling of the hour, found it impossible to devote himself to this book about which he was really serious. In May 1924 they went to Europe, not to return until the end of 1926. In retrospect he was to say that never had he tried to keep his artistic conscience so pure as during the ten months he was writing *The Great Gatsby*. It was published in the spring of 1925 to high critical acclaim, though sales dropped to half those of his first two novels. It was his one great victory and his one really sustained effort as a literary artist. But wild living set in again during their stay in Paris and on the Riviera, and continued after they came back to America. They were spending themselves as well as their money, and in 1930 his wife suffered a nervous breakdown. This was the first of a series that was soon to leave both of their lives in shipwreck, his own crack-up coming in 1936. When he saw his marriage was gone beyond repair he moved around disconsolately for several years, then settled in Hollywood for the pathetic remainder of his life. By the age of forty he was a broken old man. Four years later, in 1940, he was dead, a nearly forgotten author.

During the fifteen years that followed *The Great Gatsby* Fitzgerald continued to write furiously in a desperate uphill battle against alcoholism, mental and physical illness, and mounting expenses. Much of his work was aimed deliberately at money making, reaching a peak in the script writing that earned him $88,000 during his first eighteen months in Hollywood. But there were still valiant efforts at serious fiction. Several fine short stories appeared in his last two collections, *All the Sad Young Men* (1926) and *Taps at Reveille* (1935). And he made one remarkable comeback in *Tender Is the Night* (1934), his only novel in a decade but the second best he ever wrote. To say that he was already outmoded as an author by the time he began his final effort, *The Last Tycoon* (left unfinished at his death), is to put undue emphasis on his mere vogue, the surface popularity that he enjoyed in the twenties and would have lost in any event during the Depression years because of his exclusive concern with the wealthy leisure class. What is permanent about Fitzgerald would have always found its audience, if he had only followed up the lead of *The Great Gatsby* instead of wasting his talent and throwing his life away.

Sometimes called a Primitivists

ERNEST HEMINGWAY ✤

1899-1961

Rebelled against
manners and standards of
conservative society.

Scot College English, vol. 27, No. 3 Dec. 1965
Coopermen. "Hemingway and Old Age," pp. 215+.

Introduction

It has been customary for years to link Hemingway and Faulkner in discussions of modern fiction, not because they are alike in any way, but because they have seemed the two indisputable American giants of this century. This comparison may become less useful as the reputation of one sinks and the other rises, but the differences between them still offer a good starting point for evaluation.

Hemingway played the public role of big athlete, brawler, world traveler, and bustling newspaper man—on every war front, reporting the violence of the bull ring, making safaris to Africa, an intimate of the underworld. So he fashioned a muscular and belligerently antiaesthetic image of himself, even while behind this façade he stuck to his work as a dedicated writer. Faulkner, with the formal manners of an old-school gentleman, spent his life so privately in his native county as to seem like a recluse, strictly avoiding all publicity. He too fostered an antiliterary picture of himself, as the friend of farmers and hunters, while he was actually immersed in an almost frenzied creative life. But their masks have been so transparent both have long been recognized as serious artists: one standing in the public mind for the simple style, the other for an involuted, even tortured, style. During nearly four decades of authorship the former produced only half-a-dozen novels and fifty-odd short stories, for the most part severely limited in matter and manner. In the same period the latter published a shelf of fictions nearly three times as large, widely ranging in subject matter and experimenting with one radical technique after the other. Yet for all his productivity and varied innovations, Faulkner knew little but neglect and abuse for the first twenty years of his career, and when fame finally came he met it with the same indifference he had the obscurity. Hemingway, on the other hand, enjoyed instant success as an author, and thereafter used every trick in his bag to keep this high reputation from flagging. By setting at such opposite poles the careers of these two major novelists, it will be easier to separate their distinctive achievements.

1023

The impact Hemingway made on readers of his own generation, more electric than that of any contemporary novelist, has begun to show signs of weakening. Considering the timeliness of his appeal, the remarkable fact is that his writings should have had such staying power also. Even for readers today they are in no sense dated, like the novels of Sinclair Lewis, for instance. For, in addition to catching the exact tone of postwar disillusionment in the twenties, they also register one of the possible world views that will always be valid, and they do so with striking originality. This is something quite different from the novelty of his subject matter—the first exploration in fiction of a world fragmented by the violence of chaotic new forces, as well as cut adrift from its traditional moorings. (Joyce had already given us the latter.) And it is something over and beyond the precision with which he recorded person, place, and thing at a particular turning point in history. What is permanent in Hemingway is the new mode of fiction he hammered out to render all this: a language, a structure, and a point of view that was the exact equivalent of what he had to say. His contribution to the art of fiction, like that of Alexander Pope in verse, for example, will always be ineluctably there as an anchored light buoy, whether the tide goes with him or against him in any given period. Every creator of novels and stories will have to take into account his unique, if limited, achievement. It is the perfect embodiment of one way of seeing the world.

Hemingway discovered his special mode early and clung to it with a kind of desperate economy. This was a wise discipline for his talents, as a survey of his whole shelf quickly reveals. Cautious experimenter though he was, he did stray out of his metier on two notable occasions, but with disastrous results both times. *To Have and Have Not* (1937), caught up by the Depression in those currents of economic protest so inimical to art, is an incredible performance for the author of the early novels. It is hard to say whether this novel is more damaged by Hemingway's spleen against the rich or his indefensible effort to glamorize his outlaw hero. *For Whom the Bell Tolls* (1940) is a failure of a different kind, on a grander scale and with more that is salvageable. The trouble once again is involvement in social protest, this time sinking to the level of propaganda; the hero is committed to a cause, that of the Communist-oriented Spanish Loyalists in their gallant stand against fascism. How completely Hemingway's writing could be destroyed when motivated solely by propaganda is proved by his one attempt at a play, *The Fifth Column* (1938). In the novel, motivation is split. When his informed love of the Spanish earth takes over, he is capable of unforgettable scenes and finely etched characters. When he is moved by the cause, his language falls into bathos and his hero into absurd posturings. The intended epic of our times fails to come off.

It is an oversimplification, however, to decide that Hemingway's failures came from choosing the wrong subjects or even the wrong themes. All subjects and all themes can be valid for the artist. It is not the *what* but the *how* that really matters. Hemingway's failures came from losing his stance, and so losing both the structure and the style that matched his vision and embodied it in his best work. *Across the River and into the Trees* (1950) is a case in point. For the first time in two decades he had returned to his proven ground in a book-length fiction, and it seemed a good omen. Here again was his chosen subject of the stoic but wounded hero in a ruined world, and another variation on the familiar theme of "winner take nothing." The mediocrity of this novel might be explained by saying that both themes had been worn thin by this time, were it not for the fine comeback in *The Old Man and the Sea* two years later, with the same subject and the same theme. No, the failure in the first of these two late novels is a formal one. The artist has lost his distance from his material; he is working too close to autobiography, or at least too close to the legend Hemingway had been building up about himself. So *Across the River* is almost a parody of his own manner. The structure creaks, and the language as well as the situation seems contrived. The line between an author's actual experience of life and his imaginative reconstruction of it in fiction may be a thin one, but it must be maintained. In Hemingway it was particularly thin, but when he held it firmly it was the strategic path to his greatest successes.

I

There can be no more fruitful way to explore his best work than to follow this fine dividing line between autobiography and fiction, beginning with his first real book, *In Our Time* (1925).[1] Even in the single episode included in this anthology, "Big Two-Hearted River," one can see the pattern of all his successful novels in miniature. The diction is bare, the sentences clipped, the rhythm that of the speaking voice in cool detachment. The scene in the Michigan woods is realized before the reader's eyes by a few highly selective strokes, stripped of modifiers but resonant with symbolic suggestiveness. Plot is reduced to a minimum, but what there is of event and character fits in broad outline what is known about Hemingway's life at this period. At the age of twenty he had returned from the war in Europe, a wounded veteran, and spent his first summer in the woods of northern Michigan, fishing and trying to pull his life together again as a writer. These are exactly the outward facts, and all the important ones, given in this quiet story of Nick Adams. That he too is a bankrupt author is implied by one phrase, he had left behind "the need for thinking, the need to write," and by his careful attention to expression—in the same style as Hemingway's. But this is not the heart of the story, though it is as far as the autobiographical parallel can be taken.

[1] It had been preceded only by a privately printed pamphlet, *Three Stories and Ten Poems* (1923), and the Paris edition of *in our time* (1924), a much smaller and very different version of the book published in America in 1925.

The whole point of it is how Nick feels, about his present search for peace set over against his past experience of violence, and there is no way of knowing how Hemingway felt at this time about such matters. One is convinced that it was not the way Nick felt by the fact that Hemingway could write this story so effectively just a few years later. Nick's wound is more than physical. It is a psychic wound. He is the "sick" modern man who will never be cured, hence never capable of objectifying his own state in a fiction like this. It is all he can do to keep his emotions in control by disciplined physical activities, such as making camp and casting for trout. In the intervals of these rituals he holds on to sanity (this turns out to be his real problem) by holding grimly to a stoic's code. This is clearly not Hemingway's emotional state in 1919, but a projection of what it would be like to feel this way. It is the first draft of the representative Hemingway hero, who was immediately recognized by readers as the symbolic modern man, shattered and left alienated by the cataclysmic forces unleashed in World War I.

When we do know how Hemingway felt personally about things—as can be gathered on occasion from his interviews, newspaper writings, and nonfiction prose—it fits the rather unattractive literary personality of the man and that of the author too in his poorer fictions, where the characters seem far too close to their creator emotionally. At one extreme, he ranged from the smart aleck all the way up to an arrogant and splenetic man. At the other, he could be romantic, even maudlin, and given to foolish posturing. These characteristics of the emotional adolescent color both the author and his puppets in the novels that have been dropped from further consideration here. But they are not the traits of heroes like Jake Barnes, Lieutenant Henry, and old Santiago, who either as narrator or center of consciousness hold the author at a proper distance from his semi-autobiographical materials and enable him to dramatize the lesser characters who are emotionally uncontrolled. Nor are they the traits of Nick Adams, his first effective hero-as-point-of-view. (Hemingway's attainment of such objectivity in his best fictions may well turn out to be, when all the facts are known, the triumph of artistic discipline over his own personality.)

Even when separated out as a short story, "Big Two-Hearted River" embodies by itself much of the significance attributed to it above. This seems to be one of those Hemingway stories in which nothing happens, it is true. He must have been telling a similar one to the "elderly lady" in that comic episode in *Death in the Afternoon* (1932), when she complained, "Is there not to be what we called in my youth a wow at the end?" His reply is a fitting formula for his short fictions in general and for the river story in particular: "Ah, Madame, it is years since I added the wow to the end of a story. . . . [This particular] subject is feeble, and too hearty a wow would overbalance it." The point of "Big Two-Hearted River," its wow, is an inner one that makes itself heard only gradually. The story offers considerable interest, however, even on a surface reading. The scene is made vivid by full and precise sensory detail. The action, slight as it is, has the satisfying factual thickness of a fishing expedition recounted by an expert, for Nick's is not a city man on vacation but a fisherman who really knows. We learn how to catch grasshoppers for bait and how to put an unwanted baby trout back in the water without damaging it, exactly as in a fishing manual. But the real story is an inner one.

There are hints in the text of more than one catches at first reading. "Nick felt happy," we are told at the beginning of his expedition, because now "It was all back of him." This, of course, could refer to some trivial or merely temporary trouble he is leaving behind by going fishing. What had gone on before is never made explicit. Yet the pulsing monotony of the sentence cadence throughout the rest of the story, the droning style that comes close to setting the reader's nerves on edge, clearly echoes the hero's present state of tension. That his is an escape from something more serious than simple trouble is also indicated by the whole narrative mode. The cross-country hike, making camp, and fishing for trout are carried out almost ritualistically. Nick must follow a routine of physical activity to tire himself out so that he can keep "his mind from starting to work" and get to sleep. He must keep his emotions under strict control, as when, in the excitement and disappointment of losing his first strike, "He felt, vaguely, a little sick," then had to take a rest so he would not "rush his sensations any." The reader is naturally puzzled. Why would such normal fishing luck make a man feel "sick"? One gets no direct explanation, but has to depend instead on the presentation and the buried imagery.

For there is more than meets the eye in the scene itself. "For Hemingway the great outdoors is chiefly a state of mind," as one critic has put it aptly, "a projection of moral and emotional attitudes onto physical arenas" so that a precise rendering of the natural world as the hero sees himself reflected in it reproduces the same attitudes in the reader. In the very opening paragraphs, as Nick looks down into the stream, he sees near the surface the smaller trout "keeping themselves steady in the current"; further down he sees others in the "deep fast moving water, slightly distorted"; and at the bottom of the pool he just makes out "the big ones." This cluster of images exactly parallels the situation inside Nick himself, which is unfolded as the story progresses. Though the cause of it is withheld, readers in 1925 would have spotted it immediately as the late war. Readers today have to turn to the other Nick stories for an explicit answer, but there are two clues available in the text of "Big Two-Hearted River," one at the beginning and one at the end.

As Nick swings off the train at the station where he begins his pilgrimage back to nature, "There is no town, nothing . . . but the burned over country." This once-familiar place is now changed and all but destroyed. Reading further how nothing remained but foundations and charred timbers, "Even the surface had been burned off the ground," one finds a symbol suggesting the devastation of total war, even to the point of a scorched earth. So it is no surprise to discover, when one turns to the book of which this is the final episode, *In Our Time*, that the vignette to Chapter 6 describes Nick's near-fatal wounding in World War I. Readers of the whole volume know when they reach the fishing story (Chapters 14-15) that he is the returned veteran seeking rehabilitation. But since so many others adjusted quickly, he must be suffering from something more than the physical shock of being blown up by shrapnel.

The seriousness of Nick's condition is suggested by the second symbol. At the end of the day's fishing he looks across the river from his camp to the swamp where he knew the biggest trout would be. But "he did not want" to go in there. "In the swamp . . . the fishing would be tragic." On the literal level this is an absurd reaction for a grown man who is a seasoned outdoorsman. Nick's was clearly a psychic as well as a physical wounding. But this is no return to nature-as-healer in the Wordsworthian sense. The stream furnishes only an arena for his skill with rod and reel. And when the physical activity is over, there is no communing in the wild wood or meditation under the stars. "Nick was happy as he crawled inside the tent. . . . Nothing could touch him. . . . He was there, in the good place." Nature offers merely solitude, where he can make an envelope for hiding from a world gone bad. The key sentence in the earlier account of his battle wounding was that he had "made a separate peace." But escaping from the war, and from society as a whole, has not brought him peace. Nature must also be a setting for the therapy of exercise, so he can escape from an unbearable memory.

What made his experience traumatic is not revealed in "Big Two-Hearted River" or in the book as a whole, for this story brings *In Our Time* to a close. The reader must go outside. There are other Nick stories that fill in the gaps. Of the half dozen added later, "A Way You'll Never Be" (1933) comes closest to supplying the answer. There Nick is the shell-shocked soldier, returning to the front on a mission so eccentric that it suggests he has escaped from a convalescent hospital. Then he explicitly confesses to his former commander that he has been "certified as nutty." When a seizure threatens, he falls asleep and has his recurrent dream of a "bad place." It is described in some detail, but "what frightened him so . . . was the different width of the river" there. Readers closely acquainted with "Big Two-Hearted River" will remember that the "bad place" in that story is introduced by the sentence, "Ahead the river *narrowed* and went into a swamp." Just as the burnt-out town had set him thinking about the very war he was trying to forget, so by geographical association the swamp reminds him of the wartime bad place with all its nightmarish overtones. Hints like this led Malcolm Cowley to suspect that there are shadows lurking beneath the sunny surface of "Big Two-Hearted River," making it another of the many Hemingway stories he described as "nightmares at noonday." The final meaning of this obsessive place is not clarified until a quarter century later when the hero under a new name, Dick Cantwell of *Across the River and into the Trees* (1950), revisits ritualistically an identical one, the scene where he too was almost blown to bits.

Such casualties have been too common in the wars of this century to make the mere factual recording of their case histories a valid subject for fiction. This is why Hemingway largely avoids realistic narratives of modern war as the cause of shock and concentrates instead on the effect of such violence on his characters. The point of the Nick Adams stories is, "Why did these experiences, granting their horror, have such a disastrous effect on him?" "What manner of man is he?" "How does he symbolize the human condition today?" The whole range of them, some fifteen in all, explore the inner biography of this "wounded" modern man. His most notable trait, toughness, is a shield that was fashioned only gradually to protect an essentially sensitive person from the violence and evil of the world. In the novels, where he is a grown man, he is always wearing the shield, and many reaaders have missed what is behind it. Only in some of the short stories do we see the origin of its need. Even there the tenderness of the young hero, later to harden defensively against pain, is never commented on, only implied fleetingly in his reactions to the various experiences he undergoes.

The first five episodes of *In Our Times* sketch out Nick's boyhood and adolescence up in Michigan. The opener is his violent initiation into the pain of birth and death as he watches his father deliver an Indian woman by Caesarean section, with a jackknife and without ether, and then sees that her invalid husband in the bunk above has slit his throat because he could not bear the screaming any longer. This is followed by a much quieter story of the insolence and chicanery of a half-breed woodcutter, the real point of which is Nick's turning away from his mother in the end because she will not face the truth of what has happened, her religious idealism denying the existence of evil. In the third it is his own refusal to admit the evil in himself, his class snobbery that causes his cool break with a young sweetheart. The next is a kind of summing up so far, as Nick and an adolescent friend get drunk on his father's whisky while they boast of their initiation into the ways of the world—the corruption in big-league baseball, what they have learned about sex from their reading, and so on. This is the last of the stories in a home setting, but for a teenager brought up in a sheltered world he has made considerable progress in his knowledge of evil and suffering. The fifth story, where Nick has run away from home and is riding the rails, records the most unsettling experience of all. Slapped off a moving freight by the brakeman, he stumbles on a pair of hoboes. One is a punch-drunk ex-pugilist who threatens to thrash him, the other an obsequious Negro who is at best a leech on his white companion and at worst another kind of "queer"—homosexuality being Hemingway's recurrent symbol of ultimate evil.

There is little in Nick's heritage to provide answers to the questions raised by these contacts with the violence of the world. He has had plenty of injuries to his psyche before he ever gets to the war, and his experiences there are never detailed. On first mention, in Chapter 6, his soldiering as a volunteer in the Italian army has come to an abrupt end. He is a battle casualty who has made his separate peace. The wound is in exactly the right place, the spine, to account for Nick's psychic as well as physical wounding. The "Very Short Story" that accompanies this key vignette, telling of his abortive love affair with a nurse during convalescence, rounds out this capsule version of A *Farewell to Arms* (published four years later)—thus linking Nick to Lieutenant Henry, among other Hemingway heroes. If the war wounding threw him into shock, it was because this was the culmination of all that had gone before. Taken together, these successive blows have left him defenseless in a collapsing world. Others, less aware of the collapse, were less permanently wounded. That Nick is a special case, the symbolic modern sensibility that is shattered by all this chaos and meaningless violence, is made clear by the following story of a more average returning veteran. Krebs, who goes home to Kansas after the war, has also lost his sense of belonging to a family and a community. They are there, but they, as well as ambition and even any desire for love, are blanks to him for the time being. But the conclusion provides an all-important contrast. After just a few months Krebs has made a working adjustment to the postwar world; he is not lost psychically as Nick and his later embodiments still are years after the war is over.

Nick's own story is not taken up again until Chapter 12. The intervening four episodes are pretty far removed except as counterpoint to its theme. The first, dealing with homeless Communist agents in Europe, suggests the general breakup of society in postwar anarchy. The next three are variations on the theme of marriage as a failing institution. One shows a virginal husband and wife, past the normal age for marrying, who cannot face sex or any other reality. Another is a trivial incident about a young couple who have found boredom rather than love. The last presents a marriage gone sour, as illustrated in a fishing episode that fizzles. Their only justification in the book is that they prepare the way for the two final segments of Nick's biography. The first of these, Chapter 12, is brief, but it points up a new and important aspect of the Hemingway hero, his rather special attitude toward women. Nick is skiing in Switzerland with a friend, at a period presumably between his wounding and his return home. But he has an absent wife who is pregnant, and he must go back to the United States and get a job. Although he seems neutral toward his marriage, he is happy in this male companionship and agrees enthusiastically with George: "There's nothing really can touch skiing, is there?" Nothing perhaps for Hemingway's men-without-women, unless it is bullfighting or big-game hunts—or fishing.

The last of these is Nick's "true love" in the concluding double story, "Big Two-Hearted River," where he is alone with his rod and reel in the Michigan woods, wife and baby having faded from the picture. (One other story intervenes, "My Old Man," about a jockey and his son. It makes a serious break in the sequence, being totally unrelated to Nick. Next to the longest story in the volume, it is clearly padding to fill out to book length. It is not even good Hemingway, though it is a good story in the Sherwood Anderson manner.) Readers who have followed the spotty but subtly organized biography of Nick Adams up to this point are now prepared to get the most out of this long story that brings *In Our Time* to an end. They are also prepared to see beneath the surface of the fishing narrative the shadowy outline of the Hemingway hero who makes his long pilgrimage through the later fictions, back to whatever health and peace he can find.

There is one other feature of this first book needing mention because it adds to the total impact—the vignettes that come between the chapters, the "Introduction by the Author" and the "Envoi" that frame the whole. They are brief still-shots by a roving correspondent, rarely as long as one page, that roughly follow Hemingway's own itinerary through Europe in the early twenties. All deal with violence: battles scenes, evacuation of refugees, the bull ring, the criminal world. They range from the stylized violence of the matador, facing the victim he both hates and admires, to incidents of savage and sickening brutality. All are recorded dead pan but in the first person, as with a special reporter's privilege, and all are up-to-the-minute news. This bold experiment in structure lends a double meaning to the title. Everything about the book is insistently contemporary: this is the way it is *In Our Time*. But the phrase also refers ironically to one in the Book of Common Prayer, as Philip Young has pointed out, made notorious by Chamberlain at the time of his appeasement of the Nazis in Munich: "Give us peace in our time, O Lord." Nowhere in this world is there any peace. Though they serve as sounding boards for the stories they introduce, none of the vignettes is in any way related to Nick—with one notable exception, the one that forms the dramatic center of the book. It is the previously mentioned introduction to Chapter 6, relating the incident of his wounding. This ingenious device of inverting vignette and story welds the two disparate parts of the book into a single unit, linking the foreign-correspondent-as-narrator to the hero-as-point-of-view, and both to Hemingway's world view based on his own experiences.

In Our Time, so constructed into a fictional socioautobiography, could be subtitled "The Education of Nicholas Adams." As an initiation into the chaos of the modern world it suggests a remote parallel with *The Education of Henry Adams,* though there is no question which is the greater book. It is probably not accidental that Nick's father is actually named Dr. Henry Adams. The differences between the two books are what make the comparison instructive. Coming from the Middle West, Nick has a less traditional background either to lean on or to break from. Coming from a middle-class family, he gets an education that is less intellectual and more dependent on intuition. So his experience of both America and Europe is shallower than that of the other Adams, but more pragmatic. It is only in theme that the two fictive autobiographies come close together. Both recount the progress of a young American from a sheltered but closed life into a freer world that is falling into fragments.

There are two other parallels of more significance for the literary student. *The Unvanquished* (1938) might be called "In Another Time," by contrast with the modernity of *In Our Time*, but Faulkner's book came too late to be an influence, of course. On the other hand, the masterpiece of Sherwood Anderson, his early mentor, Hemingway admitted was his "first pattern," though it served more nearly as a point of departure. *Winesburg, Ohio* (1919) is similar in many ways to the other two, but there are important differences. For one thing, it falls between their respective concerns with a vanishing past and an emerging present, being aimed less at a specific period in American history. As parallels, all three seem closely related to their authors' biographies. All use an episodic structure, the parts separable as short stories yet linked by a single hero and the theme of his initiation into manhood. But the differences are far greater, in meaning and the mode by which it is rendered. As for the net result of their educations: young Bayard is made by his experiences, Nick is undone by his, and George is neither broken nor made whole by his, merely liberated into some degree of self discovery. Still more important is their disparity as works of art. They are miles apart in tone, style, and all the literary techniques by which an author achieves his effects and embodies his vision of the world.

In Our Time also differs from Hemingway's own later fictions in one significant way. Rarely again if ever are family, home, and community present. All the bases of society are conspicuous by their absence. A grandfather is unthinkable. There are men without women, usually on the outskirts of civilization: at war, on safaris, in the underworld. The lightly linked couples are childless. All live as transients in barracks or tents and in the anonymity of big cities—in hotels or rented rooms or at best apartments on short lease. Even when there is a semblance of family, as in *To Have and Have Not*, it is that of an outlaw who has broken with all communal ties. The past is a blank, and there is no background of order to their disordered lives. It is violence set in a world of violence, almost aesthetically pure, but raising the question whether there can be moral significance when there is no traditional code to measure from, hardly even the suggestion of a former one now abandoned.

It is beside the point, however, to use such omissions for an attack on Hemingway as being too limited in his subject matter, by the easy demonstration that even in the most modern of worlds these things are not totally lacking. This would be the fallacy of taking his "realism" as literal and sociologically representative. Instead, one must take his fictional world on its own terms and see how well it functions as a symbol, to dramatize the undeniable feeling of alienation in modern man, cut adrift from tradition and living from moment to moment in a truly fragmented real world. That Hemingway knew from his heritage this older society based on family, home, and community is sufficiently set forth in his first book to make it a touchstone for the collapse of these institutions and the values they represent. But even *In Our Time* shows them only for a moment. The break comes in Chapter 5 when the hero runs away from home, never to return. From then on he is a tramp, a soldier not only at war but in a foreign army, a footloose journalist in Europe, a returned veteran who does not come home but pitches his tent alone deep in the woods. Yet Nick Adams, the prototype of all Hemingway's isolated heroes, once belonged to an ordered society. He has a point to measure from, and through his story the reader has one. By implication it is present in the later fictions, just as the urban world Frost deleted from his poems is amply supplied by the reader.

II

In 1926 Hemingway followed up his start of the year before with a smash hit, *The Sun Also Rises*. Jake Barnes, the protagonist, is Nick Adams transformed and extended. The theme is the same, the "sick" modern man in a ruined world, but there are several important differences. Hemingway has shifted to a first-person narration, with all its advantages and dangers. Though there is no way of telling whether this novel is more autobiographical than *In Our Times* or less so, it does follow closely the next phase of the author's own life, his residence in Paris as newspaper man and hopeful author in the early twenties. The milieu is changed in much more than a geographical sense. The country or the no-man's land of war has been replaced by the big city. Also, Nick had gone through most of his experiences either alone or with a single companion. Jake is in the midst of a swirling crowd, but it is an agglomeration of characters instead of a coherent society. Yet he is trying to learn to live with people not just to make peace with himself, or, rather, he is trying to do the former as a means to the latter.

The most significant change is so minute it can easily be overlooked unless its symbolic import is underscored. Jake's wound—he also is a veteran—has been moved downward from the spine. The war has not injured him psychically, except indirectly. It has made him impotent. This makes all the difference between the two stories. Hemingway probably realized the limitations of a mental case for the novelist, or perhaps he had simply exhausted it as far as his own talents went, so he shifted his ground. Loss of the capacity to love, and the concomitant loss of religious belief, are now used to measure the destruction of values in the modern world. Jake is the only character in the book who clings to both, though he is the most deprived, an apostate Catholic and physically cut off from sex. The plot, such as it is, is a futile search to recover love and religion, failing that, to find substitutes or anodynes for their loss. How empty the world is without them is emphasized by the frenetic activity and meaningless clatter that fill the book. Although the war has been over several years, there is still no peace in our time and no health in it, except for a brief interlude. Violence may now be reduced to bickering and the evil mostly petty, at least during the first half, but this only enhances the feeling that the disease of modern times is virulent. If people behave like this in peace, when life should return to normalcy, what will they do in the next crisis? The answer is provided in the second half. The most trivial of crises explodes this little expatriate world into splinters, and no one escapes the general maiming, including the hero.

The interlude referred to comes midway in the book and provides its ethical center. It is, one discovers without surprise, a kind of duplication of "Big Two-Hearted River," this time a fishing episode in the Spanish mountains near Burgete. Its purpose likewise is to seek renewal of the spirit, to find peace by escaping from an unbearable world. But there are important differences. Since Jake is not emotionally unstable to the point of having to keep himself in tight controls, he relaxes almost at once. And since he is not so much running away from a traumatic experience in the past as from his intolerable friends in the present, he takes one choice companion with him from outside that circle and soon adds another. Here is the same retreat far from civilization, with its fine trees and streams for trout fishing, but the hero has come a long way from the lone camp of Nick in the Michigan woods. This is so clearly the "good place" there is no need of saying so explicitly. It is rendered in the happy comraderie of the three men. Together they rediscover love and religion, not in any ordinary sense but at least a concept of them that can serve as a symbol of lost values. Everything that goes on at Burgete is the antithesis of the rest of the book, so that this episode is the pivot around which the two halves swing.

The Paris section seems on the surface a continual round of drinking, but this is simply a drug for those who have lost the capacity to love. The bankrupt institution of marriage is parodied and freewheeling sex life travestied in scene after scene, crackling with a mordant irony that barely conceals the pathos of these empty lives. When a prostitute guesses Jake's condition, she offers him for consolation: "Everybody's sick. I'm sick too." That sums it up, at least as far as love is concerned. It is to escape from all this that Jake goes fishing in the mountains of Spain. When the party moves to Pamplona for the bullfights, after this interlude, the collapse of religious values gets its first dramatic embodiment, for the fiesta is both a pagan and a Christian celebration. Only Jake follows the peasants into the cathedral. Lady Bret, his unattainable love, is barred at the church door, then surrounded by the drunken street dancers and swept along with them to a wine cellar. There, seated on a cask, she presides over the revels like a very modern Circe, while her male worshipers are turned into swine. The violence of this concluding section takes two forms. The orgies of drinking and sexual promiscuity erupt in ignominious fist fights that break the thin circle of friendships beyond repair. Set against this is the formal violence of the bull ring. There the young matador performs with such skill that he becomes a symbol of the man in control of his life. (Incidentally, he is a good Catholic too.) Afterward, in his brief affair with Bret, he so conducts himself that he emerges from his sex initiation into full maturity. Romero, with his disciplined sword play, represents what Jake (and maybe the others) might have become if he were not sick with the disease of our time.

In *The Sun Also Rises* Hemingway made an even greater advance artistically than thematically. Here was the first real demonstration of his famous style—a "purified," stripped, athletic prose that was the perfect instrument for rendering the empty world of a lost generation and of a hero partly lost too, but beginning his search for the rediscovery of moral values empirically and from scratch. The two-dimensional Nick has become a character in depth, so that Jake has a life of his own quite beyond that of his prototype; and even the lesser characters create the illusion of being alive, so deftly are they drawn. Expository narrative is replaced by fast-moving action, largely expressed in dialogue of a stylized simplicity that yet gives the effect of a living vernacular. There is little more plot than formerly, but scene and story line are presented dramatically, and the chronicle form is complicated by a kind of poetic structure achieved through the fishing interlude.

It is in this direction of the novel-as-poem that A *Farewell to Arms* (1929) marked Hemingway's most distinctive development as a literary artist. Not only is it richer in allusiveness, imagery, and symbolism, but it employs a second style to counterpoint the more famous one. The theme again is the familiar one of the wounded hero in the modern world, but a new segment of Nick's story is chosen for exploration. That central episode of his wounding and his convalescent love affair, in Chapter 6 of *In Our Time*, is expanded into the whole of Lieutenant Henry's fictional life. This novel is the drama of how the modern hero was maimed by the forces that destroyed his world. The injury is again shifted, the place now being the knee, where the author himself was hit. This is less calculated to produce psychic wounding, as with Nick and Jake, though it does mean that Henry will have a permanent limp in the rest of his earthly pilgrimage. Since the novel deals with the war, not its aftermath, there was no need of a more vital wounding.

The actual clash and carnage of battle are largely off stage or in the distance, but total war encompasses the whole narrative. This gives Hemingway an opportunity to concentrate on its violent disruption of normal lives instead of on mere physical destruction. Plot once more is slight, there being none in the formal sense of conflicting forces that exert a two-way pull on the hero. Everything happens in a fairly straight line. Lieutenant Henry, an American in the Italian ambulance corps, is wounded in a minor engagement, falls in love with a nurse while hospitalized, returns to the front briefly, deserts during a retreat when the army is demoralized by an Austrian advance, escapes to Switzerland for an idyllic interlude with Catherine, then loses her in childbirth. (Incidentally, these fit the known facts of Hemingway's war experiences, all but the love affair and desertion.) If this were all there were to A *Farewell to Arms* it would not be worth serious study. Readers looking for a novel of mere plot interest will have to go elsewhere, in fact, outside of Hemingway.

The thematic structure, however, is as complex as the chronicle is simple. The best way to suggest it is by diagraming the three main lines of tension. The hero's idealism about this war-to-end-all-wars begins at a high level; he has volunteered his services in a foreign army, not to do combat, but to risk his life succoring the wounded. As the fighting drones on in its brutality and waste this idealism sinks to the dead level of just doing one's duty, from about the time of his meeting with Catherine until the retreat, when it plummets to zero in his desertion. His attitude toward love begins on the animal plane of the other soldiers, a mere biological urge to be satisfied by whores, then soars to spiritual heights at the same two climactic points that shattered his idealism. Courage with him begins on the even keel of physical bravery expected of any soldier and remains that way throughout the fighting, until it rises to moral courage in his decision to break from the meaningless war and dedicate himself to salvaging the human values represented by his love for Catherine.

This is not a structure created by events so much as a pattern of self-discovery formed by what Lieutenant Henry sees in the outward scene and with his inward eye. What leads him to desert the war is the image of utter chaos enacted, as in a tableau, on the bridge during the retreat from Caporetto. If the whole social fabric is in shreds, he will stake all on the basic relation of man and woman. What had led him upward from lust to love were his conversations with the chaplain who said, "When you love you wish to do things for, . . . to serve." He connected it with religion, and both with the life in his home town, which he pictured as so beautiful "a man may even love God" there without feeling foolish. From this point on, all Henry's thoughts about Catherine are dominated by the image of home, the one thing most conspicuously absent in a war-ravaged world. Recurrent through the book there are larger symbols for these opposed concepts of home and not-home. Heavy rains in the flatlands, washing away the very earth, represent the erosive effects of war on all the values and institutions of civilization. Cool sunny places in the mountains are associated with home, such as the priest's happy one in Abruzzi and the Swiss chalet where Catherine and Henry found the climax of their love.

The poetic effects in A *Farewell to Arms* are achieved partly by such imagery, but mainly through Hemingway's creation of a totally new style. The body of this book too, it is true, is written in the prose usually associated with him—hard and bare, secular and apparently nonliterary. But this familiar tough exterior now serves as a dramatic contrast to the rare but crucial passages written in an opposing style—warmly human, richly allusive, and at least suggestive of spiritual values. One illustration will have to serve.[2] This is the brief dream sequence that comes at the main turning point in the story, during the retreat in a deluge of rain. As Lieutenant Henry falls asleep, Hemingway takes advantage of the free association of ideas and the private symbolism expected in dreams to make his hero reveal his true feelings about Catherine.

In the space of fifteen lines there are submerged allusions to the child's prayer, "Now I lay me down to sleep," to the lullaby "Sweet and low" from Tennyson's *Princess,* and a quotation from the sixteenth-century poem, "The Lover in Winter Plaineth for the Spring." This last is especially important, for in addition to being a poignant love lyric it has religious overtones in the symbol of Christ as the gentle rain renewing the earth. Here, then, beneath the surface of the battle-weary hero's mind are images of home, married love, and Christian rebirth. They are all the more startling by reason of the tough soldier talk that frames the dream sequence. As he falls asleep, the last thing the lieutenant hears is the mock threat of the ambulance drivers that they are going to rape two young girls. As he wakes, the first words to reach his ears are their profanity and obscenity as they try to start the trucks stalled in the mud. These tender spots of sensibility, carefully nurtured in a dehumanized world, provide both a measure and a meaning for the tough exterior that encases them.

In five brief years Hemingway had staked out most of his claims to distinction as a literary artist, extended in the next five to a few superb short stories. There are some who even feel that this compact form suited his talents better than the novel did. Be that as it may, these early fictions are his real achievement.[3] If their impudent manner and pretended nihilism had

---

[2] For fuller treatment of this see the article by Charles Anderson in Reading Suggestions.

[3] To these may be added the late novelette, *The Old Man and the Sea,* another variant on his old theme but couched in an experimental semi-mythological style.

been all they had to offer, they would have dropped from the lists long ago. Perhaps their staying power derives from the occasional passages of muted lyricism sounded against the hard protective surface of his typical prose. He had one main story to tell, fabricated out of the central experience of his life, and he told it over and over, usually new. And he invented a highly original mode for rendering it, for embodying his limited but valid view of the world in memorable fiction.

One experiment in the opposite direction from autobiographical fiction, *The Green Hills of Africa* (1935), offers a valuable study in contrasting techniques: how to give literary form to a factual record. That this was Hemingway's deliberate purpose is made clear in the foreword: "The writer has attempted to write an absolutely true book to see whether the shape of a country and the pattern of a month's action can, if truly presented, compete with a work of the imagination." It is of particular interest that this project was first conceived as a short story, and that Hemingway compared it in his own mind to "Big Two-Hearted River." As it expanded to book length, a full-scale account of big-game hunting, it ran into difficulties such as a tendency to sprawl and to fall off in suspense. Another trouble was the one Edmund Wilson had in mind when he said of Hemingway, "as soon as he talks in his own person he seems to lose all his capacity for self-criticism and is likely to become fatuous or maudlin." This is particularly true of his digressions on literature and his gratuitous asides on favorite topics like war, marriage, and the flaws in modern society. In his fiction, the same situations that obsess him emotionally and engage the conflicting elements of his personality, as Wilson goes on to say, "are externalized and objectified; and the result is an art which is severe, intense, and deeply serious." The best part of *The Green Hills of Africa*, therefore, is the climax of "a month's action," which is shaped more like a fiction than other parts of the book. Here the personality of the author becomes submerged in the kudu hunter, intent on his pursuit of the large African antelope. Because of this, "Pursuit as Happiness" has been chosen for inclusion as an instructive comparison with "Big Two-Hearted River," which could have been titled "Pursuit as Escape from Despair."

Hemingway's posthumous volume, *A Moveable Feast* (1964), is an even more interesting example of how an autobiographical record can be transformed into a work of art. On the surface it seems to be a series of sketches of the author's life in Paris during the twenties, the place and time that form the milieu of *The Sun Also Rises*, but this is no mere reminiscent chronicle. Hemingway himself says in the preface, "If the reader prefers, this book may be regarded as fiction." Scenes, events, and characters are selected and maneuvered to render a single theme: his "education" as a writer. This most recent work is, indeed, Hemingway's Portrait of the

Artist as a young man, and as such it may some day take its place among his major fictions.

CHARLES R. ANDERSON

A Note on the Text. The text here followed for "Big Two-Hearted River" is that of the first American edition of *In Our Time* (New York: Boni & Liveright, 1925); for "Pursuit as Happiness," that of *The Green Hills of Africa* (New York: Charles Scribner's Sons, 1935), chapter 12.

BIG TWO-HEARTED RIVER

Part 1[1]

THE TRAIN WENT on up the track out of sight, around one of the hills of burnt timber. Nick sat down on the bundle of canvas and bedding the baggage man had pitched out of the door of the baggage car. There was no town, nothing but the rails and the burned-over country. The thirteen saloons that had lined the one street of Seney had not left a trace. The foundations of the Mansion House hotel stuck up above the ground. The stone was chipped and split by the fire. It was all that was left of the town of Seney. Even the surface had been burned off the ground.

Nick looked at the burned-over stretch of hillside, where he had expected to find the scattered houses of the town and then walked down the railroad track to the bridge over the river. The river was there. It swirled against the log piles of the bridge. Nick looked down into the clear, brown water, colored from the pebbly bottom, and watched the trout keeping themselves steady in the current with wavering fins. As he watched them they changed their positions by quick angles, only to hold steady in the fast water again. Nick watched them a long time.

He watched them holding themselves with their noses into the current, many trout in deep, fast moving water, slightly distorted as he watched far down through the glassy convex surface of the pool, its surface pushing and swelling smooth against the resistance of the log-driven piles of the bridge.

[1] This episode in the story of Nick Adams forms the concluding two chapters of *In Our Time* (1925).

At the bottom of the pool were the big trout. Nick did not see them at first. Then he saw them at the bottom of the pool, big trout looking to hold themselves on the gravel bottom in a varying mist of gravel and sand, raised in spurts by the current.

Nick looked down into the pool from the bridge. It was a hot day. A kingfisher flew up the stream. It was a long time since Nick had looked into a stream and seen trout. They were very satisfactory. As the shadow of the kingfisher moved up the stream, a big trout shot upstream in a long angle, only his shadow marking the angle, then lost his shadow as he came through the surface of the water, caught the sun, and then, as he went back into the stream under the surface, his shadow seemed to float down the stream with the current, unresisting, to his post under the bridge where he tightened facing up into the current.

Nick's heart tightened as the trout moved. He felt all the old feeling.

He turned and looked down the stream. It stretched away, pebbly-bottomed with shallows and big boulders and a deep pool as it curved away around the foot of a bluff.

Nick walked back up the ties to where his pack lay in the cinders beside the railway track. He was happy. He adjusted the pack harness around the bundle, pulling straps tight, slung the pack on his back, got his arms through the shoulder straps and took some of the pull off his shoulders by leaning his forehead against the wide band of the tump-line. Still, it was too heavy. It was much too heavy. He had his leather rod-case in his hand and leaning forward to keep the weight of the pack high on his shoulders he walked along the road that paralleled the railway track, leaving the burned town behind in the heat, and then turned off around a hill with a high, fire-scarred hill on either side onto a road that went back into the country. He walked along the road feeling the ache from the pull of the heavy pack. The road climbed steadily. It was hard work walking up-hill. His muscles ached and the day was hot, but Nick felt happy. He felt he had left everything behind, the need for thinking, the need to write, other needs. It was all back of him.

From the time he had gotten down off the train and the baggage man had thrown his pack out of the open car door things had been different. Seney was burned, the country was burned over and changed, but it did not matter. It could not all be burned. He knew that. He hiked along the road, sweating in the sun, climbing to cross the range of hills that separated the railway from the pine plains.

The road ran on, dipping occasionally, but always climbing. Nick went on up. Finally the road after going parallel to the burnt hillside reached the top. Nick leaned back against a stump and slipped out of the pack harness. Ahead of him, as far as he could see, was the pine plain. The burned country stopped off at the left with the range of hills. On ahead islands of dark pine trees rose out of the plain. Far off to the left was the line of the river. Nick followed it with his eye and caught glints of the water in the sun.

There was nothing but the pine plain ahead of him, until the far blue hills that marked the Lake Superior height of land. He could hardly see them, faint and far away in the heat-light over the plain. If he looked too steadily they were gone. But if he only half-looked they were there, the far-off hills of the height of land.

Nick sat down against the charred stump and smoked a cigarette. His pack balanced on the top of the stump, harness holding ready, a hollow molded in it from his back. Nick sat smoking, looking out over the country. He did not need to get his map out. He knew where he was from the position of the river.

As he smoked, his legs stretched out in front of him, he noticed a grasshopper walk along the ground and up onto his woolen sock. The grasshopper was black. As he had walked along the road, climbing, he had started many grasshoppers from the dust. They were all black. They were not the big grasshoppers with yellow and black or red and black wings whirring out from their black wing sheathing as they fly up. These were just ordinary hoppers, but all a sooty black in color. Nick had wondered about them as he walked, without really thinking about them. Now, as he watched the black hopper that was nibbling at the wool of his sock with its four-way lip, he realized that they had all turned black from living in the burned-over land. He realized that the fire must have come the year before, but the grasshoppers were all black now. He wondered how long they would stay that way.

Carefully he reached his hand down and took hold of the hopper by the wings. He turned him up, all his legs walking in the air, and looked at his jointed belly. Yes, it was black too, iridescent where the back and head were dusty.

"Go on, hopper," Nick said, speaking out loud for the first time. "Fly away somewhere."

He tossed the grasshopper up into the air and watched him sail away to a charcoal stump across the road.

Nick stood up. He leaned his back against the weight of his pack where it rested upright on the stump and got his arms through the shoulder straps. He stood with the pack on his back on the brow of the hill looking out across the country, toward the distant river and then struck down the hillside away from the road. Underfoot the ground was good walking. Two hundred yards down the hillside the fire line stopped. Then it was sweet fern, growing ankle high, to walk through, and clumps of jack pines; a long undulating country with frequent rises and descents, sandy underfoot and the country alive again.

Nick kept his direction by the sun. He knew where he wanted to strike the river and he kept on through the pine plain, mounting small rises to see other rises ahead of him and sometimes from the top of a rise a great solid island of pines off to his right or his left. He broke off some sprigs of the heathery sweet fern, and put them under his pack straps. The chafing crushed it and he smelled it as he walked.

He was tired and very hot, walking across the uneven, shadeless pine plain. At any time he knew he could strike the river by turning off to his left. It could not be more than a mile away. But he kept on toward the north to hit the river as far upstream as he could go in one day's walking.

For some time as he walked Nick had been in sight of one of the big islands of pine standing out above the rolling high ground he was crossing. He dipped down and then as he came slowly up to the crest of the bridge he turned and made toward the pine trees.

There was no underbrush in the island of pine trees. The trunks of the trees went straight up or slanted toward each other. The trunks were straight and brown without branches. The branches were high above. Some inter-locked to make a solid shadow on the brown forest floor. Around the grove of trees was a bare space. It was brown and soft underfoot as Nick walked on it. This was the over-lapping of the pine needle floor, extending out beyond the width of the high branches. The trees had grown tall and the branches moved high, leaving in the sun this bare space they had once covered with shadow. Sharp at the edge of this extension of the forest floor commenced the sweet fern.

Nick slipped off his pack and lay down in the shade. He lay on his back and looked up into the pine trees. His neck and back and the small of his back rested as he stretched. The earth felt good against his back. He looked up at the sky, through the branches, and then shut his eyes. He opened them and looked up again. There was a wind high up in the branches. He shut his eyes again and went to sleep.

Nick woke stiff and cramped. The sun was nearly down. His pack was heavy and the straps painful as he lifted it on. He leaned over with the pack on and picked up the leather rod-case and started out from the pine trees across the sweet fern swale, toward the river. He knew it could not be more than a mile.

He came down a hillside covered with stumps into a meadow. At the edge of the meadow flowed the river. Nick was glad to get to the river. He walked upstream through the meadow. His trousers were soaked with the dew as he walked. After the hot day, the dew had come quickly and heavily. The river made no sound. It was too fast and smooth. At the edge of the meadow, before he mounted to a piece of high ground to make camp, Nick looked down the river at the trout rising. They were rising to insects come from the swamp on the other side of the stream when the sun went down. The trout jumped out of water to take them. While Nick walked through the little stretch of meadow alongside the stream, trout had jumped high out of water. Now as he looked down the river, the insects must be set-tling on the surface, for the trout were feeding steadily all down the stream. As far down the long stretch as he could see, the trout were rising, making circles all down the surface of the water, as though it were starting to rain.

The ground rose, wooded and sandy, to overlook the meadow, the stretch of river and the swamp. Nick dropped his pack and rod-case and looked for a level piece of ground. He was very hungry and he wanted to make his camp before he cooked. Between two jack pines, the ground was quite level. He took the ax out of the pack and chopped out two projecting roots. That leveled a piece of ground large enough to sleep on. He smoothed out the sandy soil with his hand and pulled all the sweet fern bushes by their roots. His hands smelled good from the sweet fern. He smoothed the uprooted earth. He did not want anything making lumps under the blankets. When he had the ground smooth, he spread his three blankets. One he folded double, next to the ground. The other two he spread on top.

With the ax he slit off a bright slab of pine from one of the stumps and split it into pegs for the tent. He wanted them long and solid to hold in the ground. With the tent unpacked and spread on the ground, the pack, leaning against a jackpine, looked much smaller. Nick tied the rope that served the tent for a ridge-pole to the trunk of one of the pine trees and pulled the tent up off the ground with the other end of the rope and tied it to the other pine. The tent hung on the rope like a canvas blanket on a clothesline. Nick poked a pole he had cut up under the back peak of the canvas and then made it a tent by pegging out the sides. He pegged the sides out taut and drove the pegs deep, hitting them down into the ground with the flat of the ax until the rope loops were buried and the canvas was drum tight.

Across the open mouth of the tent Nick fixed cheese cloth to keep out mosquitoes. He crawled inside under the mosquito bar with various things from the pack to put at the head of the bed under the slant of the canvas. Inside the tent the light came through the brown canvas. It smelled pleasantly of canvas. Already there was something mysterious and homelike. Nick was happy as he crawled inside the tent. He had not been unhappy all day. This was different though. Now things were done. There had been this to do. Now it was done. It had been a hard trip. He was very tired. That was done. He had made his camp. He was settled. Nothing could touch him. It was a good place to camp. He was there, in the good place. He was in his home where he had made it. Now he was hungry.

He came out, crawling under the cheese cloth. It was quite dark outside. It was lighter in the tent.

Nick went over to the pack and found, with his fingers, a long nail in a paper sack of nails, in the bottom of the pack. He drove it into the pine tree, holding it close and hitting it gently with the flat of the ax. He hung the pack up on the nail. All his supplies were in the pack. They were off the ground and sheltered now.

Nick was hungry. He did not believe he had ever been hungrier. He opened and emptied a can of pork and beans and a can of spaghetti into the frying pan.

"I've got a right to eat this kind of stuff, if I'm willing to carry it," Nick said. His voice sounded strange in the darkening woods. He did not speak again.

He started a fire with some chunks of pine he got with the ax from a stump. Over the fire he stuck a wire grill, pushing the four legs down into the ground with his boot. Nick put the frying pan on the grill over the flames. He was hungrier. The beans and spaghetti warmed. Nick stirred them and mixed them together. They began to bubble, making little bubbles that rose with difficulty to the surface. There was a good smell. Nick got out a bottle of tomato catchup and cut four slices of bread. The little bubbles were coming faster now. Nick sat down beside the fire and lifted the frying pan off. He poured about half the contents out into the tin plate. It spread slowly on the plate. Nick knew it was too hot. He poured on some tomato catchup.

He knew the beans and spaghetti were still too hot. He looked at the fire, then at the tent, he was not going to spoil it all by burning his tongue. For years he had never enjoyed fried bananas because he had never been able to wait for them to cool. His tongue was very sensitive. He was very hungry. Across the river in the swamp, in the almost dark, he saw a mist rising. He looked at the tent once more. All right. He took a full spoonful from the plate.

"Chrise," Nick said, "Geezus Chrise," he said happily.

He ate the whole plateful before he remembered the bread. Nick finished the second plateful with the bread, mopping the plate shiny. He had not eaten since a cup of coffee and a ham sandwich in the station restaurant at St. Ignace. It had been a very fine experience. He had been that hungry before, but had not been able to satisfy it. He could have made camp hours before if he had wanted to. There were plenty of good places to camp on the river. But this was good.

Nick tucked two big chips of pine under the grill. The fire flared up. He had forgotten to get water for the coffee. Out of the pack he got a folding canvas bucket and walked down the hill, across the edge of the meadow, to the stream. The other bank was in the white mist. The grass was wet and cold as he knelt on the bank and dipped the canvas bucket into the stream. It bellied and pulled hard in the current. The water was ice cold. Nick rinsed the bucket and carried it full up to the camp. Up away from the stream it was not so cold.

Nick drove another big nail and hung up the bucket full of water. He dipped the coffee pot half full, put some more chips under the grill onto the fire and put the pot on. He could not remember which way he made coffee. He could remember an argument about it with Hopkins, but not which side he had taken. He decided to bring it to a boil. He remembered now that was Hopkins's way. He had once argued about everything with Hopkins. While he waited for the coffee to boil, he opened a small can of apricots. He liked to open cans. He emptied the can of apricots out into a tin cup. While he watched the coffee on the fire, he drank the juice syrup of the apricots, carefully at first to keep from spilling, then meditatively, sucking the apricots down. They were better than fresh apricots.

The coffee boiled as he watched. The lid came up and coffee and grounds ran down the side of the pot. Nick took it off the grill. It was a triumph for Hopkins. He put sugar in the empty apricot cup and poured some of the coffee out to cool. It was too hot to pour and he used his hat to hold the handle of the coffee pot. He would not let it steep in the pot at all. Not the first cup. It should be straight Hopkins all the way. Hop deserved that. He was a very serious coffee maker. He was the most serious man Nick had ever known. Not heavy, serious. That was a long time ago. Hopkins spoke without moving his lips. He had played polo. He made millions of dollars in Texas. He had borrowed carfare to go to Chicago, when the wire came that his first big well had come in. He could have wired for money. That would have been too slow. They called Hop's girl the Blonde Venus. Hop did not mind because she was not his real girl. Hopkins said very confidently that none of them would make fun of his real girl. He was right. Hopkins went away when the telegram came. That was on the Black River. It took eight days for the telegram to reach him. Hopkins gave away his .22 caliber Colt automatic pistol to Nick. He gave his camera to Bill. It was to remember him always by. They were all going fishing again next summer. The Hop Head was rich. He would get a yacht and they would all cruise along the north shore of Lake Superior. He was excited but serious. They said good-bye and all felt bad. It broke up the trip. They never saw Hopkins again. That was a long time ago on the Black River.

Nick drank the coffee, the coffee according to Hopkins. The coffee was bitter. Nick laughed. It made a good ending to the story. His mind was starting to work. He knew he could choke it because he was tired enough. He spilled the coffee out of the pot and shook the grounds loose into the fire. He lit a cigarette and went inside the tent. He took off his shoes and trousers, sitting on the blankets, rolled the shoes up inside the trousers for a pillow and got in between the blankets.

Out through the front of the tent he watched the glow of the fire, when the night wind blew on it. It was a quiet night. The swamp was perfectly quiet. Nick stretched under the blanket comfortably. A mosquito hummed close to his ear. Nick sat up and lit a match. The mosquito was on the canvas, over his head. Nick moved the match quickly up to it. The mosquito made a satisfactory hiss in the flame. The match went out. Nick lay down again under the blanket. He turned on his side and shut his eyes. He was sleepy. He felt sleep coming. He curled up under the blanket and went to sleep.

Part 2

In the morning the sun was up and the tent was starting to get hot. Nick crawled out under the mosquito netting stretched across the mouth of the tent, to look at the morning. The grass was wet on his hands as he came out. He held his trousers and his shoes in his hands. The sun was just up over the hill. There was the meadow, the river and the swamp. There were birch trees in the green of the swamp on the other side of the river.

The river was clear and smoothly fast in the early morning. Down about two hundred yards were three logs all the way across the stream. They made the water smooth and deep above them. As Nick watched, a mink crossed the river on the logs and went into the swamp. Nick was excited. He was excited by the early morning and the river. He was really too hurried to eat breakfast, but he knew he must. He built a little fire and put on the coffee pot.

While the water was heating in the pot he took an empty bottle and went down over the edge of the high ground to the meadow. The meadow was wet with dew and Nick wanted to catch grasshoppers for bait before the sun dried the grass. He found plenty of good grasshoppers. They were at the base of the grass stems. Sometimes they clung to a grass stem. They were cold and wet with the dew, and could not jump until the sun warmed them. Nick picked them up, taking only the medium-sized brown ones, and put them into the bottle. He turned over a log and just under the shelter of the edge were several hundred hoppers. It was a grasshopper lodging house. Nick put about fifty of the medium browns into the bottle. While he was picking up the hoppers the others warmed in the sun and commenced to hop away. They

ERNEST HEMINGWAY

flew when they hopped. At first they made one flight and stayed stiff when they landed, as though they were dead.

Nick knew that by the time he was through with breakfast they would be as lively as ever. Without dew in the grass it would take him all day to catch a bottle full of good grasshoppers and he would have to crush many of them, slamming at them with his hat. He washed his hands at the stream. He was excited to be near it. Then he walked up to the tent. The hoppers were already jumping stiffly in the grass. In the bottle, warmed by the sun, they were jumping in a mass. Nick put in a pine stick as a cork. It plugged the mouth of the bottle enough, so the hoppers could not get out and left plenty of air passage.

He had rolled the log back and knew he could get grasshoppers there every morning.

Nick laid the bottle full of jumping grasshoppers against a pine trunk. Rapidly he mixed some buckwheat flour with water and stirred it smooth, one cup of flour, one cup of water. He put a handful of coffee in the pot and dipped a lump of grease out of a can and slid it sputtering across the hot skillet. On the smoking skillet he poured smoothly the buckwheat batter. It spread like lava, the grease spitting sharply. Around the edges the buckwheat cake began to firm, then brown, then crisp. The surface was bubbling slowly to porousness. Nick pushed under the browned under surface with a fresh pine chip. He shook the skillet sideways and the cake was loose on the surface. I won't try and flop it, he thought. He slid the chip of clean wood all the way under the cake, and flopped it over onto its face. It sputtered in the pan.

When it was cooked Nick regreased the skillet. He used all the batter. It made another big flapjack and one smaller one.

Nick ate a big flapjack and a smaller one, covered with apple butter. He put apple butter on the third cake, folded it over twice, wrapped it in oiled paper and put it in his shirt pocket. He put the apple butter jar back in the pack and cut bread for two sandwiches.

In the pack he found a big onion. He sliced it in two and peeled the silky outer skin. Then he cut one half into slices and made onion sandwiches. He wrapped them in oiled paper and buttoned them in the other pocket of his khaki shirt. He turned the skillet upside down on the grill, drank the coffee, sweetened and yellow brown with the condensed milk in it, and tidied up the camp. It was a nice little camp.

Nick took his fly rod out of the leather rod-case, jointed it, and shoved the rod-case back into the tent. He put on the reel and threaded the line through the guides. He had to hold it from hand to hand, as he threaded it, or it would slip back through its own weight. It was a heavy, double tapered fly line. Nick had paid eight dollars for it a long time ago. It was made heavy to lift back in the air and come forward flat and heavy and straight to make it possible to cast a fly which has no weight. Nick opened the aluminum leader box. The leaders were coiled between the damp flannel pads. Nick had wet the pads at the water cooler on the train up to St. Ignace. In the damp pads the gut leaders had softened and Nick unrolled one and tied it by a loop at the end to the heavy fly line. He fastened a hook on the end of the leader. It was a small hook; very thin and springy.

Nick took it from his hook book, sitting with the rod across his lap. He tested the knot and the spring of the rod by pulling the line taut. It was a good feeling. He was careful not to let the hook bite into his finger.

He started down to the stream, holding his rod, the bottle of grasshoppers hung from his neck by a thong tied in half hitches around the neck of the bottle. His landing net hung by a hook from his belt. Over his shoulder was a long flour sack tied at each corner into an ear. The cord went over his shoulder. The sack flapped against his legs.

Nick felt awkward and professionally happy with all his equipment hanging from him. The grasshopper bottle swung against his chest. In his shirt the breast pockets bulged against him with the lunch and his fly book.

He stepped into the stream. It was a shock. His trousers clung tight to his legs. His shoes felt the gravel. The water was a rising cold shock.

Rushing, the current sucked against his legs. Where he stepped in, the water was over his knees. He waded with the current. The gravel slid under his shoes. He looked down at the swirl of water below each leg and tipped up the bottle to get a grasshopper.

The first grasshopper gave a jump in the neck of the bottle and went out into the water. He was sucked under in the whirl by Nick's right leg and came to the surface a little way down stream. He floated rapidly, kicking. In a quick circle, breaking the smooth surface of the water, he disappeared. A trout had taken him.

Another hopper poked his face out of the bottle. His antennae wavered. He was getting his front legs out of the bottle to jump. Nick took him by the head and held him while he threaded the slim hook under his chin, down through his thorax and into the last segments of his abdomen. The grasshopper took hold of the hook with his front feet, spitting tobacco juice on it. Nick dropped him into the water.

Holding the rod in his right hand he let out line against the pull of the grasshopper in the current. He stripped off line from the reel with his left hand and let it run free. He could see the hopper in the little waves of the current. It went out of sight.

There was a tug on the line. Nick pulled against the taut line. It was his first strike. Holding the now living rod across the current, he brought in the line with his left hand. The rod bent in jerks, the trout pumping against the current. Nick knew it was a small one. He lifted the rod straight up in the air. It bowed with the pull.

He saw the trout in the water jerking with his head and body against the shifting tangent of the line in the stream.

Nick took the line in his left hand and pulled the trout, thumping tiredly against the current, to the surface. His back was mottled the clear, water-over-gravel color, his side flashing in the sun. The rod under his right arm, Nick stooped, dipping his right hand into the current. He held the trout, never still, with his moist right hand, while he unhooked the barb from his mouth, then dropped him back into the stream.

He hung unsteadily in the current, then settled to the bottom beside a stone. Nick reached down his hand to touch him, his arm to the elbow under water. The trout was steady in the moving stream, resting on the gravel, beside a stone. As Nick's fingers touched him, touched his smooth, cool, underwater feeling he was gone, gone in a shadow across the bottom of the stream.

He's all right, Nick thought. He was only tired.

He had wet his hand before he touched the trout, so he would not disturb the delicate mucus that covered him. If a trout was touched with a dry hand, a white fungus attacked the unprotected spot. Years before when he had fished crowded streams, with fly fishermen ahead of him and behind him, Nick had again and again come on dead trout, furry with white fungus, drifted against a rock, or floating belly up in some pool. Nick did not like to fish with other men on the river. Unless they were of your party, they spoiled it.

[handwritten margin note: Nature lore that Hemingway knows.]

He wallowed down the stream, above his knees in the current, through the fifty yards of shallow water above the pile of logs that crossed the stream. He did not rebait his hook and held it in his hand as he waded. He was certain he could catch small trout in the shallows, but he did not want them. There would be no big trout in the shallows this time of day.

Now the water deepened up his thighs sharply and coldly. Ahead was the smooth dammed-back flood of water above the logs. The water was smooth and dark; on the left, the lower edge of the meadow; on the right the swamp.

Nick leaned back against the current and took a hopper from the bottle. He threaded the hopper on the hook and spat on him for good luck. Then he pulled several yards of line from the reel and tossed the hopper out ahead onto the fast, dark water. It floated down towards the logs, then the weight of the line pulled the bait under the surface. Nick held the rod in his right hand, letting the line run out through his fingers.

There was a long tug. Nick struck and the rod came alive and dangerous, bent double, the line tightening, coming out of water, tightening, all in a heavy, dangerous, steady pull. Nick felt the moment when the leader would break if the strain increased and let the line go.

The reel ratcheted into a mechanical shriek as the line went out in a rush. Too fast. Nick could not check it, the line rushing out, the reel note rising as the line ran out.

With the core of the reel showing, his heart feeling stopped with the excitement, leaning back against the current that mounted icily his thighs, Nick thumbed the reel hard with his left hand. It was awkward getting his thumb inside the fly reel frame.

As he put on pressure the line tightened into sudden hardness and beyond the logs a huge trout went high out of water. As he jumped, Nick lowered the tip of the rod. But he felt, as he dropped the tip to ease the strain, the moment when the strain was too great; the hardness too tight. Of course, the leader had broken. There was no mistaking the feeling when all spring left the line and it became dry and hard. Then it went slack.

His mouth dry, his heart down, Nick reeled in. He had never seen so big a trout. There was a heaviness, a power not to be held, and then the bulk of him, as he jumped. He looked as broad as a salmon.

Nick's hand was shaky. He reeled in slowly. The thrill had been too much. He felt, vaguely, a little sick, as though it would be better to sit down.

The leader had broken where the hook was tied to it. Nick took it in his hand. He thought of the trout somewhere on the bottom, holding himself steady over the gravel, far down below the light, under the logs, with the hook in his jaw. Nick knew the trout's teeth would cut through the snell of the hook. The hook would imbed itself in his jaw. He'd bet the trout was angry. Anything that size would be angry. That was a trout. He had been solidly hooked. Solid as a rock. He felt like a rock, too, before he started off. By God, he was a big one. By God, he was the biggest one I ever heard of.

Nick climbed out onto the meadow and stood, water running down his trousers and out of his shoes, his shoes squlchy. He went over and sat on the logs. He did not want to rush his sensations any.

He wriggled his toes in the water, in his shoes, and got out a cigarette from his breast pocket. He lit it and tossed the match into the fast water below the logs. A tiny trout rose at the match, as it swung around in the fast current. Nick laughed. He would finish the cigarette.

He sat on the logs, smoking, drying in the sun, the sun warm on his back, the river shallow ahead entering the woods, curving into the woods, shallows, light glittering, big water-smooth rocks, cedars along the bank and white birches, the logs warm in the sun, smooth to sit on, without bark, gray to the touch; slowly the feeling of disappointment left him. It went away slowly, the feeling of disappointment that came sharply after the thrill that made his shoulders ache. It was all right now. His rod lying out on the logs, Nick tied a new hook on the leader, pulling the gut tight until it grimped into itself in a hard knot.

He baited up, then picked up the rod and walked to the far end of the logs to get into the water, where it was not too deep. Under and beyond the logs was a deep pool. Nick walked around the shallow shelf near the swamp shore until he came out on the shallow bed of the stream.

On the left, where the meadow ended and the woods began, a great elm tree was uprooted. Gone over in a storm, it lay back into the woods, its roots clotted with dirt, grass growing in them, rising a solid bank beside the stream. The river cut to the edge of the uprooted tree. From where Nick stood he could see deep channels, like ruts, cut in the shallow bed of the stream by the flow of the current. Pebbly where he stood and pebbly and full of boulders beyond; where it curved near the tree roots, the bed of the stream was marly and between the ruts of deep water green weed fronds swung in the current.

Nick swung the rod back over his shoulder and forward, and the line, curving forward, laid the grasshopper down on one of the deep channels in the weeds. A trout struck and Nick hooked him.

Holding the rod far out toward the uprooted tree and sloshing backward in the current, Nick worked the trout, plunging, the rod bending alive, out of the danger of the weeds into the open river. Holding the rod, pumping alive against the current, Nick brought the trout in. He rushed, but always came, the spring of the rod yielding to the rushes, sometimes jerking under water, but always bringing him in. Nick eased downstream with the rushes. The rod above his head he led the trout over the net, then lifted.

The trout hung heavy in the net, mottled trout back and silver sides in the meshes. Nick unhooked him; heavy sides, good to hold, big undershot jaw, and slipped him, heaving and big sliding, into the long sack that hung from his shoulders in the water.

Nick spread the mouth of the sack against the current and it filled, heavy with water. He held it up, the bottom in the stream, and the water poured out through the sides. Inside at the bottom was the big trout, alive in the water.

Nick moved downstream. The sack out ahead of him sunk heavy in the water, pulling from his shoulders.

It was getting hot, the sun hot on the back of his neck.

Nick had one good trout. He did not care about getting many trout. Now the stream was shallow and wide. There were trees along both banks. The trees of the left bank made short shadows on the current in the forenoon sun. Nick knew there were trout in each shadow. In the afternoon, after the sun had crossed toward the hills, the trout would be in the cool shadows on the other side of the stream.

The very biggest ones would lie up close to the bank. You could always pick them up there on the Black. When the sun was down they all moved out into the current. Just when the sun made the water blinding in the glare before it went down, you were liable to strike a big trout anywhere in the current. It was almost impossible to fish then, the surface of the water was blinding as a mirror in the sun. Of course, you could fish upstream, but in a stream like the Black, or this, you had to wallow against the current and in a deep place, the water piled up on you. It was no fun to fish upstream with this much current.

Nick moved along through the shallow stretch watching the banks for deep holes. A beech tree grew close beside the river, so that the branches hung down into the water. The stream went back in under the leaves. There were always trout in a place like that.

Nick did not care about fishing that hole. He was sure he would get hooked in the branches.

It looked deep though. He dropped the grasshopper so the current took it under water, back in under the overhanging branch. The line pulled hard and Nick struck. The trout threshed heavily, half out of water in the leaves and branches. The line was caught. Nick pulled hard and the trout was off. He reeled in and holding the hook in his hand, walked down the stream.

Ahead, close to the left bank, was a big log. Nick saw it was hollow; pointing up river the current entered it smoothly, only a little ripple spread each side of the log. The water was deepening. The top of the hollow log was gray and dry. It was partly in the shadow.

Nick took the cork out of the grasshopper bottle and a hopper clung to it. He picked him off, hooked him and tossed him out. He held the rod far out so that the hopper on the water moved into the current flowing into the hollow log. Nick lowered the rod and the hopper floated in. There was a heavy strike. Nick swung the rod against the pull. It felt as though he were hooked into the log itself, except for the live feeling.

He tried to force the fish out into the current. It came, heavily.

The line went slack and Nick thought the trout was gone. Then he saw him, very near, in the current, shaking his head, trying to get the hook out. His mouth was clamped shut. He was fighting the hook in the clear flowing current.

Looping in the line with his left hand, Nick swung the rod to make the line taut and tried to lead the trout toward the net, but he was gone, out of sight, the line pumping. Nick fought him against the current, letting him thump in the water against the spring of the rod. He shifted the rod to his left hand, worked the trout upstream, holding his weight, fighting on the rod, and then let him down into the net. He lifted him clear of the water, a heavy half circle in the net, the net dripping, unhooked him and slid him into the sack.

He spread the mouth of the sack and looked down in at the two big trout alive in the water.

Through the deepening water, Nick waded over to the hollow log. He took the sack off, over his head, the trout flopping as it came out of water, and hung it so the trout were deep in the water. Then he pulled himself up on the log and sat, the water from his trousers and boots running down into the stream. He laid his rod down, moved along to the shady end of the log and took the sandwiches out of his pocket. He dipped the sandwiches in the cold water. The current carried away the crumbs. He ate the sandwiches and dipped his hat full of water to drink, the water running out through his hat just ahead of his drinking.

It was cool in the shade, sitting on the log. He took a cigarette out and struck a match to light it. The match sunk into the gray wood, making a tiny furrow. Nick leaned over the side of the log, found a hard place and lit the match. He sat smoking and watching the river.

Ahead the river narrowed and went into a swamp. The river became smooth and deep and the swamp looked solid with cedar trees, their trunks close together, their branches solid. It would not be possible to walk through a swamp like that. The branches grew so low. You would have to keep almost level with the ground to move at all. You could not crash through the branches. That must be why the animals that lived in swamps were built the way they were, Nick thought.

He wished he had brought something to read. He felt like reading. He did not feel like going on into the swamp. He looked down the river. A big cedar slanted all the way across the stream. Beyond that the river went into the swamp.

Nick did not want to go in there now. He felt a reaction against deep wading with the water deepening up under his armpits, to hook big trout in places impossible to land them. In the swamp the banks were bare, the big cedars came together overhead, the sun did not come through, except in patches; in the fast deep water, in the half light, the fishing would be tragic. In the swamp fishing was a tragic adventure. Nick did not want it. He did not want to go down the stream any further today.

He took out his knife, opened it and stuck it in the log. Then he pulled up the sack, reached into it and brought out one of the trout. Holding him near the tail, hard to hold, alive, in his hand, he whacked him against the log. The trout quivered, rigid. Nick laid him on the log in the shade and broke the neck of the other fish the same way. He laid them side by side on the log. They were fine trout.

Nick cleaned them, slitting them from the vent to the tip of the jaw. All the insides and the gills and tongue came out in one piece. They were both males; long gray-white strips of milt, smooth and clean. All the insides clean and compact, coming out all together. Nick tossed the offal ashore for the minks to find.

He washed the trout in the stream. When he held them back up in the water they looked like live fish. Their color was not gone yet. He washed his hands and dried them on the log. Then he laid the trout on the sack spread out on the log, rolled them up in it, tied the bundle and put it in the landing net. His knife was still standing, blade stuck in the log. He cleaned it on the wood and put it in his pocket.

Nick stood up on the log, holding his rod, the landing net hanging heavy, then stepped into the water and splashed ashore. He climbed the bank and cut up into the woods, toward the high ground. He was going back to camp. He looked back. The river just showed through the trees. There were plenty of days coming when he could fish the swamp.

1925

PURSUIT AS HAPPINESS[1]

THE ROAD WAS only a track and the plain was very discouraging to see. As we went on we saw a few thin Grant's gazelles showing white against the burnt yellow of the grass and the gray trees. My exhilaration died with the stretching out of this plain, the typical poor game country, and it all began to seem very impossible and romantic and quite untrue. The Wanderobo had a very strong odor and I looked at the way the lobes of his ears were stretched

[1] This episode of the kudu hunt comprises chapter 12 of *The Green Hills of Africa* (1935).

and then neatly wrapped on themselves and at his strange un-negroid, thin-lipped face. When he saw me studying his face he smiled pleasantly and scratched his chest. I looked around at the back of the car. M'Cola was asleep. Garrick was sitting straight up, dramatizing his awakeness, and the old man was tring to see the road.

By now there was no more road, only a cattle track, but we were coming to the edge of the plain. Then the plain was behind us and ahead there were big trees and we were entering a country the loveliest that I had seen in Africa. The grass was green and smooth, short as a meadow that has been mown and is newly grown, and the trees were big, high-trunked, and old with no undergrowth but only the smooth green of the turf like a deer park and we drove on through shade and patches of sunlight following a faint trail the Wanderobo pointed out. I could not believe we had suddenly come to any such wonderful country. It was a country to wake from, happy to have had the dream and, seeing if it would clown away, I reached up and touched the Wanderobo's ear. He jumped and Kamau snickered. M'Cola nudged me from the back seat and pointed and there, standing in an open space between the trees, his head up, staring at us, the bristles on his back erect, long, thick, white tusks upcurving, his eyes showing bright, was a very large wart-hog boar watching us from less than twenty yards. I motioned to Kamau to stop and we sat looking at him and he at us. I put the rifle up and sighted on his chest. He watched and did not move. Then I motioned to Kamau to throw in the clutch and we went on and made a curve to the right and left of the wart-hog, who had never moved, nor showed any fright at seeing us.

I could see that Kamau was excited and, looking back, M'Cola nodded his head up and down in agreement. None of us had ever seen a wart-hog that would not bolt off, fast-trotting, tail in air. This was a virgin country, an un-hunted pocket in the million miles of bloody Africa. I was ready to stop and make camp anywhere.

This was the finest country I had seen but we went on, winding along through the big trees over the softly rolling grass. Then ahead and to the right we saw the high stockade of a Masai village. It was a very large village and out of it came running long-legged, brown, smooth-moving men who all seemed to be of the same age and who wore their hair in a heavy club-like queue that swung against their shoulders as they ran. They came up to the car and surrounded it, all laughing and smiling and talking. They all were tall, their teeth were white and good, and their hair was stained a red brown and arranged in a looped fringe on their foreheads. They carried spears and they were very handsome and extremely jolly, not sullen, nor contemptuous like the northern Masai, and they wanted to know what we were going to do. The Wanderobo evidently said we were hunting kudu and were in a hurry. They had the car surrounded so we could not move. One said something and three or four others joined in and Kamau explained to me that they had seen two kudu bulls go along the trail in the afternoon.

"It can't be true," I said to myself. "It can't be."

I told Kamau to start and slowly we pushed through them, they all laughing and trying to stop the car, making it all but run over them. They were the tallest, best-built, handsomest people I had ever seen and the first truly light-hearted happy people I had seen in Africa. Finally, when we were moving, they started to run beside the car smiling and laughing and showing how easily they could run and then, as the going was better, up the smooth valley of a stream, it became a contest and one after another dropped out of the running, waving and smiling as they left until there were only two still running with us, the finest runners of the lot, who kept pace easily with the car as they moved long-legged, smoothly, loosely, and with pride. They were running too, at the pace of a fast miler, and carrying their spears as well. Then we had to turn to the right and climb out of the putting-green smoothness of the valley into a rolling meadow and, as we slowed, climbing in first gear, the whole pack came up again, laughing and trying not to seem winded. We went through a little knot of brush and a small rabbit started out, zig-zagging wildly and all the Masai behind now in a mad sprint. They caught the rabbit and the tallest runner came up with him to the car and handed him to me. I held him and could feel the thumping of his heart through the soft, warm, furry body, and as I stroked him the Masai patted my arm. Holding him by the ears I handed him back. No, no, he was mine. He was a present. I handed him to M'Cola. 'Cola did not take him seriously and handed him to one of the Masai. We were moving and they were running again now. The Masai stooped and put the rabbit on the ground and as he ran free they all laughed. M'Cola shook his head. We were all very impressed by these Masai.

"Good Masai," M'Cola said, very moved. "Masai many cattle. Masai no kill to eat. Masai kill man."

The Wanderobo patted himself on the chest.

"Wanderobo—Masai," he said, very proudly, claiming kin. His ears were curled in the same way theirs were. Seeing them running and so damned handsome and so happy made us all happy. I had never seen such quick disinterested friendliness, nor such fine looking people.

"Good Masai," M'Cola repeated, nodding his head emphatically. "Good, good Masai." Only Garrick seemed impressed in a different way. For all his khaki clothes and his letter from B'wana Simba, I believe these Masai frightened him in a very old place. They were our friends, not his. They certainly were our friends though. They had that attitude that makes brothers, that unexpressed but instant and complete acceptance that you must be Masai wherever it is you come from. That attitude you only get from the best of the English, the best of the Hungarians and the very best Spaniards; the thing that used to be the most clear distinction of nobility when there was nobility. It is an ignorant attitude and the people who have it do not survive, but very few pleasanter things ever happen to you than the encountering of it.

So now there were only the two of them left again, running, and it was hard going and the machine was beating them. They were still running well and still loose and long but the machine was a cruel pacemaker. So I told Kamau to speed it up and get it over with because a sudden burst of speed was not the humiliation of a steady using. They sprinted, were beaten, laughed, and then we were leaning out, waving, and they stood leaning on their spears and waved. We were still great friends but now we were alone again and there was no track, only the general direction to follow around clumps of trees and along the run of this green valley.

After a little the trees grew closer and we left the idyllic country behind and now were picking our way along a faint trail through thick second-growth. Sometimes we came to a dead halt and had to get out and pull a log out of the way or cut a tree that blocked the body of the car. Sometimes we had to back out of bush and look for a way to circle around and come upon the trail again, chopping our way through with the long brush knives that are called pangas. The Wanderobo was a pitiful chopper and Garrick was little better. M'Cola did everything well in which a knife was used and he swung a panga with a fast yet heavy and vindictive stroke. I used it badly. There was too much wrist in it to learn it quickly; your wrist tired and the blade seemed to have a weight it did not have. I wished that I had a Michigan double-bitted ax, honed razor-sharp, to chop with instead of this sabering of trees.

Chopping through when we were stopped, avoiding all we could, Kamau driving with intelligence and a sound feeling for the country, we came through the difficult going and out into another open-meadow stretch and could see a range of hills off to our right. But here there had been a recent heavy rain and we had to be very careful about the low parts of the meadow where the tires cut in through the turf to mud and spun in the slick greasiness. We cut brush and shovelled out twice and then, having learned not to trust any low part, we skirted the high edge of the meadow and then were in timber again. As we came out, after several long circles in the woods to find places where we could get the car through, we were on the bank of a stream, where there was a sort of brushy bridging across the bed built like a beaver dam and evidently designed to hold back the water. On the other side was a thorn-bush-fenced cornfield, a steep, stump-scattered bank with corn planted all over it, and some abandoned looking corrals or thorn-bush-fenced enclosures with mud and stick buildings and to the right there were cone-shaped grass huts projecting above a heavy thorn fence. We all got out, for this stream was a problem and, on the other side, the only place we could get up the bank led through the stump-filled maize field.

The old man said the rain had come that day. There had been no water going over the brushy dam when they had passed that morning. I was feeling fairly depressed. Here we had come through a beautiful country of virgin timber where kudu had been seen walking along the trail to end up stuck on the bank of a little creek in some one's cornfield. I had not expected any cornfield and I resented it. I thought we would have to get permission to drive through the maize, provided we could make it across the stream and up the bank and I took off my shoes and waded across the stream to test it underfoot. The brush and saplings on the bottom were packed hard and firm and I was sure we could cross if we took it fairly fast. M'Cola and Kamau agreed and we walked up the bank to see how it would be. The mud of the bank was soft but there was dry earth underneath and I figured we could shovel our way up if we could get through the stumps. But we would need to unload before we tried it.

Coming toward us, from the direction of the huts, were two men and a boy. I said "Jambo," as they came up. They answered, "Jambo," and then the old man and the Wanderobo talked with them. M'Cola shook his head at me. He did not understand a word. I thought we were asking permission to go through the corn. When the old man finished talking the two men came close and we shook hands.

They looked like no negroes I had ever seen. Their faces were a gray brown, the oldest looked to be about fifty, had thin lips, an almost Grecian nose, rather high cheekbones, and large, intelligent eyes. He had great poise and dignity and seemed to be very intelligent. The younger man had the same cast of features and I took him for a younger brother. He looked about thirty-five. The boy was as pretty as a girl and looked rather shy and stupid. I had thought he was a girl from his face for an instant when he first came up, as they all wore a sort of Roman toga of unbleached muslin gathered at the shoulder that revealed no line of their bodies.

They were talking with the old man, who, now that I looked at him standing with them, seemed to bear a sort of wrinkled and degenerate resemblance to the classic-featured owner of the shamba; just as the Wanderobo-Masai was a shrivelled caricature of the handsome Masai we had met in the forest.

Then we all went down to the stream and Kamau and I rigged ropes around the tires to act as chains while the Roman elder and the rest unloaded the car and carried the heaviest things up the steep bank. Then we crossed in a wild, water-throwing smash and, all pushing heavily, made it halfway up the bank before we stuck. We chopped and dug out and finally made it to the top of the bank but ahead was that maize field and I could not figure where we were to go from there.

"Where do we go?" I asked the Roman elder.

They did not understand Garrick's interpreting and the old man made the question clear.

The Roman pointed toward the heavy thorn-bush fence to the left at the edge of the woods.

"We can't get through there in the car."

"Campi," said M'Cola, meaning we were going to camp there.

"Hell of a place," I said.

"Campi," M'Cola said firmly and they all nodded.

"Campi! Campi!" said the old man.

"There we camp," Garrick announced pompously.

"You go to hell," I told him cheerfully.

I walked toward the camp site with the Roman who was talking steadily in a language I could not understand a word of. M'Cola was with me and the others were loading and following with the car. I was remembering that I had read you must never camp in abandoned native quarters because of ticks and other hazards and I was preparing to hold out against this camp. We entered a break in the thorn-bush fence and inside was a building of logs and saplings stuck in the ground and crossed with branches. It looked like a big chicken coop. The Roman made us free of this and of the enclosure with a wave of his hand and kept on talking.

"Bugs," I said to M'Cola in Swahili, speaking with strong disapproval.

"No," he said, dismissing the idea. "No bugs."

"Bad bugs. Many bugs. Sickness."

"No bugs," he said firmly.

The no-bugs had it and with the Roman talking steadily, I hoped on some congenial topic, the car came up, stopped under a huge tree about fifty yards from the thorn-bush fence and they all commenced carrying the necessities in for the making of camp. My ground-sheet tent was slung between a tree and one side of the chicken coop and I sat down on a petrol case to discuss the shooting situation with the Roman, the old man, and Garrick while Kamau and M'Cola fixed up a camp and the Wanderobo-Masai stood on one leg and let his mouth hang open.

"Where were kudu?"

"Back there," waving his arm.

"Big ones?"

Arms spread to show hugeness of horns and a torrent from the Roman.

Me, dictionary-ing heavily, "Where was the one they were watching?"

No results on this but a long speech from the Roman which I took to mean they were watching them all.

It was late afternoon now and the sky was heavy with clouds. I was wet to the waist and my socks were mud soaked. Also I was sweating from pushing on the car and from chopping.

"When do we start?" I asked.

"Tomorrow," Garrick answered without bothering to question the Roman.

"No," I said. "Tonight."

"Tomorrow," Garrick said. "Late now. One hour light." He showed me one hour on my watch.

I dictionaried. "Hunt tonight. Last hour best hour."

Garrick implied that the kudu were too far away. That it was impossible to hunt and return, all this with gestures, "Hunt tomorrow."

"You bastard," I said in English. All this time the Roman and the old man had been standing saying nothing. I shivered. It was cold with the sun under the clouds in spite of the heaviness of the air after rain.

"Old man," I said.

"Yes, Master," said the old man. Dictionary-ing carefully, I said, "Hunt kudu tonight. Last hour best hour. Kudu close?"

"Maybe."

"Hunt now?"

They talked together.

"Hunt tomorrow," Garrick put in.

"Shut up, you actor," I said. "Old man. Little hunt now?"

"Yes," said old man and Roman nodded. "Little while."

"Good," I said and went to find a shirt and undershirt and a pair of socks.

"Hunt now," I told M'Cola.

"Good," he said. "M'uzuri."

With the clean feeling of dry shirt, fresh socks and a change of boots

I sat on the petrol case and drank a whiskey and water while I waited for the
Roman to come back. I felt certain I was going to have a shot at kudu and I
wanted to take the edge off so I would not be nervous. Also I wanted not
to catch a cold. Also I wanted the whiskey for itself, because I loved the
taste of it and because, being as happy as I could be, it made me feel even
better.

I saw the Roman coming and I pulled the zippers up on my boots,
checked the cartridges in the magazine of the Springfield, took off the foresight protector and blew through the rear aperture. Then I drank what was
left in the tin cup that was on the ground by the box and stood up, checking
that I had a pair of handkerchiefs in my shirt pockets.

M'Cola came carrying his knife and Pop's big glasses.

"You stay here," I said to Garrick. He did not mind. He thought we
were silly to go out so late and he was glad to prove us wrong. The Wanderobo
wanted to go.

"That's plenty," I said and waved the old man back and we started out
of the corral with the Roman ahead, carrying a spear, then me, then
M'Cola with glasses and the Mannlicher, full of solids, and last the Wanderobo-Masai with another spear.

It was after five when we struck off across the maize field and down to
the stream, crossing where it narrowed in high grass a hundred yards above
the dam and then, walking slowly and carefully, went up the grassy bank on
the far side getting soaked to the waist as we stooped going through the wet
grass and bracken. We had not been gone ten minutes and were moving
carefully up the stream bank, when, without warning, the Roman grabbed
my arm and pulled me bodily down to the ground as he crouched; me pulling back the bolt to cock the rifle as I dropped. Holding his breath he
pointed and across the stream on the far bank at the edge of the trees was a
large, gray animal, white stripes showing on his flanks and huge horns curling back from his head as he stood, broadside to us, head up, seeming to be
listening. I raised the rifle but there was a bush in the way of the shot. I
could not shoot over the bush without standing.

"Piga," whispered M'Cola. I shook my finger and commenced to crawl
forward to be clear of the bush, sick afraid the bull would jump while I
was trying to make the shot certain, but remembering Pop's "Take your
time." When I saw I was clear I got on one knee, saw the bull through the
aperture, marvelling at how big he looked and then, remembering not to
have it matter, that it was the same as any other shot, I saw the bead centered exactly where it should be just below the top of the shoulder and
squeezed off. At the roar he jumped and was going into the brush, but I
knew I had hit him. I shot at a show of gray between the trees as he went in
and M'Cola was shouting, "Piga! Piga!" meaning, "He's hit! He's hit!" and
the Roman was slapping me on the shoulder, then he had his toga up around
his neck and was running naked, and the four of us were running now, full
speed, like hounds, splashing across the stream, tearing up the bank, the Roman ahead, crashing naked through the brush, then stooping and holding up
a leaf with bright blood, slamming me on the back, M'Cola saying, "Damu!
Damu!" blood, blood, then the deep cut tracks off to the right, me re-

loading, we all trailing in a dead run, it almost dark in the timber, the Roman, confused a moment by the trail, making a cast off to the right, then picking up blood once more, then pulling me down again with a jerk on my arm and none of us breathing as we saw him standing in a clearing a hundred yards ahead, looking to me hard-hit and looking back, wide ears spread, big, gray, white-striped, his horns a marvel, as he looked straight toward us over his shoulder. I thought I must make absolutely sure this time, now, with the dark coming and I held my breath and shot him a touch behind the foreshoulder. We heard the bullet smack and saw him buck heavily with the shot. M'Cola shouted, "Piga! Piga! Piga!" as he went out of sight and as we ran again, like hounds, we almost fell over something. It was a huge, beautiful kudu bull, stone-dead, on his side, his horns in great dark spirals, wide-spread and unbelievable as he lay dead five yards from where we stood when I had just that instant shot. I looked at him, big, long-legged, a smooth gray with the white stripes and the great, curling, sweeping horns, brown as walnut meats, and ivory pointed, at the big ears and the great, lovely heavy-maned neck the white chevron between his eyes and the white of his muzzle and I stooped over and touched him to try to believe it. He was lying on the side where the bullet had gone in and there was not a mark on him and he smelled sweet and lovely like the breath of cattle and the odor of thyme after rain.

Then the Roman had his arms around my neck and M'Cola was shouting in a strange high sing-song voice and Wanderobo-Masai kept slapping me on the shoulder and jumping up and down and then one after the other they all shook hands in a strange way that I had never known in which they took your thumb in their fist and held it and shook it and pulled it and held it again, while they looked you in the eyes, fiercely.

We all looked at him and M'Cola knelt and traced the curve of his horns with his finger and measured the spread with his arms and kept crooning, "Oo-oo-eee-eee," making small high noises of ecstasy and stroking the kudu's muzzle and his mane.

I slapped the Roman on the back and we went through the thumb pulling again; me pulling his thumb too. I embraced the Wanderobo-Masai and he, after a thumb-pulling of great intensity and feeling, slapped his chest and said very proudly, "Wanderobo-Masai wonderful guide."

"Wanderobo-Masai wonderful Masai," I said.

M'Cola kept shaking his head, looking at the kudu and making the strange small noises. Then he said, "Doumi, Doumi, Doumi! B'wana Kabor Kidogo, Kidogo." Meaning this was a bull of bulls. That Karl's had been a little one, a nothing.

We all knew we had killed the other kudu that I had mistaken for this one, while this first one was lying dead from the first shot, and it seemed of no importance beside the miracle of this kudu. But I wanted to see the other.

"Come on, kudu," I said.

"He's dead," said M'Cola, "Kufa!"

"Come on."

"This one best."

"Come on."

"Measure," M'Cola pleaded. I ran the steel tape around the curve of one horn, M'Cola holding it down. It was well over fifty inches. M'Cola looked at me anxiously.

"Big! Big!" I said. "Twice as big as B'wana Kabor."

"Eee-eee," he crooned.

"Come on," I said. The Roman was off already.

We cut for where we saw the bull when I shot and there were the tracks with blood breast high on the leaves in the brush from the start. In a hundred yards we came on him absolutely dead. He was not quite as big as the first bull. The horns were as long, but narrower, but he was as beautiful, and he lay on his side, bending down the brush where he fell.

We all shook hands again, using the thumb which evidently denoted extreme emotion.

"This askari," M'Cola explained. This bull was the policeman or bodyguard for the bigger one. He had evidently been in the timber when we had seen the first bull, had run with him, and had looked back to see why the big bull did not follow.

I wanted pictures and told M'Cola to go back to camp with the Roman and bring the two cameras, the Graflex and the cinema camera and my flashlight. I knew we were on the same side of the stream and above the camp and I hoped the Roman could make a short cut and get back before the sun set.

They went off and now, at the end of the day, the sun came out brightly below the clouds and the Wanderobo-Masai and I looked at this kudu, measured his horns, smelled the fine smell of him, sweeter than an eland, even, stroked his nose, his neck, and his shoulder, marvelling at the great ears, and the smoothness and cleanness of his hide, looked at his hooves, that were built long, narrow, and springy so he seemed to walk on tip-toe, felt under his shoulder for the bullet-hole and then shook hands again while the Wanderobo-Masai told what a man he was and I told him he was my pal and gave him my best four-bladed pocket knife.

"Let's go look at the first one, Wanderobo-Masai," I said in English.

The Wanderobo-Masai nodded, understanding perfectly, and we trailed back to where the big one lay in the edge of the little clearing. We circled him, looking at him and then the Wanderobo-Masai, reaching underneath while I held the shoulder up, found the bullet-hole and put his finger in. Then he touched his forehead with the bloody finger and made the speech about "Wanderobo-Masai wonderful guide!"

"Wanderobo-Masai king of guides," I said. "Wanderobo-Masai my pal."

I was wet through with sweat and I put on my raincoat that M'Cola had been carrying and left behind and turned the collar up around my neck. I was watching the sun now and worrying about it being gone before they got up with the cameras. In a little while we could hear them coming in the brush and I shouted to let them know where we were. M'Cola answered and we shouted back and forth and I could hear them talking and crashing in the brush while I would shout and watch the sun which was almost down. Finally I saw them and I shouted to M'Cola, "Run, run," and pointed to the sun, but there was no run left in them. They had made a fast trip uphill, through heavy brush, and when I got the camera, opened the lens wide and focused on the bull the sun was only lighting the tops of the trees. I took a half a dozen exposures and used the cinema while they all dragged the kudu to where there seemed to be a little more light, then the sun was down and, obligation to try to get a picture over, I put the camera into its case and settled, happily, with the darkness into the unresponsibility of victory; only emerging to direct M'Cola in where to cut to make a full enough cape when skinning out the head-skin. M'Cola used a knife beautifully and I liked to watch him skin-out, but tonight, after I had shown him where to make the first cut, well down on the legs, around the lower chest where it joined the belly and well back over the withers I did not watch him because I wanted to remember the bull as I had first seen him, so I went, in the dusk, to the second kudu and waited there until they came, with the flashlight and then, remembering that I had skinned-out or seen skinned-out every animal that I had ever shot, yet remembered every one exactly as he was at every moment, that one memory does not destroy another, and that the not-watching idea was only laziness and a form of putting the dishes in the sink until morning, I held the flashlight for M'Cola while he worked on the second bull and, although tired, enjoyed as always his fast, clean, delicate scalpel-ing with the knife, until, the cape all clear and spread back he nocked through the connection of the skull and the spine and then, twisting with the horns, swung the head loose and lifted it, cape and all, free from the neck, the cape hanging heavy and wet in the light of the electric torch that shone on his red hands and on the dirty khaki of his tunic. We left the Wanderobo-Masai, Garrick, the Roman, and his brother with a lantern to skin out and pack in the meat and M'Cola with a head, the old man with a head, and me with the flashlight and the two guns, we started in the dark back for camp.

In the dark the old man fell flat and M'Cola laughed; then the cape un-rolled and came down over his face and he almost choked and we both laughed. The old man laughed too. Then M'Cola fell in the dark and the old man and I laughed. A little farther on I went through the covering on some sort of game pit and went flat on my face and got up to hear M'Cola chuckling and choking and the old man giggling.

"What the hell is this? A Chaplin comedy?" I asked them in English. They were both laughing under the heads. We got to the thorn-bush fence, finally, after a nightmare march through the brush and saw the fire at the camp and M'Cola seemed to be delighted when the old man fell going through the thorns and got up cursing and seeming barely able to lift the head as I shone the flash ahead of him to show him the opening.

We came up to the fire and I could see the old man's face bleeding as he put the head down against the stick and mud cabin. M'Cola put his head down, pointed at the old man's face and laughed and shook his head. I looked at the old man. He was completely done-in, his face was badly scratched, covered with mud and bleeding, and he was chuckling happily.

"B'wana fell down," M'Cola said and imitated me pitching forward. They both chuckled.

I made as though to take a swing at him and said, "Shenzi!"

He imitated me falling down again and then there was Kamau shaking hands very gently and respectfully and saying, "Good, B'wana! Very good, B'wana!" and then going over to the heads, his eyes shining and kneeling, stroking the horns and feeling the ears and crooning the same, sighing, "Ooo-ooo! Eee-eee!" noises M'Cola had made.

I went into the dark of the tent, we had left the lantern with the meat bringers, and washed, took off my wet clothes and feeling in the dark in my ruck-sack found a pair of pyjamas and a bath-robe. I came out to the fire wearing these and mosquito boots. I brought my wet things and my boots to the fire and Kamau spread them on sticks and put the boots, each one, leg-down, on a stick and back far enough from the blaze where the fire would not scorch them.

In the firelight I sat on a petrol box with my back against a tree and Kamau brought the whiskey flask and poured some in a cup and I added water from the canteen and sat drinking and looking in the fire, not thinking, in complete happiness, feeling the whiskey warm me and smooth me as you straighten the wrinkled sheet in a bed, while Kamau brought tins from the provisions to see what I would eat for supper. There were three tins of Christmas special mince-meat, three tins of salmon, and three of mixed fruit, there were also a number of cakes of chocolate and a tin of Special Christmas Plum Pudding. I sent these back wondering what Kati had imagined the mince-meat to be. We had been looking for that plum pudding for two months.

"Meat?" I asked.

Kamau brought a thick, long chunk of roast Grant gazelle tenderloin from one of the Grant Pop had shot on the plain while we had been hunting the twenty-five-mile salt lick, and some bread.

"Beer?"

He brought one of the big German liter bottles and opened it.

It seemed too complicated sitting on the petrol case and I spread my raincoat on the ground in front of the fire where the ground had been dried by the heat and stretched my legs out, leaning my back against the wooden case. The old man was roasting meat on a stick. It was a choice piece he had brought with him wrapped in his toga. In a little while they all began to come in carrying meat and the hides and then I was stretched out drinking beer and watching the fire and all around they were talking and roasting meat on sticks. It was getting cold and the night was clear and there was the smell of the roasting meat, the smell of the smoke of the fire, the smell of my boots steaming, and, where he squatted close, the smell of the good old Wanderobo-Masai. But I could remember the odor of the kudu as he lay in the woods.

Each man had his own meat or collection of pieces of meat on sticks stuck around the fire, they turned them and tended them, and there was much talking. Two others that I had not seen had come over from the huts and the boy we had seen in the afternoon was with them. I was eating a piece of hot broiled liver I had lifted from one of the sticks of the Wanderobo-Masai and wondering where the kidneys were. The liver was delicious. I was wondering whether it was worth while getting up to get the dictionary to ask about the kidneys when M'Cola said, "Beer?"

"All right."

He brought the bottle, opened it, and I lifted it and drank half of it off to chase down that liver.

"It's a hell of a life," I told him in English.

He grinned and said, "More beer?" in Swahili.

My talking English to him was an acceptable joke.

"Watch," I said, and tipped the bottle up and let it all go down. It was an old trick we learned in Spain drinking out of wine skins without swallowing. This impressed the Roman greatly. He came over, squatted down by the raincoat and started to talk. He talked for a long time.

"Absolutely," I told him in English. "And furthermore he can take the sleigh."

"More beer?" M'Cola asked.

"You want to see the old man tight I suppose?"

"N'Dio," he said, "Yes," pretending to understand the English.

"Watch it, Roman," I started to let the beer go down, saw the Roman following the motion with his own throat, started to choke, barely recovered and lowered the bottle.

"That's all. Can't do it more than twice in an evening. Makes you liverish."

The Roman went on talking in his language. I heard him say Simba twice.

"Simba here?"

"No," he said. "Over there," waving at the dark, and I could not make out the story. But it sounded very good.

"Me plenty Simba," I said. "Hell of a man with Simba. Ask M'Cola." I could feel that I was getting the evening braggies but Pop and P.O.M.[2] weren't here to listen. It was not nearly so satisfactory to brag when you could not be understood, still it was better than nothing. I definitely had the braggies, on beer, too.

"Amazing," I told the Roman. He went on with his own story. There was a little beer in the bottom of the bottle.

"Old Man," I said. "Mzee."

"Yes, B'wana," said the old man.

"Here's some beer for you. You're old enough so it can't hurt you."

I had seen the old man's eyes while he watched me drink and I knew he was another of the same. He took the bottle, drained it to the last bit of froth and crouched by his meat sticks holding the bottle lovingly.

"More beer?" asked M'Cola.

"Yes," I said. "And my cartridges."

The Roman had gone on steadily talking. He could tell a longer story even than Carlos in Cuba.

"That's mighty interesting," I told him. "You're a hell of a fellow, too. We're both good. Listen." M'Cola had brought the beer and my khaki coat with the cartridges in the pocket. I drank a little beer, noted the old man watching and spread out six cartridges. "I've got the braggies," I said. "You have to stand for this, look!" I touched each of the cartridges in turn, "Simba, Simba, Faro, Nyati, Tendalla, Tendalla. What do you think of that?

2 The professional white hunter (head of the whole expedition) and the narrator's wife.

You don't have to believe it. Look, M'Cola!" and I named the six cartridges again. "Lion, lion, rhino, buffalo, kudu, kudu."

"Ayee!" said the Roman excitedly.

"N'Dio," said M'Cola solemnly. "Yes, it is true."

"Ayee!" said the Roman and grabbed me by the thumb.

"God's truth," I said. "Highly improbable, isn't it?"

"N'Dio," said M'Cola, counting them over himself. "Simba, Simba, Faro, Nyati, Tendalla, Tendalla!"

"You can tell the others," I said in English. "That's a hell of a big piece of bragging. That'll hold me for tonight."

The Roman went on talking to me again and I listened carefully and ate another piece of the broiled liver. M'Cola was working on the heads now, skinning out one skull and showing Kamau how to skin out the easy part of the other. It was a big job to do for the two of them, working carefully around the eyes and the muzzle and the cartilage of the ears, and afterwards flesh all of the head skins so they would not spoil, and they were working at it very delicately and carefully in the firelight. I do not remember going to bed, nor if we went to bed.

I remember getting the dictionary and asking M'Cola to ask the boy if he had a sister and M'Cola saying, "No. No," to me very firmly and solemnly.

"Nothing tendacious, you understand. Curiosity."

M'Cola was firm. "No," he said and shook his head. "Hapana," in the same tone he used when we followed the lion into the sanseviera that time.

That disposed of the opportunities for social life and I looked up kidneys and the Roman's brother produced some from his lot and I put a piece between two pieces of liver on a stick and started it broiling.

"Make an admirable breakfast," I said out loud. "Much better than mince-meat."

Then we had a long talk about sable. The Roman did not call them Tarahalla and that name meant nothing to him. There was some confusion about buffalo because the Roman kept saying, "nyati," but he meant they were black like the buff. Then we drew pictures in the dust of ashes from the fire and what he meant were sable all right. The horns curved back like scimitars, way back over their withers.

"Bulls?" I said.

"Bulls and cows."

With the old man and Garrick interpreting, I believed I made out that there were two herds.

"Tomorrow."

"Yes," the Roman said. "Tomorrow."

" 'Cola," I said. "Today, kudu. Tomorrow, sable, buffalo, Simba."

"Hapana, buffalo!" he said and shook his head. "Hapana, Simba!"

"Me and the Wanderobo-Masai buffalo," I said.

"Yes," said the Wanderobo-Masai excitedly. "Yes."

"There are very big elephants near here," Garrick said.

"Tomorrow elephants," I said, teasing M'Cola.

"Hapana elephants!" he knew it was teasing but he did not even want to hear it said.

"Elephants," I said. "Buffalo, Simba, leopard."

The Wanderobo-Masai was nodding excitedly. "Rhino," he put in.

"Hapana!" M'Cola said shaking his head. He was beginning to suffer.

"In those hills many buffalo," the old man interpreted for the now very excited Roman who was standing and pointing beyond where the huts were.

"Hapana! Hapana! Hapana!" M'Cola said definitely and finally. "More beer?" putting down his knife.

"All right," I said. "I'm just kidding you."

M'Cola was crouched close talking, making an explanation. I heard Pop's title and I thought it was that Pop would not like it. That Pop would not want it.

"I was just kidding you," I said in English. Then in Swahili, "Tomorrow sable?"

"Yes," he said feelingly. "Yes."

After that the Roman and I had a long talk in which I spoke Spanish and he spoke whatever it was he spoke and I believe we planned the entire campaign for the next day.

1935

Reading Suggestions

The best introduction to Hemingway is *In Our Time* (1925), which provides the context for "Big Two-Hearted River" and fills out the biography of Nick Adams, prototype of his later heroes. Readers will then want to go on to the major novels, *The Sun Also Rises* (1926) and *A Farewell to Arms* (1929). There are a number of fine short stories, including "The Short Happy Life of Francis Macomber," "The Snows of Kilimanjaro," "The Undefeated," and "The Killers." Of his later long fictions *The Old Man and the Sea* (1952) is the most rewarding. There is no collected edition of his works as yet, but all the above are available in either inexpensive reprints or trade editions.

Biographical material is still rather spotty for Hemingway except for the early years, which are well presented in Charles Fenton's *The Apprenticeship of Ernest Hemingway* (1954), reprinted as a Mentor paperback in 1961. Memoirs by the novelist's brother and sister have appeared, but students will have to wait for the official biography being prepared by Carlos Baker for a dependable account of his whole career. Of several books interpreting his works the most discriminating is Philip Young's *Ernest Hemingway* (1952) and the fullest is Carlos Baker's *Hemingway: The Writer as Artist* (1952, 1963).

Some of the most penetrating criticism of Hemingway has appeared in scattered articles, the best of which have now found their way into various collections where they are more readily available. R. P. Warren's "Hemingway [A Farewell to Arms]" is reprinted in *Critiques and Essays on Modern Fiction* (1952) and R. B. West's "Ernest Hemingway: The Failure of Sensibility" in *Forms of Modern Fiction* (1948). The first collection devoted exclusively to Hemingway—*Ernest Hemingway: The Man and His Work* (1950) edited by John McCaffery—contains among other important essays Edmund Wilson's "Hemingway: Gauge of Morale" and J. P. Bishop's "The Missing All." There are three later collections, all available in paperbacks, which are listed following with their most helpful articles indicated. *Hemingway and His Critics: An*

International Anthology (1961) edited by Carlos Baker—containing Lionel Trilling's "Hemingway and His Critics" and Mark Spilka's "The Death of Love in *The Sun Also Rises.*" (This volume concludes with a check list of several hundred other articles and essays from books.) *Hemingway: A Collection of Critical Essays,* edited by Robert P. Weeks (Spectrum paperback)—containing Malcolm Cowley's "Nightmare and Ritual in Hemingway" and E. M. Halliday's "Hemingway's Ambiguity: Symbolism and Irony." *Ernest Hemingway: Critiques of Four Major Novels,* edited by Carlos Baker (Scribner paperback) —containing Charles Anderson's "Hemingway's Other Style" and Clinton Burhans, Jr., "*The Old Man and the Sea:* Hemingway's Tragic Vision of Man." If these critics seem to give Hemingway too much praise, the student can find a counterbalance in the savage but witty essay by Dwight MacDonald in *Encounter* (January 1962).

Biography

Of his early life in the Middle West, the summer vacations hunting and fishing in the woods of northern Michigan made the deepest impression on Hemingway, to judge from his fictions. But his basic attitudes were equally formed by Oak Park, a small town near Chicago, where he was born in July 1899 and lived until he was eighteen. His mother was a woman of religious piety with some artistic bent. His father, a prominent doctor, was an ardent sportsman but a man of somewhat Spartan disposition. Their influences are clear and important: the son became an author and a convert to Catholicism about the same time, in the mid-twenties; he was equally famous for his code of stern discipline and his devotion to sports. Dr. Hemingway took his own life in 1928, his son in 1961. The pressures of this respectable but limited little world may have contributed to Hemingway's running away from home several times. But his years in the public schools of Oak Park seem to have been normal enough. He took part in athletics and other activities, in addition to his studies, and contributed stories to the high school publications. On graduation, too young to enlist in the army, he went to Kansas City to get a job in the fall of 1917.

Hemingway's newspaper work on the *Star,* though it lasted only half a year, was an important part of his training as a writer. There were talented young men on its staff, being put through their paces under a strict editor. The opening paragraph of his style sheet sounds like a formula for the prose of his most famous cub just a few years later: "Use short sentences. Use short first paragraphs. Use vigorous English. Be positive, not negative." And Rule 21: "Avoid the use of adjectives, especially extravagant ones." The discipline was all aimed at writing that would have immediacy, precision, and authenticity. As a reporter young Hemingway put this to work in covering his chosen assignments, those dealing with violence. Besides, many of his fellow journalists were writing novels on the side, and before leaving he himself had produced several short stories of merit.

In May 1918 Hemingway was on his way to join the Italian army as a volunteer in the Red Cross ambulance corps. Within a month he was in the midst of active fighting on the Austrian front, and less than a week later he was wounded, in July, just before his nineteenth birthday. After three months recovering in a hospital at Milan, he had a few more weeks at the front before the Armistice was signed. This was the whole of his battle experience—later to fill a novel and several short stories. But his enthusiasm to take part in a war he had considered a crusade for democracy, his heroism in combat, and the shock of his serious wounding made up for the brevity. During convalescence he could evaluate the immense psychological implications all this had for him.

Coming back from Europe in 1919 Hemingway immediately returned to his career as a writer, first in the Michigan woods and then on the Toronto *Daily Star*. With this and the *Star Weekly* he was associated for the next four years. In this second phase of apprenticeship, his journalistic experience was supplementary to that in Kansas City. For the editor of the *Weekly* was a more literary man than his previous mentors, and he helped Hemingway chiefly by giving him a free hand in writing feature material that increased his skills and his confidence as a writer. His plan being to use newspaper work only for learning and for making a living while he did his serious writing on the side, Hemingway left Canada for Chicago after a year, continuing his feature articles by mail. In the latter city he became part of a circle that included Sherwood Anderson, the first real literary influence on his work. Hemingway's interest was now turning strongly to fiction. Convinced he could support himself with part-time journalism, he took a job as roving correspondent for the *Star* and went to Europe at the end of 1921 to remain for nearly two years.

His assignment allowed him great freedom of movement and choice of materials. As a result he broadened his outlook by wide travel on the continent, and experimented in as many kinds of writing as are open to a free-lance journalist. All of this was fruitful for his creative writing too, the end toward which he was working. In Paris he met the whole group of expatriate authors, including Joyce, Pound, and Stein. It was chiefly under the tutelage of Miss Stein that he hammered his style into final form. By the time he returned to America he had launched himself with two small publications: *Three Stories and Ten Poems* (1923) and *in our time* (1924), both privately printed in Paris. The first showed a matured talent in the short story; the second, a group of vignettes sharply etching the chaos and violence in postwar Europe, showed how he could turn his newspaper reporting to literary ends.

By 1924 Hemingway was ready to break with journalism for creative authorship. The shift was made with rapid and brilliant success, five books in the next five years. The two talents were combined in the American version of *In Our Time* (1925), which set against the earlier vignettes a series of stories centered on Nick Adams. This was the prototype of the "Hemingway hero," other segments of whose biography formed the staple of the two following novels, *The Sun Also Rises* (1926) and *A Farewell to Arms* (1929). Similar characters and situations were exploited in his first collection of short stories, *Men without Women* (1927). (In between came a parody of Sherwood Anderson, *The Torrents of Spring*, exorcising the one literary influence that had hampered his originality.) These fictions, closely paralleling the author's own experiences, exactly matched the temper of the age and at the same time won wide critical acclaim. By the age of thirty Hemingway was made as an author.

The remaining thirty-two years of his career are a matter of public record. They added little to his permanent achievement except in the short story. For a decade he lived mostly in Key West, Florida. Toward the end of the Thirties, new outcroppings of violence took him back to Europe as foreign correspondent, first covering the Civil War in Spain, then World War II. The last decade of his life was spent in Cuba. The books written during these years were not impressive. Of special interest are the two volumes that attempt to bridge the gap between reporting and literature, *Death in the Afternoon* (1932) and *The*

Green Hills of Africa (1935), dealing with bullfighting and big-game hunts. His most ambitious novel was *For Whom the Bell Tolls* (1940); his most original, a novelette, *The Old Man and the Sea* (1952). There was the award of a Nobel Prize, much publicity to build up the Hemingway legend, and much talk about literary plans—but little actual production. Meantime, there were numerous trips to Europe, safaris to Africa, hunting in the American West. On July 2, 1961, the world was startled to hear of his death by a self-inflicted gunshot wound in his Idaho home. The first of his posthumous volumes has been issued under the title of *A Moveable Feast* (1964), concerned with his early writing career in Paris during the 1920's.

Great romantic genius with all
& the vitality, the exuberance, the
undisciplined ardor which the name
implies

A novelists with social themes

THOMAS WOLFE ✦

1900-1938

Reputation rest upon 4 powerful books:

1. Look Homeward, Angel (1929)
2. OR Time and the River (1935
   (both tell the story & Eugene Gant)
3. The Web and the Rock (1939)
4. You Can't Go Home Again, (1940)
   (Tell story & George Webber)

Both Gant and Webber are the author
himself.

No. 3 and 4 show growing maturity
& thought and style but less &
poetic fire, the romantic abandon.

Wolfe is closest to Coleridge
whom he often quotes, and with
Whitman whom he obviously emulated.

Wolfe re-stated the Am. dream:
"the right of every man to live,
to work, to be himself, to
become whatever thing his manhood and his vision can
combine to make him."

He is like Whitman in that he attempts to absorb America into himself and to express America subjectively and emotionally through his own life-experience. He possessed enormous capacities for feeling and passionate living.

Introduction

"I know this," young Thomas Wolfe wrote to his mother from the Harvard Graduate School in 1922; "I am inevitable." He was twenty-two years old, he had just seen his play "Welcome to Our City" produced by Professor George Pierce Baker's 47 Workshop, and his hopes were set on the writing of plays, not of novels. But he had already made up his mind that he was different from the sophisticates of Cambridge, and that he had to write out of what he was, what he knew, and what he felt. The same letter which announced his inevitability listed some of the deeply-felt people and places and events that he thought had made him an artist; significantly, they were the things that six years later he would recreate in his first novel, *Look Homeward, Angel* (1929). Except in their intensity, they were like the memorabilia of any childhood, but in Wolfe's imagination they lived with the vividness of hallucination and the portentousness of myth. "The things that really mattered sank in and left their mark," he wrote his mother, and now "I will go everywhere and see everything. I will meet all the people I can. I will think all the thoughts, feel all the emotions . . . and I will write, write, write."

Seldom has a writer addressed himself to his work with such dedication. And the memories of his family and his childhood, plus his compulsive effort to "go everywhere and see everybody," would be his total subject matter. He would write one story all his life—his own—but he must already have begun to conceive of himself as an instrument for the bringing into existence, through literature, of an American sensibility, awareness, identity, thus far unrevealed. He accepted for himself, in American terms, Stephen Dedalus' commitment to forge in the smithy of his soul the uncreated conscience of his race; and though he tried on various mythic roles during his life—Telemachus, Faust, Orestes—it was as Jason that he most figured, sailing a long voyage in search of the Golden Fleece of an unmistakably American expression. Any American writer, he said in *The Story of*

1071

a Novel (1936), "must make a new tradition for himself, derived from his own life and from the enormous space and energy of American life . . . . The labor of a complete and whole articulation, the discovery of an entire universe and a complete language, is the task that lies before him." And the only tool available for that task is the artist himself, his own sensibility and his own experience. The search that ranges outward must at the same time go inward and downward.

Throughout his career Wolfe struggled with his task like a squirrel with a coconut, constantly defeated, constantly renewing the attack. He strained language, strained fictional forms, strained the capacities of memory and observation, strained his own energies to the point of exhaustion and near-madness. He "made the best failure" of any twentieth-century American, William Faulkner said of him. "My admiration for Wolfe is that he tried his best to get it all said; he was willing to throw away style, coherence, all the rules of preciseness, to try to put all the experience of the human heart on the head of a pin, as it were."

Because many people and events of *Look Homeward, Angel* and *Of Time and the River* (1935) were transparently drawn from his own life, he was labeled (it was more an indictment than a label) "autobiographical"; but when he drew back, shrank his enormous hero Eugene Gant into an apelike five-foot-eight George Webber, and took pains to steer around identifiable situations, he found himself writing the same pilgrimage from innocence to experience all over again, following the same sort of small-town Southern mountain boy through boyhood and youth and on to the North and the City, so that in many ways *The Web and the Rock* (1939) and *You Can't Go Home Again* (1940) reproduce or continue the essential action and most of the attitudes of the Eugene Gant books. Because Wolfe wanted to examine such roots as he might claim, he gave large space in the first pair of books to Eliza Gant's eccentric family, the Pentlands. When he changed Eugene Gant to George Webber, he changed Pentlands to Joyners, but he did little otherwise to alter them; and when his own memories of the family were used up he began working back into the historical generations and the Appalachian hill society from which they came.

Because he was floundering to form an art and a tradition out of the uncreated atoms of a self, a family, and a society, he often swamped himself in details; and because Time was fascinating and mysterious to him, he waded recklessly into its quicksands. He said in *The Story of a Novel*, which he wrote to explain his relation to Scribner's editor Max Perkins and to elaborate his own intentions and methods as a novelist, that he wanted to deal simultaneously with three levels of time: the actual dramatic present, the past with its "accumulated impact" on the present, and "time immutable, the time of rivers, mountains, oceans, and the earth, a kind of eternal and unchanging universe of time against which would be projected the transcience of man's life, the bitter briefness of his day." His ambition was no less than to explore and reveal what an American was heir to, to create out of a raw continent, ancestors, faiths, actions, history, and the accumulations of time, the thing which as a living, remembering, and feeling organism he most intensely *was*. In trying to do what his mind drove him to, he paid no attention to the limits of what was customarily called the "novel." He spoke always of "the book" on which he was at work, and after the publication of *Of Time and the River*, when he was beginning to nurse his grievance against Max Perkins and Scribner's, he lamented that his publishers had insisted on taking the manuscript out of his hands prematurely, "for by God, in purpose and in spirit, that book was not episodic but a living whole and I could have made it so—the whole inwrought inweaving sense of time and man's past conjoined forever to each living present moment of his life . . . ."

Though he discovered young that he was inevitable, it took him another year of Harvard, and several of teaching at New York University and traveling abroad, to arrive at what he called a "concrete definition of his resources." He found it, not at home, but as a homesick exile in Europe. Characteristically, it is less a definition than a catalogue, and less a catalogue than an incantation. Memory was his glory and his curse; the more he floundered around France and England after the "culture" that he thought essential to him as a writer, the more America returned to him in floods of "blinding imagery." As he told it in *The Story of a Novel*,

The quality of my memory is characterized, I believe, in a more than ordinary degree by the intensity of its sense impressions, its power to evoke and bring back the odors, sounds, colors, shapes, and feel of . . . . things with concrete vividness . . . . I would be sitting, for example, on the terrace of a café watching the flash and play of life before me on the Avenue de l'Opera, and suddenly I would remember the iron railing that goes along the boardwalk at Atlantic City. I could see it instantly just the way it was, the heavy iron pipe, its raw, galvanized look; the way the joints were fitted together. It was all so vivid and concrete that I could feel my hand upon it and know the exact dimensions, its size and weight and shape. And suddenly I would realize that I had never seen any railing that looked like this in Europe. And this utterly familiar, common thing would suddenly be revealed to me with all the wonder with which we discover a thing which we have seen all our life and yet have never known before. Or again, it would be a bridge, the look of an old iron bridge across an American river, the sound the train makes as it goes across it; the spoke-and-hollow rumble of the ties below, the look of the muddy banks; the slow, thick, yellow wash of an American river; an old flat-bottomed boat half filled with water stogged in the muddy bank; or it would be, most lonely and haunting of all the sounds I know, the sound of a milk wagon as it entered an American street just at the first gray of morning, the slow and lonely clopping of the hoof upon the street, the jink of bottles, the sudden rattle of a battered old milk can, the swift and hurried footsteps of the milkman, and again the jink of bottles, a low word spoken to his horse, and then the great, slow, clopping hoof receding into silence, and the quietness and a bird song rising in the street again.

Wolfe was totally right about the quality of his memory; and he was its slave nearly as often as he was its master. Some of his worst writing is the product of total recall gone berserk, some of his best exhibits that marvelous memory working for him under control. At its worst, his memory filled pages and chapters with catalogues hardly more justified as literature than the great lists of American cities, towns, rivers, and streets which he poured into notebooks while rediscovering his native land from a London furnished room. At its best, it gave us scenes as troubled with magic as Grover's morning in the square in "The Lost Boy," or his brother's hesitant approach down King's Highway toward the house where Grover's ghost still seemed to linger in the shadowy light of the downstairs room.

Like Joyce, like Katherine Mansfield, like Katherine Anne Porter, Wolfe was self-exiled. Departing from Asheville as his hero Eugene Gant departed from Altamont, he left "the dark heart and mournful mystery of the South forever," to seek himself in the glitter of Northern and European cities. But like many another he found that there was a return as compulsive as flight: his writings led him back to Asheville as surely as Joyce's returned him to Dublin, or Katherine Mansfield's to the lost island of her childhood. Wolfe's "book" is made out of the tension between flight and return; and though he called one whole section of it *You Can't Go Home Again*, he had already done, in *Look Homeward, Angel*, what he said could not be done. For however widely he wandered, he went always picketed to his past by that relentless memory.

Sometimes he tried to fool himself, to pretend that he had escaped and emancipated himself. Three months before he died he wrote to his last editor, Edward Aswell of Harper's, a description of the manuscript he had just delivered—a mass of half-integrated sections and pieces that when stacked in one pile stood breast-high on Harper Brothers' office floor.

. . . the whole book might almost be called You Can't Go Home Again —which means back to one's family, back home to one's childhood, back home to the father one has lost, back home to romantic love, to a young man's dreams of glory and fame, back home to exile, to escape to "Europe" and some foreign land, back home to lyricism, singing just for singing's sake . . . back home to the escapes of Time and Memory.

In that last year of his life he had been trying hard to cure himself of the autobiographical excesses of his earlier work. To a degree, he had. The manuscript he was working on at the time of his death in the summer of 1938 was the long story "The Hills Beyond," whose prose is soberer—and deader—than almost anything else in Wolfe, and whose subject is the Joyner clan in the years before 1880. But these Joyners themselves were a part of "home"; they were designed to fill in some of the background of George Webber's story as the Pentlands filled in the background of Eugene Gant. However he juggled his coconut, Wolfe found that it contained only one story, that of a sensibility like his own, sprung from a town and a family like his own. Actually, the farther he got from himself, from home, from the town of Asheville, from the powerful eccentrics of his own family, the less magic and the more effort there are in his prose. He *could* go home again, and had, and should have.

Fiction is a combination of the objective world and the eye that sees it. Though Wolfe was more powerful and more passionate, as a general rule, when he wrote through a Eugene Gant or a George Webber, both essentially himself, he did in a handful of stories invent sensibilities not his own, and tell stories through them. "Web of Earth," "Lost Boy," "In the Park," "Chickamauga," and "Only the Dead Know Brooklyn" demonstrate that on occasion he was capable of the "objectivity" his critics said he did not possess. These stories make it clear that his faculty of observation was as remarkable as his memory, and that his ear for lingo, even lingo very different from the native speech of his region, was extraordinarily acute. There is in this little group a surer feel, a surer identity as stories in their own right, than in those which, like "Death the Proud Brother" or "I Have a Thing to Tell You," are episodes in the exposure of the Wolfeian sensibility to the city and to Europe. Sometimes, as in "Web of Earth," the medium is a monologue by one of the characters of the Gant-Webber saga; but "In the Park" is a childhood reminiscence of Esther Jack, George Webber's mistress; and the bewildered narrator of "Only the Dead Know Brooklyn" is one of the city's man swarm, as different in background and speech from the Gants and Webbers as he could well be.

This last story is, in fact, a triumphant act of objectification, for it deliberately reverses the customary Wolfe pattern. Instead of being the subject and the sensibility, the Gant-Webber-Wolfe figure is here the object—still passionate walker, lonely seeker in dark streets, hungry Gulliver in the million-footed city, still desperate observer of the city's meanness and despair, but now observed, not observing. The voice we hear is not shouting Wolfe's rhetoric; it is chewing out the authentic accents of Bensonhurst and Green Point and Hell's Kitchen. Though a nonentity, and nameless, the narrator is fully conceived and fully rendered, and in his own terms. His astonished incomprehension is handled with scrupulous artistry; no Tom Wolfe intrudes here; no puppeteer reveals his enormous hands and feet. Slight though it is, an incident merely, a momentary revelation of the city's depression life, this story is one of those of which Max Perkins said in praise, "You have completely imagined whole natures of people totally unlike yourself."

That Wolfe was able to do so in this instance was probably due to the intense saturation in Brooklyn to which he subjected himself for four years after March 1931. He wrote furiously, he saw almost no one except his typist, he struggled with his monstrous task until he was blind and brain-fagged, and then he walked, sometimes all night. He saw Brooklyn's shabby, depression-blasted streets, not from an outsider's comfort and safety, but from a shared precariousness. Alfred Kazin has called Wolfe the "most alert" of depression novelists because "his imagination had presented his own situation and the American situation as coeval," and the remark seems just. Wolfe may literally have felt himself drowning among Brooklyn's swarming millions, he may literally have contemplated the self-destruction toward which his lonely walker in this story is headed. The loneliness of this walker, as contrasted with the roosterish sociability and garrulity of the little cipher who reports him, is of the essence of this story and these years of Wolfe's life; for he tried to rediscover his country by himself. Though he caught a social conscience during his years in Brooklyn, he joined nothing, and had only contempt for the Union Square and Village communists. He caught only pain, not a panacea. Briefly, in "Only the Dead Know Brooklyn," we see him joining and becoming part of "the nightmare pageantry to which my consciousness lay chained a spectator."

No matter how his random writing habits or the tidying hands of his editors broke up his book, no matter whether he wrote a section as part of the book or as a story for the magazines, almost every piece turned out to fit somewhere in the mighty fabric of his story. (Max Perkins, seeing his cuts from *Look Homeward, Angel* come back to him in other contexts, said, "I began to realize that nothing Wolfe wrote was ever lost, that omissions from one book were restored in a later one.") Between January 1 and July 1, 1937, according to his agent and later biographer Elizabeth Nowell, Wolfe wrote nine short stories: "Mr. Malone," "E," "April Late April," "Katamoto," "The Child by Tiger," "The Lost Boy," "Chickamauga," "The Party at Jack's," and "No More Rivers." All but the last one were published in magazines; three later found their way into the big manuscript as parts of what Aswell published posthumously under the title *The Web and the Rock*; three others eventually became parts of *You Can't Go Home Again*; two were included in the final volume of Wolfe's work, the collection of short pieces entitled *The Hills Beyond* (1941). Of these last two, "Chickamauga" would probably have been incorporated into the large work if Wolfe had lived, for it has its natural place as a Civil War reminiscence of one of the patriarchs of the Joyner clan. Only "The Lost Boy" was destined to remain separate; for though it was written very near the end of Wolfe's life, the book of which it should have formed a natural episode had already been written and in a sense repudiated. "The Lost Boy" was an afterthought to *Look Homeward, Angel*.

Among the children of W. O. and Julia Wolfe were twin boys, Grover

Cleveland and Benjamin Harrison Wolfe, both of whom died young, as reported in *Look Homeward, Angel*. In the revision of the novel, Grover's death in St. Louis got considerably compressed, but Ben's death was built into the book's climactic scenes. The names of the brothers remained the same in fiction as they had been in life, the details of their deaths were put down straight from memory. It was as though, the more closely memory and deep feeling came together, the more trouble Wolfe had in disguising literal fact. And there is no question that the death of Grover, which happened when Thomas was three, was one of his most haunting memories— one of the first, half-retained, bright-and-dark memories, made up of a mixture of indelible images and shadowy, fading shapes and echoing sounds, a memory uneasy with the mystery of time. In the letter to his mother from Cambridge, Wolfe had listed it among the retained impressions that had helped convince him he was to be an artist:

> Then St. Louis. A flight of stairs at the Cincinnati railroad station— which must be gone up—the World's Fair, the Ferris Wheel, Grover at the Inside Inn. . . . I swallowed a fly and am sick—and one of my brothers laughs at me—two little boys who ride tricycles up and down the street— they dress in white and look alike. . . . I'll never forget it—Grover's sickness and death—I am awakened at midnight by Mabel and she says, "Grover's on the cooling board." I don't know what a cooling board is but am anxious to see.
>
> I don't know what death is but have a vague, terrified sensation that something awful has happened—then she takes me in her arms and up the hall—disappointed at the cooling board—it's only a table—the brown mole on his neck—the trip home—visitors in the parlor with condolences. . . . It gets fairly plain thereafter and I can trace it step by step.

Throughout his short life, time for Thomas Wolfe had been a mystery restless with fading faces and fading voices, haunted with lost scents and colors and sounds. It was much on his mind in the months when "The Lost Boy" was written, and almost the last words he wrote, the final paragraphs of "The Hills Beyond," reiterate the theme:

> And time passing . . . passing like a leaf . . . time passing, fading like a flower . . . time passing like a river flowing . . . time passing, and remembered suddenly, like the forgotten hoof and wheel. . . .
>
> Time passing as men pass who will never come back again . . . and leaving us, Great God, with only this . . . knowing that this earth, this time, this life, are stranger than a dream.

Fortunately for Wolfe, when his sense of the mystery of time had deepened thus, he could still reach back into his most intensely remembered childhood for an incident to express his feeling. He had always regretted the skimping of Grover's death in *Look Homeward, Angel*. In his maturity he went back and did it over.

"The Lost Boy" is testimony that the charge of formlessness often made against Wolfe should not be pressed too far. Whether or not he would have made something gigantic but shapely of his vast "book" is problematic, but some of the shorter pieces, notably this story, "Web of Earth," and "Chickamauga," achieve a form that strikes us as exactly right. This form is never bare, never stripped down or economical. In his famous letter to F. Scott Fitzgerald Wolfe stoutly defends the "putter-inners" against the "taker-outers," and in doing so he is defending his own consistent practice. But however diffuse and rambling "Web of Earth" may seem, it is a beautiful and cunningly intricate whole, made so by Wolfe's control of Eliza Gant's mind as she weaves back and forth through time, meshing living and dead, present and past, into a dense fabric. "Chickamauga," too, is a controlled single narrative, unified in action and in tone. And "The Lost Boy," which with "Web of Earth" probably represents Wolfe's highest achievement as a writer, has a structure more complicated but quite as sound, which reconciles multiple points of view into a single moment of loss, revelation, and exorcism.

Returning from a trip west in 1934, Wolfe had made it a point to go through St. Louis and hunt up the street and the house where they had lived for six months in 1903, and where Grover had died. That compulsive and troubling return got incorporated in the story of Grover's death when he rewrote it three years later, and Thomas Wolfe's search for himself got fused with the mysteries of time and loss associated with the memories of the dead brother. One way of looking at "The Lost Boy" is as a variant of the Orpheus story, an attempt through art to overcome death; another way is to view it as Wolfe's attempt to compact into an instant of revelation the three levels of time through which his mind wove as restlessly as his garrulous mother's. Still another is to see in it Thomas Wolfe's private version of an ancient primitive ritual, some echo out of *The Golden Bough,* by which he strove to call up, to know, and eventually to exorcise, the ghost of a brother more loved and more praised than he. The method of the story is one not unknown in literature, but we seldom see it practiced so consistently and persuasively. It is the method of associative magic, including ritual incantation.

It begins with a scene that might as well be a scene from *Look Homeward, Angel:* Grover in the square by the fountain, "caught upon a point of Time," the grave, quiet boy experiencing "the union of Forever and of Now." His sensuous awareness is an index of his identity; the catalogues of articles in the windows of hardware and music and candy stores, the repetitive sights and sounds of the square, the fountain that pulses and blows in spray and returns to its pulsing plume—these things, in Wolfe's phrase, "utter" Grover. They have the function less of defining Grover for us than of evoking in himself the sense of his living reality. It is possible to object to the length of these "desperately evocative" catalogues, but he who objects has refused from the outset not only Wolfe's tools but his intention; he has set himself against the working of the magic. By the same token, unless one wants to repudiate the story in advance, one must allow the incantatory rhetoric, the repetitions, the refrains. Through this scene of Grover's encounter with petty injustice, the observation is both intense and accurate and the phrasing precise ("The fire department horses drummed on the floors with wooden stomp, most casually, and with dry whiskings of their clean coarse tails"), but the realism is balanced by a sense of the mystery of life, the flow of time, the strangeness of identity, and for that a heightened rhetoric is necessary. Reality and mystery flow together in this story from first page to last; and one way to state mystery is by incantation, by repetition, by the ceremonious magic of naming things.

Another is by emphasizing, against the reality of Grover's established identity, the varying responses of others to him: his mother's pride, his sister Helen's passionate recollection, love, guilt, and bewilderment, and his brother Eugene's insistent need to *know*. This aspect of the story enforces, not rhetoric, but multiple points of view; and the combination of repetitious rhetoric and multiple points of view—the sound of the same insistent notes through several voices—doubles the effect of permanence within change, the timeless within time. Part II uses the controlled garrulous monologue of "Web of Earth," but for all her colloquial matter-of-factness Eliza Gant is made to play the themes of magic—the puzzled awareness of the strangeness of time, and the establishment of St. Louis as the city of magic when they went "down along the river, through Indiana, to St. Louis, to the Fair." Not only is the refrain picked up in later sections, but what seems comfortable and gossipy is obscurely troubled, and there are carefully planted clues that will be picked up later, such as the hinted rivalry between Eugene and the dead Grover, the best of Eliza's children.

That rivalry is suggested in Part III, too, in the monologue of Helen; for in the family photograph which stimulates her recollection Eugene is not even present—he was just a dishrag hanging out in heaven when it was taken. The photograph is as surely an instrument of associative magic as nail parings or footprints in the mud. Identity is contained in it—and the boy who does not show in it does not exist. But Grover, against whom, somehow, he must establish his existence, does exist both in the photograph and in Helen's recollections, and in a way to corroborate the mother's pride. A boy older than his years, generous, affectionate, dependable, "he was a sweet kid and he was crazy about you." Out of his sister's puzzled ruminations, out of her recollections of St. Louis, the Fair, the Inside Inn, the house where they lived, and the twins who rode bicycles up and down, emerges a Grover who is hardly so much remembered by Eugene as created for him, created as a brother who loved him, a rival against whom he has never measured himself and cannot measure himself because time and death have come between them. For him, even more than for his sister, "It all comes back as if it happened yesterday. And then it goes away again, and seems farther off and stranger than if it happened in a dream." To find

THOMAS WOLFE

and name that ghost, to track down the lost brother and thus somehow define his own identity, which is associated with Grover, Eugene makes a pilgrimage, just as Wolfe himself did for probably identical reasons, to St. Louis and the King's Highway that "wound from magic out of some dim and haunted land."

Surely this is to be taken as a visit to the land of the dead, a version of the story of all the heroes who have crossed to the Otherworld. The shape of the journey is gradual and circular, the purpose hidden at first among the garrulities of mother and sister. But now, with Eugene's section, the circling narrows to St. Louis, to the King's Highway, to the street with the forgotten name, to the remembered house. As we pass into this otherworld the rhetoric too is heightened, the namings and the repeated refrains grow more incantatory, as if the ritual were working toward its climax, as if by repeating the images retained in his memory Eugene were trying to bring back the past in all its reality, to substitute something solid for the strange, half-changed, half-forgotten present to which his search has led him. He looks back "as if the street were Time," "waiting—for a word, for a door to open, for the child to come," but there is only the unmagical street, the shabby house, the sag of disappointment that nothing is as he hoped it might be.

But memory, stimulated by the half-familiar, has begun to work in him. He seethes with remembered images—the hot backyard, the airing mattress, the smell of the cool cellar, the "sense of absence and vague sadness in the afternoons," the slick varnish and the bead curtain, the stained light from the windows—all of them seeming "to wait attentively, to be most living and most still." The catalogue is full, the details repetitive, the evocation intense, even frantic. Rhetorical as it is, this prose has the effect of magical mumbo jumbo, it lulls our disbelief and invites our participation. And when we pass the house, and turn, and speak with the woman, the remembered and the real begin to shift with the strangeness of something seen through a polarizer. We are very close to the heart of the mystery, so that Eugene feels he might sit on the stairs as he did when a child and by an act of will feel himself back bodily into his childhood's universe and thus know everything, including himself. "Here in this house, this Absence, is my core, my kernel—here am I." What he is after is exactly the feeling of intense identity, that union of Forever and of Now, that Grover had felt back in the square at the story's beginning.

It comes and goes, he almost has it and it fades again. He goes still closer to the center, to the very room where Grover died, and "it was the same." When he admits to the woman that his brother died here, the ghost of the dead boy is very close, for Mrs. Bell says, "I knew it. I don't know how. But when you told me he was here, I knew it."

There is only one further step. In that room where the ghost of Grover lies on the dusky air, at the very center of this troubling and confused pilgrimage back through time, there is a moment when "the years dropped off like fallen leaves," and passage has been made—Eugene is fully across the line that divides present from past. Quite properly, he reaches the past at a moment of ritual magic, when as a child of three he is being taught to say his brother's name. Grover's urgency is our own—"Not Gova—*Grover*. Say it!" For if that name can be plainly spoken, here, art will have overcome both death and time, contact will have been made, a knowledge gained.

It cannot be spoken. The nearest Eugene can come is his childish approximation. The adult Eugene can come no closer than the child. The effort to obliterate time and to call back the dead is an effort as doomed and partial as memory. And yet something has happened; the intensity of Eugene's search back through the "thicket of man's memory" has been in its own way a ritual assuagement and an exorcism; "the lost boy was gone forever, and would not return."

Like much in the work of Thomas Wolfe, "The Lost Boy" is at once the record of an indomitable quest and the acknowledgment of its inevitable failure. It asserts contraries, too, for in the very act of demonstrating that you can't go home again, it goes; in the anguished admission that return to childhood or the past is impossible, it utilizes that childhood and that past for what seems, thirty years after Tom Wolfe went uncertainly poking along a half forgotten street in St. Louis, his best and most evocative story.

WALLACE STEGNER

A Note on the Text.   The text here followed for "Only the Dead Know Brooklyn," in *From Death to Morning*, is that of the first edition in book form (New York: Charles Scribner's Sons, 1935); the text for "The Lost Boy," in *The Hills Beyond*, is also that of the first edition (New York: Harper & Brothers, now Harper & Row, Publishers, Inc., 1941).

❖

ONLY THE DEAD KNOW BROOKLYN

DERE'S NO GUY livin' dat knows Brooklyn t'roo an' t'roo, because it'd take a guy a lifetime just to find his way aroun' duh f—— town.

So like I say, I'm waitin' for my train t' come when I sees dis big guy standin' deh—dis is duh foist I eveh see of him. Well, he's lookin' wild, y'know, an' I can see dat he's had plenty, but still he's holdin' it; he talks good an' is walkin' straight enough. So den, dis big guy steps up to a little guy dat's standin' deh, an' says, "How d'yuh get t' Eighteent' Avenoo an' Sixty-sevent' Street?" he says.

"Jesus! Yuh got me, chief," duh little guy says to him. "I ain't been heah long myself. Where is duh place?" he says. "Out in duh Flatbush section somewhere?"

"Nah," duh big guy says. "It's out in Bensonhoist. But I was neveh deh befoeh. How d'yuh get deh?"

"Jesus," duh little guy says, scratchin' his head, y'know—yuh could see duh little guy didn't know his way about—"yuh got me, chief. I neveh hoid of it. Do any of youse guys know where it is?" he says to me.

"Sure," I says. "It's out in Bensonhoist. Yuh take duh Fourt' Avenoo express, get off at Fifty-nint' Street, change to a Sea Beach local deh, get off at Eighteent' Avenoo an' Sixty-toid, an' den walk down foeh blocks. Dat's all yuh got to do," I says.

"G'wan!" some wise guy dat I neveh seen befoeh pipes up. "Whatcha talkin' about?" he says—oh, he was wise, y'know. "Duh guy is crazy! I tell yuh what yuh do," he says to duh big guy. "Yuh change to duh West End line at Toity-sixt'," he tells him. "Get off at Noo Utrecht an' Sixteent' Avenoo," he says. "Walk two blocks oveh, foeh blocks up," he says, "an' you'll be right deh." Oh, a *wise* guy, y'know.

"Oh, yeah?" I says. "Who told *you* so much?" He got me sore because he was so wise about it. "How long you been livin' heah?" I says.

"All my life," he says. "I was bawn in Williamsboig," he says. "An' I can tell you t'ings about dis town you neveh hoid of," he says.

"Yeah?" I says.

"Yeah," he says.

"Well, den, you can tell me t'ings about dis town dat nobody else has eveh hoid of, either. Maybe you make it all up yoehself at night," I says, "befoeh you go to sleep—like cuttin' out papeh dolls, or somp'n."

"Oh, yeah?" he says. "You're pretty wise, ain't yuh?"

"Oh, I don't know," I says. "Duh boids ain't usin' my head for Lincoln's statue yet," I says. "But I'm wise enough to know a phony when I see one."

"Yeah?" he says. "A wise guy, huh? Well, you're so wise dat some one's goin' t'bust yuh one right on duh snoot some day," he says. "Dat's how wise *you* are."

Well, my train was comin', or I'da smacked him den an' dere, but when I seen duh train was comin', all I said was, "All right, mugg! I'm sorry I can't stay to take keh of you, but I'll be seein' yuh sometime, I hope, out in duh cemetery." So den I says to duh big guy, who'd been standin' deh all duh time, "You come wit me," I says. So when we gets onto duh train I says to him, "Where yuh goin' out in Bensonhoist?" I says. "What numbeh are yuh lookin' for?" I says. You know—I t'ought if he told me duh address I might be able to help him out.

"Oh," he says, "I'm not lookin' for no one. I don't know no one out deh."

"Then whatcha goin' out deh for?" I says.

"Oh," duh guy says, "I'm just goin' out to see duh place," he says. "I like duh sound of duh name—Bensonhoist, y'know—so I t'ought I'd go out an' have a look at it."

"Whatcha tryin' t'hand me?" I says. "Whatcha tryin' t'do—kid me?" *You* know, I t'ought duh guy was bein' wise wit me.

"No," he says, "I'm tellin' yuh duh troot. I like to go out an' take a look at places wit nice names like dat. I like to go out an' look at all kinds of places," he says.

"How'd yuh know deh was such a place," I says, "if yuh neveh been deh befoeh?"

"Oh," he says, "I got a map."

"A *map?*" I says.

"Sure," he says, "I got a map dat tells me about all dese places. I take it wit me every time I come out heah," he says.

And Jesus! Wit dat, he pulls it out of his pocket, an' so help me, but he's *got* it—he's tellin' duh troot—a big map of duh whole f—— place with all duh different pahts mahked out. You know—Canarsie an' East Noo Yawk an' Flatbush, Bensonhoist, Sout' Brooklyn, duh Heights, Bay Ridge, Greenpernt—duh whole goddam layout, he's got it right deh on duh map.

"You been to any of dose places?" I says.

"Sure," he says, "I been to most of 'em. I was down in Red Hook just last night," he says.

"Jesus! Red Hook!" I says. "Whatcha do down deh?"

"Oh," he says, "nuttin' much. I just walked aroun'. I went into a coupla places an' had a drink," he says, "but most of the time I just walked aroun'."

"Just walked aroun'?" I says.

"Sure," he says, "just lookin' at t'ings, y'know."

"Where'd yuh go?" I asts him.

"Oh," he says, "I don't know duh name of duh place, but I could find it on my map," he says. "One time I was walkin' across some big fields where deh ain't no houses," he says, "but I could see ships oveh deh all lighted up. Dey was loadin'. So I walks across duh fields," he says, "to where duh ships are."

"Sure," I says, "I know where you was. You was down to duh Erie Basin."

"Yeah," he says, "I guess dat was it. Dey had some of dose big elevators an' cranes an' dey was loadin' ships, an' I could see some ships in drydock all lighted up, so I walks across duh fields to where dey are," he says.

"Den what did yuh do?" I says.

"Oh," he says, "nuttin' much. I came on back across duh fields after a while an' went into a coupla places an' had a drink."

"Didn't nuttin' happen while yuh was in dere?" I says.

"No," he says. "Nuttin' much. A coupla guys was drunk in one of duh places an' started a fight, but dey bounced 'em out," he says, "an' den one of duh guys stahted to come back again, but duh bartender gets his baseball bat out from under duh counteh, so duh guy goes on."

"Jesus!" I said. "Red Hook!"

"Sure," he says. "Dat's where it was, all right."

"Well, you keep outa deh," I says. "You stay away from deh."

"Why?" he says. "What's wrong wit it?"

"Oh," I says, "It's a good place to stay away from, dat's all. It's a good place to keep out of."

"Why?" he says. "Why is it?"

Jesus! Whatcha gonna do wit a guy as dumb as dat? I saw it wasn't no use to try to tell him nuttin', he wouldn't know what I was talkin' about, so I just says to him, "Oh, nuttin'. Yuh might get lost down deh, dat's all."

"Lost?" he says. "No, I wouldn't get lost. I got a map," he says.

A map! Red Hook! Jesus!

So den duh guy begins to ast me all kinds of nutty questions: how big was Brooklyn an' could I find my way aroun' in it, an' how long would it take a guy to know duh place.

"Listen!" I says. "You get dat idea outa yoeh head right now," I says. "You ain't neveh gonna get to know Brooklyn," I says. "Not in a hunderd yeahs. I been livin' heah all my life," I says, "an' I don't even know all deh is to know about it, so how do you expect to know duh town," I says, "when you don't even live heah?"

"Yes," he says, "but I got a map to help me find my way about."

"Map or no map," I says, "yuh ain't gonna get to know Brooklyn wit no map," I says.

"Can you swim?" he says, just like dat. Jesus! By dat time, y'know, I begun to see dat duh guy was some kind of nut. He'd had plenty to drink, of course, but he had dat crazy look in his eye I didn't like. "Can you swim?" he says.

"Sure," I says. "Can't you?"

"No," he says. "Not more'n a stroke or two. I neveh loined good."

"Well, it's easy," I says. "All yuh need is a little confidence. Duh way I loined, me older bruddeh pitched me off duh dock one day when I was eight yeahs old, cloes an' all. 'You'll swim,' he says. 'You'll swim all right—or drown.' An', believe me, I *swam!* When yuh know yuh got to, you'll do it. Duh only t'ing yuh need is confidence. An' once you've loined," I says, "you've got nuttin' else to worry about. You'll neveh forget it. It's somp'n dat stays wit yuh as long as yuh live."

"Can yuh swim good?" he says.

"Like a fish," I tells him. "I'm a regulah fish in duh wateh," I says. "I loined to swim right off duh docks wit all duh oddeh kids," I says.

"What would you do if yuh saw a man drownin'?" duh guy says.

"Do? Why, I'd jump in an' pull him out," I says. "Dat's what I'd do."

"Did yuh eveh see a man drown?" he says.

"Sure," I says. "I see two guys—bot' times at Coney Island. Dey got out too far, an' neider one could swim. Dey drowned befoeh any one could get to 'em."

"What becomes of people after dey've drowned out heah?" he says.

"Drowned out where?" I says.

"Out heah in Brooklyn."

"I don't know whatcha mean," I says. "Neveh hoid of no one drownin' heah in Brooklyn, unless you mean a swimmin' pool. Yuh can't drown in Brooklyn," I says. "Yuh gotta drown somewhere else—in duh ocean, where dere's wateh."

"Drownin'," duh guy says, lookin' at his map. "Drownin'." Jesus! I could see by den he was some kind of nut, he had dat crazy expression in his eyes when he looked at you, an' I didn't know what he might do. So we was comin' to a station, an' it wasn't my stop, but I got off anyway, an' waited for duh next train.

"Well, so long, chief," I says. "Take it easy, now."

"Drownin'," duh guy says, lookin' at his map. "Drownin'."

Jesus! I've t'ought about dat guy a t'ousand times since den an' wondered what eveh happened to 'm goin' out to look at Bensonhoist because he liked duh name! Walkin' aroun' t'roo Red Hook by himself at night an' lookin' at his map! How many people did I see get drowned out heah in Brooklyn! How long would it take a guy wit a good map to know all deh was to know about Brooklyn!

Jesus! What a nut *he* was! I wondeh what eveh happened to 'im, anyway! I wondeh if some one knocked him on duh head, or if he's still wanderin' aroun' in duh subway in duh middle of duh night wit his little map! Duh poor guy! Say, I've got to laugh, at dat, when I t'ink about him! Maybe he's found out by now dat he'll neveh live long enough to know duh whole of Brooklyn. It'd take a guy a lifetime to know Brooklyn t'roo an' t'roo. An' even den, yuh wouldn't know it all.

1935

THE LOST BOY

1

LIGHT CAME AND WENT AND CAME AGAIN, the booming strokes of three o'clock beat out across the town in thronging bronze from the courthouse bell, light winds of April blew the fountain out in rainbow sheets, until the plume returned and pulsed, as Grover turned into the Square. He was a child, dark-eyed and grave, birthmarked upon his neck—a berry of warm brown—and with a gentle face, too quiet and too listening for his years. The scuffed boy's shoes, the thick-ribbed stockings gartered at the knees, the short knee pants cut straight with three small useless buttons at the side, the sailor blouse, the old cap battered out of shape, perched sideways up on top of the raven head, the old soiled canvas bag slung from the shoulder, empty now, but waiting for the crisp sheets of the afternoon—these friendly, shabby garments, shaped by Grover, uttered him. He turned and passed along the north side of the Square and in that moment saw the union of Forever and of Now.

Light came and went and came again, the great plume of the fountain

"The Lost Boy" from *The Hills Beyond* by Thomas Wolfe. Copyright 1937 by Maxwell Perkins as Executor. Reprinted with the permission of Harper & Row, Publishers, Incorporated.

pulsed and winds of April sheeted it across the Square in a rainbow gossa-
mer of spray. The fire department horses drummed on the floors with wooden
stomp, most casually, and with dry whiskings of their clean, coarse tails. The
street cars ground into the Square from every portion of the compass and
halted briefly like wound toys in their familiar quarter-hourly formula. A
dray, hauled by a boneyard nag, rattled across the cobbles on the other side
before his father's shop. The courthouse bell boomed out its solemn warning of immediate three, and everything was just the same as it had always
been.

He saw that haggis of vexed shapes with quiet eyes—that hodgepodge
of ill-sorted architectures that made up the Square, and he did not feel lost.
For "Here," thought Grover, "here is the Square as it has always been—and
papa's shop, the fire department and the City Hall, the fountain pulsing
with its plume, the street cars coming in and halting at the quarter hour, the
hardware store on the corner there, the row of old brick buildings on this
side of the street, the people passing and the light that comes and changes
and that always will come back again, and everything that comes and goes
and changes in the Square, and yet will be the same again. And here," the boy
thought, "is Grover with his paper bag. Here is old Grover, almost twelve
years old. Here is the month of April, 1904. Here is the courthouse bell and
three o'clock. Here is Grover on the Square that never changes. Here is
Grover, caught upon this point of time."

It seemed to him that the Square, itself the accidental masonry of many
years, the chance agglomeration of time and of disrupted strivings, was the
center of the universe. It was for him, in his soul's picture, the earth's pivot,
the granite core of changelessness, the eternal place where all things came
and passed, and yet abode forever and would never change.

He passed the old shack on the corner—the wooden fire-trap where S. Gold-
berg ran his wiener stand. Then he passed the Singer place next door, with its
gleaming display of new machines. He saw them and admired them, but he
felt no joy. They brought back to him the busy hum of housework and of
women sewing, the intricacy of stitch and weave, the mystery of style and
pattern, the memory of women bending over flashing needles, the pedaled
tread, the busy whir. It was women's work: it filled him with unknown associations of dullness and of vague depression. And always, also, with a moment's twinge of horror, for his dark eye would always travel toward that
needle stitching up and down so fast the eye could never follow it. And
then he would remember how his mother once had told him she had driven
the needle through her finger, and always, when he passed this place, he
would remember it and for a moment crane his neck and turn his head
away.

He passed on then, but had to stop again next door before the music store.
He always had to stop by places that had shining perfect things in them. He
loved hardware stores and windows full of accurate geometric tools. He
loved windows full of hammers, saws, and planing boards. He liked windows
full of strong new rakes and hoes, with unworn handles, of white perfect
wood, stamped hard and vivid with the maker's seal. He loved to see such
things as these in the windows of hardware stores. And he would fairly gloat
upon them and think that some day he would own a set himself.

Also, he always stopped before the music and piano store. It was a splendid store. And in the window was a small white dog upon his haunches, with head cocked gravely to one side, a small white dog that never moved, that never barked, that listened attentively at the flaring funnel of a horn to hear "His Master's Voice"—a horn forever silent, and a voice that never spoke. And within were many rich and shining shapes of great pianos, an air of splendor and of wealth.

And now, indeed, he *was* caught, held suspended. A waft of air, warm, chocolate-laden, filled his nostrils. He tried to pass the white front of the little eight-foot shop; he paused, struggling with conscience; he could not go on. It was the little candy shop run by old Crocker and his wife. And Grover could not pass.

"Old stingy Crockers!" he thought scornfully. "I'll not go there any more. But—" as the maddening fragrance of rich cooking chocolate touched him once again—"I'll just look in the window and see what they've got." He paused a moment, looking with his dark and quiet eyes into the window of the little candy shop. The window, spotlessly clean, was filled with trays of fresh-made candy. His eyes rested on a tray of chocolate drops. Unconsciously he licked his lips. Put one of them upon your tongue and it just melted there, like honeydew. And then the trays full of rich homemade fudge. He gazed longingly at the deep body of the chocolate fudge, reflectively at maple walnut, more critically, yet with longing, at the mints, the nougatines, and all the other dainties.

"Old stingy Crockers!" Grover muttered once again, and turned to go. "I wouldn't go in *there* again."

And yet he did not go away. "Old stingy Crockers" they might be; still, they did make the best candy in town, the best, in fact, that he had ever tasted.

He looked through the window back into the little shop and saw Mrs. Crocker there. A customer had gone in and had made a purchase, and as Grover looked he saw Mrs. Crocker, with her little wrenny face, her pinched features, lean over and peer primly at the scales. She had a piece of fudge in her clean, bony, little fingers, and as Grover looked, she broke it, primly, in her little bony hands. She dropped a morsel down into the scales. They weighted down alarmingly, and her thin lips tightened. She snatched the piece of fudge out of the scales and broke it carefully once again. This time the scales wavered, went down very slowly, and came back again. Mrs. Crocker carefully put the reclaimed piece of fudge back in the tray, dumped the remainder in a paper bag, folded it and gave it to the customer, counted the money carefully and doled it out into the till, the pennies in one place, the nickels in another.

Grover stood there, looking scornfully. "Old stingy Crocker—afraid that she might give a crumb away!"

He grunted scornfully and again he turned to go. But now Mr. Crocker came out from the little partitioned place where they made all their candy, bearing a tray of fresh-made fudge in his skinny hands. Old Man Crocker rocked along the counter to the front and put it down. He really rocked along. He was a cripple. And like his wife, he was a wrenny, wizened little creature, with bony hands, thin lips, a pinched and meager face. One leg was inches shorter than the other, and on this leg there was an enormous thick-soled boot, with a kind of wooden, rocker-like arrangement, six inches high at least, to make up for the deficiency. On this wooden cradle Mr. Crocker rocked along, with a prim and apprehensive little smile, as if he were afraid he was going to lose something.

"Old stingy Crocker!" muttered Grover. "Humph! He wouldn't give you anything!"

And yet—he did not go away. He hung there curiously, peering through the window, with his dark and gentle face now focused and intent, alert and curious, flattening his nose against the glass. Unconsciously he scratched the thick-ribbed fabric of one stockinged leg with the scuffed and worn toe of his old shoe. The fresh, warm odor of the new-made fudge was delicious. It was a little maddening. Half consciously he began to fumble in one trouser pocket, and pulled out his purse, a shabby worn old black one with a twisted clasp. He opened it and prowled about inside.

What he found was not inspiring—a nickel and two pennies and—he had forgotten them—the stamps. He took the stamps out and unfolded them. There were five twos, eight ones, all that remained of the dollar-sixty-cents' worth which Reed, the pharmacist, had given him for running errands a week or two before.

"Old Crocker," Grover thought, and looked somberly at the grotesque little form as it rocked back into the shop again, around the counter, and up the other side. "Well—" again he looked indefinitely at the stamps in his hand—"he's had all the rest of them. He might as well take these."

So, soothing conscience with this sop of scorn, he went into the shop and stood looking at the trays in the glass case and finally decided. Pointing with a slightly grimy finger at the fresh-made tray of chocolate fudge, he said, "I'll take fifteen cents' worth of this, Mr. Crocker." He paused a moment, fighting with embarrassment, then he lifted his dark face and said quietly, "And please, I'll have to give you stamps again."

Mr. Crocker made no answer. He did not look at Grover. He pressed his lips together primly. He went rocking away and got the candy scoop, came back, slid open the door of the glass case, put fudge into the scoop, and, rocking to the scales, began to weigh the candy out. Grover watched him as he peered and squinted, he watched him purse and press his lips together, he saw him take a piece of fudge and break it in two parts. And then old Crocker broke two parts in two again. He weighed, he squinted, and he hovered, until it seemed to Grover that by calling *Mrs.* Crocker stingy he had been guilty of a rank injustice. But finally, to his vast relief, the job was over, the scales hung there, quivering apprehensively, upon the very hair-line of nervous balance, as if even the scales were afraid that one more move from Old Man Crocker and they would be undone.

Mr. Crocker took the candy then and dumped it in a paper bag and, rocking back along the counter toward the boy, he dryly said: "Where are the stamps?" Grover gave them to him. Mr. Crocker relinquished his claw-like hold upon the bag and set it down upon the counter. Grover took the bag and dropped it in his canvas sack, and then remembered. "Mr. Crocker—" again he felt the old embarrassment that was almost like strong pain—"I gave you too much," Grover said. "There were eighteen cents in stamps. You—you can just give me three ones back."

Mr. Crocker did not answer. He was busy with his bony little hands, unfolding the stamps and flattening them out on top of the glass counter. When he had done so, he peered at them sharply for a moment, thrusting his scrawny neck forward and running his eye up and down, like a bookkeeper who totes up rows of figures.

When he had finished, he said tartly: "I don't like this kind of business. If you want candy, you should have the money for it. I'm not a post office. The next time you come in here and want anything, you'll have to pay me money for it."

Hot anger rose in Grover's throat. His olive face suffused with angry color. His tarry eyes got black and bright. He was on the verge of saying: "Then why did you take my other stamps? Why do you tell me now, when you have taken all the stamps I had, that you don't want them?"

But he was a boy, a boy of eleven years, a quiet, gentle, gravely thoughtful boy, and he had been taught how to respect his elders. So he just stood there looking with his tar-black eyes. Old Man Crocker, pursing at the mouth a little, without meeting Grover's gaze, took the stamps up in his thin, parched fingers and, turning, rocked away with them down to the till.

He took the twos and folded them and laid them in one rounded scallop, then took the ones and folded them and put them in the one next to it. Then he closed the till and started to rock off, down toward the other end. Grover, his face now quiet and grave, kept looking at him, but Mr. Crocker did not look at Grover. Instead he began to take some stamped cardboard shapes and fold them into boxes.

In a moment Grover said, "Mr. Crocker, will you give me the three ones, please?"

Mr. Crocker did not answer. He kept folding boxes, and he compressed his thin lips quickly as he did so. But Mrs. Crocker, back turned to her spouse, also folding boxes with her birdlike hands, muttered tartly: "Hm! I'd give him nothing!"

Mr. Crocker looked up, looked at Grover, said, "What are you waiting for?"

"Will you give me the three ones, please?" Grover said.

"I'll give you nothing," Mr. Crocker said.

He left his work and came rocking forward along the counter. "Now you get out of here! Don't you come in here with any more of those stamps," said Mr. Crocker.

"I should like to know where he gets them—that's what I should like to know," said Mrs. Crocker.

She did not look up as she said these words. She inclined her head a little to the side, in Mr. Crocker's direction, and continued to fold the boxes with her bony fingers.

"You get out of here!" said Mr. Crocker. "And don't you come back here with any stamps. . . . Where did you get those stamps?" he said.

"That's just what I've been thinking," Mrs. Crocker said. "I've been thinking all along."

"You've been coming in here for the last two weeks with those stamps," said Mr. Crocker. "I don't like the look of it. Where did you get those stamps?" he said.

"That's what *I've* been thinking," said Mrs. Crocker, for a second time.

Grover had got white underneath his olive skin. His eyes had lost their luster. They looked like dull, stunned balls of tar. "From Mr. Reed," he said. "I got the stamps from Mr. Reed." Then he burst out desperately: "Mr. Crocker—Mr. Reed will tell you how I got the stamps. I did some work for Mr. Reed, he gave me those stamps two weeks ago."

"Mr. Reed," said Mrs. Crocker acidly. She did not turn her head. "I call it mighty funny."

"Mr. Crocker," Grover said, "if you'll just let me have three ones——"

"You get out of here!" cried Mr. Crocker, and he began rocking forward toward Grover. "Now don't you come in here again, boy! There's something funny about this whole business! I don't like the look of it," said Mr. Crocker. "If you can't pay as other people do, then I don't want your trade."

"Mr. Crocker," Grover said again, and underneath the olive skin his face was gray, "if you'll just let me have those three——"

"You get out of here!" Mr. Crocker cried, rocking down toward the counter's end. "If you don't get out, boy——"

"*I'd* call a policeman, that's what I'd do," Mrs. Crocker said.

Mr. Crocker rocked around the lower end of the counter. He came rocking up to Grover. "You get out," he said.

He took the boy and pushed him with his bony little hands, and Grover was sick and gray down to the hollow pit of his stomach.

"You've got to give me those three ones," he said.

"You get out of here!" shrilled Mr. Crocker. He seized the screen door, pulled it open, and pushed Grover out. "Don't you come back in here," he said, pausing for a moment, and working thinly at the lips. He turned and rocked back in the shop again. The screen door slammed behind him. Grover stood there on the pavement. And light came and went and came again into the Square.

The boy stood there, and a wagon rattled past. There were some people passing by, but Grover did not notice them. He stood there blindly, in the watches of the sun, feeling this was Time, this was the center of the universe, the granite core of changelessness, and feeling, this is Grover, this the Square, this is Now.

But something had gone out of day. He felt the overwhelming, soul-sickening guilt that all the children, all the good men of the earth, have felt since Time began. And even anger had died down, had been drowned out, in this swelling tide of guilt, and "This is the Square"—thought Grover as before—"This is Now. There is my father's shop. And all of it is as it has always been—save I."

And the Square reeled drunkenly around him, light went in blind gray motes before his eyes, the fountain sheeted out to rainbow iridescence and returned to its proud, pulsing plume again. But all the brightness had gone out of day, and "Here is the Square, and here is permanence, and here is Time—and all of it the same as it has always been, save I."

The scuffed boots of the lost boy moved and stumbled blindly. The numb

feet crossed the pavement—reached the cobbled street, reached the plotted
central square—the grass plots, and the flower beds, so soon to be packed
with red geraniums.

"I want to be alone," thought Grover, "where I cannot go near him. . . .
Oh God, I hope he never hears, that no one ever tells him——"

The plume blew out, the iridescent sheet of spray blew over him. He
passed through, found the other side and crossed the street, and—"Oh God,
if papa ever hears!" thought Grover, as his numb feet started up the steps
into his father's shop.

He found and felt the steps—the width and thickness of old lumber
twenty feet in length. He saw it all—the iron columns on his father's porch,
painted with the dull anomalous black-green that all such columns in this
land and weather come to; two angels, fly-specked, and the waiting stones.
Beyond and all around, in the stonecutter's shop, cold shapes of white and
marble, rounded stone, the languid angel with strong marble hands of love.

He went on down the aisle, the white shapes stood around him. He went
on to the back of the workroom. This he knew—the little cast-iron stove in
left-hand corner, caked, brown, heat-blistered, and the elbow of the long
stack running out across the shop; the high and dirty window looking down
across the Market Square toward Niggertown; the rude old shelves, plank-
boarded, thick, the wood not smooth but pulpy, like the strong hair of an
animal; upon the shelves the chisels of all sizes and a layer of stone dust;
an emery wheel with pump tread; and a door that let out on the alleyway, yet
the alleyway twelve feet below. Here in the room, two trestles of this coarse
spiked wood upon which rested gravestones, and at one, his father at work.

The boy looked, saw the name was Creasman: saw the carved analysis of
John, the symmetry of the s, the fine sentiment that was being polished off beneath the name and date: "John Creasman, November 7, 1903."

Gant looked up. He was a man of fifty-three, gaunt-visaged, mustache
cropped, immensely long and tall and gaunt. He wore good dark clothes—
heavy, massive—save he had no coat. He worked in shirt-sleeves with his
vest on, a strong watch chain stretching across his vest, wing collar and black
tie, Adam's apple, bony forehead, bony nose, light eyes, gray-green, undeep
and cold, and, somehow, lonely-looking, a striped apron going up around his
shoulders, and starched cuffs. And in one hand a tremendous rounded wooden
mallet like a butcher's bole; and in his other hand, a strong cold chisel.

"How are you, son?"

He did not look up as he spoke. He spoke quietly, absently. He worked
upon the chisel and the wooden mallet, as a jeweler might work on a watch,
except that in the man and in the wooden mallet there was power too.

"What is it, son?" he said.

He moved around the table from the head, started up on "J" once again.

"Papa, I never stole the stamps," said Grover.

Gant put down the mallet, laid the chisel down. He came around the
trestle.

"What?" he said.

As Grover winked his tar-black eyes, they brightened, the hot tears shot
out. "I never stole the stamps," he said.

"Hey? What is this?" his father said. "What stamps?"

"That Mr. Reed gave me, when the other boy was sick and I worked there for three days. . . . And Old Man Crocker," Grover said, "he took all the stamps. And I told him Mr. Reed had given them to me. And now he owes me three ones—and Old Man Crocker says he don't believe that they were mine. He says—he says—that I must have taken them somewhere," Grover blurted out.

"The stamps that Reed gave you—hey?" the stonecutter said. "The stamps you had—" He wet his thumb upon his lips, threw back his head and slowly swung his gaze around the ceiling, then turned and strode quickly from his workshop out into the storeroom.

Almost at once he came back again, and as he passed the old gray painted-board partition of his office he cleared his throat and wet his thumb and said, "Now, I tell you——"

Then he turned and strode up toward the front again and cleared his throat and said, "I tell you now—" He wheeled about and started back, and as he came along the aisle between the marshaled rows of gravestones he said beneath his breath, "By God, now——"

He took Grover by the hand and they went out flying. Down the aisle they went by all the gravestones, past the fly-specked angels waiting there, and down the wooden steps and across the Square. The fountain pulsed, the plume blew out in sheeted iridescence, and it swept across them; an old gray horse, with a peaceful look about his torn lips, swucked up the cool mountain water from the trough as Grover and his father went across the Square, but they did not notice it.

They crossed swiftly to the other side in a direct line to the candy shop. Gant was still dressed in his long striped apron, and he was still holding Grover by the hand. He opened the screen door and stepped inside.

"Give him the stamps," Gant said.

Mr. Crocker came rocking forward behind the counter, with the prim and careful look that now was somewhat like a smile. "It was just—" he said.

"Give him the stamps," Gant said, and threw some coins down on the counter.

Mr. Crocker rocked away and got the stamps. He came rocking back. "I just didn't know—" he said.

The stonecutter took the stamps and gave them to the boy. And Mr. Crocker took the coins.

"It was just that—" Mr. Crocker began again, and smiled.

Gant cleared his throat: "You never were a father," he said. "You never knew the feelings of a father, or understood the feelings of a child; and that is why you acted as you did. But a judgment is upon you. God has cursed you. He has afflicted you. He has made you lame and childless as you are—and lame and childless, miserable as you are, you will go to your grave and be forgotten!"

And Crocker's wife kept kneading her bony little hands and said, imploringly, "Oh, no—oh don't say that, please don't say that."

The stonecutter, the breath still hoarse in him, left the store, still holding the boy tightly by the hand. Light came again into the day.

"Well, son," he said, and laid his hand on the boy's back. "Well, son," he said, "now don't you mind."

They walked across the Square, the sheeted spray of iridescent light swept out on them, the horse swizzled at the water-trough, and "Well, son," the stonecutter said.

And the old horse sloped down, ringing with his hoofs upon the cobblestones.

"Well, son," said the stonecutter once again, "be a good boy."

And he trod his own steps then with his great stride and went back again into his shop.

The lost boy stood upon the Square, hard by the porch of his father's shop.

"This is Time," thought Grover. "Here is the Square, here is my father's shop, and here am I."

And light came and went and came again—but now not quite the same as it had done before. The boy saw the pattern of familiar shapes and knew that they were just the same as they had always been. But something had gone out of day, and something had come in again. Out of the vision of those quiet eyes some brightness had gone, and into their vision had come some deeper color. He could not say, he did not know through what transforming shadows life had passed within that quarter hour. He only knew that something had been lost—something forever gained.

Just then a buggy curved out through the Square, and fastened to the rear end was a poster, and it said "St. Louis" and "Excursion" and "The Fair."

2. The Mother

As we went down through Indiana—you were too young, child, to remember it—but I always think of all of you the way you looked that morning, when we went down through Indiana, going to the Fair. All of the apple trees were coming out, and it was April; it was the beginning of spring in southern Indiana and everything was getting green. Of course we don't have farms at home like those in Indiana. The childern had never seen such farms as those, and I reckon, kidlike, they had to take it in.

So all of them kept running up and down the aisle—well, no, except for you and Grover. You were too young, Eugene. You were just three, I kept you with me. As for Grover—well, I'm going to tell you about that.

But the rest of them kept running up and down the aisle and from one window to another. They kept calling out and hollering to each other every time they saw something new. They kept trying to look out on all sides, in every way at once, as if they wished they had eyes at the back of their heads. It was the first time any of them had ever been in Indiana, and I reckon that it all seemed strange and new.

And so it seemed they couldn't get enough. It seemed they never could be still. They kept running up and down and back and forth, hollering and shouting to each other, until—"I'll vow! You childern! I never saw the beat of you!" I said. "The way that you keep running up and down and back and forth and never can be quiet for a minute beats all I ever saw," I said.

You see, they were excited about going to St. Louis, and so curious over everything they saw. They couldn't help it, and they wanted to see everything. But—"I'll vow!" I said. "If you childern don't sit down and rest you'll be worn to a frazzle before we ever get to see St. Louis and the Fair!"

Except for Grover! He—no, sir! not him. Now, boy, I want to tell you —I've raised the lot of you—and if I do say so, there wasn't a numbskull in the lot. But *Grover!* Well, you've all grown up now, all of you have gone away, and none of you are childern any more. . . . And of course, I hope that, as the fellow says, you have reached the dignity of man's estate. I suppose you have the judgment of grown men. . . . But *Grover! Grover* had it even then!

Oh, even as a child, you know—at a time when I was almost afraid to trust the rest of you out of my sight—I could depend on Grover. He could go anywhere, I could send him anywhere, and I'd always know he'd get back safe, and do exactly what I told him to!

Why, I didn't even have to tell him. You could send that child to market and tell him what you wanted, and he'd come home with *twice* as much as you could get yourself for the same money!

Now you know, I've always been considered a good trader. But *Grover!*— why, it got so finally that I wouldn't even tell him. Your papa said to me: "You'd be better off if you'd just tell him what you want and leave the rest to him. For," your papa says, "damned if I don't believe he's a better trader than you are. He gets more for the money than anyone I ever saw."

Well, I had to admit it, you know. I had to own up then. Grover, even as a child, was a far better trader than I was. . . . Why, yes, they told it on him all over town, you know. They said all of the market men, all of the farmers, knew him. They'd begin to laugh when they saw him coming— they'd say: "Look out! Here's Grover! Here's one trader you're not going to fool!"

And they were right! *That* child! I'd say, "Grover, suppose you run up-town and see if they've got anything good to *eat* today"—and I'd just wink at him, you know, but he'd know what I meant. I wouldn't let on that I *wanted* anything exactly, but I'd say, "Now it just occurs to me that some good fresh stuff may be coming in from the country, so suppose you take this dollar and just see what you can do with it."

Well, sir, that was all that was needed. The minute you told that child that you depended on his judgment, he'd have gone to the ends of the earth for you—and, let me tell you something, he wouldn't *miss*, either!

His eyes would get as black as coals—oh! the way that child would look at you, the intelligence and sense in his expression. He'd say: "Yes, *ma'am!* Now don't you worry, mama. You leave it all to me—and I'll do *good!*" said Grover.

And he'd be off like a streak of lightning and—oh Lord! As your father said to me, "I've been living in this town for almost thirty years," he said —"I've seen it grow up from a crossroads village, and I thought I knew everything there was to know about it—but that child—" your papa says— "he knows places that I never heard of" . . . Oh, he'd go right down there to that place below your papa's shop where the draymen and the country people used to park their wagons—or he'd go down there to those old lots on Concord Street where the farmers used to keep their wagons. And, child that he was, he'd go right in among them, sir—*Grover* would!—go right in and barter with them like a grown man!

And he'd come home with things he'd bought that would make your eyes stick out. . . . Here he comes one time with another boy, dragging a great bushel basket full of ripe termaters between them. "Why, Grover!" I says. "How on earth are we ever going to use them? Why they'll go bad on us before we're half way through with them." "Well, mama," he says, "I know——" oh, just as solemn as a judge——"but they were the last the man had," he says, "and he wanted to go home, and so I got them for ten cents," he says. "They were so cheap," said Grover, "I thought it was a shame to let 'em go, and I figgered that what we couldn't eat——why," says Grover, "you could *put up!*" Well, the way he said it——so earnest and so serious——I had to laugh. "But I'll vow!" I said. "If you don't beat all!" . . . But that was *Grover!*——the way he was in *those* days! As everyone said, boy that he was, he had the sense and judgment of a grown man. . . . Child, child, I've seen you all grow up, and all of you were bright enough. There were no half-wits in *my* family. But for all-round intelligence, judgment, and general ability, Grover surpassed the whole crowd. I've never seen his equal, and everyone who knew him as a child will say the same.

So that's what I tell them now when they ask me about all of you. I have to tell the truth. I always said that *you* were smart enough, Eugene——but when they come around and brag to me about you, and about how you have got on and have a kind of name——I don't let on, you know. I just sit there and let them talk. I don't brag on you——if *they* want to brag on you, that's *their* business. I never bragged on one of my own childern in my life. When father raised us up, we were all brought up to believe that it was not good breeding to brag about your kin. "If the others want to do it," father said, "well, let *them* do it. Don't ever let on by a word or sign that you know what they are talking about. Just let *them* do the talking, and say nothing."

So when they come around and tell me all about the things *you've* done—— I don't let on to them, I never say a word. Why yes!——why, here, you know—— oh, along about a month or so ago, this feller comes——a well-dressed man, you know——he looked intelligent, a good substantial sort of person. He said he came from New Jersey, or somewhere up in that part of the country, and he began to ask me all sorts of questions——what you were like when you were a boy, and all such stuff as that.

I just pretended to study it all over and then I said, "Well, yes"——real serious-like, you know——"well, yes——I reckon I ought to know a little something about him. Eugene was my child, just the same as all the others were. I brought him up just the way I brought up all the others. And," I says——oh, just as solemn as you please——"he wasn't a *bad* sort of a boy. Why," I says, "up to the time that he was twelve years old he was just about the same as any other boy——a good, average, normal sort of fellow."

"Oh," he says. "But didn't you notice something? Wasn't there something kind of strange?" he says——"something different from what you noticed in the other childern?"

I didn't let on, you know——I just took it all in and looked as solemn as an owl——I just pretended to study it all over, just as serious as you please.

"Why no," I says, real slow-like, after I'd studied it all over. "As I remember it, he was a good, ordinary, normal sort of boy, just like all the others."

"Yes," he says—oh, all excited-like, you know— "But didn't you notice how brilliant he was? Eugene must have been more brilliant than the rest!"

"Well, now," I says, and pretended to study that all over too. "Now let me see. . . . Yes," I says—I just looked him in the eye, as solemn as you please—"he did pretty well. . . . Well, yes," I says, "I guess he was a fairly bright sort of a boy. I never had no complaints to make of him on that score. He was bright enough," I says. "The only trouble with him was that he was lazy."

"Lazy!" he says—oh, you should have seen the look upon his face, you know—he jumped like someone had stuck a pin in him. "Lazy!" he says. "Why, you don't mean to tell me——"

"Yes," I says—oh, I never cracked a smile—"I was telling him the same thing myself the last time that I saw him. I told him it was a mighty lucky thing for him that he had the gift of gab. Of course, he went off to college and read a lot of books, and I reckon that's where he got this flow of language they say he has. But as I said to him the last time that I saw him: 'Now look a-here,' I said. 'If you can earn your living doing a light, easy class of work like this you do,' I says, 'you're mighty lucky, because none of the rest of your people,' I says, 'had any such luck as that. They had to work hard for a living.'"

Oh, I told him, you know. I came right out with it. I made no bones about it. And I tell you what—I wish you could have seen his face. It was a study.

"Well," he says, at last, "you've got to admit this, haven't you—he was the brightest boy you had, now wasn't he?"

I just looked at him a moment. I had to tell the truth. I couldn't fool him any longer. "No," I says. "He was a good, bright boy—I got no complaint to make about him on that score—but the brightest boy I had, the one that surpassed all the rest of them in sense, and understanding, and in judgment —the best boy I had—the smartest boy I ever saw—was—well, it wasn't Eugene," I said. "It was another one."

He looked at me a moment, then he said, "Which boy was that?"

Well, I just looked at him, and smiled. I shook my head, you know. I wouldn't tell him. "I never brag about my own," I said. "You'll have to find out for yourself."

But—I'll have to tell you—and you know yourself, I brought the whole crowd up, I knew you all. And you can take my word for it—the best one of the lot was—Grover!

And when I think of Grover as he was along about that time, I always see him sitting there, so grave and earnest-like, with his nose pressed to the window, as we went down through Indiana in the morning, to the Fair.

All through that morning we were going down along beside the Wabash River—the Wabash River flows through Indiana, it is the river that they wrote the song about—so all that morning we were going down along the river. And I sat with all you childern gathered about me as we went down through Indiana, going to St. Louis, to the Fair.

And Grover sat there, so still and earnest-like, looking out the window, and he didn't move. He sat there like a man. He was just eleven and a half years old, but he had more sense, more judgment, and more understanding than any child I ever saw.

So here he sat beside this gentleman and looked out the window. I never knew the man—I never asked his name—but I tell you what! He was certainly a fine-looking, well-dressed, good, substantial sort of man, and I could see that he had taken a great liking to Grover. And Grover sat there looking out, and then turned to this gentleman, as grave and earnest as a grown-up man, and says, "What kind of crops grow here, sir?" Well, this gentleman threw his head back and just hah-hahed. "Well, I'll see if I can tell you," says this gentleman, and then, you know, he talked to him, they talked together, and Grover took it all in, as solemn as you please, and asked this gentleman every sort of question—what the trees were, what was growing there, how big the farms were—all sorts of questions, which this gentleman would answer, until I said: "Why, I'll vow, Grover! You shouldn't ask so many questions. You'll bother the very life out of this gentleman."

The gentleman threw his head back and laughed right out. "Now you leave that boy alone. He's all right," he said. "He doesn't bother me a bit, and if I know the answers to his questions I will answer him. And if I don't know, why, then, I'll tell him so. But he's *all right*," he said, and put his arm round Grover's shoulders. "You leave him alone. He doesn't bother me a bit."

And I can still remember how he looked that morning, with his black eyes, his black hair, and with the birthmark on his neck—so grave, so serious, so earnest-like—as he sat by the train window and watched the apple trees, the farms, the barns, the houses, and the orchards, taking it all in, I reckon, because it was strange and new to him.

It was so long ago, but when I think of it, it all comes back, as if it happened yesterday. Now all of you have either died or grown up and gone away, and nothing is the same as it was then. But all of you were there with me that morning and I guess I should remember how the others looked, but somehow I don't. Yet I can still see Grover just the way he was, the way he looked that morning when we went down through Indiana, by the river, to the Fair.

3. *The Sister*

Can you remember, Eugene, how Grover used to look? I mean the birthmark, the black eyes, the olive skin. The birthmark always showed because of those open sailor blouses kids used to wear. But I guess you must have been too young when Grover died. . . . I was looking at that old photograph the other day. You know the one I mean—that picture showing mama and papa and all of us children before the house on Woodson Street. You weren't there, Eugene. You didn't get in. You hadn't arrived when that was taken. . . . You remember how mad you used to get when we'd tell you that you were only a dishrag hanging out in Heaven when something happened?

You were the baby. That's what you get for being the baby. You don't get in the picture, do you? . . . I was looking at that old picture just the other day. There we were. And, my God, what is it all about? I mean, when you see the way we were—Daisy and Ben and Grover, Steve and all of us—

and then how everyone either dies or grows up and goes away—and then—
look at us now! Do you ever get to feeling funny? You know what I mean—do
you ever get to feeling *queer*—when you try to figure these things out? You've
been to college and you ought to know the answer—and I wish you'd tell me if
you know.

My Lord, when I think sometimes of the way I used to be—the dreams I
used to have. Playing the piano, practicing seven hours a day, thinking that
some day I would be a great pianist. Taking singing lessons from Aunt Nell
because I felt that some day I was going to have a great career in opera. . . .
Can you beat it now? Can you imagine it? *Me!* In grand opera! . . . Now I
want to ask you. I'd like to know.

My Lord! When I go uptown and walk down the street and see all these
funny-looking little boys and girls hanging around the drug store—do you
suppose any of them have ambitions the way we did? Do you suppose any of
these funny-looking little girls are thinking about a big career in opera? . . .
Didn't you ever see that picture of us? I was looking at it just the other day.
It was made before the old house down on Woodson Street, with papa standing there in his swallow-tail, and mama there beside him—and Grover, and
Ben, and Steve, and Daisy, and myself, with our feet upon our bicycles.
Luke, poor kid, was only four or five. *He* didn't have a bicycle like us. But there
he was. And there were all of us together.

Well, there I was, and my poor old skinny legs and long white dress, and
two pigtails hanging down my back. And all the funny-looking clothes we
wore, with the doo-lolley business on them. . . . But I guess you can't remember. You weren't born.

But, well, we were a right nice-looking set of people, if I do say so. And
there was "86" the way it used to be, with the front porch, the grape vines,
and the flower beds before the house—and "Miss Eliza" standing there by
papa, with a watch charm pinned upon her waist. . . . I shouldn't laugh, but
"Miss Eliza"—well, mama was a pretty woman then. Do you know what I
mean? "Miss Eliza" was a right good-looking woman, and papa in his
swallow-tail was a good-looking man. Do you remember how he used to get
dressed up on Sunday? And how grand we thought he was? And how he let
me take his money out and count it? And how rich we all thought he was?
And how wonderful that dinkey little shop on the Square looked to us? . . .
Can you beat it, now? Why we thought that papa was the biggest man in
town and—oh, you can't tell me! You can't tell me! He had his faults, but
papa was a wonderful man. You know he was!

And there was Steve and Ben and Grover, Daisy, Luke, and me lined up
there before the house with one foot on our bicycles. And I got to thinking
back about it all. It all came back.

Do you remember anything about St. Louis? You were only three or four
years old then, but you must remember something. . . . Do you remember
how you used to bawl when I would scrub you? How you'd bawl for Grover?
Poor kid, you used to yell for Grover every time I'd get you in the tub. . . .
He was a sweet kid and he was crazy about you—he almost brought you up.

That year Grover was working at the Inside Inn out on the Fair Grounds.
Do you remember the old Inside Inn? That big old wooden thing inside the

Fair? And how I used to take you there to wait for Grover when he got through working? And old fat Billy Pelham at the newsstand—how he always used to give you a stick of chewing gum?

They were all crazy about Grover. Everybody liked him. . . . And how proud Grover was of you! Don't you remember how he used to show you off? How he used to take you around and make you talk to Billy Pelham? And Mr. Curtis at the desk? And how Grover would try to make you talk and get you to say "Grover"? And you couldn't say it—you couldn't pronounce the "r." You'd say "Gova." Have you forgotten that? You shouldn't forget *that*, because—you were a *cute* kid, then—Ho-ho-ho-ho-ho—I don't know where it's gone to, but you were a big hit in those days. . . . I tell you, boy, you were Somebody back in those days.

And I was thinking of it all the other day when I was looking at that photograph. How we used to go and meet Grover there, and how he'd take us to the Midway. Do you remember the Midway? The Snake-Eater and the Living Skeleton, the Fat Woman and the Chute-the-chute, the Scenic Railway and the Ferris Wheel? How you bawled the night we took you up on the Ferris Wheel? You yelled your head off—I tried to laugh it off, but I tell you, I was scared myself. Back in those days, that was Something. And how Grover laughed at us and told us there was no danger. . . . My lord! poor little Grover. He wasn't quite twelve years old at the time, but he seemed so grown up to us. I was two years older, but I thought he knew it all.

It was always that way with him. Looking back now, it sometimes seems that it was Grover who brought us up. He was always looking after us, telling us what to do, bringing us something—some ice cream or some candy, something he had bought out of the poor little money he'd gotten at the Inn.

Then I got to thinking of the afternoon we sneaked away from home. Mama had gone out somewhere. And Grover and I got on the street car and went downtown. And my Lord, we thought that we were going Somewhere. In those days, that was what we called a *trip*. A ride in the street car was something to write home about in those days. . . . I hear that it's all built up around there now.

So we got on the car and rode the whole way down into the business section of St. Louis. We got out on Washington Street and walked up and down. And I tell you, boy, we thought that that was Something. Grover took me into a drug store and set me up to soda water. Then we came out and walked around some more, down to the Union Station and clear over to the river. And both of us half scared to death at what we'd done and wondering what mama would say if she found out.

We stayed down there till it was getting dark, and we passed by a lunch-room—an old one-armed joint with one-armed chairs and people sitting on stools and eating at the counter. We read all the signs to see what they had to eat and how much it cost, and I guess nothing on the menu was more than fifteen cents, but it couldn't have looked grander to us if it had been Delmonico's. So we stood there with our noses pressed against the window, looking in. Two skinny little kids, both of us scared half to death, getting the thrill of a lifetime out of it. You know what I mean? And smelling everything with all our might and thinking how good it all smelled. . . . Then

Grover turned to me and whispered: "Come on, Helen. Let's go in. It says fifteen cents for pork and beans. And I've got the money," Grover said. "I've got sixty cents."

I was so scared I couldn't speak. I'd never been in a place like that before. But I kept thinking, "Oh Lord, if mama should find out!" I felt as if we were committing some big crime. . . . Don't you know how it is when you're a kid? It was the thrill of a lifetime. . . . I couldn't resist. So we both went in and sat down on those high stools before the counter and ordered pork and beans and a cup of coffee. I suppose we were too frightened at what we'd done really to enjoy anything. We just gobbled it all up in a hurry, and gulped our coffee down. And I don't know whether it was the excitement—I guess the poor kid was already sick when we came in there and didn't know it. But I turned and looked at him, and he was white as death. . . . And when I asked him what was the matter, he wouldn't tell me. He was too proud. He said he was all right, but I could see that he was sick as a dog. . . . So he paid the bill. It came to forty cents—I'll never forget *that* as long as I live. . . . And sure enough, we no more than got out the door—he hardly had time to reach the curb—before it all came up.

And the poor kid was so scared and so ashamed. And what scared him so was not that he had gotten sick, but that he had spent all that money and it had come to nothing. And mama would find out. . . . Poor kid, he just stood there looking at me and he whispered: "Oh Helen, don't tell mama. She'll be mad if she finds out." Then we hurried home, and he was still white as a sheet when we got there.

Mama was waiting for us. She looked at us—you know how "Miss Eliza" looks at you when she thinks you've been doing something that you shouldn't. Mama said, "Why, where on earth have you two children been?" I guess she was all set to lay us out. Then she took one look at Grover's face. That was enough for her. She said, "Why, child, what in the world!" She was white as a sheet herself. . . . And all that Grover said was—"Mama, I feel sick."

He was sick as a dog. He fell over on the bed, and we undressed him and mama put her hand upon his forehead and came out in the hall—she was so white you could have made a black mark on her face with chalk—and whispered to me, "Go get the doctor quick, he's burning up."

And I went chasing up the street, my pigtails flying, to Dr. Packer's house. I brought him back with me. When he came out of Grover's room he told mama what to do but I don't know if she even heard him.

Her face was white as a sheet. She looked at me and looked right through me. She never saw me. And oh, my Lord, I'll never forget the way she looked, the way my heart stopped and came up in my throat. I was only a skinny little kid of fourteen. But she looked as if she was dying right before my eyes. And I knew that if anything happened to him, she'd never get over it if she lived to be a hundred.

Poor old mama. You know, he always was her eyeballs—you know that, don't you?—not the rest of us!—no, sir! I know what I'm talking about. It always has been Grover—she always thought more of him than she did of any of the others. And—poor kid!—he was a sweet kid. I can still see him lying there, and remember how sick he was, and how scared I was! I don't know why I was so scared. All we'd done had been to sneak away from home and go into a lunchroom—but I felt guilty about the whole thing, as if it was my fault.

It all came back to me the other day when I was looking at that picture, and I thought, my God, we were two kids together, and I was only two years older than Grover was, and now I'm forty-six. . . . Can you believe it? Can you figure it out—the way we grow up and change and go away? . . . And my Lord, Grover seemed so grown-up to me. He was such a quiet kid—I guess that's why he seemed older than the rest of us.

I wonder what Grover would say now if he could see that picture. All my hopes and dreams and big ambitions have come to nothing, and it's all so long ago, as if it happened in another world. Then it comes back, as if it happened yesterday. . . . Sometimes I lie awake at night and think of all the people who have come and gone, and how everything is different from the way we thought that it would be. Then I go out on the street next day and see the faces of the people that I pass. . . . Don't they look strange to you? Don't you see something funny in people's eyes, as if all of them were puzzled about something? As if they were wondering what had happened to them since they were kids? Wondering what it is that they have lost? . . . Now am I crazy, or do you know what I mean? You've been to college, Gene, and I want you to tell me if you know the answer. Now do they look that way to you? I never noticed that look in people's eyes when I was a kid—did you?

My God, I wish I knew the answer to these things. I'd like to find out what is wrong—what has changed since then—and if we have the same queer look in our eyes, too. Does it happen to us all, to everyone? . . . Grover and Ben, Steve, Daisy, Luke, and me—all standing there before that house on Woodson Street in Altamont—there we are, and you see the way we were —and how it all gets lost. What is it, anyway, that people lose?

How is it that nothing turns out the way we thought it would be? It all gets lost until it seems that it has never happened—that it is something we dreamed somewhere. . . . You see what I mean? . . . It seems that it must be something we heard somewhere—that it happened to someone else. And then it all comes back again.

And suddenly you remember just how it was, and see again those two funny, frightened, skinny little kids with their noses pressed against the dirty window of that lunchroom thirty years ago. You remember the way it felt, the way it smelled, even the strange smell in the old pantry in that house we lived in then. And the steps before the house, the way the rooms looked. And those two little boys in sailor suits who used to ride up and down before the house on tricycles. . . . And the birthmark on Grover's neck. . . . The Inside Inn. . . . St. Louis, and the Fair.

It all comes back as if it happened yesterday. And then it goes away again, and seems farther off and stranger than if it happened in a dream.

4. The Brother

"This is King's Highway," the man said.

And then Eugene looked and saw that it was just a street. There were some big new buildings, a large hotel, some restaurants and "bar-grill" places of the modern kind, the livid monotone of neon lights, the ceaseless traffic of motor cars—all this was new, but it was just a street. And he knew that it had always been just a street, and nothing more—but somehow—well, he stood there looking at it, wondering what else he had expected to find.

The man kept looking at him with inquiry in his eyes, and Eugene asked him if the Fair had not been out this way.

"Sure, the Fair was out beyond here," the man said. "Out where the park is now. But this street you're looking for—don't you remember the name of it or nothing?" the man said.

Eugene said he thought the name of the street was Edgemont, but that he wasn't sure. Anyhow it was something like that. And he said the house was on the corner of that street and of another street.

Then the man said: "What was that other street?"

Eugene said he did not know, but that King's Highway was a block or so away, and that an interurban line ran past about half a block from where he once had lived.

"What line was this?" the man said, and stared at him.

"The interurban line," Eugene said.

Then the man stared at him again, and finally, "I don't know no interurban line," he said.

Eugene said it was a line that ran behind some houses, and that there were board fences there and grass beside the tracks. But somehow he could not say that it was summer in those days and that you could smell the ties, a wooden, tarry smell, and feel a kind of absence in the afternoon after the car had gone. He only said the interurban line was back behind somewhere between the backyards of some houses and some old board fences, and that King's Highway was a block or two away.

He did not say that King's Highway had not been a street in those days but a kind of road that wound from magic out of some dim and haunted land, and that along the way it had got mixed in with Tom the Piper's son, with hot cross buns, with all the light that came and went, and with coming down through Indiana in the morning, and the smell of engine smoke, the Union Station, and most of all with voices lost and far and long ago that said "King's Highway."

He did not say these things about King's Highway because he looked about him and he saw what King's Highway was. All he could say was that the street was near King's Highway, and was on the corner, and that the interurban trolley line was close to there. He said it was a stone house, and that there were stone steps before it, and a strip of grass. He said he thought the house had had a turret at one corner, he could not be sure.

The man looked at him again, and said, "This is King's Highway, but I never heard of any street like that."

Eugene left him then, and went on till he found the place. And so at last he turned into the street, finding the place where the two corners met, the huddled block, the turret, and the steps, and paused a moment, looking back, as if the street were Time.

For a moment he stood there, waiting—for a word, and for a door to open, for the child to come. He waited, but no words were spoken; no one came.

Yet all of it was just as it had always been, except that the steps were lower, the porch less high, the strip of grass less wide, than he had thought. All the rest of it was as he had known it would be. A graystone front, three-storied, with a slant slate roof, the side red brick and windowed, still with the old arched entrance in the center for the doctor's use.

There was a tree in front, and a lamp post; and behind and to the side, more trees than he had known there would be. And all the slatey turret gables, all the slatey window gables, going into points, and the two arched windows, in strong stone, in the front room.

It was all so strong, so solid, and so ugly—and all so enduring and so good, the way he had remembered it, except he did not smell the tar, the hot and caulky dryness of the old cracked ties, the boards of backyard fences and the coarse and sultry grass, and absence in the afternoon when the street car had gone, and the twins, sharp-visaged in their sailor suits, pumping with furious shrillness on tricycles up and down before the house, and the feel of the hot afternoon, and the sense that everyone was absent at the Fair.

Except for this, it all was just the same; except for this and for King's Highway, which was now a street; except for this, and for the child that did not come.

It was a hot day. Darkness had come. The heat rose up and hung and sweltered like a sodden blanket in St. Louis. It was wet heat, and one knew that there would be no relief or coolness in the night. And when one tried to think of the time when the heat would go away, one said: "It cannot last. It's bound to go away," as we always say it in America. But one did not believe it when he said it. The heat soaked down and men sweltered in it; the faces of the people were pale and greasy with the heat. And in their faces was a patient wretchedness, and one felt the kind of desolation that one feels at the end of a hot day in a great city in America—when one's home is far away, across the continent, and he thinks of all that distance, all that heat, and feels, "Oh God! but it's a big country!"

And he feels nothing but absence, absence, and the desolation of America, the loneliness and sadness of the high, hot skies, and evening coming on across the Middle West, across the sweltering and heat-sunken land, across all the lonely little towns, the farms, the fields, the oven swelter of Ohio, Kansas, Iowa, and Indiana at the close of day, and voices, casual in the heat, voices at the little stations, quiet, casual, somehow faded into that enormous vacancy and weariness of heat, of space, and of the immense, the sorrowful, the most high and awful skies.

Then he hears the engine and the wheel again, the wailing whistle and the bell, the sound of shifting in the sweltering yard, and walks the street, and walks the street, beneath the clusters of hard lights, and by the people with sagged faces, and is drowned in desolation and in no belief.

He feels the way one feels when one comes back, and knows that he should not have come, and when he sees that, after all, King's Highway is—a street; and St. Louis—the enchanted name—a big, hot, common town upon the river, sweltering in wet, dreary heat, and not quite South, and nothing else enough to make it better.

It had not been like this before. He could remember how it would get hot, and how good the heat was, and how he would lie out in the backyard on an airing mattress, and how the mattress would get hot and dry and smell like a hot mattress full of sun, and how the sun would make him want to sleep, and how, sometimes, he would go down into the basement to feel coolness, and how the cellar smelled as cellars always smell—a cool, stale smell, the smell of cobwebs and of grimy bottles. And he could remember, when you opened the door upstairs, the smell of the cellar would come up to you—cool, musty, stale and dank and dark—and how the thought of the dark cellar always filled him with a kind of numb excitement, a kind of visceral expectancy.

He could remember how it got hot in the afternoons, and how he would feel a sense of absence and vague sadness in the afternoons, when everyone had gone away. The house would seem so lonely, and sometimes he would sit inside, on the second step of the hall stairs, and listen to the sound of silence and of absence in the afternoon. He could smell the oil upon the floor and on the stairs, and see the sliding doors with their brown varnish and the beady chains across the door, and thrust his hands among the beady chains, and gather them together in his arms, and let them clash, and swish with light beady swishings all around him. He could feel darkness, absence, varnished darkness, and stained light within the house, through the stained glass of the window on the stairs, through the small stained glasses by the door, stained light and absence, silence and the smell of floor oil and vague sadness in the house on a hot mid-afternoon. And all these things themselves would have a kind of life: would seem to wait attentively, to be most living and most still.

He would sit there and listen. He could hear the girl next door practice her piano lessons in the afternoon, and hear the street car coming by between the backyard fences, half a block away, and smell the dry and sultry smell of backyard fences, the smell of coarse hot grasses by the car tracks in the afternoon, the smell of tar, of dry caulked ties, the smell of bright worn flanges, and feel the loneliness of backyards in the afternoon and the sense of absence when the car was gone.

Then he would long for evening and return, the slant of light, and feet along the street, the sharp-faced twins in sailor suits upon their tricycles, the smell of supper and the sound of voices in the house again, and Grover coming from the Fair.

That is how it was when he came into the street, and found the place where the two corners met, and turned at last to see if Time was there. He passed the house: some lights were burning, the door was open, and a woman sat upon the porch. And presently he turned, came back, and stopped before the house again. The corner light fell blank upon the house. He stood looking at it, and put his foot upon the step.

Then he said to the woman who was sitting on the porch: "This house —excuse me—but could you tell me, please, who lives here in this house?"

He knew his words were strange and hollow, and he had not said what he wished to say. She stared at him a moment, puzzled.

Then she said: "I live here. Who are you looking for?"

He said, "Why, I am looking for——"

And then he stopped, because he knew he could not tell her what it was that he was looking for.

"There used to be a house—" he said.

The woman was now staring at him hard.

He said, "I think I used to live here."

She said nothing.

In a moment he continued, "I used to live here in this house," he said, "when I was a little boy."

She was silent, looking at him, then she said: "Oh. Are you sure this was the house? Do you remember the address?"

"I have forgotten the address," he said, "but it was Edgemont Street, and it was on the corner. And I know this is the house."

"This isn't Edgemont Street," the woman said. "The name is Bates."

"Well, then, they changed the name of the street," he said, "but this is the same house. It hasn't changed."

She was silent a moment, then she nodded: "Yes. They did change the name of the street. I remember when I was a child they called it something else," she said. "But that was a long time ago. When was it that you lived here?"

"In 1904."

Again she was silent, looking at him. Then presently: "Oh. That was the year of the Fair. You were here then?"

"Yes." He now spoke rapidly, with more confidence. "My mother had the house, and we were here for seven months. And the house belonged to Dr. Packer," he went on. "We rented it from him."

"Yes," the woman said, and nodded, "this was Dr. Packer's house. He's dead now, he's been dead for many years. But this was the Packer house, all right."

"That entrance on the side," he said, "where the steps go up, that was for Dr. Packer's patients. That was the entrance to his office."

"Oh," the woman said, "I didn't know that. I've often wondered what it was. I didn't know what it was for."

"And this big room in front here," he continued, "that was the office. And there were sliding doors, and next to it, a kind of alcove for his patients——"

"Yes, the alcove is still there, only all of it has been made into one room now—and I never knew just what the alcove was for."

"And there were sliding doors on this side, too, that opened on the hall —and a stairway going up upon this side. And half-way up the stairway, at the landing, a little window of colored glass—and across the sliding doors here in the hall, a kind of curtain made of strings of beads."

She nodded, smiling. "Yes, it's just the same—we still have the sliding doors and the stained glass window on the stairs. There's no bead curtain any more," she said, "but I remember when people had them. I know what you mean."

"When we were here," he said, "we used the doctor's office for a parlor— except later on—the last month or two—and then we used it for—a bedroom."

"It is a bedroom now," she said. "I run the house—I rent rooms—all of the rooms upstairs are rented—but I have two brothers and they sleep in this front room."

Both of them were silent for a moment, then Eugene said, "My brother stayed there too."

"In the front room?" the woman said.

He answered, "Yes."

She paused, then said: "Won't you come in? I don't believe it's changed much. Would you like to see?"

He thanked her and said he would, and he went up the steps. She opened the screen door to let him in.

Inside it was just the same—the stairs, the hallway, the sliding doors, the window of stained glass upon the stairs. And all of it was just the same, except for absence, the stained light of absence in the afternoon, and the child who once had sat there, waiting on the stairs.

It was all the same except that as a child he had sat there feeling things were *Somewhere*—and now he *knew*. He had sat there feeling that a vast and sultry river was somewhere—and now he knew! He had sat there wondering what King's Highway was, where it began, and where it ended—now he knew! He had sat there haunted by the magic word "downtown"—now he knew!—and by the street car, after it had gone—and by all things that came and went and came again, like the cloud shadows passing in a wood, that never could be captured.

And he felt that if he could only sit there on the stairs once more, in solitude and absence in the afternoon, he would be able to get it back again. Then would he be able to remember all that he had seen and been—the brief sum of himself, the universe of his four years, with all the light of Time upon it—that universe which was so short to measure, and yet so far, so endless, to remember. Then would he be able to see his own small face again, pooled in the dark mirror of the hall, and peer once more into the grave eyes of the child that he had been, and discover there in his quiet three-years' self the lone integrity of "I," knowing: "Here is the House, and here House listening; here is Absence, Absence in the afternoon; and here in this House, this Absence, is my core, my kernel—here am I!"

But as he thought it, he knew that even if he could sit here alone and get it back again, it would be gone as soon as seized, just as it had been then—first coming like the vast and drowsy rumors of the distant and enchanted Fair, then fading like cloud shadows on a hill, going like faces in a dream—coming, going, coming, possessed and held but never captured, like lost voices in the mountains long ago—and like the dark eyes and quiet face of the dark, lost boy, his brother, who, in the mysterious rhythms of his life and work, used to come into this house, then go, and then return again.

The woman took Eugene back into the house and through the hall. He told her of the pantry, told her where it was and pointed to the place, but now it was no longer there. And he told her of the backyard, and of the old board fence around the yard. But the old board fence was gone. And he told her of the carriage house, and told her it was painted red. But now there was a small garage. And the backyard was still there, but smaller than he thought, and now there was a tree.

"I did not know there was a tree," he said. "I do not remember any tree."

"Perhaps it was not there," she said. "A tree could grow in thirty years."

And then they came back through the house again and paused at the sliding doors.

"And could I see this room?" he said.

She slid the doors back. They slid open smoothly, with a rolling heaviness, as they used to do. And then he saw the room again. It was the same. There was a window at the side, the two arched windows at the front, the alcove and the sliding doors, the fireplace with the tiles of mottled green, the mantel of dark mission wood, the mantel posts, a dresser and a bed, just where the dresser and the bed had been so long ago.

"Is this the room?" the woman said. "It hasn't changed?"

He told her that it was the same.

"And your brother slept here where my brothers sleep?"

"This is his room," he said.

They were silent. He turned to go, and said, "Well, thank you. I appreciate your showing me."

She said that she was glad and that it was no trouble. "And when you see your family, you can tell them that you saw the house," she said. "My name is Mrs. Bell. You can tell your mother that a Mrs. Bell has the house now. And when you see your brother, you can tell him that you saw the room he slept in, and that you found it just the same."

He told her then that his brother was dead.

The woman was silent for a moment. Then she looked at him and said: "He died here, didn't he? In this room?"

He told her that it was so.

"Well, then," she said, "I knew it. I don't know how. But when you told me he was here, I knew it."

He said nothing. In a moment the woman said, "What did he die of?"

"Typhoid."

She looked shocked and troubled, and said involuntarily, "My two brothers——"

"That was a long time ago," he said. "I don't think you need to worry now."

"Oh, I wasn't thinking about that," she said. "It was just hearing that a little boy—your brother—was—was in this room that my two brothers sleep in now——"

"Well, maybe I shouldn't have told you then. But he was a good boy —and if you'd known him you wouldn't mind."

She said nothing, and he added quickly: "Besides, he didn't stay here long. This wasn't really his room—but the night he came back with my sister he was so sick—they didn't move him."

"Oh," the woman said, "I see." And then: "Are you going to tell your mother you were here?"

"I don't think so."

"I—I wonder how she feels about this room."

"I don't know. She never speaks of it."

"Oh. . . . How old was he?"

"He was twelve."

"You must have been pretty young yourself."

"I was not quite four."

"And—you just wanted to see the room, didn't you? That's why you came back."

"Yes."

"Well—" indefinitely—"I guess you've seen it now."

"Yes, thank you."

"I guess you don't remember much about him, do you? I shouldn't think you would."

"No, not much."

The years dropped off like fallen leaves: the face came back again—the soft dark oval, the dark eyes, the soft brown berry on the neck, the raven hair, all bending down, approaching—the whole appearing to him ghost-wise, intent and instant.

"Now say it—*Grover!*"

"Gova."

"No—not Gova—*Grover!* . . . Say it!"

"Gova."

"Ah-h—you didn't say it. You said Gova. *Grover*—now say it!"

"Gova."

"Look, I tell you what I'll do if you say it right. Would you like to go down to King's Highway? Would you like Grover to set you up? All right, then. If you say Grover and say it right, I'll take you to King's Highway and set you up to ice cream. Now say it right—*Grover!*"

"Gova."

"Ah-h, you-u. You're the craziest little old boy I ever did see. Can't you even say Grover?"

"Gova."

"Ah-h, you-u. Old Tongue-Tie, that's what you are. . . . Well, come on, then, I'll set you up anyway."

It all came back, and faded, and was lost again. Eugene turned to go, and thanked the woman and said good-bye.

"Well, then, good-bye," the woman said, and they shook hands. "I'm glad if I could show you. I'm glad if—" She did not finish, and at length she said: "Well, then, that was a long time ago. You'll find everything changed now, I guess. It's all built up around here now—and way out beyond here, out beyond where the Fair Grounds used to be. I guess you'll find it changed."

They had nothing more to say. They just stood there for a moment on the steps, and then shook hands once more.

"Well, good-bye."

And again he was in the street, and found the place where the corners met, and for the last time turned to see where Time had gone.

And he knew that he would never come again, and that lost magic would not come again. Lost now was all of it—the street, the heat, King's Highway, and Tom the Piper's son, all mixed in with the vast and drowsy murmur of the Fair, and with the sense of absence in the afternoon, and the house that waited, and the child that dreamed. And out of the enchanted wood, that thicket of man's memory, Eugene knew that the dark eye and

{ the quiet face of his friend and brother—poor child, life's stranger, and life's exile, lost like all of us, a cipher in blind mazes, long ago—the lost boy was gone forever, and would not return.

1937

Reading Suggestions

Thomas Wolfe published only two full-length novels during his lifetime: *Look Homeward, Angel* (1929) and *Of Time and the River* (1935). After his death in 1938, three additional books were mined out of the mountain of manuscript he left behind: *The Web and the Rock* (1939), *You Can't Go Home Again* (1940), and *The Hills Beyond* (1941). He also published a number of short stories, many of which were collected in *From Death to Morning* (1935).

Biographical and critical studies of Wolfe are hard to separate because so much of his fiction was autobiographical. The earliest book-length essay is Herbert J. Muller, *Thomas Wolfe* (1947), devoted to an examination of Wolfe's myth-making tendency. A well-balanced critical biography is Louis D. Rubin, *Thomas Wolfe: The Weather of His Youth* (1955). Elizabeth Nowell's *Thomas Wolfe: A Biography* (1960) provides more information than any other source, but it is strongly biased in Wolfe's favor. A careful study of Wolfe's method of composition is Richard S. Kennedy, *The Window of Memory: The Literary Career of Thomas Wolfe* (1962). Wolfe's letters provide a further source of biographical and critical information; the largest collection is *The Letters of Thomas Wolfe*, edited by Elizabeth Nowell (1956).

Articles on Wolfe have not been very numerous, especially in recent years. Some of the more interesting are E. K. Brown, "Thomas Wolfe: Realist and Symbolist," *University of Toronto Quarterly* (January 1941); Frederic I. Carpenter, "Thomas Wolfe: The Autobiography of an Idea," *University of Kansas City Review* (Summer 1946); B. R. McElderry, Jr., "The Autobiographical Problem in Thomas Wolfe's Earlier Novels," *Arizona Quarterly* (Winter 1948); and Margaret Church, "Thomas Wolfe: Dark Time," *Publications of the Modern Language Association* (September 1949).

Biography

As Thomas Wolfe brooded over his experience and the problem of expressing it in his fiction, he discerned as "two of the profoundest impulses in man" the urge to wander in quest of a father, "not merely the father of his flesh, not merely the lost father of his youth, but the image of a strength and wisdom external to his need and superior to his hunger, to which the belief and power of his own life could be united," and the equally powerful desire to return to the mother, "to the female principle . . . to the womb of earthly creation, to the earth itself, to fixity." The significance of these forces in all men is perhaps debatable, but they clearly provide the best clue to the pattern of Wolfe's life.

The matrix of that life was Asheville, North Carolina, where he was born on October 3, 1900, the son of William Oliver and Julia Elizabeth (Westall) Wolfe. The youngest of eight children, Tom was treated as the baby of the family. His mother did not wean him until he was three and a half, and refused to cut his long, curly brown hair until he was eight. While she was thus abnormally prolonging the infantile relationship, she was also responsible for splitting up the boy's home life. In April 1904, she took Tom and all but one of her other children to St. Louis, where she ran a boardinghouse during the World's Fair. When one of her sons died of typhoid fever contracted at the fairgrounds where he worked, Mrs. Wolfe returned, grief-stricken, to Asheville. Then, in 1906, she bought a large boardinghouse which she called "The Old Kentucky Home" and moved into it with all of her children except one daughter, who stayed behind in the other house to take care of her father. Thus, as Tom wrote later to one of his teachers, he was "without a home—a vagabond since I was seven—with two roofs and no home."

Wolfe's father, though he often drank heavily and was obviously difficult to live with, was idolized by the children. A stonecutter from Pennsylvania who loved to recite poetry and yearned to travel, he increasingly hated and feared property as his wife became more greedy for it. They did eventually agree that Tom had talent which must be fostered by a good education at the private North State School in Asheville.

Wolfe's first real escape from his mother and Asheville came when he completed the college preparatory course at the age of fifteen and enrolled in the fall of 1916 at the University of North Carolina. Though he was miserably lonely and confused as a freshman, his talent as a campus humorist and writer made him popular as a sophomore. He edited the campus newspaper in his last two years, enthusiastically studied Elizabethan literature, and began writing poetry and stories for the *Carolina Magazine* and one-act plays for campus production. After graduating in 1920, Wolfe persuaded his mother to send him further from home, to Harvard. Obsessed with the idea of becoming a playwright, he studied in the 47 Workshop of Professor George Pierce Baker, wrote several plays, and earned a Master's degree in English in 1922. Soon after his graduation he was called home when his father died of cancer. A final year at Harvard saw the campus production of his play, *Welcome to Our City*, but he was unable to sell his plays to Broadway producers. In January 1924, he accepted an instructorship at New York University.

The remaining fourteen years of Wolfe's life were marked by a series of departures and returns, commitments and withdrawals. Although he continued teaching at New York University until 1930, his tenure there was interrupted by leaves of absence and four trips to Europe, as he strove to reconcile his driving urge to write an endless spiritual autobiography with the need to find a literary form and the even more pressing need to make a living. Aboard the ship returning from his first trip abroad in 1925 he met Mrs. Aline Bernstein, a gifted woman almost twenty years his senior. Though she was married, had two grown children, and was half-Jewish, these obstacles failed to prevent Wolfe from falling deeply in love with her. For six years they were almost constantly together, and with her background as a stage designer in the theater she helped him realize that fiction was better suited to his genius than was drama. Finally, in 1929, his first novel, *Look Homeward, Angel*, was published, provoking violent reaction in Asheville but establishing him as a writer of great promise.

By January 1930, Wolfe had committed himself to a career as a novelist. He resigned his teaching position and, having won a Guggenheim Fellowship, he also took the first agonizing step in breaking off from Mrs. Bernstein. His closest friend and supporter was now Maxwell Perkins, who had accepted and edited *Look Homeward, Angel* for Scribner's. During the next five years Wolfe spent most of his time in Brooklyn, working furiously on an ever-growing pile of manuscript. Finally Perkins told him that this part of his work was complete and should be published as his second novel. Entitled *Of Time and the River*, it was published in March 1935, and made Wolfe famous while he was in Paris on his sixth trip abroad.

Reviewers' suggestions that he was too dependent on Perkins led to a series of quarrels, and eventually Wolfe severed his contract with Scribner's. In 1937 he returned to Asheville for the first time since the publication of *Look Homeward, Angel,* and in 1938, after contracting pneumonia during a trip to the Far West, he went to the Johns Hopkins Hospital where his father had died. Operations revealed that his brain was infected by tuberculosis germs, and he died on September 15. From the prodigious amount of manuscript left behind, three novels were published posthumously: *The Web and the Rock* (1939), *You Can't Go Home Again* (1940), and *The Hills Beyond* (1941).

The Reading Suggestions for Wolfe were prepared by Richard Adams, and the Biography by Roy Male.

WILLIAM FAULKNER ✦
1897-1962

The marks of greatness in Faulkner:

1. Significant fable or myth (the fictional world that he has constructed)

2. His idiomatic language that is original and eloquent

3. a moral significance of cosmic proportions

He refused to accept the end of man. Man he declared, is "immortal... because he has a soul, a spirit capable of compassion and sacrifice and endurance."

The writer's function is to "help man endure by lifting up his heart."

See: College English, vol. 27, No. 3, Dec. 1965 Behrens, "Faulkner's Poetic Prose; Style and Meaning in The Bear, pp. 243+,

Theme of his work: "the problems of the human heart in conflict with self."

Almost all of his work is localized in the northern part of Mississippi.

Introduction

"The study of Faulkner," declared Robert Penn Warren, "is the most challenging single task in contemporary American literature for criticism to undertake." Faulkner's legacy to the world is a shelf of twenty-four volumes of novels and stories, three fourths of them dealing with the land, people, and traditions of Yoknapatawpha (pronounced "Yoćk-na-pa-táw-fa"), a legendary Southern county whose creation is one of the great feats of the imagination in this century. Half a dozen of his fictions are modern classics, and another half dozen are of major interest. But when writing at the top of his bent he does not make easy reading. Since Warren's challenge to critics in 1946, more books and articles have been devoted to Faulkner than to any other modern American author, but there are still areas of his work that provoke controversy. It has been charged against him that his ideas are reactionary; that his style is unnecessarily complex, even tortured; that his themes are sensational, morbid, and devoid of moral meaning.

Such misconceptions obstruct full understanding of his works. Perhaps the most important one arises from the failure of readers to find his moral center, the system of values that make up his world view. This failure was curiously proved by the indifferent reception given to his eloquent Nobel Prize speech in 1950, which was generally ignored in America as irrelevant to his whole career as a creative writer. But William Faulkner was never more in earnest or more consistent than when he affirmed in Stockholm his dedication to "the problems of the human heart in conflict with itself, . . . the old universal truths lacking which any story is ephemeral and doomed—love and honor and pity and pride and compassion and sacrifice." Like a refrain the list was repeated, adding, "endurance," and again adding "courage" and "hope."

These are the same words that Hemingway's hero in A *Farewell to Arms* pronounced empty and meaningless. But to Faulkner they are "the old verities" that are alone "worth writing about, worth the agony and the

sweat." They form the moral center of his fictions. Such a list is even explicitly given in one story, *The Bear* (1942), when an older man is teaching the truths of the heart to the young hero: "honor and pride and pity
and justice and courage and love." Usually they are only implicit in his
fictions, since Faulkner is too fine an artist to be didactic. And as his vision
is essentially a tragic one, these principles serve as the point from which to
measure the protagonist's fall into violence and destruction. So his great
novels illustrate the shocking failure or distortion of love, pride, compassion, honor, or endurance—and the resulting tragedy.

I

To begin with, it seems desirable to define in general terms Faulkner's
angle of vision, his attitude toward man and society. His moral principles
seem to derive, however indirectly, from ancient Rome, from Seneca and
Cicero. This has been lost sight of since the dominant morality of the last
century is humanitarian, a troubled conscience about social injustice and a
righteous zeal to uplift the oppressed. Its aim is collective, its methods are
usually economic, and its panaceas political. Faulkner is in no sense a humanitarian. If his novels deal with these matters at all, it is indirectly and as
illustrative matter only. Instead, he is a humanist, concerned with those
classical principles of conduct formulated by the Latin moralists of the
late Republic and early Empire. A book-length study showing his specific
relation to the Ciceronian tradition of the Old South and the Senecan tradition of Elizabethan England might shed light on his rhetorical style and
dramatic techniques, as well as on his moral ideas. Meantime, one can
make a tentative exploration of the function in Faulkner's novels of those
principles of human behavior generally emphasized by the moralists of ancient Rome.

The Latin classics were widely studied in the Old South, not merely for
intellectual discipline but as literal models for the formation of character
and society. Southern culture being conservative, the tradition of the old
private academies persisted in the curriculum of the modern public school
system. At least through the first quarter of the twentieth century, the
period of Faulkner's own education, classical studies remained a standard
part of the program in the high schools of Mississippi and the state university. In the absence of biographical data, it is not known whether Faulkner
in his formal education studied Cicero's *De Finibus*, Horace's *Odes*,
Seneca's *Tragedies* and *Moral Epistles*. He may have learned them second-
hand from an uncle who was a devoted Latinist, picked them up even
more indirectly through reading Shakespeare's plays (widely influential in
the South), or simply absorbed them from the very atmosphere of that conservative society. Whatever the source, several fundamental principles of

these Latin humanists—such as *virtus, gloria, pietas,* and *integritas*—seem basic to his fictions.

The concept of *virtus* was the sum of all the excellencies of manhood, all the heroic qualities. Greatly emphasized in the military sense of bravery, gallantry, fortitude, it also included moral courage, endurance, strength of character, manliness. The concept of *gloria* signified honor and fame for glorious deeds in the service of the state, the code of the aristocracy, humility being relegated to slaves. Pride in ancestry, one of the strongest influences in Roman education, inspired the young to dedicate their lives to achieving *gloria,* thus holding patricians to high standards of conduct so they could set examples for others. *Pietas* comprised one's duty to family, religion, and country—the love, the loyalty, and the kind of patriotism that produced a proper reverence for tradition and the institutions of society. In post-Augustan times it came to include what is comprehended in the Italian *pietà,* not humanitarian pity, but compassion for the suffering lot of mankind. Finally, under the concept of *integritas* may be grouped all those virtues that make up Socrates' ideal of self-knowledge—soundness of mind, purity and integrity, moderation and self-mastery—a recognition of one's capacities, limitations, and status that led to wholeness of character and a proper relation with one's fellow man.

Occasionally Faulkner writes of the old order in the South which tried to base itself on such principles and which, according to Warren, "allowed the traditional man to define himself as human by setting up codes, concepts of virtue, obligations—and by accepting the risks of his humanity." So this inquiry will begin with *The Unvanquished* and *Intruder in the Dust* since they contain his central morality, affirmatively illustrated. These two simpler works must be understood if one is to grasp the real meaning of his tragic novels, like *The Sound and the Fury,* where such principles collapse in the chaos of the modern world. Faulkner is an authentic moralist, but as an artist he does not write "Essays to Do Good." Instead, he creates dramatic characters who are struggling to *be* good, though failure is the main pattern, since he is writing tragedy. No man in any age or place has ever really succeeded, as Faulkner well knew. The human effort is what is important to him as a novelist, because he is a humanist, not a humanitarian or any other kind of idealist. Morality to him is a method of behavior for the individual aimed at a full realization of his potential character, always of course in his relation to society. It is never a collective scheme for economic and social improvement. To do good and to be good are usually interrelated in human experience, but they are poles apart in emphasis. One aims at reforming the world, the other at reforming one's self.

Given his tragic vision, Faulkner instinctively chose the morality suited to his purposes. For it is only man's struggle within himself that makes the

essential conflict of tragedy, not his struggles with other men or with society as a whole, though these may mirror his inner struggle since the world is
his arena. As a key to Faulkner's moral significance, this view of man offers
a simple and obvious way to read him—at least one way. Perhaps it will
lead closer to his central meaning than the humanitarian critics have been
able to come, so committed to the sociological view of morality that they
are puzzled by his humanism and misinterpret his fictions. There are other
ways to go astray in reading Faulkner. Many readers have simply started
with the wrong books. Either they have read only *Sanctuary*, because they
heard it was sensational, and have been disappointed to find it is not very
spicy pornography. Or they have begun bravely with *The Sound and the
Fury*, only to bog down halfway through the very difficult first section,
which is told through the gropings of an idiot's mind.

The best introduction to Faulkner's scheme of values in the saga of
Yoknapatawpha County is *The Unvanquished*. (The author himself, as
recorded in some conversations at the University of Virginia in 1959, has
confirmed this opinion.) From the title one might fear just another in the
spate of historical romances about the Civil War, like *Gone with the Wind*.
But this is no glorification of embattled cavaliers or a lament for the "lost
cause." The theme of *The Unvanquished* is the education of young Bayard Sartoris in the code of the Old South during a time of crisis and his effort to carry it over revitalized into an era of defeat. Family solidarity, loyalty to community, and devotion to country are intuitively felt in this
traditional order, without need of exposition. From his grandmother, filling
a man's role on the home front, the teenage hero learns much: her pride of
status and function as a member of the leader class, her simple acts of courage and endurance, her compassion for the plight of the freed slaves, her
unquestioning love which leads in the end to sacrificing her life.

Quite naturally, however, the hero's father, Colonel Sartoris, serves as
the shining exemplar, and also as a warning. In a much earlier novel, entitled *Sartoris*, the flaw in the family character is fully displayed in the reckless courage that Faulkner calls, in satirical allusion to the romantic hero of
the *Song of Roland*, "a glamorous fatality, like silver pennons downrushing
at sunset, or a dying fall of horns along the road to Roncevaux." The Romans also had been aware of the paradox of pride in *gloria*, which could
lead to heroic deeds of the first magnitude or to exhibitionism and vainglory. The Colonel is an embodiment of this ambiguous pride. From him
the son learns the bravery and skill of a born leader, who serves his people
selflessly during Reconstruction as well as in battle. But he is also an archetype of the leader whose role has been subverted by total war. His capacities
for leadership tempt him to make his private will into the law; what had
been daring in martial exploits becomes a habit of violence, with continued
killings even in peacetime. The final test of young Bayard's education comes
several years after the war when, as a student at the University, he receives

news that the Colonel has been murdered. Riding home, the hero knows what will be expected of him, to avenge his father's honor according to the code. In the first flush of manhood, he moves unfalteringly to his own interpretation of the tradition, and his action is accepted by all as equally effective as the *duello* in upholding honor, while at the same time more moral and more courageous. (This is the story told in the concluding episode, "An Odor of Verbena," further commentary on which appears below just before the selection itself.)

Such is the meaning of *The Unvanquished*, as well as it can be illustrated by extraction. Yet this book has been berated by a humanitarian critic as "a trivial sketch of adolescent adventure [and] coltish anecdotes." Though not one of Faulkner's major novels, it contains the central affirmation of his humanism, his fullest and clearest rendering of the moral principles in the tradition of the Old South. The Sartoris family during the period of the Civil War are responsible human beings who represent a vital morality and a sense of social obligation. Opposed to them are the codeless Snopeses, who appear once in this novel with tragic effect, representing the naturalistic forces disruptive of society—like the war itself. In between are the Negroes and small farmers. Thus all elements of his complex social scheme are sketched in, and the main lines of tension are drawn between his two worlds: the world of traditional order versus that of materialism and anarchy. In terms of the Latin concepts these stories are filled with acts of compassion and demonstrations of integrity; and since this a book about war, especially *virtus* and *gloria*. Here in full measure are pride in ancestry and heroic deeds, honor in the service of home and homeland—the patrician code that the main characters strive, however imperfectly, to live up to. But the glamour of battle is kept off stage and the martial note muted, so that the humanistic tradition here portrayed is fully applicable to the tragic novels laid in modern times.

The other chief statement of Faulkner's principles is *Intruder in the Dust*. Set in the present, 1948, it is a sufficient answer to the charge of nostalgia often leveled against Faulkner, the charge that the only efficient moral order he can conjure up for the South is in a romantic vision of the past. And it is supplementary to *The Unvanquished* rather than merely a modern restatement of its code. Courage and heroic achievement, it is true, play an impressive part in the outer plot of *Intruder in the Dust* also. This is concerned with the threatened lynching of a Negro, wrongly accused of murdering a white man, and the prevention of this crime by responsible members of the community, chief of whom is young Charles Mallison. But this episode is merely the catalytic agent that precipitates the real story, the education of a sixteen-year-old boy in good and evil and the preservation of his spiritual integrity. He accomplishes this by discovering the meaning of his heritage in a long Socratic dialogue with his uncle, Gavin Stevens, that incloses the dramatic action and interprets it. So, the inner theme is concerned with *integritas* and *pietas*—compassion for the suffering lot of mankind and loyalty to one's own sense of honor, that of his class, and of his community. Since this novel is not a tragedy but a story of rediscovery and regeneration, there is no flaw in the hero in the sense of a total failure of any of these virtues, though the characters are marked by an inadequate possession of them.

II

The full range of Faulkner's genius is brought into play only when his tragic vision is focused on the abdication of principles. Then his many-voiced prose laments like a Jeremiah, "How the mighty have fallen!" or is uplifted in appalled shriek at man's inherent capacity for evil. The tragedy that can be precipitated by a total failure of *pietas* is unforgettably rendered in the violence of *Light in August,* set in the 1930's. The sense of community is strongly felt in this novel, but it is in the background unshared by the main actors in a complex drama. The scene is the same town of Jefferson (Oxford) where the hero of *Intruder in the Dust* found his true relation to tradition, but such redeeming figures as he are off stage. The principal characters who act and suffer before the footlights are all outside the community in one way or another. In its threefold plot structure this novel dramatizes the theme of isolation by a series of collisions between virtual strangers. The downward plunge of Joe Christmas holds the center of the stage. The murder of his white mistress by this man, who does not even know whether or not he has Negro blood, and his brutal lynching by a mob make him the most alienated figure in Yoknapatawpha. Only slightly less so is the Reverend Hightower, who a quarter century before had retreated from the risk of human involvement into an absurd nostalgia for the glories of the Southern past. In spite of his efforts to isolate himself from modern violence, however, he is drawn into the horrible death of Christmas at the end and dies himself from shock.

Set against all this agony is the pastoral subplot of Lena Grove. She alone has an intuitive devotion to home and family, though she is the one most completely deprived of them. Her long search for the runaway father of her unborn child brings her to Jefferson just as the tragedies are closing in. There this natural mother is made "light" of her burden in August and wins the love of Byron Bunch, a migratory laborer. Only this couple escapes from the chaos of a fragmented world to begin their long pilgrimage back to the normal life of society. Through them the community is, by implication, pervasively suggested as the proper field for human action. They furnish the background against which is enacted a triple tragedy resulting from the failure of *pietas*. In similar manner, it could be shown that most of Faulkner's fictions yield their fullest meaning when read in terms of a humanistic morality. This brief survey permits only a concluding examination of two interrelated tragedies, generally considered his masterpieces.

Absalom, Absalom! is Faulkner's fullest rendering of tragedy in the Old South. The focus of dramatic interest is a fable that is fascinating in its accumulation of horrors, the career of the hero-villain Thomas Sutpen, spanning almost the entire nineteenth century. As an ignorant mountain boy he had suffered humiliation at the hands of a liveried slave, in a big plantation house in Virginia, symbol of a complex society he did not understand. Having no moral code of his own by which he could avenge an injured pride, he simply dedicated his life to the grandiose design of founding a dynasty; he would provide his children with the status, wealth, and prestige he never had—a lack that had made him vulnerable. In his pioneer "innocence" of the meaning of a traditional order he exalted his purposes above society, not because he hated it but because he ignored it as outside his design. Thus the history of the house of Sutpen becomes mere compulsive striving after *gloria* for its own sake.

Sutpen's ruthlessness is illustrated by his first marriage, contracted in the West Indies entirely for riches and prestige, and canceled without realization of his inhumanity when he discovered the taint of Negro blood. Wife and son were thrust aside, with a mere money settlement, lest his ambitious plans be endangered. Then with immense recuperative powers he began all over again his fanatical drive to rise to the top in Southern society, and by the outbreak of the Civil War he had achieved high estate: the wealthiest planter in Yoknapatawpha County, seated in the most pretentious mansion, with heirs of unquestioned lineage. But the vainglory of this striving is matched by his colossal inhumanity at the climactic reappearance of his mulatto son, who asked only for recognition of his kinship. For Sutpen, however, it was unthinkable to let human emotions enter into his mechanically abstract design. His refusal precipitated disaster among all his progeny, including threatened incest and actual fratricide. Meantime, his perseverance in his passion to dominate men and retrieve his worldly power was all but magnificent, both during the Civil War and after. But the folly of his ambition overtook him at last. His plantation was now in ruins, his rejected son dead, his beloved son disowned, and his daughter wasting away in the spinsterhood he had forced on her. In a final bid for a male heir at any cost, he stooped to seducing the granddaughter of his overseer, spurned her when she gave birth to a girl, and was brutally murdered with a scythe for his baseness. Forty years later retribution overtook even the haunted old house he had built at Sutpen's Hundred in a holocaust that consumed his remaining descendants, half-breed as well as white, so that not even a physical vestige was left of his once grand design.

Such is the outer plot, but not the inner theme. For young Quentin Compson, who fits the pieces of this puzzle together in 1910, it is an incredible nightmare that he desperately seeks to understand, thinking it a representative part of his Southern tradition. As the consciousness through which the fragments of Sutpen's wild story are given order and meaning, he becomes the center of dramatic revelation in *Absalom, Absalom!* After tortured probings, Quentin discovers in this violent career one of the evil forces that upholders of the Old Order in the South had tried to keep in check, though one weakness of their system was its inability to control exploiters, especially those who rose from the poor-white class by ruthless ambition. His own grandfather, General Compson, was typical of his heritage —not Thomas Sutpen. On the surface Sutpen flashed the semblance of many aristocratic virtues, but there was no moral core within. For him, *virtus* never rose above physical courage and endurance. His military exploits in the Civil War were not an expression of *pietas* but of a dangerously individualistic and dehumanized heroism. He distorted *gloria* into vainglory, pride in heroic achievement purely to further his personal ambition. Family, community, and country were made subservient to his ruthless will. Too obsessed with his selfish purposes to live by principles, he was the embodiment of an abstract evil that drove him to his doom.

To Quentin, at first, Sutpen seems like a true tragic hero—a protagonist set apart from his fellow men, with high ambitions and a strong will, who fought against his fate and failed only through an inner flaw. But this flaw was not the result of an excessive and undisciplined virtue, as in the heroes of Greek tragedy. It was his ambition to own and dominate men. He was a Macbeth without the power of self-examination. His appalling lack of self-knowledge made him incapable of that tearing out of pride which forms the cleansing ritual of tragedy. To Quentin's grandfather he had said with astonishing innocence, "Whether it was a good or a bad design is beside the point; the question is, 'Where did I make my mistake in it?'" This refusal to accept moral responsibility for the consequences of his fall is central to the meaning of Sutpen's career, making it the negation of the Sartoris tradition. This is what turns Quentin's interest away from the satanic hero to his victims. In the plight of Sutpen's children, who were capable of love and a sense of family until their father destroyed it, Quentin discovers that life in the past (his past) had human value. He learns, as well as any of Faulkner's characters, that "self-knowledge is essentially an awareness of tradition." To place such a frightening phenomenon as Thomas Sutpen in the understandable context of human history is "a continually necessary act . . . of humanistic faith," as one critic has put it. But Quentin's agonizing search for the virtues in his Southern heritage, so he can define himself in relation to it, comes too late; understanding it is beyond his capacity.

This is the theme of *The Sound and the Fury,* Faulkner's greatest tragedy set in the modern South. If *Absalom* illustrates the fall of the hero in his pride through the distortion of *gloria,* the sequel records the collapse of the house of Compson through a failure of *virtus.* The link between the two novels is Quentin Compson, one of the four children through whose consciousness the reader witnesses the deterioration of a family once the peer of the Sartorises. Quentin's disillusionment derives from the spiritual emptiness of his mother, who clings whimperingly to her pride of status as a born lady, and from the whisky and words which his father substitutes for pride of function as an aristocratic leader. Thumbing his Latin classics as a pretended source of his cynicism, he fills his son's ears with such nihilisms as "man is conceived by accident and [his] every breath is a fresh cast with dice already loaded against him"—thus shouldering off on a blind fate his moral responsibility.

The son struggles to work his way through all this quicksand back to the bedrock of the old tradition. But the constant opposition of the Snopes world of ruthless materialism has put the Sartoris world on the defensive, and tended to formalize one aspect after another of their code until it has lost vitality. Quentin finally penetrates the meaning of Sutpen's story sufficiently to separate it from his own heritage. But without adequate tutors he can find for himself only a pseudotradition by which to live—or rather to die, for he is in love with death. In his obsessive concern with his sister's honor, he convinces himself that he has actually committed incest with her and takes the weak way out through suicide, in the insane notion that he could thus cast them both into hell "where he could guard her forever and keep her intact amid the eternal fires." A Hamlet figure in his vacillation and lack of purpose, he yet lacks the strength of mind and character to face a world out of joint.

By contrast, his sister Caddy has a kind of elemental vitality, but at maturity it expresses itself only in a nymphomania which propels her into sheer promiscuousness, without even the compensation of sexual pleasure. In her crisis the family's weakness is nakedly revealed. The parents patch up a dishonest marriage as a cover for respectability, the idiot Benjy wails, Quentin offers his quixotic insistence that he has fathered her illegitimate child, and another son makes use of the scandal to extort money from her. This one, Jason, is the strongest of them all, but his strength is only animal cunning. Though born a Compson, he becomes a Snopes in acquisitiveness, turns against his whole heritage, and with undisguised pleasure watches his own family fall to pieces. He is a negation of all the old virtues of *pietas, gloria, integritas,* and the ironic inversion of *virtus.*

Jason's final insult to the family consists in committing to the insane asylum, at the age of thirty-three, the youngest brother Benjamin, born an idiot. The reader is now prepared to reread this difficult first section, Benjy's version of the Compson history, and fathom at last the full meaning of this tale told by an idiot, which gives not only the anguish but the very title to a tragic novel full to overflowing with sound and fury. The most brilliant piece of experimental prose ever undertaken in America, this opening section is too complex an achievement stylistically to fall within the limits of this inquiry. It is enough to say that Faulkner creates the illusion of taking us into the "mind" of an idiot where, for a hundred pages, we experience his past through his sensations remembered without benefit of language. Yet the tangled events of the family history caught in the spider web of Benjy's memory reveal more than do Quentin's agonized efforts to understand. This is the nucleus of the book, foreshadowing the whole in miniature, and beneath its forbidding surface recording the tragedy of a family's disintegration. The ironic suggestion that love and loyalty can survive only in an idiot is perhaps too extreme for literal acceptance. But Benjy at least stands for the collapse of the Compson mind, no longer with sufficient stamina to live in the realities of the world, just as the others represent the Compsons' physical, moral, and spiritual chaos. His castration, contrived by Jason, is the final symbol of the family's loss of the estate of manhood.

III

There are wide social implications in these fictions, suggesting Faulkner's lament over the passing of a traditional order in the South and his horror at the disorder of the modern world. But though his novels are placed in the context of Southern history, too sweeping a sociological interpretation will lead to false conclusions. It should be remembered, for example, that the survival of values in *The Unvanquished* comes chronologically after Sutpen's debacle, and the rediscovery of a tradition by the hero of *Intruder in the Dust* comes two decades after the fall of the house of Compson. Faulkner chose the South for his setting, characters, and events for two strictly literary reasons. As the region and history he knew best, he could render it with precision and vivid immediacy. As the locale of a conservative civilization which lasted right down to 1914, it offered a dramatic contrast with the modern world for authors like him who had just come of age in that time and place. The suddenness of the break with a traditional past after World War I, according to Allen Tate, "gave us the Southern renascence, a literature conscious of the past in the present." Though the South is Faulkner's subject, his theme is the condition of man today and through the ages. So Yoknapatawpha should not be taken as a county in Mississippi but as a microcosm of the modern world.

Similarly, the moral principles of the Latin humanists should not be used for a doctrinaire reading of his fictions, but only as a general approach to avoid misconceptions. Since Faulkner was an artist, the final way to his meanings will be through analysis of the language, imagery, and structure of each novel and story. This will be a long and arduous task, and only a few suggestions can be made here. Again *The Unvanquished* is a good place to start, because it lacks the complexities of his more ambitious books. Its style seems as free of radical experimentation as that of Fitzgerald, for example, yet as undeniably modern. Its dramatic concise-

ness and freshness of phrasing put it miles beyond the conventional historical romance, with hackneyed language and inflated narrative. For one
thing, though Faulkner had a real gift for storytelling, his emphasis is not
on events but their effect on his characters. This leads him to a concern
with the inside rather than the outside of his story, and style tends to follow theme in key places. This is notably true in "An Odor of Verbena,"
where the young hero is responding to the impact of the climactic event in
his life and trying to put it in relation with past events. In his search for
meaning and self-knowledge he falls into ruminative sentences that run
almost a page in length, exploratory flash-backs, and involved interior
monologues.

So, in spite of the apparent straightforwardness of its surface, *The Unvanquished* contains the germ of some of Faulkner's most experimental
styles. (It is not a question of development, since this story was written
after his three most notable experiments in language.) It is only a step
from the closing pages of this book to the stream of consciousness used with
such varied skills in *The Sound and the Fury*, the poetic evocativeness of
As I Lay Dying, and the soaring rhetoric and agonized involutions of *Absalom, Absalom!* But in these great tragedies the truth sought is so elusive,
in the final analysis such an insoluble mystery, that Faulkner developed for
his purposes the most radical techniques of linguistic exploration ever used
by a novelist in English, outside of Joyce; and they make the utmost demands on the reader's powers of comprehension. To these high complexities of style it may be only a step, but it is a long step, and their sparing use
in *The Unvanquished*, because its meaning is more patent, makes it a
much easier book to grasp.

One of the most interesting features of this simpler novel is its structure. Faulkner approached the novel as the most flexible of forms, and
played with its possibilities in all directions. His most daring experiment
was to take two stories utterly unrelated as to characters and events, and
publish them together in alternating chapters as a single book, *The Wild
Palms*, on the theory that their contrasting themes would make an effective counterpoint: giving up all for love, and refusing love at all costs.
Then, apparently deciding he had gone too far, he extracted one of them
and published it separately as a short novel, *The Old Man*. Again, his famous novelette "The Bear" was first published in a magazine with Parts I,
II, III, and V only. Then, when this story was included in *Go Down,
Moses* (1942), the long and difficult Part IV was inserted to link its
meaning with the other stories of Negro-White relations in that volume;
but it was withdrawn again when "The Bear" was grouped with a series of
hunting stories in *Big Woods* (1955). Faulkner's most effective experiments with structure are equally radical. In *The Sound and the Fury* the
same story is told four times from four distinct points of view, each retelling
adding a new dimension of understanding. In *Light in August* three dis-

tinct plots are interlocked by accidental collisions between their several casts of characters, then brought into focus by the author's omniscience to illuminate a common theme: the presence or absence of a sense of community. In *Absalom, Absalom!* fragments and contradictory parts of a story lost in the past are presented by several voices, then fitted together into a comprehensive whole by two modern narrators.

The structure of *The Unvanquished* is not nearly so radical, but it has some strikingly original features. There is some question as to when and how it took shape in Faulkner's mind as a novel, since the first six parts were published separately during 1935-1936. The seventh part was never printed until it was added as the concluding episode to the others, when they were collected out of magazine files and published as a book in 1938. The most obvious unity of the whole is that setting and characters are the same, and the events come in sequence. The first six follow each other closely, during the last two years of the Civil War, when the hero is in his teens; the seventh is laid in the 1870's, near the end of Reconstruction, when he is a mature man of twenty-four. This last is a long jump that calls for explanation.

One way in which the gap is bridged is that the earlier stories, though set in the Civil War, are not concerned with battles and soldiers except in a peripheral way. Faulkner knew that this was the first "total war" in Western history, breaking the Christian convention that limited war to the armies in combat; so his focus is on its effect on the home front, the destruction of an entire society. Hence, though "An Odor of Verbena" comes eight to ten years later, this time lapse was necessary to show the final impact of that war in the collapse of the code of behavior that held the South together, symbolized ironically in its least defensible form, the *duello*. Another important way in which the theme of total war affects the book's unity is that its scene, Mississippi, is both historically and dramatically right. The moment when the Civil War took its turn in this direction was when Grant and Sherman were put in Federal command. *The Unvanquished* begins with the siege of Vicksburg, the springboard of the former's rise to power; the fifth part ends when the Union Army under the latter has finished its depredations in Mississippi and is starting its famous March to the Sea. The last two parts deal with the wreckage that total war leaves behind.

Far more pertinent to the structural unity of *The Unvanquished*, and another bridge over the gap in time, is the fact that each of its seven episodes can be interpreted as a dramatic rendering of one of those moral principles to which Faulkner pledged his dedication in the Nobel Prize speech. The first six symbolize courage, pride, compassion, sacrifice, honor, and endurance. The experiences undergone by the teenage hero during the testing time of war, and the examples set for him by his elders, were part of his education in these principles. But he was too young then to grasp their full import, or to see how they could be salvaged when the social order they were part of had collapsed. After maturity, in "An Odor of Verbena," he surveys them all as a new crisis arises with respect to the most ambiguous and formalized of them all, the code of honor, and the closely related concept of pride. For highlighting these two, Faulkner uses a special technique that has been called the device of the "frozen moment." This is what Sartre had in mind when commenting on his use of the suspension of time: "Faulkner appears to arrest the motion at the very heart of things; moments erupt and freeze, then fade, recede and diminish, still motionless."

In the second episode, "Retreat," the ambiguous pride of the young hero's chief exemplar, his father, is preserved in the most vivid image of Colonel Sartoris recorded in *The Unvanquished*. It is the moment of his escape from the encircling enemy in a brilliant leap on horseback through the latticed doors of his own stable. As they explode into splinters the action is virtually arrested in mid-air, by adroit phrasing, symbolizing the cavalry leader's pride in his skillful horsemanship. However, it is pride not in victory but in a daring escape, with the resulting irony and the note of doom sounded. In the concluding episode about ten years later, "An Odor of Verbena," the concomitant principle of avenging the honor of his murdered father is invoked. The dramatic scene that fixes itself in the memory and symbolizes the meaning of this story is Faulkner's boldest use of the "frozen moment." For he gives it twice, in almost identical language: once as the now mature hero foresees it during the homeward ride, and again when it actually happens on his arrival. His father's regiment, mounted and in full uniform, waiting in the front yard; the old body servant standing beside the coffin where the Colonel lies in his regimentals; his stepmother, radiant in a yellow ball gown, presenting him a pair of dueling pistols. It is this freezing and framing of the scene that gives the effect of Bayard's being all but paralyzed by the stage trappings of the old code, and that heightens the drama of his refusing the *duello* as unsuited to the new age.

There is one other time strategy used in *The Unvanquished* that affects its structure. This is the long flash back in "An Odor of Verbena" that serves a dual purpose. By capsule memory flashes of the earlier episodes it links them to this later one, clarifies their meaning, and so knits the whole into a loosely unified novel. At the same time, by supplying the reader with the core of what he needs to know about the preceding events, it enables "An Odor of Verbena" to stand by itself as a separate story. With these exceptions, *The Unvanquished* employs the chronicle form of the conventional narrative. This is a far cry from Faulkner's radical maneuvering of time in his more experimental fictions. For example, in Part IV of "The Bear" the cryptic ledger entries enable the hero at age twenty-one to project himself backward through fifty years of his family's secret history and forward into a vision of his own future. In *Absalom, Absalom!* the two organizers of Sutpen's stormy history are forced, in 1910, to range back through the whole nineteenth century, following as best they can the disordered way in which bits and pieces of it have come down to them through several oral accounts. In *The Sound and the Fury*, time is chaotically scrambled in Benjy's section to create an illusion of the free association of sensations that constitute the memory process in an idiot's "mind"; and it is stopped dead in the deliberately broken watch, symbolizing Quentin's obsession to escape out of time altogether, which he finally does by suicide. The more conventional handling of time in *The Unvanquished*, since its meaning is less complex, is another of the reasons why it is easier to read.

Finally, the imagery in this novel is less pervasive and certainly less ambivalent. There is nothing comparable to the intricate variations on skin color in *Absalom, Absalom!* representing the attraction-repulsion that racial mixture holds for Sutpen, or the juxtaposed images of the "great house" that symbolize his "design." There is nothing like the Freudian suggestiveness of fence and flower, graveyard and golf ball, for Benjy in *The Sound and the Fury*, or the sexual symbolism of honeysuckle for Quentin and muddy drawers for Caddy in the same novel. Yet the use of images in *The Unvanquished* is more elaborate than might be thought at first reading. The reader will be able to work out for himself the effective use of martial paraphernalia to bring constantly to mind the war which is otherwise kept off stage; of the cavalier on horseback to symbolize the leader class in an ordered society; of the man-and-mule, linked by the plow to earth, as an image of the agrarian way of life.

Such images function throughout the novel in a rather obvious though effective way, and there are quite enough to make the search rewarding. But there is a more complex one, confined to "An Odor of Verbena" and furnishing its title, that calls for commentary. This is the sprig of verbena associated with Drusilla, the scent of which she could smell "above the smell of horses and courage." It is woven in and out of the text with multiple suggestions of submerged meaning. Once Faulkner gives a clue to its classical origin when describing her in the climactic frozen moment: "Drusilla would be waiting for me . . . , the balancing sprig of verbena above each ear, . . . the Greek amphora priestess of a succinct and formal violence." On Grecian urns the priestess is often represented garlanding her victim with verbena for the ritual occasion—just as Drusilla put a sprig of it in Bayard's lapel before his confrontation of his father's murderer and another on his pillow afterward, in spite of his bypassing the traditional code. In the Latin writers Faulkner could have found numerous examples of the sacrificial use of verbena to enrich this symbol's appropriateness to his purposes. In Horace's *Odes* (IV. 11. 6-8), for a festival celebrating the birth of Venus: "the altar, wreathed with sacred leafage [*verbenis*], yearns to be sprinkled with the blood of an offered lamb." In Ovid's *Metamorphoses* (VII. 240-242), Medea built altars to Hecate and to

Youth, "wreathed . . . with boughs from the wild wood [*verbenis sil-vaque*]," then performed a ritual sacrifice to restore her old husband to young life. In Virgil's *Eclogues* (VIII. 64-67), a neglected shepherdess burns at her shrine "rich herbs [*verbenas*] and male frankincense, that I may try with magic rites to turn to fire my lover's coldness of mood." [1]

From such clues the student may find suggestions for interpreting the enigmatic character of Drusilla, the Southern lady who symbolically un-sexed herself by cropping her hair, wearing pants, and riding as a soldier in Colonel Sartoris' troop. Also for unraveling her ambiguous relations with her stepson—she had forced him to kiss her in the garden while she "melted as women will and can"; then a few weeks later, histrionically and almost hysterically, she tried to send him to an almost certain doom as the avenger of her husband's (his father's) honor. *The Unvanquished* may be simple enough to make an easy introduction to Faulkner, but it is a richer novel than has been thought and also complex enough to prepare the reader for other and greater complexities in the more ambitious novels. And its clear affirmation of the central principles in Faulkner's view of man should pre-vent misconceptions—should keep the collapse of these principles in the tragedies from seeming like meaningless violence. His whole meaning can be arrived at only by close reading of his major fictions, and by reading them as works of art rather than of sociology.

CHARLES R. ANDERSON

A Note on the Text.   The text here followed for "An Odor of Verbena" is that of the first edition of *The Unvanquished* (New York: Random House, Inc., 1938); for the Nobel Prize Speech, the brochure issued by Random House and the Spiral Press in March 1951; for Faulkner's Com-ments on his Novels, that of *Faulkner in the University*, edited by L. Gwynn and Joseph L. Blotner (Charlottesville: University of Virginia Press, 1959).

AN ODOR OF VERBENA

1

IT WAS JUST after supper. I had just opened my *Coke* on the table beneath the lamp; I heard Professor Wilkins' feet in the hall and then the instant of

[1] All translations are from the editions in the Loeb Classical Library.

silence as he put his hand to the doorknob, and I should have known. People talk glibly of presentiment, but I had none. I heard his feet on the stairs and then in the hall approaching and there was nothing in the feet because although I had lived in his house for three college years now and although both he and Mrs. Wilkins called me Bayard in the house, he would no more have entered my room without knocking than I would have entered his—or hers. Then he flung the door violently inward against the doorstop with one of those gestures with or by which an almost painfully unflagging preceptory of youth ultimately aberrates, and stood there saying, "Bayard. Bayard, my son, my dear son."

I should have known; I should have been prepared. Or maybe I was prepared because I remember how I closed the book carefully, even marking the place, before I rose. He (Professor Wilkins) was doing something, bustling at something; it was my hat and cloak which he handed me and which I took although I would not need the cloak, unless even then I was thinking (although it was October, the equinox had not occurred) that the rains and the cool weather would arrive before I should see this room again and so I would need the cloak anyway to return to if it I returned, thinking "God, if he had only done this last night, flung that door crashing and bouncing against the stop last night without knocking so I could have gotten there before it happened, been there when it did, beside him on whatever spot, wherever it was that he would have to fall and lie in the dust and dirt."

"Your boy is downstairs in the kitchen," he said. It was not until years later that he told me (someone did; it must have been Judge Wilkins) how Ringo had apparently flung the cook aside and come on into the house and into the library where he and Mrs. Wilkins were sitting and said without preamble and already turning to withdraw: "They shot Colonel Sartoris this morning. Tell him I be waiting in the kitchen," and was gone before either of them could move. "He has ridden forty miles yet he refuses to eat anything." We were moving toward the door now—the door on my side of which I had lived for three years now with what I knew, what I knew now I must have believed and expected, yet beyond which I had heard the approaching feet yet heard nothing in the feet. "If there was just anything I could do."

"Yes, sir," I said. "A fresh horse for my boy. He will want to go back with me."

"By all means take mine—Mrs. Wilkins'," he cried. His tone was no different yet he did cry it and I suppose that at the same moment we both realized that was funny—a short-legged, deep barrelled mare who looked exactly like a spinster music teacher, which Mrs. Wilkins drove to a basket phaeton—which was good for me, like being doused with a pail of cold water would have been good for me.

"Thank you, sir," I said. "We won't need it. I will get a fresh horse for him at the livery stable when I get my mare." Good for me, because even before I finished speaking I knew that would not be necessary either, that Ringo would have stopped at the livery stable before he came out to the college and attended to that and that the fresh horse for him and my mare both would be saddled and waiting now at the side fence and we would not have to go through Oxford at all. Loosh would not have thought of that if he had come for me, he would have come straight to the college, to Professor Wilkins', and told his news and then sat down and let me take charge from then on. But not Ringo.

He followed me from the room. From now until Ringo and I rode away into the hot, thick, dusty darkness, quick and strained for the overdue equinox like a laboring delayed woman, he would be somewhere either just beside me or just behind me and I never to know exactly nor care which. He was trying to find the words with which to offer me his pistol too. I could almost hear him: "Ah, this unhappy land, not ten years recovered from the fever yet still men must kill one another, still we must pay Cain's price in his own coin." But he did not actually say it. He just followed me, somwehere beside or behind me as we descended the stairs toward where Mrs. Wilkins waited in the hall beneath the chandelier—a thin gray woman who reminded me of Granny, not that she looked like Granny probably but because she had known Granny—a lifted anxious still face which was thinking *Who lives by the sword shall die by it* just as Granny would have thought, toward which I walked, had to walk not because I was Granny's grandson and had lived in her house for three college years and was about the age of her son when he was killed in almost the last battle nine years ago, but because I was now The Sartoris. (The Sartoris: that had been one of the concomitant flashes, along with the *at last it has happened* when Professor Wilkins opened my door.) She didn't offer me a horse and pistol, not because she liked me any less than Professor Wilkins but because she was a woman and so wiser than any man, else the men would not have gone on with the War for two years after they knew they were whipped. She just put her hands (a small woman, no bigger than Granny had been) on my shoulders and said, "Give my love to Drusilla and your Aunt Jenny. And come back when you can."

"Only I don't know when that will be," I said. "I don't know how many things I will have to attend to." Yes, I lied even to her; it had not been but a minute yet since he had flung that door bouncing into the stop yet already I was beginning to realize, to become aware of that which I still had no yardstick to measure save that one consisting of what, despite myself, despite my raising and background (or maybe because of them) I had for some time known I was becoming and had feared the test of it; I remember how I thought while her hands still rested on my shoulders: *At least this will be my chance to find out if I am what I think I am or if I just hope; if I am going to do what I have taught myself is right or if I am just going to wish I were.*

We went on to the kitchen, Professor Wilkins still somewhere beside or behind me and still offering me the pistol and horse in a dozen different ways. Ringo was waiting; I remember how I thought then that no matter what might happen to either of us, I would never be The Sartoris to him. He was twenty-four too, but in a way he had changed even less than I had since that day when we had nailed Grumby's body to the door of the old compress. Maybe it was because he had outgrown me, had changed so much that summer while he and Granny traded mules with the Yankees that since then I had had to do most of the changing just to catch up with him. He was sitting quietly in a chair beside the cold stove, spent-looking too who had ridden

WILLIAM FAULKNER

forty miles (at one time, either in Jefferson or when he was alone at last on the road somewhere, he had cried; dust was now caked and dried in the tear-channels on his face) and would ride forty more yet would not eat, looking up at me a little red-eyed with weariness (or maybe it was more than just weariness and so I would never catch up with him) then rising without a word and going on toward the door and I following and Professor Wilkins still offering the horse and the pistol without speaking the words and still thinking (I could feel that too) *Dies by the sword. Dies by the sword.*

Ringo had the two horses saddled at the side gate, as I had known he would—the fresh one for himself and my mare father had given me three years ago, that could do a mile under two minutes any day and a mile every eight minutes all day long. He was already mounted when I realized that what Professor Wilkins wanted was to shake my hand. We shook hands; I knew he believed he was touching flesh which might not be alive tomorrow night, and I thought for a second how if I told him what I was going to do, since we had talked about it, about how if there was anything at all in the Book, anything of hope and peace for His blind and bewildered spawn which He had chosen above all others to offer immortality, *Thou shalt not kill* must be it, since maybe he even believed that he had taught it to me, except that he had not, nobody had, not even myself, since it went further than just having been learned. But I did not tell him. He was too old to be forced so, to condone even in principle such a decision; he was too old to have to stick to principle in the face of blood and raising and background, to be faced without warning and made to deliver like by a highwayman out of the dark: only the young could do that—one still young enough to have his youth supplied him gratis as a reason (not an excuse) for cowardice.

So I said nothing. I just shook his hand and mounted too, and Ringo and I rode on. We would not have to pass through Oxford now and so soon (there was a thin sickle of moon like the heel print of a boot in wet sand) the road to Jefferson lay before us, the road which I had travelled for the first time three years ago with Father and travelled twice at Christmas time and then in June and September and twice at Christmas time again and then June and September again each college term since alone on the mare, not even knowing that this was peace; and now this time and maybe last time who would not die (I knew that) but who maybe forever after could never again hold up his head. The horses took the gait which they would hold for forty miles. My mare knew the long road ahead and Ringo had a good beast too, had talked Hilliard at the livery stable out of a good horse too. Maybe it was the tears, the channels of dried mud across which his strain-reddened eyes had looked at me, but I rather think it was that same quality which used to enable him to replenish his and Granny's supply of United States Army letterheads during that time—some outrageous assurance gained from too long and too close association with white people: the one whom he called Granny, the other with whom he had slept from the time we were born until Father rebuilt the house. We spoke one time, then no more:

"We could bushwhack him," he said. "Like we done Grumby that day. But I reckon that wouldn't suit that white skin you walks around in."

"No," I said. We rode on; it was October; there was plenty of time still

for verbena although I would have to reach home before I would realize there
was a need for it; plenty of time for verbena yet from the garden where Aunt
Jenny puttered beside old Joby, in a pair of Father's old cavalry gauntlets,
among the coaxed and ordered beds, the quaint and odorous old names, for
though it was October no rain had come yet and hence no frost to bring (or
leave behind) the first half-warm half-chill nights of Indian Summer—
the drowsing air cool and empty for geese yet languid still with the old
hot dusty smell of fox grape and sassafras—the nights when before I became
a man and went to college to learn law Ringo and I, with lantern and axe and
croker-sack and six dogs (one to follow the trail and five more just for the
tonguing, the music) would hunt possum in the pasture where, hidden, we
had seen our first Yankee that afternoon on the bright horse, where for the last
year now you could hear the whistling of the trains which had no longer belonged to Mr. Redmond for a long while now and which at some instant,
some second during the morning Father too had relinquished along with the
pipe which Ringo said he was smoking, which slipped from his hand as he
fell. We rode on, toward the house where he would be lying in the parlor now,
in his regimentals (sabre too) and where Drusilla would be waiting for me beneath all the festive glitter of the chandeliers, in the yellow ball gown and the
sprig of verbena in her hair, holding the two loaded pistols (I could see that
too, who had had no presentiment; I could see her, in the formal brilliant
room arranged formally for obsequy, not tall, not slender as a woman is but as
a youth, a boy, is, motionless, in yellow, the face calm, almost bemused,
the head simple and severe, the balancing sprig of verbena above each ear,
the two arms bent at the elbows, the two hands shoulder high, the two
identical duelling pistols lying upon, not clutched in, one to each: the Greek
amphora priestess of a succinct and formal violence).

2

Drusilla said that he had a dream. I was twenty then and she and I
would walk in the garden in the summer twilight while we waited for Father
to ride in from the railroad. I was just twenty then: that summer before I
entered the University to take the law degree which Father decided I should
have and four years after the one, the day, the evening when Father and
Drusilla had kept old Cash Benbow from becoming United States Marshal
and returned home still unmarried and Mrs. Habersham herded them into her
carriage and drove them back to town and dug her husband out of his little
dim hole in the new bank and made him sign Father's peace bond for killing the two carpet baggers, and took Father and Drusilla to the minister herself and saw that they were married. And Father had rebuilt the house too,
on the same blackened spot, over the same cellar, where the other had burned,
only larger, much larger: Drusilla said that the house was the aura of
Father's dream just as a bride's trousseau and veil is the aura of hers. And
Aunt Jenny had come to live with us now so we had the garden (Drusilla
would no more have bothered with flowers than Father himself would have,
who even now, even four years after it was over, still seemed to exist, breathe,
in that last year of it while she had ridden in man's clothes and with her

hair cut short like any other member of Father's troop, across Georgia and both Carolinas in front of Sherman's army) for her to gather sprigs of verbena from to wear in her hair because she said verbena was the only scent you could smell above the smell of horses and courage and so it was the only one that was worth the wearing. The railroad was hardly begun then and Father and Mr. Redmond were not only still partners, they were still friends, which as George Wyatt said was easily a record for Father, and he would leave the house at daybreak on Jupiter, riding up and down the unfinished line with two saddlebags of gold coins borrowed on Friday to pay the men on Saturday, keeping just two cross-ties ahead of the sheriff as Aunt Jenny said. So we walked in the dusk, slowly between Aunt Jenny's flower beds while Drusilla (in a dress now, who still would have worn pants all the time if Father had let her) leaned lightly on my arm and I smelled the verbena in her hair as I had smelled the rain in it and in Father's beard that night four years ago when he and Drusilla and Uncle Buck McCaslin found Grumby and then came home and found Ringo and me more than just asleep: escaped into that oblivion which God or Nature or whoever it was had supplied us with for the time being, who had had to perform more than should be required of children because there should be some limit to the age, the youth at least below which one should not have to kill. This was just after the Saturday night when he returned and I watched him clean the derringer and reload it and we learned that the dead man was almost a neighbor, a hill man who had been in the first infantry regiment when it voted Father out of command: and we never to know if the man actually intended to rob Father or not because Father had shot too quick, but only that he had a wife and several children in a dirt-floored cabin in the hills, to whom Father the next day sent some money and she (the wife) walked into the house two days later while we were sitting at the dinner table and flung the money at Father's face.

"But nobody could have had more of a dream than Colonel Sutpen," I said. He had been Father's second-in-command in the first regiment and had been elected colonel when the regiment deposed Father after Second Manassas, and it was Sutpen and not the regiment whom Father never forgave. He was underbred, a cold ruthless man who had come into the country about thirty years before the War, nobody knew from where except Father said you could look at him and know he would not dare to tell. He had got some land and nobody knew how he did that either, and he got money from somewhere—Father said they all believed he robbed steamboats, either as a card sharper or as an out-and-out highwayman—and built a big house and married and set up as a gentleman. Then he lost everything in the War like everybody else, all hope of descendants too (his son killed his daughter's fiancé on the eve of the wedding and vanished), yet he came back home and set out singlehanded to rebuild his plantation. He had no friends to borrow from and he had nobody to leave it to and he was past sixty years old, yet he set out to rebuild his place like it used to be; they told how he was too busy to bother with politics or anything; how when Father and the other men organized the night riders to keep the carpet baggers from organizing the Negroes into an insurrection, he refused to have anything to do with it.

Father stopped hating him long enough to ride out to see Sutpen himself and he (Sutpen) came to the door with a lamp and did not even invite them to come in and discuss it; Father said, "Are you with us or against us?" and he said, "I'm for my land. If every man of you would rehabilitate his own land, the country will take care of itself" and Father challenged him to bring the lamp out and set it on a stump where they could both see to shoot and Sutpen would not. "Nobody could have more of a dream than that."

"Yes. But his dream was just Sutpen. John's is not. He is thinking of this whole country which he is trying to raise by its bootstraps, so that all the people in it, not just his kind nor his old regiment, but all the people, black and white, the women and children back in the hills who don't even own shoes— Don't you see?"

"But how can they get any good from what he wants to do for them if they are—after he has——"

"Killed some of them? I suppose you include those two carpet baggers he had to kill to hold that first election, don't you?"

"They were men. Human beings."

"They were Northerners, foreigners who had no business here. They were pirates." We walked on, her weight hardly discernible on my arm, her head just reaching my shoulder. I had always been a little taller than she, even on that night at Hawkhurst while we listened to the niggers passing in the road, and she had changed but little since—the same boy-hard body, the close implacable head with its savagely cropped hair which I had watched from the wagon above the tide of crazed singing niggers as we went down into the river—the body not slender as women are but as boys are slender. "A dream is not a very safe thing to be near, Bayard. I know; I had one once. It's like a loaded pistol with a hair trigger: if it stays alive long enough, somebody is going to be hurt. But if it's a good dream, it's worth it. There are not many dreams in the world, but there are a lot of human lives. And one human life or two dozen——"

"Are not worth anything?"

"No. Not anything.—Listen. I hear Jupiter. I'll beat you to the house." She was already running, the skirts she did not like to wear lifted almost to her knees, her legs beneath it running as boys run just as she rode like men ride.

I was twenty then. But the next time I was twenty-four; I had been three years at the University and in another two weeks I would ride back to Oxford for the final year and my degree. It was just last summer, last August, and Father had just beat Redmond for the State legislature. The railroad was finished now and the partnership between Father and Redmond had been dissolved so long ago that most people would have forgotten they were ever partners if it hadn't been for the enmity between them. There had been a third partner but nobody hardly remembered his name now; he and his name both had vanished in the fury of the conflict which set up between Father and Redmond almost before they began to lay the rails, between Father's violent and ruthless dictatorialness and will to dominate (the idea was his; he did think of the railroad first and then took Redmond in) and that quality in Redmond (as George Wyatt said, he was not a coward or Father would never have teamed with him) which permitted him to stand as much as he did from Father, to bear and bear and bear until something (not his will nor his courage) broke in him. During the War Redmond had not been a soldier, he had had something to do with cotton for the Government; he could have made money himself out of it but he had not and everybody knew he had not, Father knew it, yet Father would even taunt him with not having smelled powder. He was wrong; he knew he was when it was too late for him to stop just as a drunkard reaches a point where it is too late for him to stop, where he promises himself that he will and maybe believes he will or can but it is too late. Finally they reached the point (they had both put everything they could mortgage or borrow into it for Father to ride up and down the line, paying the workmen and the waybills on the rails at the last possible instant) where even Father realized that one of them would have to get out. So (they were not speaking then; it was arranged by Judge Benbow) they met and agreed to buy or sell, naming a price which, in reference to what they had put into it, was ridiculously low but which each believed the other could not raise—at least Father claimed that Redmond did not believe he could raise it. So Redmond accepted the price, and found out that Father had the money. And according to Father, that's what started it, although Uncle Buck McCaslin said Father could not have owned a half interest in even one hog, let alone a railroad, and not dissolve the business either sworn enemy or death-pledged friend to his recent partner. So they parted and Father finished the road. By that time, seeing that he was going to finish it, some Northern people sold him a locomotive on credit which he named for Aunt Jenny, with a silver oil can in the cab with her name engraved on it; and last summer the first train ran into Jefferson, the engine decorated with flowers and Father in the cab blowing blast after blast on the whistle when he passed Redmond's house; and there were speeches at the station, with more flowers and a Confederate flag and girls in white dresses and red sashes and a band, and Father stood on the pilot of the engine and made a direct and absolutely needless allusion to Mr. Redmond. That was it. He wouldn't let him alone. George Wyatt came to me right afterward and told me. "Right or wrong," he said, "us boys and most of the other folks in this county know John's right. But he ought to let Redmond alone. I know what's wrong: he's had to kill too many folks, and that's bad for a man. We all know Colonel's brave as a lion, but Redmond ain't no coward either and there ain't any use in making a brave man that made one mistake eat crow all the time. Can't you talk to him?"

"I don't know," I said. "I'll try." But I had no chance. That is, I could have talked to him and he would have listened, but he could not have heard me because he had stepped straight from the pilot of that engine into the race for the Legislature. Maybe he knew that Redmond would have to oppose him to save his face even though he (Redmond) must have known that, after that train ran into Jefferson, he had no chance against Father, or maybe Redmond had already announced his candidacy and Father entered the race just because of that, I don't remember. Anyway they ran, a bitter contest in which Father continued to badger Redmond without reason or need, since they both knew it would be a landslide for Father. And it was, and we

thought he was satisfied. Maybe he thought so himself, as the drunkard believes that he is done with drink; and it was that afternoon and Drusilla and
I walked in the garden in the twilight and I said something about what
George Wyatt had told me and she released my arm and turned me to face
her and said, "This from you? You? Have you forgotten Grumby?"

"No," I said. "I never will forget him."

"You never will. I wouldn't let you. There are worse things than killing
men, Bayard. There are worse things than being killed. Sometimes I think
the finest thing that can happen to a man is to love something, a woman
preferably, well, hard hard hard, then to die young because he believed what
he could not help but believe and was what he could not (could not? would
not) help but be." Now she was looking at me in a way she never had before.
I did not know what it meant then and was not to know until tonight since
neither of us knew then that two months later Father would be dead. I just
knew that she was looking at me as she never had before and that the scent
of the verbena in her hair seemed to have increased a hundred times, to have
got a hundred times stronger, to be everywhere in the dusk in which something was about to happen which I had never dreamed of. Then she spoke.
"Kiss me, Bayard."

"No. You are Father's wife."

"And eight years older than you are. And your fourth cousin, too. And I
have black hair. Kiss me, Bayard."

"No."

"Kiss me, Bayard." So I leaned my face down to her. But she didn't move,
standing so, bent lightly back from me from the waist, looking at me; now it
was she who said, "No." So I put my arms around her. Then she came to me,
melted as women will and can, the arms with the wrist- and elbow-power to
control horses about my shoulders, using the wrists to hold my face to hers
until there was no longer need for the wrists; I thought then of the woman of
thirty, the symbol of the ancient and eternal Snake and of the men who have
written of her, and I realized then the immitigable chasm between all life and
all print—that those who can, do, those who cannot and suffer enough because they can't, write about it. Then I was free, I could see her again, I
saw her still watching me with that dark inscrutable look, looking up at me
now across her down-slanted face; I watched her arms rise with almost the
exact gesture with which she had put them around me as if she were repeating the empty and formal gesture of all promise so that I should never
forget it, the elbows angling outward as she put her hands to the sprig of
verbena in her hair, I standing straight and rigid facing the slightly bent
head, the short jagged hair, the rigid curiously formal angle of the bare
arms gleaming faintly in the last of light as she removed the verbena sprig
and put it into my lapel, and I thought how the War had tried to stamp all
the women of her generation and class in the South into a type and how it
had failed—the suffering, the identical experience (hers and Aunt Jenny's
had been almost the same except that Aunt Jenny had spent a few nights
with her husband before they brought him back home in an ammunition
wagon while Gavin Breckbridge was just Drusilla's fiancé) was there in the
eyes, yet beyond that was the incorrigibly individual woman: not like so many

men who return from wars to live on Government reservations like so many steers, emasculate and empty of all save an identical experience which they cannot forget and dare not, else they would cease to live at that moment, almost interchangeable save for the old habit of answering to a given name.

"Now I must tell Father," I said.

"Yes," she said. "You must tell him. Kiss me." So again it was like it had been before. No. Twice, a thousand times and never like—the eternal and symbolical thirty to a young man, a youth, each time both cumulative and retroactive, immitigably unrepetitive, each wherein remembering excludes experience, each wherein experience antedates remembering; the skill without weariness, the knowledge virginal to surfeit, the cunning secret muscles to guide and control just as within the wrists and elbows lay slumbering the mastery of horses: she stood back, already turning, not looking at me when she spoke, never having looked at me, already moving swiftly on in the dusk: "Tell John. Tell him tonight."

I intended to. I went to the house and into the office at once; I went to the center of the rug before the cold hearth, I don't know why, and stood there rigid like soldiers stand, looking at eye level straight across the room and above his head and said, "Father" and then stopped. Because he did not even hear me. He said, "Yes, Bayard?" but he did not hear me although he was sitting behind the desk doing nothing, immobile, as still as I was rigid, one hand on the desk with a dead cigar in it, a bottle of brandy and a filled and untasted glass beside his hand, clothed quiet and bemused in whatever triumph it was he felt since the last overwhelming return of votes had come in late in the afternoon. So I waited until after supper. We went to the dining-room and stood side by side until Aunt Jenny entered and then Drusilla, in the yellow ball gown, who walked straight to me and gave me one fierce inscrutable look then went to her place and waited for me to draw her chair while Father drew Aunt Jenny's. He had roused by then, not to talk himself but rather to sit at the head of the table and reply to Drusilla as she talked with a sort of feverish and glittering volubility—to reply now and then to her with that courteous intolerant pride which had lately become a little forensic, as if merely being in a political contest filled with fierce and empty oratory had retroactively made a lawyer of him who was anything and everything except a lawyer. Then Drusilla and Aunt Jenny rose and left us and he said, "Wait" to me who had made no move to follow and directed Joby to bring one of the bottles of wine which he had fetched back from New Orleans when he went there last to borrow money to liquidate his first private railroad bonds. Then I stood again like soldiers stand, gazing at eye level above his head while he sat half-turned from the table, a little paunchy now though not much, a little grizzled too in the hair though his beard was as strong as ever, with that spurious forensic air of lawyers and the intolerant eyes which in the last two years had acquired that transparent film which the eyes of carnivorous animals have and from behind which they look at a world which no ruminant ever sees, perhaps dares to see, which I have seen before on the eyes of men who have killed too much, who have killed so much that never again as long as they live will they ever be alone. I said again, "Father," then I told him.

"Hah?" he said. "Sit down." I sat down, I looked at him, watched him fill both glasses and this time I knew it was worse with him than not hearing; it didn't even matter. "You <u>are doing well in the law, Judge Wilkins tells me</u>. I am pleased to hear that. I have not needed you in my affairs so far, but from now on I shall. I have now accomplished the active portion of my aims in which you could not have helped me; I acted as the land and the time demanded and you were too young for that, I wished to shield you. But now the land and the time too are changing; what will follow will be a matter of consolidation, of pettifogging and doubtless chicanery in which I would be a babe in arms but in which you, trained in the law, can hold your own—our own. Yes. I have accomplished my aim, and now I shall do a little moral housecleaning. I am tired of killing men, no matter what the necessity or the end. <u>Tomorrow, when I go to town and meet Ben Redmond, I shall be unarmed.</u>"

Decision

3

We reached home just before midnight; we didn't have to pass through Jefferson either. Before we turned in the gates I could see the lights, the chandeliers—hall, parlor, and what Aunt Jenny (without any effort or perhaps even design on her part) had taught even Ringo to call the drawing room, the light falling outward across the portico, past the columns. Then I saw the horses, the faint shine of leather and buckle-glints on the black silhouettes and then the men too—Wyatt and others of Father's old troop—and I had forgot that they would be there. I had forgot that they would be there; I remember how I thought, since I was tired and spent with strain, *Now it will have to begin tonight. I won't even have until tomorrow in which to begin to resist.* They had a watchman, a picquet out, I suppose, because they seemed to know at once that we were in the drive. Wyatt met me, I halted the mare, I could look down at him and at the others gathered a few yards behind him with that curious vulture-like formality which Southern men assume in such situations.

"Well, boy," George said.

"Was it—" I said. "Was he——"

"It was all right. It was in front. <u>Redmond ain't no coward</u>. John had the <u>derringer inside his cuff like always, but he never touched it, never made a move toward it.</u>" I have seen him do it, he showed me once: the pistol (it was not four inches long) held flat inside his left wrist by a clip he made himself of wire and an old clock spring; he would raise both hands at the same time, cross them, fire the pistol from beneath his left hand almost as if he were hiding from his own vision what he was doing; when he killed one of the men he shot a hole through his own coat sleeve. "But you want to get on to the house," Wyatt said. He began to stand aside, then he spoke again: "We'll take this off your hands, any of us. Me." I hadn't moved the mare yet and I had made no move to speak, yet he continued quickly, as if he had already rehearsed all this, his speech and mine, and knew what I would say and only spoke himself as he would have removed his hat on entering a house or used "sir" in conversing with a stranger: "You're young, just a boy, you ain't had any experience in this kind of thing. Besides, you got them two ladies in the house to think about. He would understand, all right."

"I reckon I can attend to it," I said.

"Sure," he said; there was no surprise, nothing at all, in his voice because he had already rehearsed this: "I reckon we all knew that's what you would say." He stepped back then; almost it was as though he and not I bade the mare to move on. But they all followed, still with that unctuous and voracious formality. Then I saw Drusilla standing at the top of the front steps, in the light from the open door and the windows like a theatre scene, in the yellow ball gown and even from here I believed that I could smell the verbena in her hair, standing there motionless yet emanating something louder than the two shots must have been—something voracious too and passionate. Then, although I had dismounted and someone had taken the mare, I seemed to be still in the saddle and to watch myself enter that scene which she had postulated like another actor while in the background for chorus Wyatt and the others stood with the unctuous formality which the Southern man shows in the presence of death—that Roman holiday engendered by mist-born Protestantism grafted onto this land of violent sun, of violent alteration from snow to heat-stroke which has produced a race impervious to both. I mounted the steps toward the figure straight and yellow and immobile as a candle which moved only to extend one hand; we stood together and looked down at them where they stood clumped, the horses too gathered in a tight group beyond them at the rim of light from the brilliant door and windows. One of them stamped and blew his breath and jangled his gear.

"Thank you, gentlemen," I said. "My aunt and my—Drusilla thank you. There's no need for you to stay. Good night." They murmured, turning. George Wyatt paused, looking back at me.

"Tomorrow?" he said.

"Tomorrow." Then they went on, carrying their hats and tiptoeing, even on the ground, the quiet and resilient earth, as though anyone in that house awake would try to sleep, anyone already asleep in it whom they could have wakened. Then they were gone and Drusilla and I turned and crossed the portico, her hand lying light on my wrist yet discharging into me with a shock like electricity that dark and passionate voracity, the face at my shoulder—the jagged hair with a verbena sprig above each ear, the eyes staring at me with that fierce exaltation. We entered the hall and crossed it, her hand guiding me without pressure, and entered the parlor. Then for the first time I realized it—the alteration which is death—not that he was now just clay but that he was lying down. But I didn't look at him yet because I knew that when I did I would begin to pant; I went to Aunt Jenny who had just risen from a chair behind which Louvinia stood. She was Father's sister, taller than Drusilla but no older, whose husband had been killed at the very beginning of the War, by a shell from a Federal frigate at Fort Moultrie, come to us from Carolina six years ago. Ringo and I went to Tennessee Junction in the wagon to meet her. It was January, cold and clear and with ice in the ruts; we returned just before dark with Aunt Jenny on the seat beside me holding a lace parasol and Ringo in the wagon bed nursing a hamper basket containing two bottles of old sherry and the two jasmine cuttings which were bushes in

the garden now, and the panes of colored glass which she had salvaged from
the Carolina house where she and Father and Uncle Bayard were born and
which Father had set in a fanlight about one of the drawing room windows
for her—who came up the drive and Father (home now from the railroad)
went down the steps and lifted her from the wagon and said, "Well, Jenny,"
and she said, "Well, Johnny," and began to cry. She stood too, looking at
me as I approached—the same hair, the same high nose, the same eyes as
Father's except that they were intent and very wise instead of tolerant. She
said nothing at all, she just kissed me, her hands light on my shoulders.
Then Drusilla spoke, as if she had been waiting with a sort of dreadful
patience for the empty ceremony to be done, in a voice like a bell: clear, unsentient, on a single pitch, silvery and triumphant: "Come, Bayard."

"Hadn't you better go to bed now?" Aunt Jenny said.

"Yes," Drusilla said in that silvery ecstatic voice, "Oh yes. There will be
plenty of time for sleep." I followed her, her hand again guiding me without pressure; now I looked at him. It was just as I had imagined it—sabre,
plumes, and all—but with that alteration, that irrevocable difference which
I had known to expect yet had not realized, as you can put food into your
stomach which for a while the stomach declines to assimilate—the illimitable
grief and regret as I looked down at the face which I knew—the nose, the
hair, the eyelids closed over the intolerance—the face which I realized I now
saw in repose for the first time in my life; the empty hands still now beneath
the invisible stain of what had been (once, surely) needless blood, the hands
now appearing clumsy in their very inertness, too clumsy to have performed the fatal actions which forever afterward he must have waked and slept
with and maybe was glad to lay down at last—those curious appendages
clumsily conceived to begin with yet with which man has taught himself to do so much, so much more than they were intended to do or could
be forgiven for doing, which had now surrendered that life to which his intolerant heart had fiercely held; and then I knew that in a minute I would
begin to pant. So Drusilla must have spoken twice before I heard her and
turned and saw in the instant Aunt Jenny and Louvinia watching us, hearing
Drusilla now, the unsentient bell quality gone now, her voice whispering
into that quiet death-filled room with a passionate and dying fall: "Bayard."
She faced me, she was quite near; again the scent of the verbena in her hair
seemed to have increased a hundred times as she stood holding out to me,
one in either hand, the two duelling pistols. "Take them, Bayard," she said,
in the same tone in which she had said "Kiss me" last summer, already
pressing them into my hands, watching me with that passionate and voracious
exaltation, speaking in a voice fainting and passionate with promise: "Take
them. I have kept them for you. I give them to you. Oh you will thank me,
you will remember me who put into your hands what they say is an attribute
only of God's, who took what belongs to heaven and gave it to you. Do you
feel them? the long true barrels true as justice, the triggers (you have fired
them) quick as retribution, the two of them slender and invincible and fatal
as the physical shape of love?" Again I watched her arms angle out and upward as she removed the two verbena sprigs from her hair in two motions
faster than the eye could follow, already putting one of them into my lapel

and crushing the other in her other hand while she still spoke in that rapid passionate voice not much louder than a whisper: "There. One I give to you to wear tomorrow (it will not fade), the other I cast away, like this—" dropping the crushed bloom at her feet. "I abjure it. I abjure verbena forever more; I have smelled it above the odor of courage; that was all I wanted. Now let me look at you." She stood back, staring at me—the face tearless and exalted, the feverish eyes brilliant and voracious. "How beautiful you are: do you know it? How beautiful: young, to be permitted to kill, to be permitted vengeance, to take into your bare hands the fire of heaven that cast down Lucifer. No; I. I gave it to you; I put it into your hands; Oh you will thank me, you will remember me when I am dead and you are an old man saying to himself, 'I have tasted all things.'—It will be the right hand, won't it?" She moved; she had taken my right hand which still held one of the pistols before I knew what she was about to do; she had bent and kissed it before I comprehended why she took it. Then she stopped dead still, still stooping in that attitude of fierce exultant humility, her hot lips and her hot hands still touching my flesh, light on my flesh as dead leaves yet communicating to it that battery charge, dark, passionate, and damned forever of all peace. Because they are wise, women are—a touch, lips or fingers, and the knowledge, even clairvoyance, goes straight to the heart without bothering the laggard brain at all. She stood erect now, staring at me with intolerable and amazed incredulity which occupied her face alone for a whole minute while her eyes were completely empty; it seemed to me that I stood there for a full minute while Aunt Jenny and Louvinia watched us, waiting for her eyes to fill. There was no blood in her face at all, her mouth open a little and pale as one of those rubber rings women seal fruit jars with. Then her eyes filled with an expression of bitter and passionate betrayal. "Why, he's not—" she said. "He's not— And I kissed his hand," she said in an aghast whisper; "I kissed his hand!" beginning to laugh, the laughter rising, becoming a scream yet still remaining laughter, screaming with laughter, trying herself to deaden the sound by putting her hand over her mouth, the laughter spilling between her fingers like vomit, the incredulous betrayed eyes still watching me across the hand.

"Louvinia!" Aunt Jenny said. They both came to her. Louvinia touched and held her and Drusilla turned her face to Louvinia.

"I kissed his hand, Louvinia!" she cried. "Did you see it? I kissed his hand!" the laughter rising again, becoming the scream again yet still remaining laughter, she still trying to hold it back with her hand like a small child who has filled its mouth too full.

"Take her upstairs," Aunt Jenny said. But they were already moving toward the door, Louvinia half-carrying Drusilla, the laughter diminishing as they neared the door as though it waited for the larger space of the empty and brilliant hall to rise again. Then it was gone; Aunt Jenny and I stood there and I knew soon that I would begin to pant. I could feel it beginning like you feel regurgitation beginning, as though there were not enough air in the room, the house, not enough air anywhere under the heavy hot low sky where the equinox couldn't seem to accomplish, nothing in the air for breathing, for the lungs. Now it was Aunt Jenny who said, "Bayard," twice before I heard her. "You are not going to try to kill him. All right."

"All right?" I said.

"Yes. All right. Don't let it be Drusilla, a poor hysterical young woman. And don't let it be him, Bayard, because he's dead now. And don't let it be George Wyatt and those others who will be waiting for you tomorrow morning. I know you are not afraid."

"But what good will that do?" I said. "What good will that do?" It almost began then; I stopped it just in time. "I must live with myself, you see."

"Then it's not just Drusilla? Not just him? Not just George Wyatt and Jefferson?"

"No," I said.

"Will you promise to let me see you before you go to town tomorrow?" I looked at her; we looked at one another for a moment. Then she put her hands on my shoulders and kissed me and released me, all in one motion. "Good night, son," she said. Then she was gone too and now it could begin. I knew that in a minute I would look at him and it would begin and I did look at him, feeling the long-held breath, the hiatus before it started, thinking how maybe I should have said, "Good-bye, Father," but did not. Instead I crossed to the piano and laid the pistols carefully on it, still keeping the panting from getting too loud too soon. Then I was outside on the porch and (I don't know how long it had been) I looked in the window and saw Simon squatting on a stool beside him. Simon had been his body servant during the War and when they came home Simon had a uniform too—a Confederate private's coat with a Yankee brigadier's star on it and he had put it on now, too, like they had dressed Father, squatting on the stool beside him, not crying, not weeping the facile tears which are the white man's futile trait and which Negroes know nothing about but just sitting there, motionless, his lower lip slacked down a little; he raised his hand and touched the coffin, the black hand rigid and fragile-looking as a clutch of dead twigs, then dropped the hand; once he turned his head and I saw his eyes roll red and unwinking in his skull like those of a cornered fox. It had begun by that time; I panted, standing there, and this was it—the regret and grief, the despair out of which the tragic mute insensitive bones stand up that can bear anything, anything.

4

After a while the whippoorwills stopped and I heard the first day bird, a mockingbird. It had sung all night too but now it was the day song, no longer the drowsy moony fluting. Then they all began—the sparrows from the stable, the thrush that lived in Aunt Jenny's garden, and I heard a quail too from the pasture and now there was light in the room. But I didn't move at once. I still lay on the bed (I hadn't undressed) with my hands under my head and the scent of Drusilla's verbena faint from where my coat lay on a chair, watching the light grow, watching it turn rosy with the sun. After a while I heard Louvinia come up across the back yard and go into the kitchen;

I heard the door and then the long crash of her armful of stovewood into the box. Soon they would begin to arrive—the carriages and buggies in the drive—but not for a while yet because they too would wait first to see what I was going to do. So the house was quiet when I went down to the dining-room, no sound in it except Simon snoring in the parlor, probably still sitting on the stool though I didn't look in to see. Instead I stood at the dining-room window and drank the coffee which Louvinia brought me, then I went to the stable; I saw Joby watching me from the kitchen door as I crossed the yard and in the stable Loosh looked up at me across Betsy's head, a curry comb in his hand, though Ringo didn't look at me at all. We curried Jupiter then. I didn't know if we would be able to without trouble or not, since always Father would come in first and touch him and tell him to stand and he would stand like a marble horse (or pale bronze rather) while Loosh curried him. But he stood for me too, a little restive but he stood, then that was done and now it was almost nine o'clock and soon they would begin to arrive and I told Ringo to bring Betsy on to the house.

I went on to the house and into the hall. I had not had to pant in some time now but it was there, waiting, a part of the alteration, as though by being dead and no longer needing air he had taken all of it, all that he had compassed and claimed and postulated between the walls which he had built, along with him. Aunt Jenny must have been waiting; she came out of the dining-room at once, without a sound, dressed, the hair that was like Father's combed and smooth above the eyes that were different from Father's eyes because they were not intolerant but just intent and grave and (she was wise too) without pity. "Are you going now?" she said.

"Yes." I looked at her. Yes, thank God, without pity. "You see, I want to be thought well of."

"I do," she said. "Even if you spend the day hidden in the stable loft, I still do."

"Maybe if she knew that I was going. Was going to town anyway."

"No," she said. "No, Bayard." We looked at one another. Then she said quietly, "All right. She's awake." So I mounted the stairs. I mounted steadily, not fast because if I had gone fast the panting would have started again or I might have had to slow for a second at the turn or at the top and I would not have gone on. So I went slowly and steadily, across the hall to her door and knocked and opened it. She was sitting at the window, in something soft and loose for morning in her bedroom, only she never did look like morning in a bedroom because here was no hair to fall about her shoulders. She looked up, she sat there looking at me with her feverish brilliant eyes and I remembered I still had the verbena sprig in my lapel and suddenly she began to laugh again. It seemed to come not from her mouth but to burst out all over her face like sweat does and with a dreadful and painful convulsion as when you have vomited until it hurts you yet still you must vomit again—burst out all over her face except her eyes, the brilliant, incredulous eyes looking at me out of the laughter as if they belonged to somebody else, as if they were two inert fragments of tar or coal lying on the bottom of a receptacle filled with turmoil: "I kissed his hand! *I kissed his hand!*" Louvinia entered, Aunt Jenny must have sent her directly after me; again I walked slowly and steadily

so it would not start yet, down the stairs where Aunt Jenny stood beneath the
chandelier in the hall as Mrs. Wilkins had stood yesterday at the University.
She had my hat in her hand. "Even if you hid all day in the stable, Bayard,"
she said. I took the hat; she said quietly, pleasantly, as if she were talking to
a stranger, a guest: "I used to see a lot of blockade runners in Charleston.
They were heroes in a way, you see—not heroes because they were helping to
prolong the Confederacy but heroes in the sense that David Crockett or John
Sevier would have been to small boys or fool young women. There was one of
them, an Englishman. He had no business there; it was the money of course,
as with all of them. But he was the Davy Crockett to us because by that time
we had all forgot what money was, what you could do with it. He must have
been a gentleman once or associated with gentlemen before he changed
his name, and he had a vocabulary of seven words, though I must admit he
got along quite well with them. The first four were, 'I'll have rum, thanks,'
and then, when he had the rum, he would use the other three—across the
champagne, to whatever ruffled bossom or low gown: 'No bloody moon.' No
bloody moon, Bayard."

Ringo was waiting with Betsy at the front steps. Again he did not look at
me, his face sullen, downcast even while he handed me the reins. But he
said nothing, nor did I look back. And sure enough I was just in time; I passed
the Compson carriage at the gates, General Compson lifted his hat as I did
mine as we passed. It was four miles to town but I had not gone two of
them when I heard the horse coming up behind me and I did not look back
because I knew it was Ringo. I did not look back; he came up on one of the
carriage horses, he rode up beside me and looked me full in the face for one
moment, the sullen determined face, the eyes rolling at me defiant and momentary and red; we rode on. Now we were in town—the long shady street
leading to the square, the new courthouse at the end of it; it was eleven
o'clock now: long past breakfast and not yet noon so there were only women
on the street, not to recognise me perhaps, or at least not the walking stopped
sudden and dead in midwalking as if the legs contained the sudden eyes, the
caught breath, that not to begin until we reached the square, and I thinking
*If I could only be invisible until I reach the stairs to his office and begin to
mount.* But I could not, I was not; we rode up to the Holston House and I
saw the row of feet along the gallery rail come suddenly and quietly down
and I did not look at them; I stopped Betsy and waited until Ringo was down;
then I dismounted and gave him the reins. "Wait for me here," I said.

"I'm going with you," he said, not loud; we stood there under the still cir-
cumspect eyes and spoke quietly to one another like two conspirators. Then I
saw the pistol, the outline of it inside his shirt, probably the one we had taken
from Grumby that day we killed him.

"No you ain't," I said.

"Yes I am."

"No you ain't." So I walked on, along the street in the hot sun. It was almost noon now and I could smell nothing except the verbena in my coat,
as if it had gathered all the sun, all the suspended fierce heat in which the
equinox could not seem to occur and were distilling it, so that I moved in a
cloud of verbena as I might have moved in a cloud of smoke from a cigar.

Then George Wyatt was beside me (I don't know where he came from) and five or six others of Father's old troop a few yards behind, George's hand on my arm, drawing me into a doorway out of the avid eyes like caught breaths.

"Have you got that derringer?" George said.

"No," I said.

"Good," George said. "They are tricky things to fool with. Couldn't nobody but Colonel ever handle one right; I never could. So you take this. I tried it this morning and I know it's right. Here." He was already fumbling the pistol into my pocket, then the same thing seemed to happen to him that happened to Drusilla last night when she kissed my hand—something communicated by touch straight to the simple code by which he lived, without going through the brain at all: so that he too stood suddenly back, the pistol in his hand, staring at me with his pale outraged eyes and speaking in a whisper thin with fury: "Who are you? Is your name Sartoris? By God, if you don't kill him, I'm going to." Now it was not panting, it was a terrible desire to laugh, to laugh as Drusilla had, and say, "That's what Drusilla said." But I didn't. I said,

"I'm tending to this. You stay out of it. I don't need any help." Then his fierce eyes faded gradually, exactly as you turn a lamp down.

"Well," he said, putting the pistol back into his pocket. "You'll have to excuse me, son. I should have knowed you wouldn't do anything that would keep John from laying quiet. We'll follow you and wait at the foot of the steps. And remember: he's a brave man, but he's been sitting in that office by himself since yesterday morning waiting for you and his nerves are on edge."

"I'll remember," I said. "I don't need any help." I had started on when suddenly I said it without having any warning that I was going to: "No bloody moon."

"What?" he said. I didn't answer. I went on across the square itself now, in the hot sun, they following though not close so that I never saw them again until afterward, surrounded by the remote still eyes not following me yet either, just stopped where they were before the stores and about the door to the courthouse, waiting. I walked steadily on enclosed in the now fierce odor of the verbena sprig. Then shadow fell upon me; I did not pause, I looked once at the small faded sign nailed to the brick B. J. Redmond. Atty at Law and began to mount the stairs, the wooden steps scuffed by the heavy bewildered boots of countrymen approaching litigation and stained by tobacco spit, on down the dim corridor to the door which bore the name again, B. J. Redmond and knocked once and opened it. He sat behind the desk, not much taller than Father but thicker as a man gets who spends most of his time sitting and listening to people, freshly shaven and with fresh linen; a lawyer yet it was not a lawyer's face—a face much thinner than the body would indicate, strained (and yes, tragic; I know that now) and exhausted beneath the neat recent steady strokes of the razor, holding a pistol flat on the desk before him, loose beneath his hand and aimed at nothing. There was no smell of drink, not even of tobacco in the neat clean dingy room although I knew he smoked. I didn't pause. I walked steadily toward him. It was not twenty feet from door to desk yet I seemed to walk in a dreamlike state in which there was neither time nor distance, as though the mere act of walking was no more intended to encompass space than was his sitting. We didn't speak. It was as if we both knew what the passage of words would be and the futility of it; how he might have said, "Go out, Bayard. Go away, boy" and then, "Draw then. I will allow you to draw" and it would have been the same as if he had never said it. So we did not speak; I just walked steadily toward him as the pistol rose from the desk. I watched it, I could see the foreshortened slant of the barrel and I knew it would miss me though his hand did not tremble. I walked toward him, toward the pistol in the rocklike hand, I heard no bullet. Maybe I didn't even hear the explosion though I remember the sudden orange bloom and smoke as they appeared against his white shirt as they had appeared against Grumby's greasy Confederate coat; I still watched that foreshortened slant of barrel which I knew was not aimed at me and saw the second orange flash and smoke and heard no bullet that time either. Then I stopped; it was done then. I watched the pistol descend to the desk in short jerks; I saw him release it and sit back, both hands on the desk, I looked at his face and I knew too what it was to want air when there was nothing in the circumambience for the lungs. He rose, shoved the chair back with a convulsive motion and rose, with a queer ducking motion of his head; with his head still ducked aside and one arm extended as though he couldn't see and the other hand resting on the desk as if he couldn't stand alone, he turned and crossed to the wall and took his hat from the rack and with his head still ducked aside and one hand extended he blundered along the wall and passed me and reached the door and went through it. He was brave; no one denied that. He walked down those stairs and out onto the street where George Wyatt and the other six of Father's old troop waited and where the other men had begun to run now; he walked through the middle of them with his hat on and his head up (they told me how someone shouted at him: "Have you killed that boy too?"), saying no word, staring straight ahead and with his back to them, on to the station where the south-bound train was just in and got on it with no baggage, nothing, and went away from Jefferson and from Mississippi and never came back.

I heard their feet on the stairs then in the corridor then in the room, but for a while yet (it wasn't that long, of course) I still sat behind the desk as he had sat, the flat of the pistol still warm under my hand, my hand growing slowly numb between the pistol and my forehead. Then I raised my head; the little room was full of men. "My God!" George Wyatt cried. "You took the pistol away from him and then missed him, missed him *twice?*" Then he answered himself—that same rapport for violence which Drusilla had and which in George's case was actual character judgment: "No; wait. You walked in here without even a pocket knife and let him miss you twice. My God in heaven." He turned, shouting: "Get to hell out of here! You, White, ride out to Sartoris and tell his folks it's all over and he's all right. Ride!" So they departed, went away; presently only George was left, watching me with that pale bleak stare which was speculative yet not at all ratiocinative. "Well by God," he said. "—Do you want a drink?"

"No," I said. "I'm hungry. I didn't eat any breakfast."

"I reckon not, if you got up this morning aiming to do what you did. Come on. We'll go to the Holston House."

"No," I said. "No. Not there."

"Why not? You ain't done anything to be ashamed of. I wouldn't have done it that way, myself. I'd a shot at him once, anyway. But that's your way or you wouldn't have done it."

"Yes," I said. "I would do it again."

"Be damned if I would.—You want to come home with me? We'll have time to eat and then ride out there in time for the——" But I couldn't do that either.

"No," I said. "I'm not hungry after all. I think I'll go home."

"Don't you want to wait and ride out with me?"

"No. I'll go on."

"You don't want to stay here, anyway." He looked around the room again, where the smell of powder smoke still lingered a little, still lay somewhere on the hot dead air though invisible now, blinking a little with his fierce pale unintroverted eyes. "Well by God," he said again. "Maybe you're right, maybe there has been enough killing in your family without— Come on." We left the office. I waited at the foot of the stairs and soon Ringo came up with the horses. We crossed the square again. There were no feet on the Holston House railing now (it was twelve o'clock) but a group of men stood before the door who raised their hats and I raised mine and Ringo and I rode on.

We did not go fast. Soon it was one, maybe after; the carriages and buggies would begin to leave the square soon, so I turned from the road at the end of the pasture and I sat the mare, trying to open the gate without dismounting, until Ringo dismounted and opened it. We crossed the pasture in the hard fierce sun; I could have seen the house now but I didn't look. Then we were in the shade, the close thick airless shade of the creek bottom; the old rails still lay in the undergrowth where we had built the pen to hide the Yankee mules. Presently I heard the water, then I could see the sunny glints. We dismounted. I lay on my back, I thought *Now it can begin again if it wants to.* But it did not. I went to sleep. I went to sleep almost before I had stopped thinking. I slept for almost five hours and I didn't dream anything at all yet I waked myself up crying, crying too hard to stop it. Ringo was squatting beside me and the sun was gone though there was a bird of some sort still singing somewhere and the whistle of the north-bound evening train sounded and the short broken puffs of starting where it had evidently stopped at our flag station. After a while I began to stop and Ringo brought his hat full of water from the creek but instead I went down to the water myself and bathed my face.

There was still a good deal of light in the pasture, though the whippoorwills had begun, and when we reached the house there was a mockingbird singing in the magnolia, the night song now, the drowsy moony one, and again the moon like the rim print of a heel in wet sand. There was just one light in the hall now and so it was all over though I could still smell the flowers even above the verbena in my coat. I had not looked at him again. I had started to before I left the house but I did not, I did not see him again and all the picture we had of him were bad ones because a picture could no more have held him dead than the house could have kept his body. But I didn't need to see him again because he was there, he would always be there; maybe what Drusilla meant by his dream was not something which he possessed but something which he had bequeathed us which we could never forget, which would even assume the corporeal shape of him whenever any of us, black or white, closed our eyes. I went into the house. There was no light in the drawing room except the last of the afterglow which came through the western window where Aunt Jenny's colored glass was; I was about to go on upstairs when I saw her sitting there beside the window. She didn't call me and I didn't speak Drusilla's name, I just went to the door and stood there. "She's gone," Aunt Jenny said. "She took the evening train. She has gone to Montgomery, to Dennison." Denny had been married about a year now; he was living in Montgomery, reading law.

"I see," I said. "Then she didn't——" But there wasn't any use in that either; Jed White must have got there before one o'clock and told them. And besides, Aunt Jenny didn't answer. She could have lied to me but she didn't, she said,

"Come here." I went to her chair. "Kneel down. I can't see you."

"Don't you want the lamp?"

"No. Kneel down." So I knelt beside the chair. "So you had a perfectly splendid Saturday afternoon, didn't you? Tell me about it." Then she put her hands on my shoulders. I watched them come up as though she were trying to stop them; I felt them on my shoulders as if they had a separate life of their own and were trying to do something which for my sake she was trying to restrain, prevent. Then she gave up or she was not strong enough because they came up and took my face between them, hard, and suddenly the tears sprang and streamed down her face like Drusilla's laughing had. "Oh, damn you Sartorises!" she said. "Damn you! Damn you!"

As I passed down the hall the light came up in the dining-room and I could hear Louvinia laying the table for supper. So the stairs were lighted quite well. But the upper hall was dark. I saw her open door (that unmistakable way in which an open door stands open when nobody lives in the room any more) and I realized I had not believed that she was really gone. So I didn't look into the room. I went on to mine and entered. And then for a long moment I thought it was the verbena in my lapel which I still smelled. I thought that until I had crossed the room and looked down at the pillow on which it lay—the single sprig of it (without looking she would pinch off a half dozen of them and they would be all of a size, almost all of a shape, as if a machine had stamped them out) filling the room, the dusk, the evening with that odor which she said you could smell alone above the smell of horses.

1938

FAULKNER'S COMMENTS ON
HIS NOVELS

[From 1957 to 1962 Faulkner spent several terms as writer-in-residence at the University of Virginia. While there he took part in numerous literary discussions with students and faculty and the questions and answers, first recorded on tapes, have been transcribed in a volume entitled *Faulkner in the University* (1959). The following selections from them have been arranged in four groups: his general comments on the content and form of his fictions, and his specific comments on the three novels treated at greatest length in the introduction to the present anthology. It should be remembered that these are the author's unrehearsed responses to questions from the floor, and that they are in no sense formal self-criticisms or statements of literary theory. Further, readers should be warned not to take too literally what have been aptly called "the parables in which Faulkner delights to speak to a world that so often invades his privacy." A minor feature of interest is the Southern vernacular Faulkner uses, to identify himself with his region—so different from any of his literary styles—another of his voices or masks. (Editorial matter and page references to *Faulkner in the University* are placed in brackets.)]

General: Content and Form

Q. How do you pronounce the name of your mythical county?

A. If you break it down into syllables, it's simple. Y-o-k, n-a, p-a, t-a-w, p-h-a, YOK [YOCK]- na- pa- TAW- pha. It's a Chickasaw Indian word meaning water runs slow through flat land. [74]

Q. Mr. Faulkner, . . . in your own works you keep returning to this fictitious county you've made. You don't consider that a pageant, the whole work, from the Indians through the early settlers—?

A. No, it was not my intention to write a pageant of a county, I simply was using the quickest tool to hand. I was using what I knew best, which was the locale where I was born and had lived most of my life. That was just like the carpenter building the fence—he uses the nearest hammer. Only I didn't realize myself that I was creating a pageantry of a particular part of the earth. That just simplified things to me. [3]

Q. [About the Yoknapatawpha chronicle as a whole.]

A. . . . It was not a novel. I think that anything that can't be told in one standardized book is not a novel. That is, it can't follow the fairly rigid rules . . . in which a novel has got to be compressed to be a novel. This is really a chronicle that seemed to me amusing enough or true enough to be put down no matter what rules of integrity it had to violate, so that in that sense it's not a novel, it's a chronicle. [107]

Reprinted from *Faulkner in the University*, with the permission of The University Press of Virginia.

* * *

Q. [About the setting of the short story, "Was."]
A. . . . [That story] had a certain sociological importance . . . to show
my country as it really was in those days. The elegance of the colonial plantation didn't exist in my country. My country was still frontier. The plantation,
the columned porticos, that was Charleston and Natchez. But my country was
still frontier. People lived from day to day, with a bluff and crude hardiness,
but with a certain simplicity. Which to me is very interesting because the
common picture of the South is all magnolias and crinoline and Grecian
portals and things like that, which was true only around the fringes of the
South. Not in the interior, the back wood. [131]

Q. Sir, to what extent were you trying to picture the South and Southern
civilization as a whole, rather than just Mississippi—or were you?
A. Not at all. I was trying to talk about people, using the only tool I knew,
which was the country that I knew. No, I wasn't . . . writing sociology at
all. I was just trying to write about people, which to me [is] the important
thing. Just the human heart, it's not ideas. I don't know anything about
ideas, don't have much confidence in them. [9-10]

Q. Sir, why do you sometimes satirize the South, . . . what is your general feeling for the South, I mean the deep South?
A. It's my country, my native land and I love it. I'm not trying to satirize it
. . . —that is, I'm not expressing my own ideas in the stories I tell, I'm telling about people, and these people express ideas which sometimes are mine,
sometimes are not mine, but I myself am not trying to satirize my country, I
love it, and it has its faults and I will try to correct them, but I will not try to
correct them when I am writing a story, because I'm talking about people
then. [83]

* * *

Q. Mr. Faulkner, in your speech at Stockholm you expressed great faith in
mankind . . . not only to endure but prevail. . . . Do you think that's the
impression the average reader would get after reading *The Sound and the
Fury?*
A. I can't answer that because I don't know what the average reader gets
from reading the book. . . . But in my opinion, yes, that is what I was
talking about in all the books, and I failed to say it. I agree with you, I did fail.
But that was what I was trying to say—that man will prevail, will endure
because he is capable of compassion and honor and pride and endurance.
[4-5]

Q. Sir, you say that you feel that there is hope for the South, yet the
Snopeses have taken over Frenchman's Bend, Flem is president of the bank in
Jefferson. Are those the men that are going to lead the South out of darkness?
A. They are the men that can cope with the new industrial age, but there
will be something left . . . of the old cavalier spirit that will appear, that
does appear. By cavalier spirit, I mean people who believe in simple honor for
the sake of honor, and honesty for the sake of honesty.

Q. Do you think people will band together, or how do you think they will accomplish this feat? Don't you feel that there is a curse and that it should be removed . . . ?

A. They won't band together. I doubt if people accomplish very much by banding together. People accomplish things by individual protest. [80]

*   *   *

Q. You spoke a little while ago of Greek themes. I was wondering if you think that modern literature or twentieth-century literature, so to speak, could feature the truly tragic hero that you would find in Greek times, or do you think the characters should be meaner or more simple?

A. That's a difficult question to answer. I think the writer has got to write in terms of his environment, and his environment consists not only in the immediate scene, but his readers are part of that environment too, and maybe nobody can write forever without expecting to be read, and probably a writer, whether he intends to or not, or knows it or not, is going to shape what he writes in the terms of who will read it. So maybe when there are fine listeners, there will be fine poets again, that maybe the writing that is not too good is not just the writer's fault, it may be because of the environment, a part of which is the general effluvium of the readers, the people who will read it. That does something to the air they all breathe together, that compels the shape of the book. It would be fine if people could write in the old simple clear Hellenic tradition, but then maybe that would be now obsolete, that there was a time for that, the time for that is not now, it may come back, if life does go in cycles. [41-42]

Q. Sir, what do you think of Aristotle's theories about tragedy? . . . That the hero must be a man of high place so he can fall all the further.

A. Well, I don't think Aristotle meant by high place what it sounds like. I think he meant a man of integrity, more than a man of aristocracy. . . . I think that [i.e., using characters of position and wealth as tragic heroes] was because he used the high place, the money, the riches, the title as symbols, that a king must be brave, a queen must be chaste, as simple symbols, as puppets. But tragedy, as Aristotle saw it, . . . is the same conception of tragedy that all writers have: it's man wishing to be braver than he is, in combat with his heart or with his fellows or with the environment, and how he fails, that the splendor, the courage of his failure, and the trappings of royalty, of kingship, are simply trappings to make him more splendid so that he was worthy of being selected by the gods, by Olympus, as an opponent, that man couldn't cope with him so it would take a god to do it, to cast him down. [51]

Q. Could you give us some of the titles of these books, [your favorites]?

A. Yes'm. I read *Don Quixote* every year. I read the Old Testament. I read some of Dickens every year, and I've got a portable Shakespeare, one-volume Shakespeare, that I carry along with me. Conrad, *Moby-Dick*, Chekhov, *Madame Bovary*, some of Balzac almost every year, Tolstoy, . . . Gogol. Most of the Frenchmen of the nineteenth century I read in every year. [50]

*   *   *

Q. [About critics who find symbolism, etc., in his fictions.]

A.   I can't say because I'm not aware of it. I don't read the critics. I don't know any literary people. The people I know are other farmers and horse people and hunters, and we talk about horses and dogs and guns and what to do about this hay crop or this cotton crop, not about literature. I think—I'm convinced, though, that that sort of criticism whether it's nonsensical or not is valid because it is a symptom of change, of motion, which is life, and also it's a proof that literature—art—is a living quantity in our social condition. If it were not, then there'd be no reason for people to delve and find all sorts of symbolisms and psychological strains and currents in it. And I'm quite sure that there are some writers to whom that criticism is good, that it could help them find themselves. I don't know that the critic could teach the writer anything because I'm inclined to think that nobody really can teach anybody anything, that you offer it and it's there and if it is your will or urge to learn it you do, and the writer that does need the criticism can get quite a lot of benefit from it. [65]

Q.   Mr. Faulkner, what is your objective in using long sentences over short sentences? Do you feel—is that a stream-of-consciousness effect or do you feel you can convey your thoughts easier by them?
A.   That is a matter of the carpenter trying to find the hammer or the axe that he thinks will do the best job. Another thing is, everyone has a fore-knowledge of death that is, he will have only a very short time comparatively to do the work and he is trying to put the whole history of the human heart on the head of a pin, you might say. Also, to me, no man is himself, he is the sum of his past. There is no such thing really as was because the past is. It is a part of every man, every woman, and every moment. All of his and her ancestry, back-ground, is all a part of himself and herself at any moment. And so a man, a char-acter in a story at any moment of action is not just himself as he is then, he is all that made him, and the long sentence is an attempt to get his past and pos-sibly his future into the instant in which he does something. [84]

Q.   Mr. Faulkner, do you think an author has his prerogative to create his own language? . . . —I believe Joyce and Eliot have done it—have tried to create, they found that language . . . did not suit their purposes, so they had to go beyond and make a—
A.   He has the right to do that provided he don't insist on anyone under-standing it. . . . Well, the writer, actually, that's an obligation that he as-sumes with his vocation, that he's going to write it in a way that people can understand it. He doesn't have to write it in the way that every idiot can understand it—every imbecile in the third grade can understand it, but he's got to use a language which is accepted and in which the words have specific meanings that everybody agrees on. I think that *Finnegan's Wake* and *Ulysses* were justified, but then it's hard to say on what terms they were justified. That was a case of a genius who was electrocuted by the divine fire. [52-53]

Q.   Mr. Faulkner, these characters that you follow along [making the writer run to catch up with them], do they come to a natural conclusion, or do you have to kill them off, or do they tell the story and that's the end of it, or what?
A.   No no, they exist. They are still in motion in my mind. I can laugh at things they're doing that I haven't got around to writing yet. No, that's

where the rules of the craft come in, that someone, some editor, has got to give the whole thing unity, coherence, and emphasis. To start at a decent starting place and then stop it somewhere at a logical, reasonable place. But the characters themselves are walking out of that book still in motion, still talking, and still acting. [197-198]

The Unvanquished

Q. Sir, what book would you advise a person to read first of yours?
A. Well, that's not a fair question to ask me because I would like anyone to try the one that I love best, [*The Sound and the Fury*,] which is a poor one to start on. If you are asking me to give an objective answer I would say maybe *The Unvanquished*. . . . Because it's easy to read. Compared to the others, I mean. [2]

Q. Mr. Faulkner, *The Unvanquished* was published originally as a series of short stories, I believe, and then revised for a novel form. When you were writing those short stories did you have the idea in mind that these would make a novel eventually, or did they just appear after they appeared in short story form to fit together so naturally it was necessary to make a novel out of them?
A. I saw them as a long series. I had never thought of it in terms of a novel, exactly. I realized that they would be too episodic to be what I considered a novel, so I thought of them as a series of stories, that when I got into the first one I could see two more, but by the time I had finished the first one I saw that it was going further than that, and then when I had finished the fourth one, I had postulated too many questions that I had to answer for my own satisfaction. So the others had to be—the other three . . . had to be written then. [252]

*   *   *

Q. Mr. Faulkner, . . . I'm sure there must have been a number of Confederate veterans around when you were growing up as a boy. Did you talk to them, hear their reminiscences?
A. Yes. I remember a lot of them. I was five-six-seven years old around 1904-5-6 and 7, old enough to understand, to listen. They didn't talk so much about that war, I had got that from the maiden spinster aunts which had never surrendered. But I can remember the old men, and they would get out the old shabby grey uniforms and get out the old battle-flag on Decoration, Memorial Day. Yes I remember any number of them. But it was the aunts, the women, that had never given up. My aunt, she liked to go to picture shows, they had *Gone with the Wind* in at the theatre at home and she went to see it, and as soon as Sherman came on the screen she got up and left. She had paid good money to go there, but she wasn't going to sit and look at Sherman. [249]

Q. Mr. Faulkner, could I ask a question of interest to many historians also interested in literature? You spoke of the three-fold fund—experience, observation, and imagination. When you write about—as you did in *The Unvanquished*—the period of the Reconstruction, do you find that works of historians about Reconstruction in Mississippi are useful or do they just clutter the issue and deaden the imagination? . . .

A. As far as I know I have never done one page of research. Also, I doubt if I've ever forgotten anything I ever read too. The research I did was coincidental to the fact I was doing something which was fun, that is reading. I've never gone to these things . . . for information. It's because I was reading about people in motion, alive, in the conflict of the heart with itself or with its fellows or with its environment. That what research I read, I read exactly as I do fiction because it's people, man, in motion, and the writer, as I say, never forgets that, he stores it away—he has no morals—and when he needs it he reaches around and drags it out, and if it don't quite fit what he wants to say he'll probably change it just a little. [250-251]

Q. How much did you draw on [your great-grandfather] Colonel Falkner to get the picture of Colonel Sartoris?

A. That's difficult to say. That comes back to what we spoke of—the three sources the writer draws from—and I myself would have to stop and go page by page to see just how much I drew from family annals that I had listened to from these old undefeated spinster aunts that children of my time grew up with. Probably, well, the similarity of raising of that infantry regiment, that was the same, . . . his death was . . . pretty close parallel, but the rest of it I would have to go through . . . page by page and remember, Did I hear this or did I imagine this? [253-254]

* * *

Q. Mr. Faulkner, toward the end of "An Odor of Verbena" [Aunt Jenny] says to Bayard, "Damn you Sartorises," even though she seems to approve of his not going out and getting revenge. Is it some quality of heartlessness that she feels even in an act that she approves of?

A. No no. She loves these people, and they have constantly, all of her life, they have given her anguish and trouble. That she can't help but love them and she believes in them, not in what they do, and they do these reckless, completely self-centered things that have caused nothing but anguish and grief to all their womenfolk. That's all that meant. That she's proud of this boy but he too has done something unexpected, that when she expects them to act like human beings they act like Sartorises, then when she expects the next one to behave like a Sartoris he behaves like a simple human being, and she . . . will never have any peace from them. That's all that meant.

Q. Sir, . . . why is that sprig of verbena left on Bayard's pillow right at the very end, when [Drusilla] leaves, she says she's going to abjure verbena for ever and ever, and then he goes off, he walks into town and he meets Mr. Redmond, . . . without any gun or anything, and then comes back and the sprig of verbena is left on his pillow.

A. That . . . verbena was associated with Drusilla, with that woman, and she had wanted him to take a pistol and avenge his father's death. He went to the man who had shot his father, unarmed, and instead of killing the man, by that gesture he drove the man out of town, and although that had violated Drusilla's traditions of an eye for an eye, . . . the sprig of verbena meant that she realized that that took courage too and maybe more moral courage than to have drawn blood, or to have taken another step in an endless feud of an eye for an eye.

Q.   But then why did she leave?
A.   Because she was at that time too old, she was still too involved in it to accept that morally. I mean accept it physically, that her husband had not been avenged by his own son. That is, her intellect said, This was a brave thing, but the Eve in her said, My husband, my lover has not been avenged. And she could say, You were brave, but . . . that sort of bravery is not for me.

Q.   In that final section of *The Unvanquished*, are you developing a notion of a changing and developing tradition, and that Bayard doesn't reject the whole tradition, he keeps the honor and courage but he rejects the heart of the old tradition, and that is the vendetta. And I wondered . . . if the sprig of verbena represented the old mechanical, unchanging tradition that he was building from and rejecting partly but not altogether. I notice that you present that sprig of verbena as having the petals stamped out as if by a machine. I wondered if you . . . meant that this was the mechanical, unchanging tradition that he was rejecting partly but he was growing away from, but still keeping the honor and courage.
A.   No, . . . the fact that that sprig of verbena was alive, was an accolade, that the verbena, even though it looked like it had been stamped out by a machine and was traditional, was still alive, and there would be another one next year. And that was an accolade of optimism too, that she could have left a note scrawled on a piece of paper but that would have been dead paper and dead ink. This was alive, a promise of renewal for next year.

Q.   Is there any romantic attraction between Drusilla and the boy?
A.   I don't think so. They were nearer akin in age, but I don't think so. I think certainly Drusilla would have made no effort to bring that out in that boy because her husband—older than she though he was—was her knight, he represented the best of the masculine to her. To be ruthless and brave and . . . to brook no insult, to demand blood for blood, that was exactly what she would have been if she had been a boy. And she probably never saw this boy other than someone who was close to her in age. And he had never felt of her romantically I am quite sure because his father had stamped the whole tone of that household with his, the father's, importance, that nobody would have dared tamper with his wife, for instance. And this boy, . . . the one thing he would have shot a man for, for an insult to his father's wife, not his mother necessarily, but his father's wife, because he would be preserving his father's honor. [254-255, 42, 255-256]

*   *   *

The Sound and the Fury

Q.   Sir, why do you regard *The Sound and the Fury* as your best work?
A.   It was the best failure. It was the one that I anguished the most over,

that I worked the hardest at, that even when I knew I couldn't bring it off, I still worked at it. It's like the parent feels toward the unfortunate child, maybe. The others . . . have been easier to write than that, and in ways are better books than that, but I don't have the feeling toward any of them that I do toward that one, because that was the most gallant, the most magnificent failure. [61]

Q. Mr. Faulkner, in *The Sound and the Fury* the first three sections of that book are narrated by one of the four Compson children, and in view of the fact that Caddy figures so prominently, is there any particular reason why you didn't have a section . . . giving her views or impressions of what went on?

A. That's a good question . . . —the explanation of that whole book is in that. It began with the picture of the little girl's muddy drawers, climbing that tree to look in the parlor window with her brothers that didn't have the courage to climb the tree waiting to see what she saw. And I tried first to tell it with one brother, and that wasn't enough. That was Section One. I tried with another brother, and that wasn't enough. That was Section Two. I tried the third brother, because Caddy was still to me too beautiful and too moving to reduce her to telling what was going on, that it would be more passionate to see her through somebody else's eyes, I thought. And that failed and I tried myself—the fourth section—to tell what happened, and I still failed . . . and so about twenty years afterward I wrote an appendix still trying to make that book . . . match the dream. [1, 84]

Q. You had said previously that *The Sound and the Fury* came from the impression of a little girl up in a tree, and I just wondered how you built it from that, and whether you just, as you said, let the story develop itself?

A. Well, impression is the wrong word. It's more an image, a very moving image to me . . . of the children. 'Course, we didn't know at that time that one was an idiot, but they were three boys, one was a girl . . . —and it took the rest of the four hundred pages to explain why she was brave enough to climb the tree to look in the window. . . . And the symbolism of the muddy bottom of the drawers became the lost Caddy, which had caused one brother to commit suicide and the other brother had misused her money that she'd send back to the child, the daughter. It was, I thought, a short story, something that could be done in about two pages, a thousand words, I found out it couldn't. [31-32]

* * *

Q. What is your purpose in writing into the first section of *The Sound and the Fury* passages that seem disjointed in themselves [as if the ideas are] not connected with one another?

A. That was part of the failure. It seemed to me that the book approached nearer the dream if the groundwork of it was laid by the idiot, who was incapable of relevancy. That's—I agree with you too, that's a bad method, but to me it seemed the best way to do it, that I shifted those sections back and forth to see where they went best, but my final decision was that though that was not right, that was the best [way] to do it, that was simply the groundwork of that story, as that idiot child saw it. He himself didn't know what he was seeing. The only thing that held him into any sort of reality, into the world at all, was the trust that he had for his sister, that he knew that she loved him and would defend him, and so she was the whole world to him, and these things were flashes that were reflected on her as in a mirror. He didn't know what they meant. [63-64]

Q.   Mr. Faulkner, in *The Sound and the Fury*, can you tell me exactly why some of that is written in italics? What does that denote?
A.   I had to use some method to indicate to the reader that this idiot had no sense of time. That what happened to him ten years ago was just yesterday. The way I wanted to do it was to use different colored inks, but that would have cost so much the publisher couldn't undertake it.

Q.   Doesn't that go on with Quentin, too?
A.   Yes, because he was about half way between madness and sanity. It wasn't as much as in Benjy's part, because Quentin was only half way between Benjy and Jason. Jason didn't need italics because he was quite sane.

Q.   And another thing I noticed, you don't advise that people have to have a subject and predicate . . . and all those things.
A.   Well, . . . I think that's really not a fair question. I was trying to tell this story as it seemed to me that idiot child saw it. . . . He didn't know too much about grammar, he spoke only through his senses.

Q.   I'm referring mostly to Quentin and he certainly—he attended Harvard, he should have known.
A.   Well, Quentin was an educated half-madman and so he dispensed with grammar. Because it was all clear to his half-mad brain and it seemed to him it would be clear to anybody else's brain, that what he saw was quite logical, quite clear. [94-95]

Q.   Mr. Faulkner, I'd like to ask you about Quentin and his relationship with his father. I think many readers get the impression that Quentin is the way he is to a large extent because of his father's lack of values, or the fact that he doesn't seem to pass down to his son many values that will sustain him. Do you think that Quentin winds up the way he does primarily because of that, or are we meant to see, would you say, that the action comes primarily from what he is, abetted by what he gets from his father?
A.   The action as portrayed by Quentin was transmitted to him through his father. There was a basic failure before that. The grandfather had been a failed brigadier twice in the Civil War. It was . . . the basic failure Quentin inherited through his father . . . —something had happened somewhere between the first Compson and Quentin. The first Compson was a bold ruthless man who came into Mississippi as a free forester to grasp where and when he could and wanted to, and established what should have been a princely line, and that princely line decayed. [2-3]

Q.   A few generations back, was the de Spain blood or lineage the best in the country?

A.   It represented aristocracy, yes.

Q.   Was it better . . . than that of the Compson or the Sartoris family?
A.   It was stronger, it was less prone to the aberrations, to the degeneracy into
semi-madness which the Compsons reached. It didn't degenerate into the
moral weakness of the Sartorises, it was tougher blood. It may be it wasn't
quite as exalted as theirs was at one time, [but] it kept a certain leaven of a
stronger stock by instinctive choice. It was simply stronger—not better but
stronger. [119]

* * *

Q.   Mr. Faulkner, I saw something not long ago that took *The Sound and
the Fury* in four sections and tried to draw a parallel between the id, the ego
and super-ego and the author's person. Now don't you think that is indicative
of what a lot of critics and scholars are doing today with the views of contemporary writers, making psychological inferences and finding symbols which
the author never intended?
A.   Well, I should say that the author didn't deliberately intend, but I think
that in the same culture the background of the critic and of the writer are
so similar that a part of each one's history is the seed which can be translated
into the symbols which are standardized within that culture. That is, the writer
don't have to know Freud to have written things which anyone who does know
Freud can divine and reduce into symbols. And so when the critic finds those
symbols, they are of course there. But they were there as inevitably as the
critic should stumble on his own knowledge of Freud to discern [a] symbol.
But I think the writer is primarily concerned in telling about people, in the
only terms he knows, which is out of his experience, his observation, and his
imagination. And the experience and the imagination and the observation of
a culture are—all the people in that culture partake of the same three things
more or less. The critic has a valid part in any culture. I think . . . it might
be a good thing if most writers were like me and didn't bother to read them.
That is, the writer knows what is in his book and he knows whether it failed or
didn't fail . . . —and so it's possible that reading the criticisms could do a
young writer harm because it could confuse him, it could get him to think in
terms of the symbolism which the critic, who is usually a good deal more erudite
than the writer, can find in his work. [147-148]

Absalom, Absalom!

Q.   Sir, speaking of those two books, as you read *Absalom, Absalom!*, how
much can a reader feel that this is the Quentin, the same Quentin, who appeared in *The Sound and the Fury*—that is, a man thinking about his own
Compson family, his own sister?
A.   To me he's consistent. That he approached the Sutpen family with the
same ophthalmia that he approached his own troubles, that he probably
never saw anything very clearly, that his was just one of the thirteen ways to
look at Sutpen, and his may have been . . . one of the most erroneous.
Probably his friend McCannon had a much truer picture of Sutpen from
what Quentin had told him than Quentin himself did.

Q. But it's still Sutpen's story. It's not Quentin's story.

A. No it's Sutpen's story. But then, every time any character gets into a book, no matter how minor, he's actually telling his biography—that's all anyone ever does, he tells his own biography, talking about himself, in a thousand different terms, but himself. Quentin was still trying to get God to tell him why, in *Absalom, Absalom!* as he was in *The Sound and the Fury.* [274-275]

Q. Mr. Faulkner, in *Absalom, Absalom!* does any one of the people who talks about Sutpen have the right view, or is it more or less a case of thirteen ways of looking at a blackbird with none of them right?

A. That's it exactly. I think that no one individual can look at truth. It blinds you. You look at it and you see one phase of it. Someone else looks at it and sees a slightly awry phase of it. But taken all together, the truth is in what they saw though nobody saw the truth intact. So these are true as far as Miss Rosa and as Quentin saw it. Quentin's father saw what he believed was truth, that was all he saw. But the old man was himself a little too big for people no greater in stature than Quentin and Miss Rosa and Mr. Compson to see all at once. It would have taken perhaps a wiser or more tolerant or more sensitive or more thoughtful person to see him as he was. It was, as you say, thirteen ways of looking at a blackbird. But the truth, I would like to think, comes out, that when the reader has all these thirteen different ways of looking at the blackbird, the reader has his own fourteenth image of that blackbird which I would like to think is the truth. [273-274]

Q. How much of the story of *Absalom, Absalom!* is reconstructed by Shreve and Quentin? How does the reader know which to accept as objective truth and which to consider just a [reflection] of their personalities?

A. Well, the story was told by Quentin to Shreve. Shreve was the commentator that held the thing to something of reality. If Quentin had been let alone to tell it, it would have become completely unreal. It had to have a solvent to keep it real, keep it believable, creditable, otherwise it would have vanished into smoke and fury. [75]

* * *

Q. In another class you stated that you seldom have the plot of your novels worked out before you begin to write, but that they simply develop from a character or an incident. I was wondering if you remember what character or what incident caused you to write *Absalom, Absalom!?*

A. Sutpen.

Q. You thought of that character and then—

A. Yes, the idea of a man who wanted sons and got sons who destroyed him. The other characters I had to get out of the attic to tell the story of Sutpen. [73]

Q. Is the title of *Absalom, Absalom!* taken from the passage in the Bible found in Second Samuel?

A. Yes.

Q. Did you write the novel with this episode in your mind or did you first write the novel and then realizing the similarity in name—?

A.   They were simultaneous. As soon as I thought of the idea of the man who wanted sons and the sons destroyed him, then I thought of the title. [76]

Q.   Sir, are you conscious of any similarity between Thomas Sutpen and Flem Snopes? . . . both of them have a grand design and are unscrupulous about getting in—they use people.
A.   Well, only Sutpen had a grand design. Snopes's design was pretty base— he just wanted to get rich, he didn't care how. Sutpen wanted to get rich only incidentally. He wanted to take revenge for all the redneck people against the aristocrat who told him to go around to the back door. He wanted to show that he could establish a dynasty too—he could make himself a king and raise a line of princes. . . . He'd have to have a male descendant. . . . And so he—to have a Negro, half-Negro, for his son would have wrecked the whole dream. If he . . . had thought that that would ever be exposed that Bon was his son, he may have killed Bon himself. If it had ever come to that point, he would have destroyed Bon just as he would have destroyed any other individual who got in his way. [97-98, 272]

Q.   . . . I have the impression that up until very near the end of the book that [Bon] does not realize he is part Negro. . . . At what point does he find this out and how does he find it out?
A.   I think that Bon knew all the time that his mother was part Negress, but during Bon's childhood that was not important. He grew up in the Indies or in New Orleans where that wasn't too important. His mother was a wealthy woman. She could have called herself a Creole whether she had Negro blood along with the French or not. It became important only when Bon realized that it was important to his father. I think that Bon got into that business— well, of course, because he formed a friendship with Henry and felt that Henry, the ignorant country boy, had given him a sort of worship, an admiration and a worship which he enjoyed. Then when he saw the sort of stiff-necked man that Henry's father was and knew that that was his father too, he in a way had given his father a chance to say, I will acknowledge you, but if . . . I do openly and you stay here, you will wreck what I have devoted my life to, and so take my love and go, I think Bon would have done it. But this old man was afraid to do that. And Bon tempted him . . . partly in revenge on his treatment of his—Bon's—mother, until Bon got involved too deeply. No, Bon knew that he was a Negro, but until he found it was important to Sutpen, that wasn't important to him. That he was a gentleman, had been well bred, cultured, much better bred and cultured than Henry himself was.

Q.   Did Bon love Judith, or . . . ?
A.   I think he loved her, . . . he knew that if she knew that he was part Negro, with her training and background it would have destroyed her too. [272-273]

Q.   How far do you think the relationship between Charles Bon and Sutpen parallels what you consider the general racial situation in the South?
A.   It was a manifestation of a general racial system in the South which was condensed and concentrated as the writer has got to do with any incident or any character he takes, for the reason that he hasn't got sixty years. He has got

to do his job . . . between the covers of a book, but—that is, epitomize a constant general condition in the South, yes. [94]

* * *

Q. I've been looking for . . . the reason for Sutpen's downfall, Mr. Faulkner, and it seems to me that the Civil War played a part in it. Is that true?
A. Yes.

Q. But that's not the main reason?
A. No, I used the Civil War . . . for my own ends there. Sutpen's country was wrecked by the Civil War, but that didn't stop Sutpen, he was still trying to get the son, still trying to establish a dynasty. He was still trying to get even with that man who in his youth had said, Go to the back door. [73]

Q. Mr. Faulkner, along this respectability-scoundrel line [of Flem Snopes in *The Town*], how do you explain Colonel Sutpen, who sweeps into Jefferson and grimly sets himself up and at long last decides he'll have respectability . . . ? Does he really lose his individuality or isn't this respectability just another notch in his rifle, so to speak?
A. He wanted more than that. He wanted revenge as he saw it, but also he wanted to establish the fact that man is immortal, that man, if he is man, cannot be inferior to another man through artificial standards or circumstances. . . . He said, I'm going to be the one that lives in the big house, I'm going to establish a dynasty, I don't care how, and he violated all the rules of decency and honor and pity and compassion, and the fates took revenge on him. That's what that story was. But he was trying to say in his blundering way that, Why should a man be better than me because he's richer than me, that if I had had the chance I might be just as good as he thinks he is . . . by getting the same outward trappings which he has, which was a big house and servants in it. He didn't say, I'm going to be braver or more compassionate or more honest than he—he just said, I'm going to be as rich as he was, as big as he was on the outside.

Q. And he never really attained this respectability?
A. No, . . . the Greeks destroyed him, the old Greek concept of tragedy. He wanted a son which symbolized this ideal, and he got too many sons— his sons destroyed one another and then him . . . —the only son he had left was a Negro. [34-35]

Q. Is Sutpen meant to be a completely depraved character, something like Claggart in *Billy Budd* or Iago in *Othello*, or is he meant to be pitied?
A. To me he is to be pitied. He was not depraved—he was amoral, he was ruthless, completely self-centered. To me he is to be pitied, as anyone who ignores man is to be pitied, who does not believe that he belongs as a member of a human family, of the human family, is to be pitied. Sutpen didn't believe that. He was Sutpen. He was going to take what he wanted because he was big enough and strong enough, and I think that people like that are destroyed sooner or later, because one has got to belong to the human family, and to take a responsible part in the human family. . . .

1957-1958

one of his first prose pieces

Faulkner refuses to accept the belief that man will merely "endure" rather "he will prevail"

Man is immortal

Man prevails and attains peace of mind through suffering.

THE NOBEL PRIZE SPEECH

I FEEL THAT this award was not made to me as a man but to my work—a
life's work in the agony and sweat of the human spirit, not for glory and least
of all for profit, but to create out of the materials of the human spirit something which did not exist before. So this award is only mine in trust. It will
not be difficult to find a dedication for the money part of it commensurate
with the purpose and significance of its origin. But I would like to do the
same with the acclaim too, by using this moment as a pinnacle from which I
might be listened to by the young men and women already dedicated to the
same anguish and travail, among whom is already that one who will some
day stand here where I am standing.

Our tragedy today is a general and universal physical fear so long sustained by now that we can even bear it. There are no longer problems of the
spirit. There is only the question: When will I be blown up? Because of this,
the young man or woman writing today has forgotten the problems of the human heart in conflict with itself which alone can make good writing because
only that is worth writing about, worth the agony and the sweat.

He must learn them again. He must teach himself that the basest of all
things is to be afraid; and, teaching himself that, forget it forever, leaving no
room in his workshop for anything but the old verities and truths of the heart,
the old universal truths lacking which any story is ephemeral and doomed—
love and honor and pity and pride and compassion and sacrifice. Until he
does so, he labors under a curse. He writes not of love but of lust, of defeats
in which nobody loses anything of value, of victories without hope and, worst
of all, without pity or compassion. His griefs grieve on no universal bones,
leaving no scars. He writes not of the heart but of the glands.

Until he relearns these things, he will write as though he stood alone
and watched the end of man. I decline to accept the end of man. It is easy
enough to say that man is immortal simply because he will endure; that
when the last ding-dong of doom has clanged and faded from the last worthless rock hanging tideless in the last red and dying evening, that even then
there will still be one more sound: that of his puny inexhaustible voice, still
talking. I refuse to accept this. I believe that man will not merely endure:
he will prevail. He is immortal, not because he alone among creatures has
an inexhaustible voice but because he has a soul, a spirit capable of compassion and sacrifice and endurance. The poet's, the writer's, duty is to write
about these things. It is his privilege to help man endure by lifting his heart,
by reminding him of the courage and honor and hope and pride and compassion and pity and sacrifice which have been the glory of his past. The poet's
voice need not merely be the record of man, it can be one of the props, the
pillars to help him endure and prevail.

the key to his philosophy

1950

Reading Suggestions

Those who have read "An Odor of Verbena" will want to read the rest of
The Unvanquished, as the best introduction to Faulkner's saga of Yoknapatawpha County. *Go Down, Moses* and *Intruder in the Dust* will complete the
affirmative rendering of his view of man; and, along with *The Hamlet,* they
will fill out his picture of Southern society by adding his best stories on the
Negroes and Poor-Whites. These volumes will also make excellent background
for understanding the complex tragedies—*The Sound and the Fury, As I Lay
Dying, Light in August, Absalom, Absalom!*—and valuable preparation for
their difficult techniques. Such a serious course of reading can be topped off by
The Reivers, Faulkner's best novel of pure comedy. All of these, indeed most
of his best fictions, are readily available in reprints though there is as yet no
collected edition of his works. *The Portable Faulkner* (1946) offers a good
selection of his stories plus excerpts from the novels. A very useful descriptive
bibliography can be found in James Meriwether's *The Literary Career of William Faulkner* (1961).

There is no satisfactory biography of Faulkner, though an official one is
now in preparation by Joseph L. Blotner of the University of Virginia. But
nearly a score of books about him have already appeared, mostly concerned
with interpreting his works. Of those surveying the whole shelf, the best
analyses of his fictions as literary art are Irving Howe's *William Faulkner: A
Critical Study* (1952; revised 1962) and Olga Vickery's *William Faulkner:
A Critical Interpretation* (1959). Two other studies, also full scale, deal partly
with analysis of Faulkner's literary techniques but place their chief emphasis on
his ideas and themes: Hyatt Waggoner's *William Faulkner: From Jefferson to
the World* (1959) and Peter Swiggart's *The Art of Faulkner's Novels* (1962).
More specialized, but still covering all the fictions, are two that concentrate
on a single aspect of Faulkner's art: Walter Slatoff's *Quest for Failure* (1960),
a study of his rhetorical patterns and language techniques, and John Longley's
The Tragic Mask (1963), subtitled "A Study of Faulkner's Heroes."

There has been such a deluge of articles about Faulkner that any brief
listing must be somewhat arbitrary. Frederick Hoffman and Olga Vickery's
William Faulkner: Three Decades of Criticism (1960) reprints twenty-three
of the best (including most of the ones given below) and lists over five hundred more, in a bibliography that is frankly selective. Among general essays,
readers will find the following useful: George O'Donnell, "Faulkner's Mythol-
ogy," *Kenyon Review* (Summer 1939); Warren Beck, "William Faulkner's
Style," *American Prefaces* (Spring 1941); Malcolm Cowley, Introduction to
The Portable Faulkner (1946); R. P. Warren, "Cowley's Faulkner," *The New
Republic* (August 12, 26, 1946); Charles Anderson, "Faulkner's Moral Center,"
Études Anglaises (January 1954); Richard Chase, "Faulkner—the Great Years,"
The American Novel and Its Tradition (1957); Florence Leaver, "Faulkner:
The Word as Principle and Power," *South Atlantic Quarterly* (Autumn 1958).
An interesting brief commentary by the author on his literary career can be
found in Jean Stein's "William Faulkner: An Interview," *Paris Review* (Spring
1956). Full but informal self-commentary on all the fictions is recorded in
Frederick Gwynn and Joseph Blotner's *Faulkner in the University* (1959).

From the multitude of essays on Faulkner's individual works, a few are
chosen here that relate to the three novels treated at greatest length in the

introduction to this anthology. William Poirier, " 'Strange Gods' in Jefferson: Analysis of 'Absalom, Absalom!' " in *Sewanee Review* (Summer 1945); Cleanth Brooks, " 'Absalom, Absalom!': The Definition of Innocence," *Sewanee Review* (Autumn 1951); and Ilse Lind, "The Design and Meaning of 'Absalom, Absalom!' " *Publications of the Modern Language Association* (December 1955). Jean-Paul Sartre, "A Propos de 'Le Bruit et la Fureur': La Temporalité chez Faulkner," *La Nouvelle Revue Française* (June, July 1939); Lawrence Bowling, "Faulkner: Technique of 'The Sound and the Fury,' " *Kenyon Review* (Autumn 1948); and Carvel Collins, "The Interior Monologues of 'The Sound and the Fury,' " *English Institute Essays* (1954). Andrew Lytle, essay on *The Unvanquished* in "The Son of Man: He Will Prevail," *Sewanee Review* (Winter 1955); and the chapter on *The Unvanquished* in Hyatt Waggoner's *William Faulkner* (1959).

Biography

Oxford, Mississippi, Faulkner's home from boyhood on, was the center of his life and works. Though he traveled widely first and last, and though some of his novels and stories are laid elsewhere, this small town and the adjacent country nourished the man and provided the substance of his large shelf of fictions. Born in a nearby village, September 25, 1897, Faulkner lived and wrote in Oxford so privately that no biographical sketch at this time can hope to be more than a tentative outline. His family, well established in that region for three generations before him, was reduced in affluence but not in position by the turn of the century. Local legends and the annals of his own people seem to have supplied the starting point for all those writings that, greatly transmuted, make up the saga of his mythical county, Yoknapatawpha. (The name is Chickasaw for "water runs slow through flatland.")

Perhaps closest to his family history are *Sartoris*, which inaugurated the series in 1929, and *The Unvanquished* (1938). The career of the hero's father in the latter, for example, parallels that of the novelist's great-grandfather in its main events. Colonel William Cuthbert Falkner (the name was so spelled formerly), who had served notably in the Civil War, was a leader during Reconstruction, founded a small college, built a railroad, and ran other business enterprises. Twice tried for murder and acquitted, he was shot to death in the town square by J. H. Thurmond, his former business partner turned political rival, on the same day he had been elected to the state legislature in 1889. As this same ancestor was also the author of a popular historical romance, *The White Rose of Memphis* (1881), his relation to Faulkner was probably crucial.

Such are the early influences on the novelist to be reckoned with, rather than the meagerness of his literary contacts and his spotty formal education. Faulkner's achievement is proof that these matters are not of the essence. He left high school without graduating and then, after winning a commission in the Royal Flying Corps in Canada too late for overseas service in World War I, attended the University of Mississippi from 1919 to 1920. This was the extent of his actual schooling, but he had been an avid reader since his teens and during his college years he was a constant contributor to student publications. This desultory apprenticeship as a writer, continued through the three years he served as University postmaster, was brought to an end with *The Marble Faun*, a collection of poems privately printed in December 1924.

A few weeks later Faulkner went to New Orleans, where he lived during the first half of 1925, plunging at once into a vigorous literary life. In the Vieux Carré at that time there was a small but active Bohemia, centering around Sherwood Anderson, and a ready outlet for writing was offered by *The Double Dealer*, an avant garde magazine whose contributors included most of the important new American authors. All the literary and intellectual currents that made the twenties were reaching New Orleans, and among the writers influencing Faulkner should be named Anderson, Conrad, Eliot, Joyce, Pound, and Yeats, and the French symbolists. These were heady and crowded months, and the young novelist was very productive. He contributed a group of short pieces to *The Double Dealer*, a series of sketches and stories foreshadowing his later fictions to the *Times-Picayune*, and completed his first novel, *Soldiers' Pay*, before leaving for Europe in midsummer.

Returning after six months abroad, Faulkner led a quiet life in Oxford for the next three years, an ardent hunter and fisher who supported himself by odd jobs while he immersed himself in writing. One conjectures that this was also the period when he did some of his most influential reading: Shakespeare and Greek tragedy, the Bible and Dostoevski, the old Southern humorists, and so on—extending interests he had had from the first. His first two novels had brought him small pay and no critical acclaim, but few artists have been more indifferent to both neglect and fame than he. He was engrossed with discovering his radical techniques and shaping his imaginative creation of Yoknapatawpha County—gathering the powers that burst in a frenzy of productivity between 1929 and 1932. During that brief span he published six books, including three of the most extraordinary novels of the twentieth century. But not even *The Sound and the Fury, As I Lay Dying*, and *Light in August*, appearing in successive years, brought him any reputation save as the author of sensational and morbid novels.

Instead, ironically, he won notoriety from *Sanctuary* (1931), prefaced with a bitter jibe at an apathetic public and critics who had misconceived his serious works; "it is a cheap idea," he wrote, "deliberately conceived to make money." It not only sold well itself but brought him invitations from Hollywood to do script writing, which he accepted off and on over the next two decades to free him from the need of tailoring his fictions to the market place. The double irony is that *Sanctuary*, which as his best-known book remained for years the brand of his infamy for reviewers and the general public, is anything but the novel of violence and decadence and vulgarity it has been taken for. So for another decade or so Faulkner was either derided or neglected as a serious artist, even as he added volume after volume to his great saga: *Absalom, Absalom!, The Unvanquished, The Hamlet*, and *Go Down, Moses*—all between 1936 and 1942.

When in 1946 a representative selection of his Yoknapatawpha fictions was issued as *The Portable Faulkner*, it was said that all of his novels were out of print. But a small group of discerning readers had been building up who now responded enthusiastically to the appreciative introduction by Malcolm Cowley and R. P. Warren's penetrating review-essay prompted by it. In the sixteen years that remained to Faulkner fame and honors came in place of the obscurity and misunderstanding under which he had labored during the preceding twenty. The greatest recognition came first with the award of the Nobel Prize in 1950. This was followed by the Pulitzer Prize, the National Book Award, many invitations to lecture at home and abroad, and the sudden flowering of an international reputation. A flood of articles and critical books poured from the press in a continuing effort to interpret his writings and assess his worth. Faulkner took all this in his stride, as he had the neglect and abuse, shunning all publicity to the end. He continued to produce quietly, adding some eight more volumes to his shelf though not adding substantially to the brilliant achievement of his middle period.

Faulkner's career came to its conclusion peacefully, at the height of his fame. After several pleasant terms as writer-in-residence at the University of Virginia, he returned to his home in Oxford, Mississippi, at the end of the academic year 1962. There a few weeks later he died of a heart attack, acclaimed throughout the world as one of the literary giants of the twentieth century.

INDEX

INDEX

Index of Authors, Titles, and First Lines

Note: Names of authors are in boldface type, titles of longer works in italics, titles of shorter works in roman, and first lines in quotation marks.

1171

I

J

L

M